GW01281231

Beyond the Reach of Empire

THIS BOOK IS DEDICATED TO THE MEMORY OF

Professor Richard Holmes
1946–2011

BEYOND THE REACH OF EMPIRE

Wolseley's Failed Campaign
to save
Gordon and Khartoum

Colonel Mike Snook

Frontline Books
London

Beyond the Reach of Empire
Wolseley's Failed Campaign to Save Gordon and Khartoum
This edition published in 2013 by Frontline Books,
an imprint of Pen & Sword Books Ltd,
47 Church Street, Barnsley, S. Yorkshire, S70 2AS
www.frontline-books.com

Copyright © Mike Snook, 2013

The right of Mike Snook to be identified as the author of this work
has been asserted by him in accordance with the
Copyright, Designs and Patents Act 1988.

ISBN: 978-1-84832-601-9

All rights reserved. No part of this publication may be reproduced, stored in
or introduced into a retrieval system, or transmitted, in any form, or by any
means (electronic, mechanical, photocopying, recording or otherwise)
without the prior written permission of the publisher. Any person who does
any unauthorized act in relation to this publication may be liable
to criminal prosecution and civil claims for damages.

CIP data records for this title are available from the British Library

For more information on our books, please visit
www.frontline-books.com, email info@frontline-books.com
or write to us at the above address.

Printed and bound by CPI Group (UK) Ltd, Croydon, CR0 4YY

Typeset in 11/13.5 point Arno Pro/Arno Pro Light Display

Contents

	List of Plates	vii
	List of Maps and Tables	ix
	Glossary	xi
	Preface	xvii
	Conventions Followed in the Text	xxv
	Chronology	xxvii
	The Course of the Mahdist Uprising, 1881–1883	
	Prologue	3
Chapter 1	**All Men Worship the Rising Sun**	31
	Strategic and Political Background to the Nile Campaign	
Chapter 2	**Quandary**	61
	Gordon at Khartoum: February–April 1884	
Chapter 3	**Novel Expedients**	81
	Wolseley's Plan of Campaign	
Chapter 4	**Delays and Decisions**	117
	Prosecuting the Campaign: November–December 1884	
Chapter 5	**Leap in the Dark**	139
	The March of the Desert Column	
Chapter 6	**Go Strong into the Desert**	171
	Composition, Organization and Capability of Stewart's Force	
Chapter 7	**Approach to Battle**	200
	Jakdul Wells to Abu Klea: 14–16 January 1885	
Chapter 8	**Under Fire**	222
	The Battle of Abu Klea: Phase I – On the Defensive	
Chapter 9	**The Valley of the Shadow**	241
	The Battle of Abu Klea: Phase II – The British Advance	
Chapter 10	**England's Far and Honour a Name**	265
	The Battle of Abu Klea: Phase III – The Climax	

Chapter 11	**Walking Amongst Vipers**	305
	Abu Klea: The Aftermath	
Chapter 12	**Endless Confusion**	329
	The Night March of 18/19 January	
Chapter 13	**The Fight to the Nile**	344
	The Battle of Abu Kru: 19 January 1885	
Chapter 14	**The Fort of the Infidels**	390
	Gubat and Metemmeh: 20–23 January 1885	
Chapter 15	**Boy's Own**	421
	The River Dash: 24 January–4 February 1885	
Chapter 16	**Too Late: Lies, Myth and Reality**	466
	Analysis and Conclusions	
	Epilogue	502
	Appendices	
Appendix A	Composition of the Nile Expedition	515
Appendix B	Organization of the Camel Corps	517
Appendix C	Movement Plan to Ambukol and Korti	520
Appendix D	Order of Battle: Abu Klea, 17 January 1885	521
Appendix E	Order of Battle: Abu Kru, 19 January 1885	523
Appendix F	Casualty Return: Abu Klea, 17 January 1885	525
Appendix G	Casualty Return: Abu Kru & Metemmeh, 19–21 January 1885	529
Appendix H	Lt. Col. J. D. H. Stewart's Notes on the Suakin–Berber Route	533
	Notes	535
	Bibliography	564
	Index	568

Plates

Plate 1: Major General Charles Gordon; Prime Minister Gladstone; General Lord Wolseley; Colonel William Butler.

Plate 2: Brigadier General Sir Herbert Stewart (*Royal Collection*); Colonel Sir Charles Wilson; Colonel Fred Burnaby; Captain Lord Charles Beresford RN.

Plate 3: The British *zariba* position at Abu Klea; the view down the Abu Klea Valley.

Plate 4: The 7-pounders at Abu Klea; hand-to-hand fighting at Abu Klea.

Plate 5: The stone wall on Trafford's hill; the conical hill viewed from the area of the hospital fort.

Plate 6: The Battle of Abu Klea. View along the valley from the *zariba* towards the wells; looking across the British line of advance.

Plate 7: The area of the attack on the left face of the square; dead ground on the approaches to the square.

Plate 8: The view from the left rear corner of the square; the author paying his respects at the remains of Burnaby's cairn.

Plate 9: The night march of 18/19 January; Melton Prior's drawing of the defence of the *zariba* at Abu Kru.

Plate 10: The climax of the Battle of Abu Kru.

Plate 11: The British zariba position at Abu Kru; the fight to the Nile.

Plate 12: The Battle of Abu Kru. The view from the gravel ridge towards the square; the loss of the *Bordein*.

Plate 13: The steamers fighting at the confluence of the Niles; the action at Wad Habeshi.

Plate 14: The steamer *Bordein* re-floated by the Mahdists; the heavily fortified *Bordein* of January 1885 (*West Sussex Records Office*).

Plate 15: Location of the wreck of the *Bordein*; Captain Trafford's watercolour of the wreck.

Plate 16: G. W. Joy's portrayal of the death of Gordon.

Maps and Tables

Maps

1.	The theatre of operations – The Sudan 1884–5	2
2.	Gordon's reading of the situation in February 1884	62
3.	Khartoum and the South Front defence line, from Sandes's *The Royal Engineers in Egypt and the Sudan*	68
4.	The Nile from Wādī Halfā to Dongola	106
5.	The axis of advance across the Bayūda Desert	118
6.	Lieutenant Lawson's sketch map of the *Zariba* at Abu Klea	215
7.	The square at Abu Klea	247
8.	Verner's map of the Abu Klea battlefield, as it appeared in Macdonald's *Too Late for Gordon and Khartoum*	268
9.	Verner's section drawing of Abu Klea	276
10.	The British approach to Metemmeh	336
11.	Verner's map of Abu Kru, Gubat and Metemmeh	400
12.	Verner's map of the 21 January Operation at Metemmeh	406

Tables

The Desert Column's marching-out state, Korti, 8 January 1885	172
The Desert Column's marching-out state, Jakdul, 14 January 1885	207

Maps and Tables

Glossary

adjutant – regimental appointment usually held by the senior lieutenant. The adjutant worked as a personal staff officer to the commanding officer.

AMD – Army Medical Department.

amīr – a senior leadership figure in the Mahdīst movement, akin to an appointed prince.

anṣār (singular: *anṣāri*) – literally 'followers'; the name given to the Mahdīst faithful in imitation of the Prophet's retainers and supporters.

ardeb – an Egyptian unit of measure, equivalent to 5.62 Imperial bushels.

Baqqāra (or **Baggara**) – literally 'cowman'; a grouping of ethnically Arab Kordofani tribes that for the most part lived as cattle-owning nomads. Certain clans were both renowned as horsemen and feared as brigands.

bāshi-būzuq – irregular mercenary soldier in the service of Khedival Egypt.

bazinger – black African irregular soldier. Typically rifle-armed mercenaries or slave-soldiers, they could be found both in government service and in the private employ of prominent Arab *shaikhs*, warlords, slavers, and traders.

Bays – British heavy cavalry regiment; nickname or abbreviated form of '2nd Dragoon Guards (Queen's Bays)'.

bearer company – ad hoc medical unit intended to transport casualties.

Bey – honorary title customarily bestowed upon Egyptian officers in the ranks equivalent to colonel and lieutenant colonel.

Bija – the predominant indigenous ethnic group along the Red Sea littoral. Renowned for his ferocity in battle and his eccentric hairstyle, the Bīja fighting man was immortalized by Rudyard Kipling as the 'fuzzy-wuzzy'.

bluejackets – nickname given to members of the Royal Navy operating ashore as a 'naval brigade'. The sobriquet should not be regarded as an indicator of dress; even shore parties clad in tropical whites might be referred to as 'bluejackets'.

Blues – see RHG.

Boxer (cartridge) – bottle-necked rolled brass cartridge invented by Colonel Edward Boxer and adopted for use with the .450-inch Martini-Henry rifle. The case was of .577-inch calibre.

cacolet – a pair of counterbalancing seats suspended from the flanks of a baggage camel, used by bearer companies and field hospitals for transporting casualties capable of sitting upright.

Camel Corps – brigade-sized force of British troops, consisting of four composite camel-borne regiments intended always to dismount and fight as infantry.

Camerons – abbreviated form of 'Cameron Highlanders'.

cataracts – stretches of river characterized by the presence of white-water rapids, sub-surface obstacles and narrow channels or 'gates'. There were six major cataracts between Cairo and Khartoum, though in practice there were numerous other perilous stretches of water, in addition to the best known half-dozen.

Commissariat & Transport Department – parent corps of the Army's non-commissioned logisticians – a forerunner of the later Royal Army Service Corps, Royal Corps of Transport and today's Royal Logistic Corps.

company – infantry sub-unit, intended to be commanded by a captain, with a typical strength of 3 officers, 1 colour sergeant, 4 sergeants, 4 corporals, 2 drummers and 70–85 privates. A company consisted of four sections and could if required operate as two half-companies each of two sections. There were eight companies in a full-strength battalion, each of which was assigned to one of the two 'wings' or half-battalions. Companies could be known by numbers or letters.

DCLI – Duke of Cornwall's Light Infantry.

DG – Dragoon Guards.

dhura – a type of sorghum or cereal grass, also known as 'Egyptian corn'; the kernels can be made into flour, while the green plants can be used as animal feed.

fellaheen (singular: *fellah*) – the rural poor of the Nile Delta. Also used loosely to mean Egyptian other ranks in the Khedival Army.

frock – an unadorned field version of the tunic. Home service frocks were red or blue according to arm: the collar and only rarely the cuffs, by this period, were in the regimental facing colour. Foreign-service versions of the frock were completely plain and could be khaki or grey.

Gardner – five-barrelled machine gun in service with the Royal Navy.

GCR – Guards Camel Regiment.

GOC – General Officer Commanding.

Gordons – British infantry regiment; abbreviated form of 'Gordon Highlanders'.

Greys – British heavy cavalry regiment; nickname or abbreviated form of '2nd Dragoons (Royal Scots Greys)'.

H – Hussars.

Hadendawa – major tribal sub-grouping of the Bīja people.

HCR – Heavy Camel Regiment.

HLI – Highland Light Infantry.

Ja'līyīn (singular: **Ja'alī**) – prominent Arab tribe from the Nile Valley north of Khartoum; the majority population in the region of Metemmeh, Shendy and Berber. Often rendered as Jaalin.

jazīra – literally an island, but commonly used to mean the expanse of territory between the Blue and White Niles south of Khartoum.

jihādīya – a specialist corps of Mahdīst riflemen, consisting in large part of black Africans, most of whom had been bazingers in Kordofan or Darfur before the rebellion, or had been taken prisoner whilst serving in Sudanese units of the Egyptian Army.

khalīfa – title bestowed by the Prophet on his four principal subordinates, a practice emulated by Muḥammad Aḥmad.

khor – watercourse, typically dry and sandy-bottomed for all but a few weeks a year.

kourbash – whip or flail.

KRRC – King's Royal Rifle Corps.

Krupp – German arms manufacturer which made many of the guns in service with the Egyptian military.

'lunger' – British soldiers' nickname for the 22-inch 1876-pattern bayonet.

L – Lancers.

LCR – Light Camel Regiment.

LG – Life Guards.

Mahdī – the 'divinely guided' one, Islamic prophet and saviour.

Martini-Henry – the service-rifle on general issue to British infantry and engineer units at the time of the Mahdīst uprising. A short-barrelled carbine version was in service with the cavalry and artillery.

Medical Staff Corps – the parent corps of the Army's non-commissioned medics, which had formerly been known as the Army Hospital Corps.

MICR – Mounted Infantry Camel Regiment.

mudir – A senior civil appointment in the Egyptian service equating to a state governor e.g. the Mudir of Dongola, Mudir of Berber, etc.

mounted infantry – soldiers seconded from infantry battalions to form ad hoc units mounted on camels or ponies. They were armed with the rifle and bayonet and invariably dismounted to fight.

Naval Brigade – contingent of Royal Navy personnel landed for service ashore. There was no correlation between the arbitrary strength of a naval 'brigade' and an army brigade of three or more battalions.

nuggar – native sailing vessel used on the Nile.

Nordenfelt – early machine gun in service with the Egyptian Army (often incorrectly rendered as 'Nordenfeldt').

Officer Commanding – the senior officer in a unit; today the expression would be reversed as 'Commanding Officer'.

oke – an Egyptian unit of measure equivalent to 2.75 lb or 1.24 kg.

Pasha – honorary title bestowed upon senior Egyptian officials and general officers, including British officers holding Egyptian ranks equivalent to brigadier general and above.

PMO – Principal Medical Officer.

Quartermaster (QM) – a regimental officer with specific responsibility for logistic support, who would typically have been commissioned in early middle-age, after first rising through the ranks from private to sergeant-major.

RA – Royal Artillery.

RBL – Rifled Breech Loader (used of artillery pieces).

RE – Royal Engineers.

reis – river pilot.

Remington – the standard 0.433-inch rolling-block rifle in service with the Egyptian military until late 1885.

RHG – Royal Horse Guards: the formal title of the Household Cavalry regiment also known as 'the Blues'.

RM – Royal Marines (consisting of RMA and RMLI).

RMA – Royal Marine Artillery.

RML – Rifled Muzzle-Loader (used of artillery pieces).

RMLI – Royal Marine Light Infantry.

RMO – Regimental Medical Officer.

Royals – British heavy cavalry regiment; nickname or abbreviated form of 1st (Royal) Dragoons.

sarāya – palace or grand building.

screw gun – a light artillery piece or mountain gun which could be disassembled for carriage aboard mules or camels, the barrel of which literally screwed into the breech mechanism. The standard gun of the type in the Royal Artillery was a rifled muzzle loader (RML) of 2.5-inch calibre firing a 7-pound shell. Ammunition types included common shell, shrapnel and case-shot.

section – tactical sub-grouping within an infantry company. There were four sections in a company. Sections were commanded by a sergeant and consisted of a corporal and about 20 privates. Two sections could operate as a half-company under the command of a subaltern officer.

shaikh – an Arab tribal chief or headman.

Shā'iqīa (singular: **Shā'iqī**) – loyalist Arab tribe from the Nile Valley north of Khartoum. Often rendered as Shaggiya, Shaggieh or other variations.

Sirdar – the Commander-in-Chief of the Egyptian Army.

squadron – cavalry sub-unit commanded by a major or a captain and consisting of two troops. There were four squadrons in a full-strength regiment, although it was not uncommon to proceed on active service with only three. A strong squadron would consist of around 150 officers, NCOs and men.

subaltern – junior officer.

sword bayonet – Rifle battalions and the senior NCOs in line battalions carried the 1860 Pattern sword bayonet which, having originally been designed for use with the Snider rifle, was 'bushed' to fit the Martini-Henry. The Camel Corps received a universal issue of the P1860 sword bayonet for the Nile expedition.

Tarbush, tarboush or **tarboosh** – the name given to the simple black-tasselled red headdress worn by Egyptian public figures, soldiers and officials; often erroneously referred to as a fez.

troop – tactical sub-division of a cavalry squadron. A troop might be commanded by a captain or a lieutenant. A strong troop might field around 70 NCOs and men.

voyageur – civilian Canadian boatman enlisted to provide the watermanship skills necessary to pilot British troops up the Nile aboard small boats.

whaler – specially commissioned shallow-draught rowing boat designed by Colonel William Butler. The boats were also fitted with mast and sails, although the high banks of the Nile meant that these did not see as much use as had been anticipated.

wing – half-battalion, typically of four companies.

Yataghan – the British P1860 sword bayonet was designed in the 'Yataghan' style, which is to say with a slight wave or curve in the blade.

zariba – thornbush perimeter originally conceived by indigenous inhabitants of East Africa and South Sudan as a defence against wild animals, but later adopted by the Egyptian and British military as an obstacle to attack.

Preface

THE EXPEDITION UNDERTAKEN by General Lord Garnet Wolseley for the relief of Major General Charles 'Chinese' Gordon at Khartoum was one of the great adventures of the High Victorian era, an epoch of British history which it is no exaggeration to say is littered with dramatic military episodes, from the cavalry charges at Balaclava to the dawn of modern warfare on the South African *veldt*. Wolseley wrote of the Nile Expedition, 'It is the biggest operation the English Army has ever undertaken. I think those engaged in it, are now beginning to realise that fact, and to feel they have the honor [sic] of taking part in an operation the like of which has never been undertaken before.'[1] Not untypically Wolseley was over-egging his case but, even so, that the expedition was a grand, ambitious and complex military undertaking cannot be denied. It may indeed have been too grand, too ambitious and far too complex, for ultimately it was to prove an abject failure. Towards the end, with the writing on the wall, Wolseley had changed his tune somewhat, remarking in his journal, 'O what a campaign of anxieties is this!'[2] By the time it had run its course the popular expression 'All Sir Garnet', implying that everything was organized and under control, no longer had quite the same ring to it and duly dropped out of common usage.

Beyond the Reach of Empire is grounded not merely in conventional historical research alone, but is also underpinned by an extensive programme of fieldwork designed to achieve the best possible understanding of what soldiers refer to as 'ground'. Khartoum is no longer quite the same of course, although the *sarāya* (Gordon's palace) and the Mahdī's tomb have been restored, the Khalīfa's house is intact and not even man can interfere with the confluence of the Niles. For the most part the major desert battlefields of 1884–5 are pleasingly unspoiled. The ability to bring to mind the terrain, going, distances, obstacles, views, inter-visibility and so on has enabled me to develop a much better understanding of precisely what the primary sources are and are not saying in respect of the campaign. This has been more than a little useful, for the pen when it is wielded by men more accustomed to the sword is not invariably the mightier instrument and can sometimes confuse, mis-sequence and mislead. Military historians will readily acknowledge that the anomalies across any array of participant accounts will almost always be legion but, if I have learned nothing else from tramping battlefields, it is that there is a direct correlation between a historian's familiarity with the battle-space and his mastery of the nature and sequence of the fight. In other words, a great many mysteries will be eradicated when one has a firm grip of the ground. I hope to succeed in passing this on to the reader.

My travels in the Sudan took me to all the historic sites in and around the capital, north into the Bayūda Desert, including numerous visits to the Abu Klea (Abū Ṭulaiḥ) and Abu Kru (Abū Kurū) battlefields, to the riverside towns of Shendy and Metemmeh, and to a number of other important points along a 100-mile stretch of the Nile. The latter included the Sixth Cataract, the Sabalūka Gorge, the 'Narrows of the Nile', Mernat Island, Wad Habeshi and Jabal Royan. Quite what the historic significance of these places is will become apparent as the story unfolds.

To digress briefly, it dawned on me after I had completed my long sequence of pilgrimages that these were all places upon which Garnet Wolseley never once gazed. It is true on the other hand that I have never been to Korti, the site of his lordship's forward-most headquarters, although I have not so far found this much of an impediment. The point, though, is a serious one, for the reason that Metemmeh is some 174 miles from Korti, while Khartoum lies the best part of 100 miles south of Metemmeh. That the army commander could site himself 174 miles to the rear of his main force and 274 miles behind his vanguard bespeaks the extraordinary extent to which Wolseley allowed himself to become dislocated from the main focus of his operations. Such great distances were without precedent in the 'small wars of empire' and would not even be allowed to open up today, notwithstanding the advantages conveyed by modern communications systems. In order to make consistently sound judgements a commander has to be able to 'touch' the situation for himself. If he cannot do this, he is both mal-located and failing in his duty. Even in January 1885, even in so remote a spot as Korti, the wonders of telegraphy made it possible for Wolseley to communicate his thoughts to the War Office in Whitehall within a matter of hours. To talk to his fighting men, however, or perhaps more crucially for them to talk to him, the message had to be conveyed by camel-mounted couriers, for whom 174 miles represented a four-day journey. An every-day military process, every bit as relevant to Hannibal as to Schwarzkopf, is for the operational-level commander to seek the views of the tactical commander before deciding whether the latter should enact Option A, B or C; and yet in January 1885, Wolseley contrived a situation in which a process of forward consultation could not fail to consume nine days.

Little wonder, then, that the final phase of operations in the Bayūda Desert saw the army commander issuing a number of sets of orders which, even before the ink had dried, had already been overtaken by events and rendered inappropriate. There is no question but that Wolseley lost control of his campaign, that he ceased to be the director of operations and became a spectator instead. The remarkable thing is that his campaign journal, with its references to long, frustrating waits for news, shows that he sensed this happening – albeit his vanity precluded any possibility of him recognizing that he was in any way to blame – but failed to do anything about it. While it is true that Lord Hartington, the Secretary of State for War, had earlier asked that Wolseley remain at the end of the telegraph, this does not come up to the mark as mitigation: no politician has the right to ask a general in the field to command his force ineptly, and, since the object of the expedition was to get to Khartoum, Hartington knew full well that Wolseley was going to have to leave Korti sooner or later. It was a simple matter of timing and judgement and it was the army commander who got it wrong.

Of less direct relevance to British operations in the Nile Valley, but no less fascinating for all that, I was also able to reach the Red Sea coast and visit Suakin, Tokar and the battlefields of El Teb, Tamai, Tofrek and Hasheen. For me these were moving, meaningful and memorable experiences from beginning to end. I was guided to places I might otherwise have struggled to find by Ja'līyīn and Bīja tribesmen, whose names I never knew and whose modern-day lives are no less arduous than were those of their forebears, 125 years and more ago. My hosts drew water from holes in the ground for me, took me to their mud-baked houses, introduced me to their families and would, I sensed, willingly have shared all that they had with me. The Hadendawa man who guided me to the scene of Valentine Baker's defeat, seemingly through a portal in time, was fuzzy-haired, dressed in the simplest of robes, rode a camel and was armed with a cross-hilted sword. It is certain that neither he nor anybody else who helped me in those far-flung places will ever read these words, but to such noble and generous-spirited men as these I am most profoundly grateful.

I was at that time serving as the Senior Staff Officer, Operations, with the UN Mission in the Sudan. I found myself occupying a busy job at an anxious time, for not only was the Sudanese head of state indicted by the International Criminal Court, precipitating an all-round escalation in tension, but there were also a number of nasty internecine battles within so-called Joint Integrated Units, as well as a cruelly violent three-way tribal war in the south between Murles, Dinkas and various Nuer clans. Fortunately, amidst all the drama and misery, there were also some quiet weekends, so that on occasion the professionalism of my right-hand men allowed me, with a tolerably clear conscience, to slip away into the desert to identify and explore the battlefields of the 1880s. Without exception the dedication of my subordinates in 'J3 Ops' to the cause of peace in the Sudan brought great credit upon their respective nations.

As it would have been both inadvisable and disallowable to roam too far from safety on my own (though I did through force of circumstance have to go solo through the Red Sea Littoral), I owe a particular debt of gratitude to those of my colleagues who accompanied me on my dusty desert forays, whether from historical interest, a sense of adventure, or some combination of both these things. I would emphasize to readers from the Western World that the Sudan is not, regrettably, to be regarded as a tourist destination and that UK citizens travelling there, for any reason, should not fail to pay all due heed to the prevailing Foreign and

Commonwealth Office Travel Advice (*see* www.fco.gov.uk/en/ travel-and-living-abroad/travel-advice-by-country/sub-saharan-africa/sudan1). Citizens of other countries should similarly consult their respective national authorities. Please bear in mind that as a lifelong regular soldier I have developed a professional 'nose for danger' and, moreover, was able to travel within the protective umbrella of overlapping national and international security systems. Even then there were difficulties upon which it would be inappropriate to expand here. I emphasize that nobody should lightly attempt to undertake battlefield tours in the region on the basis of anything I was able to do. Doubtless the security situation will change for the better one day, but that time is not now, nor is it for the immediately foreseeable future.

To turn now to acknowledgements, I owe a debt of gratitude to Neil Aspinshaw, one of the world's foremost experts on the Martini-Henry rifle, for allowing me to experience the merits and the foibles of the rifle for myself and for drawing my attention to the Arbuthnot report, which specifically addressed its performance in the Sudan. I am grateful too to the Egyptian Army officers at the Citadel in Cairo, who were kind enough to show me around a fascinating collection of artefacts. Alan Readman of the West Sussex Records Office in Chichester was kind enough to make a key unpublished primary source, Captain Lionel Trafford's diaries, available to me. In 2003 James Whitaker made a significant contribution to the historiography of the Nile campaign in transcribing and publishing *The Military Diary of Colonel W. W. C. Verner*. Verner was a key player in the campaign, so that almost anything written before 2003 will have missed points of importance raised by his account. Carrying a copy of his diary in the Bayūda Desert, as I invariably did during the course of my fieldwork, was to have Willoughby Verner guiding me, in much the same way as he had guided Sir Herbert Stewart's brigade in January 1885. I am most grateful to Andy Lonergan for providing me with access to his transcribed copy of 'Mounted Infantry in the Desert Campaign 1884–5', the MS account of Thomas D'Oyly Snow. Similarly Mat Toy was most generous in providing me with access to a personal account by Sergeant Charles Williams DCM of the Medical Staff Corps. David and Julia Hollands were kind enough to draw my attention to a letter written from the Bayūda by Sergeant William Stakings of the Royal West Kents.

Without doubt the most significant documentary find during the course of archival research was that of the Orders Book and War Diary of the Desert Column. The staff of the National Archives of Scotland could not have been more helpful in dashing an obscure file from the Airlie Papers across the fair city of Edinburgh at my urgent request, only days ahead of my departure for Khartoum. It was a chance reference on their website to Abu Klea which led to the unearthing of documents never before tapped in the published literature of the Sudan campaigns. David Stanley William Ogilvy, or Captain Lord Airlie (the 11th Earl), was Sir Herbert Stewart's brigade major in the Bayūda Desert and evidently never quite got around to handing over the contents of his saddlebags to the authorities. So fresh and well preserved were these documents that there was still sand between the pages. Tucked away with the two crucial hard-backed notebooks were a number of handwritten letters received by Stewart from, amongst others, Wolseley and Colonel Sir Charles Wilson. Also present, and crucially important in developing a more sophisticated understanding of the Battles of Abu Klea and Abu Kru, were the handwritten casualty returns submitted to Airlie by commanding officers on 23 January 1885. As I have on around a dozen occasions been asked by descendants of men who were killed in action in the Bayūda Desert if I know anything of the circumstances of their death, these returns were to prove a particularly useful find.

I must also extend my grateful thanks to the staff of Frontline Books, most especially my friend and publisher, Michael Leventhal, who as usual has been unfailingly supportive throughout the project. Thanks are also due to my editor, Stephen Chumbley. I would also like to acknowledge important enabling contributions made in the Sudan by Johnny Rollins, Armin Wagner, Ansgar Glatzel, Graham Townsend, Jason Davies, Andrew Banks, Andy Barnes, Ken Renaud, Liam Jones and Dave Anderson. Finally, the striking photograph of Sir Herbert Stewart in the plate section is archived in the Royal Collection at Windsor; I am most grateful to Her Majesty, Queen Elizabeth, for her gracious permission to publish it here.

I should provide the reader with a few words of introduction about my subject matter and approach. What is *Beyond the Reach of Empire* all about? Why was it written and what does it offer that is new? It will perhaps be easier to answer those questions forthrightly by stating at the outset what the book is not about. It is not intended to serve as a complete campaign history of the Gordon Relief Expedition, though it does major on its most important phase and also reflects in its concluding chapter on why the relief expedition failed, who was to blame and what might have been done differently to save General Gordon and his people. Because nothing in war takes place in splendid isolation, I have broken down the discussion of failure and culpability into the strategic, operational and tactical levels of command. The wider expedition, though, serves only as a backdrop to the all-important culminating phase of the campaign. We will not, therefore, be battling our way through the cataracts in painstaking detail. The book is not about Gordon Pasha either, the subject of countless biographies, nor is it about his nemesis, Muḥammad Aḥmad ibn al-Saiyid ʿAbd Allāh,[3] who in May 1881 proclaimed himself the Mahdī,[4] and proceeded to lead the disenchanted in a bloody and ultimately successful attempt to throw off the yoke of Turco-Egyptian misrule. Ironically Gordon Pasha had been sent to effect precisely the same thing, ideally without further bloodshed. Neither is the book about William Ewart Gladstone, Islamic theology, colonialism or the history of the vast African space known as the Sudan, all of which are subjects which have been admirably covered elsewhere.

So far so good. *Beyond the Reach of Empire* is a military history: it *is* about Garnet Wolseley in the twilight of his career and seeks to refine our understanding of his military ability, his personality and his failings; it also describes a dramatic but these days somewhat overlooked episode in the history of the British Army and, in the process, reflects in some detail on the tactics and conduct of colonial warfare in the late nineteenth century. At the heart of the book, however, is to be found the story of the British officers and soldiers who in January 1885 departed the riverside town of Korti and set out on camels to fight their way across the Bayūda Desert. They would thus be short-cutting the 400-mile Great Bend in the Nile, a huge question-mark-shaped deviation in the river's otherwise straight-line course from Lake Victoria to the Mediterranean. They would emerge from the desert at the town of Metemmeh, a place of no great importance, then or now, where they could expect to marry up with a small flotilla of Gordon's steamers, in concert with which they would push south across the last 100 miles, defeat the Mahdī, relieve Khartoum and shield the evacuation of the garrison and loyalist citizenry.

In short *Beyond the Reach of Empire* is a detailed examination of the operations of Sir Herbert Stewart's 'Desert Column' – the culminating phase of the Nile Expedition and a subject which has not previously been afforded a book all of its own. I have tried not only to reflect the gallant deeds of the British, but also to give all due prominence to the extraordinary courage of the ordinary Sudanese *anṣār* who resisted them, and to acknowledge the undoubted military skill of the Mahdīst *amīrs*. It is these two factors which made the advance across the Bayūda Desert such an uphill struggle. While the first has been reflected by writers many times, not least within the accounts of those who were there, the second, the tactical guile of Mūsā wad Ḥilū and Nūr 'Anqara in particular, has been almost entirely overlooked. I am by no means convinced that the British officers present at Abu Klea ever quite understood that they had been led into a trap, but ensnared and surprised they most assuredly were – which is why the battle suddenly went so horribly wrong for them. They were fortunate that the last card in their hand was the indomitable British 'Tommy' and his bayonet.

While it is true that there are a few accounts of the Battles of Abu Klea and Abu Kru tucked away on less accessible library shelves, they are without exception wrapped inside something else, be it an autobiography of a great life, the story of Gordon and the siege, or broad-brush coverage of Wolseley and his grand expedition. Some authors have made so bold as to attempt all three of these things in the same book. As a result their writing did not, could not, incorporate substantive examination and analysis of the two fascinating general actions fought by the British Army in the Bayūda Desert. I concluded that there were two principal reasons why the fighting had not been addressed in any great detail. The first is that the complexity of the geopolitical situation in Egypt and the Sudan in the 1880s, considered in combination with the plethora of British, Egyptian and Mahdīst military operations preceding the relief expedition, has tended to consume authors' word counts at so prodigious a rate that more often than not there was next to no space left for what was actually the climax and the crux of the matter. Secondly, because Abu Kru and Abu Klea were fought by hastily assembled composite regiments, they became in the end nobody's property. Because they were not cherished by living regiments, they had been all but forgotten within a generation.[5] Time and again I have come across regimental histories which, to speak metaphorically, devote far more space to the 2nd Battalion's concurrent stint of garrison duty in Allahabad, than to the heroic endeavours of thirty or forty detached members of the regiment fighting for their lives in the Sudan. Small detachments do not of course return home with famous battle honours: hence, nobody's battles, nobody's heritage. British soldiers died in significant numbers all the same and have no less a claim to their rightful place in history than the widely extolled heroes who fell with their regiments at Waterloo, the Somme or El Alamein. The object of this book is to tell their story and bring their experience of battle to life.

But there is something else too. As we shall see, Sir Herbert Stewart's soldiers were amply possessed of courage, resolve and bloody-minded grit. Their story epitomizes everything that is good about the British national character. Nobody with the Desert Column was more courageous or resolute than Colonel Sir Charles Wilson RE the expedition's head of intelligence, a thoughtful, scholarly officer who, though he had a first-class brain and was regarded as an expert Arabist, was both light on charisma and short of combat experience. To some younger officers these were sins. In truth they were nothing of the sort. Instead they were but facts of life, which Wilson overcame, to put in a perfectly acceptable performance as a tactical-level commander.

It was Sir Charles who took command when Stewart was wounded and who subsequently battled his way through to Khartoum with a brace of 'penny-steamers' on the morning of 28 January 1885. It should have been General Gordon's fifty-second birthday. Instead it was, the history books tell us, 'Too Late!' – two days too late to be precise, for Khartoum had fallen and been given over to pillage, rapine and massacre in the early hours of the 26th. If it was surprising that the steamers had made it through to the confluence of the Niles in the first place, remarkable that they were able to survive the extremely heavy crossfire which greeted their arrival, and noteworthy that both vessels were fated to founder deep inside enemy-held territory on the return journey, the fact that Wilson and the great majority of his officers and men lived to tell the tale can be counted little short of a minor miracle.

Some weeks later, Wolseley made a concerted attempt to pin the blame for the failure of the relief expedition on Wilson, who could easily, it was asserted, have set off for Khartoum two days earlier than he did. The way in which Wolseley contrived to have Wilson's 'failure' raised in the newspapers and enshrined in the historical record was devious, simple and brilliant. For a long time I, like everybody else, blithely accepted the premise that the Gordon Relief Expedition had amounted to the narrowest of misses: that it was a matter of recorded history that it had arrived only forty-eight hours too late; that Wolseley did his best but was unlucky at the end. I know now that this is a contrivance. The book's other major object, then, is to give Sir Charles Wilson a fair hearing and present evidence which will permit the reader to make an informed judgement on just who was to blame for the failure of the Nile Expedition.

The conception behind the last part of the book is to lift the rocks for the reader, see what emerges and in so doing set the historical record straight. My reason for taking this tack is that it has been clear to me for some time that the facts of the matter have been much obfuscated over the years, including intentionally by Lord Wolseley, in whose case, I am prepared to own, it may have been a function of cognitive dissonance and a pathological fixation with reputation. I am not altogether convinced that his ego ever allowed him to understand just how disingenuously he began to behave after the fall of Khartoum, which is to say that in some sense he could not help doing what he did – that he lost control of both his reasoning and his sense of honour. Whatever the underpinning psychological reasons might have been, they drove the self-obsessed Wolseley to misrepresent what had happened in the Sudan. The result was an unwarranted and fundamentally unjust attack on Sir Charles Wilson's character, courage and judgement. But even if I can show that Wilson was unfairly blamed, the possibility would still remain that it was all down to the bloody-mindedness of Prime Minister Gladstone and plain bad luck in the field. Wolseley would be happy enough with such a verdict. But there was more to it than that. Military campaigns are not prosecuted by prime ministers or colonels, but by general officers. As I have, so to speak, already gone ahead of the reader, have already tried the case comprehensively and objectively in my own mind over the course of the past five years, and have duly arrived at a clear-cut set of findings, it would be futile to pretend that I intend to act as anything other than the prosecutor against Lord Wolseley. In laying out my case I have endeavoured not to make casual recourse to hindsight, but rather have attempted to represent the situation faithfully as the campaign progressed through all its key decision points. Wolseley's defence is to be found in his campaign journal (transcribed by Adrian Preston and published in 1967 under the title *In Relief of Gordon*), a document I would encourage anybody with a close interest in the subject to read, but not necessarily to take at face value.

In bringing these prefatory remarks to a close, I should like to take the opportunity to dedicate *Beyond the Reach of Empire* to the memory of the late Professor Richard Holmes, the perfect gentleman, senior TA officer, brilliant intellect and globally renowned military historian, under whom I several times over the course of my lifetime had the privilege to study. It is hardly necessary to extol the achievements and virtues of so well-known and so widely admired a figure. Suffice it to say, to be able to hold an audience of professional fighting men spellbound on the subject of war is a rare gift indeed, but Holmes's style and persona was such that he was able to pull it off as a matter of course. 'Enthralling' was Richard's default setting. His lecturing, writing and TV appearances inspired countless numbers of people to take a keen interest in history. I daresay much water will have to pass under the bridge before we see his like again.

Mike Snook
London
April 2013

Conventions Followed in the Text

I have chosen to transliterate Arabic proper names in conformity with Richard Hill's classic text *A Biographical Dictionary of the Anglo-Egyptian Sudan* (Oxford, 1951). The names of prominent figures in both the Mahdīst movement and the Egyptian Army, including Turks and Turco-Circassians, are in almost all cases rendered in accordance with his lead. I have made exceptions in the cases of 'Uthmān abū Bakr Diqna and Aḥmad 'Urābī Pasha or, as I have preferred, Osman Digna[6] and Arabi Pasha, whose importance in history has resulted in the anglicized forms of their names entering into common usage. As Arabic is a field in which I am supremely inexpert, I have been obliged to follow Hill slavishly, meaning that the blame for anything which was allowable in 1951 but considered passé or erroneous today is self-evidently mine alone. In the case of place-names I have given the typical transliterated Arab-Sudanese rendering at first mention, again mostly based on Hill, but have resorted thereafter to what I consider to be the most readily recognizable anglicized forms. It is worthy of note that 'Abu Klea' is meaningless to the inhabitants of Shendy and Metemmeh and that the adventurous traveller is best advised to ask for Abū Ṭulaiḥ, with a very distinct 'to' sound in lieu of what we westerners might in our naiveté be inclined to mistake for a 'k'. Spellings in quoted matter have been left in the form in which they originally appeared.

The matter of officer's ranks in the High Victorian Army can be confusing to the uninitiated and necessitates the adoption of some clear-cut conventions within the text. Acting rank, local rank and honorary rank are the least difficult to grasp and can be dealt with case by case as they crop up. Much more confusingly a good many officers held a substantive regimental rank, in which they drew their pay, and a 'brevet' or 'army' rank, quick-step promotions which would typically have been awarded for courageous conduct or distinguished campaign service. Save in so far as an officer in a brevet rank was always automatically junior to any officer holding the same substantive rank, there was nothing second-rate about a brevet. 'Brevet' was, so to speak, a silent word. (Brevet) Colonel Sir Charles Wilson was a colonel plain and simple. He was addressed as 'Colonel', he wore the rank badges of a colonel and he exercised the authority of a colonel.

Hence officers are referred to within the text in the rank which they wore on their uniforms, and by which they were known at the particular point in question. For example, the commander of the Desert Column, Brigadier General Sir Herbert Stewart KCB, ADC appears in the *Army List* of 1884 amongst the majors of the 3rd Dragoon Guards – the lieutenant colonel's and colonel's posts resting with officers who were his regimental seniors, but not necessarily senior 'in the Army', which is to say outside the close confines of the regiment. The practice followed by some historians of prefixing an officer's army rank with the word 'brevet', as if somehow to caveat his authority, is unsound, as anybody who had walked up to Stewart and addressed him as anything other than 'General' would swiftly have found out. Only in the appendices of this book is the word 'brevet' discreetly inserted as a prefix to officers' ranks.

Another potential source of confusion is the practice of rendering rank informally, as for example in the case of 'General Gordon' who was actually a major general and thus two grades junior to a full general. He was nonetheless referred to in the third person and written about as if he was a full general, although this was merely a reflection of the way in which he would have been addressed in person. Because the constant repetition of an officer's formal rank (e.g. lieutenant colonel, major general, etc.) can become wearisome to the reader over the course of a work of this length, I have, after invariably citing formal rank at the first mention of an officer's name, typically lapsed into informal renderings subsequently; thus Lieutenant Colonel the Honourable R. A. J. (Reginald) Talbot becomes simply 'Colonel Talbot', which is how the officers and men of the Heavy Camel Regiment would have referred to their 'OC' or 'officer commanding'. At the point at which I consider the reader will be comfortable with exactly who he is, I have even gone so far as to call him 'Reggie Talbot', which is how his peers and superiors would have referred to him.

It should be noted that 'brigadier general' was at this period an army *appointment* held by senior colonels and not a *rank* in its own right as is the case today. An officer holding such an appointment would be addressed and referred to as 'general', a practice still followed by many of the world's armies, albeit no longer in the British service where 'brigadier' has been adopted in its stead. Similarly 'brigade major', the brigade commander's right-hand man (or chief of staff in today's currency), was an appointment which might well be held by a senior captain, as was the case with the Earl of Airlie. It was actually the practice for much of the Victorian period to entrust the command of powerful, full-strength brigades not to brigadier generals, but to major generals.

In order to obviate the need for a ready-reckoner I have not rendered Egyptian Army ranks in their original Ottoman form, but in their closest English equivalents, making use also of the suffixes *pasha*, applied to brigadier generals and upwards, and *bey*, applied to colonels and lieutenant colonels.

Finally, I have retained imperial measures for distances in accordance with the conventions of the day. Artificially converting the intervals between Queen Victoria's soldiers into centimetres, or the sight settings on their rifles into metres, whilst I have seen it done, seems to me to be a peculiarly inappropriate thing to do. To young readers, I apologize in advance for any resultant air of mystery.

Chronology

The Course of the Mahdīst Uprising 1881–1883

Preliminary History

1820	Muḥammad Ali Pasha, the Ottoman ruler of Egypt, orders a Turco-Egyptian invasion of Sudan.
1833	Khartoum, a relatively insignificant village at the confluence of the Niles, is chosen as the colonial capital.
1843/4?	Birth of Muḥammad Aḥmad ibn al-Saiyid ʿAbd Allāh near Dongola.
1861–5	Sir Samuel Baker's exploratory expedition to southern Sudan.
1863–79	Reign of the Khedive Ismāʿil Pasha.
1863	Ismāʿil Pasha orders the suppression of the slave trade in Sudan.
1870	Muḥammad Aḥmad moves to Abā Island 160 miles south of Khartoum.
1870–3	Sir Samuel Baker serves as Governor of Equatoria.
1874	Colonel C. G. Gordon appointed in April as Governor of Equatoria in succession to Baker. War breaks out between prominent Sudanese slavers and the Sultan of Dār Fūr.
1875	Disraeli purchases 44 per cent interest in Suez Canal from a bankrupt Ismāʿil Pasha. The Khedive sends troops to join in the campaign of conquest being waged by the notorious slaver al-Zubair Raḥma Manṣūr (Zubair Pasha), against the Sultan of Dār Fūr.
1876	Gordon is elevated in December to be Governor-General of the Sudan.
1877–8	Russo-Turkish War.
1878	Gordon despatches Romolo Gessi to deal with a rebellion in the Bahr el Ghazal. It is led by Zubair Pasha's son, Sulaimān. Gessi victorious and executes Sulaimān.
1879	At Anglo-French instigation the Sultan deposes Ismāʿil Pasha for his financial profligacy. Accession of Méhémet Tawfīq Pasha, Ismāʿil's eldest son, as Khedive.

xxviii • *Chronology*

1880

January — Angry at the treatment of Ismā'il Pasha, Gordon resigns his post. Gessi follows. Muḥammad Ra'ūf Pasha succeeds Gordon as Governor-General.

1881

May — Muḥammad Aḥmad proclaims himself publicly as the Mahdī.

11 August — 200 Egyptian troops under Abū Su'ud routed by the Mahdī's *anṣār* followers at Abā Island. Rebels capture 120 rifles.

12 August — Muḥammad Aḥmad proclaims *jihad* against the Turco-Egyptian colonial regime.

Aug.–Nov. — Mahdīst long march south to Jabal Qadīr in the Nuba Mountains, in staged fulfilment of an ancient prophecy.

September — Beginning of nationalist-inspired disturbances in the Egyptian Army, under the leadership of Colonel Aḥmad 'Urābī Bey (Arabi Pasha).

4 December — Colonel Rāshid Bey Aymān, the Mudir of Fashoda, marches against the Mahdī with 400 troops and 1,000 Shilluk irregulars under Reth (King) Kaiku.

8 or 9 December — Battle of Jabal Qadīr: Rāshid Bey, Reth Kaiku and the German Carl Berghof (all KIA) are defeated by the Mahdīsts. Rebels capture 400 rifles.

1882

March — Brigadier General Yūsuf Pasha Ḥasan al-Shallālī marches from Khartoum with strong government force, but makes it no further than Kawa, where he remains inactive for some weeks. Ra'ūf Pasha is dismissed as Governor-General and temporarily replaced by Giegler Pasha (a German in khedival employ).

April — Senaar besieged by rebels in the *jazīra* under Aḥmad al-Makāshfī. Giegler Pasha takes the field.

15 April — Minor defeat of government irregulars near Messalamia. A further 150 rifles lost to rebels.

3 May — Giegler Pasha defeats Mahdīsts at Abu Haras on the Blue Nile.

11 May — 'Abd-al-Qādir Pasha Ḥilmī arrives in Khartoum as Governor-General.

25 May — Giegler Pasha wins a second victory in the *jazīra*, this time near Senaar.

7 June? — Battle of Massa (precise date uncertain). Having finally moved south from Kawa, Yūsuf Pasha's (KIA) force is routed by the Mahdī. 4,000 rifles lost to rebels. Tens of thousands of Kordofanis now flock to the Mahdī's standard.

11 June — Alexandria riots: massacre of Europeans and indigenous Christians.

Chronology • xxix

July	ʿAbd-al-Qādir Pasha raises additional irregular troops and concentrates existing military resources.
11 July	Admiral Sir Beauchamp Seymour orders naval bombardment of Alexandria. Captain Lord Charles Beresford distinguishes himself in command of HMS *Condor*.
28 August	Egyptian victory over the rebels near Duem.
September	When summoned to surrender El Obeid, the provincial capital of Kordofan, Major General Muḥammad Saʿīd Pasha Wahbī (Governor of Western Sudan) hangs the Mahdīst emissaries out of hand.
8 September	Failed Mahdīst assault on El Obeid: several thousand rebels killed. Town invested and starved until January 1883.
Late September	Battle of El Kona. Colonel ʿAlī Bey Luṭfī (KIA) defeated *en route* to Bāra with 3,000 troops by Jawāmaʿa Arabs under Raḥma Muḥammad Manūfal. Rebels capture 1,100 rifles.
13 September	Battle of Tel-el-Kebir. Following a night approach-march and dawn attack, Lieutenant General Sir Garnet Wolseley crushes the Egyptian Army. Colonel Herbert Stewart leads the cavalry pursuit to the gates of Cairo.
3 December	Arabi Pasha sentenced to death by Egyptian court martial; sentence is commuted to a comfortable banishment to British Ceylon.
1883	
2 January	ʿAbd-al-Qādir Pasha leaves Khartoum and leads an expedition into the *jazīra*.
6 January	Capitulation of Bāra: town surrendered to ʿAbd-al-Raḥmān wad al-Najūmī. About 2,000 rifles lost to rebels.
17 January	Major General Saʿīd Pasha capitulates at El Obeid, only to be murdered subsequently. Some 6,000 rifles and five guns are lost to the rebels.
February	Fundamentalist rule established throughout Kordofan and Dār Fūr.
13 February	ʿAbd-al-Qādir Pasha marches from Kawa to relieve Senaar, which is once again besieged by Aḥmad al-Makāshfī.
20 February	ʿAlāʾ al-Dīn Pasha Ṣiddiq arrives in Khartoum to assume ʿAbd-al-Qādir Pasha's civil duties as Governor-General. He is accompanied by Sulaimān Pasha Nyāzī, a Circassian general who is to be C-in-C Sudan.
28 Feb/1 Mar	ʿAbd-al-Qādir Pasha defeats the rebels near Senaar.
4 March	Egyptian irregulars defeat al-Makāshfī's rebels again.
7 March	Colonel William Hicks, late of the Bombay Army but now contracted to the Khedive as an Egyptian general officer,

	arrives in Khartoum as the nominal chief of staff to General Sulaimān Pasha Nyāzī.
3 April	Hicks Pasha leads the Soudan Field Force (SFF) into the field for the Senaar Expedition.
29 April	Battle of Marabieh; Hicks inflicts a heavy defeat on Aḥmad al-Makāshfī (KIA) and the *jazīra* rebels.
13 May	Hicks telegraphs Cairo declining to take responsibility for forthcoming Kordofan expedition unless given supreme military authority.
July–August	'Uthmān abū Bakr Diqna (Osman Digna) attempts to raise the Bīja tribes in the east, at first meeting with only limited success.
5 August	Osman Digna attacks Colonel Muḥammad Tawfīq Bey at Sinkāt and is repulsed.
22 August	General Sulaimān Pasha Nyāzī is appointed as Governor of the Red Sea Littoral; Hicks Pasha withdraws his resignation and assumes the mantle of C-in-C.
9 September	The 10,000-strong Kordofan Expedition departs Khartoum for El Obeid under the command of Hicks Pasha.
10 September	Tawfīq Bey scores a minor victory over the eastern rebels at Ghabbat.
20 September	Kordofan Expedition reaches Duem.
16 October	Major Muḥammad Khalīl and two companies massacred in the Khor Abent en route to Sinkāt.
4 November	A battalion-strength Tokar relief expedition under Brigadier General Maḥmūd Ṭāhir Pasha is routed at El Teb (known locally as Andatteib). The British consul for the Red Sea region, Commander (retd.) Lynedoch Moncreiff, is KIA.
5 November	The Shaikān (or Kashgil) disaster: Hicks Pasha and 'Alā' al-Dīn Pasha Ṣiddiq KIA; 10,000+ souls massacred; 8,000 rifles, fourteen guns and six machine guns lost.
Dec-Jan 84	Lieutenant Colonel Henry de Cöetlogon, one of Hicks's British officers, begins work to improve the 'South Front' defences at Khartoum.
2 December	Acting under the orders of Generals Sulaimān Pasha Nyāzī and Maḥmūd Ṭāhir Pasha, Lieutenant Colonel Kassim Bey (KIA) attempts a sortie from Suakin with a black Sudanese battalion but is defeated with heavy loss near Tamai.
19 December	Lieutenant General Valentine Baker Pasha, head of the Egyptian Gendarmerie, leaves Cairo bound for operations in the Red Sea Littoral.
23 December	Baker Pasha arrives at Suakin.

Beyond the Reach of Empire

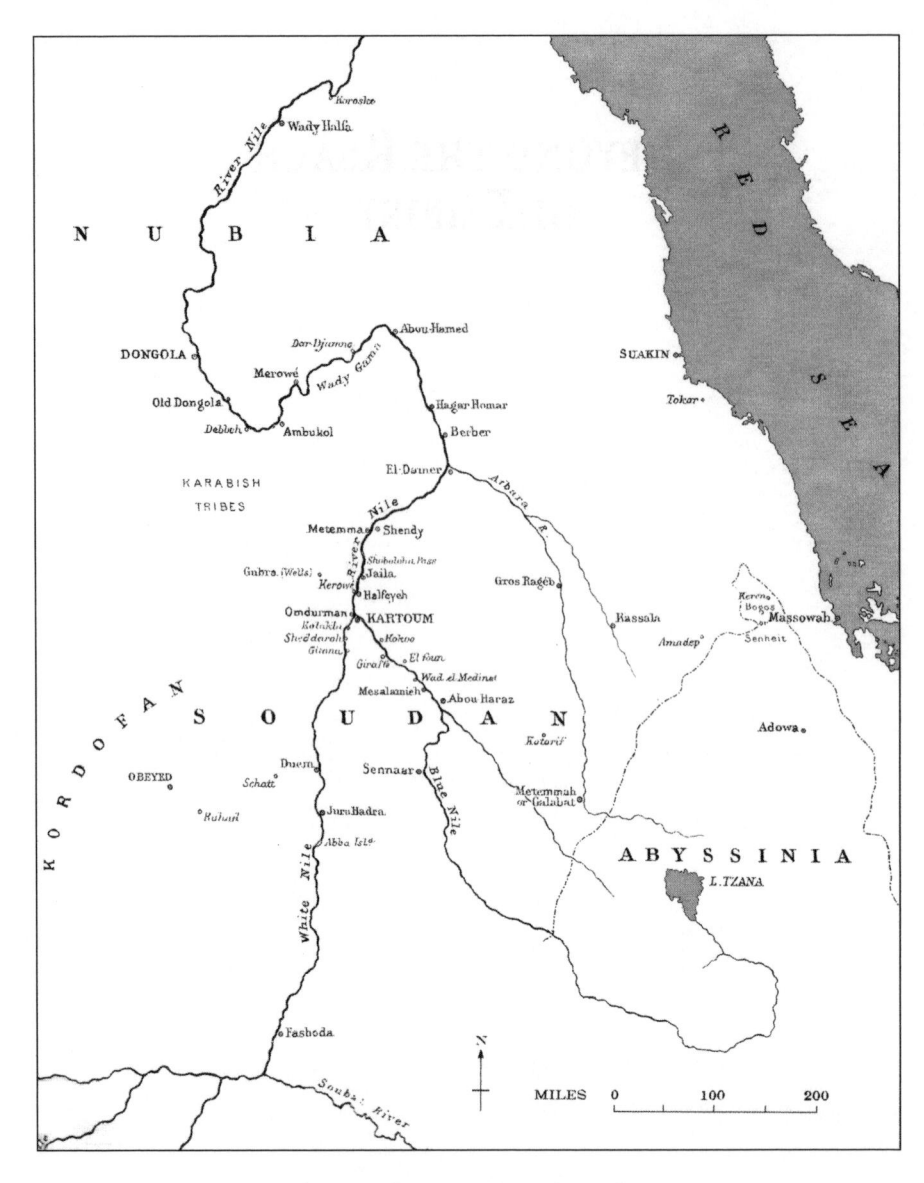

Map 1: Theatre of Operations – The Sudan 1884–5

Prologue

BY THE SPRING OF 1884 General Lord Garnet Wolseley was holding high office as the Adjutant-General, was widely regarded as Britain's most able soldier and, as a result of his lightning-quick conquest of Egypt, enjoyed a degree of global renown. Above him in the War Office hierarchy he need only kow-tow to the Commander-in-Chief, the Duke of Cambridge, and to the Secretary of State for War, Spencer Cavendish, Marquess of Hartington, later the 8th Duke of Devonshire. The Gordon Relief Expedition, which at first appeared unlikely by dint of Wolseley's great seniority to come his way, would in the end prove to be his last field command. It was also the only campaign in which he did not attain a notable victory. For a man pathologically obsessed with his reputation and standing, this came as the cruellest of blows.[1] It was never meant to turn out like that. The Relief of Khartoum was to have been a crowning triumph. Now, instead of a Wolseley–Gordon handshake on the jetty at the rear of the *sarāya*, a moment in history which was certain to have triggered an avalanche of congratulatory telegrams from the great men of Europe, America and the Colonies, gentlemen's studies and schoolrooms across the Empire would be adorned with an iconic painting set on the other side of the building – G. W. Joy's haunting portrayal of Gordon's last moments at the head of the palace stairs. Wolseley never quite got over it and for the rest of his life failed to accept one iota of personal responsibility for the campaign's unsuccessful outcome.

The Nile Expedition was of note for its dependence on what might be termed operational originality. Two measures in particular were characterized by Wolseley as 'novel expedients'.[2] The first was moving two brigades of infantry from Wādī Halfā to Khartoum aboard a fleet of specially commissioned whalers, small boats provided with both oars and sails, which were capable of carrying a crew of twelve and sufficient rations to sustain them for 100 days. This particular expedient had a sub-plot too: if 'Tommy' was not a natural boatman, Wolseley would provide him with helpers who were. A corps of civilian *voyageurs*, Native Americans and Canadian backwoodsmen, would be brought across from the New World to the Old to provide the Army with small-boat expertise. A second and smaller party of boatmen, made up of black African *krooboys* from the Gold Coast, would also be shipped around North Africa to Cairo. The presence of these contingents was owed to Wolseley's experiences in the Red River Campaign of 1870[3] and the Second Anglo-Ashanti War of 1873–4.[4] The second of his clever ideas would be providing his mounted brigade not with hardy Levantine ponies, but with dromedaries. There was much to commend both 'novel expedients', although they each had distinct disadvantages too. If one could strip out *time* as the single most important factor in the equation, Wolseley's campaign plan could probably be held up as a masterpiece of military improvisation and a classic exercise in achieving operational 'reach'. Unfortunately for the great man successful application of the military art relies not on grandstanding one's originality, but on the most important operational factors being afforded the prominence which is their due. From beginning to end it was always about the balance between time, risk and logistic sustainability. But the greatest of these was time.

The question of whether Wolseley's more innovative measures were indeed expedient, or instead amounted only to mere novelty, is not something we should try to address without having properly contemplated the evidence, although in the summer of 1884, before a boat had been built or a camel had been purchased, there was a positive rush to judgement. The campaign plan was deeply controversial and far from widely supported when its general outline became public. If the odd expression of doubt was articulated in the Home Army, there was positive dissent in the Army of Occupation in Cairo, while armchair generals, 'clubmen' and retired officers were moved to outright scorn, much of which they felt compelled to share with the newspapers.[5] Colonel William Butler, the architect of the whaler scheme, wrote, 'Day after day, the columns of the London Press held letters denouncing or ridiculing our arrangements.'[6]

Contrasting Military Careers: 1 – The Life and Times of Garnet Wolseley

At the opposite end of his distinguished career, the young Garnet Wolseley, then a frantically ambitious ensign in the 80th Regiment, first saw action against irregular, jungle-dwelling *dacoits* in the Second Anglo-Burmese War of 1852–3. His youthful conviction that there must surely be a direct correlation between battlefield gallantry and rapid advancement, resulted in his being both mentioned in despatches and badly wounded in his first fight.

Wolseley was descended from an old Anglo-Irish family well known for having done good service under William of Orange, since which time a good many Wolseleys had been drawn to soldiering. He was born at Golden Bridge House, County Dublin, on 4 June 1833, the eldest of seven children born to the unremarkable and recently retired Major Garnet Joseph Wolseley, and a young wife some twenty-five years his junior. Major Wolseley died when his eldest son was only seven, leaving his offspring to be raised in relatively straitened circumstances. There was no grand public-school education, nor was there money enough to buy the teenaged Garnet a commission. Instead, he and his mother set out to badger the ageing Duke of Wellington into granting the rare privilege of a Commander-in-Chief's bursary. After a number of their pleas had gone unacknowledged, they had all but given up hope, when the boy was appointed out of the blue to a vacancy in the 12th Regiment. The Army's newest officer was slightly built, was of average height at five feet seven inches tall, and had been brought up on all the worst prejudices of the Anglo-Protestant ascendancy. He was very determinedly not an Irishman and had no great fondness for those raised on the 'wrong' side of Ireland's great divide. He would quickly have learned to moderate his views, as just about all the regiments of Queen Victoria's army contained a significant proportion of Catholic Irishmen, who for the most part were good men and true.

Ensign Wolseley quickly arranged a transfer to the 80th Regiment, as it was bound for active service in Burma. Thus it came about that he was shot in the thigh, whilst leading an attempt to storm the stronghold of a *dacoit* chieftain called Myat Toon. He was fortunate not only to have avoided the ravages of a cholera outbreak which had decimated the British force during its approach march through the jungle, but also to have survived the return journey nursing a severe wound. Young Wolseley was promoted to lieutenant and sent home to Ireland to recuperate.

He next transferred into the 90th Light Infantry, which at the time was stationed in Dublin, but soon found itself committed to the second half of the Crimean War. Not long after he arrived in the theatre of operations, Wolseley was promoted to captain at the tender of age of twenty-one. Because all the action was to be found in the siege lines, he applied for secondment to the undermanned Royal Engineers. It was in the grim trenches before Sebastopol that he met and struck up a firm friendship with an impressive young officer of Royal Engineers called Charley Gordon, with whom he happened to share the same year of birth. Wolseley spent 1855 in the siege lines, where he consistently displayed conspicuous, if not foolhardy, bravery which ought to have seen him killed. Instead, he was wounded three times. On what proved to be his last day in the trenches, he and others were shredded by the gravelly contents of a wicker gabion upon which the Russian gunners had scored a direct hit with round-shot. Wolseley's head injuries were so severe that for a while it looked like he would be blind for the rest of his days. After a few weeks recuperating in hospital, he regained the sight in one eye and promptly returned to duty as a member of the headquarters staff. His other eye was indeed permanently blind, although there was no outward sign that this was so. In the summer of 1856 Wolseley helped organize the army's re-embarkation at war's end and was one of the last away from Balaclava harbour. If it was evident that he had evolved into a professionally competent and unswervingly brave young officer, it was also the case that by the time he left the Crimea he had grown psychologically habituated to the horrors of war.

In 1857 the 90th Light Infantry embarked more than 1,000 strong for China. Three of the companies, including Captain Wolseley's, sailed aboard the troopship *Transit*. The officer commanding embarked troops was Lieutenant Colonel Frederick Stephenson, whom we shall meet again. The vessel had to undergo repairs in Cape Town, where strangely there were rumours abroad that the sepoy regiments in India had mutinied, although no formal despatch to that effect had yet arrived. In all likelihood it was the imminent intention to mutiny which had found its way across the ocean with migrant workers. The *Transit* survived a succession of severe storms in the Indian Ocean, only to strike a rock and founder off the coast of Sumatra. The troops were able to scramble onto the reef without loss of life and were recovered in the ship's cutters to a nearby island. They were rescued by the Royal Navy, only to learn that the Bengal Army had indeed mutinied and that the main body of the 90th was already bound for Calcutta. Though not conventionally thought of as an India-hand, Wolseley subsequently marched up the Grand Trunk Road, passed through Cawnpore, where the evidence of Nana Sahib's abominable massacre of women and children was still fresh, and then participated in the Second Relief of Lucknow under the command of Sir Colin Campbell. Wolseley's company was the first to link up with the besieged garrison, somewhat to the chagrin of the army commander, who expected the honour to fall to the 93rd Highlanders – his particular favourites since the glorious 'thin red line' episode at Balaclava. Wolseley was involved in much of the subsequent heavy fighting in the environs of Lucknow. In the spring of 1858 he joined the staff of Sir Hope Grant, for operations aimed at the pacification of Oudh, during the course of which he took part in another half-dozen general actions. By the time the suppression of the Mutiny was complete he had made his way to lieutenant colonel, but was still four years shy of his thirtieth birthday, making him the youngest officer of his rank in the service. Wolseley remained on Grant's staff for the Second China War of 1860, participating in the action at Sin-ho, the storming of the Taku Forts, the fall of Tientsin and the Battle of Pa-to-cheau. He was present at the campaign's denouement when Peking fell.

Wolseley spent most of the 1860s as a staff colonel in Canada. During the course of the American Civil War, he took a long-leave and slipped unobtrusively through Federal territory to visit the Army of Northern Virginia. He was afforded a warm welcome and spent time in the company of Lee, Jackson and Longstreet, all of whom left a deep impression on him. He would later say that he had only two heroes in life: one of them was Gordon, but at the top of the tree was Robert E. Lee.

Wolseley's rise to public renown began not unnaturally with his first independent command, a relatively low-key affair of 1870, when he led the 'Red River Expedition' through the wilds of Manitoba to Fort Garry, scattering Louis Riel's irresolute Métis rebels in the process. Crucially it was a waterborne operation, in which great distances were conquered swiftly with the aid of small-boats and *voyageurs*. His fame was secured by the workmanlike Ashanti Campaign of 1873–4, in what is today Ghana. The fighting took place in a festering, disease-ridden forest environment and was invariably tense, confusing and physically exacting. Whenever the well-armed and numerous Ashanti pressed hard, it also became perilous in the extreme, as the British had no other recourse but to lock horns with them at terrifyingly short ranges. The victory was hard-won but resounding. No sooner had the Ashanti capital at Kumasi been torched than Wolseley turned back for the coast, so as to prevent his regular battalions being consumed by malaria.

On his return to England he was feted on all sides as the man of the moment. A parliamentary vote of thanks was accompanied by a cheque for £25,000, a sum sufficient to secure a gentleman's prosperity for life. He was invited to an audience with the Queen at Windsor Castle and later got to parade his Ashanti veterans in her presence. In 1875 he was sent to South Africa as the Lieutenant Governor of Natal, with the primary object of putting the colony's administration on a sound footing. It was not a lengthy tour of duty, but time enough nonetheless to develop a thoroughgoing dislike of rough-hewn Afrikaners. When, in the wake of the Russo-Turkish War, Disraeli persuaded the Turks to cede Cyprus to Britain, Wolseley was sent to take possession of the island and establish an administration there.

In the aftermath of the Battle of Isandlwana (22 January 1879), which saw 600 officers and men of the 24th Regiment annihilated by a Zulu army, the Duke of Cambridge shrewdly saw past the obfuscating despatches of Lieutenant General Lord Chelmsford, to conclude that it was his complacency which had in large part set the conditions for tactical-level disaster. The Duke's response to the crisis was to direct that Wolseley should proceed to South Africa and supersede Chelmsford at the earliest opportunity. On 4 July, with only a matter of days in hand, Chelmsford was able to conclude his uphill struggle by gaining a decisive victory at the Battle of Ulundi. He departed the theatre of operations immediately, leaving Wolseley to deal with the capture of King Cetshwayo and the imposition of a peace settlement. Later that year there was a hasty redeployment to the newly annexed Transvaal, to resolve a long-running conflict, inherited from the Boers, with Sekhukhune, the paramount chief of the baPedi. Although the tribe had earlier thwarted a succession of irresolute burgher commandos, they were ill-equipped to confront a coordinated British offensive. Following a futile defensive action around his principal kraals, Sekhukhune found himself bound for a prison cell on Robben Island.

The greatest challenge of Wolseley's career came when Gladstone, much against the general tenets of his political creed, ordered a full-scale military intervention in Egypt. Although Wolseley had not long since been appointed as the Adjutant-General, he was the only credible choice to be the commander of land operations and duly handed over his desk in Whitehall to a stand-in. Following a short but brilliant campaign of manoeuvre, he routed the rebellious Egyptian military at the Battle of Tel-el-Kebir (13 September 1882) and occupied Cairo the following day.[7]

Always an ardent advocate of professionalism and modernization, Wolseley had for some years been referred to by newspapermen and caricaturists as 'our only general'. He was notorious for making repeated use in his campaigns of the same circle of talented subordinates, referred to at first as the 'Ashanti Ring' and later as the 'Wolseley Ring'. Excluded rivals were less charitably disposed towards the chosen few and labelled them the 'Wolseley Gang'.[8] By the time the Khartoum crisis blew up, the great man was at the height of his powers and in his second year as Adjutant-General. There were few subjects upon which he was in complete accord with the Commander-in-Chief.[9] Since 1856 the venerated desk at Horse Guards, once that of the Duke of Wellington, had been occupied by Field Marshal His Royal

Highness Prince George, Duke of Cambridge, a grandson of George III and a first cousin to the Queen Empress. By 1884 the Duke was sixty-five years of age and more than a little set in his ways. To Wolseley he was an arch-reactionary plain and simple. Thirty years earlier, though, the Duke had commanded the 1st Division (Guards and Highland Brigades) in the Crimea, where he had experienced more than a whiff of grapeshot in the two great infantry triumphs at the Alma and Inkerman. Wolseley always sneered that he had been in a 'funk' at Inkerman, the Victorian Army's term for frightened and showing it.

Instinctively conservative he may have been but, contrary to the picture painted in Wolseley's private correspondence, the 'incompetent old crocodile'[10] was far from stupid. What is more he knew the Army inside out and cared passionately for its well-being. Ultimately the C-in-C and the AG were like chalk and cheese. Both possessed attributes which could drive the other to distraction. Perhaps unsurprisingly they were both capable of barking energetically up the wrong tree. The Duke had opposed the abolition of both purchase and flogging. On the other hand he had earlier enacted regulations to ensure that only mutineers and hard-core repeat offenders could ever be flogged, with the result that the incidence of corporal punishment had gone into steep decline long before abolition was imposed. Wolseley, for his part, not content merely with mobilizing the Ring every time he took the field, was also inclined to request the services of composite units of hand-picked men, a measure which the Duke perceived as prejudicial to the wider interests of the service. He had refused to accede to such a request for the Ashanti campaign which in the event was fought to a conclusion by perfectly ordinary battalions of the Royal Welsh Fusiliers, the Black Watch and the Rifle Brigade.

In a strangely curious way the bickering duo did not make an entirely ruinous or irreconcilable combination. In an age of military transition, when the best road ahead might not always be immediately apparent, it was by no means a bad thing to have the worst excesses of the arch-radical checked or choked by the caution of the arch-reactionary and vice versa. The Duke had no choice but to respect Wolseley's ability, while the rank of field marshal and the Duke's royal lineage similarly demanded due deference from the Adjutant-General. There were no shouting matches or tantrums in so formal an age and there were even times when they seemed to be rubbing along well enough.[11] Nonetheless, to an arch-snob like Wolseley, the Duke's private life was a matter for scorn. There was no Duchess of Cambridge, but there was Mrs FitzGeorge, a Drury Lane actress with whom the Duke had two illegitimate sons in the 1840s. The couple married in 1847, in contravention of the Royal Marriages Act, so that the Queen was both unable and unwilling to acknowledge the union. There had been a longstanding mistress too, Mrs Louisa Beauclerk, the true love of the Duke's life for more than thirty years, but she had passed away in 1882.

Wolseley's record of service demonstrated that he was innovative, a thoughtful planner and more than merely a safe pair of hands as a field commander. He had stepped down from the post of Adjutant-General to command in Egypt, but having stepped back up again his career as a fighting soldier seemed to have run its course. And yet his insatiable ambition and love of campaigning drove him to covet still more active service. It is no exaggeration to say that he could perceive only glory in war – that he was all but blind to its horrors. His 1862 visit to the Army of Northern Virginia had brought him into contact with men who were widely recognized as 'great captains' of the modern age. The problem for Wolseley's ego was that while he knew in his heart of hearts that he too was a great captain, he had only ever triumphed in what his Continental and North American contemporaries would have regarded as minor colonial skirmishes.

In the aftermath of the Second Anglo-Afghan War, fought in two bouts of hostilities between 1878 and 1880, Wolseley's jealously guarded pre-eminence in British military circles was threatened by the rise in the Indian service of Fred Roberts VC, or 'Bobs' as he was known, a nickname coined by the soldiery in Afghanistan and proliferated across the Empire by Kipling's verse. The burgeoning rivalry between the Queen Empress's greatest generals, driven in large part it must be said by the vainglorious streak in Wolseley's character – Roberts was much more the gentleman – goes some way to explaining why he strove quite so hard to shift the blame for the failure of his last field command, the Gordon Relief Expedition, onto the shoulders of others.

At the strategic level Wolseley successfully deflected the blame in the direction of the Prime Minister, possibly his least difficult piece of politicking, for in the unsophisticated court of public opinion Gladstone's protracted intransigence made for the shortest of trials and the easiest of convictions. As Lord Cromer (formerly Sir Evelyn Baring, the British Consul-General in Cairo at the time of the Nile Expedition) later so powerfully articulated in his *Modern Egypt*, it was not an altogether unreasonable verdict. 'In a word the Nile expedition was sanctioned too late, and the reason why it was sanctioned too late was that Mr Gladstone would not accept simple evidence of a plain fact, which was patent to much less powerful intellects than his own.'[12] A question mark remains over the extent to which this also takes care of what we would now call the operational level, as Gladstone did not dictate how the relief of Khartoum should be effected, and advancing along the Nile was not the only option on the table. That said, we should not lose sight of the fact that even by the beginning of August 1884 he had not yet given his willing consent to a relief expedition, and that it proved necessary at that juncture for Lord Hartington to force his hand politically.

At the tactical level Wolseley jabbed the finger of blame in the direction of an officer who, were it not for his involvement in the Nile Expedition, would otherwise have enjoyed a relatively obscure career, albeit by no means an unworthy one.[13] He was not slow to arrive at his judgement, but in his heart of hearts must have known that there was no formal case to answer, and that any impartial enquiry which delved too far into the detail would be bound to acquit Wilson and make some damning observations on his own management of the campaign. He resolved, accordingly, to salve his reputation by roundabout means.

Contrasting Military Careers: 2 – The Life and Times of Charles Wilson

Charles Wilson was born at 8 Wesley Street, Princes Park, Liverpool, on 14 March 1836. His childhood home was Hean Castle, situated on Carmarthen Bay, a few miles from Tenby, which Wilson's father, Edward, had purchased from his wife's family. Young Charles was educated at St David's School from the age of seven, the Collegiate Institute in Liverpool (later Liverpool College) from the age of nine, and Cheltenham College from the age of sixteen. In the school holidays he acquired a great fondness for field sports; he was only eight years old when he rode to hounds for the first time. In June 1854 the eighteen-year-old Wilson was sent to live in Bonn, in order to hone his German-language skills. He had always had an interest in joining the Army and hurried back from Germany after a year, on learning that the under-manned Royal Engineers was about to admit a special cohort of officers by examination. He sailed through the test papers and in October 1855 was commissioned as a lieutenant and called forward for young officer training at Chatham. In April 1857 he was posted to an engineer company stationed at Shorncliffe. A little over a year later he was transferred to Portsmouth to work on the Gosport defences.

In February 1858 Wilson was appointed to his first tour of duty overseas. The task of the North American Boundary Commission, a joint Anglo-US body, was to determine, chart and mark the ill-defined boundary between Canada and the United States from the Rockies to the Pacific. The 21-year-old Wilson was to act as the 'Secretary and Transport Officer', a post which entailed commanding a small party of Royal Engineers and toiling across the North American wilderness with convoys of pack-mules. Wilson was employed with the mission for more than four years, from April 1858 to July 1862. On his return to England he was posted to work on the Medway fortifications. In September 1864 he volunteered to lead a small privately sponsored expedition tasked with surveying Jerusalem. While engaged in his mapping work, Wilson developed a fascination for the cultures and ancient sites of the region and took up archaeology in his spare time. A return journey to the Middle East ensued in November 1865, at the behest of the newly formed Palestine Exploration Fund. Such was the quality of Wilson's survey work that, when he came home in June 1866, he was promptly elected to the fund's executive committee. His next official posting was to the Ordnance Survey of Scotland. In June 1867, at the age of thirty-one, he married Olivia, the daughter of Colonel Adam Duffin, late of the 2nd Bengal Cavalry. The newlyweds made their home at Blythefield near Inverness. A little over a year later Wilson sailed from Southampton at the head of the Sinai Survey Expedition (October 1868–May 1869). He might not be fighting his way around the globe like Wolseley, but he had at least grown accustomed to hard living in wild, dangerous corners of the world.

Between May 1869 and August 1876, the era of the Cardwell Reforms, Wilson undertook seven years of hugely significant staff work at the War Office. At the outset he was posted in the rank of captain to the Topographical Department in New Street, Spring Gardens, from which the Ordnance Survey, no longer of a purely military bent, had only recently been hived off. Still *in situ* were the Topographical and Statistical Sections, formed in the immediate aftermath of the Crimean War, of which Wilson now became the director. In addition to researching and printing accurate maps of places of geostrategic or developing interest, the department was meant to act as a fount of knowledge on foreign armies – to have an intelligence function in other words. Unfortunately the outbreak of the Franco-Prussian War served only to expose its inadequacies. Wilson's greatest contribution to the British service would be as an intelligence reformer. This was the period in his career which most historians of subsequent events in the Sudan have casually dismissed as 'office work', but it was much more than that.

There had been precious little harmony in War Office affairs in the period between the end of the Crimean War and the point at which Wilson took over the Topographical Department, not least because successive secretaries of state had concluded that the time had come to assert their primacy over the C-in-C and Horse Guards. Because the politicians had need of a properly functioning strategic intelligence branch, they more readily appreciated the potential of the Topographical Department than did their senior military colleagues at Horse Guards. But the generals still called the shots when it came to posting officers hither and thither and Wilson took over an organization which was undermanned, disorganized and not very good at its job. Working in the department's favour was that it had strong ties with the Staff College, an organization of comparable post-Crimean vintage, and had established itself as an attractive career path for intelligent and energetic officers from the engineer and artillery branches.[14]

If it was clear that the Topographical Department would benefit from a radical overhaul, it quickly became apparent that Captain Wilson was just the man for the job. A strikingly intelligent new arrival, Captain Evelyn Baring RA, an officer deeply committed to modernization and reform, would prove to be the perfect foil. Together Wilson and Baring pressed the Secretary of State for War to expand the role and responsibilities of their office. Cardwell appointed his Under Secretary, Thomas Baring, 1st Earl of Northbrook, a former Viceroy of India (1872–6), to look into the matter and in due course endorsed most of the recommendations of the Northbrook Report, a document in large part authored by Wilson. Cardwell pressed ahead and at the beginning of 1873 announced that the Topographical Department would henceforth be known as the Intelligence Branch of the War Office and would now have a major general at its head. A year or so later it became a branch of the Quartermaster-General's department. The first man to be known as the Director of Military Intelligence (DMI) was Major General Henry Brackenbury, who assumed the office on 1 January 1886 and occupied it for a period of five years. By the early 1890s the retitled 'Intelligence Department' enjoyed virtual autonomy and was of the first importance in matters of strategy and imperial defence. Brackenbury's role as one of the founding fathers of British military intelligence is well recognized, but less well remembered is that he was building on foundations laid by Captains Wilson and Baring in the first half of the 1870s.

On 23 May 1873 Wilson was promoted by seniority to major.[15] He had been one of only two serving officers in the Topographical Department when he began his tour of duty, but was one of 17 officers (supported by 11 military clerks and 14 civil servants), when in August 1876 it came to an end. Shortly afterwards he was made a Companion of the Bath in recognition of his services. Out of office hours he had remained heavily involved with the Palestine Exploration Fund, and by the time he left the War Office had been elected as a fellow of both the Royal Society and the Royal Geographical Society.

Wilson's new post was as the Director of the Ordnance Survey in Ireland, but he had caught the eye of many influential figures in London and after only two years in Dublin was diverted into the grey area between intelligence and diplomacy, to work on issues arising from the cessation of the Russo-Turkish War. He was first sent to be the British representative on a multinational commission tasked with fixing the boundary between Serbia and Turkey. In December 1878 he departed Belgrade to join a new network of British consuls-general deploying across Asia Minor, where Ottoman governance had come to be regarded as notoriously venal and hopelessly inept in equal measure. Widespread brigandage and inter-ethnic violence had contributed to an atmosphere of lawlessness, and was in large part to blame for the dire condition of the rural poor. Now the proposition was that the British consuls-general, military men all, would tender their advice to local officials and in the process strive to exert a beneficial moral influence over their districts. They were also to gather information and submit regular progress reports. They enjoyed no executive authority and where they were unable to make any headway were to report the local situation to the British ambassador in Constantinople, so that top-down pressure could be applied. In other words they were to work as both political officers and intelligence officers. Wilson's area was Anatolia. He was given four subordinate vice-consuls, amongst them Captain J. D. H. Stewart of the 11th Hussars and Lieutenant H. H. Kitchener RE, later to distinguish themselves in the Sudan. In practice the group was so widely dispersed that they saw very little of one another. Their mission was 'reform of the administration, the welfare of the people, and justice and protection for all classes without distinction of race or creed'.[16] It was a tall order for men who could never be more than sages, counsellors and honest-brokers. In April 1879 Wilson received a brevet promotion to lieutenant colonel.[17]

Between August 1879 and January 1881, he was virtually constantly on the move, covering vast distances on horseback, attempting always to dispense sagacity and goodwill wherever he passed. Contrary to the popular perception of him as an office man, Wilson diced with danger on a daily basis. He was allowed two months' leave in Britain between January and March 1881, at which point he returned to Turkey to continue his work. His reports had been consistently intelligent, thorough and perceptive and that summer his services were recognised with the award of a knighthood (KCMG). His substantive lieutenant colonelcy by seniority came with effect 31 December 1881.[18]

By the spring of 1882 the futility of a mere handful of men attempting to reform the administration of so vast an area had been recognized and the hard-riding consuls-general were on the point of being withdrawn. With Egypt in crisis and British troops already ashore, Wilson and two of his subordinates, Stewart and Chermside, received instructions to leave Turkey and report for duty under Sir Edward Malet, the British Consul-General in Egypt. Wilson arrived in Alexandria on 3 September to find that Wolseley had moved the bulk of his army to Ismailia, leaving Sir Evelyn Wood's brigade behind to screen the city and keep the enemy occupied. Two days later Wood took Wilson out to visit his deployed troops. An artillery exchange developed during the course of the day – the first occasion on which Wood's visitor had been under fire. A few days later Wilson received orders from Wolseley, instructing him to report for duty in Ismailia. There was meant to be a Turkish contingent coming to fight alongside the British and it would be Wilson's job to act as a political go-between when they arrived. When Wolseley's force advanced on Tel-el-Kebir, Wilson was not permitted to accompany it, but was required to continue holding himself in readiness at Ismailia. Of course the decisive phase of the campaign was to be so brief in duration that the Turkish contingent never did materialize.

As we have seen Wolseley defeated Arabi Pasha on 13 September and seized Cairo the following day. On 15 September Wilson was called forward to join the army headquarters. Wolseley saw him the following day, appointed him as his political officer and directed him to manage the victorious army's interaction with the Egyptian civil authorities. In addition to many other wide-ranging duties, Wilson was to assume responsibility for Arabi Pasha and a number of other senior captives. He was also to review the cases of the hundreds of prisoners unfortunate enough to have been incarcerated by the nationalists at the Citadel. It was Wilson who formulated the proposal to found a new Egyptian Army, under the leadership of a small cadre of British officers.

Wilson proved to be a considerate gaoler and spent the rest of the year concocting a pragmatic arrangement under which Arabi and his confederates would be arraigned before an Egyptian court-martial, admit a charge of rebellion, be sentenced to death, and then have their punishment commuted by the Khedive to banishment for life. It was a far more intelligent solution than the hanging widely anticipated by many of Wilson's colleagues. After the trial Sir Charles busied himself with organizing the departure of the detainees and their families for a comfortable exile in British Ceylon. On 27 December 1882, Arabi wrote to Wilson to express his gratitude:

I surrendered myself to the generosity and honour of the British people, feeling that I would be well treated at the hands of England. This hope has been realised. You have been to us all in the days of our captivity, kinder than a father to his children. Your constant care of us, your untiring vigilance on our behalf, your visits to us, the activity and kindness you always displayed in seeing that we should be treated with fairness and justice, have imposed upon us all a debt of gratitude which we can never sufficiently acknowledge.

> We hope, sir, you will accept the heartfelt expression of our gratitude and respect for you,
> *Ahmed Arabi, the Egyptian*[19]

Some months prior to Arabi's departure, the Earl of Dufferin, who had formerly been the British ambassador in Constantinople, arrived in Cairo to take office as the British political and diplomatic supremo. He knew Wilson well, had a high opinion of his personal qualities and duly co-opted him onto his staff as his principal political adviser. It is noteworthy that when, in January 1883, Dufferin became aware that Wilson was due to go back to Dublin as head of the Irish Ordnance Survey, he tentatively enquired how he would feel about going to the Sudan as Governor-General instead. At this juncture El Obeid was on the point of falling to the Mahdists, while the Hicks disaster was still some nine months away. In a letter to Lady Olivia, Sir Charles remarked that:

> I hardly know what to do; the Sudan is a tempting offer, it would be great work to pacify it, and it is a country which has a great future before it. A railway will probably be commenced this year, and I believe I could do good, as well as save enough in a couple of years to provide a good education for all the children. Then, on the other hand, it is utter banishment from you and the children, and, if anything happened in Europe while I was out of the way I would feel it terribly.[20]

In the end nothing came of the idea and in late February Wilson departed for Ireland as planned. His valuable service in Cairo was recognized with a brevet promotion to colonel dated 19 April 1883.[21] Lord Dufferin left Egypt in May, and four months later Evelyn Baring, no longer a soldier, relieved Malet as the consul-general. In the meantime Wilson followed the disastrous turn of events in the Sudan as best he could from Dublin.

Then, in mid-August 1884, he received a letter from Wolseley asking if he would be willing to serve as the Nile Expedition's chief of intelligence. Above all else Wolseley liked to surround himself with proven, battle-hardened heroes, although he also had it in him to admire cleverness. That he had asked for Wilson was a tribute to his intellect, his reputation, his experience of intelligence work, his empathy with the Islamic world, his understanding of the Arab mind and his industriousness. There could be no better candidate to head the Intelligence Department. Sir Charles left London on 3 September and sixteen days later reported at Wolseley's headquarters in Cairo.[22]

The Wilson Controversy

The Gordon Relief Expedition was a huge story in its day, even on the far side of the Atlantic. The *New York Times* reported to its readership that such was the public clamour in the environs of the War Office when the news of Abu Klea broke, that it was quite impossible to make headway through Whitehall for the crowds. The death of the martyr and the heroic struggle against the clock to save him survived in the popular imagination for a great many years. It became, as they say, a story 'known to every schoolboy'. As will be explored below the essential outlines of that story are of questionable veracity.

The romanticized outline of the Gordon Relief Expedition would, to take my own lineage as a metaphor, have been learned by my maternal grandfather in the Edwardian era, by my slightly younger paternal grandfather in the 1920s, by my father around the time of the Second World War and, to switch from metaphor to the literal truth, in my own case in the early 1970s, by which time only a minority of schoolboys would have been quite so interested in the heyday of empire as formerly. The story learned by three generations of Britons was that a lone British general, the heroic 'Chinese Gordon', somehow held out against the overwhelming military might of the Mahdī for almost a year, but despite the conspicuous gallantry of the Tommies sent to his rescue was killed only two days before the relief expedition attained its goal. 'Too late!' was the cry; even the great contemporaneous howl of grief raised by the newspapers had survived down the generations. I cannot say whether my forebears were as attentive to their history as young men as I was, but if they were they would also have known that the blame for the failure of the expedition lay with Prime Minister Gladstone, who dithered about sending British troops to Gordon's aid, and with some nameless colonel who likewise dithered needlessly on the banks of the Nile for two days, before eventually embarking aboard a brace of Gordon's steamers and setting forth on the final stretch of the journey. Of course two days' dithering and two days 'Too Late' went hand in glove. These then were the essential outlines of the story known to successive cohorts of schoolboys.

The hapless colonel, I later learned, was Colonel Sir Charles Wilson KCMG, CB, RE. I also came to recognize that it was a précis of Wolseley's version of events which had survived down the generations. By the time he made his journal entry of Saturday 6 June 1885, he had lapsed into denial and contrived a substantially fictitious interpretation of recent events:

My effort to relieve Gordon and the Khartoum garrison was a failure; an hour in such matters is as fatal as a month and therefore I have no right whatever to any reward. And yet such is life that I don't expect ever to do anything better in the way of plans than that formed to save Gordon, designed to make up for the valuable time dawdled away though Mr Gladstone's folly and ministerial incapacity. The conception from first to last was a most daring one, partaking of the romantic in many ways. Had it succeeded, it would have been I think the most memorable military event of the kind ever achieved. However it failed, and there is no use in crying over the few days, few hours indeed, by which it missed being a glorious success.[23]

Even a cursory examination of the Nile Campaign reveals that the historic reality was altogether more complex than Wolseley suggests. As I got older I read more, became a tolerably serious student of military history and joined the Army. Try as I might I could not as a military professional see what it was that Sir Charles Wilson had done wrong. The accusation of dawdling could only hold water provided the

Desert Column was positively engaged in a dash for Khartoum. While the 'story known to every schoolboy' clearly implied that this was so, the contemporary documentary evidence appeared, when one delved into the detail, to suggest otherwise. At length I drew the inference that Wilson had been very harshly treated. After that successive layers of the myth I had learned in school began to unravel.

To my eyes the evidence tended to suggest that ground-truth had been given a good hard spin long before it found its way into school texts and generalist history books. These duly went into print on the basis of a gross misinterpretation of the facts, which is to say that two days were all that separated Gordon from salvation. The notion is very directly reflected in Wolseley's journal entry for Friday 22 May 1885 where, anticipating his return to England, he observes, 'In what a different position I am returning home from that in which I went home in 1882. And yet I deserved success more in 1885 than in '82. Forty-eight hours too late at Khartoum has made all the difference!!.'[24] The premise was quickly adopted by Wolseleyites as the settled party line. At best it represented questionable subjective opinion, although plenty of perfectly honourable men were drawn into taking it at face value. But there is a case to be made that it actually amounted to a barefaced misrepresentation, intended to conceal an unpalatable truth – that those who had condemned Wolseley's seemingly eccentric campaign plan at the outset had been right all along.

The bibliography identifies history-defining books by Brackenbury (*River Column*, London, 1885), Butler (*Campaign of the Cataracts*, London, 1887), and of course Colonel H. E. Colvile's three-volume (Official) *History of the Sudan Campaigns*, published under the auspices of the Intelligence Division of the War Office in 1889, by which time Brackenbury had become DMI and Wolseley was still firmly ensconced in Whitehall as the Adjutant-General and the second-most-powerful soldier in the land.[25] It is instructive to note that neither Brackenbury nor Butler felt the need in their near-contemporaneous accounts to denigrate Wilson in any way, something which was also true of the memoirs they wrote late in life – works which in both cases post-dated Wilson's death. The same was also true of Sir Evelyn Wood's autobiography, *From Midshipman to Field Marshal* (London, 1906). Clearly the most senior members of the Ring felt no compulsion to support a whispering campaign against Wilson. Rather, the open criticism directed at him in the immediate aftermath of the fall of Khartoum emanated from three principal sources. First and foremost there was Wolseley himself, well supported by certain members of his staff; second, there was a vocal section of the press; and third, there was the disloyal chatter emanating from some of the younger officers who had served with the Desert Column.

Wilson first became aware that he was being set up as a scapegoat on 23 March 1885, some two months after the fall of the Khartoum, by which time the campaign was still afoot but had entered an operational pause. Unsurprisingly Wolseley had sought political direction from the Secretary of State for War following the tragic news from Khartoum. Gladstone, the 'Grand Old Man', or 'G.O.M.', as certain sympathetic sections of the press were given to calling him, was on the political rack at this juncture and was now being openly referred to as the 'M.O.G.' or 'Murderer of Gordon'. This was a period in which the Prime Minister was more often than not jeered at and booed whenever he appeared in public. Much to Wolseley's 'extreme astonishment'[26] his recommendations to the government were accepted in full: he was directed to resume his advance on Khartoum after the hot season and 'smash' the power of the Mahdī once and for all. He was asked what additional assets he would need and what could be done from the direction of Suakin on the Red Sea coast. There is little doubt that Lord Hartington, the Secretary of State for War, was pursuing the matter in all sincerity. Whether Gladstone, the arch-politician, was quite so sincere is another story. On 13 April 1885, by which time the political firestorm over Khartoum had abated and Afghanistan had begun to dominate the foreign news, Hartington telegraphed Wolseley indicating that the government was likely to change its mind, an intimation confirmed on the floor of the House of Commons some eight days later.[27]

The so-called 'Pendjeh Incident' of 29 March 1885, which saw Russian and Afghan troops clash on the Kushk River, provided the backdrop to the government's change of heart. A war scare developed, in consequence of which it was argued that the Army could ill-afford to be distracted by on-going operations in the Sudan. It was in many ways the perfect excuse for disengagement, a policy which both Wolseley and Wilson alike regarded as foolish. Wilson predicted that if the British disengaged it would inevitably become necessary to return to the Sudan at some future point in order to break up the Mahdīst movement.[28] So 23 March, the day on which Sir Charles received his rude awakening, preceded the Pendjeh Incident by a week and the cancellation of the renewed campaign by not quite a month. As yet oblivious to the coming u-turn, Wolseley still had his headquarters at Korti and was supervising the withdrawal of his force to rough and ready summer quarters in the riverside towns and villages of Dongola Province. His correspondence with Lady Louisa at this period shows that he was both tired and dejected.

Wilson was also present at Korti and was stunned on the day in question to receive a note from Wolseley requiring a written explanation of the two-day delay in setting off from Metemmeh for Khartoum. He wasted no time in drafting a robust and compelling report dated the same day. It concluded, 'No one can regret the untimely death of General Gordon more than I do, or could have been more anxious to relieve him, but I do not think that any action of mine could have saved his life or averted the fall of Khartoum.'[29] It is obvious from the tone of Wilson's report that he felt wounded by the necessity to account for his actions, a fact amply confirmed by a private letter to his wife penned later the same day:

> I see I am to be made the scapegoat for this failure. Even Lord Northbrook in his speech on the Vote of Censure assigns me a role which the Government distinctly refused to allow me to play. He tries to make me a political agent, whereas they insisted on making me a staff officer under Lord Wolseley. Being on active service I cannot resign, though I clearly

see that the political part of the Sudan question is going to end in a fiasco just as the Zulu settlement did and, in my position, I am unable to prevent it.

You must not trouble about my not being praised by the Chief [Wolseley]; I care nothing for it, but I did care very much when I found he had discredited the account I brought of the fall of Khartum and the death of Gordon.[30]

If Wilson regarded this as the beginning of his nightmare then he was slow to catch on, as the hare had been set running in London anything up to a month earlier, albeit by highly irregular means.

Wolseley was devoted to his wife and knew her foibles well. In a letter written in the immediate aftermath of the fall of Khartoum, he confided to Lady Louisa that he could barely stand to be in Sir Charles Wilson's presence.[31] He knew of course that she was active in high society and frequently drew on his letters to gossip about events at the front in the best London drawing rooms.[32] Indeed, something around three weeks earlier she had remarked in one of her letters that ever since the news of the fighting in the Bayūda had broken, their Hill Street home had been subject to tea-time invasions by 'Camel Corps mammas',[33] the mothers, wives and fiancées of officers serving with the Desert Column, many of whom came from the smartest, best-connected families in the land. If Lady Wolseley was as good a gossip as her letters suggest, then the fact that her husband held Wilson to blame for Gordon's death must have been spreading through London society within days of her receiving the offending letter.

By now Sir Gerald Graham's Second Suakin Campaign was in full swing in the Red Sea Littoral: the Battle of Hashīn was fought on 20 March, and the Battle of Tofrek two days later. With his campaign on the Nile stalled for a few months, Wolseley decided the time had come to visit Graham and set out for Cairo on 30 March.[34] He did nothing with Wilson's report until 13 April, by which time he had gained the Egyptian capital. At this point he composed a short, sniffy covering note and despatched the two documents for the attention of the Secretary of State for War:

> Cairo,
> 13th April, 1885
>
> My Lord,
>   I have the honour to forward a letter from Colonel Sir C. Wilson, R.E., giving the reasons for the delay in the departure of the steamers from Gubat.
>
>   I do not propose to add any remarks of my own to this letter. The reasons given by Sir Charles Wilson must speak for themselves.
>
>   I have, etc,
>   *Wolseley*,
>   General

Even as Wolseley was sat at his desk penning these words, Lord Hartington was sat at his, drafting the telegram heralding the coming governmental u-turn, thereby putting paid to any dreams Wolseley might still be harbouring of a redeeming victory yet to come.

It was the inclusion of one little word in the last line of Wolseley's note, the word 'must', which sets the tone of the document and conveys its connotation; dispense with it and the meaning would otherwise be entirely supportive. That the report should be asked for in the first instance and then subsequently be forwarded to the Secretary of State for War shows that this was no mere chance grammatical ambiguity. It was subtle, non-actionable, but quite intentional and the inference was clear. Because it was an official report Wilson's submission was published in a Parliamentary Blue Book and entered the public domain on 20 May 1885.[35] The following day his justification of his actions received nationwide press coverage.[36]

The interview of 23 March and its aftermath was when Wolseley showed his hand. Careful examination of his campaign journal reveals, however, that it had been preceded by a behind-the-scenes attempt to besmirch Wilson in the eyes of the Secretary of State for War – and for that matter for posterity, as sooner or later almost all military despatches of significance ended up in the public domain. Writing in his journal on Tuesday 17 March, Wolseley noted:

A telegram [has arrived] from Hartington saying my despatch in which I describe Wilson's proceedings when en route from Goubat to Khartoum and back casts a slur upon Sir C. Wilson & that he cannot publish it until Wilson has had a chance of rebutting the slur. The fact is, I pass no comment whatever upon Wilson, but my despatch shows up the Govt. very strongly & the Cabinet does not therefore want it published. I have replied, I did not see how despatch blamed Wilson & that I wished it published in justice to myself & to those under my command. Several of my recent despatches will be disagreeable reading to Govt. and I must have them published in vindication of my reputation as a General and of this Army the men of which have done all that men could do to carry out my plans. I foresee some trouble with Hartington on this score.[37]

It was almost certainly this exchange with Hartington which precipitated Wolseley's demand of six days later that Wilson formally account for his actions. In this particular journal entry we get to see Wolseley's fixation with his reputation paraded in all its nakedness. Here too we see how he is strongly inclined to regard all other men as fools, for there can be little doubt that Hartington's objection was both sincerely motivated and firmly grounded in Wolseley's spiteful inferences. No doubt the slur referred to by Hartington was subtle and deniable, much like the one Wolseley would shortly employ in the icy covering note of 13 April.

It would be difficult if not impossible for anyone to read Wolseley's journals and come away from the experience filled with admiration for him. His vanity, self-obsession and arrogance leap from the page with almost every entry. The frankness with which he writes does have a thousand-and-one historical uses, however. In this instance we are able readily to trace the officers who contributed to his hostility to Wilson. One of the culprits was Wilson's namesake, Lieutenant Colonel Mildmay

Willson of the Guards Camel Regiment. In writing up his journal on Wednesday 11 March, Wolseley launched into a cruel tirade:

Mildmay Wilson [sic] of the Scots Guards dined with me, and as I know him to be a good sensible man with plenty of nerve and pluck, I gently drew him out on the subject of the delay in sending the steamers to Khartoum. It seems there were about four hours lost in moving the square forward to the river. The camels were laden several times & every preparation made for marching upon the Nile, but as often were counter-orders issued.

Kasm el Moose [sic] with 4 steamers arrived at Goubat about 9.00 a.m. on 21st Jany. & two steamers might have started that afternoon for Khartoum: instead of doing so they did not start until 8.00 a.m. on the 24th Janry. and then only went a few miles (about 13) when they halted for the night to take in wood although they had plenty on board.

Sir Charles Wilson is clearly responsible for all those delays, but poor devil he had lost any nerve he ever possessed: Abu Klea did for him in that respect: he must never again be employed on active service: the Irish [Ordnance] Survey is better suited to men of his mettle. It is too dreadful to think of the fearful consequences that have resulted from his unfitness. He could have reached Khartoum quite easily on the 25th Janry. & had he done so, Gordon would still – in all human probability – be still alive.

Great God, it is too dreadful to dwell upon the hairbreadth by which we failed to save Gordon and Khartoum. I still think if Stewart had not been wounded, we should have saved Khartoum. Is it then to be wondered at that I hate the sight of Sir C. Wilson? I have asked that he may be recalled as wanted for his Survey, and when he goes, I hope I may never see him again. He is one of those nervous, weak, unlucky creatures that I hate having near me on active service; yet he is clever.[38]

Wolseley had received the news of the fall of Khartoum nine days after the fact, on Wednesday 4 February. He had thirty-seven days to come to terms with the failure of his campaign before he made the spiteful and unjust remarks quoted above. Such was the deep-seated and unshakeable arrogance of Garnet Wolseley.

There is a clear inference that Mildmay Willson was asked leading questions, so it is only fair to point out that he may have inadvertently reinforced the worst of Wolseley's prejudices. The same cannot be said of Captain Charles Berkeley 'Bloody-Minded' Pigott, a company commander in the Mounted Infantry Camel Regiment, who was the first officer to gain Wolseley's headquarters in the aftermath of the Battle of Abu Kru. As we shall see Pigott was a fearless blood-and-thunder merchant of the sort greatly admired by Wolseley. He arrived at Korti at 3.00 a.m. on Wednesday 28 January, at which point he was immediately interviewed by the anxious army commander who had received no news of the Desert Column for more than a week.[39] It follows that any interpretation recorded in Wolseley's journal that day is entirely grounded in Pigott's opinions:

Wilson has proved a great failure as a soldier: he succeeded to command when Stewart was wounded. On 21st instant Wilson made a foolish reconnaissance of Matammeh moving his men about in square and then fell back, a line of conduct that of course has encouraged enemy. During this silly operation four steamers arrived from up river, landed men and guns to cooperate in attack on village...[40]

Recorded in these two journal entries is the substance of the case against Wilson. He was nervous, weak, vacillating and even afraid. He was unfit to command; his operations were so 'foolish' and 'silly' that they encouraged the enemy; he was a 'great failure'; he lost his nerve at Abu Klea; he was responsible for a four-hour delay in advancing at Abu Kru; he could readily have started for Khartoum on the afternoon of 21 January; it was his fault and his alone that the expedition had failed. Such was his negligence that he might as well have murdered Gordon by his own hand. True, part-true or wicked calumny?

In May 1885 the prestigious periodical the *Fortnightly Review* published an article entitled 'How We Lost Gordon'. The author was the well-known war correspondent Charles Williams, who had accompanied the Desert Column into the Bayūda as the representative of the *Daily Chronicle* and the Central News agency. Not quite thirty years earlier, in 1856, the eighteen-year-old Williams had participated in a filibustering expedition mounted from New Orleans for the relief of 'General' William Walker, the notorious freebooter who had installed himself as the president of Nicaragua. Following the military rout of the expedition Williams was repatriated to England, where he enlisted in the burgeoning Volunteer movement and underwent military training. The first campaign he covered as a war correspondent was the Franco-Prussian conflict of 1870–1. After having worked as the editor of the *Evening Standard* for a few years, he again took the field to cover the Russo-Turkish War. In the autumn of 1878 he accompanied the British advance on Kandahar at the commencement of the Second Anglo-Afghan War. He was the editor of the *Evening News* at the time of the Egyptian intervention and in his running commentary on the campaign predicted the timing and mode of Wolseley's attack on Tel-el-Kebir some sixty hours in advance.[41]

Although the article was published in May, it had been in fact been written and signed off at Korti on 9 March. 'How We Lost Gordon' was stridently hostile to Wilson: after attacking his character, military pedigree and lack of combat experience, Williams went on to insist that had he pushed on from Metemmeh with all possible speed, Gordon would undoubtedly have been saved. In a remarkable personal attack sustained over more than 6,000 words, Williams asserted that Wilson had lost his nerve and turned the steamers far too early to be certain of Gordon's fate; this particular piece of intelligence he attributed to the Royal Navy 'bluejackets' and members of the twenty-strong Royal Sussex detachment which had been aboard the steamers. Williams then proceeded to 'prove' his point by observing that no casualties had been incurred in the fight at the confluence of the Niles, a statement which, whilst it was true of the British personnel, did not apply to the loyalist Sudanese. We shall see in due course that 'How We Lost Gordon' directly contradicted a number of earlier generous observations on Wilson's conduct incorporated by Williams in his *Daily Chronicle* coverage of the Battle of Abu Kru.[42]

A number of other newspapers, all of them sympathetic to Gladstone but ill-placed to judge the truth of the matter, took up Williams's refrain. At Korti, meanwhile, a telegram from home advised Wilson that the attack in the *Fortnightly Review* had taken place,[43] although it remains unclear whether he actually got to see the full text of the article prior to returning to England. A good many newspapers chose to spring to Wilson's defence.[44] The 20 May publication of the Parliamentary Blue Book enclosing both Wilson's explanation of 23 March and Wolseley's covering note, followed hard on the heels of the May edition of the *Fortnightly Review* and served to fuel the fire kindled by Williams. The 21 May edition of the *Sheffield and Rotherham Independent*, though only a provincial publication, provides an excellent example of just how much heat the affair generated that summer:

Lord Wolseley's curt refusal to make any comment upon the report, and his dry remark that Sir Charles Wilson's reasons must speak for themselves admit, obviously, of two diametrically opposite interpretations. But whether this be intended as praise or censure, we see no reason why others should display the same reticence, and, for our own part, we are bound to say that Colonel Wilson's apology [sic – it was hardly that] is altogether unsatisfactory, and signally fails to remove the grievous belief that when Gordon was still within reach of prompt succour, the golden opportunity of relieving him was lost through inconceivable dawdling, and through a want of push so deplorable as to be little short of criminal.[45]

According to his biographer, Colonel Sir Charles Watson, Wilson received a great many letters of support from friends and acquaintances over the ensuing few weeks, 'expressing in strong language' how angry they were at the unfounded accusations which had been levelled against him.[46] On the same day that the editor of the *Sheffield and Rotherham Independent* ran amok with Wilson's reputation, the London based *Standard* took a more perceptive tack, condemning the very fact that the government had seen fit to publish Wilson's defence of his actions.

Is it intended that Sir C. Wilson is to be tried before the bar of public opinion, and acquitted or condemned, not only informally but without evidence taken on either side? And is military discipline to act or hold its hand, moved by a mere gust of popular displeasure or checked by popular good nature, like the victorious gladiator of an old Roman Amphitheatre? The whole proceeding appears to us eminently unsatisfactory. We should be sorry to accept the bait thrown to the public and condemn or acquit an officer who has not even been charged by the authorities with any offence. But this we may say – that the day or two lost or saved at the end of a long operation, which lingered over several months, cannot, and must not, be allowed to make us forget the far longer delays and hesitations which preceded the expedition.[47]

Other London papers, such as the *Morning Post*, merely quoted extracts of Wilson's explanation without making any editorial comment, a seemingly neutral stance which actually served to favour Wilson.

Free at last to come home, Sir Charles reached Cairo on 8 June and two days later embarked at Alexandria for Venice. While he was journeying across the

Continent, Gladstone's administration was in the process of collapse and duly fell on 9 June 1885. By the time Wilson landed in England eight days later, a Conservative government had taken office with Lord Salisbury as Prime Minister and W. H. Smith as Secretary of State for War. The new government gave brief consideration to reversing its forerunner's decision to disengage from the Sudan. Wilson was summoned to see Smith, so that he could give his view of the matter.[48] Like Wolseley, Sir Charles believed that the security of Egypt demanded that Mahdīsm should be crushed without delay. In the end, however, the new government was forced to conclude that the evacuation of Dongola had gone too far to be reversed and that it had no choice but to persist with a policy of abandonment. The Secretary of State for War telegraphed Wolseley confirming this on 2 July 1885.[49] It was around this period, most likely on 20 June, that Muḥammad Aḥmad died, most probably of typhus but conceivably of poisoning,[50] to be succeeded by the Khalīfa 'Abd Allāhi.

The day after Wilson landed in England, General Sir Lintorn Simmons, the Governor of Malta, felt moved to send him a long, perceptive and forcefully expressed letter of support.

> Of course if possible a scapegoat must be found. I have just read your report of March 23rd and Lord Wolseley's letter forwarding it to the Secretary of State. No doubt that letter may be read in two ways. 'Your reasons which speak for themselves' may be satisfactory or the reverse. But there can be no doubt that the tone of that letter is contemptuous, and intended to let the blame of failure rest on you.[51]

Simmons concluded his observations with, 'I write this from deep conviction and in the firm belief that the dastardly act of trying to make you the scapegoat will, ere long, meet the reward and exposure it deserves.' It is in large part because he was not entirely right on this last point that *Beyond the Reach of Empire* revisits the Khartoum crisis, with the aim of establishing and asserting the objective truth.

On Monday 22 June Wilson gave an interview to a sympathetic representative of the Press Association[52] in which he remarked of Williams's criticisms, 'There is hardly one correct statement in the whole article.'[53] There then followed a twelve-point repudiation of the allegations, which appeared in a question and answer format in the *London Daily News* and certain provincial papers the following day.[54] Because his 23 March report to Wolseley had been published and widely discussed in the press so soon after the May edition of the *Fortnightly Review*, Wilson used the Press Association interview to correct the apparently widely held misconception that his report had been written specifically as a response to the Williams article.

On Tuesday Williams sent a lengthy and strongly worded telegram to the Press Association in which he stood by his remarks and disputed everything Wilson had said. The text of his telegram was carried in newspapers across the country the following day.[55] He began by disputing the point on the Nile at which Wilson had ordered the steamers put about, first noting that Lieutenant Stuart-Wortley had told him that they had been, 'near the south end of Tuti Island'. Williams next quoted an article he had read in the *Daily News* the day before. It had been written by Colonel (Retd.) the Hon. John Colborne, who had gone to Khartoum as a member of Hicks Pasha's staff in the summer of 1883, but had not in the end accompanied the ill-fated Kordofan Expedition. Colborne had since turned his hand to the role of war correspondent and in January 1885 had accompanied the River Column forward of Korti. Wolseley's journal entry for 10 January observes that he was representing 'some German Illustrated Paper',[56] although he also seems to have been in the employ of the *Daily News*, which in addition to Harry Pearse's coverage of the operations of the Desert Column also carried reports from a special correspondent who had been present at the Battle of Kirbekan. Colborne's article of 22 June had reprised a lengthy account by a Greek who had survived the fall of Khartoum, from which Williams had cherry-picked a few choice words in his turn:

> The Greek, whose statement has been sent home by Colonel Colborne from Dongola to the Daily News, says – 'The steamers arrived at Halfiah. I saw them about one mile and a half from Khartoum: they turned back directly.' How about reaching the junction of the Blue and the White Niles now?

In fact Ḥalfaiya was about three miles from the confluence of the Niles (not that the steamers had turned there anyway),[57] but Williams had evidently failed to realize in any case that in order for there to be a very large island at the confluence of the Niles, there must perforce be two river junctions. He was also directly disingenuous in punctuating the passage in question with a full stop. In reality the Greek's narrative ran,

> The steamers arrived at Halfiah. I saw them about one mile and a half from Khartoum. They turned back directly; but I say this – if they had come on then every man would have been destroyed.[58]

This did not convey anything like the same connotation. Evidently a man who had to have the last word, Williams continued his selective rejoinder in breathtakingly arrogant vein:

> If the presence of our English officers, a detachment of the Royal Sussex, and a number of black troops, with a quantity of grain aboard the steamers, would not in effect have been a relief of Khartoum, words seem to me have lost their meaning . . .
>
> Under the tenth head Sir C. Wilson states that he was not induced by anybody to leave the zariba and march to the Nile on the 19th of January. Perhaps he will deny that he was told by an officer that if he would not form the camp on the Nile that officer would do it on his own responsibility . . .
>
> Perhaps if he desires to continue the controversy he will make public the terms of the correspondence from Lord Wolseley to which his paper of the 23rd of March was an answer. I have said Sir C. Wilson disobeyed written orders. I say so again. To disobey orders about which there could be no mistake used to be a high military offence. I suppose it is not now.[59]

We will return to contemplate the matter of orders in due course.

On Saturday that same week, Williams himself came under heavy fire when the *Saturday Review* published an article entitled 'The War Correspondent':

> There is no need to enter here on the merits of the dispute between Sir Charles Wilson and Mr. Williams: neither would it be just in the absence of information which will not easily be got at in our time. What we have to deal with here is the illustration the quarrel affords of the evils arising out of the presence of war correspondents with our armies. On the one side is the servant of a newspaper – a private speculation, which exists to sell – who rushes into print to accuse an officer of gross negligence. On the other hand is an English general [sic], who has allowed himself to be provoked into a wordy war, and has condescended to give and take the lie by merely entering into the dispute. Sir Charles has proved how low the standard of professional pride in the army has sunk. At an earlier period it would have been a matter of course to a gentleman in his position that he had no answer to give except to his official chiefs.[60] Mr. Williams cannot be said to have offended against professional etiquette. It was his business to produce an effect –the more striking the better. He has succeeded. We think it will, however, prove that one of the means he has selected to attain this effect should not be forgotten. It throws a useful light on a war correspondent's work in the army. On his own showing, then, Mr. Williams has accused Sir Charles Wilson of gross misconduct chiefly on the authority of private soldiers. He has gone to the ranks in search of ill-natured and partially mutinous gossip about a commander . . . it is unnecessary to explain that the existence of people engaged in this sort of intrigue in a camp is destructive of all discipline . . . The lesson will be learned if the next of the tribe who is caught at this trick is sent back to the base of operations tied by the wrists to the tail of an ammunition wagon.[61]

Williams dined that evening with fellow members of the 'Gallery Lodge of Freemasons'. After dinner the 'worshipful master', W. M. Duckworth, proposed a toast to brother Williams who happily, Duckworth observed, had recently returned safely from the Sudan. Williams was then invited to speak. There was only limited reporting of the speech, but what little exists shows that Williams claimed that those who knew him well could not possibly apprehend that he had intended to make a personal attack on Sir Charles Wilson, and that the 'sole purpose' of his article was to convey the lesson that officers who had spent the bulk of their careers in diplomatic appointments should on no account be permitted to succeed to a field command in the face of the enemy. Williams then proceeded to repeat a point he had made in the *Fortnightly Review*, by singling out the Guards and the Royal Engineers as corps where officers of that ilk were to be found in abundance. This, then, was the gist of the speech as reported in the press the following Monday.[62] Assuming it constitutes a reasonably accurate précis, Williams very plainly misrepresented what he had written back in March, as there can be no doubt that his article incorporated a multi-faceted, sustained and vicious personal attack on Wilson.

The following Saturday (4 July) Williams went to the Bow Street Police Court to initiate libel proceedings against Alexander James Beresford Hope, the proprietor of the *Saturday Review*.[63] Cleverly, he argued that 'The War Correspondent' contained an inference that he had committed a criminal offence in military law by eliciting insubordinate remarks amongst the troops in respect of a superior. The case would not come to court until late October 1886.

It can be no mere coincidence that Captain Fred Gascoigne's account 'To Within a Mile of Khartoum' appeared in the July 1885 edition of *The Nineteenth Century*, suggesting that it would have been written and submitted not long after the publication of Williams's attack on Wilson. Gascoigne would no doubt have felt slighted by association. Although his article is in no sense a direct response to Williams and makes no mention of any notion of controversy, it incorporates three particularly eye-catching elements. One was its title, which made a very strong point of itself; the second was a compelling list of reasons why Wilson and he had concluded, on the basis of what they could see from the gun turret of the *Bordein*, that Khartoum had fallen; the third was the fact that the captain and *reis* (pilot) stopped *Bordein*'s engines at one point, to insist that it was obvious that Khartoum was in the hands of the enemy, only for Wilson to order the vessel forward again – hardly the act of a man who lacked 'nerve', as Williams had suggested.

Sir Charles, meanwhile, was due to move in short order to Dublin, to resume his duties as the head of the Irish Ordnance Survey. He was visited by a good many friends prior to his departure, amongst them General Sir Edward Hamley, who three years earlier had commanded a division under Wolseley at Tel-el-Kebir. There had been a very public falling out between the two generals, when Hamley complained noisily that Wolseley's official despatches paid insufficient attention to his services. Hamley was instrumental in persuading Wilson to publish the journal he had kept during the desert march,[64] although given the ill-informed libels and slanders abroad at the time he probably did not require a great deal of persuasion.

On top of the misrepresentations appearing in print, there was the cruel gossip of the junior and middle-ranking officers to contend with, many of whom were well-connected blue-bloods from Guards and cavalry regiments and carried considerable sway in the smart London drawing rooms in which they were now being feted. Their experiences had been genuinely harrowing and they were doubtless frustrated that their heroic endeavours had come to nothing. Many of them had lost close friends and regimental colleagues along the way. It was the carping criticism from this quarter which set the seal on Wilson rushing *From Korti to Khartum* into print. How far the young blades of the Camel Corps were egged on and encouraged in their not altogether balanced opinions by members of the Ring is probably not a matter we shall ever get to the bottom of. Evidently Wolseley himself would have done nothing to discourage such talk.

Prior to his departure for Dublin, Wilson was received cordially by both Lord Hartington, now out of office of course, and by the altogether more immoveable Duke of Cambridge. Both expressed their compliments on so gallant an attempt to gain Khartoum. Indeed the Duke had already written to Wilson in the Sudan, expressing his complete approbation of the way in which he had handled the Desert

Column following Stewart's wounding. After a busy fortnight in London, Wilson reached Ireland on 1 July to find that he had only narrowly beaten a telegraphic summons to Buckingham Palace. He raced back to London to be presented to the Queen Empress on 3 July. Victoria was enthralled by his account of the 'river dash' and amply demonstrated that she for one found no fault with his actions. The following day she sent for a photograph of Wilson, so that he could be included in the royal albums now archived at Windsor Castle.[65]

According to Sir Charles Watson (to whom Lady Wilson gave full access to her late husband's private papers), Wilson wrote to the [acting] Adjutant-General in the summer of 1885, to draw his attention officially to misleading statements being bandied about in the newspapers and to press for a public inquiry. He received a reply which stated that the C-in-C was perfectly satisfied with all that he had done and which went on to 'request' that he did not press the matter further.[66] On 12 August 1885, a little over a year after he had been permitted by Gladstone to fire the starting-gun on the race for Khartoum, Lord Hartington addressed the House of Commons to second a parliamentary vote of thanks to the servicemen who had gone up the Nile. In his speech he went to great pains to emphasize that Sir Charles Wilson had performed gallantly and warranted none of the criticism which had been lately and unjustly levelled at him.[67] It was clear that Hartington, only too keenly aware of Wolseley's haughty opinions and machinations, wanted no room left for doubt. In November the Queen Empress invested Wilson with a KCB at Windsor Castle – and that should have been the end of the matter.

The Williams *v* Beresford Hope libel case was tried before the Lord Chief Justice of England and a special jury of the Queen's Bench Division on Thursday 28 October 1886.[68] While Beresford Hope had engaged the Attorney General as his defence counsel, Charles Williams chose to press his case in person. His contention was that any notion that he had suborned the troops into making disloyal remarks about an officer not only implied the commission of a military crime, but also besmirched his good standing as a journalist. He set the price of his anguish at £2,000 in damages. It was always inevitable that at some point in the proceedings the Lord Chief Justice would be obliged to remind the court that Sir Charles Wilson was not on trial and that the issue was whether Williams had been libelled by the *Saturday Review* or not. A reminder to that effect having been duly dispensed, Williams proceeded to argue that he had been obliged to talk with the rank and file about the events at the confluence of the Niles because Lieutenant Stuart-Wortley had been far too busy writing a despatch for the attention of Lord Wolseley to talk to him.[69] This, then, was a particular reference to 1 February, the date on which Stuart-Wortley had returned in a rowing boat to break the news that Khartoum had fallen, that both steamers had since foundered, and that Sir Charles Wilson and his command were awaiting rescue on Mernat Island.

If the Attorney General had taken the trouble to read *From Korti to Khartum* he would have been able to sway the jury by pointing out that there were no 'bluejackets' (specifically referred to in Williams's article) with Stuart-Wortley that day, only four members of the Royal Sussex and eight Sudanese soldiers. In order to speak to the three sailors who had been aboard the steamers, Williams would have had to wait until Wilson's return on 4 February, when he would in any case have had the opportunity to lay his questions before any one of four officers – a cast consisting of Sir Charles himself, Captains Fred Gascoigne and Lionel Trafford, and Stuart-Wortley, who had gone back upriver with Beresford to participate in the rescue. The Attorney General might also usefully have pointed out that Williams's article was dated 'Korti, 9 March', some five weeks after the events at issue. He might further have helped his client's cause by pointing out that Khartoum is on the south bank of the Blue Nile, which is to say around the corner from the general line of the White Nile, and then going on to query quite how Williams imagined that naval artificers in their engine rooms, or infantrymen volley-firing at the banks of the White Nile, with a smoke-generating black-powder round, from narrow firing-ports running down the sides of the vessels at maindeck level, could possibly have been in a position to judge what Sir Charles Wilson and the other officers had been able to see from the elevated gun turrets with the aid of their field glasses.

Where the Attorney General had failed to line up any witnesses, Williams had the 11th Earl of Airlie up his sleeve. David Airlie testified that he could recall Stuart-Wortley beavering away at his despatch, that relations between the headquarters staff and the war correspondents had been good – which he added they would not have been had any of them been suborning the troops – and that there had been no suggestion that Williams was given to behaving improperly in the field. The jury duly found for the prosecution and awarded Williams £300 in damages, sufficient in those days to sustain a gentleman comfortably for about six months. If ever the law is an ass, this was one of its especially asinine moments: if anybody should have been in the dock facing libel charges it was Charles Williams.[70] He continued his journalistic career, went on to publish a biography of Sir Evelyn Wood in 1892 and six years later returned to the Sudan to cover Kitchener's campaign of reconquest; he was unfortunate enough to be wounded at Omdurman. He died in 1904 at the age of sixty-six, a year or so before Sir Charles Wilson.[71]

From Korti to Khartum was published in January 1886 and proved a runaway best-seller. Wilson duly covered much the same ground in the text of his book as had been addressed by his 23 March report to Wolseley;[72] he allowed his story to speak for itself and made no reference to the controversy of the summer months. His report, already included in a Parliamentary Blue Book, reared its head again in November 1889 when the Intelligence Division of the War Office finally released Colonel Henry Colvile's long-delayed official history of the campaign. Colvile had declared his work complete as early as March 1887, since which time it had been circulated for comment and tinkering, a process in which Wolseley would undoubtedly have played a part. In the final version, Wilson's 23 March report was given its own appendix and cited in full. The subject heading was no more boldly emphasized than any other, but it was in block letters and ran, 'Sir C. Wilson's Explanation of Delay at Gubat'. And there sitting above it, where covering notes always sit, was Wolseley's icy note of 13 April: 'The reasons given by Sir Charles Wilson *must* [emphasis added] speak for themselves.' Thus was Wolseley's disdain for Sir Charles Wilson's actions permanently enshrined in the official record.[73]

The doyen of Victorian Britain's war correspondents, Archibald Forbes of the *Daily News*, had not been present in the Sudan, but had provided a military commentary on the relief expedition in the London papers while it was in progress. He had been obliged by his remoteness from the proceedings to be reasonably cautious in his observations, although it was clear that he was to be numbered amongst the commentators who had doubted the wisdom of Wolseley's plan from the outset. Forbes took time to sift through the *Official History*, until he felt sufficiently at home with the facts of the case to launch a blistering attack on Wolseley's management of the campaign:

The whole business was one of amazing ineptitude, of strange miscalculations, of abortive fads, of waste of valuable time, of attempted combinations which, devised in ignorance of conditions, were never within measurable proximity of consummation, of orders issued only to be changed and positions indicated only to be altered, of lost opportunities, wrecked transport, and squandered supplies.[74]

After Charles Williams's effort the next most public criticism of Wilson by a participant in the expedition, while Sir Charles was still alive, emanated from one of the Desert Column's medical officers, Surgeon Thomas Parke, who became a well-known figure when he accompanied H. M. Stanley on the Emin Pasha Relief Expedition, a private enterprise undertaking of 1893 designed to rescue the German-born governor of Equatoria, long since cut off in the Sudanese deep south. In May 1892, when Parke had either left or was about to leave the service to work for Stanley, he penned a piece in *The Nineteenth Century* called 'How General Gordon was Really Lost', a title very close to that of Charles Williams's article of May 1885. Parke arbitrarily dismissed any notion that Gladstone or Wolseley were in any way to blame and asserted instead that, 'the indisputable fact remains that our force arrived at Metemmeh and was actually met there – as if by intervention of Providence – by Gordon's steamers, within such a very short distance of the beleaguered city, five whole days before the latter yielded to the enemy'.[75] If Doctor Parke had read *From Korti to Khartum* or had any sort of grasp of Wolseley's campaign plan, he gave no sign of it. Critical his article may have been, compellingly well-argued it was not. The apparently curious timing of Doctor Parke's contribution to the debate can be accounted for by the fact that Forbes had entered the lists only four months earlier, triggering a minor stir in the press in which Parke evidently felt the need to involve himself. Wilson did not trouble himself to respond to Parke in any way, although his friend Watson did pen a piece for the next edition of the *Royal Engineers Journal*.

The Wilson controversy was given a new breath of life after his death when some of the gossiping junior officers of the 1880s committed their memoirs to print in the early decades of the twentieth century. In *My Army Life* (London, 1926), and

Rifleman and Hussar (London, 1931) Lieutenant General the Earl of Dundonald and Colonel Percy Marling VC respectively, both offered disparaging comments on Wilson's performance and temperament. Neither of them was generous enough to make allowance for the fact that the leadership of the Desert Column had devolved upon a man who was quite unqualified to exercise it, by dint of enemy action alone. In the mid-1960s Adrian Preston was responsible for unearthing Wolseley's long overlooked journal for the Nile Campaign, which he published in 1967 under the title *In Relief of Gordon*. This was a major historical find without which Wolseley's harshest criticisms of his political and military contemporaries, including Sir Charles Wilson, might quietly have turned to dust. As it is they have been revitalized and proliferated within the historical record, requiring that they are not simply taken as read but are also probed for veracity. In a sense Wolseley attacked Wilson's reputation far more cruelly from beyond the grave than he was ever able to get away with in life.

To get to the truth of the matter we must journey back to 1884 and travel upriver, initially in the train of 10,000 British servicemen, until at length, in January 1885, there are only twenty-eight of them still with us and Khartoum is in sight.

Chapter 1

All Men Worship the Rising Sun

Strategic and Political Background to the Nile Campaign

It is all very well to decide that the entire evacuation of the Soudan is the easiest way out of the difficulty, but the first condition of a complete evacuation is ability to evacuate, and that, if General Gordon is correct, is exactly what we do not possess.

W. T. Stead, *Pall Mall Gazette*, 9 January 1884

DOMESTIC POLITICAL AFFAIRS were what William Ewart Gladstone excelled at. His principal preoccupations during his second premiership were electoral reform and Irish Home Rule. As much as he would have liked to have left the intricate affairs of empire to his Cabinet colleagues, Egypt and the Sudan just refused to go away. The role of Secretary of State for War had fallen to Spencer Cavendish, Lord Hartington (later the 8th Duke of Devonshire), an old-style political grandee and the de facto leader of the powerful Whig faction within the Liberal Party. The War Office, over which the industrious Hartington presided, was located on Pall Mall at Cumberland House, since demolished, and was a purely Army department. The Royal Navy, commanded and administered by the Admiralty, had no connection with the Secretary of State for War or the War Office, but was presided over instead by Lord Northbrook as First Lord of the Admiralty, a Cabinet appointment not to be confused with the First Naval Lord[1] who was the professional head of the service. At the time of the Khartoum crisis this was Admiral Sir Astley Cooper Key GCB, ADC, FRS. A short hop across Whitehall at the Foreign Office was another political grandee by the name of Granville Leveson-Gower, the 2nd Earl of Granville.

The 1882 intervention to restore khedival rule in Egypt had left the British administering Tawfīq Pasha's realm in all but name and required that Lords Granville, Hartington and Northbrook pay close attention to political and military developments in Cairo. The Prime Minister on the other hand, though he had sanctioned the intervention of eighteen months earlier, took no great interest in Egyptian affairs and did his best to remain determinedly aloof. The essence of his instructions to Granville was to spare no effort to get Egypt back on its feet, terminate British suzerainty as soon as possible, and on no account become embroiled with the troublesome Mahdīst movement in the meantime. The Prime Minister could not have made the position of Her Majesty's Government any more clear in respect of the burgeoning difficulties south of Wādī Halfā: if it was a fact of life that Great Britain now had de facto responsibility for governing Egypt, this did not imply that it had inherited one iota of responsibility for its vassal's vast colonial hinterland. As a foreign policy line it was loose, untidy and difficult to justify, but it was all too easy to imagine the unstable Sudan turning pink on the world map and becoming just one more unwarranted burden on the Exchequer, something Gladstone was determined to avoid at all costs, even at the expense of what his Conservative opponents were given to calling 'Britain's honour'.

The Foreign Secretary's agent in Cairo was the 43-year-old Sir Evelyn Baring, formerly of the Royal Artillery, the Army Staff College and the old Topographical Department of the War Office. Originally the British 'Controller-General' under the old arrangements for Anglo-French 'Dual-Control' of the bankrupt Egyptian economy, Baring had now been appointed to the all-powerful role of Consul-General, a post he would occupy for twenty-five years, 1882–1907 (as Lord Cromer from 1892 onwards). Lord Hartington's man on the ground was Lieutenant General Sir Frederick Stephenson, a well-regarded veteran of the Crimea, who as GOC Cairo had the none too onerous task of commanding the 'Army of Occupation', two large brigades quartered on Cairo and Alexandria with not a great deal to do.

There were a number of other key military men in Cairo. Major General Sir Evelyn Wood VC, KCMG, CB,[2] late 90th Regiment, had been appointed as the first Sirdar, or commander-in-chief, of Egypt's new model army, a body of men who had been left in no doubt that their first duty was to the Khedive. Evelyn Wood was able, fearless, enjoyed a distinguished fighting record and was one of the most senior members of the Wolseley Ring. He was a veteran both of the Crimea, at which point he had been serving in the Royal Navy, and the Mutiny, by which time he had transferred into the Army. It was in India that he gained the Victoria Cross. He had gone on to serve under Wolseley in Ashantiland and later held senior command appointments in South Africa during the 9th Cape Frontier War, the Zulu War and the closing stages of the Transvaal Rebellion. His victory at Khambula had served as a turning point in the war with the Zulu. Although the disaster at Majuba Hill (27 February 1881) had been squarely the work of Wolseley's particular favourite, the late Major General Sir George Colley, the job of negotiating a peace settlement with Kruger and his republican henchmen had fallen to Brigadier General Wood. The British side of the proceedings was directed from London by the Gladstone government, which had no intention of crushing the resistance in the Transvaal by military force, once the strength and relative unanimity of Boer sentiment had been made so apparent. Disregarding the fact that modern telegraphic communications had rendered commanders in the field quite powerless to gainsay their political masters in Whitehall, Wolseley blamed Wood for what he saw as a humiliating end to the conflict. During the course of the Nile Expedition he would make the mistake of referring to 'Wood's ignominious peace' in a letter to the Queen Empress, a remark to which she took great exception. A scathing reply put Wolseley firmly in the picture about Mr Gladstone's role in the proceedings and caused him to sulk in a letter to Lady Louisa about how little the Queen appreciated him. The fact of the matter was that Evelyn Wood was one of Victoria's favourite generals; that no blame could be attached to him in respect of the recent humiliation in South Africa in any case; and that Wolseley's interpretation of events was nothing less than irrational.

To ensure that the new Egyptian Army, or 'EA' as it was known for short, was markedly different from its woefully led and ineffectual predecessor, Wood had enlisted the services of a few dozen British officers, all of whom had been bumped up an acting rank or two and had thrown themselves into their work with a passion. They were supported by a cadre of top-notch British NCOs. Because secondment to the EA attracted a hike in pay, the Sirdar could afford to pick and choose only the most talented candidates. As a consequence the new army was coming along well, although Wood was of the view that it was still some way from being ready for fully fledged combat operations. London had left Baring and Wood in no doubt that the EA was intended for the security of Egypt and was not to be frittered away in the Sudan. The transformation was helped along by the fact that the British officers and NCOs not only liked their enthusiastic *fellah* recruits, but also set them an example and went to great pains to explain precisely what was expected of them as professional soldiers. This sort of treatment contrasted starkly with the way in which the Turco-Circassian elite had so lightly taken the *kourbash* (whip) to the soldiers of the old brutalized, dispirited and ultimately mutinous Egyptian military. Although the old army had been defeated and disbanded in Lower Egypt by the British, and had been either massacred or assimilated by the Mahdīst movement in Kordofan and Dār Fūr, a few demoralized remnants lingered on in the Sudanese capital and a handful of garrison towns in the Red Sea Littoral and Equatoria.

Sir Evelyn Wood was not the only distinguished VC holder in Cairo. There was also the towering Major General Sir Gerald Graham VC, KCB, late of the Royal Engineers. Graham was one of Sir Frederick Stephenson's principal subordinates and a personal friend of 'Chinese' Gordon, the living legend who had led the 'Ever Victorious Army' to victory over Taiping rebels in the 1860s, before entering the service of the Khedive a decade later, initially as the Governor of Equatoria (1874–7) and subsequently as Governor-General of the Sudan (1877–January 1880). Graham and Gordon became firm friends in the siege lines at Sebastopol, where Graham was awarded the Victoria Cross for his role in the costly and ultimately futile attack on the Redan. He missed the Mutiny but sailed from India in 1860 to take part in the Second China War. By 1882 Graham had risen to the rank of major general. He commanded the 2nd Infantry Brigade in the Egyptian intervention and at Tel-el-Kebir played a leading role in driving the enemy from their defences. The men of Graham's brigade took collective note that their commander had been in the thick of the fight from beginning to end and in the aftermath of the battle cheered him wherever he went.

Sir Evelyn Wood had not been the Khedive's original nomination as Sirdar. Instead the first-choice candidate was the controversial Lieutenant General

(Ottoman rank) Valentine Baker Pasha, younger brother of Sir Samuel Baker, the renowned Nile explorer and first Governor of Equatoria. As the commanding officer of the 10th Hussars, a leading cavalry theorist and a personal friend of the Prince of Wales, the regiment's colonel-in-chief, Val Baker had once been the most promising and fashionable cavalry colonel in the service.[3] On 17 June 1875, however, Baker's world came crashing down about his head, when he was alleged to have molested an un-chaperoned 22-year-old by the name of Miss Rebecca Dickinson in a first-class railway carriage. Although nothing approaching an 'indecent assault' as we would understand it today seems to have occurred, an overblown police charge-sheet insisted otherwise. A howl of public outrage at the antics of the upper crust virtually guaranteed a conviction. The incident attracted a year-long prison sentence and a fine of £500. Baker immediately tendered his resignation, as he was honour-bound to do, but the Queen intervened through the Duke of Cambridge to insist that he be cashiered and discharged with ignominy instead. After his release from prison Baker fled the country for Constantinople, where the Russo-Turkish War of 1877–8 was in the offing. In August 1877, four months into the war, he accepted an invitation to serve on the staff of the Ottoman C-in-C in Bulgaria. Following the defence of Plevna, which had long delayed the Russian advance, Baker commanded a crucial rearguard action at the Battle of Tashkennan. After the war he took up an administrative appointment in Armenia. When, in the aftermath of the British intervention in Egypt, it became known that a Sirdar would be required for the new EA, Baker prevailed on the Sultan to release him and crossed the Mediterranean in the belief that the job was as good as his. He had not counted on the personal veto of the Queen Empress who, quite rightly it must be said, refused to countenance British officers serving under a cashiered colonel – a man whose lawful status was akin to a private soldier dishonourably discharged the service. 'General' Baker was forced to content himself with a second-best consolation prize and was duly appointed by the Khedive to command the Gendarmerie.

The Egyptian Occupation of the Sudan

The ill-defined 'Soudan' had been an Ottoman–Egyptian possession since the 1820s, when Muḥammad ʿAlī Pasha sent his son Ismāʾil Kamil up the Nile at the head of an army. The primary object was to seize a large swathe of the interior, fit to yield rich sources of gold and black slave-soldiers. Ironically, by the time Muḥammad ʿAlī got to make his first and only trip to the Sudan, the best part of twenty years had passed and one of the main purposes of his visit was to announce that henceforth Egypt would be committed to the suppression of the slave trade. He did not announce emancipation and nobody in the south paid much attention to the new policy anyway. The regime established by the pashas had been notoriously venal from the outset and over the ensuing sixty years had shown but scant sign of improvement. To be appointed to a government post in some remote corner of the Sudan was something nobody in his right mind would seek. If the worst came to the worst, however, service in the south at least represented an opportunity to line one's pockets by way of consolation. If a repressed indigenous population had risen bloodily against the 'Turks', as the Sudanese still termed the Egyptians, then as far as Gladstone was concerned that was a problem for Méhémet Tawfīq Pasha and his ministers, not one for Victoria Regina and hers. That each of Tawfiq's ministers was 'shadowed' by a senior British administrator, answerable to Sir Evelyn Baring, was neither here nor there – at least not in the Prime Minister's eyes. If Muḥammad Aḥmad ibn al-Saiyid 'Abd Allāh, who in May 1881 had proclaimed himself the Mahdī, or the 'divinely guided one', had managed to overwhelm a number of powerful punitive expeditions with a mere rabble of ill-armed *anṣār* followers, then good luck to him; God probably was on his side.

One of the factors the Prime Minister failed to understand was just how many indigenous Sudanese were living perfectly contented lives as wholehearted collaborators with the Egyptian administration; whatever its faults, the occupation had been a fact of life for more than sixty years and people had to get by somehow. Nowhere was this more obvious than in Khartoum, where a bustling merchant class was doing very nicely out of Egyptian colonialism. Similarly there was a great deal of collaboration in the military domain, where there were whole regiments of black African regulars from the south who had no domestic ties whatever with Egypt. Unhappily for the good standing of the Khartoum government, the most obvious manifestation of its authority was not the regular battalions it could bring to bear in a crisis, but the ill-disciplined, parasitic contingents of *bāshi-būzuq* irregulars quartered all over the country.

In the early days of the occupation Ottoman suzerainty over Egypt had drawn a good many Balkan mercenaries down the Nile. Military ties with Constantinople having worked progressively looser over time, it was now the case that almost all new recruits to *bāshi-būzuq* units came from Lower Egypt or the Levant. Of course these were hard times and many recruits were men who had formerly lived from hand-to-mouth in the Cairo, Alexandria or Damascus bazaar, where they had necessarily evolved into expert survivors. As such they knew how to get by and were instinctively inclined to put themselves first. It did not help that they received only rudimentary training, were absorbed into the service of an institutionally corrupt regime, and might be obliged to survive without pay for months at a time. Following the lead of the men already *in situ*, they lost no opportunity to profit by the abuse or plunder of the indigenous population. Service as a *bāshi-būzuq* was a way of life and the ticket to the Sudan usually a one-way one, so that, in addition to taking in new recruits from the big cities, irregular units also sired their own replacements. There were still some Albanians, Bosnians, Bulgarians, Greeks and others of eastern European origin about in the 1880s, many of whom had lived most of their adult lives in the Sudan and had risen to become venerable old officers, but there were far greater numbers of sons, grandsons and even some great-grandsons – the offspring or second- and third-generation descendants of the original Eastern European mercenaries and local black or Arab wives and concubines. There were also several thousand irregulars who were not outsiders domiciled in the Sudan, but rather were genuinely of the Sudan. This was particularly the case with the Shā'iqīa tribe which, while it had offered fierce resistance to the Ottoman–Egyptian invasion of the 1820s, had since thrown in its lot with the 'Turks'. Now most Shā'iqīa of fighting age earned their daily crust as heavily armed government tax collectors, in consequence of which they were detested by most of the other tribes in the principally Arab north.

Like most conflicts of its kind there was more than a hint of civil war about the Mahdīst Uprising. On the side of the government were to be found: two or three generations of Ottoman–Egyptian officials who had made their home in the Sudan; the relatively prosperous indigenous mercantile and artisan classes based on the larger towns; the remnants of the old Egyptian Army, including a number of Sudanese black battalions; a domiciled class of irregular soldiers and former soldiers; and committed loyalist tribes like the Shā'iqīa. All these vested-interest groups came with extended families of course. A certain amount of support could also be hired in from some of the black African tribes in the south. On the rebel side were to be found: a self-proclaimed messiah and his band of disciples, together with their respective clans and families; a military hard-core based on the nomadic tribes of Kordofan; the fractious Hadendawas and other desert-dwelling Bīja clans of the Red Sea Littoral; and the downtrodden poor of the Nile Valley. In many ways it was not so much a conflict between fundamentalist jihadists on one side and orthodox Muslims on the other, so much as a war between government-supporting 'haves' and a loose alliance of impoverished 'have-nots'.

From an Egyptian perspective the situation in the Sudan took a dramatic turn for the worse on 6 January 1883, when General Muḥammad Sa'īd Pasha surrendered El Obeid, the provincial capital of Kordofan, after a siege lasting the best part of five months. With this latest capitulation around 6,000 Remington rolling-block rifles were added to the several thousand modern weapons already in rebel hands following a seemingly endless string of Egyptian military disasters. When first summoned to surrender, the stubborn Muḥammad Sa'īd Pasha had hanged the Mahdī's emissaries from the nearest tree. Now that the shoe was on the other foot, the humbled general met a grisly end at the hands of old enemies.[4] Monitoring the unhappy course of events from Khartoum was a British intelligence officer, Lieutenant Colonel J. D. H. Stewart of the 11th Hussars. Slightly built and sharp as a razor, Hammill Stewart had been assigned to snoop around the Sudan and report back to London on the military position there. His reports, though fascinating and far-sighted, made for depressing reading and made it plain that there was next to no hope of the Egyptians emerging on top. For Gladstone the solution was obvious and simple: the Khedive and his ministers should gather in their incompetent generals, their crooked officials and their vile *bāshi-būzuqs* and bring them home to Egypt, leaving the liberated Sudanese free to determine their own destiny. Like so many half-baked imperial policies before it this latest utterance failed to take account of the fiddly little details prevailing on the ground, but in Whitehall would have assumed the guise of an admirable strategic plan.

If the Prime Minister had any grasp at all on the despotic character of Muḥammad Aḥmad's fundamentalist creed, or the grandiose nature of the ambitions induced by his trances, dreams and visions, then it was tenuous at best. That the false prophet's goals could have included leading a host of devoted *anṣār*[5] from Khartoum to Constantinople, via Cairo, Damascus, Mecca and all the other great cities of the Arab world, would to Gladstone have seemed preposterous. It might be a notion fit to frighten children, but was not something to be taken seriously in government circles. Gladstone was not to know that God had appeared to Muḥammad Aḥmad in a dream and granted him forty years in which to accomplish his mission.[6] Mere scorn alone can do nothing to alter the fact that the flames of jihad are wont to burn fiercely and, in the right conditions, can spread like wildfire across vast distances. No matter how deluded his ambitions might appear from afar, Muḥammad Aḥmad was bent on nothing less than the direct subordination of orthodox Islam to his personal will and so far, inside the Sudan at least, his tactics were paying dividends. What Gladstone failed to comprehend was that the Mahdī was ruthless, unscrupulous, driven and, like all the other fanatics who have ever ridden the tiger of self-proclaimed divinity, unlikely to go away of his own volition: somebody, somewhere, would have to stop him. Any antigovernment insurrection needs to gather and maintain momentum: above all else it can never afford to stall. It was Gordon's year-long defence of Khartoum that stopped the domino effect south of the Egyptian frontier. But all that lay a year and more in the future. In the meantime the Khedive and his ministers had prepared a last desperate attempt to dispense with the false prophet once and for all.

Hicks Pasha and the Kordofan Expedition

Colonel J. D. H. Stewart tarried in Khartoum long enough to be on hand when, on 4 March 1883, Colonel William Hicks, a 53-year-old retired Indian Army man, arrived in the city at the head of a small European staff of no great distinction. All the new arrivals had been elevated a rank or two in the Egyptian service, though Hicks himself had rocketed from colonel to lieutenant general, in order to become the chief of staff of what was left of the old Egyptian military in the Sudan. After a long desert journey from Suakin on the Red Sea coast to Berber on the Nile, a distance of 245 miles, Hicks and his officers embarked aboard a government steamer for a 200-mile southbound cruise to the confluence of the Niles. They disembarked in front of the Governor-General's palace, the *sarāya*, where Hicks was greeted by his civil and military superiors, 'Alā' al-Dīn Pasha Ṣiddiq, the Governor-General, and the army commander, an elderly Circassian by the name of General Sulaimān Pasha Nyāzī. Colonel Stewart passed all his observations on to Hicks over the next few days, wished him the best of luck and, with his work in the Sudan complete, set off for home. Little did he realize, as he strolled up the gangplank to take ship for Berber, quite how soon he would be back.

It was a particular source of irritation to Gladstone that 'Hicks Pasha' conspired to have the interfering and incompetent Sulaimān Pasha Nyāzī sent away to the

Red Sea Littoral, so that he could himself assume the mantle of C-in-C Sudan. When Hicks began sending telegraphic reports directly to Sir Evelyn Baring, the Prime Minister instructed Lord Granville to put a stop to it. The reports of an 'Egyptian' general should be submitted to Egyptian ministers, not to the British consul-general. The measure served to reaffirm the Prime Minister's position in respect of the Sudan for everybody involved. After a brief flourish of success with the Senaar expedition of April 1883, including the Battle of Marabieh (29 April) in which he had trounced the Mahdīst forces operating in the *jazīra* (the broad swathe of fertile territory between the two Niles), Hicks turned his attention to the rebel heartland in Kordofan. Having concentrated and part-trained a numerically powerful army of dubious quality, Hicks marched out of Khartoum on 9 September, bound for the de facto Mahdīst capital at El Obeid. It was an unhappy enterprise from beginning to end and on 5 November 1883 was terminated by the cruelly one-sided Battle of Shaikān,[7] in which Hicks, the Governor-General and the best part of 10,000 Egyptian and Sudanese soldiers were killed. Fourteen artillery pieces and half-a-dozen machine guns were lost into the bargain. Mahdīst casualties ran to a few hundred men at most. Father Josef Ohrwalder, an Austrian priest who had been captured by the rebels at his mission in the Nuba Hills, described the Mahdī's triumphant return and the effect the great victory had on his standing:

The Mahdi's entry into El Obeid was a scene of wild enthusiasm and excitement. The many-coloured flags came first, then followed thousands upon thousands of Dervishes moving to the ever swelling murmur of 'La Ilaha il'lallah' [*sic*] ('There is no god but God'), whilst others danced out from the ranks and shook their blood bespotted spears, uttering fearful yells. After them followed the cavalry with the three Khalifas. Every now and then a halt was made, when a number of riders would dash forward at full gallop, poising their spears ready for the thrust, and then would return to the ranks amidst the loud applause of the others. After the cavalry followed a few prisoners, the wretched remnant of Hicks's army. Most of them were naked, and were being dragged forward under the continual insults of the Dervishes; then came the guns drawn by wounded mules, and last of all came the Mahdi himself, riding a magnificent white camel, and surrounded by his most fanatical adherents ... Clouds of dust filled the air, and as the Mahdi passed by, the spectators threw themselves down and kissed the ground. Such a scene of wild triumph had never before been witnessed.

The Mahdi was now honoured almost as a god. The victory gained for him an enormous increase of power and respect. The fear of his name sped like wildfire throughout every province and district in the Sudan. He was now regarded as the true Mahdi, every Moslem believed in him, and all doubt was put aside. At the battle near Shekan numbers of people said they saw the angels whom the Mahdi had summoned to fight against the Turks. He now became the object of almost superhuman veneration; even the water with which he washed himself was handed by the eunuchs to the believers, who drank it with avidity as an antidote to all ills and diseases.[8]

Particularly galling for Gladstone was that Hicks's staff officers had turned out to be mostly British and were now mostly dead, to the consternation of their grieving

families, the outrage of the Conservatives and the ire of a good many London newspapers.

It did nothing for the Prime Minister's temper to learn that only the day before Hicks died, the British diplomatic representative in the Red Sea region had gone and got himself killed by Hadendawa rebels at a middle-of-nowhere place called El Teb (locally Andatteib). Ironically Commander Lynedoch Moncrieff, a retired naval officer, was well known in the Red Sea Littoral and on cordial terms with most of the Bīja clans. Evidently an adventurous spirit, Moncrieff really had no business accompanying General Maḥmūd Ṭāhir Pasha's ill-fated attempt to relieve the insignificant government outpost at Tokar. Moncrieff is said to have died well, defending himself with a brace of pistols and fighting back to back with a knot of three or four Greeks, although this was just about the only serious act of resistance mounted by a battalion-sized force. Consequently the butcher's bill had been extremely heavy, serving further to undermine the government's tenuous hold on the coast. Fortunately for Maḥmūd Ṭāhir Pasha's person, if not his military repute, he jabbed his spurs into the flanks of his horse early in the proceedings and was carried safely in the direction of Suakin.

Lieutenant Colonel Henry de Cöetlogon had been fortunate that Hicks Pasha had not cared much for his company and had left him in Khartoum as the garrison commander. In the wake of the Shaikān disaster de Cöetlogon turned his attention to improving the 'South Front', an improvised line of defence which ran between the left bank of the Blue Nile and the right bank of the White Nile. Although the capital had not as yet been pressed in any way, it was nonetheless an act of great foresight, something the next Governor-General would have good reason to be thankful for. In the meantime the garrison commander was egged on in his endeavours by Frank Power, the special-correspondent of *The Times*, whose drooping moustache and monocle belied his youth. The 25-year-old Power had departed Khartoum with Hicks, but had fallen ill and been obliged to turn back. For want of an alternative candidate, Baring had wired him asking that he assume the mantle of British consul. If Power could count himself lucky to have avoided the Kordofan Expedition's long march to oblivion – unlike his much better-known colleagues, Edmund O'Donovan of the *Daily News* and Frank Vizetelly of the *Illustrated London News* – he was not out of the woods yet. His editor aside, there was nothing to stop him steaming downriver whenever he chose, as there were no British interests to speak of in Khartoum. In reality he was little more than Baring's eyes and ears in the south; the Consul-General's background in intelligence should not be forgotten. Power's resolve was fortified by the brash courage of youth and speculation amongst the Egyptian officers and officials that surely, now, Gordon Pasha would come.

The Hicks disaster set the seal on what was to be done about Egyptian rule in the Sudan. Save for the few thousand soldiers in Khartoum there was nothing to prevent the Mahdīst ascendancy spreading across the length and breadth of the land. Such a development would risk fundamentalist insurrection spilling over the border into

Upper Egypt. In the circumstances nothing would have pleased the Khedive and his ministers more than the commitment of British troops, a proposition which immediately met with a flat refusal. In desperation the Egyptian Cabinet contemplated asking Constantinople to provide Turkish troops, a retrograde measure which would contribute nothing to the cause of modernization. It might conceivably have been a bluff designed to force the hand of the London government, but nonetheless obliged Baring to seek the Foreign Secretary's direction. What was he to say to the Egyptians if they turned to him for guidance? 'If consulted,' came Granville's reply, 'recommend the abandonment of the Sudan within certain limits.'

'Send Gordon'

In the meantime Granville had been quietly nudged about the possibility of sending Chinese Gordon to Khartoum. He was by no means averse to the idea and wrote to Gladstone to seek his opinion. The Prime Minister too could see some merit in the proposal. On 1 December Granville telegraphed Baring to ask, 'If General Charles Gordon were willing to go to Egypt, could he be of any use to you or the Egyptian government, and, if so, in what capacity?'[9] Baring sounded out Chérif Pasha, the head of the khedival government, and found him more than a little lukewarm. Baring proceeded to despatch his reply on 2 December: 'The Egyptian Government are very much averse to employing General Gordon, mainly on the ground that, the movement in the Soudan being religious, the appointment of a Christian in high command would probably alienate the tribes who remain faithful.' This plausible-sounding explanation avoided any necessity for Baring to give vent to his deep-seated doubts about Gordon's temperament and suitability. With Christmas fast approaching, the Consul-General advised the Foreign Secretary that if Her Majesty's Government insisted on a policy of abandonment, Chérif Pasha and his ministers were likely to resign. Baring concluded by adding that if the ministry did fall, the dire situation in the Sudan might, after all, warrant the despatch of a British officer 'of high authority'. Early in the New Year, London replied that it stood by its insistence on abandonment. On 7 January this triggered precisely the mass resignation Baring had warned of. Thankfully before the day was out Nubar Pasha had agreed to form a new administration.

W. T. Stead and the Press Campaign

The proposal 'Send Gordon!' was first mooted publicly in the New Year's Day edition of *The Times*, when Sir Samuel Baker reflected on the disastrous situation in the Sudan in a letter to the editor. The refrain was quickly picked up by W. T. Stead,[10] the editor of the *Pall Mall Gazette*, and an early pioneer of the personal interview, who proceeded to track Gordon down to his sister's home in Southampton. The general had only just returned from Brussels, where he had concluded an arrangement to serve as the principal administrator of King Leopold's burgeoning personal fiefdom in the Congo. Unsurprisingly, his request that he be allowed to sign a contract with the Belgians, whilst at the same time continuing to serve as a British officer, had been turned down. Leopold's financial offer was sufficiently generous, however, to render the sacrifice of an Army pension inconsequential. Thus, when Stead interviewed Gordon in Southampton on Tuesday 8 January, a letter tendering the resignation of his commission had only just gone off in the post. The *Pall Mall Gazette* ran the interview the following day. It was clear, his recent discussions with the Belgians notwithstanding, that Gordon was itching to return to his old stamping ground and set things straight. Stead heralded his scoop with a front-page leader urging that Gordon be sent back to the Sudan in the role of governor-general:

It is a rare piece of good fortune that at the critical moment in the destinies of the Soudan and the Nile Valley the ablest Englishman who ever held command in Equatorial Africa should be once more within two hours of London. It is therefore, with peculiar satisfaction that we direct the attention of our readers to our eleventh page, where we are privileged to set forth in considerable detail the views of Chinese Gordon on the question of the Soudan. It will be found in more than one important point they directly conflict with those which prevail in high quarters in this country. General Gordon not only impeaches directly the policy of ordering the evacuation of the Soudan, but he absolutely denies its possibility, unless we are willing to admit that when we say evacuation we mean massacre . . .

In common with the ex-khedive, of whom he speaks with remarkable cordiality, General Gordon deprecates the despatch of either Indian or English troops to the Soudan. But if we have not an Egyptian Army to employ in the service, and if we must not send an English force, what are we to do? There is only one thing that we can do. We cannot send a regiment to Khartoum, but we can send a man who on more than once occasion has proved himself more valuable in similar circumstances than an entire army. Why not send Chinese Gordon with full powers to Khartoum, to assume absolute control of the territory, to treat with the Mahdi, to relieve the garrisons, and do what he can to save what can be saved from the wreck in the Soudan?[11]

Gladstone would not have much cared for Stead's use of 'we', by which he meant the British state, but he was under a good deal of pressure over the evacuation policy and had to be seen to have some sort of tenable plan for its execution. The text of the interview throws some interesting light on how Gordon perceived Egyptian rule in the Sudan.

During the three years that I wielded full powers in the Soudan I taught the natives that they had a right to exist. I waged war against the Turks and Circassians who had harried the population. I had taught them something of the meaning of liberty and justice, and accustomed them to a higher ideal of government than that with which they had previously been acquainted. As soon as I had gone the Turks and Circassians returned in full force; the old bashi-bazouk system was re-established; my old employés were persecuted; and a population which had begun to appreciate something like decent government was flung back to suffer the worst excesses of Turkish rule. The inevitable result followed; and thus it may be said that the egg of the present rebellion was laid in the three years which I was allowed to govern the Soudan on other than Turkish principles.

The Soudanese are a very nice people. They deserve the sincere compassion and sympathy of all civilised men. I got on very well with them, and I was sincerely sorry at the prospect of seeing them handed over to be ground down once more by their Turkish and Circassian oppressors. Yet, unless an attempt is made to hold on to the present garrisons, it is inevitable that the Turks, for the sake of self-preservation, must attempt to crush them. They deserve a better fate. It ought not to be impossible to come to terms with them, to grant them a free amnesty for the past, to offer them security for decent government in the future. If this was done and the government entrusted to a man whose word was truth, all might yet be re-established.

There is one subject on which I cannot imagine anyone can differ about. That is the impolicy of announcing our intention to evacuate Khartoum. For even if we were bound to do so, we should have said nothing about it. The moment it is shown we have given up the game every man will go over to the Mahdi. All men worship the rising sun. The difficulties of evacuation will be enormously increased, if, indeed, the withdrawal of our garrison is not rendered impossible.[12]

It was Thursday 10 January, the day after the publication of the Gordon interview, before Granville got around to replying to Baring's telegram of 22 December. 'Could General Charles Gordon or Colonel Sir Charles Wilson be of assistance in altered circumstances in Egypt?' he enquired.[13] Baring once again consulted with the Egyptians and once again declined the Foreign Secretary's offer, without ever articulating his reservations about Gordon's suitability. Over the next few days most of the big London newspapers picked up Stead's refrain, until Chinese Gordon was the name on the lips of just about every opinion-former in England. The despatch of Gordon very quickly became a done deal, whether Baring and the Egyptians liked it or not. In the event the new Egyptian Minister for War, 'Abd-al-Kader Pasha, who had agreed to go to the Sudan as governor-general, suddenly changed his mind, pulling the rug from under Baring's feet. This coincided with the arrival of a telegram from Granville enquiring just how the new Egyptian government intended to go about conducting the evacuation. On Wednesday 16 January, a week after the publication of Stead's interview, Baring sent two telegrams to Granville, the first of which was of an official nature and requested that a British officer be identified to go to Khartoum, 'with full powers, both civil and military, to conduct the retreat'. The second was a private message which conceded that Gordon was probably the best man for the job, provided that he was prepared to pledge himself to a policy of evacuation and accept that he would be subject to the Consul-General's instructions. Such had been the extent of the public and governmental clamour for Gordon's despatch that Baring concluded that he personally must have become 'unconsciously prejudiced' against him. The fact that Sir Evelyn Wood was all for the appointment went a long way towards tipping the balance.[14]

The London End

Only the day before Baring finally relented, Gordon had presented himself at the War Office in response to a summons from his old Crimean comrade and ardent admirer, the Adjutant-General. The ostensible reason for the interview was to discuss Gordon's letter of resignation, although Wolseley had already written back to discourage any idea of his going to the Congo, urging him instead to focus his thinking on the Sudan. The real reason for the interview was that Wolseley was under orders to sound Gordon out on the whole question of evacuation and to put a somewhat half-hearted measure to him. The proposal was that he should go to Suakin without any executive authority, to enquire on behalf of Her Majesty's Government into just how the evacuation of Khartoum might best be carried out. Wolseley had received his instructions from Lord Hartington but may not have been aware that Granville was also in on the act and had already secured the Prime Minister's assent to such a mission. Gladstone had fallen ill before Christmas, was not in London at this time and contrary to popular myth did not speak with Gordon at any point prior to his departure for Khartoum. By the time the discussion in Wolseley's office had drawn to a close, Gordon had pronounced himself wholeheartedly in favour of evacuation and had agreed to go to Suakin. It is impossible to know what private words passed between the two generals on how Gordon's role might develop subsequently. What is certain is that they cannot have avoided the subject. At the perfectly innocent end of the spectrum their conversation might have been something along the lines of 'We'll just have to wait and see.' At the more conspiratorial end of the spectrum, however, they might have reflected that such a mission might readily be manipulated to become merely an interim step towards Gordon resuming the governor-generalship. Either way Wolseley must have briefed Hartington on the outcome straight away, as the Foreign Office telegraphic traffic makes it plain that Granville was fully abreast of the proceedings before the day was out. In a telegram dated the same day he advised Baring that,

> I hear indirectly that Gordon is ready to go straight to Suakin without passing through Cairo on the following rather vague terms. His mission to be to report to Her Majesty's Government on the military situation of the Soudan, and to return without any further engagement towards him. He would be under you for instructions and will send letters through you under flying seal. You and Nubar Pasha to give him all assistance and facilities as to telegraphing, etc. . . . He might be of use in informing you and us of the situation. It would be popular at home, but there may be countervailing objections. Tell me your real opinion with or without Nubar Pasha.[15]

Granville's telegram crossed with the two drafted by Baring the following morning, which in effect requested Gordon's appointment to an executive position. Even as Granville was reading them through at the Foreign Office, Gordon was on his way back to Brussels, presumably to advise the Belgians that his resignation had not been accepted and that there would be an indeterminate delay before he could go to the Congo. It is not inconceivable that the post-evacuation fate of the Sudan's southern provinces also came under discussion. On Thursday Wolseley wired Gordon to insist that he return to London post-haste to meet with ministers. He was back by breakfast-time the following day. Apart from Granville and Hartington, the only other members of the Cabinet in town were Lord Northbrook, the First Lord of the Admiralty, and Sir Charles Dilke, the President of the Local Government Board. Wolseley brought Gordon along to Hartington's outer office, briefly left him outside while he went through to speak with the ministers, and a few minutes later called him in to join their deliberations. Wolseley then took his leave, as the meeting's only object was to rubber-stamp the plan he and Gordon had agreed three days earlier. Thus its primary focus was on Gordon going to Suakin in a non-executive capacity to report. Crucially, passing reference was also made to his taking on any other duties that the Egyptian government might require of him. It would appear that Granville did not make plain to Northbrook and Dilke that this might entail the general assuming an executive appointment, even though this was very clearly implied in Baring's message of two days earlier. There is a faint aroma here that Granville, Hartington, Wolseley and Gordon himself, all either suspected or knew that he was likely to be appointed as governor-general sooner or later, but temporarily glossed over the matter as Gladstone had not yet given his assent and was likely to be difficult about it. It also appears that the ministers asked Gordon to draft his own instructions.[16] These stipulated that:

Her Majesty's Government are desirous that you should proceed at once to Egypt to report to them on the military situation in the Soudan, and on the measures which it may be advisable to take for the security of the Egyptian garrisons still holding positions in that country, and for the safety of the European population in Khartoum.

You are also desired to consider and report upon the best means of effecting the evacuation of the interior of the Soudan, and upon the manner in which the safety and the good administration by the Egyptian Government of the ports on the sea-coast can best be secured . . .

You will consider yourself authorised and instructed to perform such other duties as the Egyptian Government may desire to entrust to you and as may be communicated by Sir E. Baring.[17]

If anybody present at the 18 January meeting did not grasp that the third paragraph of Gordon's orders was potentially of far greater import than the first, then he should not have been holding a great office. If it was a report the government wanted there could be no better man to send than Colonel Hammill Stewart, who had carried out just such a mission in the first half of 1883. Gordon Pasha was not a man one sent anywhere to write reports, but a man of action, a miracle-worker and a one-man army. The meeting concluded with handshakes all round and an agreement that Gordon would leave for the Sudan that night. In some of the earlier telegraphic traffic Baring had suggested that Stewart might be a suitable candidate to organize the evacuation of Khartoum. Instead it had now been arranged that he would be hauled in to act as Gordon's aide. This entailed cancelling his imminent departure for Canada where he was due to undertake a six-week staff project.[18] In the event Stewart would be much more than an aide; indeed his work would be of such a nature that he not only acted as the general's chief of staff but also came to be regarded as his deputy. Granville hastened away to fire off a telegram advising Baring that Gordon and Stewart would be leaving London within hours. He added that it would be helpful if Baring would meet them at Ismailia, as the general wanted to go directly to Suakin without diverting through Cairo.[19] In the meantime Wolseley had taken his old friend back to his house in Hill Street for the afternoon. Gordon already had a dinner engagement with his friend Captain John Brocklehurst of the Blues which there would be just time enough to keep. Before Gordon left Hill Street that evening, Wolseley established that he had no cash with which to meet his travelling expenses, so undertook to tour the military clubs, borrow what he could from the members and meet him at Charing Cross in time for the departure of the boat-train. In the end Wolseley's impromptu fund-raiser turned up £300 which he duly turned over to Colonel Stewart at the station.[20] Gordon arrived in the company of Brocklehurst, to find the Commander-in-Chief, the Foreign Secretary and the Adjutant- General waiting on the platform to bid him farewell. It is said that Granville bought the train tickets and that the C-in-C held the door of the carriage as Gordon boarded.

Ten days had elapsed since the general had been interviewed for the *Pall Mall Gazette* at his sister's home in Southampton. Gordon's mission owed more than a little to William Thomas Stead. Already well known in London, Stead went on to become one of the most celebrated newspapermen in the world. Unhappily he was one of the unfortunate souls who took passage aboard RMS *Titanic* in April 1912; by one account he was seen near the end quietly reading a book in the first-class smoking lounge.

The Cairo End

Gordon and Stewart hastened across the Continent for Brindisi, where they intended to take passage for Port Said aboard the mail-steamer SS *Tanjore*. There was a three-way exchange of telegrams as they travelled. At one point Gordon wired Granville with the text of two proclamations he felt should be immediately promulgated in the Sudan. The first of them should emanate from the Khedive and announce, first, that his highness had decided to restore the Sudan's independence; second, that the Egyptian garrisons were to be withdrawn; and third, that Gordon Pasha had been appointed as Governor-General of the Sudan for 'the time necessary to accomplish the evacuation'. The second proclamation was to emanate from Gordon himself and was to the effect that he had been pleased to accept the post of Governor-General. Granville forwarded the text of the message to Baring on 22 January (by which time Gordon was already steaming across the Mediterranean), adding a footnote to the effect that,

Her Majesty's Government have not sufficient local knowledge to enable them to form an opinion as to the practicability of these suggestions, and I therefore authorise you, as time is valuable, either immediately to make the arrangements suggested, or to await General Gordon's arrival, and consult with him as to the action to be taken.[21]

Of course the notion of the governor-generalship going to a British officer was a much hotter potato than Granville's rather casual postscript might have implied.

Another three-way piece of traffic saw Granville, at Baring's request, overrule Gordon's intention of travelling straight through the canal to Suakin, without stopping in at Cairo first. There was precious little point in his going to Suakin anyway as there could be no question of his travelling the Suakin–Berber caravan road in safety. That Gordon should call on the Khedive was an important point of protocol in any situation – notwithstanding any embarrassment he might be feeling over certain intemperate remarks he had made about Tawfīq Pasha in the past – but was doubly important if he was to enjoy any legitimacy as the civil–military supremo in Khartoum. Sir Evelyn Wood was duly despatched to Port Said to intercept Gordon and escort him to Cairo. The captain of SS *Tanjore* knew Wood well and, on learning the object of his mission, struck a wager with him to the effect that he would never be able to get Gordon to go to Cairo.[22] Unfortunately for Captain Briscoe his gamble turned out to be a bad investment. The party duly arrived at the Sirdar's house at 9.30 p.m. on the evening of 24 January.[23] After dinner they called on Sir Evelyn Baring at the British Agency and sat talking with him into the early hours of the morning.[24] The following morning Baring took Gordon and Stewart to see Tawfīq Pasha at the Ismailia Palace. Once an apology for past indiscretions had been dispensed, the rest of the audience passed off smoothly.[25] The prime movers then adjourned to Baring's office to discuss what additional instructions should be issued to Gordon. Present at the meeting were Baring himself, who had such a sore throat that he could only speak with difficulty,[26] Nubar Pasha, Wood, Gordon and Stewart. They agreed to meet again the following day to approve a formal written record of their deliberations and decisions.

The Zubair Pasha Affair

That evening Gordon and Baring paid a courtesy call on Chérif Pasha, at whose home a chance encounter took place between Gordon and an old adversary by the name of al-Zubair Pasha Raḥma Manṣūr. Now around fifty-four years of age, Zubair Pasha[27] was a Sudanese Jaʿalī who a decade or so earlier had been the most powerful warlord, slaver and power-broker in the Bahr al-Ghazāl (today Bahr el Ghazal). In 1874 he had set out at the head of a private army of *bazingers* and freebooters to conquer Dār Fūr in the name of Ismāʿil Pasha. Having defeated the Fūr Sultan in battle, he proceeded to annex most of his realm. It was not long before he had fallen out with the Egyptian authorities in the Sudan, leading to his journeying to Cairo to press his grievances. Ismāʿil Pasha heard him out, and in the end ruled that he should not be allowed to return to the south but instead be held in a loose form of house-arrest. He had been obliged to live in the capital ever since, comforted only by a generous government pension. In June 1878 Zubair's son Sulaimān raised a slaver's rebellion in the Bahr el Ghazal which began with the massacre of 200 of Gordon's black troops. The Governor-General responded by sending an Italian contract officer called Romolo Gessi to suppress the rising. After an arduous, bloody and brutal campaign, which for a long time looked as if it might go against the government, Gessi succeeded in surrounding Sulaimān's encampment by night and compelling his surrender. Sulaimān and other henchmen were shot by firing squad the following day.[28] His captured papers included a letter from his father said to have incorporated an incitement to rebel. The letter was produced in evidence at an *in absentia* court-martial convened by Gordon in Khartoum shortly afterwards. Despite the seriousness of the charges and the fact that Zubair was in Cairo, the court proceeded to pronounce a sentence of death. Suspecting rightly that the Khedive would fail to act on the sentence, Gordon sequestered Zubair's wealth and property in the Sudan.

The accidental meeting of the two old antagonists at Chérif Pasha's house led to a cold conversation of a few minutes' duration. It concluded with Gordon expressing a desire to meet with Zubair at the British Agency the following day, in order to hear out his grievances. It was widely known that he held Gordon to blame for the death of his son. When later that night Gordon adjourned to his quarters, he gave vent on paper to the 'mystic feeling' which had come over him while he was talking to Zubair. He wrote a long memorandum to Baring, commending that he be allowed to take Zubair with him to Khartoum. If the British and Egyptian governments were content that he should pull out the garrisons and leave a state of anarchy behind him, ran Gordon's argument, then all well and good: but if they wanted some sort of resolution to the Mahdīst Uprising, then Zubair was the one man influential enough to subvert Muḥammad Aḥmad's following and win the rebellious tribes over to a 'settled state of affairs'. The note was tantamount to a proposal that Gordon should invest Zubair as some kind of Sudanese head of state. The final paragraph of the general's memo ran:

I will, therefore, sum up my opinion, viz. that I would willingly take the responsibility of taking Zobeir [*sic*] up with me, if after an interview with Sir E. Baring and Nubar Pasha, they felt the mystic feeling I could trust him, and which mystic feeling I had for him tonight when I met him at Chérif Pasha's house. Zobeir could have nothing to gain in hurting me, and I would have no idea of fear. In this affair my desire, I own, would be to take Zobeir. I cannot say exactly why I feel towards him thus, and I feel sure that his going would settle the Soudan affair to the benefit of Her Majesty's and Egyptian Governments, and I would bear the responsibility of recommending it.[29]

What made the proposition all the more remarkable was that while he had been in transit across Europe, Gordon had telegraphed Granville to recommend that Baring should order Zubair's deportation to Cyprus.[30] As Baring so aptly put it in his memoirs,

A few minutes conversation with Zobeir Pasha, and a 'mystic feeling' which that conversation had engendered, had led General Gordon to jump from one extreme to the other. Instead of being considered an enemy, Zobeir Pasha was to be treated as a trusted ally, on whose conduct the success of the mission was to depend.[31]

The affair reflected precisely the judgmental inconsistency Baring had worried about prior to Gordon's appointment.

The meeting with Zubair went ahead the following afternoon.[32] Present were Baring, Nubar Pasha, Wood, Gordon, Stewart, Colonel Charles Watson, Carl Giegler Pasha,[33] Zubair himself and an interpreter called Mr Aranghi. The meeting was substantially sterile, Gordon insisting that Sulaimān's execution and the confiscation of Zubair's property were just acts arising from their treachery, while Zubair denied that he had been implicated in the rising and claimed to have been treated shamefully. Both men, Baring noted, 'spoke with vehemence'. The case hinged on the letter found in Sulaimān's camp, which Gordon had forwarded to the Khedive as part of the court-martial proceedings. The meeting closed with Baring deputing Sir Evelyn Wood to have the archives searched for the incriminating letter.[34]

After Zubair had withdrawn there was a discussion of Gordon's memorandum proposing his secondment to the mission. Nobody was for it, while even Gordon himself now seemed uncertain. Colonel Stewart was vehement in his opposition. Baring, ultimately the decision-maker, could not help wondering whether Gordon's 'mystic feeling' might not actually be one of guilt and could not overlook that only a few days earlier he had urged Zubair's deportation, for fear he might be in cahoots with the Mahdī.[35] At the same time it was true that Zubair's name still carried a great deal of weight in the Sudan. In the end the Consul-General took a measured non-decision. Zubair would not be allowed to go immediately, but might possibly be sent once Gordon had taken some time to think the matter over.[36] Nobody had yet ascertained what Zubair himself thought of the idea.

Cairo's Orders to Gordon

The most substantive item of business conducted that afternoon was the approval of Gordon's written orders from Baring. The most important passages ran as follows:

It is believed that the number of the Europeans at Khartoum is very small, but it has been estimated by the local authorities that some 10,000 to 15,000 people will wish to move northwards from Khartoum only when the Egyptian garrison is withdrawn. These people are native Christians, Egyptian employés, their wives and children, etc. The Government of His Highness the Khedive are earnestly solicitous that no effort should be spared to ensure the retreat both of these people and of the Egyptian garrison without loss of life. As regards the most opportune time and the best method for effecting the retreat, whether of the garrisons or of the civil population, it is neither necessary nor desirable that you should receive detailed instructions . . .

You will bear in mind that the main end to be pursued is the evacuation of the Sudan. This policy was adopted, after very full discussion, by the Egyptian Government on the advice of Her Majesty's Government. It meets with the full approval of His Highness the Khedive, and of the present Egyptian ministry. I understand, also, that you entirely concur in the desirability of adopting this policy, and that you think it should on no account be changed. You consider that it may take a few months to carry it out with safety. You are further of the opinion that the restoration of the country should be made to the different petty Sultans who existed at the time of Mehemet Ali's conquest, and whose families still exist; and that an effort should be made to form a confederation of those Sultans. In this view, the Egyptian Government entirely concur. It will, of course, be fully understood that the Egyptian troops are not to be kept in the Soudan merely with a view to consolidating the power of the new rulers of the country. But the Egyptian Government have the fullest confidence in your judgement, your knowledge of the country and your comprehension of the general line of policy to be pursued. You are therefore given full discretionary power to retain the troops for such reasonable period as you may think necessary, in order that the abandonment of the country may be accomplished with the least possible risk to life and property. 66A credit of £100,000 has been opened for you at the Finance Department, and further funds will be supplied to you on your requisition when this sum is exhausted.[37]

In addition to his orders Gordon was given a khedival *firman* dated the same day, appointing him as Governor-General of the Sudan.[38] It would later be suggested by both press and politicians, and by Gladstone in particular, that the nature of Gordon's mission underwent a fundamental transformation between his leaving London and his leaving Cairo. This was perfectly true, as his appointment to the most senior executive position in the Sudan necessarily implied. What was not true was the oft-twinned assertion that Baring changed Gordon's role and object without reference to London. It is of note that the texts of the two proclamations proposed by Gordon, with their unequivocal references to the governor-generalship, were omitted by the Foreign Office from the relevant Parliamentary Blue Book.[39] No matter how politically expedient the notion that Cairo had in some way gainsaid London's intent later became to Gladstone, the events of the previous few days left no room for any retrospective debate about precisely what Gordon's legal position and responsibilities were. Tawfiq Pasha lawfully constituted Gordon as Governor-General of the Sudan at the request of Sir Evelyn Baring, Her Britannic Majesty's Consul-General in Cairo. His resignation having been declined by the office of the Adjutant-General, he was still a serving major general in the British Army. The Khedive had also appointed him to hold supreme civil and military authority over Egyptian and Sudanese officials, soldiers and citizens in the south. The end result of the proceedings was that he remained a Briton and at the same time became an Egyptian. He was beyond all cavil the lawful head of government in the Sudan. This might not have been what William Ewart Gladstone had wanted or expected, but was what had come to pass all the same.

Gordon's Departure

The political formalities having been dispensed with over the course of a frantically busy couple of days, Gordon and Stewart set off up the Nile on the evening of 26 January, accompanied by Major General Sir Gerald Graham and his ADC.[40] As a member of the Army of Occupation Graham had no official role to play in the Gordon mission, but was intent simply on spending a few days in the company of an old friend. Baring saw them off at the station. Although Gordon was 'in excellent spirits and hopeful of success', the Consul-General bade him farewell with a heavy heart:

I knew the difficulties of the task which had to be accomplished. I had seen General Gordon. Nothing could have been more friendly than his behaviour. The main lines of his policy appeared wise and practical. Nevertheless, I was not relieved of the doubts which I had originally entertained as to the wisdom of employing him. Manifestly, in spite of many fine and attractive qualities, he was even more eccentric than I had originally supposed. However, the die was cast. A comet of no common magnitude had been launched on the political firmament of the Soudan. It was difficult to predict its course. It now only remained for me to do my best to help General Gordon, and to trust to the shrewd common sense of his companion, Colonel Stewart, to act in some degree as a corrective to the impulsiveness of his wayward chief.[41]

Also aboard the train that evening was one of the exiled sons of the late Sultan of Dār Fūr, together with his twenty-three wives, who somebody in authority had decided would make an excellent political figurehead in a newly independent Sudan. Gordon saw through him quickly, ticked him off for comporting himself like a king, when he did not as yet have a kingdom, and threw him off the train at Aswan.

The long river leg of the journey would terminate at the town of Korosko, where Gordon and Stewart would transfer to camels for the long overland haul to Abū-Hamed at the northernmost tip of the Great Bend. Graham recounts that while they were in transit, Gordon telegraphed Khartoum to let it be known that salvation was at hand: 'Don't be panic-stricken; you are men, not women; I am coming.'[42] Two it seems can play at messiahs. It was on the evening of Saturday 2 February that Graham parted company with his old friend:

About eight o'clock he mounted his camel and said, 'Good-bye,' but I walked beside him, and he shortly after got down and walked with me. At last I left him, saying 'Good-bye,' and 'God bless you.' Then he mounted again, and a handsome young Arab, Ahmed, son of the Sheikh [sic – mudir] of Berber, rode beside him on a beautiful white camel. At the head of the caravan rode Ahmed's brother, both armed with great cross-hilted swords and shields of rhinoceros hide... These swords together with a couple of very old double-barrelled pistols with flintlocks, made up the Arab armament. Gordon carried no arms, but Stewart had a revolver... The place where I last saw Gordon is wild and desolate... I climbed up the highest of these hills with Scott [his ADC], and through a glass watched Gordon and the small caravan as his camels threaded their way along a sandy valley, hoping that he would turn round that I might give him one more sign; but he rode until he turned the dark side of one of the hills, and I saw him no more. Sadly we returned to our steamer, and I felt a gloomy foreboding that I should never see Gordon again.[43]

On Friday 1 February, five days after Gordon left Cairo, Baring sent Granville a telegram covering the texts of four other documents, all of which were dated 26 January.[44] Two of the enclosures were khedival *firmans* addressed to Gordon personally, while the other two were khedival proclamations which Gordon had been told he could promulgate at a time and place of his choosing. One of the *firmans* was that specifically appointing him as governor-general, while one of the proclamations instructed officials and citizens to give their obedience and loyalty to Gordon Pasha as the newly appointed head of government. After what was no doubt a pleasant weekend, Lord Granville read Baring's telegram at the Foreign Office on Monday afternoon. Incredulous, it would seem, at what had been placed on the desk in front of him, at 3.50 p.m. he replied, 'Has General Gordon accepted any appointment from the Khedive?' He must surely have worked out the answer for himself by the end of his second reading of the documents. If it had dawned on the Foreign Secretary that he would have a lot of explaining to do at his next meeting with the Prime Minister, at the other end of the wire Sir Evelyn Baring had every right to be confident that his political superior had given him carte blanche on this point, three days before Gordon so much as set foot in Cairo. Baring's reply to the Foreign Secretary's enquiry was a model of brevity and propriety.

Cairo,
February 5, 1884

My Lord

In reply to your Lordship's telegram of yesterday, I have the honour to inform your Lordship that General Gordon was given, at his own request, a firman from His Highness the Khedive, appointing him Governor-General of the Sudan with full powers civil and military.

Under the circumstances it was very necessary that this step should have been taken.

I have, &c.
E. Baring[45]

A little further down in Lord Granville's in-tray was a short message sent by Baring on Saturday. 'I have the honour to inform your Lordship that General Baker Pasha has telegraphed that he will advance with 3,200 men to the relief of the garrison of Tokar on the 3rd instant. He says that there is every chance of success.' Even as Granville was running his eyes over these words, two-thirds of Baker's men were strewn across a few hundred yards of blood-soaked sand.

The Tokar Expedition and First Battle of El Teb

It was on the second full day of Gordon's journey to Abū-Hamed, just as Lord Granville was making his way back to the Foreign Office after the weekend, that the Egyptian cause in the Sudan was once again overtaken by bloody disaster. The scene was the Red Sea Littoral where Baker Pasha had spent the past six weeks concentrating a scratch field force on Suakin. Only too keenly aware that the Mahdīst enemy was in the ascendant and that little could be expected of the demoralized Egyptian military, the two Sir Evelyns, Baring and Wood, had gone to great lengths to ensure that the Khedive's written instructions to Baker were unambitious and plainly articulated the need for caution.[46] In the meantime the small inland garrisons at Sinkat and Tokar had been besieged by Osman Digna for some weeks and were now certain to be coming to the end of their tether.

As Baker put his battalions through their paces around Suakin, he allowed himself to be taken in by a tolerably competent performance. The missing ingredients in the training were the sense of mortal fear and blind panic almost invariably induced in *fellaheen* soldiers by the sight of hard-charging Bīja tribesmen. The Cairo and Alexandria gendarmerie battalions were in large part made up of old soldiers from Arabi Pasha's army, but the Senhit and Massowah battalions were hearty black regulars who gave Baker grounds for hope. He may have also have taken some comfort from the presence of a handful of British officers. With one notable exception they were retired from the British service and had taken up contract employment under the Khedive. The exception was the Commanding Officer of the Royal Horse Guards (the Blues), an old friend of Baker's who had come out to Suakin on a long-leave in response to a worried letter from Baker's wife. Colonel Fred Burnaby, a six-foot four-inch man-mountain, was one of the best known hero-adventurers of the age and like Wolseley, Gordon, Graham and others of that ilk, knew not the meaning of fear. The companionship of a living legend can only have served to lift Baker's spirits. Unfortunately he came to believe that his army was in better shape than Baring and Wood imagined. He might have done better to accept the general tenor of the reports being filed by John 'Jack' Cameron, the well-known war correspondent in the employ of the *Standard*, who despaired at the quality of the troops and openly asserted that disaster was to be anticipated. Having decided on a relatively unambitious operation designed to effect the relief of Tokar, less than twenty miles from the sea, Baker embarked his troops and sailed down the coast to an indifferent natural harbour known as Trinkitat.

The Tokar Expedition[47] came to grief on the morning of 4 February 1884, in almost exactly the same spot at which Commander Moncrieff had lost his life some eight weeks earlier. The rout started within minutes of a numerically inferior rebel force advancing to the attack. The *bāshi-būzuq* cavalry became over excited at an early glimpse of a handful of camel-mounted *anṣār* and went charging off en masse, intent on their slaughter. Burnaby and another British officer called Major Harvey went chasing after them and in due course succeeded in wheeling the squadron back in the direction of the heavy firing now emanating from the main body. Burnaby expected to find the infantry battalions formed up in the three echeloned squares in which they had so repeatedly been rehearsed. Instead the onset of a live enemy had induced only wild, ineffective firing, rapidly followed by an irredeemable outbreak of panic. 'The sight was one never to be forgotten,' wrote Burnaby, 'some four thousand men running pell-mell for their lives with a few hundred Arabs behind them spearing everyone in reach.'

Of the 3,650 officers and men who had taken the field that morning, 112 officers (including sixteen Europeans), and 2,250 NCOs and men were killed. It was extraordinary that such slaughter had been inflicted by fewer than 1,200 Bīja.[48] Baker and Burnaby were lucky to escape with their lives, as were Jack Cameron and Frank Scudamore of *The Times*. Melton Prior of the *Illustrated London News* was fortunate enough to have fallen ill and was still aboard one of the ships in Trinkitat harbour. Burnaby's Nubian cook escaped by holding on for grim death to the tail of a riderless horse, while his batman, Private Henry Storey, had been thrown from the saddle, but somehow clung on to the neck and collar-chain of his horse over the course of a mile-long gallop. At length Colonel Fred came galloping up beside the frightened animal, quickly brought it under control and then dismounted to heave an exhausted Storey back into the saddle. Fortunately there was too much loot lying about for the enemy to harry the survivors all the way back to the coast. Despite the best efforts of the surviving British officers, the evacuation from the beach was also conducted in an atmosphere of high-panic.[49] History would designate the Baker fiasco as the First Battle of El Teb, although in truth it was actually the second encounter on the same spot and, much like the first, more a massacre than a battle. The action known to history as the Second Battle of El Teb, in reality the third fight on substantially the same piece of ground, would be fought before the month was out, this time by troops of an altogether different mettle.

The rout of Baker's force meant that even Suakin was now in peril, so much so that Rear Admiral Sir William Hewett immediately landed British marines to 'take charge of town and allay panic'.[50] Although there was a mainland suburb called al-Geif, with some rudimentary landward defences, behind which the remnants of Baker's army were now cowering, the hub of Suakin was to be found on a small oval-shaped island in the harbour.[51] Because almost all of the principal buildings had been built from bricks of coral, the claustrophobic streets and alleyways glistened white against the deep blue of the lagoon. The harbour provided a safe anchorage, albeit it was small and entered through a dangerously narrow channel in the coral. The island town was linked to al-Geif by a seventy-five-yard causeway raised by Gordon some years earlier. The island should have been safe enough but to emphasize that the town was now under the control and protection of the Royal Navy, Commander W. E. Darwall of HMS *Coquette* and Lieutenant-Commander F. H. E. Crowe of HMS *Ranger* anchored their ships so as to be able to sweep the causeway with their guns.

The London papers got wind of the Baker disaster late on Tuesday 5 February. While some evening editions hinted that something might be amiss, the story broke in full force the following day. The government quickly found itself under heavy attack from the press and the opposition. There could be no mistaking the public mood of the country either. Gladstone's abrogation of Sudanese affairs was so loudly condemned that the outcry served to get Granville off the hook over the governor-generalship issue: Gordon's appointment was allowed to assume the air of a decisive measure directly instigated by the Prime Minister. There was still a need to take substantive military measures if the situation in the Littoral was to be restored. Even Gladstone could not pretend that there was no strategic British interest in the region. The fall of Sinkat, news of which arrived at Suakin on 12 February to be promptly telegraphed home, served to pour fuel on the flames. The context of the town's fall only made the furore worse. The garrison was commanded by Colonel Muḥammad Tawfiq Bey, an able and courageous officer of Cretan origin. It transpired that the news of Baker Pasha's defeat had driven Tawfiq Bey to conclude that there was no longer any prospect of outside help. Rather than face the inevitability of capitulation through starvation, he resolved to spike his guns and attempt to cut his way out. Having formed his troops in a loose square, around a frightened cluster of wives and children, Tawfiq began marching for the coast. For all that it was a brave attempt, it ended in annihilation after only a few miles. Those of the women and children who survived were enslaved by the victorious rebels.

The First Suakin Expedition

Sir Frederick Stephenson now received orders to mount a British expedition for the relief of Tokar. Although the stated objective was limited in the extreme, it nonetheless implied London's acceptance that the Hadendawa and their confederates could expect to be on the receiving end of British bullets. The speed with which Stephenson assembled a divisional-sized force of two infantry brigades and a cavalry brigade was commendable. Command of the force went to Sir Gerald Graham. Five major units, a company of Royal Engineers and a camel-borne battery of screw guns were shipped down from Cairo and Alexandria, while SS *Jumna* was diverted into Suakin on its way home from India with the 10th Hussars and the 2nd Battalion, The Royal Irish Fusiliers. The 1st Battalion, The York and Lancaster Regiment, was shipped across the Red Sea from Aden and arrived just in time to participate in the first action of the campaign. The Royal Navy for its part supplemented the Army's endeavours by landing a small battalion of Royal Marine Light Infantry (RMLI) and a 150-man naval brigade equipped with half-a-dozen machine guns. The units yielded by the Army of Occupation were the 19th Hussars; 1st Battalion, The Black Watch; 3rd Battalion, The King's Royal Rifle Corps; 1st Battalion, The Gordon Highlanders; and a composite company of mounted infantry.

Command of the 1st Infantry Brigade went at Wolseley's instigation to Major General Sir Redvers Buller VC, KCMG, CB, ADC, late King's Royal Rifle Corps,[52] one of the original and now best-known members of the Ring. Buller had first served under Wolseley as a company commander on the Red River Expedition and four years later was handpicked to be an intelligence officer in the Ashanti Campaign. His next extended spell of active service came in South Africa at the end of the decade, this time without Wolseley on hand. Buller served in the closing stages of the 9th Cape Frontier War and throughout the Zulu War, for the first few months of which he found himself commanding the mounted troops with Colonel Evelyn Wood's No. 4 Column. In March 1879 Wood contrived to get his horsemen tangled up in a bloody affair on Hlobane Mountain, obliging Buller to get them untangled again via the 'Devil's Pass', a treacherous descent which failed to live up to the second part of its name. Buller showed great and formidable example throughout. The following day the decimated cavalry were back in the saddle for the Battle of Khambula, where Buller again displayed great courage in demonstrating in front of the Zulu right horn, with the object of provoking an uncoordinated attack. His gallant conduct over both days earned him the Victoria Cross.[53] His most recent spell of service under Wolseley had been in the Tel-el-Kebir campaign. Graham's other infantry brigade was in the hands of Major General John Davis, who was to play no part in the Nile Expedition and on whose biographical details we need not dwell. The cavalry brigade on the other hand was commanded by a man destined to become one of the central figures in the Gordon Relief Expedition.

Colonel Herbert Stewart CB, ADC, 3rd Dragoon Guards, was a relative newcomer to the Ring but had quickly established himself as Wolseley's particular favourite. He is often portrayed as a dyed-in-the-wool cavalryman, but in fact had spent the first half of his career in the infantry. Wolseley had come across him as a disenchanted staff captain in Zululand, at which stage he had been on the point of resigning his commission. He was revitalized by the campaign against the baPedi, the quick promotion which followed and Wolseley's generous words of encouragement. In December 1880 the Transvaal Rebellion broke out. The campaign to advance from Natal to the relief of the tiny garrisons besieged on the high *veldt* of the Transvaal was commanded as we have seen by Major General Sir George Colley. Colley, another Ashanti man, was well known for having put in an exceptional performance at the Staff College and had preceded Stewart as foremost in Wolseley's estimation. On 28 January 1881 Colley fumbled an attack on the Boer positions on Laing's Nek, the gateway between Natal and the Transvaal. On 8 February he suffered a second mauling at the Battle of Ingogo (locally Schuinshoogte), and was lucky to get a brace of guns and the remnants of 3rd KRRC away under the cover of a storm. He was obliged to leave his wounded and medical staff behind. By this stage in the campaign most members of Colley's original headquarters staff had been killed or incapacitated. Not long afterwards Brigadier General Sir Evelyn Wood VC arrived to take up the duties of second-in-command.

By the time Herbert Stewart joined the Natal Field Force as its new chief of staff, the general was contemplating an ill-conceived plan to seize Majuba Hill, an offensive manoeuvre which flew in the face of new and conciliatory political direction emanating from London. Notoriously, Colley sent Wood off on a weeklong errand and discussed his plan for Majuba with nobody but Stewart. Colley lost his life in the ensuing shambles, or rather surrendered it when it became clear that all was lost. The last man with his face to the foe, he advanced on the enemy firing his revolver, only to be shot in the forehead. It is said that Wood, not invariably the most sensitive of characters, sent his late chief's helmet to Lady Edith, Colley's widow, in order that the hole in front would conclusively disprove the rumour that her husband had been shot down in flight. In the meantime the chief of staff had been wounded and captured. Eighteen months after Majuba, Stewart had participated in the altogether more creditable Egyptian Campaign, where he had spearheaded the cavalry dash from Tel-el-Kebir to the gates of Cairo. There were plenty of officers at Suakin in the spring of 1884 who had not forgotten his part in the unnecessary and disastrous secrecy preceding the Majuba fiasco, including inevitably a whispering faction from 3rd KRRC who very much held it against him. Overwhelmingly, though, Stewart was a popular and well-regarded figure. A natural leader, amply possessed of charm, charisma and winning ways, he was tall, distinguished in appearance and sported a bristling military moustache after the Prussian fashion.

Having assembled his force at Suakin, Graham embarked it for Trinkitat, just as Baker Pasha had done a little over three weeks earlier. All told Graham could field 2,850 infantry, a small 750-man cavalry brigade, 150 sailors, 100 gunners, eighty sappers, six machine guns and eight 7-pounders.[54] As a courtesy to Val Baker, Graham allowed him to join his staff as an intelligence officer, an offer which was also extended to Colonel Burnaby. It was they who set the direction when, on the morning of 29 February, Graham commenced his advance on Tokar.[55] The putrid scene of Baker's defeat was only a couple of hundred yards to the British left, when Stewart's cavalry detected the enemy, arrayed along a low ridge, just in front of the village of El Teb. There were guns and there were earthworks, suggesting that the Bija intended, somewhat unusually, to fight a defensive action. The reason that this was so was that the authorities had let it be known that British troops would be advancing on Tokar, giving the rebels ample warning that this time they could expect to have a much tougher fight on their hands. In command were the Amīrs Madanī ibn ʿAlī and ʿAbd Allāh ibn Hamid, who had concentrated something between 6,000 and 8,000 men from the Hassanab, Atreiga, Gemilab, Hadendawa, Ashrab and Demilab tribes. Hardy, psychologically tough and courageous beyond reason, these were Kipling's 'fuzzy-wuzzies', men whose eccentric hairstyles were their pride and joy. While there were many captured Remingtons on the field, the Bija weapons of choice were broad-bladed spears of between six and eight feet in length, cross-hilted swords and hardwood throwing sticks, which they could throw with unerring accuracy to about thirty yards. Many were also equipped with round shields manufactured from rhinoceros skin. There were also four Krupp field guns, three brass howitzers, a Gatling gun and two rocket troughs, a mixture of ordnance captured at First El Teb and at Tokar, which, as was already known in Cairo and London, had capitulated some days earlier. The Krupps had captured Egyptian crews chained to them, operating the pieces under pain of death, though some of the other heavy weapons including the Gatling and the rocket troughs seem not to have been fired at all, most likely from want of ammunition rather than expertise.

Graham had his infantry and artillery arrayed in a single great square which he steered to the right of the enemy position, before turning through a right angle to attack from the flank. The manoeuvre resulted in what had originally been the square's left face becoming its new front face. Thus it was that the break-in battle fell to Lieutenant Colonel Byam's 1st York and Lancaster, six companies strong, and a lone company of RMLI deployed on Byam's left. The two Highland battalions, resplendent in kilts, sporrans, hosetops and spats, found themselves occupying the side faces of the square, with 1st Black Watch on the left and 1st Gordons on the right. Many of the Bija chose not to await the British assault but emerged from their defences to attack the front face of the square. They were driven back by rifle fire, after which the front-face companies counter-charged with the bayonet. Fred Burnaby was the first man up the parapet and would almost certainly have lost his life had not the infantry rushed to his assistance. Once the York and Lancaster were inside the principal enemy bastion, the Highland battalions came up on their flanks to commence fighting through the rest of the position in line. The enemy fought from the cover of rifle-pits and trenches and periodically made madcap charges. At the sort of ranges at issue, they stood little chance against such large concentrations of Martini-Henry rifles.

Colonel Stewart had been given instructions not to make a mounted charge until the enemy was broken and in flight but, like so many cavalry officers before him, proved a little too eager to 'Draw swords' and may have gone off anything up to fifteen minutes too early. The 10th and 19th Hussars ran into fresh bodies of Bija secreted in the scrub to the flank and rear of the main position and were left with little choice but to cut their way through them. They took unnecessarily heavy casualties in consequence and in the end were forced to dismount and drive the enemy from the field with carbine fire. Graham took the view that the loss in the cavalry brigade had marred what would otherwise have been a handsome victory and in his official despatch left little room for doubt just whose fault he considered this to be.[56]

When it was all over the British had suffered a fatal loss of 4 officers and 26 NCOs and men. A further twenty officers and 142 NCOs and men had been wounded, amongst them Baker Pasha, with a large shard of shrapnel in his cheek, and Fred Burnaby, who had been shot in the arm. The loss on the Bija side is less clear-cut; Graham's official despatch remarks, 'I am informed they admit a loss of 1500 killed.' By one count, however, they left only 825 bodies on the field. Most British estimates put their total casualties at between 1,500 and 2,000 men. There is a broad-order rule of thumb in military history which suggests that in any battle there will generally be two men wounded to every man killed. If that is so and there were 800+ dead, then this would suggest that there were 1,600 wounded and an overall loss of 2,400. This sounds a little excessive and takes no account of one of the more dreadful aspects of Sudanese warfare now unfolding for the first time, if not for the Egyptians, then at least for the British.

Why it should be so I am neither psychologist nor theologian enough to state with authority, but the sources tell us that a wounded *anṣāri*, no matter how badly hurt he was, simply would not be helped and would do anything within his power to kill anybody who came within reach. This included a practice which the British came to refer to as 'shamming', which is to say feigning death until a Good Samaritan came within striking distance. Kind-hearted souls, scouring the field to bring succour to the injured, lost their lives in just this fashion at Second El Teb. It does not take many such incidents before the enemy wounded are adjudged by angry soldiers to have sacrificed their right to be regarded as non-combatants. At the time the British attributed this behaviour to the fact that the *anṣār* had been taught to believe that anybody who killed an infidel gained automatic admission to paradise. They may well have been right; such is the power of religious fervour. Whatever its origin, the practice of shamming led to the Sudan campaigns being characterized by ugly scenes played out in the aftermath of battle. A well-known war correspondent, Bennet Burleigh of the *Daily Telegraph*, would liken the experience of crossing a Sudanese battlefield to 'walking amongst wounded vipers'. This is a point to which we will return in more detail when we come to contemplate the operations in the Bayūda Desert. The evidence would suggest that some proportion of the 800 Bīja fighters left dead on the field were wounded men who were finished on the ground with a shot or a bayonet thrust. If only three-quarters of the dead had been killed outright, then the overall Mahdīst loss would be reduced to something around 1,800 which on balance sounds more plausible.[57] We will come later to more detailed consideration of the Mahdīst style of command, but for now it is enough to note that the Amīrs Madanī ibn ʿAlī and ʿAbd Allāh ibn Hamid both lost their lives in the battle.

Graham despatched his wounded for the coast the following morning and resumed his advance on Tokar. It took some little time to find such an inconsequential place in broken scrub country, but once the cavalry screen had homed in on it the mud-built town was secured without further resistance. Around 700 liberated Egyptians and loyalist Sudanese accompanied the British on their return journey to Trinkitat.[58] It was from the loyalist citizenry that Graham obtained his questionable estimate of 1,500 Bīja dead, said to have been admitted by the rebels as they passed through the town in retreat.[59]

A fortnight later Graham gave battle again, this time some fourteen miles southwest of Suakin, near the temporary desert settlement of Tamai, no more than a cluster of straw huts and a sea of tents. Nonetheless it was home to several thousand rebels, who called in all the reinforcements they could muster from the hills and deployed to contest the British advance along the line of a dry watercourse known as the Khor Ghob, a feature wide enough and deep enough to be a small valley unto itself. On the night of 12/13 March 1884, the British passed the hours of darkness under a heavy fire in an overly exposed *zariba* position. The following morning Graham advanced in two brigade squares. The formations stepped off in echelon, albeit not altogether intentionally, with Davis's 2nd Brigade forward and to the left of Buller's 1st Brigade, which had been a few minutes late in getting under way. Stewart's cavalry regiments were kept well back, although his mounted infantry company and a few dozen Abyssinian scouts led by a Suakin trader called Augustus Wylde were thrown forward to screen the infantry. The enemy's main position was obvious, as not only were there several thousand warriors deployed in front of the *khor*, but there were several thousand more manoeuvring through the scrub on the British right. The Bīja attacked both brigades bravely, but could make no headway against a heavy defensive fire. Graham and his staff were in the thick of things and accompanied Davis's brigade to within a few hundred yards of the *khor*. The brigade was formed with the RMLI battalion occupying the rear face of the square and the other three sides divided between two much larger units, 1st Black Watch, which had been assigned the left face and the left half of the front face, and 1st York and Lancaster, deployed on the right face and the right half of the front face.

Graham was conscious that he had caused mortal offence to Colonel William Green and the officers of the Black Watch by suggesting in his official despatch for Second El Teb that the battalion had been briefly 'out of hand'. He had attempted to make amends by making a ham-fisted pre-battle speech, in which he had promised that the battalion would be given the opportunity to 'redeem' itself. It was this which lay behind the sudden mad impulse that impelled Graham to order the battalion to charge the enemy lining the lip of the *khor*. No attempt was made to communicate what was about to happen to Colonel Byam, so that the York and Lancaster company commanders, while they eventually took it upon themselves to charge in conformity, were somewhat slower off the mark than the Highlanders. This served to weaken the front face of the square around its centre point and, after a few moments, to detach Byam's left-wing companies from the right face. It just so happened that there was a body of around 1,500 Bīja concealed beneath the lip of the *khor*, at the very point where the front-right corner of the square had suddenly dissolved. The outcome was bloody chaos and a vicious close-quarter brawl which resulted in Davis's brigade being driven back 600 yards, before it was able to rally and re-form. The *Daily Telegraph* correspondent was caught up in the melee and attempted to encapsulate the scene for his readers:

> The Arabs were all over that side and corner of the square, bounding like deer out of the khor by hundreds... With hair on end, eyes glistening and their white teeth shining, more like infuriated demons than men, they seemed to bound out of the battle-smoke upon the soldiers like figures in a shadow pantomime. In an instant they were at the guns and among our men, thrusting, cutting, stabbing with desperate energy. The men recoiled before the avalanche of fierce savages; but to our soldier's credit, be it ever told, they retired mostly with their faces to the foe, loading and firing with the courage of heroes.[60]

As desperate as the situation in Davis's brigade became, there were simply too many Martinis in action for the enemy to retain their advantage for long. Buller also rendered good service by bringing his brigade up smartly and pouring in a flanking fire. While Davis was re-forming his battalions in line, to counter-attack and recover the abandoned naval machine guns, Buller's brigade shot a great crescent-shaped Bīja assault to pieces.

Having regained the initiative on their respective sectors, the infantry brigadiers were at last able to push across the *khor*, by which time the fierce enemy resistance was all but spent. The British had suffered a fatal loss of 5 officers and 110 NCOs and men. There were also 111 wounded, 8 of whom were officers. The Bīja had taken the field with something between 9,000 and 12,000 men, of whom 1,500–2,000 were said at the time to have been killed. If we were to go in at the lower end of these estimates, at say 1,600 bodies strewn across the field, and again make allowance for only three-quarters of them having been killed outright, then, in addition to the 1,200 immediate fatalities and the 400 men who might or might not have been 'despatched', there would also have been a further 2,000 wounded – which is to say some 3,600 casualties in all. There is no way of knowing how many of the wounded might have succumbed subsequently to shock, blood loss or infection.[61]

A fortnight after Tamai, Graham again advanced into the desert in full force, this time to attack Osman Digna's other stronghold at Tamanieb. The only resistance was some long-range rifle fire from the hills. The huts at Tamanieb were put to the torch, just as the encampment at Tamai had been. The Bīja casualties across the two battles had been so crippling that the back of the rebellion in the east could be counted as broken. All that remained was to harry the tribes with Stewart's cavalry and press them politically to conclude a negotiated peace. Long-term pacification of the Red Sea Littoral was there for the taking. Instead Gladstone decreed that Graham's force should be withdrawn. Even before the last troopship had departed Suakin, Osman Digna was touring the desert, boasting how he had driven the British back into the sea. As outrageous as his rhetoric might have sounded to the departed victors, this was jihad, whipped up and sustained in the usual way by lies, propaganda, threats and intimidation. If there was no British military presence to fear, the Littoral was bound to remain in Osman's hands. So it was that the Red Sea rebellion limped on, rendering the terrible loss of life at El Teb and Tamai meaningless and, by extension, morally reprehensible.

If William Ewart Gladstone imagined for one moment that he had now done with the Sudan, the Sudan, alas, had not yet done with him.

Chapter 2

Quandary

Gordon at Khartoum: February–April 1884

It would be cowardly and shameful for me to leave Khartoum now in the face of the enemy and because there is danger here; even for your sake I would not do it.

Frank Power, letter to his mother, 24 January 1884

THE CORE INGREDIENTS of Gordon's thinking in the early days of his mission have been too often obscured by historians, albeit for the most part unintentionally, notwithstanding the fact that his plan was clearly articulated in a memorandum to Baring penned while he was travelling upriver to Korosko. The document was accompanied by a sketch map on which the three principal rebel-held areas had been delimited by hatching and designated A, B and C (*see Map 2*). Rebellion A was Kordofan where the situation could be regarded as beyond redemption; rebellion B embraced the *jazīra* south of Khartoum; while rebellion C covered the Red Sea Littoral from Suakin to Kassala. The accompanying memorandum outlined six lines of operation:

The rebellion in the Soudan is situated as on the accompanying sketch. The programme of operations I propose to carry out is as follows:
1. To get down to Egypt all Egyptian employés' families and their belongings.
2. To replace these Egyptian employés by native Soudan officials under myself, thus forming the foundation of the future Government of Soudan.
3. To concentrate the neighbouring tribes against the Hadendowa (Rebellion C) and to open the road from Suakin to Berber and Suakin to Casala.
4. To relieve Sennar and the triangle between Blue and White Niles (Rebellion B).
5. To send up expedition of five steamers to bring down families of the troops of Equatorial Province and Bahr Gazelle.
6. To arrange at Dongola for the exodus of those who remain in Darfour if they still exist.

For this programme I need five officers to assist me . . . I shall need them for six months. I would wish Lord Wolseley to choose them . . . These five officers to be my agents; they are not to lead troops or enter into active operations, but merely hold together the well-disposed Soudan tribes against these pillaging tribes, and to insure harmony amongst the well-disposed.

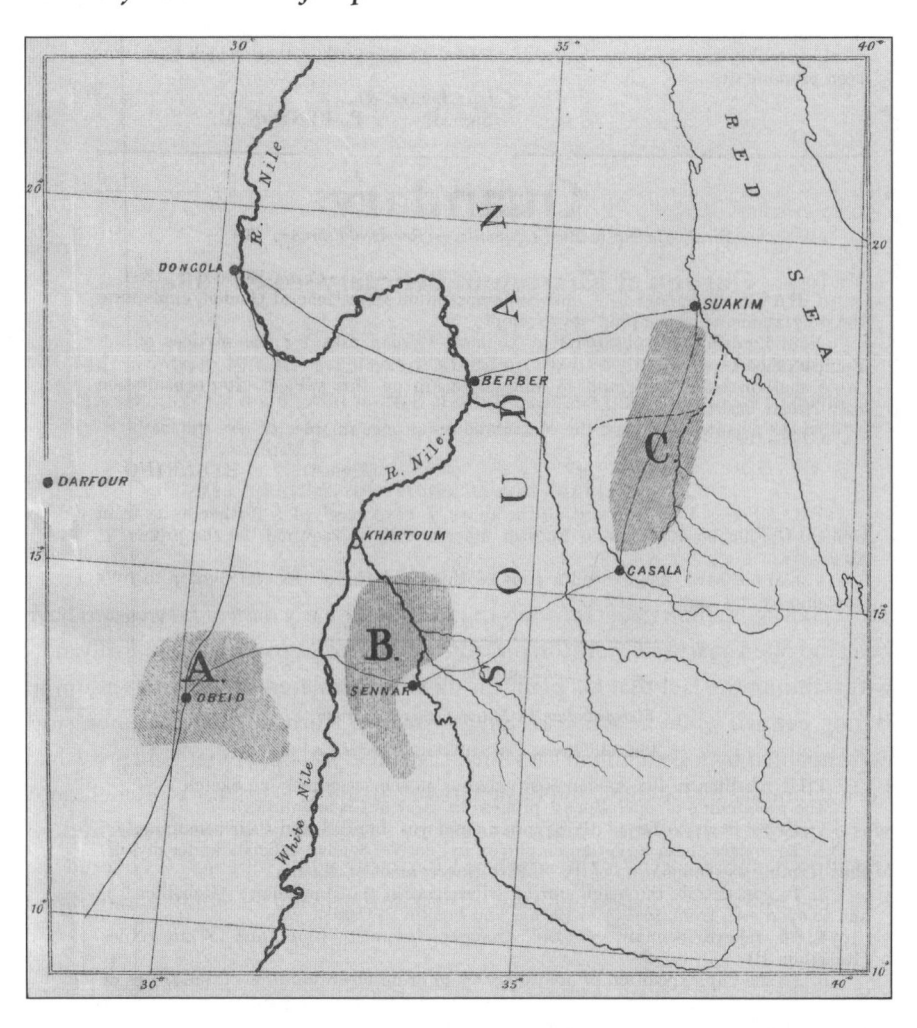

Map 2: Gordon's reading of the situation in February 1884

I particularly point out that these officers are in no way supposed to lead troops, that the suppression of the Rebellion (B) and (C) will be the act of the Soudanese themselves (who are rendered independent of Cairo), and on which suppression depends the establishment of the independent Soudan government which Her Majesty's Government desires.

If your Excellency feels any difficulty about these officers, or thinks that it would lead to trouble, never mind sending them, for I humbly believe we will manage without them, only it may take a longer time than if they were sent, and I may mention that, to me, it is of far greater import not to raise an outcry in England than to have these officers.

Anyway, this Memorandum will show you what I design, and give you to understand that if fighting occurs it is the Sudanese conservatives of their property fighting the Sudanese communists, who desire to rob them, and that in the fighting, if it occurs (which is not certain and I hope may be avoided), there is no idea of asserting the Khedive's authority over the Soudan, but only of forming a form of conservative Soudan government, which I believe Her Majesty's Government has in view.[1]

Such was Gordon's concern to avoid any difficulty with the London government that he almost immediately fired off a telegram dropping his request for the services of other British officers. The memorandum reflects the essence of the approaching disarray in British decision-making. Gordon had set out to do a difficult job well and intended to attain at least a semblance of a structured end-state. Having divested himself of the Egyptians, he would breathe life into a self-governing Sudanese state centred on the Nile Valley and the Red Sea Littoral and would then proceed to pacify the littoral and the *jazīra* with the help of loyalist tribes and indigenous regular troops. Kordofan and Dār Fūr would be cast off to become ungoverned space, ruled *ipso facto*, for a period at least, by the Mahdī. Once the situation had been stabilized he would set up a confederation of semi-autonomous traditional leaders under the chairmanship of a local strong-man, a role in which he now intended to cast Zubair Pasha. Finally, after providing a few months of mentoring to Zubair, he would hand over supreme authority to him and go on his way. Given Gordon's standing as a hero of the anti-slavery movement, the alacrity with which he dismissed the possibility of a return to slave-raiding under Zubair is of note.[2] In essence Gordon had spent his time on the Nile drawing up something which would pass for a strategy. Although he hinted to Baring that it might all be wrapped up in six months, this was assuredly an expedient designed to mollify the London government. In reality his several lines of operation could not have failed to consume at least eighteen months.

Looking back with the sort of hindsight not granted to its architect, it was a wildly unrealistic, unachievable plan, but then again it could hardly be otherwise when one man is sent to do the work of thousands in a geographic space which, until it was partitioned in 2011, constituted the largest territory in Africa. Today such lofty objectives would more than likely trigger a UN-led multi-dimensional governance intervention involving thousands of officials, soldiers, humanitarians, aid workers and logisticians. In 1884 the most powerful nation in the world managed to stretch to a major general, a lieutenant colonel and a 25-year-old newspaperman. Far better that Her Majesty's Government had not bothered at all, as it is an inescapable fact of life that the establishment and citizenry of a superpower are unlikely to be overly taken with the idea of abandoning a national hero to his fate. The problem was that while the Consul-General in Cairo and a supine Foreign Secretary had signed up to all this, after a fashion at least, it was not at all what the Prime Minister had in mind. If Gladstone had come to accept that Gordon had by fait accompli come to occupy an executive position in the Sudan, he nonetheless still saw his task as extending no further than gathering up the Egyptians at Khartoum and cutting and running with them – a strategy of hasty retreat, rather than measured withdrawal. What became of Sennar, Kassala and the garrisons in Bahr el Ghazal and Equatoria, Gladstone simply did not care. Such places were manifestly beyond the reach of even the British Empire. The same could not be said of the Sudanese capital – or so it seemed.

Gordon at Abū-Hamed and Berber

After a gruelling six-day camel ride from Korosko, Gordon and Stewart reached Abū-Hamed on 8 February. From there the new Governor-General telegraphed Baring to say, 'It is evident that the country is far less disturbed than has been reported.'[3] This was a sweeping statement, based it would appear on not much more than the fact that the authorities in Abū-Hamed were still receiving solicitations for government appointments and contracts. Gordon went on to make the point that there was in place a telegraph system, a postal system, courts and a series of government departments, upon which large parts of the Sudanese population depended. 'To disturb, if not annihilate, this system at a moment's notice', he wrote, 'would appear to me to hand over the country to complete anarchy.' This was not an unreasonable point and plainly hinted that the timetable for pulling out key Egyptian employees ought to be the subject of further contemplation. Gordon then proceeded to advocate something which the prime movers in the London government would have regarded as a significant divergence from their stated policy. 'Hence I would suggest that the Government of Egypt should continue to maintain its position as a Suzerain Power, nominate the governor-general and *mudirs* and act as a Supreme Court of Appeal. Its controlling influence should, however, be a strictly moral one, and limited to giving advice.' Gordon's object in suggesting this was to prevent the *mudirs*, or provincial governors, turning over time into regional warlords and contributing to a downwards spiral into anarchy. Again there was rational substance to such concerns.

Almost straight away, then, we can detect a fundamental divergence between Gordon's assessment of the situation and the perspective of the London government. The new Governor-General was anticipating dealing on a practical level with people he cared about and was responsible for, whereas Gladstone and Granville were concerned only to evade embroilment in a troublesome African hotspot. British liberals had to some extent been thrown into a quandary over whether it was better to permit venal Egyptian governance to continue, or to have no governance to speak of across a vast swathe of the African interior. In the latter scenario there would be a strong likelihood that overt slaving in the Bahr el Ghazal and Equatoria would resume and quickly become widespread. Gladstone and Granville wanted both to have their cake and eat it; they did not want the Egyptians in the Sudan, but neither did they want to bear any responsibility for a resurgence of slavery in the benighted southern provinces. What they had not yet grasped was that the choice was not, in fact, between bad government and no government, but between bad government which might perhaps be influenced to become better, and the relentless tyranny of theocracy and 'warlordism' in dreadful combination. What price the prospects of the African population in the Bahr el Ghazal and Equatoria then? Even Gordon had not yet grasped just how pervasive and immediate the Mahdist threat had already become.

He would discover these things soon enough but in order to do so had to be not in sleepy Abū-Hamed, but 337 miles further south in jittery Khartoum. Importantly the Sudan strategy of Her Majesty's Government drew a distinction between the Red Sea coast, in which the British had a very obvious strategic interest, namely the security of the direct sea-lane to India, and the Sudanese interior, where just as obviously there was no particular national interest at stake – assuming that is that Britain would be abdicating its suzerain role in Egypt in the next two or three years as Gladstone intended. Strategic factors aside, there were a great many powerful British opinion-formers who took a strong humanitarian interest in the Sudanese interior, a factor which the fractious Liberal Cabinet could ill afford to ignore.

By 11 February Gordon and Stewart had reached Berber, 192 miles north of Khartoum, where the Mahdīst threat and the deteriorating government position was much more tangible, not least because it was here that they learned of the Baker disaster, the best part of 250 miles to the east. It was in Berber that the new Governor-General was at last able to get down to business. On the afternoon of the 12th Gordon read the khedival proclamations he was carrying to an assembled audience of government officials and tribal elders. 'The people, great and small,' he wired Baring, 'are heartily glad to be free of a union which had only caused them sorrow.'[4] Colonel Stewart, who had been separately mandated to provide a running commentary to Baring, was nothing like as sanguine, observing the following day that, 'Gordon has taken his great leap in the dark and shown his secret firman. How it will act, and what will be the result, goodness only knows.'[5] Stewart was right to have doubts, as the only effect that a public announcement of intent to withdraw could ever have had was to undermine still further the already ruinously weak authority of the in-place government. For the uncommitted and wavering there was now only one side to be on. While it is true that Gordon could not have kept the issue of withdrawal under wraps for much longer, announcing it before he had even reached the capital and taken some time to weigh up the situation, and doing so at *the* key waypoint on the line of retreat, was in some sense tantamount to severing his own lines of communication.

Still brimming with optimism in the face of a gradual accrual of evidence to the contrary, Gordon also sent Baring a telegram which urged, 'Do not fear for Khartoum garrison. It can come by Berber if necessary, but neither the men who attacked Berber nor those who attacked Hicks will ever leave their tribal limits.'[6] He was right about the eastern rebels at least and, if these had been ordinary times, would also have been justified in doubting that the fractious Kordofani clans could ever share the unity of purpose required to menace Khartoum. But the revelations still to come included the power of jihad and the mettle and mysticism of his nemesis. That said, Gordon was fully attuned to the fact that the rebellion in Kordofan was 'too strong to be touched',[7] a deduction made manifest by the scale of the Shaikān disaster. It was this unavoidable conclusion which would lead Gordon to extend a conciliatory but supremely pragmatic offer to recognize Muḥammad Aḥmad as the Sultan of Kordofan.

Khartoum – Hearts and Minds

When, amidst scenes of great rejoicing, Gordon Pasha disembarked from the steamer *Tawfiqiyeh* on 18 February 1884, he had no intention of leaving his suite of rooms at the *sarāya* until a reasonably stable situation had been attained. Gladstone, on the other hand, expected to see his emissary back in London within two or three months, come what may. Gordon lost no time in sending away the 'sick, widows and orphans' associated with the Egyptian element of the garrison, but quickly detected that there was already a battle afoot in the capital for the hearts and minds of the people. On 27 February he reported that he did not feel able to send away his 1,400 *fellaheen* regulars for fear of the signal it would send. 'Supposing I sent down these fellaheen soldiers,' he wired Baring, 'in a few days the town would send to the Mahdi its submission, and all the machinery of government would be caught. It would not be for the love of the Mahdi, but because they are hopeless [i.e. in the sense of without hope]. They would be perfectly right to do so.' The core of the problem he encapsulated as, 'Two-thirds of the people are terrorized over by one-third, excited by emissaries of the Mahdi.'

Gordon moved straight into what counter-insurgency theorists would later term a 'hearts and minds' offensive. In the most substantive proclamation made in the early days of his mission he announced that, 'The Soudan has now become an independent State to govern itself without the intervention of the Egyptian Government in any way whatever.'[8] He heralded the dawn of a new age by emptying the city jail, where many of the inmates had been incarcerated by the pashas for the most trivial of reasons, and followed up with proclamations designed to remedy the major grievances against the government. A large proportion of the city's inhabitants were black slaves whom Cairo had pledged itself to emancipate towards the end of the decade. As welcome as such a development would have been to the subjugated Africans, it was also a source of rancour amongst the slave-owning Arab citizenry. Remarkably Gordon now made it clear that emancipation was no longer on the government agenda. To some extent this was a red herring, as clearly the slaves would not have been emancipated in an autonomous Arab-dominated Sudan anyway. Nonetheless, when at length news of the proclamation became known in London, it did not play at all well with the liberal-minded establishment. Gordon went on to dismiss all the tax arrears for 1883 and to reduce the taxes due for 1884 by 50 per cent. He was not above bolstering his personal standing with the odd white lie:

> It should be known to you that the Sultan had the intention of sending an expedition of strong Turkish troops to subdue the rebellious provinces, but this knowledge of your condition and of my kindness to you during the four years I was Governor-General of the Soudan has prevented him from sending such an expedition and I have come in person, by the will of God, to prevent war between the Moslems and the shedding of blood, which is contrary to the will of God, his Prophet and the Saints.

The Military Position at Khartoum

So long as the Mahdī remained in Kordofan with the main rebel host clustered about him, the military situation in Khartoum could not be considered desperate. Colonel de Cöetlogon had gathered in all the outlying garrisons capable of reaching the capital and, before departing for Cairo with the first tranche of evacuees, handed over a force of something around 10,500 men, about half of whom were regulars. Writing in his journal on 19 October 1884, some eight months after his arrival, Gordon summarized the garrison's strength at that point as 1,421 Egyptian regulars, 2,316 black Sudanese regulars, 1,906 *bāshi-būzuqs* and 2,330 Shā'iqīa irregulars. In addition ther were also 692 citizens under arms, for a total of 8,665 men. His journal entry for 22 November, however, estimates the garrison's losses up to that point as 1,800–1,900 men, most of whom seem to have been black regulars. As there would appear to have been no major losses between these two dates, it seems reasonable to tally the two figures to give the total size of the garrison at the beginning of the siege.

The ordnance available to Gordon is nowhere specifically listed, although a reconciliation of various sources would suggest that he had two Krupp 20-pounders, two or three *Mitrailleuse* machine guns (Gordon could have been using the French term in its generic sense and might actually have been referring to Nordenfelts), eleven 7-pounder mountain guns and around sixteen brass guns and howitzers. At least a third of the guns were mounted aboard the all-important flotilla of steamers, of which there would seem to have been nine or ten at the outset of the siege. With water on two of the city's three sides, the improvised gunboats served as the garrison's quick-reaction force. Colonel Stewart devoted considerable time and attention to ensuring that they were as well 'armoured' as possible, but while he was able to make their superstructures proof against small-arms fire with timber sleepers and whatever limited quantities of plate metal he could lay his hands on, they remained essentially defenceless against artillery.

Gordon meanwhile turned his mind to improving the landward defences and outlying forts. He was building on good work done in the first half of 1883 by 'Abd-al-Qādir Pasha Ḥilmī, then the Governor-General, and to a lesser extent by Colonel de Cöetlogon since November. Contrary to 'movie history' there were no great city walls sealing off the apex of the *jazīra* and no wet moat between the Niles (*see Map 3*). Rather, the 6,000 yards of 'South Front' consisted successively of a dry ditch, a berm and an earthen rampart with a firing-step. The ditch was six to eight feet deep, and about 10 feet wide and would not be lightly crossed under a heavy fire. The berm behind it was designed to protect the base of the rampart from artillery fire and was about three feet thick. The main rampart and firing-step had been raised from the spoil of the excavated ditch and was around seven feet high and up to fourteen feet thick. It incorporated three gates and four large protruding bastions to facilitate enfilading fire. In front of the ditch there were successively (from an attacker's perspective) a thick belt of broken bottles and spiked iron

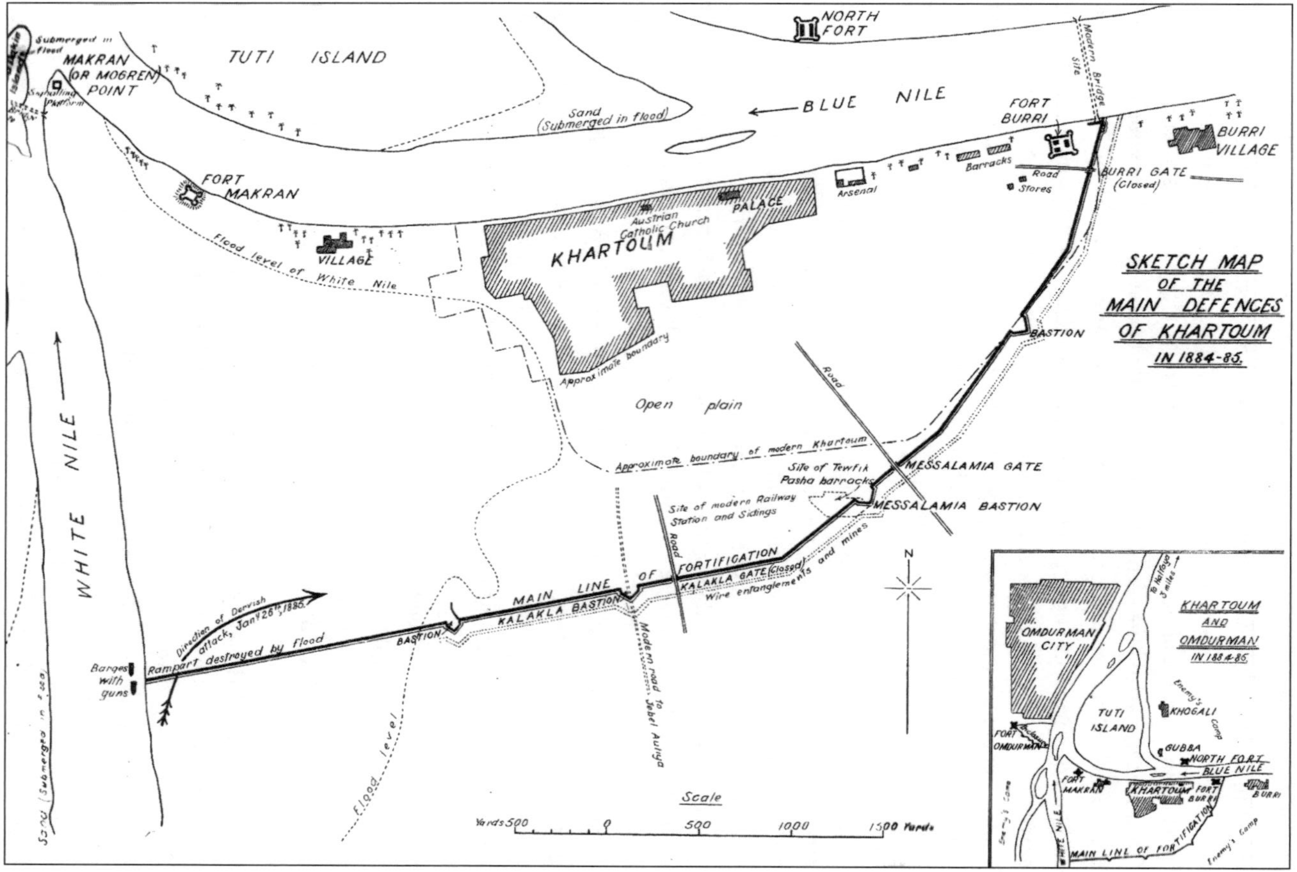

Map 3: Sandes's plan of Khartoum's defences

'crow's feet', a minefield of fuze-wire or pressure-initiated explosive charges and a low wire entanglement designed to function as a trip-hazard and so slow the momentum of an assault.

The city was further shielded by five principal outposts. Fort Omdurman, the only purpose-built defensive structure, stood on the far side of the White Nile, some 1,200 yards from the riverbank, and was capable of commanding the confluence of the rivers with artillery fire. Fort Moghran, a basic earthwork with corner bastions, is often shown on sketch maps at the western end of the South Front, but this is incorrect. It actually stood at the confluence, on a spit of land pointing towards Omdurman (*see Map 3*). On the other side of the Blue Nile from Moghran was a large triangular-shaped island called Tuti, where there was a small village of the same name. On the far side of Tuti, a subsidiary branch of the Blue Nile had carved a short-cut to the White Nile and created a slightly more northerly confluence of its own. Commanding the point at which the subsidiary branch diverted behind Tuti, at the southern tip of what is now North Khartoum but was in those days open desert, was a position known as the North Fort. This consisted of two double-storey buildings standing about sixty yards apart and an earthwork perimeter with corner bastions.

The double-storeyed *sarāya*, the Governor-General's home and the seat of government, was directly across the river from the North Fort and mounted a Krupp 20-pounder on the roof. Other buildings of note included the stone-built Catholic cathedral, a barracks and a brick-built government arsenal and dockyard. Because the cathedral was much stronger and less exposed than the arsenal, Gordon leased it to serve as the garrison's magazine. The best houses were to be found lining the south bank of the Blue Nile, on either side of the *sarāya*. The rest of the mud-built city, home to around 34,000 people, was laid out in front of the *sarāya* and was both claustrophobic and unsanitary. The handful of European residents found the smell of the back streets unbearable and if forced to visit them invariably went about with handkerchiefs clapped over their noses. Protecting the eastern end of the South Front, just beyond the barracks and the arsenal, and about 1,200 yards from the suburbs, was Fort Burri, an earthwork with corner bastions surrounding a cluster of ordinary mud-built buildings. There was a Burri Gate, with a village of the same name located about 400 yards in front of the defences. Here, as was the case at the western end of the defence line, Gordon had moored three 'castellated' barges in midstream, his own word for the two-storey timber structures he had erected aboard the boats to house well-protected parties of riflemen.

Groping for a Mature Plan

General Charles Gordon was perfectly capable of presenting a coherent argument on paper, but also had a bad habit of firing off short, unreferenced telegrams espousing apparently random thoughts and ideas. Baring recognized the problem fairly quickly and advised Granville not to take everything he was passing on from Gordon at face value. It was necessary in other words to look beyond the noise and clutter of his passing thoughts, for the general drift of his substantive plans and propositions. Far better to have sent fewer, better collated and structured communications, but unfortunately that was not Gordon's way. One senses that the traffic between Khartoum, Cairo and London might have gone much better had Baring and Granville made recourse to more robust language earlier than they did.

There was no room to doubt that the new Governor-General had inherited a critical situation in which government authority was balancing on a knife-edge, but in resorting almost immediately to requests which ran counter to the policies of his political lords and masters in London, Gordon succeeded only in causing irritation. On 2 March, less than a fortnight after his arrival, Gordon wired Baring proposing that Zubair be sent up to Khartoum without delay. He also urged that Zubair be promised a financial subsidy to run over a number of years and that 200 British troops should be sent up the Nile to the frontier town of Wādī Halfā. In respect of the troops Gordon explained, 'It is not the number but the prestige which I need. I am sure the revolt will collapse if I can say that I have British troops at my back.'[9] He had already publicly announced by proclamation that British troops were on their way to Khartoum.

Later the same day Gordon followed up with a single-sentence telegram which stated that if Zubair was sent upriver it would be 'absolutely necessary' to remain alongside him for a period of four months. The following day Gordon sent Baring a telegraphic 'digest of the state of affairs' which did not bode well for the hasty evacuation anticipated by the London government:

In the present state of affairs it is impossible to withdraw the Cairo employés from Khartoum without its falling into the hands of the Mahdi's emissaries, and if this took place then of course all hope of saving the Cairo employés of Kassala and Senaar and the garrisons of Equator[ia] and Bahr Gazelle fails, and Berber and Dongola must fall also, not by the force of the Mahdi but by sheer collapse. I am strongly against any permanent retention of the Soudan, but I think we ought to leave it with decency, and give the respectable people a man to lead them, around whom they can rally, and we ought to support that man by money and by opening road to Berber. Pray do not consider me in any way to advocate retention of Soudan; I am quite averse to it, but you must see that you could not recall me nor could I possibly obey until the Cairo employés get out from all the places. I have named men to different places, thus involving them with Mahdi; how could I look the world in the face if I abandoned them and fled? As a gentleman, could you advice this course? It may have been a mistake to send me up, but [this] having been done I have no option but to see evacuation through, for even if I was mean enough to escape I have no power to do so. You can easily understand this; would you do so?[10]

Later that day Gordon returned specifically to the matter of Zubair in two short telegrams, the first of which stated,

The combination at Khartoum of Zebehr and myself is an absolute necessity for success, and I beg you and Lord Granville to believe my certain conviction that there is not the slightest danger of our quarrelling, for Zebehr would know that the subsidy depended on my safety. To do any good, we must be together, and that without delay.

The second message ran,

About a policy of a hurried evacuation of the Soudan, pray abandon fear of Zebehr's hurting me. His interests are bound up with mine. Believe me I am right, and do not delay.[11]

On 4 March Colonel Stewart tried to amplify and support the general's thinking.

The principal desire of General Gordon is to have Zebehr here as soon as possible. His reasons are: Zebehr is the only man with sufficient prestige to hold the country together, at any rate for a time, after the evacuation. Being a Pasha among the Shagié irregulars he will be able to get at sources of information and action, now closed to us. He will be opposed to the Mahdi. I agree with Gordon. It seems evident to me that it is impossible for us to leave this country without leaving some sort of established Government which will last at any rate for a time, and Zebehr is the only man who can insure that. Also that we must withdraw the Senaar and other besieged garrisons, and here also Zebehr can greatly assist us. The principal objections to Zebehr are his evil reputation as a slave-dealer and his enmity to General Gordon. As regards the first, it will have to be defended on the plea that no other course is open except British annexation or anarchy. As regards the second, if precautionary measures are taken, such as making the subsidy payable through General Gordon, I think Zebehr will see that his interests are in working with General Gordon.

Of the secondary measures proposed by General Gordon to assist the evacuation, they are: (1) When the Berber–Suakin road is clear to send a small force of Indian or British cavalry to Berber. (2) To send a small force of British cavalry to Wady Halfa. These measures showing that we had forces at our disposal would greatly assist negotiations with rebels, and hasten evacuation. I assure you that none are more anxious to leave this country than myself and General Gordon, and none more heartily approve the Government's policy of evacuation. Unless, however, Zebehr is sent here, I see little probability of this policy being carried out. Every day we remain finds us more firm in the country, and causes us to incur responsibilities towards the people which it is impossible for us to overlook.[12]

Sending troops to Wādī Halfā was less of an issue for London than sending them to Berber. Even so, such a deployment would be of questionable utility, while getting even a small force into position on Egypt's southern frontier was bound to entail considerable expense. Berber on the other hand was regarded as a non-starter. While it was true that the presence of British troops there would bolster government authority and strengthen Gordon's negotiating hand, both of which were desirable outcomes, the proposition disregarded the fact that despatching troops into the Sudanese interior was precisely what the Gladstone government intended to avoid at all costs. With Osman Digna still rampaging around the Red Sea Littoral with 10,000–12,000 men at his disposal (the Battle of Tamai would not be fought for another nine days), Baring's covering note to Granville served to scupper the second of Gordon's 'secondary measures', not that it would have survived endorsement by the Cabinet anyway: 'I cannot agree with the proposal mentioned in Colonel Stewart's telegram that a force of British or Indian cavalry should be sent through from Suakin to Berber.'[13] The following day Baring ruled out the Wādī Halfā option also: 'General Gordon has on several occasions pressed for 200 British troops to be sent to Wadi Halfa. I agree with the military authorities [i.e. Stephenson and Wood] in thinking that it would not be desirable to comply with this request.'[14] Conscious that the Nile Valley would otherwise be left wide open, Stephenson gave orders on 11 March for the 1st Battalion, The Royal Sussex Regiment, to entrain for Assiut, 229 miles south of Cairo.[15]

On 6 March Gordon struck a more conciliatory note on the Zubair issue, wiring Baring to say,

Be assured that whatever is decided by Her Majesty's Government . . . I honestly accept it, as I should look on it as ruled by a Higher Power, and it will be sure to come right. As I have been inconsistent about Zebehr, it is my fault, and I should bear the blame if Zebehr is sent, and should put up with the inconvenience if he is not.[16]

In the growing realization that there simply had to be some sort of medium-term plan, Baring was prepared to compromise over Zubair and lent strong support to Gordon's proposal.[17] Even as his telegram was sitting on Granville's desk, the British and Foreign Anti-Slavery Society entered the fray. On 10 March the society's chairman, Edmund Sturge, wrote to the Foreign Secretary to express strident disapproval of any measure designed to empower the notorious Zubair.

The antecedents of Zebehr Pasha are well known to your Lordship. In the records of the devastations and murders inflicted by the Slave Trade on North-eastern Africa this man has stood the foremost and the principal actor, and his career is specially marked by perfidy and crime. The Committee are unanimous in the feeling that countenance in any shape of such an individual by the British government would be a degradation for England and a scandal to Europe . . .

As yet, however, the Committee are unable to believe that Her Majesty's Government will thus stultify that anti-slavery policy which has so long been the high distinction of England, or that they will thus discharge a trust which they have undertaken on behalf of the British people and of Europe.[18]

In London, if not in Cairo, it was clear that Gordon's plans for Zubair were a political non-starter. In the meantime Baring had wired Gordon to say, 'So far as I know, there is no intention on the part of the Government to send an English force to Berber.' As usual he copied the message to Granville, but there was a temporary break in telegraphic communications with the south and he added that he could not be sure that Gordon had received the message.

When telegraphic traffic resumed on 12 March, Baring received a series of seven telegrams from Gordon which he had originated on the 9th and 10th.[19] They included three written between 11.00 p.m. and midnight on 9 March which sought to press the government into deciding whether Khartoum should be evacuated immediately, or should be held onto, pending the arrival of Zubair in the capital and of British troops at Berber. He went on to propose that if the decision was for immediate evacuation, he would send Stewart out via Berber with the Egyptians, while he himself, having resigned his commission, would set off for the south with the Sudanese troops and the steamers. He would then aim to secure Bahr el Ghazal and Equatoria in the name of King Leopold. He added that he had the King's written assent to the assumption of sovereignty and financial responsibility for the region.

The existence of such a document might serve to explain Gordon's otherwise curious and fleeting visit to Brussels of 16 January, the day after his initial meeting with Wolseley. It is possible that incorporation of the Sudanese south into the so-called 'Congo Free State' always represented Gordon's favoured solution to averting the danger of a regional resurgence of the slave trade. An earlier exchange with Baring confirms that Gordon intended that the newly autonomous Sudanese state would be restricted to the Arab-dominated north, thus denying Zubair jurisdiction over the mainly black population of the Bahr el Ghazal and Equatoria, the scene of his worst depredations and the source of his wealth.[20] Perhaps if Gordon had gone on to become the principal administrator of the Belgian King's private fiefdom, the Congo Free State might not have come to the disgraceful pass that it did. It goes without saying that nobody in London or Cairo had said anything to Gordon about leaving Sudan via Equatoria and handing the sovereignty of the south to another European power. If there were indeed such wildly eccentric schemes running through Gordon's head, even before he left London, it is little wonder that Baring had been so worried by the prospect of his coming. Although the Consul-General fired off an immediate veto on Gordon's going south, the position in the interior was already far too fragile for such a plan to be tenable.[21] All Gordon could do for the present was concentrate on maintaining his precarious hold on the capital.

Commencement of the Siege

The fight for the confluence of the Niles opened not quite a month after Gordon's arrival, when a holy man from Umm Dibbān, the Shaikh Muḥammad Badr al-'Ubeid, together with his sons al-Ṭāhir and 'Abbās, brought a strong force of *anṣār* up the Blue Nile to invest Khartoum loosely from the east and north. Gordon's optimistic prediction that the Kordofani tribes would never leave their home areas was given the lie at the same time, when one of the Mahdī's fathers-in-law, Muḥammad al-Ṭaiyib al-Baṣīr, also closed in from the west to take up a position about twenty miles from Omdurman. The first serious clash took place at the furthest-flung of the government outposts. The village of Ḥalfaiya was located on the east bank of the merged Nile, about three miles north of Khartoum. Gordon had left 500 Shā'iqīa irregulars to hold it, in large part because he was unsure whether or not they could be trusted. On 12 March 1884 Shaikh al-'Ubeid and about 4,000 of his followers struck unexpectedly between Khartoum and Ḥalfaiya. Three companies of black regulars, about 250 men, had been sent out to the north in boats, to gather wood for the steamers, and now found their line of retreat severed. Their attempt to withdraw resulted in the loss of eight out of eleven boats and the death or capture of about 120 men. The rebel force then moved on to attack the Shā'iqīa at Ḥalfaiya. The following morning Gordon sent three steamers to the rescue, two of which were towing large grain barges with hundreds of troops concealed in their holds. In all there were about 1,200 men aboard the flotilla. The expedition reached Ḥalfaiya safely, extricated the hard-pressed Shā'iqīa and steamed back to Khartoum with the loss of only four men.[22] Even as the evacuation of Ḥalfaiya was afoot, Sir Gerald Graham was locked in battle at Tamai.

Three days later, Brigadier Generals Ḥasan Pasha Ibrāhīm al-Shallālī and Sa'īd Pasha Ḥusain al-Jimī 'ābī, both of whom were black Sudanese, marched out of the city to counter-attack and regain Ḥalfaiya. At their disposal was a mixed force of around 1,200 *fellaheen* and Shā'iqīa *bāshi-būzuqs*, supported by two steamers. Both men owed their exalted ranks to Gordon, but nonetheless were already engaged in secret negotiations with the enemy. With the steamer *Talahawiyeh* covering their left, the faithless pashas advanced to contact with their regular infantry in square on the left, a lone gun in the centre and the *bāshi-būzuqs* extended in line on the right. A charge by a paltry sixty rebel horsemen resulted in the loss of the gun and the rout of the *bāshi-būzuqs*. Having next charged and broken up the regulars, the same sixty horsemen then harried the fleeing troops to within a mile of Khartoum, cutting down stragglers at so rapid a rate that they managed to inflict around 350 casualties. The defeat had been so indecently quick that the *anṣār* infantry played no part in it. The survivors of the fiasco were quick to report that their commanders had betrayed them by giving irrational orders at critical moments, testimony which led to the two pashas being court-martialled and shot six days later.[23] Ḥalfaiya would eventually be recovered at the second attempt, but in the meantime the execution of two Sudanese generals for treachery hardly betokened the best of starts on the road to self-government.

Negotiating with the Mahdī

Not long after reaching Khartoum, Gordon had sent a courier to the Mahdī with a letter offering to recognize him as the sultan of an autonomous Kordofan. The message was accompanied by the gift of an ornate Chinese silk robe. Father Ohrwalder was present when the Governor-General's letter was read in public at El Obeid:

The Mahdi laughed at Gordon's proposals and thought him a very cunning unbeliever, who was attempting to delude him with vain promises merely to gain time. He could not understand how it was Gordon came to offer him what he already possessed . . . and he remarked that the very ground on which Gordon was standing was practically in his hands.[24]

Gordon's man returned to Khartoum on 22 March, the day on which the treacherous pashas met their end, bringing with him two Mahdīst emissaries. Gordon received them in the *sarāya* that afternoon. They declined to hand over their swords at the door of his office and stood with their hands on the hilts of their weapons throughout the interview. Gordon found their manner insolent, or 'exceedingly cheeky', as he put it in the summary of the meeting he later sent to Baring.[25] The first thing the emissaries did was to return the Chinese robe. They then handed over the Mahdī's written reply. While it was being translated and read to the Governor-General by his clerk, the emissaries placed a bundle in front of him. Gordon had no idea what it might be and was much more interested in listening to how the Mahdī had responded to his overtures. The emissaries kept nudging the mysterious object across Gordon's desk, until at length his temper snapped and he hurled the object across the room. It turned out to be 'a filthy, patched dervish's coat', a cotton *jibbeh* in other words, the poor man's apparel soon to be adopted as the uniform of the Mahdīst faithful. The accompanying letter urged Gordon to recant his faith, an exhortation which would have angered him still further, as there was nothing he despised more than an apostate, before then proceeding at great length to assert Muḥammad Aḥmad's credentials as the expected one. Gordon dictated a peremptory dismissal of the Mahdī's solicitations, which unlike his first letter addressed his antagonist as a mere shaikh, rather than as the Sultan of Kordofan. He handed his note to the emissaries with a show of scorn fit to trump their arrogance and waved them from his presence. The clerk was sent scurrying after them to hand back the rejected *jibbeh*.

Unlike the rest of his Cabinet colleagues, the Secretary of State for War enjoyed the advantage of being advised in matters of imperial strategy by the far-sighted General Lord Wolseley. The Adjutant-General had no difficulty in predicting that Gordon would be hemmed in at Khartoum and that sooner or later the government would come under pressure to get him out. Wolseley's solution to the developing predicament was that Gordon should be allowed to announce that the British would be sending in officers to help him run the Sudan as a protectorate, and that a brigade of troops should immediately be moved up to Wādī Ḥalfā to provide the Governor-General with moral support. Such a strategy would, the Adjutant-General felt, encourage wavering shaikhs to treat with Gordon, rather than immediately going over to the Mahdī. Implying as they did the assumption of British authority over the Sudanese interior, something which was diametrically opposed to government policy, Wolseley's ideas were scarcely worth the paper they were written on, but in his reading of the runes at least, the Adjutant-General hit the nail on the head – public opinion mattered.

The March 1884 Decision Point on Berber

Gordon was not much inclined to expend time and energy on carefully composing his despatches. His relatively short reports on the events of mid-March would have suggested to the reader that there were already powerful enemy forces in the vicinity of Khartoum, but in fact there seem to have been only a few thousand men, leaving the local military balance tilted in favour of the government. There would be later reports from Gordon which spoke, perhaps unwisely and certainly inaccurately, of the 'trumpery nature' of the revolt, but for the time being the principal decision-makers were running their eyes over reports which not only described the rout of 1,200 men, but also indicated that some of Gordon's most senior lieutenants were in cahoots with the enemy. Depending to some extent on the eye of the beholder, Gordon's position already appeared serious. All this coincided and conspired with Graham's second victory in the Red Sea Littoral to generate a major decision point. Should Sir Gerald Graham be tasked with opening the 245-mile caravan road to Berber and advance some part of his force to secure a foothold on the Nile? Graham, whose close friendship with Gordon should be borne in mind, thought that it could and should be done.[26] Stephenson and Wood advised Baring that such an operation would be difficult due to shortage of water along the road, but that it was by no means impossible. What really mattered was what the Prime Minister and Foreign Secretary thought.

In the event they had to be pressed even to allow Graham's operation against Tamanieb. At first they 'deprecated' the despatch of an expedition 'for fighting purposes' and stated that they were 'disposed to recommend, if possible, treating [with Osman] on the basis of his submission, and rendering himself answerable for the safety of the Berber road and the protection of traders and other travellers'.[27] This might come close to qualifying as the most naive suggestion ever to emanate from a British Foreign Secretary and amply illustrates just how wide of the mark was the Gladstone/Granville vision of poor, downtrodden Sudanese 'natives'. Sensibly Baring brushed his lords and masters aside, as always with remarkable politeness, replying that he intended to depute the military commander on the ground to act as he thought best.[28] Graham of course attacked, but as we saw at the end of the last chapter met with virtually no opposition.

Baring now posed the exam question on Berber. His object was to try and get Gladstone and Granville to acknowledge that they simply had to do something to succour Khartoum. His telegram of 24 March is an important one and worth quoting in full. It was addressed as usual to the Foreign Secretary:

My Lord,
In my despatch of the 18th instant I had the honour to inform your Lordship that the instructions contained in the telegrams of the 13th and 16th had been forwarded to General Gordon. I have not heard from him since he received my telegram, but it appears to me that under the present circumstances he will not be able to carry out your Lordship's instructions, although those instructions involve the abandonment of the Senaar garrison on the Blue Nile, and the garrisons of Bahr Gazelle and Gondokoro on the White Nile.

The question now is how to get General Gordon and Colonel Stewart away from Khartoum. In considering this question it should be remembered that they will not willingly come back without bringing with them the garrison of Khartoum and the government officials.

I believe that the success gained by General Graham in the neighbourhood of Suakin will result in the opening of the road to Berber, but I should not think that any action he can take at or near Suakin would exert much influence over the tribes between Berber and Khartoum.

Unless any unforeseen circumstances should occur to change the situation, only two solutions appear possible.

The first is to trust General Gordon's being able to maintain himself at Khartoum till the autumn, when by reason of the greater quantity of water, it would be less difficult to conduct operations on the Suakin–Berber road than it is at present. This he might, perhaps, be able to do, but it of course involves running a great risk.

The only other plan is to send a portion of General Graham's army to Berber with instructions to open communication with Khartoum. There would be very great difficulty in getting to Berber, but if the road were once open it might be done by sending small detachments at a time.

General Gordon is evidently expecting help from Suakin, and he has ordered messengers to be sent along the road from Berber to ascertain whether any English force is advancing.

Under present circumstances, I think that an effort should be made to help General Gordon from Suakin, if it is at all a possible military operation.

General Stephenson and Sir Evelyn Wood, whilst admitting the very great risk to the health of the troops, besides the extraordinary military risks, are of the opinion that the undertaking is possible. They think that General Graham should be further consulted.

We all consider that, however difficult the operations from Suakin may be, they are more practicable than any operations from Korosko and along the Nile.

I have, &c.
Baring[29]

In the light of subsequent events, the telegram's final sentence is of particular note.

On 28 March Granville signed off two lengthy letters to Baring dealing with the Zubair issue and the question of despatching troops to Berber.[30] They reprised the recent telegraphic traffic between London, Cairo and Khartoum and went on to outline the logic underpinning the government's refusal to comply with the two requests. The documents are so comprehensive and well-reasoned as to suggest that they were prepared specifically with a view to publication. They demonstrate perfectly adequately why the Cabinet had arrived at the conclusions it had. One key point made in respect of Zubair was that, 'The chivalrous character of General Gordon appeared to be likely to lead him into the generous error of trusting too much to the loyalty of a man whose interests and feelings were hostile to him.'[31] By 7 April Gordon had gleaned that the government had no intention either of sending Zubair to Khartoum or of advancing any troops to Berber. It was enough to trigger an angry telegraphic tantrum, fired not altogether fairly at Baring:

As far as I can understand, the situation is this: you state your intention of not sending any relief force up here or to Berber, and you refuse me Zobeir. I consider myself free to act according to circumstances. I shall hold out here as long as I can, and if I can suppress the rebellion I shall do so. If I cannot, I shall retire to the Equator, and leave to you the indelible disgrace of abandoning the garrisons of Sennar, Kassala, Berber and Dongola, with the certainty that you will eventually be forced to smash up the Mahdi under great difficulties if you would retain peace in Egypt.[32]

While Gordon's ire caused a stir in Whitehall, Gladstone as usual took from it only what suited him. Gordon, he noted, could get out to the south if he wanted to. It did not happen to be true, but Gladstone was particularly adept at assuming an air of innocence and pretending that he had taken a protagonist's words at face value. The Prime Minister had been unwell for most of March and missed the two meetings of the Cabinet which had addressed the Zubair issue; ironically he had not at first been personally inclined to deny Gordon his services, but in the end fell into line with the majority view prevailing in the Cabinet.[33] It is more than likely that he allowed himself to be swayed by the political necessity to avoid outraging the anti-slavery lobby.

On 8 April, five days after Graham and his staff had sailed for Suez, Granville indicated to Baring that the government was prepared to consider moving a detachment of troops up to Wādī Halfā.[34] Having consulted as instructed with Generals Stephenson and Wood, Baring duly replied, 'On the whole we are disposed to think that the objections to undertaking this movement outweigh the benefits likely to accrue from it. Those benefits are of a very doubtful nature.' Indeed they were: Wādī Halfā is more than 850 miles from Khartoum.

Covering Upper Egypt

Baring and Wood agreed to cover the frontier by sending two EA battalions into Upper Egypt. Korosko and Wādī Halfā were to be garrisoned and fortified by half-battalions, while the second unit was to remain concentrated in depth at Aswan.[35] Three British officers of the EA were also sent south in a role which was part political officer, part intelligence officer and part commander of irregular forces. Their task was to gather information and enlist the services of the friendly Bedouin tribes in monitoring the desert approaches to southern Egypt.[36] The trio comprised Majors (EA Rank) Herbert Kitchener RE, Henry Rundle RA and Edward Stuart-Wortley KRRC. In the Queen's service, as opposed to the Khedive's, Kitchener was a captain while his two colleagues were lieutenants: hence Major Stuart-Wortley, who ended up attached to an all-British force, will have to be demoted in the course of the narrative.[37]

Kitchener in particular would prove to have great aptitude for this sort of work, as he spoke some Arabic and, his striking blue eyes notwithstanding, soon turned himself into the apocryphal 'master of disguise'. But these were not japes or high jinks; rather it was extremely dangerous work which called for nerves of steel and great strength of character. While Kitchener and Rundle set off for Korosko to cover the road from Abū-Hamed, Stuart-Wortley was sent to watch the Darb el Arba'in, literally 'the forty day's route' – a caravan road by which it was possible to travel through the Libyan desert from Assiut to Kordofan.[38] Within a few weeks Kitchener and Rundle had enlisted the services of around 1,500 'friendlies' drawn from the Foggara, 'Abābda and Ashiabab tribes. From time to time Kitchener sallied into the desert in the hope of apprehending the Mahdīst agitators reported to be stirring up the 'Abābda and Bisharin.[39] In due course he was sent a khedival *firman* which authorized him to negotiate with the Bisharin _shaikhs_ and was successful in retaining the loyalty of six of the nine clans.

In early April the Robatab Arabs, whose territory lay between Berber and Abū-Hamed, rose against the government. Amongst a number of other unhelpful developments this led to the telegraph between Berber and Khartoum being cut, though for the time being the line from Berber to Abū-Hamed remained operational. Baring's communications with Khartoum now depended on couriers travelling the best part of 200 miles through enemy territory. Losing direct touch with Gordon was not something Gladstone and Granville had made any allowance for. Even less had they contemplated the possibility of Berber falling into enemy hands, but no sooner had Graham's force re-embarked at Suakin than the *mudir*'s telegrams began to assume a frantic tone. It is impossible to read them without feeling a twinge of pity for their author.

Sixty-four years old, a notable of the local 'Abābda tribe and a faithful servant of the government, Ḥusain Pasha Khalīfa pointed out to Cairo that the Mahdī's nomination for his post was reported to be coming in great strength and that he had too few troops and insufficient ammunition at his disposal. On 14 April he reported that the town of Shendy, 102 miles north of Khartoum, was already under attack and likely to fall within the next few days.[40] The *mudir*'s erstwhile replacement was somebody he knew well, a venerable Berberine theologian called Muḥammad al-Khair 'Abd Allāh Khūjalī, under whom Muḥammad Aḥmad had studied in his youth. More recently the one-time pupil had elevated his former master to be a Mahdīst *amīr*. Ḥusain Pasha Khalīfa bombarded Cairo with increasingly frantic pleas for help, to receive not a word of encouragement in response. Also firing in worrying reports from Berber was Giuseppe Cuzzi, a 41-year-old Italian soldier–adventurer turned merchant, who had been taken onto the government payroll when Gordon passed through in February. On 16 April Baring received a petition from the 'Egyptian Employés, Merchants and Foreigners at Berber':

We, Europeans, Turks, Egyptians, Hedjazites, Algerians, came to the Soudan relying on the support and protection of the Government. Now if it abandons us to-day, through indifference or weakness, its honour will be everlastingly tarnished in thus handing over its servants and subjects to death and dishonour.

If Egypt has given the Soudan up to England, we implore that great, chivalrous, and humane Power to come to our help, for it is full time. Can it raise us again after our death? We await help from England, from our Government, or from any charitable Power, for if the same state of things continues for ten days or a fortnight more our country will be ravaged, and we shall be lost.

We implore you then to quiet our minds by announcing the immediate dispatch of a force to our assistance. If not certain death awaits us.[41]

Having been forbidden from sending the EA into the Sudan there was literally nothing Baring could do to help Berber, apart from forwarding the impassioned pleas of its citizenry to the Foreign Secretary. On 21 April he left for London anyway, where there was to be a major international conference on Egyptian finance and governance. In his absence his duties in Cairo would fall to a deputy named Edwin Egerton.[42]

With Berber under threat and communications with Khartoum lost, Baring had by now become firmly convinced of the necessity for a relief expedition. This was motivated at the time by concern for Gordon's safety and a sincerely held feeling of moral responsibility for having sent him into the lion's den, a responsibility very clearly shared by Gladstone and Granville. With the benefit of twenty years' hindsight Baring would argue in his memoirs that Gordon behaved irresponsibly in not immediately focussing on the evacuation of Khartoum, supposedly his primary object.[43] Evacuation was possible, argued Baring, up to the end of May. In stating this, however, Baring failed to give sufficient weight to the several significant adjustments to the tenor of Gordon's instructions which had been conceded over the first few weeks of the mission. To talk of unauthorized departures from orders, or even wilful disobedience, is to pretend that London and Cairo maintained a consistent line throughout.

Chapter 3

Novel Expedients

Wolseley's Plan of Campaign

In my little wars I generally hit upon some novel expedient, and it frightens many; the foolish don't understand it, and my enemies hope it may ruin me. This is now the case with my boats and Camel Corps.

General Lord Wolseley, Campaign Journal, Gemai, 18 October 1884

AT THE WAR OFFICE Wolseley was one step ahead of the game, knowing full well that the weight of public opinion would eventually swing against the government and compel it to act. As early as the first week of April he started working on options for the relief expedition he regarded as inevitable. As the Adjutant-General, it would not, it could not, be his campaign. That was a responsibility which would fall to Sir Frederick Stephenson as GOC Cairo. But London would have to fire the starting gun and, as the principal military adviser to the Secretary of State for War, it would be Wolseley who would have to do the early brainstorming. He outlined his initial thoughts in a lengthy memorandum to Hartington dated 8 April 1884.[1]

With Berber still in the hands of the government, Wolseley began by nominating Shendy, almost 100 miles further south, as the first point at which resistance could be anticipated. The immediate object should be to concentrate a force of 6,500 men there. This he anticipated would consist of a regiment of cavalry, a regiment of mounted infantry (which could be mounted either on local horses or on camels), two brigades (eight battalions) of infantry, a battery of camel-borne light guns, a company of Royal Engineers and 400 departmental troops.

The force should be exclusively British, Wolseley added, on the grounds that, 'It is very doubtful if even the very best of our Indian regiments would stand the charges of the Arabs, such as those which our troops recently had to encounter at Suakin.' He went on to argue that Indian Army units were incapable of taking the field without encumbering themselves with large numbers of camp followers, an assertion in which there was a good deal of truth, and that the allowances paid to its British officers always bred resentment when Home Army and Indian Army units were brought together. He conceded that if it was absolutely necessary to send Indian troops for political purposes, then the best course would be to incorporate a battalion of Sikhs into each of the infantry brigades.

Options

The memo then went on to consider the route by which the force should be moved to Shendy. There were four possible choices, only three of which warranted serious contemplation. The option rejected out of hand was a 500-mile overland advance from Massowah on the Red Sea coast to Abu Haras on the Blue Nile, via Kassala, Girri and Kedaref, a vast distance across which the difficulties of water and transport were certain to be insurmountable. Strangely, notwithstanding that he had nominated Shendy as the concentration area, his memo actually cited the distances between the possible start-points and Berber. In all cases, then, it is necessary to add another 100 miles to his figures to obtain the true distance to the concentration area, or 200 miles to obtain the distance from the start-points to Khartoum. The viable start-points were the ports of Massowah and Suakin on the Red Sea Coast, and Wādī Halfā on the land frontier between Egypt and Sudan, options 1, 2 and 3 in that order, covering distances of 603, 245 and 666 miles respectively. He had chosen Wādī Halfā as the assembly area for the river option because, 'The Nile even when low, presents little obstacles [sic] to the collection of the troops, stores, &c., required, at that place, and at full Nile no obstacles at all.' The Wādī Halfā of 1884, since submerged by the construction of the Aswan High Dam in the 1960s, was located on the east bank of the Nile and consisted of only a handful of railway buildings and a few dozen hovels clustered in the shade of a palm grove.[2]

Option 1, Massowah to the junction of the Atbara River and the Nile, a distance of 603 miles, would require a baggage train of 5,000 camels for provisions alone, 'not making any allowance for baggage, camp equipment, hospitals ammunition &c.' and would require a desert march of eleven weeks' duration. Although the Atbara River generally ceased to exist in September, Wolseley considered that there would be sufficient waterholes left along its course for the force to sustain itself.

In considering Option 2, Suakin to Berber, an eye-catching 245 miles, Wolseley noted that, 'the water difficulties are so great along this route, that not more than 300 cavalry or 400 infantry could move along it daily between the several places where drinking water is at present obtainable'. Wolseley does not explain why infantrymen are apparently thirstier than ponies; why, that is, 300 cavalrymen do not translate into 600 or more infantrymen. He continued,

> Our recent experience has shown us the warlike character of the tribes living about it; their hostility would make the march of small detachments along it extremely dangerous ... If the Suakin–Berber road were safe, of course the force might be passed over it in small detachments; but as it is now, the march of such a force as that contemplated, by this route, would be an extremely difficult and dangerous operation.[3]

Surprisingly, Option 2 is ranked behind Option 1, with its inherently daunting prospect of marching across a wilderness for no fewer than eleven weeks.

On top of the pile, however, was Option 3, Wādī Halfā to Berber, a distance of 666 miles, including the transit of the Great Bend in the Nile. Of course an army cannot just pop up in Wādī Halfā; there is the small matter of the 560 miles (as the crow flies) from Cairo to Wādī Halfā, which Wolseley completely failed to discuss. Nonetheless his advice to the Secretary of State for War was unequivocal.

Although much longer than either of the other two routes, it has, in my opinion, numerous advantages over them. In the first place, an ample supply of good drinking water, the most serious want in a tropical and desert region, is always at hand. Then again the difficulty of transport is reduced to very narrow limits.

I would propose to send all the dismounted potion of the force up the Nile to Khartum in boats, as we sent the little expeditionary force from Lake Superior to Fort Garry on the Red River in 1870 . . . Of the total distance by river from Wady Halfa to Berber (666 miles) 224 miles of that distance is navigable by steamers at one stretch, and a railway is finished for 33 miles, and only requires the rails to finish 22 miles further. There are also two stretches of about 70 miles each, easily navigable by light draft steamers at high Nile, and by ordinary sailing boats. In fact there would only be about 200 miles of difficult navigation between Wady Halfa and Berber.

Remembering the great superiority of river over land transport, the ease with which stores of all sorts are carried in boats, the great distance, comparatively speaking, that can be traversed daily in boats, and the vast saving that there would be in expense, I have no hesitation whatever in saying that the river route from Wady Halfa to Khartum is infinitely preferable to any other.[4]

When Wolseley wrote these words in the first week of April 1884, they constituted a compelling enough argument. For reasons we will come to they would have constituted an even stronger one had they focussed not on reaching Khartoum via Berber, but on using water transport only as far as Ambukol or Korti, places from which it was possible to strike out across the Bayūda Desert for Metemmeh, a town located just across the river from Shendy.

The purpose of the thirty-three miles of railway running south from Wādī Halfā to a hamlet called Sarras was to bypass the Second Cataract. What Wolseley evidently did not know, or did not let on, was that the railway had seen barely any maintenance since it was first laid in 1877 and was now in a poor state of repair. There were three locomotives and some twenty to thirty carriages and trucks *in situ*. There was a once weekly service when one of the locomotives was serviceable. This short stretch of track and the twenty-two miles of prepared ground beyond was all that had been accomplished in fulfilment of Ismā'il Pasha's vision of a railway from Wādī Halfā to Khartoum. Ironically it had been Gordon who, in his first tour as Governor-General, had put an end to the scheme after the wasteful expenditure of around £450,000. If there was one piece of good news in respect of the railway, it was that an adventurous British engineer called C. E. Fowler had surveyed the optimal route in 1871–2 and that it ran across the Great Bend from Korti to Metemmeh. As a result Fowler's mapping of the centre-line across the Bayūda Desert, including the location of all the principal sources of water, was available in London and Cairo.[5]

Lord Hartington's response to Wolseley's first memorandum was to pose the obvious question, 'Is there no point on the Nile between the southern end of the Wady Halfa railroad and Berber where further progress in boats becomes impossible?' Much depended on the seasonal rise and fall of the Nile: high between the months of June and September; falling after that; low from Christmas onwards; and at its very worst by April and May. Wolseley's advice had been penned in the reasonable expectation of exploiting high-Nile to good advantage. He responded to Hartington's question with a second memorandum dated 14 April, in which he suggested that Sir Redvers Buller, a veteran of the Red River expedition, should be consulted. Crucially the memo also addressed the question of time. Wolseley identified 15 November as the latest date to which Gordon could reasonably be expected to hold out. Working backwards from his cut-off point, he considered that the relief expedition should be at Berber by no later than 20 October. In the event that the government decided to send an expedition via Suakin, then the force should be assembled there by not later than 1 September. Ironically at the time these words of advice were written, a British field force had only just departed Suakin.

The bona fide answer to Hartington's question was that nobody in London was quite sure how difficult navigation became if one continued past Merowe into the Great Bend. The Fourth Cataract lay between Merowe and Abū-Hamed, at the northernmost tip of the bend, while the Fifth Cataract intervened between Abū-Hamed and Berber. The Sixth or Sabalūka Cataract lay between Berber and Khartoum, but did not come under discussion at all as a possible further cause of delay. 'Don't know' was not an answer the politicians ever got. Instead they would be presented only with the unshakeable confidence of the Red River clique within the Wolseley Ring who believed that they could get small boats anywhere they chose. The techniques used in Canada had included pulling from the bank, poling and circumventing difficult rapids by portage. Poling of course relies on shallow water, while portages cannot be too lengthy, nor can they be conducted over impossible terrain. Canadian portage frequently relied on the labour-saving technique of moving boats on log rollers, but rollers cannot work if there are no forests to cut them from, nor can they work over exceptionally rocky ground. In addition to the back-breaking work of portaging the boat itself along the riverbank, its cargo also has to be carried overland somehow.

Indecision

It was only right and proper that Sir Frederick Stephenson, as the senior officer in Egypt and erstwhile theatre commander, be consulted. He too addressed a long memorandum to Lord Hartington, in which his thoughts did not differ materially from Wolseley's in respect of the size and type of force. In the matter of the axis of advance, however, there was a fundamental divergence of opinion. For Stephenson the winning advantages of the Suakin–Berber road included the fact that it was far shorter than any of its rivals; that the operation would be based on a defended seaport only 4½ days steaming from Cairo, enabling large tonnages of supplies to be built up and maintained comparatively close to the front; that the arrangements for evacuating the sick and wounded by sea would be infinitely superior; that reinforcements could be deployed quickly; and that the relief expedition and the Khartoum evacuees could be extricated far more rapidly at the close of the campaign. Because nobody had yet raised with him the idea of using a specially commissioned fleet of small boats of the sort Wolseley had in mind, Stephenson imagined the relief column marching 860 miles along the banks of the Nile from Wādī Halfā to Khartoum via the Great Bend. 'Four months, at least, would be required before Khartum was reached,' he pronounced. 'Under the circumstances I consider this route quite unsuited for the purpose intended.'[6]

Wolseley's advice was not accepted immediately, if for no other reason than because it looked illogical on the map. Moreover, GOC Cairo evidently did not agree with it, while as far as the Prime Minister and Foreign Secretary were concerned, the War Office might as well have been playing at wargames. The Admiralty was invited to comment on the feasibility of the Nile route and duly tasked Vice Admiral Lord John Hay, C-in-C Mediterranean, to look into the matter. On 1 May Hay gave orders for a team of officers, under Captain Robert Molyneux RN, to set forth and reconnoitre the Nile. The man tasked with going furthest south was an able 36-year-old officer called Commander Tynte Ford Hammill of HMS *Monarch*, who arrived at Wādī Halfā on 15 May and whose particular job was to look at the 212 miles of river between the foot of the Second Cataract and the open water on the far side of the Third Cataract. In the event telegraphic toing and froing about whether it was safe for him to proceed south of Wādī Halfā, prevented him setting off for Hannek for another fortnight.[7]

The Crisis Spreads to Dongola

By mid-May it was becoming increasingly clear that the rebellion was spilling over into Dongola, Sudan's northernmost province. If Dongola fell the next domino to go would be Upper Egypt, but even this prospect did not suffice to stir the British government to action. The Mudir of Dongola, a notably devout Circassian called Muṣṭafa Yāwar Pasha, joined the Mudir of Berber in pleading with Cairo for help. Submitted with his telegraphic reports of Mahdīst encroachment and widespread disaffection was an appeal to the Khedive's ministers from the officers of the garrison. The only troops available in the *mudirieh* were four companies of regular infantry at Dongola itself, together with a small contingent of *bāshi-būzuqs* at Debbeh under the command of al-Nūr al-Dīn Pasha. Having reminded the ministers of the dire fate which had befallen much larger garrisons in Dār Fūr and Kordofan, the officers inquired,

> Does the government consent to see us seized by the enemy, ourselves killed, our wives dishonoured? We cannot protect the loyal subjects, their goods and their honour. The enemy is pitiless. If our august Sovereign has any regard for us, let him send us quickly a large force, with artillery and provisions; if not, we are lost.[8]

Nubar Pasha and his colleagues were powerless to do anything so long as the EA remained under British control and could only turn to the acting consul-general for guidance. Egerton in turn could only appeal to the Foreign Secretary, though it was clear that hell would have to be at least close to freezing over before Gladstone and Granville consented to military action south of Wādī Halfā. The extent of their intransigence was illustrated in a chillingly aloof reply sent by Granville to Egerton on 13 May.

I have received your telegrams of yesterday, inquiring on behalf of the Egyptian Government, whether in the opinion of that of Her Majesty's the population and garrison of Dongola should be instructed to hold out, with the view of their being relieved later on; or whether the Mudir should fall back towards the north, or else make the best terms he can for his safety and that of his people.

Her Majesty's Government can give no pledge with reference to their future action, and they are of the opinion that the Mudir should be instructed to adopt the last alternative, and to arrange the best terms he can.[9]

Fortunately for Dongola Province and embattled Khartoum, Muṣṭafa Yāwar Pasha and his officers were made of sterner stuff. As might be expected of a man who had risen from khedival slave to provincial governor, the *mudir* was an old fox who knew how to play a weak hand well. He received the Mahdī's emissaries and gave them every reason to believe that he admired their master and could be counted on to change sides when the time was right. A letter from the Mahdī flattered Muṣṭafa Yāwar's devotion to the faith and indicated that he would be allowed to continue governing the district as a Mahdīst *amīr*. That the *mudir* had sent a reply to this overture was known in Cairo. This, coupled with a sequence of bewildering and contradictory reports which made it difficult to know quite what was going on in Dongola, served to raise doubts about Muṣṭafa Yāwar's loyalty. With the benefit of hindsight there is no reason to believe that he did anything other than make instinctive recourse to the tactics of stratagem. As Sir Reginald Wingate put it in his history of Mahdīsm, 'it must have been evident to him that his nationality alone would have been sufficient to prevent his ever retaining his high position in a community whose motto was "Death to the Turk"'.[10]

In the meantime Egerton, on the advice of Stephenson and Wood, had also pressed the Foreign Office for permission to ask C-in-C Mediterranean to take over three khedival steamers and undertake reassurance patrols on the Nile. It was proposed that two of the vessels would operate between Assiut and Aswan and the third between Aswan and Wādī Halfā. Lord John Hay was supportive, sent Captain Frederick Bedford of HMS *Monarch* to Cairo to make all the arrangements and wired the Admiralty for permission to proceed. It took three days and a reminder to elicit a response from Lord Granville, but it turned out that riverine patrols were acceptable to Her Majesty's Government.[11] The vessels duly taken into the service of the Admiralty at the end of May were *Gizeh* under Lieutenant William Reid RN, *Mahmoudieh* under Lieutenant Gordon Ede RN, and *Nasif-el-Kheir* under

Lieutenant Richard Poore RN. Each of them was armed with a Gardner machine gun borrowed from the fleet at Alexandria. Captain Bedford had overall command of the flotilla and took *Gizeh* as his flagship. All the vessels hoisted the White Ensign.[12] In order to avoid any confusion over command and control, all military assets operating south of Cairo, including those owned by the Sirdar or the Admiralty, were subordinated to Sir Fredrick Stephenson with effect 20 May.[13]

After all the strained signals traffic between Cairo and London, a report came in from the Mudir of Dongola which at last enabled Egerton to lighten the mood a little. There was it seemed a second Mahdī on the loose in Dār Fūr, who in the best tradition of successor prophets had declared that Muḥammad Aḥmad had merely been sent to herald his coming. As proof of his divinity the new chosen one was able, it was said, to fly about on an *angareb*, which is to say one of the low latticed bed-frames much beloved of Sudanese village loafers on a hot afternoon.[14]

Investment of Berber

By the middle of May, Muḥammad al-Khair had closed in on Berber and loosely invested his home town in the name of the Mahdī. Included in the rebel force were the Robatab, Muḥammad al-Khair's own people, and a body of turncoat Shā'iqīa under the Amīr Aḥmad al-Heddai. Ḥusain Pasha Khalīfa disposed something over 2,500 men, comprising roughly 1,000 fellaheen regulars, 600 Cairene *bāshi-būzuqs*, 800 Berberine irregulars and 400 of his 'Abābda kinsmen. While he had two steamers available, he was critically short of artillery, with only a single fieldpiece and ten gunners at his disposal. Although he built three outworks and made an effort to clear the garrison's fields of fire, he failed to demolish a garden belonging to one of the town's spiritual leaders. This was duly used by the enemy as a forming-up place. An attack mounted at 3.00 a.m. on 26 May quickly succeeded in breaching the defences. Survivors recounted that the 'Abābda and *bāshi-būzuqs* were the first to be broken and that the latter lost their colonel in the fighting.[15] Those who survived the break-in were driven into the open, where they were rallied by a cavalry officer and formed square beside the Nile. The rebels left them alone for about two hours, while they busied themselves with murder and pillage. The *mudir*, meanwhile, had been wounded in the leg and had taken to a hiding place. When the rebels located him, he was forced to send an order instructing his men to lay down their arms. According to Wingate a terrible massacre lasting the best part of two days then ensued.[16]

It is often said that such had been the deafening silence from central Sudan for the past several weeks that Cairo and London remained oblivious to the fall of Berber for the best part of a month. What actually happened, though, was that Egerton and the British consul in Suakin both wired Granville with the news on 1 June,[17] only four days after the fact, but while the authorities in Suakin never doubted the report, Egerton changed his mind on the basis of rumours presented by the Mudir of Dongola as intelligence. Several of his telegrams suggested that Berber was still resisting, when in reality Ḥusain Pasha Khalīfa had been clapped in irons and despatched on the gruelling journey to the Mahdī's encampment at Rahad in Kordofan. Giuseppe Cuzzi had fared little better. Having disguised himself as an Arab, he attempted to escape into the desert with his Sudanese wife, but fell into the hands of the rebels the following day. He would later be sent to Khartoum as a Mahdīst emissary, although because he had turned apostate Gordon refused to see him.

Covering the Frontier

On 29 May Kitchener wired Sir Evelyn Wood from Korosko to say that travellers had arrived there to report that Abū-Hamed was in the hands of the enemy, and that they had seen a large rebel force made up of Rowat, Bisharin and Hassaniyeh tribesmen at Murad, a set of wells half-way between Abū-Hamed and Korosko. Kitchener went on to say that he saw no reason to disbelieve the report and had sent parties of friendlies to watch all the usual routes across the desert. In addition Shaikh Saleh, one of the sons of Husain Pasha Khalīfa, present with the ʿAbābda contingent, had been sent with a stronger patrol to investigate the situation at Murad.[18] Although Kitchener's intelligence had not yet been confirmed, Egerton and the generals made an immediate decision to send two more EA battalions to Aswan, with supporting elements of cavalry and artillery.[19] By 3 June Saleh had returned to Korosko to report. The enemy had indeed been at Murad, but had since fallen back to Abū-Hamed. He had followed them up and had left 140 ʿAbābda camped in the desert about three hours north of the town.

On 9 June Kitchener submitted a report advising Wood that an old retainer of Husain Pasha Khalīfa had arrived at his outposts, bearing news of Berber's fall. The story went that Muhammad al-Khair had allowed the old man to go on his way so that he could advise the *mudir*'s sons what had become of their father. Of course this was no act of magnanimity, but rather was designed in typical Mahdīst fashion to secure their defection, a tactic which on this occasion was firmly rebuffed: Saleh and his brothers reported every detail to Kitchener and remained scrupulously loyal to the government. In forwarding Kitchener's despatches to London, Egerton added the caveat, 'Information received from other sources [i.e. the Mudir of Dongola] makes this news difficult to credit.' When the Sirdar wired Korosko suggesting that there were grounds to doubt that Berber had fallen, Kitchener expressed bemusement:

I do not think you need doubt accuracy of news I sent. The effect on the tribes has been considerable, and there was wailing all night. A well-known retainer of Khalifa's family brought the news. Khalifa's sons are much affected, and declare themselves responsible that the news is true [i.e. they vouch for its accuracy]. I have done my utmost to give you the news first, but it must be all through Egypt tomorrow. What is the reason for your doubting it?[20]

It was not until 26 June, more than a fortnight after Kitchener had wired in the news, that Egerton finally notified Granville that there was no longer any reason to doubt that Berber had fallen.[21]

The time had come for the Army of Occupation to support the Sirdar's defensive measures in the south, regardless of any concerns the medical officers might previously have articulated for the health of the troops. On 22 June Stephenson notified Lord Hartington that he was moving 1st Royal Sussex up from Assiut to Aswan, to bolster the Egyptian battalions quartered upriver, and was contemplating sending a second British battalion to take station at Keneh, an insignificant town midway between Assiut and Aswan.[22] The Royal Sussex set off upriver on 26 June and arrived at Aswan on 7 July, while the 2nd Battalion, The Duke of Cornwall's Light Infantry, left Cairo on 4 July and reached Keneh five days later.[23]

The British government had in the meantime been drawn into contemplating the Suakin–Berber road as an axis, as all the other advice they had been given diverged from Wolseley's. A senior Royal Engineer called Colonel Sir Andrew Clarke, at the time the Inspector-General of Fortifications, had advocated the construction of a Suakin–Berber railway in a memorandum dated 19 May but, like all the other ideas being bandied about, it was contemplated too long by ministers, so that in the end it was mid-June before Stephenson was instructed to embark a company of sappers for the Red Sea Littoral. The 17th Field Company, RE, under Lieutenant Colonel Elliott Wood, arrived at Suakin on 1 July. The idea of laying a railway through enemy-held territory was plainly vacuous, however, and under scathing attack from Wolseley quickly fell out of favour. In the event Colonel Wood and his men were able to busy themselves with improving the port and water-condensing facilities, a far more practical use of their skills.[24]

Like his colleagues at Korosko, Stuart-Wortley had successfully drummed up a force of friendlies, in this case 500 camel-mounted Jowasi Bedouin under Shaikh Djelani. In light of growing concerns about the Arba'in road and the Libyan desert, Stuart-Wortley was instructed to set out from Assiut and establish outposts at two key oases west of the Nile.[25] These were Beris, located 150 miles south of Assiut and the best part of 200 miles west of Aswan, and the Selima Oasis, around 100 miles south-west of Wādī Halfā. In effect the expedition would constitute right-flank protection to the defensive deployments in the Nile Valley. Lieutenant Colonel Henry Colvile, Grenadier Guards, later to become the official historian of the campaign, was sent with Stuart-Wortley to assess the viability of the Arba'in road as an enemy invasion route. The two British officers and their flock of Bedouin followers set off into the desert on 1 July. They reached Beris eight days later, where they left 400 of the Jowasi *in situ*. The long haul to the Selima Oasis took until 25 July, but by the end of the month they had emerged from the desert and made their way in to Wādī Halfā. Colvile's report advised that scarcity of water rendered the Arba'in axis impracticable for anything in excess of a thousand men.

In the meantime the Amīr Aḥmad al-Heddai had put June to good use by advancing around the Great Bend from Abū-Hamed to Ambukol, acquiring several thousand adherents as he went. Many of the newly enrolled rebels from the Merowe and Korti districts had been told that they were marching on Dongola to attend a great gathering at which Muṣṭafa Yāwar Pasha would be presented with the Mahdī's *firman* as the *amīr* of Dongola. One man, on discovering that al-Heddai's intentions were hostile, hastened ahead to warn the garrison of the old fort at Debbeh. Al-Nūr al-Dīn Pasha and his men had fended for themselves in the usual *bāshi-būzuq* way by plundering the district and were in no position to throw themselves on the mercy of the rebels. When al-Heddai attempted a surprise attack at 3.00 a.m. on 5 July, he ran into fierce resistance, took heavy casualties and was forced to fall back on Merowe. Gaudet Bey, the deputy *mudir*, harried the rebels back into the Great Bend from a government steamer. At length al-Heddai took to a place of refuge in the north-west corner of the Bayūda Desert, from whence he wrote to the Mahdī begging for reinforcements. Still bemused by the *mudir*'s flowery reports, the authorities in Cairo agreed Kitchener's suggestion that he leave Harry Rundle in charge at Korosko and make his way upriver to Dongola. He arrived there on 1 August to find Muṣṭafa Yāwar fully in control of the situation. A few days later Kitchener accompanied the *mudir* upriver to Debbeh and saw for himself the hundreds of unburied Mahdīst dead strewn around the fort.[26]

'The Battle of the Routes'

Commander Hammill had returned to Wādī Halfā on 9 June and set off for Cairo the following day. Evidently an extremely professional officer, he produced a comprehensive report covering every conceivable aspect of navigating the Second and Third Cataracts, including the maximum length and beam of suitable vessels. He concluded at the end of his herculean task that the 212-mile stretch of river he had reconnoitred could be divided between 190 miles of open water and 24½ miles of rapids. While the Second Cataract could be deemed to be 8½ miles long and the Third or Hannek Cataract 3 miles long, intervening between them were the marginally less formidable cataracts of Semneh (2 miles long), Ambako (1 mile), Tanjur (3 miles), Akasheh (1 mile), Dal (4 miles), Amara (1 mile) and Kajbar (1 mile).[27]

As interesting as Hammill's report is, one should not lose sight of the fact that to get to Wādī Halfā it is first necessary to travel the entire length of Egypt; that the stretch of river he surveyed from Wādī Halfā to Hannek is less than one third of Wolseley's 666 miles to Berber; and is less than one quarter of the full-length journey from Wādī Halfā to Khartoum. On 3 August, after consulting with Hammill, Lord Hay signalled from HMS *Helicon* at Alexandria that he had 'formed the opinion that the 400 boat proposal was not practicable'.[28]

Wolseley seems to have had some inkling of what was coming from the Admiralty and quickly assembled a three-man committee of Red River men to beat the Royal Navy to the draw. The committee submitted its own findings four days ahead of Hay's verdict.[29] At the beginning of their short and generally superficial submission, the Red River triumvirate stated that they had read the recent reports of Captain Molyneux and Commander Hammill and had been able to engage in discussions at the Admiralty with the First Naval Lord, Admiral Sir Astley Cooper Key. The committee was made up of Redvers Buller, Major General Sir John McNeill VC, KCMG, CB and Colonel William Butler CB.[30]

McNeill, an old India hand in his early fifties, had served in the Bengal European Regiment (later the 107th Foot and subsequently the 2nd Battalion, Royal Sussex Regiment) before and during the Mutiny. On 30 March 1864, during the Second New Zealand War, he rode back into a group of fifty Maoris to rescue a wounded private, an act which had earned him the VC. He would go on to command a brigade during the Second Suakin Campaign, but that particular phase of operations still lay the best part of eight months in the future.

Colonel William Butler, late of the 69th Regiment, was a handsome man of forty-six, whose moustache and mutton-chop whiskers suggested a pillar of the established order. In fact he was unusual amongst his Army peer-group in that he was a Jesuit-educated Catholic from County Tipperary. A gallant and able soldier to be sure, Butler was also ambitious, opinionated and mercurial by disposition. He was also a poor team player, although his devotion to Wolseley usually served to hold this most unhelpful of traits in check.[31] Married since 1877 to the prodigiously talented artist Elizabeth Thompson (later better known as Lady Butler), he had served with the Ring in Canada, Ashantiland and Egypt. When Colonel Hammill Stewart's trip to Canada had been cancelled so that he could accompany Gordon to Khartoum, it was Butler who had been sent in his stead. He had sailed from Liverpool in the first week of February, worked with the Government of Canada for something around six weeks and was back in England again by April.[32] Butler remarks in his autobiography that he saw a good deal of Wolseley at this time: 'With him I had many interviews after my return . . . and we discussed at length the various routes by which Khartoum could be reached by troops.'[33] Evidently the 8 and 14 April memoranda addressed to Lord Hartington relied as much on Butler's input as Wolseley's. The colonel's energy, resolve and past experience of small-boat work would make him the ideal candidate to run any re-enactment of the Red River expedition on the Nile, for if nothing else was certain it was that the Royal Navy had no intention of assuming the responsibility.

The submission of the Red River men was little short of amateurish in comparison with the offerings of their naval counterparts, but they insisted nonetheless that, 'In our opinion the question really resolves into this: is it possible to procure and place on the Nile at Sarras 500 boats by the 5th October?' They proceeded to answer their own question with, 'Surely this would be possible.' It will be recalled that Wolseley's memo of 14 April, which is to say some three and half months earlier, had identified 15 November as the latest date to which Gordon could be expected to hold out. From this it follows that the triumvirate were allowing 41 days to cover 860 miles of river, including the Third to Sixth Cataracts inclusive, or an average rate of 21 miles a day against the current. This was the first of the minor miracles they would need to perform. Given that this would all have to be done from a standing start, the other tall order was to get, within 67 days or 9½ weeks, some or all of the boatyards dispersed around the British Isles to construct several hundred specially designed boats; to gather them up into batches; have them shipped from an island in the North Sea to the north-east corner of Africa; and then get them moved up the Nile to a point beyond the Second Cataract. The actual requirement would later evolve to become two batches each of 400 boats. McNeill would play no part in the expedition, but we shall return later to reflect on just how well Buller and Butler performed against the targets they set themselves.

It was probably because the Red River memorandum was so light on substance that Butler followed it up five days later with a note to Wolseley of his own.[34] He posted it from Plymouth on the morning of Monday 4 August. Because he was evidently at or near a naval station and addresses poling and tracking in detail, two small-boat techniques rejected as impractical in Lord John Hay's comments of 3 August, it seems certain that a copy of the admiral's remarks had either been shown to him or had been specifically wired through to him the same day. It might well have been Wolseley who arranged for this to happen.

Butler made the perfectly sensible observation that the Royal Navy had reported from the point of view of getting steamers and *nuggars* through the first three cataracts, but that this was not what he was proposing. The case he proceeded to lay out in favour of a small-boat scheme was much after the fashion of the story of Major General Phillips, Burgoyne's gunner in the Hudson Valley campaign of 1777. Faced with a seemingly impossible hill, from the summit of which Fort Ticonderoga could readily be pounded into submission, Phillips is said to have remarked, 'Anywhere a goat can go, a man can go; and anywhere a man can go, he can drag a gun.' Phillips duly lived up to his boast and, with a single shot, succeeded in triggering the abandonment of one of the strongest forts in the Americas. Butler's corresponding mantra was to be found in his third last paragraph:

> I have not yet seen the Nile above Cairo and its neighbourhood, and so far, I labour under a disadvantage in writing these rough notes, but I have had considerable and varied experience in ascending rapid and dangerous rivers. Water is water, and rock is rock, whether they lie in America or in Africa, and the conditions which they can assume towards each other are much the same all the world over.[35]

'Water is water and rock is rock': it was hardly the most scientific of arguments but then again it no longer mattered what Butler thought for while the final act in the 'Battle of the Routes' had yet to play itself out, its outcome had already been ordained.

The long-running argument had been resolved by the nagging calls of the Adjutant-General on the office of the Secretary of State for War, coupled with the seemingly imminent collapse of khedival authority in Dongola Province. The crisis in north Sudan allowed Wolseley to contend that a Nile expedition would serve not only to save Gordon, but would also shield Upper Egypt and regain lost territory as it went. It was a sustainable argument, up to a point at least, although throwing only one stone does not invariably serve to kill two birds. There had been a period when the two objectives were eminently compatible, but so much time had been squandered in the interim that the relief of Khartoum now depended above all else on rapidity. Even so, day after day the leading professional soldier in the land had pressed the case for boats; and who was Lord Hartington to overturn the professional judgement of the conqueror of Egypt?

Gladstone Gives Way

On the evening of the same day, Monday 4 August, Butler received a telegram from Wolseley which read simply, 'I want to see you here tomorrow.' Butler guessed correctly that the government was on the verge of folding, in the face of a mounting storm of protest over its continued inaction. The newspapers had been up in arms for weeks, with the result that it was now commonplace for the Prime Minister to be booed and jeered whenever he appeared in public. The Queen Empress had already urged action on him in the strongest possible terms and was doubtless pleased at the eminent good sense of her subjects. What Butler could not have guessed at was quite how Gladstone's hand came to be forced.

The agent of change had been the Marquess of Hartington, long since driven to distraction by a succession of Cabinet meetings in which he had been afforded only five minutes at the end of the proceedings to discuss the deteriorating military situation in Egypt and the Sudan. He changed tack in advance of the meeting due for Friday 25 July, by circulating a memorandum to his Cabinet colleagues laying out the clear necessity to take military action in the Nile Valley. The military provisions outlined in the note had been conceived in large part by Wolseley, and pressed the urgent need to send a brigade of British troops up the Nile in small boats as far as Dongola, against the contingency of operations for the relief of Khartoum eventually becoming necessary. Hartington and Wolseley knew only too well that such operations were already long overdue, but even now had to pander to Gladstone's perception that Gordon could leave Khartoum any time he chose, but had wilfully elected to thwart governmental intent. There was an element of truth in the first part of the Prime Minister's viewpoint: Gordon could always have stolen away in the dead of night aboard one of his steamers, but as Governor-General of the Sudan and a holder of the Queen's Commission was honour-bound to remain in Khartoum, even at the cost of his life. Unfortunately ethereal precepts like the honour code of the British officer corps were not the Prime Minister's forte. The cost of moving a brigade of 3,000 men up to Dongola had been provisionally estimated by the War Office at £300,000, although all the senior figures in the department knew that this was far too small a force to effect the relief of Khartoum. Nonetheless 3,000 men and £300,000 were the quantities tabled before the Cabinet.

When Hartington and other ministers insisted on the provisions of the memorandum being put to the vote, the Cabinet divided nine votes to three in favour of proceeding with the military preparations it advocated. One of the hold-outs, predictably enough, was the Prime Minister himself, who tried to mollify Hartington by promising to write to him over the weekend, outlining his personal reading of the situation. The promised note turned out to be an exercise in Gladstonian obfuscation and led Hartington to anticipate only continued inaction. No longer prepared on a point of honour to be brushed aside, to abandon General Gordon to his fate or to return to the War Office to face a contemptuous Wolseley, Hartington channelled an indirect threat of resignation through Granville and awaited Gladstone's response. Lord Selborne, the Lord Chancellor, similarly deprecated the Prime Minister's position and made it clear that he too was prepared to resign.

This was not a bluff Gladstone could afford to call. Hartington was not merely the principal Whig, but during the last parliament had led the Liberals in opposition. Moreover, in the aftermath of the 1880 election victory, he had magnanimously declined the premiership in favour of Gladstone, who had made it plain that his return to the campaign trail was conditional upon his leading the new government in the event of victory. Blending Liberals, Whigs, Peelites and Radicals in one party had not made for an easy political alliance; it was well within Hartington's gift to rally his adherents, vote with the Opposition, bring down the government and sink the Prime Minister's programme of electoral reform. Wearily Gladstone tried to pretend to Hartington that he had never been opposed to making reasonable preparations for a relief expedition. At the next meeting of the Cabinet he conceded that a 'Vote of Credit' in the sum of £300,000 could be put to Parliament during the course of the coming week. The measure sailed through the Commons on Thursday 7 August. It is broadly true to say that from this point on the whole Gordon issue passed out of the control of the Prime Minister and Foreign Secretary, to become the particular preserve of the Secretary of State for War. There was nothing official about this arrangement; it was simply the way it was going to be, whether Hartington's colleagues liked it or not. The decision to relieve Khartoum had been made, not by the Cabinet collectively, but by the country – by the Queen Empress, by the newspaper editors, by the Army, by the Conservatives, by Hartington and the Whigs, but first and foremost by the settled will of the people.

Butler and the Whaler Scheme

When Butler reported to Wolseley at the War Office on Tuesday morning, two days ahead of the Vote of Credit, he was handled a bundle of papers containing all the correspondence so far transacted between the War Office and the Admiralty in respect of the small-boat proposal. The Royal Navy was of the certain opinion that it would take two to three months to construct 400 boats of the sort Wolseley proposed. Butler was told to find boats suited to the role or, if they simply did not exist, to scope their construction from new. Lieutenant Colonel James Alleyne RA, another Red River hand, had been called in to assist Butler in the enterprise. By lunchtime the following day the duo had concluded that the boats would have to be manufactured. An early morning visit to a Lambeth boatyard had convinced them that such small enterprising firms would be perfectly capable of building a modest number of boats inside a month. The recipe for success, therefore, would be based not on engaging a few firms to build large numbers of boats, but on inviting a large number of firms each to build a relatively small number of boats. For Butler forty times ten worked nicely. What he did not yet have was a design. Butler considered that the boat he sought would have to be, 'large but light, safe in cataract but swift in smooth waters, fast-sailing but easy to row, roomy but small of draught, strong but portable, heavy with cargo but light of build, staunch but elastic, slight but lasting'. It amounted to a daunting list of seemingly irreconcilable attributes.

The best place to search for such a boat was surely the naval dockyard at Portsmouth. Butler and Alleyne spent Wednesday afternoon and evening firing off telegrams to prepare the ground for a meaningful visit the following day, including instructions to all the local boat-building firms to send along a representative. The two colonels left London on the morning train and reached Portsmouth just before noon. The handful of ship's boats presented on the basin for inspection met with short shrift. In the nearby boat-loft Butler proceeded to reject ship's cutters, captain's gigs, life-boats, jolly-boats and just about every other kind of boat. Next he walked through a large store-shed, where at last his eye fell by chance on a useful-looking whale-gig resting across the rafters above his head. By now the mysterious quest of the two army colonels had drawn a small crowd of naval officials and dockyard men curious to see what all the fuss was about. The gig was taken down to the basin to be loaded with the 100 days' worth of rations and stores Butler had requisitioned in preparation for a trial. A dozen dock-hands took their places and rowed the gig out into the basin. Although the boat was unduly heavy and too small for so large a cargo, it appeared satisfactory in almost every other respect. Butler made a note to the effect that he needed a boat which was 4 feet longer, 18 inches wider in the beam and a few inches deeper. This meant that the perfect Nile whaler would be 30 feet in length, 6 ft 6 in across the beam and 2 ft 3 in draught. It was to come with two collapsible masts and sails, a dozen oars and all the requisite fittings. The overall weight of boat and accessories was not to exceed a thousand pounds. There was no question but that constructing a bigger, lighter boat represented a tall order.

Ten boats each, inside a month, queried Butler. The boat-builders sucked their teeth and scratched away in their notebooks, but they were enterprising Britons and there was a profit to be turned. Provided the terms of the contract were generous enough to allow them to take on extra hands and work around the clock, of course they could do it. Butler and Alleyne did not as yet have the authority to spend a five pound note so, with grateful thanks to everybody involved and a promise that they would be in touch shortly, they took their leave and hastened back to London. Over the next three days, which included a weekend, they proceeded to have design drawings made and despatched to every boat-building firm the Admiralty knew of. All were invited to tender by return and most did so, with firms distributed along the Thames and the Clyde to the fore. There were to be four points of delivery at the end of the twenty-eight days allowed: London, Portsmouth, Liverpool and Glasgow.

On Tuesday 12 August Butler was summoned to attend upon 'a high Government official'.[36] Neither in his *Campaign of the Cataracts*, nor in his later autobiography does he say who this was, although in the latter he adds that it was a parliamentarian – a minister in other words. He was ushered in to find the principal figure surrounded by officials of the contracts and finance departments. Butler was asked if he really thought it was possible that the work could be completed inside twenty-eight days, as the minister had read in the colonel's most recently submitted paper. Butler replied that he was sure it could, before going on to explain that all the preparatory work was already complete and that the only thing he still needed was the authority to commit to expenditure. The minister scratched out a note and handed it to the colonel. It said simply, 'Colonel Butler, You may proceed with the construction of four hundred boats.' The minister then turned to the assembled civil servants and said, 'Gentlemen, I have assembled you here to tell you that Colonel Butler has a blank cheque for the building and equipment of these boats, and his decisions as to expenditure are not to be questioned.' Butler placed orders with a total of forty-seven firms that evening.[37] With that the clock started running on the relief of Khartoum. There were three months to go before the expiry of the 15 November deadline Wolseley had set back in April, one of which would now be consumed by boat-building in Britain.

Stephenson Demurs

The reason why Lord Hartington, assuredly the minister in question, had felt the need to ask Butler if he was quite certain he could deliver on his twenty-eight-day guarantee was that Sir Frederick Stephenson had not lamely fallen into line with the small-boat proposal. At 10.00 p.m. the previous Thursday, Hartington had wired Stephenson with news of the vote of credit and to enquire what size of force he would be able to deploy from the Army of Occupation:

Am sending by next mail instructions as to preparations consequent on vote of credit obtained from Parliament. General scope is to enable brigade to be despatched at short notice from Halfa to Dongola. Proposal to use small boats above Cataracts as in Red River expedition. I gather from Egerton's telegram of 6th that you are prepared at once to move English troops beyond Halfa. What could you do with force and resources now at your disposal? The additional battalion asked for is already placed under orders.[38]

The detailed written instructions drafted the following day, Friday 8 August, ran to several pages and would have been prepared for the Secretary of State's signature, a process in which Wolseley and his staff would have had a hand. Hartington also signed a second letter dated the same day which devolved the detail to Stephenson:

I have further to add, that having in my despatch of this date given you a general outline of the operations which Her Majesty's Government consider may become necessary, and of the preparations which should be undertaken, I desire to leave the details of these, as much as possible, to your judgement, acting on your knowledge of the circumstances, and of the resources at your disposal.[39]

In subsequent paragraphs Hartington instructed Stephenson to report fully on any expenditure he incurred, and prohibited him from advancing beyond Wādī Halfā without the further sanction of the government. The two letters would not make it to Cairo until late the following week.

Hartington's telegram, however, was on Stephenson's desk on Monday 11 August. At 1.10 p.m. the same day he replied as follows:

Yours 7th. Can move to Wady Halfa 4 battalions 2,200 bayonets, two squadrons 200 sabres, 1 battery horse or field artillery, 2 batteries mountain [artillery], mounted infantry. No Royal Engineers to spare. Can leave detachment Wady Halfa and move on remainder as far as Semneh right bank.

Small boats proposed not suitable. Can procure large amount water transport locally.[40]

After everything he had gone through to convince his Cabinet colleagues of the merits of Wolseley's plan, this was not what Hartington wanted to hear. It was undoubtedly this telegram which resulted in Butler being called in to reassure the minister the following day. Having authorized Butler to proceed, Hartington replied to Stephenson at 8.40 p.m. on Tuesday evening:

Yours 11th. You will receive Thursday my despatch of 8th containing instructions as to movement of troops. But in the possible contingency of necessity of advance to Dongola, or even Khartoum, Admiralty reports lead me to doubt whether operation could be conducted with local land or water transport within next winter and without enormous expense. Experienced officers here confident of practicability of boat plan, and I propose to adhere to it, and provide 400 at once. General Earle returns tomorrow [to Egypt from home leave] to take command under you of force at Wady Halfa. General Buller will go next week as his Chief of Staff. Report your proceedings fully.[41]

The appointments announced in the last paragraph represented a compromise proposed by Wolseley in the wake of what he termed 'a regular turn up' with the Duke of Cambridge. Wolseley had originally urged that Buller be appointed as the commander of the expedition, in the local rank of lieutenant general. The Duke, who believed that promotion should come strictly on the basis of *Army List* seniority, had been reluctant enough to see Buller raised to major general after El Teb and Tamai, over the heads of colonels who were his senior, and now made it plain that he was not prepared to countenance his appointment as a lieutenant general only a matter of months later. Although Wolseley liked Earle, and counted him an old friend, he strongly objected to 'entrusting any independent command to an untried unproved man as long as I have available one who has proved himself in the field to be a capable General'. The Duke stood his ground, however, compelling Wolseley to accept that Buller would be chief of staff to Earle, rather than vice versa.[42]

On Thursday Stephenson sent a routine telegram designed to comply with the injunction to report his proceedings. On Friday Hartington and Wolseley drafted another long letter designed to explain the merits of the boat plan more fully. It incorporated what for Wolseley was a key point: if the troops were moved from Wādī Halfā to Dongola, it would in all likelihood be because they had been ordered to proceed to Berber or Khartoum. To achieve their object they would have to be provided with a means of transport which was going to get them to their destination and back again, before the cooler weather turned over to high summer. The letter also advised that a company of sappers had been ordered to Egypt, together with two newly formed companies of mounted infantry. The latter would be added to the two Stephenson already had under his command to create a composite camel-mounted regiment.

Stephenson had not seen any of the Secretary of State's long letters, when on Saturday 16 August he pressed for permission to start passing steamers and other craft through the Second Cataract. He went on, 'Early occupation of Dongola moreover desirable from political as well as military grounds. If approved prompt reply necessary.' He again stated that 'sufficient and suitable craft can be obtained here, and further supply from Dongola if necessary'. The hire or purchase of suitable boats, he estimated, was likely to cost about £30,000.[43] It was obviously necessary that Hartington's reply should clear up any lingering confusion.

Before replying to your telegram of the 16th instant, it is desirable to avoid any misunderstanding. Her Majesty's Government wish to be in a position to send a force this season to Dongola, and if necessary to Khartoum. The force to be so equipped that it shall be able to return from Khartoum this winter. From Hammill's reports we believe that it is impossible to effect our object if we employ only steamers and Nile boats; also that to effect it at all there must be at least twelve good steamers on Nile below Assouan, and eight between that place and Wady Halfa. Consequently, until twenty steamers are thus distributed, it appears wrong to pass any steamer above Wady Halfa. In these circumstances we are organizing an expedition in small boats, propelled by their crews beyond Wady Halfa.

You disagree but what do you propose? What force do you propose to send to Dongola, and how would you get it there? If obliged to send a force to Khartoum, what, in round numbers, do you propose it should consist of? How would you send it to Khartoum, and how bring it back? State approximate number of camels you would require to assist in each operation. How many steamers would you keep north of Wady Halfa before you send any to the south. Report fully.[44]

Stephenson telegraphed his reply on 21 August.[45] His first sentence did not sound a particularly positive note in respect of time. 'Possible to send force New Dongola Ordeh this season, but impossible, owing to distance, for a force to proceed to Khartoum via Dongola, and return this winter.' Subsequent events would show that Stephenson was perfectly right on this point; it was also something which should have been apparent even from London. He next addressed the size of the force and proceeded to impugn the advisability of advancing a single brigade:

Force to proceed from New Dongola to Khartoum should not be less than 8,000 . . . If small force you propose to send to New Dongola in first instance does not realise hopes of Government, it will be placed in false position, and difficulties of reinforcing it later with men and stores will be very great, owing to fall of Nile and consequent amount of land transport required.

Next came an outright dismissal of the small-boat scheme, followed rapidly by a preference for the Suakin–Berber axis:

Believe expedition to New Dongola by means of small boats impracticable. Difficulties on this river too great. Naval opinion here is in this sense. Can be best done by steamers and local craft, but prompt decision urgent to secure craft for force you propose in yours of 8th. Already arranged that eight steamers be placed above Assouan and twelve below. More available if required. Former fit to pass Second Cataract . . .

My own opinion still is in favour of Suakin–Berber route if friendly tribes were armed and subsidized, and would procure sufficient camels, which I believe they easily could. With troops now in Egypt, those coming from Gibraltar and India, and three battalions in addition, should leave force sufficient for Suakin route.

If Hartington was frustrated by the disagreement between the generals, Wolseley was furious that GOC Cairo should presume to question his judgement. On 22 August he lambasted Stephenson in the privacy of his journal, although there can be little room for doubt that he had shared broadly the same thoughts with the Secretary of State for War earlier in the day:

In his telegrams of the last few days Stephenson has shown the greatest confusion of ideas & want of plan: they are worth studying as specimens of confused English and as an illustration of the misfortune of having men of small mental calibre in positions where the power of taking in all the phases of your position both as it exists and will be further on when influenced by change of season, high or low Nile for example, or by easily forseen [sic] eventualities – such as the end of Gordon's ammunition having been reached – where the grasp of thought required for the solution of such problems is absent.[46]

Only that morning Hartington had wired Gladstone and Granville to say that he wished to send the Adjutant-General to Egypt on the grounds that the War Office and Headquarters Cairo were not in agreement, that the plan under contemplation was Wolseley's anyway and that it was neither fair nor prudent to ask Stephenson to accept responsibility for an operation in which he appeared to have no faith. At 2.00 p.m. the Secretary of State for War sent for Wolseley to tell him what he had done. Hartington would not have been surprised to learn that he was perfectly prepared to take the job on, as Wolseley had written to him in May volunteering his services as the commander of the Suakin–Berber expedition then under contemplation by the government.[47] It can be no mere coincidence that the quantity of whalers on order with the boatyards was increased from 400 to 800 during the course of the afternoon.[48] The following day the Prime Minister and Foreign Secretary each sent messages consenting to Wolseley's appointment, though it was clear that both men harboured reservations. Gladstone thought that the announcement should be handled in such a fashion as to avoid any inference that an advance on Khartoum would now automatically follow. Granville for his part made an observation to the effect that he concurred in Wolseley's despatch only with a heavy heart, as he felt sure the general would contrive the necessity for just such an advance as soon as he was in Egypt.[49] After obtaining the assent of his Cabinet colleagues, Hartington wrote at length to the Queen Empress to secure her endorsement. There was a delay while Victoria conferred with a reluctant Duke of Cambridge, who did not want to lose Wolseley's services in the role of Adjutant-General, but by 26 August the matter had been settled. It was to be announced in the newspapers the following day.[50]

At midnight on 26 August Hartington telegraphed Cairo to notify Stephenson that he would shortly be superseded.

After anxious consideration, Her Majesty's Government have come to the conclusion that it is unjust to ask you to be responsible for directing an operation which, after full knowledge of plan, you consider to be impracticable. They have therefore decided to send Lord Wolseley to take temporarily the chief command in Egypt. Government highly appreciate the manner in which you have carried out the important and difficult duties of your command, and earnestly hope that you will feel able to remain in Egypt whilst Lord Wolseley is there, and assist him with your advice.[51]

Notwithstanding the poisonous remarks in Wolseley's journal, Sir Frederick Stephenson was a popular and highly regarded figure in Cairo and had done an excellent job as GOC in difficult circumstances. It was inevitable that his first thoughts were of resignation. He had pretty much made up his mind to go, when he received a letter written by Wolseley something around a week earlier, before he knew that the expedition was to be his. The letter saw Wolseley at his charming best: he could quite understand why, not having been on the Red River, Stephenson found the small-boat scheme unconvincing. Indeed without his Canadian experience to draw on, he might have arrived at the same conclusion. Nonetheless he was quite sure that Stephenson would throw as much energy into the scheme as if he had devised it himself.[52] The letter had been rapidly overtaken by events, but was enough to make the difference between Stephenson resigning and staying on to help. Instead of firing off the resignation letter he had been contemplating, he wired Hartington with a simple acceptance of his lot: 'Yours 27th. Will willingly remain here as you wish.'[53] Wolseley had been in this position once before, when in 1879 he superseded Lord Chelmsford in Zululand. On that occasion there had been a good deal of wounded pride and sulkiness on show. Recollecting the episode in his journal, Wolseley described Chelmsford as 'that very silly noble Lord'.[54] In the event Stephenson would be so welcoming and helpful that even Wolseley could have no grounds for complaint.

Wolseley Takes Command

Wolseley sailed for Cairo aboard HMS *Iris* in company with Lord Northbrook, newly appointed as the British High Commissioner to Egypt, and Sir Evelyn Baring, returning to his duties after the long London conference. They docked in Alexandria at noon on Tuesday 9 September, where they were met by Generals Stephenson, Buller and Dormer (Stephenson's chief of staff). By 8.00 p.m. the same day Wolseley and his entourage had been quartered at the Kasr el Noussa Palace, where

Lord John Hay was amongst the first-night dinner guests. Wolseley found the admiral 'as pompous as usual' and was irritated to be asked by him whether he had come to Egypt as the 'Commander in Chief' or the 'General Commanding in Chief', not least because nobody in London had given any thought to the matter. The following morning Wolseley called at the Abdin Palace to pay his respects to Tawfiq Pasha, who afforded him a cordial welcome and promised that one of the best khedival yachts would be placed at his disposal for the journey up the Nile. From there Wolseley moved to the British agency for a meeting attended by Northbrook, Baring, Egerton, Stephenson and the two principal British officers of the Cairo Police. Amongst other things they agreed a level below which the Cairo garrison could not be denuded.

Later in the day Wolseley dealt with all the senior command and staff appointments. Stephenson would command all troops north of Assiut, which meant that he would remain in charge of the garrisons in Cairo and Alexandria much as before. Buller would be Wolseley's chief of staff, while Major General William Earle CB, CSI, ordinarily the garrison commander in Alexandria, would command the fighting echelon at Wādī Halfā and points south. Command of the mounted troops would rest with Colonel Sir Herbert Stewart KCB, who was thus subordinated to Earle in his role as the tactical-level commander. Evelyn Wood would act as GOC Lines of Communication south of Assiut. Colonel Sir Charles Wilson KCMG, CB, RE would be the Deputy Adjutant-General (DAG) Intelligence Branch, while the role of DAG General Staff, Buller's right-hand man in effect, would go to Colonel Henry Brackenbury CB, RA, another of the Ring's core members. Though he was by no means universally popular with the other senior disciples, it was 'Brack' who had the keenest brain of them all.

By 11 September Wolseley was ready to commit himself to an outline plan and wrote to Lord Hartington to press for the urgent despatch of the additional men and materiel he would need to succour Khartoum.[55] He began by enumerating the forces available in Egypt or en route there:

1 Regiment of Cavalry (mounted)	365
13½ Battalions of Infantry	8,887
1 Battery Royal Horse Artillery	159
1 Field Battery	135
1 Camel Battery	119
2 Garrison Batteries	225
3 Companies of Engineers	569
Mounted Infantry	423
Total	10,882

Omitted from this list were the battalion of Royal Marines and company of Royal Engineers based at Suakin. Wolseley next went on to say that his consultations with Northbrook, Baring and Stephenson had shown that Alexandria would require a garrison of 1½ battalions and a heavy battery, while Cairo would consume 3 battalions, a squadron of cavalry, a battery of horse artillery, a field battery and the second garrison battery. This would leave a balance of 3 squadrons, a regiment of mounted infantry, 9 battalions and a camel battery available for operations south of Cairo, or 300 sabres, 423 MI, 6,000 bayonets and 6 mountain-guns. Six of the nine battalions would be required to secure the lines of communication, one of them between Cairo and Hannek in support of Sir Evelyn Wood and the EA, and five between Hannek and Berber. This would leave an inadequate three battalions for the final push on Khartoum.

In his tenth paragraph Wolseley went on to request the reinforcements he would need if he was to adhere to the outline proposals he had submitted in April. His requirement included the manpower needed to breathe life into the second of his 'novel expedients', an elite brigade-sized Camel Corps:

10. To place ourselves, therefore, in a position to be able to meet the possible contingency of having to send a force by the Nile route to Khartum, it is in my opinion absolutely necessary to send here with the least possible delay two battalions of infantry from Malta, and the following detachments from England, to be here converted into a camel corps. This camel corps should be based on the same principle that was lately adopted in raising a corps of 200 mounted infantry from the line battalions at home, namely by obtaining so many men and one or two officers as volunteers from each of the following regiments or battalions:

	Rank and File
From the seven battalions of Foot Guards, 40 men from each	280
From the 16 regiments of cavalry of the line at home, 40 men from each	640
From the three regiments of Household Cavalry	100
From the two battalions of the Rifle Brigade at home	80

Wolseley next moved on to describe the composition of the 5,000-strong force he intended to assemble at or near Shendy:

11. This would enable a fighting force to be placed in line somewhere about the neighbourhood of Shendi, composed (in round numbers) as follows:–

	Rank and File
Five battalions of infantry	3,500
19th Hussars	300
Mounted Infantry now existing	400
Camel Corps which Admiral Lord J Hay will place at my disposal from Royal Marines	100
Camel Corps coming from England	1,100
	5,400

Say 5,000 fighting men with 6 guns.

12. I have given this subject the deepest thought during my journey from England, and have had the advantage of obtaining the views of the authorities here as to the

military position in the Sudan, and, as at present informed, I am decidedly of the opinion that with no smaller force would it be safe to advance upon Khartum.

Wolseley's final paragraph was designed to secure prompt compliance with his requirements and preclude any possibility of further political procrastination.

18. I should be wanting in my duty if I did not point out in the clearest terms that, unless the force in Egypt be augmented forthwith to the extent I have proposed, we shall not be able to relieve General Gordon this year if the force now surrounding him remains where it is; and it is a certainty, in my opinion, that want of ammunition would prevent him from holding out for another 12 months. I cannot, therefore, too strongly urge upon your Lordship the necessity for immediate action if his relief is to be provided for this coming winter.

The abridged essence of the letter was telegraphed to the Secretary of State for War the same day. The matter of Wolseley's title would also seem by now to have been resolved. At his signature block he styled himself, 'Wolseley, General, Commander-in-Chief of the Forces in Egypt'. Hereafter we will adopt the abbreviation C-in-C to mean Wolseley, rather than the Duke of Cambridge.

At some point during the course of the afternoon telegrams containing some long overdue good news reached Cairo from Colvile and Kitchener. The Mudir of Dongola, it seemed, had brought the rebels to battle near Korti and visited a serious defeat upon them in which the Amīr Aḥmad al-Heddai, the leader of the turncoat Shā'iqīa, had been killed. Verification continued to flow in over the next few days, but such was the extent of the victory that it now looked as if the whole *mudirieh* of Dongola, as far as Merowe on the Great Bend, could be considered to be firmly under government control.

The staff planning and calculations continued apace over the next few days in order to put flesh on the bones of an already logistically complex outline plan. The arrival of the quick-witted Colonel Brackenbury on 17 September was a great boon. With all their meals being delivered from Shepheard's Hotel, the headquarters staff lived well at Kasr el Noussa. Wolseley fancied the name translated closely enough as the 'Palace of Victory', which he regarded as a good omen. The 19th Hussars found a small guard at the palace, enabling the C-in-C to borrow a horse whenever he needed to get out and about. Between Wednesday 17 September and Friday 19 September he inspected the three Highland battalions in Cairo over consecutive days, in the order 1st Black Watch at the Kasr el Nile Barracks, 1st Gordons at the Citadel, and 1st Camerons at the Abdin Barracks. While the Black Watch 'looked very well' and the Gordons were 'a splendid battalion', 1st Royal Irish, not long since landed from India and inspected on Sunday were a 'very varmint looking lot all truly Irish in appearance'. Quite what Wolseley meant to convey by such a curious remark is anybody's guess, but 1st Royal Irish was certainly a very fine battalion which by dint of its 'band-box' appearance caught the eye wherever it went. Even a thousand miles and more up the Nile, the Irishmen would manage a notably smarter turnout than anybody else.

The good news from the south meant that a little over a week after he had asked for an additional two battalions from Malta, Wolseley concluded that the requirement could now be dropped. At around this time the Mudir of Dongola also wired in a number of misleading reports suggesting that the rebels at Khartoum had given up the ghost and gone home. The resultant confusion was so serious that on the evening of 21 September Wolseley noted in his journal, 'It is now tolerably certain that the siege of Khartoum has been raised.'[56] The 'news' had a predictable effect in London, causing the Secretary of State for War to wire Wolseley to ask whether the despatch of the Camel Corps ought to be delayed. The reply was a courteous but unequivocal no. A telegram also came in from Kitchener on the 22nd, stating that he had just returned from Merowe and now proposed leading the Mudir of Dongola's 'army' (amounting to 500 men at best) in an advance on Berber. It was a gallant offer, but one the C-in-C had no hesitation in declining. The major was to stay on the end of the telegraph at Debbeh as the voice of reason, until such time as the first of the troops came up to join him and Sir Charles Wilson was safely ensconced at Dongola. Kitchener's return to the telegraph quickly resulted in the nonsense about the siege having been raised being exposed for what it was. On Thursday 25 September a bouyant William Butler arrived from England; the first consignment of whalers had docked at Alexandria only three days earlier.

Contrary to Wolseley's expectations it had quickly become clear that the Duke of Cambridge had no intention of resisting the despatch of so many small regimental detachments from home, although given the choice he would certainly have preferred to send two formed battalions in their stead. Indeed the Duke had expressly resolved not to gainsay a commander in the field and had thrown the full weight of his office behind the preparations. The camel corps detachments were hurriedly selected by commanding officers, grouped into Guards, Heavy Cavalry and Light Cavalry Divisions, were each inspected and addressed by the Duke at their assembly points and on 26 September embarked aboard the steamships *Australia* and *Deccan*. They would dock at Alexandria on 7 October.[57] Wolseley got precisely what he had asked for: a hand-picked body of men, universally range-qualified as marksmen, not one of whom was less than twenty-two years of age. Most commanding officers had provided their best men as instructed, although one or two undoubtedly took the opportunity to unburden themselves of their least favourite reprobates into the bargain.

In the meantime the call for *voyageurs* had gone out in Canada. It took only twelve days, commencing on 1 September, to enlist a contingent of 380 men. It was comprised of 36 Englishmen or Scotsmen, 158 Anglo-Canadians, 93 French-Canadians, 77 Caughnawaga Indians and 16 others. Fifteen years on from the Red River Expedition, the old river ways were already receding into history and not all the *voyageurs* were the real thing. They left Quebec on 15 September under the command of Lieutenant Colonel Fred Denison, who had been Wolseley's ADC on the Red River. Amongst the other half-dozen Canadian officers were a doctor, a paymaster and a Catholic priest.[58] They would reach Wādī Halfā on 26 October.

The efforts of the Canadians would be supplemented by 266 West African *krooboys*, raised on the Gold Coast by Major Charles Smyth of the Welsh Regiment.

The Journey Ahead

Wolseley's outline plan called for the whaler-borne troops to marry up with their boats at Gemai, a beach located just above the Second Cataract, so near the Sarras terminus of the thirty-three-mile stretch of railway as to be virtually synonymous with it. Unfortunately there was a journey of almost 800 miles to cover first. Colvile remarked in the *Official History* that the preparations required over this distance, 'entailed great expenditure of energy and power of organization, but were at the same time of an ordinary character'.[59] The first 229 miles would be covered by a straightforward railway journey from Cairo to Assiut. The next leg, from Assiut to Aswan, was a long river journey of some 318 miles and would be traversed using standard Nile craft, a combination of coal-burning steamers, towed barges and native sail-boats such as *nuggars* and *feluccas*. It would then be necessary to disembark men and stores alike in order to bypass the First Cataract by means of a nine-mile rail journey to Philae. At Philae everything could be re-embarked on boats for a 210-mile river trip to the forward assembly area at Wādī Halfā.

The railway from Wādī Halfā to Gemai/Sarras would take care of the next thirty-three miles, bypassing the Second Cataract in the process, although the poor capacity of the line, coupled with low availability of rolling stock, would mean that a proportion of the whalers would have to run through the cataract in the care of Butler's civilian workforce. From Gemai onwards the whaler-borne troops would be at the oars, while the Camel Corps detachments paralleled their advance on land. It was twenty-nine miles from Gemai to the head of the Dal Cataract, 102 miles from Dal to Kajbar and thirty-one miles from Kajbar to Hannek. The boats would have to be portaged at both Kajbar and Hannek. Hannek to Dongola, the expedition's immediate objective, was a further thirty-nine miles, meaning that the total length of the journey from Cairo to Dongola was 1,033 miles. If the whaler-borne troops went forward of Dongola to Belal, on the Great Bend just beyond Merowe, they would have a further 176 miles of rowing ahead of them. Of the formidable logistic difficulties of the undertaking the campaign's official historian said,

The Nile Expedition was a campaign less against man than against nature and against time. Had British soldiers and Egyptian camels been able to subsist on sand and occasional water, or had the desert produced beef and biscuit, the army might, in spite of its late start, have reached Khartoum in November. But as things were, the rate of progress of the army was dependent on the rate of progress of its supplies.[60]

In fact there was no set of circumstances in which a Nile Expedition starting so late and proceeding by way of Abū-Hamed and Berber in small boats could ever have reached Khartoum in November.

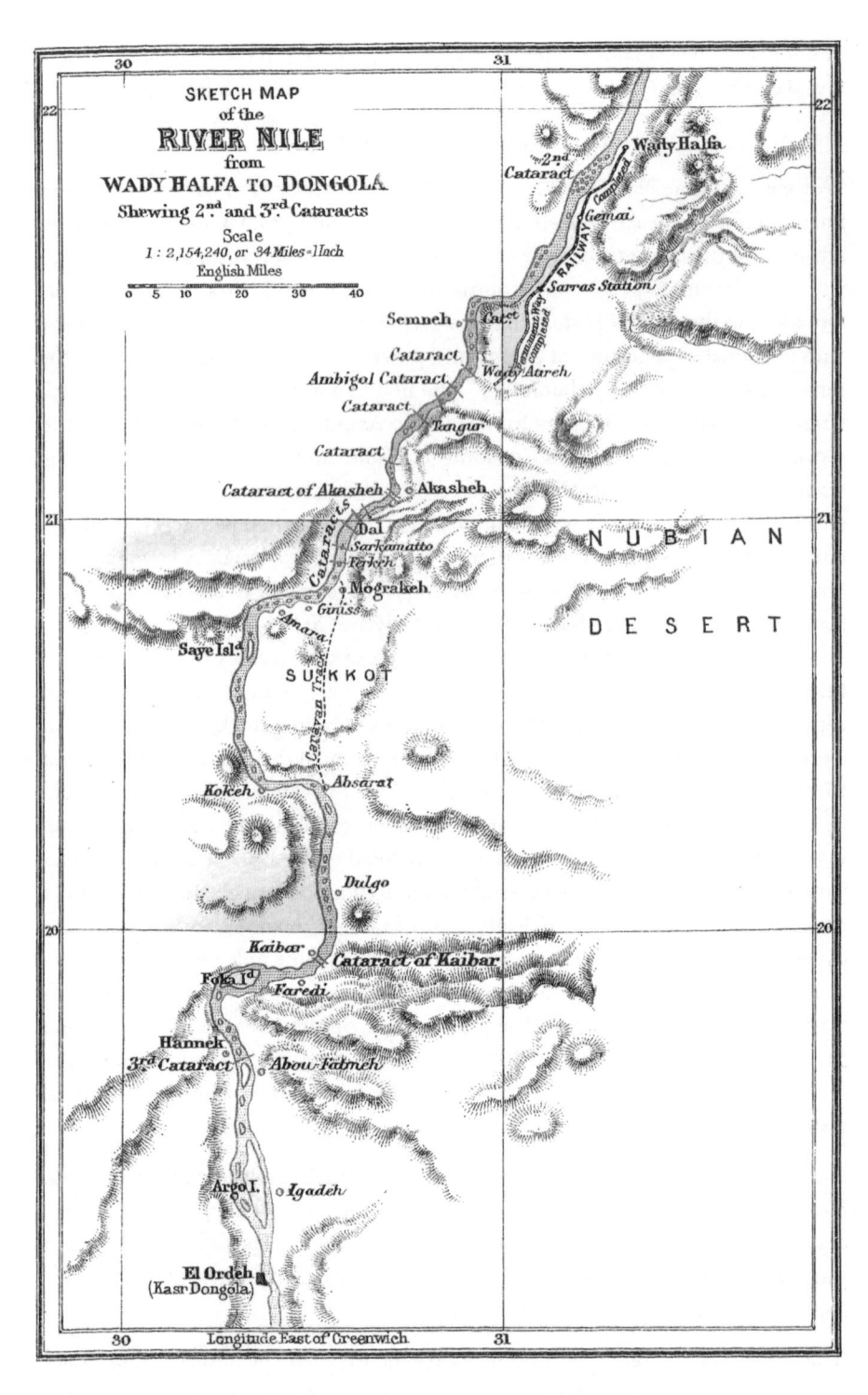

Map 4: The Nile from Wādī Halfā to Dongola

Establishing the Lines of Communication

By the middle of September, a month after Butler had placed his initial order, the first 400 whalers had been completed and loaded aboard vessels bound for Alexandria. The first to sail was the steamship *Pelican*, which left England on 10 September with thirty whalers in its hold and docked in Egypt some twelve days later. The second batch of 400 had departed England by 3 October, with the result that all 800 were in Egypt by the 18th of the month. There were nineteen consignments in all, each of which was accompanied by a special service officer whose job it was to hurry the whalers upriver to Wādī Halfā as quickly as possible. Although military orders had been given to the effect that the boats were on no account to be separated from their ancillaries, Thomas Cook & Sons, contracted to deliver the boats to Wādī Halfā, paid no heed to the injunction with the result that considerable time and effort had to be expended on marrying items up at the end of the journey. Some ancillaries, including masts, never did find the boat they had originally been made for and had to be adapted by carpenters to fit others.

From 27 September onwards an average of forty boats a day left Alexandria by rail for Assiut, with the final batch being despatched on 20 October. At Assiut they were transferred into barges, specially fitted to carry them in tiers. On arrival at Aswan the barges were moored off Elephantine Island, where the boats were unloaded into the water and, in strings of twenty, towed behind a steamer to the foot of the First Cataract. A native crew of six then rowed or poled them through the cataract to Philae, a passage of about five hours' duration. At Philae they were tied in strings of twelve to the sterns of steamers bound for Wādī Halfā. While a proportion of the boats bypassed the Second Cataract by rail, the majority were taken through the rapids by native crews operating under the direction of Captain Lord Charles Beresford RN, originally appointed to the expedition as Wolseley's naval ADC. There was also a 1¼ mile portage running in parallel, a task assigned to a 400-man contingent of the EA under Lieutenant Colonel Charles Holled Smith, ordinarily a KRRC major. With thirty men to a boat it was possible to complete the carry in about two hours: the most Smith ever got through in a day was twenty. At Gemai the boats were inspected and repaired at an ad hoc workshop, commanded by Lieutenant Colonel Coleridge Grove of the East Yorkshire Regiment.

The task facing Sir Evelyn Wood as GOC Lines of Communication was a daunting one, although he had been well into his stride for the past several weeks. While the order to push through to Khartoum had still not been given, there was no longer any doubt that it must come. If the 'fighting base' of the expedition was to be at or near Korti or Ambukol as Wolseley now conceived, then it would be more than a thousand miles from the sea. The whalers would each leave Gemai with 100 days' worth of sealed rations for the ten soldiers on board, but these were the provisions intended to supply the troops during the culminating phase of the campaign and were not to be touched in the meantime. While they were in transit the troops would have to be fed from a chain of way-stations and food depots, many of which would be located along remote stretches of river where local purchase was unlikely to yield significant quantities of livestock or other foodstuffs. The Camel Corps was certain to represent a significant additional burden, as it too would need to have 100 days' rations available for the fighting phase of the operation, but unlike the whaler-borne infantry battalions would be incapable of moving the requisite quantities forward itself. A particular difficulty was the sheer volume of *dhura* required to feed large numbers of camels in such barren countryside.

All this meant that huge tonnages of foodstuffs, fodder and other supplies would have to be pushed up the Nile through a succession of barriers to navigation. The whalers would prove themselves well capable of handling most of the river obstacles forward of Wādī Halfā, although passing them through so many chokepoints in large numbers was certain to slow the overall rate of progress. In terms of the wider logistic task facing Sir Evelyn Wood, the troop-carrying whalers would be of little use. The first of them would reach Wādī Halfā on 14 October, meaning that Wood had a six-week window up to that point in which he would have only local river craft available to him. At some point after that he could look forward to the river becoming unnavigable in places.

Through the good offices of the Mudir of Dongola, Wood wasted no time in buying up all the local river craft between Merowe and Wādī Halfā. This produced fifty *nuggars*, twin-masted sail-boats capable of carrying about eight tons of supplies apiece. The sixty-eight 'Nubian' boats purchased north of Wādī Halfā were smaller, less robust and more problematic, as the local men best qualified to handle them were reluctant to travel south of Wādī Halfā. Only fifty-four of the sixty-eight had been passed through the Second Cataract before it became unnavigable, which at a capacity of three tons apiece gave the commissaries an additional 162-ton lift, to supplement the 400 tons which could be collectively carried aboard the *nuggars*. When at last, from mid-October onwards, the whalers began arriving in numbers, Wood purloined ninety of them to help with the logistic effort on the Second and Third Cataracts. There were thirty-six government steamers on the Nile north of Wādī Halfā, two of which, the armed patrol vessels *Nasif-el-Kheir* and *Gizeh*, Wood successfully passed through the Second Cataract, albeit with some difficulty and at considerable risk. The parts to build two Yarrow stern-wheeler steamers had also been ordered from England. The *Lotus* went up the river as freight, to be assembled and launched above the Semneh Cataract, while the *Water Lily* was assembled in Alexandria and moved up to Wādī Halfā under her own steam. The two upcountry stretches of railway, the nine miles from Aswan to Philae and the thirty-three miles from Wādī Halfā to Sarras, were taken over by the Royal Engineers and by hook or by crook kept operational, although for the want of materiel Wolseley's plan to extend the line twenty miles beyond Sarras could not be effected before the bulk of the expedition had passed through to the south.[61]

Resourcing the Camel Transport

The provision of sufficient camel transport was to prove a headache for the transport staff. It was not just a question of buying animals; the complete span of the task took in the provision of native drivers, riding camels, baggage camels, riding-saddles and pack-saddles, all of which were resources which proved far less easy to come by than expected. Prior to being superseded by Wolseley, Sir Frederick Stephenson had got the enterprise off to a good start by wiring the British resident in Aden to request the services of 500 camel-drivers. Eventually 590 men would be enlisted at eighteen rupees *per diem* and found. Together with the 300 camels Stephenson had asked for, the Adeni contingent was shipped to Kosseir on Egypt's Red Sea coast, where it was met and organized by Lieutenant Edmund Bartellot of the Royal Fusiliers. A march of about 120 miles brought the Adenis to the British line of communications at Keneh and Aswan. The officers of the transport staff quickly came to view them as dutiful and willing workers.

It was normal to put one driver in charge of three baggage camels, so that 500 men was far too small a number to meet the expedition's overall requirement. It was intended that the shortfall be made up with Egyptians or Dongolāwī Sudanese, although in the event there was no great rush for the work. Those who did come forward were often not camel-drivers at all. It transpired that many of the local Esneh and Aswan men had been press-ganged into service by the respective *mudirs*, so that inevitably there was a high incidence of desertion in transit. Others proved to be bone idle and could not be trusted to do work for which the generally reliable Adenis were being paid far less. The contrast between the imported drivers and the locals was highlighted in the official report penned by Lieutenant Colonel G. A. Furse, the expedition's Director of Transport:

A smart boy from Aden was worth a dozen of the latter [Esneh and Aswan Egyptians]. Always cheerful and ready to work, with a supreme contempt for the natives of Egypt, these Aden drivers gave satisfaction to everybody, and their willingness to work was attested by every officer who had anything to do with them during the expedition.[62]

When eventually the Mudir of Dongola was asked to provide men in the south, his officials fielded a very high preponderance of old men and boys.

There were a number of patterns of camel-saddle in use in Egypt, but such was the scale of the sudden demand for them that Colonel Furse's department could only adopt for service those patterns which were easy and quick of manufacture. A contract was placed for 2,506 lightweight riding-saddles, lashed together with rawhide. There was considerable uncertainty, however, as to the date by which they could be delivered. By the time a consignment of saddles reached Aswan, where the majority of the riding camels were being assembled, it was often the case that a proportion of the lashings had tightened in the sun and been cut by the outside edges of the woodwork. Fortunately it proved easy enough to repair the damage by replacing the rawhide with telegraph binding wire. Generally the riding-saddle was found to suit its purpose well.

The same could not be said of the regulation pack-saddle, the only design the Ordnance Store Department was capable of mass-producing at speed. It was too easily broken and, worse still, was inclined as a function of the length of its rear pads and its sharp hard corners to press on the hips and loins of the animal and 'after many hours of continuous travelling generate severe galls'. Writing in July 1885, six months after Sir Herbert Stewart's operations in the Bayūda Desert, Colonel Furse recommended that no more saddles of this pattern should be manufactured.[63]

By the time the Nile Expedition had run its course some 7,990 camels had been purchased to support the enterprise, at an average price of £13 6s 11d (£13.35) apiece. Many of these animals, however, were used in portaging duties and never left Upper Egypt, so that in the event there would be too few available in Dongola when the crunch came.

Amongst the administrative details leaving England with the Camel Corps detachments were sufficient members of the Commissariat & Transport Corps to form Nos. 9 and 11 Transport Companies, and enough medics to man a 'moveable field hospital' and a 'medical bearer-company'. All four of these sub-units were intended to be camel-borne and would contain more native drivers than British soldiers.

Wolseley Departs for the Front

Having readied themselves for the field and done everything they could in Cairo, the C-in-C and his personal staff officers left the capital at 8.00 p.m. on the evening of 27 September. At the instigation of the British diplomatic representatives, the Cairene authorities had taken the precaution of secretly vesting Wolseley with authority over Gordon prior to his departure. He carried in his pocket an as yet undisclosed khedival *firman* which relieved Gordon of his duties and appointed Wolseley in his stead. This potentially controversial document would only be served on Gordon in the event of his attempting unreasonably to assert his khedival authority as Governor-General over a man who was otherwise two grades senior in the service of the Crown.[64] At this juncture the leading element in the expedition was the 1st Battalion, The Royal Sussex Regiment, under Lieutenant Colonel John Vandeleur, which thanks to Sir Frederick Stephenson's foresight had arrived at Dongola by *nuggar* a week earlier. Sir Herbert Stewart had gone on ahead of the staff, married up with the leading companies of the Mounted Infantry and assumed command at Dongola on 29 September, only two days after the C-in-C departed Cairo. Wolseley and his entourage would be four days in transit to Assiut by rail, and a further four days from Assiut to Wādī Halfā by steamer, arriving there on 5 October 1884. The journey gave Wolseley plenty of time to ponder Lord Hartington's most recent political direction:

My Lord,

Before you leave Cairo, Her Majesty's Government think it desirable that you should receive general instructions as to the course which you are to pursue in connection with the affairs of the Soudan. The primary object of the expedition up the Valley of the Nile is to bring away General Gordon and Colonel Stewart from Khartoum. When that object has been secured no further offensive operations of any kind are to be undertaken. Although you are not precluded from advancing as far as Khartoum should you consider such a step essential to secure the safe retreat of General Gordon and Colonel Stewart, you should bear in mind that Her Majesty's Government is desirous to limit the sphere of your military operations as much as possible. They rely on you, therefore, not to advance further southwards than is absolutely necessary in order to attain the primary object of the expedition. You will endeavour to place yourself in communication with General Gordon as soon as possible. In respect to all political matters, you will communicate with Her Majesty's Government and receive their instructions through the Consul General in Cairo. You are aware that the policy of Her Majesty's Government is that Egyptian rule in the Soudan should cease. It is desirable that you should receive general instructions on two points which necessarily arise in connection with the method of carrying this policy into execution. These are (1) the steps to be taken to insure the safe retreat of the Egyptian troops and the civil employés; (2) the policy to be adopted in respect of the future government of the Soudan, and especially of Khartoum. The negotiations with the tribes for endeavouring to secure the safe retreat of the garrison at Kassala may most conveniently be treated from Suakin and Massowah. You need not, therefore, take any steps in connection with this branch of the subject. The positions of the garrisons in Darfour, the Bahr-el-Gazelle and Equatorial Provinces renders it impossible that you should take any action which would facilitate their retreat without extending your operations far beyond the sphere which Her Majesty's Government is prepared to sanction. As regards the Sennaar garrison, Her Majesty's Government is not prepared to sanction the despatch of an expedition up the Nile in order to insure its retreat.

From the last telegram from General Gordon, there is reason to hope that he has already taken steps to withdraw the Egyptian portion of the Sennaar garrison.

You will use your best endeavours to ensure the safe retreat of the Egyptian troops which constitute the Khartoum garrison and of such of their civil employés, together with their families, as may wish to return to Egypt.

As regards the future government of the Soudan, and especially of Khartoum, Her Majesty's Government would be glad to see a government at Khartoum which, so far as all the matters connected with the internal administration of the country are concerned, would be wholly independent of Egypt. The Egyptian government would be prepared to pay a reasonable subsidy to any Chief, or number of chiefs, who would be sufficiently powerful to maintain order along the Valley of the Nile from Wady Halfa to Khartoum, and who would agree to the following conditions: 1. To remain at peace with Egypt and to repress any raids on Egyptian territory. 2. To encourage trade with Egypt. 3. To prevent and discourage by all possible means any expeditions for the sale of and capture of slaves. You are authorised to conclude any arrangements which fulfil these general conditions.

The main difficulty will consist in the selection of an individual, or a number of individuals, having sufficient authority to maintain order. You will, of course, bear in mind that any ruler established south of Wady Halfa will have to rely solely on his own strength in order to maintain his position. I have already mentioned that under certain conditions the Egyptian Government would be prepared to pay a moderate subsidy in order to secure tranquillity and fairly good government in the Valley of the Nile. Beyond the adoption of this measure, neither Her Majesty's Government nor the Egyptian government are prepared to assume any responsibility whatsoever for the government of the Nile Valley south of Wady Halfa.[65]

What nobody, including the Governor-General of the Sudan, yet knew was that by the time Wolseley left Cairo, Colonel Hammill Stewart was already dead.

The Loss of the *Abbas*

August had been a good month for the defenders of Khartoum. The pick of the Sudanese officers was a young man called Muḥammad ʿAlī Ḥusain who in typical fashion Gordon had raised to brigadier general at an uncommonly young age. The 'fighting pasha' led a number of successful steamer raids which served to keep the rebels off-balance for a period of some weeks. This culminated on 31 August with the defeat of Shaikh al-ʿUbeid and the recapture of Ḥalfaiya. The secret of Muḥammad ʿAlī's success was that Gordon had assigned him the pick of his troops, a force of around 1,200 black African regulars. Following the success at Ḥalfaiya, Gordon turned his thoughts to the recapture of Berber, a high-risk operation he intended entrusting to Colonel Stewart. Muḥammad ʿAlī Pasha prevailed upon Gordon to let him follow up his success against Shaikh al-ʿUbeid by raiding down the Blue Nile into the shaikh's home territory, prior to turning their attention to Berber. His proposal having been agreed, he raided the village of al-ʿĀilafūn on 4 September and dispersed a small enemy force. Unfortunately Muḥammad ʿAlī now overstretched himself, by deciding to stay out overnight and the following morning strike a village called Om Dubban, twenty miles from the river, where he had reason to believe Shaikh al-ʿUbeid had taken refuge. On the morning of the 5th the command was ambushed on the line of march by a Mahdīst force under the Faqī Medawi and all but annihilated.[66] With the death of Muḥammad ʿAlī Pasha and the loss of a thousand of his best men, Gordon was forced to come to terms with the fact that he no longer enjoyed any sort of offensive capacity. From this point on the defence of Khartoum became entirely passive in character. There could be no question of making an attempt on Berber.

Gordon was greatly disheartened by the al-ʿĀilafūn disaster and, in the absence of any news about a relief expedition, determined to evacuate the small diplomatic community, together with the miscellany of Greek, Jewish and Syrian civilians who had temporarily made their homes in Khartoum but had somewhere else to go. It was arranged that the steamer *Abbas* would depart on 10 September under Stewart's command. Whilst it would be useful to get letters and despatches through to the north, and particularly to have Stewart explain the exact situation to the authorities in Cairo, Gordon's primary object might have been sending his two British companions away to safety. Although the relationship between Gordon and Stewart had been difficult at first, in large part because the colonel was under orders to report independently to Baring, they had since arrived at an accommodation and grown much closer together. Gordon also thought highly of young Frank Power who, although he was no soldier, had nonetheless participated in a good many sorties and shown conspicuous courage. The despatch of Stewart and Power would also serve to demonstrate to London that Gordon regarded his own destiny as irrevocably linked with that of Khartoum; that there were no circumstances in which he would steal away and leave his people to their fate. The other evacuees included the French consul, Henri Herbin. The Austrian and Greek consuls, Martin Hansal and Nicola Leontides, were not career diplomats, had acquired Sudanese families and had no better life to return to, so that nobody was surprised when they announced their intention to stay.

Abbas left the city at the appointed hour, escorted by two other armed steamers. The principal risks lay in the possibility of running aground inside enemy territory and in running past Berber, where the rebels might have emplaced guns to cover the river. Once the two consorts had seen *Abbas* safely past Berber and well on the way to Abū-Hamed, they were to put about and return to Khartoum. The *Abbas* had three *nuggars* in tow, with an unknown number of Jews, Syrians and other Levantine refugees aboard, who had been left under no illusion that they were coming at their own risk and might at any point be cut adrift. On board *Abbas* were Stewart, Power, Herbin, an Egyptian called Hassan Effendi (a member of the telegraph department acting as Stewart's interpreter), 19 Greek merchants, 5 Egyptian gunners, 7 crewmen and 8 women, 4 of whom were slaves and probably did duty as ship's cooks.

Although there were minor ship-to-shore clashes north of Khartoum, the flotilla arrived safely at Berber and commenced running past the town under a heavy small-arms fire. The steamers replied with their brass guns and Remington fire. Stewart would have spent an anxious minute or two scanning the riverbank for any sign of enemy artillery coming into action, but it quickly became apparent that there were no guns present and hence nothing to prevent the steamers running the gauntlet without mishap. The following day the flotilla was pursued downriver by the steamer *El Fasher*, a vessel which with the loss of Berber had fallen into the hands of the enemy. It was afterwards ascertained by the Egyptian Intelligence Department that the Amīr 'Abd-al-Mājid Nasr al-Din abū' l-Kailak[67] and a man called 'Abd al-Mājid Khūjalī, both of whom appear to have been nephews of Muḥammad al-Khair, were in charge of the pursuit.[68] If *Abbas* was to stay in front, Stewart had to make all possible speed. As the escorts turned in midstream to give battle, he gave the order to cast the *nuggars* adrift. Quite what happened in the ensuing action and quite what befell the Levantine refugees is unclear, although all three steamers involved in the fight made it back to their respective home bases. *Abbas*, meanwhile, continued running downriver at top speed. By 18 September, a week after setting out from

Khartoum, *Abbas* was well into the Great Bend, inside Mānāsir territory and near the village of Hebbeh, when she struck a rock and foundered. Another day or two's steaming would have seen the vessel regaining territory newly restored to government control by the Mudir of Dongola's recent offensive.

Historians have not generally made the connection, but it should be borne in mind that the loss of the *Abbas* occurred only a week after the Mānāsir and others had received a drubbing near Korti, at the hands of Muṣṭafa Yāwar's spirited little army. Stewart of course was oblivious to recent developments this far north and could not have guessed that the Mānāsir were grieving their losses and smarting for revenge. Having spiked the ship's gun and thrown it overboard, he proceeded to evacuate his party to a nearby island. By mid-morning he had entered into negotiations for the purchase of camels with the village headman from Hebbeh, a blind man by the name of Fakri wad Otman. The old villain appeared cordial enough and promised to send a message to his near relative Shaikh Sulaimān wad Gamr, the chief of the Mānāsir, asking that he send camels as soon as possible. In reality the message said something quite different.

Shaikh Sulaimān arrived during the course of the afternoon at the head of a band of armed men, whom he proceeded to secrete about the village in the vicinity of Fakri wad Otman's house. Hassan Effendi went ashore first, with an escort of four men. His companions were either seized or immediately murdered in the village, after which he was sent back to the river, presumably under pain of death, to lure the Europeans across to the west bank and into the headman's house. Unfortunately he played his part to perfection, so that Stewart, Power and Herbin walked straight into the trap. They were sat talking to Shaikh Sulaimān over coffee, when he suddenly leapt to his feet, threw open the door and called on his gang of assassins to strike. It is said that Stewart thought that the *shaikh* had been alarmed by the revolver in his waistband and tamely handed the weapon over, before finally it dawned on him that there was treachery afoot. After a brief tussle, the trio of white men were cruelly done to death. Other rebels hastened towards the river to attack the Greeks and the crew, most of whom threw themselves into the water and struck out for the east bank under a heavy fire. Of something around forty people, only thirteen survived being shot or drowned. Thus ended the ill-fated voyage of the *Abbas*.

Wolseley Arrives at Wādī Halfā

The news of Stewart's death was awaiting Wolseley when, on 5 October, he steamed into Wādī Halfā aboard the khedival steam-cutter *Ferooz*. 'Poor Stewart,' he wrote in his journal that evening, 'His loss just at this moment is a national one. A fine chivalrous fellow to die at the hands of a murderer. May that murderer fall into my hands.'[69] Wolseley had been reunited with Sir Evelyn Wood during the course of the day and reserved the greater part of his journal entry for a long and vitriolic attack on his vanity and ambition. He found Wood's propensity to flatter him particularly annoying. Although there were four generals at Wādī Halfā – Wolseley,

Earle, Buller and Wood – they did not even now, in the first week of October, have a brigade of troops or a whaler between them.

Wolseley was anxious that Muṣṭafa Yāwar Pasha should move his troops up from Dongola to Merowe as soon as possible. He was advised by Stewart and Wilson that the *mudir* considered it too dangerous and was likely to resort to delaying tactics. A protracted exchange of telegrams ensued over the course of a week, at the end of which the *mudir* was still safely ensconced at the provincial seat of government.[70] On 11 October the headquarters issued telegraphic orders detailing the composition of the fighting force to be concentrated on Shendy:[71]

Royal Engineers	50
19th Hussars (3 squadrons)	360
Mounted Infantry	400
Camel Corps	1,050
Royal Marine Light Infantry	100
1st Bn., Royal Irish Regiment	550
1st Bn., Royal Sussex Regiment	550
1st Bn., Black Watch	550
1st Bn., Berkshire Regiment	550
1st Bn., Royal West Kent Regiment	550
2nd Bn., Essex Regiment	550
1st Bn., Gordon Highlanders	550
British Camel Battery (6 screw guns)	50
Egyptian Camel Battery (6 screw guns)	50
	5,910

In addition to these units, 1st South Staffords would be left at Dongola and 2nd Duke of Cornwall's Light Infantry (DCLI) at Berber. A week later, on the 19th, Wolseley took the decision to concentrate Sir Herbert Stewart's mounted troops at Debbeh (337 miles from Wādī Halfā), against the eventuality of a camel-borne dash across the Bayūda becoming necessary. It was planned that Stewart would have about 2,250 men at his disposal, made up of the 19th Hussars, four camel regiments, the two camel-borne batteries, Nos. 9 and 11 Transport Companies, the camel bearer-company and a 100-bed moveable field hospital.[72] In addition to 2,250 riding camels, something around 2,000 baggage camels would also be required. On 26 October a general order was issued which formally assigned names to the camel regiments: they were to be called the Heavy Camel Regiment (HCR), the Light Camel Regiment (LCR), the Guards Camel Regiment (GCR) and the Mounted Infantry Camel Regiment (MICR). It was not for another two days that the first of the Camel Corps detachments from England arrived at Aswan and took over their camels.[73]

By 28 October Wolseley had grown bored with trying to decipher what was going on at the front so, leaving Buller in charge at Wādī Halfā, he departed for Dongola. With the exception of MICR and 1st Royal Sussex, the rest of the force was still strung out behind him. At Wādī Halfā were 1st South Staffords, two companies of 2nd Essex and the newly arrived *voyageurs*. The 19th Hussars, the camel-borne batteries and the transport and medical companies were echeloned in marching detachments along the east bank of the Nile from Aswan to Dongola. Another two companies of 2nd Essex were in transit on the river between Aswan and Wādī Halfā. There were 2½ battalions (1st Black Watch, 2nd DCLI and the other half-battalion of 2nd Essex) camped at Aswan, while still waiting to be called forward from Cairo were 1st Gordons, 1st Royal Irish, 1st Berkshires and 1st Royal West Kents. Three of the Camel Corps regiments were still in transit between Cairo and Aswan.[74]

If Wolseley had long since been compelled to abandon any idea of relieving Khartoum by mid-November, his correspondence with his wife serves to identify the revised target date he set himself, once he was in Egypt and his preparations were in full swing. Writing from Cairo on 13 September, which happened to be the second anniversary of Tel-el-Kebir, he had linked his last great triumph with what he eagerly imagined would be his next:

This day two years ago, thank God, ended brilliantly. I can remember my feeling of growing anxiety all through the hours from 1.00 a.m. until I stood on the bridge at Tel-el-Kebir, with a defeated army flying from us in all directions. If I am equally blessed, I ought to shake hands with Gordon near Khartoum, about 31st January next. Remember that Khartoum by the Nile is over 1700 miles from Cairo.[75]

Two days after Wolseley left Wādī Halfā the calendar turned over to November, at which point eighty-five days had elapsed since the Vote of Credit had been approved by the House of Commons. Remarkably around 85 per cent of the force had not yet commenced the 666 miles of Wolseley's Option 3. It will be recalled that his April options paper had said nothing about eighty-five days being required to get less than a fifth of the force to the start point. Four of nine infantry battalions had not yet left Cairo, seventy-five per cent of the infantry were no further south than Aswan and three-quarters of the Camel Corps had not so much as stroked a camel. It was some consolation that according to Wolseley's revised timetable there were still ninety-two days to go. According to his appreciation of April, however, the food would run out in Khartoum seventy-seven days too soon for his revised timetable to be considered tenable. Sir Frederick Stephenson could be forgiven for reflecting that the interval between the two Battles of El Teb was a paltry twenty-five days, proof positive of how quickly a force of three brigades could have been concentrated at Suakin, and that marching from Suakin to Berber took a fortnight at the most. If Gordon could somehow eke out his rations to allow Wolseley's ninety-two days to run their course the city might yet be saved, but the margin was tight and only timely, thoroughly sound decisions would serve to pull it off. One false step and it was over.

Chapter 4

Delays and Decisions

Prosecuting the Campaign: November–December 1884

The only useful work done by this force was the punishment of the Monnasir tribe for their treacherous murder of Colonel Stewart and his companions, and probably also in diverting to some extent the attention of the enemy in the region through which it passed . . . In fact this was all the crack regiments composing it contributed towards the great end of the expedition. So far as any direct effort to rescue Gordon was concerned, two thirds of the Nile Column might safely have been left behind.

Alex Macdonald, Too Late for Gordon and Khartoum,
on the role of the River Column

WHILE THE BAYŪDA FULFILS all the necessary criteria to be categorized by geographers as a desert, it is a label which can readily lead the uninitiated astray, for the landscape inside the Great Bend in the Nile is not much akin either to the Sahara in the west or the Nubian desert to the north. The Bayūda can certainly be fairly described as a wilderness area, but is by no means a 'howling wilderness'. There are trees, even groves of trees, but no forests; there are bushes and thickets, but no great expanses of scrubland; one might encounter small groups of antelope, but there are no large herds of game. There are extended periods when the Bayūda is insufferably hot and gives every appearance of being bone dry, but where there is life there is subterranean water and where there is water desert nomads will usually have sunk wells. Outsiders are unlikely to stumble across such places by chance, for in the desert it pays to know the way, but locals will know exactly where they are and how to reach them from any given point. The Bayūda is veneered by sand but boasts no great sea of dunes, as the greater part of its surface is formed by hard-packed dark grey shale. In places the surface is so dark in colour that from a distance the desert might be taken for a played-out coalfield, while in others the golden glow of late afternoon can appear to turn the rocks and boulders a neutral shade of purple. The surface is intersected by sandy *khors* which spend most of the year dry, but periodically bear rainwater through the wilderness allowing areas of grass, if not to flourish, at least temporarily to adorn in verdant green an otherwise puritanical landscape. The breeze in the Bayūda can readily transform itself into a wind and has the power to switch between icy cold and stifling hot according to time of day and season. From time

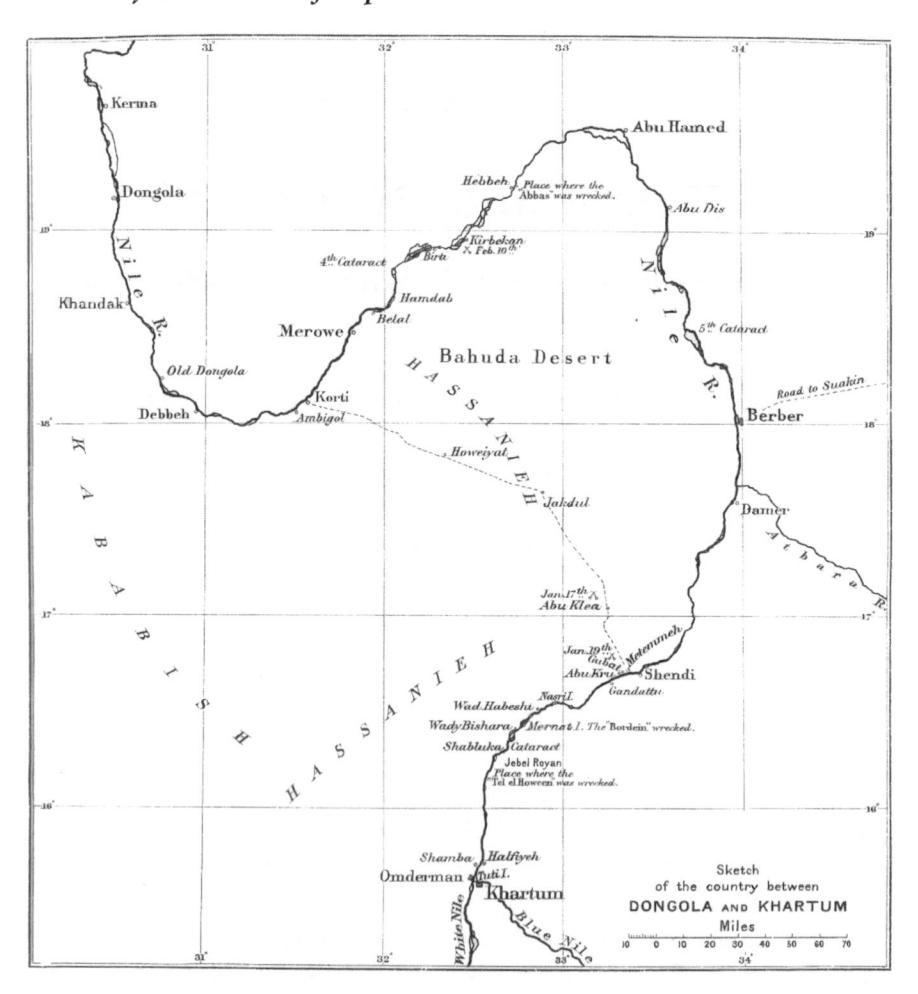

Map 5: The axis of advance across the Bayūda Desert

immemorial the Nile has been both lifeblood and artery to the wing of humankind known to the modern world as the Sudanese. Cultures rose, flourished and fell along the banks of the great river, but the laws of geostrategy and of commerce dictated that the region's predominant civilization would always be based around the Nile Delta, the maritime gateway between a flourishing Mediterranean world and an inhospitable African interior. Thus the draw was always to the north and the Nile the means of getting there. But the fabled river is characterized by a seemingly perverse 400-mile deviation in its journey to the sea, the so-called Great Bend, inside which lies the Bayūda Desert (*see Map 5*). It was the Bayūda's 400-mile outer boundary which before the coming of the aeroplane conveyed great importance upon its centre-line, for here was to be found an overland short-cut between north and south. The Bayūda is spanned by a range of hills running diagonally from the north-west to the south-east. These hills feed rainwater into the handful of rocky hollows in the centre of the desert, which function all year round as natural reservoirs. Desert-dwelling nomads had only to sink their wells in the intervals to forge a 174-mile caravan route from one side of the Great Bend to the other. River settlements sprang up at either end of the line and by the nineteenth century had flourished to become the mud-baked towns of Ambukol and Korti, in the northwest, and Metemmeh and Shendy, to the south-east.

When the Khartoum crisis blew up it was inevitable that the Bayūda crossing would attract the attention of the British military. It was impossible for Wolseley to contemplate the plans for a great Nile Expedition over his maps, without his gaze falling upon the Korti to Metemmeh caravan road. Of course Butler's whalers would get up the Nile in good time, carrying the infantry battalions and the huge tonnages of commissariat stores the expedition would require if it was to reach Khartoum in time, just as in 1870 they had made it to Fort Garry expeditiously. Of course they would. But in the unlikely event they did not, there was always the Bayūda. It might have been the word 'desert' that did it, or perhaps the word 'caravan', or possibly both words in compelling combination, but whenever Wolseley looked at his map and contemplated the caravan road across the Bayūda, his mind conjured up an image of men on camels. Thus was the second of the 'novel expedients' called into being.

The Campaign's Key Decision Point

As the autumn wore on it became increasingly apparent that things were moving too slowly on the Nile if the late January deadline was to be adhered to. The desert crossing to Metemmeh represented the only possible means by which progress could be accelerated. Although Wolseley had always had the contingency in mind, Buller's private correspondence would suggest that the C-in-C was slow to arrive at a committed decision to throw part of his force across the short-cut. It may have been the bitterness of the opposition to the whaler scheme and the amount of reputational capital that Wolseley had invested in winning the 'Battle of the Routes' which precluded his committing to a desert march at the correct decision-point. On the other hand it is inherently improbable that an officer of Wolseley's experience could ever lose track of time and space. Buller was the first of the Ring's 'big-hitters' to break ranks and urge that the whaler-borne phase of operations be terminated short of the Great Bend. In a letter home, written from Wādī Halfā on 8 November, he refers to an important item of military correspondence he had penned the previous day:

I still do not think it is possible for us to be concentrated at Debbeh or Ambukol, which latter Wolseley now rather seems to favour, before Christmas. I wrote Wolseley yesterday proposing the following plan. Concentrate at Ambukol, and later perhaps at Abu Dom. From those two places roads lead to Shendi. Move one regiment on camels to Abu Halfa [in fact nearby Jakdul Wells was the superior source of water and would be substituted for Abu Halfā], which is the junction of the two roads, and about half way to Shendi; make a fort there and fill it with provisions. Then, based on that fort, move across to Shendi and thence up the Nile to Khartoum. I think we should do an advance quicker that way than all the way round by Abu-Hamed and Berber. The objection is that we should have to reduce our fighting force to 3,000 men at the outside, and it is a question whether that is enough. I think that it should be. I have not an idea what Wolseley means to do, but I think that he must do something of that sort.[1]

Wolseley left Wādī Halfā for Dongola some nine days before Buller wrote to him commending this change of plan. He reached his destination on 3 November, at which point there were still only two fighting units that far forward: Colonel Vandeleur's 1st Royal Sussex, which as we have seen had come upriver from Sarras by *nuggar*; and the larger part of the Mounted Infantry Camel Regiment (MICR), which had come up on camels. Having lost its commanding officer to sunstroke en route, MICR was now under the command of its senior major, Major the Hon. George Gough, 14th Hussars. It was not until 9.15 a.m. on 6 November that the 1st Battalion, The South Staffordshire Regiment, under Lieutenant Colonel Phillip Eyre, became the first of the infantry battalions to embark aboard whalers at Gemai and depart for the front.[2]

Wolseley's first political priority now that he was well inside the Sudan was to secure the wholehearted cooperation of the Mudir of Dongola. Sir Herbert Stewart and Sir Charles Wilson, the first senior officers to arrive at Dongola, had found the *mudir* arrogant, offhand and obstructive. Stewart had been at Dongola for two days before the *mudir* even agreed to see him. Wilson had formed the view that his reticence was rooted in a deep-seated hatred of Gordon, who had once dismissed him from office. Forewarned of the difficulty, Wolseley had decided to make early recourse to flattery. Having borrowed the KCMG from Buller's dress uniform, he proceeded to invest Yāwar Pasha as an honorary knight of the realm. 'Sir Muṣṭafa' seemed much more ready to deal meaningfully with the conqueror of Egypt than with mere colonels and for a while Wolseley allowed himself to believe that the expedition would now be able to count on the unstinting support of the civil power. With the political sphere seemingly back on track, there was not much else to do but wait for the troops to come up. Wolseley passed his time riding, keeping up his prolific correspondence with Lady Louisa (which in addition to his private letters included the page-by-page despatch of his campaign journal), reading occasional telegraphic progress reports and poring over maps in the company of his personal staff officers. From time to time he visited the Mounted Infantry and the Royal Sussex as they were being put through their paces on the training ground and soon pronounced himself well-pleased with both units.

Reviewing the Situation: Wādī Halfā 17 November

Buller's letter of 7 November took four days to make its way to Dongola. Although Wolseley did not immediately buy into the idea of terminating the whaler-borne advance at Ambukol or Korti, he was so displeased by unsatisfactory progress reports that he decided to return to Wādī Halfā to investigate the causes of delay. 'Something is wrong,' he confided to his journal, 'and I must examine into it myself. This is a horrid bore.' Accompanied only by Major Frederick Wardrop, his Egyptian ADC Colonel Zohrab Bey, and a native servant, Wolseley left Dongola aboard his steam launch at 7.25 a.m. on Thursday 13 November. Four hours later the party transferred to camels to begin a hard-riding, rough-living desert adventure of four days' duration.

The general and his travelling companions regained civilization at Sarras at 9.00 p.m. on the evening of 16 November and quickly transferred to a train for the final leg of the journey.[3] A halt at Gemai to take on water presented Wolseley with an ideal opportunity to consult with Colonel Butler. Why were the troops not moving south of the Second Cataract in greater numbers? Why were the companies that had embarked moving so slowly? Butler reported that he had despatched more than 200 boats already, but was able to point to more than 200 others waiting idly not sixty yards from where he and the general were talking.[4] The problem with critical mass evidently did not lie this side of the Second Cataract, where there were no more troops to embark, but somewhere to the north. The reasons for this Wolseley would have to establish with the chief of staff when he reached Wādī Halfā.

Butler was quick to attribute the unexpectedly slow progress of the embarked troops to the extra weight imposed on the boats by the QMG's branch of the staff. As we have seen his original conception had called for the whalers to carry 100 days' worth of rations for the embarked troops only, but it now turned out that no alternative provision had been made for the stores needed to sustain the camel-mounted troops. The commissaries' only plan was that the additional burden would have to be evenly distributed across Butler's flotilla. As a result individual boats were now carrying anything up to 126 days' worth of rations; in other words the boat crews were pulling 26 per cent more weight than had ever been intended. To make matters worse the number of embarked personnel per boat had been reduced from twelve to ten. This had come about as a result of a decision not to place two *voyageurs* permanently aboard each of the boats as originally intended, but to keep them concentrated in groups at the cataracts, in order that each such party could master the vagaries of a particular stretch of river. Thus the whalers were not only sitting much lower in the water due to the additional cargo, but were also much harder work for a reduced complement of men. Butler felt sure that if they could agree to lighten the load by even a thousand pounds that instances of grounding would be minimized and the embarked companies would start flying upriver.[5] Butler being Butler he cannot have failed to make clear his strongly held perception that there was a great deal of obstructionism and apathy in play on the lines of communication.[6] Wolseley heard the colonel out, noted his concerns and as soon as his train was ready departed for Wādī Halfā.

Wolseley spent Monday 17 November in conference with Buller and Brackenbury. The progress reports from the staff indicated that to date some 212 whalers had left Gemai with embarked troops and stores, and that another 222 were waiting for units to come up and take them over. Of these fifty-two were undergoing repairs for minor damage incurred in transit.[7] The most significant item on the agenda, however, was an impromptu one, for a long letter from General Gordon had arrived at Dongola three days earlier, having spent only ten days in transit from Khartoum. Lieutenant Colonel Leopold Swaine, Wolseley's military secretary, lost no time in telegraphing a synopsis of the letter's contents to Wādī Halfā and Cairo. Sir Evelyn Baring read the telegram on the morning of the 15th and immediately had it forwarded to Lord Granville at the Foreign Office. It was rushed across Whitehall the same day, with the result that the Secretary of State for War got to read it at least twenty-four hours ahead of the army commander in the field, a sign of changing times for the military.[8]

Gordon's letter was dated 4 November and began by referring to the fact that messages from Wolseley, dated 20 September, and Kitchener, dated 14 October, had found their way through to him only the previous day. Irritated to learn that Gordon had been unable to read his letter, as he had for some unaccountable reason sent his Foreign Office cipher books downriver aboard the *Abbas*, Wolseley seethed into his journal, 'That any man could have been so idiotic is to me a puzzle.' Gordon had not long since learned of the loss of the *Abbas* and went on to reflect on the sad demise of Stewart and Power. On the reverse of his letter he provided a list of the nineteen Greeks who could also be presumed lost. There was also a sketch map showing in very general terms how the enemy were disposed around the city.[9]

By far the most critical piece of news conveyed by the letter was Gordon's estimate of just how long he would be able to sustain the defence of the city. 'We can hold out 40 days with ease, after that it will be difficult,' ran the operative sentence. This should have made it abundantly clear that Wolseley's 31 January timeline could no longer be regarded as tenable. Gordon's remarks should by extension have dictated that all the C-in-C's thinking now be focussed on reaching Khartoum as close to mid-December as possible. It should in turn have been apparent that this would demand precisely the sort of dash across the Bayūda which Buller had recommended in his letter of 7 November.

Other important news was that the Mahdī had come up from Rahad, that he was now directing the siege in person, and that the main enemy strength lay to the west and south. The north, the direction from which the British would make their approach, appeared not to be strongly held. Gordon also went on to offer simple, unequivocal advice on which route Wolseley should follow: 'I should take the road from Ambukkol to Metemmeh, where my steamers await you.'[10]

That the news from Khartoum was of great operational import was so blatantly apparent that Hartington immediately sent Wolseley a one-sentence telegram enquiring, 'Should like to know how information in Gordon's letter affects your plans, also what announcement safe or desirable to make.'[11] The Secretary of State would not get a reply until the 22nd of the month, almost a week later, which was the day after Wolseley got back to Dongola. 'Yours of the 15th,' ran his response.

'News from Gordon makes no change in my plans, but it seems to indicate the almost impossibility of his relief without fighting.'[12]

Hartington's telegram had been sent two days before Wolseley's eight-hour meeting at Wādī Halfā with Buller and Brackenbury. It is inconceivable in the circumstances that the chief of staff's Bayūda proposal did not come under consideration. It is no less clear, as evinced in Wolseley's reply to Hartington, that the proposition was firmly rebutted in favour of proceeding via the Great Bend. As far as the C-in-C was concerned the logistic advantages of the river route still outweighed any countervailing considerations of time and space.

The most important decision to emerge from the conference had two strands. The first of these was that Korti would now become the expedition's 'fighting base', or forward concentration area. The second was that the staff would continue feeding whalers upriver until all 600 boats destined for service south of Wādī Halfā had dropped off their embarked troops at Korti. Coupled with 2,500 cavalry and camel-mounted troops, this would provide a fighting echelon of around 8,500 men.

At the time this decision, or rather non-decision, was taken, there were only 1,355 men at Dongola. Working back along the lines of communication from south to north, there were 970 men in transit between Dal and Dongola: 1,955 somewhere between Gemai and Dal; 1,895 at Wādī Halfā, Sarras or Gemai; 1,379 making their way from Aswan to Wādī Halfā; 1,840 at Aswan; 500 traveling between Assiut and Aswan; and a last seventy-five who had not even departed Assiut.[13] This represented an all-up total of 9,969 men.

Instead of moving on to forge a new and bold plan fit to meet a new and urgent timeline, the rest of the meeting was dedicated to discussing the causes of delay up to that point. It transpired that the principal difficulty had been inadequate stockpiles of coal at various key stations above the Second Cataract. Wolseley reflected on the reasons for the mistake and its operational implications.

The coal question had never been looked into by Buller who assumed that Dormer had made all the necessary arrangements before he, Buller, had arrived in the country. Dormer it seems had made very few arrangements & those few were not very good. However Buller is of course to blame for not having made certain that all was right on this most vital point. All was wrong hence the delay. I blame myself too, for although I trust Buller fully, I should not have relied upon my trust in him on such a vital question, & ought personally to have gone into it. I know from my own personal experience when I was a staff officer, how inconvenient and difficult it was to serve a general who wished to command, & to be his own staff officer at the same time. At the beginning I told Buller I looked to him for all details which I unreservedly left in his hands & that I had no intention of keeping a dog and barking for myself. The result has been in this one respect unfortunate. However the difficulty is now over, but instead of having the Army concentrated at Debbeh–Ambukol about the middle of December, it cannot possibly be so until the 7th or 10th January.[14]

The 17 November meeting at Wādī Halfā represented a perfect opportunity to revise a faltering plan and yet Wolseley seems to have failed to grasp either the compelling nature of the problem before him, or the fact that it allowed of only one solution: moving fewer, less well-provisioned soldiers over a faster route. It is inconceivable that he left Wādī Halfā believing that there was still time aplenty to journey to Khartoum via the Great Bend, as the most rudimentary calculations must have shown that he needed to be in Khartoum in four weeks' time, or if Gordon's luck held, six weeks at the outside. If this was not achievable, and it was not, as only two-fifths of the force had yet gained Wādī Halfā or points beyond,[15] then he had to strain the expedition's every sinew to get a viable fighting force to the city as soon as possible thereafter. Everything cried out that this was a vital decision point and yet the army commander set out for Dongola that evening without having made one.

A number of routine but nonetheless important directives would be promulgated in the aftermath of the Wādī Halfā meeting. For reasons of internal command and control, Colonel Eyre had not unreasonably been attempting to operate the South Staffords by 'wings' or half-battalions. This was judged to be one of the factors contributing to slow progress. The new guidance issued by Sir Evelyn Wood as GOC Lines of Communication was that a group of four boats, the tactical equivalent of a half-company, was to be regarded as the optimal working unit. A mandatory daily routine for embarked troops was also stipulated. Reveille was to be one hour before daylight: the troops were to take coffee before starting upriver with the dawn; the only breaks before sunset were to be a forty-five-minute halt between 8.00 and 9.00 for breakfast and a one-hour halt in the early afternoon. The hundred days' rations on board the boats were on no account to be broken open this side of Korti. Instead embarked troops would be issued with fifteen days' worth of consumable rations at Sarras, twenty days' worth at Sarkamatto and five days' worth at Abu Fatmeh.[16] Other directives sought to ensure that Camel Corps units paid all due care and attention to the condition of their animals. The rate of advance was to be regulated at not more than 120 miles a week, while the officers were left in no doubt that they would be held to account for any avoidable losses:

The efficiency of a mounted force in the field is estimated by its powers of locomotion.

The General Commanding in Chief, Egypt, impresses most strongly upon all officers, non-commissioned officers and men, that as the camel requires as much assiduous care and constant attention as does the horse, the most energetic and unremitting efforts are necessary for maintaining the condition of these animals.

Officers are held personally responsible for all casualties which may occur from preventable causes. In their marching-in states commanding officers will give the number of animals unfit and the cause.[17]

Wolseley Returns to Dongola

On the second day of a no less punishing return journey to Dongola, Wolseley and his aides ran into a detachment of the Guards Camel Regiment under Lieutenant Colonel Charles Rowley, Grenadier Guards, who unhappily failed to get his campaign off to a very good start. Once again Wolseley's journal was pressed into service for the purpose of eternal damnation.

Passed en route in the desert the first lot of the Guards Camel Corps, about 120 men under a fellow called Rowley, who struck me as being of little use – I believe he plays cricket well. Glad to know he does something well for soldiering does not seem to be his forte.[18]

Just as the general thought he was trotting nonchalantly into the desert to resume his journey, his camel, with the characteristic bloody-mindedness of its kind, decided it still had other business to transact with the Guards and came to an abrupt halt. Wolseley went flying, landing hard on his right hip, grateful if nothing else not to have been thrown on the other side of his body where his sword hilt might have done untold mischief. Nothing appeared to be broken, although it had been a nasty fall for a man past his physical prime. Wounded pride drove the general to remount quickly. He was back in the saddle before any of the men rushing to his assistance could reach the scene. Amongst the group of erstwhile rescuers was Melton Prior, the well-known artist–correspondent of the *Illustrated London News*. Wolseley was quick to fix the newspaperman with an icy glare. Prior took the hint immediately and said, 'I did not see you fall, sir.' 'Thank you, Prior,' came the reply.[19] With that Wolseley hastened on his way as if nothing had happened, but by the time the party pitched camp that evening he was so badly bruised as to be barely able to walk. The following day's ride proved extremely painful, though in typical fashion the old man gritted his teeth and pushed the pace as hard as ever.[20] As Prior later recollected, 'It was generally acknowledged out there that the vitality of Lord Wolseley was something beyond the ordinary run of mortals.'[21]

Wolseley and his aides reached Dongola on Friday 21 November, to find that General Earle had come up in their absence and that ten members of the Royal Sussex had been hospitalized with smallpox. Wisely Earle had directed Colonel Vandeleur to move his camp some distance apart from the other units and had put the battalion into quarantine. The *mudir* had again been giving Sir Charles Wilson and the intelligence department trouble, by sending a number of 'impudent' messages upriver to Major Kitchener. Colonel Zohrab Bey was despatched to tell the *mudir* that Wolseley would not tolerate any more of his antics and returned bearing an abject apology. Two days later Zohrab Bey was again sent to see the *mudir*, this time to sound him out on the idea of his taking over from Gordon as the first sultan of a newly independent Sudan. Wolseley's first choice in this somewhat improbable role was Ḥusain Pasha Khalīfa, but there were a number of intelligence indications, based on the questioning of merchants and other travellers from the south, that he was still being held as a prisoner in the Mahdī's camp. Zohrab returned to report that Yāwar Pasha appeared much taken with Wolseley's proposition, but had failed to give any real indication whether or not he would be able to hold his own in the long term without the assistance of British troops.[22] Sir Herbert Stewart, meanwhile, had been ordered to move MICR a few miles upriver to Khandak, to escape the smallpox outbreak. Infantry companies coming upriver were ordered to proceed straight through to Stewart's new camp, without landing anywhere near the pestilent Royal Sussex.

If Wolseley appeared to Buller to have very firmly rebutted the idea of on overland advance, there is a clear-cut indication in his journal from around a week later, either that he changed his mind fairly quickly, or that Buller had got the wrong end of the stick. The entry in question ran, 'I have telegraphed home about forming a small Naval Brigade... I shall send two gardiners [sic – Gardners] with them and may possibly send them on camels across desert to Shendy from Ambukol to man the guns in Gordon's steamers there.'[23] It would appear that Wolseley's insistence that they persevere with the river route had the effect of convincing his chief of staff that he intended going only by the river, whereas what he actually meant was that he did not intend only to go overland, which is not at all the same thing. If there was confusion on this point then the blame must rest with Wolseley, as an army commander is duty bound to make his intent quite plain to his staff. If he was disingenuously concealing some part of his intent, a point we shall come to shortly, then he can only be regarded as doubly culpable.

Within a few days of Wolseley's return to Dongola, the staff had been able to fit a timetable around the army's forward concentration at Korti. It was based on the transit times of 1st South Staffords, the leading whaler-borne unit, and allowed ten days for a battalion to get from Aswan to Gemai and embark all its companies; eighteen days to get from Gemai to the upper end of the Dal or Second Cataract; twelve days to transit the 152 miles of relatively clear water between Dal and Dongola; and seven days to cover the remaining 132 miles between Dongola and Korti. This aggregated total of forty-seven days in transit between Aswan and Korti enabled the staff to project that 1st South Staffords would arrive at Korti on 15 December; 2nd Essex on 30 December; 2nd DCLI on 31 December; 1st Black Watch on 5 January; 1st Gordons on 9 January; 1st Royal Irish on 14 January; 1st Royal West Kents on 18 January; and 1st Camerons on 22 January.[24] Because the camel-mounted regiments were all capable of making faster progress than the boats, 22 January could be fixed as the date by which the concentration of the army's fighting echelon would be complete. The staff projections proved broadly accurate (although 1st Camerons would be held at Korosko), but did not bode particularly well for General Gordon, whose most recent communication had suggested that the game would be up around a month earlier.

The Butler Rebuke

By now the pressure of slow progress was beginning to tell. There were a number of military reputations riding aboard the whalers, none more so than that of C-in-C Egypt himself. The next greatest vested interest was that of Colonel Butler, who was not only the prime advocate and architect of the whaler scheme, but now found himself responsible for driving it forward. On Saturday 29 November Wolseley was notified that Butler had moved upriver to Abu Fatmeh at the head of the Third Cataract and was waiting to 'speak' to him over the telegraph. Long bothered by the overloading of the boats and the apparent indolence of many of the personnel working the lines of communication, Butler finally ran out of patience at Dal on 21 November and fired off a telegram to Wādī Halfā insisting that certain steps be taken to reform the management of the lines of communication. The message was probably addressed to Buller as the chief of staff and, taking Butler's fiery temperament as read, was almost certainly intemperate in tone. Butler then decided to push on to Abu Fatmeh, about forty miles short of Dongola, where there was a telegraph office, in the belief that if only he could spend an hour 'talking' over the wires with the army commander he would be able to persuade him to revert to the original loading plan for the boats.

The telegraph office at Dongola was almost four miles from the headquarters camp, though for the time being the distance had been temporarily bridged by heliographic relay, pending the arrival of the Royal Engineers with more telegraph wire. Keen to be able to interact with Butler 'live', much after the fashion of a telephone conversation, the general called for his camel and set off for the telegraph office. He was only about half-way there when he met one of his ADCs, Lieutenant John Adye RA, coming the other way. It transpired that Butler had been waiting since the previous evening and, having obtained no reply to his initial message, had since telegraphed to say that he had set off in his whaler to talk with the general face-to-face. Wolseley had no greater anxiety than the seemingly slow progress of the embarked infantry battalions and was counting on Butler to keep things moving. That he should have raced ahead of everybody else and even now be widening the gap still further drove Wolseley to anger. He penned a stiff note instructing Butler to adhere to his orders and return at once to Dal. The message was taken downriver by the *Ferooz*.

Butler could not have been more wounded by the suggestion that he had disobeyed orders, or more insulted by the general's refusal to see him. Before he turned his crew back downriver, he wrote a hot and hasty eight-page letter which he entrusted to the captain of the *Ferooz*. By the time he pulled his boat into the riverbank that evening he was overwrought and had quite forgotten the disparity in rank between full colonels and full generals. Butler's second emotional outpouring did him even fewer favours than his first. Always keen to be in the right, he felt moved to cite it at length in his autobiography of 1911:

You have known me long enough to know that disregard of orders, much less disregard of your orders, is not my line of conduct, but I would have thought that there was enough in the past to show you that when you set me a task it was best to let me work it in my own way. Had you tied me down six years ago [*sic* – 14 years] on the Red River you would not have known at Fort Francis that the Winnipeg River was only a week's work for the expedition, and the men would have been committed to the swamps of the north-west angle of the Lake of the Woods as all the experts and others, save myself, counselled and advised. Again, if you had not given me own head in Ashanti eleven years ago, you would have had ten thousand more fighting men arrayed against you at a very critical moment in the battle of Amoaful; and coming down to our work of yesterday and today, was it not through your letting me work this boat idea on my own lines that you have at the present moment six hundred boats ready above the Second Cataract, that I have one above the Third Cataract, and that there might have been fifty above it today had the old order of time and despatch of troops been adhered to? And that all this had been done within the limit of time, please remember, which the highest naval authorities in England had declared would be required only for building the boats in England. I go back over the past and speak of the present work now only because your words and actions today have forced these recollections upon me. It had never entered my head for a moment to remain more than a few hours in Dongola. I should have gone down the river again in a very different position and armed with a very different authority from that which I shall now do; not that I shall not use every effort, sparing myself in no way to effect the more rapid movement upriver; but my words will not be heard for the noise of the slap in the face I have been given today, the sound of which will be grateful to many to whom I am distasteful because I have been identified with this expedition by ceaselessly furthering its interests. I freely admit that the orthodox English staff officer would have stopped at Hafir today, tomorrow and the day after, eyeglass in eye and cigarette in mouth; but on the other hand, he would have taken sixteen to eighteen days to ascend the river from Sarras to Hafir, and when acting on your orders to go back on the seventeenth or nineteenth day to try and galvanise the slow moving mass of boats into quicker work, his words would have had about as much effect upon Tommy Atkins as his cigarette smoke would have had in dulling the Egyptian sky. Unfortunately perhaps for me, these were not my methods of work; and I fear they never will be. I realised from the first that we were dealing with a lot of unwilling horses at these Nile fences, and that the only chance of getting them quickly over the water-jumps was to give them a lead over.[25]

When Wolseley wrote up his journal that night, he had not yet received either of Butler's written messages. After reflecting briefly on the difficulty with his emotional Irish subordinate, he went on to pen an unduly optimistic passage which ran, 'I am now very hopeful of being able to do a great deal by negotiation & possibly ending the business without any fighting.'[26] By cross-referring with his telegraphic correspondence with Baring of the same date, we learn that a messenger he had sent to Khartoum, in reply to Gordon's letter, had been captured by the enemy and spent four days in their camp before escaping. Wolseley's sudden burst of optimism was based on the courier's account of his adventures:

Mahdi's troops suffering from disease; food very dear; Arabs deserting, but Kordofan men faithful to him. Gordon sent to Mahdi inviting him, if he were the real Mahdi, to dry up Nile and cross over. Five hundred regulars recently went over to Gordon; the regulars still with Mahdi are discontented. On 14th he saw attack made on Khartoum between Blue and White Nile; it was repulsed; Mahdi, who was looking on, very angry because it had been made without his orders.[27]

While Gordon's journals show that there were elements of truth in the report, taken in the round it by no means constituted an accurate portrayal of the situation at Khartoum, where the Mahdists were increasingly in the ascendant.

Incentivizing Progress

The following day was a Sunday which Wolseley began by attending the 6.45 a.m. church parade with the Royal Sussex. He then returned to his headquarters to find the first of the Butler missives amongst his correspondence. While he did not at all care for its tone, it was almost certainly references made by Butler to late starts, early finishes and half-hearted endeavour that drove Wolseley to spend the rest of the morning drafting a pompous General Order designed to elicit the army's best endeavours. It was decreed that it should be read at the head of every unit over three successive days and be repeated in all regimental, corps and station Daily Orders. It would doubtless have become rather wearing to both the commanding officers and their captive audiences by the third reading:

To the soldiers and sailors of the Nile Expedition,

The relief of General Gordon and his garrison, so long besieged in Khartum, is the glorious mission that the Queen has entrusted to us.

It is an enterprise that will stir the heart of every soldier and sailor fortunate enough to have been selected to share in it, and the very magnitude of its difficulties only stimulates us to increased exertions.

We are all proud of General Gordon's gallant and self-sacrificing defence of Khartum, which has added, if possible, to his already high reputation. He cannot hold out many months longer, and he now calls upon us to save his garrison. His heroism and patriotism are household words, wherever our language is spoken; and not only has his safety become a matter of national importance, but the knowledge that a brave comrade is in need of help, urges us to push forward with redoubled energy.

Neither he nor his garrison can be allowed to meet the sad fate which befell his gallant companion in arms, Colonel Stewart, who, when endeavouring to carry out an enterprise of unusual danger, was cruelly and treacherously murdered by his captors.

We can, and, with God's help, we will, save Gordon from such a death.

The labour of working upriver is immense. To bear it uncomplainingly demands the highest soldierly qualities, that contempt for danger, and that determination to overcome difficulties which in previous campaigns have so distinguished all ranks of Her Majesty's Army and Navy.

The physical obstacles that impede our rapid progress are considerable; but who cares for them when it is remembered that General Gordon and his garrison are in danger.

Under God their safety is now in our hands, and come what may we must save them.

To British soldiers and sailors, it is needless to say more.

Wolseley
General Commanding in Chief[28]

As is readily apparent rhetoric was not an art that came easily to Wolseley. In his journal entry of the same day he worries that his grandiloquent language might be mocked for its grammar or its sentiment in the *Pall Mall Gazette*, a newspaper he regarded as habitually cynical in tone. 'It is a difficult thing', he mused, 'for an Englishman to compose an order of this sort. For a Frenchman & perhaps all other foreigners the task is easy; he can afford to be heroic and pompous in his expressions without being thought ridiculous.'[29]

If a string of clichés were unlikely to exert any real effect on the spirit or endeavours of the troops, drafting them at least kept the C-in-C's troubled mind occupied for a few hours. The first General Order of the day was accompanied by a shorter and rather less heroic one to the effect that the battalion which made the best time between Sarras and Debbeh could expect to draw a cash reward of £100 and would be afforded an 'honourable' role in any fighting to come.[30] The Queen Empress was not taken with the idea of her soldiers being offered financial incentives to do their duty and, in replying to a letter from Wolseley some weeks later, made her displeasure abundantly clear.[31]

Dividing the Army

Wolseley's journal entry for the first day of December confirms how heavily the slow progress upriver was now weighing on his mind. 'How my hopes have been disappointed', he wrote, 'as to the time when I should have been in a position to do something. I expected to have been at Ambukol by this date with a force large enough to have walked through the Monassir Country with fire and sword.'[32] This of course is a reference to taking punitive action for the murders which followed the loss of the *Abbas* and is arguably the first real indication to be found in the journal that the penny had at last dropped. By now it was clear that the expedition was not just a little behind time, but had drifted a long way off course. At some point over the course of the next ten days, Wolseley concluded that the time had come to mount the camel-borne thrust across the Bayūda heralded by Buller more than a month earlier. That such an operation would have to involve the newly elevated Brigadier General Sir Herbert Stewart,[33] the four regiments of the Camel Corps and appropriately sized detachments of gunners, engineers, logisticians and medics was obvious. As yet there was no suggestion that the whaler-borne infantry battalions would do anything other than continue the journey around the Great Bend, although there was nothing to prevent their being used in support of the Camel Corps. On 7 December Stewart received orders to begin moving the Guards and Mounted Infantry Camel Regiments from the advanced camp at Khandak to Korti, a journey of about 100 miles, in four days' time. He could expect to be joined in short order by 1st South Staffords, 1st Royal Sussex and the headquarters staff.

Colvile states in the *Official History* that by the time Wolseley left Dongola for Korti on 13 December, he was firmly resolved to lead a camel-borne column across the Bayūda to seize Metemmeh, there to rendezvous with Gordon's steamers.[34] Wolseley's journal entry for 15 December provides the first real confirmation of

Delays and Decisions • 131

Colvile's assertion: 'If I can only reach Shendy safely with 1500 men on camels & with 30 days' provisions for them, I think I could tickle up the Mahdi.' In the meantime the inadvisable separation of army commander and chief of staff had continued unabated, causing Buller to complain in a letter dated 18 December:

I have not seen Wolseley, except for 8 hours, for two months, and am really absolutely ignorant of his information and his plans, while he has left the working of the troop part entirely to me, and I have equipped, fed, and forwarded, or rather superintended these actions, almost absolutely without reference to him. Now I trust the time for action has come. I really do think we shall go into Khartoum without much further difficulty, but how we shall go there, I mean by what route, I am ignorant as the babe unborn. I still, though, expect we will only go with camels across the desert: I shall soon know.[35]

It is hard to know why this extended divorce between commander and chief of staff was considered in any way desirable. Sir Evelyn Wood was meant to be GOC Lines of Communication after all, and both General Earle and Colonel Butler were hastening things along forward of Gemai. Despite the fact that Wolseley and Buller had telegraphic communications and sometimes 'talked together' over the wires, the chief of staff appears to have been caught flat-footed by the decision to strike out across the Bayūda. It was not until 16 December, three days before the last of the whaler-borne troops were embarked at Gemai, that Buller finally got away from Wādī Halfā.[36] He was more than a week in transit and arrived at Korti on Christmas Eve.

Here a surprise awaited me. I found that Wolseley had just made up his mind to act on the lines . . . I sketched out to him in November last, viz. to go with the camels across the desert to Shendi, and to send the infantry by boat to Abū-Hamed and Berber. Earle will command the force by water, and Brackenbury goes as second in command. Herbert Stewart will command the Mounted Force. Wolseley will go with it, and so do I, as fifth wheel to the coach, to command vice Stewart or Wolseley if one of them is shot. I am sorry that Wolseley did not make up his mind sooner. I could have done him much better than he will be now, but he has so persistently said that he must go by water, and that he must have at least 5,000 men at Shendi, that I have been put off my idea, and have been doing my best to prepare for his. Consequently he has not here either the men, the camels or the food I should have liked to have had for the operation he proposes. However, we must do the best with what we have and risk the rest . . . The expedition we are going on will be severely criticised, and partially justly so, for Lord Wolseley has I think quite forgotten that I was not in touch with his mind during the last two months, and consequently that it was out of my power to follow his line of thought. Fact is, in a few words, that we are now undertaking an expedition which we have not properly provided for, but which we ought to have foreseen and fully provided for two months ago. Of course it is a bore: one does not like to do bad work, when one is conscious that one could have done better. However, I have patched it up as well as may be, and we shall do pretty well, I think. As for the Mahdi, he is a fraud, and I really do not anticipate that we shall have any fighting at all. At the same time, I anticipate that we shall have very serious difficulties, and perhaps shortness of supply. But it is a poor heart that never rejoices, and I do rejoice to see the end of the long journey, though at the same time I cannot help regretting that Wolseley did not give me the chance of doing him as well as I should have liked to, and indeed as I could have. But it is no use crying over spilt milk.[37]

It seems extraordinary, if Buller is to be believed, and his tone appears both sincere and compelling, that Wolseley failed to notify his chief of staff and heads of department of a major operational-level decision he can be shown to have made at least as early as 12 December. At least twelve invaluable days were lost in consequence which might otherwise have been used to staff-check the C-in-C's plan and resolve any shortfalls or deficiencies.

The issue was not so much the availability of key elements of the fighting echelon, which in all cases were continuing to make their way to Korti by the fastest possible means, but resourcing the transport and logistics assets necessary to support a major push across the desert. The most under-resourced commodity was baggage camels, which the army staff had stopped purchasing on the basis of Wolseley's apparently firm rebuttal of Buller's 7 November proposals. It was not a shortfall which could be readily or rapidly addressed in Dongola Province, where there were simply not the requisite numbers of animals to be had, even if it had been possible to count on the wholehearted support of local *shaikhs* and merchants. At Dongola a good many Sudanese had been taken on to the British payroll as camel-drivers, although a proportion of them had deserted as soon as the animals were moved upriver, leaving a significant shortfall in the number of native workers. It was also proving impossible to acquire additional camel saddles in any significant quantities. Perhaps the most serious difficulty, however, was that of procuring and moving the great volumes of *dhura* required to feed such atypically large concentrations of camels.[38] If we accept that Buller identified the right decision point as being 7 November or thereabouts, then Wolseley squandered the best part of five weeks' worth of priceless lead-time which might otherwise have been used to make up the shortfall in camels, saddles and fodder.

In confirmation of Buller's remarks about poor passage of information, it is clear that Butler had also been kept in the dark. He received a summons to come forward to Korti on 28 December. Although he was as yet unaware of his new role, it had been agreed at Wolseley's headquarters that he should command the cavalry assets assigned to General Earle's 'River Column'. The following passage from Butler's *Campaign of the Cataracts* describes the situation confronting him when, having only just been ordered forward, he again reached Abu Fatmeh at the head of the Third Cataract:

What the ultimate route of the expedition would be beyond Korti, no one could yet tell for certain. At Korti began that singular bend in the river which carries it, for a distance of 160 miles, in an opposite direction to its proper north course. Not only did this change of direction double the distance from Korti to Berber, but some sixty miles beyond Korti a second series of rapids began, neither the nature nor extent of which were known to the modern world. These cataracts were variously called the 'Fourth Cataracts', the Shagghieh Cataracts, and the Cataracts of Dar-Djuma. Men on the Lower Nile shook their heads when these wild rapids were spoken of. The few experts in Nile travel whose opinion could be asked in London had taken an even gloomier view of them.

'You will get over the cataracts of the Batn-el-Hager and of Dar-Mahass,' said a traveller who had visited Dongola and the Bayuda Desert, to me, when we were building our boats; 'but you will never pass with these boats the cataracts of Shagghieh.'

Between us now and these terrible rapids of Shagghieh lay a perfectly open waterway of 240 miles. Korti was about 175 miles distant along that open river. Once at that point, the choice would lie between crossing the desert to Metemma, or moving by the long detour of the river, taking the cataracts as they came.[39]

It was not until 1 January, when Butler spoke with a Royal Sussex officer quartered on the old fort at Debbeh, that he finally learned that an overland thrust across the Bayūda was definitely afoot. Butler was a colourful, florid author and wrote with the kind of energy that sometimes led to him exposing the contradictions inherent in his own arguments. Here for example we get a glimpse of the disingenuousness employed by the Ring during the 'Battle of the Routes'. As Butler himself observes, 'some sixty miles beyond Korti a second series of rapids began, neither the nature nor extent of which were known to the modern world'. And yet Wolseley and his acolytes had insisted that Her Majesty's Government need have no fear about the whalers getting up the Nile to Khartoum: water is water and rock is rock, after all.

Wolseley's 'Grand Conception'

Save in so far as there may have been faster strategic alternatives, such as advancing via the Suakin–Berber axis, there was nothing inherently unsound about using whalers to concentrate men and supplies at Korti, in readiness for an overland thrust across the Bayūda. On the other hand, the broader dictates of time and space were such that pushing boats around the Great Bend and beyond was never going to be timely enough to affect the outcome at Khartoum. But the notion had always been a central tenet of the grand conception devised by Wolseley in London. By mid-December it should have been abundantly clear to him that this phase of the plan could no longer have any possible bearing on the attainment of his mission. Yet still he felt an irresistible compulsion to send a large part of his force via Abū-Hamed and Berber. Why was this? How could the chief of staff conclude as early as 7 November that the Bayūda route was the only tenable option and be content with aborting any further river movement, whilst at the same time the army commander, faced with precisely the same set of factors, continued to insist that a manifestly irrelevant phase of operations be persevered with? There can be only five possible answers to this conundrum. The first is that an army commander renowned for his military acumen had failed to grasp a very basic time and space equation. This is so far-fetched a premise that it can be readily dismissed. The second is that the army commander considered the shorter overland route to be too high-risk. If this was the case there would not have been a Desert Column and British forces would not have been within 100 miles of Khartoum until March 1885; it follows that this notion can likewise be dismissed. The third is that the army commander intended evacuating the Khartoum garrison along the Berber–Suakin caravan route to the sea. It is a matter of record, however, that thousands of tons of foodstuffs were in the process of being stockpiled to facilitate the garrison's extrication via Wādī Halfā and Aswan.[40] The fourth possibility is that the chastisement of Colonel Stewart's murderers was considered to be of such vital political importance that it needed to be undertaken at all hazards. This too is hardly likely.

The fifth, final and most credible proposition is that the army commander had always had a phase of operations in mind which would not readily have commanded the Prime Minister's support: something set distinctly apart from the relief of Khartoum; something fit to feed Wolseley's burning ambition; a phase of operations he could portray as a military necessity, thereby evading any undue political interference in its execution. If there was to be a substantially contrived phase of operations, then it is little wonder that Wolseley had not yet laid all his cards on the table. What Buller failed to appreciate is that his chief's insistence on pushing the whaler-borne brigade around the Great Bend had a subsidiary purpose. It did not follow, as Buller had evidently inferred, that there was to be no overland push from Korti. Wolseley had always had just such a contingency in mind and had even formed the Camel Corps expressly for the purpose.[41] Once Khartoum had been relieved, Gordon and his Egyptians were clearly going to be evacuated across the Bayūda, the only route by which they could reach the depots of food being stockpiled along the Nile for them. What Buller nor anybody else knew was that Wolseley had set his heart on extracting his British troops by an altogether different route. The C-in-C's as yet undeclared intent was to march to the sea along the Berber–Suakin caravan road: the undeclared phase of operations was the defeat of Osman Digna and final pacification of the Red Sea Littoral. This was indeed a grand conception, an extraordinary campaign fit both to be Wolseley's last and to secure his place amongst the 'great captains' of the nineteenth century. He was to reveal a glimpse of the grandiose nature of his scheming in a plainly delusional journal entry of 8 January 1885:

This is certainly a strange episode in our military history. It is the biggest operation the British Army has ever undertaken. I think those engaged in it, are now beginning to realise this fact, and to feel they have the honour of taking part in an operation the like of which has never been undertaken before.[42]

Thus were the great campaigns of Marlborough, Clive, Wolfe and Wellington consigned to obscurity.

In order to chastise the rebellious Bīja 'on the way home', so to speak, it would first be necessary to get a large quantity of supplies to Berber. Prior to that there would be a point of 'logistic no-return', somewhere along the course of the Great

Bend, where pressing on to Berber and marching to the sea would become the best, indeed the only, course of action: a point where it was manifestly more practical to press forward than to turn back; a point where the politicians would be unable to gainsay the best military judgment of the commander in the field. Incontrovertible proof of the existence of such a scheme is hard to come by, but on or about 18 January Lieutenant Colonel Hugh McCalmont of LCR, Wolseley's particular friend and confidante, wrote in a letter home, 'I fancy the advance from Shendy on Khartoum will come off about 14th of February, but it is rash to prophesy. The camels [by which he means the Camel Corps] will return by Suakin. This is a secret.'[43] This constitutes the first item of 'smoking gun' evidence of the grand conception. We shall come to a second in due course.

Christmas at Korti

As we have seen in Buller's own words the plan outlined to him on Christmas Eve, when at last he caught up with the army commander, was for Sir Herbert Stewart and the Camel Corps to push across the Bayūda to Metemmeh and there marry up with Gordon's steamers. None of this was yet generally known to the force. Wolseley intended to accompany the movement in person, which to all intents and purposes would mean his assuming tactical command of the Desert Column. At this stage he was still of the view that the rebel movement was neither militarily nor morally strong enough to do anything other than abandon the siege and retreat into Kordofan at the near-approach of the British. In the meantime General Earle would lead a whaler-borne River Column into the Great Bend with the aim of capturing, first, Abū-Hamed, which would serve to open the caravan road north to Korosko, and subsequently, Berber, which would open the route to Suakin and the sea. At Korosko 200,000 rations of groceries, 100,000 of biscuits and 500,000 of tinned meat had been stockpiled in the care of Major Rundle. Rundle was to convoy a large consignment of rations across the desert to Abū-Hamed, in the care of his Abadeh friendlies, within four days of the town falling to Earle.[44] Once the existence of the grand conception is recognized, it becomes obvious that these were the rations intended to support it. Wolseley took the view that in the meantime the presence at Korosko of the 1st Cameron Highlanders would be regarded by the enemy as a standing menace to Abū-Hamed.[45]

By turning to Wolseley's journal entry for Christmas Eve we are able to ascertain the proposed timetable for these plans, although his language is a touch vague in places. The Desert Column was to cross the Bayūda in two echelons, a first and larger echelon, which he would accompany in person, and a second less powerful echelon under Buller. He and Stewart would set out on 2 January with the aim of reaching Metemmeh five days later. Buller would be 24–48 hours behind them and would join them on the river on either 8 or 9 January. General Earle for his part would set off upriver on 7 or 8 January, with the aim of taking Abū-Hamed by 1 February. Importantly the journal entry concludes by remarking that 1 February is,

... the date when I hope with God's aid to be in Khartoum. I may be there some days earlier. If I can I shall avoid fighting until I reach Khartoum and will attack the Mahdi's position D.V. [*Deo volente* – God willing] the day after I can ferry my troops across the White Nile to the neighbourhood of Omdurman.[46]

The last part of this passage is curious in so far as Omdurman and Metemmeh both lie on the west bank of the Nile, and could be taken to imply that at this point in the proceedings Wolseley envisaged using Gordon's steamers to ferry the Desert Column across to the east bank in the vicinity of Shendy, so as eventually to gain the city through the stretch of desert upon which North Khartoum has since sprung up. This makes perfect tactical sense although interestingly there are no other traces of the notion to be found anywhere else in the primary sources. But the real significance of the 24 December entry is that it constitutes proof positive that when the River Column was despatched into the Great Bend, Wolseley knew perfectly well that it would be playing no part in the relief of Khartoum. This makes it plain that the purpose of advancing the River Column was to get to Berber and thus accommodate the final phase of the grand conception.

It was not long before Wolseley had to some extent been forced into the open by enquiries from Lord Hartington about the merits of sending a second expedition to cooperate with him along the Suakin–Berber axis, operations which would plainly serve to torpedo his grand conception. Wolseley began by replying that such an operation would only help if it could be effected within sixty days and that he very much doubted that this was possible. The next objection he turned to was that it could only be undertaken by 2,000 troops 'picked' after the fashion of the Camel Corps, something he knew the Duke of Cambridge would never consent to for a second time. At length the Secretary of State's enthusiasm for a second front forced the admission, 'I have always contemplated the possibility of sending all mounted troops back by Berber and Suakin, to open road and crush Osman Digna. There can be no tranquillity in the Sudan as long as he remains defiant. Of course I may not eventually be able to do that.'[47] This is the second item of 'smoking gun' evidence – the final sentence was clearly designed to throw Hartington off the scent of a pre-ordained plot. In fact, as Wolseley's Christmas Eve journal entry shows, he was actively planning to contrive precisely the right conditions for such an operation.

Christmas Day was a working day, save for divine service first thing in the morning and a few festivities held around blazing bonfires after sunset. A double-issue of rations would serve as the troops' Christmas present.[48] Buller and his staff subordinates slipped quickly into overdrive to try and address all the unanticipated logistic shortfalls and kept the telegraph operators busy all day. Sir Evelyn Wood was instructed to send forward all the camel transport at the portage points on the river and backfill the resultant gaps with newly purchased animals. Similarly the commandants at all the posts on the lines of communication were to buy up every camel they could find and hasten them to the front. The commandant at Abu Fatmeh was to move all the food stockpiled there forward to Korti. The officer commanding at Dongola was to send up the 800 *ardebs* of barley, 1,600 *ardebs* of *dhura* and 170 *ardebs* of dates known to be stored in the *mudir*'s warehouses. Colonel Colvile, who was upriver at Merowe, was instructed to procure large quantities of *dhura*, barley and firewood.[49]

After completing a few basic staff computations, Buller approached Wolseley to say that he very much doubted whether it would be possible to start the Desert Column as early as 2 January and that it might be advisable to put its departure back by a week. Wolseley's journal shows that he was anxious not to get to Metemmeh with part of the column, only to be faced with a long delay while he waited for the second echelon, on the grounds 'That would give the Mahdi time to arrange his plans. What I should really like best would be move across the desert with the whole of my force in one body or in two echelons one behind the other at a day's interval.' In the event, the scheme he eventually enacted gave the Mahdī so much time to 'arrange his plans' that Stewart would be compelled to fight two battles en route to Metemmeh. Crucially, in terms of ascertaining his precise intent, he then went on to say, 'I should then be able to push on to Khartoum without halting.' Here, then, we see that the advance of the Desert Column was intended at this point to be one flowing movement all the way through to Khartoum. In so far as Gordon's steamers had any part to play, it was to support an overland advance. In other words Stewart's brigade was going to ride 174 miles to Metemmeh, storm the town and then ride the final 100 miles south to Khartoum, there to give battle and relieve the city.

Wolseley ate early that evening so as to be in good time for one of the great traditions of the British Army, the impromptu Christmas concert. Around his dining table were Major General Sir Redvers Buller, Colonels Henry Brackenbury and Zohrab Bey, Lieutenant Colonels Leopold Swaine and Hugh McCalmont, Surgeon William Pratt (the headquarters' physician) and the three remaining ADCs, Major Arthur Creagh and Lieutenants John Adye and Edmund Childers. On the menu were 'two very fat wild geese' and an apparently rather good plum pudding.[50] Major Frederick Wardrop, who until 17 December had also been employed as an ADC to Wolseley, had now been appointed to be the DAAG (Deputy Assistant Adjutant-General) on Stewart's brigade staff.[51] Wardrop had landed the job of master of ceremonies for the concert and was doubtless far too busy firing up his performers to worry about his Christmas dinner. The Royal Engineers had lashed a stage together and the two-hour performance proceeded by the light of two huge bonfires. Jack Cameron of the *Standard* described for his readers how a Life Guardsman gave a speech which purported to be on temperance, but bewailed the fact that there 'remained not another drop of rum in the Commissariat department'. There were many songs and parodies of native dances. 'There are few British regiments', wrote Cameron, 'whose ranks do not include one or more whilom professionals in the art of entertaining.'

The show was attended by all the troops at Korti. Stewart's brigade was represented by all three squadrons of the 19th Hussars (15 officers and 283 NCOs and men); all four companies of MICR (22 & 392); three out of four GCR companies (15 & 286); two out of five HCR companies (10 & 156); but only one of the three companies in LCR (6 & 113). The most serious deficiency in the mounted brigade was the camel-borne battery, 1st Battery/1st Brigade, Southern Division, Royal Artillery, with its six 7-pounder screw guns, but this it turned out was only a day's march away. Of the seven infantry battalions coming upriver only 1st South Staffords (18 & 535) had yet reached Korti, though 1st Royal Sussex was represented by 3 officers and 163 NCOs and men, or about two-fifths of the battalion. Counting the staff, 17 Egyptians soldiers and minor details from the Commissariat & Transport Corps and the Medical Staff Corps, there were some 134 officers and 2,086 NCOs and men in the concentration area that Christmas evening.[52] With the exception of the general officers and a handful of the most trusted staff officers, everybody else present at the festivities remained oblivious to the fact that the majority of them would be plunging into the Bayūda Desert in a few days' time. Cameron concluded his coverage of the evening's entertainment by flattering the vanity of the army commander – never a bad idea for a war correspondent anxious to learn what the next twists and turns in the campaign might be:

Lord Wolseley was there all the time with his cheery, confident mien and manner. One has only to glance at our sprightly Commander in Chief to feel sure that the difficulties and dangers of the campaign will disappear, if necessary, by magic the moment he confronts them. No trace is there to be seen of the tremendous responsibility which really sits on his shoulders, and if any one doubts our ultimate success, he has only to make his way to Headquarters Camp and wait for a glimpse of the general, to feel completely reassured.[53]

As generous a portrait as it was, the special correspondent of the *Standard* derived no benefit from it: by the time it appeared in the 22 January edition of his paper, Jack Cameron had been dead for three days.

Chapter 5

Leap in the Dark

The March of the Desert Column

> The march of Sir Herbert Stewart yesterday into this incomprehensible desert was really very imposing. The slow, steady, and measured pace of the camels, the silence of the big men who sat upon them, and the order and regularity of the formation all conspired to make it a scene the remembrance of which will long be impressed upon the memory.
>
> General Lord Wolseley to his wife, Korti, 31 December 1884

THE CHRISTMAS FESTIVITIES having been duly dispensed with, there was tremendous bustle up and down the lines of communication from Boxing Day onwards. If no detailed orders had yet been disseminated, the multiplicity of telegraphed imprecations that this asset or that item should be hurried to the front served to suggest that there was something afoot. Wolseley recorded in his journal that the battery of camel-borne screw guns arrived on 27 December, but Boxing Day had been a busy day for him and he had failed to notice the battery marching in late that afternoon. Accompanying the guns were ninety-six members of the RMLI under Major William Pöe, destined to take their place in the order of battle as the fourth company of the Guards Camel Regiment.

The reason why Wolseley remained oblivious to the latest arrivals was that he was now preoccupied with the intimate detail of the next phase in his plan. He spent most of Boxing Day in company with Buller and Stewart, working up a detailed scheme of manoeuvre for the overland advance, or the 'great leap in the dark' as he referred to it in his journal.[1] On 27 December Buller was able to telegraph the latest thinking back to Wood.

As I have already informed you by telegram in cipher, Lord Wolseley has decided on dividing his force at Korti. One division will proceed by water and one by land. The force proceeding by water will consist of 1½ squadrons 19th Hussars, and 4 regiments of infantry, viz., the Staffordshire Regiment, the Royal Highlanders, the Gordon Highlanders, the Duke of Cornwall's Light Infantry (it is possible some of these may be changed for others), battery of Egyptian Artillery, Egyptian Camel Corps, headquarters and about 400 camels of the 11th Transport Company.

Major General Earle will command the force, with Colonel H. Brackenbury as his principal staff officer and second in command. This force will be concentrated at Hamdab, just above the Gerendid Cataract, and will move thence, taking 100 days' whaler supplies with it.

As you are aware, Major Rundle, E.A., has been directed to take steps to have a further supply of rations at Abu-Hamed within four days of the arrival there of this force. Major General Earle will have one regiment placed at his disposal, in addition to the above named force, from which to detail such posts on his line of march as he may require. As to these he has been directed to inform you.

The force proceeding by land will be under the command of Brigadier-General Sir H. Stewart, and will consist of 1½ squadrons of 19th Hussars, the four Camel Regiments, one battery of the Royal Artillery, and a portion, or perhaps the whole, of the Royal Sussex Regiment. All the transport camels, not detailed for the water force, will accompany this force. General Lord Wolseley and his staff will accompany this force. The intention is to form a post at the Jakdul Wells, which will be garrisoned by the Sussex Regiment, and there to collect 60 days' of supply for the whole force. The mounted troops will then attack and occupy Metemmeh, and either proceed at once to Khartoum, or else bring some more supplies, and a garrison from Jakdul to Shendi as circumstances may direct.[2]

There were four items presaged in Buller's telegram which did not in the end come to pass. First, the 19th Hussars would not be evenly divided between the two columns: instead Stewart was to get two squadrons and Earle only one. Second, the River Column was not assigned any additional infantry battalions to secure its lines of communication. Instead it would be designated a 'flying column', which meant that it had no lines of communication and would have to carry its supplies aboard the boats, at least until such time as it took Abū-Hamed and Rundle was able to come up from Korosko.[3] Third, the River Column would be assigned nothing like 400 baggage camels, but instead was given only a few dozen. Finally, and perhaps most importantly, Wolseley never got to go forward of Korti. When Lord Hartington was notified that the C-in-C intended plunging into the Bayūda with the Camel Corps, he effectively vetoed the proposal by insisting that he remain at the end of the telegraph.[4] With the army now diverging into two brigade-sized wings and many of the 'force troops' still to come upriver, there was no better place for the overall commander to be located than Korti. It did mean, however, that unless the Desert Column left a line of vulnerable heliograph stations to its rear, Wolseley would be out of touch with events at the front for as long as it took camel-mounted couriers to hasten across the Bayūda. From Metemmeh, on the far side of the desert, this would entail a four-day journey, or a round trip of more than a week. Hartington was happier that this should be so than that the War Office should lose touch with the senior officer in the field, an illustration of how increasingly sophisticated communications systems were changing the face not only of continental warfare, but also drawing the curtain on the semi-autonomous way in which the 'small wars of empire' had long been waged. Even so there was an onus on the army commander not to lose touch with his subordinate commanders, least of all with the commander of his foremost elements. Wolseley's instincts should have told him that there would inevitably come a time when it would no longer be tactically sustainable for him to remain at Korti, whether the Secretary of State liked it or not.

In the meantime the Guards and Mounted Infantry had been honing their camel-handling skills with a succession of early morning training sessions. The ever observant Jack Cameron watched the two units at work and observed to his readers at home that they had become 'extremely expert in the management of their animals'. What he should have said was they had become tactically proficient as camel-mounted regiments, which was not at all the same thing, as the one thing the British had most assuredly not become was expert managers of camels:

I do not exaggerate when I say that no body of Arabs in the Orient could ride or manoeuvre camels with so much skill as can now our English soldiers, and even the camels themselves seem changed in nature, and are developing qualities hitherto not credited to them. Several of the Mounted Infantry officers have taught their camels to trot, canter and even jump at will; and the men like their mounts immensely . . . From half past six every morning until nine the corps is busily drilling. And no mere barrack-square manoeuvres are they which are practised; but stern workmanlike evolutions, likely to prove effective when their alert and rapidly-moving Arab foe is encountered. Continually do the column halt, dismount, and prepare to meet the enemy; and on these occasions there is always a race between the Mounted Infantry and Guards Regiments as to who shall be first in square.[5]

The most vital planning consideration in crossing the Bayūda was the amount of water available at each of the recognized staging posts, as a brigade-sized column was sure to be many times larger than the traders' caravans which from time to time plied the route. It was known that by far the greatest quantity was to be found about ninety-eight miles into the desert at a place called Jakdul Wells, though this was something of a misnomer as the water there was to be found in a series of natural rock-pools distributed along a steeply descending watercourse. The staging posts en route to Jakdul were Hambok, Howeiyat and Abu Halfa. Fifty-one miles beyond Jakdul and about twenty-five miles shy of Metemmeh and the Nile, lay the Abu Klea Valley where a cluster of bona fide desert wells would provide a much less generous supply of water.

After water the next most important factor was the intelligence picture. Major Kitchener had been monitoring the situation in the Bayūda for a number of months and thus far had been unable to detect any indications that an overland advance was likely to meet with heavy resistance north of Metemmeh. The town itself, on the other hand, was known to be strongly held. A traveller who passed that way on 15 December, subsequently to be questioned by Colvile at Merowe on Christmas Day, reported that were about 3,000 Ja'līyīn and Awadiyeh of fighting age quartered there. He added that the *anṣār* seemed to be well supplied with Remingtons and fowling pieces and moreover could dispose two brass mountain guns. He had also been told that the Mahdī was sending them a third mountain gun and a Gatling.

The town of Shendy, a little way downstream on the opposite bank, was believed by Colvile's informant to house about 1,000 rebels.

The staff computations carried out by Buller and his assistants had shown that there were nothing like enough camels in hand to permit a single-phase advance all the way through to Metemmeh. The Mudir of Dongola had promised that Shaikh Saleh of the Kababish would bring large numbers of camels in to Korti, but he had not so far put in an appearance, nor was there any indication that he could be expected to arrive any time soon. The best that could be done in the circumstances would be to mount a preliminary operation to secure Jakdul Wells and pre-position a large quantity of stores there. These would be used to sustain an in-place garrison, for the passage of the main force, and to support the subsequent phase of operations around Metemmeh. This would necessarily entail the same animals shuttling back and forth to Jakdul with heavy loads and might potentially reduce through attrition the number of baggage camels available for the main advance.

On 28 December 1st South Staffords set off for the village of Hamdab, newly selected as the River Column's concentration area and jumping-off point. The battalion was played aboard its flotilla of fifty-five boats and out of sight around a bed in the river by the band of the Royal Sussex.[6] Jack Cameron was again on hand to capture the scene for the benefit of his readers:

From Wady Halfa to Ambukol the boats have progressed in parties of threes and fours; but today five hundred and fifty hardy soldiers fell in on the banks of the Nile and by word of command filed down together to the fifty [*sic*] whalers, wherein, and without confusion they were soon seated . . . Practised oarsmen are our soldiers now; and with long, steady, measured stroke they make headway against the stream with not even a single Canadian or native pilot to aid them – a strange and impressive sight, and pleasing withal to the Briton who, proudly watching them, is conscious that with the soldiers of no other nation in the world would such a feat be practicable. Very soon after beginning the voyage from Sarras are the weakly men weeded out and invalided, and by the time Korti is reached the Regiments consist all of strong, healthy soldier-boatmen, inured to fatigue and proof apparently against sickness . . . So the river route if it is hard, long, and wearisome, promises, at least, to be a healthy one.

But it is also a dirty one in some respects. Judged by their outward appearance only, Her Majesty's really fine Regiment of South Stafford Infantry would be pronounced on their arrival at Korti, after their fifty days or so of river navigation from Sarras, a unique collection of seedy, out-at-elbow blackguards. Officers and men looked like a lot of disreputable Seven-Dials roughs. There was not a thoroughly sound garment in the Regiment, nor, I make bold to remark, a clean countenance either. Scrubby beards of a month's growth, coats and trousers sometimes patched and sometimes not, tattered mud-stained helmets, and faces from which the skin peeled off in great ugly patches, testified to hard work in the sun from daylight to dark.[7]

Having at last decided that the time had come to take the plunge into the desert, Wolseley ordered that Sir Herbert Stewart should march for Jakdul Wells with two

Camel Corps regiments and a baggage train of more than a thousand animals on the morning of Tuesday 30 December. It is worthy of note that the cabal of newspapermen accompanying the expedition, not all of whom had yet reached Korti admittedly, had been given no official intimation that a dash across the Bayūda was imminent, although the sharper ones like Cameron and Burleigh would doubtless have succeeded in eliciting hints to that effect from their conversations with members of the army staff. Some of the others were still, even at this late stage, forwarding copy to London describing how the Camel Corps would soon be moving upriver with General Earle. This was typical of Wolseley who, while he might entertain the odd correspondent at his dinner table, also viewed them as fair game and seemed to take perverse pleasure in seeing them submit confused or inaccurate reports. Alex Macdonald, representing the *Western Morning News* and a syndicate of smaller newspapers, felt certain that they were deliberately misled in accordance with notions propounded in Wolseley's *A Soldier's Pocket Book*.[8] In the event, Mr Piggott of Reuters, not to be confused with either the naval officer (Alfred) or the army officer (Charles Berkeley) of the same name, would be the only correspondent to accompany Stewart's first march to Jakdul.[9]

Having unloaded the stores and left GCR to secure the wells, Stewart could be expected to return on either 6 or 7 January. After a day's rest, Wolseley would then take over and lead the main body's move via Jakdul to Metemmeh. It was now anticipated that the full-strength fighting force would consist of two squadrons of the 19th Hussars (operating as a single enlarged squadron of four small troops), three Camel Corps regiments, 1st Royal Sussex, a number of Royal Artillery screw guns, one five-barrelled Gardner machine gun and a fifty-man Naval Brigade. The supporting arms would consist of a small detachment of 26 Field Company, RE, four medical sections and Nos. 9 and 11 Transport Companies. With the exception of Lieutenant Colonel Percy Barrow's 19th Hussars, which had been mounted on matched-grey Syrian ponies expropriated from the EA's recently formed cavalry regiment, and the native camel drivers, who were meant to walk but were already showing a strong disinclination to do so, the rest of the force would be entirely camel-borne. The logistic units were all ad hoc in nature, with rather more native workers on their strength than British officers and soldiers. At least three-quarters of 1st Royal Sussex would be assigned to garrison duty at Jakdul Wells and Abu Klea, in order to secure the column's water supply. Once the infantry battalion had been in large part detached, the number of sabres and bayonets remaining would amount to barely 1,500.

This then was the feeble military force with which Garnet Wolseley intended not merely to cross the Bayūda to Metemmeh, but subsequently to defeat the Mahdī's cohorts in a decisive battle on the outskirts of Khartoum. If it was true that he would also be able to count on the support of a small flotilla of steamers, there was little prospect of the garrison of Khartoum providing any meaningful help. The aptly named 'great leap in the dark' undoubtedly constituted a high-risk operation of war, but this was the unhappy pass to which Wolseley's adoption of the Nile Route had brought him. It is all the more remarkable, given the great numerical disparity in favour of the enemy, that his plan still called for General Earle to head off into the Great Bend without the remotest prospect of being able to support the overland thrust through to Khartoum.

Even now there was a workable answer to the conundrum, although it would have called for the abandonment of both the much vaunted 'novel expedients' and the still closeted grand conception alike. Save in so far as the proposition was a vital enabler to the grand conception, there were no legitimate grounds for sending the bulk of the infantry past Korti in whalers. It was perfectly possible at this time of year to march across the Bayūda on foot, as 1st Royal Irish would later demonstrate by gaining Abu Klea Wells without incurring a single heat casualty. A camel-borne column with a heavily laden baggage train was no faster-moving than marching infantry and it had always been intended that the Camel Corps would dismount to fight in any case. There was indeed an answer, if only Wolseley could bring himself to swallow his pride. The best course of action in the situation now confronting the British was to re-role the Camel Corps as infantry and re-assign its riding camels to the commissaries. This would not only have enabled the Desert Column to mount a single-phase advance to Metemmeh, but would also have allowed some of the infantry battalions to follow up and lend close support to Stewart's brigade. Indeed 1st South Staffords, some 550 additional bayonets, could have been brigaded under Stewart's direct command without the loss of a single day. A one-phase crossing of the Bayūda would have allowed the British to avoid any heavy fighting in the desert and effect a rendezvous with Gordon's steamers by the end of the first week of January. The enemy force in Metemmeh could have been defeated by means of direct assault, or alternatively could have been fixed in place by entrenching one of the infantry battalions on the Nile to the south of the town. There would still at that juncture have been more than a fortnight in hand for a somewhat stronger and substantially intact fighting column to cover the last 100 miles and effect the relief of Khartoum. Unhappily for Gordon Pasha none of these things would come to pass. Indeed it is to be doubted whether anybody on the staff ever had the temerity to mention the notion of dismounting the Camel Corps.

Stewart Marches for Jakdul Wells

Sir Herbert Stewart gave orders for his preliminary operation on the afternoon of 29 December. For many, even the officers, this was the first indication that a desert march was definitely afoot.[10] The following day Stewart began assembling his column on a low plateau just to the south-east of Korti, in readiness for a 3.00 p.m. departure, a late start predicated on the premise of marching by night. The cavalry component would comprise 2 officers and 32 NCOs and men from the 19th Hussars. Captain Hew Fanshawe, said to be the youngest captain in the service, would split his troop between an advance guard of 1 & 20 and a rearguard of 1 & 12, the latter commanded by Lieutenant Edward Craven.[11] The fighting escort would consist of all four GCR companies (21 & 360) under Lieutenant Colonel the Hon.

Evelyn Boscawen, and the comparably structured MICR (23 & 358) under Major the Hon. George Gough. A small detachment of 2 officers and 27 NCOs and men from 26 Field Company, RE, commanded by Major James Dorward, had been attached to the Guards and would also be staying behind at Jakdul to install pumps, pipes and water troughs. Dorward had divided his sappers into four small specialist sections, tasked with Watering, Demolition, Entrenching, and Materials & Miscellaneous.[12]

Between the two full-strength camel regiments, GCR at the front and MICR to the rear, came a ponderous thousand-camel baggage train. Ordinarily Colonel Stanley Clarke was the Commanding Officer of the Light Camel Regiment, but only one of his three companies had yet come up to Korti and he duly found himself temporarily assigned to the unenviable post of baggage master. Always more a high-society man than a serious soldier, Stanley Clarke was a personal friend of the Prince of Wales and had never before seen active service. His appointment as CO LCR had been pretty much forced on Wolseley, who was obliged in consequence to disappoint Lieutenant Colonel Hugh McCalmont of the 7th Hussars, a close personal friend and his preferred candidate for command of the regiment. Clarke epitomized the sort of officer that Wolseley loathed and for all his royal connections would have to step carefully around an army commander all too ready to find fault with inexperienced colonels.

Numbers 9 and 11 Transport Companies, under the overall direction of Assistant Commissary-General Robert Nugent CB,[13] made up the bulk of Clarke's baggage train with 5 officers, 26 NCOs and men, 140 native drivers and some 540 baggage camels. In addition to the larger, more robust baggage camels, 320 riding camels had also been pressed into service as beasts of burden and were being led in strings of three by camel-mounted detachments of LCR (10 & 81) and HCR (7 & 91). The Royal Artillery paraded 2 officers, 20 British NCOs and men, 21 natives and 155 camels, but had been committed to transporting stores rather than guns, all six of which were left behind at Korti. The medical units fielded 6 officers, 16 NCOs and men, 35 native drivers and 80 camels, under the command of the Principal Medical Officer, or PMO, Surgeon-Major Frederick Ferguson.[14] In addition to ammunition, medical comforts and all sorts of other miscellaneous stores, Nugent had managed to load something around 50,000 rations aboard a total of 1,095 camels.[15]

Stewart's brigade headquarters consisted of 5 officers, 3 NCOs and men, 2 native servants and 11 camels. The general's personal staff officers were Major Fredrick Wardrop of the 3rd Dragoon Guards, an able and experienced soldier with 26 years' service; David Ogilvy, the 11th Earl of Airlie, a 29-year-old captain in the 10th Hussars, serving as the brigade major; and Captain Frank Rhodes (the elder brother of Cecil John Rhodes) of the Royal Dragoons, employed as the general's ADC, a role he had also fulfilled in the Suakin Campaign nine months earlier. Lord Airlie had served with his regiment in the Second Afghan War, had fought in the Battle of Ali Masjid, and in the aftermath of the Maiwand disaster of July 1880 participated in Roberts's famous march from Kabul to Kandahar. In addition, the adventurous and well-connected correspondent of the *Morning Post*, St Leger Herbert, was also working as the general's private secretary. He was evidently a striking figure as Brackenbury remarked in his memoirs that, 'He was as handsome as a young Greek God.'[16] Herbert was not in the Army, but had worked for Wolseley in a civil capacity in Cyprus and South Africa and had been much attracted to the military way of life. He and Stewart became firm friends during the war against the baPedi. Herbert had again been present during the Egyptian Campaign where he had done duty with the mounted infantry as a volunteer. More recently he had also been with Stewart and Rhodes in the Red Sea Littoral and had been wounded at Tamai.[17] In short 'Sankey' Herbert enjoyed the complete confidence of the generals and with their blessing was now comporting himself as just another officer on the staff. By the autumn of 1884 he was thirty-five years of age and was to be counted amongst Sir Herbert Stewart's closest personal friends.[18] Kitchener was also attached to the brigade staff as the Intelligence Department representative.

The column marched punctually at 3.00, with the two Camel Corps regiments riding on section-strength frontages. All told the command consisted of 83 officers, 1,014 British NCOs and men, 233 native workers, 2,158 camels and 46 horses.[19] Wolseley had ridden out to see Stewart off and was greatly pleased by the formidable appearance of the Guards and Mounted Infantry. Riding with Kitchener at the head of the column was a group of seven locals from the town of Ambukol, who had been all but press-ganged into acting as scouts. Their headman was a son of 'the old King of Ambukol, dispossessed when the Turks [*sic*] first occupied the country'. The apparent reluctance with which they had undertaken their duties saw them surrounded by 'an escort of Mounted Infantry with their rifles unslung and ready for instant use, silently, but grimly hinting, that any attempt to abandon the column in the desert, or play false, would meet with immediate retribution'.[20]

Lieutenant Douglas Dawson of the Coldstream Guards was riding well forward of the main body and able to obtain a good idea of just how imposing the column looked from a distance.

From my position with the scouts in front of the column it was indeed a striking sight, and one not easily forgotten. The force looked at least ten times its real size, owing to the large space occupied by the camels; the grey coats, brown helmets, and red saddles gave a most picturesque effect, while the enormous mass moving over a . . . boundless plain, gave an idea of the infinite grandeur of nature compared with the puny efforts of man. Our faces were now turned towards the sandy plain, relieved here and there by sharp-cut hills in the distance; behind us lay the valley of the Nile, green fields and palm trees, beyond which rose the mountains, the other side of the river – that river which so many now saw for the last time.[21]

Jack Cameron watched the column depart and in his coverage of the event for the *Standard* went on to reflect on some of the vulnerabilities of a camel-borne brigade.

It was a strange sight to see the two thousand camels, with their necks stretching out like ostriches, and their four thousand pairs of long legs moving along in military array, until the rising dust first blended desert, men, and camels in one uniform grey hue, and finally hid them from the sight of those who remained in camp. Broad as was the face on which this strange column marched, it extended fully a mile in length, and would be an unwieldy body in case of an attack by the enemy. The Camel Corps and Mounted Infantry could form up quickly enough, but confusion would be likely to prevail among the baggage animals, for camels are the most obstinate of creatures, and object particularly to sudden and hurried movements. Their Somali [*sic* – Adeni] drivers, too, could scarcely be expected to be very cool or steady if suddenly assailed by a large body of yelling tribesmen.

In case of attack the Guards will form square echeloned on the left front of the column, the Mounted Infantry will do the same on the right rear. The column is, however, so long that their fire would hardly cover the entire line, unless the enemy were perceived approaching long enough before their attack to give time for the baggage camels to close up into a compact body.[22]

Cameron went on to muse how, for the first time in his experience, there was a wholesale absence of native friendlies marching beside the British. In Afghanistan and even at Suakin there had been local allies aplenty, but here in the Bayūda the British would be all alone save for a paltry handful of reluctant scouts. Right at the end of his piece Cameron described how Wolseley and the staff rode alongside the column for two or three miles, before at length bidding their comrades farewell and turning back for Korti. His penultimate sentence foreshadowed many of the difficulties ahead.

Short as had been the distance marched from camp it had been long enough to show that some at least of the camels had been badly loaded, for several were already falling out of line in order to have their burdens repacked.

General Stewart led on for two hours, before calling a supper halt from 5.00–7.00 p.m. Then, having doubled the frontage and halved the length of the baggage train in preparation for night marching,[23] he pushed the force on through a still and uneventful night, halting periodically to give the slower-moving baggage camels time to close up on the head of the column. At 8.00 the following morning the general at last initiated a 7-hour rest halt.[24] Thus far the caravan road had been tolerably good going and had remained readily discernible even by night.[25]

New Year's Eve: Gordon's Last Message

At around the same time as the men bound for Jakdul were throwing themselves down to sleep some thirty-four miles into the Bayūda, one of the ADCs brought Wolseley a telegram from Merowe reporting that a courier from General Gordon had arrived there the previous evening. The man had, it seemed, been entrusted with letters addressed to the C-in-C and was even now on his way downriver in a launch. Merowe was located about thirty-five miles upstream of Korti, so that the wait for Gordon's news was drawn out until noon. Wolseley passed some of the time by writing to Lady Louisa.

Last night messengers from Gordon carrying letters for me, reached Merawi . . . and I am as you may imagine anxiously expecting them. They say that Gordon has plenty of food to enable him to hold out, and told them to tell me I was not to divide my force. [This passage must refer to some gist of the message telegraphed ahead of the courier (in the singular), but in respect of Gordon's food stocks was quite incorrect.] If he gives me in his letters good reason why I should not operate as I had just made up my mind to do in two separate columns, each entirely independent of the other, I shall have to change all my plans. Gordon of course wants to keep at least some of our soldiers here all the year, so his advice may be biased by that wish.[26]

Wolseley's reference to Gordon manipulating the situation to suit some long-term political agenda was less than worthy, as Gordon's siege journal demonstrates that by this point his mind was preoccupied only by the betrayal visited upon him by the British government.

When at length the courier arrived and was brought into the headquarters, Wolseley recognized him as the same man he had sent to Khartoum from Dongola at the end of October.[27] The only physical message in his possession was a slip of paper about the size of a postage stamp, on one side of which was Gordon's gubernatorial seal. On the other was a tiny handwritten message which read, 'Khartoum all right. 14/12/84. C. G. Gordon.'[28] It was evidently not for this alone that the messenger had risked his life. Then the man began to utter the text of a carefully rehearsed oral message:

We are besieged on three sides: Omdurman, Halfiyeh and Hoggiali. Fighting goes on day and night. Enemy cannot take us except by starving us out. Do not scatter your troops, enemy are numerous. Bring plenty of troops if you can. We still hold Omdurman on the left bank and the fort on the right bank. Mahdi's people have thrown up earthworks within rifle shot of Omdurman. Mahdi lives out of gunshot. About four weeks ago Mahdi's people attacked that place and disabled one steamer. We disabled one of the Mahdi's guns. Three days after fight was renewed on the south, and the rebels were again driven back. Saleh Bey [a prominent Shā'iqī loyalist] and Slatin [the Austrian-born Mudir of Darfur] are chained in Mahdi's' camp.

Secret and Confidential. Our troops are suffering from lack of provisions. The food we still have is little, some grain and biscuit. We want you to come quickly. You should come by Metemmeh or Berber. Make by these two roads. Do not leave Berber in your rear. Keep enemy on your front, and when you take Berber send me word from Berber. Do this without letting rumours of your approach spread abroad. In Khartoum there are no butter, no dates, little meat. All food is very dear.[29]

This is the full text of the message as recorded in a telegram sent by Wolseley to Baring the same day. Although it is nowhere stated as fact, it is safe to assume that this represents a translation from Arabic conducted through an interpreter. The message had a deeply unsettling effect on Wolseley, whose first response, as recorded in his journal entry of that night, was to complain that his plans had been imperilled. The rather more awkward reality was that his thinking had been based all along on a gross underestimation of Muḥammad Aḥmad and the Mahdist movement, in consequence of which his plans had never been militarily sound to begin with.

The messenger brings me a long rambling message which I cannot depend on, saying I am to come very quickly, that I must have a large force as the enemy is very numerous &c. &c. He adds Khartoum can only be taken by starvation & that food is scarce. Altogether this is most unsatisfactory, & unsettles my plans without giving me any information which is worth having. The fellow was five days in Mahdi's camp . . . Slaten Bey [Rudolf Slatin] is there in chains – Husain Pasha Khalifa [Mudir of Berber] is there but free. All the people with Mahdi have their families & their cattle with them: his army covers an immense space of country: there is much sickness in Mahdi's camp, but the people there have enough to eat.[30]

By the time night fell, Wolseley was racked with uncertainty and went to bed, 'with a heavy heart – Oh God how heavy!'[31]

Sir Herbert Stewart, meanwhile, had resumed his march at 3.30 p.m. that afternoon, with sixty-four miles still go to go. To some the terrain did not seem unduly hostile:

We now marched through a beautiful country, and one very characteristic of the best part of the Bayuda Desert. Great spreading plains, covered with mimosa and scrub, succeeded one another, bounded by black rocky mountains, through the gorges of which we passed, only to emerge on fresh tracts of the same nature. Every now and then herds of gazelle could be seen galloping off, as they were disturbed by our cavalry scouts, who, at a considerable distance from the column, kept appearing on every bit of advantageous ground, and, with the well known dash and knowledge of this work for which the 19th Hussars are renowned, scoured the whole country both to the front and flanks. One could not help thinking, if only it were watered, what a country this would be; and indeed from its appearance in many places it is hard to understand the absence of water.[32]

Stewart halted for a supper break from 5.15–8.00 p.m. and, half an hour into his second night march, reached the wells at Hambok to find that there was only a limited quantity of muddy, white-coloured water to be had.[33] The column pushed on through the evening bound for the wells at Howeiyat, which it was hoped would prove more bountiful. Some of the officers were keeping a close eye on their watches and in due course announced the imminent arrival of *Anno Domini* 1885. The temptation to break into a chorus of 'Auld Lang Syne' proved irresistible. A miscellany of other popular songs followed, amongst them 'My Grandfather's Clock', a particular music-hall favourite of the period.[34] An hour into the New Year the column reached Howeiyat Wells, where the troops were permitted to bivouac for the rest of the night. Major Dorward's sappers were less fortunate than everybody else, as they were required to work until 3.00 a.m. setting up water pumps and troughs.[35] The column had covered seventeen miles since the last long halt and was now fifty-one miles forward of Korti.[36]

New Year's Day: Adapting the Plan

The army commander slept badly, got up at 4.00 a.m. and immediately woke his chief of staff to cancel the dawn departure for Merowe of a squadron of the 19th Hussars. With that he retired to his tent to ponder the implications of Gordon's message.[37] While we know little of the staff to-ing and fro-ing of New Year's Day, Wolseley's journal provides a good overview of its outcome. It is clear that Gordon's latest advice completely transformed the C-in-C's estimation of the Mahdīst threat. That Wolseley had been drawn into the timeless trap of despising his enemy was to some extent Gordon's fault, as many of his early despatches had displayed a strong tendency to belittle the Mahdī's hold over his followers, creating an impression of fragility which had no foundation in reality. It had not helped either that the siege had not been prosecuted particularly vigorously for the first few months, during which period by far the greater part of the rebel host had remained in Kordofan. Thus Gordon's early estimates of the enemy's strength had failed to encapsulate the Mahdīst movement's formidable military capacity.

The most important injunctions in Gordon's message were: come quickly because food is running out; bring plenty of troops because the enemy is numerous; keep the enemy in front and do not leave Berber in your rear. Wolseley's current plan complied only with the first of these injunctions and was in danger of positively flying in the face of the others. It is hard, even with the benefit of hindsight, to know what caused Gordon to set so much store by the enemy presence at Berber. The Amīr Muḥammad al-Khair 'Abd Allāh Khūjalī was an ardent and fiery Islamist, but in no sense a gifted military commander. Moreover it was doubtful if the local tribes, the 'Abābda, Barabra and Bisharin, could put more than 2,000–3,000 men in the field. Gordon might conceivably have been worried by the prospect of the Berberine rebels striking west against the British lines of communication across the Bayūda, albeit no such threat was ever to materialize.

At some point in his New Year's Day deliberations, Wolseley resolved to switch two-thirds of his infantry away from the river axis to the desert one. His journal entry of that evening is an important one, as it is the only place where this change of heart manifests itself.

All along I have been counting on an expression which occurs more than once in Gordon's letters, that the whole attack upon Khartoum would collapse if he had a few hundred determined soldiers upon whom he could depend. I have been basing my calculations on this view of the position & had therefore determined upon forcing my way into Khartoum with about 1500 of the finest men in our or any other army. Now this message from him tells me not to advance unless I am strong. I have therefore determined upon sending four battalions to Matemmeh across the desert, one to be the garrison of that place, the other three to go on with the Camel Corps, 19th Hussars and 10 guns to Khartoum. I shall have to hold the wells at Abu Klea, Gakdul and Hambok as well as Korti. So including Matemmeh & Korti I shall have three Battalions [sic] on this desert line of commns. leaving only two Battalions & detachments of Cavy., Artillery & R.E. for operations up the river to Abu Ahmed. This will be a safer plan of operation than that I had previously determined upon but it will take more time & prevent me perhaps from being in Khartoum as I had hoped to be with a fighting force on the 31st Jany., at latest. However, God is great, in Him is my trust & with his aid I shall yet be in Khartoum on or before that date. The new year has not opened brightly for me, but I don't believe things are nearly as bad as they look: Gordon's nerve cannot be fresh and vigorous after all he has gone through during the last eight months as they were when he & I last met.[38]

It might indeed have taken some additional time to bring up the infantry, but nothing like as much as sending them 400 miles by rowing boat in completely the wrong direction. Importantly this new scheme of manoeuvre would not have precluded a rapid advance by a leading echelon based on the Camel Corps. Since it preserved the potential to make best speed across the desert and avoided the unnecessary dissipation of combat power, this was undoubtedly a better plan than that which preceded it. We should note in passing Wolseley's reiteration of his target date and observe that he would later feel no compunction about damning Sir Charles Wilson for gaining Khartoum on 28 January.

While Wolseley was pondering his change of plan, Sir Herbert Stewart had resolved to press on from Howeiyat without delay. The wells had proved to be around twenty feet deep and despite the best efforts of the sappers, there was no practical means of watering such large numbers of animals quickly. The column was roused at 6.00, breakfasted, loaded up the camels and set off again at 8.00 a.m., this time with MICR leading and GCR bringing up the rear.[39] The first long halt of the day was from 1.00–3.30 p.m. Douglas Dawson recalled that, 'We were now on the edge of a vast plain stretching to our right as far as the eye could see, while on our left, at the distance of a mile or so, rose the line of black, barren-looking mountains that we were to follow the whole way to Gakdool.'[40] The next leg of the march lasted from mid-afternoon until dusk. The supper break ran from 6.30–8.00 p.m., at which latter point the moon rose, cueing another lengthy night march.[41]

Friday 2 January: The Death Knell of General Gordon

When Wolseley rose on Friday morning to meet with Buller and the rest of the staff, some unknown factor caused him to reverse his New Year's Day resolutions. By the time the cabal had broken up the C-in-C was no longer intent on mounting a more powerful thrust across the Bayūda, but instead had fixated on Gordon's injunction, 'Do not leave Berber in your rear.' Wolseley's answer to this particular conundrum was to keep the infantry on the boats as he had originally intended and mount a much slower-moving pincer movement against Muḥammad al-Khair. The Desert Column would be tasked to gain Metemmeh as before, but instead of immediately dashing south for Khartoum would secure a lodgement on the Nile and push an emissary ahead by steamer, in order to confer with Gordon and ascertain just how long he could hold out. Only when the emissary returned to Korti to make his report would Wolseley decide whether to launch Stewart to the north, to cooperate with Earle against Berber, or to the south, so as to attempt to reach Khartoum as quickly as possible. In an ideal world Gordon would declare that he could hold out for a good while yet, so that the relief of Khartoum could be effected by the River and Desert Columns advancing south from Metemmeh in concert. Earle's four battalions were to be committed to rowing all the way round the Great Bend after all. From being momentarily relevant, they had once again been consigned to oblivion. The key point, though, is that despatching an emissary from Metemmeh to Khartoum by steamer represented an entirely new and necessarily time-consuming phase of operations. It followed that the earliest date by which British troops could reach Khartoum in brigade strength would inevitably shift some considerable distance to the right: just how far to the right we will come to in due course.

These latest changes amounted to a truly remarkable piece of procrastination, as there was absolutely nothing to suggest that there was any likelihood of an emissary returning to report that everything in General Gordon's garden would remain rosy for some weeks to come. On the contrary, everything pointed to the fact that the worst-case scenario, famine in Khartoum, must already be afoot. Wolseley's journal entry for 2 January describes his new plan thus:

Another morning's study of the problem before me, going carefully into distances and dates, and Buller's calculations of the several problems I have set him, has caused me to fix upon the following plan of campaign. As I originally intended, I shall move all the mounted troops and the Battery of R.A. & provisions for them to Matemmeh & there create a post which I shall eventually garrison with a Battn. of Infry. This will enable me to communicate direct by steamer with Gordon & to arrange for our final advance upon Khartoum with him. At the same time Earle will advance upriver and punish Monassir tribe & then on to Abu Ahmed where I hope he may receive supplies direct from Korosko. He will leave a Battn. or half a Battalion at Abu Ahmed & then move to attack Berber in which operation I hope some of Gordon's steamers may be able to assist, the Naval Brigade manning them. Berber taken and a Battn. left there as a garrison, Earle to move on with all haste with three Battalions, the Egyptian Camel Corps & Egyptian Camel Battery & a Squadron of XIXth Hussars to join me at Matemmeh. The united force them to march for Khartoum. Of course our relief of Gordon will be thus greatly postponed, but this will enable me at any moment if Gordon sends to tell me he is in extremis, to push on with all the camel Regts to Khartoum. The risk would perhaps be great, but no risk would be too great under those circumstances . . . Baring asked me if I was confident of success: I replied yes, provided Gordon would hold out until my infantry going by river could reach Khartoum.[42]

It should be noted that Wolseley still makes allowance at this stage for the contingency of pushing through to Khartoum with the Desert Column only, should news come in at any point that Khartoum was at the end of its tether. The rest of the journal entry for that day goes on to invoke divine intervention, as well it might, but concludes with the truly remarkable statement, 'I still feel that I shall be in Khartoum before the end of the month.' Wolseley's faith, it would seem, was stronger than his reason.

The Seizure of Jakdul Wells

The final leg of Sir Herbert Stewart's march to Jakdul Wells was completed at 7.00 a.m. on 2 January. The only excitement to speak of had occurred in the early hours of that morning. Not that long after midnight the column had been brought to a halt to allow a party of 19th Hussars to investigate a distant campfire. They returned half an hour later to report that they had surprised and scattered a small caravan carrying a consignment of dates. At about 2.00 a.m. Major Kitchener, Major Thomas Phipps one of the wing commanders in MICR, and B Company, MICR, under Captain Henry Walsh were detached from the column to go and investigate the wells at Abu Halfa, some three or four miles north-east of Stewart's line of march.[43]

The rest of the ninety-eight-mile journey had been in large part uneventful, although there had been periodic encounters with small parties of travellers and nomads. Most had been quick to disappear over the horizon the moment they clapped eyes on the great mirage-like phalanx moving across the desert towards them. From time to time, though, a handful of more curious souls had hung around for a closer look, only to be rounded up and herded in by hard-riding hussars. Kitchener's questioning had failed to elicit any information of particular intelligence value. Before being sent on their way the detainees had been encouraged to come in again in a few days' time with whatever cattle and goats they were prepared to sell.

An exception was made in the case of a notorious robber called Ali Loda,[44] who had been found by the hussars skulking in long grass and was immediately recognized by the knot of local guides.[45] Bennet Burleigh described him as, 'a big burly Berbereen, with a pleasant round face and bushy, curly black hair'.[46] Pleasant looking or not, he was blackguard enough for the Ambukol men to want to execute him on the spot. He owed his life to Stewart and Kitchener, who felt sure he would know the desert like the back of his hand and thus make an invaluable guide. Ten minutes later the habitually half-naked Mrs Loda had also been brought in by one of the hussars. One of the GCR officers described her as 'a decidedly handsome young woman', although his sketch of the camel-borne family Loda would hint at a tinge of irony.[47] Faced with little alternative but to enlist in the service of the British, the Lodas persuaded their captors to escort them to a nearby grass hut to collect their possessions. These consisted of a camel, a sack of corn, some cooking pots and a babe in arms.[48] Thus did the sublimely mobile family Loda up sticks to enter the service of the Queen Empress.

The troops had been in good heart throughout the march and so far seemed to be paying all due care and attention to the loading of the baggage camels. Nothing was more likely to induce unnecessary losses than the sort of carelessness that could result in an animal's flanks being rubbed raw to the ribcage. It was precisely to avoid such difficulties that local drivers tended to break boxed stores open and transfer the contents into baggage nets. But this was just one aspect of camel management for which the British had come ill-prepared; cases of bully beef, hardtack biscuit and Martini ammunition were all sharp corners, while netting and decent load-carrying pack-saddles were in extremely short supply. In consequence improvisation became the order of the day. The necessity to take particular care over loading and then remain constantly alert for slipped loads was the principal reason why marching by night did not necessarily represent the best of ideas: it was not something the Arabs did. Stewart had set what was a brisk pace for heavily laden baggage camels, covering 98 miles in 63 hours and 45 minutes, of which some 32 hours and 45 minutes, roughly half the total journey time, had been spent on the move. Douglas Dawson noted that the last 38½ miles of the journey had been completed in 14 hours.[49] Fourteen animals had been driven into the ground and had been destroyed, while another seventeen had been turned loose to die or recover. A handful of the latter would be rounded up on the return journey to be gently coaxed back to Korti.[50]

Stewart had no intention of loitering at Jakdul Wells a moment longer than was necessary and directed his staff to pass the word that the return march to Korti would begin not long after sunset. The first priority was to get the slow process of watering more than 2,000 camels under way. The gorge in which the three main reservoirs were located was anything up to 300 feet deep and was commanded at a distance by a range of black hills. It lay some 2¼ miles north of the caravan road, at the head of a steep-sided cul-de-sac of high ground, which some officers described as a 'natural amphitheatre'. The reservoirs were positioned one above another in the bed of a watercourse which drained the distant hills down through the gorge to the plain. The two upper pools could only be reached by scrambling up the rocks which, though inconvenient, at least precluded their being fouled by animals. The lower pool was positioned amongst the rocks in such a way that only a small number of animals could be watered at one time. This might suffice for passing caravans, but fell a long way short of General Stewart's requirements. The first job for Major Dorward and his sappers, therefore, was to pump water down into the low ground so that a significant number of animals could be watered simultaneously. This would take time and ingenuity, so that for the present the tortuous business of watering the animals by the handful would have to suffice.

The lowest and largest pool was 85 feet long by 55 feet wide and about 12 feet deep. Dorward calculated that it held 420,000 gallons of water, but judged that passing caravans and flocks had rendered it all but unfit for human consumption. This pool he reserved for watering the animals and washing. The middle pool was 50 feet long by 16 feet wide, but only 6 feet deep. This gave it a capacity of around 34,970 gallons. The upper pool was long and narrow, some 85 feet by 15, but at something around 12½ feet deep was estimated to hold 84,080 gallons. Dorward pronounced himself content that the middle and upper pools contained good clean drinking water with a combined capacity of 119,050 gallons. There were three much smaller pools nearby which the staff designated as 'Gazelle', 'Jackal' and 'Pothole', and which together contained an additional 10,432 gallons of drinking water.[51] Though Dorward did not yet know it, there was in fact a fourth and a fifth pool further up the watercourse, with a combined capacity more than 2½ times as great as that of the second and third.

The business of watering the camels and unloading the baggage had been under way for about three hours when, at about 11.00 a.m., B Company, MICR, rode in from Abu Halfā with a handful of prisoners.[52] Unlike the temporary detainees of the past few days, these men were clad in the so-called 'Mahdī's uniform': the Nile Expedition had at last made contact with the enemy and taken its first prisoners of war. It transpired that Walsh and his men had surprised about twenty Arabs encamped at Abu Halfā and in the ensuing hue and cry had succeeded in rounding up four men and eleven camels. Whether the forlorn quartet were quite the fervent supporters of Muḥammad Aḥmad that the British imagined them to be is a moot point; it is known that the fanatic hard-core in Metemmeh required everybody else in the town to dress as a Mahdīst whether they liked it or not.

Primary source references from the Nile Campaign to the 'Mahdī's' uniform' are commonly and mistakenly taken to refer to the symmetrically patched dervish *jibbeh*, but these were mass-produced items rolled out in Omdurman during the reign of the Khalīfa 'Abd Allāhi, the Mahdī's right-hand man and successor, and were not in widespread use before the fall of Khartoum. In fact the patching of clothes had always been prevalent amongst the Kordofani poor, but had been declared by the Mahdī to betoken godliness and humility. Once El Obeid had fallen and the rebel movement had a capital of its own, the *amīrs* had taken to easy living and had been quick to adopt ornate and symmetrically patched *jibbehs* of the later 'dervish' pattern.[53] The ordinary *anṣār*, however, continued patching their clothes much as before, out of necessity. Hence the patches of the unwashed were not necessarily rectangular, cut from the same piece of cloth or positioned with any regard to the dictats of Mahdīst high-fashion or the rules of symmetry. Many Kordofanis, indeed, chose not to wear *jibbehs*, but preferred to wrap a length of white cotton around the waist like a skirt or kilt. Others wore the *tobe*, a much longer cotton wrap worn over one shoulder, not unlike a half-length Roman toga.[54]

Contemporary sketches show that the riparian rebels north of Khartoum, who had not yet come into contact with the Kordofan-based mainstream of the movement, had adopted an entirely different 'uniform'. Captain Willoughby Verner, an able and perceptive Rifle Brigade officer, was not the only artistically gifted eyewitness to capture their mode of dress in his sketches, but is certainly to the forefront of those who did. Verner was one of the officers who had originally been tasked with supervising the movement of a consignment of whalers as far as Wādī Halfā. His primary task fulfilled, he then, as a graduate of the Staff College, found himself temporarily attached to General Earle's personal staff as he dashed back and forth chivvying the whaler-borne battalions upriver. Earle and his band of helpers only reached Korti on New Year's Day, at which point Verner was transferred by Buller to the Intelligence Department under Sir Charles Wilson.[55] Verner enjoyed drawing, was not without talent and fortunately never went anywhere without his sketchbook. Not long after he returned home, he published a volume called *Sketches in the Soudan*. Not only do his watercolours and drawings amount to one of the most important visual sources for the campaign, but they are also accompanied by facing-page captions incorporating facts and figures which are not to be found anywhere else in the sources. The Mahdīst 'uniform' portrayed by Verner and others was based on a white knee-length garment, cut much after the fashion of a modern-day ladies' cocktail-party dress. It could be short-sleeved or sleeveless and was typically decorated at the round collar and bottom hem with a trim of coloured rhomboid shapes or triangles. Some of the British participants took to referring to this as a 'vandyke' trim, parodying its passing resemblance to the eccentric lace collars portrayed in the works of the seventeenth-century master. Usually there was also a piece of coloured cloth sewn onto the left breast, which appears more often than not to have been a rhomboid shape. Vandyke trims were typically black, red, blue or green.[56]

According to Colvile's official history the prisoners captured at Abu Halfā were emissaries from the Mahdī, intent upon crossing the desert to stir up one of the more troublesome Dongolāwī shaikhs. Colvile would appear to have derived this information from a report sent by Stewart to Wolseley on 4 January, in which the shaikh is specifically named as 'Sheikh Wad Kinkain'.[57] One of the best-known participant accounts of the Nile Expedition, Count Edward Gleichen's *With the Camel Corps up the Nile*, would tend to suggest that the 'emissaries' turned out not to be the hardened *agents provocateurs* portrayed by Colvile. Later a divisional commander in the Great War, but at the time a young lieutenant in No. 1 (Grenadier Guards) Company, GCR, Gleichen recounts that the four captured 'emissaries' tore off the Mahdī's uniform, stamped it underfoot and spat on it.[58] They were detained nonetheless, and subsequently taken back to Korti for further questioning. As we shall see shortly, they were interrogated by Verner, whose diary would tend to support Gleichen's interpretation rather than Colvile's.

Not counting Major Kitchener and his band of scouts, Colonel Boscawen would have a total of 437 officers and men available to secure the wells. His command included six hussars to act as scouts, 21 & 360 from GCR, 2 & 25 from 26 Field Company, including Dorward and his number two, Lieutenant Henry Lawson, and some twenty-two members of the medical staff.[59] Quite how many of the latter were doctors is not known. Having secured himself decent lodgings in a cave, Kitchener intended to spend the next few days prowling the desert in the direction of Metemmeh. All but ten of the GCR riding camels would be returning to Korti with the convoy, in order that 1st Royal Sussex could be mounted for the main body move to come.

Having unloaded the stores, watered the camels and snatched a bite to eat, Stewart was on the move again by 8.00 p.m. that evening, although he was to cover only four miles before coming to a long halt. At 3.45 on the morning of 3 January the column set off again. Although there were ninety-minute halts for breakfast, lunch and dinner, it marched all day and through the evening, until at 1.00 a.m. on the 4th it reached Howeiyat Wells and bivouacked for the rest of the night.

After a few hours' rest Stewart resumed his march at 7.00 a.m. and reached Hambok about two hours later.[60] Captain Richard Fetherstonhaugh,[61] the officer commanding C (Rifles) Company, MICR, was summoned to see the general, only to be told that he would be staying behind to garrison the wells with part of his company when the rest of the column moved off.[62] He could expect to be relieved when the main body returned in a few days' time, but in the interim was to do what he could to improve the water supply. Fetherstonhaugh's party consisted of four other officers, including a doctor, and fifty-eight NCOs and men.[63] The other company officers were Captain the Hon. Henry Hardinge of 3rd Rifle Brigade ('Punch' Hardinge to his friends),[64] Lieutenant Max Sherston of 2nd Rifle Brigade and Lieutenant W. P. 'Johnny' Campbell of 1st KRRC.[65] As the average rank and file strength of sub-units in MICR was around eighty-five and only fifty-eight men were left behind, it seems likely that only three of C Company's four sections remained at Hambok. The detachment retained only twenty-two camels, which means that there must have been an additional forty riderless animals to go back to Korti.[66] This is almost certainly why Lieutenant Archie Miles of 2nd KRRC, the company's only remaining officer, would appear not to have been left behind with everybody else. If the 2nd KRRC men were indeed involved in leading the riderless camels back to camp, then they were not the only ones, as Percy Marling makes a clear-cut reference to the fact that the 3rd KRRC section in A Company also had charge of some C Company camels.[67]

While everybody else was settling down to rest or brew tea, Stewart sat down and wrote a report describing his progress to date. The message went away in the care of Captain Lord Cochrane of No. 1 Company, HCR, at about noon, an hour or so before the column resumed its march. He was accompanied by Lieutenant the Hon. George Bryan, 10th Hussars, a LCR officer who had been obliged to seek out his regimental colleague, Lord Airlie, to swap his camel for the brigade-major's pony. The escorting cavalry detail consisted of Lieutenant Edward Craven and two privates.[68] It was about fifty miles back to the Nile, but the party was tolerably well mounted and covered the distance in about eight hours.[69] Embarrassingly for Bryan, Airlie's pony expired not long after completing the journey.[70]

Cochrane arrived at the straw hut which served as the C-in-C's mess not long after Wolseley and his staff had finished dinner. One of the aides was sent scurrying away to fetch Buller, so that he too could listen to the news of Stewart's progress. Alex Macdonald, the war correspondent, happened to be present as a dinner guest.[71] Quite how Lord Wolseley imagined that the Mahdī would get to read the *Western Morning News* over the course of the coming week is not altogether clear, but he felt the need nonetheless to usher Cochrane into the privacy of his tent before allowing him to proceed with his report. When a little later that evening Wolseley came to write up his journal, he remarked of Stewart's operation, 'all this is very satisfactory'. He also noted the arrival of two interesting telegrams from London. The first was anonymous and offered the eminently sensible advice, 'Don't despise your enemy, go strong into desert.'

This was not merely good advice but was also very opportune, as the failure to mount a single-phase crossing of the Bayūda had already actively compromised British intent. A letter written by Muḥammad al-Khair the same day, 4 January, makes it clear that news of Stewart's advance had already reached both Berber and Metemmeh. It is certain therefore that well mounted couriers were dashing south for Omdurman to impart the intelligence to the Mahdīst high command. The object of Muḥammad al-Khair's letter was to get Berberine fighters moving towards Metemmeh without delay, in response to an urgent appeal for assistance from the Amīr 'Ali-wad-Saad. Theologian or not, Muḥammad al-Khair also had some good military advice to offer: 'Warn all your followers to take their water-skins, their leathern sacks and food for the road; for if you meet the enemies of God, it will be in the desert and not in houses.'[72]

The second and rather more important telegram from London had originated with the Cabinet and like the first was also referred to in the C-in-C's journal:

Also from the Govt. in answer to a question I put to them as to the propriety of my attempting to relief Gordon with an insufficient force in the event of his being in extremis. They say such a risk should not be entertained as any reverse to my Force would be a greater disaster than the fall of Khartoum & the capture of Gordon by the Mahdi.[73]

The inference, nay governmental direction, was clear. Wolseley was not to put hundreds of lives unreasonably at risk merely to save one general officer. The notion that thousands of other lives were also at risk in the embattled Sudanese capital does not seem to have troubled the Cabinet unduly. How much influence this clarification of the governmental position may have had on Wolseley's prosecution of the campaign is a moot point: on the face of it none of the plans hatched two days earlier seem to have changed. What this second telegram seems to have done, however, was relegate a dash by the Desert Column from a strong possibility to an option of last resort. We will examine this premise further, when we come to consider Wolseley's orders for the advance on Metemmeh.

At noon the following day, Monday 5 January, Lord Wolseley rode three miles into the desert with Buller and a knot of aides and staff officers to see Stewart in. He was in an excellent mood and greeted the return of his favourite subordinate with a shower of compliments.[74] The three generals then took station for the column to 'march past' as it made its way into camp. It did so to the musical accompaniment of MICR's regimental march, sounded from the head of the column by the Mounted Infantry buglers.[75] The tune would have been instantly recognizable as 'The Campbells are Coming', although as far as the MICR wags were concerned the operative word was not 'Campbells' but 'camels'. When Major Gough rode past at the head of the regiment, Wolseley is said to have remarked to him that MICR was the finest body of men he had ever seen and would assuredly be able to march from one end of Africa to the other.[76] The 196-mile round trip had been effected in the end with the loss of thirty-one camels out of 2,195.[77] If the number of dead animals was not a particular cause of concern, it was apparent that the succession of long night marches had taken a severe physical toll of many, if not most, of the remainder. Some already had serious sores on their backs and flanks, while others were very obviously developing them.[78] All but the very strongest animals were exhausted. Yet come what may they would all be going back into the Bayūda inside a matter of three days, for a repeat performance in which they would see precious little water or food. Hence it was certain that any loss of condition or chronic fatigue occasioned by the first journey would be magnified many times over by the rigours of the second.

Major Alfred Turner RA, only recently assigned to the Intelligence Department, witnessed Stewart's return.

> I rode out to meet him with Lord Wolseley, Sir Redvers Buller and others, and a most depressing sight was offered to our eyes. I was told that the camels were in first rate condition a few days before, when the force left Korti on 30th December. A forced march of a hundred miles had been made to Gakdul, which was reached early on 2nd January. The column left that place the same evening, and reached Korti on 5th January – that is to say, two hundred miles in less than 6 days. There is no animal living which can endure so much and last so well as the camel, but he is exceedingly delicate, and needs expert care. His pluck is great, and he will go till he drops to rise no more. The camels were handed over to our men, who were quite ignorant as to how they should be treated; and this they did in the last way in which it should have been done. I was actually told myself, by a Staff officer to whom I said I watered my camels twice daily, that a camel only needed water every three days – the fact being that a camel will survive without water, under press of circumstances, for that time.
>
> I am sorry to say I fear that the unfortunate animals were treated under the regime propounded to me, and that large numbers died of thirst. Napoleon managed his camel corps much more sagaciously. His camels were left in charge of their Arabs, and the French soldier was carried as a burden, having nothing to do with the animal except when on his back.
>
> The camels we met were drooping and dead-beat, dragging themselves along with manifest difficulty – every now and then one falling to rise no more, while as far as the eye could reach, one saw along the track of the column ominous looking heaps, soared over by foul vultures, the number of which were increased every moment by others . . . Nearly all the transport had been given to this force – the advanced portion of the desert column – and it was but too clear that it had suffered irreparable damage, if not destruction, owing to this forced march.
>
> Lord Wolseley said to Sir Redvers Buller, alluding to the seizure of the Gakdul wells and his rapidity, that Herbert Stewart had done splendidly. Upon which Buller replied, in his blunt straight way, something about deserving a court martial for destroying the transport of the army. There was much to be said in favour of a rapid march to Gakdul, in order to

seize the wells; but once seized, there was no reason whatever for making an equally forced march back to Korti, as there were none of the enemy within appreciable distance.[79]

Turner's account offers an invaluable insight into the consequences of not resting the animals properly and failing to ensure that they were watered and fed at more realistic intervals. It is certain, given the logistic shortfalls in play, that they had also been overloaded. Turner's testimony would argue that Stewart's movement, which in itself was a preliminary operation, should have been preceded by a much more low-key movement to secure and improve the wells at Hambok and Howeiyat, in order that large numbers of camels could be watered tolerably quickly whilst in transit. A second alternative would have been to feed troops and supplies forward in smaller convoys from an earlier start date. Since Dorward's detachment of 26 Field Company had arrived at Korti as early as 10 December,[80] an operation to improve the wells could have been mounted without prejudice to Stewart's 30 December departure (although Dorward was ill-provided with water pumps, another significant but avoidable failure in staff-work). Buller's reaction to the state of the baggage train is genuinely illuminating and stands in stark contrast to the very brief entry in Wolseley's journal for that evening which reads, 'I rode out to meet Herbert Stewart's column which marched back in very good order. Charlie Beresford arrived.'[81] In order to be certain that Turner's version of events represents the more accurate portrayal, we should also note the following passage in Colvile's *Official History*:

This first march . . . at the beginning of which the animals were comparatively fresh . . . had told, however, very severely on the camels generally. Most of them had been marching for a long time and were in low condition. Many returned to Korti with large sores and were incapacitated for service for the remainder of the campaign.[82]

There is, then, no reason to doubt the authenticity of Buller's irritated response to Wolseley's acclamation of Stewart. Having watched the convoy in a furious Buller probably derived some much-needed cheer from the arrival of his old Wādī Halfā mess-mate, 'Charlie B'.

Having initially been left downriver to supervise the passage of the Second Cataract, Captain Lord Charles Beresford RN was now to assume command of the newly authorized Naval Brigade. 'Charlie' was the second of five sons born to the 4th Marquess of Waterford. The family estate was at Curraghmore, County Waterford, and embraced the best part of 100,000 acres. Three of the Beresford brothers had joined the Army, one of whom, William, had won the Victoria Cross in Zululand. Charlie, though, had joined the Royal Navy at the tender age of thirteen and had been in the service since 1859. In the Victorian era there was no bar on serving officers standing for parliament and in 1874 Beresford became the member for Waterford. As a member of the Anglo-Irish ruling elite he was squarely aligned with Disraeli and the Tories. He became an ADC and close friend of the Prince of Wales at about the same time. Beresford's reputation as something of a rake guaranteed that the Queen Empress would disapprove of his inclusion amongst her son and heir's circle of confidants. In truth he was just one more aristocratic bon viveur amongst a generally badly behaved bunch. From time to time he also made himself unpopular at the Admiralty by presuming to make speeches in the House on naval affairs. He retained his seat, nonetheless, for the best part of six years. In 1882 he commanded HMS *Condor* during the Bombardment of Alexandria. Famously he had steered his ship inshore to engage a troublesome battery called Fort Marabout at very close range, eliciting the signal 'Well done *Condor*' from Admiral Sir Beauchamp Seymour aboard the flagship. In the immediate aftermath of the action, Beresford was appointed as the provost-marshal ashore and played a prominent role in restoring order to the city.[83] Now thirty-nine years of age, he had been appointed to Wolseley's staff at the particular request of the Prince of Wales. Unlike Stanley Clarke, however, Beresford was a man with a famous fighting record. Together with his blue blood and winning ways, this sufficed to gain him ready admission to the Ring's inner circle. In short Charlie Beresford was both a naval hero and fun to have around. Writing in his journal on 8 January, Wolseley described him as 'a really first-rate man all round'.[84] Given that two of the most important founding fathers of military intelligence, Wilson and Brackenbury, were serving alongside Beresford at this juncture, it is worth digressing momentarily to observe that on his return from the Sudan he would become one of the leading advocates for a Naval Intelligence Department.

It was 5.30 p.m. before Lieutenant Percy Marling finished his work for the day and retired to his tent, intent on catching up on a week's worth of lost sleep. Not long afterwards Lieutenant Lord Freddy Fitzgerald KRRC, a brother of the Duke of Leinster and Buller's ADC, called by to invite him to dine with the chief of staff. Marling treated himself to a much-needed bath and at the appointed hour made his way to the general's tent. He arrived to find that his CO, Major Gough, was also a guest. Champagne was in plentiful supply, as was always the case whenever Buller took the field, and kept flowing over the course of what turned out to be a lengthy repast. 'Fizz *ad lib* and about seven courses,' Marling recorded in his diary.[85]

Final Preparations for the Bayūda Crossing

There were just a little over seventy-two hours intervening between Stewart's return to Korti and the second march of the Desert Column at 3.00 p.m. on Thursday 8 January. It was a period of great bustle and rising tension. Wolseley was becoming increasingly irritated by a running exchange of telegrams with Lord Hartington over whether or not a second Suakin expedition could possibly help. He convinced himself that somebody in London was whispering against the conduct of the campaign and frightening the Secretary of State for War, when in fact sending a concurrent expedition to crush Osman Digna and the Hadendawa was no more than an eminently sensible piece of strategic thinking. Wolseley continued to obstruct the proposal, stating that he was confident of success and implying that such an expedition would be no more than an expensive luxury.[86]

A total of seven prisoners had been brought in with Stewart's column, four of whom were dressed in vandyke-trimmed *jibbehs*. The intelligence staff interviewed them at length over the ensuing forty-eight hours. Captain Willoughby Verner was one of their principal interrogators and noted, 'They of course lied like true "Believers", but one of the seven, a lad, split on them, and by a little judicial pressure, his brother also came to a more sensible frame of mind.' It was established that they hailed from the Metemmeh area, were members of the Awadiyeh tribe and were engaged in nothing more sinister than transporting dates to the Mahdi's camp at Omdurman. On the second day of questioning Verner pressed the more co-operative members of the group to talk about Metemmeh. They described 'a strongly built town of considerable size', which they said stood several hundred yards from the river at this time of year. Verner also gleaned that there were two or three mountain guns in the town and about 2,000 fighting men, although a lower estimate of around 1,200 was also bandied about. The guns, said the prisoners, had been brought down from Berber to protect the town from Gordon's steamers, which it appeared were still operating north of the Sixth Cataract.[87]

Even after Sir Herbert Stewart's first journey there was still a large quantity of commissariat stores to be ferried out to Jakdul. It was arranged that Colonel Stanley Clarke would march out at sunset on 7 January with a second thousand-camel convoy. Of these, 100 animals were laden with Martini ammunition, 80 with medical stores and 30 with artillery stores. The remainder carried rations. With the Guards already out in the desert, the escort could be much lighter and would consist of the three regimental detachments of LCR which had so far come up to Korti,[88] a total of 10 officers and 106 NCOs and men.[89] This time Clarke was his own master but, without Stewart and his brigade staff scurrying about to make sure that everything was just so, he made a hash of his preparations and attracted the C-in-C's opprobrium:

Nothing could be worse managed: he had had the advantage of being with the previous convoy and seeing what a well conducted convoy should be like & how it should be managed, but it was of no use to him. His heart was in Marlborough House or some Court circle. Any old woman who shines in such society would have done quite as well as he did. This is the first & it shall be the last time that he follows my fortunes.[90]

Alex Macdonald learned of the convoy's imminent departure only that morning and made a hasty decision to leave for Jakdul with Clarke. Having readied himself in good time for 1.00 p.m., he was then notified that there would be a two-hour delay while the loading of the baggage camels was completed. With nothing much else to do, Macdonald walked through that part of the camp where the transport was being readied and found the scene 'anything but assuring'. His narrative confirms that there were bigger problems in play than can reasonably be attributed to the hapless Colonel Clarke alone.

'Confusion worse confounded' seemed to prevail, and from all I saw and heard, I could not but feel painfully convinced that this contemplated dash across the desert had never been thought through as a possible contingency in the expedition . . .

In the scramble and hurry I witnessed in getting the convoy ready, it was painfully evident to me then, and more so now, when I look back on all that subsequently occurred, either that this forethought in planning the expedition had not been duly exercised, or, as appears to me to be more likely, that if it had been the details decided upon had been most inefficiently carried out. Some of the prime necessities for such a dash across the desert as this was to be, were wanting when it came to be undertaken. For example, we had plenty of riding-saddles made for the expedition at the arsenal in Cairo, although much less cumbersome and much better ones could have been manufactured in England, and in less time. The question of pack-saddles, however, and their lashings became a very serious one when the troops reached Korti. Attempts were made to increase the small supply in hand by purchase from the natives, and even by manufacturing them ourselves on the spot. The deficiency in rope lashings had to be made good by native manufacture. Nor were the saddles, either bought or manufactured, very suitable for the transport of British stores, contained in wooden and tin cases, as the sore backs of the pack camels plainly showed, as well as the scores of their dead carcases scattered along the line of our march.[91]

In the event it was well past 5.00 p.m. before the convoy finally got under way. By the time the tail of the procession had covered the short distance from the picturesque camp beside the Nile to gain the desert plateau to its south, it was just about dark and time to make a supper-halt until such time as the moon rose and the march could be resumed. Some of the LCR officers were heard to remark that they might just as well ride back to camp for supper. All in all it had not been a good day for CO LCR.

Wolseley's Orders

By the time Clarke went stumbling into the desert, Wolseley had already completed his written orders for Sir Herbert Stewart, Sir Charles Wilson and Lord Charles Beresford, each of whom had a vital role to play in the next phase of operations, the first as the commander, the second as the newly nominated special emissary to General Gordon and the third as the commodore of a flotilla upon which he had not yet clapped eyes. The precise nature of their orders is vital to any objective assessment of Wolseley's management of the campaign, and in gauging whether or not any of his subordinates failed him at the tactical level as he was later to assert. On 6 January[92] he wrote to Sir Herbert Stewart as follows:

On the 8th you will arrange to start yourself with the following force:

>Half Battery Royal Artillery
>1 Squadron 19th Hussars
>Heavy Camel Regiment
>Mounted Infantry Camel Regiment

> Headquarters and 400 all ranks, Sussex Regiment
> 1 Company, 50 men, Essex Regiment
> All the Naval Brigade now here
> 2 Sections Bearer Company
> 1 Section Moveable Field-hospital
> As many transport camels carrying supply as can be provided

Of this force, you will leave the 50 Essex at El Howeiya, and take on the mounted infantry now there. After such rest as your animals require [at Jakdul], you will proceed to Matemmeh with the following force:

> 1 Squadron 19th Hussars
> 3 Guns Royal Artillery
> Guards Camel Regiment
> Heavy Camel Regiment
> Mounted Infantry Camel Regiment
> 250 Men Sussex Regiment
> Naval Brigade
> Detachment Royal Engineers

and a convoy taking eight day's supply for the force, 25,000 rations for the post at Matemmeh, and 3,000 rations for a post to be established at Abu Klea, as hereafter ordered; 400 boxes small-arms ammunition, 1 section if possible, 2 sections, Moveable Field-hospital; 2 sections Bearer Company.

On reaching Abu Klea you will establish a post there garrisoned by from 50 to 100 men, Sussex Regiment, as the nature of the ground may require, 300 rounds per man, and 3,000 rations.

You will then advance on Matemmeh, which you will attack and occupy. For this it may be advisable to laager your convoy at the wells of Shebakat.

Having occupied Matemmeh, you will leave there the Guards Camel Regiment, the detachment Sussex Regiment, the Naval Brigade, detachment Royal Engineers, and three guns Royal Artillery, 25,000 rations, and 300 rounds small-arm ammunition per rifle; and return with the convoy to Jakdul.

You will give strict orders to all officers commanding posts that a cordon is to be established round their several posts, within which no Arabs may be allowed to come.

You will post at all stations a detachment of Mounted Infantry as express riders. For the present it is not advisable that less than four men should be sent with a message. Arrangements should be made to keep a supply of water in each post.

You will be particular to use every endeavour to keep me as well and as quickly informed of your movements as possible. On your return to Jakdul you will continue to forward stores by convoy to Matemmeh.

It may be necessary for you to leave Jakdul with more camels than you leave Korti with, in that case you will take camels from Colonel Clarke's convoy.

Colonel Sir C. Wilson, DAG, and Captain Verner, DAAG, will accompany you for intelligence duties. Sir C. Wilson has been directed to show you his instructions. He will be in command of Matemmeh when you leave.[93]

It will be observed that in accordance with the 4 January entry in the War Diary of the Desert Column, we left C Company, MICR, at Hambok, but that Wolseley's orders refer to recovering the Mounted Infantry detachment from Howeiyat. Stewart's report on his second march to Jakdul makes it clear that it was indeed from the latter location that he recovered the mounted infantry.[94] On the face of it, then, there would appear to be an anomaly in play here. Stewart's report describing his first march to Jakdul, the despatch ridden in by Lord Cochrane, was written from Hambok, makes no mention of anybody being left at Howeiyat, and goes on to say, 'A post will be established for the improvement of the water supply *here* . . .'[95] What had happened in fact, as is made rather clearer by Macdonald's *Too Late for Gordon and Khartoum*[96] and Willoughby Verner's *Diary*,[97] is that Fetherstonhaugh had originally been detached from the column at Hambok but remained there only until 9 January, when Clarke's second convoy passed through. Having been unable to effect any marked improvement in the water supply, Fetherstonhaugh had come to the conclusion that it was about to fail and would no longer suffice to sustain the needs of C Company, let alone the rest of the brigade. Accordingly he sought and obtained Clarke's permission to accompany his convoy as far as Howeiyat Wells and await the main body there. Since he had only twenty-two riding camels, forty of his men must either have marched on foot or have been temporarily mounted aboard baggage camels. It is not inconceivable that there had been some prior discussion of just such a contingency before Stewart and Fetherstonhaugh parted company at Hambok, but when Wolseley wrote the orders for the Desert Column on 7 January, there would not appear to have been any mounted infantrymen at Howeiyat.

Much more importantly it will also be observed that Stewart's orders make no reference to despatching Sir Charles Wilson to Khartoum aboard Gordon's steamers, stating rather that he was to be left in command of Metemmeh. Clearly this must have been subject to oral amendment not long after the ink had dried. Wilson's orders were written on 7 January, were read to him during the course of the day and handed to him the following morning. The original idea of communicating with Gordon in advance of relieving Khartoum dated from 2 January and hence was only a few days old at this stage. As Wolseley prepared Stewart's orders on 6 January, he must have selected Wilson as the most appropriate emissary either that evening or early the following morning. Sir Charles had always been the ideal choice, since he was not only one of the most senior officers available to Wolseley, but was also a personal friend of Gordon. It was the news that Colonel Fred Burnaby was now within striking distance of Korti that served to free up Wilson in the role of emissary. Although Burnaby was unlikely to arrive in time for the Desert Column's departure, he could give chase and in all likelihood catch up with Stewart before he pressed on from Jakdul Wells. Burnaby was not only an experienced regimental officer, but was renowned as a great warrior; Wilson by contrast was somewhat condescendingly regarded as a map-maker and information-gatherer, though in truth there was much more to him than that. Nonetheless there was no question in Wolseley's mind which of them would make the better deputy to Stewart. Ultimately neither candidate could be formally appointed to the role, Wilson by dint of his important primary role as chief of intelligence, and Burnaby because he was not even supposed to be in the Sudan. The new arrangement was that Burnaby would become the commandant of Metemmeh, while Wilson steamed up the Nile to see Gordon. The orders issued to Sir Charles ran as follows:

Camp, Korti

You will accompany the column under the command of Brigadier-General Sir Herbert Stewart, K.C.B., which will leave Korti tomorrow for Matammeh. Your intimate knowledge of Soudan affairs will enable you to be of great use to him during his operations away from these headquarters.

You will endeavour to enter into friendly relations with the Hassaniyeh tribe, and to induce them if possible to carry supplies for us across the desert, and to sell us sheep, cattle, etc.

As soon as Matammeh is in our occupation, Sir H. Stewart will dispatch a messenger to Korti with an account of his march, etc; and you will be good enough to send me by same opportunity all political information you may have obtained, all news of General Gordon, the so-called Mahdi, etc.

I am sending Captain Lord Charles Beresford R.N., with a small party of seamen, to accompany Sir H. Stewart to Matammeh, where, if there are any steamers, Lord Charles Beresford will take possession of one or two of them, as he may think best. Any Egyptian (fellaheen) soldiers on them can be converted into camel-drivers and come back here with unloaded camels.

As soon as Lord Charles Beresford reports that he is ready to proceed with one or more steamers to Khartum, you will go to that place with him, and deliver the enclosed letter to General Gordon. I leave it open so you may read it.

Orders have been given to Sir H. Stewart to send a small detachment of infantry with you to Khartum. If you like, you can, upon arriving there, march these soldiers through the city, to show the people that British troops are near at hand. If there is any epidemic in the town you will not do this. I do not wish them to sleep in the city. They must return with you to Matammeh. You will only stay in Khartum long enough to confer fully with General Gordon. Having done so you will return with Lord Charles Beresford in steamers to Matammeh.

My letter to General Gordon will explain to you the object of your mission. You will confer with him both upon the military and upon the political position. You are aware of the great difficulty of feeding this army at such a great distance from the sea. You know how we are off in the matter of supplies, the condition and distribution of the troops under my command, the dates when Major-General Earle will be able to move on Abu Hamed, etc.

I am sending with you the three officers named in the margin who will accompany you to Khartum, and will remain there to assist General Gordon until I am able to relieve that place.

It is always possible that when Mohamed Ahmed fully realises that an English army is approaching Khartum he will retreat, and thus raise the siege. Khartum would under such circumstances continue to be the political centre of our operations, but Berber would become our military objective. No British troops would be sent to Khartum beyond a few red coats in steamers for the purpose of impressing on the inhabitants the fact that it was to the presence of our army they owed their safety. The siege of Khartum being thus raised, all our military arrangements would be made with a view to the immediate occupation of Berber, and to a march across the desert to Ariab, on the Suakin road.

Upon arrival at Matammeh, it is very possible you may find papers or letters from General Gordon awaiting us. You will be good enough to send them to me by the first messenger coming here. Upon your return to Matammeh from Khartum you will rejoin my Headquarters at your earliest possible convenience.[98]

By the time Wilson received these orders only two officers had been pencilled into the margin to accompany him. They were Major John Dickson of the Royal Dragoons and Lieutenant Edward Stuart-Wortley KRRC, both of whom were members of the Intelligence Department.[99] On 11 January Wolseley sent a telegram to London in which the identity of the third officer was mentioned. It was to be Captain Fred Gascoigne, late of the Blues, who would arrive at Korti in company with his old friend and one-time regimental colleague, Fred Burnaby.

It is noteworthy that while Colvile's *Official History* includes a full transcript of Wilson's orders, it fails to incorporate the text of the memorandum from Buller which accompanied them – the document detailing the 'dates when Major-General Earle will be able to move on Abu-Ahmed, etc.' This is not merely a curious omission but actually rather a suspicious one, as the gist of the note is essential to any bona fide understanding of how the campaign would ultimately have played itself out had it not been brought to so precipitate an end. It is unsurprising that Sir Charles felt no hesitation about incorporating the memo into *From Korti to Khartum*.

The following is my estimate of approximate times:

General Earle's force should with luck, be in a position to commence its forward movement on the 20th January. The whole of that force should have moved by the 25th January. It will, I hope, reach Abu-Ahmed about the 10th February, Berber about the 22nd February and Shendy about the 5th of March. I have not calculated on its meeting with any serious opposition before Berber.

Lord Wolseley's force will commence to reach Matemmeh the 16th January, and should be concentrated there with sixty day's supplies by the 2nd March. If we hire many camels this date may be anticipated.

Redvers Buller
Major-General [100]

Thus it can be seen that the final push south from Metemmeh by a reunified British force had been projected by the staff for the second week of March.

It should now be very plain that when on 8 January 1885 the Desert Column marched out of Korti, it was not, contrary to popular myth, engaged in a dash for Khartoum. Its objective was the capture of Metemmeh, and it was not anticipated that it would move south from there for another six weeks or so. Despite all the fine talk about still being able, *in extremis*, to push through to Khartoum with the Desert Column, Wolseley's written orders actually served to preclude the column doing anything *in extremis*. They contained no provision for Stewart to assume personal responsibility for dashing south from Metemmeh, should either the intelligence picture or further desperate pleas from Gordon demand urgent, decisive action. They also required that having been to Khartoum and back, Wilson should then ride all the way back to Korti to make his report to the C-in-C in person.

The absence of any provision for a 'do or die dash' by the Desert Column hints at the possibility that something had changed since the staff conference of 2 January. If we jump ahead to the evening of 8 January, some hours after Stewart's departure, we find Wolseley writing to Lady Louisa in the following vein:

You will see by my journal that I have given up all intention of forcing my way into Khartoum with a small column owing to the warning that Gordon sent me by his messenger. I expect Sir Charles Wilson back here on the 28th instant, having been into Khartoum. He will be able to tell me what Gordon's prospects and wishes really are. In the meantime, I am collecting supplies at Matammeh so as to be prepared for all contingencies. This delay is provoking, but it all leans towards increased safety, or rather, I should say, less risk.

The key issue is whether the first sentence of this extract was literally true. Had Wolseley changed his mind again, by accepting that he could only push through to Khartoum in full strength and recognizing that such an operation could not possibly take place before March? Was there *any* prospect of his leading the Desert Column south from Metemmeh in a do-or-die dash? Unfortunately the collateral evidence one way or the other is sketchy. In the knowledge that any such operation would represent an extremely risky venture, Wolseley had telegraphed Hartington to seek the government's view. He couched the question by saying that he presumed the Cabinet would regard the fall of Khartoum and the death of Gordon as a far greater calamity than the relief expedition sustaining some kind of reverse in the desert. It is curious that he chose to pose the question in quite this fashion, as he must have known that the government would take the opposite view. Of course that is precisely how the Secretary of State for War replied. In a later letter to his wife, this time dated 15 January, Wolseley again refers to Wilson getting back to Korti on either 27 or 28 January. Ignoring the fact that this represented an absurdly optimistic projection,[101] we should note that he then adds the crucial remark, 'On the news he brings will depend all my future movements.'[102] This would tend to suggest that he still regarded a dash as something which might eventually be forced upon him by a worsening situation at Khartoum. What is quite clear, however, is that in the meantime he had no intention of delegating the authority to make a decision to anybody else. This precluded any possibility of Stewart and Wilson conferring on the latter's return to Metemmeh and pruning back on wasted time by pressing south without waiting for orders to do so. In terms of the inherent import of the decision, there can be no question but that such weighty matters would ordinarily rest with the army commander; but if the army commander was located at Korti, not less than four days' journey-time from Metemmeh, then a minimum of nine days would be wasted before a time-critical decision could be implemented.

The practical effect of Wolseley's orders was to shift to the right by not less than three weeks any prospect of the Desert Column racing south in a worst-case scenario. The arguments to support this assertion will unfold at a later point in the narrative. It is also clear that while Wolseley recognized that a dash might still be forced upon him, he had now come to view it as an option of last resort. The practical outcome of this latest change of heart was to impose a new and entirely arbitrary timeline for the relief of Khartoum. If Wolseley had one shred of evidence which led him to believe that Gordon could hold out until mid-March, his strategy might have been vaguely justifiable. But there was no such evidence: there could be no such evidence by reason of the simple fact that it happened not to be true. Gordon had done himself no favours by apparently failing to affix a timeline to his message of 14 December. The message had said only, 'We want you to come quickly', whereas 'We want you to come not later than . . .' would have been an eminently more meaningful plea. What cannot be overlooked is that Gordon might well have provided a timeline, as the message was an oral one and could conceivably have been garbled in the transmission or the translation. But the long and the short of it was that by the time the ink had dried on Sir Charles Wilson's orders, General Gordon was as good as dead. The writing, of course, was in Lord Wolseley's hand.

The final set of instructions was the grammatically tortuous set issued to Beresford.

The Section Naval Brigade now here, will march with Sir H. Stewart's convoy on the 8th for Metemmeh. You will report yourself to Sir H. Stewart to receive instructions regarding the march. On arrival at Metemmeh, you will at once take over and man any steamer, or, if you can, steamers that are there or in the vicinity; and you will use every means in your power to put one or more of the steamers that will, it is believed, be available into an efficient state.

You will do this under the direction of the senior military officer at the post, and will take his instructions regarding the steamers when ready.[103]

Thursday 8 January 1885 – March of the Main Body

The Desert Column started for Jakdul Wells at around 3.20 p.m. on Thursday 8 January.[104] The C-in-C and his staff were out in force to see the troops off. It was an impressive if somewhat curious military spectacle which served to swell Wolseley's ego to such an extent that in his journal entry of later that day we encounter him at his narcissistic worst.[105] All the heartache and worry of the previous few weeks had now been consigned to history. Sir Herbert Stewart, his particular favourite, a man he, the supreme judge of a military professional, had pushed on ahead of others, was now on the march at the head of a hand-picked fighting force drawn from across the smartest regiments in the service. It must have seemed to Wolseley that his plans had at last come to fruition and that success was assured. He felt so pleased with the events of the day that he was tempted to revert to the invariably inadvisable practice of despising his enemy: 'I have for long thought the enemy's power was a great bubble that only required pricking with a stout bodkin – a pin would not be strong enough – to collapse entirely.'[106]

In truth it was all an illusion as nothing had occurred to alter the most vital factor in play – the reconciliation of time and space – the very issue which had been causing Wolseley such anguish for the past several weeks. No matter how impressive a spectacle a camel-mounted brigade on the march might be, if the supporting staff computations have been done properly a real-world military formation can advance no faster than the map-pin which in the planning phase had once represented it. Wolseley had taken no meaningful measures to accelerate progress in the interim. On the contrary he had applied a brake by inserting the ill-conceived idea of sending Sir Charles Wilson to Khartoum and back, before proceeding with the main order of business. Famously, the Confederate cavalry general Nathan Bedford Forrest is said to have characterized the secret to the art of war as 'getting there the fastest with the mostest'. For all that he must have been an abhorrent character, the founder of the Ku Klux Klan was much too erudite to have put it quite like that. Whatever form of words Forrest actually used, the underpinning premise bespeaks concentration of force and rapidity of manoeuvre. It would thus have served admirably as a guiding mantra for the Nile Expedition. Instead Wolseley had flown in the face of military logic by inserting a new and unnecessary phase of operations into a time-critical scenario. In so doing he had also devised a scheme which, while it would have been hazardous enough at high-Nile, was likely to be near-suicidal now that the river had fallen and was sinking lower by the day. That Sir Charles Wilson was able both to execute his orders faithfully and live to tell the tale can be counted as something of a minor miracle.

Neither had Wolseley done anything to concentrate his combat power to a single decisive purpose. On the contrary, after toying briefly with the right answer – which is to say diverting the infantry across the Bayūda in support of the Camel Corps – he had, on second thoughts, reverted to quite the wrong answer.

But Korti was a pleasant spot, all seemed well with the world and for the time being at least, the C-in-C was brimming with optimism.

Chapter 6

Go Strong into the Desert

Composition, Organization and Capability of Stewart's Force

> Anonymous telegram to me just received from London saying, 'Don't despise your enemy, go strong into desert.'
>
> General Lord Wolseley, Campaign Journal, Korti, 4 January 1885

THE MARCHING-OUT STATE of the Desert Column when it left Korti is shown in Table 1, overleaf. The figures cited are drawn from the War Diary of the Desert Column and ought to be accurate.[1] It is curious, therefore, that MICR is said to have paraded 21 officers and 336 NCOs and men on the day of departure, as the highest unit strength cited during the course of the campaign is 24 & 366, and some 4 officers and 58 NCOs and men of C Company were still at Hambok at this juncture. This last figure is derived from Stewart's official report on his second journey to Jakdul and is stated unequivocally.[2] Beresford's memoirs, on the other hand, give the strength of the Hambok detachment as thirty-three. Although he does not cite a source, his figure dovetails precisely with the marching-out state of MICR in a way that Stewart's does not. But then again we should not overlook the possibility that Beresford simply calculated a figure of thirty-three by subtracting the regiment's marching-out state from Korti, from its later marching-out state from Jakdul. Ultimately Stewart's contemporaneous and official figure has to be regarded as more historically authoritative than an un-sourced remark of almost thirty years later. Accepting the possibility that the strength of MICR on departure might well be overstated by something around twenty-five to thirty NCOs and men, then counting the 437 guardsmen, sappers and medics already at Jakdul Wells, and the sixty-one members of the Mounted Infantry at Howeiyat, Stewart had just over 2,000 British officers and soldiers under his command. Because Colonel Vandeleur was able to bring only seven companies of 1st Royal Sussex into the field,[3] Captain William Carter's company of 2nd Essex had been incorporated into the column to complete a full-strength battalion. For the time being the eight infantry companies had been mounted on a combination of vacant GCR riding camels and less heavily laden baggage animals.

Table 1: The Desert Column's Marching-Out State, Korti, 8 January 1885

	Officers	NCOs & Men	Natives	Camels	Horses
Army HQ	3	3	8	11	
Stewart's HQ	5	3	5	15	5
Naval Brigade	5	53	11	91	
19th Hussars	9	121	19	73	146
HCR	24	376	5	420	
MICR	21	336	4	424	
1st Royal Sussex	16	401	7	442	4
2nd Essex	3	55	2	58	
1/1 Battery, SD, RA	4	39	12	90	
C & T Corps	5	72	160	431	
No. 1 Field Hospital	1	10	6	27	
Medical Bearer Company	2	40	57	146	
Total	98	1,509	296	2,228	155

Dress and Equipment

The Desert Column might have been a formidable military spectacle, but had it not been for the striking red leather saddle-covers of the camel regiments would have been almost entirely devoid of any martial splendour. On their arrival in Egypt, the scarlet undress frocks in which the home-based detachments of the Camel Corps had sailed from England had been stowed away in the men's kitbags, in favour of a grey serge replacement. In HCR there was always a splash of colour on a cold morning, as one source reference reveals that the Household Cavalry detachments took their home-service greatcoats up the Nile. These were red in the case of the Life Guards and blue in the Royal Horse Guards. Wolseley had devised a drab, grey campaign uniform for the Ashanti War and had intended that grey would again be the order of the day for his Egyptian Campaign. Although a contract had been placed for 30,000 suits of grey serge, they had failed to arrive in time for the fighting and had subsequently gone into storage in Cairo. Two years on they were now servicing the needs of regiments passing through Cairo and Alexandria bound for the Sudan. The grey undress frock was single-breasted, had a low round collar and fastened to the throat with five brass buttons. It quickly became de rigueur in some of the Camel Corps detachments to sew a red cloth regimental acronym, such as '1 GG' for 1st Grenadier Guards, or '4 DG' for 4th Dragoon Guards, onto the right arm of the frock. While the expedition's infantry battalions had been issued with full-length grey trousers to match, anybody destined for mounted service, including the Camel Corps regiments, the 19th Hussars and the camel battery, had been issued with buff-coloured Bedford-cord riding breeches. Contemporaneous sketches show that all the mounted units, including the Hussars, wore ankle-length ammunition boots, with navy-blue puttees wrapped neatly to the knee.[4]

The cork foreign-service sun helmet was worn with a fitted pugaree and was both comfortable and effective. It was worn universally throughout the force, including by the Naval Brigade. Uniquely General Stewart had adorned his helmet with an orange pugaree, while the officers of the HCR had adopted a distinctive regimental pugaree in alternating diagonal bands of red and yellow, an adornment which was not worn by the regiment's rank and file. The only other coloured pugaree in use was the navy-blue one worn in the Naval Brigade by officers and men alike. Eyewitness sketches suggest that these were not akin to the fitted items worn by the Army, but rather had been improvised from lengths of cloth tied into a knot at the back of the helmet, so as to leave a trailing end. Although the foreign-service helmet was pipeclayed white in peacetime, it had long been standard practice in the field to stain it a dirty brown colour using tea, coffee or local substitutes such as boiled mimosa bark. Wolseley had insisted that everybody be issued with padded spine protectors and a set of blue-tinted goggles of much the same design as modern-day swimming goggles. While the latter proved popular and were generally worn perched on the front of the helmet, ready for use, the spine protectors were not taken seriously and had long since been consigned to the men's kitbags.

The Camel Corps soldier had only a basic issue of fighting-order equipment on the basis that his camel would always be close at hand, with his blanket, spare clothes and personal effects stowed in the saddlebags. An 'Oliver' pattern water-bottle and a white canvas haversack, the latter containing a day's rations and sundry miscellaneous items, were worn slung over the right shoulder. A brown leather P1882 Mounted Infantry Bandolier, holding fifty rounds of ammunition, was worn over the opposite shoulder. A full bandolier weighed more than 6 lb and when worn for any length of time became uncomfortable on the neck and chest. The waist-belt supported a P1860 sword-bayonet over the left buttock and a twenty-round expense pouch on the right hip; both the belt and the pouch came in brown leather, while the bayonet scabbard was black with a brass tip. Originally used in conjunction with the Snider-Enfield rifle, the P1860 sword-bayonet had since been modified to fit the Martini-Henry and had a Yataghan-style blade of just over twenty-two inches in length. As the name suggests the expense pouch was the soldier's first recourse for loose ready-to-use ammunition. Because the seal between the 0.450-inch calibre bullet and the bottle-necked 0.577-inch coiled brass cartridge case could not be regarded as completely watertight, Short Chamber Boxer-Henry rounds came in waxed paper packets of ten for protection against the elements. A single packet weighed something around 1 lb 2 oz. If orders required that more than seventy rounds were to be carried on the person, the additional packets had to go into the haversack. The Camel Corps regiments began the crossing of the Bayūda with an issue of 170 rounds per man, seventy of which were carried on the person, with the additional ten packets stowed in the saddlebags. These were nothing akin to the type carried by cavalrymen over the rump of a horse, but rather were yard-long holdalls with a drop-down top flap. Manufactured in both red leather and white canvas, such bags were known locally as *zuleetahs* and were carried on both flanks of the animal. They were suspended from the camel saddle parallel to the ground and protruded from under the bottom edge of the red leather saddle cover.

In addition to a standard 'Oliver' pattern water-bottle, always worn on the person, the Camel Corps soldier was also given a long Egyptian water-bottle called a *mussek*, which held about six pints, and a dark brown water-skin, known as a *gerbah*, which held six or seven gallons. These he hung from the rear horn of his saddle, so that the *mussek* was suspended on the animal's left flank and the *gerbah* was hanging directly rearwards down the line of its spine, where it rested on a yellow leather saddle flap. Provided the *mussek* and *gerbah* were sound and a good standard of water discipline was exercised along the way, the total quantity of water available to each man was more than enough to see him through to Jakdul Wells. In reality, however, many of the items leaked badly and could be counted next to useless. Suspended from the front horn of the saddle, so as to hang to the rider's right-front, was a canvas feed-bag capable of holding about 15 lb of fodder. For his bivouac the soldier had a waterproof ground sheet, a grey army blanket and a half-share in a *tente d'abri*, a very basic ridge tent long enough to lie down in, but nothing like high enough to sit up in. If as a result of marching by night he was required to sleep by day, the Camel Corps soldier probably had an uncomfortable few hours ahead of him, as there could be no question of his lying in the open, unprotected from the sun, while the inside of his tent was virtually certain to heat up like an oven. On the march the Martini-Henry rifle was carried to the rider's right-rear, inside the brown leather 'Namaqua' rifle-bucket. This was deep enough to shroud the lower third of the weapon and at least part-protect the breech mechanism against the ingress of sand; of course this was not the case if there was any sort of breeze, or if the day's march saw the column crossing loose sand and throwing up dust. The *tente d'abri* was carried rolled up and suspended from the saddle, beneath the *zuleetah* on the camel's right flank, while the rolled-up waterproof sheet and greatcoat went in the corresponding position on the left. The girths, basic strips of leather with an iron ring stitched at one end, were separate from the saddle and were passed front and rear over the framework and tightened with a knot. Similarly the stirrup leathers were not an integral part of the saddle, but were secured either by being nailed or knotted to the framework.[5]

With the Camel Corps up the Nile contains an interesting passage describing the arrival of the RMLI company at Korti, in which Count Gleichen particularly notes the 'band-box' appearance of the Marines. He goes on to observe that while they were dressed in the same fashion as the rest of the Camel Corps, they were sporting snow-white helmets and freshly pipeclayed belts and pouches.[6] As was the case in the rest of the force, the Guards companies had already stained their helmets to what Gleichen describes as a 'coffee-colour'. His narrative is often cited as proof that the RMLI marched into the Bayūda in spotless white helmets. In fact it had long been recognized that wearing an unstained helmet in the age of the long-range rifle was an act of madness and there can be no doubt that the Marines would have conformed to the rest of GCR prior to leaving Korti. Had they not done so such dangerous eccentricity is bound to have elicited comment in the sources, but no such references exist. It seems more than likely that Major Pöe, knowing he was about to marry up with a regiment of Foot Guards, wanted his men to cut a dash on parading with their new unit for the first time and that thereafter he would have dressed his men down, in line with the practices prevailing in the rest of the regiment.

The Gleichen narrative does demonstrate that the RMLI had not received an issue of the same brown leather waist-belts and expense pouches used by the rest of the Camel Corps, but instead were wearing the corresponding items from their valise pattern equipment.[7] This came in light buff-coloured leather and could be pipeclayed white for parade purposes or allowed to regress to its natural condition for field service. Although not definitively sourced as fact, it can be safely assumed that the Marines had been issued with P1882 bandoliers, probably when they passed through Wādī Halfā, for it was there that they are known to have been provided with Bedford-cord riding breeches and puttees, the items that particularly singled out members of the Camel Corps as mounted troops. Had they not been so equipped, it is certain to have elicited comment amongst Gleichen's series of detailed observations. Before leaving the subject of the physical appearance of the column, it is noteworthy that the Adeni camel-drivers had been issued with red turbans and navy-blue undress frocks, an expedient designed to distinguish them from the enemy.[8] It is unlikely that the logistic system had coped with dressing drivers recruited in the south in the same fashion.

Although eight companies of line infantry were now riding into the desert on camels, they were not formally roled as mounted troops and accordingly had not received an issue of riding breeches, puttees, Yataghan sword-bayonets or P1882 MI bandoliers. Instead they wore full length grey serge trousers, carried standard straight-bladed twenty-two-inch P1876 'lunger' bayonets and wore buff-coloured P1871 or P1882 valise equipment consisting of waist-belt, braces, left and right ammunition pouches, together with the universal 'Oliver' Pattern water-bottle and haversack.

While all infantry officers were required to qualify annually with the Martini-Henry, they were not issued with rifles and armed themselves at personal expense with swords of the appropriate pattern and revolvers acquired according to taste, fashion or the personal recommendation of friends. Many officers were enthusiastic shooting men and carried double-barrelled game guns and sporting rifles in their baggage. Officers' personal equipment was also privately purchased but, because there were only so many gentlemen's outfitters in London, there was a high if not altogether intentional degree of uniformity increasingly based around Sam Browne type designs. Although a few Camel Corps officers wore puttees like the men, most preferred riding boots, if nothing else as a status symbol. With the exception of the Rifle regiments, who wore black, officers' equipment and riding boots were made of dark brown leather. An infantry officer's dress uniform included a red sash, worn over the shoulder: although it was no longer common practice to wear such items in the field, the officers of 1st Royal Sussex seem to have done so.[9]

If the 1st Division of the Naval Brigade had appeared very much at home in whalers, they looked altogether less comfortable now that they were on terra firma and mounted on camels. If the sketches of Frederic Villiers are free of artistic licence, the 'White Ensign' was carried at the head of the Naval Brigade on the line of march. Charlie Beresford thought better of trotting about on a lofty dromedary and had procured a large white donkey which he named 'County Waterford' after his ancestral home. Beresford had half a mind that he might have to use his beast to tow the Gardner around the battlefield, although the Navy's standard practice was to haul disembarked machine guns about using drag-ropes and relays of ten burly sailors. On the march the disassembled Gardner would be distributed across four strong baggage camels: the first animal carried the barrels, the second, the wheels and the training and elevating gear, the third, the trail, and the last, four boxes of 'hoppers' (the magazine as it were) and ammunition. If the crew raced through their drills at best speed, the weapon could be dismounted, assembled and brought into action in less than four minutes. Ordinarily the gun would have been accompanied by a limber, but Beresford regarded the item as an unnecessary encumbrance and sensibly left it behind at Korti.[10]

In truth the five-barrelled Gardner was not so much a machine gun as a volley gun, although the interval between five-round volleys was fleeting enough to permit the maintenance of a tolerably high cyclic rate of fire. As was often the case with early machine guns, the weapon's Achilles heel was the extraction of spent cartridge cases. Stoppages were not uncommon and could take a couple of minutes to get at and rectify. That said it is not to be imagined that the Gardner jammed with monotonous regularity; its mechanism was actually regarded as reasonably reliable. Another Villiers sketch for *The Graphic* shows that both the Gardners sent up the Nile (one of which was still travelling up the lines of communication with the Second Division of the Naval Brigade) were fitted with a small steel shield designed to protect the crew from small-arms fire, albeit it was so small that it was likely to deflect incoming rounds more by chance than design. The pressure on the baggage train was such that Beresford had been allowed to bring only a thousand rounds of Gardner ammunition; sufficient to sustain only about ten minutes' worth of rapid-fire.[11] Looking ahead to the possibility of having to overhaul Gordon's steamers, Beresford's chief engineer had taken care to scrounge a quantity of engineering stores, including eight boiler plates, some lubricating oil, various useful tools and a quantity of nuts, bolts and rivets.[12]

Contemporaneous sketches by Villiers and Verner show that for the Bayūda crossing the Royal Navy ratings were dressed in their tropical whites, with brown leather boots and gaiters, but that they also had their temperate blue uniform packed away in their kit. During the later operations on the Nile they seem to have mixed blue and white freely, according to which items of clothing were still serviceable or more presentable. The naval waist-belt and ammunition pouches also came in brown leather. Suspended from the left hip in a black leather scabbard was a cutlass-bayonet, purportedly designed to fulfil both roles. In fact it was far too heavy to be fixed as a bayonet without exerting an adverse effect on the men's musketry, while anybody who drew a three-foot cutlass and sought to attack an Arab wielding an eight-foot spear would plainly be asking for trouble. The naval officers, Captain Lord Charles Beresford, Lieutenants Alfred Pigott and Rudolph de Lisle, and Sub-Lieutenant Edward Munro were dressed in their usual navy-blue blazers, with gold rings around the cuff denoting their respective ranks. Beresford rounded his campaigning outfit off with a non-regulation broad-brimmed sola topee, breeches, riding boots, haversack and waist-belt. His sword was suspended from a broad tan-leather shoulder belt. The Royal Navy contingent had been drawn from across the Alexandria squadron of the Mediterranean Fleet and included men from Her Majesty's Ships *Alexandra, Helicon, Inflexible, Invincible, Iris, Monarch, Superb* and *Temeraire*.[13]

The shortage of baggage camels had driven the division of 1st/1st Battery, Southern Division, Royal Artillery, into half-batteries each of three guns, only one of which would immediately cross the desert with Stewart. It is not clear why the battery commander, Major Woodburn Hunter, did not take command of the leading half-battery in person, but instead delegated the job to Captain Gilbert Norton. Norton's command consisted of three other Royal Artillery officers, Lieutenants Charles Lyall, Noel Du Boulay and James Guthrie, and thirty-nine NCOs and gunners. In addition there was one officer (name unknown) and seven men from the Egyptian Army attached to the half-battery. Whilst their precise role is not specifically mentioned in the sources, it would seem more likely than not that they were employed as additional camel-drivers, if nothing else because the battery would later depart Jakdul with ninety baggage camels but only twelve civilian drivers.[14] Norton had been permitted to pack only 100 rounds per gun, which given the relatively benign intelligence picture would probably not have been an immediate cause for concern.[15] The 2.5-inch screw-gun fired a seven-pound shell out to ranges of 3,400 yards, or roughly two miles, and was capable of great accuracy even at maximum range. Seven-pound 'common shell' sat very decidedly at the light end of the spectrum, so that whilst it might inflict a significant number of casualties on a massed target, it tended to be much less effective if the enemy were dispersed or in hard cover. It was unlikely to be of much use in reducing walls or buildings, as there was every possibility that a round fired over open sights would pass straight through the sort of mud-brick structures typically found in the Sudan.

The 19th Hussars

The participant accounts are littered with compliments on the work of the 19th Hussars in their role as the column's reconnaissance screen. Ordinarily part of the Army of Occupation, the regiment had served under Stewart in the First Suakin Campaign and fought with distinction at Second El Teb where it was called upon to make a series of gallant if not altogether prudent charges in concert with the 10th Hussars. Lieutenant Colonel Percy Barrow, now the commanding officer, but at the time only the second-in-command, had been extremely fortunate to survive the regiment's second charge through a still unbroken mass of Hadendawa. Only moments after he had been hit by a throwing-spear which penetrated his arm and ribs, his horse was brought down and he was sent tumbling to the ground. With the hard-pressed squadrons sweeping past at the gallop, he was in grave danger of being left in the midst of the enemy. Clambering to his feet he stretched out an arm in desperation. It was seized by Quartermaster Sergeant William Marshall who, by some miracle, was able to keep a firm grip of the slightly built colonel and drag him clear of any immediate danger. After a short gallop Marshall deposited Barrow on the ground and rode away to find a riderless horse. He quickly returned with an animal which had not long since fallen under Private Boseley. Boseley was unharmed as it turned out and gamely ran across to help QMS Marshall lift the colonel onto his horse. Once Barrow and Boseley were clear of the fray, Marshall rode back into the maelstrom to re-join his squadron. His gallantry and devotion to duty had subsequently attracted the award of the Victoria Cross.

Barrow's wound was an ugly one and, although he professed to have recovered from it in the intervening nine months, was still causing him great discomfort.[16] For his service in the Eastern Sudan he was mentioned in despatches and made a Companion of the Most Honourable Order of the Bath (CB). Barrow had earlier commanded a mounted infantry squadron in the Zulu War, fought in the Battles of Nyezane and Gingindlovu and over the course of the campaign had acquired a great deal of practical experience in the art of reconnaissance. His service in Zululand earned him a brevet promotion to major and a CMG, which is to say admission as a Companion of the Order of St Michael and St George. Two years later he found himself in command of a mounted infantry squadron during the later stages of the Transvaal Rebellion. In short Barrow was an extremely able cavalry officer with a wealth of recent campaign service.

The next most senior officer in the enlarged four-troop squadron (two squadrons operating as one) was Major John French, whose qualities as an officer are more than amply evinced by his distinguished service as a brigade and divisional commander in the Boer War, his subsequent rise to the rank of field marshal and his appointment to command the BEF in 1914. Although French had been in the Army for eleven years at this point, the Nile Expedition was his first serious spell of campaign service. Barrow's other officers were Captain Hew Fanshawe, Lieutenants Harold De Pledge, Hugh Young and Edward Craven, and Quartermaster Arthur Lima (not long since commissioned after riding in the charge at El Teb as the regimental sergeant major). With the exception of Young, who had been at Tamai only, and French, who missed the campaign altogether, the other officers had been present at both the recent battles in the Red Sea Littoral. In 1882 Fanshawe had been at Kassassin and Lima at Tel-el-Kebir. Most of the NCOs and men had fought in both the Egyptian Campaign and the First Suakin Campaign.

The 19th Hussars was the only horsed cavalry unit concerned in the Nile Expedition and carried the weaponry appropriate to the role. Where the infantry battalions, sappers and camel regiments carried long-barrelled Martini-Henry rifles of the Mk II pattern, Barrow's troopers were armed with the short-barrelled Martini-Henry carbine, an infinitely more manageable weapon in the saddle. Although the two weapons had an identical action, the carbine was not capable of consistently accurate fire much beyond 300 yards. Contemporary sketches show that the 19th Hussars were not issued with P1882 MI bandoliers, but carried their ready-to-use rounds in a black pouch worn with a white leather crossbelt.[17]

In lieu of bayonets Barrow's men carried P1864/1882 cavalry swords, conveying, theoretically at least, the capacity for mounted shock-action. In practice the regiment's experience at Second El Teb had shown that bodies of unbroken *anṣār* were not to be trifled with, even by two regiments charging in concert, let alone by a single squadron. Relying on the facts that most horses will not intentionally trample a man underfoot and that a sword-wielding trooper cannot generally reach a man lying on the ground, many of the Hadendawa had thrown themselves down in front of the charging British squadrons, only then to leap back to their feet as they passed to make great hamstringing slashes at the horses' hindquarters. This had proved so troublesome a tactic that when the battle was over Stewart had ordered that all the eight-foot spears recovered from the enemy dead should be distributed amongst his hussars as makeshift lances. As the practice was not carried forward into the Nile Expedition, it is probably safe to assume that with so small a cavalry element at his disposal, Stewart had resolved not to initiate any shock-action charges – a case of 'Once bitten, twice shy.'

The Mounted Infantry Camel Regiment

Like the 19th Hussars, MICR contained a significant number of veterans of the First Suakin Campaign, some of whom had been in the mounted infantry company in Stewart's brigade, while others had fought on foot with their parent battalions and joined the MI later. The concept of moving infantrymen about the battlefield on horseback was by no means a new one; the regiments of dragoons extensively employed in the Civil War were but one early example of the genre. Over the course of the eighteenth century the British Army's dragoons had evolved to become full-blooded cavalrymen, no longer carrying long-barrelled firearms as a primary weapon, but short-barrelled carbines as a secondary one. Now it was all sabres and shock action like everybody else. More recently the pressures of policing the Queen Empress's vast and expanding empire had brought the mounted infantry concept back into vogue, particularly in Southern Africa where the prevalence of the tsetse fly could spell the rapid destruction of a cavalry regiment mounted on expensive Irish chargers. From the late 1880s onwards infantry battalions would be formally chartered to maintain a mounted infantry section. The underpinning concept was that sections could then be brought together from across a four-battalion brigade to provide the brigadier with a composite mounted infantry company. The first MI school would be established in 1888, but in the meantime mounted infantry companies were scratch organizations with no formal structure, locally purchased mounts and an issue of begged, stolen or borrowed equipment. They might at this stage be called 'companies' or 'squadrons' according to whim. The formation of MICR, the first battalion-sized body of its kind, would turn out to be a significant stride in formalizing the existence of a mounted infantry arm.

Sir Frederick Stephenson had drawn on the garrison battalions in Cairo and Alexandria to form a second MI company in June 1884, appointing Major Edward 'Curly' Hutton of 3rd KRRC as the commanding officer of the new two-company unit. Hutton had seen a good deal of active service in Zululand and the Transvaal, and in the Egyptian Campaign had been ADC to Major General Sir Archibald Alison, in which capacity he had been present at Tel-el-Kebir.

Hutton's first adjutant was Lieutenant Percy Marling, a fellow member of 3rd KRRC.[18] Though still young, Marling had already gained a wealth of fighting experience and had a Victoria Cross to show for it. He had seen his first campaign service in the Transvaal Rebellion and fought at both Laing's Nek and Ingogo. In the latter action 3rd KRRC had received a serious mauling at the hands of Boer marksmen. Marling was fortunate not to be intimately concerned in the campaign's third and worst fiasco at Majuba Hill, although he did witness the disaster unfolding from the nearby British encampment. A reconstituted 3rd KRRC went on to serve in Egypt, where Marling participated in the actions at Tel-el-Mahuta, Kassassin and Tel-el-Kebir. The battalion stayed on subsequently as part of the Army of Occupation. Marling was a keen horseman and an enthusiastic amateur jockey, so was the natural choice to lead his battalion's MI section when the First Suakin Campaign cropped up. He fought under Stewart at both Second El Teb and Tamai, in which latter action he caught the general's eye. His VC citation read:

For his conspicuous bravery at the Battle of Tamai, 13th March 1884, in risking his life to save that of Private Morley, Royal Sussex Regiment, who, having been shot, was lifted and placed in front of Lieutenant Marling on his horse. He fell off almost immediately, when Lieutenant Marling dismounted, and gave up his horse for the purpose of carrying off Private Morley, the enemy pressing close on to them until they succeeded in carrying him about 80 yards to a place of comparative safety.[19]

Having served with General Stewart in three arduous campaigns, Marling had come to hold him in high estimation, a feeling which would appear to have been mutual.

The two original companies of Curly Hutton's command became A and B Companies, MICR, the former commanded by Captain Charles 'Daddy' Payne of the Gordons,[20] and the latter by Captain Henry Walsh of the Somerset Light Infantry, another of the officers who had served with the Mounted Infantry in the Zulu War.[21] C and D Companies, MICR, were newly formed composite companies which had come out from England with the rest of the Camel Corps. The formation of MICR resulted in Hutton being granted local promotion to lieutenant colonel.

C Company, as we have seen, was commanded by Captain Dick Fetherstonhaugh and contained sections from the 1st and 2nd Battalions of the King's Royal Rifle Corps, together with sections from the 2nd and 3rd Battalions of the

Rifle Brigade. C Company quickly took to calling itself the 'Rifles Company'. D Company was drawn from line infantry units, with sections from 1st Somerset Light Infantry, 2nd Connaught Rangers, 1st Royal Scots Fusiliers and 2nd Royal West Kents. Its company commander was Captain Charles Berkeley Pigott, a former 3rd KRRC officer in the process of transferring to the 21st Hussars (later re-roled as the 21st Lancers). Pigott was fierce by disposition and liked to comport himself as a hardened warrior. On the voyage out to Egypt he had frequently gathered his company together, not so much to lecture them as to berate them on the finer subtleties of hand-to-hand fighting. Although one of his subalterns noted that he was not particularly popular with his soldiers, his fighting credentials commanded their respect.[22] Pigott had previously campaigned with 3rd KRRC in Zululand and with the mounted infantry squadrons in the Transvaal Rebellion and the Egyptian Campaign. He had been present at Laing's Nek and Ingogo and in 1882 was severely wounded at Kassassin. Pigott's temperament had earned him the nickname 'Bloody-minded Pigott', a sobriquet which his brother officers often foreshortened to the even less endearing 'Bloody Pigott'. A fanatical shooting man, he was accompanied everywhere he went by his beloved fox terrier 'Smoke' and by a civilian servant called Pegrum whose job it was to carry 'an assortment of weapons such as a rifle, a gun or a spear, ready to hand his master according to his requirements'.[23]

Percy Marling had been on leave in England for three weeks, when at the end of September a telegram arrived recalling him to Egypt. He caught up with Colonel Hutton at Wādī Halfā on 26 October. The adjutancy of the enlarged regiment having gone in the meantime to Captain John Sewell of the Norfolks, Marling took over the 3rd KRRC section in 'Daddy' Payne's A Company, dislodging Lieutenant Bobby Bower, his regimental junior, as its commander. A MICR training session conducted with newly allotted riding camels the following day seems to have started well enough, with only a handful of soldiers taking a tumble, but soon went rapidly downhill:

Curly Hutton sounded the trot, and in two minutes the air was thick with Tommies flying about at every angle. Twenty-three camels got loose and went off with their tails in the air, towards the setting sun, and we never got back five of them. Curly Hutton came off on his head.[24]

On 28 October MICR's leading element, seven officers and fifty NCOs and men, commenced the long march upriver. By the end of the day Hutton had been laid low with sunstroke,[25] although the nasty-sounding fall of the previous day might also have had something to do with his condition. Either way the doctors pronounced him unfit to proceed and in due course sent him home to England to recuperate. With Hutton gone, command of the regiment immediately devolved upon its next senior officer, Major the Hon. George Gough, who was actually a cavalry officer from the 14th Hussars.

For all that there were sixteen different infantry battalions represented within MICR, the fact that it was full of experienced and battle-hardened officers and soldiers enabled it to come together very quickly as a first-rate fighting unit. At a strength of 1 officer, 2 sergeants, 2 corporals and 25 privates, the regimental detachments in MICR were somewhat smaller than those of the other camel regiments and acted as tactical sections in their own right, with a standard four sections to the company. Although the sections were regimental, they were known for simplicity's sake by numbers, for example No. 1 Section, A Company, MICR. One of the major reasons for the regiment stealing a march on the camel-mounted cavalry units was that these were all professional infantrymen employed in their stock-in-trade role. They spoke the same language, were completely at home with their weapons and knew the 'infantry drill' inside out. By contrast the cavalry detachments had been provided with new weapons, had a huge amount to learn about fighting on foot and very little time in which to learn it, a point to which we will return in due course.

The Guards Camel Regiment

Even with an RMLI cuckoo in the Foot Guards' nest, GCR shared many of the same advantages as the Mounted Infantry. It was easy for a composite regiment of guardsmen to unify around their status as Household troops. Added cohesion was derived from the fact that battalion detachments had been grouped by parent regiment into companies: No. 1 Company was made up of detachments from 1st, 2nd and 3rd Grenadier Guards; No. 2 Company from the 1st and 2nd Coldstream Guards; and No. 3 Company from 1st and 2nd Scots Guards. A proportion of the rank and file would have been veterans of the Egyptian campaign and Tel-el-Kebir, while the RMLI men in No. 4 Company had come directly from Suakin.

The seven battalion detachments making up the first three companies of GCR each paraded 2 officers, 2 sergeants, 2 corporals, 1 bugler and 38 privates. Although it is nowhere sourced as fact, it seems logical that detachments of this size would have divided to form two twenty-man sections, each with an officer, a sergeant and a corporal, in accordance with the tactical norms of the day. With only two battalions represented in Nos. 2 and 3 Companies, this would have given the requisite four sections of the standard infantry company. No. 1 Company, however, had three constituent detachments and was half as strong again as Nos. 2, 3 and 4 Companies.

There was a curious anomaly still in play in the Foot Guards, which for the avoidance of confusion it would be as well to explain here. In the days of purchase officers' commissions in the Foot Guards carried a capital value far in excess of their direct equivalents in the line infantry. Coupled with the high social standing of Household troops, this had given rise to the so-called 'double-rank' system, in which, for example, an officer holding a captaincy in the Foot Guards also ranked in the wider Army as a lieutenant colonel. This was denoted in the *Army List* with the term 'Captain & Lieutenant Colonel'. Such arcane practices had no place in a modernized army and came to an end with the abolition of purchase. But although the practice had been abolished, the term lived on. The difference now was that Guards officers only became 'Captain & Lieutenant Colonel' according to their proper place in the Army seniority roster. In other words while they are shown in the various Regimental Gazettes of the 1885 *Army List* as 'Captain & Lieutenant Colonel', they were in every sense substantive lieutenant colonels. It follows that the Foot Guards had sent out a number of officers who were overly senior for the appointments they held in the field. When GCR formed up, No. 1 (Grenadier Guards) Company was commanded by Lieutenant Colonel Charles Rowley. Worse still one of the regimental detachments within Rowley's company, the forty-five-strong contingent from 2nd Grenadiers, was commanded by Lieutenant Colonel Ivor Herbert who only two years before had been the brigade major of the Guards Brigade in the Egyptian Campaign. No less bizarre was the idea that a regimental signals officer should be a lieutenant colonel, but in GCR the post was held by Lieutenant Colonel Harry Bonham of the Grenadiers. Although Rowley seems by this stage in the campaign no longer to have been in command of the Grenadier Guards company, the Coldstream and Scots Guards companies were still headed by 'double-rank' men, the former by Lieutenant Colonel Francis Graves-Sawle and the latter by Lieutenant Colonel Mildmay Willson, one of the most senior members of the cabal. As we now have two Colonels Wilson/Willson to contemplate, it will be as well to note the double-L spelling in the case of the Scots Guardsman. Serving under Willson, in command of the 1st Scots Guards detachment, was Lieutenant Colonel Sir William Gordon-Cumming Bart., who would later be swept up in the Baccarat Scandal of 1890 and be ignominiously discharged the service as a card-cheat. For the time being, though, there was precious little time for cards and Sir William was just one more Guards officer trying to do his best by Queen and Country.

Quite why Charles Rowley was no longer in charge of No. 1 Company is nowhere definitively stated, but it is clear that on a personal level the first phase of the campaign had not gone well for him. He was certainly still fit for duty and present with GCR up to and including at least as far as 17 January 1885. As we have already seen he had attracted Wolseley's displeasure on 19 November and exactly a week later was unfortunate enough to make a second appearance in the C-in-C's journal:

Colonel Rowley with 121 men of Guards Corps arrived – crossed the river to see them – such a magnificent lot of real soldiers! The world could not produce finer. I felt a hundred per cent pluckier as I looked at them, for I felt with a thousand of such men I could and would face 25000 of any men the Mahdi could bring into the field. I was worried to see them under so inexperienced and incompetent a man as Rowley whose ignorance of what his first duties are has resulted in his having one third of his camels with sore backs.[26]

It is also of note that Airlie's War Diary entry for 11 December contains the passage, 'Lt Col. Rowley with part of baggage column went astray.' It seems not inconceivable in the circumstances that Colonel Boscawen had chosen to employ Rowley in a staff rather than a command appointment. He might even have been compelled to do so by either Wolseley or Stewart. Gleichen's narratives in *With the Camel Corps up the Nile* and *A Guardsman's Memories* suggest that by the time GCR left Jakdul Wells, Captain Eyre Crabbe was in command of No. 1 Company. Although he was but a conventional regimental officer from the Grenadiers, Crabbe had originally been appointed as the quartermaster of GCR. It is possible that there was a straight swap between Rowley and Crabbe. Quite why command of No. 1 Company did not go to Lieutenant Colonel Ivor Herbert, originally one if its company officers, is unclear, but he does not appear to have been sick and can be shown to have been a member of the regimental headquarters on 23 January.[27] Because a number of the other double-rank men were senior to him, it seems improbable that Herbert had been appointed as second-in-command. He might possibly have been designated as a wing commander or, given his former service as one of the brigade majors at Tel-el-Kebir, might simply have been pulled into regimental headquarters as a particularly useful aide to the commanding officer.

The tricky job of leading GCR, with its cabal of colonels, had fallen to Lieutenant Colonel the Hon. Evelyn Boscawen (later Lord Falmouth), a Coldstream Guardsman since 1866. Boscawen had served with the 2nd Battalion in the Egyptian Campaign and had seen action at Tel-el Mahuta and Tel-el-Kebir.[28] Although he still held a major's appointment in his regiment, his Army seniority as a lieutenant colonel dated back to 1878. Quite where this left him in the pecking order within the Desert Column we will come to later. Like many of his colleagues in the Camel Corps, Boscawen had been born with a silver spoon in his mouth and was neither a rampant careerist, nor a military genius. He had, however, been a guardsman long enough to know the 'infantry drill' inside out, had experienced his metaphorical whiff of grapeshot and would prove to be a cool customer.

To the men of No. 1 Company, GCR, the next most important member of the regiment after the commanding officer was the much adored 'Jacky' the dog, who had attached himself to the Grenadier Guards in Aswan and had been marching south with the regiment ever since. Jacky's technique on the line of march was to scurry on ahead to a shaded spot and wait for his friends to catch up with him, before dashing on to the next piece of cover. Towards the end of the day, when he showed signs of flagging, one of the men would take him up and carry him on to the next bivouac. Alex Macdonald thought that he 'resembled a colley dog in appearance, but was much smaller in size'.[29] Naturally everybody was firmly convinced that a dog as game as Jacky must have found his way to Egypt from England.

The Heavy Camel Regiment

The Heavy Camel Regiment was commanded by Lieutenant Colonel the Hon. Reginald Talbot of 1st Life Guards. 'Reggie' Talbot had been in the Army since 1859, but had to wait the best part of twenty years for his first spell of campaign service. It came in the closing stages of the Zulu War, when he served as a staff captain under Colonel Baker Russell. He had gone on to command a Life Guards squadron in the famous 'Moonlight Charge' at Kassassin, and also saw action at El Magfar and Tel-el-Kebir. Not long afterwards he became a substantive lieutenant colonel.[30] If the 'infantry drill' was second nature to Evelyn Boscawen and his ilk, it was lost on Reggie Talbot, a cavalryman of twenty-five years standing. Nor was the commanding officer alone in his blissful ignorance. There are no source references to suggest that anybody ever thought of attaching a handful of infantry sergeants to the Heavies, in order that they could be initiated into the mysterious ways of the dismounted arm during the course of their long journey up the Nile. Some last-gasp training was carried out at Korti, but it was too little and too late for the Heavies miraculously to transform themselves into infantry automatons. Unfortunately they would shortly be meeting an enemy more than capable of giving the very best infantry professionals a run for their money.

Ten regiments of cavalry had provided detachments to HCR, although only eight of them were bona fide 'heavy' units, not that this was any longer a reflection of any sort of tangible tactical reality. Each of the detachments consisted of 2 officers, 2 sergeants, 2 corporals, 1 trumpeter and 38 troopers or privates. This is a mirror image of the Foot Guards detachments and suggests that HCR was likewise intended to divide its regimental contingents down the middle to form two sections. With two detachments to the company, Talbot had sufficient manpower to form five sub-units, one more than either GCR or MICR. The detachments were assigned to companies according to their seniority in the *Army List*. Hence No. 1 Company was manned by the 1st and 2nd Life Guards; No. 2 Company by the Royal Horse Guards (The Blues) and the 2nd Dragoon Guards (The Queen's Bays); No. 3 Company by the 4th (Royal Irish) Dragoon Guards and the 5th (Princess Charlotte of Wales') Dragoon Guards; and No. 4 Company by the 1st (Royal) Dragoons and the 2nd Dragoons (Royal Scots Greys). Finally, No. 5 Company included the two detachments of light cavalry interlopers, namely the 5th (Royal Irish) Lancers and the 16th (The Queen's) Lancers.

With some of the smartest regiments in the land, including the Household Cavalry, finding its constituent companies, HCR boosted the blue-blood quotient of the Camel Corps, but hardly to the point that Sir Herbert Stewart was tripping over aristocrats as some historians have chosen to imply. The adjutant was one John Jervis, or more properly Captain the Viscount St Vincent, 16th Lancers. In the Life Guards company were Major the Hon. Charles Byng, Lieutenant the Lord Rodney (George Dennett) and Captain Lord Cochrane (Douglas Hamilton), eldest son of the Earl of Dundonald and heir to the title. Number 2 Company was commanded by Major Lord Arthur Somerset, a son of the Duke of Beaufort, while the Blues detachment was in the hands of Lieutenant Lord George Binning, a veteran of the 'Moonlight Charge' and Tel-el-Kebir. Other peers or sons of peers with the column included Airlie, Beresford, Boscawen, Gough, Talbot, Hardinge and Gleichen, all of whom we have already encountered, and finally Lieutenant the Hon. Hugh Amherst of No. 2 Company, GCR. Stewart, Wilson and Gordon-Cumming were of course knights of the realm. Social mobility being what it was in Victorian Britain, it goes without saying that many of the commissioned commoners came from backgrounds no less privileged than the officers bearing titles. The majority of officers, though, were sons of the minor gentry, men who had been born comfortably rather than to great privilege. Although the social gulf between officers and men could not have been wider, these were increasingly enlightened times and the relationship was nothing akin to the British Army in which Wolseley and some of the other senior officers had cut their teeth at the time of the Crimean War.

The Light Camel Regiment

The Light Camel Regiment was destined to be the Cinderella outfit of the Camel Corps but, much to the chagrin of its officers and men never did get to the ball in any meaningful way. It was drawn from nine hussar regiments, namely the 3rd (King's Own), 4th (Queen's Own), 7th (Queen's Own), 10th (Prince of Wales's Own), 11th (Prince Albert's Own), 15th (The King's) and the 18th, 20th and 21st Hussars. Detachments again consisted of 2 officers, 2 sergeants, 2 corporals, 1 trumpeter and 38 privates. Because the regiment played such a minor role, the source coverage of its activities is generally poor. It appears to have had only three large companies, though whether these were A, B or C or Nos. 1, 2 and 3 Companies is unclear. As was the case in HCR, it is likely that companies were formed by grouping regimental detachments in order of *Army List* seniority.

1st Battalion, The Royal Sussex Regiment

The Royal Sussex Regiment had been born from the Childers amalgamations of 1881 and was a merger of the old 35th, which dated to 1701 and brought with it the county affiliation, and the 107th Regiment, which until 1858 had been one of the European regiments in the employ of the Honourable East India Company. Probably the best known incident in the history of the old 35th had taken place in 1757, during the French and Indian War, when the regiment defended Fort William Henry at the southern end of Lake George. The post-capitulation atrocities perpetrated by the Marquis de Montcalm's Huron allies famously provided the backdrop to Fenimore Cooper's *The Last of the Mohicans*. Two years later the 35th exacted its revenge as one of the regiments which fought under Wolfe at Quebec.

As reflected in Wolseley's orders to Stewart, it was intended that 1st Royal Sussex, sixteen officers[31] and 401 NCOs and men, would hold the staging posts across the Bayūda. The first link in the chain, Howeiyat Wells, would be guarded by the attached company of 2nd Essex. The central hub would be Jakdul Wells, with its plentiful supply of water and stockpiles of commissariat stores, where Colonel Vandeleur would be left in command. Much as he might have wanted to go on with the other half of his battalion, this would be commanded by the senior major, an officer by the name of Marsden Sunderland. Although Vandeleur had a thirty-three-year career behind him and was in his fifties, and Sunderland had been in the service for twenty-three years and was in his forties, neither had seen active service. While most other members of the battalion had participated in the recent Egyptian Campaign, the unit had played only a peripheral role and had missed Tel-el-Kebir and all the other significant actions leading up to it. Otherwise the preceding decade had been consumed by uneventful stints of garrison duty in Jamaica and Malta, so that by 1884 there was very little combat experience residing in the battalion. Sunderland's four-company 'wing' would go on to Abu Klea Wells with the Camel Corps regiments, where it would sub-divide again in order to provide a garrison for the third and final staging post on the lines of communication. Whatever residue of the half-battalion was left with Sunderland after Abu Klea had been taken care of would go on to Metemmeh and form part of the garrison there.

Because there were insufficient camels both to carry all the baggage and to mount Sunderland's companies for the advance on Abu Klea, a proportion of the Royal Sussex men would have to ride aboard some of the more lightly laden baggage camels. Typically this meant that in addition to the man and his kit, a heavy enough burden, the animal might also be carrying two 600-round boxes of small-arms ammunition. As these were constructed from a hardwood and weighed more than 80 lb apiece, they imposed a significant extra strain on animals already approaching the end of their tether. Others carried a pair of biscuit-boxes or cases of tinned bully beef, items which were even heavier than ammunition boxes.

The Royal Sussex officer fated to play the most prominent part in the story of the Gordon Relief Expedition was Captain Lionel Trafford, the officer commanding C Company, who wrote an important diary of his regiment's adventures which now resides in the West Sussex Records Office at Chichester.[32]

The Medical Sections

In addition to the Regimental Medical Officers (RMOs) serving with each of the major units, Surgeon Major Frederick Ferguson, the Principal Medical Officer (PMO), would be able to dispose two sections of No. 1 Moveable Field Hospital under Surgeon William Briggs, and two sections of the Medical Bearer Company under Surgeon Arthur Harding. Both assets were camel-borne and, counting the men already at Jakdul, would be able to field more than sixty hospital orderlies and administrators from the Medical Staff Corps. The bearer-company camels came equipped with either a pair of stretcher-litters, suitable for more serious cases, or a pair of counterbalancing seats known as *cacolets*. In addition to Ferguson, Briggs and Harding, there would appear to have been at least seven and possibly eight more Army Medical Department (AMD) doctors serving with the Desert Column.[33] Amongst them were Surgeons William Dick, Thomas Lucas, James Maconachie (RMO 1st Royal Sussex), Thomas Parke (RMO Naval Brigade), James Magill (RMO GCR), John Robertson (RMO MICR) and John Falvey (RMO HCR).[34]

Stewart's Second March to Jakdul Wells

The Desert Column moved off 'amid a chorus of good wishes'[35] at 3.20 on the afternoon of Thursday 8 January 1885,[36] at which juncture there were only sixteen full days remaining before the fall of Khartoum, though for the time being not even Muḥammad Aḥmad, the 'divinely guided one' himself, could have guessed that this was so. If there was one man in all the world who knew quite how fast the sands of time were draining from the hour-glass, it was the mildly eccentric British general whose name would forever be coupled with the place of his death.

As we have seen the distance from Korti to Metemmeh was 174 miles, from Metemmeh to Khartoum all but a hundred more. Although Stewart had already driven his camels hard to cover 198 miles in six days, it by no means followed that he would now be able to cover 274 miles in a mathematically feasible eight or nine days. This was dictated not only by the deteriorating condition of the camels, but by the fact that this time the enemy knew he was coming.

If it was at least theoretically possible in terms of time and space for the Desert Column to make it all the way to Khartoum in sixteen days, there were five major factors in play which guaranteed that this would never be so. First, instead of being bypassed to the south on a right oblique from Abu Klea Wells, Wolseley's orders required that Metemmeh be stormed. With a garrison of 3,000 anṣār known to be *in situ* this was certain to consume time and in all likelihood prove costly. Second, because the overland advance had been compromised so far in advance, the enemy commanders were already deploying forces to resist it. Though the British did not yet know it, this meant that there would now have to be a major fight in the desert. This again would be time-consuming, costly and, as battles against a numerically superior foe usually are, more than a little risky. Third, there was every danger that the near-approach of a relief column would drive the enemy high command to order an all-out assault on Khartoum. Fourth, and fundamentally, dashing 274 miles is not what Wolseley's orders required Stewart to do. Even if there was a battlefield triumph in the desert and Metemmeh fell quickly, the orders called not for the rapid exploitation of success but rather for a continued logistic build-up and a cautious exploratory mission which, because it required Wilson to make his report in Korti, could not fail to consume an additional fortnight. Fifth and finally, Stewart had not been granted any freedom to act at discretion: nothing in his orders envisaged a scenario in which the Desert Column would immediately advance south from Metemmeh. This would be the C-in-C's business, and his alone, and Wolseley was set to remain dislocated at Korti for the foreseeable future. Cut it any way you will, when the Desert Column left Korti it was not that the game was afoot, but rather that it was already up. In other words the operational-level constraints were such that there was nothing that could be done at the tactical level to affect the outcome.

Stewart was accompanied by his usual cabal of staff officers, Wardrop, Airlie, Rhodes and Herbert, but had also been joined by three additional officers from the Intelligence Department, its chief, Colonel Sir Charles Wilson, and two of his five assistants, namely Major John Dickson and Captain Willoughby Verner. Of the others, Major Herbert Kitchener was already at Jakdul, Lieutenant Edward Stuart-Wortley had gone on ahead with Clarke's convoy[37] and Major Alfred Turner had taken over Wilson's duties at army headquarters and would be staying behind at Korti. Only that morning Turner had received a brief visit from the column commander. 'Just before starting Sir Herbert Stewart confided to me a few small articles which I undertook to hand to his wife, if he did not survive the campaign ... He seemed to have a presentiment of coming fate.'[38]

We noted earlier that the news blackout on Stewart's first march to Jakdul had been so effective that only Piggott, the Reuters man, had got wind of it early enough to tag along. There was huge public interest in the salvation of Gordon and now that the cat was out of the bag there would be no fewer than nine war correspondents accompanying Stewart's second march. They included some of the best known war artists and correspondents of the age. Melton Prior (*Illustrated London News*), Frederic Villiers (*The Graphic*), Jack Cameron (*The Standard*), St Leger Herbert (*Morning Post*) and Charles Williams (*Daily Chronicle* and Central News) were already established names, while Alex Macdonald (*Western Morning News*), though less experienced than some of his colleagues, was a particularly keen-eyed observer. Also present were Harry Pearse of the *Daily News* and Walter Ingram, the son of Sir William Ingram, the proprietor of the *Illustrated London News*, who had tagged along more for the adventure than for the edification of the reading public.

Macdonald and Cameron were not the only Scots amongst the cabal of journalists. Bennet Burleigh of the *Daily Telegraph*, now in his mid-forties, was a tough Glaswegian with a remarkable past. Two decades earlier young Burley (as he was then known) had travelled to Civil War America to peddle innovative underwater charges intended for acts of naval sabotage. Carried away by his youthful sense of adventure, he ended up enlisting in a cloak-and-dagger wing of the Confederate Navy. He was taken prisoner at one point and might well have been summarily executed, had he not made a daring jail break and escaped to Canada. After an ill-fated piratical escapade on Lake Erie, Burleigh again escaped to Canadian territory, where this time he was detained for violating British neutrality. The Federal authorities applied for his extradition and a high-profile court hearing to decide the matter duly ensued. He was turned over to face relatively low-key robbery charges, although there was a widespread expectation that the Americans would eventually add piracy to the charge sheet, with the consequent danger of a capital sentence. Nobody had counted on Burleigh charming his gaoler to such an extent that he was regularly permitted to exercise by walking about town. Needless to say, one sunny day he elected not to return from his afternoon stroll and next raised his head in England. He began his journalistic career in Texas in the 1870s, where nobody in authority seemed interested in his past misdemeanours, before eventually returning to England to take up a job with the Central News. He migrated onto the staff of the *Daily Telegraph* in time to cover the Tel-el-Kebir campaign and had gone on subsequently to cover Graham's first Suakin campaign. He was present at both El Teb and Tamai, and in the latter action had played a part in rallying the troops in Davis's brigade when the square was driven in.[39]

Burleigh had already come close to losing his life on the Nile, when on 1 December 1884 his privately hired *dahabieh* had capsized in crocodile-infested waters near the village of Akhashieh. Though his native servant was drowned, Burleigh was able to save himself by swimming for the bank using two oars as flotation aids. From time to time he clattered them together as noisily as possible in the hope that the sound would frighten any lurking crocodiles away. Although all his kit had gone to the bottom, Burleigh was fortunate still to have some money in a pouch on his waist-belt. He was even more fortunate that Major Alfred Turner had been attracted to the scene by the peculiar sound of the clattering oars and was at hand to provide succour. Even now, not quite six weeks later, Burleigh was still clad in the assorted items of clothing Turner had been kind enough to lend him.[40] Burleigh's remarkable past, bluff character and physical courage meant that he commanded the unequivocal respect of his colleagues. What they did not yet know was that, professionally speaking, he was extremely hard-edged and determined to 'scoop' them at any and every opportunity. Many more campaigns yet lay ahead of him. It is a moot point whether Russell, Forbes or Burleigh was the greatest of the Victorian war correspondents, but Burleigh must certainly be counted somewhere near the top of the pecking order.

Strangely, the Reuters correspondent, having initially stayed behind at Jakdul Wells with GCR, was even now riding back to Korti accompanied only by a native servant. It was noted by Wolseley that he was able to do so without running into any hostile bands of Arabs. He arrived at the headquarters camp only hours after the rest of his press colleagues set off in the opposite direction with Sir Herbert Stewart.[41]

With the 19th Hussars cantering on ahead, the camel-borne units lurched silently into the desert, marching on a front of camel corps sections, some twenty to twenty-five animals abreast. The column made about nine miles, before the onset of darkness brought an end to the day's proceedings at about 6.00 p.m. Although it had not been a long or arduous march, Percy Marling was already beginning to have doubts about how the camels would fare in the days ahead.

January 8th. Started from Korti at 1 p.m. [sic]. The camels kept breaking down. I don't think they will stick it, they are already losing condition, and consequently getting fearfully sore backs; some of them have holes you can put your fist into.[42]

Having cooked their suppers, the troops then slept through to a 1.30 a.m. reveille,[43] apart that is from one 'minor' disturbance when Verner and Dickson were obliged to chase a runaway camel through most of the bivouac, much to the disgust of hundreds of rudely awakened Tommies.

While the rest of the force was forming up ready to resume the march under a bright moon and a cold clear sky, Sir Charles Wilson, Major Dickson and the Ambukol guides took their usual station at the head of the column. They were still waiting for the order to march when 'the whole of the right wing marched across our front, in a direction nearly at right angles to our proper road'.[44] Who originated the movement was never discovered, but a long delay ensued while the confusion was sorted out and the wandering companies re-formed in the right place. It was 3.30 a.m. before the column got properly under way.[45] The ensuing leg of the march lasted until 9.30 a.m., when a breakfast halt was called at the Wādī Abu Gir. At

2.00 p.m. they were off again, marching on through a hot Friday afternoon until 5.45 p.m. With darkness approaching Stewart brought the column to a halt in a rugged valley with a good covering of grass. Allowing the camels to graze was out of the question and they were once again knee-haltered en masse. Reveille was meant to be sounded by HCR at 1.20 a.m., but for some unknown reason was forty minutes late.[46] There was some difficulty in getting going in broken ground and the column twice missed its way in the gloom of early morning.

The wells at Hambok were reached not long after sun-up on Saturday, but according to Sir Charles Wilson were good only for 'a few cupfuls of water'.[47] As had been the case on the first journey, the general decided to push through to Howeiyat, nine miles further on. A proportion of the troops, particularly some of the Royal Sussex companies, had already run very low on water. Lord Airlie was probably being less than charitable in noting in the War Diary that 'some of this Regiment had used more [water] than was allowed'. A more compelling explanation is offered by Sir Charles Wilson in *From Korti to Khartum*. Because the men of the Royal Sussex had never been intended for mounted duty they received an issue of water-skins only at the last minute, by which time the pick of the items had already gone to the camel regiments, leaving a residue which were in generally poor condition and inclined to leak badly. Willoughby Verner adds in his account that the Royal Sussex had not in fact been provided with skins on the same scale as the camel regiments.[48] Everybody, though, was jealous of the Naval Brigade, which had brought along 'large indiarubber bags' expressly designed to carry water and which with a little foresight could have been provided as a universal stores item.[49] The native drivers seem to have been left particularly short of water, though whether this was because they failed to show restraint, or because they had not been as well provided for as the troops, is impossible to tell. As a result there were instances of water-skins and water-bottles being stolen.[50] Melton Prior took to concealing the water-skins aboard his baggage camels inside potato-sacks. At a bivouac halt he would have the 'potatoes' put under his camp-cot and slept in his pistol belt, having first given due warning to his servant and drivers that he would 'shoot them like dogs' in the event he caught them stealing water.[51]

Sir Charles Wilson rode on ahead of the toiling column and arrived at Howeiyat just in time to see Colonel Stanley Clarke's thousand-camel convoy disappearing over a distant ridgeline. Unsurprisingly the wells had been all but drunk dry, a predictable eventuality which does not seem to have occurred to the army staff in advance. Having pushed on ahead of the main body overnight, Colonel Percy Barrow and the 19th Hussars had been in residence beside Fetherstonhaugh and his riflemen for some hours. The rest of the column came up at about 10.00 a.m.[52] and was halted just short of the wells, so that there would be time for them at least partially to recharge themselves from the water table. In the meantime sentries would be posted over them. A quantity of reserve water was issued out from the forty-gallon tanks with the baggage train, in order that the troops could at least wash down an unappetizing breakfast with a mug of tea. At length the men were marched across to the wells by companies to take a modest drink of muddy water.

Although the fighting troops behaved faultlessly, maintaining order when it came to the turn of the native drivers proved something of a challenge.[53] While Fetherstonhaugh and his men were delighted to be re-joining the rest of their brethren, Captain William Carter and his 2nd Essex lads would have been rather less taken with the prospect of being left behind in so remote a spot. The enemy would have to strike very deep indeed if they were going to do any mischief at Howeiyat Wells, but in the event that they did Carter would have two subalterns and fifty-five NCOs and men with which to keep them at bay. Much more realistically, Carter knew that his main job for the next few weeks would be preventing his men losing their minds through unrelenting tedium. Stewart visited Carter to describe the work he wanted undertaken with a view to securing the outpost and improving the water supply. Eight members of MICR would also be staying at Howeiyat with their camels, in order to provide two four-man courier parties on the lines of communication.

The main body had been at the wells for about ninety minutes by the time the rearguard, Major Lord Arthur Somerset's No. 2 Company, HCR, four officers and eighty NCOs and men strong, caught up. In line with Marling's remarks about the state of the camels, a delay of such length would suggest that there had been a good deal of trouble at the rear of the column with broken-down camels.

As the passage of Clarke's convoy had unexpectedly left Stewart without the wherewithal to water his own animals, he concluded that he would have to divert into the Abu Halfâ valley the next day and take on water there. Barrow and the 19th Hussars departed not long after noon,[54] followed by the main body at 2.30 p.m.[55] Because 'Podge' Somerset's company had come in so much later than everybody else, it would be permitted stay at Howeiyat overnight and resume the march first thing in the morning.[56]

Stewart led his brigade past some hills on the left, across 'a plain of black flints'[57] and on through another hot, thirsty afternoon, until at length, with darkness fast closing in, he caught sight of campfires in the distance. Convinced that he was looking at Stanley Clarke's encampment, Stewart decided to press on through the gloom in order to be able to bivouac in front of the convoy. Sir Charles Wilson noted that without the moon illuminating the desert, night marching quickly turned into an ordeal. 'The way in which the unfortunate camels tumbled about in the dark, and loads came off, and the strong language that was used, were things to see and hear.' A treacherous stretch of rough, stony ground brought the march to a precipitate halt in the floor of a *khor* long before Clarke's encampment had been reached. It turned out in the end that the campfires off to the flank were not Clarke's but Barrow's. There was little choice on so dark a night but to bivouac in column of march. Once again a quantity of water was issued from the reserve tanks,[58] although it was nothing like enough to meet the needs of the men who had begun the march with only a part-share in a defective water-skin. By Willoughby Verner's estimation the bivouac was some sixty-seven miles from Korti. At no point to date had the column's rate of advance topped 2½ miles in the hour.

Reveille on the morning of Sunday 11 January was sounded ninety minutes in advance of a 4.00 a.m. start.[59] As usual Colonel Barrow pushed his squadron on half an hour ahead of everybody else.[60] Once again there was a good deal of confusion at the outset, leading to part of the column moving off in quite the wrong direction.[61] Once the disarray had been rectified, a gruelling five-hour march ensued. Percy Marling's diary notes for the day were succinct but convey a great deal: 'Camels breaking down in all directions, and the native drivers falling down and shrieking for water.'[62] Riding at the head of the column with the scouts, Verner came upon a number of cases of biscuit and tinned beef, dropped and abandoned by Clarke's more feckless drivers. Worse still than the odd dropped item, the cavalry flankers also brought in a number of fully laden baggage camels which had been abandoned altogether.[63] After a ninety-minute breakfast halt, the next leg of the journey got under way at 11.00 a.m.[64] At the appropriate point near a low rocky hill, the line of march swung through ninety degrees towards the 'prettily wooded' valley of Abu Halfa. The wells were reached at about 2.00 in the afternoon. Again, whilst the quantity of water available would have amply serviced the needs of a passing caravan, there was nothing like enough for a brigade of camel-borne troops. Sir Charles Wilson described the scene:

. . . we found much less water than we expected. There was one pond of dirty water almost black with mud, and a few holes in the gravel with better water. We set to work to open new holes, into which the water ran quickly; but the men were so wild with thirst that, directly the water began running in, we had to give the holes up and begin digging others. The men behaved admirably. Officers and men were marched up, and each received a pint; they then moved off to their camping grounds, and were afterwards allowed to come and draw water for cooking. We managed to get three tin biscuit-boxes[65] sunk in the ground, to act as rough filters and reservoirs, from which the men could bale out water; but it was hard work. It was a curious scene, as the camels, donkeys and ponies rushed for the water directly they arrived, and had to be kept back by main force. All the afternoon there was a continuous stream of men going down for water, and it was kept up the whole night. Some of the officers worked hard in the hot sun digging new wells and distributing water to all comers.[66]

Wilson was struck by the quiet professionalism of the Mounted Infantry, 'all old soldiers, looked after by picked officers', as he put it.[67] The NCOs had taken particular care in advance to ensure that the men's water-skins were sound to begin with and properly maintained thereafter: in particular they needed to be kept wet in order to prevent their drying out and cracking. From the moment the column left Korti, the MICR companies were allowed to drink only by the order of their captains. In consequence the regiment experienced none of the hardship undergone by the Royal Sussex. Wilson noted that Gough's men still had a good deal of water left in their skins when they reached the end of the journey.

Although Jakdul Wells was now only a few hours' march away, Stewart did not intend moving off on the final leg until sun-up the following morning. This was excellent news as far as Sir Charles Wilson was concerned, as he had already seen more than enough night marching to conclude that it was a thoroughly bad practice. He decided to raise the matter with Stewart during the course of the afternoon and attempt to win him over to his own way of thinking.

He [Stewart] says truly that the camels march much better at night, and that men and camels suffer from the heat when they march by day. I contend that sleep by day is not so refreshing as sleep by night for the men; that when the camels are loaded in the dark the loads are badly put on, and that sore backs are started before the loads can be properly adjusted by daylight; that owing to the constant long halts, necessary to keep the column together in the dark, the loads remain on the camels' backs for an excessively long time, fifteen or sixteen hours out of the twenty-four; that the camels start on empty stomachs, contrary to the habit of the beast; that much harm is done to the camels by marching in close order, in the dark over rough ground; that the camels get neither rest or food; and that the men cannot stand marching from 2 A.M. to 10 or 11 A.M with nothing inside them. I cannot think why we violate all the dictates of common sense in our treatment of the camel, and believe we should get much more out of ours if we worked them as the Arabs do. The desert is not a desert in the proper sense of the term. There is ample water, abundant vegetation, and an almost limitless supply of savas grass, the best of feeding for camels: and here ours are failing before we have commenced, simply because we will not give them time to feed, and when in camp tie them down so tightly they cannot move. I do not think more than 500 camels should ever travel together, and 300 would be a safer limit. It would be heresy to say the camelry is a mistake; but if Tommy Atkins cannot march in such a climate as this, we had better give up fighting.[68]

These were telling arguments to be sure, although Wilson fails to indicate how the general responded to them. Perhaps he agreed to sleep on the advice, as the day was wearing on and everybody was tired. No attempt seems to have been made to water the animals that evening, probably to prevent what little water there was being polluted while the men were still trying to re-charge their skins and bottles. Verner woke with a start during the course of the night, when one thirsty beast came trotting through the bivouac of the intelligence staff. Believing it to be his own animal, he jumped up and gave chase in the direction of the wells.

There I found an extraordinary spectacle. There was a bright moon shining on the small pool and on the bank was a piquet to guard the water. All round were dozens of horses and camels which had broken loose and made for the water. The men were keeping them off with their bayonets. As a rule the camels halted at a few yards distance and looked solemnly at the men, but the horses were far more enterprising. Some of the men had the sense to tie down the camels which kept arriving in unceasing procession. I found mine by sheer luck and led him back to our lines. The whole night I was disturbed by other people's animals wandering over our bivouac.[69]

Reveille on Monday 12 January came at 4.15 a.m., in readiness for a 6.00 a.m. start. It was about twelve miles to Jakdul Wells and an abundant supply of water. While the camel regiments and baggage train moved out with the dawn, the cavalry squadron stayed on to water its ponies and did not in the end set out until 12.45 p.m.[70]

By 10.30 a.m. the main body had completed the journey and arrived at Jakdul to find that the Guards and Royal Engineers had been hard at work over the past week. The regimental camping grounds were neatly marked with signboards and had been completely cleared of stones. There was also a network of cleared pathways, which the Guards officers explained would serve to prevent any undue wear and tear on the men's boots. Three strong outworks had been raised on commanding high points above the wells: Forts Stewart, Boscawen and Flagstaff. Even more importantly, Dorward had successfully devised ways and means of delivering water into the low ground: three hand-operated tripod pumps brought water down from the lower pool to a 'puddled mud trough', long enough for fifty camels to be watered at a time, while the drinking water was brought down from the upper pools by means of a length of hose.[71] Count Gleichen had made a particularly useful contribution by wandering past what everybody thought was the upper pool, to find that there were in fact two more large reservoirs about three-quarters of a mile further up the gorge. These had not as yet been drawn upon but were estimated to hold around 320,000 gallons.[72] There were of course still two bodies of troops some way behind the main body when it rode into Jakdul. Lord Arthur Somerset brought his company in at 2.30 p.m., while Colonel Barrow rode in at the head of the 19th Hussars a little under two hours later.[73]

Colonel Clarke and his men had reached Jakdul at 3.30 p.m. the previous day, Sunday, and had occupied a *zariba* built by the Guards astride the main caravan route in readiness for their arrival. They had spent the rest of the day bringing relays of camels down the track to be watered at the wells. The operation took about 4½ hours in all and drew to a close at about 9.00 that evening.[74] On Monday morning Clarke's camels had again been watered. Now, over the course of Monday afternoon and evening, it was the turn of the long-suffering camels with the main body. The Guards and Marines were standing by to manage the operation and did sterling work over the course of about seven hours, toiling even by lamplight at the end to ensure that all two and a half thousand camels were attended to.

Sir Charles Wilson and Willoughby Verner tracked down Kitchener at his cave and spent much of the afternoon talking the intelligence picture through with him. It was the first time that Kitchener and Verner had met.[75] Having daily scoured the desert with a handful of hussars, the Ambukol guides and the occasional bored Guards officer, Kitchener had succeeded in capturing a few more prisoners but had gleaned no new intelligence to speak of. *The Standard* carried a Reuters report, dated Saturday 3 January, which described one of Kitchener's desert adventures.

On Sunday, Major Kitchener, Colonels Sawle [Graves-Sawle] and Bonham, Captain [*sic* – Lieutenant] Dawson, and two corporals of Hussars, while reconnoitring in the direction of the Abu Halfa Wells, met a small party of natives, with camels and asses laden with grain.

These they captured, and while returning with them to the camp they sighted on their right a large convoy of about seventy camels, with fifty natives. Major Kitchener and his party at once galloped after them. On coming to close quarters with the natives, half of the latter cut away the loads from their camels, and let them loose, while the other half halted, and forming in front of the camels, showed fight. Major Kitchener's party, observing this, galloped hard, shouting at the top of their voices. This scared both the camels and the rebels, and scattered them, thus enabling the British to capture nine camels laden with grain and flour. As Major Kitchener's party was small, and it was near sunset, they returned to the camp with their spoil. At midnight a stronger party went out, and brought back eight camel loads of dates, one camel and some donkeys; but they did not sight any of the rebels. This captured convoy was bound for the Mahdi's camp.[76]

Wilson was obliged during the course of his long talk with Kitchener to break what he knew would be most unwelcome news: when Colonel Clarke set off to return to Korti, it was Lord Wolseley's express wish that the major accompany him. Quite what good this would do, when so resourceful an officer might otherwise have been of inestimable service to General Stewart, was far from clear. Although the order left Kitchener hopping mad, an order it remained. Later on Sir Charles was one of the lucky guests invited to dine with Boscawen and the officers of GCR. The general would doubtless also have been present. Sir William Gordon-Cumming enjoyed a reputation as a fine shot and over the previous few days had been out after gazelle and sand-grouse. Wilson wrote that he and his fellow guests did 'full justice' to 'a capital dinner'.[77]

Alex Macdonald had been in residence since the previous day. His account of his journey to Jakdul reveals that Clarke's convoy had been managed every bit as badly as Wolseley had feared. Quantities of stores had been lost, there was a good deal of straggling and more than twenty animals had died of exhaustion en route. At one point in the march Macdonald had fallen back to the rear in search of his baggage camels and the not altogether trustworthy Greek servant he had been foolish enough to take on. The unlikely duo then tarried rather too long over breakfast and failed to notice the column moving off ahead of them. As a result they were lost in the desert for a while, but at least learned to keep their wits about them in future.

Having recounted the story of his own tribulations, Macdonald goes on to describe the mysterious disappearance of a war correspondent called Gordon (no relation), who was reported as having left Korti on 9 January, the day after Stewart's main body, intent on catching up with a third and much smaller convoy, consisting of 125 camels loaded with *dhura*, with which Colonel Burnaby and Captain Gascoigne were making their way to the front. Macdonald concluded that the convoy must actually have left Korti after Gordon and that he remained oblivious to the fact that he was chasing a chimera; but he might just as readily have set off on a different bearing, only to overtake Burnaby in the desert without realizing it. On 13 January, the day after the main body reached Jakdul Wells, Gordon and his

Greek servant ran into an officer by the name of Douglas, who at the time was conducting survey work about eight miles west of Howeiyat Wells. Douglas later recounted the story of his curious chance encounter to Macdonald.

He [Gordon] told Lieutenant Douglas that he had been without water for two days. His eyes glazed with excitement. During the evening he said he had a great deal on his mind, for he had volunteered to carry despatches to General Stewart, and then rambled on about having lost his sword. Such an adventure, he said, as he had had only occurred once in a man's lifetime, and he must write it down. During nearly the whole of the night, Lieutenant Douglas informed me, Gordon's light was burning. Early in the morning Douglas rode with him some distance, when Gordon spoke about the landmarks in connection with finding his way. In reply he was told to keep his eye more on the broad well-marked track so recently made by our thousands of camels. After parting with Douglas he was never heard of again, and it was supposed that he had either perished of thirst in the desert or been killed by wandering Arabs.[78]

The mysterious Gordon is more fully identified in a Reuters report dated Korti, 11 February 1885, as Captain (retired) W. H. Gordon, formerly of the Royal Welsh Fusiliers and latterly the representative of the *Manchester Guardian*. He was reported by Reuters as having last been seen on 18 January, a few days later than is stated by Macdonald.[79]

It should be noted that Macdonald asserts in his book that MICR arrived at Jakdul not long after he did, having come straight on without going via Abu Halfā like the rest of the main body. He goes on to describe how he was camped out on ground allotted to the officers of the Mounted Infantry, when Major Gough rode up and told him in no uncertain terms to move somewhere else. Macdonald's ruffled feathers were smoothed by the much more kind-hearted Major Thomas Phipps and Captain Henry Walsh.[80] Whilst the anecdote sounds compelling enough, somewhere along the way Macdonald has overlooked a night's sleep, as MICR *did not* in fact come straight on, *did* go via Abu Halfā and *did not* arrive on the 11th but on the 12th, with the rest of the main body.[81]

Final Preparations

Before going to dinner with the Guards, General Stewart outlined his plan for the next phase of operations.[82] The following day, Tuesday 13 January, would be given over to watering, feeding and resting the animals, recharging water containers and the miscellany of other administrative preparations necessary to sustain a rapid advance on Metemmeh. GCR would need to take its riding camels back from 1st Royal Sussex at some point. Colonel Vandeleur, meanwhile, would assume command of Jakdul Wells and take the forts over from the Guards. He would have his battalion headquarters and three of his seven companies available to him, a total strength of eight officers and around 150 bayonets. In addition a proportion of the medical staff would stay behind to provide a necessarily rough and ready base-hospital facility.[83] Major Sunderland would go on with the other half-battalion and would be able to dispose eight officers and 250 bayonets. As had been the case at Howeiyat Wells, MICR was to leave behind a party of eight camel-mounted NCOs and men to provide courier parties.[84] Colonel Clarke and his LCR detachments would depart for Korti first thing on Wednesday morning, while the main body would begin its march to the Nile at 2.00 that afternoon. It was anticipated that the column would next see a fresh supply of water at Abu Klea Wells on Friday 16 January, and that the attack on Metemmeh would take place on Sunday.[85] Verner's diary is the one primary source to reveal the hugely significant fact that at this juncture Sir Charles Wilsons's journey to Khartoum was still 'a profound secret from all'.[86]

When Colonel Vandeleur came to assigning troops to task, he decided that his D, E and H Companies would stay behind, and that B (Major George Harden), C (Captain Lionel Trafford), F (Major Arthur Gern) and G (Major Marsden Sunderland) Companies would be the ones to go on.[87] With an average strength of about sixty officers and men, the Royal Sussex companies were about 25 per cent weaker than their Camel Corps counterparts.

Tuesday was quickly consumed by the flurry of administrative preparations for the march. Colonel Vandeleur took his three company commanders to look around the forts and to contemplate how they might best dispose their troops. We have noted already that the wells were located in a narrow gorge within a natural amphitheatre of high ground. Fort Flagstaff was a minor outpost, constructed only over the past couple of days, and was located atop a spur on the left-hand side of the amphitheatre. By contrast Forts Stewart and Boscawen were much larger redoubts which the Guards had worked on from the outset.

Fort Stewart, the outermost position, was sited at the head of a spur on the right-hand side of the cul-de-sac and was designed to take a garrison of up to two companies, although Major Dorward, its architect, felt sure that *in extremis* a conventionally sized half-company would have no difficulty in holding it. As Vandeleur's companies were so small, this more than likely became a company-strength outpost. Fort Boscawen, the innermost position, directly commanded the rock pools from a high point on the right-hand side of the gorge.[88] Evidently smaller than Fort Stewart, it was designed to be garrisoned by a half-company. The two original forts now had dry stone perimeter walls which were five feet high, three feet thick and incorporated corner bastions designed to permit enfilading fire. They had only been raised with a great deal of back-breaking labour on the part of Boscawen's guardsmen and marines. Gleichen observed that by the end of the fourth day all the loose stones in the vicinity of the forts had been used up and that for the rest of the time the men had been breaking rocks using only three pickaxes and two crowbars per fort. In fact Dorward, whose tools they were, stated in his official report that the work had been done with two crowbars and three sledgehammers in total.[89] Although Dorward seems not to have recorded their dimensions, Gleichen estimated the size of the two larger forts as 20 yards x 23 yards, and 30 yards x 15 yards, although he fails to specify which was which.[90] Fort

Flagstaff was essentially a look-out post and may have been nothing more complex than a rough stone sangar capable of protecting perhaps a dozen men. Between labouring all day and mounting a strong picket of two officers and sixty-five NCOs and men by night, the rocky ground had taken a severe toll of the guardsmen's ammunition boots, many sets of which would not see out the campaign.

The allotment of baggage camels was supervised by Assistant Commissary-General Nugent. In addition to the animals already allocated as regimental transport, some 1,118 more were subsumed into Nos. 9 and 11 Transport Companies, the largely nominal organizations which together made up the baggage train. There would have been more than enough baggage camels left over for all the men in Sunderland's half-battalion to be provided with animals of their own, had not Stewart, who was only too keenly aware that Buller had next to no camels left at Korti, decided to send back as many as possible with Colonel Clarke. This meant that for the time being some 256 of Nugent's 1,118 animals would have to carry not only a standard load of bully beef or biscuit, but would also have a member of 1st Royal Sussex perched on top.[91]

Everybody's spirits received a lift when the famously lion-hearted Commanding Officer of the Blues rode in at the head of the *dhura* convoy during the course of the afternoon. When Conductor Joseph Pritchard walked across to greet the colonel and assume responsibility for the baggage animals strung out behind him, Burnaby's first words to him were, 'Am I in time for the fighting?'[92] Pritchard doubtless took great pleasure in informing the colonel that he had not missed anything so far and that the column would be marching out the following afternoon in the reasonable expectation that there would be a fight at Metemmeh before the week was out.

In logistic terms the arrival of the *dhura* was crucial, as it permitted Stewart's animals to be properly fed before departing Jakdul. Lord Cochrane estimated that since leaving Korti the camels had each consumed about 16 lb of grain, and not quite twice that amount of 'dry wiry grass', gathered in by the soldiers and native drivers at halts. Unfortunately the nutritional value of the grass was negligible.[93] Gleichen wrote that 'the camels had to sustain themselves on mimosa shoots and long, dry yellow grass, a hundredweight of which would barely produce a pound of nourishment'.[94] In other words the camels were already malnourished when they reached Jakdul. Such was the shortage of transport that it was decided that the 125 animals brought in by Burnaby would be pressed into service for carrying commissariat stores, rather than ferrying a bulk supply of *dhura* forward with the column. Sufficient fodder would be distributed around the force for each man to move out with two feeds of 8 lb in the grain-sack on his saddle.[95]

Chapter 7

Approach to Battle

Jakdul Wells to Abu Klea: 14–16 January 1885

I don't like unnecessary slaughter, but I'm afraid we shall have to kill five hundred or so of the poor devils before we can establish ourselves in Metemmeh.

> Brigadier General Sir Herbert Stewart, quoted by Lieutenant
> Count Gleichen in *With the Camel Corps up the Nile*

COLONEL FREDERICK GUSTAVUS BURNABY was not merely a senior officer of the sovereign's bodyguard, but was also a swordsman, pugilist, strong-man, man-about-town, daredevil adventurer, war hero, long-distance balloonist, Conservative parliamentary candidate and father. He was in short a swashbuckling icon of the Victorian age and literally a legend in his own lifetime. Now forty-two years of age, he had been in the Household Cavalry all his adult life. He stood more than 6 ft 4 in tall and as a result of a youthful predilection for boxing, weight training, fencing and sundry other sporting pursuits was both powerfully built and formidably strong. It was said that in his prime he had sported a 46-inch chest and a 30-inch waist. Over the past few years, however, he had been much troubled by ill-health, had sunk into the inexorable physical decline of middle age and now weighed in at something around nineteen stone. In 1870 the French artist Tissot had captured a tall, elegant and athletic 27-year-old in a famous and much-loved work which now hangs in the National Portrait Gallery in London. Tissot portrays Burnaby at repose over a quiet cigarette in his rooms, clad in a shell jacket and tight-fitting overalls, with his cuirass and helmet laid out on the furniture behind him. The navy blue and red of his Royal Horse Guards' uniform contrasts vividly with the drabness of an everyday domestic setting. The subject's magnificent pointed moustache and the splendour of his uniform bespeak fastidiousness and elegance. It is a compelling portrait, although the real Fred Burnaby, while he scrubbed up like a latter-day god of war at the hands of his soldier-servants, was not overly attentive to his appearance. When he was not on show in the capital as a member of the Sovereign's bodyguard, which was about five months in every twelve (such was the generous officers' leave entitlement in the High Victorian Army), his tastes were distinctly bohemian and his turnout sometimes a little frayed around the edges.

'Fred' was a gregarious soul, with a ready smile and winning ways. He was also possessed of a well-developed sense of fun which in certain quarters of Victorian high society was not always appreciated. If he was strongly inclined not to take himself too seriously, he was also a little too ready to provoke people who did: he once told the Prince of Wales that his own lineage, which could purportedly be traced to Edward I, gave him the stronger claim on the throne. It was intended as a joke but instead served only to offend the Prince needlessly. If he could not be counted a noted intellect, he was no fool either and possessed an impressive talent for languages. He was able to speak French, German and Italian fluently and could get by in Spanish, Arabic, Turkish and Russian. He was not much given to turning the other cheek in the face of an insult or a provocation and knew only too well how formidably strong he was, so that there were occasions when he was tempted to throw his weight around a little too readily. One of the least damaging rumpuses cropped up when he encountered a man beating his wife in the street, to which unhappy scene he responded by throwing the bounder head-first over a wall.

Burnaby held stridently patriotic political views but was inclined to trumpet them rather too publicly for the taste of many of his regimental colleagues. A colonel of Household Cavalry he may have been, but grand, aloof or pretentious he most assuredly was not. In some ways he was not quite right for the Blues, too rumbustious, perhaps, for an officer's mess which affected fashionable disinterest in soldiering and which for the most part knew nothing of the empire's wilder corners, places most senior members of the regiment hoped never to see. To prise the Blues out of London the enemy would have to be fashionably worthy of the inconvenience: the French or the Prussians might just about come up to the mark. Although the Household Cavalry officers of today might speak fondly of the Burnaby legend, and rightly so, many of their antecedents heartily disapproved of the man who gave rise to it.

A famous story of Burnaby's younger days had it that he had once been Captain of the Guard at Windsor, when a horse-trader brought two Shetland ponies into the castle for the Queen Empress's approval. By way of a jape the other officers of the guard had the animals brought upstairs to the Captain's apartments. They were delighted to find the door ajar and shooed the ponies through it. When, joke over, the time came for them to be taken into the Queen's presence, they could not be prevailed upon to walk back down the staircase they had earlier ascended contentedly enough. The solution was obvious; Burnaby positioned himself between the animals, picked one up under each arm and walked downstairs with them.[1]

By the mid-1870s Burnaby had been in the Household Cavalry for fifteen years, had grown bored with the monotony of public duties in London and took it into his head to use his long-leaves for seeing something more of the world. As a result he was all but unique in the British Army of January 1885, in that he had already been to see Gordon Pasha in Khartoum, albeit his visit had taken place during his long-leave of 1874/5,[2] at which time the then Colonel Gordon was in his first tour of duty in the Sudan. As was customary Burnaby had travelled to Khartoum by crossing the desert from Suakin to Berber and taking passage aboard a south-bound steamer. The journey through the Sudan had been interesting enough, although Gordon seems to have been a little stand-offish, if not downright inhospitable. It was a year later that the gallant Captain Burnaby shot to fame. In the winter of 1875/6 he had undertaken a hard-riding foray into Central Asia, a solo escapade undertaken in climatic extremes and in open defiance of Tsarist Russia. He recounted his adventures, including the tale of how a party of friendly Cossacks prevented the loss of his hands through frostbite,[3] in a runaway best-seller called *A Ride to Khiva*. The following year Burnaby set off from Constantinople and rode east for a thousand miles. *On Horseback through Asia Minor* also became a best-seller. During his leave of 1877–8 Burnaby went to see something of the Russo-Turkish War, ostensibly as the representative of a London-based humanitarian organization known as the 'Stafford House Committee'. In Bulgaria he met and befriended Valentine Baker, by now a Turkish divisional commander. Burnaby assumed a strictly unofficial role as an aide to Baker in the ensuing heavy fighting.

In 1879 the 36-year-old Fred married an 18-year-old Anglo-Irish heiress from County Wicklow called Elizabeth Hawkins-Whitshed. A son, Harry Arthur Gustavus St Vincent Burnaby, was born the following year. It was contempt for timorous Liberal government which drew Burnaby into the political arena. For the general election of 1880 he was adopted by the Conservatives as the man to turn Joe Chamberlain out of his Birmingham stronghold. It was a tall order. Although Burnaby polled 15,716 votes, more than twice the Tory share at the previous election, it was still 4,000 too few to topple the sitting member. The Liberals also gained the day nationwide, resulting in Gladstone assuming the premiership for the second time. The following year Burnaby was appointed as the Commanding Officer of the Blues and set about changing the ways of a notoriously indolent officer's mess. His endeavours were resisted by an effete and disloyal cabal of officers much set in its ways, although the colonel's renown and his gift for the common touch meant that he commanded the devotion of his NCOs and men.[4]

In March 1882 Burnaby completed a solo-crossing of the English Channel[5] in the hot air balloon 'Eclipse', only to attract a rebuke from the Duke of Cambridge for departing the country without leave. Although this has typically been presented by historians as if Burnaby had been subjected to serious censure, the interview was good natured and done more for the sake of 'form' than anything else. In fact the Duke admired the exploit and on one occasion remarked that he wished he could go up with Burnaby, only he feared 'there would be such a hullabaloo'.[6] Although there were occasional run-ins with the C-in-C, it is doubtful whether the Duke actively disliked Burnaby as much as Wolseley's journals would imply. It was probably more the case that he had resolved to curtail Burnaby's buccaneering disregard for military formalities, rather than that there was any great personal difficulty between them.

Not long after his cross-Channel adventure Burnaby's young wife 'Lizzie' left the country on doctor's orders, to go and live in Switzerland for the sake of her health.

Fortified by the mountain air, she appears to have climbed Mont Blanc the following year. The couple remained on cordial terms and exchanged letters often, while Fred visited whenever he could. Lizzie would outlive her first husband of course, but married twice more in the course of a long life and, as Mrs Aubrey Le Blond, became well known in her own right as an alpinist, author and pioneer of women's mountaineering.

Later that year all the talk was of war in Egypt. Wiser heads than the cabal of blockheads in the Blues decided that after some sixty-seven years of peacetime soldiering in England, it was high time the Household Cavalry went to war again. It was decided to send a composite regiment, consisting of a squadron each from 1st Life Guards, 2nd Life Guards and the Royal Horse Guards, a measure intended to restore the credibility of all three regiments at one fell swoop. With the Queen Empress herself heartily supporting the despatch of one quarter of her bodyguard, Arabi Pasha suddenly became every bit as fashionable an enemy as the French or the Prussians, with the result that there was a positive clamour to be sent to war. Nobody was keener to go than Burnaby, but he was not the senior commanding officer and, agitate as he might, he was left kicking his heels in England. In the spring of 1883 he went speech-making in Birmingham, but was swiftly laid low with a bout of bronchitis and severe inflammation of the lungs. In November that year the situation in the Sudan boiled over with the annihilation of the Kordofan expedition. By Christmas Val Baker was in Suakin attempting to piece together a force capable of holding the ring in the Red Sea Littoral. It was now that Fanny Baker wrote the letter that brought Burnaby rushing to her husband's assistance and saw him caught up in the El Teb disaster. A little over three weeks later, still officially on leave, clad in mufti and carrying a double-barrelled game gun borrowed from Commander Crawford Caffin RN,[7] Burnaby found himself out in front of the 1st Battalion, The York and Lancaster Regiment, as it pressed towards the enemy defensive positions hard by the scene of Val Baker's earlier humiliation.

Immediately in front of the battalion was a large redoubt jammed with untold numbers of Hadendawa. The enemy launched a sudden counter-attack on the advancing British infantry, obliging the men at the forefront of the assault to fall back on their comrades. It was said afterwards that Burnaby shot thirteen men with twenty-three cartridges at this point.[8] Once the short-lived enemy assault had been repelled, the men of 1st York and Lancaster again surged towards the earthworks. Burnaby was the first man to the top of the parapet and for a moment stood silhouetted against the sky in gallant and glorious solitude, before suddenly emptying both barrels of his gun into the sea of faces below. Quite how many times he was able to load and fire nobody can say for sure, but when after a few moments he was attacked at close-quarters, he was obliged to reverse his gun and hold his assailants at bay with the butt-end. A few seconds more and he must have been killed. Fortunately the infantry now came bustling through the position, shooting and stabbing at everything in sight. Somebody started the story afterwards that Burnaby was rescued by a Gordon Highlander, and he might well have been, but today the tale cannot be traced to a primary source and it was overwhelmingly the men of the York and Lancaster Regiment who were right behind him and pushed past to drive the enemy from the redoubt. At some point in the fracas Burnaby was shot in the left arm, a relatively severe injury which necessitated his being sent home before the campaign reached its denouement at Tamai.

While Sir Gerald Graham saw fit to mention Burnaby's name in despatches, he did so in the context of valuable service and not of great gallantry. The newspapers, though, were full of it. If Burnaby had momentarily forgotten that he was not only a soldier but a politician too, his Liberal Party enemies lost no time in reminding him. In a sublimely cynical piece of politicking he was denounced in the Commons for using a shotgun in battle, an issue which was then hotly debated in the press until it became a full-blown controversy. In truth this was as illogical and irrelevant in 1884 as would be an identical case today. Shooting other men on the battlefield is what soldiers do; quite how many projectiles they happen to shoot them with is neither here nor there. Unsurprisingly a large sector of the press sprang to Burnaby's defence and the affair quickly died a death.

On his return to England the wounded hero again went speech-making in Birmingham. Though it had yet to dawn on Gladstone, his stubborn inaction over Gordon and Khartoum was rapidly developing into a political Achilles heel. There could be nobody better placed to denounce the lily-livered premier than a living legend not long since returned from grappling with the Queen's enemies. Burnaby's impassioned, sometimes spiteful rhetoric was widely reported and hurt the government badly, even in the eyes of its most ardent supporters. In June Burnaby again fell ill with a congested lung, respiratory difficulties and violent coughing fits. In the meantime there had been another grave falling out within the Blues, with the commanding officer again ostracized and 'sent to Coventry' in all but matters of business by his most senior subordinates. Gasping for breath and depressed by the petty disloyalty of his field officers, the ailing man-mountain saw his life all but grind to a halt. His condition improved only very slowly. He at least had the consolation of being promoted to colonel, with effect 11 September 1884.

Burnaby was at home in London when a note arrived from Wolseley saying that he had been to look for him at the Junior Carlton, his favourite club, to recruit him for the Nile Expedition, but had evidently missed him. Wolseley went on to intimate that so long as he was still in his Whitehall office not even he was powerful enough to sway the C-in-C's most firmly held prejudices, but that as soon as he was in Egypt he would telegraph home to press for Burnaby's appointment as a special service officer. It would be much harder, Wolseley explained, for the Duke to refuse such a request when it came directly from a commander in the field. It is a moot point, when the Duke did actually decline the request, whether he did so to spite Burnaby or because it was just one more 'Ring' appointment. It should not be forgotten that Burnaby had a regiment of cavalry to command in London – a perfectly justifiable reason for his application to be refused. If Wolseley required the services of a special service colonel, there were dozens of more readily available officers to choose from.

If it was also true that most members of the Cabinet would not have wished to see another triumphal Burnaby homecoming – an eventuality which was likely to result in Chamberlain being unseated by his fickle constituents – none of them would have dared to approach the C-in-C on the matter, as it would have been quite improper for them to have done so and there was in any case no love lost between the Duke and the sitting administration.

To Burnaby it didn't altogether matter what the C-in-C's position was. The great Wolseley had asked for his services and he intended living up to the compliment. Having allowed a suitably diplomatic interval to elapse, he applied to take his annual long-leave in South Africa. The request was duly approved, although somebody at Horse Guards took the precaution of wiring the military authorities at the Cape, where Sir Charles Warren's Bechuanaland Expedition was in the offing, to say that on no account was Colonel Burnaby to be allowed to involve himself in any unofficial soldiering. Burnaby proceeded to close up his London house and asked Val Baker to become his young son's guardian in his absence. It was said afterwards that he had dropped hints to his servants that he might not be coming back. Of course soldiers have a keen sense of their mortality and each time they go off to war have to make contingencies against the worst eventuality. It is in this context that premonition stories are often dreamt up in hindsight. The suggestion that Burnaby's ill-health led to him leaving for the Sudan on some kind of suicide mission is very plainly belied by his letters to his wife and by the fact that as soon as he got into Egypt's hot, dry climate his health took a marked turn for the better. It was not long before he was back to his old self. By the time the Duke found out that he was on the loose in Egypt, it was too late to do anything but fire off another stiff note to the absentee Adjutant-General. Thus it was that the mightiest of the Queen's warriors arrived at Jakdul Wells in good time for the fighting.

Seniority and Command Succession within the Desert Column

Sir Herbert Stewart's seniority as a full colonel dated from 18 November 1882. After Stewart, newly appointed as a brigadier-general, the next most senior Army officer at Jakdul Wells was Burnaby, with his substantive colonelcy dated 11 September 1884. After that came Colonel John Vandeleur of 1st Royal Sussex, elevated to the rank even more recently, with effect 26 November 1884. Sir Charles Wilson was also a full colonel, but only by brevet. Thus whilst Sir Charles had commenced the Nile Campaign as Vandeleur's senior (at which juncture Vandeleur had been a substantive lieutenant colonel with seniority dating to 1 July 1881), he had for the past six weeks been his junior. It is of passing interest that Vandeleur had been in the Army longer than any other officer with the column. As a naval captain Beresford ranked alongside Colonels Burnaby and Vandeleur and, technically at least, slightly above Sir Charles Wilson in his brevet colonelcy. As the Desert Column was a land command, a naval officer would be excluded from taking over so long as there were any credibly senior Army officers on their feet. More than anything else this was a simple matter of good manners and common sense.

Wilson's substantive lieutenant colonelcy was dated 31 December 1881 and his brevet colonelcy 19 April 1883. Burnaby had been a double-rank 'Major & Lieutenant Colonel' in his regiment, with seniority in the Army as a lieutenant colonel, since 11 September 1880. He had since been promoted into a regimental lieutenant colonelcy with effect 6 April 1881, which although it made him eligible to command the Blues was in large part irrelevant as far as the rest of the Army was concerned, where he had already been a lieutenant colonel for the past nine months. Burnaby had thus always been senior to Wilson as a lieutenant colonel, but between April 1883 and September 1884 became the junior of the pair by dint of Wilson's brevet as a colonel. Burnaby's recent promotion to substantive colonel had put him back in front of Sir Charles for the past four months, with the result that it was Burnaby who was now the de facto second-in-command of the Desert Column.

The next most senior officer after Wilson was Evelyn Boscawen, nominally a major in the Coldstream Guards, but a lieutenant colonel in the Army since 18 February 1878. Next came the string of Foot Guards officers who held regimental vacancies as 'captain & lieutenant colonel' but were also substantive lieutenant colonels in the Army. After Boscawen came Mildmay Willson of the Scots Guards, with seniority dated to 14 December 1878. After that the sequence was Charlie Rowley of the Grenadiers (7 June 1879); Sir William Gordon-Cumming, Scots Guards (28 July 1880); and Francis Graves-Sawle, Coldstream Guards (10 December 1881). Next came Reggie Talbot of HCR, with a 1st Life Guards lieutenant colonelcy dated 21 July 1882, after which it was back to the Foot Guards with Ivor Herbert, Grenadier Guards (21 May 1883); Harry Bonham, Grenadier Guards (22 July 1883); and finally Percy Barrow with a lieutenant colonelcy in the 19th Hussars dated only two days after Bonham. It will not immediately be clear to the reader why it has been necessary to belabour the issue of seniority in such detail. We shall see, however, that the matter of command succession cropped up several times in the Desert Column and that the sequence of succession has the potential to bewilder unless one has a firm grasp on how the Army's seniority system worked at this period.[9]

Final Composition of the Desert Column

The marching-out state of the Desert Column when it left Jakdul Wells is shown in Table 2. It consisted ostensibly of 2,153 souls, of whom some 1,802 were British military personnel. Included amongst the 351 non-European personnel are the one officer and seven other ranks of the Egyptian Army attached to 1st/1st Battery, Southern Division, Royal Artillery. The 2,153 figure is, however, only a cumulated total of servicemen and locally engaged civilians in the employ of the Crown, Her Majesty's Government or the khedival government. In addition there was also the cabal of war correspondents, travelling with an unknown number of privately employed servants and camel-drivers. It is not known whether or not Ali Loda and the seven local guides from Ambukol are incorporated in the figures, perhaps with the headquarters staff or the 19th Hussars, or whether they have been omitted altogether. Either way, allowing for the newspapermen and their retainers, the all-up total of human souls is likely to have been close to 2,200.

Table 2: The Desert Column's Marching-out State, Jakdul, 14 January 1885[10]

	Officers	NCOs & Men	Natives	Camels	Horses
HQ Staff	10	6	13	26	5
Naval Bde	5	53	11	91	
19th Hussars	8	127	19	73	155
HCR	24	376	5	420	
GCR	19	365		406	
MICR	24	359	4	424	
1st Royal Sussex	8	250	4		2
1/1 Battery, S.D., RA	4	39	20	90	
26 Field Company, RE	2	25	4	40	
Medical Bearer Company	2	40	57	146	
No. 1 Field Hospital	2	20	12	54	
C & T Corps	7	33	202	1,118	
Total	115	1,687	351	2,888	162

At 7.00 a.m. on Wednesday 14 January, Stanley Clarke moved out for Korti with his LCR detachments, close to 500 un-laden baggage camels and a deeply disappointed Major Kitchener. Stewart's fighting force spent the day watering the animals unit by unit and moving out to a rendezvous point about two miles from the camp in readiness for a 2.00 p.m. start. Sir Herbert Stewart took the opportunity while he was waiting to sit down and pen a private letter to Wolseley.

Jakdul,
January 14th,
1885

My Dear General,

I have endeavoured to give you everything up to this officially, but I write one line privately to tell you that everything is going on swimmingly except as to time. In the absence of dhura, I am sure you would not have wished the camels to be tried beyond what they ought to be called upon to bear, and this, coupled with the operation of watering the number of camels and horses now here, has consumed time which I would wish had been employed marching.

To see 3,000 camels and more watered from a pool, all water-skins, tanks and water-bottles filled up, is a sight to be seen to be appreciated. I am sorry to tell you a considerable amount of Nile stores are useless. It seems incredible, but whilst flour has been soldered down, the tea had only been fastened up with canvas, so has easily got wet. That which has got wet is spoiled. Fortunately the loads thus spoiled have not used up much transport, but most unfortunately they are our most valuable stores.

I am very much obliged for the 29 red coats which arrived quite safely.[11]

The more I see of this road and its work, the more convinced I am that you will have largely to supplement the supply of camels. The camels with my force are very well, but the transport animals will want a deal of replenishing, and we are also bound with time to make calls upon you.

The water on the road could be vastly improved. Bad as Hambok turned out, I still think it is capable of improvement. If a little shafting such as is used for mines was sent here in the shape of a few planks, I am sure a supply might be obtained for small convoys. El Howeiya will afford a really good supply, and at Abu Halfâ where I halted, there could soon be an unlimited quantity. There are also other places on the road where we found water. I won't bother you with any more, but hope to write to you from Metemmeh and send off Sunday afternoon.

> Yours very truly,
> Herbert Stewart[12]

Stewart's letter does two things of substance. It first draws attention to the fact that administering a camel-borne force in the desert is more time-consuming than might be imagined. It then goes on to urge Wolseley to ensure that the army staff is well-positioned to provide replacement baggage camels for the animals which Stewart has realized are in the process of being driven into the ground by relentless marching on short commons. It can sometimes be difficult to tell what sort of physical condition a camel is in, but even so, the statement 'the camels with my force [the riding camels] are very well' was edging towards the disingenuous.

Just before the march got underway, a Remington rifle was recovered from amongst nearby rocks.[13] The column had not been on the move for very long before Captain Verner spotted the tracks of unshod ponies and deduced that at some point in the previous few days, a body of Arab cavalry had prowled very close to Jakdul Wells.[14] Although the column was on the march, 'over a vast gravelly plain, with gentle undulations',[15] for only about four hours, Airlie's War Diary entry for that day incorporates the remark, 'Sussex camels very bad', suggesting that even over the course of about ten miles, the double load of baggage and rider was too much for some animals. At sunset the column halted on a hard, sandy slope to eat and snatch a few hours' sleep. Outlying sentry posts were established and orders given that, in the event of an attack, four regimental squares were to be formed at the corners of the great mass of knee-haltered camels. As usual supper was preceded by the time-consuming and tedious task of unloading all the baggage camels and laying a few handfuls of *dhura* under their noses. As a result the night was pitch-black long before any of the soldiers were able to huddle around their campfires and attend to their own needs. Once again there was to be a pre-dawn reveille at 3.20 a.m. and a first light start at 5.00. In between came the sort of snatched breakfast described by Count Gleichen:

It is very cold in the early morning in the desert, especially during January, and the comfort of a steaming cup of cocoa or tea, with biscuit and cold 'bully' beef, must be felt to be appreciated. Although I own 'bully' is not inviting at midday, when floating about the tin in red, warm, stringy masses, yet it has its period of beauty, in the early mornings, when the cold night has solidified it into respectable-looking cold beef; at that time a quarter of a pound of it inside you, washed down with hot drink, makes a deal of difference in the way you are disposed to look at things on a dark and cold morning.[16]

The morning march got under way, 'over a tract of loose sand where the track was occasionally quite covered by drift-sand'.[17] Gleichen remarked of this leg of the journey that, 'Several camels went head over heels down the soft slopes, and lay there with their legs in the air, unable to right themselves with their loads on.'[18] At length the column came in sight of a well-known Bayūda landmark, a tall conical hill called the Jabal El Nus. At 10.30 a.m. Stewart was obliged to call an hour-long halt in order for the rearguard company to catch up, an indicator that yet more overburdened camels had given up the ghost.[19] The rearguard, which on this particular morning happened to be Colonel Willson's No. 3 (Scots Guards) Company, GCR,[20] was always strictly enjoined not to overtake anybody, so that stragglers and breakdowns would continue to be protected. The unenviable task of commanding and shepherding the baggage train along had fallen to Captain Lord Cochrane, who for the time being had handed his 2nd Life Guards detachment over to Lieutenant Rowland Beech. As 'baggage master' Cochrane had the authority to sound the 'Halt', although Sir Herbert had emphasized that he should do so as seldom as possible. He began the day's march with a dozen un-laden camels in reserve, such was the rate of breakdowns that in next to no time they had all been pressed into service.[21] More often than not the hands-on work of sorting out stragglers and breakdowns fell to the officers and men of the baggage guard. Today the painful duty had fallen to No. 1 (Grenadier Guards) Company, GCR, under Captain Eyre Crabbe, in which Gleichen was one of the subalterns:

My company, worse luck, was detailed for baggage-guard that morning: this irksome duty consisted in keeping a short way behind the baggage train, and whacking up any camel or driver who lagged behind. Every five minutes a load would slip off, or a camel fall down sick; in that case a couple of men were at once detailed to dismount, help load up the camel, and whack it along again. As all the baggagers were in strings of three, tied nose to tail, each string in charge of one native driver, the downfall of one meant the stoppage of the three; the other two camels generally did not comprehend why they should stop, and hauled away until their headgear or tail ropes gave way, or else got themselves so entangled with each other that their loads dropped off, and then the whole thing had to be done again; it was an endless business, and provocative of much swearing. Generally by the time the three camels were reloaded and set going again, the column was nearly out of sight, with nothing behind but the rear-guard, who had strict orders not to allow any one behind them . . .

If a camel dropped in his tracks, his load and saddle were taken off him and loaded on another (already loaded) camel. The few spare camels had been used up long ago, so the stores had to be packed at any cost on animals already weakened by fatigue and short rations. The way the poor brutes toiled on was something marvellous; you would see one go slower and slower, till the tail of the animal in front he was tied to seemed nearly coming off; then he would stop for a second, give a mighty shiver, and drop down stone-dead. If he fell alive, but could not go on, he was left there. It sounds cruel not to have shot them at once, but the majority of those thus left rested for some time, then staggered up to browse on the dry grass and mimosa trees, and thus prolonged their life some days. A great many recovered sufficiently to travel to various small wells, guided by their marvellous instinct for finding water.[22]

The march was resumed at 11.30 a.m., only for the problems with Sunderland's overburdened camels to become even more marked. Verner noted in his diary,

In the afternoon the camels began to drop in the most alarming manner, chiefly those ridden by the Sussex men which carried two boxes of beef or biscuit, as well as their riders. Several of the Mounted Infantry camels, which have always been well looked after, dropped dead. This is a tolerably good gauge of the general condition of the brutes and makes one anxious to get to a place where they can rest a bit and get food.[23]

There was again ground-sign to indicate the passage of Arab horsemen to and from Metemmeh, while at one point a party of three or four camel-mounted Arabs was spotted in the distance. Stewart called a halt to a long day's march at 5.20 p.m.[24] and bivouacked astride the caravan road, about thirty-four miles from Jakdul and half a mile west of the Jabal Sergain.[25] All the usual precautions were taken against night-attack.[26] The soldiers' cooking fires were on the go, when Lieutenant Lord Binning of the Blues received a message instructing him to report to Colonel Burnaby at the headquarters bivouac.

I found him at his evening meal and in high spirits at the prospect of fighting. Bennet Burleigh and [Charles] Williams of the Chronicle were with him, and to them he was detailing the steps he intended to take to maintain order and discipline in Metammeh when we arrived there, it being understood that he was to be appointed governor of the place. After some conversation and speculation as to the force we were likely to encounter, the Colonel turned laughingly to me and said, 'I want you to give the men a message. Tell them I shall be disappointed if each of them does not account for at least six of the enemy tomorrow.' The fight, however, was not destined to be the next day. I delivered the message, and the men were delighted.[27]

Friday 16 January began with a 3.00 a.m. reveille in advance of a 5.00 a.m. start. As usual Barrow and the cavalry slipped away early. The main body again had a false start, with part of the force heading off in the wrong direction some little while before the order to march had been given. Sorting out the confusion took more than thirty minutes. The column ran into rough ground almost immediately and Sir Charles Wilson again noted the camels 'tumbling' about amongst the 'high tufts of grass'. 'When daylight broke,' he continued, 'we found ourselves on a vast plain, scantily clad with savas grass, with the hills of Abu Klea ahead of us in the distance.'[28] Verner noted that the plain was marked 'Ohmithandel' on C. E. Fowler's map.

Enemy in Front

Some way out across the plain, the 19th Hussars had been divided between an advanced patrol under the command of Major French, and the squadron main body under Colonel Barrow. It was about 9.00 a.m. when French spotted a small party of camel-mounted Arabs to his right-front. Barrow had just come up to join the forward patrol and ordered French to take a few men in hot pursuit. He appears to have ridden off at the head of two corporals and ten or eleven privates. The chase took French and his party up into the hills in front and through the gorge leading down into the Abu Klea Valley. A second party of nine camel-mounted *anṣār* was encountered on the divide, together with a number of spear- and rifle-armed infantry, all of whom fled in the direction of the valley floor. This would tend to suggest that French's rapid offensive manoeuvre had surprised and driven in what was a look-out post, rather than any sort of forward fighting position. French might well have sent a galloper back to his commanding officer at this juncture, as Stewart's official despatch states that Barrow first reported the presence of around fifty of the enemy on the high ground. The patrol pushed on into the valley where French quickly singled out a fleeing *anṣāri* as a prospective prisoner. Leaving a corporal and ten men in a covering position, he ordered his other corporal to accompany him and set off to ride his man down. French was in the act of reaching down to grab his victim by the shoulder, when suddenly a nearby swathe of long grass came alive with *anṣār* spearmen. The intrepid duo could only yank their ponies about and ride for their lives in the opposite direction.[29]

Once he had re-joined the rest of his men, French fell back towards the divide, pausing occasionally to take in what was going on behind him. The patrol was being trailed by parties of enemy cavalry, but soon encountered Barrow and the squadron main body in the gorge. It seems likely that this was the point at which Barrow rode back to brief the general, as Stewart's official report reflects something of what French had seen in the valley, but says nothing about his activities over the next hour. Realizing that he would need to secure the defile for the main body, French galloped the squadron back to the valley, drew carbines and threw out a dismounted skirmish line. Not long afterwards parties of enemy horsemen, totalling something around 200 men, came up and proceeded to probe the skirmish line on both flanks.[30] They did not press the squadron hard, were held in check by its fire and after a short-lived skirmish fell back into the valley and out of sight.[31]

At about 10.30 the main body halted for breakfast in the Wādī um Keteer where as usual the general established his headquarters under the shade of a mimosa tree. Verner calculated that they had marched twelve miles so far that day and were now about forty-five miles from Jakdul, although the general was of the opinion that they had come a few miles more than Verner thought.[32] Gleichen noted that the lines of hills that had formerly been a mile or so to either flank, now arced around to form a defile in front. 'The track ahead we saw led up a steepish hill over rocky ground, and then through a regular pass commanded by the hills on each side.'[33] Harry

Pearse's report to the *Daily News* indicates that the sound of distant firing was heard while the troops were preparing their breakfast.[34]

At about 11.15 am Colonel Barrow rode in to Stewart's headquarters to report that the cavalry screen had made contact with what appeared to be a significant Mahdist force a few miles short of Abu Klea Wells.[35] Alex Macdonald was resting in the shade about fifty yards away from the general's headquarters, when Jack Cameron called across that Barrow had come in and that they should go and see what was afoot. Barrow seems not to have tarried long before turning back for the high ground to re-join his command. Sir Herbert greeted the approach of the curious war correspondents with, 'Well, gentlemen, the enemy is ahead of us. Barrow has exchanged shots with his outposts, and I am going to attack him at once.' Macdonald noted that he uttered the words with a 'tone of quiet determination'. With that the general gathered his staff around and began sketching the formation of advance into the sand with his swagger stick.[36] A minute or two later the staff officers trotted away to pass the orders on to the regimental commanders. According to Stewart's official despatch the plan called for the camel regiments to form on 'a broad front in line of [regimental] columns at half-distance',[37] with MICR on the left, HCR in the centre and GCR on the right. The artillery was to move behind the Heavies. The baggage train was to close up on a broad front so as to keep it concentrated not far behind the camel regiments, while the Royal Sussex companies and the Naval Brigade were to dismount and cover the rear.[38]

In common with just about everybody else Gleichen was trying to snatch forty winks in the shade, when the tranquillity of the bivouac was rudely disturbed:

The rest of the force had finished their dinner in comfort, and were resting peacefully, when the order came to fall in at once and examine arms and ammunition. Then like a flash the report spread from mouth to mouth that the enemy were in sight on the hills commanding the pass, and were evidently prepared to make a fight of it . . . The column mounted and fell in at once, much pleased at such an unexpected bit of luck. At last we were actually coming to blows with the enemy that so many had regarded as a phantom.[39]

As soon as the orders had been disseminated and the force had formed up, the general led off in the direction of the gorge and the Abu Klea Valley beyond. He remained with the main body until it was within 400 yards of the high ground, at which point he gave the order to halt and rode on ahead with an entourage of staff officers and war correspondents to reconnoitre the situation on the far side of the divide.[40]

Major French had followed up his repulse of the enemy cavalry by pushing a number of patrols forward to size up the enemy's strengths and dispositions. It took only a few minutes for them to gain a good view along the line of the Abu Klea Valley. The most obvious feature within the confines of the broad, grey-black valley was a sandy-bottomed *khor* of several miles in length, presently bone-dry, which for about two or three weeks a year drained torrents of rainwater from the hills above the divide, in the broadly southerly direction of the wells. The general and his party, most of them on ponies but some on camels, spotted Colonel Barrow and a knot of his men on a commanding high point and rode uphill to join them.[41] Without the report written by Charles Williams for the *Daily Chronicle* there would be considerable doubt about quite where the general's vantage point was located, but on the basis of Williams's description and my own interpretation of the lie of the land, it would seem fairly certain that it was atop the whale-backed hill later occupied as a British outpost.

Accompanying Stewart at this juncture were Sir Charles Wilson, Majors Wardrop and Dickson and Captain Verner. They were joined in their vantage point by a knot of war correspondents which included Jack Cameron, Melton Prior, Harry Pearse, Alex Macdonald and Charles Williams. It is possible that Captains Lord Airlie and Frank Rhodes were also present, although neither is specifically mentioned in the sources save in so far as Verner remarks that Stewart was accompanied by 'the staff'.[42] It is certain that Stewart would also have been followed by an orderly carrying a small, square-shaped, red pennant, the purpose of which was to denote the commander's position on the battlefield.[43] Tagging along at the back came the somewhat incongruous spectacle of Colonel Fred Burnaby mounted on a donkey.[44] His steed might have been somewhat lacking in style but, as befitted a colonel of Household Cavalry, Burnaby was clad as usual in his black-braided, navy-blue patrol jacket and red-seamed overalls.[45] The only other officer in the force dressed in a home-service uniform was Major Pöe, who habitually turned out in a red undress frock.

Looking directly along the line of the valley, the general and his entourage could see that the hills on both flanks were strongly held and that the high-ground positions were sited to support a blocking position in the valley floor. The main or 'sandy *khor*', let us call it, ran down the centre of the valley for about two miles, until it met and merged with a second watercourse which ran into it from the left, at a prominent junction best characterized as an inverted letter Y. Running broadly south from this point was another three miles or so of grey-black valley, its sides much lower-lying on the left than the right, before the golden stripe of sand running through the heart of the landscape finally petered out in the vicinity of the wells.

Just in front of their confluence the two major watercourses were separated by a narrow gravel spit, atop which the British could make out a line of twenty Qur'anic flags and banners.[46] Although one or two participant accounts particularly mention green flags, Percy Marling wrote that they were 'of every colour under the sun – white, green, red etc.'[47] In at least partial confirmation of Marling, Alex Macdonald reported to the *Western Morning News* that there was one green flag and that the remainder were red and white.[48] Just to the rear of the flags was a large Bedouin-style tent which appeared to be functioning as a command post. It was clear that the spit marked the rough centre of the Mahdīst position. Without quoting a figure, Verner observed in his diary that a number of the enemy were 'congregated' in its vicinity. The Mahdīst right, also denoted by the presence of banners, straddled the caravan road and from a British viewpoint lay just to the left of the merged *khor*.

There also appeared to be a strong position on the enemy left, which from the general's vantage point was half-way up the gentle gravel slopes to the right of the *khor*.[49] It was obvious that the enemy had deployed with the intention of denying the wells four miles or so to their rear, but it was too early to tell whether they intended to take the offensive or simply stand their ground. If they chose to remain where they were for any length of time, Stewart would have no choice but to attack and fight his way to water.

While the rest of the staff were taking in the panorama below, Burnaby leant across to Alex Macdonald and muttered, 'If any disaster happens to us, not one will ever see London again.'

'Why Colonel,' replied Macdonald, you are the very last man here that I should suspect of dreaming of disaster. What do you mean?'

'Well, our chances of pulling through all right are twenty to one,' came the retort.[50]

It is impossible to know whether there was something about the scenario which genuinely worried Burnaby, or whether he was simply having some fun at Macdonald's expense. Scanning the broken ground to the right of the *khor*, Macdonald identified a string of enemy riflemen running in the direction of the high ground. Cameron judged that they were heading for a towering conical hill about 1,500 yards away and drew the general's attention to the movement. According to Macdonald, a conversation then ensued between Stewart and Burnaby over whether, with only three hours of daylight remaining, it would be advisable to attack immediately or wait for morning. Burnaby thought it best to wait, advice which Stewart was content to accept.[51] The immediate imperative, therefore, was to secure a strong defensive position in which to sit out the hours of darkness.

The *Zariba*

While Sir Charles Wilson and his officers rode deeper into the valley to join the most advanced cavalry patrols, Stewart and the rest of the staff rode back downhill to decide on the layout of a *zariba* position, the local name for a thorn-bush perimeter designed for defence against wild animals and human enemies alike. It would be sited on flat ground on the near side of the *khor*, leaving the splayed head of the watercourse and its feeders a few hundred yards to the British right-rear. Because the *khor* was carved deep into the surface of the desert in its upper reaches, the British position would be elevated about twenty-five feet above it on a low, flat plateau. The plateau reached back to the hills from which the camel regiments were even now emerging and was constrained, to the left, by the whale-backed hill, to the right by the line of the *khor* and, in front, by a low gravel ridge. At about fifteen feet above the general lie of the land, the ridge would serve to shroud the main position from enemy riflemen located in the valley floor. While the edge of the plateau commanded a view across the *khor*, which here in its splayed upper reaches was anything up to 300 yards wide, there were a number of low-lying ridges and hillocks on the far side with the potential to provide cover to enemy marksmen.

Approach to Battle • 215

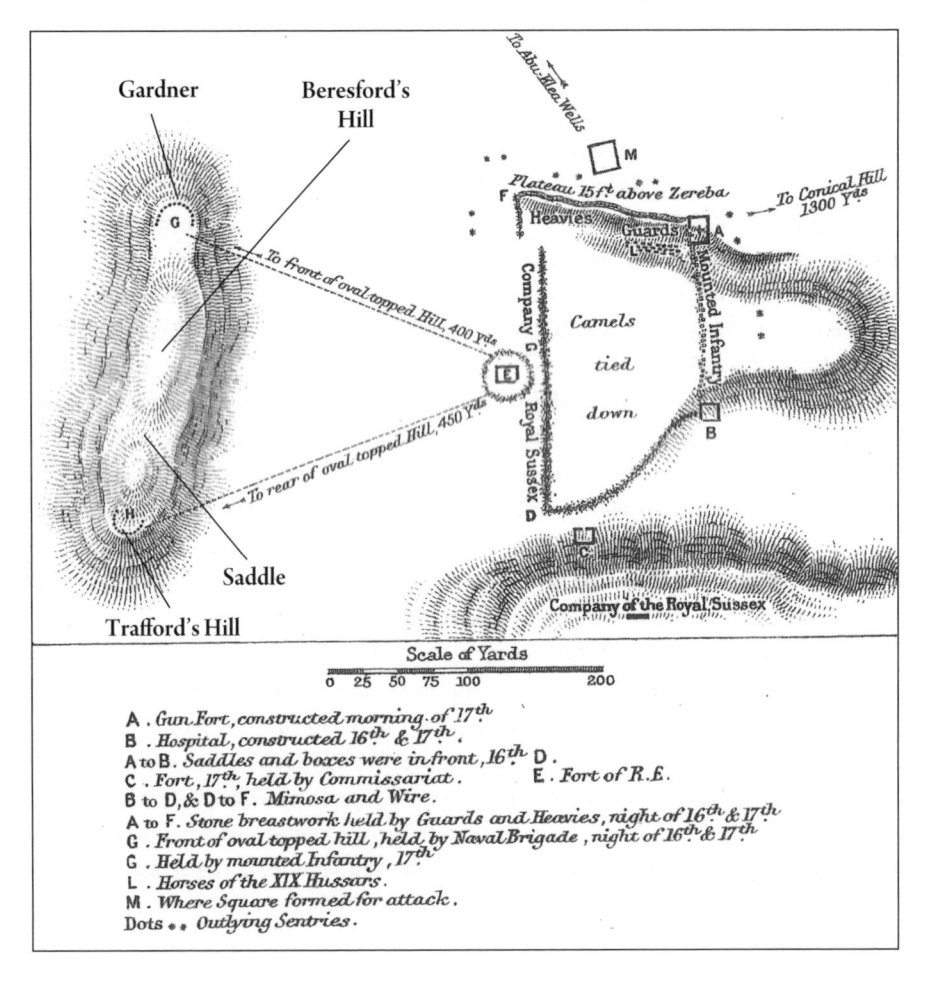

[Map showing the zariba at Abu Klea with the following labels: Gardner, Beresford's Hill, Saddle, Trafford's Hill, To Abu Klea Wells, Plateau 15ft above Zereba, To Conical Hill 1300 Yds, Heavies, Guards, Mounted Infantry, Camels tied down, Company G Royal Sussex, Company of the Royal Sussex, To front of oval topped Hill, 400 Yds, To rear of oval topped Hill, 450 Yds, points G, H, F, E, A, B, C, D, M, L]

Scale of Yards: 0, 25, 50, 75, 100, 200

A. Gun Fort, constructed morning of 17th.
B. Hospital, constructed 16th & 17th.
A to B. Saddles and boxes were in front, 16th.
D.
C. Fort, 17th, held by Commissariat.   E. Fort of R.E.
B to D, & D to F. Mimosa and Wire.
A to F. Stone breastwork held by Guards and Heavies, night of 16th & 17th
G. Front of oval topped hill, held by Naval Brigade, night of 16th & 17th
G. Held by mounted Infantry, 17th
L. Horses of the XIX Hussars.
M. Where Square formed for attack.
Dots •• Outlying Sentries.

Map 6: Lieutenant Lawson's sketch map of the *zariba* at Abu Klea, with additional annotation.

Behind these low features, perhaps 1,300 yards from the edge of the plateau,[52] was the commanding high ground which served to delimit the right-hand side of the valley. Although the range was long, riflemen positioned atop the prominent conical hill to the right-front of the position would be able to see and fire on every British movement. The conical hill jutted from the side of the valley like a bastion. Running away to its right was a long, straight ridgeline which ran parallel to the British right at a range of around a thousand yards. Stewart gave at least fleeting consideration to occupying the commanding ground along the side of the valley, but concluded that the intervening distance rendered the proposition impractical.

The general now proceeded to describe to his staff how he envisaged the *zariba* being laid out. The perimeter would be rectangular, with its shorter sides facing front and rear. The front face would run along the low gravel ridge and would need to be strongly held against the eventuality of a powerful enemy rush under the cover of darkness. The right face would run along the edge of the plateau, looking out across the *khor* towards the conical hill and the long ridge. The left face would run across the centre of the plateau, set back from the foot of the whale-backed hill by about 400 yards.[53] Finally the rear face would cover the high ground through which the column was now making its approach.

The whale-backed hill on the left was elevated about seventy-five feet above the plateau and about 100 feet above the valley. While the feature screened the *zariba* from the main enemy position admirably, it also commanded the British position from so short a range that it would have to be held at all hazards. Because the crest offered an unimpeded view in the direction of the wells, its possession would make it all but impossible for the Mahdists to manoeuvre aggressively by day without being seen. The immediate problem, though, was the onset of darkness. If a powerful storming party got even half-way up the slope before the alarm was raised, there would be very little prospect of containing the attack. Separated from the whale-backed crest by a low saddle was a much smaller piece of high ground, perhaps sixty feet in elevation, which would lie to the left-rear of the main position and would similarly have to be denied to enemy marksmen.

The overall dimensions of the *zariba* were about 150 x 400 yards.[54] The camels would be knee-haltered en masse in the centre, while the horses of the 19th Hussars would be concealed in the floor of a re-entrant running from the plateau into the floor of the *khor*, about half-way down the right face of the perimeter. The substantially unaltered lie of the land is illustrated in the modern-day photographs incorporated in the plate section. The only known sketch-map of the position drawn by a participant is that made by Lieutenant Henry Lawson RE which is similarly incorporated here (*see Map 6*) and can be readily reconciled with the photography.

Down in the valley Wilson, Dickson and Verner had reached Barrow's forward patrol. Leaving their camels in the care of the hussars, they made their way to the top of a nearby knoll. The new vantage point offered a reasonably good view of the Mahdist position across a distance of about a mile, although the intelligence officers were conscious that the mimosa bushes and long grass in the *khors* might be concealing any number of lurking *anṣār*. In addition to the two main *khors*, there were a good many tributaries feeding into them from both sides of the valley. Tell-tale puffs of white smoke told Wilson and his companions that they were being fired on, but in the absence of any cracking sounds overhead they concluded that they must still be safely out of range. 'There could be no doubt about it,' wrote Verner, 'but that the enemy were present in strong force, very much stronger than anybody had expected. By the method they showed in their arrangements and occupation of the ground, they were no mere assemblage of river tribes from Metemmeh etc. as might have been reasonably expected.'[55] Sir Charles Wilson decided to ride back to the main body to brief the general, while Dickson and Verner worked their way across to a spur on the right of the valley where another of Barrow's patrols was surveying the scene.[56]

In the meantime Lord Cochrane had been shepherding the baggage train forward behind the camel regiments.

> The track wound through and over some rugged hills, then into a rocky defile some 4 miles from Abu Klea [Wells], a black and forbidding-looking valley, almost surrounded by fairly high hills, through which the track to the wells lay. I thought at the time it looked like a veritable Valley of the Shadow of Death.[57]

For all that the metaphor might have been coined in hindsight, the Abu Klea Valley does indeed have a strangely forbidding appearance.

The three camel regiments came onto the position at about 2.30 p.m.[58] As they arrived the commanding officers received orders to throw a company of skirmishers each onto the low gravel ridge in front. Colonel Boscawen assigned the task to Captain Eyre Crabbe and No. 1 Company. Formerly his battalion's musketry instructor, Crabbe reckoned it would be possible to bring section volleys down on the enemy at the extraordinary range of 2,000 yards and sought leave to open fire. His request must have been addressed to an officer of a markedly less optimistic disposition and was duly refused.[59]

By now the chief of intelligence had made his report to the general. With the staff galloping about the position to get things into a semblance of order, Sir Charles rode back into the valley to take another look at the enemy. In the meantime Dickson and Verner had gained an excellent vantage point on the right and had begun sketching the layout of the enemy position. By the time Sir Charles rode up to join them, they had been brought under fire by a small party of riflemen located on a low ridge immediately to their front. Verner made all possible haste to complete his sketch, while the nearby cavalry vedette fell back into better cover. Not long after Wilson had re-joined his officers, the general also rode up with a small escort of hussars under the command of Lieutenant Hugh Young.[60] Observing that the Mahdīsts had made no significant moves in his absence, Stewart spent a few minutes discussing enemy intent with the chief of intelligence before leading the party back to the *zariba*.[61]

The general's return brought a string of fresh orders for the occupation of outpost positions. Beresford was directed to take the Naval Brigade to the top of the whale-backed hill, which for the sake of clarity will henceforth be referred to as 'Beresford's Hill'. Although hauling the Gardner up the rocky slopes made for hard toil, the gun reached the crest without undue difficulty. The Naval Brigade was soon joined by a half-company from B Company, MICR, under the command of Captain Arthur Morse.[62] The two sections concerned were Morse's 1st Royal West Kents[63] and Lieutenant Robert Tudway's 2nd Essex men.[64] Beresford and Morse would have about a hundred bayonets in all with which to hold the outpost. Beresford left the crest to the MICR sections and moved his own men down to the right-hand end of the feature, where he could not only see directly down the line of the sandy *khor* but would also be able to cover the conical hill on the far side of the valley with the Gardner, albeit at extreme range.

Across the saddle from Morse's half-company, Captain Lionel Trafford was leading C Company, 1st Royal Sussex, something around sixty bayonets, to the crest of the second and lower feature – henceforth referred to as 'Trafford's Hill'.[65] A second Royal Sussex company was making its way onto the high ground at the rear of the position. Quite which company this was we cannot be altogether certain but, as Lawson's diagram shows Sunderland's G Company inside the perimeter, it can only have been either B or F Company.

Once the outpost companies had taken up their positions, they began throwing up rock sangars and walls. While none of the defences would be more than about 2½ feet high, they would at least serve to protect men lying in the prone position from incoming fire. Trafford elected to construct a single wall of about sixty feet in length, which survives intact to this day and is shown in the plate section. When it was finished he had his men throw their blankets over it, in order to prevent incoming rounds sending splinters of rock flying about.[66] Beresford raised what he called a 'breastwork of loose stones'[67] to house the Gardner on the point of the hill.[68] This likewise survives intact and can also be seen in the plates. It is apparent from its small size that the forty or so rifle-armed ratings must have been dispersed about the position in natural cover. Down in the valley parties of *anṣār* were now infiltrating around the right flank of the cavalry vedettes. It was not long before Barrow's officers were obliged to break clean and fall back to the *zariba*.[69]

With the light beginning to fade, the main position was the scene of much frenetic activity. Having tied down their camels, the Heavies and the Guards had deployed along the gravel ridge at the front of the position and were gathering all the loose rocks into a low wall, the officers toiling every bit as hard as their men, Heavies to the left, Guards to the right. When the rocks ran out the 'wall' was barely two feet high;[70] by one account there was also a thirty-yard gap around its centre point.[71] Captain Norton, meanwhile, had dismounted his screw guns at the right-front corner of the position so as to be able both to see down the long gravel slope into the valley floor and to cover the high ground on the right.[72] Along the right face of the perimeter, facing the upper reaches of the *khor*, the 19th Hussars and some of the MICR companies were throwing up a 250-yard barricade of camel saddles and commissariat stores. The left and rear faces of the perimeter were defined only by improvised thorn-bush hedges constructed by the Royal Engineers. The heat had been such that two of Dorward's men had collapsed during the course of the afternoon. Once all the mimosa on the plateau had been cut down by the Engineers, work parties descended into the *khor* to cut more.

Just before last light, orders were given for a string of pickets to be thrown seventy-five yards forward of the position and for two biscuit-box redoubts to be raised. There were still significant gaps between the ends of the low stone wall and the defences on the flanking faces of the perimeter which would have to be filled with thorn-bushes. As a result a good many men were committed to work parties well into the evening. The first and larger of the two redoubts would serve as a combined hospital and fort and was to be located at the right-rear corner of the position. It would be occupied by the surgeons and their helpers, but defended by a section of Captain Pigott's D Company, MICR.[73] The second redoubt was to be located half-way down the thinly held left face of the perimeter and would be built and defended by elements of Captain Payne's A Company, MICR.[74]

Now that the British had committed themselves to ground, the Mahdist commanders had begun manoeuvring parties of riflemen into commanding fire positions. The party of riflemen spotted by Macdonald and Cameron had indeed made their way onto the conical hill and in the afterglow of sunset could be seen scurrying about to throw up a low stone breastwork of their own. Even had they been twice as far from the 7-pounders they would still not have been safe. As it was they were just under a mile away, which for Royal Artillery professionals represented the easiest of targets. Just before the light failed altogether Norton landed a sniping round squarely amongst them, a shot which Macdonald claimed later to have learned had inflicted some twenty-seven casualties.[75] Charles Williams reported that the guns fired three rounds in all before sunset.[76]

Not long after the artillery had come into action, the conical hill came alive with rifle-fire, compelling all but the last of the work parties to sink behind the cover of the barricades and keep low. After several hours toiling on the thorn-bush defences, Dorward and his sappers now had to turn their attention to setting out low wire entanglements in front of the more vulnerable sectors of the perimeter.[77] Those who were not otherwise engaged hurried to heat up some bully beef before the order came to extinguish fires. Efforts to rustle up a meal for the members of the 'intelligence mess', Wilson, Dickson, Verner and Stuart-Wortley, were hampered when bullets twice struck and scattered the sticks of their campfire. The order to douse fires came too soon for many men even to get a drink of hot tea.[78] The instructions for night routine insisted that there were to be no lights, no smoking and no talking. The men were to lie down in their greatcoats, with their bayonets fixed and be ready to spring to their feet at the first sign of an alarm.[79] The GCR and HCR companies deployed along the front of the position, nine companies in all, lay down behind their wall in two ranks, where the relatively short overall frontage must have resulted in the men being jammed together like sardines.

The uneasy repose of the British was disturbed not only by the sound of cracking bullets but by the enemy's tom-toms, or *noggara*, which throbbed their nagging, monotonous rhythm for most of the night. Bennet Burleigh wrote that their sound was 'beyond all discordant noises successful in irritating and worrying a sensitive ear'.[80] The drums also exerted an unsettling effect as they were pounded gradually towards a crescendo, creating the impression that the enemy was stalking ever closer.[81] Stewart had sited the headquarters bivouac in the cover of a small hollow just to the rear of the Guards. The staff lay on the deep side of the depression with their backs to the enemy, but nonetheless found themselves squarely in the line of fire. They were much disturbed throughout the evening by rounds passing over their heads to bury themselves in the embankment on the far side of the hollow.[82] Burnaby and Burleigh, Tory and socialist, ignored the bullet strikes opposite and spent a considerable amount of time talking politics together. The ravages of his recent respiratory illness seemingly behind him, Burnaby declared:

> I have got to that stage in life where the two things that interest me most are war and politics; and I am equally exhilarated and happy whether holding up to odium an unworthy politician or fighting against my country's foes. I shall take up politics again on my return, for, next to war and fighting, there is more fire and go in that than anything else. Besides wars are going out of fashion. Politics give me a course and stir my blood.[83]

Politics was not the only thing on Colonel Fred's mind, as he revealed in the course of the conversation that his next great adventure would be a ride to Timbuktu. The duo prattled on at such length that eventually the general, who was trying to sleep, had to ask them to be quiet. Later in the evening Burnaby toured the perimeter to check that all was well. Captain William Hippisley, commanding the Royal Scots Greys detachment in No. 4 Company, HCR, asked him if he thought the enemy would attack. 'No such luck,' replied Burnaby. 'We shall have to go and attack them.'[84]

The column's other ardent warrior, Captain Charles Berkeley 'Bloody' Pigott, had laid down to rest beside the hospital-fort in the company of two of his subalterns, Lieutenants Thomas Snow and Edwin Alderson, when a sudden commotion behind the biscuit-boxes gave notice that a night-panic had broken out. With the men rushing around a confined space with fixed-bayonets, there was every possibility that serious injuries would occur. Snow recalled that,

> I was much struck by Pigott's method of allaying the panic. He leant over the parapet, struck a match and lighted a cigarette. Then holding up the match to throw a dim light on the interior of the fort, he said, 'What are you silly devils doing, having a dance or what?'[85]

Alex Macdonald was woken by false alarms at times he estimated at around 9.00 p.m. and midnight. On both occasions the source of the consternation was the line of HCR pickets deployed to the left-front of the position. Just around the corner from the Heavies was a sector on the left face manned by G Company, 1st Royal Sussex. Not unnaturally the alarm to their right brought the G Company pickets running in too. On the second occasion they were met by the imposing figure of Fred Burnaby. The colonel was wrapped up against the cold in 'a big pilot jacket lined with astrakhan'[86] and would doubtless have been wearing the peaked regimental forage cap he seems to have preferred ahead of a helmet once the sun had gone down. When Burnaby asked one of the Royal Sussex lads why he had seen fit to leave his post, he was told that it was because the HCR sentries had raised the alarm. 'Never mind those fellows,' retorted the colonel. 'There is no danger. Stick to your post my man.'[87] During a later alarm, again caused by the deceptive sound of the enemy's drums, Burnaby was rather less sure of the situation. Passing 4411 Corporal J. R. Payne of No. 3 Section (2nd Rifle Brigade), C Company, MICR, he asked, 'Are your men awake? Is their ammunition ready?' Passing a little further down the line he gave the order, 'Don't fire, men, until you see the whites of their eyes.'[88] There would appear to have been at least four false alarms in all.[89] During the last of them Lord Binning and the men of the Blues were staring into the darkness from behind the low stone wall, when they heard a horse walking up the gravel slope towards them. Next they saw the end of a cigar glowing in the darkness, at which point one of the men exclaimed, 'It must be the colonel.' It was indeed the colonel; Burnaby had been down into the valley to see for himself what the enemy was up to.[90]

After the bitter chill of a desert night had settled over the *zariba* Lord Cochrane felt the need, heedless of any danger from stray rounds, to warm himself up by walking about for a few minutes. After a while he came upon the officer commanding No. 5 Company, HCR, Major Ludovick Carmichael, who was 'very down about things and said that he felt sure he would be killed tomorrow'. When Cochrane laid down to rest again, he did so beside Lieutenant Rudolph de Lisle of the Naval Brigade. As de Lisle had no blanket and was doubtless freezing cold, Cochrane was kind enough to share his with him.[91]

After the midnight alarm the fire from the conical hill tailed away significantly, although from time the time the night was punctuated with fusillades of three or four shots.[92] Although nobody, save perhaps the surgeons, could be quite sure in the dark what effect the enemy fire was having, there were actually very few human casualties. Percy Marling thought that 'three men, some horses, and several camels were hit' during the course of the night.[93] Gleichen on the other hand heard that only two men, one a hussar and the other a native driver, had been wounded.[94] When at length a casualty did arrive at the hospital-fort, one of the surgeons was foolish enough to forget himself and show a light. Mercifully the ensuing fusillade failed to hit anybody.[95] At some point in the proceedings 381 Private C. Wilford of the 2nd Essex section was hit and killed atop Beresford's Hill.[96] From 2.00 a.m. the dropping fire from the conical hill had been carried out to the irksome accompaniment of bouts of furious drumming and wild war-dances silhouetted against the orange glow of the enemy's watch fires.[97] Somebody on the staff had convinced the general that it was common practice amongst the Arabs to use the appearance of Venus as the signal for a night attack. Thus the morning stand-to was to be predicated on an old wives' tale.

Chapter 8

Under Fire

The Battle of Abu Klea: Phase I – On the Defensive

Had they been going into a sing-song, instead of into a life and death struggle with a savage foe, they could hardly have evinced more cheerfulness. The tired and weary travellers of our desert caravan had all at once been transformed into a band of stern warriors, ready and anxious for the fray.

Alex Macdonald, *Too Late for Gordon and Khartoum*

THE WAR DIARY OF THE DESERT COLUMN reports that it was 3.30 a.m. when the British force stood to its arms in readiness to face an assault. Venus came up without incident, however, heralding only a long, cold wait for the approaching dawn. Another six hours would elapse before Stewart began his advance upon the all-important wells at the far end of the valley, the only source of water in a barren landscape of sand, gravel and grey-black outcrops of rock. The incoming fire from the conical hill increased in both intensity and accuracy as the light came up. It is from Sir Charles Wilson that we learn, 'Stewart had talked about occupying this hill last evening, but thought it too far off for the enemy to do us any harm; we did not realise that we had such good shots in front of us.'[1] Other primary source evidence would suggest that there had been around 300 riflemen on the hills the previous evening and there is nothing to suggest that this number fluctuated in any way between sunset and sunrise.[2]

When eventually the light improved and it became clear that it was no longer possible for a lightning-quick assault to surge suddenly from the half-gloom, the general had the word passed to 'stand down', not that the prevailing situation allowed for much more than shedding greatcoats and continuing to lie quietly in the cover of the barricades exactly as before. Within half an hour of sun-up, the sniping, all but ineffective by night, had come to constitute a serious hazard to life and limb. In part this was because a good many *anṣār* riflemen had left their positions atop the conical hill, crossed a shallow saddle of a few hundred yards in width, and established themselves along the long ridge delimiting the right-hand side of the valley. The manoeuvre left many of the firers no longer at a forty-five-degree angle to the *zariba*, as had been the case from the conical hill, but in a position of perfect defilade, at a right angle to it. The new enemy fire positions served to reduce the range to the *zariba* and exposed even the mouth of the re-entrant in which Colonel Barrow had until now been able to shelter his Syrian greys from harm. The great mass of knee-haltered camels, which overnight had been afforded some protection by a combination of darkness and the 1,300 yards separating the animals from the conical hill, had now become a great deal more vulnerable. Even by night a few of the camels had been killed, while it was just about impossible to tell how many had been wounded. For most human members of the Desert Column that morning, their world, for the time being at least, would be only two or three feet high. Few of the officers risked kneeling up to use their field glasses, but those who did were quick to spot that the enemy had utilized the hours of darkness to raise a second low stone wall along the crest of the long ridge; Verner estimated that the position was sited about 900 yards away.[3] Down in the valley the line of flags was still *in situ* on the gravel spit between the two big *khors*, although the absence of any massed *anṣār* formations suggested that the enemy's blocking position of the previous afternoon had been left unattended during the hours of darkness.

Strengthening the Position

Against the contingency of having to fight a general action from within the *zariba*, in effect Stewart's best-case scenario, he now gave orders for the strengthening of the defences. As had been convincingly demonstrated at the Defence of Rorke's Drift almost exactly six years earlier, the heavy commissariat boxes containing hardtack biscuits or tinned bully beef made ideal improvised defence stores. The first priority was the front-right corner of the perimeter, where a redoubt would command fields of fire forward into the Abu Klea Valley and at the same time provide protection for the gun-crews and riflemen involved in returning the fire from the high ground. The members of the Royal Engineer work party tasked with raising the fort were forced to dash back and forth under a 'hot cross fire', but were fortunate enough not to suffer any casualties in the process.[4] Whilst it can be established that the 'gun-fort', as it was called, was constructed from commissariat boxes and camel saddles,[5] there is no written source which describes its shape. As luck would have it Gleichen captured the work in one of the sketches he used to illustrate *With the Camel Corps up the Nile*. This shows that it had been constructed in the shape of an inverted letter V.[6] Incredibly, for something which was in place for only a little over twenty-four hours, the weight of biscuit boxes piled two high was sufficient to leave an indentation in the ground of precisely the right shape, in precisely the right position, which even some 124 years later I was readily able to identify. The gun-fort was capable of housing only one of Captain Gilbert Norton's 7-pounders at its apex, but would also have provided shelter to the crews of the other two guns as they awaited fire orders. Safely beyond the danger range of even the best enemy shots, a second work detail proceeded to raise another new biscuit-box redoubt facing the commanding high ground at the rear of the *zariba*.

Some of the officers affected the sangfroid expected of their caste and went about their business, paying little or no heed to the incoming fire. Melton Prior found himself engaged in polite conversation with Colonel Burnaby and another unnamed officer. After a number of successive rounds had passed over their heads, Burnaby remarked, 'I think some rascal has got our range; we had better continue our conversation some distance apart.' Prior admitted, 'I was not sorry when we separated altogether and I was able to take a little shelter.'[7]

Early Skirmishing on the British Right

Only a small minority of men were involved over the course of about two hours in raising the gun-fort and the new redoubt at the rear. For everybody else it was a matter of hug the ground harder, hope for the best and wait. As is always the way in such situations some men chose to close their minds to danger and were able to snooze amidst all the excitement. By contrast Captain Norton's gunners, equipped with 2.5-inch screw guns and the power to influence events up to 3,400 yards away, were amongst the most important men on the position and were required to remain fully alert in case any worthwhile targets presented themselves only fleetingly. Whilst pounding the enemy fire-positions along the western side of the valley would be child's play for experienced artillerymen, Norton was mindful of the need to conserve his ammunition against an array of future eventualities. If sustained bombardment of the opposite hillside was not to be contemplated, a few well-placed sniping rounds might at least serve to dampen the enemy's ardour. Norton obtained permission to open fire on that basis. His first shell landed in the centre of about forty *anṣār*.[8] A further two rounds were enough to exert a noticeable effect.[9] If a fully fledged lull was too much to ask for, a marked reduction in the volume of incoming fire was much appreciated by everybody inside the *zariba*, even if the respite was only ever likely to be temporary.

For the men in the fighting companies breakfast was a less than ceremonious affair, eaten lying on their sides in the lee of the improvised perimeter defences. Not for them the fried bully beef and pots of tea and coffee that a lucky few were able to rustle up in the better-sheltered spots in and around the redoubts. For the great majority of men it was a matter of munching on a few hardtack biscuits scrounged from the bottom of their haversacks, which they washed down with a slug or two from half-drained water-bottles.[10]

At length parties of enemy riflemen on the right, perhaps 200 men altogether,[11] began descending from the conical hill and the long ridge, intent on gaining the valley floor. In its upper reaches the sandy *khor* was both wide enough and shallow enough for the MICR companies lining the right face of the perimeter to see into the floor of the feature and command it with fire. On the far side of the watercourse, though, there were more than enough rises, hollows and undulations for scores of riflemen to stalk ever closer to the British perimeter, improving the accuracy of their fire with every hundred yards they were able to gain. Stewart decided to counter the developing threat by deploying a skirmish line on the far side of the *khor*.

The natural candidates for such a task were the professional light infantry of C (Rifles) Company, MICR. Willoughby Verner's diary contains a wealth of detail not to be found elsewhere and is the only source to cover the ensuing skirmish in any detail. A Rifle Brigade man himself, Verner noted that Dick Fetherstonhaugh[12] was accompanied in his sortie by Captain the Hon. Henry 'Punch' Hardinge[13] and Lieutenant Max Sherston, both of whom commanded Rifle Brigade sections in C Company. While Verner's diary can be read to imply that the whole company went out, something which is positively asserted by Colvile in the *Official History*,[14] it is curious that Verner would mention Sherston and Hardinge and yet omit any mention of Lieutenants William 'Johnny' Campbell and Archie Miles,[15] the company's KRRC officers, both of whom were fit for duty and played an active part in the battle. Stewart's official despatch throws no light on the matter, failing even to mention the deployment. Given that the MICR companies were holding a defensive perimeter at this juncture and that the absence of all four sections would necessarily create an extended gap which other companies would be compelled to fill, it would seem much more likely that Fetherstonhaugh took only his two Rifle Brigade sections into the open, leaving the KRRC sections to hold the company sector. Ironically further credence to this notion is lent by the captions Verner wrote to accompany his watercolours in *Sketches in the Soudan*, where in contradiction of his own diary he writes, 'At dawn on the 17th January the fire from the enemy on the hills to our right increased, and *a portion* of the Rifle Company of the Mounted Infantry was sent out to engage them.' Further tipping the balance in favour of the half-company construct is that Charles Williams specifically states in his *Daily Chronicle* report that 'two sections' went out.[16]

A little further along in his diary account Verner states that the C Company riflemen 'skirmished *up the hill* for about 200 yards and opened fire. The enemy, well under cover, replied briskly and soon hit two of our men. They shot very well.'[17] It would be tempting to infer from Verner's language that C Company's action took place on the far side of the valley, on or near the lower slopes of the long ridge. At something around two-thirds of a mile from the *zariba*, however, this would have entailed Fetherstonhaugh deploying his men in an extremely exposed position. Verner then clears up the seeds of confusion he has sown with some uncharacteristically loose language by adding:

Sir Herbert now ordered me go out to the Rifle Company and caution Fetherstonhaugh to watch his left flank, where there was a wady. I had a decidedly unpleasant walk across the open to him and came to the conclusion that a staff officer on foot was a poor creature, for he must not run and walking is very slow![18]

The reference to a 'wady' confirms that Fetherstonhaugh had in fact advanced only about 200–300 yards from the *zariba* and had deployed his firing line just on the far side of the watercourse, a position which would have allowed him to beat a hasty retreat in the event his left flank was menaced.

Advance of the Mahdist Main Body

The reason for the general's warning and Verner's errand was that over the previous thirty minutes the grey-black gravel ridges of the Abu Klea Valley had once again come alive with enemy activity. A number of white-robed masses in the distance were seen to manoeuvre over the ridgelines and undulations in such strength and with such precision that some British observers quickly concluded that they could not possibly be in the presence of a mere local levy. Verner for example wrote, 'I don't know what Sir Herbert thought of this business, but I at once made up my mind that we had a big job on hand and that the force opposed to us must be some of the Mahdī's regulars.'[19] This is a point to which we shall return later; suffice it to say for the time being that Verner's use of the word 'regulars' is inappropriate and that he means merely to suggest some element of the Mahdī's main field army.

The men atop Beresford's Hill had an excellent view of the developing threat from the valley floor, but in the event they were themselves menaced would be quite unable to derive any meaningful fire support from the blind-sided *zariba*. Stewart concluded that the outpost was too exposed simply to stay put and decided to recall Beresford and Morse to the main defensive perimeter. With the two Mounted Infantry sections covering them from the crest, the officers and men of the Naval Brigade set about manhandling the Gardner back downhill. A recall order also went out to Captain Trafford, who similarly fell back to the low ground. Interestingly Trafford's campaign diary indicates that he left Lieutenant Rhys Jones and fifteen men to continue manning the stone wall.[20] It is not clear how long they remained there but because the position is known to have been occupied later in the day by a detached section of B Company, MICR,[21] the assumption can be safely made that Jones and his men were called in to re-join the rest of the company at some point preceding the battle's climactic phase.

The abandonment of the hilltop outposts on the British left is an interesting tactical decision. Had either of them been occupied by the enemy, and Stewart had now conceded ideal dead-ground approaches to them both, the *zariba* would have been exposed both to a crossfire and to an even more galling plunging fire over far shorter ranges than was the case from the conical hill and long ridge. While the two abandoned outposts were certainly reoccupied later, there is no source evidence to suggest that their original garrisons had been relieved in place and strong enough grounds to infer that they had not.

Having made their way in safely, the officers and men of the Naval Brigade were quickly assigned to a new position 'on the right front'.[22] This placed them alongside the Guards on the low ridge, looking down a long gentle slope into the floor of the Abu Klea Valley, where for the present the enemy were maintaining a safe stand-off distance. That there would be a significant general action during the course of the day was now obvious; what was less clear was which side would be doing the attacking.

As a rule general officers do not much care for their battlefield tactics being decided by logistic factors, but the conduct of desert operations must inevitably be swayed by the availability of water. Stewart knew that the wells, which his map told him were some four miles down the valley, must be in his hands by sunset, not least for the sake of the camels and ponies, many of which were showing signs of distress from near-continuous deprivation over a succession of long desert marches. His assessment though, as he surveyed the scene through his binoculars, was that the enemy host was working itself up to an attack. If the Mahdīst *amīrs* intended playing into his hands in this way, his long-suffering animals would just have to wait a while yet. In his official despatch, penned the following day, Stewart wrote:

In our front the manoeuvring of their troops in line and column was apparent, and everything pointed to the probability of an attack on our position being made. Under these circumstances no particular hurry to advance was made, in the hope that our apparent dilatoriness might induce the enemy to push home.[23]

Verner describes how the enemy main body advanced down the valley in the direction of the *zariba*, 'in two lines, the second very strong and reckoned at about 5,000 men', although he omits any suggestion that the two lines appeared at separate points in time. According to Charles Williams's report for the *Daily Chronicle*, however, the first enemy advance came at about 7.00 a.m. on 'a front of two divisions'. The Mahdīst formations, he noted, were 'well in hand and well worked'. He estimated their strength at 2,500–3,000 men. Williams also adds the useful detail that it was another hour and a half before the second line appeared; 'At half past eight there were signs, according to Colonel Burnaby and others, of a second line coming up, but I confess I could see nothing of it myself.'[24] Evidently Williams was either in the wrong place or had no field glasses. For the time being, then, it would appear that only the enemy vanguard was in plain view.

For the most part the flags and banners floating above the two leading divisions of *anṣār* were red and white.[25] It was a longstanding convention amongst the Arab tribes that *shaikhs* would ride into battle, with their position on the field marked by a mounted attendant carrying a distinctive personal banner. Now that Muḥammad Aḥmad held sway over most of the Sudan's Arab population, almost all flags and banners were painted with verses from the Qur'an, although they still served as the personal standards of great men. While the *shaikhs*, their standard bearers, their personal attendants and a smattering of holy men were mounted, the overwhelming majority of the *anṣār* were arrayed behind their leaders as shock-action infantry. Only here and there did small dust clouds indicate the presence of insubstantial parties of cavalry.

Long before their advance began to pose any immediate threat to the *zariba*, the *anṣār* halted.[26] To Verner it seemed at this juncture that they began dressing their ranks, although Charles Williams thought that they were dancing; they may indeed have done both these things. There was a great deal of furious tom-tomming and the odd wild shot at a range of about a mile. As the Mahdīst army had been forward in roughly the same positions the previous afternoon but, with the exception of the few hundred men on the high ground, had not been present at sun-up, it is clear that the *amīrs* had pulled their men back to the wells for the night and that these most recent manoeuvres represented their early morning return to pre-selected battle positions.

Composition of the Mahdīst Force

We should now digress to ponder just who it was that Stewart and his officers were studying so intently through their binoculars. A strong popular myth has grown up to the effect that the Mahdīst forces present at the battle belonged almost exclusively to an ill-defined classification commonly termed the 'Nile Arab', an expression used in the context of Abu Klea to mean local men from the towns of Metemmeh, Shendy and Berber, together with their respective satellite villages and rural surrounds. The predominant tribes in the Nile Valley north of Khartoum were the Ja'līyīn, the Awadiyeh, the 'Abābda, the Barabra and the Shā'iqīa.

Whilst it is true that local men played a prominent part in resisting the British advance across the Bayūda, it is of singular importance that they had also been reinforced by a strong Kordofani contingent detached from the Mahdī's main force at Omdurman a few days earlier. The more cosmopolitan nature of the Arab force is reflected by an important passage in Wilson's *From Korti to Khartum*, which he based on his personal interrogation of a group of four Mahdīst 'prisoners' – in reality press-ganged members of the Kordofan expedition who had purportedly been fortunate enough to survive the slaughter at Shaikān. In fact the climactic disaster had been so all-consuming that there is a strong likelihood that Wilson's informants were amongst the men known to have defected to the enemy in the days preceding the final catastrophe. Without the interrogation of the four prisoners by Wilson and Verner to draw upon, historians might well have found themselves mystified as to the exact composition of the Mahdīst force:

The gist of the information was, that we had fought Arabs and regulars from Berber, Arabs from Kordofan, some of the Mahdi's troops from Omdurman, and local levies from Matemmeh, with Jalin and Awadiyeh Arabs from the country round – in all, from 9,000 to 11,000 men. The enemy's sharpshooters were black soldiers of Hicks's army, and of the garrisons of Obeid and Bara, which had surrendered to the Mahdi, and a few Kordofan hunters. The great charge was delivered by Duguaim, Kinana and Hamr Arabs from Kordofan, whose contingents with their sheikhs and emirs were almost annihilated. The Jalin and Matemmeh men were in reserve, and the Awadiyeh did the cavalry scouting.[27]

Collation of the data proffered by the intelligence officers and other less crucial sources suggests that the Mahdīst host was configured as follows. The Amīr 'Abd-al-Mājid Nasr al-Din abū' l-Kailak, a nephew of Muḥammad al-Khair, had marched south from Berber at the head of around 250 horse and 1,750 foot, drawn primarily from the Abadeh, Barabra and Bisharin tribes. In addition the Berber contingent fielded about sixty turncoat Egyptians under the command of Muḥammad Effendi Wahabi and Beshir Agha. Interestingly, 'Abd-al-Mājid Nasr al-Din abū' l-Kailak was himself a turncoat, who until the fall of Berber had been on the staff of Ḥusain Pasha Khalīfa. The Amīr 'Ali-wad-Saad of Metemmeh had marshalled around 2,000 Ja'līyīn and Awadiyeh, mainly local townsmen, while the fierce Kordofani contingent, something between 4,000 and 6,000 men from the Daghaim, Kināna and Hamr tribes, had been brought north from Omdurman by the Amīr Mūsā wad Ḥilū.[28] Around 1,000 men from other tribes, some 400 of whom were reported as rifle-armed, had also accompanied the three principal Kordofani groupings. There are no compelling reasons to disbelieve or distrust Wilson's estimate of 9,000–11,000 men. Mūsā wad Ḥilū, said to be a 'small broad man with a very pleasant smile', a member of the Daghaim Baqqāra and a younger brother (age unknown) of the Khalīfa Alī wad Ḥilū, was in overall command.[29] An order of battle for both British and Mahdīst forces is given in Appendix D.[30]

Interestingly there were significant differences in the dress and appearance of the Nile Valley locals and that of the Kordofani tribes. These are reflected in key visual sources such as Verner's watercolours and Gleichen's pencil drawings. Because of the popular assumption that the Mahdīst host at Abu Klea was made up exclusively of local men, the much wider availability of Gleichen's book (reprinted for the first time in 1975 and several times subsequently) has led over the intervening period to his sketch of the hand-to-hand fighting at Abu Klea becoming associated with the costume and general appearance of 'Nile Arabs'.[31] In fact the primary sources, including the passage from Wilson quoted above, tell us that it was the Kordofanis who broke into the square, meaning that it was actually they who are captured in the foreground of Gleichen's drawing. In order to visualize authentically clad riparian Arabs such as the Ja'līyīn or Awadiyeh, one needs to turn to a key watercolour in the less readily accessible work of Verner.[32]

Of course none of the close detail on the enemy host later acquired by Sir Charles Wilson was in the hands of the British prior to the battle. All they had to go on in advance was Colvile's Christmas Day report from Merowe, which had suggested that there were about 3,000 fighting men at Metemmeh and 1,000 at Shendy. In addition there was the Mudir of Dongola's rather more dramatic report of 30 December, to the effect that the Mahdī intended sending a force of 20,000 men to meet the British in the Bayūda, a scenario which the Intelligence Department had rightly judged not to be credible.[33] Wilson, Colvile and Kitchener had done their best to develop a reasonably accurate intelligence picture in the build-up to the Bayūda crossing, but can hardly be blamed for the fact that the shuttle-run to and from Jakdul Wells had all but telegraphed British intent to the enemy. As a result the Mahdīst high command had been allowed more than enough time to move a blocking force northwards from Omdurman. The long and the short of it was that Sir Herbert Stewart would now be obliged to fight his battle against an enemy defined not by a coherent intelligence picture collated by Wilson and his team, but by the view through his field glasses.

Mahdīst Minor Tactics

Abu Klea was to be the first clash between the British military and the main rebel movement, both sides having only recently converged on central Sudan. Although some of the officers and war correspondents present, including Stewart, Burnaby, Burleigh, Cameron, Prior, Herbert, Marling and the officers of the 19th Hussars, had been at Second El Teb and/or Tamai a little under a year earlier, there could be no real certainty that the western and riparian Arabs would fight in quite the same way as a distinctly separate ethnic grouping like the Bīja. In fact, while there was a good deal of military commonality between Bīja and Arab, there was also one key difference, a factor which would exert a significant influence on Stewart's operations in the Bayūda.

The tactical mainstay shared by the two halves of the rebel movement was the blood-curdling massed charge intended to come to close quarters, which in both cases was usually coupled with the guileful use of ground to minimize charge distances and maximize shock effect. It was the intelligent use of dead ground and covered approaches at the tactical level which distinguished a Mahdīst army from a Zulu *impi*, that other great exponent of massed shock action in the high-colonial era. Whereas Zulu commanders might use ground to manoeuvre a striking force to advantage at the operational level, often leaving the enemy blissfully ignorant of their primary avenue of approach to the battlefield, Mahdīst *amīrs* typically marched their force mob-handed along desert caravan routes, their movements being necessarily constrained by the ready availability of water. Indeed, in order to contest the British advance across the Bayūda, the Kordofani contingent had moved north from Omdurman following the west bank of the Nile. The key difference at the tactical level, however, was that where Zulu commanders were often content to fight battles of decision on ground of the enemy's choosing, their Mahdīst counterparts would generally seek to contrive a situation in which they would be able to fight on carefully selected ground of their own choosing. Typically this would be terrain characterized by deceptive hills, rises, hollows and undulations with the potential to convey battlefield surprise. Put simply Mahdīsts of all persuasions, Bīja and Arab alike, were past masters of the tactical trap.

So much for military commonality in the two major seats of the rebellion: what then of the principal difference? According to Augustus Wylde, a British trader who was a long-term resident of Suakin, the Bīja tribes had been almost entirely ignorant of modern firearms prior to Osman Digna's rebellion.[34] There being no illicit gun trade to speak of at that point, breech-loading rifles were the preserve of the Egyptian garrison and passing parties of eccentric Englishmen who from time to time disembarked at Suakin and proceeded into the interior in search of game. For the most part the English sportsmen had been crack shots and left everybody who came into contact with them in awe of their marksmanship. The situation had changed with the succession of Egyptian disasters. Even so the manly contempt felt by hardened desert warriors for the miserable performance of the Egyptian military served to ensure that the several thousand captured Remingtons now in Bīja hands would remain a mere adjunct to shock action.

In Kordofan it had been different. There, in what had until relatively recently been ungoverned space, the Arab warlords had employed small armies of black African slave-soldiers known as *bazingers*, with which they terrorized the indigenous tribes and made war on one another's commercial interests. There had also been a profitable ivory trade which had called into being a breed of professional hunters, men who like the *bazingers* were capable shots and generally carried the same Remington rolling-block rifle as the Egyptian military. Most of these men, hunters and slave-soldiers alike, with their experience and understanding of modern firepower, had now been subsumed into the Mahdīst movement. Together with all the surrendered black soldiers of the defeated Egyptian military, they had been incorporated by the Amīr Ḥamdān abū 'Anja into a body of full-time rifle-armed troops known as the *jihādīya*. While ordinary tribal adherents of the movement were grouped under the 'flags' of the three Khalīfas, Abū 'Anja's men functioned as a corps of quasi-professional soldiers. It is worth observing in passing that although there literally were great battlefield flags – famously the Khalīfa 'Abd Allāhi's was black – the word 'flag' can also be taken to be synonymous with 'division'. The Daghaim, Kināna and Hamr Kordofanis present at Abu Klea would ordinarily have been grouped under the Khalīfa Alī wad Ḥilū's red flag.

That there were at least a few hundred competent riflemen amongst the Mahdīst host at Abu Klea would seem on the basis of events shortly to unfold to be incontrovertible. It is distinctly possible that the 400 riflemen who accompanied Mūsā wad Ḥilū and the Kordofanis north from Omdurman were in fact a detached wing of Ḥamdān abū 'Anja's *jihādīya*. To arrive at an estimated total of trained Remington-armed riflemen present on the battlefield that day, the contingent of Egyptian turncoats from Berber must be tallied alongside the probable *jihādīya*, so that something close to 500 men would seem a reasonable estimate. It would be surprising if there were not in addition another several hundred men, from the Berber contingent in particular, let us say for the sake of argument another 500, who, while they were armed with captured Remingtons, possessed no particular aptitude for military marksmanship. If this postulation is sound, giving the Mahdīst force at Abu Klea something around a thousand Remingtons, then for every three Martini-Henrys fielded by Sir Herbert Stewart there would have been two rifles of comparable quality in *anṣār* hands. If one was to subtract 250 Martinis to allow for the defence of a temporary base like the *zariba*, then Stewart's deployable fighting force would have been able to field only 20 per cent more rifles than the Mahdīst enemy, in addition to which the latter also enjoyed an overall numerical advantage of not less than six or seven to one. From this it can be seen that the hackneyed argument that superior firepower invariably gave the British a decisive advantage in the general actions of the High Victorian period is once again not actually endorsed by case study. Interestingly St Leger Herbert's report for the *Morning Post* noted that the rebels fielded '900 special riflemen who were negroes and proved themselves to be good shots'.[35] If Herbert's numerical estimate is perhaps a little high, the inference that a body of Ḥamdān abū 'Anja's *jihādīya* was indeed present is clear.

It was, so to speak, the 'combined-arms' integration of shock action with concentrated modern firepower that would eventually prove to be the undoing of the Desert Column. It is worth adding in passing that the events of January 1885 are instructive if we seek a bona fide understanding of the nature of colonial warfare in the Victorian age. The notion of 'native-bashing' so emphatically propounded in the middle decades of the twentieth century by the liberal establishment and historians of the political left, whilst it might fairly be applied to the imperial era after the coming of the Maxim gun, is not an accusation that can be justly sustained in respect of the first five decades of Victoria's reign. As we shall see the military reality of the colonial battlefield has very little in common with a politically inspired and arguably still prevalent popular myth.[36] Back then to the harsh reality of the Abu Klea Valley.

Events Between 7.30 and 9.30 a.m.

While the primary-source coverage of events between sunrise and the point at which Stewart decided to take the initiative is thin, in large part because most participants focussed their accounts on the climactic phase of the battle, it is clear nonetheless that there was a considerable amount of activity around the *zariba* between dawn and 9.00 a.m. Of particular use in covering what would otherwise be a significant gap in the history of the battle is the account written for the *Daily Telegraph*. Bennet Burleigh estimated that around 200 Arab riflemen had descended into the valley floor. He is also the only source to mention that a troop of the 19th Hussars went out in support of Fetherstonhaugh's half-company and that at length this combined force succeeded in driving the enemy riflemen down the valley in the direction of the Mahdīst vanguard. Given that this entailed turning the enemy skirmishers through more than ninety degrees, the chances are that this represented a line of retreat of their own choosing. None of the sources describe the point at which Fetherstonhaugh returned to the *zariba*, but return he must have and this would seem the most obvious point for him to have done so. Burleigh goes on to lend collateral to Verner's description of the enemy main body, but was evidently a rather better judge of distance. Where Verner's diary account places them 1,000 yards from the front face of the *zariba*, which would have put them within range of company volleys, the newspaperman gives a much more realistic estimate of the stand-off distance:[37]

At about 1,800 to 1,900 yards on our left front could be seen masses and lines of rebels, their bright broad spear-heads and two-edged swords glittering in the sun's rays. With tom-toms fiercely thumming [*sic* – thumping?], and scores of heathenish banners fluttering in the fresh northerly breeze, they swarmed everywhere along the crests of the rolling foothills, and threatened to rush us. Close to the wady on our left there were probably 3,000 or 4,000 of them deployed in two not very irregular lines of men four to five deep. Their leaders, sheikhs or dervishes in conspicuously embroidered Mahdi shirts, were stationed at intervals of about 25 yards apart, and mounted on fleet little horses. The lines were at least half a mile long...[38]

It is difficult to be absolutely certain quite what it was that the British were looking at. We have seen that Charles Williams refers to two lines, one of which appeared at 7.00 a.m., the other an hour and a half later. He could see the first line, split between two divisions, and estimated its strength at 2,500–3,000 men. He could not see the second line, suggesting that this particular formation was at least two or three miles down the valley and obscured by a heat-haze penetrable only with field glasses. Verner is imprecise in respect of time and space, but suggests that the second line was at least 5,000 strong. Burleigh on the other hand could see two lines and estimated their combined strength at 3,000–4,000 men in all. He excludes from his estimate, though, the separate bodies swarming 'along the crests of the rolling foothills', which is to say the right-hand side of the valley (the left-hand side being simply too far away to have had any relevance to the battle). It is distinctly possible that Burleigh is describing two 'lines' or bodies of troops deployed side by side, which is to say the same two 'divisions' described by Williams, rather than two lines echeloned one behind the other. In other words the second big formation, that described by Verner and spotted in the far distance by Burnaby and others at 8.30 a.m., did not come up the valley to join the first line, but rather kept its distance and in due course disappeared into a place of concealment. This construct would suggest that only about half the Mahdīst force, approximately 5,000 men, was committed to demonstrating in front of the British position and that the other half was still much further up the valley approaching only very slowly, until such time as it gained its hiding place. Of the 5,000 men on show from 7.00 a.m., about two-thirds were committed to the two Mahdīst divisions in the floor of the valley, while the remainder were moving about on the ridges to the right-hand side of the valley, in a number of much smaller bodies. Although the two divisions in the valley were within easy range of the screw guns, Stewart declined to engage them. This doubtless sprang from a desire to offer the enemy every possible encouragement to 'come on'.

We have seen that about half of the Mahdīst force was made up of Kordofanis and the other half of locally levied riparian townsmen and villagers. We have no source evidence from the Mahdīst side to say definitively which half was now visible and which was out of sight, or for that matter if the force on show was made up of some combination of the two components. From the British side we have Verner's assertion that the blocks of infantry manoeuvring in the valley could not possibly be local levies and must therefore be 'regulars' from Omdurman. Of course he misuses the term, so that it forms no basis on which to make so emphatic a judgement. Why should a general levy of Kordofani Arabs be any more proficient at manoeuvring around the countryside than their riparian cousins? After all with a day or two's practice, the director of an 'epic' movie will be able to pass his extras off as a well-drilled Greek or Roman phalanx. In fact there are strong enough grounds to infer that the Mahdist high command was operating a stratagem at this juncture and that, for reasons we will come to, it is far more likely that it was the riparian Arabs who were disporting themselves in front of the British and the Kordofanis who were tucked away out of sight.

Inevitably the senior officers had to move around the *zariba* to assess the developing tactical situation from different points of observation. The relatively extended nature of the position tempted both Stewart and Burnaby to remain mounted as they did so. Thankfully Stewart was dressed rather more anonymously on this occasion than had been the case at Second El Teb, where he alone in the entire cavalry brigade had charged into the midst of the Bīja wearing a red tunic. Burnaby on the other hand was still conspicuously clad in his blue patrols. Observing the gallant pair from his new position alongside the Guards, Charlie Beresford ran across and implored the two of them to dismount but, as a function of the ingrained and sometimes foolish bravado of the Victorian officer corps, neither paid him any heed. By the time Beresford returned to his position they had at least parted company on separate errands, but even now, as Beresford turned around to survey the scene once more, Burnaby's horse went down, apparently tumbling its rider onto the ground in the process. Beresford left his position to run across and 'help Burnaby to his feet', to be greeted with the remark, 'I'm not in luck today Charlie.'[39] This at least is old man Beresford's version of events – writing in 1914 he is quite emphatic that Burnaby was unhorsed.

The balance of the evidence suggests, however, that Burnaby was already afoot when his horse was shot. Willoughby Verner records, with no mention of a fall or of any assistance being rendered, that, 'Colonel Burnaby who was standing amongst us had his horse hit in the forelock joint.'[40] Gleichen's reference to the incident, whilst made only in passing, likewise makes no mention of a fall and tends to support Verner's version: 'Colonel Burnaby's horse next received a bullet in the fetlock, and was led limping to the rear.'[41] Charles Williams remarks only that, 'Among the animals hit at the same time was Colonel Burnaby's grey horse; and, saying with a grim smile, "I am not in luck today," he led the limping creature away to procure a fresh charger.'[42] Not only does Beresford unhorse Burnaby in his memoirs, he also goes on to state that the general's bugler was shot shortly beforehand. This is not corroborated by any other source, although Macdonald does make passing reference to Stewart's bugler becoming a casualty during the battle's climactic phase, which is to say a good deal later in the day than Beresford suggests. Similarly St Leger Herbert's account for the *Morning Post* fixes the fall of Stewart's mounted 'orderly', who may or may not have been a bugler, at precisely the same point as Macdonald. Herbert, moreover, was an eyewitness to the incident.

Whether or not Beresford was resorting to poetic licence when he published his memoirs, or has simply mis-sequenced certain events as a function of fading memory, a remount for Burnaby was forthcoming in the form of 'Moses', a grey polo pony included in Sir Herbert's string of horses as a kindness to Percy Marling, the animal's owner.[43] Such was the difficulty of transporting fodder to the front that Wolseley had been angered by the fact that many of the company officers in MICR had come up the Nile with privately owned horses. A general order had prohibited them being taken forward of Korti on the basis that camels had been provided for all Camel Corps officers. 'Moses', though, had been reprieved and placed in the care of the general's groom. Now the poor animal would have to ferry a nineteen-stone man-mountain around the battlefield.[44]

At this stage in his coverage of the early morning skirmishing, Burleigh introduces a separate body of 'five hundred spearmen, with a few Baggara cavalry', which he says 'came sweeping down as if to attack our right'. Although Verner makes no mention of the event, Sir Charles Wilson noted, 'Some horsemen now came round our right . . .',[45] while Alex Macdonald wrote, 'About this time a body of the enemy's horse were noticed moving in the direction of our right flank.' That these slightly different descriptions represent one and the same incident is demonstrated by their common outcome. Burleigh wrote that the attack was checked when 'a round of shrapnel, which was burst over their heads, knocked over three or four Arabs, and scattered the others'. Wilson noted that, 'they were soon dispersed by a few rounds of shell', while Macdonald for his part generously observed that the enemy cavalry,

. . . were soon sent to the rightabout by two or three of Captain Norton's skilfully fired shells. If all our artillery officers are as efficient as those with our half-battery of screw-guns were, we have good reason to be as proud of that arm of the service in the present as we have been in the past.[46]

Despite having shown a bold front to the British, Mūsā wad Ḥilū and the other *amīrs* had no intention of closing the final mile now separating the two sides. Rather they were seeking to draw Stewart into the open for a stand-up fight in the valley floor. In effect both sides were now waiting for the other to make the first move. Observing the enemy's apparent hesitation, Stewart decided to resort to a ruse, the same 'stratagem of feigned withdrawal' so successfully employed by Sir Evelyn Wood at Khambula. The Zulu right horn having arrived before the laagered British position somewhat ahead of the left, Wood had sent Buller's cavalry out to stir things up with carbine fire, before then staging an apparently panic-stricken retreat to the laager. Wood's idea was that by provoking a premature attack by one wing of the Zulu army, he would confound the simultaneity of the whole. Once Buller and his men had attained their object, the outcome of the battle was never in doubt.

Electing not to use his cavalry as Wood had done, Stewart instructed the officers commanding the Guards and Mounted Infantry Camel Regiments to throw skirmish lines down the slope.[47] None of the sources describe the strength of the sortie, but it was a high-risk ploy and Stewart would not have wished to imperil any subsequent defence of the *zariba* by throwing forward too many of its erstwhile defenders. It cannot have involved fewer than two sections (approximately 40–50 men), might conceivably have involved two half-companies (80–100), but almost certainly did not involve two whole companies. The skirmishers were to bring the enemy under fire and, at a given signal, turn on their heels and run for the sanctuary of the *zariba* as if the devil himself was hard on their heels. It was worth a shot. Burleigh tells us that the skirmishers advanced 600 yards down the slope and brought the enemy under fire at 1,200 yards, which is to say pretty much the limit of the Martini-Henry's range. Over the next few minutes they made a further 200 yards and began engaging at a marginally less aspirational 1,000 yards. All of a sudden the prearranged signal was given and the Tommies began running for their lives. There was a brief forward surge from the Arab host in response, but the *amīrs* checked the movement after about 200 yards. Undeterred the British tried their ruse again, this time to absolutely no avail.[48] The preparation and execution of the attempted provocations cannot have consumed less than half an hour.

With the skirmishers trudging back up the long slope to the *zariba*, probably not all that disconsolately, Stewart decided to resort to artillery fire. Far from provoking the uncontrolled charge he hoped for, Norton's fire triggered a prompt but orderly withdrawal in the direction of the wells. Now, at perhaps a little shy of 8.00 a.m., it had become abundantly clear that it was the British who would have to do the attacking. It was at this point that one of the newspapermen heard the general remark, 'Well if they won't come on, I must go out.'[49] Before long the *anṣār* had withdrawn past the line of flags on the spit, beyond which point distance and glare obscured their further movements.

Although the contention cannot be substantiated on the basis of source evidence from the Mahdīst side, it seems logical, if not indeed obvious, that Mūsā wad Ḥilū and the other Mahdīst commanders were now executing precisely the gambit they had been planning on since the previous afternoon. If so then they too were operating a stratagem of feigned withdrawal, but on a much grander scale. The plan was for the seemingly nervous local contingents to withdraw along the valley ahead of the British, so as to allow the main strike force suddenly to fall upon the infidel from a place of concealment. If this was to work then the Daghaim, Kināna and Hamr contingents had to be concealed about the landscape already and hence cannot have been involved in the demonstration in front of the *zariba*. The British had in fact been observing a Mahdīst false front since the previous afternoon. Located a mile or so down the valley and centred on the line of flags, it was manned by the Abadeh, Bisharin, Ja'līyīn and Awadiyeh contingents. It was never intended that this advanced position should be seriously contested or that the main action should be fought around it. Rather it was the job of the demonstrating contingents to lure the British half a mile further down the valley, where the Kordofanis would spring the trap. There is no great secret to this construct; it merely represents a considered interpretation of what was about to unfold. But it is time to vest the Mahdīst commanders with the shrewd tactical brains they evidently possessed, something which no British officers who fought in the battle, nor any historian writing since, has taken the trouble to acknowledge. The point is this: the Battle of Abu Klea did not simply happen the way it did by chance; it happened the way it did for a reason; and that reason was Mahdīst generalship. There is a corollary pertaining to the generalship of Sir Herbert Stewart which we will come to in due course.

Preparing to Advance

Although the enemy commander had now withdrawn his numerically powerful bodies of infantry along the line of the valley, Stewart could see that his riflemen and horsemen had been left behind and would plainly be bent on harassing the British advance. Divided amongst numerous separate bands, they could be seen deployed along the right-hand side of the valley and on high points either side of the sandy *khor*. In the meantime the riflemen who had remained on the conical hill and the long ridge, perhaps a hundred men in all, had begun to concentrate their fire on Norton's guns, in retaliation for the earlier spitefulness of the Royal Artillery. Curious as to what the next move might be, Alex Macdonald spotted the small red flag customarily carried beside the general and began making his way towards it on horseback. Stewart was down near the gun-fort at the time, a vantage point which offered an excellent view over his only practicable line of advance. Major Dorward was also nearby, supervising the improvement of the defences, and on spotting Macdonald shouted that he should get off his horse at once.[50]

By now the interplay between commander and staff had begun to focus on the necessity to advance a fighting square. While the proposition would have been straightforward enough for formed infantry battalions, for a composite force like the Camel Corps it would constitute a matter of some complexity. In addition it would be necessary to divide the column's combat power prudently, between an offensive element strong enough to defeat an evidently powerful and well-handled enemy main body, and a defensive element capable of holding the *zariba* against anything which might descend upon it in the meantime. One of the greatest worries would be the danger of an infinitely more mobile enemy bypassing a cumbersome British square, to fall upon the thinly defended camel transport and commissariat stores.

By dint of the harassing fire still pouring in from the right flank, Macdonald never did get to complete his journey towards the headquarters staff. Just as he was about to descend into the ravine in which the 19th Hussars were sheltering their ponies (the gun-fort was just the other side of the feature), a mounted infantry soldier came staggering back from the barricade. He had been hit,

> . . . by a bullet in the left breast, which came out of his back and whizzed past me. The poor fellow turning round exclaimed, 'I am badly hit, sir,' and fell into my arms. As I laid him down I noticed that the hole made in his grey tunic by the bullet had a scarlet and a black ring round it. A file of the bearer company soon came along with a stretcher and carried him off to the hospital. I then heard several voices calling out to me to get under cover, 'or sure as anything you'll get hit!' These friendly warnings were almost immediately emphasised by the whiz of a bullet past my head. This decided the matter, and hoping the squall of lead would soon blow over I sought cover.[51]

As serious as the injury sounds, examination of the 23 January casualty return for MICR confirms that no members of the Mounted Infantry died inside the *zariba* on the morning of the 17th, so that the man can be assumed to have survived his wound. Although the number of casualties was not serious in relation to the amount of time the column remained exposed to the fire from the right, scurrying stretcher-bearers were becoming too commonplace a sight for comfort.

Captain Lord Cochrane was one of the smartest of the HCR 'swells' and in his first fight. Originally appointed to command the 2nd Life Guards detachment in Major the Hon. Charles Byng's No. 1 Company, HCR, he had since leaving Jakdul Wells been diverted into the unglamorous but important role of baggage master. Learning that there was now to be a sortie in strength, he made his way to the headquarters and obtained permission to re-join his detachment for the coming fight. He then moved across to No. 1 Company's position on the front face of the *zariba*, where the order to form square was now eagerly anticipated. Cochrane assembled his men in a hollow to the rear of the low stone wall and sat down to await further instructions. After a minute or two Burnaby appeared leading 'Moses' and:

> . . . asked if he could put his horse in the hollow with my men. He sat down beside me on the bank. We had only just sat down when a bullet came between his head and mine and went through the pocket of a man named Murray of my regiment who was lying on the ground in front of us. We then talked of our casualties and he said, 'Unluckily you can't make omelets [*sic*] without breaking eggs.'[52]

If it had been a close shave for the two officers, it had been closer still for 1224 Trooper J. Murray,[53] who quickly recovered the bullet from his clothing and held his trophy aloft. When Cochrane asked Murray if he might have the bullet, the latter replied, 'I think, sir, I have the best right to it as it has gone through my pocket.'[54] It was a fair point.

Cognizant that preparations for an advance were under way, Alex Macdonald caught sight of Jack Cameron as he was making his way towards the hospital-fort and hurried after him to ask whether he intended going out with the square. The reply reflected the black mood that seemed to have settled over Cameron of late. 'No. I do not think it is the right thing to do. It will be a mob of camels, sailors, cavalry and artillery, all mixed up together . . . We are going to have a hot time of it here, for those fellows on the hill and those horsemen on our left mean mischief.'[55] Cameron had every right to consider himself no mean judge of a military situation. In 1881 he had accompanied the ill-fated Sir George Colley through Laing's Nek, Ingogo and Majuba Hill, and the following year had been aboard Admiral Sir Beauchamp Seymour's flagship during the ship-to-shore fight at Alexandria. In the spring of 1884 he was lucky enough to survive the Baker disaster in the Red Sea Littoral and only weeks later had the courage to go back into the desert to cover Second El Teb and Tamai. In a short pen-picture in his *Campaigns of a War Correspondent*, Melton Prior described Cameron as 'a well-tried man from north of the Tweed, who was never tired of letting us know it with pride'. Prior further described his friend and colleague as 'sharp-eyed, impetuous, but keen as a razor at his work'.[56]

On the basis of Cameron's concerns about the square, Macdonald agreed his proposal that one of them should stay at the *zariba* while the other accompanied Barrow and the 19th Hussars. As the two correspondents were talking things through in the lee of the hospital-fort, stretcher-bearers continued ferrying in the latest casualties. Amongst them was Major John Dickson who would evidently not now be one of the three officers going to Khartoum to assist General Gordon. Dickson had been sat in the cover of the barricade, barely five yards from Charles Williams. Williams mistakenly thought that the major was in 'apparent complete shelter',[57] when he was hit just below the knee. Fortunately the bullet hit neither bone nor artery, so that Dickson was not too seriously injured.[58] Wilson had gone across to see him just before he was taken away by the stretchers-bearers and found him 'very cheery' in the circumstances.[59]

Major Marsden Sunderland had already had his horse shot through the nostrils, when unhappily his native groom was also badly hit. He too was carried away by the stretcher-bearers, but had been shot through both thighs and was losing a great deal of blood. The surgeons established that the bullet had severed the major arteries in both lower limbs and concluded that there was nothing they could do to arrest such severe bleeding. Macdonald observed that the man was in great pain until at length he expired.[60] He departed the unhappy scene, passing seven bodies laid neatly in a row beside the hospital, their faces covered by blankets. He next made his way to a spot near the redoubt on the left face of the perimeter, where he had earlier left his Greek servant, his horse and his baggage camels. By dint of the mile or more to the high ground on the right, this was one of the safest parts of the position. Having saddled his horse, presumably under the impression that he would be the one sallying forth with the 19th Hussars, it now transpired that Cameron wanted to go out with them instead. Macdonald decided to return to the hospital-fort as its position, on slightly raised ground, 'afforded a good view of everything going on'. Judging by the sketch he drew for the *Illustrated London News*, Melton Prior had much the same idea. While the hospital-fort offered a good view across the *zariba* and towards the high ground on the right, what it did not do, contrary to Prior's sketch, was offer any view forward of the HCR and GCR positions into the Abu Klea Valley. For Bennet Burleigh, half correspondent and half old soldier, positioning himself anywhere but at the centre of the action was unthinkable; he too proceeded to saddle his horse, but with the intention of accompanying the square, whether to death or glory. 'Sankey' Herbert was of a like mind and also intended accompanying his friends on the staff.[61]

A little after 8.00 a.m. the same body of enemy horsemen which had earlier attempted to get round the British right, only to be thwarted by the screw guns, could be seen positioning themselves amongst the succession of low ridges and gullies to the left of the *khor*. Stewart decided to send the 19th Hussars out early, so that they could fend off any threat the enemy cavalry might pose to his advance.

Barrow himself would immediately take out three-quarters of his men to operate on the open left flank, while the fourth troop would stay behind for the time being and move out to cover the square's right flank as soon as it was ready for the off.[62] Burleigh estimated that the arrangement split the squadron into bodies of about ninety men on the left and thirty on the right.[63] Barrow rode out at about 8.30 a.m.,[64] moving slowly to conserve what little energy his enfeebled ponies could still muster. With his animals in such poor condition he would have to operate his command not as dashing hussars, but instead place his reliance on dismounted carbine fire. After Second El Teb both he and Stewart had good reason to be cautious in matters of cavalry 'dash' anyway.

The rifle fire concentrated on the gun-fort had resulted in the wounding of two of Captain Norton's gunners, one of whom lost a finger to a shot in the hand. For some unfathomable reason the man in question had been holding a large iron key at the time, which was reckoned by nearby bystanders to have saved him from a much more severe wound elsewhere in his body.[65] Now, Lieutenant Charles Lyall, one of the battery's subalterns, was severely injured by a shot in the back which pierced his lungs. Once more the stretcher-bearers were called into action. By the time patient and carrying-party reached the hospital-fort, the small interior space was crowded with surgeons, medics and wounded men. Macdonald was again present when Lyall was brought in and at this point in his account states that the row of blanket-shrouded bodies outside the hospital had now doubled in size to fourteen.[66] If there really were fourteen bodies, then ten of them were native camel-drivers, as the casualty returns submitted to Lord Airlie reflect that only four soldiers in all were killed in or near the *zariba* during the course of the battle: one from the 19th Hussars, one from MICR (Private Wilford who had been killed on Beresford Hill the previous day), and two from the Heavies. Ten native drivers, it must be said, seems an improbably high number and compels the conclusion that Macdonald was in some way mistaken.[67]

Thus far the enemy had been more a nuisance than a serious menace. But it was now time to fix bayonets, forsake the barricades and face them in the open.

Chapter 9

The Valley of the Shadow

The Battle of Abu Klea: Phase II – The British Advance

This was the first time that all our force had worked together in a square on the move and surrounding 150 camels. But no blame can attach in connection with faults of practice or preparation, [for] there was no time to aim at perfection in detail; the one thought was to be in time to save Gordon.

Lieutenant General The Earl of Dundonald, *My Army Life*

QUEEN VICTORIA'S ARMY WAS HEIR to a tradition dating back to the Restoration of the Stuarts, but in the second half of the nineteenth century found itself operating in an age of dramatic military transition – five decades which embraced far more change and innovation than had the previous two centuries together. Our cast of characters lived out their professional lives sandwiched between the end of the 'horse and musket' era and the dawn of modern warfare. Many historians are inclined to nominate the American Civil War or the Franco-Prussian War as the 'first modern war', arguments which in both cases possess undeniable merit. Much depends upon the criteria by which the matter is judged, but if one particularly hones in on battlefield tactics it seems not unreasonable to suggest that these two conflicts actually represented pseudo-Napoleonic transitional wars and that the first truly modern war was waged in South Africa from 1899 to 1902. Here for the first time we see blended the 'less dense battlefield', reliable belt-fed machine guns and 'pom-poms', entrenched lines of defence running over frontages of many miles, quick-firing artillery, smokeless powder and the all but invisible rifleman. Moreover barely identifiable defensive positions were now capable of engaging the attacker at unprecedentedly long ranges. It was the war on the *veldt* which resulted in a radical overhaul of British Army training, organization and tactics and which over the course of the ensuing decade gave rise to the British Expeditionary Force of 1914, an army which was to display demonstrable superiority over its far mightier continental counterparts and which would deny German militarism the crushing victory it sought and expected in the first few weeks of the war. Had the British Army not been overhauled when it was – 'reformed' would be too emphatic a word – there might otherwise have been a triumph of militarism over democracy which would have altered the course of world history in ways we can scarcely begin to contemplate.[1]

Contrary to popular perception, the British Army had not in any case been in doctrinal and conceptual stagnation in the half-century between the Alma and Spion Kop. The officer class might not have been very democratic or even particularly meritocratic, even after the abolition of purchase, but it was expected to know its business inside out – to be professional in other words. Even a notorious dunderhead like Cardigan, one of the worst products of purchase, was capable of handling a regiment of cavalry tolerably well. Conscious of being isolated by 'Pax Britannica' from the transitional military mainstream, a cabal of progressive officers took care to study the great American and European wars of the era for transferrable lessons in the art of war. Colonel Wolseley's visit to the Army of Northern Virginia was but one example of the effort made to stay abreast of the most recent developments. Baker, Brackenbury, Wilson and Kitchener were amongst the reform-minded officers who had either been sent or had found excuses to snoop around the Franco-Prussian War. The writing and lecture scripts of figures like Colonel G. F. R. Henderson, 'Henders' to his students at the Staff College, bear witness to how much serious conceptual thought was taking place in the High Victorian Army.[2] At the same time it is true that the scale, if not the quality, of British conceptual thinking was put to shame by the major continental armies. Even so this was not mere idle intellectualism; the Army changed and its tactics changed, although as is always the way in the military there was an ever-sceptical reactionary wing which had to be overcome with a combination of patience and reason. But the lessons of 1861–5 and 1870–1 were studied and adapted by a serious-minded elite, before being promulgated into the British military mainstream through the medium of such publications as the 1877 and 1884 editions of *Field Exercise and Evolutions of Infantry*. This particular manual repays careful study because with a cursory glance the eye will inevitably fall upon the many sections and diagrams concerned with the old close-order drill dating back to Wellington's day. But those sections of the manual which addressed how to go about the business of fighting were markedly different from what had gone before, reflecting the necessity in the face of improved weapons technology to skirmish in open order, make good use of natural cover, and maintain a system of supports capable both of blunting the enemy's offensive manoeuvres and exploiting the success of one's own. For all that, however, it was not change or modernity which came to dominate the British military iconography of the era but, rather, heroic episodes from the small wars of empire.

In some small part the first glance or clichéd view of the High Victorian Army owes its origins to the iconic image of the 'British square' being assailed by a horde of 'native' enemies. In Wellington's day there had been nothing particularly 'British' about the square – in the first two decades of the century just about everybody used the formation – rather it was the small wars of empire which served to make it so. It is well-nigh impossible to browse a library shelf dealing with the Victorian military without coming across a powerful image of 'our men' standing heroically back-to-back against a numerically superior foe. To what might be termed the Anglo-Saxon mind-set it is a powerful and in many ways appealing image, but it represented, and here is the point, not an outmoded army struggling to leave the 'horse and musket' era behind, but rather a transitioning army which had been forced back upon a battlefield tactic which it already regarded as a thing of the past. Because the American Civil War had convincingly demonstrated that horsed cavalry would be forced in future to adapt to the role of mounted infantry, the 'receive cavalry' square had come to be viewed as at best obsolescent, if not entirely defunct. In the face of greatly improved infantry firepower, the shock-action cavalry charge could be regarded as near-suicidal, not that all the senior cavalry colonels could yet bring themselves to accept such heretical notions. Similarly the close-order infantry square would not now be exposed to the odd roundshot bouncing through the ranks and taking down perhaps half a dozen men, but to shrapnel rounds, fired from well beyond small-arms range, which were likely to burst overhead and kill or maim by the half-company. In short neither the cavalry charge nor the infantry counter-measure, the receive cavalry square, could any longer be regarded as viable acts of war.

It would be the supremely mobile tribal fighters of late nineteenth-century Africa who, for the British at least, came to constitute the new 'cavalry' threat. The British Army had often been compelled to make war in distant lands with too few assets on hand and the start of the Anglo-Zulu War had been no exception. Whilst there were a great many firearms in Zulu hands by 1879, neither the weaponry nor the men carrying it could be considered the equal of trained regulars equipped with the breech-loading Martini-Henry. Taking astonishing courage and terrible ferocity as read, by far the most deadly capability of a Zulu *impi* was the rapidity of its tactical manoeuvre. At the Battle of Isandlwana the 1st Battalion, The 24th Regiment, had faithfully followed the strictures of the 1877 manual and had been left exposed to a crushing double envelopment as a result. The annihilation of the 24th sent a shudder through the nation and the Army. Eighteen months later the same fate befell the 66th Regiment at the Battle of Maiwand in southern Afghanistan, for broadly the same reasons. It was clear that extended-order formations were failing to cut the mustard on the colonial battlefield. Lord Chelmsford's tactical guidance to his column commanders on the eve of the Zulu War had contained contradictory injunctions to regard the Zulus as cavalry and yet fight in line, with the regular battalions in the centre and the African levies on the flanks. He was forced back to the doctrinal drawing board within a fortnight of crossing the border. Such was the shock of the Isandlwana disaster that his every move thereafter was characterized by extreme caution. Campsites were now ringed by great defensive wagon laagers which could take a day to establish, while tactical advances and general actions, including the final victory of 4 July 1879, utilized huge fail-safe squares which by dint of having no flanks could never be undone by rapidity of manoeuvre alone. The human walls of the ponderous great square at Ulundi were manned by no fewer than thirty-three companies of infantry, whilst its corners bristled with Gatling guns and field pieces.[3] But it worked. Thus was the Napoleonic 'receive cavalry' square reincarnated as the colonial battle-square.

When Sir Gerald Graham's force was committed to the Red Sea Littoral in the spring of 1884, it was in the wake of a string of wretched Egyptian performances, in which the shock-action tactics practised by the Bīja had induced moral and tactical disintegration amongst barely trained and badly led troops. It was unsurprising, given their mobility, numerical advantage and rapidity of manoeuvre, that Graham felt an irresistible compulsion to confront the Bīja in square. At both Second El Teb and Tamai the British had advanced to the attack in square – in the first action in one vast divisional square, and in the second in two brigade squares deployed in echelon. In both battles the initiative had appeared to rest with the British, although as earlier described this was because the Mahdīst commanders had chosen the ground and had a number of nasty surprises concealed about the landscape. In both instances advancing squares had fallen into disarray. The original concept of the 'receive cavalry' square had been entirely defensive in nature, as famously exemplified by the protracted stand of the British and Allied infantry against Ney's massed cavalry at Waterloo. Now, seven decades on, in attempting to move across trying desert terrain, while at the same time maintaining a cohesive close-order formation capable of delivering a heavy fire on all sides, the Army was striving to do something infinitely more challenging. If anybody could do it the still peerlessly drilled British infantryman could, but it was a tall order even so. It was decidedly not a sport for the occasional amateur.

State of Training in the Heavy Camel Regiment

And so we return to the Abu Klea Valley on the morning of 17 January 1885 where, amongst other interesting ideas, a hastily assembled composite regiment comprising elements of the sovereign's bodyguard and a miscellany of other representatives from the heavy cavalry arm were, with next to no training to speak of, attempting to pass themselves off as a small infantry battalion. It would be vacuous to suggest that a squad of thirty dismounted Household Cavalrymen could not bang and crash its way around Horse Guards Parade as well as, if not better than, a comparable number of infantrymen, but that was not the issue. What mattered was not close-order drill per se, but the ability of the HCR officers to give effect to the 'infantry drill' – the formations and manoeuvres espoused in *Field Exercise and Evolutions of Infantry* – in such a way as to be able to control five companies as a single tactical entity, whilst at the same time inter-operating, without impediment, alongside units whose officers and men had a near perfect grasp of the techniques and procedures at issue.

Two other important points bear down on the utility of the Heavies as infantry. Again it would be vacuous to suggest that the transition from the Martini-Henry carbine to the long-barrelled infantry rifle was in any way difficult, as the weapons had an identical action. Although it was true that the sights were different, so basic a soldiering fundamental could be addressed with a few minutes of instruction. There remained, nonetheless, two other important issues associated with the adoption of the long-barrelled weapon. First, because it was the principal weapon of their arm, when the men of an infantry battalion went onto the range they did so with all appropriate seriousness. Shooting was important and was supervised by the battalion musketry instructor, usually the second senior lieutenant after the adjutant, and a hand-picked team of NCOs, who were almost always fanatics for their subject. In addition to live firing there was a great deal of classroom and parade-ground instruction. In the cavalry, however, the carbine came only a poor second to lance or sabre and musketry tended to be taken altogether less seriously. In part this was because, prior to the advent of the Martini-Henry, the cavalry arm had struggled to procure a carbine with which it was at all happy; carbines came and carbines went, but lance and sabre seemed eternal. Medium-range engagements for the infantry took place at distances which the Martini-Henry carbine was incapable of attaining. Infantry company commanders would look to begin engaging massed targets at around 800 yards. If by contrast a carbine round struggled its way to 300 yards, it was because the wind was set in the right direction. Secondly, the infantry also had a secondary weapon, the bayonet, which it by no means regarded as a ceremonial adornment. Everybody was regularly trained in its use, while inter-company and inter-battalion bayonet-fighting competitions, conducted with spring-loaded stand-ins for 'cold steel', were as keenly contested as any other sport. To the cavalry this was a black art, in much the same way as 'tent-pegging' would have been to the infantry.

There is one more matter to ponder in considering the enforced conversion of heavy cavalry to infantry – the all-important issue of battlefield discipline – 'steadiness' in other words. Once the order to form square had been given, for the Victorian infantryman that was an end to the matter. In concert with the mate or mates assigned to the self-same yard of real estate,[4] he was required to stand his ground. He need not give any thought to the situation. He was expected not to flinch in the face of danger but, if it came to it, to hold the line with his bayonet and if necessary die where he stood, rather than give ground. Rock steadiness, an atmosphere of calm resolve, the maintenance of silence (so that range settings and other key words of command could be heard) and accurate musketry were the four key attributes which would prevent it ever coming to that. The belief that a calm, well-ordered square was impervious to anything the enemy might throw at it was a given, something deeply ingrained in the infantryman's psychology. This was not the case in the cavalry of course, where every officer and sergeant was given to theorizing on how to go about breaking a square. Two apposite quotations, the first of them from Lord Cochrane's memoirs, will serve to illustrate the challenge presented by HCR's conversion between roles.

During our journey up the Nile it had again been impressed upon us that we were to learn infantry drill. One or two of the officers of other detachments said they would be d____d if they would learn infantry drill, and I'm afraid they did not like doing it, but they did it all the same. Cavalry dismounted drill is too loose a formation for working in a square, also when mixed up with infantry one drill is advisable and that must necessarily be the one practised by the infantry.[5]

Despite the reticence in some quarters, it is evident that some basic attempt at learning the infantry drill was made in HCR. It is instructive to reflect though that whatever training did take place occurred during the journey up the Nile, when the main business of the day was conducting long desert marches by camel. In *From Korti to Khartum* Sir Charles Wilson observed, 'The Heavy Camel Corps had marched straight up from Aswan in detachments, and its organization was changed from troops to companies only just before leaving Korti; it had also had little drill as infantry.' In other words HCR had next to no opportunity to train by companies and no training at all at regimental level. Neither was there any time available to train once the regiment had been concentrated. 'We arrived at Korti on Tuesday, 23 December, 1884,' says Lord Cochrane. 'On 29 December we heard that we were to march into the desert on the following day.' Even had all six days had been available for training, it still would not have been possible for HCR to re-role itself as a competent mounted infantry unit in anything like in so short a period of time. Inevitably most of the week was consumed in any case by the essential administrative preparations for a long desert march. It necessarily follows that the blame for whatever failings would be exposed in the cauldron of battle should be laid at the door of the man who conceived a hastily thrown together composite camel corps, designed to fight in the infantry role, of which one half consisted, for no good reason, of cavalrymen.[6]

The second quotation throws light on just how effectual HCR's ad hoc training regime had actually been. It obliges us to make a chronological leap to the battlefield of Abu Kru, where Captain Lionel Trafford, the Royal Sussex company commander, found his company abutting the Heavies in an advancing square. The rear face was:

> . . . also rather harassed by an officer in the Household Cavalry who happened to be senior to Major Sunderland,[7] taking command and giving words of command that do not appear in the book; he commenced by trying to make the rear face march in fours and, not content with giving many wrong words of command, abused the men for doing right . . . [Later] The officer who had taken command of the rear ordered us to fire a volley, but giving the word 'Fire' before 'Present' the volley was a failure.[8]

Forming Square

The order to form square had at last been given. No source mentions how it was done; it may have been by means of a face-to-face conference between Sir Herbert and his regimental commanders, which seems the most likely scenario, or alternatively by the rapid circulation of a written or oral message, perhaps with an accompanying sketch-plan. One by one the companies detailed to the task peeled away from their sector of the perimeter to gather at the designated 'forming-up place' in the dead ground behind the gravel ridge. The area was 'dead', however, only to the Abu Klea Valley; from the conical hill and the long ridge it was in plain view. Accordingly each newly arrived company was ordered to lie down, immediately it had taken its place. Even in the prone position there could be no guarantee of safety.

The Valley of the Shadow • 247

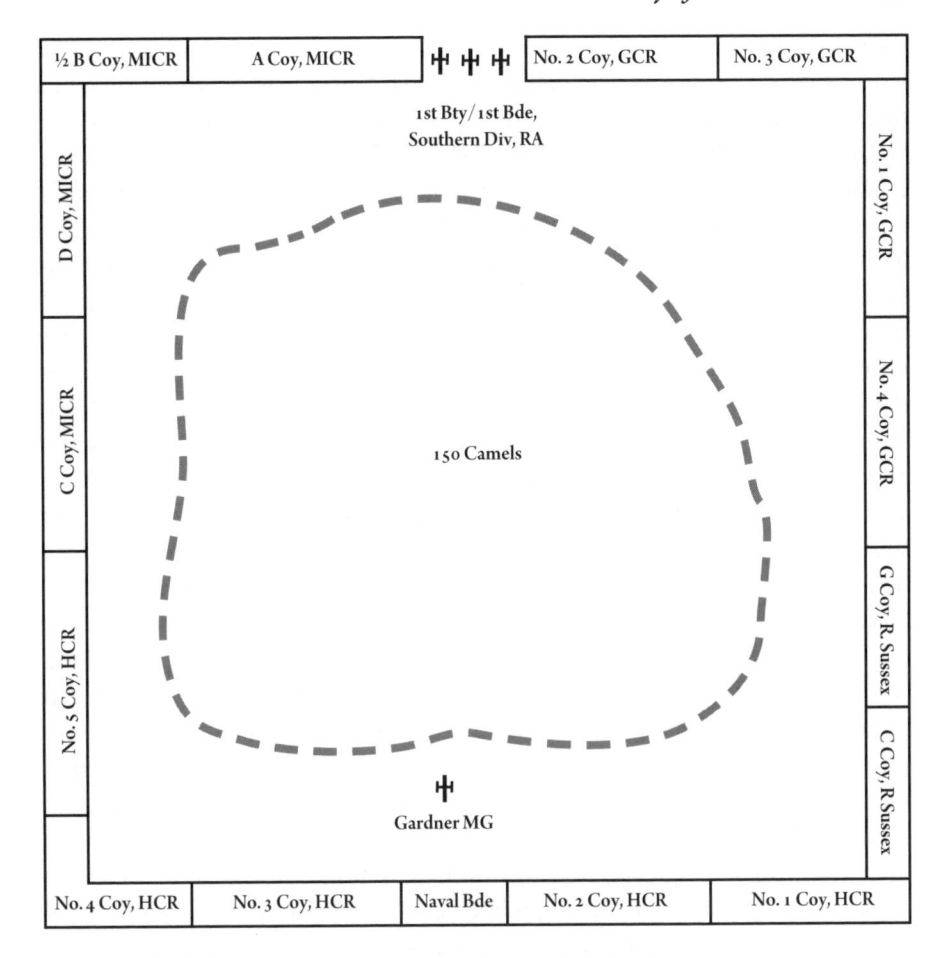

```
┌─────────────┬──────────────┬─────────┬──────────────┬──────────────┐
│ ½ B Coy, MICR│  A Coy, MICR │ ╬ ╬ ╬   │ No. 2 Coy, GCR│ No. 3 Coy, GCR│
├─────────────┴──────────────┴─────────┴──────────────┴──────────────┤
│                      1st Bty/1st Bde,                               │
│                      Southern Div, RA                               │
```

Map 7: The square at Abu Klea

A last-minute change of command in MICR became necessary when a spent round hit Major Gough on the back of the helmet with 'a crack that was audible for yards round'.[9] Burleigh and others close at hand were convinced that the sickening sound meant that Gough must be dead, but as Gleichen put it he was lucky enough only to have been 'knocked senseless'.[10] Alive he might be, but Gough was in no sort of shape to continue, nor would he be in his right mind for some time to come. The next senior officer in MICR was Major Charles Barrow of the Cameronians, Percy's younger brother, who now took command of the regiment.

Working from the front-left corner in a clockwise direction the square was configured as follows.[11] Along its front face from left to right were: two sections of B Company, MICR (the company's other two sections having been detailed to the defence of the *zariba*); next A Company, MICR; then, slightly left of a true centre point, Norton's half-battery with all three 7-pounders; then No. 2 (Coldstream Guards) Company, GCR; and finally No. 3 (Scots Guards) Company, GCR. Down the right face from front to rear were: No. 1 (Grenadier Guards) Company, GCR; No 4 (RMLI) Company, GCR; and then G and C Companies, 1st Royal Sussex in that order. Along the rear face from right to left were: No. 1 Company, HCR (1st and 2nd Life Guards); No. 2 Company, HCR (the Blues and the Bays); next forty Royal Navy personnel;[12] then No. 3 Company, HCR (4th and 5th Dragoon Guards); and finally No 4 Company, HCR (the Royals and the Scots Greys). The left face from rear to front consisted of: No. 5 Company, HCR (5th and 16th Lancers); C (Rifles) Company, MICR; and last D Company, MICR. A diagram of the layout can be seen in Map 7. Such was the enemy's fire potential that the order went out for the companies to form only two ranks deep.[13] The screw guns were carried disassembled, each of them split, barrel, carriage and wheels, between three strong baggage camels. The initial rifle strength of the Naval Brigade would be reduced by the necessity to provide two relays each of ten ratings to haul the Gardner on drag-ropes. For the present the gun would be positioned inside the square, a few yards in front of the centre-point in the rear face, although Beresford had been told that he could use his best judgement in deploying it for action.

The principal subordinate commanders in the square were Lieutenant Colonel Evelyn Boscawen, commanding GCR; Lieutenant Colonel Reggie Talbot, commanding HCR; Major Charles Barrow, commanding MICR; Major Marsden Sunderland, commanding the Royal Sussex companies; Captain Lord Charles Beresford, commanding the Naval Brigade; and Captain Gilbert Norton commanding the Royal Artillery. Quite what Colonel Fred Burnaby's precise role was on the morning of the battle is a matter of some interest. As we have seen he had a long talk with Burleigh the previous evening, during the course of which he apparently said that he had been appointed, 'to the command of the left face and rear of the square, and on the morrow would be virtually discharging the duties of a brigadier-general'.[14] Burleigh's assertion begs the question, who then was in command of the front and right faces? This is a conundrum to which there is no obvious answer. The only officers ranking alongside Burnaby were Colonel Sir Charles Wilson and Captain Lord Charles Beresford, neither of whom would have been regarded as qualified for the role. Both men left a clear record of their involvement in the battle and neither mentions being vested with so important a task; indeed, it can be plainly inferred from their accounts that they had not. Neither does commanding two faces of a square in any way equate to the duties of a brigadier general. On the evening of the 16th advancing in square was but a future contingency, whereas the following morning it became an imminent reality. Lieutenant Douglas Dawson who, like his brother Vesey, was serving in No. 2 (Coldstream Guards) Company, GCR, commented in his November 1885 article for *The Nineteenth Century* magazine that Burnaby was 'in immediate command of the square'. The Burleigh and Dawson interpretations are separated by something in excess of twelve hours, so that it is perfectly possible for both to be true, Burnaby having been afforded a wider role by Stewart in the interim. The general would certainly have wanted to pass executive command of the formation to a senior subordinate, leaving him free as the GOC to concentrate on the wider command of the force and the tactical conduct of the battle: as the key decision-maker, he could not also function as the general manager. In the absence of a second figure of comparable standing, it seems clear that Dawson's statement more accurately reflects Burnaby's role in the battle.

Whilst we can never be sure precisely how many men were in the square, we can gain a broad feel for the numbers in each face by working with unit start states and average strengths of sub-units. Importantly we can also ascertain whether the square was correctly balanced, as there are suggestions in the sources, most notably in Lord Cochrane's memoirs and Captain Trafford's diary, that it was not. Commencing with the parade states of each of the regiments, and subtracting a consistent three men from each sub-unit to provide company rear details at the *zariba*, we find that the average strength of an HCR company is around seventy-two, an MICR company about eighty-eight and a Royal Sussex company about sixty. GCR is atypical in that No. 1 Company, with its three battalion detachments, is one third larger than Nos. 2 and 3 Companies, while the RMLI stand alone with approximately 85 men. Subtracting the Marines from the overall bayonet strength of the regiment leaves 268 bayonets to be divided between seven Guards detachments, three of which are made up of Grenadier Guardsmen. This gives a strength of 117 NCOs and men for No. 1 Company and seventy-eight each for Nos. 2 and 3 Companies. From Beresford's official report we know that forty is about the right figure for the Naval Brigade.

If one then tallies the companies or half-companies on each of the faces, we find that there are theoretically 288 bayonets in the front face and 328 in the rear face. Although at first glance this looks like a marked discrepancy, forty men would equate to twenty yards of frontage, an interval which would have been more than adequately covered by the three screw guns. The necessity to detach two relays each of ten ratings to haul the Gardner while the square was on the move, amounted only to a minor and temporary discrepancy well within manageable limits. Front to rear, then, there is relative symmetry at the outset. Turning to the flanking faces, average strength calculations would suggest that there were roughly 322 bayonets on the right face, compared with something around 248 on the left. Here then is a serious discrepancy of seventy-four bayonets – the equivalent of another HCR company, or around thirty-seven yards of frontage. The left face comprised only two companies of MICR and one of HCR, while on the right was the enlarged Grenadier Guards Company, the RMLI Company and two Royal Sussex companies. The last, although they were the smallest companies in the force, each had only about a dozen men fewer than an HCR company. Accepting that they represent necessarily broad-brush calculations the figures nonetheless serve to corroborate the testimony of Cochrane and Trafford, both of whom assert that the right face was longer than the left.

The four faces tallied together come to a total of 1,186 bayonets in all, to which must be added the aggregated total of staff, regimental, company and departmental officers, probably around eighty-five officers altogether. In addition there were about thirty artillerymen and perhaps forty departmental soldiers from the Medical Staff Corps and the Commissariat & Transport Corps. Thus the all-up number of officers, NCOs and men inside the square was probably only just shy of 1,350. It had been decided to take along 120–150 baggage camels, most of which were devoted to carrying reserve rifle and artillery ammunition. According to Burleigh, fifty-two of the animals belonged to the medical bearer-company and would thus have been fitted with either *cacolets* or stretcher-litters.[15] It can be inferred that 40–50 native drivers would also have been present. With everybody prone or crouched in the last few minutes before the off, the dimensions of the formation would not have been readily apparent, but once the order to stand up and close up had been given, the sprawl would have contracted to leave a neat rectangle of approximately 150 x 125 yards. With close to 1,400 human souls and, allowing for the horses of the staff, 130–160 quadrupeds jammed into a space equating to seven cricket pitches by six, the square would be the easiest of small-arms targets. And by now every Mahdist north of Metemmeh, from the grandest *amīr* to the humblest *anṣāri*, knew that the British were coming.

Defending the Zariba

The task of keeping the *zariba* safe had fallen to Major Arthur Gern, ordinarily the company commander of F Company, 1st Royal Sussex, who had been assigned B and F Companies of his own battalion, two sections of B Company, MICR, and the 26 Field Company detachment. The mounted infantry sections had already left the *zariba* to re-occupy the rough stone redoubt on Beresford Hill and the low stone wall on Trafford Hill.[16] The commanding view from Beresford Hill would at least permit any developing threat to the *zariba* to be promptly identified. It is likely that Captain Morse as the senior of the two officers in the half-company would have occupied the superior vantage point with his 1st Royal West Kents, leaving Trafford Hill in the care of Lieutenant Tudway and the 2nd Essex section.[17]

It would be impossible for Major Gern to defend the lengthy faces of the *zariba* with only two small Royal Sussex companies, mustering at best 125 officers and men between them. His effort would have to be concentrated instead on the four biscuit-box redoubts, while every man-jack within the perimeter would have to be prepared to stand to his arms and play his part. Unfortunately the men of the Medical Staff Corps had not been provided with rifles and were only slowly acquiring them as casualties in the fighting companies mounted. There is little doubt that, medics or not, they would all have wanted a Martini in the face of such an enemy. The officers of the transport staff and the remaining Commissariat & Transport Corps men, of whom there might perhaps have been twenty, were assigned to the redoubt at the rear of the position. Major James Dorward and his twenty-six-strong party of Royal Engineers were posted in the redoubt half-way down the left face, but found it too large and quickly set about reducing its dimensions better to suit their numbers.[18] That left the gun-fort, forward right, and the hospital-fort at the right-rear. The sources fail to recount precisely how the Royal Sussex companies were deployed, although thankfully Macdonald gives us the key to what might otherwise be an insoluble conundrum in stating that forty-seven Royal Sussex men under the command of Lieutenant Kane were stationed in the gun-fort.[19] As this is clearly an entire company, but evidently not Major George Harden's B Company, we can deduce that Richard Kane,[20] one of the most junior subalterns in the battalion, had temporarily assumed command of F Company in order that Major Gern could attend to the wider command.

Macdonald also states that the hospital-fort was held by 'a few of the Mounted Infantry'. This could conceivably account for some element of the half-company from B Company, MICR, although it is of note that Verner's diary contradicts Macdonald by assigning the hospital-fort to the Royal Sussex. Macdonald, to be fair, was in or near the redoubt, while Verner had gone out with the square. Major Harden's B Company gets no definitive mentions in the sources but may have been manning the right face of the *zariba*, a principal direction of threat, including the outside perimeter in the vicinity of the hospital-fort, a disposition which would permit the views of Macdonald and Verner to be reconciled. It is worth noting that there are one or two passing references in the sources to small details left behind by the camel regiments: this is likely to have been a party of two or three men per company, whose job would have been to prevent their comrade's kit being pilfered by the 300-strong native workforce lurking amongst the knee-haltered camels. Usefully for Major Gern such an arrangement would have left another 32–48 riflemen scattered about the position. It is possible that some of these men accounted for the MICR detail which Macdonald places in the hospital-fort. Ultimately a paucity of source coverage means that the precise dispositions of the assets committed to the defence of the *zariba* is by no means cut and dried. In all Gern may have had close to 250 fighting men at his disposal, with which he had to protect the surgeons and medics, their patients, the little knot of war correspondents, the huge mass of camels and the commissariat stores.

Advance of the Square

At the southern edge of the Bayūda Desert, Saturday 17 January 1885 was now turning into what Verner termed a 'cruel hot day'. For the British and Mahdīsts alike, everything was now in place. Buller had not assigned any of the expedition's chaplains to Stewart's command, but if there had been a man of the cloth present it was now that he would have felt moved to raise a prayer for the success of the Queen's arms and the preservation of her soldiers.[21] Sensing that there would be hard fighting ahead, Bennet Burleigh was preoccupied with more worldly matters and felt driven to enquire of Burnaby where his shotgun was. 'He told me he had given to his servant to carry that double-barrelled shotgun which he had used so well against the Hadendawas at El Teb, in deference to the noise made in England by the so-called humanitarians against its use.' Burleigh claimed to have replied, 'That was a mistake. I should have seen them damned first.'[22] Characteristically

'Bloody' Pigott was unaffected by such qualms of conscience and, anticipating a good day's sport, had his best English gun cradled under one arm, his pockets full of cartridges and his devoted fox-terrier 'Smoke' dancing at his heels.[23] Pigott's would not be the only dog marching into battle that morning, as 'Jacky', the game little 'colley' much beloved of the Grenadier Guards, had fallen in with his regiment as usual.[24]

Down in the valley the distant popping of carbine fire indicated that Barrow and French were now doing their best to shield the left flank of the advance. At a nod from the general, the officer commanding the remaining troop of hussars kicked up his pony and led his men down the long gravel slope in front of the gun-fort towards the valley floor. This was it then. The decisive and most dangerous phase of the battle was about to get under way. The bellowed order 'Stand Up!' came moments later. It was followed by a cacophony of yapping and barking from the company officers and sergeants, as they bustled about dressing their ranks from left to right and their files from front to rear. A minute or two more and they were off down the cruelly exposed slope towards the 'Valley of the Shadow', which for all the blazing sunshine overhead still appeared somehow dark and sinister. On the conical hill and the long ridge excited Arab riflemen loaded and fired as fast as they could. There were three or four immediate casualties who were left where they fell, to be recovered by carrying-parties dashing the relatively short distance from the *zariba*. Staff Sergeant O'Malley of No. 9 Transport Company, a man described by his officers as 'cool and business-like under fire',[25] rushed back and forth on the open slope recovering the rifles of the wounded. When Lieutenant Rowland Beech of No. 1 Company, HCR, went reeling to the ground, it was O'Malley who ran downhill to help him back inside the perimeter and on to the surgeons.[26]

The long slope reaching down to the sandy *khor* was free of natural obstacles and readily permitted the men in the ranks to get into their stride. It was not long before the distance to the rear was such that it would be necessary to carry any further casualties aboard the *cacolets* and litters. After only a few hundred yards of tolerably good progress, two significant problems became apparent. First, there were so many camels in the notionally hollow centre of the square that it was impossible to see from one side of the formation to the other. Alex Macdonald wrote that, 'More than one officer assured me that it was almost impossible for anyone at the front to be usefully cognizant of what was taking place in the rear.'[27] This would inevitably prove a significant nuisance to the maintenance of cohesion. Secondly, the discrepancy in the strengths of the flanking faces had also become obvious. It is no coincidence that Lord Cochrane, marching at the right-rear corner, should be the participant who best articulates the problem, as he was commanding one of the regimental detachments most affected by it.[28] In essence his men were now attempting to keep station behind a right face that was the best part of forty yards longer than the face opposite. This would have resulted in the rear-face companies being dressed not in a straight line from the right-rear corner to the left-rear corner, but obliquely between these two points, with the extreme left-hand file way in advance of the extreme right-hand file, a sight which had it not been for the presence of the camels might have reduced the infantry colour sergeants to near-apoplexy.

Colonel Reggie Talbot addressed the problem promptly by shuffling the Royal Scots Greys detachment of No. 4 Company, HCR, around the left-rear corner to extend the frontage of the left face,[29] although what should have happened of course is a transfer of manpower from the right face to the left. The incorporation of the Greys half-addressed the shortfall on the left, but would also have required the rear-face companies to stretch the intervals between their files in order to cover an additional 18–20 yards of ground. This was by no means the end of the world, but neither was it a particularly helpful contribution to the cohesion of the square, when maintaining the solidity of all four faces was a matter of vital importance. Talbot and his officers probably accepted the weakening of the rear on the basis that it was the infantry companies on the front and flanking faces which were going to be doing the serious fighting. The Heavies were there to watch the back door and were fated, so it appeared, not to see too much of the action. But that is not how fighting in square worked – one formed square as a counter-measure against an agile enemy and the point about such an enemy was that one could never be quite sure where he might strike.

In the meantime Willoughby Verner, his intelligence work temporarily laid aside, was playing his part as a supernumerary company officer. As a Rifle Brigade man he began the advance marching alongside his regimental colleagues in C Company, MICR, but soon drifted a few files to the rear to assist Major Ludovick Carmichael with No. 5 Company, HCR. 'The Heavies', wrote Verner, 'also had to be looked after to lock up their fours very often as they were apt to cover too much ground.'[30] Our average-strength calculations have shown just why it was that the files in No. 5 Company, which unlike its sister companies was marching as a column of course, were opening up front to rear. At the same time Verner's account reflects the anxiety he felt as an infantry officer to keep things tight, as his every instinct demanded. Ultimately it was more important that the rear face remained solid than that the square be made symmetrical. It could be argued that, for the time being at least, Talbot had struck a tolerably happy medium by repositioning the Scots Greys.

Out on the low ridges to the British left, Percy Barrow had dismounted his troops to engage an enemy body of around 200 horse and 300 foot which he encountered infiltrating down the side of the valley towards the *zariba*.[31] It was a significant skirmish conducted at odds of around six to one and would serve to keep the main body of the 19th Hussars preoccupied for a considerable time, in large part negating Stewart's plan for the protection of his left. There were other large bodies of *anṣār*, one or two of them running to four-figure strengths, manoeuvring in the distance on both sides of the valley.

Just ahead of the square the *khor* now described a wide arc to the left of the conical hill, before straightening again to run south towards the wells. Continuing on a straight-line course would necessitate crossing the watercourse and then moving parallel with it on its right-hand side. Steering a line which kept the *khor* a few hundred yards to the left would give all four faces of the square good fields of fire and at the same time maintain a healthy distance from the high ground running down the right-hand side of the valley. Dickson and Verner had been out on this ground the previous afternoon and it was largely on the strength of their recommendations that Stewart had selected his line of advance.[32] Crossing the *khor* itself would not be difficult, but was sure to slow things down and break the easy rhythm that had been established in the first half-mile of the advance. While the gentle right-to-left slope on the far side looked from a distance like good going, it was characterized by occasional low ridges, a multitude of shallow hollows and a number of tributary *khors* lying directly across the line of advance. Veterans of the Red Sea Littoral would have realized instinctively that these were precisely the sort of features in which Mahdīst *amīrs* could hide thousands of men. Fortunately most of the soldiers in the accompanying troop of hussars fell into this category and could be relied upon to probe areas of dead ground for any lurking danger long before the square came within striking distance.

Thankfully the dry water features intersecting the landscape did not share the same characteristics as the *dongas* which had proved so vexatious to British operations in Zululand; in particular their banks were gentle not vertical, while none of them was more than a few feet deep. They were the sort of easy obstacle that a lone rambler might cross by running quickly into the bottom and straight out the other side, free to continue on his way in a matter of twenty seconds or so. For a battle square of 1,350 people and a large contingent of bloody-minded baggage camels they would constitute a rather different though still not unduly difficult proposition. Colonel Reggie Talbot described the going thus:

The route taken was parallel to, and a few hundred yards from, the wadi, or shallow ravine, that ran on our left to the wells at Abu Klea, in which were stunted trees, and thick high grass concealing deep watercourses, giving admirable cover for the enemy. Our course was up and down, and across steep hillocks of sand, which sloped towards the wadi and it was commanded by hills to the right and rear occupied by Arab riflemen. It was trying ground for camels, hardly a yard of it being level, and also for the Gardner gun, which was hauled by the bluejackets with an energy and activity that deserves all praise.[33]

As Macdonald observed, the principal irritant for the British at this stage of the proceedings was still incoming rifle fire:

Many of the enemy's sharpshooters followed the square along the ridges on the right of the line of its advance, and from 400 to 800 yards distant from it. Taking every advantage of every rock and tree, they kept up a hot and telling fire on it from their safe commanding positions. Others of them, moving along the same flank, availed themselves of the inequalities of the ground and of the cover afforded by the sparsely scattered shrubs and grass. On the left flank the Arab sharpshooters had plenty of cover among the tall grass in that direction and also kept up a hot fire.[34]

From his position at the rear of the right face, Captain Trafford estimated the range to the enemy fire positions as 'roughly 500 yards'.[35]

Not long after the time-consuming process of crossing the main *khor* had been completed the adjutant of HCR, John Edward Leverson Jervis, or more properly Captain the Viscount St Vincent, fell victim to one of the enemy riflemen.[36] It was a curious remark but Lord Cochrane thought that the bullet which felled him, 'made a noise such as is caused by striking a sack of oats with a stick'.[37] The remorseless advance of the square soon left the badly wounded peer some little distance to the rear. Sergeant Charles Williams of the Medical Staff Corps (not to be confused with the war correspondent of the same name) recalled that:

> ... prior to the actual [climax of the] battle, we of the medical corps, assisted by regimental [stretcher] bearers, had [to] run some distance from the halted square to bring [in] men who had been wounded; [the] dead were left where they fell. Not a very pleasant job, bullets whistling round your ears like so many flies, [but] luckily our casualties were very few. On one occasion in particular I carried a wounded Major on my shoulders, some 100 yards from where he lay badly wounded, into the square.[38]

Williams only got around to describing the fight late in life, but as it is a certain fact that only two officers fell between the point at which the square moved off and the battle's denouement, one of whom, Lieutenant Rowland Beech (recovered to the *zariba*), can be ruled out, it can only have been Lord St Vincent that he brought in.

The wounded could expect to receive only fleeting and rudimentary attention at the hands of one of the surgeons, before being rushed into a seat or litter aboard a bearer-company camel. Thereafter they were necessarily left to their own devices and, in their dangerously elevated box-seats, found themselves in far greater danger than anybody else on the battlefield. Reggie Talbot remarked in his account of the battle that one of his men was unfortunate enough to have been shot three times. Another of Talbot's observations, to the effect that, 'the camels in the square also received many a bullet which would otherwise have found its way into the leading portion of the square',[39] would suggest that there was a good deal of fire pouring in from the conical hill which, as the British advanced down the valley, was slipping ever more to their right-rear. A wounded soldier placed in the *cacolet* seat opposite Lord St Vincent was not long afterwards shot again, this time in the wrist, although even this was not the end of his tribulations.[40]

St Vincent was an able, experienced soldier and a great loss to HCR, although some of his regimental colleagues had found him 'a little inclined to be fussy'. They had exacted their revenge by nicknaming their overly fastidious adjutant 'Martha'.[41] Deprived of his 'most gallant and promising'[42] right-hand man, Talbot now pressed Major Charles Byng of 1st Life Guards into the role of acting adjutant, obliging him in turn to hand No. 1 Company over to Lord Cochrane as its next senior officer.[43]

Across on the right face Lance Sergeant Parker of No. 3 Company, GCR, had been shot through the chest. After being briefly fussed over by one of the doctors, Parker insisted on re-joining his section. It was only some time later that his strength gave out and he had to be ushered into a *cacolet*. His selfless conduct would later attract the award of a DCM.[44]

The necessity to halt periodically, in order to pick up casualties and urge harassed bearer-company camels back to their feet, meant that the advance down the valley was necessarily a tortuous stop–start affair. Lionel Trafford captured something of the scene in his diary:

> As each man fell the few words, 'Man down!' was called and the doctors with one or two Army Hospital Corps ran to him.[45] If life was left a camel was halted and the wounded man was put on it; the square by this time would have got 50 or 60 yards, so the rear face was constantly being broken by camels going in and out . . . McSorley, D Company attached to C [Trafford's], was sent flying out of the ranks struck in some vital place; he fell at least two feet clear of where he was marching.[46]

Private John McSorley, dead when he hit the ground, was left where he fell. In the case of wounded men the surgeons had only moments to try and patch up their patients as best they could. Although it was common practice amongst the war correspondents to phrase their reports as if they personally had been in the thick of the fight, when this might not necessarily have been the case, Harry Pearse of the *Daily News* does appear to have been inside the square and reported that, 'The medical staff under Surgeon-Major Ferguson worked splendidly under the heaviest fire. There were frequent stoppages for those purposes. They made progress slow.'[47] During one such halt Cochrane watched the RMO of HCR, Surgeon John Falvey, 'that brave and devoted officer', as he called him, 'who was near to me dressing wounds; how coolly he was working, shot at all the time, his whole thoughts on his case. The square, ordered from the front face, would recommence its onward move before he was ready.' Whether the doctors were ready or not was the last thing on General Stewart's mind. There was a battle to win first and it was high time something was done about the intolerable weight of incoming small-arms fire.

Shielding the Advance

It was apparent that there were a good many enemy riflemen down in the sandy *khor*, where they were benefiting from relatively short engagement ranges and good cover from view in the long grass.[48] Stewart decided that it would be prudent to screen the square by deploying skirmishers from the Guards and Mounted Infantry. In the style of a conventional infantry battalion MICR had been organized with two wing commanders on its establishment, Major Charles Barrow, now commanding the regiment, and Major Thomas Phipps.[49] Phipps was assigned to command the skirmish line. Once again it was a task for which C (Rifles) Company was ideally suited, but this time it was the turn of the two KRRC sections under Lieutenants 'Johnny' Campbell and Archie Miles.[50]

It is not clear how the departure of a half-company of about forty men from the middle of the left face was handled. Clearly if the KRRC men were driven in by an enemy rush they would have to fall back into the left face somewhere. It seems unlikely that a gap would have been left to accommodate them, as this would have had an adverse effect on the cohesion of the formation. It is far more likely that the two Rifle Brigade sections reconfigured themselves from two ranks to one, so as to extend themselves over what had formerly been a four-section frontage. This would enable the KRRC skirmishers simply to run in individually and, on reaching sanctuary, adopt a kneeling position beneath the bayonet of a Rifle Brigade man, in effect taking post as the company's front rank. This was both simple and workable and would serve to preserve the integrity of the square in the meantime. The use of skirmishers around a square was an unconventional tactic which did not feature in *Field Exercise and Evolutions of Infantry* for the simple reason that they must perforce mask the fire of the formation during their withdrawal. That being so it was vital that in going about their business the skirmishers did not wander too far from sanctuary.

With a troop of hussars already rendering good service to the right-front, Colonel Evelyn Boscawen of GCR chose to throw forward only one section of Lieutenant Colonel Mildmay Willson's No. 3 (Scots Guards) Company, a job which fell to Lieutenant Frederick Romilly and his men.[51] The skirmishers on both sides of the square pushed forward and commenced trading shots with the white-robed figures darting about the ridges and gullies in the middle distance.

The sources leave no room for doubt that the deployment of MICR and HCR skirmishers was the work of General Stewart himself. What is less certain is precisely who took the decision that the units at the back of the square should likewise conform. Lionel Trafford wrote that, 'As no orders were given to send out scouts to cover our flanks, individual commanders took the responsibility of doing so.'[52] In the case of the Royal Sussex, at the rear of the right face, this would have been Major Sunderland's decision. In the case of HCR it has to be presumed to be the work of Colonel Talbot, not least because the HCR skirmishers are known to have been commanded by Major Charles Byng, now standing in as the adjutant, albeit it was a curious role for the colonel's new right-hand man to play. The soldiers assigned to the task were Captain Joseph Darley's detachment of the 4th (Royal Irish) Dragoon Guards, one of the half-companies in No. 3 Company.[53] As a result the rear face was now even more thinly spread than before. It is worth briefly contemplating the scale of this problem. Feeding the Scots Greys into the left face had served to leave the rear face deficient by one half-company. With the 4th DG contingent departing as skirmishers there were now around seventy-two men too few for the rear face to constitute the solid wall of humanity it ought to have done. For his part Sunderland sent out Colour Sergeant Kelly with a party of only ten men.[54] Before leaving the subject of the skirmishers it is only fair to note that in his January 1886 article for *The Nineteenth Century*, Talbot implies that he too was told by Stewart to send out skirmishers. On the other hand, the emphatic nature of Trafford's remark must at least raise a question mark over whether Talbot received a direct order, or merely assumed that the order given to the Guards and Mounted Infantry must also apply to his own regiment.

The score of flags fluttering from the long gravel spit between the two big *khors* were within easy range of the screw guns. It appeared to the British that the position represented some sort of focal point for the enemy. The square was brought to a halt so that the 7-pounders could be assembled and brought into action. For well-drilled gunners like Norton's this was the work of only three or four minutes. From his position just to the right of the guns Lieutenant Douglas Dawson watched the ensuing engagement and its effect. 'The guns sent four or five shells right among them, and we saw hundreds of them spring up and bolt.'[55] Marling too saw several shells 'pitch right into' the parties of *anṣār* near the flags and observed 'most of them . . . trekking away to the hills on the left'.[56] The screw guns were not disassembled again at the end of the engagement but instead were each towed on drag-ropes behind a baggage camel.[57]

The various details of skirmishers were already doing good work on all sides of the square. Not only were they shooting well, some of the better shots scoring hits on individual targets at ranges of anything up to 800 yards, but much more importantly they were also drawing a good deal of fire away from the tight-packed square. At the right-rear a dozen *anṣār* spearmen suddenly sprang from cover and charged the Royal Sussex skirmishers. Colour Sergeant Kelly called his ten men up into the present for a volley at 400 yards. The ensuing salvo crumpled seven of the enemy into the gravel, but did nothing to deter the remaining five. A second volley brought down three more men, at which point a brace of fortunate survivors thought better of the enterprise and disappeared into the nearest cover. Ten hits scored for twenty rounds expended on moving targets at between 300 and 400 yards: an interesting insight into the battlefield efficacy of the Martini-Henry in the hands of trained British infantrymen.[58]

Out on the GCR skirmish line one of Lieutenant Romilly's men had gone down wounded, prompting the Guards RMO, Surgeon James Magill, to go dashing forward to render first aid. As he crouched over the wounded guardsman, Magill himself was shot in the leg. Gleichen observed that recovering both doctor and patient was a matter of 'some difficulty'.[59] Only three Scots Guardsmen were wounded that day. Lance Sergeant Parker was one, but he was hit not long after the square set out. The man to whom Magill was attending can therefore only have been either 3317 Private J. Fox or 5020 Private W. Smith. We know that Fox was shot in the thigh, but that like Lance Sergeant Parker before him he refused to acknowledge his injury and returned to his place in the ranks. While Parker's strength eventually gave out, Fox somehow hobbled his way through to the end of the day, an act of dogged determination which, like Parker's, would also be recognized with the award of a DCM.[60] In all likelihood then it was Private Smith, returned as severely wounded, who had to be helped in with Magill.

The incident served as one more contribution to the stop–start nature of the advance. Everybody present that day would recall how slow across the ground the movement of the square had been. When yet another call for a halt was passed forward from the rear, the general despatched Captain Verner to find out what on earth was going on behind the baggage camels. Having pushed his way through to the rear face, Verner found the naval lieutenants, Alfred Pigott[61] and Rudolph de Lisle, trying to get two recalcitrant dromedaries back to their feet, the latest episode in a string of problems caused by the animals and drivers. Beresford wrote that the camels 'lagged behind, slipping and falling, and we of the rear face were all tangled up with a grunting, squealing, reeking mass of struggling animals'.[62] Although Beresford himself omits the detail, Reggie Talbot noted in his account that straggling camels often obstructed the naval ratings hauling the Gardner.[63]

Devoid of any training for the task in hand the camel-drivers had no real grasp of what was expected of them, much beyond the necessity to stick close to the troops. The Adenis alone were admired by the British for their 'pluck'.[64] As for the Egyptians and Dongolāwīs there were bullets coming from their left and bullets coming from their right, but, if it felt like the great majority of them were coming from the right, then it was only natural that they should drift in the opposite direction so as to increase their distance from harm.[65] They had several times come close to forcing the left face of the square asunder.[66] Even if they could tell that the fighting men were becoming irritated with them, few of them had English enough to comprehend the bad-tempered injunctions being hurled in their direction by the handful of Commissariat & Transport Corps NCOs accompanying the square. It seemed to Lord Cochrane that the native drivers almost always failed to step off promptly after a halt;[67] the possible connection with his having temporarily abandoned the role of baggage master seems not to have occurred to him. Inevitably the combination of the camel-drivers both hanging back and drifting to the left was making life a misery for the officers and soldiers at the left-rear corner of the square. Once the two naval lieutenants had succeeded in getting the recalcitrant camels moving again, the advance was resumed.

A small body of enemy cavalry, probably about fifty strong, now put in an appearance in a wide gully to the British right-rear. Yet another halt was promptly called for. Sensing an opportunity to bring the Gardner into action at last, Beresford jumped down from 'County Waterford' and began manoeuvring the gun into position. Nearby HCR officers bellowed and gesticulated for Captain Darley's skirmishers to clear the fields of fire. It took only a few thunderous five-round volleys from the machine gun to scatter the distant horsemen into a panic-stricken retreat. With the cavalry threat disposed of, the HCR skirmishers went back out to resume their dispute with the scattering of Arab riflemen tailing the square.

The further along the valley the British went, the stronger the parties of *anṣār* lurking on the flanks became. Burleigh reported to his readers that it became necessary to keep them in check with company volleys:

The Arabs appeared more numerous every moment, sometimes showing in lines of battle array as if they meant to charge the square, and anon disappearing behind a ridge, or sinking out of sight in the water scored lumpy ground, covered with scrub and bunch grass – just as Roderick Dhu's clansmen vanished at a wave of their chieftain's hand.[68] There was no questioning now among old campaigners whether the Arabs would fight, and General Stewart and his personal staff consisting of Major Wardrop, Lord Airlie and Captain Rhodes galloped to right and left to keep the force in readiness to repel any attack. With all deference to the gallant Heavies, it was felt to be a trial for them, a much mixed cavalry force, fighting on foot as infantry and with the long rifle, to which they were unused. Onward our fighting square moved, the enemy forming up as if to charge and after a volley or two, given by companies, getting again out of sight.[69]

At one point a massed formation of about 1,500 *anṣār* appeared to the right of the square.[70] The <u>shaikhs</u> leading it made no immediate move to attack, but failed to appreciate that they would not be able to loiter inside effective small-arms range. A sequence of volleys from the Grenadier Guards, RMLI and Royal Sussex, each company firing in its turn, sufficed to drive the enemy into retreat.

So far so good: despite the weight of incoming fire, casualties had been relatively light up to this point. Although the British had gained less than two miles in something around an hour's worth of fighting, they were nonetheless making steady progress in the direction of the wells. Alex Macdonald was amongst the knot of officers and war correspondents observing the advance from an elevated vantage point back at the *zariba*:

Up till then I had my misgivings as to the prospects [of the advance], but these were soon dispelled by the appearance which the square itself now presented. How grandly imposing was that mass of armed men! At first sight it suggested a moving fortress, but with walls of such material as to bid defiance to the assaults of any ordinary foe. Then, under the ocular deception produced by the prevailing mirage, it was lifted above the ground and seemed to float away from us, now firing a gun from one side and then the other, when an enthusiastic fancy converted it into a line-of-battle ship sailing into action.[71]

For Bennet Burleigh, standing on the quarterdeck of Macdonald's metaphorical man-of-war, it seemed that, 'our progress was like that of some huge machine, slow, regular, compact, despite the hail of bullets pouring in'. The hyperbole of the newspapermen was all very well, but to a professional infantryman like Lionel Trafford things looked rather different. 'The square was not in very good order: the right face was very crowded and the left very thin. This might be from the front and rear faces not being parallel. The rear face was constantly being broken by the camels.'[72]

The Qur'anic banners which had earlier proved so useful to the gunners in marking their target were now only 300 yards to the left-front of the square, on the far side of the sandy *khor*. From this distance it was apparent that they were not fluttering over large bodies of *anṣār*, but had been planted in the ground. Although the area around the confluence of the *khors* had earlier seemed likely to be a focus of enemy resistance, it was clear that it had since been abandoned. A scattering of bloody corpses bore testament to the efficacy of Captain Norton's gunnery.[73] There were more banners planted in the long grass a few hundred yards along the merged *khor*, but this area appeared likewise to be deserted.[74]

It had become apparent that the spit between the two *khors* was the last significant rise on the British left. Beyond the junction of the watercourses there was a relatively flat and featureless stretch of plain, bounded at a distance of about two miles by a series of significant hill features which could have no possible bearing on the fight to the wells. It was an altogether different story on the right, where the high ground along the side of the valley was a lot closer and still had a mile or more to run. From the point at which the two watercourses collided, the merged *khor* became a good deal wider but no deeper. Nowhere did its banks drop more than about four feet below the general lie of the land. The caravan road to Metemmeh ran parallel to the *khor*, on the far side of the feature from the British, although it was by no means easy to discern. Anticipating that the 'enemies of God' would follow the time-honoured route to the Nile, the Mahdīsts had erected a number of loop-holed stone sangars designed to command the road from a range of about 150 yards.[75] By advancing to the right of the *khor*, largely a function of the juxtaposition of his overnight position and the general line of the valley, Stewart had contrived to leave the enemy's defences on the blind side of the spur where they could now have no tactical relevance. The marked contrast between the open ground unfolding to the British left and the high ridges running along the near side of the valley led many of Stewart's officers to infer that the principal threat must now lie on the right,[76] where small groups of horsemen and strong bodies of *anṣār* infantry were continuing to dog the advance. On the left there was only the inevitable scattering of *jihādīya* marksmen.

Immediately in front of the square was a shallow, flat-bottomed *khor* of about seventy-five yards in width, one of a succession of tributaries lying directly across the British line of advance. Stewart and Burnaby cannot have anticipated any significant difficulty in crossing it and in all likelihood pushed forward without giving the matter a second thought. The ground on the far side of the feature also looked like tolerably good going, although after the square had gained another 300 yards or so it would be necessary to steer a course around the heads of two smaller *khors* lying to the left of the axis. About 150 yards in front of these features was a fourth, much longer tributary which the British would have no choice but to cross. Some 600 yards further on again was another big *khor* of comparable dimensions to the first and the fourth, although intervening rises meant that this particular feature was not yet visible to the British.

Major Phipps and the KRRC skirmishers had done such good work to the left-front of the square that they were now getting only intermittent opportunities to trade shots with enemy riflemen. Phipps could see no sign of any strong enemy force on his sector and sent Lieutenant Cyril Martyr of 2nd DCLI running back to the square to report the coast clear. Phipps also seems to have told Martyr to seek permission for some of the skirmishers to dash forward and seize the apparently abandoned Qur'anic banners in the *khor*.[77] Stewart already had his binoculars trained on the proceedings and was heard by Percy Marling to remark, 'There's old Phippy; he'll have some of those flags in a minute.'[78] Lieutenant

Dawson was also watching the left flank and similarly found himself within earshot of the general:

> ... so little could be seen of the enemy there that the skirmishers sent word to ask if they might go down and take them [the flags], and seemed to think that the Arabs were gone. One of our officers, who had been at Teb and Tamai, said to me, 'There is no one there; it is merely a burial ground,' and Sir Herbert Stewart laughingly said to Burnaby who was in immediate command of the square, 'Move a little more to the left; I want that green flag.'[79]

It is one of the truisms of military history that general officers are vested in their own despatches with something akin to papal infallibility. The reality of course is that they are as prone to human failings as the next man, even if they are not given to admitting them quite as readily. In his official despatch for Abu Klea, Stewart would imply that he directed an intentional bypassing movement to the right of a clearly identified enemy position.[80] The plain inference to be drawn from Dawson, however, is that there were next to no enemy in sight on the left, that the general had at this juncture been seized by the prospect of obtaining trophies and that he actually wanted the square steered towards them – which is to say closer to the main *khor*. There was at least a reason for such apparent eccentricity, albeit not a particularly good one in the circumstances. It had long been traditional to send captured enemy standards to the army commander who in turn would forward them to the sovereign, a practice which had originated on the formal European battlefield, but which had since been carried with somewhat less credibility into the more remote corners of the globe by the officers of the Queen Empress. It was unlikely, after all, that Muḥammad Aḥmad would feel quite the same humiliating sting at the loss of an anonymous painted banner, as had Bonaparte at the loss of an imperial eagle, cast in gold and presented by his own hand. It would be tempting to dismiss Dawson's story as a single-source curiosity and give Stewart the benefit of the doubt were it not for the fact that Lieutenant Thomas Snow of D Company, MICR, lends strong collateral to his assertion:

> Sir Herbert Stewart and Colonel Burnaby were mounted just behind where I was. I twice heard Sir Herbert say, 'Don't you think we might move on and capture those flags?' and twice Burnaby answered, 'No, let's edge off to the right a bit until they show what is under them.'[81]

Thus are born the shrewd bypassing movements of illustrious general-officers.[82]

The front face of the square was now nearing the top of the slope on the far side of the first of the feeder *khors*. Perceiving the necessity to increase the distance between the main *khor* and the left face, Burnaby passed the word for the Scots Guards company, on the right of the front face, to begin steering a gradual right oblique.[83] The new course would also avoid the two shorter watercourses away to the left. Events now conspired to create heightened difficulties for the Heavies and the Naval Brigade at the rear. Burnaby's touch of the tiller was quickly sensed and responded to by the troops, who marching in close order had only to maintain their dressing by a directing flank in the usual way. Unfortunately the disorganized mob of native drivers and camels moving in the centre of the formation was nothing like as responsive. To borrow a metaphor from the Battle of the Atlantic, it was as if a flotilla of sleek destroyers escorting a sluggish convoy of tankers had altered course without so much as signalling their intention to do so. A baggage master possessed of the tactical acumen to read the situation unfolding about him might have been worth his weight in gold at this juncture.

Even if the native drivers at the front of the disorderly mass of animals observed the right oblique taking effect, those at the back could not immediately feel it in the same way as the men in the ranks. This dispelled any prospect of them conforming smartly to Burnaby's change of course. With the troops proceeding forward and to the right, the tail of the baggage column was suddenly thrust through the left-rear corner of the square.[84] Several heavily laden camels chose this moment to lower themselves onto their haunches. It has long since become conventional to attribute the problems with the baggage train to the characteristic moodiness of the dromedary, but this is to overlook the fact that by this stage in the advance many of the animals had been wounded and were probably in great distress.

Oblivious to the difficulties at the rear, the companies on the front and flanking faces of the square strode on another 300 yards, quickly passing the heads of the two smaller *khors* to the left. Soon the front face had begun crossing the fourth and longer *khor*, a relatively shallow feature of about 25–30 yards in width. By now the camels were straggling so badly that an eighty-yard interval soon opened up between the rear face and the rest of the formation.[85] Realizing that the situation had become dangerous and needed to be brought rapidly under control, Beresford instructed a nearby bugler to sound 'Halt'. Having no doubt shouted instructions for everybody at the rear to keep moving, he then made his way forward to explain the urgent necessity for the halt to the general. Stewart endorsed his actions with a brusque, 'Quite right' and sat patiently in conversation with his staff, while Beresford hastened back to the rear to help Reggie Talbot and his officers sort out the disarray.[86] It seems highly likely that it was either Beresford's bugle-call or his report to the general which acted as a catalyst for Burnaby to leave Stewart's side and ride to the left-rear corner.[87] It was probably as he was making this very journey that he passed Verner, 'and giving me a hearty slap on the back, ejaculated "Isn't this fine sport, my boy!"'[88]

Despite being in overall command of the Royal Sussex half-battalion, Major Sunderland had retained immediate command of G Company, now operating in concert with Trafford's C Company at the rear of the right face. On this sector some of the Royal Sussex sections were now being compelled to march in four ranks, which to an experienced infantryman like Sunderland made the discrepancy between the length of the flanking faces all the more glaringly apparent. He decided to go and see the general to seek permission to move his company from the right face into the left. Stewart having duly given his assent, Sunderland began making his way back towards the rear of the square.[89]

Doubtless the combined efforts of Burnaby, Beresford, Talbot and Sunderland would soon have brought the situation under control had it not been for the fact that only a few hundred yards away several thousand wild-eyed Kordofanis had just risen to their feet in the floor of the sandy *khor*. The time was 11.00 a.m.[90] To Lieutenant Douglas Dawson it was, 'as if they had risen from the earth',[91] a metaphor also adopted by Lord George Binning who wrote that they, 'sprang up as if from the bowels of the earth'.[92] In fact they had been concealed beneath the lip of the *khor* or in the swathes of long grass to its rear. They were, observed Sir Charles Wilson, 'in the most perfect order ... a beautiful and striking sight'.[93] Another eyewitness thought that there were 'at least a hundred large parti-coloured banners' on show.[94]

The spectacle was probably rather more striking and considerably less beautiful from a distance of 200 yards. Thomas Phipps, Johnny Campbell and the forty-odd KRRC skirmishers, separated from the lip of the *khor* only by a gentle and horribly bare gravel slope, were in the gravest peril. The regimental history of the King's Royal Rifle Corps recounts an interesting tale, which although it is not sourced nonetheless sounds authentic enough:

When the dervishes rose up and charged, a Cavalry Officer who had been studying the Infantry drill-book drew his sword and called out, 'Form rallying square!' (the formation laid down for skirmishers to assume when attacked by Cavalry). If this had been done, not one of the skirmishers would have been alive two minutes later. Johnny Campbell saved the situation by shouting 'No! Run like hell!'; the moral of which is that a difficult situation is more likely to be saved by presence of mind and common sense than by looking for a ready-made solution among the text-books.[95]

The free-thinking gentlemen of the KRRC were far too polite to name the dunce in the corner of their regimental history, but there was only one cavalry officer out with the skirmishers. Although he was serving as a MICR field officer, Major Thomas Phipps was actually a member of the 7th Hussars.[96] The idea of the skirmishers trying to make any sort of stand was of course crassly stupid. There could be only one course of action, 'fire and retire', and this the skirmishers duly did – as fast as their legs could carry them. In a trice the enemy were also on the move.

Chapter 10

England's Far and Honour a Name

The Battle of Abu Klea: Phase III – The Climax

If any man had said four years ago that it was possible for naked Arabs armed with swords and spears to break into squares of infantry armed with the most effective breech-loading rifle, such a man would have been laughed to scorn.

Colonel William Butler, *Campaign of the Cataracts*

MŪSĀ WAD ḤILŪ HAD SPRUNG HIS TRAP, leaving the British a miserly 430 yards of reaction time.[1] For a force intent upon the tactics of shock action it was a masterstroke. Without Burnaby's timely right oblique the distance might have been even shorter. The only participant in the battle openly to acknowledge the notion of a trap was Harry Pearse of the *Daily News* who remarked, 'The rebels fought with the most reckless and admirable courage, and displayed great tactical skill. They harassed the zareba all the previous night, and endeavoured to lead us into a skilfully laid trap.'[2] By contrast General Stewart's official report made recourse to obfuscating language which denied the enemy their due. It is nonetheless plainly apparent that the British had no idea that the main Mahdīst strike force was positioned where it was. It necessarily follows that Stewart was in no sense directing an intentional bypassing movement as he was later to claim. The more awkward truth was that he had marched straight into a well-sited ambush, initiated at a time and place of Mūsā wad Ḥilū's choosing. The word 'ambush' precisely describes what had just happened, and yet does not once crop up in the accounts of the military participants.

It is interesting to contemplate the reason why Colonel Percy Barrow and his officers were not doing their customary excellent job of scouting ahead of the rest of the force. As earlier described they had become unavoidably embroiled in a sustained skirmish on the far side of the *khor*, in a position which by now had been left more than 1,200 yards to Stewart's left-rear. Whether or not the 500-strong body of *anṣār* confronting Barrow had been intentionally deployed to block the hussars, so as to blind the British commander and shield the Mahdīst ambush site, we shall never know for sure. Although it could conceivably have come about by chance, it would seem ungenerous not to credit Mūsā wad Ḥilū with having set in hand arrangements to shield his right, in anticipation of the British advancing along the general line of the valley. The beauty of the ambush site was that it would have served just as well to strike an advance on the opposite side of the *khor*, in the event the British had chosen to follow the caravan road.

As far as a dearth of credible Arabic primary sources and the haze of 125 intervening years allow, these observations on how the *amīrs* planned and fought their battle go at least some way towards establishing a better understanding of the fight from a Mahdīst perspective. Importantly the Battle of Abu Klea was not merely 'done to' the Mahdīst side. They were not only every bit as influential as the British in determining its shape and form, but actually anticipated, planned and regulated the proceedings from the outset. The only spanner the British had succeeded in throwing into the works was to delay the execution of the Mahdīst battle-plan by something just shy of twenty-four hours; otherwise they had played their part to perfection. If in essence the troops had blundered into a pre-planned ambush, it was going to take a surfeit of British 'pluck' to fight their way out again.

The Mahdīst Formation

Sir Charles Wilson had rather more time than Major Phipps and his men to take in the extraordinary sight unfolding at the foot of the gentle incline separating the square from the *khor*. 'It was as if there were portions of three phalanxes with rows of men behind. At the head of each rode an emir or sheikh with a banner, accompanied by personal attendants, and then came the fighting men. They advanced at a quick pace as if on parade.' By way of illustrating his point, Wilson included a diagram of the Mahdīst formation in *From Korti to Khartum*. The drawing reflects three triangular bodies of men protruding from a rectangular main body.[3] The instinctive association of the word 'phalanx' with the rigid close-order formations adopted by the hoplites of Classical Greece or the legionaries of Ancient Rome renders it a singularly inappropriate descriptor for a body of hard-charging Mahdīst *anṣār*, so with all due respect to Sir Charles I shall adopt 'division' in its stead. The early popularity of *From Korti to Khartum* and its subsequent ready accessibility has resulted in Wilson's description of the Mahdīst formation asserting itself as the pre-eminent interpretation. Beresford's memoirs, for example, merely plagiarize Wilson's description. In his official report of almost thirty years earlier, however, Beresford paints a quite different picture:

> The square had halted when abreast the flags, and immediately the enemy, to the number of about 6,000, sprang up from the vicinity of the flags, and formed a v-shaped column with the apex towards the square. They were accompanied by about 40 horsemen, who all carried flags, and came on at a hard gallop; the footmen who carried spears, swords or axes kept pace with them however.[4]

In fact none of the near-contemporaneous accounts entirely endorse Wilson's description of the enemy. Everybody it seems saw things from a different perspective. When Willoughby Verner drew the official map of the battle, he charted the Mahdīst position as a single rectangular block and reflected not three but five main lines of advance (*see Map 8*). When in 1908 Lord Binning wrote his account of the battle for Thomas Wright's *The Life of Colonel Fred Burnaby*, he suggested that the unmasking of the main Mahdīst host had been preceded a matter of moments earlier by the sudden appearance of 'two large bodies' of *anṣār* who initially moved down the *khor* away from the square, with 'banners flying and drums beating'.[5] Lieutenant Thomas Snow for his part described a 'very dense' line of spearmen 'some six or seven hundred yards in width'. Burleigh was also observing events carefully and in his account reflects neither three nor five divisions, but rather the same two lines earlier adopted in front of the *zariba*.

Just as the front of the square had crossed a narrow depression and gained the top of the little crest on the other side, we saw a force of 4,000 to 5,000 of the enemy echeloned in two lines on our left, or opposite the part of the square maintained by part of the Mounted Infantry and Heavy Camel Regiments. They were four hundred, or perhaps five hundred, yards distant, and looked like coming on. Dervishes on horseback and on foot marshalled them, standing a few paces in front of the fanatic host. With fluttering of banners, clamour of 'tom-toms' and shouts of 'Allah,' they began to move towards our square. At first they came slowly, not quicker than a fast walk. Our skirmishers' fire appeared to have very little effect on them... Very few of the Mahdi's forces fell, their lines were scarcely marred, and the miscarriage of our bullets must have inspired them with the hope that Mohammed Ahmed had at last conferred upon them charmed lives. They were soon within three hundred and fifty yards of the square, and now they commenced to run towards us, coming over the rolling ground like a wave of black surf.[6]

By far the most detailed description of the Mahdīst attack formation is to be found in Macdonald's *Too Late for Gordon and Khartoum*. Although he was at the *zariba* and could not possibly have seen with his own eyes how the Mahdīsts were arrayed, it is clear that Macdonald went to considerable lengths to tease out as accurate a picture as possible from those who had been present with the square. He includes an only slightly adapted copy of Verner's official Intelligence Division map in his book (*Map 8*) and drew heavily upon it for his description of the battle. He also draws on the sketch in Wilson's book, although in his own version Macdonald chooses to show only a single, typical wedge-headed column. The reason for this is that he is at variance with Wilson in stating emphatically that there were five columns not three. Although strictly speaking Macdonald has ceased to be a primary source at this juncture his account owes so much to well-placed witnesses, including Wilson and Verner, that it would be inappropriate to disallow his observations:

The Arabs advanced to the attack in compact, oblong columns of spearmen, each having a wedge-shaped front or head... The oblong form of the columns which closely followed these wedge-shaped heads, made them less vulnerable to fire as they advanced, but when they charged they did so on a broad front, bringing up their right shoulders. Each column was led by either an Emir or a Sheik on horseback carrying a flag, and accompanied by

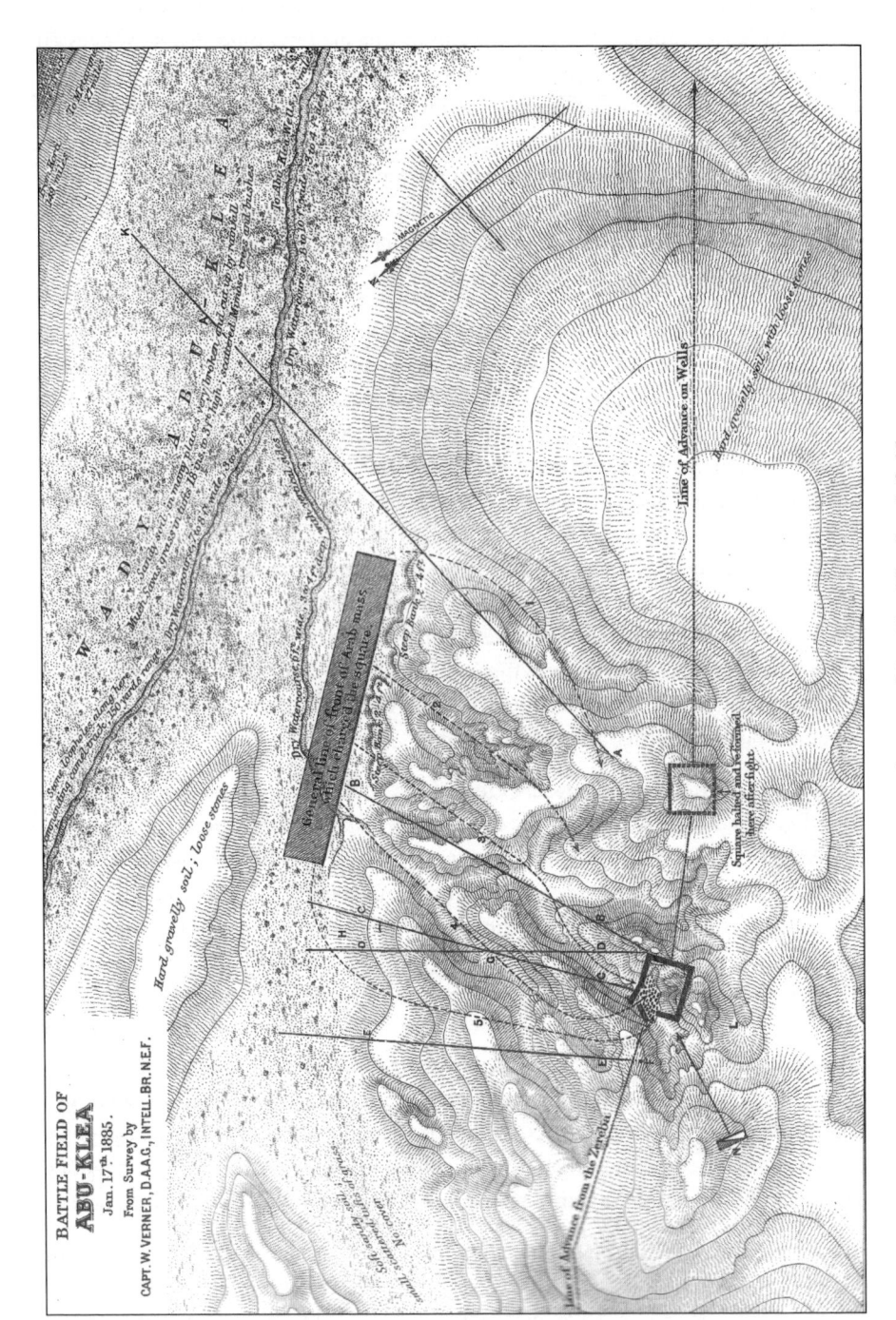

Map 8: Verner's map of the Abu Klea battlefield

mounted attendants. There were five of these columns, three of which had evidently been formed up under cover of the steep bank . . . The enemy came on very rapidly, in fact a quick run, and in such regular order as to excite general admiration.[7]

The different ways in which the witnesses reported the Mahdīst formations are not necessarily wholly incompatible. A little further on in his account Binning tells us that the two bodies of *anṣār* observed as if retreating down the valley, turned and joined the attack as soon as the Kordofani main body showed itself. This tends to suggest that he ought not to have interpreted them as retreating at all, but might more accurately have portrayed them as the Mahdīst left wing manoeuvring into position. It is possible for Wilson, Verner, Binning and Burleigh all to be right, and is a credible construct on the ground, if the rectangular block shown in Wilson's drawing was actually a further two divisions, echeloned behind the leading three, in preparation for the attacks reflected by Lines 1 and 2 on Verner's map (*Map 8*). Burleigh's reference to two echeloned lines of *anṣār* would tend to lead credence to the postulation that there was a leading assault wave consisting of three wedge-shaped divisions, and a second echelon of two divisions tasked with moving out to the left where it would pivot on the leading echelon and attack the front-left corner of the square. Macdonald puts only three of the five divisions under the lip of the *khor*, suggesting that two of them were somewhere else, although less than helpfully he does not say where. Arguably the construct described above lends collateral to Binning's description. His assertion that the left wing showed itself some time in advance of the rest does not chime with the other participant accounts, however, and remains difficult to reconcile with the rest of the evidence. It is perhaps instructive to reflect that Binning was not only writing more than twenty years later, but that his company was positioned in the rear face behind the camels, where he would certainly have struggled to see with his own eyes anything going on to the left-front of the square.

In the official despatch he wrote the following day, Stewart would estimate the strength of the enemy main body at a modest 3,000 men, although most other observers gave higher estimates clustered around the 5,000 mark. The general's considered assessment was that, 'The strength of the enemy is variously estimated from 8,000 to 14,000 men. My opinion is not less than 2,000 operated on our right flank, 3,000 in the main attack, and 5,000 in various other positions; but it is difficult to estimate their numbers with any exactness.'[8]

The men charging the square were of course the fierce and fanatical Daghaim, Kināna and Hamr tribesmen brought north by Mūsā wad Ḥilū. It seems improbable that the principal *amīr* would have divided his main striking force when there were two other large contingents, the combined Abadeh, Barabra and Bisharin force under 'Abd-al-Mājid Nasr al-Din abū' l-Kailak of Berber, and the combined Ja'līyīn and Awadiyeh one under 'Ali-wad-Saad of Metemmeh, both of which were around 2,000 strong, to fulfil supporting roles. In the intelligence report enclosed with Stewart's despatch, Sir Charles Wilson put the strength of the Kordofanis at

4,000–6,000. While this high-end estimate relied on intelligence acquired from deserters, the low-end one adopted by Stewart is based on the evidence of his own eyes. Ultimately there is no way of knowing which is the more reliable. Perhaps the best we can do is content ourselves with the notion that Mūsā wad Ḥilū was now charging at the head of between 4,000 and 5,000 men, precisely the bracket cited by the experienced Burleigh. It would be tempting to think of five divisions each around a thousand strong, although this comfortable and arguably rational construct cannot be directly substantiated from the sources.

I conclude, however, that Verner's map constitutes near incontrovertible evidence that there were five columns, or principal axes of advance, rather than three. The onus on him to provide an accurate representation for the War Office history would have been such that he would have taken great pains to verify his interpretation of the battle with fellow veterans. He is in any case to be regarded as an excellent witness in his own right. In contrast to Verner's much more deliberate approach, we have seen that there were good reasons for Sir Charles Wilson rushing his book into print, without going through the time-consuming process of circulating the manuscript around a selection of other participants in advance of publication.

British Musketry

We have seen that wherever their fields of fire allowed them to do so, infantry company commanders at this period would seek to begin engaging a mass target with company volleys at around 800 yards. The serious killing could be expected to begin at about 600 yards, while from 400 yards and closing company volleys could be expected to become devastatingly effective. Provided the firer kept his head, hitting a moving man-sized target at 100 yards with the Martini-Henry could just about be taken as read. Contrary to popular perception, the act of blunting and defeating a frontal assault by masses of hard-charging 'fanatics', such as Afghan *ghazis*, Zulu warriors or Mahdīst *anṣār*, was never the work of a single short-range volley fired, as the cliché would have it, at 'the whites of their eyes'. Rather it was a process of literal and psychological attrition which would ideally commence in the bracket between 800 and 600 yards. In practice the broken landscapes of Afghanistan, North-West Frontier Province, Zululand and the Sudan only rarely permitted such extended fields of fire. This meant that the 400–300 yard bracket was typically where battles were won or lost, so that maintaining adequate fields of fire out to at least 400 yards was always a vital tactical consideration for the British.

Juxtaposing in ten-second windows a rate of fire of one volley for every fifty yards gained by the attacker meant that a hard-charging enemy breaking cover at 430 yards, as was now the case, could expect to receive a 'killing' volley at 400 yards and five 'devastatingly effective' volleys at 350, 300, 250, 200 and 150 yards, before then entering a zone in which it was just about impossible to remain upright and expect to live. In theory it would be necessary to make allowance for the necessity to adjust sights at 100-yard intervals, but in practice, and this is where psychological factors came into play, the enemy rate of advance would get progressively slower with each volley. Clicking one notch on the rear-sight was in any case the work of only about three seconds. In a close-order square formed two-deep there were eighty Martinis for the forty yards of frontage typically occupied by a company. Such was the psychological impact of volley-fire, with men being killed and horribly maimed on all sides, that no matter how courageous the attacker, he and his surviving brethren would be driven to their bellies long before they were within 200 yards of the firing line. Here was the invisible 'wall', so to speak, in front of every British infantry company. The point at which the enemy reached the metaphorical wall could be regarded as the point at which the attack had been 'broken' and usually served as the signal for company officers to slow their rate of fire in order not to waste ammunition. All that was needed now was a suppressive rate sufficient to remind the enemy that renewed forward movement would be ill-advised. Generally this meant the company commander handing fire control over to his four sergeant section commanders, to fire successive section volleys from a directing flank. Once an attack had been 'broken' in this way, it was generally only a matter of time before the enemy bolted for the rear. So much for the theory: back once again then to the Abu Klea Valley, where the British were by no means particularly well poised to defeat a massed attack in the approved fashion.

Decisions, Decisions

With the not inconsiderable help of Fred Burnaby, General Stewart had succeeded in maintaining good fields of fire on all sides, nowhere more so than at the left-front corner and along the left face of the square, the sectors upon which the weight of the Mahdīst assault appeared certain to fall. The trouble was that the KRRC skirmishers, formerly so useful, had been caught off-guard and were now well and truly in the way. Had Beresford not sounded the halt when he did, the front face of the square would have been up and over a low rise to its left-front a matter of only seconds later: but as things stood the feature was now inhibiting the fields of fire for the front face. This gave the company officers affected no option but to push their men forward thirty yards so as to gain the crest.[9] With the square already disordered and badly strung out at the rear, the sudden forward lurch rippled down the flanking faces to make an awkward situation even worse. As unhelpful as it was to the Heavies and the Naval Brigade, the short advance was nonetheless a tactical necessity. From this point on the troops were no longer marching in line (front and rear faces) or column (flanking faces), but were in all cases facing outwards, so that what was formerly described in the narrative as, for example, the rear of the left face, will now become the left half of the left face.

Other officers were also responding to the crisis as they thought best, but not necessarily with such readily defensible decisions as the front-face company commanders. It is important to bear in mind that the next series of events happened both concurrently and very quickly, in a window in time and space so fleeting that it allowed next to no opportunity for considered thinking. Describing these occurrences to the reader's satisfaction will occupy far more time than did the occurrences themselves.

Captain Norton's snap response to the dramatic development on the left was to order that his left-hand gun be moved from the centre of the front face to the front-left corner of the British position. The other two guns were advanced some yards ahead of the front face companies, in order that they could be trained half-left in the direction of the assault.[10] It is not clear whether Lieutenant James Guthrie and his crew manhandled their piece up to the corner of the square by moving it in front of the six sections of mounted infantrymen arrayed to the left of their start point, or behind them. In the former scenario they would temporarily have masked the fields of fire of parts of A and B Companies as they moved along the line, but would not have had to burst through the ranks anywhere, whereas in the latter they would have kept clear of the fields of fire but would then have thrown at least one section of D Company into momentary disarray as they unmasked the gun. Simultaneously Beresford had much the same idea as Norton and quickly had the Gardner run across the middle of the square to the imperilled left. The arrival of a machine gun and a party of around fifteen sailors did nothing for the coherence of the three cavalry detachments struggling to do the right thing on the left side of the left face. More than amply vexed by the challenge of comporting themselves like infantrymen, the officers and men of the 5th Lancers, 16th Lancers and Scots Greys now had to contend with a string of other tribulations competing simultaneously for their attention. Not only were the very hounds of hell bearing down upon them, with the intervening fields of fire cluttered by fleeing skirmishers, but the mounted infantry company to their right was evidently shifting its ground still further to the right, while at the same time the animated naval captain newly arrived in their midst clearly didn't care what they did, so long as they got out of the way of his precious machine gun. Willoughby Verner, who was 'helping to close up the Heavies' at this point, wrote that he 'was somewhere in the rear of the 5th Lancers, when Beresford came bursting through the mob with a Gardner to bring it into action on that face. As he ran it out I pulled back two lancers who were then on the knee and whose heads were in the way of the gun.'[11]

It is curious that almost all secondary accounts of Abu Klea place the Gardner outside the left-rear corner of the square, as there is more than enough evidence to show that Beresford actually ran the gun through the left face only a few files shy of its centre point. If we allow roughly eighteen files per HCR regimental detachment, Verner's anecdote, with its reference to the 5th Lancers, would suggest that the gun was around thirty-six files away from the left-rear corner, a notion further supported by the rough diagram he drew into his diary. Beresford's widely read memoirs are the principal source of confusion. In the paragraph immediately preceding the operative one he talks of 'the appalling danger of this open corner'. In the subsequent paragraph he goes on to say, 'Then I ordered the crew of the Gardner to run it outside the left flank.' He dropped the trail, he tells us, some five or six paces outside the square.[12] It would be easy to fall into the trap of conjoining these remarks were it not for the infinitely less ambiguous language of his contemporaneous official report. 'Immediately I perceived the enemy coming down, I ran the gun from its position in the rear face of the square, to a position in the centre of the left flank [not strictly accurate or he would have been amongst the Mounted Infantry], about five paces out from the square, and at once commenced firing.'[13] Given that Beresford's move would have been concurrent with the forward lurch of the front face, it is likely that Carmichael's No. 5 Company would have been taking ground to the right at this juncture, so as to conform with C and D Companies, MICR, which had themselves closed up on the new front-left corner only a matter of moments beforehand. The effect of the movement would have been to shift Carmichael's men to Beresford's right-rear and pull the right hand file of the Scots Greys detachment directly behind him. In the process the Gardner would have slipped from thirty-six files to the right of the left-rear corner to around eighteen files, although such figures must be understood as illustrative of a broader range of possibilities. As we shall see shortly, as far as some of the Heavies were concerned, the corner of the square was a moveable feast in any case.

Lieutenant Colonel Charlie Rowley, Grenadier Guards, was positioned somewhere near the rear of the square, where the sudden appearance of the enemy had caused the handlers of the more stubborn or injured dromedaries to abandon their charges and flee for sanctuary amongst the troops. Observing that two or three of the forsaken camels were bearer-company animals with casualties aboard them, Rowley and a brace of gallant privates from the Heavies dashed to the rescue. In no mood to tolerate any further displays of truculence, the tiny rescue party brutalized the offending animals into a reluctant trot and began hauling them across the hundred yards of open ground separating them from safety. The *anṣār* could not have been very far behind.[14] For all Wolseley's reservations, Rowley was evidently a courageous man. The onset of the enemy was so formidable that the wounded Private Fagan picked up his rifle and re-joined his 2nd KRRC mates in the left face; he would remain in the ranks for the rest of the day, earning himself a DCM in the process.[15]

Concurrently with all the other excitement, Phipps, Campbell and the KRRC skirmishers were making the best of the 200-yard head-start they had on the *anṣār*. The 250 yards back to the square would have taken them safely less than a minute, although one officer's batman was too slow off the mark or in too awkward a spot to keep up with everybody else and was done to death by his pursuers. A tentative identification of this man as 1932 Private J. Bowles is explained in the note.[16] Marling was positioned with A Company, MICR, on the left of the front face and, with scant regard for the true ethnicity of the enemy host, recalled that, 'We in the square shouted out to the skirmishers to lie down and we would fire over them, as if anybody would lie down with 4,000 fuzzy-wuzzies prancing behind them with six-foot spears. Old Johnny Campbell shouted, "No, no, run like hell," and he was quite right too.'[17]

The hiatus on the left-front notwithstanding, Lieutenant Romilly's Scots Guardsmen probably barely broke into a sweat on the opposite flank. There is no mention at all in the sources of what the scouting troop of 19th Hussars did at this juncture, but they cannot have returned to the square and gone unremarked in the sources, from which it can be inferred that they must have either have been engaged in a skirmish further along the valley, or that they rallied on a distant ridge to watch the high drama unfolding around the square.

If the great majority of the infantry skirmishers looked like they were going to make it home comfortably, the situation was far more perilous at the rear of the square where Byng and Darley had most of the HCR skirmishers orientated so as to cover back down the valley. As a result they were still preoccupied with exchanging fire with parties of enemy riflemen and had their backs turned to the sudden appearance of the Kordofanis.[18] Bellowed warnings from the square and a sudden cacophony of Islamic chants and war-cries probably meant that the 4th DG skirmishers remained oblivious to the threat for only a few moments longer than the KRRC sections, but over such short distances any sort of delay had the potential to prove fatal. There were after all anything up to a hundred well-mounted horsemen,[19] amīrs, shaikhs, standard bearers and bodyguards, riding in the van of the great host, for whom fleeing stragglers would represent easy pickings. According to Lord Cochrane a number of the horsemen also had spearmen clinging on to their saddles and harness.[20]

Still down upon us the dark Arab wave rolled [wrote Burleigh]. It had arrived within 300 yards almost undiminished in volume, unbroken in strength. It was a rush of spearmen and swordsmen, scarcely any carrying guns. Their rifle-fire had practically ceased, and the other Arab forces surrounding us . . . all stood eager on the hillsides watching the charge upon the British square.[21]

Commence Firing

Thus far the only shots to have come from the square were eight five-round bursts from the Gardner, fired by Beresford in person. A few men at the rear of the Mahdīst formation fell to this fire, allowing Lord Charles to spot his fall of shot and conclude that 'the gun had too much elevation'. With a shout of 'Cease firing!' to alert the rest of the crew, he began lowering the elevation, so as to be able to play on the leading ranks of the assault at a range of about 250 yards. Fortunately the breathless KRRC sections were even now scrambling home to take up fire positions alongside their Rifle Brigade brethren. On the opposite side of the square Romilly's men were also safely home. The reunification of GCR's No. 3 Company meant that all the front-face companies now enjoyed completely clear fields of fire. The same was true for the two mounted infantry companies on the right half of the left face – with only one minor exception – like the good skirmisher he was, Pigott's terrier 'Smoke' was still out in front contesting the advance of the enemy by dancing ahead of them and yapping his disapproval.

The type, nature and effect of the British fire at Abu Klea is a matter of some interest. We have seen how the typical model for breaking a mass attack demanded that a sequence of controlled and progressively more devastating company volleys be fired, in the confident expectation that the resultant mauling would break the back of the attack and drive it to ground at something over 200 yards. Stewart's decision to deploy skirmishers into the square's primary fields of fire, ultimately an ill-advised measure, would render the Battle of Abu Klea atypical. It is worth noting at the outset that the word 'volley' is conspicuous only by the paucity of times it occurs in the primary sources – our first pointer to the fact that very few volleys were fired.

Percy Marling wrote, 'The skirmishers came running in and only got into the square about 250 yards in front of the enemy, preventing us firing until they were comparatively close.'[22] This meant that the *anṣār* were less than a minute away from charging home by the time the fields of fire in front of the four MICR companies were clear. Major Charles Barrow now found himself squarely in the box-seat at the front-left corner of the square. With his A Company and a half-strength B Company to the left of Norton's guns, he had six sections, or not more than 140 officers and men, on the left side of the front face. Around the corner on the right side of the left face, where D and C Companies were at full strength, he had eight sections, or around 185 officers and men. While the left wing of the Mahdīst assault would lap around the front of the square and present A and B Companies with a reasonable array of targets, there would be only a limited amount of pressure on the two Guards companies to the right of the guns. By far the greatest strain would fall on Pigott's D Company and Fetherstonhaugh's C Company in the left face. It seems entirely logical that it was they who were first into action.

Bennet Burleigh witnessed the first British salvo from a vantage point near the Gardner. Immediately to his front were HCR sections which, for reasons we will come to shortly, failed to commence firing as promptly as the MICR sections to their right. Judging by its effect the volley, in the singular, described by Burleigh was probably two simultaneous company volleys initiated by a single word of command. In other words Barrow must have preceded his executive with a preliminary fire order stipulating that the regiment was to volley by wings:

> A volley was sent into the enemy at one hundred and fifty yards as they rose over the last crest between our opposing lines. A hundred or more Arabs dropped, and for a moment I saw their force waver and halt, as a man stops to gasp for breath at any sudden surprise. Had that volley been repeated there would have been little more of the Battle of Abu Klea to tell except the rout and slaughter of the Mahdi's troops, but somehow the firing that followed from our ranks was dropping, irregular, scattering, wild, without visible effect.[23]

Other sources, including Colvile's *Official History*, put the first volley at 200 yards.[24] That the deadly broadside described by Burleigh came from the mounted infantry companies to his right is confirmed by a letter written by Sergeant William Stakings of D Company, MICR, a little under three weeks later. 'They came madly rushing on right on our left face (of which the 2nd West Kent division formed the

Explanation.

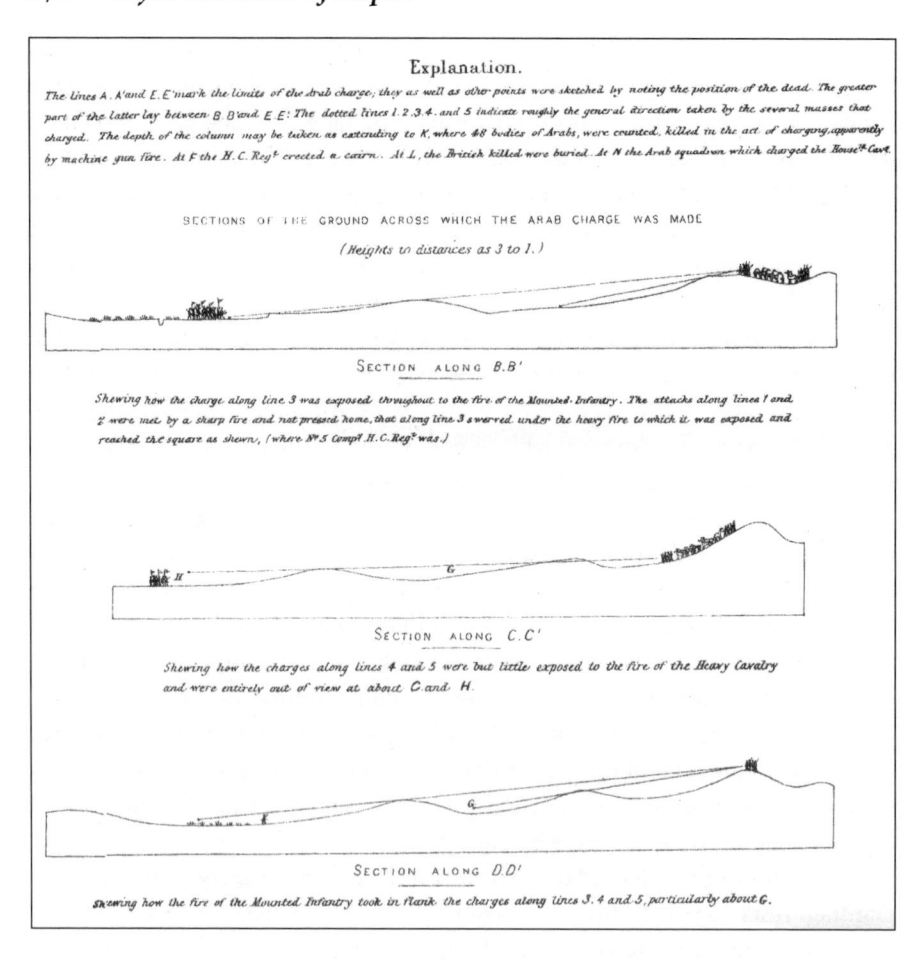

The lines A, A' and E, E' mark the limits of the Arab charge; they as well as other points were sketched by noting the position of the dead. The greater part of the latter lay between B, B' and E, E'. The dotted lines 1, 2, 3, 4, and 5 indicate roughly the general direction taken by the several masses that charged. The depth of the column may be taken as extending to K, where 48 bodies of Arabs, were counted, killed in the act of charging, apparently by machine gun fire. At F the H.C. Reg.t erected a cairn. At L, the British killed were buried. At N the Arab squadron which charged the House.td Cav.t

SECTIONS OF THE GROUND ACROSS WHICH THE ARAB CHARGE WAS MADE
(Heights to distances as 3 to 1.)

SECTION ALONG B.B'

Shewing how the charge along line 3 was exposed throughout to the fire of the Mounted Infantry. The attacks along lines 1 and 2 were met by a sharp fire and not pressed home, that along line 3 swerved under the heavy fire to which it was exposed and reached the square as shewn, (where N° 5 Comp.y H.C. Reg.t was.)

SECTION ALONG C.C'

Shewing how the charges along lines 4 and 5 were but little exposed to the fire of the Heavy Cavalry and were entirely out of view at about C and H.

SECTION ALONG D.D'

Shewing how the fire of the Mounted Infantry took in flank the charges along lines 3, 4 and 5, particularly about G.

Map 9: Verner's section drawing of the Abu Klea battlefield

second section from the right). We then opened fire on them, the first volley leaving about a hundred on the ground, but still they kept coming and still we kept firing...'[25]

It would have taken very little additional time for the Mahdist left to have wheeled around against the front face. In all likelihood it would have been only a matter of seconds later that A and B Companies, MICR, also volleyed as a wing. Describing this stage of the battle Gleichen wrote, 'The moment the skirmishers were in, a terrific fire began from the left and rear faces [*sic* – the left face undoubtedly came into action well ahead of the rear face] upon the Arabs, volleys rapidly merging into independent firing.'[26] In fact it is clear from Burleigh's account that there was no subsequent volley – that after their first shot the troops immediately resorted to independent fire, as was the drill, indeed, for desperate short-range engagements. If Burleigh's range estimate is correct and the initial volleys – left wing, right wing, in that order – were delivered at 150 yards, then it follows that the enemy were within thirty seconds of breaking into the square. It is hardly surprising in the circumstances that the Mounted Infantry began loading and firing as fast as they could. Predictably enough the result was a deafening cacophony, a rapid build-up of smoke and a certain amount of wild firing. Lieutenant Douglas Dawson[27] was quick to notice that a good many men were firing high:

> ... the advancing mass came nearer and nearer undeterred by the tremendous fire they were exposed to. That the firing at this point did not stop the front ranks of the enemy is shown by the fact that all the flags coming on, high up in the air, were being riddled with bullets, and seeing this I found myself near the left face trying with others to induce the men to aim lower.[28]

There are a number of reasons why fire goes high, including difficulty seeing the target, failure to adjust sight settings and failure to aim. Addressing such issues fell to the handful of men distributed behind the firing line in a third, thinly spread supernumerary rank, made up of company officers and sergeant section commanders.

Obscuration by smoke could conceivably have been part of the problem. The Martini-Henry might have been the first purpose-made breech-loader to enter service with the British Army, but its rolled-brass cartridge was still a black-powder round. This meant that at the moment of discharge the firer was briefly blanketed by billowing white smoke and generally had little idea whether he had hit his suddenly invisible target or not. It took a few seconds for the smoke to rise above the firer's line of vision, although if there was no breath of wind the build-up of smoke from large numbers of rifles could become a significant nuisance. In a controlled situation the infantry drill required company commanders to slow down their rate of fire so that the smoke could disperse between volleys. In a situation like Abu Klea, where the enemy were closing fast and rapid independent fire had broken out, there was next to no prospect of the officers being able to manage the smoke problem in the approved fashion. It is unsurprising that in a set of notes he prepared for a lecture on the Nile Expedition, Verner refers to 'the dense smoke which soon gathered round us'.[29]

It was important that the rear sight of the Martini was properly adjusted for range. In the particular context of Abu Klea sights would initially have been set at a medium range around the 500–600 yards mark, although the skirmisher nuisance would soon have rendered this inappropriate. It was the job of the company commanders to prefix their fire orders with a range setting. The descriptions of the first volley by Burleigh and Sergeant Stakings make it plain that Fetherstonhaugh and Pigott had not fixated on the drama of the fleeing skirmishers, but rather on the consequences for their men's musketry and that they had the presence of mind to order a new range setting before opening fire. This was meat and drink to infantry officers, but would not necessarily have been instinctive to HCR officers brought up only on the carbine. In truth the real reason for some of the subsequent MICR fire going high was a fairly widespread failure to aim. In their understandable anxiety to load and fire at the looming menace as rapidly as possible, some of the Mounted Infantry had overlooked their soldiering basics.

In the space of only about two or three minutes, Sir Charles Wilson had gone from feeling pity for the enemy to grave concern at their seemingly unstoppable momentum:

When the enemy commenced their advance, I remember experiencing a feeling of pity mixed with admiration for them, as I thought they would all be shot down in a few minutes, I could not have believed beforehand that men in close formation would have been able to advance for 200 to 400 yards over bare ground in the face of Martini-Henrys. As they advanced the feeling was changed to wonder that the tremendous fire we were keeping up had so little effect.[30]

Although C and D Companies, MICR, had come into action as promptly as the skirmisher nuisance allowed, Carmichael's No. 5 Company, HCR, was slower off the mark. There were two main reasons for the interval. First, while the KRRC skirmishers were quick to get home, many of Darley's 4th DG men had been slower in starting. Thomas Wright, Burnaby's biographer, asserts that the colonel gave the order, 'Don't fire yet; you'll hit our men!' Although Wright fails to substantiate his remark with a primary source, it sounds a credible enough story. The second and probably more substantive reason for the delay was that No. 5 Company's fields of fire were much more undulating than the relatively flat ground in front of the mounted infantry.[31] In other words, no sooner had the *anṣār* directly in front of Carmichael commenced their charge, at which point they had been in plain view, than they suddenly vanished into a depression. The feature was little more than head-height in depth and they were certain to emerge from it soon enough, but there must have been a short period in which the men of No. 5 Company, while they were fully aware that the enemy were out there and closing fast, did not have any viable targets inside their primary arcs. This is reflected in the section drawings accompanying Verner's February 1885 survey of the battlefield (*see his Line C–C in Map 9*).[32]

Interestingly Verner, who was with No. 5 Company of course, does not discuss the dead-ground problem either in his diary account or in *Sketches in the Soudan*, suggesting that it would be a mistake to make too much of it. On the other hand something about his experiences that day moved him to make a section drawing. Having walked the ground repeatedly, my reading of it is that C and D Companies had unlimited fields of fire, but were prevented by the skirmishers from coming into action at anything beyond 150 yards, while No. 5 Company could also see the *khor*, but was hindered by intervening undulations and depressions to such an extent that it had a short-range field of fire out to only 75–90 yards. I tend to think that it was this which delayed No. 5 Company coming into action. Carmichael's problem would have been shared by the detachment of Scots Greys to his left.

To Break a British Square

If there were difficulties in developing a meaningful weight of defensive fire along a sector running from the centre of the left face to the square's left-rear corner, there was at least a machine gun on hand to save the day.[33] Beresford was seated on the trail operating the gun in person, with the assistance of the actual 'captain of the gun', Chief Boatswain's Mate William Rhoods, Armourer Walter Miller and an oversized sixteen-stone rating affectionately known as 'Jumbo'.[34]

They were tearing down upon us with a roar like the roar of the sea, an immense surging wave of white-slashed black forms[35] brandishing bright spears and long flashing swords; and all were chanting as they leaped and ran, the war song of their faith 'La ilaha ill Allah Mohammedu rasul Allah'; and the terrible rain of bullets poured into them by the Mounted Infantry and the Guards stayed them not. They wore the loose white robe of the Mahdi's uniform, looped over the left shoulder, and the straw skull cap. These things we saw and heard in a flash, as the formidable wave swept steadily nearer. I laid the Gardner gun myself to make sure. As I fired, I saw the enemy mown down in rows, dropping like ninepins; but as the men killed were in rear of the front rank, after firing about forty rounds (eight turns of the lever), I lowered the elevation. I was putting in most effective work on the leading ranks and had fired about thirty rounds more when the gun jammed. The extraction had pulled the head from a discharged cartridge, leaving the empty cylinder in the barrel. William Rhodes, chief boatswain's mate, and myself immediately set to work to clear the barrel or to take out its lock.[36]

Beresford states in his official report that the enemy were about 200 yards away when the gun jammed. If that is the case he was probably firing along a half-right oblique at the *anṣār* attacking C and D Companies, MICR, which would have placed the lip of the troublesome depression in front of No. 5 Company about seventy yards to his left.

The 1st Royal Dragoons detachment, commanded by Lieutenant John Burn-Murdoch,[37] was part of Major Wilfred Gough's No. 4 Company, HCR. Its sister half-company was the Scots Greys detachment, now positioned on the left face. In the heat of the moment the men of the Royals probably did not have a good reason between them for doing what they were now about to do, so it would be futile to try and second guess what might have been running through their minds. They were excited, they were not trained infantrymen and they wilfully broke the golden rules of fighting in square. It is not impossible that the arbitrary nature of the recent halt, rapidly succeeded by a last-moment lurch, left them partway down the gravel slope of the fourth tributary *khor*, or even in a worst-case scenario standing in its sandy floor. This would not have been a comfortable situation in which to find oneself. Looking across from the right-rear corner, Lionel Trafford saw them, 'in their eagerness to get engaged', leaving their position on the right of the rear face, 'first by twos and threes and then en masse', to prolong the line of the left face. Had they done this on a training ground in sight of an apoplectic colour sergeant instructor, there is little room for doubt that they would never have done it again. But the Royals had never once been entrusted to the tender care of an infantry instructor and this was not a training ground but a battlefield, where men who have not been properly prepared for the ordeal can sometimes do the strangest things.

Fred Burnaby was still riding about at the left-rear corner trying to restore a modicum of order, when suddenly he was seized by the same fit of madness which had possessed the Royals. He now began right-wheeling No. 3 Company, HCR, out of the rear face to conform with the errant Royals.[38] At least this is the conventionally stated interpretation of his actions, but with Darley and the 4th Dragoon Guards detached as skirmishers, it would be more accurate to say that Burnaby was wheeling not No. 3 Company, HCR, but rather the 5th DG half-company.

Where an excuse is proffered in justification of Burnaby's actions, as for example in Alex Macdonald's *Too Late for Gordon and Khartum*,[39] it is commonly to the effect that he considered Beresford and the Gardner crew to be too exposed in their position outside the left-rear corner of the square and was seeking to support or protect them. Innocently and sincerely proffered though this explanation always is, it has nonetheless served over the years to conceal a serious failure of judgment on Burnaby's part. The plain fact of the matter is that Beresford was not outside the corner of the square, but rather was on the left face just in front of the Scots Greys, where, with a hedge of levelled bayonets only a matter of five or six paces to their rear, the naval machine gunners could not possibly have been better protected than was already the case.

Again it must be emphasized in the interests of balance that all this was happening extremely quickly, against the backdrop of a lightning-quick enemy assault. This meant that it would be impossible to adjust snap decisions – there was time to do one thing and one thing only – after that it would be necessary to live with the consequences. Regardless of any mitigating circumstances, such as the possibility that part of the rear face found itself disrupted by the *khor*, wheeling the 1st Royals and 5th DG detachments to the right represented the gravest possible infringement of the infantry's golden rule: whatever fell to the lot of individuals, or even whole sections, it was the integrity of the square as a whole which always had to come first.

Thus was the 3½-company left face of the square extended to become a 4½-company firing line with an open left flank. From right to left it comprised, D Company, MICR, C Company, MICR, No 5. Company, HCR (5th and 16th Lancers), No. 4 company, HCR (Greys and Royals), and finally a half-strength No. 3 Company, HCR (5th DG only), whose other detachment was still scattered across the back of the square sprinting for sanctuary. Whilst some of Darley's 4th DG men would have been able to run in and re-form on their parent company, the majority would have been scattered in small knots amongst all the other HCR companies. The rear face, formerly consisting of 3½ companies plus the Naval Brigade, the rough equivalent of another half-company, had suddenly been slashed to just Nos. 1 and 2 Companies, HCR, plus the rifle-armed sailors, in effect reducing it from eight half-companies to five. Straggling and disordered as it already was, the rear face no longer had a right-hand side. That the back door should now be standing ajar had nothing whatever to do with the enemy and everything to do with a combination of impulsiveness, indiscipline and want of training.

The sudden thirty-yard lurch of only a minute or two earlier had left Captain Trafford and the rest of the men at the right-rear corner standing atop a low knoll. Trafford needed only to turn about to get a grandstand view of the Mahdīst attack. He might only have been about ten feet above the general lie of the land, but it was enough to make him grateful that the enemy rifle fire had lifted to facilitate the charge. From his elevated vantage point, Trafford was quick to realize the danger of the situation. His superior, Major Sunderland, having for some minutes been absent at the front of the square, was now on the return journey. On nearing the right-rear corner, Sunderland gave shouted instructions for his G Company sergeants to double their sections across the interior of the square, from the right face to the left, as agreed by the general. Trafford failed to hear the order and intercepted Sunderland's men in transit, an intervention which served to arrest the manoeuvre for a few moments. Once the confusion had been resolved, Sunderland and Trafford then tried to feed both Royal Sussex companies into the gaping hole to the right of the Naval Brigade.[40] Lord Cochrane spoke to Sunderland as he passed and quipped that the onset of the enemy looked like 'a Hyde Park meeting coming towards us'.[41]

Burnaby might have erred but was at least quick to realize his mistake. Glancing to his left he could see masses of Mahdīsts surging from the cover of nearby *khors* and undulations, seemingly intent on outflanking the 5th DG detachment and bursting tempest-like into the centre of the square. No sooner had the 5th DG men occupied their new position on the end of the elongated left face, than Burnaby rode out in front of them and began barking orders for them to fall back into the rear face. Any lingering hesitation in Nos. 4 and 5 Companies, HCR, about opening fire with the skirmishers still in front evaporated with the near approach of the enemy. If the last few 4th DG men were going to get home at all, they would do so only by a short head, whereas delaying any longer was going to get everybody killed. A sputtering fire broke out from the left side of the left face. Some of Darley's men dropped to their hands and knees and crawled the last few yards to safety with friendly fire passing only a foot or so above their heads.[42]

At the left-front corner of the square the critical moment had arrived for C and D Companies, MICR. The enemy had taken some heavy punishment but were still coming on at full tilt. With bellowed admonishments and exhortations from the supernumerary rank ringing in their ears the men seemed suddenly to shoot straighter,[43] but at least part of the truth was that the range was now so short and the enemy so concentrated that it was just about impossible to fail to hit something. Sir Charles Wilson and Lieutenant Thomas Snow both described the moment the leading *anṣār* elements hit the metaphorical wall. 'When they got within 80 yards,' wrote Wilson, 'the fire of the Guards and Mounted Infantry began to take good effect, and a huge pile of dead rose in front of them. Then to my astonishment the enemy took ground to the right as if on parade, so as to envelop the rear of the square. I remember thinking, "By Jove, they will be into the square!"[44] Snow reflected precisely the same manoeuvre: 'Just as the whole mass of dervishes, which had now assumed more the shape of a wedge, seemed to be going to strike the corner of the square where I was, it swerved to its right.'[45]

Even in its extended form, with four companies arrayed along it, the left face of the square still would not have exceeded 150–175 yards in length. The change of direction referred to by Wilson and Snow was not, then, some great flowing manoeuvre as is commonly portrayed. What it actually represented was a sudden shying away from the evidently dangerous blanket of smoke shrouding C and D Companies, MICR, in favour of an apparently far less deadly sector slightly further to the right. In other words the *anṣār* were not so much manoeuvring shrewdly to gain tactical advantage, as instinctively taking evasive action. The distance at issue was to be counted in tens of yards only. It is perhaps understandable that almost all secondary accounts of Abu Klea make a direct connection between the manoeuvre described by Sir Charles Wilson and the difficulties at the left-rear corner of the square, but go deeply enough into the sources and it becomes clear that they represent two distinctly separate episodes.

It is at this point, then, that we encounter probably the most significant of the several myths which hinder the faithful reconstruction of the battle. In the conventional interpretation the Mahdists wheel to the right in order to attack the left-rear corner of the square. We are variously told either that they were making for the gap in the square, or that they instinctively know that the corners of a square are its weakest point; sometimes indeed we are told both these things. In a trice the adroit manoeuvre is executed to perfection and the *anṣār* penetrate the British formation at its angle precisely as planned. In truth such a construct flies in the face of the source evidence, the first authoritative sketch-map of the action and the practical realities of battle.

Taking the last aspect first, the proposition calls for the *anṣār* intentionally to veer along the left face of the square at a range of less than a hundred yards, for a distance approaching 150 yards, with the best part of 150 Martini-Henrys blazing away at them as they do so. Not only is this inherently far-fetched, it also requires the attacking *anṣār* to be vested either with telepathic powers of communication or an instinctive and collective genius for the military masterstroke. In reality it would have been quite impossible for men charging uphill against the left face of a square to see a gap in its rear face. Furthermore, if the minds of the *anṣār* had been seized by anything, it was not minor tactics but rather visions of paradise and the red mist of fundamentalist fervour. In such a frame of mind their only thought was to get to close quarters and begin killing infidels. Why then would they veer away from the attainment of that goal when its fulfilment was only a matter of seconds away? Moreover the proposition calls for a level of tactical sophistication which, as the wider history of the Mahdīya relates, formed no part of the blood-chilling Mahdist charge. Nor would it have been possible for the handful of *amīrs* and shaikhs riding in the van to control changes of direction over so fleeting a window in time and space: while they might conceivably have managed to steer a 20–30 degree oblique over 400 yards, to suggest that they had sufficient control to be able to do it over a distance of 100 yards and closing cannot be regarded as credible. Added to that many of the mounted *amīrs* and shaikhs were amongst the first to go down, some of them shot out of the saddle, others merely unhorsed.[46]

In short the Mahdīst charge was a blunt implement, a one-shot option which was not in any way amenable to tactical finesse or the split-second impulses of the men leading it. Its timing and its rough bearing at launch were the only aspects which the *amīrs* had it in their power to control. After many years of studying the battlefield performance of highly manoeuvrable and disciplined Zulu *amabutho*, I take the view that even the Zulus, regimented from adolescence and drilled annually thereafter, could not have performed the manoeuvre so lightly attributed by historians to a general levy of Arab nomads.

What then of the enemy's 'instinctive' awareness that the corners of a square represented its weak points? The only estimate of the Mahdīst frontage available to us is the one provided by Snow: at 700 yards it chimes tolerably well with Verner's map. From this we can readily infer that the Mahdīst frontage was not less than three times greater than that of the square's left face. That the square would be heavily attacked at the two corners most exposed to such an onslaught was but a function of geometry and as inevitable as sunrise. The same is true of every other battle in which the Queen Empress's soldiers faced numerically superior hard-charging masses; British frontages were so short that it was well-nigh impossible specifically to attack the corners of a square: they were going to get attacked come what may. It was for precisely this reason that it had become an unofficial tactical norm to site artillery pieces and machine guns at the angles, a practice which had the added advantage of maximizing their fields of fire. Stewart had seen fit to deviate from the conventional, both in his employment of skirmishers and in the siting of his artillery, decisions for which there would now be a price to pay. The square would indeed be penetrated at its left-rear, but not by the men described by Wilson and Snow. In truth these men veered only as far as the sector occupied by No. 5 Company, HCR, as illustrated by the slight deviation in Verner's Line 3 (*see Map 8*). It should be noted that Verner himself was in the best possible grandstand seat, directly behind Carmichael's men, at precisely this time. He had good reason to recall the Mahdīst manoeuvre vividly, as it very nearly cost him his life.

The sources indicate clearly that the Heavies were not coping at all well with the ordeal unfolding around them. Sir Charles Wilson noted in his book that, 'Those who were near the Heavies told me that as the men fired they moved back involuntarily – not being taught as infantryman are to stand in a rigid line; they thus got clubbed together.'[47] Reggie Talbot took particular exception to the expression 'clubbed together' and specifically repudiated the notion in his January 1886 article for the London periodical *The Nineteenth Century*. The evidence that a number of things went badly wrong in HCR is overwhelming, however. When Percy Marling wrote to his father a little over a week after the battle he said of the Heavies that they 'were very unsteady and fired wildly'.[48] While Lionel Trafford was gallant enough to recognize the undoubted courage of the *anṣār*, he likewise attributed the success of their charge to the indifferent musketry of the cavalry detachments:

> The Arab charge was a glorious sight. Trained as infantry are to believe that unless it [a square] has been broken with fire nothing can approach it over clear ground, we believed that no Arab could get within a hundred yards of us; we thought they were charging to certain death yet they not only reached the square but penetrated it; this was in a great measure owing to the random shooting of the Heavies. It required the bravery of the Arabs even under these circumstances to have done so.[49]

Willoughby Verner went much further than the grudging respect for the *anṣār* articulated by Trafford. 'No words can do justice to the gallantry of the enemy,' he wrote. 'Nothing daunted them.' It was a fair and widely echoed sentiment.

The Battlefield Performance of the Martini-Henry Rifle

The participant sources record that the Martini-Henry suffered a good many stoppages at Abu Klea. This may account, at least in part, for the poor fire-effect on the HCR sector. At this early stage in the fight it cannot have been anything to do with the commonplace problem of fouling, as even the slickest infantry rifleman would not have been able to get away more than about five or six shots in the time available, while the cavalry detachments had been late in opening fire and might have fired as few as two rounds in the same short window. The amount of fouling in the barrel only began to become significant after about fifteen rounds and affected recoil rather than operation. Sir Charles Wilson made the point that the principal problem was that the cartridges were 'made on economical principles' and that they did not 'stand knocking about'. 'I saw myself', he continued, 'several men throw their rifles down with bitter curses when they found them jammed and useless; and if the infantry did this, the cavalry using the long rifle for the first time must have been worse.'[50] Regardless of Sir Charles Wilson's statement it is not be imagined that he saw large numbers of soldiers throwing down their rifles, for the obvious reason that the enlisted man had no other recourse save to his fixed bayonet or the butt-end of his weapon, so that discarding it would be akin to an act of madness. One man who definitely did throw down a Martini in disgust was Burleigh, who managed to get off only three rounds before the weapon jammed, but he was a newspaperman and, unlike the men in the ranks, was also carrying a privately owned revolver which he proceeded to draw and put to good use.

By 1885 the Martini had been in service for more than a decade, so that the fragility of its soft rolled-brass cartridge was a widely recognized issue. As is usual in such cases, a number of mitigating measures had been evolved, foremost amongst them taking care of one's ammunition as a matter of course and, secondly, not attempting to load damaged rounds at the height of a battle. Problems of the sort referred to by Wilson generally occurred not with rounds yet to be broken out of the waxed paper packet, but with the ready-to-use rounds carried loose in the soldier's expense pouch, which could easily get dented during the rough and tumble of life on campaign.

We have already noted that the first-line scale of ammunition was seventy rounds a man, carried in the case of the camel regiments in a twenty-round expense pouch and a fifty-round bandolier. This meant that all seventy cartridges had been removed from the waxed paper intended to protect their eighty-five grains of black powder from the elements. The Boxer-Henry cartridge was reasonably waterproof in its own right, save in worst-case scenarios such as torrential rain or immersion during a river crossing. Clearly neither of these eventualities had cropped up in transiting the Bayūda. On the plus side, the fifty rounds in the bandolier were unlikely to be badly dented, save through outright abuse. Experienced riflemen who knew that they were about to go into action, as had been the case in the *zariba* earlier that morning, would have quickly sifted through their ready-to-use ammunition for questionable-looking rounds and would have rotated them with undamaged rounds from the bandolier. It was not uncommon, however, for brass cases carried in a leather bandolier gradually to accumulate a layer of dirt, making it doubly important in desert conditions that ammunition received a quick wipe-over prior to battle. It was important also that rifles were dry cleaned – which is to say not heavily lubricated with oil – in order to minimize the ingress and retention of sand.

Assuming that a Short Chamber Boxer-Henry round was moisture-free and could be made to chamber, the odd indentation in the case counted for nothing; it was going to go off regardless. What the empty case might not do subsequently, however, was eject when the lever behind the trigger guard was operated to open the breech and engage the extractor. It was important that the jerk on the lever was a sharp one; this was a matter of drill and would have been a particular point of emphasis amongst infantry musketry instructors. The immediate action on a jammed cartridge was to try the lever again, jerking it harder and sharper at the second and third attempts.

One of the popular myths which has sprung up around the Martini-Henry is the image of hard-pressed soldiers drawing pocket knives to try and prise jammed cartridge cases free. This is a scenario which has migrated in the popular imagination from US Cavalry troopers struggling to bring Springfield carbines back into action at the Little Big Horn, to apply just as readily to British infantrymen fighting at Isandlwana with the Martini-Henry three years later. From there it is only a short hop in the popular imagination to the Abu Klea battlefield. Whether or not cartridges can be prised from a Springfield carbine is not remotely relevant to the matter in hand. What does matter is that the rim of the Boxer cartridge rested flush in the chamber of the Martini-Henry and simply could not be prised out in this way; try as one might there was simply no purchase to be had.

Inexperienced riflemen could continue wrestling with the lever all they liked, a measure which if it failed to work at the second or third attempt was almost certainly not going to work at all. The old sweat, on the other hand, knew that he had only to draw the steel cleaning rod from under the muzzle and impel it hard down the barrel to send the jammed case flying from the open breech every time. The rifle then had to be upended to recover the cleaning rod, not something one would want to do with the enemy twenty yards away admittedly, but in less immediate scenarios it was a quick and effective way of getting a jammed rifle back into action. The technique wasn't to be found in the book, but it can be safely assumed that the old sweats demonstrated it to the younger soldiers and that the practice was universally employed in the infantry. That said, there is evidence to suggest that there was a mark of cleaning rod in existence with a head too large to fit down the bore, allowing its tail end only to be applied to the barrel:[51] in quite what numbers these were supplied to the troops in Sudan is impossible to know; indeed, there might not have been any.

These then were the ways in which the widely recognized problems with the soft rolled-brass cartridge were mitigated; but while such nitty-gritty techniques were an essential part of a professional infantryman's skill-base, they were by no means meat and drink to members of the cavalry arm. If the Heavies oiled their rifles, failed to inspect for doubtful-looking rounds in advance, failed to wipe over their ready-to-use ammunition, failed to jerk their levers sharply in the approved fashion and were less well versed in unconventional weapon-handling skills, they would undoubtedly have suffered a higher incidence of stoppages and might have struggled to clear them as quickly as the men in the infantry companies.

All of the foregoing needs to be contextualized by recognizing that it does not take very many stoppages at the height of a crisis for such incidents to be afforded a degree of prominence in the sources which might not be entirely warranted. From there it is but a short hop to exaggeration in secondary narratives, and only one more bound after that to a fully fledged myth. That Martinis did jam at Abu Klea at particularly inopportune moments and in exceptionally difficult circumstances is beyond doubt; that the overwhelming majority functioned faithfully throughout the action, no less so in HCR than in other regiments, is clearly evinced by the outcome of the battle and so heavy a Mahdist loss in so short a space of time. Beresford's assertion of 1914 that 'Nearly half the British rifles jammed, owing to the use of leaf cartridges,' can be safely dismissed as hyperbole.[52] If that was anything near a reflection of the truth, Beresford would almost certainly not have been around thirty years later to pen these words.

Writing only two years after the battle, Alex Macdonald spotted a myth in the making and articulated an altogether more balanced view:

That the fire of these companies as well as that of the whole force was weakened by the jamming of the cheaply made regulation cartridges with which they were supplied, and also by some imperfection in the cartridge extractors of their rifles, has been abundantly proved. But that these defects contributed, to the extent which has been alleged, to the giving way of a portion of the square, cannot be fairly maintained . . .[53]

Macdonald was quite right in identifying the design of the cartridges and extractors as the factors at the heart of the issue.

It was inevitable that there would be something of a furore over jamming in the aftermath of the campaign, in large part because Wolseley returned home fuming about the issue and Burleigh had complained about it in the pages of the *Daily Telegraph*. Such matters rested within the staff domain of Brigadier General H. J. Alderson in his capacity as Director of Artillery and Stores. Some 538 rifles which had been in service with units of the Camel Corps were called in to the Royal Small Arms Factory when the troops returned to England. On 17 September 1885 Colonel H. T. Arbuthnot, the military superintendent at the facility, submitted his inspection report to General Alderson. He identified that 248 of the rifles, close to half, were Mark Is manufactured prior to 1875, which had subsequently undergone the upgrading process to convert them to the Mark II pattern. The remainder were newer rifles specifically manufactured as Mark IIs. The former were not a direct facsimile of the latter, however, as the Mark II had a stronger extractor which had not formed part of the Mark I upgrade.

Arbuthnot could not be sure which individual rifles had jammed and which had not, but did identify that significant numbers of the old extractors were 'slightly sprung'; in other words they had been strained in such a way as to be no longer capable of applying the same force to the cartridge case as formerly. This he attributed to attempts to clear jams. By contrast the stronger extractor supplied with the Mark II appeared not to have suffered in the same way. That is not to say that converted Mark Is would have jammed any more often than Mark IIs; at the root of the problem was the soft brass cartridge case, which would have caused jams in equal measure, regardless of the mark of rifle. The difference was that there was a greater chance of a Mark II clearing a jammed case at the second and third attempts, as the new extractor was much more likely to continue functioning normally. On the other hand the effectiveness of the old extractor might have been degraded by any previous jam, including conceivably by a stoppage which had occurred on a rifle range in England some months before the troops departed for Egypt. No data has surfaced to suggest which units were carrying the older converted rifles and which were carrying newer purpose-made Mark IIs, or for that matter, whether and in what proportion they might have been mixed within the same unit.

The Crisis

Less than thirty yards to the left-rear of the jammed Gardner, Major Walter Atherton was trying desperately to respond to Burnaby's most recent order and wheel his men back into the rear face, whilst at the same time maintaining a bold front to the Mahdīsts bubbling out of the *khors* to the rear of the square. 'The order was obeyed,' wrote Talbot, 'the men stepping steadily backwards.'[54] The *anṣār* though were moving fast and getting close. Lionel Trafford, meanwhile, was attempting to deploy the Royal Sussex into the yawning gap on the right-hand side of the rear face, precisely the same piece of real estate that Atherton had vacated only moments earlier and was now striving to reoccupy.[55] Burnaby was still out in front of Atherton's bayonets, urging haste and steadiness in the rearwards wheel, when the plight of Charles Byng and a last desperate handful of skirmishers caught his eye. Collation of the sources would suggest that there was one man behind Byng and two to his left-front, with a hard-riding _shaikh_ bearing down on them. Ever the warrior, Burnaby could no more help himself than could a tourney knight in the lists. Kicking 'Moses' into a trot, he braced his sword and went thundering to the rescue. While the rearmost soldier was suddenly caught and killed, Byng and the other two men succeeded in sprinting home.[56]

Forty yards or so from the impending crisis at the rear, scores of Mahdists now crashed with demoniacal ferocity into No. 5 Company. Verner found himself squarely in the path of the assault, when the thin grey line in front of him was hewn apart by a wave of stabbing, hacking Kordofanis:

At the moment when the enemy reached the square, I was with the Lancers and close to the Gardner gun; all the men in front of me were down in a moment, and I had just time to shoot an Arab coming at me, when another hurled a long spear past me killing a man on my right (I believe Major Carmichael), and something hit me in the face, and I fell.

Pinned to the ground by two bodies which fell across his legs moments later, Verner saw a 'wicked looking old Dervish with a grizzly beard' running towards him with a broad-bladed Baqqāra spear poised to strike. With the British line recoiling past him, his only resort was to feign death. Whether his immediate assailant ran straight past him or was promptly brought down, he never did find out.[57] Harry Pearse's despatch for the _Daily News_ contains an otherwise unexplained remark to the effect that, 'When Carmichael of the 5th Lancers fell, his death was immediately avenged by Shoeing-Smith Austin of the same regiment.'[58] We do know that 2130 Private G. Austin of the 5th Lancers was returned as slightly wounded at Abu Klea and would later be awarded the Distinguished Conduct Medal. Whether Beresford and the Gardner crew were overrun a few seconds before Austin brought down his company commander's assailant, or a few seconds afterwards, it is not possible to say, but the two events must certainly have been near-simultaneous in time and space:

The next moment the enemy were on top of us. The feed plate dropped on my head, knocking me under the gun and across its trail. Simultaneously a spear was thrust right through poor Rhodes, who was instantly killed at my side.[59] Walter Miller the armourer was speared beside the gun at the same time. I was knocked off the trail of the gun by a blow with the handle of an axe, the blade of which missed me. An Arab thrust at me with his spear, and I caught the blade, cutting my hand, and before he could recover his weapon a bullet dropped him. I was carried bodily backwards by the tremendous impact of the rush, right upon the front rank of the men of Number 4 Company, who stood like rocks. I can compare the press to nothing but the crush of a theatre crowd alarmed by a cry of fire. Immediately facing me was an Arab holding his spear over his head, the staff of his weapon being jammed against his back by the pressure behind him. I could draw neither sword nor pistol.[60]

This particular passage of Beresford's memoirs is corroborated by his official report of March 1885, in which he wrote of these first few seconds that 'the crush was so great ... that few on either side were killed'.[61] It was only a matter of moments later, however, that the two sets of adversaries drew sufficiently far enough apart to begin wielding their weapons effectively. If Beresford was lucky to scramble away in the confusion with only cuts and grazes, the huge able seaman known as 'Jumbo' enjoyed nothing like the same good fortune. Knocked flat in the near vicinity of the gun, he was repeatedly stabbed in the back by passing spearmen.[62]

As more and more Mahdists came up to exploit the breach in the left face, the frontage of the assault broadened to overlap the left-hand sections of C Company, MICR. Bracing their bayonets, the riflemen readied themselves for the onslaught. When it came, 'it made no other impression on that portion of the face than to force it back a couple of paces, but when bayonet crossed spear these companies [more accurately sections] stood their ground like a wall of rock'.[63] While the men in the front rank lunged and parried, the rear rank men fired over their shoulders at point-blank range, or thrust into the fray with their bayonets wherever the situation called for it. The brawl lasted only seconds but on the C Company sector at least, the line was held.

The break-in to the left of Fetherstonhaugh's men soon undid their good work, however, and brought a scrum of No. 5 Company men crashing into C Company's left-hand section. This was precisely the danger of such a penetration; unless the sections held together and kept their heads, there was every danger that the entire left face would be rolled up from the flank. The only counter-measure was to establish a pivot point further along the company's frontage to the right, and then wheel everybody to the left of that point back through ninety degrees so as to 'refuse' the threatened flank. Good infantry soldiers would have grasped this precept instinctively and, with only a minimal amount of bawling from the officers and sergeants to their rear, would immediately have begun shuffling themselves into roughly the right places. The main concerns of the individual soldier were to keep his bayonet braced in front and maintain shoulder to shoulder contact with the mates left and right of him. In this way an intimidating 'hedge' of bayonets could be maintained. Fortunately the riflemen of C Company were more than up to the challenge; bellowing instructions to the intruding members of No. 5 Company, they quickly absorbed them into their own ranks. While the left half of C Company was no longer a pretty sight, all that mattered was that it had been successfully refused.

On the right side of the rear face Atherton's 5th Dragoon Guards and Burn-Murdoch's Royals had struggled frantically to undo the self-inflicted damage and to some extent had succeeded in shuffling themselves into line. If the metaphorical back door had not quite been slammed shut, it was at least no longer fully ajar. Burnaby though had been left stranded on the wrong side of the bayonets, not that he seemed to pay the slightest heed to his predicament. A few seconds before he could come to blows with the mounted shaikh, his opponent was sent reeling from the saddle by a shot from the square. As Bennet Burleigh recounts, a wave of *anṣār* infantry were hard on the heels of the shaikh and quickly swarmed towards the mounted infidel in blue. Lord Binning thought he saw his colonel with his four-barrelled Lancaster pistol in his hand, but if he did it can only have been moments before he fired off the last of the barrels and unsheathed his sword.[64] Burleigh was also nearby and provides the best account of Burnaby's last stand:

The enemy's spearmen were close behind, and one of them dashed suddenly at the colonel, pointing the long blade of his spear at his throat. Checking his horse and slowly pulling it backward, Burnaby leaned forward in his saddle and parried the Moslem's rapid and ferocious thrusts; but the length of the man's weapon – eight feet – put it out of his power to return with interest the Arab's murderous intent. Once or twice, I think the colonel touched his man, only to make him more wary and eager. The affray was the work of three or four seconds only, for the savage horde of swarthy negroes from Kordofan, and the straight-haired, tawny complexioned Arabs of the Bayuda steppe, were fast closing in on our square.

Burnaby fenced smartly, just as if he were playing in an assault-at-arms, and there was a smile on his features as he drove off the man's awkward thrusts. The scene was taken in at a glance – with that lightning instinct which I have seen the desert warriors before now display in battle while coming to one another's aid – by an Arab who, pursuing a soldier, had passed five paces to Burnaby's right and rear. Turning with a sudden spring this second Arab ran his spear-point into the colonel's right shoulder. It was but a slight wound – enough, though, to cause Burnaby to twist round in his saddle to defend himself from this unexpected attack. Before the savage could repeat his unlooked for blow – so near the ranks of the square was the scene now being enacted – a soldier ran out and drove his sword-bayonet through the second assailant. [This would appear to have been 2445 Private G. Laporte of the Scots Greys.[65]] As the Englishman withdrew the steel the ferocious Arab wriggled round and sought to reach him. The effort was too much however even for his delirium of hatred against the Christian, and the rebel reeled and fell. Brief as was Burnaby's glance backward at this fatal episode, it was long enough to enable the first Arab to deliver his spear point full in the brave officer's throat. The blow drove Burnaby out of the saddle, but it required a second one before he let go his grip of the reins and tumbled upon the ground. Half-a-dozen Arabs were now about him. With the blood gushing in streams from his gashed throat, the dauntless Guardsman leaped to his feet, sword in hand, and slashed at the ferocious group. They were the wild strokes of a proud, brave man, dying hard, and he was quickly overborne, and left helpless and dying. The heroic soldier who sprang to his rescue [this time, 1076 Corporal John McIntosh of the Blues[66]] was, I fear, also slain in the melee for – though I watched for him – I never saw him get back to his place in the ranks.[67]

'Moses' had been hacked to the ground, even as the unseated and badly wounded Burnaby somehow mustered the strength to climb back to his feet. Reggie Talbot

Major General Charles Gordon, Governor-General of the Sudan.

Prime Minister Gladstone.

General Lord Wolseley, the Army Commander.

Colonel William Butler, the principal architect of the whaler scheme.

Brigadier General Sir Herbert Stewart, Commander of the Desert Column. *(Royal Collection)*

Colonel Sir Charles Wilson, Head of Intelligence.

Colonel Fred Burnaby, living legend and Commanding Officer of the Blues.

Captain Lord Charles Beresford RN, Commanding Officer of the Naval Brigade.

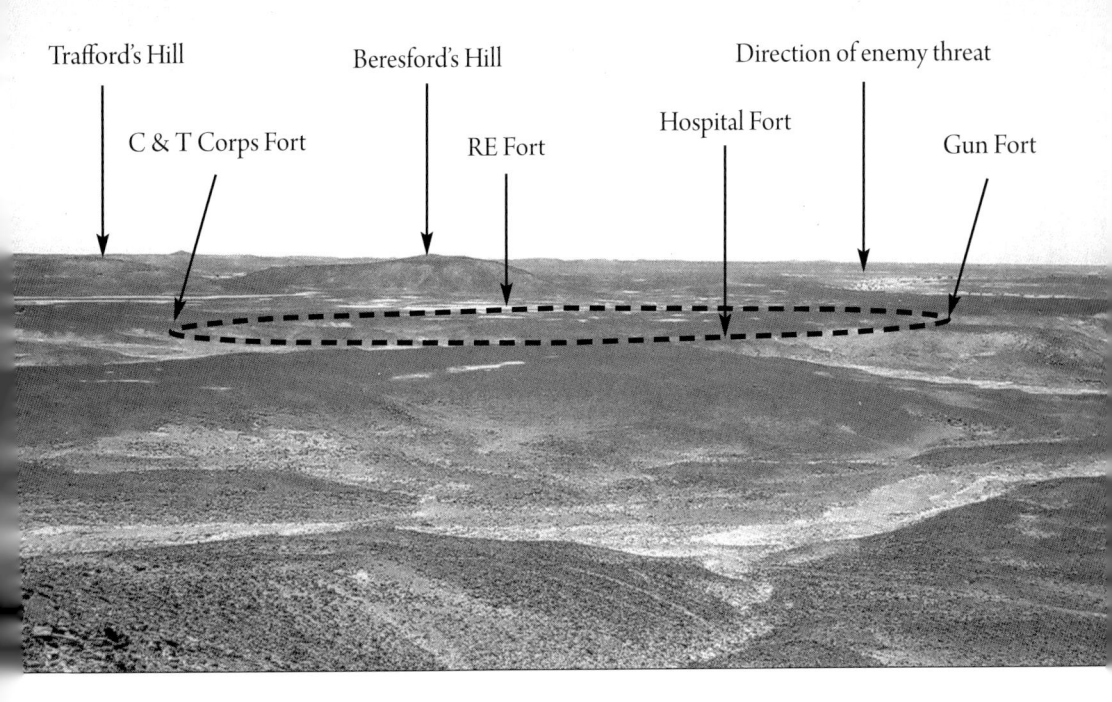

Trafford's Hill — Beresford's Hill — Direction of enemy threat

C & T Corps Fort — RE Fort — Hospital Fort — Gun Fort

The British *zariba* at Abu Klea: the site of the Desert Column's bivouac on the night 16/17 January 1885. The position was subject to harassing fire throughout the night and for much of the next day.

The 'Bedouin' tent and flags, p.m. 16 Jan. — General line of the Mahdist demonstration, a.m. 17 Jan.

The view down the Abu Klea Valley from the Gardner sangar on Beresford's Hill.

An *Illustrated London News* portrayal of the 7-pounders being brought into action in the front face of the square at Abu Klea.

A stirring *Illustrated London News* depiction of the hand-to-hand fighting at Abu Klea. Reality, of course, was altogether more nightmarish.

Beresford's Hill

Gardner sangar

Abu Klea Valley

Trafford's Hill

The low stone wall raised by C Company, 1st Royal Sussex. Captain Trafford had his men throw their blankets over the wall to minimize the danger from splintered rock thrown up by enemy fire.

The conical hill (the left-hand high point) and associated high ground viewed from the area of the hospital fort. The Abu Klea Valley stretches away to the left of this point. Captain Fetherstonhaugh's two-section skirmish line fought in the low ground at the foot of the plateau.

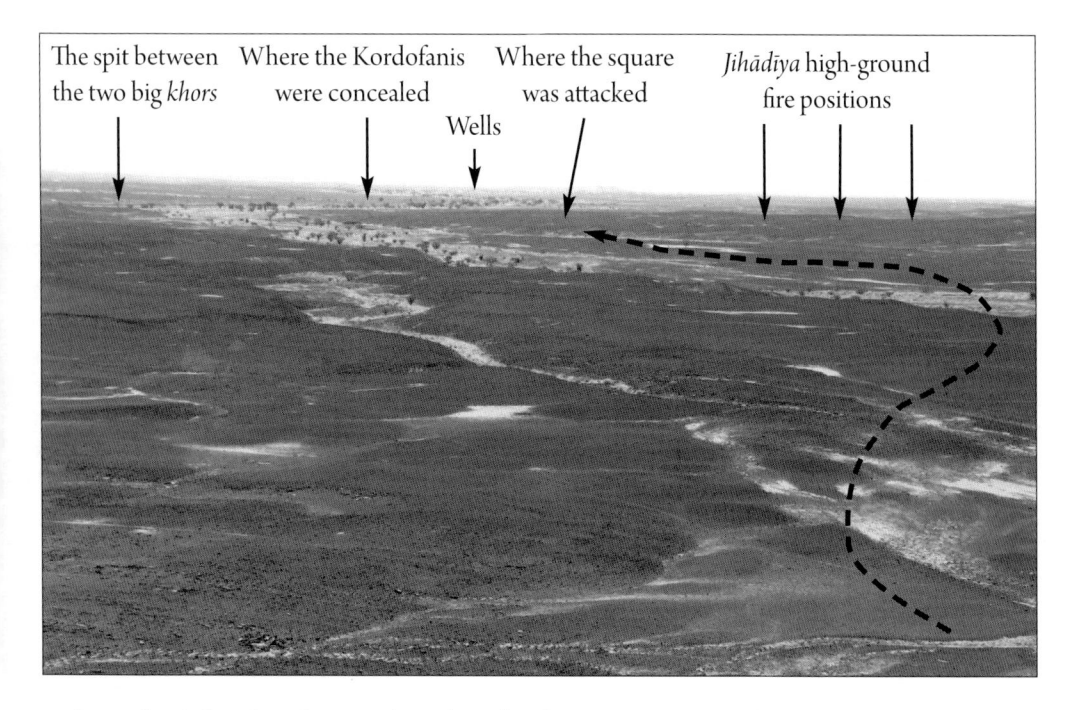

The Battle of Abu Klea. The view along the valley from the *zariba* towards the wells. The line of flags was located on the spit. The head of the arrow denoting the line of advance rests on the tributary *khor* which disrupted the square in the last few minutes before the onslaught.

The view across the British line of advance (left to right) from the right-hand side of the Abu Klea valley. Burnaby steered the square on a slight right oblique after crossing the tributary *khor* in the centre.

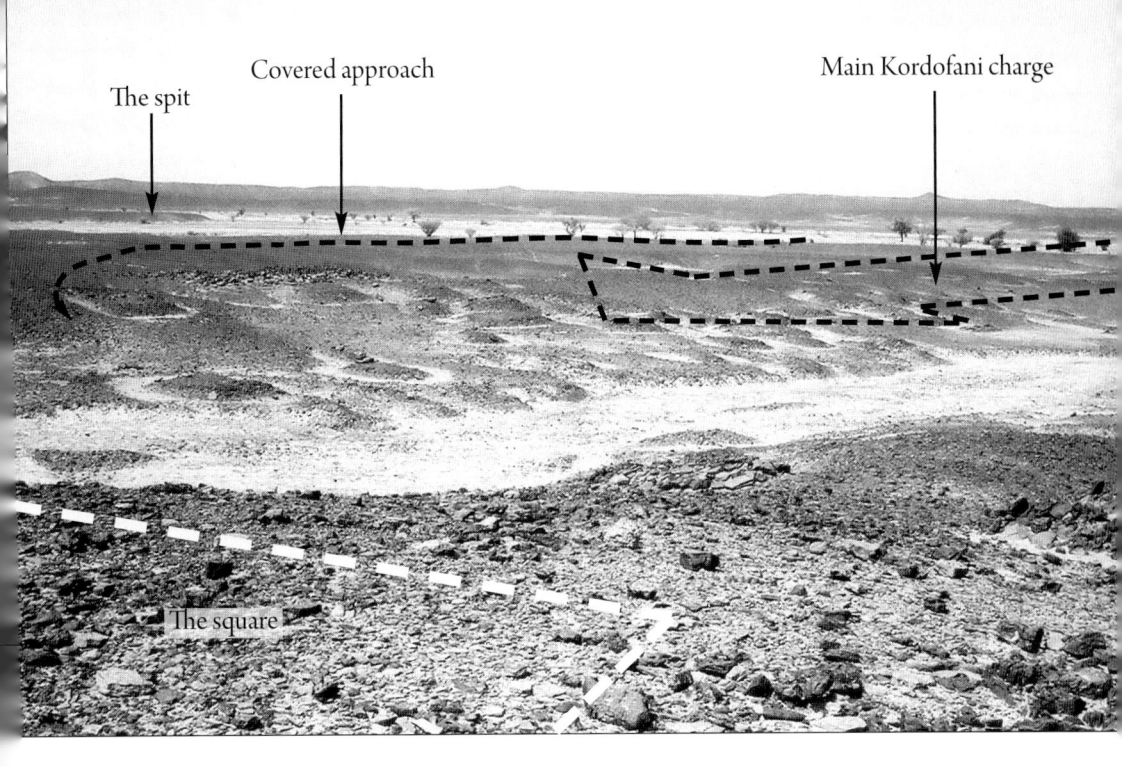

View of the attack on the left face of the square. The remains of Burnaby's cairn are visible on the far side of the *khor*. The other graves are Mahdist ones. With only a few exceptions the British dead were buried in a trench-grave outside the right face of the square.

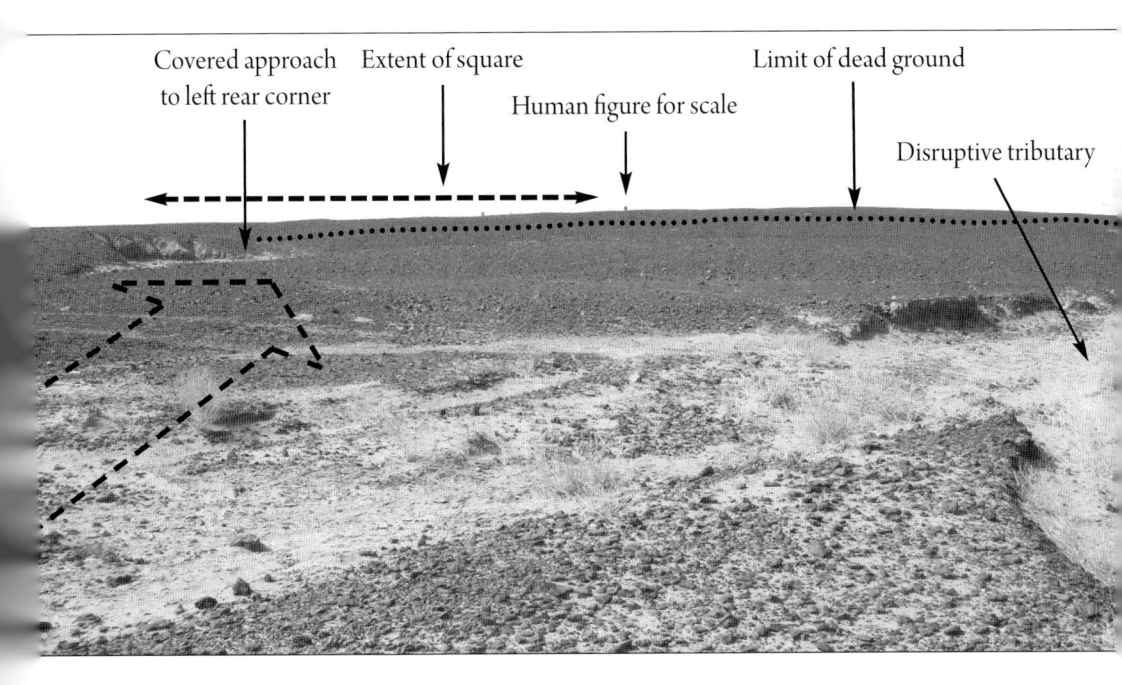

The real reason why the square was broken into at the left rear: note the amount of dead ground available to an attacker and in particular the tributary *khor* labelled as a covered approach.

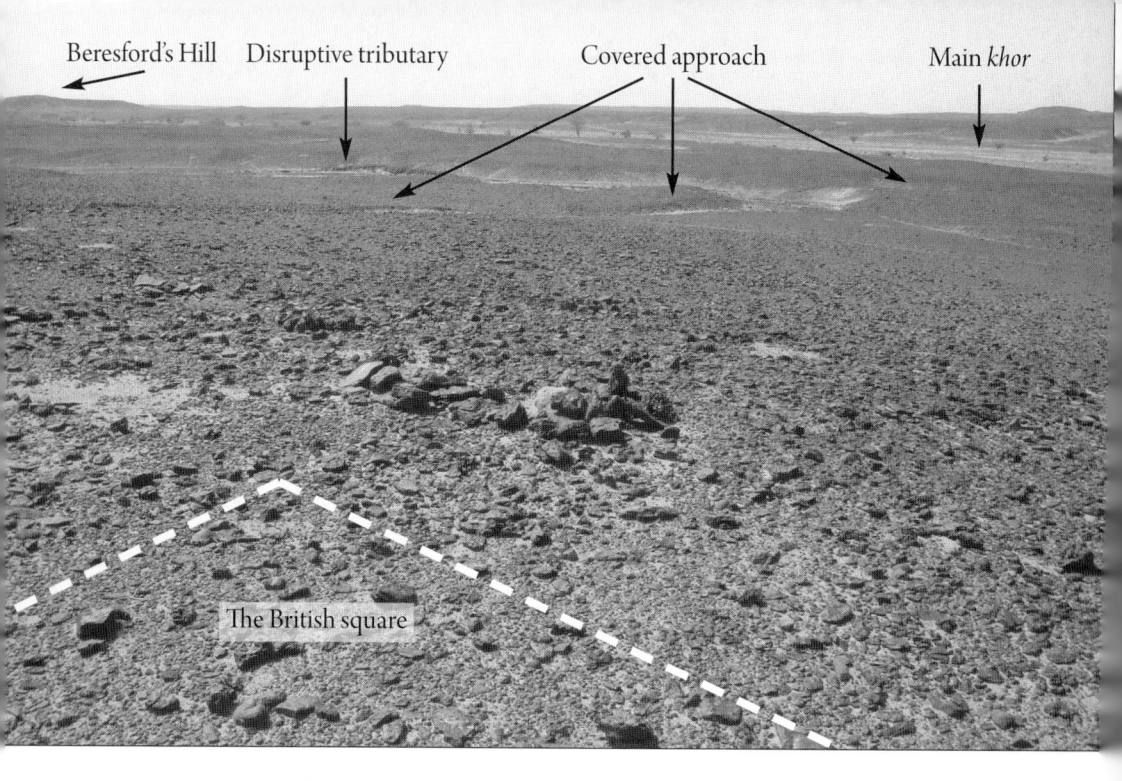

The view from the left rear corner of the square. Note how close to the corner the covered approach runs.

The author paying his respects at the remains of Burnaby's cairn. The cairn was raised by officers and soldiers of the Desert Column depositing stones as they filed past Burnaby's grave.

Without the benefit of moonlight, the night march of 18/19 January degenerated into disarray. Having failed to reach the Nile under the cover of darkness, the British were forced to halt and give battle for the second time in two days.

Melton Prior's drawing of the defence of the *zariba* at Abu Kru. Colonel Percy Barrow has clambered onto the barricade to make himself heard, while in the far distance the square is coming under attack from the gravel ridge. The mortally wounded Stewart can be seen, centre left.

The climax of the Battle of Abu Kru. After being exposed to a heavy fire throughout their approach march, the British 'Tommies' greeted the onset of the Mahdists with a cheer.

The British *zariba* position at Abu Kru, the point at which Sir Herbert Stewart finally halted his overnight march and established a defensive perimeter. Although the knoll offered a good view towards Metemmeh and the Nile (behind the camera), it was badly exposed to incoming fire from the surrounding scrub.

The *zariba*

The fight to the Nile. Captain Verner navigated the square using the bare gravel patches as a zig-zag axis of advance through the scrub (rather sparser here than was the case in January 1885). The advance was well supported by long-range artillery fire from the *zariba*.

Approximate position of the square

The *zariba*

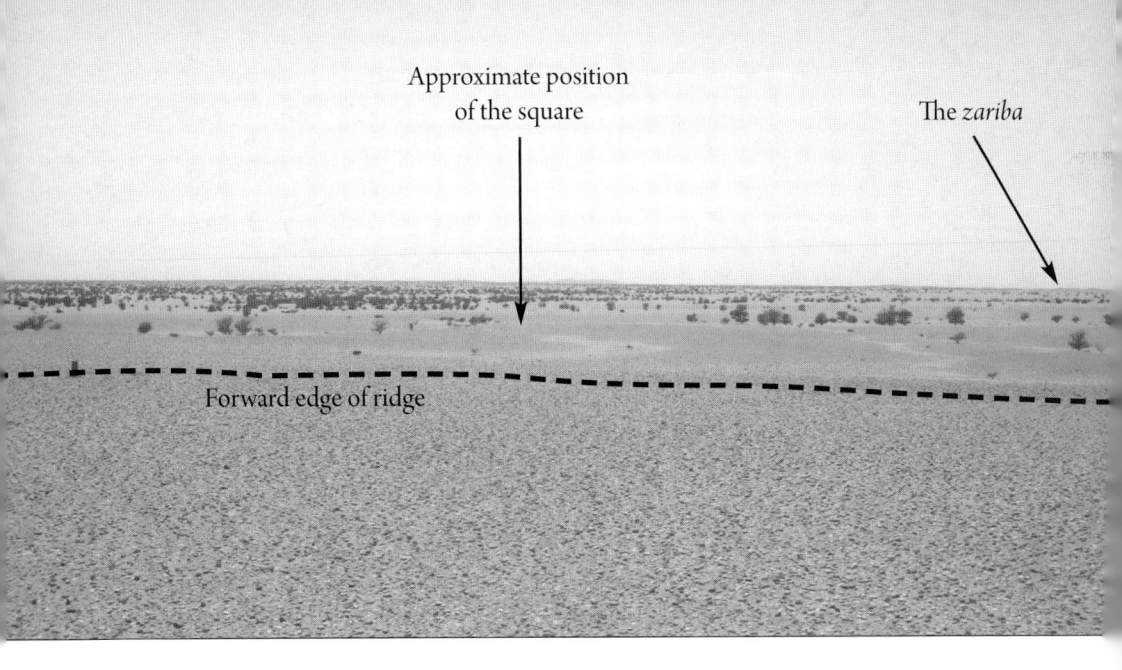

Forward edge of ridge

The climax of Abu Kru showing the view from the gravel ridge towards the square. The main Mahdist onslaught came from the right of this point and fell on the front and left faces of the square.

Old tip of Mernat, now a new island

Wilson's *zariba* on Mernat Island

East bank

Where *Bordein* foundered

The loss of the *Bordein*. The point at which Sir Charles Wilson had the steamer run onto a sandspit after striking a rock. Direction of travel was downstream, from right to left. The offending rock is about 400 yards upriver to the right. The river is higher in the photograph than it was in January 1885. Note that a new channel has been carved between the old north tip of Mernat and the rest of the island.

The steamers fighting at the confluence of the Niles, being fired on from Tuti island to their port side, Omdurman to starboard, and Khartoum dead ahead.

The action at Wad Habeshi. Wilson's men cover the immobilized *Sāfia* with fire, while below decks Chief Engineer Henry Benbow toils to effect repairs to the boiler. In reality *Sāfia* was much closer to the opposite bank.

The steamer *Bordein* was re-floated by the Mahdists and subsequently recaptured during Kitchener's re-conquest. Here she is seen at anchor in front of the *sarāya* on the fiftieth anniversary of Gordon's death. Tuti island is to the rear, while Omdurman and the confluence of the Niles lie downstream to the left. The armour cladding does not reflect how *Bordein* appeared in 1885.

The heavily fortified *Bordein* of January 1885: a watercolour from Captain Lionel Trafford's diary. (*West Sussex Records Office*)

Mid-river island

Where *Bordein* grounded and foundered

West bank

North tip of Mernat, now a new island

To Wad Habeshi and Gubat

New channel

Mernat Island

The view from Mernat Island.

A watercolour from Captain Trafford's diary showing the wreck of the *Bordein* from Mernat Island (compare with the modern-day photo above). Unless Trafford thoughtlessly painted the steamer facing the wrong way, it would appear that *Bordein*'s stern swung around with the current at some point.

Once G. W. Joy had painted this moving portrayal of Gordon passively awaiting his martyrdom at the head of the palace stairs, it ceased to matter that the balance of the primary source evidence would suggest that Gordon went down fighting: no mere historian has the power to gainsay such powerful iconography.

seems to have witnessed the blow that finally drew a line under the adventures of a great British hero: 'Burnaby, whose horse had fallen, was one of the first to be attacked, and as he lay on the ground he received a mortal wound in the neck from a sword-cut.'[68] While Private Laporte would survive the scrimmage around the fallen colonel, Corporal McIntosh had indeed been killed.

Burnaby fell at the heart of a sudden, terrific and bloody collision between the *anṣār* charging along Verner's Lines 4 and 5 and the 5th DG half-company. The square had now been broken in two places, the points of penetration separated by perhaps forty yards and twenty seconds. When in battle one side charges maniacally en masse into a static linear defence, a combination of the attacker's momentum and a certain amount of nervous flinching from the fray on the part of the defenders will almost always drive the latter back a few yards. At that stage the time for flinching has passed. One of two things must now happen: either the defending side will become seized by a contagious panic and collapse into rout or, if the men in the ranks are made of sterner stuff, they will rally, club together and begin fighting like demons to turn to back the tide. These were British soldiers, imbued by the lustre of their nation and the proud traditions of their regiments with an innate sense of superiority over any 'native' foe. For men such as these, flight was not an option. Nor did the example of their officers fall short of anything but the highest standards. Major Walter Atherton, Captain Joseph Darley and Lieutenant Charles Law all stepped forward to defend the breach in the square with their swords and pistols. All were cut down. Atherton was last seen backed against the flank of a camel, blazing away with his revolver.[69] Provoked by their survival instinct and the gallant example of their officers to a fighting fury that overmatched even the red mist of fundamentalist fervour, the Heavies collectively clenched their teeth and began brawling as only Tommies can. For all the grit they displayed that day, many of their number would not survive the ordeal.

It would be as well to summarize the overall situation at this juncture. On the left face No. 5 Company, HCR, had been penetrated at roughly its midway point and broken into two groups of survivors. While a larger cluster of men on the right had made a fighting retreat in the direction of C Company, MICR, a somewhat smaller party on the left had rallied on the Scots Greys of No. 4 Company. Scores of *anṣār* were interposed between the two groups. While many had wheeled left or right to attack the nearest infidels, others had charged into the centre of the square where, thankfully for the British, their further progress was arrested by a barrier of tight-packed baggage camels. Only seconds after No. 5 Company was penetrated, the left half of C Company, MICR, had been subject to a frontal assault. The company had succeeded in standing its ground with the bayonet, but had been forced by the break-in to its left to refuse its left flank.

In the meantime the parties of *anṣār* spilling from the *khors* to the left-rear of the square had thrown themselves against the bayonets of the Greys and the Royals. Only moments later the Mahdīst right wing (*Verner's line 5*), delayed fractionally by the slightly greater distance it had to cover, came crashing into the 5th Dragoon

Guards. This drove the detachment back in disorder compelling the Greys and Royals to fight front and rear.[70] A proportion of the men in these two detachments found themselves in a virtually hopeless position from which only the luckiest of them would escape. With both Nos. 3 and 4 Companies recoiling onto the baggage camels and the Naval Brigade, the left-rear corner of the square was no more.

The combined momentum of the Mahdist onslaught and the resultant British recoil brought a heaving, struggling mass of more than 150 Heavies into collision with the forty Royal Navy personnel deployed to their left and around 120 members of 1st Royal Sussex moving up behind them.[71] The crush was such that some soldiers in the centre were briefly lifted off their feet. At the front of the mob, officers and men alike did their best to wield their weapons effectively. As the Naval Brigade became swept up in the brawl, both of Beresford's lieutenants, Pigott and de Lisle, were cut down and killed.[72]

In stark contrast to the chaos on the far side of the baggage camels, the men of the Guards Camel Regiment had been deprived of targets for some minutes. While the furious musketry to their rear alerted them to the fact that the left face had come under heavy attack, they remained oblivious to just how critical the situation had become until all of a sudden they felt a 'terrific shock'.[73] Immediately alive to its meaning, Colonel Evelyn Boscawen and his officers ordered their rear rank men to right-about-turn to confront the threat from within. Sir Charles Wilson was 'much struck by the demeanour of the Guards officers. There was no noise or fuss; all the orders were given as if on parade, and they spoke to their men in a quiet manner, as if nothing was unusual was going on.'[74] Perhaps Wilson's impression was true of the Guards colonels, but Gleichen and Dawson both recount that they shouted themselves hoarse over the next few minutes. As the press from the rear drove the camels ever closer to the front face, Douglas Dawson thought that, 'it looked as if the two remaining sides of the square must be swallowed up'.[75] The situation appeared so serious that he suddenly felt moved to rush across to his brother Vesey for a farewell handshake. To the left of the Guards, the officers of A Company, MICR, also turned their rear rank about.[76]

The Heavies, meanwhile, were in the thick of the fray. When, a year later, Reggie Talbot wrote his article defending the conduct of his men in *Nineteenth Century* magazine, he not only took exception to Sir Charles Wilson's use of the word 'clubbed', but also rounded on the author of another participant account:

Sir C. Wilson speaks of the Heavies being clubbed. When it is remembered that there was a severe hand-to-hand fight, and eighty-six officers and men in that portion of the square were killed and wounded, it will readily be understood that some confusion was inevitable, but as the men never lost their heads, and the officers retained control over their men, the expression is hardly accurate or fair. Some people, [including] apparently the writer of the article in the November number of this Review, seemed to have thought that the battle was lost, and that it only remained to sell our lives as dearly as possible. I can only say that it never occurred to me that the fight was lost, and in evidence of this I never drew sword or pistol. Most determined fighting was going on, but there was no sign of giving way, still less of demoralisation.[77]

Talbot's thinly veiled reference was to Douglas Dawson, whose piece 'Sir Herbert Stewart's Desert March' had appeared two editions earlier and recounted the story of the farewell handshake. It was not as if the Dawson brothers had been alone in imagining that the game was up. In his *Daily News* report on the battle Harry Pearse had stated quite accurately that, 'For a while the fate of the whole force trembled in the balance.' It is true to say that the first few published accounts of the battle had laboured the failings of the Heavies as infantrymen, at the expense of extolling their courageous conduct in the close-quarter fighting. In that context Reggie Talbot's sensitivity was at least understandable. But there could be no altering the essential fact that his regiment's heavy casualties occurred as a direct consequence of what the infantry officers present that day regarded as 'unsteadiness'. The compliments showered on other regiments served only to annoy Talbot further. Pearse for example had written, 'The steadiness of the Guards, Marines and Mounted Infantry prevailed . . .', adding also, 'The Sussex Regiment, though taken in rear [untrue], rallied and fought desperately.'[78]

Talbot was the first officer to point a finger of blame at Burnaby, although Charles Williams had already let the cat out of the bag in the pages of the *Daily Chronicle*, so that Burnaby's error of judgement, while it had been discreetly omitted from Stewart's official despatch, had in fact been common knowledge for the best part of a year by the time Talbot chose to raise it. As one of his major concerns was to protect the reputations of the contributing regiments, it is only fair to cite his remarks on the subject. (His references to the 'left wing' of his regiment are to its organization in order of regimental seniority, not to its tactical deployment; rather it should be borne in mind that the technically more 'junior' companies of the left wing were actually on the right of the rear face once the square had halted and faced outwards.)

In the events that happened no credit belongs to one corps more than another. The brunt of the attack at Abu Klea fell on the left wing of the Heavy Camel Regiment and Naval Brigade and they acquitted themselves to the satisfaction of their General, but not a whit better did they acquit themselves than others of the column would have done. They all did their work in the several places in which they found themselves. Sir C. Wilson remarks that not a single Arab penetrated the ranks of the 1st and 2nd Life Guards or Blues (he might have added Bays). It is perfectly true; but, like the other parts of the square, they did not bear the chief force of the main attack; they only had to resist portions of the surging force whose fury chiefly spent itself on the left-rear corner of the square. They were able moreover to meet the attacks with fire, and they were not impeded to the same extent by lagging camels. They would be the last to accept credit which implies undeserved criticism of the left wing of their regiment. It cannot be admitted that the fate of the day depended upon any one portion of the force more than another, and that had it not been for the front and right faces of the square, or, as Lieutenant Dawson puts it, the Guards, all would have been lost. All credit to their right good behaviour; but it is not a fact that the whole of the rear face or left face were driven back and only prevented from retreating by the steadiness of the other faces . . . It has been asked how it was that the Arabs entered the square: the cause was that it was not closed up when the attack took place. It was not broken because it was not properly formed. No doubt the masking of the fire from the rear of the square by our skirmishers enabled the enemy to approach comparatively unharmed. The jamming of the rifles was a very serious matter, and added to the difficulties and diminished the volume of fire from all portions of the square; but, on the other hand, it caused the men to use their bayonets, which in a hand-to-hand fight are safer and more effective weapons. It has been hinted that cavalry, fighting on foot, were not suited to the work they were called upon to perform, and again that the Heavy Camel Regiment was wanting in cohesion and in esprit de corps. No cavalry soldier ever wishes to be separated from his horse, except when being honoured by being selected for some exceptional service like the advance across the Bayuda desert . . . Certain it is that no one regiment, either cavalry or infantry, could have supplied an equal number of highly trained, active, strong, efficient men, selected from their regiments for general efficiency and good shooting. As to the esprit de corps which bound together and supported this regiment on many a trying occasion, it was as if it had been the growth of years instead of weeks. Nothing could have exceeded the cordial feelings that existed between each detachment, or the belief and confidence that they had in each other.[79]

This at least was how Reggie Talbot saw the events of a supremely confusing and violent ten minutes. If there is truth in some of his contentions, it is also the case that there are sins of omission inherent in his article.

Amongst the very first of the Mahdists to break through the gap carved in No. 5 Company, HCR, was a venerable Daghaim *amīr* who galloped into the square with a Qur'anic banner in one hand and verses of scripture in the other.[80] Sir Charles Wilson was watching him during the charge and thought that he 'never saw anything finer':

The old man never swerved to the right or left and never ceased chanting his prayers until he planted his banner in our square. If any man deserved a place in the Moslem Paradise he did. When I saw the old sheikh in the square, and heard the wild uproar behind the camels, I drew my revolver, for directly the sheikh fell, the Arabs began running in under the camels to the front part of the square.[81]

Safe in Dublin some months later, Wilson could afford to indulge in a little romantic sentiment as he sat writing *From Korti to Khartum*, although on the day of the battle an altogether more savage reality had been played out on the other side of the camels. Recognizing that the *amīr* was an important leadership figure, Corporal Yetton of the 2nd Rifle Brigade section raised his rifle to the aim and shot him out of the saddle. But the old man had not placed his well-being in the hands of God alone; he was surrounded by fierce Daghaim bodyguards, four of whom instantly turned on Yetton, inflicting no fewer than seventeen spear wounds upon him.[82] It is of note that Wilson attaches the name 'Musa' to the *amīr*. Whilst this was a relatively commonplace name, it seems more than likely that Corporal Yetton had brought down Mūsā wad Ḥilū himself.

Beresford had escaped to relative safety amongst the men of C Company, MICR. As he watched scenes of slaughter being played out around him, he was struck by the extraordinary bravery of the average *anṣāri*.

Their desperate courage was marvellous. I saw a boy of some twelve years of age, who had been shot through the stomach, walk slowly up through a storm of bullets and thrust his spear at one of our men. I saw several Arabs writhe from out a pile of dead and wounded, and charge some eighty yards under fire towards us, and one of them ran right up to the bayonets and flung himself upon them and was killed.[83]

Beresford now found himself fighting beside the officer commanding D Company, MICR. Shotgun at the ready, 'Bloody Pigott' was in his element. With Arabs 'crawling and twisting under the camels', he was responding to target indications from a handful of naval ratings who had somehow managed to rally on their captain. 'Here's another joker, sir!' cried one sailor, as a Kordofani emerged from behind a mound of bodies. A split second later Beresford saw his 'bald crown riddled like the rose of a watering pot'.[84] Effective it may have been: pretty it was not. Nor was Pigott the only man wielding a shotgun to good effect. According to Marling his native servant, 'Old Saich', brought down three Arabs with his master's best 'scatter-gun'.[85]

As the hand-to-hand fighting intensified, a number of soldiers found to their horror that the Camel Corps had been issued with a batch of P1860 sword-bayonets which had been so poorly tempered that a violent thrust could buckle the steel. To make matters worse they had been issued unsharpened and without grindstones, though this latter deficiency might conceivably have been addressed by the infantry units on their arrival in Egypt.[86] Lord Cochrane's batman, a Downpatrick Irishman called Private David Gilligan, 'the best and truest man ever born', stood beside his master throughout the Arab break-in, emerging from the fight with his bayonet 'twisted like a corkscrew'.[87] Beresford observed that some of the soldiers cursed aloud as the 'shoddy bayonets twisted like tin'. Some of the Naval Brigade cutlass-bayonets failed in like fashion, although the Navy had at least 'sharpened for action'.[88] The Royal Sussex companies were better off with the standard P1876 'lunger' bayonet but, arrayed as they were behind the recoiling Heavies, had only fleeting opportunities to put it to good use. Failed bayonets attracted a great deal of attention in the aftermath of the battle and in due course triggered a minor storm in the press, although the incidence of failure needs to be kept in perspective. Writing in later life as a general officer, Gleichen remarked of the P1860 bayonets only that, 'in several cases [they] bent when it came to hand to hand fighting'. Although failures were potentially life-threatening, they seem not to have been that widespread.

If there was any good news at all for the British, it was to be found on Major Charles Barrow's sector, where alone of all the left face companies Pigott's

D Company had been unaffected by the Mahdīst break-in and was maintaining a deadly and unrelenting fire. The largely instinctive refusal of C Company's left-hand sections had sufficed both to meet the immediate crisis and to absorb a good many No. 5 Company men and naval ratings back into the British ranks. Over the next minute or two the pivot-point at the centre of Captain Walsh's C Company gradually rippled its way through the right-hand sections and then continued down the line into D Company. One by one the Mounted Infantry brought their left shoulders and bayonet points around, until the angled pivot finally came to a halt at the corner of the square. Where previously C and D Companies had been separated from B and A Companies by a right angle, the interval between the two wings of the regiment had reduced to forty-five degrees, so that MICR was now fighting in something akin to a V-shaped wedge. The realignment of C and D Companies was a simple enough manoeuvre, requiring the men only to shuffle back a few paces, whilst at the same time maintaining their dressing by the right. As such it would have exerted no noticeable effect on the heavy and telling fire pouring forth from both companies. Sergeant Small of D Company's 2nd Connaught Rangers section preferred to put his trust in the bayonet and on a number of occasions charged singlehandedly into the throng around the dead and dying camels to fight at close quarters. His DCM citation would observe that, 'his personal courage and leading contributed much to the ultimate expulsion of the enemy'.[89]

Around the corner on the front face, the excellent fields of fire enjoyed by A and B Companies were proving just about impossible for the *anṣār* of the Mahdīst left wing. With scores of them lying dead and maimed on the open slope and their surviving brethren driven to ground, it was apparent that on this sector at least the attack was not going to be pressed home.[90] In the meantime the new alignment of C and D Companies left them ideally placed to continue inflicting heavy punishment on the Mahdīst centre. The significance of this fire lay not only in the sheer numbers of *anṣār* being shot down on the open slope, but in the fact that it served to prevent any significant reinforcement of the break-in. So long as Major Barrow stood his ground the Mahdīst left and centre would be neutralized, leaving only the right wing still in play at the rear of the square.

Although Barrow's C and D Companies had wielded the bayonet to excellent effect, the pressure on the left face of the square had forced them back a few yards, exposing the 7-pounder at the corner of the formation. Lieutenant James Guthrie had been so intent on fighting his gun that he had still not drawn sword or revolver when a Mahdīst came running up to set about him with a long knife. Albert Smith, a 24-year-old gunner, was more keenly aware of the danger and rushed to Guthrie's rescue, parrying his assailant's first thrust with a trail-spike. This sufficed to buy the second or two Guthrie needed to draw his sword and run the man through. As the dying *anṣāri* sank to the ground he lashed out suddenly with his knife, wounding Guthrie severely. Smith brained the man with a blow from his trail-spike and then stood at bay over his wounded officer. His selflessness was to earn him the only Victoria Cross of the battle.[91] There could and should have been more.

In addition to the Mounted Infantry there was one other component of the British force working hard to confound the Mahdīst break-in. As Lord Cochrane put it:

> Thus the camels which had been a source of embarrassment to us when the square was advancing, now became a source of strength. They did not take fright, they did not plunge or kick, they did not seem to mind a bullet, they acted as a living wall. When the enemy spearmen reached this living traverse in their rush, they raised their spears in the air and did not seem to know what to do: some crept under the camels, but were shot down on the other side.[92]

Other Mahdīsts began venting their blood-lust by hacking away at the animals. Perhaps the cruellest scenes occurred where bearer-company camels were brought down and the occupants of the *cacolets* were butchered as they lay on the ground. This terrible fate befell the soldier opposite Lord St Vincent, though the 34-year old peer was fortunate that the dying camel fell on top of him, leaving only his head showing from under its flank. Miraculously not one of the rampaging Mahdīsts spotted him, though he had to endure a moment of sheer terror when one *anṣāri* came so close that his foot struck St Vincent in the mouth – fortunately without causing him to look down.[93] A few moments later Privates Newton and Inglis of the 16th Lancers came charging out of the recoiling British ranks. Even as they were attempting to heave his lordship free, they came under attack and were obliged to stand their ground with rifle-butt and bayonet.[94]

Captain Trafford, meanwhile, had made use of his slight stature to slip through the chaos at the rear of the square into the forefront of the hand-to-hand fighting. Like Beresford, he was intimately exposed to the extraordinary courage of the enemy. He particularly noted one mounted *amīr* who, having galloped around the left-rear corner of the square, was now riding along the broken rear face. He seemed not to have full control of his horse and was pulling hard on the bit to turn the animal towards the British:

> The horse had his mouth open and his neck bent towards us, but was galloping across our front. Suddenly the rider got him in hand, and turning his head dashed the shovel stirrups into his flanks and came at the square alone. When he was about 30 yards off his horse fell but the man sprung up and dashed at the square, only to fall wounded. Then on his hands and knees he crawled up that he might kill one man before he died – he died a yard from my feet, as he raised himself for his last effort.[95]

Although he urged the Heavies to stand firm and fire low, Trafford's rallying cries failed to prevent yet more ground being conceded. He soon became isolated in front of the bayonets. Darting back to safety, he was suddenly squeezed between 'two huge dragoons', was lifted off his feet and found himself being carried backwards and forwards in the crush. Fortunately he had just enough use of his arms to fire his revolver when needed.

With a scrimmage of battling soldiers, struggling sailors, bellowing officers, maddened *anṣār* and bewildered camels moving closer and closer to the Guards and Mounted Infantry, some of the men in the about-turned rear ranks began firing into the mayhem. Doubtless a proportion were still calm enough and good enough shots to draw a careful bead on an individual *anṣāri*, although the slightest carelessness had the potential to strike down anybody in the general line of fire. It was inevitable in so frightening a situation that for every man in icy cool control of his faculties, there were two or three others who were over-animated and firing wildly. That Britons were hit by bullets from Birmingham is beyond all doubt. Verner wrote that 'a great many deplorable accidents must have occurred',[96] while Sir Charles Wilson was certain that both Majors Ludovick Carmichael and Wilfred Gough lost their lives to friendly fire, albeit that in Carmichael's case he was probably wrong.[97] Several of the Adeni camel handlers were also killed and wounded by British fire, notwithstanding their distinctive blue frocks and red turbans.[98] It was impossible in the tumult for the company officers to bring the firing under any sort of control. Lord Cochrane recalled that 'an order at the top of one's voice could only be heard a yard or two away'. 'I shouted myself hoarse,' wrote Gleichen, 'trying to get the men to aim carefully, but my voice was lost in the din. A rain of bullets whizzed dangerously close past my head into the fighting mass in front. Numbers of the Arabs went down in that hail, and I fear several Englishmen too.'[99] Indeed the firing brought down so many men and animals that the threat of the front face being swept away by the approaching tidal wave of hand-to-hand fighting suddenly abated. Many of the officers who had been in the thick of the fray spoke afterwards of the whole square shifting its ground, but this was an illusion arising from the recoiling movement in the HCR companies, the Naval Brigade and the Royal Sussex. In fact the GCR companies stood rooted to the spot and would close the fight in precisely the same positions in which they had started.[100] Lance Sergeant Pearson of No. 2 Company was one of the Guards NCOs who performed sterling work in holding the front of the square together. His DCM citation observed that, despite being severely wounded, he 'set an example of steadiness and coolness to the men and rendered most valuable assistance to the officers'.[101]

Whether Sir Herbert Stewart's horse was brought down by a British or a Mahdist bullet is impossible to say. In his despatch for the *Morning Post*, St Leger Herbert noted, 'At the same time his orderly was killed beside him.' As the general went crashing to the ground near the left-front corner of the square, three Mahdist swordsmen rushed to finish him as he lay powerless to resist. Fortunately a ripple of pistol shots from the chief of intelligence and nearby MICR officers felled all three assailants before they could do any harm. The closest of them was brought down at a range of only three paces by Sir Charles himself.[102] Wardrop, Airlie, Rhodes and others quickly clustered around Stewart to drag him back to his feet and away to a marginally safer spot. It is not clear how or when Lord Airlie was injured, but he would end the day sporting two 'slight' spear wounds in one hand. The chances are that the injury occurred in the fracas around his unhorsed chief.

In a campaign where it could be taken as read that the enemy would show no regard for the Red Cross, it was more than a little remarkable that the soldiers of the Medical Staff Corps had been sent into the field unarmed. In an article of 1892, Surgeon Thomas Parke, who seven years earlier had been ministering to the medical needs of the Naval Brigade, remarked that this state of affairs, 'elicited from Sir Herbert Stewart an expression of extreme astonishment'.[103] Such a thing really ought not to have come as a surprise, least of all to the general officer commanding, and should have been addressed prior to leaving Korti. Caught up in the havoc as they now were, Sergeant Charles Williams and his bearer-company colleagues were obliged to pick up discarded weapons with which to defend themselves. The AMD surgeons, at least, had been sensible enough to arm themselves at private expense like any other officer. Surgeon William Briggs, the officer commanding the field hospital, was observed in the thick of the fray with his sword drawn and his helmet knocked from his head, rallying soldiers about him like a line officer.[104]

On the left-hand side of the rear face HCR's Nos. 1 and 2 Companies, comprising the Queen's Bays and the three Household Cavalry detachments, had fared altogether better than the broken and badly mauled companies to their right. The Blues and Bays were under the command of the towering, splendidly bewhiskered Lord Arthur Somerset, one of the officers who had long been at odds with Burnaby. The latter's nomination of Lord Arthur as the officer to command No. 2 Company appears to have generated something of a rapprochement between the two Household Cavalry giants. Sad to say Lord Arthur's sexual predilections would later embroil him in one of the most notorious scandals of the age, ruining him utterly. Four years after Abu Klea, by which time he was holding a Household Cavalry sinecure as the master of horse in the Prince of Wales's household, he was caught up in the so called 'Cleveland Street Scandal', an affair in which the Metropolitan Police broke up a male prostitute ring, some of whom were minors. Warned by a well-placed acquaintance that Scotland Yard was closing in and intended to arrest him for pederasty, Somerset fled to the continent and thereafter was obliged to live in permanent exile in the south of France. The best part of 125 years after his spectacular fall from grace, he should at least receive credit as the brave soldier and selfless leader of men he showed himself to be at Abu Klea. That he was 'slightly wounded' in unspecified circumstances but continued thereafter to parade for duty is a fact which, although it is not widely known or referred to, is recorded in one or two primary sources. The unpublished account of the medic Sergeant Charles Williams having kindly been made available to me by his descendants, we now know that Somerset was actually quite seriously injured during the hand-to-hand fighting inside the square. Although we cannot be precisely certain how it came about, it is clear that as he was leading the defence of No. 2 Company's refused right flank, a Mahdist either slashed a sword or thrust a spear at him in such a fashion as to cut his chest from one side to the other, leaving a wound half-an-inch deep. Paying no heed to the injury, Lord Arthur saw the battle through at the head of his men.

The stout resistance offered by the Blues and the Bays was substantially their own doing, but was also materially aided by the men of the Royal Sussex who, having first attempted to support Nos. 3 and 4 Companies, had gradually been pushed back towards their former position where the small knoll offered a commanding view across the mayhem at the back of the square. Protected by a dense wedge of Heavies, naval ratings and their own regimental comrades fighting hand-to-hand at the foot of the slope, a proportion of the Royal Sussex found themselves in elevated fire positions and commenced a heavy overhead fire. Lord Cochrane observed that they 'did great execution and splendid service'.[105] The two Life Guards detachments under Lord Cochrane's command were still occupying substantially the same ground as at the outset, when suddenly about fifty Awadiyeh cavalry mounted on black horses came charging along a shallow re-entrant to assail the remnants of the rear face. They were unfortunate in running squarely into the only HCR company still capable of receiving cavalry. The troopers of the Life Guards kept their nerve and at a range of fifty yards loosed a fusillade which brought down about twenty-five of the horses.[106] The remaining riders thought better of pressing their attack and wheeled away to safety. The men left unhorsed in front of the Life Guards did not long survive a swift reload.

Turn of the Tide

The close-quarter killing match of the past ten minutes had been so intense that most of the British had little or no idea just how quickly Mahdīst losses were mounting. A sudden easing of the pressure came as a surprise to many. It was the Royal Sussex men atop the knoll who were the first to grasp what was going on. 'They are going! They are going!' came the cry. Nobody can have been more relieved at the sound of those words than the brace of gallant rescuers who against all the odds were still standing unharmed over Lord St Vincent. Both Newton and Inglis would be awarded the DCM.[107] Douglas Dawson thought that it was now, with the flags of the enemy receding from the rear face, that the wildest British firing took place:

> Then began the most indiscriminate firing of the whole time, and I fear at this time many of our poor fellows lost their lives. Among my own men I was surrounded by representatives of nearly every regiment in the force, who all began firing into the square at the retreating enemy. I should think twenty or thirty rifles went off just in my ear, fired over my head, past my head, anywhere.[108]

A ripple of shots sufficed to clear the immediate environs of the crumpled British perimeter of a last handful of *anṣār* still intent on coming to close quarters. Anxious both to allow the smoke to clear and to make themselves heard, some of the HCR officers bellowed the order to 'Cease Firing!' Their hearing rendered inoperative by the incessant firing, two or three 'half-crazed' troopers got hold of the wrong end of the stick and rushed towards Lord Cochrane shouting 'Retire! Retire!' He quickly barred their way, proceeded to roar the correct word of command at them and sent them scurrying back to their places.

Realizing that he could now afford to show himself, a dazed Willoughby Verner dragged himself free of the corpses piled on top of him and crawled towards the nearest soldiers. A bugler dragged him to safety beneath the bayonets and quickly replaced his lost helmet with a discarded one lying near at hand. Back on his feet at last, Verner checked himself over and was relieved to find that his only injury was a bleeding nose. Glancing about the battlefield, he realized that just about every *anṣāri* who had come near enough to wield a weapon at close quarters had been clubbed, bayoneted or shot down. The remainder, amounting to not less than two and a half thousand souls, had been driven to ground on the gravel slope, or pinned down in the *khors* by the heavy fire from Barrow's C and D Companies.

Although the long incline between the square and the *khor* was alive with retreating *anṣār*, a last few aspirant martyrs remained fixated on paradise:

I shall never forget [wrote Douglas Dawson] the slow sullen way in which the Arabs retired, every now and then turning to stop and look as if anxious to come on again, and often ten or twelve would jump up from the ground and rush on till the rattle of rifles stopped them forever. A last three or four would rush on the square and finally one man alone.[109]

Whilst many *anṣār* were nursing wounds or helping their badly injured brethren to safety, the majority seemed to be in no great haste to quit the field.[110] With thousands of as yet uncommitted warriors at other points of the compass, Stewart and his officers could have no great confidence that the ordeal was at an end. As the square was in utter disarray, the first priority for the company officers was to rally, steady and re-form their men, so as to be ready to face any renewed onslaught. One of the staff officers ordered a nearby bugler to sound 'Cease Firing', so that orders could be heard. By the time the last note of the call had tailed away, the sudden silence was all but tangible. Although the battlefield was carpeted with dead and dying *anṣār*, many of the living gave no audible vent to their pain, in the belief that they might yet gain paradise by slaying an unwary infidel with the last of their strength. Nine months earlier Burleigh had described walking across the battlefield of Tamai as 'like walking among wounded vipers'.[111] Abu Klea would be no different. At what had been the back of the square were hundreds of crumpled human forms, fifty dead camels, numerous dead horses, two unharmed Arab ponies and a couple of wounded camels, the latter still standing but, 'riddled with bullets'.[112]

Such was the euphoria amongst the soldiers that restoring an atmosphere of calm was not easily accomplished. Sir Charles Wilson observed that the men were 'somewhat out of hand, wild with excitement. It was for a few moments difficult to get them into their places; and if the enemy had charged again, few of us would have escaped.'[113] Glad simply to be alive, the wild-eyed Tommies broke into cheers of exultation. The fighting rage which had stood them in such good stead at the height of the crisis, dissolved with the first rousing cheer. In a matter of only a few moments they had reverted to type. The grinning handshakes and back-slapping suggested that they had done little more than triumph in the last over of a cricket match. A bare few hundred yards down the slope, the realization that they had somehow been bested by infidels was only now settling over many of the *anṣār*. With their pride deflated and their fighting rage burning less fiercely, they simply turned their backs on the scene of their humiliation and began trotting into the distance. At the sound of the British cheering, a last few die-hards were seen to turn on their heels and shake their fists in the direction of the square.[114] Private Burge of GCR was just one of many men who could not help feeling great admiration for the foe:

> I for one was glad that they went away unmolested. Of their kind they were the bravest of the brave. They did not know the meaning of fear. I was glad and relieved, too, and I do not think that there was either officer or man in the broken square who had not a feeling of thankfulness to see the backs and not the faces of them.[115]

The Blues lost no time in fanning out in search of their commanding officer. Lord Binning was one of the first to reach his side. Remarkably a last flicker of life still lingered:

> I made my way as best I could to the spot where I had last seen him, foreboding in my heart. But I was not the first to find him. A young private in the Bays, a mere lad, was already beside him trying to support his head on his knee; the lad's genuine grief, with tears running down his face, was touching as were his simple words: 'Oh sir, here is the bravest man in England, dying, and no one to help him.' It was too true; a glance showed that he was past help. A spear had inflicted a terrible wound on the right side of his neck and throat, and his skull had been cleft by a blow from a two-handed sword – probably as he fell forward on his pony's neck. [Talbot's testimony would suggest that this blow was probably inflicted once Burnaby was lying on the ground.] Either wound would have proved mortal. The marvel was that he was still alive. As I took his hand, a feeble pressure and a faint look of recognition in his eyes, told me he still breathed, but life was ebbing fast, and it was only a matter of a few moments before he was gone. Amid the slain Arabs he lay there, a veritable Colossus, and alone of the dead his face wore the composed and placid smile of one who had been suddenly carried away in the midst of a congenial and favourite occupation.[116]

Some of the Blues were so overwrought at the passing of their lion-hearted colonel that they sat down and cried.

The natural line of withdrawal for the Kordofanis lay to the British half-right, in the direction of Metemmeh. For the present they were on the wrong side of the valley and would have to make a long detour to the south, in the direction of the wells, before it would be safe enough to cross the *khor* and start the long march back to the Nile. The Ja'līyīn and Awadiyeh similarly sought to fall back to Metemmeh, but from their positions on the right-hand side of the valley were better placed to do so than the Kordofanis. Conversely if the Abadeh and Bisharin were to withdraw directly to Berber, they too would have to move in the direction of the wells before crossing the *khor* in the opposite direction to the Kordofanis.

While the company officers were shuffling their men about and striving to impose some semblance of order, Norton and his gunners got on with the business of hastening the Kordofanis on their way, opening fire at a range of 500 yards.[117] Firing on the Mahdist withdrawal was probably the most protracted artillery engagement of the day. All told the gunners fired thirty-eight rounds of shrapnel, nineteen of common shell and six of case-shot.[118] While the case-shot would certainly have been fired from the square at the charging enemy (two rounds per gun presumably), the common shell would have been expended in the longer-range engagements, such as firing on the conical hill and the spit of land between the *khors*. The bulk of the shrapnel rounds were probably fired now, as the enemy were streaming into the distance. In the meantime the withdrawal of the Kordofanis had cued a resumption of the long-range sniping from the high ground on the right of the valley.

Harassing fire from the artillery was one thing, but the most effective means of turning a defeated enemy's disengagement into a costly rout was a vigorous cavalry pursuit. According to Burleigh the enemy were now presenting themselves as 'three long streams of Arabs, afoot and on horse, camel and donkey back . . . making off, one in the direction of Berber, another towards Metemmeh and a third for Khartoum'.[119] That there must indeed have been three clearly discernible lines of retreat for Burleigh to have said that is clear; whether they were pointing in quite the directions he says they were is another matter, as it would have been quite impossible from a vantage point on the floor of the Abu Klea Valley to distinguish between a line of retreat bound for Metemmeh and a second one bound for Khartoum. Burleigh may simply have guessed at the enemy's destinations, on the basis of the intelligence gleaned from the liberated survivors of the Kordofan expedition the following morning. But regardless of the route by which they left the valley, the fact of the matter is that most of the surviving Mahdists rallied on Metemmeh. For the time being, though, their straggling lines of retreat were a sight fit to tempt any cavalry officer worth his salt.

When Stewart and his staff rode within earshot of the Life Guards, perhaps to take advantage of the elevated view from the nearby knoll, Lord Cochrane heard the general lament, 'Why don't the 19th Hussars charge?' For all that he had proved himself to be an aggressive leader of cavalry, Stewart must have known in his heart of hearts why not. If riding down fleeing Mahdists sounded fine in theory, there were still a number of large bodies of *anṣār* moving about which had suffered but few casualties and were no less dangerous now than at the start of the fight. That as few as 120 horsemen could have any significant effect in harrying so great a host was doubtful. Apart from the enemy's numerical advantage, Barrow's exhausted ponies were in no fit state to charge anything. Instead he had to content himself with cantering about on the far side of the *khor*, doing everything he could to harass the enemy with carbine fire. At the back of his mind he was cognizant that the general's first priority simply had to be water and that it would fall to the 19th Hussars to push on ahead and secure it. After that there were another twenty-five miles of desert to be crossed, in the course of which the column would need to be shielded by its light cavalry squadron. The damage or destruction of that squadron in return for a few more dead Mahdists was simply not worth the candle. It was absolutely the right call.

Beresford rushed back to the Gardner as soon as the Kordofani wave began to recede, but clearing the jam proved more time-consuming than he had hoped. By the time he was ready to come back into action, the fire of the screw guns and the harassing operations of the 19th Hussars had spurred on the enemy withdrawal to such an extent that there were barely any worthwhile targets still in sight.[120] A few of Beresford's trademark five-round ripples at least affirmed that the Royal Navy remained undaunted.

There was a short-lived scare not long after this, when the cry went up amongst the Guards, 'Close up! Close up! They are coming again!'[121] In the event it proved to be a false alarm occasioned by elements of the Berber and Metemmeh contingents manoeuvring some distance to the right-front. The renewed fire from the ridges on the right proved to be largely ineffective, except where an occasional sniper stalked down into the low ground before opening fire. For the most part they were picked off by Guards or RMLI marksmen within a minute or two of their position being betrayed by their smoke. These short-lived exchanges of fire were not entirely one-sided however. As Private George Ormiston of the 3rd Grenadiers was passing his water-bottle to one of his comrades, a bullet cracked through the other man's hand and into Ormiston's chest. He fell on top of Count Gleichen, 'a torrent of blood gushing from his mouth', and was dead within a minute. A short while later a Mahdist horseman made a single-handed charge against the right face. He was not immediately brought down and appeared to Gleichen to be coming straight towards him. Raising his revolver into the aim he calmly bided his time and waited for the range to close. Much to his disgust, 'a marine bowled him over an awful "crumpler" at an unfairly short range for a rifle'.[122] It was not to be the last futile gesture of the day.

Chapter 11

Walking Amongst Vipers

Abu Klea: The Aftermath

'Put down our spears, infidel dogs! By God and the Prophet, never!'

Response attributed to four Kordofanis,
challenged after Abu Klea to surrender[1]

WITH THE WITHDRAWAL of the Berber and Metemmeh contingents across the high ground, it was clear that the battle really was over. Even the gravel ridges which had for so long harboured the *jihādīya* marksmen had now fallen silent. As it would be neither practicable nor desirable to reorganize amidst such scenes of carnage, Stewart gave orders for the square to advance 200 yards to the south, where a flat-topped rise offered uninterrupted fields of fire in all directions. Fully recovered from his close scrape, Verner once again lent a hand to Reggie Talbot and the HCR officers, many of whose colleagues were conspicuous by their absence. When Verner ran across the remnants of No. 3 Company, he found 'Podge' Somerset forming the men up and felt moved to enquire why. 'All their officers are killed,' came the explanation.[2] Relocating to the new position was the work of only a few minutes. Once the regimental commanders were content that everything was in order, the troops were allowed to sit down in formation, while the battlefield to their rear was scoured for survivors. When the GCR officers gathered to fraternize they marvelled that, with the unfortunate exception of their RMO, they were all unhurt. Laying their weapons aside, the surgeons and medics reverted to their proper role and began gathering in the wounded. In addition to dozens of serious cases, scores of other men had emerged from the fight with cuts, bruising and grazes which they would have to self-treat until the medics could get to them. In most cases that would not be until the morning of the following day. Observing the often dreadful plight of the casualties being ferried across from the battlefield, Lord Somerset said nothing of his own injuries. Despite being twice wounded, 3603 Private G. Woods of the 3rd Rifle Brigade section had remained in the ranks until the fight was over. Now, instead of seeking medical attention himself, he was hurrying about helping the surgeons attend to others. His selflessness subsequently attracted the award of a Distinguished Conduct Medal.[3]

Having been obliged by the state of their horses to draw a line under their harassment of the Mahdīst retreat, Barrow and French now came trotting in at the head of the left-flank guard. From a distant vantage point, three-quarters of a mile back down the valley, they had heard all the firing and seen something of both the Mahdīst charge and retreat, although the intervening break-in and brawl had not registered with them. Instead the battle had all the appearances of being a handsome victory. Now the scenes of destruction around the square and the frantic bustle of the medical staff came as a shocking revelation. After a brief conference with the general, Barrow took his other troop back under command and led the consolidated squadron off in the direction of the wells. The condition of the ponies, the presence along the route of retreating and wounded *anṣār*, and the difficulty of locating a series of sunken gravel pits on an otherwise featureless plain, threatened slow progress in the quest for water.

Verner borrowed a few troopers of the Blues from Lord Binning and led them back to the battlefield to gather water-skins from a miscellany of dead, dying, injured and unharmed baggage camels. They encountered an almost indescribable scene of destruction. At one spot there was a great heap of dead camels, some of which were bearer-company animals with some of the early casualties now lying dead in the *cacolets* and litters. The slain baggage camels were surrounded by a 'wild confusion' of water-tanks, boxes of reserve ammunition and other stores. Some 110 officers and soldiers 'were jammed close together and crowded with dead Arabs under and over them, whilst around lay over 800 Arabs, with horses and camels in all directions'.[4] Around forty soldiers or sailors were found still to be breathing and were hurried across to the surgeons, who were already well into their stride treating a broadly comparable number of walking wounded. When Captain Beresford and Able Seaman Laker rolled over the blood-soaked form of poor 'Jumbo', they were amazed to find him still breathing, notwithstanding the seventeen stab-wounds in his back. Beresford's tunic was covered in blood by the time he got the grievously hurt sailor into a *cacolet* and away to the doctors. Despite the ferocity of the attack upon Corporal Yetton, he too was still alive. As he was going about his duties Sergeant Charles Williams, the medic, happened to pass by No. 2 Company, GCR, where he caught sight of his old friend, 2445 Colour Sergeant George Kekewich, 1st Coldstream Guards, who had been much troubled before the battle by a premonition of death. It was time to snap him out of it. 'There you are,' grinned Williams, as he passed, 'alive and kicking in spite of presentiment!' A still troubled Kekewich shook his head, but made no other reply.[5]

Marling had come through the battle without a scratch, although his appearance somewhat belied his state of health. The left arm of his tunic was literally 'drenched in blood from the shoulder to the wrist'. Happy in the realization that at least it wasn't his own, he never did work out where it had come from. Like many other officers he found himself irresistibly drawn to the gruesome scene of the close-quarter fighting. After a while he came upon the slain 'colossus' of the Blues. A few yards away from Burnaby's body was the carcass of Marling's little grey polo pony, 'stabbed and cut to pieces'. Though not easily given to sentiment, Marling felt moved to cut off a piece of Moses's tail as a memento. Lord Cochrane also wandered over the field and came across the body of his old friend Major Ludovick Carmichael: 'I did not recognise him at first; his face looked as if he had been dragged face downwards over a flinty road for miles.'[6] Unlike Colour Sergeant Kekewich, Carmichael's eve of battle premonition had come to pass. His death was doubly tragic in that his wife had died in childbirth only weeks before he embarked for the Sudan, so that a still tiny baby had now been left orphaned.[7] Burnaby's face, Cochrane noted, was drained white through loss of blood. A short while later Lord Binning and others returned to the scene to shroud their late colonel in a Union Flag.[8]

By now Burleigh's 'vipers' had started to wriggle. One wounded *anṣāri* fired a Remington at Verner from a range of only five yards but missed; his erstwhile victim quickly drew his revolver and proved himself much the steadier shot. Not long afterwards, half-a-dozen *anṣār* who had been shamming amongst the dead suddenly leapt to their feet and charged the square. All were quickly shot down, though the last man standing got close enough to swing his sword at some soldiers, fortunately without doing any harm. In another incident a wounded Mahdīst suddenly sat up and fired on a pair of medics, knocking one of the legs off the stretcher they were carrying.[9] Having already recovered two wounded ratings to the square, Beresford was scouring the position for any more Naval Brigade survivors when he heard a cry of, 'Look out Charlie!' Turning rapidly on his heel, he saw a resurrected Kordofani running directly at him with his spear raised. 'I ran to meet him, sword in hand, parried his spear, then held my sword rigid at arm's length. He ran right up the blade to the hilt, against which his body struck with so great force that he fell backward.'[10]

As the old hands from the Red Sea Littoral knew only too well, there was no morally comfortable solution to the viper problem. In trying to help the enemy wounded, the usual smattering of Good Samaritans were taking their lives in their hands. A man whose leg was hanging to his body by only a thin sliver of flesh was cautiously approached by medics intent on helping him, but despite his condition he still felt the compulsion to snatch up a spear.[11] Nobody on the British side wanted to kill wounded men for whose courage they had so much respect, but time and again injured *anṣār* forced them to it. Sergeant Williams and his medics were faced with the difficult task of making a thorough check amongst the dead or dying *anṣār* for any remaining British wounded:

So soon as we could pull ourselves together, the work of searching the field of battle for our wounded men was undertaken. Whilst so engaged, many of the enemy lying about apparently dead made efforts to spear our men when stepping over them, even if it was their last effort in life. Consequently any Arab that showed a spark of life was shot at once. I myself had to do so, dozens of times. It was a ghastly business, turning over heaps of Arabs to find one or perhaps two of our men underneath – very, very few were living.[12]

The sailors assisting their captain in his quest for survivors were surprised when one unusually placid Kordofani allowed himself to be placed aboard a *cacolet*. When a few moments later Beresford located another badly wounded sailor, he had him placed into the seat on the opposite flank of the same camel. Having turned away to continue the search, Beresford heard a sudden howl of pain from behind him. Spinning around, he saw that the Kordofani had reached across to the wounded sailor, grabbed his arm and was now trying to bite his thumb off. Lord Charles did not specify in his memoirs whether, after hauling the ungrateful prisoner from the camel, he 'disposed' of him with his sword or his pistol.[13] Sadly the 'wounded viper' was to remain an intractable problem throughout the thirteen years of campaigning around the Sudan still to come.

Having given over some of his rescued water-skins to Surgeon Major Ferguson,[14] Verner issued the balance around the Heavies, before then returning to the battlefield with a party of troopers from the Life Guards. This time he focussed on weapons. First, seventeen boxes of small-arms ammunition were recovered. Then, once Beresford had kindled a good fire, the work-parties started feeding it with all the Mahdist swords and spears they could find. There was a conspicuous and curious absence of shields,[15] later explained by one of the captured letters brought in to the intelligence staff by the 19th Hussars. It transpired that Muḥammad Aḥmad had urged his commanders in the north to ensure that the faithful armed themselves only with spears and swords, so as not to be encumbered in the fight.[16] Their faith, he insisted, would protect them in a way that mere shields never could. There were also the rifles of the British casualties to consider. Many would have been retained by members of the Medical Staff Corps, but at least thirty had to be rendered useless by having their butts smashed. To make doubly sure of the job the barrels and stocks went into the fire. As there were insufficient baggage camels left to carry the reserve ammunition recovered by Verner, the boxes were broken open so that the cartridges could be served out around the men.[17] According to the War Diary maintained by Lord Airlie, some remaining balance of the 10,200 rounds recovered from the field was deemed surplus to the immediate requirement and also went on the fire. It soon transpired that Lord Charles had not chosen a particularly good spot for his bonfire. A number of dead baggage camels were lying too close to the leaping flames: it was not long before the fire had spread to their saddle-covers and loads and the carcasses themselves began to burn, the unpleasant smell of their consumption further contributing to the ghastliness of the setting.

Sir Charles Wilson also walked across the battlefield, finding the scene 'too horrible for description'. Even so *From Korti to Khartum*, published before the year was out, contained an observation that Major Carmichael had been 'accidentally shot through the head by one of our own men'. The Verner, Pearse and Cochrane accounts would tend to suggest that Carmichael had been killed at close quarters during the break-in. After a while the chief of intelligence started to wilt, with symptoms which are recognizably those of heat exhaustion. He was obliged to retire to the square and lie down with his head 'in such shade as a kneeling camel could give'.[18]

More than three hours would pass in scouring the field, gathering in the wounded and preparing to advance on the wells. It might have taken even longer had it not been for the pressing want of water spreading through the force.

The Mahdist Loss

Shortly before he was obliged to go and lie down, Wilson had reclaimed Verner for the intelligence department and instructed him to estimate the number of enemy dead. He first reported 'about 800', but finding himself with time in hand then took a second and closer look.

I counted roughly about 400 close up to the square and lying in heaps, with some 300 more towards the wady and 200 on the left front. On the left rear were 25 horses all together and I heard there had been a regular cavalry charge there. The horses were within 50 yards of the square. Colonel Barrow told me the wady was full of dead men and I put the number down at close on 1,200.[19]

Verner's identification of four significant concentrations of enemy dead is interesting and tells us something of the fire effect achieved by the British force. That no fewer than 400 Mahdists had been killed at close quarters, whether by bayonet, bludgeon or point-blank blast, bespeaks the ferocity of the hand-to-hand fighting. In all likelihood the 300 men shot down 'towards the wady' were primarily the victims of the heavy fire maintained by C and D Companies, MICR, throughout the crisis. The 200 to the left-front were probably attributable in the main to A and B Companies, MICR, with some help from D Company around the corner to their left, and No. 2 (Coldstream Guards) Company, GCR, to the right of the guns. A proportion of the *anṣār* killed to the left and left-front of the square would have fallen to the six rounds of case-shot fired by the screw guns, although it is impossible in the absence of any source references to know just how effective the short-range artillery fire had been. Verner seems to have made allowance for the best part of another 300 dead in the floor of the *khor*. These men could have fallen to one of a number of causes. Some could have been victims of early bursts from the Gardner, while others could have been shot down by the left face, or been killed or wounded by shrapnel during the retreat: but the majority were probably men who had been wounded in the charge and stumbled or crawled back into the *khor* to die.

While it is impossible to establish with any degree of certainty just how many Mahdists left the field wounded, the usual rule of thumb is that for every man killed in a battle, two others are wounded, one of them seriously. In this case, taking an estimated 1,200 'dead' as a start point, we need at the outset to subtract 400 from the number of fatalities, to reflect that there were virtually no survivors amongst the men struck down during the close-quarter fighting. If 800 other men were also killed, it follows that there ought to have been 1,600 wounded to match them. This would give a total of 1,200 dead and 1,600 wounded, but would mean that more than half the Kordofanis were killed or wounded, even at the 5,000 high-end estimates of their start-state. At Sir Herbert Stewart's low-end estimate of only 3,000 men, it would mean that virtually all of the participants in the charge had been shot down. This, then, is almost certainly too high a figure. Let us suppose that 400 of Verner's 1,200 'dead' – the men who fell at close quarters – really were dead after the scouring of the battlefield, but that the 800 bodies left lying further afield were in fact a combination of dead and badly wounded. This latter figure would divide half and half, as 400 dead and 400 seriously wounded, to which must be added another 400 slightly wounded who walked or were helped away from the field and thus would not have been tallied by Verner. The Mahdist loss in this scenario would amount to 800 men killed outright, 400 seriously wounded and left for dead, and a further 400 walking wounded strong enough to quit the field. This would tally as a total loss of 1,600 men, less than one third of the 5,000 high-end start-state, or just over half of the low-end 3,000. This rings fairly true, suggesting that Verner did not in fact count the dead, but rather all of the bloody forms left lying about the field, one third of whom were still alive at some distance from the British position.

This begs the question how many of the Mahdist walking wounded would have died subsequently? The wounds inflicted by the 0.450-inch Boxer round were ghastly if they hit a bone, and only marginally less horrible if they did not. In other words almost anybody shot with a Martini-Henry could die subsequently of shock or blood loss. The risk of death by infection was also high. The ultimate fate of the 400 men left for dead in a desert wilderness may, sadly, be rather easier to compute. The small nomadic population of the Bayūda had been aware that war was marching its way along the Korti–Metemmeh caravan road and had been steering well clear of it for some days. There simply were no nearby villages or itinerant communities to help the wounded. Having lost control of the local water supply, the defeated army had to fall back to the Nile or die; there could be no question of it loitering in the desert to succour its wounded. The closest inhabited place was Metemmeh, twenty-five miles to the south. The hostile British had been left in possession of the field and would shortly be advancing on the town along the caravan road. Bypassing the advancing column and its umbrella of scouting cavalry to get to Abu Klea would represent a high-risk undertaking. There was one more nail to be hammered into the coffins of the sorely wounded: for the most part they were Kordofanis – men whose families were encamped 100 miles away at Omdurman. Those who did not die of shock or blood loss that night would have been slowly broiled the following day. An unlucky few might have crawled their way agonizingly to shade and lasted a second night. The ultimate fate of almost all of them was to be rendered carrion for the gorged hyenas, jackals and vultures prowling the field by that time.

Even at a tally of 1,200 dead and 400 walking wounded the computations are incomplete, as Verner's estimate makes no allowance for Mahdists killed around the *zariba* or on the flanks of the advance. The fight along the line of the valley had entailed artillery fire, sniping, company volleys and half-company skirmish lines, in addition to which a substantial part of Major Gern's force had been in action for an hour or more. It would be surprising if there were not at least another 150 dead and 300 wounded *anṣār* to be added to Verner's estimate. All told, then, the Mahdist loss in the two-day action around Abu Klea was probably around 1,350 killed or died of their wounds, and 700 or so wounded.

The British Loss

The British fatal loss in the Battle of Abu Klea was given officially as 9 officers and 65 NCOs and men.[20] The deceased officers were: Colonel Frederick Gustavus Burnaby (HQ Staff/RHG [Blues]); Major Wilfred Arbuthnot Gough (HCR/Royals); Major Walter Hyde Atherton (HCR/5th DG); Major Ludovick Montefiore Carmichael (HCR/5th L); Captain Joseph Watkins William Darley (HCR/4th DG); Lieutenant Richard Wolfe (HCR/Scots Greys); Lieutenant Charles William Albert Law (HCR/4th DG); and Lieutenants Alfred Pigott and Rudolph Edward Lisle March Phillipps de Lisle (Naval Bde). Gough, Darley and Wolfe were all from prominent Anglo-Irish families. The officially stated number of wounded was 9 officers and 85 NCOs and men. Verner is the only source who cites a figure for the number of casualties incurred at the *zariba*, giving 4 men killed, and 4 officers and 13 NCOs and men wounded. We can conclude then that, subject to the caveats given in the next endnote, the casualties incurred during the advance and the close-quarter brawl totalled something around 9 & 61 killed and 6 & 72 wounded.[21]

The nine 'officially' wounded officers were: Major Hon. George Hugh Gough (MICR/14th H), severely; Major John Baillie Ballantyne Dickson (Intelligence Staff/Royals), severely; Captain (John Edward Leverson Jervis) Lord St Vincent (HCR/16th L), dangerously; Captain (David Stanley William) the Earl of Airlie (Brigade Major/10th H), slightly; Surgeon James Magill (GCR/AMD), severely; Lieutenant James Dunbar Guthrie (RA), dangerously; Lieutenant Rowland John Beech (HCR/2nd LG), slightly; Lieutenant Henry Costello (HCR/5th L), slightly – contusion;[22] and Lieutenant Charles Noel Lyall (RA), dangerously. Of these Captain Lord St Vincent and Lieutenant Guthrie were destined to die of their wounds, raising the true fatal toll of officers to eleven and reducing the number of wounded to seven. Lord Somerset was not listed at all, but on the basis of Sergeant Charles Williams's evidence, to which we shall come in due course, should be counted as an eighth wounded officer.

Inevitably the heaviest regimental loss by far fell on HCR, which had suffered 6 officers and 45 NCOs and men killed, and a further 4 officers and 30 NCOs and men seriously wounded. The disproportionate ratio between fatalities and injured reflects the merciless way in which the Mahdists had hacked at anybody they happened to pass lying on the ground. For the most part the seriously wounded were men who had managed to keep their feet despite their injuries and fall back amidst the recoiling British ranks. The fatalities by parent regiment included: the Royals, Major Gough, Sergeant Philps[23] and 11 private soldiers; the Scots Greys, Lieutenant Wolfe, Lance Corporal Sheals and 9 privates; the 4th Dragoon Guards, Captain Darley, Lieutenant Law and 4 privates; the 5th Dragoon Guards, Major Atherton, Sergeant Heverin and 5 privates; the 5th Lancers, Major Carmichael, Sergeant Percival, Corporal Parker and 2 privates; the 16th Lancers, Lance Corporal Jacques and 3 privates. The breakdown lends collateral to certain elements of the reconstruction. The figures show, for example, that most of the regimental detachments in HCR were initially swept backwards in the crush by the two Mahdist penetrations, losing only a handful of fatalities in each contingent. There were two predictable exceptions, one of which was No. 4 Company, HCR, where the Royals and the Greys, having been attacked both in front and rear, had lost a total of 2 officers and 23 NCOs and men killed, and a further 10 NCOs and men seriously wounded. Similarly No. 3 Company was also badly knocked about, with 3 officers and 9 NCOs and men killed, and 16 NCOs and men seriously wounded. By contrast the losses in the 5th and 16th Lancers show that No. 5 Company had escaped relatively lightly despite being penetrated, and demonstrate that most of its members had been able to rally on the KRRC and Rifle Brigade sections to their right. Of the other units most intimately swept up in the fight, the Naval Brigade had lost 2 officers and 6 men killed, with 7 men seriously wounded, while the Royal Sussex had only 2 men killed. The loss in GCR was also negligible in the circumstances, each of the four companies losing one man killed apiece. Although MICR had only 5 men killed, including Private Wilford, shot dead on Beresford Hill the previous day, it also had 1 officer and 28 NCOs and men wounded, a reflection of the hand-to-hand to fighting to which the Guards had not been exposed. Appendix F lists all the casualties by name and unit. For a variety of reasons it is seldom wise to regard such lists as the final word on the subject.

Defence of the *Zariba*

Far from being substantially undisturbed during the battle, as Count Gleichen and most derivative secondary accounts would imply, there had been a good deal of fighting around the *zariba* from about 10.00 a.m. onwards. Although the relentless sniper fire from the right had continued much as before, the Mahdists first pressed the British left, where several successive parties of *anṣār* attempted to pick their way towards the *zariba* via the dead-ground approach beyond Beresford Hill. Captain Arthur Morse and the men of the 1st Royal West Kents enjoyed a commanding view from the crest and were able to flay the would-be infiltrators with hard-hitting section volleys. At length a much stronger party tried to work its way around the left flank by stealth, but was soon spotted, hammered with a volley or two and driven back in confusion.

In the meantime Alex Macdonald and a knot of other observers had been monitoring the progress of the square until 'suddenly it disappeared from our view behind an intervening swell'.[24] A distant crescendo of gunfire suggested that the battle had reached some sort of denouement and for a while made the uncertainty unbearable. From the top of Beresford Hill, Morse and his men would certainly have had an excellent view of the Mahdist charge, although on all the occasions I have myself been atop the hill, the heat-haze has made it difficult to tell whether or not they would have been able to see the square itself; because the battle was fought on an exceptionally hot day, on balance I suspect probably not.

After a while the Mahdist pressure on the *zariba* switched from the British left to the opposite flank, albeit the great physical separation between the two sectors would suggest that this apparent change of emphasis occurred more by accident than design. The delay in attacking the right, coupled with the fact that there were only about a hundred riflemen operating on that side of the *zariba* tends to argue that some new Mahdist reinforcement had used the intervening period to make its way into the upper reaches of the valley. Conjecturally it may have entered the battle-space via the saddle between the conical hill and the long ridge. Thereafter a succession of relatively small groups of *anṣār*, perhaps a few dozen men on each occasion, descended from the high ground and threw themselves forward across the valley floor. The approach was cruelly bare and well covered from the gun-fort by Lieutenant Kane and the men of F Company, 1st Royal Sussex, with the result that none of the *anṣār* got within 600 yards of the British position.[25]

The valley in front had been silent for some time, when shortly before 2.00 p.m. a plume of smoke was observed rising from the ridge behind which the square had earlier disappeared. The group of spectators at the front of the *zariba* detected that the smoke was blue. They inferred from this that it must be caused by burning wood and concluded that Stewart had triumphed and must now be putting the enemy camp to the torch. They would have been hard-pressed to guess that the smoke had been caused by burning ammunition boxes and camel flesh. Not long afterwards they caught sight of some of the 19th Hussars, who appeared to dismount and engage targets with carbine fire. This of course would have been part of Barrow's cautious harassment of the Mahdist retreat.

That a victory had been gained was soon confirmed by the enemy disengaging on all sides and by the blissful silence that finally settled across the *zariba*. Peace and quiet could mean only one thing – there was time in hand to brew some tea. As if to betoken the changed situation, the breeze shifted, the oppressive afternoon air cleared and the sunshine seemed somehow to become more agreeable. After a while the four survivors of the Hicks expedition, who were to provide so much useful intelligence on the composition of the Mahdist force, came in from the high ground on the right to surrender. Their principal spokesman was a former sergeant,[26] a one-time resident of Cairo, who rather improbably had acquired a passing acquaintance with bad Italian by dint of having crossed the Mediterranean to work in a Naples hotel. After assuring his new British friends that he and his comrades had spent the night intentionally firing high, the flow of intelligence began. The bad news from the south was that Omdurman Fort had fallen, meaning that Gordon Pasha no longer enjoyed complete control over the confluence of the Niles. The rather better news was that a flotilla of his river steamers had for some time been operating well to the north of Khartoum, in the vicinity of Sabalūka and the Sixth Cataract.[27] This meant that they were almost certainly within easy striking distance of Metemmeh.

Occupation of Abu Klea Wells

Airlie's War Diary states that the re-organized square moved off in the direction of the wells at 3.00 p.m. With around 140 fewer bayonets to man its faces, it was a significantly smaller formation than formerly. The 19th Hussars having long since disappeared into the plain, infantry skirmishers were again thrown forward to screen the advance. This time the job fell to the stray section of riflemen in A Company, MICR, the 3rd KRRC detachment, under Marling.[28] Because there were insufficient camels left to carry all the seriously wounded, the Grenadier Guards Company was assigned to carry the balance on stretchers. 'The men were fearfully weak themselves through fatigue and thirst,' wrote Gleichen, 'but stuck to their burdens manfully all the same.'[29] In truth, where some men did precisely that, others were unable to cope and fell out exhausted. Getting all the stretchers to their destination required Colour Sergeant Ditchfield to chivvy the men to still greater endeavours. His DCM citation noted that he led by 'brilliant example' and did not rest until the last casualty was safely home.[30] The walking wounded struggled along as best they could, with the assistance of the able-bodied.

As all the remaining water had gone to the medical staff, the men still under arms were suffering the agonies of raging thirst, including cracked, blackened lips and painfully swollen tongues.[31] A number of played-out Tommies fainted during the march and had to be helped along by mates who were every bit as exhausted themselves. Observing Sir Charles Wilson's fragile state, 'Sankey' Herbert lent him his pony.[32] The Naval Brigade was so short-handed that even Beresford took a turn on the Gardner's drag-ropes. All in all the straggling, bloodied procession made a sorry sight. Some participants recalled that the march to the wells seemed to go on forever. Marling, for example, wrote, 'I thought we should never find the wells; they were four miles from where we fought – 4 such miles!'[33] Verner, on the other hand, said that the wells were three miles ahead and observed that the journey was, 'painfully slow'. In truth the distance was not much more than two miles and the journey, though slow, took only about an hour and three-quarters.[34]

Feeling a little better now that the worst of the heat had passed, Wilson rode on ahead in company with a small party of other officers. Though Wilson does not mention Verner, nor vice versa, it seems apparent from their accounts that they must have been together at this time. Following the line of the *khor*, they came upon the debris of the retreating Mahdist host, including prayer-mats, flags, discarded weapons, water-skins (which were swiftly sent back to the square for the wounded), camel saddles and a good many stray donkeys. The detritus of defeat was punctuated at intervals by dead and dying Arabs whose wounds had finally laid them low.

At one point the skirmishers came upon six dead and four wounded *anṣār* lying under a mimosa tree. An interpreter with the soldiers called on the quartet to come out and surrender. This they insisted they were physically unable to do; why did the British not come and take them? According to Burleigh they were told, 'Very good, put down your spears, and we will see you are well treated, and do all we can to cure your wounds.' 'Put down our spears infidel dogs!' came the angry reply, 'By God and the Prophet, never!' Once again the peremptory solution had to be applied.[35]

In due course a messenger from Colonel Barrow rode in to report that the wells had been occupied without opposition. Though Wilson describes the approach to the wells in a matter of fact way, suggesting that he simply came upon Barrow and his men watering their ponies, Gleichen injects a distinct note of desperation into the proceedings. He describes how, notwithstanding their head-start, the 19th Hussars had still not located the wells when the square closed up behind them. With Barrow's troopers still ranging through the scrub and daylight fading fast, he implies that hearts had started to sink, as minute after agonizing minute ticked fruitlessly by. Gleichen even maintains that Sir Herbert Stewart was on the point of turning the force back to the *zariba*, where there were still a few water-skins in reserve, when at last a hussar came galloping in from the left with the welcome news that the squadron had found and secured the wells.[36] Nor is Gleichen alone in this assertion; Douglas Dawson paints much the same picture.[37]

The wells turned out to be 'simply deep holes in the sand, thirty or forty in number, and mostly with one or two feet of water in them'.[38] The wounded were once again afforded priority, while the fighting troops stood patiently by, in perfect discipline, waiting for the staff to allocate unit watering holes. At last they were able to slake their thirst. To Count Gleichen and his exhausted Grenadier Guardsmen, the questionable quality of the water mattered not a jot:

One of my men, a great six-foot-three private called Rooke, who had taken me under his special protection, soon picked me out in the dusk, and presented me with a huge calabash full of cool milky-tea-coloured water of the consistency of thin mud. It was delicious! I drank till I was full to the brim, and then felt annoyed that I couldn't hold any more, for the roof of my mouth wasn't soft yet.

Lord Cochrane described his drink as sweet, yellow and muddy but 'very nice after the horrible water in my goat skin'.[39] Burleigh, the old campaigner, was more inclined to be generous, ignoring the mud and applying only the adjectives 'cold', 'pure' and 'inexhaustible', although the last was untrue. For Beresford, 'the water was yellow and of the consistency of cream; but it was cool, sweet and delicious'.

Sir Charles Wilson was interested in any potential sources of intelligence and was already perusing the captured letters and documents brought in by the 19th Hussars. The bag of prisoners was miserable, however, Barrow's sweep to the wells having netted only two wounded *anṣār* tame enough to be taken alive. The correspondent of the *Daily Telegraph* helped bring in a third uninjured man:

. . . but he was hardly a captive, for the man gave himself up. He had a Remington and 100 rounds of ammunition. His story was, that he had been one of the Berber Egyptian garrison, and since the fall of that place had been forced into the Mahdi's army. He was glad to escape from them he declared; and the fellow looked cheerful at being taken. A trooper of the 19th conducted him to General Stewart.[40]

When everybody had drunk their fill, Stewart moved the force onto an elevated, rocky piece of ground about 200 yards from the wells and gave orders for the defence of the position.[41] The troops would lie down in square around Surgeon Major Ferguson's makeshift hospital, where the doctors and medics were already frantically busy, setting up awnings and moving the wounded into some sort of shelter. The fighting units made a half-hearted attempt to cut down mimosa bushes for a *zariba*, although the result was unconvincing and would have done little to hinder a hard-pressed charge. Fires were lit for tea, but once again there were no hot rations and precious few hardtack biscuits left in the men's haversacks. The Royal Sussex were tasked to man an outlying picket to the left-front of the position.[42] Having been on duty the previous night, Lionel Trafford was relieved when Major Sunderland announced that he would command the outpost himself.[43]

Orders were given that at 8.00 p.m. Major Phipps was to march back to the *zariba* with a hundred volunteers from each of the camel regiments, 300 men in all, and fifteen bearer-company camels with *cacolets*.[44] Lord Cochrane, reinstated as baggage master, was to accompany Phipps and help supervise the forward move of the camel transport and stores. Burleigh decided that he too would go back, in order to write up his report for the *Daily Telegraph* and despatch it back across the desert to Jakdul Wells ahead of the offerings of his rivals.

We now come to perhaps one of the saddest elements in the story of the fight across the Bayūda. Earlier reference was made to the unpublished manuscript account of Sergeant Charles Williams. Of singular note is an open admission by Williams to an unpleasant reality which goes unmentioned in any other source. It is to the effect that lethal doses of opiates were administered by the surgeons to some of the most badly wounded. It had been in the nature of the battle that any man who fell amongst the *anṣār*, rather than at the feet of his mates where he could be protected beneath a hedge of bayonets, was doomed to be repeatedly stabbed with spears and hacked about with swords. We have seen how, coincidentally, both 'Jumbo' and Corporal Yetton each suffered no fewer than seventeen wounds. Sorely hurt as the pair were, there were others in an even more pitiful condition. The surgeons struggling manfully to patch up the six officers and sixty-five NCOs and men who had walked or been carried to the re-formed square were Doctors Ferguson, Parke, Briggs, Dick, Falvey and Maconachie. If Sergeant Williams is to be believed, and there is no compelling reason why he should not, they had started their ministrations with a slightly higher number of patients. Quite how many of the sixty-one other ranks technically killed in action had their passing eased by the doctors is impossible to know, although it was not likely to have been more than a handful. Here, then, are the words with which Sergeant Williams recorded the harrowing deed:

Whole night was so occupied – burying the dead [possibly a handful who had died of their wounds, but otherwise the dead had been left where they fell], dressing wounds, feeding and unfortunately placing by themselves officers and men who were considered past medical relief. To these a merciful drug was administered that permitted them to die in peace. Medical science and surgical aid had not reached present day heights at those times.

It was doubly unfortunate that the night was bitterly cold and that none of the medics had thought to pack blankets amongst the medical stores. Some officers judged that it was the coldest night of the campaign, but the combined effects of fatigue, hunger, dehydration, shock, dejection, damp clothing and the absence of greatcoats and blankets might have made the night seem more relentlessly cruel than might otherwise have been the case. For Charlie Beresford, though, 'it was the coldest night in my remembrance';[45] for Dawson, 'the coldest night I ever felt'.[46]

Huddled into a tiny square, Phipps and his 300 picked their way back across the starlit desert. From time to time the silence was broken by the groaning of wounded Mahdists. The journey back to the *zariba* was perhaps four or five miles in length and was completed in about two hours. Ever the professional, Burleigh trotted on ahead over the final mile, so as to be able to get on with his work. He arrived at about 9.30 p.m., about half an hour before Phipps and his troops, and promptly set about drafting a telegraphic report by candlelight.[47]

Jack Cameron must have talked to Burleigh about the events of the afternoon, because he too wrote his copy for the *Standard* that night rather than waiting for the morrow. Melton Prior had been sketching all day and was now sat on the ground adding the finishing touches by candlelight. Cameron joined him to share the light and to discuss how they were going to get their material back to London. They had jointly made an arrangement with a civilian meat contractor called Rees, who had been commissioned by the military to move beef cattle down the Nile to Korti. Rees had undertaken to honour cheques or chits from Cameron and Prior up to the value of £100. When the pair had completed their work, they went in search of a native camel driver, 'who was not wanted', as Prior put it, and willing to take their material via Jakdul Wells to Rees at Korti. In truth the mischievous duo were actually inciting a desertion and the theft of a government camel. They had to promise an exorbitant £50 sterling before they found their man – undertaking to pay £15 up front in gold, and give him a cheque for the balance, to be drawn on Rees at Korti. Unfortunately, the readers of the *Standard* never did get to read Cameron's report. Prior later established that their none too shrewd courier had been unable to resist flashing his handful of shiny sovereigns around amongst the native drivers at Jakdul. Although he began the second leg of his journey in perfect health, he failed to put in an appearance at Korti.[48]

Alex Macdonald had not long since fallen asleep on a pile of flour sacks inside the engineer redoubt, when he was woken by the bustle that broke out with Major Phipps's return. With the work of disassembling the biscuit-box forts and gathering in the stores for loading going on about him, he instructed his servant to saddle his horse and load up his camp gear. It was a bad judgement call as, unsurprisingly, Majors Gern and Phipps had resolved not to move off until sun-up. Macdonald now had to keep warm for the rest of the night using only the highland plaid he customarily carried in his kit. The braying of the camels, the chatter of a group of shivering Adeni drivers gathered around a nearby campfire and the banter of toiling soldiers served to keep him awake for most of the night.

Back at the wells, Charlie Beresford was freezing cold and in a disproportionate amount of pain from the cut across his fingers. Unable to sleep he 'sat on an

318 • *Beyond the Reach of Empire*

ammunition box and shivered'. After a while Douglas Dawson dropped by to scrounge some tobacco:

> I told him that my tobacco, together with my field-glasses, had departed into the desert with my steed County Waterford, which had run away. Dawson had six cigarettes, of which he gave me three. I would cheerfully have given a year's income for them, as I told him. We agreed that it was hard to have to die without knowing who had won the Derby.[49]

After spending some hours interviewing the prisoners and poring over captured letters and documents, Wilson, Verner and Stuart-Wortley decided to turn in for some much-needed rest. They did their best to keep warm by lying together under an abandoned prayer-mat that Stuart-Wortley had picked up in the *khor* that afternoon. 'I think we spent most of the time in trying to pull it off each other,' wrote Wilson, 'for none of us did more than doze for a few moments at a time.'[50] The men of the Royal Sussex dug themselves scrapes in the sand, but in the end were no warmer than anybody else.[51] Gleichen decided to squeeze himself between two camels, 'but directly I began to get warm the brutes would feel me and lurch over on top of me, till I was driven into the open again.' In the end he and half-a-dozen others gave up all hope of sleep and sat huddled together taking turns to suck on a pipe, in the hope that smoking might help soothe their pangs of hunger.[52] All the while Frederick Ferguson and his colleagues were toiling over the wounded by lamplight. The hours of darkness ticked slowly but surely by, until at length the near approach of a new day called the force to arms once more.

Sunday 18 January

Rather than a stalking enemy, the dawn betrayed nothing more menacing than the near-presence of a small herd of cattle, a remnant of the now abandoned Mahdīst commissariat. The native drivers were sent out to give chase but raised such a 'diabolical haroosh'[53] in the process that they succeeded only in spooking the cattle deeper into the desert. So jumpy were the cattle after their first fright that even a party of 19th Hussars was unable to round them up and had to be content with shooting a few animals on the hoof. There was plenty of nearby ground-sign to confirm an extended Mahdīst occupation of the wells, including old camp fires and discarded items of pottery. A little while later a roving patrol discovered a veritable village of rough straw shanties concealed in a nearby hollow.

Majors Gern and Phipps marched not long after dawn. Most of the camels were already in a sorry state, having been pushed hard on the shuttle-run and fed a paltry 8 lb of *dhura* on the return march to Jakdul. Since setting out for Abu Klea they had been given very little to eat and for understandable tactical reasons had been kept knee-haltered at halts, a measure which precluded any question of them grazing for themselves. Sunday 18 January was their fourth consecutive start without water. Alex Macdonald had ridden on ahead of the troops in order to pick over the scene of the previous day's fight, but was disturbed by a sudden outbreak of firing behind him. He raced back to the baggage train in the belief that it was under attack, only to find that a number of exhausted and badly wounded camels were being put down at the tail of the column.[54] The attrition of the transport through sustained mismanagement would only get worse over the days ahead.

Macdonald's brief glimpse of the battlefield included a number of curiosities:

I soon reached the place where the square had repulsed the charge of the enemy. Their dead lay in heaps, and in all imaginable forms of contortion. A few, however, had died without a struggle, for they lay on their gravel death-bed as if they had been laid out by loving hands. Others, who had crept away from where they received their mortal wounds, were seen kneeling in the Mohammedan attitude of prayer.

Some were aged men, but the majority of the slain were in the prime of life. One of the former, who lay dead near the watercourse where so many of the Arabs had lain in ambush, had a wooden leg of the rudest description.

Amongst the slain were also many mere lads, armed only with the short curved [throwing] stick commonly carried by the natives. [It should be borne in mind of course that most of the Mahdīst weapons had been gathered in and burned the previous afternoon.] One of these poor fellows, lying with his arms outstretched, still grasped his little stick in his right hand. His face was turned towards me as I rode past, and his unclosed eyes seemed to look up piteously at me.

Near the body of this lad was that of a man in the Mahdi's uniform, lying in a reclining position against a bush. He presented a terrible sight. For someone had driven a native battle-axe into his skull between his eyes, and left it there with the handle sticking out from his face! Who killed him? From the weapon used for the purpose, certainly none of our soldiers.[55]

A letter written by Percy Marling to his father makes it clear that a small number of wounded Arabs were shot dead as the column passed the battlefield, though in quite what circumstances is unclear.[56] Although no other source mentions the continued presence of the enemy, the ever-observant Burleigh spotted small bodies of *anṣār* watching the progress of the baggage train from distant vantage points.[57]

In the column's War Diary, Lord Airlie fixes the reunification of the force at 8.00 a.m.[58] The first priority was to get some hot food on the go, as the great majority of officers and men had not eaten a square meal for more than thirty-six hours. The first man Macdonald ran into at the bivouac was Sir Herbert himself. Anxious to get his report away, Macdonald offered the general his congratulations and enquired whether he would be sending despatches back to Korti: 'No, my orders are to take Metemmeh and secure a position on the Nile, and when that is done it will be time enough to communicate with Lord Wolseley.'

Something happened subsequently to change the general's mind. At 11.00 a.m. Macdonald got a message from him saying that he would be sending a courier to the C-in-C after all, and that if he had anything to go back down the wires to London it must be ready by 2.00 p.m. There was almost certainly a direct connection between the general's change of heart and the actions of the senior correspondents, for not only had Cameron and Prior managed to get a courier away, but so too had Burleigh. The general duly retired to a quiet corner to write up his own report. As earlier discussed it included a distinctly disingenuous passage which implied that the climax of the battle had incorporated an intentional bypassing movement by the British:

The enemy's main position was soon apparent, and by passing that position well clear of its left flank, it was manifest that he must attack or be enfiladed. As the square was nearly abreast of the position the enemy delivered his attack in the shape of a singularly well organised charge, commencing with a wheel to the left.[59]

Interestingly the despatches of the other correspondents appear to have been vetted before being sent away in the care of the general's couriers. While Macdonald's innocuous and in places inaccurate report for the *Western Morning News* passed muster, the one penned by Charles Williams for the *Daily Chronicle* found its way into Lord Airlie's haversack and duly went forward with the column rather than back with the couriers. It seems clear that this can only have been uncovered by Williams himself, perhaps on the basis of a tip-off from an officer who disapproved of such dealings. The offending report would not in the end be published until 25 February, more than five weeks after the events it described.

The editorial staff at the *Chronicle* felt no compunction about implying that the report had been intentionally suppressed on General Stewart's orders, though the report was lengthy and appears according to its header not to have been started until noon, which if the mail really did go at 2.00 p.m. might have left Williams hard-pressed to meet the general's deadline. If it was genuinely suppressed it may have been because Williams included the line, '. . . to tell the truth, we very narrowly escaped a very great disaster'. This was indeed the truth, but of course in no way chimed with the much more positive interpretation enshrined in General Stewart's version of events. It is not clear whether the postscript to the report, cited below, was always there, or whether it was added after Williams had retrieved his report from Airlie. Quite when he got it back is also uncertain, but it was not for at least two days and may have been up to two weeks or more. The inclusion within the postscript of the qualifying statement 'at Abu Klea' would tend to support the notion that it was not present in the original version and could not have contributed to the report's suppression. It certainly touched on a sensitive subject which, while it also happened to be true, was no less unpalatable than Williams's intimations of near disaster:

P.S. It has, I regret to say, been definitely ascertained that the order which resulted in the breaking of the square at Abu Klea, and the loss of life in the Heavy Camel Corps, was given by Colonel Burnaby, who had no position in the regiment, and was merely acting as a staff officer. He ordered the men to leave their positions, and he then ordered them back, but, unfortunately, too late for the square, for the Heavies, and for himself.[60]

While the battle for history got under way on paper, the officers and men of the 19th Hussars had more pressing business to attend to. Having disposed of a welcome hot breakfast, they rode back to the battlefield to bury the British dead, where they were joined by a number of HCR officers intent on saying a few prayers over the graves of their fallen friends. The hussars are said to have dug a long trench-grave about seventy yards forward of where the square's right face had been, a position plotted on Verner's map as Point L. I could detect no sign of this during my field work and was left doubting whether this was actually the case. Major Wilfred Gough of the Royals and Lieutenant Richard Wolfe of the Scots Greys are said to have been buried separately at Point F, roughly fifty yards from the position of the rear face. It is difficult to know why this should have been so, as the other deceased officers were not in this instance buried separately from the men, as was often the case at this period, and no explanation for their special treatment is offered in any of the sources. It is conceivable that the mortal remains of Gough and Wolfe had been attacked by scavengers and dragged to the spot at which they were interred, though why such a fate should have befallen two officers, but nobody else, is hard to imagine. Burnaby was interred a short distance away from the two stray officers, above the lip of the feeder *khor*, not far from where he fell. Major Byng read the funeral service over the British dead, with unburied Mahdīsts lying strewn on all sides.[61]

Intelligence, Decisions and Doubt

In the immediate aftermath of the battle, Stewart had been so shaken by the heavy British loss that for a while he had contemplated a long halt at Abu Klea to wait for reinforcements.[62] His doubts soon passed, however, and he seems never to have arrived at a serious or final resolution to that effect. His revitalized determination to push on may have originated with a crucial piece of intelligence presented to him by Sir Charles Wilson during the course of the morning. The four black soldiers who had surrendered at the *zariba* the previous afternoon had come in with the baggage train, presenting the intelligence officers with the opportunity to question the garrulous Italian-speaking sergeant. Wilson found him 'an intelligent man' and, for some unstated reason, 'an altogether most comical fellow to look at'. One potentially vital piece of information imparted by the sergeant was that the Kordofani contingent was only the advanced guard of a much stronger army which was even now marching north from Khartoum. It appears to have been a sincerely proffered statement, although it also happens not to have been true, an issue to which we will return later. Regardless of its questionable reliability the information nonetheless exerted a profound effect on Stewart's thinking. He now determined to press on to Metemmeh with all possible speed, with the idea of establishing himself on the Nile before the new Mahdīst force could come up. As he sat writing his despatches and mulling things over, he set his heart on making a long night march, commencing at 2.00 that afternoon. As there was a great deal of work to be done before the column would be fit to move anywhere – weapon cleaning, cooking, re-stowing baggage, replenishing water skins and fortifying the wells, to name but a few of the more essential activities – this sort of timetable would leave precious little time for the troops to enjoy so much as a catnap.

Wilson was similarly busy, drafting an intelligence report to accompany Stewart's despatch. Interestingly the idea that a fresh Mahdist force was even now on its way up the Nile, whilst it was being treated as hard intelligence by the general, was not portrayed in anything like the same light in Wilson's otherwise comprehensive report. Indeed it is only mentioned by implication in the passage, 'Prisoners captured report that the fort of Omdurman has been taken by the Mahdi's troops, and a portion of his army is thus set free for operations northwards.'[63] This is not the same thing at all as words to the effect of 'a freed-up portion of the Mahdi's army is now reported to be marching northwards'. It might be tempting to suspect, in the light of subsequent events, that Wilson had 'spun' the intelligence picture in writing *From Korti to Khartum* if it was not the case that, first, Macdonald dwells at length on the implications of the intelligence in his book, and second, that Verner's diary also confirms the substance of the prisoner's debriefing: 'They said that the great bulk of the force had arrived at the wells the day before we did and that another force was following from Omdurman.'[64] That Wilson failed properly to articulate this key information in his official report can perhaps be attributed to a combination of fatigue and the after-effects of heat exhaustion. In the event it proved not to be a serious omission, but only because it happened not to be true. The real significance of the intelligence, however, lay in the effect that it exerted on Stewart's decision-making, and indeed, subsequently, on Wilson's own.

The short extract from Verner quoted above is doubly significant in that it also establishes that the Kordofanis arrived at Abu Klea Wells on the 16th. Wilson's report, by contrast, is ambiguous on this point, stating that 'various tribes from Kordofan arrived on the morning of the action', failing to state whether he is referring to the start of the wider 'action' on the 16th or the general action fought on the 17th. The combination of Verner and Wilson enables us to conclude that the most likely scenario is that they arrived on the morning of the 16th, and that the Mahdist army was complete by the time the British cavalry screen made contact that afternoon. Wilson was rather more precise in respect of the other enemy contingents, stating that the force from Berber arrived at the wells on the 12th and that from Metemmeh on the 14th.[65] The length of the local contingents' stay at the wells accounts for the improvised village of shanties located by the 19th Hussars.

Orders and Intent

At about 1.00 p.m. Stewart called in the commanding officers to outline his plan.[66] When the intelligence concerning the imminent arrival of a second enemy host was disseminated, it caused a certain amount of consternation amongst the assembled colonels. Of the newspapermen, Macdonald alone would seem to have been within earshot. He describes in his book how one of the commanding officers, 'on the ground of this rumour advised him to fall back on Jakdul and wait for reinforcements. The only notice of this suggestion taken by our lion-hearted general was a contemptuous stare at the man who ventured to make it.'[67] There seems to have been much more widespread opposition to the idea of a night march.

According to Macdonald:

Several of the commanding officers had strongly advised General Stewart to postpone marching until early next morning, in order that the men might have a rest after their two sleepless nights and the excitement of the battle on the previous day. He resolved, however, to push on in order not to give the enemy time to recover from the effects of their recent defeat.[68]

Stewart heard the colonels out politely and then, as was his perfect right, discarded their advice. It must have been not long after the orders group broke up that Stewart, sensing the dented morale of his force, took time out to dictate an appropriately rousing special order of the day. It was scribbled into the column's Daily Orders book by Lord Airlie and was the last entry to appear under General Stewart's authority.

Brigade Orders by Brigadier General Sir H. Stewart, KCB,
Commanding Mounted Bde,
Abu Klea 18th Jany 85.

No. 1. The Brigadier expresses his most sincere thanks to the officers and men under his command for the great exertion that they have made during this march from Korti. Their exertions were crowned yesterday by a triumphant victory which proved once again what has so often been proved before that the courage of British soldiers when united with discipline is more than a match for any number of savages. The Brigadier General knows well what work the men are doing and he regrets most truly the exceptional labour which he is forced to ask from them in a trying climate under privation of food and water, but he is confident that they are animated by the same spirit which supports him and feel that if the trials are exceptional the honor [sic] of being called upon to undertake such work is exceptional also. The General deplores deeply the loss of so many brave comrades and laments that they were not spared to share the high reputation for fearlessness and discipline which was earned by them equally with the living.

The General asks the men for another display of courage and self-denial. We have to reach the Nile a distance of 25 miles and when that is done a large part of our work will be ended and a feat will have been achieved at the end of which every man can say that he has indeed striven to do his duty.

> By Order
> *Airlie*
> Captain
> Bde Major

Daily Orders commonly included the coordinating instructions for the following day's activities. In this instance Daily Order No. 1 was the only entry in the ledger for Sunday 18 January, confirming that Stewart gave his detailed instructions for the coming night march while he was face to face with the regimental commanders. There are no source references to the lonely written order being read at the head of the troops, which is not to say that it was not done, perhaps by regiments or companies. It is not clear what the standing mechanism for the dissemination of daily orders was. A strong possibility is that regimental adjutants were summoned to the brigade major by the bugle-call 'Report for Orders', in order to take notes to Airlie's dictation. Judging by Macdonald's remarks, the doubters amongst the commanding officers may have been as much the intended target audience of Daily Order No. 1 as their men.

As can often be the way with overruled cabals of colonels, the regimental commanders were probably, on balance, in the right. Aside from the urgent necessity to give their exhausted soldiers a decent night's rest, there was a second and particularly compelling reason to wait for morning. There may have been as many as fifty waterholes[69] sunk into the gravel, but they were all shallow and of limited capacity. By the time they had satiated the needs of Barrow's ponies and the human members of the column, there was insufficient water left to go round two and a half thousand dehydrated camels. The wells would gradually refill by percolation, but it was certain to be a time-consuming process and Stewart's decision was that he could not afford to wait. As logistic decisions go, this was about as big as they come. By failing to water his animals the general had started a stop-clock running.

The advance across the Bayūda had now reached the point where the operative sentence in Stewart's orders was, 'You will then advance on Metemmeh, which you will attack and occupy. For this it may be advisable to laager your convoy at the wells of Shebakat.' Although he had expressed himself sufficiently loosely to allow of a certain amount of latitude, clearly Wolseley could foresee the necessity to have a ready supply of water available prior to commencing operations against Metemmeh. Stewart, though, no longer intended halting at Shebacat, where the water supply might be dubious and the enemy could be waiting, but instead would strike out on a right oblique designed to bring him directly to the west bank of the Nile. Of all the wells on the axis so far only Jakdul had contained an ample sufficiency of water. There was every possibility that Shebacat might also disappoint and leave him critically short of water in close proximity to the enemy. The strike for the Nile would obviate any such risk.

Stewart's overriding concern, though, was to avoid a second general action by using the hours of darkness to achieve surprise. He would do this by keeping out of sight of Metemmeh and hitting the Nile about three miles upstream of the town. He would then be able to ensconce himself in a strong defensive position, with an infinite supply of water at this back, prior to undertaking further offensive operations. In *From Korti to Khartum* Sir Charles Wilson states that Stewart's intention was to breakfast on the river and attack Metemmeh later the same morning.[70] If it could all be relied upon to go unfalteringly well, then there was considerable merit in the scheme.

The problem lay in the inflexibility of the plan, for only rarely do operations of war work themselves through precisely as conceived. Insert a night march and the potential for things to go awry increases exponentially. If Stewart marched on without watering his camels for a fifth successive day, he was necessarily committing himself to reaching the river by sunset on Monday. He was, in other words, putting all his eggs in one basket. Also bearing down on the tactical conundrum was the apparently imminent arrival of the second Mahdīst force. In the lecture notes he prepared at some point in the 1890s, Willoughby Verner wrote, 'Another piece of news of serious import to us was that the Mahdi had sent a second contingent to bar our road to the river which still lay 24 miles ahead of us. Sir Herbert at once decided to push on at all risks and thus gain the river before this new force could oppose us.'[71] In essence Stewart wanted to be established on the Nile before having to fight anybody else, although in assessing his decision-making we should keep in mind that there was absolutely no intelligence to suggest where the second Mahdīst army actually was. It might, for all he knew, already be at Metemmeh.

A general seized by the compulsion to 'dash' must be able to gauge at which point the balance of risk tilts towards the inadvisable. While the boldness of Stewart's plan was commendable, he appears not to have fully contemplated the implications of failing to reach the river under the cover of darkness. If the night march fell even a few miles short of its object, he was certain to find himself short of options. By failing to water his camels prior to departing Abu Klea, he would be leaving himself with no alternative but to fight his way to the Nile by Monday evening come what may. Once the column was in sight of Metemmeh, with more than twenty miles of waterless desert to its rear and the camels on their last legs, any form of delay would very quickly become intolerable. Similarly retreat would be impossible, without killing hundreds of irreplaceable camels to the wider prejudice of Stewart's mission and Wolseley's campaign plan. Retreat, however, was the last thing on Stewart's mind. Balanced, reasoned risk-taking is one thing, an essential part of the military art, but there is seldom a valid justification for a commander at the tactical level acting in such a way as to jeopardize the C-in-C's whole plan of campaign. Therein lies the distinction between 'dash' and an irresponsibly cavalier approach. Taken in the round, Stewart was hovering over the dividing line.

If the night march was to proceed and there was any sort of fight short of the river, it was now certain that it would be fought in daylight on the 19th by troops who had last enjoyed a decent night's sleep on the night of 15/16 January. If it turned out to be anything other than a swift and handsome victory, the baggage train would be all but destroyed for want of water and there would be no stockpile of stores at Metemmeh with which to sustain the final approach to Khartoum. On top of that there was the danger of an unwieldy and vulnerable column being attacked in the dark to weigh. Such was the dramatic nature of Stewart's gamble. The alternative was to delay by about fourteen hours, march on Metemmeh in daylight and arrive in good order – with refreshed troops, high morale, camels fit to endure another four or five days in the desert and an infinitely greater array of tactical options still open. The downside to this otherwise attractive course of action was that it entailed a strong likelihood of a second general action in front of Metemmeh.

The commanding officers were not the only ones who doubted the wisdom of the plan. The ferocity and strength of the Mahdīst resistance to date was both surprising and daunting, and whatever moral ascendancy the British now enjoyed was about to be undone by the arrival of a second and apparently stronger Mahdīst force. Three of the war correspondents had been in the Red Sea Littoral, where Sir Gerald Graham had confronted comparably sized Bīja armies with three brigades of British troops. Even then the two big fights had incorporated moments of near-catastrophe, just as the previous day's victory had, in truth, amounted to little more than a narrowly averted disaster. Now Stewart intended pushing on with a single weak brigade of barely 1,300 effectives. In the circumstances it is perhaps unsurprising that there was a momentary loss of nerve amongst the war correspondents. Macdonald was approached by some of his colleagues and asked what he thought about returning to Jakdul Wells. His first instinct was that it was safer to go on with the column than to risk running into parties of enemy cavalry in the desert. Under pressure, he agreed to go back if the idea commanded the unanimous support of the press corps. It did not.

Cameron, to my surprise, was not amongst those who had made this proposition, because I knew he felt more keenly than any of us our critical and dangerous position. To his credit be it recorded that when approached on the subject he refused to return. His keen sense of duty made it a matter of honour with him to go on and face all the dangers that he feared still threatened us. And so this proposition to return broke down and we all went on together.[72]

Cameron might have deemed it his duty to stand by the troops, but was evidently gravely worried about the prospects of success. During the course of the early afternoon he approached Beresford and enquired, 'Lord Charles, have you any influence with General Stewart? If so for God's sake implore him not to go on without reinforcements. I know these people and he does not.' Beresford was generous enough to observe that Cameron 'was not alarmed for his own safety, for he was a most gallant man; but he feared for the column'.[73] His memoirs do not go on to say whether or not he actually made any such approach to the general.

Notwithstanding the lack of unanimity, a cabal of journalistic fainthearts evidently did seek permission to depart. It is hard to imagine that Bennet Burleigh or Sankey Herbert would have been amongst them. Frederic Villiers had not been approached and was still oblivious to the wavering of his colleagues, when a messenger arrived to say that General Stewart would like to see him.

He was flicking the dust from his boots with his whip; in spite of the dust and state of piggery we lived in for want of water, the general was always the most smartly groomed of all. I remember the picture made by his handsome figure, smiling face, and dark blue eyes, somewhat weary by want of sleep, and his smart Guards helmet, with the distinctive pugaree of orange silk, as he looked at me and said,

'You will wait until we get through this business, Mr. Villiers?'

'What do you mean general?' I replied.

Then he told me that the rest of the correspondents had asked permission to go back. If I had given a thought to returning, which I had not, I don't think I could have entertained the idea for a moment after that short conversation with Stewart.[74]

In the event all the correspondents persevered.

While the wounded would have to be moved back across the desert to Korti at some point, there would be no immediate opportunity to commence their evacuation. Instead they would have to be bedded down in the hospital tents beside the wells, until Metemmeh was safely in British hands and the trans-Bayūda lines of communication were fully operational. Airlie's War Diary notes rather vaguely that the garrison left behind at the wells consisted of 100 anonymous members of 1st Royal Sussex under the command of Major Harden. In fact it was the same B and F Company combination, a theoretical 4 and 125, which had earlier garrisoned the *zariba* under Majors Harden and Gern respectively, with the latter rather than the former in overall command. The Army List shows that Arthur Gern's majority was dated November 1883, and George Harden's August 1884.[75] That the brigade major[76] was in error is confirmed by Lionel Trafford's diary and by one of Burleigh's reports for the *Daily Telegraph*,[77] which in both cases specifically identify Gern as the officer in charge. In addition to the two infantry companies some small element of Major Dorward's detachment of Royal Engineers was also left behind; doubtless this would have been to work on improving the water supply.[78] A stone enclosure was hastily erected around the hospital tents to serve as a fort.

In the meantime 2.00 p.m. had come and gone: the difficulty in filling a multitude of water-skins from depleted desert wells compelled a temporary postponement of the column's departure. The general's couriers, a party of five camel-mounted *bāshi-būzuqs*, who had been given more than £100 in coin to race across the 149 miles separating Stewart from Wolseley, departed not long after 2.00. They would not reach Korti until Wednesday 21 January.[79] Between them they were bearing the GOC's despatch, Sir Charles Wilson's intelligence report,[80] the accounts and sketches of some of the war correspondents and a clutch of private notes from officers asking that well-placed friends on the staff send telegrams home on their behalf.[81] Verner's wife Leila would receive the brisk but no less welcome reassurance, 'Alright. Stop.' Happily there was also a rather more comprehensive letter travelling slowly behind the telegram.[82]

With the column forming up for the off, Stewart rode across to the baggage train to speak with Lord Cochrane. His instructions were that halts were to be called for only if broken-down camels or the onset of disarray made them absolutely unavoidable. As bugle-calls would not be allowed after dark, Cochrane arranged that the left-hand men of each section would act as a relay chain between himself and the head of the column. For the avoidance of 'Chinese whispers' the only permissible words of command would be 'Halt in front', or 'All right behind'. The baggage train would be moving thirty animals abreast, with the native drivers riding the lead animal in a string of three or four.[83] At the back there would be a reserve of fifty riding camels, now surplus to the requirements of the decimated Heavies, which Cochrane intended would quickly take over the loads of played-out animals.

With the death of Burnaby, Sir Charles Wilson now found himself the de facto second-in-command, and as such felt compelled to make one last attempt at talking Stewart out of a night march:

> I had always been dubious about the advisability of these night-marches, and before starting spoke to Stewart about this one, and pointed out that the men had had no sleep for two nights. He was, however, very sanguine; said that the men were in capital spirits, and that as it was only a matter of 25 miles, we should be at the Nile long before daybreak, and in time for the men to have a good rest before fighting.[84]

It was a bold assessment. It is hard to think of an example of a cross-country night march pre-dating the age of mechanization which succeeded in gaining anything like twenty-five miles. And yet the staff calculations, as is so often the case in these situations, seemed in advance to add up. According to Lord Cochrane the baggage train was capable of making 2½ miles in the hour;[85] Metemmeh was a mathematically convenient twenty-five miles away. The theoretical transit time, then, was ten hours. Building in two one-hour halts would mean that the column, had it departed Abu Klea promptly at 2.00 p.m., ought theoretically to hit the river at 2.00 a.m., some four hours before sunrise.[86] But the Desert Column did not depart promptly. It marched, in the end, at 4.20 p.m.[87] Had it left on time it would have enjoyed about 4½ hours of daylight at the beginning of the march, an itinerary which would have seen it about eleven miles closer to the river by the time the light failed. Instead, the delay left Stewart only two hours and ten minutes of daylight to play with. The 4.20 p.m. departure suggested a theoretical arrival time at the river of 04.50 a.m., a mere one hour and forty minutes before sunrise.

It would have been a tight schedule, with barely any margin for error, under a clear sky and a full moon. Unfortunately the night of 18/19 January would be illuminated only by faint starlight.[88]

Chapter 12

Endless Confusion

The Night March of 18/19 January

A longer or more exhausting nightmare I never suffered.

Admiral Lord Charles Beresford, *Memoirs*

THE EXHAUSTED, MAULED BUT VICTORIOUS Desert Column marched from Abu Klea Wells with its fighting regiments deployed 'in column of sections at close interval',[1] which is to say with its animals packed virtually nose to tail and a frontage of 25–30 files. The Guards Camel Regiment, sixteen ranks deep, took the lead, with the similarly arrayed Mounted Infantry following in their train. Next came Lord Cochrane's baggage train, with something around a thousand heavily laden camels in all. Immediately behind the baggage animals was the sombre and much depleted Heavy Camel Regiment. Major Sunderland's two-company detachment of 1st Royal Sussex brought up the rear. Excluding the advanced-guard and rearguard companies, the main body was around 600 yards in length. There would be times during the night ahead when the column would struggle to three or four times this distance. Ranging far ahead and two or three miles to either flank as long as the light lasted were the widely dispersed troops of the 19th Hussars. It took about three-quarters of an hour for the head of the column to make its way from the wells to the top of a low spur, beyond which point a rocky desert plain reached south for Metemmeh. The limits of the plain were marked by parallel low-lying ranges of hills, separated by an undulating expanse of about six miles. Whilst it was an unremarkable piece of terrain, the sand-coloured vistas unfolding ahead of the column were altogether more pleasing to the eye than the sinister grey-black shale of the Abu Klea Valley. Instead, a marginally less barren landscape was enlivened by dark outcrops of rock, occasional belts of savas grass and the inevitable scattering of mimosa trees. Some miles ahead there was a very distinct green belt of mimosa scrub and acacia trees.

Captain Willoughby Verner had been assigned by Sir Charles Wilson to act as the column's navigator. With his compass bearings prepared, the caravan route well defined and the Ambukol guides riding beside him, Verner could afford to relax for the time being. Though some of the guides were not overly familiar with this southern swathe of the Bayūda, Ali Loda, the 'celebrated thief'[2] captured near Jakdul on Stewart's first approach to the wells (no longer accompanied by his wife and child), claimed to know it well. Also present at the head of the column was

Colonel Percy Barrow, with a small party of 19th Hussars, and Lieutenant Edward Stuart-Wortley, the junior member of Wilson's intelligence team. Sir Charles himself rode with Stewart and the staff at the head of the Guards until sunset, but thereafter forged ahead to join Verner. From time to time the little scouting party of officers, guides and hussars came across the stiffening corpses of Mahdists who had been mortally wounded the previous afternoon and expired beside the caravan road during the course of the night.

It was probably fatigue which kept the war correspondents clustered together beside the baggage, instead of ranging up and down the column in two and threes as had been their wont up to this point. Lieutenant Count Gleichen, meanwhile, had drawn the short straw and found himself in charge of GCR's regimental baggage, a small and inglorious command consisting of seven native drivers, twenty-one baggage camels tied in strings of three and an escort of precisely eight Grenadier Guardsmen.[3] His task was easy enough while the light lasted, but would test his patience to breaking point after dark. By sunset the column had gained only 3½ miles at a rate of 1¾ miles in the hour, a slower pace than might reasonably have been anticipated in daylight.[4]

The point at which General Stewart discussed the route ahead with Ali Loda is not entirely clear: it may have been before setting out from Abu Klea Wells, or might conceivably have taken place at the head of the column. It would appear from their respective accounts that Wilson and Verner also participated in the same conversation. What is certain is that after his captors had described what they required of him, Ali Loda expressed reservations about the column being able to pass through the wide belt of scrub around Shebacat on a dark night.[5] His concerns were brushed off with the promise of a handsome reward if he brought the troops safely to the river. Although he appeared cooperative enough, content it seemed to assist the British in return for a handful of silver, he was nonetheless both a prisoner and a pressed man. Even now, many days after his capture, two precautions against his absconding were still in effect: not only was his camel firmly tethered to Verner's saddle, but his legs were tied together beneath the beast's neck.[6] It would in fact have been perfectly possible for the column to have diverged from the caravan road and in so doing bypass the Shebacat bush around its western or right-hand extremities, a route which would have taken the British over relatively flat, open desert, yet for some reason Ali Loda never thought to suggest this, nor did Stewart, Wilson or Verner press the right buttons in questioning him. Conversations carried on through an interpreter and across cultural divides are seldom all that illuminating, but this one seems to have been particularly uninformative. The irony was that diverging from the caravan road on a right oblique was precisely what Stewart intended to do anyway. That he should attempt to do so *after* passing through a belt of dense bush, instead of changing tack two or three miles earlier, made no sense at all, but such are the frailties of Man and the fortunes of war.[7]

Stewart ordered a halt around sunset, but any hope that it would be long enough to take a hot meal and rest for a few hours was dispelled when the order went round that henceforth there was to be no talking, no lights, no smoking and no bugle calls. In a matter of only minutes, the march resumed.[8] The caravan road continued broad and distinct even after dark, so that for about two hours the rate of progress remained substantially unaltered.[9] Verner calculated that by 8.00 p.m., they had come the best part of eight miles. Alone among the sources, Macdonald reports that not long after sunset a small fire suddenly appeared about half a mile to the right of the column, to be followed shortly afterwards by a second conflagration some distance to the right-front. His assertion that they can only have been beacons announcing the coming of the British is feasible but unsubstantiated: they could just as readily have been something to do with the 19th Hussars and a 'poor Arab lad'[10] who was brought in wounded not long after the fires appeared. Stewart ordered that the prisoner be placed aboard a bearer-company *cacolet* and later sent a message that he should be roped in to prevent his escaping. For a while the lad raised a racket that was audible half a mile away.[11] He must have passed out, calmed down, or have been gagged, drugged or beaten into submission, as he soon lapsed into silence.

For dozens of wounded, overladen or badly loaded camels, many of which had appalling maggot-ridden gunshot wounds or saddle-sores, the ardours of a relentless night march meant the end of the road. It was not long before the message 'Halt in front' was being relayed forward with monotonous regularity.

For five days they had been without water, and almost without any other food excepting an occasional bite of the long grass through which the column was passing at the time, or when it halted for the night.

It is not therefore to be wondered at that during this night's march one tenth of their number gave out and had to be left behind. I have already described the manner in which they were tied together head and tail. Often as I rode along the column by daylight I saw the poor tired brutes towed along thus, with their necks drawn out forward and at such a tension as to suggest that soon their heads might part company with them, or that the tail to which the halter of the lagging brute had been tied would give way. By-and-by some exhausted camel, though apparently willing enough to go forward, could not. With his forelegs he appears to be marking time. At last his utmost limit of endurance is reached, and down he goes gracefully enough, for he sinks kneeling as is his wont. The column is asked to halt until his load and saddle are hastily removed, often from a bruised and bleeding back . . . Relieved from this used-up means of transport, the word was passed up to the front: 'The rear is ready,' and on we marched again until some other camel had to be similarly abandoned.[12]

After the first few hours, Lord Cochrane's reserve of camels began rapidly to dwindle. When the last of them had been committed, there would be no alternative but to begin abandoning commissariat stores in the desert.

Disarray

The real trouble began when the native drivers did what they always did when they were tired and purposely dropped off to sleep in the saddle. Soon rudderless strings of baggage animals were proceeding much as they pleased. Any last vestige of regularity was quickly and irredeemably lost when the camels began 'crowding out of their places and streaming up both flanks to the front'. Macdonald went on to describe how the gaggle of war correspondents did their best to help:

> My colleagues and myself, who were then riding together on the left flank, attempted to drive back those which came up that side; but our efforts, I need hardly say, were useless, excepting when we came across a sleeping Aden driver and woke him up. The officers of the Mounted Infantry now became very anxious; for in the case of attack their movements would have been hampered by the crowding round them of this mass of camels.[13]

The demands of good order and military discipline carried the exhausted British soldiery a little further than the shameless civilian workers, but at length chronic fatigue and the gentle rocking of the camels overpowered even the most hard-core professionals. At any given moment from about 9.00 p.m. onwards, hundreds of soldiers were asleep in the saddle. Often they were inadvertently straggling away from their parent sections and companies; indeed some awoke to find themselves plodding along with completely the wrong regiment. It was not long before so many men were out for the count, that there was no longer any prospect of Lord Cochrane getting muttered messages passed to the head of the column. Melton Prior was one of the many unfortunates who fell asleep and took a tumble from a high-rise saddle:

> Camels are a good height, and it is not at all a pleasant sensation to roll off and come thumping down on the ground. Twice did I go through this silly performance; the first time I held on to the head-rope of the animal and easily hauled him down and remounted, but my second experience was bad: I rolled over on the sand and my camel was gone. I picked myself up quickly and ran in amongst the crowd of animals calling out, 'Lost my camel! Lost my camel!' until at last I heard what seemed to me a heavenly voice – 'Here you are, sir!'. . . No one, unless he has been in the same straits, would appreciate my feelings when I once more got hold of my camel's head-rope. A bluejacket had caught him. The reward of a good pull at my whiskey flask brought forth the simple thanks, 'Aye, aye sir, that's jolly fine; I'd like to be catching camels all night, sir.'[14]

Bennet Burleigh was a little more fortunate: 'Along with others, I nodded in my saddle, and narrowly escaped two or three bad falls in consequence. 'Go on! Go on!' was the cry incessantly uttered; and, heavy-eyed, half-dozing, the force mechanically moved forward.'[15]

Only rarely were the old desert caravan routes defined by what might be reasonably described as a road or a track. Much more typically they were characterized by a miscellany of trails. Most of the time, they ran broadly parallel to one another but there were also many junctions, crossroads and other points of divergence. In daylight it was easy enough for a traveller to scorn a false trail and maintain a consistent direction of travel. By night, not that many people felt moved to travel after sunset, it was a different matter. The caravan route to Metemmeh was of precisely this common or garden variety: there was no road to speak of. In the run up to midnight the increasing prevalence of long grass made it more and more difficult to tell the main trail apart from any other. It also served to conceal a multitude of ruts and depressions which tripped and harassed the camels and served to slow the rate of advance still further.

It is curious to think of something as innocuous as grass exerting an effect on an operation of war, but the camels were now so hungry that whenever the opportunity to make a bid for freedom presented itself, they went drifting into the desert to graze. For the most part their somnolent riders would wake with a start and, after a panic-stricken minute or two finding their bearings, were able to make their way back towards the column. Two soldiers and at least three or four native workers ran out of luck, however, and were borne away into the night. The first of the missing soldiers was 4717 Private W. Dodd of No. 2 Company, GCR, whose mishap happily came right in the end. Spotted not long after dawn by a party of enemy spearmen, Dodd managed to keep them at bay with his rifle and in due course made his way back to join Major Gern at Abu Klea Wells. 2185 Private C. Peters of the 5th Lancers was less fortunate, somehow fell into the hands of the enemy and was taken to Metemmeh to be murdered. The manner of his death is not known. According to Burleigh's *Daily Telegraph* report of 24 January, Peters died in company with 'two or three' native drivers.[16] On 6 February, some eighteen days after he was taken, the native lad employed as a servant by Charles Williams escaped his captors and rejoined the British. It was he who bore witness to the death of a soldier inside Metemmeh.[17]

Through the Shebacat Bush

After around five hours plodding through the dark, the thorn trees closed in around the column and the trail narrowed considerably. This obliged the commanding officers to halve their frontages, by moving their sections into two ranks from one. This, declared Ali Loda, was the Shebacat bush he had warned of: from here on the density of the thorn-bushes was only going to get progressively worse. Verner felt moved to pass the observation on to Sir Charles Wilson, who in turn dropped back to notify the general. Concerned that Shebacat Wells might be occupied by a lurking Mahdīst force, Stewart instructed Colonel Boscawen to dismount the Guards. Half the regiment was thrown forward on foot, while the rest of the men each led a pair of camels, a less than ideal tactical posture which, as Douglas Dawson observed, 'caused endless confusion'.[18] Although it is difficult to be sure quite how this was managed, it might well have been executed by odd and even numbers within sections. This would have left the regiment's fighting element configured in the usual four companies, but with half-strength sections. The ground allowed for nothing more complex than GCR's dismounted element marching in column of route behind Barrow, Verner and the guides. The tactical situation in which the Desert Column now found itself had all the hallmarks of a military disaster in the making. Fortunately for Sir Herbert Stewart, there was no enemy force lurking in the vicinity of Shebacat Wells.

It was not long before the vegetation overhanging the trail started catching on the rope-netting packs of the baggage camels, causing bewildered strings of animals to tie themselves in knots and obstruct the passage of others.[19] Wilson described the ensuing bedlam:

> The trees now began to increase in number, and at last we got into the thicket of acacia which Ali Loda had described. The tracks which had been numerous, began to diminish in number, until there was only room for a half-section of cavalry to pass between the scrub on either side. I was riding close to the guides at this time, so had a clear view ahead and few people near me; yet even then I had some little trouble in avoiding the long sharp thorns of the bushes.
>
> The column got into terrible disorder here. The mounted portion got through fairly enough, but the baggage-camels got jammed and entangled in the bush; many were left behind, others were extricated with difficulty. The confusion was endless, and the noise of swearing men and 'grousing' camels could have been heard miles away. The passage through the bush would have been troublesome enough in daylight for a convoy as large as ours; at night, with no moon, it was exceedingly difficult. Halts were frequent, and for a long time we made little progress.[20]

The loss in tangled, abandoned baggage camels appears to have been considerable. Macdonald noted that 'some said' afterwards that it had been, 'a hundred at least'.[21] Sir Charles Wilson wrote, 'No one will ever know the number of camels lost during the march, but it is supposed that over 100 disappeared with their loads.'[22] If these estimates were broadly accurate, then the night march cost the Desert Column 10 per cent of its commissariat stores. As Lord Cochrane had used up the last of the reserve camels, each new break-down was also costing a payload of provisions.

Breaking Track – The Right Oblique

When at length the head of the column broke free of the Shebacat bush and found itself on relatively open ground, Ali Loda advised Wilson and Verner that there was now a straight run into Metemmeh ahead of them, though marching directly on the town was not what Stewart intended. There would inevitably be a long halt while the rest of the force cleared the thick cover and closed up on the head of the column. Many soldiers dismounted as soon as their sections came to a halt and laid down on the ground to rest. It was about 1.00 a.m. when Verner reported to Sir Charles Wilson that in his judgement they had come fifteen miles. Aware that the GOC intended to leave the caravan road and push into the open desert on a right oblique, Verner represented to his chief, 'the difficulties likely to arise from such a proceeding'.[23] Wilson was not unsympathetic and rode across to speak to the general:

> I was in favour of going along the road to within two or three miles of Matammeh, and then halting to let the men have a good rest before daylight, after which we could attack

the town; and I pointed out that the men and animals were very tired, and that a long halt on the right road would enable the transport animals to close up and stragglers to come in. Stewart was, however, determined to go on and get to the river without fighting. He was quite opposed to the idea of fighting before reaching the Nile, and thought that we would be in a much better position if we fought with our backs to the river and made sure of water.[24]

Verner and Ali Loda were summoned to join the conversation, which was conducted where appropriate through Wilson's interpreter. Ali Loda appeared certain that the worst of the thorn bush lay behind them. Importantly, from the general's point of view, he was adamant that he could lead the column over the open desert to the river, without passing in sight of Metemmeh.

Although this was a critical decision point, nobody seems to have taken the trouble to do the time and space calculations necessary to support rational decision making. If Verner's estimate of distance was correct – and Stewart had nothing better to go on – the column had taken eight hours and forty minutes to gain fifteen miles. This equates to thirty-four minutes per mile, or safely less than 2 mph. With another ten miles to go, it could not possibly reach the river for another five hours and forty minutes. If Stewart could make an immediate start, maintain the same rate of advance (regardless of worsening fatigue), take no further rest-halts, check-navigate on the move and steer a perfect course from beginning to end, his command would arrive at the river at 6.40 a.m. Unfortunately, life, as they say, is not quite like that – soldiering even less so. If the column forged ahead its advance was now certain to be compromised some miles short of the river; if this happened there would in all likelihood be a stiff fight at the edge of the Bayūda. The options had now resolved themselves into push on, fail to reach the river and be forced to fight a battle with exhausted troops or, alternatively, halt while the column was still ten miles from the enemy, use the remaining five hours of darkness to sleep, and fight not long after midday at the head of rested troops. Being able to water the camels and rest the troops beside the Nile was an attractive notion, but at 1.00 in the morning of 19 January 1885 could no longer be regarded as a realistic proposition. Unfortunately Stewart chose to place his faith not in rational time and space calculations, but in that eternal and ardent agent of military disaster, wishful thinking.

Many of the men resting on the ground were so fast asleep that they had to be kicked or shaken awake. A great grumble of reluctance arose from the camels as their riders clambered aboard and urged them back onto their feet. Wilson penned a vivid portrayal of the next couple of hours:

Stewart decided to go on, and the guide was told to take us well clear of and out of sight of Matammeh. A bearing was taken from the map for Verner to use, and I picked it up on the stars to keep a check on both. At 1.15 am we moved on over a fair country, with scattered trees and no path. The column, which had become disorganised during its passage through the bush, seemed now to have got into hopeless confusion; men and animals were quite

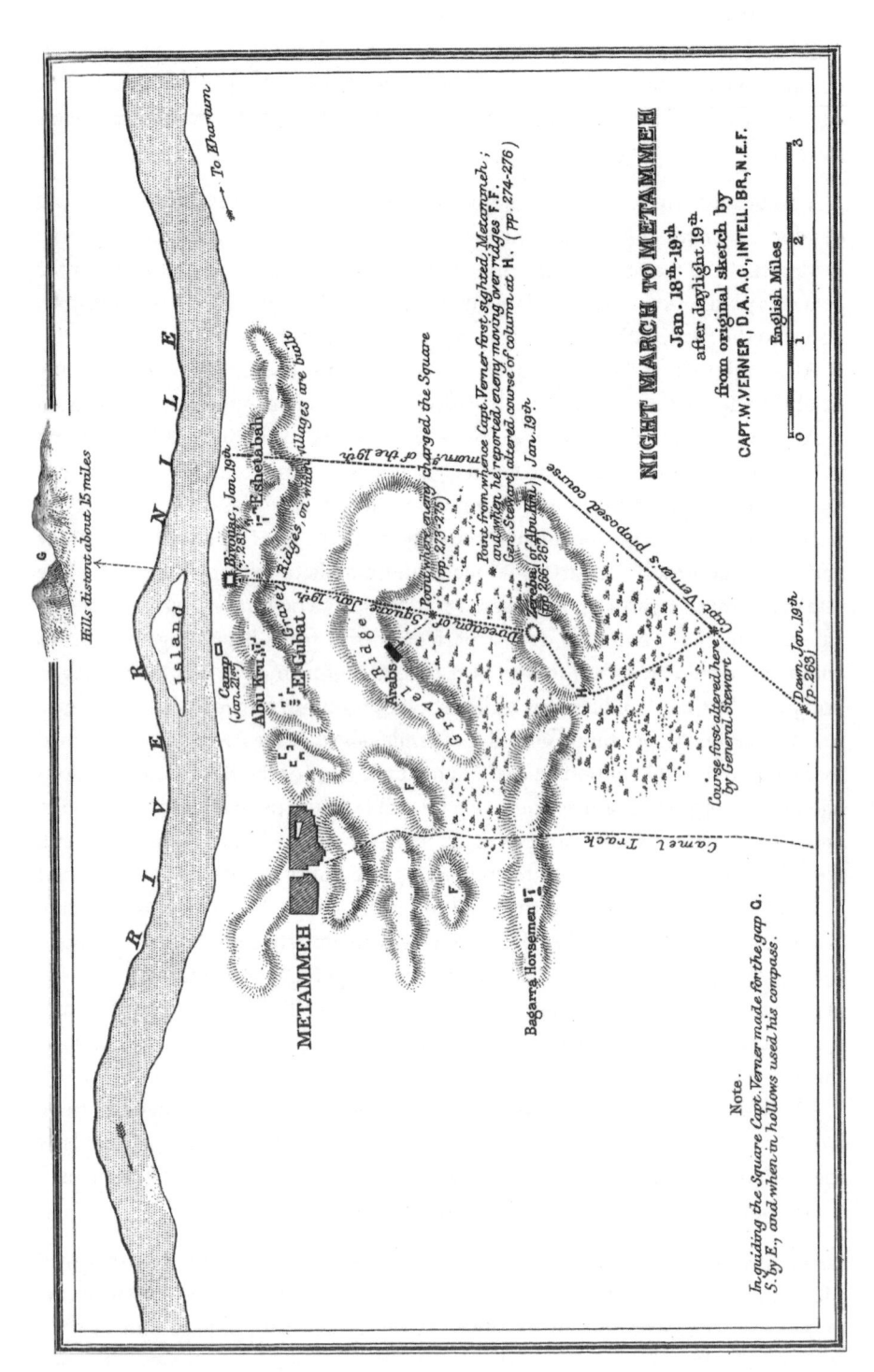

Map 10: The British approach to Metemmeh

worn out, progress was slow, and there were frequent and long halts. I rode with or close to the guides, and during the halts generally went back to Stewart, who rode near the leading company of the Guards.

It was a strange experience. During the halts loaded camels, whose drivers had fallen asleep or allowed them to get loose in the dark, kept moving on until they reached the head of the column, and appeared before us gaunt, spectre-like, in the dim starlight. Then, as we moved they moved, so that at last the head of the column was a mob of guides, hussars and driverless camels. We tried to get rid of the brutes, but had to give it up as hopeless, for we could get hold of no drivers, and the animals would not be driven back. So great was the confusion, that at one halt part of the column, following some of these loaded camels, came up from near the rear to the front. All this was very wearying for the men, and those marching were rather done up with their struggle through the savas grass and bushes. Directly the halt sounded,[25] every man lay down, to snatch, if he could, a few minutes sleep. But the most extraordinary feature was the noise. From the transport animals and their drivers a loud continuous roar rose up to the sky, which must have been easily heard at Matammeh, and probably gave the enemy their first notice of our flank march.[26]

When in 1926 the ageing Earl of Dundonald (formerly Captain Lord Cochrane) wrote *My Army Life*, he felt moved to suggest that the column had been led astray by treacherous guides, in much the same way, he asserted, as Hicks Pasha in Kordofan. He fails, however, to offer any evidence in support of the contention. By contrast Willoughby Verner's account serves to make clear that Ali Loda served the British faithfully:

From the start he showed a tendency to work off to his right, i.e. to steer a more westerly course than I deemed expedient. This I checked at first, but as I found that he invariably returned to his course as soon as he could, I decided it was best to leave him to his own line as long as I was satisfied that he kept true to it and, when daylight appeared, to wheel to the left if necessary and make for the river at the most suitable point.

I was strengthened in this resolve by Lieutenant Colonel Barrow who, with his Hussars, was near me during the whole of the night-march and was of the opinion that Ali Loda's course was a perfectly true one. Generally the course taken was south by west by half west. At times it was more to the westward to avoid rocky spurs running into the wady we were following. I may here state that Ali Loda's reason for not taking the course I wished was that it would lead over high ground where we would be visible when day broke. A subsequent inspection of the ground has proved this to be perfectly correct.[27]

Dawn, Monday 19 January 1885

When at about 5.30 a.m. the first signs of dawn appeared in the east, the general again brought the column to a halt and held a lengthy consultation with the knot of officers leading the way. Stewart and Wilson thought that the column should now be within striking distance of the Nile and were disappointed to find Ali Loda talking as if it were still some distance away. Wilson wrote that, 'we began to think he was taking us too far away from Matammah [*sic*], as Stewart did not want to strike the river more than three miles above the town.'[28] Verner's diary would suggest, however, that the column had made as few as four miles in the preceding 4¼ hours.[29] If his estimate was correct, the British were still around six miles shy of the river at this juncture, a distance endorsed by both Wilson's and Macdonald's accounts. Here, then, was another key decision point. It was still not too late to draw a line under the night march and rest the troops at a safe distance from the enemy, but wishful thinking was once again set to triumph over logic. Verner described the outcome of the consultation:

> It was generally decided that the course I had taken was far too much to the westward and would bring us to the river many miles above Metemmeh. Eventually the general ordered the column to move in a direction which may be described as south-easterly. I told him that I was firmly convinced that this course would take us right on top of Metemmeh. The general, however, said he wished to go the nearest point of the Nile, and Ali Loda was given, through the general's interpreter, fresh orders to conduct the column there.[30]

There then appears to have been a delay of about half an hour while Stewart waited for the sun to come up.[31] Having mislaid his regiment's baggage for most of the night, Gleichen now took the opportunity to herd his command back together. Only two camels could not be located. Somebody advised him that the reason they were missing was that they had been cut adrift by the Egyptian driver who had charge of them, in order that he could sleep better on the march. Gleichen had one of his burly Grenadiers take the *kourbash* to the villain and told him he would be walking the rest of the way.[32] Most other people, meanwhile, had taken the opportunity to throw themselves down beside their camels for a catnap. Long before they had managed anything like forty winks, they were on the move again. The change of direction imposed by Stewart served to swing the column off its right oblique, onto a slight left oblique (*see Map 10*). Verner remained convinced that the new bearing would bring them directly to Metemmeh in precisely the manner Sir Herbert sought to avoid. 'From this time,' he wrote, 'I did not consider that Ali Loda had a fair chance; as he still tried to work off to the west, he was more or less compelled to follow the cavalry party who escorted him.'[33] Though it was now light and everybody was awake, the camels were far too tired to pick up the pace and progress continued to be painfully slow. After making about two more miles, Stewart finally accepted that the Nile was nothing like as close as he had imagined and again called a halt. Verner asked if he could take a party of hussars to scout over the next few rises and was duly given an escort of a sergeant and four men.[34]

Before the column resumed its march, a party of Barrow's men came in with a prisoner, a black African goat-herd, whose animals the 19th Hussars had also annexed to the Crown and which now supplied some of the officers and men at the head of the column with a refreshing drink of milk. The bewildered prisoner proved a poor conversationalist and failed to provide any information of note.[35] The barking of the man's dog betrayed the near presence of his shack, together with a shed housing several fully charged water-skins, which were passed around at the head of the column and quickly drained. Another detachment of 19th Hussars brought in a second prisoner, a young man dressed in 'the Mahdi's uniform'. By now the intelligence officers were aware that all male residents of the area were required to dress in this fashion as a sign of fealty to the movement. The young Arab was effusive in his compliments to the British but, like the goat-herd, had no intelligence of import to offer. He was evidently not taken seriously as an enemy combatant, as he was not placed under guard and disappeared soon afterwards. Not long after the column had moved off again, the scouts stumbled across a black slave-boy, who was so amazed by the sight of so many camel-mounted and apparently friendly white men that he followed the line of march for some time.[36]

The View into the Nile Valley

Having pushed about two miles ahead of the main body, Verner trotted onto a low gravel knoll from which he gained an expansive view into the Nile Valley. He was at no great elevation, however, so that the slightest obstruction to his line of sight made it difficult to tell what might lay beyond. The familiar sound of throbbing *noggara* told him at once that the enemy around Metemmeh were alive to the near-approach of the British. The course of the great river was marked by the usual belt of green, although the lie of the land was such that it was much more readily discernible in some stretches than others. Beyond the river lay an irregular line of precipitous-looking whale-backed hills. There were no corresponding high features on the near side. Instead there was an almost dead flat plain of about 3½ miles in width, bounded at its southern extremity by a low, flat-topped gravel ridge which served to separate the Bayūda Desert from the cultivated flood-plain astride the Nile. The ridge was anything up to seven miles in length and generally about three-quarters of a mile wide, though at its eastern extremity, to Verner's half-left, it broadened in the environs of mud-brown Metemmeh into a plateau of about 1½ miles in width. While there was a scattering of green mimosa bushes across an otherwise gold-coloured plain, the distant ridge was all but devoid of vegetation, save in one or two places where there were small groves of acacia trees. There was a string of primitive mud-built settlements along the narrower stretch of ridge west of Metemmeh. Most of the British did not worry too much about which proper name applied to which cluster of buildings, so that our best tactic in understanding the layout of the habitation is to follow one of Verner's maps (*see Map 11*). Confusingly 'Gubat' was a name which could be applied both to a mid-river island and a village. The village of Gubat, located only about two-thirds of a mile from the walls of Metemmeh, was the left-hand or easternmost cluster of buildings atop the ridge. Abu Kru, the right-hand settlement, lay around two miles west of Gubat, not far from a prominent re-entrant, where a glimpse of green suggested to Verner that the Nile ran relatively close to the village. There were two hamlets, the names of which seem not to have been recorded, lying between the two more substantial villages, as well as a scattering of dwellings on the reverse slopes of the ridge which for the present were not visible to the approaching troops. It should be noted that the British would come to refer to the defensive position they eventually established on the river as 'Gubat': notwithstanding that the village of that name was more than a mile away; the site was actually equidistant between Abu Kru and Gubat; and the closest cluster of buildings was in fact one of the unnamed hamlets. The riverbank position would be sited directly opposite Gubat Island, however, so that in that sense at least, it represented as good a name as any. Where most officers and soldiers would confuse matters – as Verner pointed out in his *Sketches in the Soudan* – was in also referring to the nearby hamlet as 'Gubat'.

Although he did not for the moment enjoy a particularly good view of it, Verner knew that the town of Shendy lay a mile or two downstream of Metemmeh, on the opposite side of the river. Because the British had been led to believe that Metemmeh was the smaller of the two towns, Verner found its dimensions surprising. In fact they had been misinformed and the reverse was true, albeit this is no longer the case today. Scanning the landscape for the source of the distant tom-tomming, Verner spotted two substantial bodies of *anṣār* in front of Metemmeh, both of which appeared to be moving forward, 'to occupy what looked like trench work facing north'.[37] There were also parties of horsemen galloping about between the villages and hamlets atop the ridge. When he felt certain that he had taken in everything there was to see, Verner turned his horse and cantered his little knot of cavalrymen back towards the column.

In the interim the main body had been plodding slowly forward. The growing suspicion that he was probably riding towards yet another costly general action in the Sudan did little to improve Jack Cameron's black mood. Melton Prior was riding beside him and innocently remarked, 'By Jove, old chap, we are in for another fight, and I don't like the idea of it at all.' 'If you don't like it, if you are funking, why did you come? You had better go back!' came a somewhat testy reply.[38] Cameron then rode on ahead of the rest of his colleagues in company with Macdonald: 'He seemed unusually anxious and depressed, and said to me; "Well, I would give a five pound note if our backs were to the Nile; wouldn't you?"' When they gained a minor rise from which Metemmeh and Shendy were just discernible, Cameron seemed to brighten a little. Not long afterwards the general and his staff trotted up behind the war correspondents and they all rode on together towards another nearby rise. It was about 6.40 a.m. when they came to a halt to take in the view.[39]

While the course of the Nile was plainly identifiable away to the far right, the low elevation of the new vantage point made it difficult to tell what line they ought to take if they were to reach the river by the shortest possible route, or for that matter quite how long it would take to get there. After a few moments scanning the landscape ahead, Macdonald lowered his binoculars, drew everybody's attention to one of the hamlets on the ridge and declared that he could see the westernmost tip of a river island just to its right-rear. He then opined that it would take about an hour and a half to get there. Sir Charles Wilson appeared doubtful and asked Macdonald if he really thought that they could cover the distance so quickly: 'Feeling that an important crisis had arisen requiring decisive action, I reaffirmed my opinion with all the vehemence allowable to one in my position.' The curious slave-boy, whose continued attentions were doubtless attributable to some tasty titbit proffered by one of the officers, was still trailing along beside the headquarters staff. The fact that General Stewart was desperate enough to call the lad over and enquire through his interpreter whether he knew the best way to the river is indicative of just how difficult it can be to 'read' the Nile Valley without the benefit of a commanding view.

Before the conversation, such as it was, had run its course, a renewed bout of tom-tomming drew everybody's attention back towards Metemmeh. Large crowds of *anṣār* were now pouring out of the town and moving along the gravel ridge to the west. 'After all,' observed Stewart, 'we shall have to fight our way to the Nile. We ought to have been here two hours ago, and should have been but for those unfortunate camels.' There is something of the poor workman blaming his tools about the remark; the more awkward truth was that Stewart himself had ruined his baggage animals in a gamble he was always going to lose. The general and his staff now trotted back to the head of the approaching column.

At around 7.00 a.m. Captain Verner and his five-man detail of hussars came riding in. The oral report given by Verner to the general made it abundantly clear that there was next to no prospect of getting to water without fighting for it, and included the important observation that one of the settlements on the ridge looked like it would offer a strong defensive position and be within relatively easy reach of water. Stewart asked Verner whether he had identified any good commanding positions en route to the river and on hearing his description of the high point from which he had been observing Metemmeh directed him to lead the column towards it. Sir Charles Wilson asked the general what he intended to do and was told in reply that, 'he was going to close up the transport, and then march for the river, with his fighting men on the left between the transport and Matammah [*sic*]'.[40] Colonel Barrow was then instructed to push the 19th Hussars out to protect the left, while the camel regiments and baggage train resumed the march. Wilson decided to accompany the cavalry and would not play a role in any of Stewart's subsequent decision-making. The course now set by Verner was a pronounced right oblique (*see Map 10*). It is clear from Percy Marling's account that A Company, MICR, was also thrown out to the left of the column at this juncture, to act as a flank guard.[41] There is no suggestion that it dismounted at any point.

It was at around 7.45 a.m. that Stewart made the first major modification to his plan. The sound of musketry popping in the distance indicated that Barrow's cavalry screen was skirmishing to the column's left. The head of the column was still about half a mile shy of Verner's high point, when all of a sudden enemy riflemen opened a 'smart fire' from the British left.[42] At a range of more than a mile the fusillade was all but pointless as an act of war: its real significance was that it served to notify Stewart that the enemy had no intention of waiting limply at Metemmeh while he teed up an attack. If the enemy were all over the plain, instead of only to the left of the British axis, attempting to push the baggage train through to the river was bound to be fraught with danger. To Stewart's mind there was nothing aboard the baggage camels which the fighting troops could not afford to forgo for a few more hours. The obvious solution was to leave the animals in a defended position on this side of the plain and push ahead with the fighting echelon only. A low round-topped knoll just to the right of his line of march caught Stewart's eye, obviating any need to reach the high point earlier commended by Verner. Melton Prior heard the general announce to the staff, 'This position will do for me.'[43] As the column stuttered to a halt, a staff officer galloped away to tell Lord Cochrane that the general was anxious to speak to him:

When I came, he said, 'I am taking the column straight on to the Nile, but am leaving the transport here under you,' pointing to a spot some 250 yards to the right; 'I will send you the company of the Sussex Regiment, and with the regimental baggage-guards you will be able to hold your own.'[44]

Major Sunderland duly assigned Trafford's C Company to stay behind with the baggage.[45] Once the native drivers had moved their strings of grumbling camels onto the knoll, Cochrane and his NCOs started dropping them onto their haunches in the shape of a hollow square, each face consisting of several parallel lines of animals. Cochrane then had all the animals' head-ropes tied to the saddle in front, so as to create an improvised entanglement which he hoped would at least slow down an enemy rush. He left an entrance at the right-rear of his square, which he covered with a traverse of biscuit-boxes. Clearly this was not the work of five minutes; quite what the fighting troops were doing while Cochrane and Trafford were preparing their defensive position on the knoll is not plainly stated in the sources. I can find no hint that they actually moved off into the plain. That being so, the most likely scenario is that they were forming up in front of the knoll, in preparation for enacting Stewart's battle plan.

It was now that an important intervention described in Alex Macdonald's book took place. Quite what was said in the close detail is not clear, but it appears to have been the brigade major who did much of the talking. After spending some little while watching the enemy through their binoculars, Airlie and other unnamed members of the staff arrived at the conclusion that the general's plan was no longer tenable. The advice they now placed before their chief probably centred on three key points. First, there was the physical condition of the troops to consider; their chronic fatigue aside, they had last eaten at around midday the previous day. If they were now to be exposed to the same sort of violent physical exertion that had characterized the action at Abu Klea, it was imperative that they be allowed to fortify themselves with a decent meal first. Second, it would be tactically prudent in the face of such a strong and determined enemy to give battle in square. The third and decisive factor was that the *anṣār* were already deployed in strength directly across the British axis. This meant that fending off the enemy on the left flank alone would no longer suffice. In other words the direction of enemy threat now lay across a frontal arc of more than 180 degrees.

After thinking things through for a few moments, Stewart nodded towards the baggage train and announced, 'I will occupy that position. I intend attacking the enemy as soon as the men get something to eat.' The low knoll was only ever intended as a temporary defensive position but looked, even to a mortified Alex Macdonald who had nothing but his common sense to draw upon, 'like an uncanny and dangerous place to halt in under the circumstances'. 'For any sake,' Macdonald suddenly interjected, 'do not halt the column here, but defend your left flank and boldly advance.' He wrote later that, 'I received no reply to my impulsive appeal, excepting an anxious look.'[46] The staff were already on their way to tell the colonels to move their units to the foot of the knoll.

We might ask ourselves, admittedly somewhat idly as the decision had now been made, which of the two courses of action, halt, fortify and eat, or alternatively fight straight on through to the river, was the correct one in the circumstances. On the one hand, there was every possibility that any attempt to push through to the Nile with the ponderous baggage train in tow might result in its wholesale destruction. On the other, a successful holding action would require a more readily defensible piece of terrain than was presently on offer. The night march had been a sound enough idea but failing to draw it to a close before now, when for the past five hours at least it had been perfectly obvious that it could not possibly succeed, amounted to woefully bad judgement. And herein lies a key point: by 7.30 a.m. Stewart had put himself in a position where *all* of his options were in some way unsatisfactory. Indeed, they might yet prove to be pregnant with disaster. Sad to say the price of Stewart's wishful thinking would now have to be paid in that costliest of commodities, the lives of British soldiers.

Sir Charles Wilson had been against the idea of a night march from the beginning and in *From Korti to Khartoum* would make the telling point that Metemmeh might actually have been attacked earlier, if only the night march had been terminated at Shebacat:

So ended the night-march, which I cannot think was necessary, for the days were not hot, and the men would have fought much better after a night's sleep and a good breakfast. Had we halted when the column came to grief in the bush, every one would have been fresh in the morning; we should have had our fight close outside Matammeh, and been into it and on the Nile by mid-day. As it was, we were in laager, with camels and horses that could scarcely walk, and men who had been marching all night, and who had had no rest for three consecutive nights. Men under such circumstances get into a nervous 'jumpy' state, which might lead to a grave disaster.[47]

It was fortunate then that the men of the Camel Corps were made of stern stuff.

Chapter 13

The Fight to the Nile

The Battle of Abu Kru: 19 January 1885

> If ever a little British army looked like walking to certain death, it was that thin square of infantry.
>
> Admiral Lord Charles Beresford, *Memoirs*

THE POSITION IN WHICH STEWART finally brought his march to the Nile to a halt was in no sense a strong or particularly commanding one. It was nothing more, in fact, than a low, oval-shaped knoll covered with a veneer of wind-blown sand and a scattering of grey-black gravel rocks. Nothing much grew there, nor were there any hollows, rocky outcrops or good-sized boulders, so that it offered not a whit of cover, either from view or from rifle fire. It stood proud of the general lie of the land by barely twenty-five feet at its highest point and was perhaps 300 yards in diameter. It nonetheless enjoyed an extensive view to the south, both half-left towards Metemmeh and dead ahead towards the long gravel ridge shrouding the flood-plain. The fields of fire took in a dead flat desert plain dotted with mimosa bushes and occasional belts of long grass; ground cover fit to provide skulking enemy riflemen with any number of well-concealed fire positions. The view to the right of the axis was fine for the first sixty or seventy degrees, but was then obstructed by a low spur of perhaps 200 yards in length, which originated just to the right-rear of the knoll and arced round in front of it. It was so insignificant a feature that Burleigh remembered it as 'a little double-crested pebbly mound'.[1] Only about a third of its overall length jutted forward of the knoll to impede the view into the plain. Because the highest point on the spur was marginally higher than the crest of the knoll, there was an almost limitless amount of menacing dead ground away to the British right. The two features were separated by a shallow re-entrant of 70–80 yards in width. It was glaringly apparent that the spur could not be left unoccupied; apparent, indeed, for those with the eyes to see, that it would have to be fortified and held at all hazards. About 350 yards in front of the knoll, running across it at something close to a right angle, there was an extremely low ridge of around 300 yards in length. At its highest point the feature stood barely fifteen feet proud of the plain and tapered away to significantly lower elevations at both extremities. Like the spur, this was not a ground feature Stewart could afford to cede to the enemy, for fear of enemy marksmen ensconcing themselves in good cover.

Those officers who took the trouble to raise their binoculars in the direction of the river could see that there were already hundreds of white-robed forms flitting towards them through the scrub. Beresford estimated their strength at 'about 600'.[2] It was hardly necessary to be an avid student of the Mahdīst way of war to grasp that the Remington rolling-block rifle would shortly be intervening in the fortunes of the day. Any idea that the troops would be able to enjoy a revitalizing hot breakfast before having to give battle was fast receding. While the rifle-armed *anṣār* were evidently intent on harassing the British at the earliest possible opportunity, the fact that the Mahdīst main bodies were still resolutely installed on the long gravel ridge above the flood-plain, the best part of two miles away, suggested that the *amīrs* again intended to wait for the British to take the initiative. All the early evidence hinted that the coming action would have much in common with Abu Klea.

Digging In

Company by company the fighting regiments moved back towards the knoll, where they dismounted and knee-haltered their riding camels around the outer edge of the great square of transport animals already *in situ*. The constraints of space meant that hundreds of camels ended up in the low ground at the foot of the knoll. The troops were then allocated regimental and company arcs in what might be characterized as a loose square, although it very much conformed to the lie of the land and seen from above would have had a distinctly irregular shape. Its northern half faced back into the Bayūda, while its southern half overlooked the Nile Valley and the principal direction of threat.

Starting in the north, at the rear of the position, and moving clockwise around the perimeter, Stewart deployed his command in the order: 19th Hussars; Royal Engineers; the Naval Brigade; MICR; GCR; HCR; Royal Sussex.[3] Hence the three Camel Corps regiments found themselves at the front of the position, with the Mounted Infantry on the left, facing south-east, the Guards in the centre, facing due south, and the Heavies on the right, facing south-west. Beresford and the Naval Brigade were at the left-rear corner, where they emplaced the Gardner to cover the British left flank. The Royal Artillery screw guns were deployed to the left-front of the position with arcs facing the river and the principal direction of enemy threat.[4] The 19th Hussars, whose skirmish line had for the past hour or more been supported by A Company, MICR, were the last to fall back to the perimeter. Major John French had his men tether their ponies to the north of the knoll, its blind side, where for the present they would be much better protected than the camels atop and in front of the feature to the south.

With a good many long-range shots dropping onto the knoll, Stewart gave instructions that the commissariat stores and camel saddles be unloaded and arrayed around the transport animals as a low breastwork. Most of the riding camels would have to be left outside the perimeter, where they could be covered by fire and would serve as an impromptu obstacle to an *anṣār* charge. The jutting spur to the west of the knoll meant that they would at least be in dead ground to riflemen sniping from the British right. The elevation and convex slope of the knoll meant that the animals inside the defences would be far more exposed to incoming fire than the ones left outside the perimeter in the low ground. Cochrane's baggage camels were so densely jammed together that the troops found it extremely difficult to move around amongst them: lugging heavy saddles and boxes of provisions about only served to make it a doubly difficult proposition. In consequence the work of erecting the defences was both labour-intensive and time-consuming, and served to preclude any possibility of the British quickly transitioning to the offensive. While the barricades were being thrown up on the south side of the perimeter, the Engineers and others set about cutting down and dragging in all the thorn-bushes within a practicable striking distance, but the enemy were closing fast and time was short. In the event the improvised defence stores stretched far enough to create a perimeter wall of only about 2½ feet in height.[5] At the rear and on parts of the left face mimosa-bushes were dragged into a poor excuse for a thorn-bush fence.[6] In the meantime a small detachment of Heavies had been sent out to occupy the high point on the spur and cover the dead-ground to the right.[7] They had come into action almost immediately. By this point Ferguson and the other surgeons had positioned themselves inside the vacant space at the centre of the baggage animals, where one of the medics drove a triangular red-cross pennant into the ground to make the position of the hospital clear to the rest of the force.[8]

The enemy skirmishers were quick to develop their attack. Burleigh wrote that, 'In less than ten minutes, the Arabs were not only all over our front and flanks, but had drawn a line around our rear.'[9] Space on the congested knoll was at such a premium that the only place Macdonald could find to leave his horse was on the crest where, standing high above the kneeling camels, it appeared certain to provide a 'capital mark' for enemy marksmen. Macdonald next went in quest of his Greek servant and baggage camels and was lucky enough to locate them without too much difficulty. It transpired that one of his three camels had died during the night march, but that his man had nonetheless managed to bring on most of their kit. Macdonald found him 'very coolly' boiling some water. With bullets cracking about the position with ever greater frequency, the staid young Scot settled down amongst the camels to enjoy a mug of hot tea. When he had done he made his way to the right-front of the perimeter, to try and ascertain what was likely to happen next. He emerged from amongst the camels on a sector manned by No. 5 Company, HCR, to find a good deal of lead flying about. One nearby member of the 5th Lancers was crouched over a small fire, trying to patch up a bullet-hole in his kettle. As Macdonald happened by, a second soldier approached the first to ask if he might share some of the tea. In the blink of an eye the new arrival was killed by a head-shot.[10]

Inevitably a great many 'overs' were raining down amongst the camels. Lieutenant Snow of D Company, MICR, observed that, 'If a camel is hit in a vital spot, his neck curls round till his head touches his body and he dies quickly. If not hit in a vital spot, he does not seem to mind and merely grouses in the same way as he does when you hit him or for that matter offer him food. There seems no betwixt and between.'[11] Captain Lionel Trafford saw one camel take a bullet in the head, but was astonished to note that after giving its head a shake, it showed no further sign of distress.

Percy Marling breakfasted on bully beef and biscuit in the company of two Gordons officers, his company commander, Captain Charles Payne, irreverently known to his subalterns as 'Daddy' Payne,[12] and Lieutenant Harry 'Bimbash' Stewart, a popular character with a hard-earned reputation as a rogue, philanderer and light-fingered 'borrower' of his brother officers' kit. Marling would later observe in his memoirs that 'Bimbash' plundered so much gear during the course of the campaign that he was obliged in the end to add Lieutenant 'Bobby' Bower's kit-bag to his collection. Marling was so exhausted after the night march that no sooner had he finished eating than he fell fast asleep in the cover of the barricade. Scores of other men doubtless followed suit.

Ordeal by Fire

By now Stewart's command was well and truly hemmed in. 'Gradually the enemy's skirmishers worked in force round our flanks,' wrote Verner, '*i.e.* along the eastward side first [the British left] and then along the westward, and before long the circle was completed and every available bit of scrub or grass was tenanted by riflemen.'[13] Sir Herbert Stewart's experience at Majuba Hill ought to have taught him that occupying the high ground was no longer the defensive panacea it had once been, especially where low-lying cover offered rifle-armed attackers a wealth of well-concealed fire positions. Lieutenant Douglas Dawson perfectly articulates the dangers of entrenching oneself on a hilltop in the age of the long-range rifle:

We had a fair position as regards defence from a rush, for we were in open ground with a view to our front everywhere, except on our right front, where forty yards off [closer to 80 yards] was some rising ground behind which the enemy could congregate unseen. As regards defence from sharpshooters I should call our position bad, but it is not easy in a moment to combine both. We had beyond the open ground, 200 or 300 yards wide, miles of scrub, thin, but sufficient for cover. Thus the marksmen could fire at us in the open, themselves concealed. Also what I look on as worse still, the section of ground we were on was convex instead of concave; consequently anyone leaving the immediate shelter of the boxes was more and more exposed. From this cause the hospital in the centre was much exposed, and our camels were shot in hundreds.[14]

Notwithstanding the heavy ammunition expenditure of two days earlier, the enemy appeared still to have plenty of cartridges in hand. One particular *anṣāri* threw himself down beneath a mimosa bush and proceeded to make life a misery for the Naval Brigade by peppering their position over the course of the morning with more than 200 rounds. Though he succeeded in wounding only one rating, he also knocked a spoke from one of the Gardner's wheels and made certain that the Royal Navy contingent went without a hot breakfast. Beresford would later find the troublesome *anṣāri* lying amongst his cartridge cases with a bullet in his head.[15]

It was not long before the British position had been invested, not only by enemy riflemen but also by significant bodies of horse and foot which had picked their way through the scrub to occupy nearby positions of advantage. Burleigh's *Daily Telegraph* report of 24 January captures this phase of the battle:

Our mound or crest was dominated by the high ground 2,000 yards [actually 2 miles] on our front; whilst to the right and the right rear there were two low ledges of rock, not 1,700 yards distant, which overlooked our position and afforded good cover for the enemy. Every vantage point they quickly occupied with bodies of from 300 to 500 men. Upon our rear a force of between 200 and 300 Baggara-Soudanese horsemen, and as many foot men deployed.[16]

With no pressing intelligence work to occupy him, Willoughby Verner moved around the perimeter lending a hand wherever he could. On the GCR sector Major William Pöe's Royal Marines were returning section volleys at a troublesome band of *jihādīya* infesting the bush to the south.[17] Across such a flat and featureless landscape it was proving difficult to gauge range accurately. Recognizing that an experienced infantryman like Verner might prove an invaluable foil, Pöe asked him to spot the company's fall of shot with his binoculars, while he got on with directing the fire of his men.

We tried one [volley] at 850 yards [wrote Verner], and then some at 800. At about 750 yards we 'got onto' the enemy, for they at once ceased fire. It was almost impossible to keep on a point, for the enemy were invisible and the numerous mimosa trees intervening between us and them rendered aiming most difficult for us.[18]

A little later on Verner came across Jack Cameron, who had emerged from amongst the camels to take up a fire position on the barricade, where he was now sniping back at the *jihādīya* with a Winchester repeating rifle. As Verner passed Cameron made a remark about 'bearing a hand in such a desperate situation'. He was certainly dressed for the part; a Prior sketch for the *Illustrated London News* shows that he was clad that day, in best military style, in a battered foreign-service helmet with a dark-coloured pugaree, a navy-blue officer's-pattern patrol jacket, Bedford cord riding breeches and boots with knee-length gaiters. Less than generously Verner observed that, 'He went off somewhere with a most lugubrious face on him.'[19] In fact Cameron was on his way to re-join his European servant, who like all the other non-combatants had found what he hoped was a well-sheltered spot amongst the camels. The long engagement ranges, combined with the high trajectory of the Remington round were, however, conspiring to ensure that safe spots were few and far between.

At something around 10.15 a.m.[20] General Stewart was moving around on the left face of the perimeter in company with Captain Frank Rhodes, his ADC. Having talked briefly with Bennet Burleigh, the general turned away to move along the front of the position. A minute or so after leaving Burleigh, he paused to survey the battlefield through his binoculars. Frederic Villiers was somewhere close at hand and recounts in his memoirs that the general suddenly stepped onto a box to gain a better view. A matter of seconds later he went reeling to the ground, shot in the groin. Rhodes and Villiers bellowed for one of the surgeons and rushed to the general's assistance.[21] Though conscious and still fully in control of his faculties, he was clearly very badly hurt. He was carried away to the hospital with as little fuss as possible, although it was impossible inside so small a perimeter to prevent word of his injury spreading rapidly through the force. Verner got wind of it almost immediately and not long afterwards broke the news to Sir Charles Wilson. As far as Verner was concerned the Desert Column was now under the command of the scholarly head of intelligence. He would probably not have been aware that his chief held his colonelcy by brevet only. Sir Charles on the other hand would have known that Charlie Beresford was technically his senior.

Wilson was only too acutely aware that he had precious little command experience to draw upon. He went at once to the next-senior Army officer, Evelyn Boscawen, commanding the Guards, to talk the situation over. They decided to go to the hospital to ascertain what sort of condition the general was in. They found him lying on a stretcher in the shelter of some commissariat boxes, being 'very tenderly nursed' by Frank Rhodes and Sankey Herbert.[22] Wilson observed that Stewart was 'very cool and collected, and apparently not in great pain'. When he attempted to console the general by remarking that he hoped he would make a swift recovery, Stewart responded with words to the effect that 'he was certain the wound was fatal and that his soldiering days were over'.

'I asked', wrote Wilson, 'what he had intended doing if he had not been hit. He said he thought the best thing to be done was to go straight at Matammah or to repeat the Abu Klea plan of going out to fight for the water, and then returning to the zeribah to carry the wounded, stores, etc, down to the Nile.'[23] Interestingly, Verner would place a rather different interpretation on Stewart's mind-set, although it would appear that the relevant passage in his diary refers to a second and quite separate conversation between Stewart and Wilson which took place some 3¾ hours later. In order to demonstrate that this is the case it will be necessary to trace Verner's movements around the battlefield and return to the issue at the appropriate point.

Verner had followed his chief towards the hospital, but stopped en route to talk briefly with Lieutenant Archie Miles of C Company, MICR, who had been shot in the arm some little while earlier. Miles had a pair of binoculars which Verner at once recognized as the ones he had lost at Abu Klea. 'He told me his servant had picked them up and given them to him. Across the end of one glass was a deep notch apparently caused by a sword. I suppose they were knocked out of my hand.' Continuing on to the hospital, Verner picked his way through the casualties to the place where the general lay and raised an arm in salute. Stewart managed a smile in return but then indicated the seriousness of his condition with a shake of the head. Although the doctors had pronounced that he might well recover, he told Verner that, 'he felt he would only last a few hours'. Once Verner had expressed his sad regret at the general's misfortune and excused himself, he was sent by one of the colonels to fetch Lord Charles Beresford.[24]

When Alex Macdonald heard that the general had been shot, he concluded that there were unlikely to be any immediate developments and decided to seek the shelter of the little bivouac site established by his servant amongst the knee-haltered camels. Jack Cameron and Melton Prior were only a matter of yards away. Exhausted by the overnight proceedings, Macdonald eschewed the banter of his fellow correspondents in favour of an hour's sleep. Because it was once again a blazing hot day, he propped a stick under a box of provisions suspended from the flank of one of his camels and lay down with his head resting in its shade. It was not long before he dozed off and became oblivious to events unfolding nearby.

As he made his way past the Mounted Infantry, Verner was intercepted by Captain 'Punch' Hardinge of C Company, a fellow Rifle Brigade officer, who was keen to learn from a member of the headquarters staff quite what the latest tactical thinking was. As they were talking the screw guns away to their left came into action against long-range targets in the direction of Metemmeh. As usual Captain Norton and his gunners attracted a good deal of return fire from an enemy, 'who showed a remarkable aptitude for picking up any new point to fire at'.[25] Over the noise of the booming 7-pounders Verner told Hardinge that in his view the only possible course of action was to improve the defensibility of the current position, by raising redoubts on the knoll and the spur, before then sending out a fighting square to cut its way through to the river. Hardinge was in full agreement and urged Verner to do everything possible to press this course of action upon the colonels. A little further down the line Verner also shared a few words with the other Rifle Brigade officer in C Company, Lieutenant Max Sherston. When at last he reached Beresford he outlined his personal reading of the situation and was pleased to find that the senior naval officer concurred with everything he said. Verner recounts that Lord Charles then made his way to the hospital to confer with Wilson and Stewart. It is of note that Beresford makes no reference to participating in a council of war in either his official report or his memoirs. Similarly Sir Charles Wilson gives no indication in any of his official reports or his book that his assumption of command was anything other than automatic. In his *Daily Telegraph* despatch of 24 January, however, Burleigh suggests that there was a formality to be gone through before anybody began issuing orders.

When General Stewart was wounded the command of the column I understand by seniority devolved upon Lord Charles Beresford, but he being a naval officer and far from well, although personally standing by his Gardner gun all day, passed on the honour and it fell to Sir Charles Wilson. The latter officer held a council of war at which Colonels Boscawen, Barrow, Lord Charles Beresford and others were present.[26]

For Beresford the question of command succession would have been easy. Lord Wolseley had assigned him only a very limited role and it would have been presumptuous of him to assume a far greater one over the heads of his Army colleagues. His job was to take command of Gordon's steamers when they reached the Nile, not to command a camel-mounted brigade of soldiers. As chief of intelligence Sir Charles Wilson was at the heart of things, had a far better understanding of Wolseley's intent and, ultimately, was Beresford's senior by appointment. Ceding the command to Wilson was only a formality, but the regulations governing seniority demanded that it be gone through nonetheless. That particular conversation dispensed with, Sir Charles Wilson would have announced to the lieutenant colonels that he was now formally assuming command. He immediately appointed Boscawen as his chief of staff. The knock-on effect of the arrangement was that command of GCR devolved upon its senior company commander, Lieutenant Colonel Mildmay Willson, who in turn would have handed Number 3 (Scots Guards) Company over to Lieutenant Colonel Sir William Gordon-Cumming.

It was probably about 10.45 a.m. when Marling woke up to find his section under a hot fire. Over the course of the next thirty minutes or so, Private Wareham was shot in the head and mortally wounded, Private Winter was hit in the face (probably by a spent round as he was returned as only 'slightly wounded'), and Lance Corporal Thorward was shot in the back, even as he was talking to Marling.[27] This was just one section; across the position as a whole, scurrying stretcher-bearers seemed to be in virtually constant motion. Marling hero-worshipped Stewart and the moment he heard he had been hit, dashed away to the hospital to pay his respects. Evidently intent upon saying his goodbyes while he still could, the general shook his young protégé's hand and wished him the best of luck.[28]

Having forsaken his Winchester, for which he would have had only a finite supply of ammunition, Cameron was sat quietly amongst his baggage camels, while his servant scratched about in their camp-gear for something to eat: latching on to some tinned sardines, he peeled back the lid and proffered them in the direction of his employer. As Cameron reached out an arm to take the tin, a bullet came sailing over the camels and hit him squarely in the back.[29] 'With one gurgling sigh' he fell back dead. 'At first I could not believe it,' wrote Prior, 'but turning him over I found a small hole in his coat where the bullet had entered and broken his vertebrae.'[30] Cameron probably died at something around 11.00 a.m. Macdonald remained fast asleep throughout the incident.

Sergeant Charles Williams was tending to the wounded, under the supervision of Surgeon William Briggs. His unpublished account is once again of great interest, indicating as it does that at least one mercy killing took place at Briggs's behest. Rather than litter the extract below with grammatical and factual corrections, it is rendered warts and all:

Another casualty that is worth relating occurred to an AS Corps WO well known to myself. He was in charge of ammunition well under cover, simply had to hand out boxes to troops on demand. Little or no danger had he not in the goodness of his heart gone out of way to assist. Stood up to help two weary Tommies to lift a box of ammunition and received a bullet in the abdomen. Our chief medical officer (Captain Briggs) in trouble some time later in India in connection with the Viceroy's staff – said put him away, his case is hopeless. He poor chap, asked me what chance he had? Saying am not afraid to die – have made my peace with God – but if it is hopeless I should like to die in peace. Here again he received a 'merciful drug', covered with a blanket and found quite dead an hour or so later with a beautiful smile on his face.[31]

Examination of the column's casualty returns leave little room for doubt that Williams is referring to Conductor of Supplies A. C. Jewell of the Commissariat & Transport Corps.[32] Even at this long remove and taking all due account of the limitations of field surgery at this period, the idea of army surgeons 'putting away' wounded soldiers makes for uncomfortable reading.

Strengthening the Defences

By now the impromptu council of war had broken up. Verner's advice seems to have exerted an influence, as orders were given for the knoll and the spur to be fortified. In the meantime two companies of infantry, one from MICR and the other from the Guards, would be thrown forward as skirmishers while the work was in progress.[33] The sources contain virtually nothing of substance in amplification of this bald fact, though fortunately the accounts of Marling and Gleichen make it plain that both officers were involved in fighting forward of the main position at around this time.[34] It seems safe on that basis to conclude that the two companies in question were A Company, MICR, and No. 1 (Grenadier Guards) Company, GCR. Marling's account states that A Company went out to what he terms 'our left', which almost certainly places it on the low ridge some 350 yards in front of the knoll – the only feature capable of providing a prone skirmish line with any sort of cover. Gleichen, on the other hand, says he was 'with my company on the ridge, covering the building of that work', evidently a reference to the outpost on the spur. The Grenadiers, then, were deployed along the crest of the spur facing west, covering what would otherwise have been a vast swathe of dead ground to the British right. When at length both skirmish lines were in position and returning fire into the mimosa scrub, the work of construction got under way. In the meantime Charles Williams had been struck by the calm demeanour of the new brigadier, noting in his *Daily Chronicle* coverage of the battle that, 'Sir Charles Wilson was now in command, cool, collected, meeting each move of the enemy and noting weak points.'[35] Here, then, is one of the stark discrepancies in Williams's contemporaneous reporting and his highly critical *Fortnightly Review* article of some weeks later.

Although the top of the knoll already housed the makeshift field-hospital, it was still relatively uncongested thanks to Lord Cochrane's earlier decision to array the baggage camels in a hollow square. There would be room enough to raise an improvised fort of about forty feet square,[36] which could serve both as a hospital and as an inner bastion. In the interests of clarity the work will henceforth be referred to as the 'hospital fort'. Major James Dorward, the senior Royal Engineer, took charge of its construction. In order to generate the requisite quantities of defence stores, it would be necessary to take camel saddles and commissariat boxes from the outer perimeter.[37] This meant they would have to be manhandled through serried ranks of densely packed camels, an awkward, dangerous and time-consuming process.

Fortifying the highest point of the spur, a spot which could be brought under fire across an arc of over 220 degrees, was certain to be an even more hazardous proposition. The Grenadiers ferried a few commissariat boxes across to the spur as they deployed. These they configured as a low breastwork, capable of sheltering perhaps a dozen men. It quickly became clear that so rudimentary an outwork would not suffice and that a fully fledged redoubt would be required. Lord Cochrane took responsibility for getting the requisite quantity of biscuit boxes out to the knoll and quickly assembled a party of forty volunteers from the 2nd Life Guards and the Scots Greys. Lugging heavy boxes across eighty yards of bullet-swept ground, in plain view of the enemy, was a risky business and unlikely to be completed without loss. Quite how many men were hit while the work was under way is nowhere definitively stated, although Sir Charles Wilson makes reference in his official despatch to 'several' casualties having occurred at this point. Lieutenant Henry Lawson and a handful of Royal Engineers went out to the spur to supervise the construction work and found themselves labouring under a heavy fire.[38] Lance-Corporal Dale and Sappers Bennet and Leitch did so with such remarkable disregard for their own safety that all three would later be awarded the DCM.[39] To set the seal on his distinguished conduct, Lance Corporal Dale continued to do duty after being wounded. The fact that Burleigh also lent a hand in dashing boxes across to the knoll says much about his character, but also suggests something of just how desperate the situation had become. Burleigh's conduct was to attract a mention in despatches, the first time that a war correspondent had been so honoured.[40]

The Grenadiers, meanwhile, were lying prone on the spur, sniping at the puffs of smoke billowing from the scrub. Initially Gleichen was content to lie on his belly like everybody else, but after a while took it into his head to sit up and scan the plain with his field glasses. He was 'prospecting round satisfactorily', when suddenly he received, 'a violent blow in the pit of the stomach'. He rose to his feet instinctively, but immediately fell flat on his back gasping for breath. Two of his men dashed to his assistance and, in response to a cry of 'Take him away!' from Captain Crabbe,[41] hauled him to his feet and doubled him towards the hospital. By the time the trio reached the defences on the knoll, Gleichen had recovered his breath sufficiently to blurt out that he didn't think he was too badly hurt.

So I clambered over the wall of saddles and things, and sat down to get my wind and see what damage had been done. It was chiefly to my clothes; the brass button that had saved my life was carried away, ditto watch and compass (that had been connected by a steel chain through the button hole), and my pockets were half torn away. Further investigation only revealed a large bruise just over my wind. It must have been a ricochet bullet (Crabbe[42] said he saw it hit the ground in front of me) coming obliquely, but, 'racco' [sic] or not, it was as near a squeak as I ever wish to have.[43]

It was not long before Gleichen was back on the spur with his men. When Lawson pronounced the redoubt complete, the sappers and three of the four Grenadier Guards sections fell back to the main perimeter. The fourth section, about twenty men, stayed behind to garrison the new outpost.[44]

Alex Macdonald had been sleeping the sleep of the dead. He woke to find his Greek servant waving a recently perforated water-bottle about in annoyance. It transpired that while he had been out for the count, the camel beside which he had been stretched out had been grazed by a bullet which travelled on to wound a nearby Adeni boy. If Macdonald's man knew of Cameron's death, he failed to mention it to his master. Not long afterwards the box beneath which Macdonald had been resting his head was hit twice in rapid succession.

This was a hint to move, and after changing my position several times with as many narrow escapes I caught sight of a breastwork and made a dash for it. It was the hospital redoubt, which had been constructed under the heavy fire while I had been asleep. It was full of wounded men lying on stretchers, some of them in great agony. General Stewart was amongst them, and, although not suffering very much pain, was very weak and apparently much depressed.

Outside of the hospital redoubt there was another breastwork, where two of the screw-guns were then in position, and where the Gardner was placed later on. Looking in the direction of Metemmeh, two large masses of the enemy with flags could be seen on the gravel ridge, one in the rear of the other. Another mass, nearer to us, could be seen to the right of what appeared to be the direct road. All were in the regular wedge-shaped formation we had noticed at Abu Klea . . .

Glancing at the ridge on our left rear, I noticed that it was now occupied by a squadron of Baggara horsemen . . . The enemy's sharpshooters on our right and front were keeping up a hot fire, but it was seldom any of them could be seen. Our only guide in replying to it was the puffs of smoke from their rifles, and volley after volley was fired from the redoubt [the hospital-fort], and from the fort on the knoll [or rather the spur], at all such indications of their whereabouts.[45]

Riding the Storm

Melton Prior had known Jack Cameron for years and of all the war correspondents was probably the closest to him. He was sat lamenting the death of his friend in the company of Bennet Burleigh and Harry Pearse, when all of a sudden their conversation was interrupted by the sound of a sharp crack. Although the big Glaswegian began clawing frantically at his neck, Prior was slow to realize that a spent bullet had struck him an 'ugly blow' in the side of the throat. 'Pick it out, Prior! Pick it out!' Burleigh demanded. Unable to discern any sign of an injury, Prior responded with, 'There is nothing to pick out.' 'Pick it out, idiot!' came the disbelieving response. In the event the blow did nothing more than raise 'a great black lump half the size of a chicken's egg' just under Burleigh's ear, though the shock and pain were so great that it took a minute or two for Prior to convince him that the skin had not been broken and that there really was nothing to pick out. Burleigh reported to his readers at home that, 'Luckily it was not enough to put me on the sick list or prevent me attempting to carry out my duties.'[46] His misfortunes had not yet run their course, however, as a short while later another spent round hit him in the leg. Harry Pearse was likewise struck a painful blow on one of his lower limbs during the course of the afternoon.

After a while Melton Prior moved across to join Frederic Villiers. As they sat chewing the fat, Prior could not help noticing the sangfroid of Lord Charles Beresford who 'walked by us with as happy a smile as though he were in the park, quite indifferent to the lumps of lead flying about him'. Prior himself now enjoyed some remarkable luck. First a bullet struck the instep of one of his riding boots, tearing the upper from the sole. Villiers was sat cross-legged at Prior's side and a split-second later was hit in the heel of his own boot by the ricocheting round.

'I'll tell you what, Villiers, it is looking very nasty', I said, and as I stretched out my hand to emphasise my remark I received a ricochet bullet on the ball of my thumb, the effect of which I can still feel to this day [Prior was writing in 1912], for it injured the muscle. Then turning round I received another in a softer part of my body, so I had my share of the entertainment, though luckily nothing very serious.[47]

If some of the war correspondents enjoyed more than their fair share of luck, several dozen members of the camel regiments had been altogether less fortunate. Amongst the many casualties was Quartermaster Arthur Lima of the 19th Hussars, who was shot in the head and killed as he was moving about the position. Reggie Talbot's quartermaster, Lieutenant Gerald Leigh of the Blues, was also hit, although the nature of his injury is not clear. The source coverage would indicate that there may by now have been close to sixty casualties. Burleigh captured something of the harrowing scene around the hospital fort:

As stretcher after stretcher with its gory load was taken to the hospital, the space was found too little, and the wounded had to be laid outside. Surgeon-Major Ferguson, Doctor Briggs, and their colleagues had their skill and time taxed to the utmost. Want of water hampered their operations; doctors and patients alike were exposed to the enemy's fire. More harrowing battle scenes in the course of a long experience I never saw.[48]

Unaccountable Delay?

The combination of mounting casualties with what many officers and soldiers experienced as unfathomable inaction was beginning to fray people's nerves. Some of the young officers inferred, quite unfairly, that Sir Charles Wilson must be to blame. Beresford notes in his memoirs that he grew so impatient that he felt moved to scribble a note advising Wilson that, 'unless we marched against the enemy at once, we were done'. His first messenger was apparently killed en route; though quite who this might have been is impossible to know as the Naval Brigade suffered no fatalities in the battle. His second, Sub-Lieutenant Edward Munro, was hit by a bullet which bounced around his body to leave him wounded in no fewer than seven places.[49] What then was the cause of the delay? Did Sir Charles Wilson hesitate or procrastinate? Were there other factors in play? Might Beresford's remarks be misleading?

Fortunately Burleigh's *Daily Telegraph* report of five days later describes precisely what the outcome of the earlier council of war had been. 'It was resolved to wait until two p.m. the enemy's assault upon our position, and if by that time they did not assail it, to march out with a square of about 1,200 men which should fight its way on foot to the Nile.'[50]

Sir Charles Wilson observes in his book that, 'It was this difficulty of getting around amongst the camels that caused so many delays, and it was quite 2.00 p.m. before the units of the square began to disentangle themselves after leaving the two redoubts in a state in which they could be completed by the garrisons left in them.'[51] It can be presumed, then, that Sir Charles gave orders for the square to form up not long after 2.00 p.m., although another hour would elapse before it would be ready to advance. It would seem more than likely that Beresford wrote and despatched his note at some point between these two times. Because he affixes no time to his message, the story serves to present him as an advocate of urgency and Wilson as the architect of delay. In truth Beresford was party to the decision to make no forward move before 2.00 p.m., so that his memoirs are somewhat disingenuous in suggesting that it became necessary for him to hurry Wilson along. It is of note that Wilson died in Tunbridge Wells in 1905, nine years before Beresford published his memoirs.[52]

In order to contextualize further the issue of decisiveness and delay, it is now necessary to establish that a second conversation about the tactical situation took place between Wilson and the technically *hors de combat* Stewart, and that it had a markedly different tone to the first. The following passage from Verner's diary establishes that the conversation took place *after* the outlying redoubt had been completed, which is to say up to 3¾ hours after Stewart had been wounded, precluding any possibility of it being the same and only conversation described by Wilson in *From Korti to Khartum*.

The mound had meanwhile been roughly and rapidly fortified by the Engineers and a party of volunteers from the Guards. Mr. Burleigh, the Daily Telegraph correspondent, lent a hand. I went across to this point and found it rather a warm corner, the enemy being able to concentrate a considerable amount of fire on it. I then went back to the hospital and found Sir Charles kneeling beside Sir Herbert discussing the situation. From what I could gather the latter wished us to remain where we were until the enemy should summon courage to attack us and deliver a charge. There can be no doubt but that Sir Herbert justly feared the risk that a small square might be rushed by the enemy's overwhelming numbers and so preferred to keep the force together to repel an attack. As, however, he had been wounded tolerably early in the action, he was not a witness to the effect of the enemy's all round fire on our zeriba and to which we had now been exposed for some four hours.

In the lecture notes he drafted at some point in the 1890s, Verner reiterated the remarks he made in his diary. 'It was about now that Sir Herbert received his mortal wound and, believing that he could not live many hours, his only orders were for us *on no account to advance* [emphasis added], but to wait until the Dervishes should charge and then defeat them. Unfortunately this is exactly what they would not do . . .'[53]

Verner is telling us, then, that the grievously wounded General Stewart played a role as an advocate of delay. He was evidently of perfectly sound mind and felt entitled to express an opinion. If Wilson was indeed the ditherer that so many secondary sources have chosen to portray, he would surely have covered his trail by reflecting Stewart's hesitancy in his book. After all, the doubts attributed to the general by Verner were entirely rational. The essence of the problem was that no matter how the cake was divided between offence and defence, an advancing square was unlikely to contain even a thousand rifles. It was certain on that basis to be the smallest and least powerful battle-square the British had yet deployed in the Sudan. In two of the three previous encounters, significantly larger formations had been penetrated by the *anṣār* charge. Even at Second El Teb the largest infantry square so far deployed had fallen into disarray whilst fighting through a Mahdīst defensive position. On that basis it was logical to conclude that advancing in such meagre numbers might well result in the same sort of supremely violent denouement as Abu Klea. If the enemy again got to close quarters, there would be a strong possibility of annihilation. Launch a high-risk attack, or sit tight suffering mounting casualties in the hope that the enemy would come on? It was a tough judgement call. The time-consuming process of constructing redoubts, which lasted from approximately 11.15 a.m. to 2.00 p.m., deferred the necessity to jump one way or the other; but in the meantime sitting tight had slowly but surely turned into a nightmare.

Verner's testimony places the second conversation between Wilson and Stewart at some point after 2.00 p.m., the time at which work on the forts stopped. What, then, is the evidence telling us? It suggests, first, that Wilson went to tell Stewart that he was about to give, or had already given, the order to advance in square; second, it suggests that the wounded general pressed his successor to delay further; and third, that Wilson chose to reject the advice. The reason why Wilson did not report this second conversation in his book is probably plain and simple humility. Had he done so it would tend to make it look as if he was extolling his own bravado and powers of decision over those of the much lamented General Stewart. Wilson was simply too modest and too much the gentleman to intrude on such territory. The *Daily Chronicle* correspondent reported of the coming advance that, 'The movement was strikingly bold. A commander made of weaker fibre might well have hesitated, but not so Colonel Wilson, who did not fear to realise the risk must be taken.'[54] Once again the contrast with Williams's later piece for the *Fortnightly Review* is remarkable.

It is apparent that historians have set too much store by the ill-informed carping of junior officers like Marling and the misleading testimony of an ageing Beresford. In truth Wilson was working to a pre-ordained plan agreed by a council of colonels not long after Sir Herbert Stewart was wounded. The decision to erect the forts was entirely reasonable, for without them there could have been no hope of a small garrison standing its ground in such an indifferent defensive position. Had the work been finished sooner it might have been possible to review the decision to wait for 2.00 p.m., but the plain fact of the matter is that the forts were not finished until 2.00 p.m. and that the advance took place as soon as was reasonably practicable thereafter. There was no long and pointless delay at Abu Kru: rather a tactically prudent plan had been put into operation on the basis of decisions made by a cabal of experienced officers. Put simply the 3.00 p.m. 'H-Hour', of which so many were to complain, was in no way attributable to procrastination on the part of Sir Charles Wilson. The sullying of Wilson's reputation would begin with the bloodthirsty Captain Pigott, who would no doubt have had at the enemy at the first possible opportunity, but that is a side-trail which still lies some way ahead of us.

Composition of the Square

The forming-up place would be a hundred yards or so north of the *zariba*, where the incoming fire was marginally less severe and the knoll would be interposed between the assembling troops and the hundreds of enemy riflemen to the south.[55] Even so the weight of enfilading fire from the flanks was such that it would be necessary for the companies to lie down in formation as they took their places. The enfeebled state of Barrow's ponies meant that the 19th Hussars would be quite incapable of supporting the advance and could be much more usefully left behind to defend the *zariba*. All the infantry companies, Guards, Mounted Infantry and 1st Royal Sussex alike, received marching orders, while Colonel Reggie Talbot was instructed to divide the Heavies into two wings, only one of which would accompany the square. Two of Norton's 7-pounders were already occupying embrasures built into the barricade. The maximum range of the guns would suffice to cover the square as far as the gravel ridge above the river. The only advantage to be derived from manhandling the guns forward was that they would at least be on hand to punish an enemy charge with a last-moment salvo of case-shot. On the other hand, they would enjoy only limited fields of fire in the scrub and were certain to slow the advance and exhaust the gunners into the bargain. In the circumstances it made eminent sense to leave them where they were. Even though the third gun was standing idle, Wilson felt no compulsion to take it out with the square. Similarly there would be little or no point in flogging the Gardner across the plain, when it could just as well engage targets from the high ground, where the occasional stoppage was unlikely to prove catastrophic. Besides, it too had been manhandled into an embrasure and was already playing a major role in protecting the British left. The fighting strength at the *zariba* would amount in round figures to 100 men of the 19th Hussars under Major John French, 150 Heavies under Major Thomas Davison,[56] 25 rifle-armed naval ratings and about 40 gunners and sailors manning two 2.5-inch guns and a machine gun. If it came to it the logisticians and medics could also lend a hand on the barricades. Lieutenant Colonel Percy Barrow would be in command of the troops, albeit Captain Beresford was technically the senior man present.

Unfortunately there is no one primary source which comprehensively describes the configuration of the square, nor indeed does the totality of the source coverage contain sufficient clues to permit it to be deduced with any great degree of certainty. Much of what follows therefore is hypothesis and remains amenable to amendment in the light of fresh evidence.

HCR presents a particular difficulty, for we are told only that half the regiment went out with the square and half stayed behind in the *zariba*, a less than helpful start-point in contemplating a regiment of five companies. None of the participant accounts reflect any internal reorganization of HCR in the aftermath of Abu Klea. If none took place, then five regimental detachments went out and five were left behind, implying that one of the companies was sub-divided. As Davison must now have been in command of No. 5 Company, vice Carmichael, it seems safe to assume that the two lancer detachments stayed at the *zariba* with him. We know for sure that the 2nd Life Guards detachment under Lord Cochrane stayed behind to garrison the redoubt, but have no evidence one way or the other in respect of 1st Life Guards. A letter written by Lieutenant Robert Hibbert of the Bays establishes that No. 2 Company, HCR, comprising the Blues and Queen's Bays detachments, definitely went with the square, a fact which is corroborated by the known presence of Lord Arthur Somerset.[57] Another important clue is to be found in the newly uncovered 23 January casualty return for HCR. This shows that the 5th DG detachment suffered fatal casualties inside the square, but then again does not preclude the possibility that the other half of No. 3 Company, the 4th DG detachment, might not have been alongside it.

In the absence of any worthwhile source coverage of the issue, we can only second-guess how Colonel Reggie Talbot would have responded organizationally to the heavy losses incurred at Abu Klea. We have seen that, unlike the Guards and Mounted Infantry, the Heavies began the campaign with a fifth sub-unit. The overall unit strengths of the three camel regiments were broadly similar, however, meaning that the HCR companies had a lower average strength at the outset than their infantry counterparts. Both No. 3 Company (4th and 5th DG) and No. 4 Company (Royals and Scots Greys) were badly cut up at Abu Klea, though it was No. 4 Company which suffered the greater loss. No. 3 Company had three out of four officers killed – Major Atherton, Captain Darley and Lieutenant Law. While No. 4 Company had lost Major Gough of the Royals and Lieutenant Wolfe of the Scots Greys, it still had Captain William Hippisley and Lieutenant John Burn-

Murdoch fit for duty. In other words Talbot had two half-strength companies, capable of fielding only three officers between them. By contrast both No. 1 Company (1st and 2nd Life Guards) and No. 2 Company (Blues and Bays) had emerged from the fight relatively unscathed. Although No. 5 Company had lost Major Carmichael, it was in the fortunate position of having a second major (Davison) on its strength. The company's two subaltern officers were also unharmed.

In the circumstances it would have made no sense for Talbot to interfere with the internal organization of Nos. 1, 2 or 5 Companies, but a great deal of sense to merge the remnants of Nos. 3 and 4 Companies. If this postulation is correct, the new sub-unit – let us call it 'No. 3/4 Company' – consisted of four weak regimental detachments, from 4th DG, 5th DG, the Royals and the Scots Greys, and was under the command of Captain William Hippisley. There would be no good reason to delay such a reorganization and every reason to implement it right away. If it was not in effect before the square moved off from the Abu Klea battlefield to the wells, it might well have been enacted either that evening or the following morning. There is some circumstantial evidence in support of the construct which will be deployed shortly.

In reconstructing the composition of the square, what follows is the best that can be pieced together from some decidedly fragmentary source coverage. References to left, right, front and rear should be understood in the context of the square standing at the halt, with its sub-units facing outwards. It will again be necessary to resort to average strength calculations, this time making allowance for the casualties incurred at Abu Klea. It will be recalled that previously we allowed average bayonet strengths per sub unit of 88 for MICR, 72 for HCR and 60 for the Royal Sussex. In GCR we allowed 117 for No. 1 Company, 78 for Nos. 2 and 3 Companies and 85 for the RMLI. The calculations below allow HCR strengths of 69, 68, 47, 40 and 61 for Nos. 1–5 Companies respectively; in GCR 112, 76, 74 and 81 for Nos. 1–4 Companies respectively; in MICR 86, 82, 70 and 81 for A–D Companies respectively; and in 1st Royal Sussex 58 each for C and G Companies. None of these figures should be regarded as exact, but only as a tolerably accurate illustration of a slightly broader range of possibilities. To arrive at a number of files we simply divide by two, while the number of files also provides a frontage in yards.

The Guards Camel Regiment, under the command of Lieutenant Colonel Mildmay Willson, occupied the entire front face and the left half of the right face, with its sub-units arrayed from left to right in the order No 4. (RMLI) Company, No. 1 (Grenadier Guards) Company, No. 2 (Coldstream Guards) Company and No. 3 (Scots Guards) Company. As usual Jacky the dog had fallen in with the Grenadiers.[58] The accounts of Gleichen of the Grenadiers and Dawson of the Coldstream are both accompanied by sketch-maps of the square. Unhelpfully both officers major on GCR at the expense of other units and even then disagree on the deployment of their own regiment. While Gleichen shows only the Marines and Grenadiers in the front face, Dawson also includes the Coldstream Guards company, a significant discrepancy to which we will return shortly.[59] A third map is to be found with Burleigh's 24 January despatch for the *Daily Telegraph*, but while this indicates the position of the RMLI, it fails to distinguish between the regiments of Foot Guards.[60]

The right half of the right face and, around the corner, the left half of the rear face was occupied by a wing of HCR under the command of Colonel Talbot. If this was literally half the regiment, Talbot would have had some 132 bayonets with him. Lord Arthur Somerset's No. 2 Company (Blues and Bays) was certainly present in full strength. The fact that the 5th DG detachment was also present (as demonstrated by the 23 January casualty return), argues that the second company must have been the newly merged No. 3/4 Company under Hippisley. That said, it can also be argued that of all Talbot's companies this was the one most likely to have been left behind at the *zariba*, after its terrible experience of two days earlier. But if neither the Life Guards nor the Lancers were present, *vide* the known locations of Cochrane and Davison, and barring some inherently improbable sub-division of one of the three combat-effective companies, it is the only possible candidate remaining. It is by no means inconceivable that Talbot came under pressure to let the company 'show what it could do', or that it might be allowed to 'avenge its fallen comrades' – such attitudes crop up elsewhere in the history of the High Victorian Army.[61] It should also be borne in mind that it would still have had sufficient men on parade to make it the largest company in the regiment. The sources tend to suggest that Somerset's No. 2 Company was in the rear face, which if it is true would imply that the other HCR sub-unit, conjecturally the merged No. 3/4 Company, was in the right face. We can be certain that the two under-strength companies of 1st Royal Sussex, around 116 bayonets in all, occupied the centre and right of the rear face, with Sunderland's G Company adjoining Somerset's Heavies, and Trafford's C Company to Sunderland's right.[62]

Around the left-rear corner from Trafford the entire left face was in the hands of Major Charles Barrow and the Mounted Infantry.[63] Quite how Barrow's companies were arrayed is also unclear, although it is possible to construct a reasonable working hypothesis. Marling wrote a long letter to his father on 28 January 1885, in which he describes how he and Lieutenant Charles Hore were standing together, 'in the left-front corner, when a bullet came right between us and hit a marine in front of us in the head, killing him dead'.[64] Like Marling, Hore was a company officer in A Company, MICR; this would suggest that A Company was on the right of the regiment, adjoining Major William Pöe's RMLI company. This might reasonably be viewed as a fairly tenuous assertion were it not for the fact that it was traditional in the infantry for the senior company to occupy the right of the line and the junior company the left. Moreover, Barrow had deployed his regiment in conformity with this convention at Abu Klea.[65] By the time Marling got round to publishing his *Rifleman and Hussar* of 1931, his comrade was no longer Hore, but 'Bimbash' Stewart, an anomaly which offers an interesting insight into the reliability of autobiographies penned late in life.

Of particular note is a remark in the manuscript account of Lieutenant Thomas Snow to the effect that, 'My company was in reserve inside the square and we had to help to get the wounded on to the camels.'[66] Snow was serving under 'Bloody-minded' Pigott in D Company. The notion of one of the MICR companies being held in reserve, inside the square, is not reflected anywhere else in the sources, not even by Sir Charles Wilson, who does mention the presence of reserve details made up of sappers and hussars, of which more in a moment. And yet Snow's remark could not possibly be more emphatic. It seems also to make perfect sense when the respective strengths of the square's faces are contemplated. All four MICR companies would amount to something in the region of 320 bayonets, a figure which would far outstrip the maximum possible strength of the right face, which calculates at around 216 bayonets. It seems reasonable, then, to conclude that the left face consisted, from left to right, of C (Rifles) Company, B Company and A Company only, and that Pigott's D Company was dispersed by sections inside the square. This would leave only 238 bayonets or 119 files in the left face and allow broad symmetry between left and right.

In *From Korti to Khartum* Wilson states that, 'At each angle there were small reserves, dismounted hussars and sappers, to meet a sudden rush.'[67] A little further on he lists the units and commanders present in the square, itemizing amongst others, 'R.E. [of unstated strength] with Lawson; and a few dismounted 19th Hussars under Craven'.[68] In fact Lawson's article for the *RE Journal* states that he had only nine NCOs and sappers with him and that his men had taken a number of entrenching tools along. Remarkably the already wounded Lance Corporal Dale was one of Lawson's nine and in the words of his DCM citation again 'rendered good service'.[69] If there were small reserves at all four corners of the square as Wilson suggests, they could not all have been meaningfully covered by a 'few' dismounted hussars and a party of ten sappers. Snow's account would suggest that the other two corners must have been covered by sections of D Company, MICR, which if that were the case would also have had sufficient manpower left over to provide a general reserve of perhaps forty men. Assuming that the idea of the corner reserves emanated from Boscawen or one of the other senior infantry officers, it is not inconceivable in the light of Snow's account that Wilson was mistaken in identifying the sappers and hussars as the only reserves; he might merely as a matter of coincidence have caught sight of Lawson and Craven at or near different corners of the formation. The notion of D Company being dispersed by sections to cover all four corners certainly has neatness to commend it.

Turning to the Dawson–Gleichen conundrum in respect of the Coldstream Guards, the comparison of the right and left faces outlined above compels the conclusion that No. 2 Company has to have been in the right face. We can confirm the finding by means of a similar comparison front to rear and by taking a wider view of the square's dimensions. The composition of the rear face is well sourced at two Royal Sussex companies and half of the approximately 132 Heavies.[70] This would have amounted to around 182 bayonets, arrayed in two ranks of 91 files. The dimensions of the square, then, were something around 91 files x 119 files. To be more geometrically precise the so-called square would actually have been an oblong, with front and rear only four-fifths as long as the sides. It follows that only the RMLI (81) and the Grenadiers (112), a total of 193 bayonets in 96 files, can have been in the front face and that it is Gleichen's map which is the more accurate.[71] If, flying in the face of Dawson, we move the Coldstream Guards around the corner into the right face as Gleichen suggests, it would consist of 216 bayonets in 108 files, a frontage which balances within manageable limits with the three MICR companies on the opposite face, thus serving to vindicate Gleichen.

These admittedly rough estimates suggest that there were around 829 Martini-Henrys in the walls of the square. The reserve elements, D Company, MICR, the tiny RE contingent and a small party of 19th Hussars, brought the total bayonet strength to about 925. Allowing for regimental officers, the headquarters staff and a handful of doctors and medics, the square probably contained about a thousand officers and men in all. There seems to have been some discussion between Wilson, Boscawen and the staff as to what had gone wrong at Abu Klea, as the plan incorporated a number of mitigating measures. First, there was the presence of a small reserve at each corner of the square; second, no skirmishers would be thrown out; third, the Gardner and the guns would not be present to disrupt the integrity of the formation; and finally, a much smaller number of camels would be taken along.

Once the fighting companies detailed to the square had extricated themselves from the perimeter, Barrow, Beresford and Davison supervised the re-distribution of the men who were to be left behind. At some point the Grenadier Guards section on the spur was relieved by Lord Cochrane and the 2nd Life Guards detachment.[72]

There seems at this juncture to have been a distinct sense of foreboding abroad. Marling thought the enterprise 'just like a forlorn hope'. Gleichen was similarly doubtful about the outcome:

> It was neck or nothing, for the fighting force could muster only 900 bayonets, and the enemy were swarming round in thousands. I must say it looked as risky a business as it well could; we all felt it was exceedingly doubtful if the two halves of the force would ever see each other again, but yet it was the only thing possible to be done.[73]

It would appear that even the gallant Burleigh had been shaken by his narrow scrapes and a generally ugly situation. As the square was forming up he approached Harry Pearse and Melton Prior in turn, to enquire if they would join him in galloping back to Abu Klea and Jakdul Wells. Both agreed to go. Their subsequent adventures are comprehensively described in Prior's *Campaigns of a War Correspondent*, although it is of note that Burleigh's account contains only a passing reference to the caper. According to Prior his *Daily Telegraph* colleague was anxious to get his latest despatches back to London, but this is surely no more than a generous attempt to cover up Burleigh's anxiety – he was simply too good a newspaperman for such an excuse to hold water. The 'story' was in full flow around him and its outcome far from certain; if he were to depart now, he would be in no position to report its denouement. For his own part, Prior was honest enough to admit that he had concluded that the game was up and that his only chance of salvation lay in what he termed, 'a ride for life to the rear'. While Burleigh and Pearse clearly concurred with this pessimistic reading of the situation, some of the other newspapermen thought the scheme ill-advised:

We then went in search of our ponies, but before mounting we three shook hands and swore that we would get through or die together. If one was wounded the others were to stand by him to the death – a much more awful situation than I realised at the time, but we were all very determined to carry out our word. Villiers and Ingram thought the risk we were taking even worse than remaining, and with tears in their eyes shook my hand and wished me God-speed. Having mounted our animals, we started quietly at first, Burleigh riding on my left and Pearse on my right. We knew we had to pass through a small forest and then we quickened our pace, Burleigh saying, 'There is a line of skirmishers in front, and once we get through them we are all right.' Putting our animals at a hard gallop, we did get safely past them, though the bullets rained around us, but on emerging from the other side of the forest I espied cavalry. 'Great heavens! Look, Burleigh, there's cavalry on the right – and yes, more on the left; they are trying to surround us! We can't face that lot; we shan't have the smallest chance; we must return.' And the others, seeing the impossibility of us three getting past fifty fanatical Arabs well mounted, agreed that we should return to the square.

Once more we had to face those skirmishers, who were no doubt closing up, and we this time put our ponies into a mad gallop. Just as we were coming out of the forest into the open I saw a fallen tree in front of me. Momentarily I questioned whether my animal would jump it or not. There was, however, no time to stop and go round it, so lifting up his head he cleared it like a deer – another short gallop and we had safely arrived within the zareeba.[74]

The hard-riding trio were lucky not to be shot down by members of the 19th Hussars who, having taken them for Arabs, were about to give them a volley, when a nearby regimental officer realized they were Europeans and roared at the men to hold their fire.[75] Interestingly the less than heroic behaviour of this particular group of war correspondents did not attract a great deal of adverse comment in the primary sources: perhaps the military participants were simply too polite or embarrassed to mention a momentary loss of nerve by fellow Britons. There was absolutely no compulsion on the newspapermen to participate in the fight, despite which Burleigh had already displayed great courage. In fact Dawson is the only military source to lend any sort of collateral to Prior's story, although in his version of events Colonel Barrow would appear to have played a part in turning the correspondents back:

During the forming up of the square, so hopeless did our case appear to some civilians free to act for themselves, that they started for Abou Klea, but were turned back, partly by our cavalry sent out by Barrow, partly by that of the enemy, who by this time were well in our rear – a wise precaution on Barrow's part, for the doleful account they would have given of us would have been an unnecessary alarm to those at home.[76]

Within forty-five minutes of Wilson giving the order, the square was just about ready for the off. We have seen that it was usual for infantrymen to carry 70 rounds of ammunition into battle on the person. According to Sir Charles Wilson the men were issued with 150 rounds on this occasion,[77] which meant that they were carrying a 17-lb burden in ammunition alone. The only place in which an additional eight packets of ammunition could be carried was in the haversack. Whilst the additional weight would have been uncomfortable on the hip, the greater nuisance value was in the sheer volume of the ammunition, as there would have been precious little room left in the men's haversacks for the biscuits and bully beef necessary for them to sustain themselves over the course of an extended operation. Since it was already mid-afternoon, guaranteeing that come what may the troops were certain to be out overnight, somebody on the staff ought to have had the sense to load up a few camels with cases of beef and biscuit, but foresight can be a rare commodity in the middle of a battle. The Guards, at least, thought to take along a couple of their regimental baggage camels loaded with two days' rations.[78] About sixty camels in all were taken out with the square, half of them with the usual loads of reserve ammunition, medical supplies and water-tanks, and the other half with *cacolets* and litters.[79]

At the last gasp somebody on the staff did manage to think ahead to digging in on the Nile and brought up the subject of entrenching tools. Verner dashed back to the knoll to see what he could scrounge from the small party of sappers working there, only to find them 'digging themselves in like demons'.[80] Unsurprisingly he was unable to get any of them to part with their tools. Verner's failure resulted in the adjutant of GCR, Lieutenant Charlie Crutchley of the Scots Guards, being despatched on much the same errand. Crutchley decided to go to the horse's mouth and cast about for Major Dorward. Even Sir Charles Wilson, a fellow engineer, afterwards expressed surprise that Dorward should insist in such extreme circumstances that a few picks and shovels be signed for, but for some officers 'rules are rules' and insist he did. Crutchley was probably on the point of giving his officious superior a piece of his mind when he was shot in the thigh and severely wounded.[81]

Just before moving across to join the square, Wilson made his way to the hospital fort to speak to Stewart for a third time. Given the general's condition, Sir Charles probably expected it to be a final goodbye. He found 'Sankey' Herbert, wearing an all too conspicuous red undress frock, sat beside the general taking down a private letter to his dictation, an indication perhaps that Stewart held out little hope of seeing another sunrise. It is likely that Verner was with Wilson at this time as his diary records that he saw 'Sir Herbert dictating a letter to St. Leger Herbert who was quite broken-down with grief'. His business at the hospital concluded, Sir Charles set off downhill, clambered over the perimeter defences and walked across to join Boscawen at the centre of a great ring of grimly resolute British Tommies.

I fully felt the gravity of the situation, but from the moment I entered the square I felt no anxiety as to the result. The men's faces were set in a determined way which meant business, and I knew they intended to drink from the Nile that night. I was never so much struck by the appearance of the men; they moved in a cool, collected way, without noise or any appearance of excitement. Many, as I afterwards heard, never expected to get through, but were determined to sell their lives dearly.[82]

As he had only the feeblest grasp of the infantry drill, Wilson sensibly asked Boscawen to assume executive command of the square. This in no way suggests weakness or military incapacity on Wilson's part, as some secondary accounts imply: even an infantry colonel acting as the brigade commander would have vested executive command of the square in a second party. Indeed if Stewart had not been hit, there is every likelihood that he too would have entrusted the close management of the proceedings to Boscawen, just as two days earlier the task had fallen to Burnaby. In short it was not the force commander's place to manage the square.

In the meantime Sankey Herbert had said his own farewell to the general and was now walking downhill to join the square. When it occurred to him that he had left his water bottle behind, he quickly turned on his heel to go and fetch it. Villiers, meanwhile, had gone to collect his pony from the horse lines, intending to take it with him for fear the animal might die of thirst if it did not get a drink soon. He was told, however, that no horses would be permitted inside the square. As he made his way towards the forming-up place on foot, he chanced upon Herbert searching through his kit for the water bottle. The two correspondents then walked towards the square together, descending the reverse slope through a phalanx of knee-haltered camels. A number of bullets went whistling overhead, prompting Villiers to complain, 'You are drawing the fire with that infernal jacket: take it off!'

Receiving no reply I looked round; poor Herbert was lying on his back with a bullet through his brain. I knelt by his side. His large blue eyes were staring up at me, but with no speculation in them. He was dead. Then in a frenzy of grief I began to drag his body toward the square, but an officer crawled up to me on his knees and said: 'Hurry up, Villiers, leave the body where it is; they will pick him up from the zereba. We don't want dead men with us.'[83]

Herbert's death meant that Villiers would now be the only war correspondent accompanying the square.[84]

Percy Marling's *Rifleman and Hussar* contains a retrospective account of Herbert's demise which is irreconcilable with references to the event made by Wilson, Villiers and Macdonald. Not only that, it is also irreconcilable within itself as Marling puts himself squarely in two places at once. It is clear that additional passages have been inserted, probably late in life, into what purports to be a contemporaneous journal of events. If nothing else the fact that his book has two adjacent entries for 19 January tends to give the game away. In the first of them Marling marches out with the square at 2.00 p.m.,[85] but in the second, he is concerned in the burial of St Leger Herbert at 2.30 p.m.[86] He also suggests that Herbert was immediately buried in a lone grave, whereas we know from other sources that he was actually buried in the smaller of two mass graves dug the following day. Not only that, but Alex Macdonald asserts that he was unaware of the death of either Cameron or Herbert until he passed their bodies laid out beside the hospital.[87] Lying with the correspondents at the time were two other bodies alongside which they are known to have been buried at noon the following day. Heavily caveated with a pinch of salt, then, Marling's story goes as follows:

Sankey Herbert was shot through the head dead about 1.00 p.m. [it was actually much closer to 3.00 p.m.]. Bennet Burleigh, the celebrated War-correspondent of the Daily Telegraph, and I buried him about 2.30 p.m., at least we got two Tommies to scratch a shallow hole in the sand and covered him up. He had on a pair of new brown field boots, which he got up by the last post before we left Korti. Bennet Burleigh wanted to take these boots, as his own were worn out, and he said it was a sin to waste a good pair of boots on a dead man. I, being young and more squeamish in those days, protested and said, 'Damn it, Burleigh, you can't take the boots off poor old Sankey,' and so we buried him. Next day, when we came back from Matemmeh [more accurately the position on the river] to pick up the wounded, and stores, and camels, I passed the spot where we had buried Sankey, and there were his poor old feet in a pair of Tommy's grey stocks sticking out of the sand. When I saw Burleigh about two hours afterwards he had on a new pair of field boots which, however, were too tight for his fat calves, and he had slit them up behind.[88]

The pragmatic Burleigh might well have acquired Herbert's sharp new boots, but the certain fact that Marling went out with the square necessarily implies that he was never in a position to bury Herbert or raise an objection to the removal of his footwear. Nor does Burleigh seem to have had sufficient time on his hands for the inherently unlikely pastime of casually digging graves under a heavy fire. Much as described in his last sentence, Marling might well have spotted that Burleigh was sporting Herbert's boots the following day, but the rest of the story has all the hallmarks of an old age yarn.

Willoughby Verner had already joined the square, when he suddenly felt the need to fetch the photograph of his wife Leila and his young son Rupert he customarily carried in his kit. He dashed back to the knoll to retrieve it from his saddlebag and took the opportunity to gather up all the empty water skins belonging to the intelligence department, with the idea of getting them filled and sent back to the troops at the *zariba*, once he had reached the Nile. He quickly rejoined the square, and was handing the skins over to one of the medics to be stowed aboard a camel, when he heard a voice say, 'Which is the way to the Nile? Who knows?' A second voice replied, 'Verner does.' With that he found himself being called for by Sir Charles Wilson. 'Verner, will you give the square a point to march on to bring us to the Nile?' asked the colonel. Politely expressed it may have been; a request it was not.

I moved out by the left corner and placed myself about 30 paces in front of the left file of the front face. I could see the undulating ground which I knew must hide the river from my view and the tops of the villages seen in the morning. In the far distance beyond the river a range of blue hills were visible with a remarkable gap or pass through them. This gave me a bearing by compass south ¼ east, easterly, and was as near as could be what I wanted to bring me down to the river on my original point.[89]

Verner drew the v-shaped gap at the top of the map he later made of the final stages of the British approach march (*Map 10*) and also portrayed it in a watercolour included in his *Sketches in the Soudan*.

Moments later the order to stand up boomed around the square. Verner recalled that the words of command were, 'Rise! The square will advance; by the left, *slow* . . . march!'[90] Most sources agree that it was now about 3.00 p.m.[91] No sooner had the men clambered to their feet and closed up their files than a heavy fusillade of Remington fire came pouring in. As the square rounded the spur to sally into the open plain, scores more enemy riflemen came into play. Several men dropped, but as they were still only thirty yards from Lord Cochrane's outpost they were left where they fell. As the square continued to press south, carrying-parties from the Life Guards went dashing out from the redoubt to recover the casualties to safety.[92]

Only a couple of minutes after setting off, the square came to the first of many halts. It may conceivably have been to pick up Colour Sergeant George Kekewich of No. 2 Company, GCR, he of gloomy presentiment, although there are conflicting accounts of quite what befell him. Looking back from his dotage, Sergeant Charles Williams says at one point in his account that his friend was shot in the head and was amongst the first to be killed. The GCR casualty return of 23 January shows, however, that Kekewich did not die immediately but lingered until at least the following day. A little further on in the same account Williams contradicts himself by asserting that Kekewich was wounded just after the square set off and was recovered to the *zariba*. 7498 Private William Burge of No. 1 Company, GCR, left an altogether more coherent (probably ghost-written) account than that of Williams, in which he asserts that Kekewich was wounded during the advance and placed aboard a *cacolet*. Abu Klea had shown that being raised above ground level left the wounded more exposed than ever. Burge adds that the colour sergeant was hit twice more, including a mortal wound, which it would seem safe to assume is likely to be the point at which he was hit in the head.[93]

Whether it was the unfortunate Kekewich or somebody else who was the cause of the first halt, the men of C Company, 1st Royal Sussex, found themselves standing on a slightly elevated sand-hill. Just at that moment a fusillade of shots came raining down on the left-rear corner of the square. Captain Trafford thought that, 'the ground seemed torn up all round with bullets', and spun around to see how his men had fared. No fewer than a dozen of them were down: two had been killed, several more were badly hurt and a few got away with grazes.[94] The wounded were looked at briefly by the medical staff and then hurried aboard *cacolets* so that the advance could be resumed. As we noted in an earlier chapter, Trafford remarked in his diary that he and the other Royal Sussex officers grew increasingly vexed by 'an officer in the Household Cavalry who happened to be senior to Major Sunderland, taking command [of the three companies in the rear face] and giving words of command that do not appear in the book; he commenced by trying to make the rear face march in fours and not content with giving many wrong words of command, he abused the men for doing right'.[95] It is clear that Trafford can only be referring to Colonel Reggie Talbot.[96]

Although there were mimosa bushes and swathes of long grass on all sides, there were also a number of bare gravel patches, several hundred yards in width, where there was next to no vegetation growing. In most cases the corner of one patch ran into the corner of the next, like a string of giant stepping stones. Mercifully for the British, they lay pretty much directly along the axis of advance and Verner had been quick to grasp their tactical significance. By steering the square from one patch of gravel to the next it would be possible to avoid the thorn-bushes which might otherwise disrupt the formation, and at the same time stay well clear of the long grass where any number of *anṣār* might be lurking. Keeping to the gravel patches would also guarantee relatively clear fields out to ranges of at least 200 yards. As at Abu Klea many of the enemy riflemen were moving parallel with the square, from one fire position to the next. The scrub was also alive with large parties of sword- and spear-armed *anṣār*. Douglas Dawson wrote, 'I am told by those who remained in the zariba that there were many, many more all-round us than at Abou Klea, and that it looked as if the square was going to certain destruction; we in the low ground could not, of course, see their movements and numbers.'[97]

Back on the knoll Captain Gilbert Norton and Lieutenant Noel Du Boulay were scanning the plain with their field glasses and periodically directing the fire of the screw guns onto points in the scrub where they could see the enemy had congregated in strength. Their fire was both accurate and punishing. It also conveyed the added advantage of indicating the locations of significant Mahdīst concentrations to the officers in the square.[98] The importance of this fire in sapping the morale and resolve of the *anṣār* is not to be underestimated. Whenever a round landed with visible effect amongst the enemy, scattering them 'like a flock of starlings',[99] the gunners received a hearty cheer from the nearby knot of war correspondents.[100] Beresford, described by Macdonald as being stripped to his shirtsleeves and 'in his element', did not enjoy quite the same reach with the Gardner as did Norton with the 7-pounders, but was doing everything he could to add to the discomfiture of the enemy, many of whom were still firing on the *zariba* from positions about 700 yards away. The Gardner was an excellent weapon for clearing snipers out of soft cover. One turn of the handle sent a burst of five 0.450-inch rounds crashing through the scrub; anybody who was foolish enough to annoy his lordship unduly got two or three turns for their trouble. The fire of the Gardner was supplemented by volleys from the Heavies and the Naval Brigade. Equipped only with short-ranged carbines, the 19th Hussars had to content themselves with keeping a weather-eye out to the north.

Every so often Colonel Barrow would have the call 'Attention' sounded by his bugler, whereupon he would step onto a camel saddle and brief everybody on the progress of the square. Macdonald recounts how he invariably terminated his performances with, 'Now, men; no single firing! Give them volleys!'[101] The fire from the *zariba* was of course pouring forth over the heads of the best part of 2,000 camels, who took it in their stride as usual, making a mockery of an experiment conducted at Korti in which the 19th Hussars had ridden around the animals firing blank cartridges and whooping like banshees.

The courageous Captain Verner, still moving thirty yards in front of the square and steering it from one patch of open ground to the next, was beginning to feel the strain. 'The hard gravelly soil in front and around me was cut up by numerous bullets and I believe I was honoured by an unfair share as the enemy evidently looked on me as a "sheik" who had better be got rid of.'[102] It came as a great relief when the square halted and he was called in by the RMLI officers to his rear. Colonel Boscawen had decided that the time had come to give the enemy marksmen a taste of their own medicine. 'The square will halt!' he boomed. 'The square will fire a volley at two hundred yards. Ready!'[103] The effect of the ensuing thunderclap was perhaps more moral than physical, though doubtless a few of the enemy lost their lives to it. More importantly the sound was deafening, intimidating and served notice on the *anṣār* that any sudden rush they cared to make could expect to be met with a wall of fire. History relates that to be on the receiving end of a British volley is to be in the wrong place, but on the other side of the psychological battle-lines the thundering salvoes served to lift the spirits of the Tommies and inspire the belief that the victory might yet be theirs.

Their moral superiority duly re-asserted, the British resumed their advance. Verner returned to his position in front, where he was soon joined by 'Bloody-minded' Pigott.[104] Sadly history does not relate whether on this occasion the gallant 'Smoke' was dancing along at his master's heels or not, although 'Jacky' was certainly on parade with the Grenadiers and is sourced as chasing after the bullets striking the ground in and around the square.[105] After a while, Douglas Dawson, who seems to have had something of a propensity for wandering away from his company, also joined Verner and Pigott.[106] Because the close-packed square to the rear of the trio was not by any stretch of the imagination a difficult target, losses were mounting fast.

Wilson's principal interpreter was Muḥammad Effendi Ibrahim, a close friend of Arabi Pasha and one-time enemy of the British. Doubtless Wilson would have made his acquaintance whilst acting as Arabi's gaoler two years earlier. Sir Charles had secured Ibrahim's services as he passed through Cairo and, at all the way-stations between Wādī Halfā and Korti, had been in the habit of sending him into the bazaar to do a little amateur spying. The wily Ibrahim now took a round in the side of his abdomen but proved not to be too badly hurt and only minutes later was observed enjoying a soothing cigarette from the comfort of a *cacolet* seat.

A short while later Lord Somerset suddenly went reeling to the ground. When the medics reached him, he was clutching at his chest and in so much pain that he was quite convinced he had been mortally wounded. In fact he had been hit over the heart by a spent round, but of course was still concealing the vicious sword-cut of two days earlier– little wonder that he was in such great pain. Nor was this the end of it. It is unclear whether Lord Arthur was nicked in the arm before or after he was hit in the chest, but he also ended the day with his arm in a sling. The next senior officer in No. 2 Company was Captain Arthur Gould of the Bays, but he was 'disabled by gout' and had been left behind at the *zariba*. Accordingly the command of No. 2 Company now devolved upon Gould's subaltern, Lieutenant Robert Hibbert.[107]

Villiers had not managed to get his pony into the square, but had brought his youthful driver and one of his baggage animals along. A sudden salvo of bullets hit both boy and beast. While the lad fell dead with a bullet in his heart, Villiers noted that the camel, 'simply turned his long neck in my direction and opened his gazelle-like eyes to their full extent, as much to say, "Did you do that?" Then a shiver shook his body, and he lumbered steadily forward, continuing to chew the cud as if nothing had happened.'[108] Even to hardened campaigners, used to the fear and panic of injured horses, the insouciance of a wounded camel was a constant source of wonderment. Not long afterwards Villiers himself had a lucky escape when a bullet passed through a slight bulge in one of his puttees.

From the redoubt on the spur, Lord Cochrane's troopers had a huge swathe of ground to the south-west to cover and were blazing away with their Martinis to good effect. At length they began running low on cartridges. A number of boxes of reserve ammunition had been brought across from the main position and Cochrane now directed that one of them be opened. Much to everybody's surprise it was found to contain Maria Theresa silver dollars, the currency of the Egyptian colonial regime, which much to the bemusement of the British were prized by the locals above comparable quantities of gold sovereigns. A second box was opened and also found to contain treasure. Trooper Hodges, regarded by Lord Cochrane as 'one of the best of men', had only just exclaimed, 'We don't want this stuff here', when he was felled by a bullet which somehow passed clean through one of the commissariat boxes to inflict what would turn out to be a mortal wound. Fortunately the third ammunition box to be opened contained not a precious metal, but the usual mundane combination of brass and lead.

There was now sufficient movement in the scrub to the right of the square to suggest that the *anṣār* were contemplating a charge. The three officers out in front were brought in, from which point onwards Verner set the direction from the right-hand file of the front face. As no charge materialized the square marched on, pausing occasionally to pick up its wounded, but leaving its dead where they fell. Whenever he felt the incoming fire was becoming intolerable, Boscawen brought the troops to a halt, gave the order to lie down and then instructed the relevant captains to direct company volleys into the scrub.[109] This invariably had a salutary effect and after one or two broadsides left the British free to resume the advance. The enemy marksmen, who manifested themselves only as darting white shapes and puffs of smoke, were not the only targets engaged during the square's stately progress towards the Nile; every so often a cluster of flags and banners betrayed the presence of a powerful body of Mahdīst infantry. An overly racy account of the battle by Burleigh suggests that no fewer than four major charges against the square were defeated by volley fire.[110] He was safely ensconced in the *zariba*, however, and this version of events is not sustained by the accounts of officers inside the square. It might perhaps be true that on occasion bodies of spearmen were *prevented* from charging by pre-emptive volley fire, but no major attacks seem to have manifested themselves up to this point.

All the while the rate of advance had been kept deliberately slow, in order that the square retained its integrity and there could be no possibility of the difficulties experienced at Abu Klea recurring. Marling wrote that, 'We moved slowly, oh so slowly, first to the right and then to the left [a reference to the square moving from one gravel patch to the next], all this time under a heavy fire.' It may have been too slow for Marling's taste, but his elders and betters were bearding an enemy force with a numerical advantage of not less than 10:1. Such scenarios called for prudence and required that no chinks be left in the armour. Such thinking was lost on the likes of young Marling. At some point in the next few hours he would note in his journal, 'Sir Charles Wilson is rather an old woman who doesn't know anything about drill, and funks the responsibility, and Boscawen, though an awfully good chap personally, has not much experience.'[111] Wilson and Boscawen might have lacked the 'dash' of Sir Herbert Stewart and others of his ilk, but they had safe pairs of hands and it was they who were slowly but surely extricating the Desert Column from a mess of the general's making. A day later Marling had mellowed a little and duly noted, 'Boscawen is a right gallant fellow and really did A.1 yesterday in a very difficult position.'[112]

Ninety minutes of steady marching and fighting had brought the British to within half a mile of the edge of the Bayūda. Ahead lay the flat-topped gravel ridge which served to separate the barren desert from the cultivated flood-plain. The top of the ridge stood perhaps forty feet above the almost dead flat plain across which the embattled square was making its approach. The downhill slope facing the British was long, gentle and veneered with a layer of sand. Only a mile or so beyond the ridge was an infinite supply of cool clean water, the like of which the Tommies had not tasted for the past five days. Even if they could not see it, their every instinct told them it was there. Their lips were cracked and black, and their water bottles dry, but they were not done yet and this final half-mile of wilderness represented the Mahdī's last chance to deny them the Nile.

As the square continued relentlessly to close the distance, it became apparent to the British that were marching directly towards a horseshoe-shaped indentation in the general line of the ridge. The feature was sufficiently wide that provided they steered a course through the centre, they would still have tolerably good fields of fire to either flank. While the spur to the left had only a sparse covering of mimosa, the one on the right was all but wooded.[113] Many officers were keeping a weather-eye to the left-front which, while it now appeared to be deserted, was the direction in which two large bodies of *anṣār* had been visible for most of the day. There were also a good many red, white and green-coloured Qur'anic banners moving about in the scrub on the right, betraying the presence of a number of 'large bodies of spearmen'.[114] It was not long before a handful of mounted *amīrs* came riding onto the forward slope of the ridge, suggesting to Verner that they were 'evidently arranging matters for a rush'. They disappeared back into dead ground before the best shots in the front face could draw a bead on them. When the manoeuvring on the right started to look menacing, the Grenadier, Coldstream and Scots Guards companies loosed a number of volleys into the scrub. As the smoke lifted, it became apparent that the firing had checked the enemy movement.

With the battle obviously approaching some kind of denouement, the weight of incoming fire seemed to the British all of a sudden to double, pouring in from both arms of the horseshoe, the ridge in front and the scrub on the right.[115] Verner recalled that, 'the bullets came over us like a storm'.[116] The British volleyed back at the high ground from three of the square's faces, but took a significant number of casualties all the same. Sir Charles Wilson was walking along behind Pöe's company, when one of the marines in the rear rank fell dead at his feet. Over the next few minutes another six men were shot dead, in addition to which there may also have been a score of wounded. The doctors and medics would have been at least momentarily overwhelmed. Indeed there were now so many casualties that there were no longer any vacant litters or *cacolets* left. 'Things began to look ugly,' wrote Wilson. 'Some of the officers told me afterwards that they thought we should have been obliged to turn back without reaching the Nile. That, however, we should never have done as failure meant annihilation.'[117] Verner perceived that, 'the square was a little shaken and things looked very serious indeed'.[118] If the troops were rattled they nonetheless kept their heads, gritted their teeth and gave no outward sign of it. 'The steadiness of the front and left face of the square was most remarkable and did great honour to the Mounted Infantry, Guards and Marines composing them.'[119] Succinct as always, Marling noted that, 'The men behaved A1.'

The British picked up their wounded and kept coming. It had been a long wait, but now, at about 4.30 in the afternoon, they were exactly where the Mahdīst *amīrs* wanted them: surrounded, softened up and only a few hundred yards from two great masses of shock troops. History does not relate how the signal was given, but the gentle reverse slope behind the gravel ridge suddenly came alive with *anṣār*, a swarming human wave of several thousands, collectively fixated on sweeping the desert clean of infidels. Down below eagle-eyed marines at the front-left corner of the square spotted a sudden flicker of movement on the ridge. They had barely taken in the fact that they were looking at the top of a line of flags, when the shaikhs and *amīrs* came cantering over the skyline to plunge down the forward slope. 'Here they come!' cried the NCOs.[120]

The Mahdist Charge

The word of command 'Halt!' was largely superfluous, but was raised on all sides just the same. 'I could have shouted for joy when I saw them coming on,' wrote Marling. Most men did precisely that. It was remarkable that only two days after Abu Klea, British Tommies could raise a spontaneous cheer at what should by all rights have been a blood-curdling sight. The spectacle might indeed have sent a shudder through the Heavies, but the men doing the cheering were guardsmen, marines, riflemen, line and light infantrymen, men for whom a mob of wild-eyed fanatics at 600 yards represented not something to be feared, but a perfect target. Verner said of this moment, 'This was just what we wanted,'[121] while Marling observed, 'By Jove, the men did buck up.'[122] A Guards officer told Macdonald afterwards that the officers quickly silenced the cheering, 'as we were afraid the enemy would then turn back without coming on'.[123] We have already seen that it was standard practice in any case that the men in the ranks should remain silent, so that range settings and other words of command were audible. Verner observed that, 'As the roar of cheers subsided, the clear sharp words of command to fire volleys by companies was to be heard.'[124] One of the most succinct eyewitness descriptions of the shape and form of the Mahdist charge appeared in the 30 January edition of the *Standard*.

For two miles the Arabs made no attack, but kept up an incessant rifle fire from a distance. When the square emerged from the bush-covered ground into an open flat at the foot of some low hills, two bodies of Arab footmen, some thousands strong, each in crescent formation, were seen approaching. The troops were halted, and in two minutes the enemy charged down upon them. One body made for the left angle of the front face, where the Guards and Mounted Infantry were posted; the other charged the left rear. The first attack looked the most serious.[125]

The British Army had not yet succeeded in defeating a Mahdist charge with fire alone. One of the major *anṣār* masses was now charging straight over the ridge at the front face. It would be met by only 193 Martinis: forty files of Royal Marines and fifty-six files of Grenadier Guardsmen; front rank kneeling, rear rank standing. A second *anṣār* swarm was descending the left arm of the horseshoe and heading straight for the left face, where the three Mounted Infantry companies fielded a marginally more formidable 238 Martinis.[126] The science of operational analysis had not yet been 'invented' but, if it had been practised in the 1880s, the evidence of the three previous Anglo-Mahdist encounters would have suggested to analysts that with only 420 rifles trained on the enemy, the badly outnumbered British could expect the square to be penetrated. One way or another the climax of the Battle of Abu Kru was sure to be short and bloody.

When, thirty years later, Charlie Beresford penned his memoirs, he suggested that the battle's denouement could not be seen from the *zariba*.[127] He might personally have struggled to see what was going on at a remove of almost two miles, after all 'County Waterford' had run off with his field glasses, but there were others who experienced nothing like the same difficulty, the eagle-eyed Lieutenant Noel Du Boulay RA amongst them. Having laid his gun in person Du Boulay proceeded to throw a shell just to the left of the square, so that it exploded amongst the charging *anṣār* on the left arm of the horseshoe.[128]

If Norton and Du Boulay were capable only of harassing the *anṣār* from afar, it was the five company commanders on the front and left faces of the square who would have first to check their momentum and then break their spirit. Having reined in the men's cheering, they began barking out their fire control orders, commencing with the cautionary words of command, 'At 600 yards . . . volley fire . . . present!' With the men's rifles levelled in the aim, all that remained was the one word executive, customarily given after a pause of only a few seconds. Sir Charles Wilson thought that the companies volleyed much as they would have done on an Aldershot field day. Even so, the first five carefully sequenced thunderclaps – ordered by Eyre Crabbe, Bill Pöe, 'Daddy' Payne, 'Tommy' Walsh, Dick Fetherstonhaugh, or perhaps some other variation on a theme – did little to cool the ardour of the Mahdīst faithful. Just as the *imams* had foretold, the bullets of the godless 'Ingliz' had turned to water. A cacophony of angry voices was raised in praise of Allah, the Prophet and the divinely guided one. For the Tommies the air was thick with white smoke and the pungent odour of burnt black powder. Although 400 spent brass cartridges had gone tumbling into the sand, the effect on the enemy seemed negligible. In a matter of only five or six seconds fresh cartridges had been thumbed home and breeches snapped shut. Before the company commanders could begin a second round of volleys, the bugle-call 'Cease Firing' was drifting in the air. If nothing else Colonel Evelyn Boscawen was a cool customer. Much to Sir Charles Wilson's surprise, there was a flawless response to the call. Now the only sounds were the chants of the enemy and the calming exhortations of the company officers and sergeants – 'Steady boys, steady.'

The pause was probably of around forty-five seconds' duration, as it allowed the enemy to close the interval to 300 yards.[129] In doing so the *anṣār* had gained the level ground at the foot of the ridge, an important tactical consideration in terms of fire effect. A bullet fired uphill at men on a skyline has only one chance to hit something before it goes sailing harmlessly into the ether: similarly a bullet fired at men running downhill has only one chance to hit before it buries itself into the ground behind them; but a bullet fired across a flat plain, if it misses the men in front, has as many chances to strike home as there are ranks arrayed to their rear. But the real significance of the pause lay in the way in which it served to concentrate the minds of the men in the ranks. There was next to no incoming fire now, save a few wild shots from rifle-armed *anṣār* in the front rank of the charge. As the Tommies stood shoulder-to-shoulder awaiting the onset of the enemy, their minds were unburdened of the anxiety of a long and harrowing advance. They might as well now be on the barrack square rehearsing the firing drill. Satisfied that all was now well, Boscawen snapped the order for his bugler to sound 'Commence Firing'.

Major William Hutcheson Pöe had been a soldier for eighteen years and would have been word-perfect in the infantry drill: 'Number 4 Company. . . At 300 yards . . . Volley fire . . . Present!' To the right of the Royal Marines the same familiar, rhythmic sequence of commands was being given to the men of the Grenadier Guards, culminating with the fatal executive, 'Fire!' According to Sir Charles Wilson the volleys struck home with 'deadly effect', so much so that the mounted shaikhs, their standard bearers and 'the whole of the front ranks were swept away'.[130] Lieutenant Thomas Snow wrote that the oncoming Arabs were 'mowed down like grass', precisely the same metaphor adopted by Gleichen in his account.[131] Snow himself was struck in the legs only moments later and was sent reeling to the ground with the impact. It transpired that like so many others that day he had been struck a vicious blow by a ricochet. It hit him six inches above the ankle and left him with a severely bruised shin. Incapacitated he may have been, but maimed he was not.[132]

Prior to the charge the amīrs and holy men had whipped the anṣār into a wild-eyed frenzy which the ineffectiveness of the first few British volleys had done nothing to curtail. The downhill slope had served to impart added speed and momentum to the charge, while the seemingly long pause during which the anṣār had not been fired on at all served further to inflame their pounding hearts and racing brains, until they attained a state of mind somewhere betwixt violent rage and spiritual rapture. All this meant that they were running full tilt at the metaphorical 'wall', in the sure and certain expectation that the opportunity to cut down an infidel and thus be assured of a place in paradise was only seconds away. The shock of actually hitting the 'wall' must therefore have been all the more psychologically traumatic. By the time the tiny British square disappeared from view amidst clouds of billowing smoke, the Mahdīst charge had been decapitated by a storm of bullets. In a trice the desert was strewn with dead and dying ponies and the crumpled forms of well-known shaikhs and amīrs. Scythed down with the great men were the Qur'anic banners at the head of the charge.

Even so, downhill momentum and fundamentalist fervour carried many anṣār on towards the square. Long before they could gain another hundred yards, scores more of them had been brought down. The British company commanders had more than enough time to complete a second ripple of company volleys, before then bellowing the order to initiate independent fire. With the men loading and firing at will, there was now a continuous cacophony of rifle fire. Frederic Villiers, who was not above spinning a yarn or two, would later claim in his memoirs that he hurried about with a haversack of cartridges, although it is quite impossible that anybody in the square had any immediate need for more ammunition.[133] To be sure of his place in history, he drew himself handing out cartridges in one of his own sketches.

We have referred before to a short-range zone where the accuracy of the Martini-Henry made it just about impossible for an upright human figure to move unharmed across the ground. This is endorsed by the testimony of the un-named Guards officer fighting on the front face of the square who later described the scene to the attentive Macdonald. 'What struck me most,' reported his informant, 'was that during our firing there seemed a particular zone beyond which no one could pass, viz., from about one to two hundred yards; and of all the men that entered that zone I don't think more than half-a-dozen got away.'[134] If the no-go zone to their front was so obvious to the Guards, it must have been all the more painfully apparent to the charging *anṣār*. The dead and maimed now lay on all sides, making it plain that faith alone could never carry the day.

The tide seems to have turned in a moment. Villiers wrote that, 'the sudden collapse of the attack was almost beyond realization'.[135] Some faint-hearts, stung by Du Boulay's shrapnel and cowed by the accuracy of his gunnery, had hesitated on the left arm of the horseshoe, where they displayed little enthusiasm for advancing to the support of the leading wave.[136] The surviving brave-hearts, none of whom had made it to within fifty yards of the square, now right-wheeled in the low ground and fled along the foot of the ridge towards Metemmeh.

Just how many men had participated in the charge is a moot point. Most secondary accounts casually imply that there were some 5,000 *anṣār* present on the field and that most of them came piling over the ridge. The primary sources recount a different tale, however. There would seem in reality to have been considerably more men on the battlefield, but rather fewer committed to the charge. As we have seen the spectators in the *zariba* were convinced that the Mahdīst host was larger than the one at Abu Klea. That said, estimating the strength of massed bodies of troops from a distance was notoriously difficult at the best of times and they could easily have been wrong. Whether the assertion was literally true or not is of no great consequence, although it certainly points towards a five-figure number. The spectators are vindicated, or more accurately almost vindicated, by an observation from Sir Charles Wilson to the effect that, 'The number of the enemy on the gravel hills and round us – that is to say on the field of battle – was I should think, very nearly as great as at Abu Klea.'[137] With only one important exception the participant accounts fight shy of estimating the strength of the charge. The exception is Wilson himself to whom, as the force commander, we are duty bound to listen carefully. He was to write two official despatches on Abu Kru, a preliminary despatch of 22 January and a more considered supplementary report dated 14 March. In neither document does he offer a numerical estimate. Towards the end of the year, however, when he was writing *From Korti to Khartum*, he observed that, 'the number of spearmen who charged was only about 800, as against about 1500 at Abu Klea'. This is a surprisingly conservative figure, which tends to be further discredited by the glaring underestimate in respect of Abu Klea. Whilst we need not dwell on the latter, the 800 figure is one to which we must return in due course.

The British sealed their victory with a fusillade of parting shots and three resounding cheers. Only about six or seven minutes had elapsed since the enemy first broke over the skyline. A number of officers stepped across to congratulate Sir Charles Wilson on his victory. He was modest enough to thank Boscawen in turn and to praise the prominent part he had played.[138] With some of the more determined *jihādīya* beginning to resume their sniping from the nearby scrub, Boscawen stepped the square off again to gain the top of the gravel ridge. From the high ground thousands of *anṣār* could be seen streaming back towards Metemmeh, including a body of 3,000–4,000 men which seems not to have played a particularly significant part in the fighting. The last of the *jihādīya* felt moved to break off the fight as soon as the British had ensconced themselves in a commanding position on the ridge.[139] For the ordinary Tommies the sight of the routing enemy was gratifying, but the wider landscape, which they had imagined would incorporate a downhill view to a limitless supply of water, proved more than a little disappointing. Instead the ridge merged into a flat-topped plateau which seemed to stretch on forever. Sir Charles Wilson felt much the same sense of disappointment as the men but was pleased to note 'the line of green vegetation and the houses of the villages. We knew the Nile must be there, but it seemed a long way off to weary men.'[140]

According to Marling, who alone of the participants records the incident, Boscawen almost undid his good work by splitting the force, when the enemy threat had by no means completely subsided:

After we had repulsed the niggers [sic] he actually wanted to march the front face of the square away to water in the river two miles off, and the other three sides to go back to the zariba, although the enemy's cavalry were threatening us some 500 yards to the rear. The front face had actually marched off 100 yards from the remainder, but everyone shouted 'Halt', and Johnny Campbell went and expostulated with old Wilson, and used such awful language that it was stopped and we all went on together.[141]

In truth the square was only a little over a mile from the river at this juncture, although dividing the force would have been a foolhardy thing to do regardless of the distance at issue.

At length the party of Arab cavalry, the strength of which is nowhere reflected in the sources, but would probably have been between fifty and a hundred, closed the distance and came within range of the rear face. Verner noted that, 'Some of the enemy's cavalry now threatened our rear and the square halted and fired at them and they made off.'[142] Lionel Trafford's diary reveals, however, that the vexatious HCR field officer, who we can only assume was Reggie Talbot, had again made a hash of things by jumbling the sequence of commands required to initiate a volley.[143] The sputtering half-strength broadside did at least serve to frighten off the cavalry predators and thus pretty much marked the moment at which the Battle of Abu Kru, sometimes called Gubat, drew to a close. While the action had been an ordeal for an already hard-pressed force, it was nonetheless remarkable as the first battle in the Sudan in which not a single British soldier had been killed or wounded in hand-to-hand fighting. Nor had a single British life been lost during the enemy's main assault. Lieutenant Snow may have been the only man to be hit during the battle's denouement.

The Mahdist Loss

In his first despatch, written only three days after the battle, Wilson stated that 250 of the enemy had been killed in the charge, while in his supplementary report of six weeks later he cited a figure of 250–300. He then went on to add that, 'It was ascertained afterwards that many more were killed in the long grass and in rear of the ridge, and that a number of wounded were carried off to Metemmeh.' Whatever the precise number of deaths, there is no reason why the 'two wounded to one fatality' rule of thumb should not apply. Even if we take only modest account of the bodies hidden in the grass, the total number of fatalities incurred in the charge cannot have been any fewer than 300.

On this occasion the 'wounded viper' problem was not a major factor, as there was no requirement for the British to scour the field searching mixed mounds of humankind for wounded comrades. As a result the participant sources do not contain any references to the necessity to despatch wounded Mahdists. Even so, let us for a moment be hard on the British and imagine that one third of the 300 fatalities were men who had been left wounded on the ground and were subsequently shot dead on showing some sign of life. This would mean that there had been around 600 casualties in all. If the charge had been only a paltry 800 strong, as Wilson suggests, the loss of so high a proportion as three-quarters of the men involved is certain to have elicited comment in other accounts. The average strengths of massed Mahdist formations over the course of the two battles in the Bayūda also tend to argue against so low a figure. Nowhere else have we seen a shock-action formation of fewer than 2,000 men. Two possibilities present themselves: first, Wilson's numerical estimate might simply be some way wide of the mark; alternatively, he may have failed to make clear that he is describing only the leading wave of a much larger formation; the men who kept coming when others held back. Ultimately the total number of men who charged over the ridge remains uncertain. That there were no fewer than 4,000–6,000 *anṣār* within striking distance of the square when the charge took place is clear from a number of other sources.

Composition of the Mahdist Force

It is readily apparent that the majority of the men who fought the British at Abu Kru had been present two days earlier at Abu Klea. What is less obvious, as it has to be deduced from a number of less than emphatically expressed sources, is that a fresh contingent of *anṣār* arrived at Metemmeh on 18 January, which is to say the day intervening between the two battles. It appears to have been around 2,000 strong and was under the command of a prominent Mahdist *amīr* called al-Nūr Bey Muḥammad 'Anqara. With Mūsā wad Ḥilū dead and the rest of the senior command structure devastated, it was Nūr 'Anqara who led the Mahdist host at Abu Kru.[144]

Nūr 'Anqara was an interesting though somewhat unsavoury character. Born a Sudanese Dongolāwī, he had enlisted with the Egyptian colonial garrison as a cavalry irregular. He had risen to much greater prominence as a military freebooter under Zubair Pasha, whose chief of staff he was during the 1874–5 conquest of Dār Fūr. He went on to serve in slave-raiding expeditions under Zubair's son. When the troublesome Sulaimān rose against Gordon in 1878, Nūr 'Anqara deserted to the government side with about 2,000 men. Gordon rewarded his defection with elevation to the rank of colonel and a succession of government appointments. By 1882 he was in command of the garrison at Bāra. The hopeless military situation prevailing in Kordofan at that time left him with little choice but to capitulate. Changing sides had worked for him before and again paid dividends when Muḥammad Aḥmad appointed him as an *amīr*.[145] He threw himself into his new allegiance with a passion. Father Ohrwalder, the captive missionary, reports an occasion early in 1884 when he personally beheaded three Nuba captives in cold blood.[146] An ogre he may have been, but given Nūr 'Anqara's military pedigree it is little wonder that the Battle of Abu Kru proved quite so testing for the British.

Following its mauling at Abu Klea, the Mahdīst host can only have been less than buoyed up by the prospect of fighting the British for the second time in three days. Mūsā wad Ḥilū we must remember was not just a Mahdīst *amīr*, but a brother of the Khalīfa Alī wad Ḥilū, a member of the 'divinely chosen one's' innermost circle. The combination of being defeated at the hands of godless infidels, and having so prestigious a leadership figure killed in the process, cannot have done much for the average *anṣāri*'s faith in the *imams*' invocations of divine intervention. In addition to Mūsā wad Ḥilū, the commanders of the Metemmeh and Berber contingents had also been casualties of Abu Klea. According to the intelligence report written by Sir Charles Wilson on 18 January,[147] a document based largely on the interrogation of prisoners taken the day before, the Amīr 'Ali-wad-Saad of Metemmeh had been killed in the battle. This turned out not to be true, however. Intelligence gathered by Verner, a little under a fortnight later, indicated that he had in fact been wounded in the leg and side and made his way to Metemmeh.[148] The Amīr 'Abd-al-Mājid Nasr al-Din abū' l-Kailak, the commander of the Berber contingent, was said by the prisoners to have been wounded in the arm. While Wilson's report has him wounded and retiring towards Berber, the later Verner report confirms the nature of his injury but places him in Metemmeh alongside 'Ali-wad-Saad on or about 30 January.[149] It is clear, then, that by the time Abu Kru was fought, the riparian Arabs had been deprived of their most notable leaders and must have found themselves under the command of much less celebrated figures. In addition to their battle casualties of two days earlier, the strength of the three Berberine tribes, the 'Abābda, Barabra and Bisharin, would have been further reduced by the large numbers of men who had accompanied the wounded back to the north. This might even have rendered the Berber contingent all but non-effective in the second battle. By contrast the Ja'līyīn and Awadiyeh fighters had retired onto their home turf, with the British only a day's march behind them. They would thus have had the opportunity to top up their fighting contingents to full strength with a new levy of older men, teenaged boys and men of more conventional fighting age who had earlier come up with a good enough excuse not to be mobilized in the first wave. The arrival of the British on the doorstep would have negated virtually all such excuses. Thus the Metemmeh contingent, which does not seem to have sustained a particularly heavy loss at Abu Klea anyway, would probably still have been around 2,000 strong at Abu Kru.

The Kordofani contingent at Abu Klea had been so badly mauled that Rudolf Slatin, at the time a prisoner in the Mahdī's camp, records in his *Fire and Sword in the Sudan* that he was told that, 'The Degheim and Kināna had been almost annihilated.'[150] Allowing for a certain amount of hyperbole, the original Kordofani contingent cannot have been much more than 3,000 strong in the second fight. It is distinctly likely that they would have been much less enthusiastic about charging a British square for a second time. As far as the *jihādīya* contingent is concerned, it might well have been reduced through the losses of two days earlier to something around 250–300 men.

When it comes to determining the exact movements of Mahdīst reinforcements, the various elements of Sir Charles Wilson's testimony conspire to generate a picture which is less than crystal clear. Fortunately Verner's diary provides a little more lucidity.[151] Particularly useful is the fact that Verner records the defection to the British on 7 February of two rebels who had formerly been Egyptian soldiers. One of them was a man called 'Achmet Mohamed', who reported that he had come north from Omdurman with 'Nur Anga' (Verner's rendering of Nūr 'Anqara) and had fought at Abu Kru. He estimated the strength of the new contingent as 2,000 men, a figure which, while it cannot be regarded as absolutely reliable, certainly has a realistic air about it. There are no clues as to the tribal make-up of this contingent, but there would have to be a reasonably strong likelihood that they were also Kordofanis. Achmet Mohamed's testimony would have it that nearly three-quarters of Nūr 'Anqara's men were killed in 'the battle of the square which reached the river'.[152] While this cannot literally be true, as it would imply a fatal loss of 1,500 men, it does tend to support the notion that the charge on the square was spearheaded by the new arrivals.

Although the attack from the gravel ridge appears not to have fallen *exclusively* to Kordofanis, there is good reason to believe that the western tribes again provided its mainstay. Sir Charles Wilson's supplement to his official report states that, 'amongst the killed were five sheikhs or emirs of the Baggara Arabs'.[153] This could be taken to indicate that the Daghaim, Kināna and Hamr again participated in strength, or alternatively that the new arrivals were also of Baqqāra stock. Achmet Mohamed's testimony, considered in combination with Slatin's remarks about the 'annihilation' of the Daghaim and Kināna in the first battle, argues in favour of the latter scenario. Wilson's account of his wandering across the battlefield the following day shows that in all likelihood a body of Ja'līyīn also participated in the culminating attack.

During the night the Arabs had buried their principal men, but I counted over 200 bodies still lying on the ground; they all had the Mahdi's uniform, and the string of ninety-nine beads round their necks. Some of them were fine men, Arabs from Kordofan, like those who fought at Abu Klea; whilst others were black regulars, and a few were Jalin from the neighbourhood. We found two or three wounded, whom we carried on with us. From these we had confirmation of the fall of Omdurman, and heard that another force under Feki Mustafa[154] was on its way from Khartum to fight us, and that one was also coming up the river from Berber; so we had every prospect of more fighting.[155]

Nūr 'Anqara's Battle Plan

If one takes a wider view of the admittedly fragmentary evidence, the following postulations would seem plausible. Nūr 'Anqara took command of a Mahdīst army only one day after it had taken a great many casualties, been beaten by a numerically inferior foe and lost most of its senior leadership figures. This much is certain fact. The army's belief in the Mahdi's divine credentials would have left it collectively disheartened by so adverse a turn of events. Many Berberines may have gone home with the wounded in the knowledge that a second British force was moving around the Great Bend to menace their home territory. Nūr 'Anqara had accumulated sufficient military experience, from opposite sides of the fence, both to understand the capacity and capability of the army he now commanded and to foretell the tactics of disciplined regular troops like the British. He knew that it would be wise to defend the river as far forward as possible, so as to deny his enemy access to water, and at the same time make optimal use of harassing fire. Hence he threw the *jihādīya* and other rifle-armed troops forward as soon as the British appeared at the edge of the Bayūda. This first offensive movement initiated the protracted fight around the *zariba*. He knew also that a shock-action charge should be a tactic of last resort and that the only troops who might be readily amenable to making one were the new arrivals from Omdurman. These he would keep concentrated at the river as his strike force. Because there were as few as 2,000 of them he probably supplemented them in echelon with bodies of local Ja'līyīn and Awadiyeh, contingents which had not suffered particularly badly at Abu Klea.

When the British square began its advance to the river, he committed the 3,000 remaining Daghaim, Kināna and Hamr Kordofanis to the plain in the hope that they might once again give the British a run for their money. Although they massed, manoeuvred and threatened, the British halted periodically to pour forth the same sort of heavy fire which had proved so ruinous only two days earlier. The British fire exerted a marked deterrent effect, with the result that the three worst-mauled tribes were unable to muster the collective courage required for an all-out charge.

Anticipating a certain amount of hesitancy amongst the survivors of the grand charge at Abu Klea, Nūr 'Anqara assigned the shock-action phase of his battle plan, the downhill assault from the gravel ridge, to the new arrivals, with the Ja'līyīn and Awadiyeh arrayed behind them as a second wave. While Nūr

'Anqara's men charged hard, none of the other contingents could be persuaded to follow suit and, as soon as the first echelon had been repulsed, lost no time in quitting the field.

Having taken care to demarcate the line between demonstrable fact and hypothesis, this would seem to represent a not unreasonable reconstruction of Abu Kru from the Mahdist side of the fence. At the same time it has to be freely owned that one or two elements in a reconstruction of this kind could be wide of the mark.

The British Loss

Up to this point historians have had only a limited amount of data available on the British casualties, and in particular on how they divided between the square and the *zariba*. Unhelpfully the War Diary throws no light on the matter. Verner notes in his diary that 10 men were killed and 30 wounded with the square, and that there were 15 killed and 60 wounded 'before starting'. He then goes on to list the killed and wounded officers and concludes by saying that the total loss was 25 killed and 105 wounded, rendering his earlier division of the wounded between square and *zariba* deficient to the tune of 15.[156] In his *Sketches in the Soudan* he contradicts his diary, albeit only marginally, by saying that, 'the total losses in the day's fighting amounted to 2 officers and 19 men killed and 9 officers and about 100 men wounded. Two war correspondents, St. Leger Herbert and Jack Cameron, were killed in the zariba before the square advanced.' This amounts in total to 23 killed and 109 wounded.

Macdonald, for his part, offers a description of the burial of the casualties at the *zariba* the following day:

Before marching our dead were buried in two pits, one of which was filled with fourteen bodies, laid side by side, and another in line with it by those of Quartermaster Lima of the 19th Hussars, Conductor Jewell of the Commissariat, St. Leger Herbert (correspondent of the 'Morning Post'), and Cameron of the 'Standard'.[157]

Macdonald, then, places no fewer than eighteen of the dead in the *zariba* – an implausible-sounding three-quarters of the total loss. Burleigh tends to support Macdonald, by noting that 'our approximate loss in the day's fighting was, in and about the works, sixteen killed and sixty wounded; with the square twelve killed and forty wounded'.[158]

Turning to the official account we find that Colvile, who excludes the two war correspondents from his figures, gives the casualties as one officer and twenty-two NCOs and men killed, and eight officers and ninety NCOs and men wounded.[159] This is the most authoritative set of figures we have to work with, but incorporates a number of soldiers who were mortally wounded on 19 January and died of their wounds subsequently. Added complications in attempting to divide these figures between square and *zariba* include the fact that some men were shot with the square but were then hastily recovered to the *zariba*.

Fortunately the 23 January casualty returns residing amongst the Airlie Papers permit us to flesh out some of the detail.[160] The returns do not itemize the wounded, but do divide the fatalities and mortally wounded (or at least those of the latter who died in the period 19–23 January), between those who were killed in the *zariba* and those who were killed with the square. According to their commanding officers, the following personnel lost their lives in the *zariba*:

> Quartermaster Arthur Lima (19th Hussars)
> Conductor A. C. Jewell (Commissariat & Transport Corps)
> 16774 Sapper William Chapman (26th Field Coy., RE)
> 21 Private Arthur Holland (RMLI, No. 4 Coy., GCR)
> 1657 Private W. H. Jones (2nd DCLI, B Coy., MICR)
> 2308 Private W. Powell (Queen's Bays, No. 2 Coy., HCR)
> 1446 Trumpeter W. Wilson (Royals, No. 4 Coy., HCR)
> St Leger Herbert (*Morning Post*)
> Jack Cameron (*Standard*)

At one officer, two correspondents and six NCOs and men, or nine in all, this is a much smaller number than is suggested by Macdonald's description of the funeral service on the 20th.

Buried with these nine would have been perhaps two or three men who were killed near the *zariba* rather than inside it: we know for sure that the bodies of two members of the Royal Sussex were recovered back to the position. Even if we tally an additional three there would still only be twelve bodies to bury, rather than the eighteen cited by Macdonald. It is not inconceivable that the balance were native drivers and servants whose names went unrecorded. Nor is it impossible that Macdonald simply got his facts wrong, or that he calculated a figure retrospectively and inaccurately whilst writing his book. Not listed in the HCR return is 953 Trooper W. Hodges, mortally wounded beside Lord Cochrane in the redoubt on the spur, who, it follows, must have clung to life beyond the point at which the regiment submitted its paperwork. 1751 Private R. Wareham of Marling's 3rd KRRC section is reported as having died a week after the battle and similarly does not appear in the MICR return.[161]

The essential deduction from the casualty returns is that only nine British lives were lost to incoming small-arms fire prior to the advance of the square. That is not to say that the fire was any less heavy than has been described, for no fewer than sixty men were wounded by it. The low ratio of killed to wounded is attributable to the long engagement ranges, which saw many men struck by spent rounds and ricochets. Notwithstanding the good fortune experienced by Somerset, Snow, Gleichen, Burleigh, Villiers, Prior, Pearse and others, even spent rounds can cause severe bruising and break bones, while a great many ricochets retain more than enough energy to kill and maim.

The regimental casualty returns tell us that the following personnel were killed in the square:

1732 Sergeant W. H. Hinton (1st South Staffs, A Coy., MICR)
37 Corporal Mark Carey (RMLI, No. 4 Coy., GCR)
2204 Corporal J. Newton (5th DG, No. 3 Coy., HCR)
25 Private Edward Arnold (RMLI, No. 4 Coy., GCR)
1769 Private John Daly (1st Royal Sussex)
7224 Private Philip Hickey (2nd Gren. Gds., No. 1 Coy., GCR)
1763 Private Richard Leppard (1st Royal Sussex)
41 Private Edwin Meade (RMLI, No. 4 Coy., GCR)
24 Private William Mitchell (RMLI, No. 4 Coy., GCR)
19 Drummer Edward Rogers (1st Royal Sussex);
7712 Private William Rogers (1st Gren Gds, No. 1 Coy., GCR)
2000 Private T. Rose (1st South Staffs, A Coy., MICR)
2139 Private A. Russell (5th Lancers, No. 5 Coy., HCR)
1410 Private G. Thornhill (5th DG, No. 3 Coy., HCR)
5074 Private William West (2nd Scots Gds., No. 3 Coy., GCR)

In addition the following personnel died subsequently of their wounds:

2445 Colour Sergeant George Kekewich (1st Coldm. Gds., No. 2 Coy., GCR)
8587 Private Daniel Bailey (1st Gren. Gds., No. 1 Coy., GCR)
1304 Private R. Blake (2nd Connaught Rangers, D Coy., MICR)[162]

This amounts to a total of eighteen men, fifteen of whom were killed outright. This is a higher figure than has usually been cited.

All this means that the total British loss in the battle was actually one officer, two war correspondents and twenty-four NCOs and men killed, with 8 officers and some 85–90 NCOs and men wounded. One more officer would linger for the best part of a month and should of course be added to the final tally.[163] The wounded officers were:

Brig. Gen. Sir Herbert Stewart (3rd DG, General Officer Commanding), mortally
Major Lord Arthur Somerset (Blues, No 2. Coy., HCR), slightly
Captain the Earl of Airlie (10th Hussars, Brigade Major), slightly
Lieutenant Charles Crutchley (Scots Guards, Adjutant, GCR), very severely
Lieutenant Gerald Leigh (Blues, QM, HCR), extent of injury unknown
Lieutenant Charles Livingstone (Black Watch, A Coy., MICR), extent of injury unknown
Lieutenant Archie Miles (2nd KRRC, C Coy, MICR), severely
Sub-Lieutenant Edward Munro (RN, 1st Division, Naval Brigade), severely
Lieutenant Thomas Snow (Somerset LI, D Coy., MICR), slightly

Quite what befell Leigh and Livingstone is not known. Airlie, who for a second time remained on duty despite a battlefield injury, must have been hit by a spent round or ricochet, though where in the body he was struck and at quite what point in the fighting is similarly unclear. Villiers drew a sketch of the climax of the battle for the *Graphic* in which Airlie is portrayed standing inside the square, on duty, gesticulating with his right arm, while he carries his other arm in a sling. What we cannot infer from this piece of evidence alone is whether the sling dated back to the hand injury he sustained at Abu Klea, or whether it had been newly applied to an injury sustained at Abu Kru. If it was the latter, we cannot know either whether he was hit during the defence of the *zariba* or the advance of the square. It is interesting that the Orders Book went unsigned for a couple of entries after Abu Kru, before the signature block changed as a matter of routine to that of Major Wardrop; but there is nothing specific to link the change to Airlie's injuries and it could have taken place for a range of other reasons.

The casualty return in Appendix G is based on a list which accompanied Wolseley's telegram to Hartington of 23 January and which was published in the *Standard* six days later. Because it incorporates without distinction all the casualties incurred between 19 and 21 January inclusive, it is not possible to separate definitively the Abu Kru casualties, the overwhelming majority, from the balance, although where it is possible to do so the casualties of 21 January have been annotated as such.

The Nile at Last

Once the enemy cavalry had been frightened off by the stammering volley from the rear face, the square was free to resume its march to the Nile. The indispensable Verner once again took up position in front and led off across the plateau beyond the gravel ridge. The exhausted and heavily laden bearer-company camels were slower than ever. An order to push on with all possible speed so as to beat the onset of darkness had little effect.[164] The sun had already set when the presence of a naked flame in the distance betrayed the presence of a cluster of dwellings. Verner went back to report to Sir Charles Wilson and suggested that it might be prudent to steer a slight south-westerly oblique, in order to avoid any danger of a sudden fusillade from the buildings. Wilson agreed the proposal. Not long afterwards Verner struck the head of a wide re-entrant. This could only mean that they had reached the far side of the plateau. Verner set off downhill and, sure enough, as he reached the mouth of the feature, two wild geese took to the air honking their alarm call. Although he did not yet know it they had in fact been put up from the western tip of Gubat Island. At last it dawned on Verner that the bank of white, taken by his exhausted mind for mist, was actually a great stretch of water. He was the first to enjoy the long drink that everybody in the Desert Column had been craving all day. Not long afterwards Sir Charles Wilson and Stuart-Wortley also appeared on the riverbank in company with a few other officers. The last glimmer of daylight was fading fast as the square came down to the water. Amidst the ensuing scenes of jubilation, Captain Verner climbed back to the top of the riverbank and promptly passed out in a pea-field. Count Gleichen describes how, despite all the excitement, good order and military discipline were maintained to the last.

The men were as wild with joy as their exhausted condition would allow. The wounded were held up for one look at the gleaming river, and then hurried to the banks. Still, perfect discipline was observed. Not a man left his place in the ranks until his company was marched up to take its fill. The front face having drunk itself full was marched to relieve the rear face and so on, in order that, in case of attack, no flank should be left undefended. However all was silent as the grave and the enemy disturbed us not. In the distance was still heard the faint noise of tom-toms, but most of us were too sleepy to pay any attention to them.[165]

As Sir Charles Wilson recounts, Verner was not the only one to pass out with exhaustion.

Directly everyone had had a drink, I sent Lawson and his sappers to cut brush for a zariba and had pickets posted on each side of the ravine we had come down. The men were so exhausted that when they came up from their drink at the river they fell down like logs, and we had some trouble rousing them and getting them into their places for the night.[166]

By the time two burly soldiers dragged Captain Verner back to his feet, the rest of the force had watered itself, established a line of sentries along the ridge, turned the camels out to graze on the villager's crops and re-formed the square on the riverbank. Verner was quickly back to his normal self, but was irritated to find that his binoculars had again disappeared along with the blue sailor's guernsey, 'a companion of 12 years', which he had been carrying in his haversack. 'The bivouac was a very rough one and the night was bitterly cold,' he observed, 'but nothing to compare to that after Abu Klea.'[167] There was still plenty of ammunition to hand but, except in the case of the Guards, next to no food. Lionel Trafford went to see Colonel Boscawen to ask if his men might draw on GCR's second days' worth of rations, to which the colonel was happy to agree. Unfortunately it transpired that the Guards' second camel had been killed during the advance, as a result of which Trafford and his men ended up going hungry after all.[168]

While others slept the sleep of the dead, the doctors had roughly thirty wounded men to treat. Sir Charles Wilson made a point of visiting the medical staff and their patients before turning in:

The doctors behaved splendidly; nothing could have been better. They had been up three nights and through two fights, and here they were again working on the fourth night. One of them, I believe, fainted from exhaustion, but they went on until every wounded man had been attended. The bearer-company also behaved admirably: not a wounded man was left on the ground; everyone was at once picked up and put into a cacolet on a camel or on to a stretcher. The hospital after a fight is a horrible sight, but the men bore their wounds nobly, and were much quieter than I expected.[169]

Brigade commander he may have been, but the intelligence officers were Wilson's mess-mates and it was in the company of Verner and Stuart-Wortley that he finally lay down to sleep. His second interpreter had failed to bring along the colonel's ulster overcoat as instructed, so that the trio were once again glad of Stuart-Wortley's plundered prayer-mat. Wilson wrote that he slept 'very soundly at first but as the night wore on, it got bitterly cold and one could only sleep in snatches'.[170]

Lieutenant Snow was on picket duty and felt his injured leg stiffening. In the absence of any excitement on the picket line, he hobbled down to see one of the doctors, but found them so busy with the seriously wounded that he about-turned and hobbled back to his post.[171]

So did the Desert Column finally ensconce itself on the Nile. If the casualties incurred in the square had been the only losses, the Nile might have been regarded as relatively cheaply won, but the hospital at the *zariba* was twice as crowded as the one on the river. Taken in conjunction with the heavy losses at Abu Klea, there could be no denying that the Desert Column had been badly mauled in fighting its way across the Bayūda. Lord Wolseley took his breakfast the following morning quite oblivious to the fact that his army had fought two major battles.

The *Zariba*: Late Afternoon to Nightfall

The enemy marksmen loitering in the vicinity of the *zariba* broke off the fight at about 4.30 p.m. and scuttled away after the rest of the defeated army. Norton, Du Boulay and the gun crews were able for some time to continue pitching shells amongst the enemy, as they made their way back towards Metemmeh. Had there been more 7-pound shells available they might have upped their rate of fire and made life a misery for the shattered Mahdist host. Instead they did what they could, ever mindful of the likely need to lend fire support to an assault on a walled town.

The fighting troops had been so preoccupied with defending their posts that they had failed to notice the native workers, ably assisted by two or three reprobates from the Medical Staff Corps, plundering the baggage behind their backs. General Stewart's kit was pilfered, as was that of a good many other officers, while somebody had also turned over the medical stores and made off with a quantity of medicinal brandy. Macdonald was unable to find his Greek servant and soon worked out that he was one of the culprits. He was lucky that his kit had been incorporated into the barricade and thus escaped being raided. As the sun began setting over the position he was forced to rely on the 'charity of friends' for a meal, and was given a tin of bully beef and some biscuits by Deputy Assistant Commissary-General Marcus Rainsford.[172] Some time elapsed before he got to enjoy his frugal supper, however, as he fell asleep with his back to the barricade, bully in one hand and hardtack in the other. He slept that night in the hospital fort where around sixty men were being treated for gun-shot wounds of varying severity.

There were two alarms during the course of the night, but on neither occasion did the enemy actually put in an appearance. The rudely awakened Macdonald was much disturbed by the suffering of the wounded.

One poor fellow who had been hit in the abdomen had become delirious. Late in the evening I noticed him getting up on his knees and heard him raving – talking of friends at home, as I gathered from what he said; and then in his agony he would lie down again and moan. The first time we were roused I heard him still. The second time not hearing him, I learned upon enquiry that he was dead. I could not help thinking then, as I have often done in similar circumstances in the past, that a night alongside of a field hospital after a battle would do much to moderate the tone of those who clamour for military expeditions in defence of national interests or for the maintenance of British prestige.

We had no chaplain with us, although there were two of them at Korti. The reason of this was that the chief of the staff [Buller] refused permission for either of them to accompany the Desert Column . . . Surely more consideration ought to have been shown to the spiritual wants of our troops, when exposed to wounds and death, than was manifested on this occasion. Our chaplains are appointed and paid by the British public for certain religious purposes; and where could their services be more useful or appreciated than in a field hospital after a battle? Our wounded men were nevertheless allowed on this occasion to suffer or die without the consolations of religion so far as chaplains were concerned. Many of them I was glad to see however, had their Bibles with them; and some of the officers as well as others did all they could to make up for this mistake of those in authority – to call it by its softest name.[173]

Lord Charles Beresford was also sleeping in the hospital fort, but was woken twice during the course of the night by the adjutant of GCR, who on both occasions asked him for water. The senior naval officer was doubtless bemused that a mere lieutenant should pester him so, as Charlie Crutchley was made of such stern stuff that Beresford remained oblivious to his condition. The following afternoon Crutchley's leg was amputated high above the knee.[174]

Chapter 14

The Fort of the Infidels

Gubat and Metemmeh: 20–23 January 1885

This is the fort of the infidels, the liars, the enemies of God. God curse them.

Annotation on a captured Mahdist sketch-map,
showing the British position at Gubat

WITH THE COMING OF THE DAWN the officers and men of the Desert Column were shaken awake and ordered to stand to their arms. Having lain down to sleep amongst the men of his company, Captain Trafford was perplexed on waking to find himself surrounded by guardsmen. Instructed during the course of the night to shift their position slightly, the C Company sergeants had been quite unable to wake their captain and left him to slumber on in the tender care of the Guards.[1]

In the event neither the *zariba* nor the lodgement on the river was threatened from the morning gloom, leaving the senior officers free to concentrate on the pressing need to reunite the column. The *zariba* was a scene of great confusion, with wounded men lying on all sides and most of the camel saddles, ration boxes and other baggage incorporated into the low barricades encircling the knoll. Around a hundred dead camels were scattered amongst the surviving animals.[2] Alex Macdonald was surprised to find that the horse he had left on the crest was still alive, with only a graze across both forelegs and a bullet lodged in the flap of its saddle.[3] Beresford and Barrow could not allow the barricades to be disassembled or the baggage animals to be loaded, until such time as it became clear that the main body was marching back to their succour. In the meantime there was nothing to prevent the troops enjoying a hasty breakfast. At the bivouac on the river, where there were next to no rations to be had, the officers were turning their thoughts to securing the position against the possibility of counter-attack. Neither British force could be entirely confident about the fate or state of the other, though the clear-cut victory at the foot of the gravel ridge, coupled with the absence of any subsequent heavy firing, gave Beresford and Barrow good reason to believe that Wilson had succeeded in gaining the river.

Securing the Lodgement on the Nile – a.m. Tuesday 20 Jan

Willoughby Verner woke, 'quite frozen and stiff as can be'[4] but quickly pulled himself together and set off for an outpost on the right flank manned by C Company, MICR. He was greeted by 'Punch' Hardinge, who lost no time in pointing out that there was a deserted but potentially bothersome cluster of buildings just in front of his position. This was one of the hamlets lying between Abu Kru and Gubat. Having given the place a wide berth in the twilight of the previous evening, its presence came as no surprise to Verner. Casting about to assess the defensibility of the low-lying lodgement on the Nile, he concluded that certain commanding stretches of the long gravel plateau would have to be denied to the enemy. The hamlet lay some 780 yards from the river and about 3,500 yards upstream of Metemmeh. It consisted of fifteen square-shaped dwellings and a handful of round ones. It was clear to Verner that the site would make both a good high-ground strongpoint and a tolerably good hospital, where if nothing else the wounded could be sheltered from the sun. All twenty or so buildings were detached and constructed from baked mud. The square houses were about eleven feet high, varied in size from twelve feet square to thirty feet square and had strong flat roofs made from *dhura*-stalks, baked mud and wooden beams. The larger ones were typically divided into two rooms. By contrast the round huts had pointed thatched roofs which could be of no possible use as elevated fire-positions. Doorways were small, generally about five feet high by two feet wide, and there were no windows. About 300 yards west of the hamlet was another small cluster of dwellings. Both sets of residents had fled with almost all their possessions, save fortuitously for a few *angareb* bed-frames.[5]

Sir Charles Wilson, meanwhile, had given orders for work parties to fill all the empty water-skins and tanks, so that in due course they could be taken back to the troops holding the *zariba*. As soon as the light came up he also despatched small reconnaissance patrols to probe up and down the riverbank. The upstream patrol duly returned with a black slave who had been content to surrender quietly. Questioned through Wilson's interpreter, the man knew of no significant Mahdist presence upriver. The downstream patrol recorded no significant sightings of the enemy and brought in no prisoners, but was able to report that all the habitation between the British position and Metemmeh had been abandoned.[6] Wilson now gave orders that GCR and MICR should prepare to march back to the *zariba*. Reggie Talbot's detachment of Heavies, perhaps 125 bayonets, and the two small Royal Sussex companies under Major Sunderland, around 100 more, would remain at the river to secure the lodgement and protect the wounded.

When Verner re-joined the headquarters, he outlined his tactical concerns to Sir Charles and suggested that he order the occupation and fortification of the hamlet on the ridge. When the colonel declined the advice, Verner pressed him harder, suggesting that he be allowed to take some men and go and secure the buildings himself. Wilson again expressed reservations, doubtless in the belief that the main imperative was to keep a firm hold on the Nile. Verner briefly busied himself with other business, but on discovering that Lord Arthur Somerset had returned to duty and would be staying behind with Colonel Talbot, decided to try and win him over to his way of thinking. This time Verner's arguments met with a positive reception: Somerset gave him Lieutenant Lord Binning and a twenty-five-man detachment of the Blues. At some point in the proceedings Sir Charles must have relented and endorsed the measure. As soon as the detachment reached the buildings, Verner took the young peer to one side to give him a thorough briefing on the lie of the land and the defensive measures he considered appropriate.[7]

It was at about 6.30 a.m. that the main body moved off for the *zariba*.[8] The return journey quickly took the force onto the high ground around the hamlet. No doubt the earnestness with which Verner had pressed his advice had been preying on Wilson's mind in the interim. Now that he was able to scan the surrounding terrain from an elevated vantage point, the vulnerability of the riverside position and the hamlet's merits as a strongpoint both became apparent. He promptly gave orders that Talbot's command and the wounded should be brought up from the riverbank to the ridge. Lieutenant Henry Lawson and his handful of sappers were detailed to stay with the Heavies and Royal Sussex and assist them with the fortification of the buildings. Moving the wounded was always going to be a time-consuming process and if Percy Marling's watch is to be believed seems to have taken about 2½ hours in all.[9]

A number of officers occupied themselves in the meantime by scanning the general area of the *zariba* with their field glasses, but at a range of more than three miles found it impossible to say for sure whether it was held by friend or foe. To the right 'crowds of the enemy' could be seen 'hanging about' in the direction of Metemmeh.[10] At one point two Camel Corps riding camels, identifiable by their red saddlecloths, were led into the town, though the watching officers were quick to conclude that they could easily have been lost on the night march and did not necessarily betoken any sort of disaster at the *zariba*. Gleichen suggests that there was talk at this juncture of making an immediate attack on Metemmeh, but as Wilson makes no mention of any such discussion, it is likely to have been mere idle chatter amongst the Guards officers. For some unknown reason, where originally Talbot was to have been left in command at the river, it was now to be Lord Somerset, twice wounded but soldiering on regardless, who would command the position centred on the hamlet.[11] While it is not explicitly stated anywhere in the sources, Talbot can be presumed to have travelled back to the *zariba* with Wilson, in order to attend to the forward move of the other half of his regiment.

Reuniting the Column

At around 9.30 a.m. the main body moved off again. The Guards and Mounted Infantry marched in separate regimental squares, with GCR leading and MICR echeloned diagonally to the left-rear. At the mid-way point between the two squares was a small cluster of baggage camels, most of which were laden with freshly filled water-tanks.[12] The British movement triggered a rapid concentration of *anṣār* on the open ground in front of Metemmeh, an unexpected development which left Wilson and his staff anticipating an attack. Unable to march away and leave Somerset's command to shift for itself, Wilson decided to change direction and offer battle. In the event the mere sight of the British advancing along the gravel plateau caused the rebels to break up and begin falling back into the town. A few long-range volleys from the Guards served both to inflict a few casualties on them and to hasten their retreat.[13]

Moving back into square, the British swung the line of march back towards the *zariba* and descended from the gravel plateau to the expanse of desert beyond. At the foot of the slope they found themselves interposed between Metemmeh and the scene of the previous day's climactic fight. A significant number of locals, who had been scouring the battlefield, were caught unawares by the arrival of the troops. Because they seemed intent only on carrying away their dead and wounded and there were women and children present, the British held their fire and went quietly on their way.[14]

The march back into the desert proceeded apace. Officers with binoculars quickly confirmed that all was well at the *zariba*. Lengthening their stride, the troops made light work of the two miles separating them from a hearty breakfast. The garrison of the *zariba* greeted the return of their victorious comrades with cheers, backslapping and congratulatory handshakes all round.

Back at the river the injured Somerset had asked Verner to devise a plan of defence. He began by torching the small group of buildings to the west of the hamlet. Because the five or so thatched huts dotted around the immediate position were not defensible and might provide cover for an assaulting enemy, they were in some cases demolished and in others burnt to the ground. Numerous small shanties and goat-pens were similarly disposed of. The flat-roofed houses were retained intact, provided with stockpiles of ammunition and water and each assigned a garrison of between six and twelve men according to size. Over the course of the morning the troops used logs and stones to raise low defensive parapets around the rooftops. In order that they could man their elevated stand-to positions in relative safety, they used picks to mouse-hole the ceilings and made ladders to go inside each of the buildings. Finally makeshift hospital wards were readied by gathering all the abandoned *angarebs* into the largest rooms.[15]

After slaking their thirst from the newly arrived water-tanks, the men who had remained at the *zariba* made an immediate start on the work of disassembling the barricades and loading the baggage camels. The Guards and Mounted Infantry were allowed to fall out to an eagerly anticipated breakfast of tea and bully beef, but were soon toiling hard beside everybody else. Sir Charles Wilson made his way to the little shelter which Frank Rhodes and the medics had erected over the grievously injured General Stewart: 'I found he had passed a fairly good night, and was not quite so low about himself. The doctors, too, gave a favourable account of his symptoms, and he had not much pain except when moving.'[16] When Sir Charles proceeded on his way to visit the rest of the wounded, he was enraged to stumble across a medic who was 'hopelessly and noisily drunk' on looted medicinal brandy: 'I was very wroth and longed for a return of the days when a man could be triced up and given four dozen lashes. All I could do was to have the brute tied up to a tree in the sun.'[17] When at length Wilson moved on in search of his kit, his 'most stupid of servants' and a belated breakfast, it was to find that his possessions had been thoroughly rifled. Not only had his ulster gone absent, but so too had all the little campaigning comforts he had allowed himself – small quantities of cocoa, condensed milk and compressed tea. A few sheets of foolscap writing paper were the only items to survive the attention of the more light-fingered drivers.[18]

Gleichen's account reflects something of the difficulty entailed in restoring a semblance of order to the administrative chaos:

. . . orders were given to load up all the camels left with the stores, and return as soon as possible. The work was hard, for all stores, boxes and saddles were built up round the zeriba, and over a hundred camels were dead. The contents of many of the boxes were lying scattered about, and the camels were stiff and tired with fatigue and hunger; added to this many of the saddles were broken, so several hours elapsed before everything was ready to start. I looked eagerly for my own camel, Potiphar, and found him calmly grazing about him in the same spot where I left him, not damaged in the least, and as bad-tempered as ever. Only my sheepskin and blankets had disappeared, but since they had probably gone for the wounded I did not mind: several of the others had their zuleetahs rifled, probably by the native drivers on the look-out for loot: so I was in comparative luck.[19]

If 'Potiphar' appeared game enough, most of the other animals on the position were in a state of considerable distress. The camels had been knee-haltered for more than twenty-four hours, had not eaten for four days and had been the best part of a week without water. Colonel Barrow's ponies, so vital to the Desert Column's scouting, early warning and intelligence-gathering functions, were all but on their last legs. Percy Marling always took a keen interest in horseflesh and noted that most of the Syrian greys had not had a drop of water for fifty-six hours. There was even one group of about 20 ponies which had gone without for seventy-two hours.[20] Nobody was more conscious of this than Barrow himself, one of the most fastidious managers of horse-flesh in the Army. In addition to the 100 or so camels which had been killed outright, a great many more had been wounded; quite how many the habitual insouciance of the dromedary made it impossible to tell. Lord Cochrane found that his camel had been shot through the head a few inches below its eye-line, but observed that it, 'ate as usual when it could get anything'.[21] Macdonald noted that even the unwounded camels were in 'wretched condition'.[22] As a result the officers of the transport staff advised Sir Charles that it would be impossible to move all the baggage to the river in one go. Wilson decided that Major Thomas Davison would stay behind with a detachment of fifty Heavies to garrison the outlying redoubt on the spur, until such time as sufficient baggage camels could be sent back to pick up the balance of the stores. Because this was unlikely to be until the following day, the redoubt was quickly strengthened in such a way as to make it impervious to an enemy rush. Davison's garrison would almost certainly have been based on No. 5 Company, HCR (5th and 16th Lancers).

At midday, Wilson, Beresford, Barrow, a handful of other officers and the six surviving war correspondents gathered around two shallow pits, one large and one small, in which the dead had been laid out. In the smaller of the graves were the mortal remains of St Leger Herbert, Jack Cameron, Quartermaster Lima and Conductor Jewell. Cameron's body had been carried to the graveside by a party of his peers: Alex Macdonald, Melton Prior, Harry Pearse, Charles Williams, Frederick Villiers and Bennet Burleigh.[23] Beresford asked if he might be allowed to read the Burial Service, a prerogative which in the absence of a chaplain was traditionally that of the senior officer present, a request to which Wilson readily gave his consent. Macdonald noted that Beresford read 'in feeling tones',[24] while Burleigh observed that Melton Prior was desperately upset.[25]

As soon as the moving graveside scene had played itself out, the officers in attendance returned to their duties. Cognizant of the poor state of his ponies, Percy Barrow was particularly anxious to make a start for the river. Having urged all possible haste on his men, he was able to depart some little while in advance of the main body. A few baggage camels, laden with enough food to provide Somerset's command with a much-needed meal, were hurried along in the wake of the cavalry.[26]

Slowly but surely the commissariat and transport staff assembled the baggage train at the foot of the knoll. The riding camels would be led in strings, so that the Guards and Mounted Infantry could be ready to fight at a moment's notice. At the last gasp the section of Somersets in D Company, MICR, lost the services of their officer. Thomas Snow had limped back from the river with his men, but on rousing himself for the return journey found that he was no longer able to walk. He was obliged to seek leave to ride back with the baggage train.[27] In order that he would not be unduly exposed to the sun, Sir Herbert Stewart was the last of the wounded to be brought down from the knoll. Before leading the column off, Sir Charles Wilson dropped in on the redoubt to check that the position had been made as secure as possible. In the course of his conversation with Major Davison he gave orders that all the debris left lying around the position should be burned, 'so that the enemy might not know how much we had suffered'.[28]

Wilson gave no time of departure in either his official report or his book. Macdonald put it at 2.30 p.m.,[29] while Marling went for 3.15 p.m.[30] The War Diary split the difference with, 'Started about 3p.m.'[31] The Guards and Mounted Infantry led the way in a 700-man fighting square, with the balance of the force, consisting of No. 1 Company, HCR, the Naval Brigade and Dorward's handful of sappers, echeloned to its right-rear in a much smaller square.[32] The baggage train, rendered even more unwieldy than usual by the presence of string upon string of riding camels, marched between the two bodies of troops. There was also a small rearguard, the composition of which is nowhere stated in the sources, but might conceivably have been a party of 19th Hussars.[33]

Progress across the desert was necessarily slow, as there were far too many serious casualties for the number of bearer-company litters. Some fifty-five officers and men had to be carried by stretcher-parties.[34] Although Sir Herbert Stewart and Lieutenant Charlie Crutchley were accorded the privilege of travelling in the centre of the fighting square, all the other casualties travelled with the baggage train. In order to avoid depleting the fighting units, volunteer stretcher-bearers had been called for from amongst the non-combatants. A number of the war correspondents had come forward, volunteering not only their own services but those of their servants too. In another somewhat bizarre anomaly in the sources, Melton Prior would later claim in his *Campaigns of a War Correspondent* that he and Burleigh carried a wounded private between them. He even recalled occasional interjections to the effect of, 'Come on, Prior, wake up!' from his partner. Burleigh's contemporaneous *Daily Telegraph* report, however, has the two of them carrying separate stretchers, each with the assistance of their respective servants. According to Burleigh the soldier he carried was a 'stalwart Marine named Lorraine',[35] although in fact 8086 Private H. Loraine was a member of the Grenadier Guards. Prior goes on to recount that four years later, while he was covering the war in Burma, a soldier approached him and said, 'Will you excuse me, sir, for the liberty of stopping you.' Prior did not know the man but indulged him all the same. 'Possibly you do not recollect me, but I am the man you and Mister Burleigh carried wounded from the fight at Abu Klea [*sic* – Abu Kru] to the Nile. I thanked you then, sir, but now that I am well I should like to take the opportunity of again thanking you for the careful way in which you carried me.'[36] Barring any inherently improbable half-way reshuffle in the carrying parties, whoever this man was, he was not Private Loraine, was not carried by Burleigh and cannot have said quite what Prior claims he said. As Burleigh put it in the *Daily Telegraph*, in a report written only five days after the fact, 'Prior convoyed another.' Of course it was 1912 before Prior got round to writing *Campaigns of a War Correspondent*.

On coming up level with the scene of the previous day's culminating fight, Major Pöe was told to take a few of his marines to bury the British dead. Sir Charles Wilson was anxious to confirm that no badly wounded men had been left behind when the square moved off, and accompanied the burial party in scouring across the battlefield. There were probably seven British bodies at issue. 'I was relieved,' wrote Wilson, 'to find that all of them had bullet-wounds which must have caused immediate death; and though the bodies had been stripped,[37] and three of them had been much cut about with spears and swords, there was none of that mutilation which is such a horrid feature in fights with some savages.'[38] Although the bodies of the amīrs, shaikhs and other notables had already been carried away, we have seen that Wilson counted more than 200 others still lying on the field. Three wounded Arabs were picked up and carried along with the column.[39] Questioned through interpreters, the prisoners let slip three important pieces of information. First, they corroborated the fall of Fort Omdurman. Next they confirmed that a fresh force of anṣār under the command of the Faqī Muṣṭafa was on its way downriver from

Omdurman. Finally, they added that there were also more Mahdīst reinforcements on their way upriver from Berber. Sir Charles Wilson gives no indication as to how he gauged the veracity of this information, but was certainly seized by the idea that two enemy forces would shortly be converging on his command. We do not know a great deal about the Faqī Muṣṭafa, who does not even attract an entry in Hill's *Biographical Dictionary of the Anglo-Egyptian Sudan*. What we do know is that he was a Ja'alī headman, 'of much repute for sanctity, and had commanded the Arabs on the Omdurman side from the very commencement of the siege'. Wilson adds that, 'his fighting capacity was not equal to his religious fervour'.[40]

Once Pöe and his men had interred the handful of British corpses the column moved on. Not long afterwards it broke the crest of the gravel ridge to come in sight of the fortified hamlet. Verner vaguely noted that it came up between 4.00 and 5.00 p.m., preceded some little while earlier by Barrow and the 19th Hussars.[41] The War Diary was much more precise in noting the column's time of arrival as 4.45 p.m.[42] Alex Macdonald was in such a sorry-looking state as he came in that a handful of spectators from the Heavies felt moved to adopt him temporarily. The Good Samaritans had been fortunate enough to acquire a part-share in a ewe found wandering amongst the buildings, so, sitting their weary guest down against the wall of one of the houses, they treated him to a revitalizing bowl of mutton broth. The headquarters staff, meanwhile, had been trotting about assigning unit tasks. The 19th Hussars and the camel lines would be located to the rear of the buildings, nearest the Nile, while the camel regiments were to bivouac around the other three sides of the hamlet, with GCR in the centre, HCR on the left, and MICR on the right facing Metemmeh. The strongpoint based on the buildings at the heart of the position would be held by Sunderland's brace of Royal Sussex companies. The Commissariat & Transport Corps men would also be in amongst the buildings with the stores stockpiled around them.[43]

Condition of the Command

Like the deadbeat Syrian ponies before them, the camels were ushered straight through to the Nile to be watered. Inevitably there was something of a stampede. Gleichen noted that 'Potiphar' drank from the river for fourteen minutes, before then setting about the nearby shrubbery as if he intended never to stop eating. This might tend to suggest a case of 'all's well that ends well' with the animals, until one contrasts Potiphar's condition with that of one of Gleichen's baggage camels. This second animal 'was so much affected by the sight of the river, that he took a mouthful and dropped stone dead'.[44] Of course an animal does not immediately recover its condition after days of deprivation and the cavalry ponies, for example, would be fit only for short patrols for some time to come. While the camels and horses were drinking their fill, the human casualties of war were being moved into the makeshift hospital wards dotted about the buildings on the ridge. Altogether there were now 104 battle casualties in the care of the medical staff, ten of whom were officers.[45] There would also have been several dozen sick, the number varying daily.

When Sir Charles Wilson wrote *From Korti to Khartum*, which of course was not merely a facsimile of his campaign journal but also intended as a vindication of his actions, he inserted a passage which reflected on the condition of the Desert Column when it reached the river. Although it was meant to encapsulate something of the difficulties he had inherited and was never intended as a criticism of Stewart's generalship, it nonetheless offers a number of interesting insights into just how badly the crossing of the Bayūda had backfired.

We had now secured ourselves on the Nile, and this is the place to consider the state in which we got there. First as regards the men. They had had no proper sleep on the night of the 16th–17th. On the 17th they had been roughly handled by the enemy, and fully realised they had had a narrow escape. On the night of the 17th–18th no sleep, and many of them employed all night on fatigue-duty, moving and loading up stores at the zeribah. On the 18th filling up water-tanks and waterskins at the wells; then the weary night-march through the thick grass and mimosa bush from 3 P.M. to 7 A.M. After this the trying time in the zeribah, and the march to the Nile, with its fight,* followed by a bivouac without blankets, and with little food. [*Wilson's footnote reads: On the 19th the men were under fire from about 8 A.M. till 5 P.M. – about nine hours.] Lastly the march back to the zeribah on the 20th, with the heavy work of dismantling the zeribah, loading up the camels, and carrying the wounded down. It may be said that the men arrived at the Nile after four days of exceptional exertion under a tropical sun, without having had one night's rest, and having lost, in killed and wounded, more than one-tenth of their number. They were in capital spirits, and the complete success of the previous day's fight had quite restored their confidence in themselves, which had been a little shaken at Abu Klea. Still they needed rest; and we knew no reinforcements were going to be sent or would start until we could get a message through to Lord Wolseley.

Next as regards the camels. They had been watered on the 13th and 14th, and did not get water again until the 19th and 20th. They had therefore been without water for from six to seven days, having been previously accustomed to water every second or third day. The camels started from Jakdul with about 12 lb of dura each or 3 lb a-day for four days, the usual allowance being 9 lb. They were thus on one-third rations, which they did not always get, for four days only out of six. From 2 P.M. on the 16th to 3 A.M. on the 18th, some thirty-seven hours, they were tied down so tightly in the zeribah, before Abu Klea, that they could not move a limb, and I doubt if they were fed at all during that time. Then from 3 P.M. on 18th to 7 A.M. on 19th, or sixteen hours, they were on the march, part of the time struggling through savas grass and mimosa by night; and they probably had their loads on for seventeen or eighteen hours. This was followed by another tying down in a zeribah for over twenty-four hours without any food. Can it be wondered at that the poor beasts were hardly able to crawl down to the river with their loads, and that they were practically useless without some rest and food? The result almost justified the *mot*, that we thought we had found in the camel an animal that required neither food, drink, nor rest: we certainly acted as if the camel were a piece of machinery. The sore backs from careless loading in the dark, and from tumbling about during the night-marches, were sickening to look at.

The cavalry horses were also quite done up. The way in which Barrow managed to bring the 19th Hussars across the desert is one of the best things in the expedition; but the horses had only a short drink at Abu Klea, and then they had barely enough to wash their mouths out until they got to the Nile on the 20th. The scouting of the Hussars during the march was admirably done; they were ubiquitous. But want of food and water no horses can fight against, and they were but a sorry spectacle as they moved out of the zeribah to go down to the river. They reached the Nile almost useless as cavalry, and could only be employed for scouting purposes, at short distances from the camp.[46]

This then was the state of the 'flying column' which might at any point be ordered to dash 100 miles south to Khartoum. It is apparent that the baggage camels and ponies would need a significant period of rehabilitation before marching anywhere else. We have seen that around 100 baggage animals had been lost during the night march, that another hundred more, this time a mixture of riding camels and baggage camels, had been shot dead in the recent battle and that an unknown number (speculatively 300–400), had been wounded. Many of the animals which had been chafed raw to the rib-cage by ineptly loaded baggage were still walking for the present, but would be destined in the fullness of time to expire from a fatal combination of distress and infection. The animals with bullets lodged somewhere in their bodies were only marginally less likely to succumb than the more obviously injured animals. If the Desert Column received orders to go anywhere in a hurry, it now looked as if it was going to have to walk.

The Walls of Metemmeh

Wilson had given some considerable thought as to whether it was advisable to make an immediate attack on Metemmeh the following day. The situation was much changed from the benign scenario imagined by Lord Wolseley when he penned Stewart's orders. For one thing the town seemed to be much bigger and more populous than had been anticipated. Furthermore, there was every reason to believe that the number of *anṣār* fighters still loitering in the town ran into several thousands. Given that the column was ensconced on the Nile and already capable of effecting a junction with Gordon's steamers, whenever they deigned to put in an appearance, there was a reasonable case to be made that Metemmeh could and should be left alone until such time as reinforcements came up. Wilson recollected that:

I thought over the whole question, and considered that the political effect of not taking Matammeh would be so bad that its capture ought to be attempted. Besides, as we had seen no signs of the approach of the expected reinforcements to the enemy, I hoped we might be able to establish ourselves in the town before they arrived. I had heard that on the north side of the town, and near its centre, there was a large government building; and I determined if possible to attack this, feeling sure that if it were once secured the place would be ours.[47]

In view of the accusations of procrastination that would later be levelled at Wilson, the rapidity with which he intended marching on Metemmeh is worthy of note. The

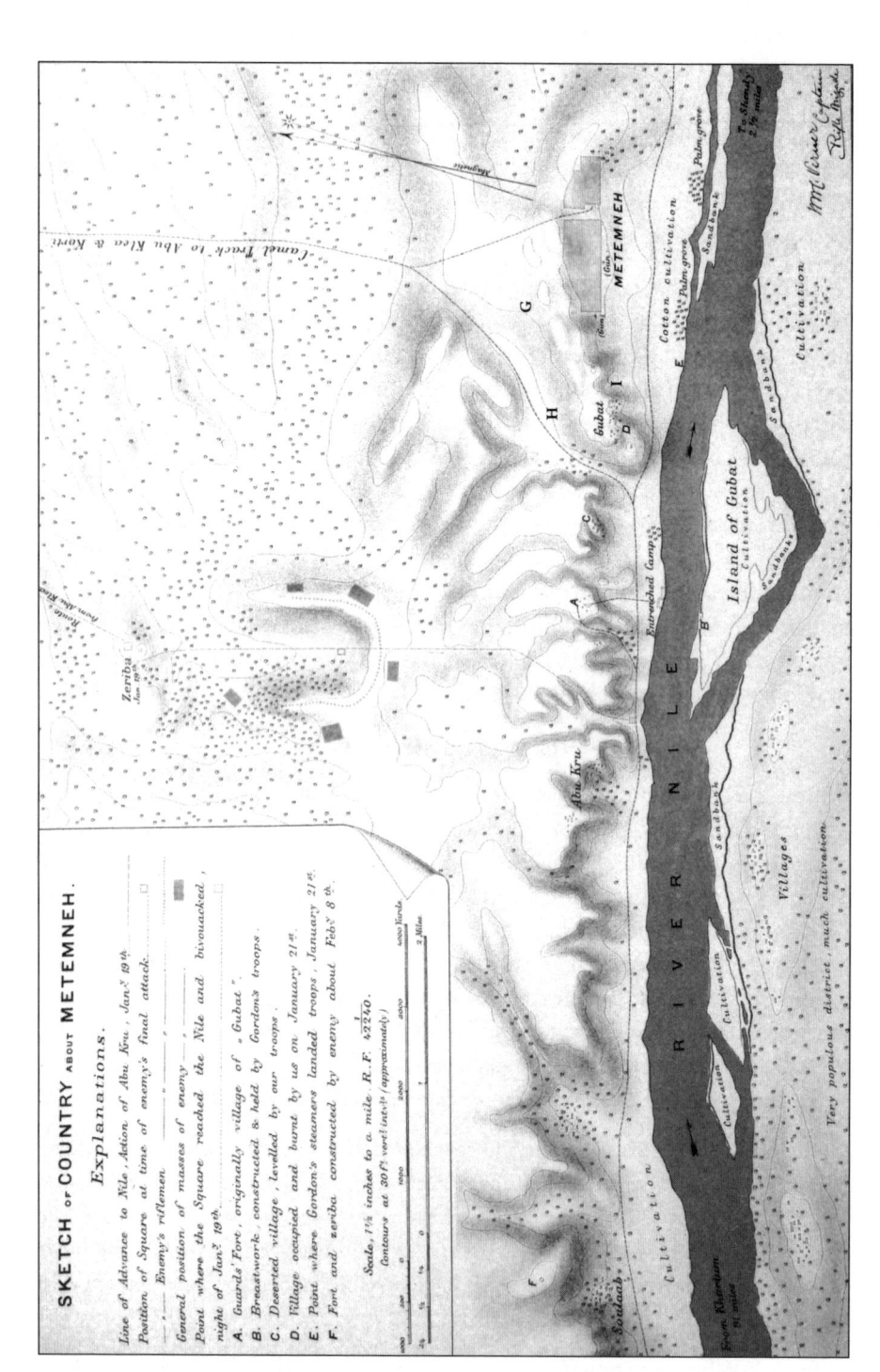

Map 11: Verner's map of Abu Kru, Gubat and Metemmeh (points G, H, I added)

commanding officers were duly called in for orders. The 19th Hussars, GCR, MICR, two HCR companies, the guns, the Naval Brigade and a slice of the medical staff would be committed to the operation. The units concerned were to parade in front of GCR's position at 5.00 the following morning, with full water-bottles, a day's rations and 100 rounds a man. Each company was to take a baggage camel with an additional (unspecified) quantity of reserve ammunition. It is likely that the animals would each have been loaded with four boxes, or 2,400 cartridges, sufficient to provide an additional 30–40 rounds per man. Reveille would be at 3.45 a.m.[48]

As Beresford had now been incapacitated by an excruciatingly painful boil on the backside, which prevented him walking anywhere, and Edward Munro, the only other naval officer still alive, was amongst the seriously wounded, the Naval Brigade would be under the command of Boatswain James Webber, who Beresford was later to observe, 'did admirably well'.[49]

Lieutenant Colonel Harry Bonham of the Grenadier Guards, GCR's signals officer, would be in charge of the fortified position while the main body was away.[50] The mainstay of the guard force would be C and G Companies of the Royal Sussex.[51] Major Sunderland's principal task was the protection of the wounded, the camel transport and the stores. Column Daily Orders, promulgated that evening, stated that his companies were also to act as a reserve. In addition he was instructed to post a strong picket to the west of the position and keep a weather-eye upriver, in order to give as much early warning as possible of the Faqī Muṣṭafa's approach. Finally he was to provide such stretcher-parties as Surgeon Major Ferguson might require for the morrow. These additional tasks may have left Sunderland and Trafford with as few as sixty men. It was not remotely realistic to imagine that they would be able both to defend the position and function as a reserve.

Having been told to detail only half of his regiment to the coming operation, Colonel Reggie Talbot selected Nos. 1 and 2 Companies, his least badly mauled. The merged No. 3/4 Company would not be committed, but was to hold itself in readiness to escort a convoy of baggage camels back to the old *zariba* and recover Major Davison's detachment and the balance of the stores.[52] Column Daily Orders stipulated that the troops were to make the journey mounted and indicated that they would be sent on their way only once Metemmeh had fallen.[53] With the details settled the commanding officers returned to their units to brief their officers, eat their suppers and snatch a few hours' sleep. There was one problem with Wilson's intent to attack from the north: getting into position would draw the force around a mile into the desert and so preclude its remaining interposed between the enemy and the thinly defended cluster of buildings to the west.

While his commanding officer was away at headquarters, an exhausted Percy Marling was consoling himself with his first square meal for four days. On the menu was bacon, bully beef, jam, brandy, tea and biscuits. As an extra treat Marling had a wash and took off his boots, the first time he had the chance to do either of these things since leaving Jakdul Wells. He must have received his orders for the following day not long afterwards. If he was looking forward to snatching a few hours of undisturbed sleep before the off, he had failed to allow for the noisy neighbours in Metemmeh. Once again the 'infernal tom-toms' throbbed throughout the night.[54] For Gleichen the problem was not noise but cold: his blankets having gone missing in the recent confusion, all he could find to cover himself with was a straw mat, which unsurprisingly proved ineffective. Fortunately 'Jacky', the unofficial regimental mascot, 'came sniffing about' and was coaxed into lying curled up by Gleichen's midriff for the rest of the night.[55] If there truly is no rest for the wicked, the exhausted surgeons must have been very wicked indeed, as even the onset of darkness brought no let-up in their endeavours. It was about now, by lamplight, that Charlie Crutchley lost his leg.

The little cabal of war correspondents had been assigned one of the smaller houses, but decided to bivouac around it in the open air. Having polished off a frugal supper they were settling down to sleep, when the interior of an adjacent dwelling caught fire.[56] Although Major Pöe and his marines turned out to fight the flames, by the time Willoughby Verner came rushing onto the scene the building was well and truly ablaze. Recollecting that he had given orders that a box of ammunition should be stowed on the roof, Verner clambered up the outside of the building to recover it. The roof was hot under his feet, but he could see no sign of the ammunition and quickly lowered himself back to the ground. He found the missing box just inside the door and dragged it clear only moments before the roof fell in.[57] The marines ensured the flames did not spread beyond the confines of the building's mud-walls and once the rafters had burned themselves out the alarm subsided.[58]

Reveille, in its usual unforgiving way, came all too soon. Breakfast was eaten in the dark, and with the first streaks of dawn the senior NCOs began mustering their men for another day's fighting. Thomas Snow knew from the moment he opened his eyes that it was not going to involve him. A couple of his men helped him to hobble away to the hospital, where one of the doctors broke the news that he would be playing no further part in the campaign.[59]

The War Diary entry for the day itemized the morning parade-states of the units committed to the operation.[60] The necessity both to leave a viable guard force under Sunderland and at the same time be prepared to bring in Davison, meant that only 842 fighting men would be involved in the attack on Metemmeh. Unit strengths were as follows:

RN	24	(with Gardner machine gun)
HCR	120	(Nos. 1 & 2 Companies only)
GCR	269	
MICR	285	
19th Hussars	67	
RE	19	
RA	36	
Medical Bearer-Company	22	(2 sections with *cacolets* and litters)

The presence of the headquarters staff, some of the war correspondents and perhaps a score of native drivers from the medical bearer-company would still not have edged the force above 900 men all told. The much-reduced strength of Major French's squadron, a mere sixty-seven men, was in part a reflection of how many ponies were unfit for duty, though it should also be noted that Barrow had despatched a separate patrol of unknown strength to scout upriver for any sign of the Faqī Muṣṭafa's approach.[61]

By the time the 19th Hussars led off along the gravel plateau, the men of the Royal Sussex were already hard at work, loopholing the walls of their strongpoint buildings. Accompanying Barrow at the head of the advance was one of the black slaves earlier taken prisoner, whose job it would be to take a written summons to surrender into the town. Given that we hear no more of him it can be safely assumed that he failed to return from his errand. There can be no certainty that a humble slave ever handed Wilson's letter to anybody, let alone to someone in authority. If there was no real expectation that so fanatical an enemy would suddenly give up the ghost and surrender, there was every likelihood that it would prove necessary to bombard the town. Wilson's main concern may have been to pre-warn the civilian population of the coming bombardment in accordance with the rules of war. He might also have entertained the hope that the enemy might be frightened into abandoning the town without a fight and falling back on Berber. In the event there was some significant refugee movement out of the town, initially to the north, but later to the east, although it is impossible to say whether this was triggered by Wilson's warning or by the first salvo from the artillery.

The infantry component, meanwhile, formed up in line of quarter columns, MICR to the left, GCR to the right, with a twelve-pace interval between regiments. The remainder of the force was echeloned thirty paces to the rear, with the two HCR companies covered off to the rear of the Guards and the Naval Brigade behind the Mounted Infantry.[62] The thirty-pace interval was for forming up and would have been allowed to open a little once the force had stepped off. In the meantime it was occupied by a few dozen camels carrying the usual assortment of litters, *cacolets*, water tanks and reserve ammunition. The Royal Artillery carried their 7-pounders disassembled aboard baggage camels and were under orders to fall in on the right of the Guards. They probably moved into the interval between the two fighting echelons for added security once the advance was under way.

The sources contradict each other in respect of whether there were two or three 7-pounders on parade. The War Diary states plainly that there were three. Moreover all the gunners were included in the parade-state for the operation. Colvile's official history, on the other hand, states that one gun was left behind.[63] Gleichen and Dawson in their respective accounts suggest that only two guns were brought into action during the course of the morning, which does not preclude the possibility that the third was also present but remained disassembled aboard the camels.[64] Arguably Alex Macdonald's account tips the balance. The young Scots correspondent was still played out and woke from a deep slumber at the sound of the troops marching past. He had not had any breakfast, nor was he ready to take the field, so he decided to watch the proceedings from a nearby rooftop, where the presence of a party of signallers with heliograph equipment indicated he would gain a good view. It seems certain that if there had been a 7-pounder present at the hamlet, Macdonald would have seen it. Instead he definitively asserts in his account that all three guns went out with Wilson.[65] It seems likely that Colvile drew directly on the published accounts of Dawson and Gleichen in preparing the official history, but misinterpreted them in suggesting that one of the guns had been left behind. He certainly erred in stating that the Naval Brigade were left behind. The balance of the evidence, then, is that all the guns were taken, but that only two were assembled and brought into action.

The manner in which the troops had formed up was designed to combine easy cross-country movement, with the ability quickly to form square. The only mounted officers with the main body were Sir Charles Wilson and Lord Airlie, the former because he intended having a good look at Metemmeh in the company of Percy Barrow before finally deciding on his point of attack.[66] Bennet Burleigh appears to have been the only other horseman present, with the result that he would later be pressed into service as a galloper.

The ground over which the operations of Wednesday 21 January were conducted is best illustrated by two of Verner's maps (*Maps 11 & 12*). All subsequent references within this chapter to lettered reference points relate to the more readily legible Map 11. The general line of the Nile at this point is west–east. Metemmeh lay downstream of the British defensive position by about two miles as the crow flies. The town was located on the left bank and at low-Nile stood about 1,200 yards away from the water's edge. The mapping shows that it was distinctly divided into two main residential areas. To the west was the main walled town and Arab quarter, while 200 yards to the east was an unfortified merchant's quarter known as Sanahir, where the inhabitants were less than wholehearted supporters of Mahdīsm, something of which the British were as yet unaware.[67] The town was much longer, west to east along the river, than it was deep, south to north into the desert. There was no shortage of good well-water inside the walls. Because the town was not atop the low gravel plateau like the British-held hamlet (Point A), or the other settlements lying upstream (Points C & D), it was to some extent commanded by rising ground lying just to the north-west (Point G and general area). This was the ground that Sir Charles Wilson was most interested in and the ground towards which Percy Barrow was now steering the advance. Two GCR companies and two MICR companies were thrown forward to screen the main body.[68] The men on the skirmish line cleared through all the mud-baked dwellings along the line of the plateau, including a deserted hamlet around a thousand yards east of their start point (Point C).[69]

Though the British were uncertain at this juncture how many *anṣār* were in the town, it appears on the basis of intelligence later acquired by Verner[70] that there were perhaps 3,000 of whom about a third were equipped with rifles. If this estimate is not hugely wide of the mark, it would suggest that as many men again had dispersed in various directions after the battle of two days earlier. In addition to the 3,000 fully fit fighting men there were also a great many wounded. There would seem to have been four pieces of artillery, two of which had been emplaced to cover the river, while the other two were facing the landward approach from the desert. Amongst the Mahdīsts believed to have been present that day were Nūr 'Anqara, Ali-wad-Saad and 'Abd-al-Mājid Nasr al-Din abū' l-Kailak, though as we have seen the last two were recovering from wounds and probably did not play an overly active part in the day's proceedings. An intelligence report of 30 January[71] suggests that there were six *amīrs* in the town at that slightly later date, though one of the three additional names listed was 'Abd-al-Raḥmān wad al-Najūmi, who is extremely unlikely to have been present at that stage and was certainly not there on 21 January, at which point he is known to have been at Khartoum.[72]

Verner had been left behind to manage the intelligence function in the absence of Wilson and Stuart-Wortley. Not long after the main body of the troops had moved off for Metemmeh, he looked up from his work to find that there were no longer any outlying pickets around the buildings, a task which had fallen by default to No. 3/4 Company, HCR. He made an immediate beeline for the Heavies bivouac and found them 'all dispersed cooking etc'.[73] He quickly located the senior officer present, Captain William Hippisley of the Greys. Acting on his own authority, Verner told Hippisley that he was to move his men up to the buildings immediately. Beresford meanwhile had risen from his sickbed to discover much the same situation as had rattled Verner some minutes earlier. Bellowing for a bugler, Beresford promptly had the 'Assembly' sounded, obliging everybody in earshot to come doubling onto parade fully armed and accoutred. When Verner returned from mustering the Heavies, he was instructed by Beresford to take the defence of the position in hand. It would seem unlikely in the circumstances that Sunderland, Verner's senior, was present at this time. In all probability he had taken personal command of the Royal Sussex picket to the west of the main position.

Verner's swiftly conceptualized plan of defence called for a cluster of centrally located buildings, including the impromptu hospital wards, to serve as an inner redoubt. The houses concerned would be linked with a parapet of boxes and camel saddles. The outlying houses he divided into four groups, each of them under the command of an officer. It was not long before some satisfactory progress was being made with the barricades and other defences.[74]

At some point between 7.00 and 8.00 a.m. the 19th Hussars encountered a force of about sixty Mahdīst cavalry on the high ground north-west of Metemmeh. Barrow dismounted his men to engage the horsemen with carbine fire and quickly succeeded in driving them into the desert. The enemy did not break visual contact, but instead loitered a safe distance to the north-east observing the movements of the British cavalry (now at Point G). In the meantime Wilson had been marching the rest of his force across the gravel plateau on an arcing axis of about two miles in length, with the object of marrying up with the cavalry on the high ground behind the town.

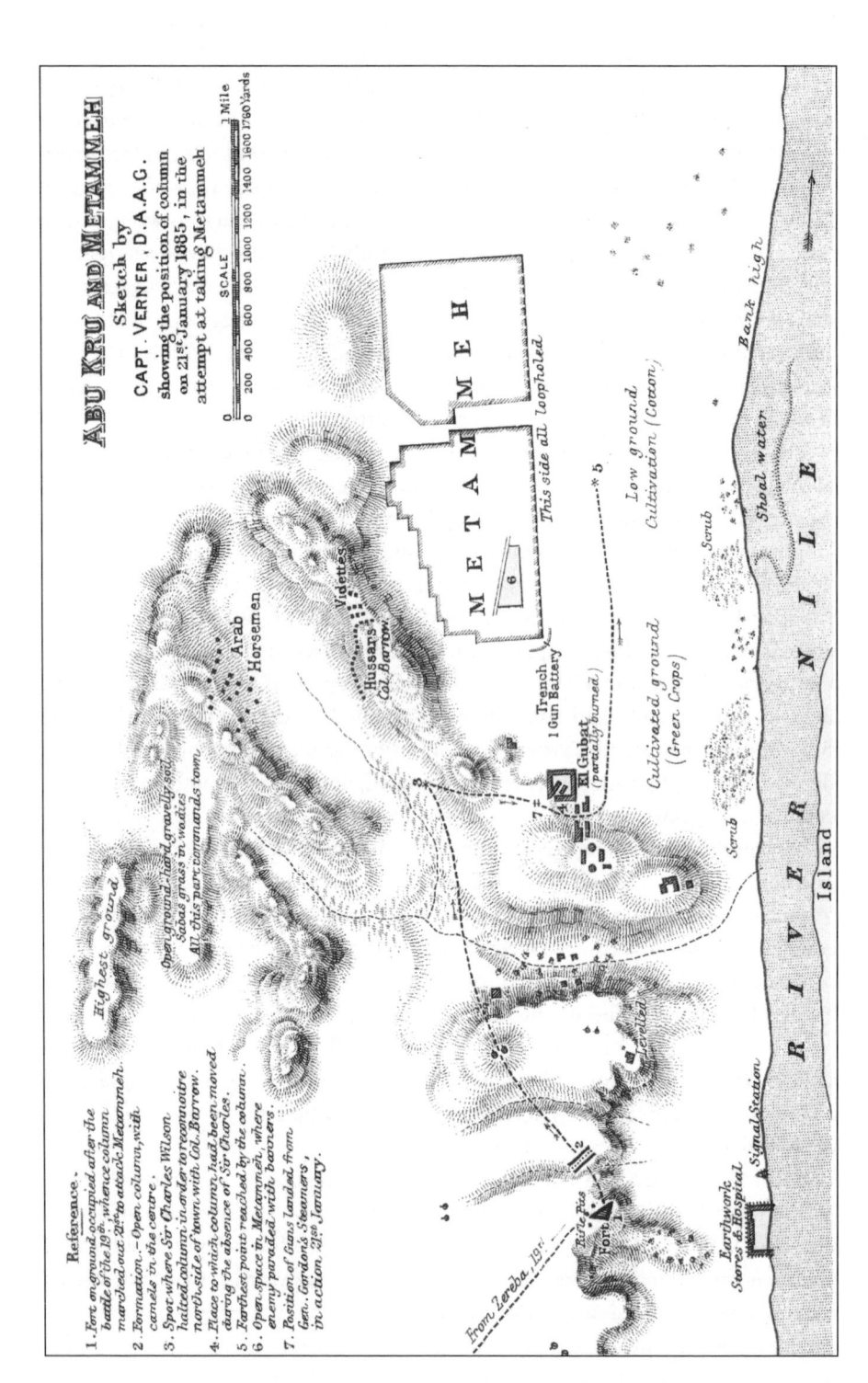

Map 12: Verner's map of the 21 January operation at Metemmeh

By 8.00 a.m., at which point a cavalry galloper brought in a short report from Barrow describing his recent skirmish, the infantry and artillery were about two-thirds of the way through their advance. Scanning Metemmeh with his field glasses, Wilson could discern 'no regular openings in its mud walls'.[75] Just in front of the western end of the town, however, he could see a row of enemy banners and what appeared to be a defended trench, though it was actually an outlying earthwork. He decided to ride on ahead to join Barrow, leaving Boscawen and the main body at the halt (Point H). If Sir Charles had any sort of escort over his mile-long ride, it was the trooper or brace of troopers who had ridden in with Barrow's message. When at length he reached the 19th Hussars he found them, 'in a capital position on some gravel swellings of ground which quite commanded the town, and from whence artillery-fire would take the trench . . . with its defenders, in reverse'.[76] His hunch vindicated and his mind made up, Wilson set off to bring up the main body. Unfortunately his mount, in all likelihood a Syrian pony borrowed from the hussars, was just about on its last legs. He had not gone far before he was obliged to dismount and lead the animal.[77]

Not long afterwards Wilson noticed that Boscawen had thrown a line of skirmishers forward and that firing had broken out. In *With the Camel Corps up the Nile* Gleichen reveals that the firing originated with Captain Eyre Crabbe, who brought twenty picked men of No. 1 Company, GCR, into action at the extraordinary range of 2,000 yards. The target would appear to have been the crowds of people now leaving Metemmeh – not an altogether legitimate engagement even in 1885. Burleigh's reporting for the *Daily Telegraph* confirms that there were indeed fugitives fleeing the town to the north at this point – which is to say they were heading into the open desert.[78] Crabbe's experience as his battalion's musketry officer had evidently left him with a high opinion of the Martini-Henry's capabilities.[79]

As we passed through the second village and got in sight of Metemmeh, crowds of Arabs were seen running about just outside the town. 'Here's a grand chance thought C____ the former musketoon, who was in command of the extended company of Grenadiers, and he forthwith called out twenty of our best marksmen. 'Fire five volleys at 2,000 yards – ready,' and down they went, taking careful aim at the masses . . . The effect of the volleys was extraordinary. At that enormous distance we saw with the help of our glasses two or three Arabs drop, and the rest skedaddle as fast as their legs would carry them into the town, dropping their household goods as they went. The moral effect must have been great, for in two minutes, with the help of a few shells from the guns, they had all disappeared within the walls.[80]

Although Gleichen flows seamlessly into an artillery bombardment at the end of this passage, there was actually a significant interval between Crabbe's volleys and the point at which the guns came into action.

What makes Gleichen's anecdote so interesting is that the Martini-Henry was sighted only to 1,450 yards, at which extreme setting the barrel had to be raised to what was virtually a skywards angle. In order to engage a target at 2,000 yards, the shot could only be guesstimated rather than aimed, so that to hit anything in such a fashion was an extraordinary piece of soldiering.

Sir Charles probably took little interest in the musketry exhibition. Of much more concern was that not long after Crabbe's fifth and final salvo had crashed out, the main body came to life, swung away from the original axis of advance and began making a bee-line in the direction of the river. Hurrying on as best he could, Wilson bumped into a messenger. For some reason he chose to blank out the man's name in *From Korti to Khartum*, failing even to give an initial letter. This tells us that it was not an anonymous trooper from the 19th Hussars, but more than likely Airlie or Burleigh. Whoever the courier was, he relayed a message from Boscawen to the effect that he was manoeuvring to interdict a body of the enemy moving west along the riverbank towards the British-held hamlet.[81]

By the time Wilson caught up with Boscawen, he had moved the force a thousand yards to the south and come to a halt behind the deserted village of Gubat (Point D). The nearby buildings were located towards the edge of the gravel plateau and commanded a good view both of Metemmeh and of the flat cultivated land lying between the town and the Nile. Pressed by Sir Charles to indicate the position of the force manoeuvring against the camp, Boscawen was unable to do so. It was suggested that the enemy must be hidden amongst the belt of palm groves and *dhura* lining the river.[82] Alex Macdonald would discover the truth of the matter later in the day, when the troops returned to camp. 'As we were advancing,' his informant told him, 'we saw some flags below one of the villages near the river, and the column was diverted in that direction so as not to leave the camp open to attack. As we advanced we found only a few of the enemy, the flags we had seen being stuck over the graves of some of the chiefs who had fallen on the 19th.'[83] It would seem that nobody shared this explanation with Sir Charles Wilson at the time, suggesting that Boscawen either failed to realize what had happened or chose not to admit it.

It is seldom a good idea for a commander to counter-march his troops, as there are few things more likely to suggest indecision amongst the officers and instantaneously damage morale. Instead Sir Charles chose to accept that he would have to keep the force interposed between Metemmeh and the defended hamlet. Accordingly, he now abandoned his first-choice plan to attack from the north, in favour of operating to the west and south of the town.

About 400 yards to the north-east of the point at which Boscawen had halted there were two mud-houses atop a low knoll. (Point I). As this feature commanded the short western face of the town from a range of only 800 yards, it would make an excellent fire position for the artillery and simultaneously serve as an admirable blocking position against any Mahdīst attempt to move west towards the camp. One of the Mounted Infantry companies was detailed go forward to the knoll and protect the gunners while they went about breaching the town's western wall.[84] A party of sappers was also sent along to assist in fortifying the nearby houses. The enemy remained largely passive, until Burleigh rode too far forward and drew a good deal of fire from the earthwork at the south-west corner of the town.[85]

It was not long before the Royal Artillery gun crews were scoring good hits on the mud-baked town western wall. If anybody was anticipating dramatic results from so light a gun as the 7-pounder RML, they were to be sorely disappointed. To those observing the proceedings with the naked eye, the bombardment produced no effect at all. Officers with field glasses thought that the shells were passing through the wall without detonating.[86] In fact there were two walls around the town, an outer one about six feet high, and an inner one just inside the first. The interval between them having been filled with sand and gravel, it was certain that Norton's supply of common shell would give out long before any sort of Jericho-effect could be achieved.[87] As to the threat of fire, Gleichen remarked that, 'there was nothing combustible but the roofs, and, even when one did catch fire, for all practical purposes a hut without a roof was nearly as good as a hut with one'.[88] None of the other participant accounts mention burning buildings, suggesting that such instances as occurred were few and far between.

At around 9.00 a.m. Wilson decided to move the force around to the south of the town, in search of a place where it might be possible to carry the enemy's defences by storm without incurring too heavy a loss. In order to avoid being caught flat-footed by the Mahdist force supposedly secreted along the riverbank, it would be necessary to advance in square. While the 7-pounders were withdrawn from the knoll to accompany the main body, the MICR company and the sappers appear to have been left *in situ*.[89] The sources are completely silent as to how precisely the square was configured, although precedent would suggest that the Guards and Mounted Infantry occupied the front and flanking faces and that the Heavies were stationed at the rear. With only nine Camel Corps companies deployed around its faces, three of MICR, all four of GCR and Nos. 1 and 2 Companies of the Heavies, it was a markedly smaller formation than that employed at Abu Klea where there had been fifteen companies, or even for that matter at Abu Kru where there had been twelve.

As soon as the square exposed itself on the flood plain in front of the town, land which for the most part had been given over to the cultivation of cotton, it came under a heavy fire from a line of loopholes in the obviously well-defended south wall fronting the river.[90] Skirmishers were deployed to return fire and protect the left flank of the square, as it continued what turned out in the end to be a slow and substantially pointless mile-long perambulation between the town on its left flank and the river on its right. From time to time the order was given for the troops to halt and lie down in formation, while the skirmishers potted away at the puffs of smoke billowing from the south wall. It would be surprising in the circumstances if more than a handful of Arab riflemen were hit, and not at all surprising to find that none of them were. Whenever the square came to a halt, the gunners would again try their luck with the dwindling stock of common shell, but always without any meaningful effect.

410 • *Beyond the Reach of Empire*

Percy Barrow had moved his sixty-six-strong detachment of cavalrymen back to the south-west in conformity with Wilson's change of axis, but was still dutifully securing the open desert flank with a line of vedette posts strung across the gravel ridges west of Metemmeh. In response to a sudden exclamation from one of his troopers, he turned and trained his field glasses upriver. Distance, shimmering heat and unhelpful graze angles did much to hinder the view, but there were definitely flags in the distance . . . red flags. Barrow squinted hard into his field glasses and declared that they were unusually large Ottoman flags. Surely it simply had to be Gordon's steamers. What else could it be? Summoning one of his best-mounted troopers, Barrow indicated the position of the tiny square, a thousand yards and more into the middle distance, and proceeded to rehearse the man in the message he was to repeat to Sir Charles Wilson. With a jab of his spurs, the galloper was off. He must have had an exhilarating canter past the loopholed south wall of the town, but his pony ran the gauntlet gamely and at around 9.30 a.m. brought him face to face with the acting brigadier.[91] After all the tribulations of the past few days, the arrival of Gordon's steamers was exhilarating news. Burleigh immediately rode away in the direction of the river to greet them.

Arrival of the Steamers

A little while earlier Gordon's officers had heralded their arrival by firing off one of their cannon. The unexpected sound caused consternation amongst the hussar vedettes posted upstream of the British position, who came cantering in to Colonel Bonham to report the near approach of the enemy.[92] Momentary alarm quickly turned to rejoicing. By the time the leading vessel in a flotilla of four had pulled in to the riverbank, Verner and his interpreter were waiting to go aboard. It is not altogether clear whether he boarded the *Talahawiyeh* or the *Tawfiqiyeh*, but he was afforded a joyous reception by a medley of Egyptian and Sudanese soldiers and quickly ushered into the presence of Nushi Pasha, the Egyptian brigadier general in overall command of the flotilla,[93] and Khashm al-Mūs Bey, a prominent Shā'iqī headman and colonel of irregulars. Given that the steamer crews had in effect being living as river pirates since October, it is little wonder that Verner was afforded the warmest of welcomes. As far as his hosts were concerned, this was the turning point of the war. When the backslapping and handshaking abated, Verner quickly let it be known that the British main body was even now hotly engaged at Metemmeh.

Colonel Muḥammad Khashm al-Mūs[94] was a short, dark-skinned Sudanese Arab in his early fifties. A son of Shaikh Muḥammad Sibair, he had been born at Korti in the 1830s and had spent most of his life as a cavalry irregular. He sported a neat grey beard and the pairs of v-shaped scars on either cheek that identified him as a Shā'iqī. Verner later captured his appearance in one of the watercolours in his *Sketches in the Soudan*. An orange cummerbund and a loose turban with a pattern of orange, sky blue and white wrapped into its folds, added a touch of colour to an otherwise all-white ensemble of loose-fitting Arab clothes. The brace of flintlock pistols tucked into his cummerbund seemed somehow to give the old colonel an appropriately piratical air. Nushi Pasha, on the other hand, was a light-skinned native of the Nile Delta, sported a bristling white moustache and was probably a little older than his Sudanese comrade. As an Egyptian regular he was conventionally clad in a white summer uniform and the inevitable red *tarbush*. The duo encapsulated the dilemma that had dogged Gordon's mission from the outset. While Nushi Pasha and his men had somehow to be evacuated to their homes in the far north, Khashm al-Mūs and his men had no ties to Egypt, save in so far as they had for many years earned their living in the employ of the Khedive. Their homes and their families were in Khartoum or in the riparian villages to the north of the city. Gordon had somehow to find a solution that would prevent the Shā'iqī and other loyalists being put to the sword by a vengeful fundamentalist enemy, a moral complication which Gladstone and his Cabinet had failed to allow for.

When Verner spoke of the fight downriver, Khashm al-Mūs was quick to pronounce, 'We will go and help.'[95] It transpired that were more than 500 men aboard the steamers, most of whom had no real role in crewing or fighting the vessels and could readily be put ashore as landing parties.[96] Some concern was expressed, probably by Nushi Pasha, about the possibility of the British mistaking them for the enemy. Knowing full well that his comrades downriver were expecting the steamers to put in an appearance at some point, and observing that they had great Ottoman flags flying at the bow, stern and masthead, Verner agreed to stand on top of the covered battery amidships and head off any unduly precipitate action by his countrymen. With that the little flotilla got underway again. The vessels and commanders were:

Talahawiyeh	Brigadier General Nushi Pasha
Tawfiqiyeh	Colonel Khashm al-Mūs Bey
Bordein	Colonel 'Abd al-Ḥamīd Bey
Sāfia	Colonel Maḥmūd Bey

While the steamers were in transit, one of the officers in the wheelhouse handed Verner a short note to the effect that British officers coming aboard should treat the soldiers and crewmen '. . . with forbearance and not be harsh to them. I know that their manners and customs are different to ours but they are good fellows and do their best.' The signature was Gordon Pasha's. Shortly after this a Shā'iqī civilian was ushered into Verner's presence and, after fumbling about in his clothing for a moment, produced a tiny slip of paper on which was written, 'Khartoum is all right. Could hold out for years.' It was dated 29 December and bore Gordon's signature.[97] Historians have tended to be somewhat bewildered by this note and have generally been inclined to advance the notion that it can only have been written with the intention of deceiving the Mahdī. If the courier had been intercepted the note could not have achieved such an effect because Khartoum was riddled with spies, as Gordon well knew. Deception, then, was clearly not its primary purpose. The real point of the note was surely not the sentiment it expressed, but rather the signature it bore. In other words it was probably intended to serve as a passport with the

British. It seems likely that the object of the courier's daring journey through enemy-controlled territory was either to deliver an oral message, the details of which have not come down to us or, more probably, that the man had been sent to act as a fount of knowledge when questioned by the intelligence staff. Verner, for example, noted in his diary that, 'I took the paper and told him he was to tell me all about Khartoum after the fight.'[98]

Khashm al-Mūs now proceeded to impart some worrying news. Two hours prior to their arrival with the British the steamers had sighted a strong Mahdīst force, including guns, marching downriver. Verner concluded that the Faqī Muṣṭafa could only be about eighteen miles away. This meant that it was by no means impossible for the British to be attacked from the west that afternoon. It was clear that there was no time to lose in getting this vital new intelligence through to Sir Charles Wilson. Verner now went outside to stand in plain sight of the British as he had promised.

We steamed away downstream with our red flags flying gallantly and in a few minutes were opposite the west end of the town. An Englishman on a horse now appeared on the bank, the irrepressible Burleigh of the D.T. [*Daily Telegraph*]. I hailed him and asked him if he would take a message for me and he readily assented. So I wrote a line to Sir Charles Wilson that I had arrived with four of Gordon's steamers and 500 men, and could land 250 men and four guns at once to cooperate with him. Meanwhile I hastened the disembarkation and sent back to camp for ten camels to carry up my guns and ammunition. The troops soon got their guns ashore. They were about 8 or 9 pounders, M.L. [muzzle loading] rifled, of an Egyptian pattern and fired common shell.[99]

By the time Burleigh rode in with Verner's message, Wilson had concluded that the square was doing nothing more than promenading along the strongest sector of the enemy's defences to absolutely no avail. Because the incoming fire had been nothing like as severe at the western end of the town, he decided to about-turn and develop his attack from there. Calling Stuart-Wortley over, he instructed him to dash down to Verner and tell him to move his force up to join the detached company on the gravel ridge to the west of the town. That Verner's request for camels was relayed quickly and efficiently to Bonham is clear, although the means by which this was effected is not known for sure. There was certainly heliographic communication between Wilson's force and the camp, although Verner cannot have been anywhere near the signals post at this time. Its most likely position was on the reverse slope of the knoll earlier occupied by the guns (Point I). It is possible that there were members of the 19th Hussars down at the river by now and that one of the troopers rode to the heliograph post with Verner's message. Another possibility is that having passed Verner's message to Sir Charles, Burleigh then rode on to deliver a second message to the signallers. Either way, Lieutenant John Burn-Murdoch of the Royals was quick to set off from the camp with a string of camels and a small escort.[100]

As the men in the square took their first steps back to the west, a Mahdīst gun position unmasked. A loud report from the town wall took everybody by surprise and sent a stone cannonball sailing over the top of the square.[101] A minute or so later a second shot fell short,[102] but the third tore the lower jaw off one of the Royal Artillery baggage camels, before burying itself in the centre of the square. Sir Charles Wilson noted that the 'poor brute' barely broke its stride and faithfully carried its load to the end of the day.[103] The fourth shot wounded a soldier and killed a camel. Doubtless the men in the close-packed ranks of the Camel Corps companies lengthened their stride to get clear of the gun's arcs as quickly as possible.

The miscellany of infantry aboard the steamers included *fellaheen* conscripts from the Nile Delta, black African *bazingers* many of whom were slaves, Shā'iqī irregulars and a melange of other *bāshi-būzuqs* from Cairo, the Levant, Turkey and the Balkans. Some wore badly tattered white summer uniforms, but most were clad in long white smocks known as *galoubiehs* and went about their business with bare legs and feet. While many wore the distinctive red *tarbush* of the Egyptian military, others preferred loose-wrapped Sudanese turbans. Most men were draped with a bandolier or two of brass cartridges, be it over the shoulder, round the waist or both. They all carried Remington rolling-block rifles, which some supplemented with a government-issue sword-bayonet, others with a cross-hilted sword, and still others with a broad-bladed spear.

Verner marshalled around 250 of Gordon's river-marauders behind the cover of the grove of trees (Point E) which Boscawen had earlier imagined was concealing a Mahdīst force. While the two Sudanese colonels, Khashm al-Mūs Bey and 'Abd al-Ḥamīd Bey, accompanied the troops ashore, the Egyptian officers were nowhere to be seen. Sir Charles Wilson observed, 'Only blacks came up, as the Egyptian Pasha with his fellahin preferred to remain on board.'[104] When Burn-Murdoch and his party arrived with the string of baggage camels Verner had asked for, the Sudanese rushed to get them loaded up with artillery ammunition. Verner's axis of advance lay from the grove of trees above the riverbank, across the cotton fields and up a gentle gravel slope, to some deserted buildings lying about 600 yards from the south-west corner of Metemmeh.

My mob followed me at a great pace and as soon as we topped the riverbank we were greeted by a brisk long fire from the Remingtons of the enemy. As we advanced their fire increased and presently they opened on us with roundshot, one of them coming very unpleasantly near me. I soon found that the white coats of my men were drawing all the fire so I got well ahead of them and had a comparatively easier time of it.[105]

Some of the *bazingers* and *bāshi-būzuqs* positioned themselves around the cluster of deserted buildings and began exchanging fire with the men at the loopholes along the south wall. Others pushed on with the baggage camels and guns and at length succeeded in emplacing them on the knoll formerly occupied by the British 7-pounders. Verner's Sudanese gunners made 'capital practice'[106] at a range of 800 yards, though for all the proficiency of their crews the slightly heavier field guns proved no more capable of breaching the walls than had the hopelessly ineffective mountain guns of the Royal Artillery.

Only now did the square return from its futile march to the south of the town. Once the force had reoriented itself to face east, and the main body was in cover behind the gravel ridges, the screw guns were moved back onto the knoll. Two new skirmish lines were also thrown forward. Major Pöe's No. 4 (RMLI) Company, GCR, was committed to the general area of the knoll, tasked with suppressing the incoming rifle fire now being concentrated on the toiling gun-crews.[107] Pöe's deployment suggests that the detached MICR company had not long since been withdrawn into dead ground to re-join the rest of the regiment. Having been in position on the knoll for some considerable time the Mounted Infantry company is likely to have used up a good proportion of its first-line ammunition, so that Pöe's deployment might conceivably have been executed as a direct relief in place, one company coming up as the other fell back – there is insufficient source coverage of the day's proceedings to know for sure. As there was not a great deal of cover to be had on this sector, most of the marines threw themselves down in prone fire positions. The major, however, calmly walked back and forth behind his firing line, barking fire control orders and shouting encouragement to his men. At a range of only 800 yards from the town, it would not have been an altogether prudent way to behave even if he had been wearing an inconspicuous grey frock. William Pöe had crossed the Bayūda wearing a red one.[108] To the right of Pöe's position, Lord Cochrane's No. 1 Company, HCR, was fed into the gap between the RMLI and Verner's Sudanese.

Hoping that sooner or later the combination of four 9-pounders and two 7-pounders would suffice to demolish a stretch of wall, Sir Charles Wilson left the artillery officers to their business and got on with his. With rifle fire rattling incessantly and guns booming periodically in the background, he had a long talk with Khashm al-Mūs and 'Abd al-Ḥamīd. The ubiquitous Verner was also on hand to show his chief the note from Gordon and to impart the critical news from the south: the Faqī Muṣṭafa could be expected to arrive that afternoon or, if their luck was in, the following morning.[109] It transpired that while three of the steamers had been loitering just north of the Sabalūka Gorge and the Sixth Cataract since October, the fourth, *Bordein*, had been sent downriver by Gordon as recently as 15 December.[110] This means that the steamer captains as a collective were under no illusions about how desperate the situation at Khartoum had become. On board *Bordein*, said the Sudanese colonels, were journals and letters which Gordon Pasha had said should be given to the 'English'.

Wilson had more than enough food for thought to be going on with and now brought the conversation to a close. Sending for a cavalry galloper, he quickly composed a note to Bonham. It first warned that the enemy were closing in from the south and might conceivably attack during the course of the afternoon, and then went on to direct that the plan to bring in Major Davison and No. 5 Company, HCR, be enacted without delay. With the message safely on its way, Sir Charles went to see how the gunners were faring. The view from the knoll was less than encouraging. The west wall was riddled with small holes but otherwise intact. Quite how much damage was done to the buildings inside the walls is unclear. The fact that there were now large numbers of refugees fleeing to the north[111] suggests that the bombardment had at least caused a certain amount of alarm and despondency. Ammunition for the 7-pounders was running low and, if there was to be a big fight with the Faqī Muṣṭafa, it would be prudent to conserve what little was left. When Wilson went to confer with Boscawen, they were quick to agree that the time had come to break off the fight and fall back on the camp. Moments later the order was given for the guns to cease fire. When the signallers flashed 'Force withdrawing' to the rooftop heliograph station, Alex Macdonald and the other spectators gathered there could not help feeling a mixture of surprise and disappointment.[112]

Retreat to 'Gubat'

Lord Cochrane had his dander well and truly up and felt sure that it would be possible to carry the town by storm. When the brigade major rode up with orders for him to retire, he expressed outrage and insisted that Airlie tell Sir Charles that he felt they 'ought to go on and burn the place down'.[113] Airlie sympathized but no doubt told Cochrane that he had best get on and withdraw as ordered. Cochrane's view was that of a company commander only and decidedly ill-informed to boot. When in the 1920s he wrote his memoirs, he gave vent to the following indictment:

The great mistake made by Sir Charles Wilson on this day was to show his teeth and then not bite; it disheartened our men and emboldened the enemy. Once embarked on the enterprise, to my mind it was folly to leave the town in the enemy's hand untouched, close to us and our line of communication, a centre for enemy forces, and from which nightly large bodies of men issued and marched close to our bivouac beating defiance on their tom-toms.[114]

There might be some excuse for the young Lord Cochrane to think these thoughts, but the older, wiser Earl of Dundonald, a retired general officer writing with the benefit of hindsight, really ought to have known better. The mission was to save Khartoum, not to beat up Metemmeh and the several thousand *anṣār* fighters secreted about its dingy streets and alleyways. The Desert Column itself was already badly bruised and could ill afford the sort of losses which would inevitably be incurred in clearing house-to-house through an endless sequence of close-quarter engagements. Moreover, Dundonald made no allowance whatever for the facts of the tactical situation as Wilson understood them when he took the decision to withdraw. What sort of commander would allow himself to be attacked by a numerically superior enemy force from the rear, whilst still obsessively engaged with a strongpoint in front? What sort of commander would leave a hundred wounded men to be massacred in the west, while he was fighting for a non-essential objective in the east? Wilson had every reason to assume that reinforcements would soon be on their way across the Bayūda. There would be time enough to deal with Metemmeh when fresh troops came up. In the meantime the gravely weakened Desert Column had to retain its feeble lodgement on the Nile at all hazards and get on with the business of communicating with General Gordon. With the arrival of the steamers, the means of doing so was at hand.

Major Pöe almost got away with it: he was shot in the thigh only minutes before the order to retire was given. Verner noted in his diary that, 'Eyewitnesses say that he was deliberately picked off by a man at a loophole some 600 yards off who had several shots at him.'[115] Later in the day the surgeons would be obliged to amputate the major's leg, virtually at the groin. On the opposite flank a sulking Lord Cochrane had his spirits revived by one of the Life Guards' regimental wags:

When we commenced to retire by alternate troops, we could hear a loud murmur from the town, whether of relief or derision I do not know. But I do know what the men felt, and a trooper of the Life Guards who stopped behind in the open when his company retired and whilst being fired at all the time, showed his contempt for the enemy and the proceedings in a most amusing manner.[116]

The withdrawal across the plateau was skilfully handled by Boscawen. Moving slowly and steadily as if to suggest that the British were quite unafraid of anything the *anṣār* might do, he succeeded in deterring any question of a counter-attack. Gleichen observed that the infantry retired 'by alternate battalions',[117] GCR covering MICR for a certain distance, then vice versa and so on. The dwellings lying along the line of retreat were fired by the troops as they passed, sending plumes of black smoke drifting into a simmering sky. The rest of the return march was easily and quickly accomplished, so much so that the infantry beat Verner and the steamers back. It was something after 3.00 p.m. before everybody was safely in.[118] The only life lost before the walls of Metemmeh was that of Sergeant Cowley, a member of the 1st Royal Sussex section in B Company, MICR, shot dead inside the square.[119] Some six to eight men seem to have been wounded.[120]

There was a certain amount of alarm and consternation abroad at the camp when Sir Charles Wilson rode in.

When I returned to camp between three and four, I found they had made preparations for moving the wounded down to the river, and were waiting orders to do so. There was some excitement about the expected attack, and _____ was much excited, declaring the position a bad one, too far from water for the thirsty British soldier, &c.

I was at first averse to moving the wounded to a place where they would have no shade except such as tents could give; but after talking to Stewart, and finding that he thought it the best plan, I gave the necessary orders.[121]

Usefully Verner's diary enables us to identify the name in the blank with a high degree of certainty:

I did not get back to the camp until some time after the column and on my arrival found a scene of great confusion. Beresford and some others were urging on Sir Charles to shift down to the riverbank below so as to prevent the enemy cutting us off from water. There were many counsellors and eventually the common-sense view was taken of occupying the village and shifting the camp to the riverbank so as to deny the heights to the enemy.[122]

Wilson decided that GCR would garrison the buildings, but that the rest of the force would shift to the riverbank. This was undoubtedly the right course of action, as both the water and the high ground overlooking it were vital. Quite why the wounded could not have been left in the relative comfort of the buildings is less clear, particularly given that the new position would be sited beneath the seasonal high-water mark, on damp ground. Because the village of Gubat has no further part to play in the narrative, the British defensive position on the river, including the fortified hamlet on the ridge above, can henceforth safely be referred to in the wider sense as 'Gubat'.

Twenty yards from the lip of the riverbank there was an irrigation embankment of about eighteen inches in height, which would give some added substance to the usual barricade of commissariat boxes and camel saddles. It was obvious that such a pathetic line of defence would have to be replaced at the earliest possible opportunity with ditching and earthworks. Orders were given that the force was to stand to its arms in square, in the event the Faqī Muṣṭafa attacked while the construction of the barricade was still in progress.[123]

The News from Khartoum

Having done all the work of a stand-in force commander, Sir Charles now turned back to his role as chief of intelligence and sat down in a quiet spot with Gordon's journals and letters.

Whilst the move was being made, I opened and read the letters which Gordon had sent down at various times, the last lot having been forwarded on the 14th December by the 'Bordein,' the last steamer to leave Khartum: this mail, with the last volume of the 'Journal,' had been entrusted to a Greek. The first two letters I opened were addressed to the officer commanding Her Majesty's troops: one was an order to Nashi Pasha, the Egyptian commanding the four steamers, to deliver them over to the English; the other a most characteristic letter telling us to remove all Egyptians, whether pashas, beys or privates – 'those hens,' he called them – and not to allow one of them to go up to Khartum again. In other letters he wrote in strong terms of the uselessness and cowardice of these men, and begged that if the steamers were not manned by British sailors, they should return to him with none but Sudanese soldiers and sailors. These letters were dated in October, when he first sent the steamers down to await our arrival, which he then expected weekly. I next opened two letters from Gordon to Lord Wolseley, which did not give much news; and at last opened one to Watson, knowing Gordon would write openly to him on the situation. The letter was dated 14th December, and in it Gordon said he expected a crisis within the next ten days, or about Christmas-day. He evidently had given up all hope of help from outside, and asked Watson to say goodbye to his friends and relations. This agreed with his letter of the 4th November, which said he had provisions enough to hold out until the middle of December, but that after that it would be difficult to do so.[124]

Twenty-seven days had passed since Christmas.

By the time he had finished perusing the letters Wilson must have known in his heart of hearts that it was already too late for Gordon. Even so, as long as there was glimmer of hope, he would have no choice but to proceed from a position of weakness with Wolseley's ill-conceived river dash, an operation which at low-Nile stood a better than even chance of ending in disaster. Before he could possibly depart for the south, however, it would first be necessary to ascertain whether there really were two powerful enemy forces converging on Gubat, and, if it proved to be true, somehow confront and overcome the problem.

The key operational imperative in the meantime was to ensure that the lodgement on the Nile remained secure, for without it there would be no prospect whatever of saving Khartoum. Military norms dictated that there could be no question of the force commander throwing up his responsibilities if another engagement fit to imperil the very survival of his command was in the offing. As Wilson himself put it, 'I had every reason to believe that forces of the enemy were advancing against us from the north and the south, and I could not leave the small force in its position on the Nile without ascertaining whether it was likely to be attacked.'[125] There were also good reasons why Wolseley had nominated his chief of intelligence as the best man to open face-to-face communications with General Gordon, so that despatching a stand-in could not be regarded as an option. In the circumstances the need to verify wider operational reality, by scouting the enemy's avenues of approach, would preclude Wilson making an immediate start for Khartoum. Instead he would send the 19th Hussars to probe upriver first thing in the morning and, if they reported no immediate danger of a powerful enemy thrust from the south, would then take a brace of steamers downriver to reconnoitre the approaches from Berber. Two MICR companies would go along to provide extra firepower and act as landing parties. Wilson intended paying particular attention to the village of Sayala where, the steamer captains had heard tell, a substantial enemy force had been concentrated.[126]

In order to formulate a truly objective assessment of Wilson's decisions and actions, it is necessary to recognize that five key factors were in play at this juncture. First, it appeared more than likely that at some point within the ensuing 12–48 hours the British would find themselves compelled to fight a major defensive action against fresh and powerful Mahdīst forces. Second, Gordon's injunction not to send any Egyptians back to Khartoum implied the need to reorganize four randomly mixed steamer crews in such a fashion as to produce two entirely Sudanese ones. Third, the heavy losses in men and camels, combined with the played-out state of the remaining baggage animals, meant that the Desert Column could no longer be regarded as a hard-marching manoeuvre asset. Moreover it was now incapable of fighting its way into Khartoum. Fourth, Wolseley's orders to Stewart included an injunction to the effect that as soon as the column had gained the river, it was to despatch a major convoy for Jakdul Wells and bring up more supplies. Fifth, the only higher intent articulated in the same set of orders was for the Desert Column to hold its ground at Metemmeh and wait for the River Column to come up. As we have seen a separate note from Buller forecast that this would not be for some weeks to come, while Stewart's orders made no allowance for the Desert Column to press south for Khartoum in the interim.

His reading complete and his mind made up, Wilson went to inform Boscawen that his examination of Gordon's papers would compel him to make a river dash for Khartoum as soon as was practicably possible, but that the sacrifice of at least one day to reconnaissance and intelligence gathering would be unavoidable. Boscawen was to take command of the main body in Wilson's absence and see to it that the river lodgement was properly entrenched while he was away. As soon as he had briefed his deputy, Sir Charles turned his thoughts to communicating all the recent developments to the C-in-C. The journey back across the Bayūda would not be easy. Wilson selected 'Bloody-minded' Pigott to act as his courier, his role as a company commander notwithstanding.[127] It might have been a tribute to Captain Pigott's soldierly qualities, but from Wilson's personal point of view would turn out in the end not to be the wisest of choices. In the event it was decided that Pigott should not start out until the following day, as none of the horses or camels looked like they were up to making an immediate start on so arduous a journey.

As usual Willoughby Verner had been taking a wider view of the tactical situation and concluded that it would be necessary to deny Gubat Island to enemy snipers. He was given Lieutenant Max Sherston and the 2nd KRRC section of C Company, MICR, twenty strong at best, and told to transport it across the intervening 500 yards of water aboard the *Bordein*. By the time the Rifles had gathered their kit together and Colonel 'Abd al-Ḥamīd Bey had ferried them across the channel, the evening had turned pitch black. Verner had to content himself with posting a double sentry ashore and waiting for daylight.[128]

Before turning in for the night an exhausted Wilson had one last duty to perform. It was dark by the time he reached the hospital to make his customary round of the wounded. He found Lieutenant Charlie Crutchley 'very cheery after his amputation' and took special care to share his news, thoughts and plans with the still frail Stewart.[129]

Wolseley Receives News of Abu Klea

One hundred and seventy-four miles away from the scene of the action, the C-in-C had completed the business of the day and was as usual giving vent to his innermost thoughts in his journal. It was only that morning that the party of *bāshi-būzuqs* had come in with news of Abu Klea. Sir Charles Wilson had sharpened their sense of urgency with the promise of a cash reward. They had been told that if they reached Korti by 4 p.m. on 23 January, they would each receive £5 in gold. The corporal in charge stood to earn twice as much for urging his men on. In addition to their basic reward, the couriers had been further incentivized by the promise of an extra pound for every four hours they saved against the deadline. Having covered 149 miles in three days, to arrive at Wolseley's headquarters on the morning of Wednesday 21 January, they qualified for a total haul of £110. The details of the deal were almost certainly included in a separate letter known to have been sent by Wilson in the same mail to Wolseley's military secretary. The contents of Wilson's letter have not come down to us, but they enabled Wolseley to sneer into his journal, 'I have been rather amused at a letter written by Sir C. Wilson to Swaine. This has been his first fight and it has evidently from his letter shaken his nerves a good bit.'[130] Stewart's official despatch had of course also been included in Wolseley's reading that day, as had all the copy sent back by the war correspondents for the attention of their London editors.[131]

Ever judgmental, Wolseley was quick to latch on to the failings of the Heavies:

Our loss has been heavy arising from the unsteadiness of the Heavy Camel Regt. which allowed the enemy to break into the square . . . I am very sorry about this Heavy Camel Regt. The men and officers were magnificent, but not being drilled as Infantry, they did not have their confidence in their rifles that an Infantry Regt. would have had. It is a dangerous experiment, using cavalry as foot soldiers under such a trial, but being picked men they ought to have done better.[132]

Wolseley wrote as if somebody else had conceived the 'dangerous experiment'. He was at his most obnoxious when he mused, 'How delighted the Prince of Wales & the Duke of Cambridge will be that poor Burnaby is killed. His high military spirit, energy, zeal and remarkable personal courage were not sufficient in the eyes of those Royal tailors to cover up the fact that socially Burnaby was distasteful to them and their set.' Ironically Wolseley observed of Stewart that, 'he and his staff were for some minutes in great danger: I believe they were knocked down in melee and Stewart had his horse killed. His loss would have been irreparable, and I dread to think of his being killed in some of these early affairs.' Little did he know as he penned these lines that the worst of his fears had already come to pass and that these were not 'early affairs' but the high-water mark of his campaign.

Chapter 15

Boy's Own

The River Dash: 24 January–4 February 1885

As we got nearer we could make out the White Ensign flying bravely in the breeze, a pleasant sight for hard-pressed Britishers.

Colonel Sir Charles Wilson, *From Korti to Khartum*

NOT LONG AFTER SUN-UP on the morning of Thursday 22 January, Verner, Sherston and the 2nd KRRC section disembarked from *Bordein* and began scouring across Gubat Island. They found a few huts, some goats and a luxuriant crop of barley and *dhura*, but failed to encounter a single person. The channel on the far side of the island was only 150 yards or so wide, but the presence of a few small boats confirmed that it was not fordable and could safely be trusted to function as a defensive moat. Leaving Sherston and his men to raise a small earthwork commanding the channel, Verner returned to *Bordein* and made his way back to camp to report his findings to his chief. During the course of the day Sherston and his men were relieved by a much stronger party of Egyptians.[1]

Major Dorward, Lieutenant Lawson and the men of the Royal Engineers made a prompt start to constructing a fort overlooking the defensive position on the river. Having identified a spot which was up to sixty feet above the general lie of the land, they demolished a few of the nearby houses with gun-cotton and began ferrying the debris up the slope to buttress a small triangular-shaped earthwork. The site lay about 800 yards from the main position. As elevated as it was, it was commanded in turn by a horseshoe of slightly higher ground at a range of 1,500–2,000 yards. Verner later observed that if the enemy to the south brought up artillery the fort would be 'a perfect shell trap'.[2] For all that, there was no better position to be had on the plateau.

In the meantime some element of the 19th Hussars had made an early departure to reconnoitre upriver. How many men were included in the patrol, who commanded it and just how far upstream it went, the sources fail to recount. What we do know is that at some point during the course of the morning, the patrol commander reported that he could detect no sign of an approaching enemy force. This was the cue to launch a downriver reconnaissance by *Talahawiyeh* and *Bordein*. On the basis of Gordon's unkind references to Egyptian 'hens', Wilson left Nushi Pasha behind and turned command of *Talahawiyeh* over to Khashm al-Mūs.

Beresford, still incapacitated and in great pain, was also taken along but had to be helped aboard and spent most of the trip lying on an *angareb*. Two companies of MICR[3] under the overall command of Major Thomas Phipps, perhaps 150 bayonets in all, went aboard the flagship.[4] Verner would take charge of *Bordein* with 'Abd al-Ḥamīd Bey, but would have only Sudanese troops at his disposal. It was arranged with Boscawen that if during the absence of the steamers any heavy firing was heard from the direction of Gubat, Sir Charles would at once put about and hasten back upriver to assist.

The Downstream Reconnaissance

Talahawiyeh and *Bordein* got under way at around noon.[5] In the event Colonel Maḥmūd Bey took it upon himself to tag along at the back with *Sāfia*.[6] The fourth and smallest vessel, *Tawfīqiyeh*, was nothing like as well armoured as the other three and remained at anchor off Gubat. During the course of the afternoon Frank Rhodes commandeered its salon as a hospital room and had the general stretchered aboard.[7]

As the other three steamers cruised past Metemmeh they were engaged by enemy riflemen posted in the date-palm groves along the riverbank. The British and Sudanese infantry returned fire, but it was a short-lived exchange in which neither side appears to have suffered any casualties. A little further downstream, also on the left bank, lay the village of Sayala (or Sayal),[8] the purported enemy strongpoint and concentration area. The settlement was set back from the river and almost entirely concealed by trees. The lookouts aboard *Talahawiyeh* spotted what they suspected was an entrenched gun position dug into an old water-wheel (or *sakieh*) pit, but could detect no other tell-tale signs of an enemy presence. A landing-party was thrown ashore and quickly confirmed the existence of an abandoned battery. As his men set about destroying it, Sir Charles waved *Bordein* on towards Shendy.[9] Verner recalled:

I was soon opposite the town, the main portion of which consists of a solid mass of mud buildings on some rising ground about 1,000 yards from the riverbank. The latter is steep and about 15 feet high. To the eastward a ruined suburb runs down to the river and on the bank of the river are two considerable blocks of buildings, with a long wall in front and some fine trees in the rear of them.

We steamed right in under the high bank and made fast. I landed with about 50 of Gordon's troops under Abdul Hamid Bey. The ground was broken and there were ruins scattered up the slope towards the town. As soon as we showed ourselves on the bank, a dropping rifle fire was opened on us from the town. There was a regular entrenched position in the centre of the front of the town, consisting of a strong-looking wall parapet, well loopholed, about 100 yards in length and with its flanks resting on loopholed houses.

Inside of this, seven banners were now displayed, and several more at other portions of the town. As I was desirous of being able to report on the probable strength of the enemy, I ordered the Soudanese to advance and took a Martini rifle myself. At about 800 yards from the wall we established ourselves and opened fire. I put a couple of bullets into the earthwork.

Rather to my disgust the enemy now opened a brisk fire on us and greeted my next advance with a well-meant volley of some 15 rifles from one point, which sent the dust and gravel flying all round us. So I halted, as it was evident there was some force in the town.[10]

In the meantime Wilson had re-embarked his landing party and was on the move again. Not long after passing another well-concealed but abandoned gun position on the right bank, *Talahawiyeh* was hailed by a Shendy loyalist, who was quickly taken aboard and questioned about Mahdīst troop movements. He reported that a fresh wave of reinforcements from the north had halted when they encountered groups of fellow Berberines marching home from Abu Klea with their wounded. He went on to say that there was a large loyalist faction in Shendy and not more than about 300–400 anṣār fighters.[11] Although it was not to be relied upon as authoritative, this was precisely the sort of information that Wilson was seeking. Some of the Sudanese must have gone ashore to secure the riverbank while this conversation was taking place, as Verner remarks in his diary that he was expecting Wilson to come up and cooperate with him. This formed no part of the colonel's thinking, however. He remarks in *From Korti to Khartum* that he was urged at this point to land and capture Shendy, but does not specify whether it was the British or the Sudanese officers who were behind the proposal; it is by no means inconceivable that it was a vested-interest proposition from Khashm al-Mūs and the other Shā'iqīa officers. Either way it was a bad idea as Shendy was on the wrong side of the river, was of no tactical importance and could not possibly have been garrisoned ahead of so many other competing priorities. Wilson rightly dismissed the notion out of hand.

When at length the troops 600 yards to Verner's rear showed no sign of moving up to join him, he decided to disengage and re-embark. No sooner had he done so than *Talahawiyeh* and *Sāfia* came steaming past, firing on Shendy with their guns as they went. *Bordein* hastened after them. It was as well that Verner cleared out when he did, as a significant body of Mahdīst cavalry under the Amīr Wad Hamza now came riding towards Shendy from the south. Quite how many horsemen there were is not clear, but the absence of any particular excitement in the sources would suggest that there could not have been more than a couple of hundred at the most. Wilson was told, presumably by Khashm al-Mūs, that these were the same riders who had been upriver watching the steamers for some considerable while.

Not far downstream the flotilla came across a ruined government warehouse, where *Talahawiyeh* stopped to take another Shā'iqī loyalist aboard. The answers given by the second man corresponded precisely with the earlier interrogation, enabling Sir Charles to conclude, 'it was now therefore certain that we had nothing to fear from any force advancing from the north, at any rate for several days'.[12] His mission accomplished, he ordered the steamers put about for Gubat. The flotilla hauled off in midstream when once again it arrived at Shendy, this time to pummel the town with small-arms fire and a barrage of ten rounds from each of the guns – which is to say some sixty shells in all.

When at length the steamers continued on their way, they made only slow progress against the current. This did not augur well for the ninety-eight-mile journey to Khartoum. Beresford took the opportunity to ask Wilson to grant a field commission in the Royal Navy to young Walter Ingram, who although he was purportedly representing some minor newspaper had found his way to the Sudan more for the adventure than anything else. Ingram held a Volunteer commission in the Middlesex Yeomanry but had fought in the ranks at Abu Klea and Metemmeh, in effect as a gentleman-volunteer, and had caught the eye of some of the regular Army officers as a 'cool and collected' customer. With a wave of Wilson's magic wand he instantly became an acting lieutenant in the Royal Navy; quite what their Lordships at the Admiralty would have thought of such irregular proceedings we can only imagine.[13]

Never one knowingly to undersell himself, Beresford would later submit in his official report 'Proceedings of the Naval Brigade' that he had been in command of the steamers on 22 January:

After some repairs to the engines reported the steamers ready to proceed to Khartoum at 3 p.m. Took command of Gordon's steamers. Proceeded to Shendy, distance seven miles, in 'Bordein' and 'Tull-Howeiya,' taking Bashi-Bazouks and the crews I found in the vessels. Fired a few shells into Shendy and cleared a small earthwork. Received no opposition.[14]

One would have to spend a good deal of time in the archives of the Admiralty to find a more disingenuous report than this, as the reality was that Beresford had spent most of the day flat on his back in great pain, quite incapable of commanding anything. The real problem, however, lies in the first sentence of the report where a falsehood of significance needs to be highlighted. Beresford was first rumbled by Alex Macdonald, not entirely politely, in his *Too Late for Gordon and Khartoum*:

Lord Charles Beresford unaccountably exaggerates the part he played in the proceedings of this day . . . he was also inaccurate in stating at the same time that he had on the 22nd reported the steamers ready for Khartoum, for to my personal knowledge the naval artificers did not touch them until the following day, and Lord Charles, when I called his attention to the matter, frankly acknowledged his error in date and said that I was correct in my statement.[15]

The Egyptians dug in on Gubat were fortunate that the steamers returned before nightfall, as there was chicanery afoot at the eastern tip of the island, where several boatloads of *anṣār* had crossed unobserved from the right bank. Wilson and Verner steamed to the rescue, panicked the enemy in their approach and quickly threw a large party of Sudanese troops ashore to clear through the undergrowth. There was a good deal of wild shooting, as was always the case whenever the ill-disciplined steamer crews went into action, although most of the enemy were already back aboard their boats and paddling furiously for the right bank. They were fired on by the guns and the MICR riflemen, but it was a short crossing, the light was fading and the majority managed to run the gauntlet safely. It was dark by the time the Sudanese had been re-embarked and the flotilla was able to drop anchor beside *Tawfīqiyeh*. Before going ashore Wilson gave orders that *Bordein* and *Talahawiyeh* should be readied for a dash upriver, to commence as early as possible the following day. It was generally anticipated that this would probably mean getting under way at about noon.

Much good work had been done on the defences in the absence of the steamers. The triangular fort up on the plateau had not only been completed but was now ringed by GCR rifle-pits. In addition Captain Norton had emplaced two of the screw guns inside. He had also taken the opportunity to count his ammunition and found that he had a total of eighty-three rounds left. Within a day or so the new position had become known as the 'Guards Fort'.[16] In the meantime one of the larger buildings left standing in the village had been adopted by the GCR officers as their mess. As was their wont they worked hard to make themselves as comfortable as possible, and it was not long before their home away from home had acquired the name, 'The Guards Club'.[17]

Down on the Nile, where most of the force was bivouacked between the lip of the riverbank and the water's edge, strong fatigue parties had been busily throwing up earthworks. In due course this main defensive position would be designated the 'River Fort'. By the time the steamers returned there was already a strong defensive parapet of about 140 yards in length running along the edge of the cultivated flood plain, only twenty yards from the riverbank. The excavation required to raise the parapet had created a ditch about twelve feet wide and up to eight feet deep, in front of which there was a strong thorn *zariba* and a low wire entanglement. The next phase of construction, to be carried out over the course of the next two days, would be to add left and right faces running down to the water's edge.[18] The horse-lines of the 19th Hussars were outside the eastern face of the perimeter, where the animals could be sheltered between the water's edge and the high-water riverbank. Just beyond was an old *sakieh* mound which within a few days would be converted into a redoubt, the purpose of which was to allow Major French's men to stand to with their carbines and protect the tethered ponies.[19] This position duly became known as the 'Hussar Fort'.[20] For the time being crude shelters with *dhura*-stalk roofs had been erected over the wounded, though within a few days Surgeon Major Ferguson would pronounce them unhealthy and have them replaced with awnings made from tent canvas and hospital sheets.[21] That the British had struck the river at Gubat proved to be a particular blessing, as the island served to screen the River Fort from the east bank of the Nile. As a result the nearest potential enemy fire positions on the far side of the river were 1,300 yards distant.[22] Ferguson had been keeping a careful tally of the casualties and calculated that in all the fighting to date the Desert Column had suffered 101 fatalities and 167 wounded.[23]

On disembarking Wilson learned that it had still not been possible for 'Bloody-minded' Pigott to make a start for Korti. He had circumvented the poor condition of the animals by buying a reputedly fast, strong camel owned by Melton Prior for the princely sum of £35,[24] but had again been thwarted when his native guides declared themselves too frightened to start out with so small a party in such close proximity to the enemy. It was not an altogether unreasonable viewpoint. It was decided that Pigott should go out the following evening, when Colonel Talbot was due to set off for Jakdul with a convoy of around 900 baggage camels and a 400-man escort.[25] It was anticipated that Pigott and his party would accompany Talbot as far as Major Gern's outpost at Abu Klea Wells and then hasten ahead from there.[26]

Orders were also given in preparation for the coming river dash. Sir Charles would travel aboard *Bordein*, said to be fastest and most manoeuvrable of the steamers, which would be commanded by Colonel Khashm al-Mūs Bey. Wilson would be accompanied by Captain Fred Gascoigne, the late Colonel Burnaby's travelling companion, who although he had spent a decade in the Blues from 1870-80 had never seen action and was no longer a regular Army officer. He was, however, listed in the Reserve of Officers[27] and also held a commission in a part-time Volunteer unit. In quite what official capacity Gascoigne was present in the Sudan, if any, is not clear. He is certainly not to be found amongst the special service officers listed in Colvile's *Official History*. On 11 December Burnaby had written to his wife from Dal, 'I sleep on the ground in a waterproof bag, and have as aide-de-camp Captain Gascoigne, late of my regiment.' While he was at Dal he is also reported to have said to Mr J. R. M. Cook, 'If the British Government had not sent an expedition to Khartoum, I and my friend, Captain Gascoigne, would have gone out alone with the intention of cutting our way through to Gordon.'[28] Sir Charles Wilson observed in his book that Burnaby had introduced Gascoigne to him as, 'a young man who knew his way about in the Sudan', although in truth he was better acquainted with the eastern swathe of the country and the Abyssinian frontier than with the Nile Valley.[29] If, as it would appear, Gascoigne's presence was more than a little irregular, he seems nonetheless to have been accepted by the column's hierarchy as just another officer serving in the Sudan.

Stuart-Wortley would travel aboard *Talahawiyeh* with Colonel 'Abd al-Ḥamīd Bey. Gordon had confided in his journals that he thought highly of both Khashm al-Mūs and 'Abd al-Ḥamīd, who appear to have been related. The latter was much the younger and may conceivably have been a nephew to Khashm. Gascoigne described him as a 'handsome young man of about twenty-six',[30] while Wilson observed that he much given to dressing elegantly, 'in some flowing garment of gorgeous hue'. He was very young to hold the rank of bey and had evidently been pushed on quickly, as was Gordon's wont wherever he encountered young men of talent. By contrast Sir Charles Wilson would form the opinion that he was altogether too young for the level of responsibility he now enjoyed, observing that, 'he had the petulant manners of a spoiled child, amusing to watch, but annoying when work has to be done'.[31]

It had originally been intended that fifty British soldiers would go aboard the steamers, but as Talbot would shortly be taking 400 men away from Gubat, leaving

Boscawen with barely 600 bayonets, Wilson decided to reduce his escort to one officer and twenty men from 1st Royal Sussex.[32] It will be recalled that Sir Charles was under orders to bring the soldiers back from Khartoum, but leave three officers to assist General Gordon until such time as Wolseley could effect the relief of city. Gascoigne and Stuart-Wortley were still squarely in the firing line, but the final member of the trio, Major John Dickson, had been wounded at Abu Klea. Having read Gordon's journals and gained a sense of the dire situation which must now be prevailing at Khartoum, Wilson chose not to nominate a substitute. In the circumstances Gascoigne and Stuart-Wortley deserved gallantry awards for even stepping foot aboard the steamers. Some of the newspapermen, including certainly Burleigh and Prior, pressed to be allowed to go, but Wilson knew better than most that if Gordon was still alive when he reached his destination there would be a strong likelihood of emotional words fit to embarrass even the thick-skinned Mister Gladstone. Besides, Wolseley appears to have anticipated the problem and somewhere along the line had given specific instructions that the correspondents were to be excluded.

Final Preparations

Friday 23 January began with great bustle. Verner, Stuart-Wortley and Gascoigne had their work cut out if they were to sift out Gordon's Egyptian 'hens' from the Sudanese blacks and Shā'iqīa Arabs. It was not only a question of getting all the Egyptians off *Bordein* and *Talahawiyeh*, but of transferring eligible Sudanese from *Sāfia* and *Tawfīqiyeh* in their stead. Everybody had his particular spot in the darkness of the hold, where he slept and kept a precious pile of personal possessions. Nor was it easy to work out who did what – who was a boiler-man and who was a gunner. Amidst all the toing and froing, the Naval Brigade artificers were doing their best to service the boilers so that the little vessels could give a good account of themselves in running past enemy batteries against the current. By now Beresford was laid up in hospital and unable to move at all. He offered to accompany the steamers even so, but the doctors were of the view that the previous day's voyage had done him no good at all and that he was likely to get worse before he got better. Above all he needed to go under the knife. A good deal of time was lost over the course of the day by the necessity to pass queries through interpreters, as the only Briton capable of transacting his business in bad Arabic was Stuart-Wortley.

The chaos aboard the boats was further compounded by the presence of a significant number of women – wives, concubines and slave-girls – who amongst other things attended to the on-board catering. Quite how they were able to cook over open fires without igniting the carelessly stowed artillery ammunition and blowing the heavily armed vessels to pieces was a source of wonderment to the British officers. In the event, about twenty-five women, some of whom had babes in arms and infants in tow, would inveigle themselves aboard *Bordein* and *Talahawiyeh* for the coming voyage. Verner recollected the events of the morning thus:

General Gordon sent us very urgent instructions on no account to send up any Egyptians, but to select a crew of his Soudanese soldiers. This operation, simple as it sounds, was a work of untold agony and worry and nearly sent Gascoigne, Stuart-Wortley and myself out of our minds. Every Egyptian and Soudanese had some belongings in the shape of a woman slave or goat or boxes of loot or figs or dried meat. The confusion and fights arising out of the shifting of some 400 of these men from the four steamers and selecting some 250 of them to man two, was simply indescribable.[33]

In the meantime Wilson, Boscawen, Barrow and the officers of the staff had come together to refine their plans. One of the first decisions to emerge was that Captain Trafford would be the officer in charge of the Royal Sussex party. He was told to nominate the twenty best shots in his company and, in accordance with Lord Wolseley's very particular order, to kit his men out in red. Try as they might, however, Trafford and Colour Sergeant Wellstead were unable to locate the consignment of red frocks brought up by Burnaby with the *dhura* convoy. The chances are that they had been lost during the chaotic night march to the river. Trafford was obliged to return to the headquarters bivouac and report his difficulty. The commanding officers of the Guards and the Heavies knew that their men had their red serge in their *zuleetahs* and, anxious to further the glory of their own regiments, took the opportunity to try and dislodge the Royal Sussex. Left to their own devices Reggie Talbot would doubtless have detailed the 1st Life Guards section from his No. 1 Company, and Evelyn Boscawen a section of Coldstreamers from his No. 2 Company. Percy Barrow, though, was having none of it and spoke up strongly for the Royal Sussex. They were the regiment ordered to go and go they must. It was only their just deserts after being used and abused as the column's odd-job men. The other regiments would just have to hand over sufficient red serge and have done with it.

Barrow won the day and later that afternoon Trafford's party was provided with a mixed assortment of Guards and heavy cavalry frocks. Although some primary accounts and almost all secondary sources talk of there being red-coated men aboard the steamers as a matter of fact, it would appear that this is nothing more than an assumption. The point, after all, was to march the infantry detachment through the streets of Khartoum in red serge, not necessarily to fight upriver in it. At no point in the comprehensive participant accounts of Wilson, Trafford or Gascoigne is there a reference which confirms that the Royal Sussex men were actually clad in red during their river adventure. Even more compellingly Captain Sir George Arthur's *The Story of the Household Cavalry* quotes a letter from Stuart-Wortley which positively asserts that red was not worn.[34] It is possible that the Royal Sussex filed up the gangplank in ill-fitting scarlet frocks for the benefit of jealous onlookers, before quickly changing back into their grubby grey ones as soon as they were out of sight – but perhaps far more likely that those who were not there simply imagined them fighting in red. In the event Trafford and his men had to wait to file up the gangplank. So prolonged were the twin difficulties of sorting out the steamer crews and of gathering in enough firewood for the boilers that in the end Wilson was obliged to give up any idea of setting out on the 23rd and postpone his departure until first light the following morning.

Talbot's Convoy – Night 23/24 January

Not long after sunset, Reggie Talbot slipped quietly into the desert at the head of a long convoy of unladen baggage camels. The principal guide and navigator was Lord Cochrane, specially appointed to the task because he had made his way back from Jakdul Wells to Korti in the first week of January and was evidently no slouch with map and compass. Deployed on the point, along the flanks and at the rear were no fewer than six companies of the camel corps – two from each regiment. We know from Percy Marling's account that MICR sent its A and B Companies, but that young Marling himself had been laid low by severe stomach pains and was prevented from going by the RMO, Surgeon John Robertson.[35]

Riding with Cochrane at the front of the convoy was 'Bloody-minded' Pigott. 'I liked Pigott,' recalled Cochrane, 'he amused me and was a gallant fellow.' True to form Pigott remarked as they rode along, 'If the enemy springs up out of the scrub you are bound to miss him with that revolver of yours; carry a shot-gun like I do, and blow their heads off.' After the column had gone about seven miles into the desert Pigott cut loose with his batman and a native guide and disappeared into the gloom.[36]

Cochrane was navigating in the direction of Abu Klea Wells by dead reckoning and concentrating hard on his compass accordingly. He was irritated not long after sun-up when two un-named 'senior officers' rode up beside him to insist that a well-beaten track diverging from the line of march to the right was the correct direction of travel. Cochrane snapped that he could guide or not guide, but if it was to be the former he was not prepared to brook any compromise with the advice of his 'trusty compass'. For Cochrane to make such a remark, one of the vexatious duo must have been Talbot; quite who the other man was is a matter of no consequence. Talbot gave way, enabling Cochrane to lead the column straight and true, so that after some 10½ hours on the march they reached Major Gern's outpost. Cochrane gloated in his memoirs, 'If only our night march of 18–19 January had been done in 10½ hours, how different things might have turned out!'[37]

The convoy had not been at Abu Klea Wells for long when Pigott and his companions came riding back in. It transpired that there was a small party of *anṣār* burying bodies on the nearby battlefield, so it was agreed that Talbot would provide Pigott with an eight-man escort. The enlarged party picked its way cautiously along the Abu Klea Valley with no further sightings of the enemy. Unfortunately Pigott became hopelessly disorientated over the course of the next twenty-four hours, with the result that Talbot and his convoy reached Jakdul Wells ahead of him.[38]

Wilson Departs for Khartoum – a.m. Saturday 24 January

Like Sir Charles Wilson, Captain Trafford and his men slept beside the steamers and embarked bright and early the following morning. Melton Prior, it seems, had stowed away in *Bordein*'s 'forecastle' or forward gun-turret, but was soon discovered and ordered ashore.[39] That he failed to get away with his caper is a pity, as there would doubtless have been some fascinating sketches to show for it. It was not until about 7.45 a.m. that the vessels finally got up steam and pulled away from the bank. For a while Wilson was able to empty his head of worldly concerns and relax for the first time in days. It was not long, though, before his brain once again started racing through the military situation, the factors in play and the numerous eventualities which might flow from them.

Also aboard *Bordein* were: Colonel Khashm al-Mūs Bey; Captain Fred Gascoigne and his native servant, Sulaimān; Wilson's batman, 16014 Driver R. Sutton (RE); the colonel's interpreter, Muḥammad Effendi Ibrahim, still nursing a flesh wound from Abu Kru; a petty officer and an artificer from the Naval Brigade, whose names would appear not to have been formally recorded for posterity; 110 Sudanese officers, soldiers and crewmen; and the following members of C Company 1st Royal Sussex:

> 003 Colour Sergeant E. Wellstead
> 318 Corporal W. Othen[40]
> 512 Private G. Benford
> 688 Private E. Dale[41]
> 506 Private J. Gausden
> 93 Private H. Ings[42]
> 534 Private J. Jones
> 2054 Private W. Leggett
> 2076 Private M. Patching
> 1591 Private H. Temple

Aboard *Talahawiyeh* were: Captain Lionel Trafford, Royal Sussex; Colonel ʿAbd al-Ḥamīd Bey; Lieutenant Edward Stuart-Wortley KRRC; his batman, also a member of KRRC;[43] an unknown Royal Navy artificer; an unknown army signaller;[44] the unknown Greek who had brought down the last volume of Gordon's journal and was anxious to return to his family; eighty Sudanese officers, soldiers and crewmen; and the following members of Trafford's company:

> 478 Corporal T Smith
> 520 Private J. Cannings
> 1440 Private S. Cowstick[45]
> 795 Drummer Gilbert
> Private Mitchell (whether 1913 G. Mitchell or 759 W. Mitchell is unclear)
> 1318 Private H. Nealan
> 1434 Private C. Paine[46]
> 742 Private M. Poole
> 1144 Private G. Woods
> 1 x other private soldier unknown

Talahawiyeh was also towing a dismasted *nuggar* loaded with grain for Khartoum and about fifty additional black *bazingers* and Shā'iqīa *bāshi-būzuqs*. In tow behind *Bordein* was a much smaller native boat of a type known locally as a *felucca*.

It is a pity that Beresford was thoughtless enough not to name the seamen who went with Wilson, either in his *Memoirs* or in his official report 'Proceedings of the Naval Brigade'. Rather less culpably Trafford made a slip in his journal by listing Private Ings with both detachments, implying that he must have accidentally omitted the name of another soldier.

Wilson had kept his orders simple. The steamers were to make best speed for Khartoum, with *Bordein* leading and *Talahawiyeh* conforming to its movements. There was next to no prospect of controlling the fire of the excitable Sudanese, but the Royal Sussex detachments were under orders that whenever the vessels encountered emplaced guns they were to fire volleys at the embrasures. The steamers flew their great red Ottoman flags as usual. Wilson remarked in *From Korti to Khartum* that he did not much care for the idea of fighting under the Egyptian flag and gave brief consideration to having them lowered, but he had nothing else to raise in their stead and in the end left well alone.[47]

It had been Colonel Hammill Stewart who, not far shy of a year earlier, had been principally responsible for overseeing the conversion of the steamers from everyday river-craft to makeshift gunboats. It was clear that within the limits of the resources available he had done an impressive job. Both vessels were armed with two brass 9-pounder howitzers, one in the bow and the other amidships.[48] The guns had been emplaced in open topped 'turrets' – fixed structures constructed from baulks of timber – which were turrets only in the sense of a castle turret rather than of a traversing gun-platform. Instead the howitzers had to be adjusted for bearing the old-fashioned way, by heaving them around with a trail-spike. Of course wheeled artillery pieces need deck-space to accommodate their recoil. While the piece mounted in the bow had insufficient room to do anything other than fire forwards through a single embrasure, the turret amidships had been raised above the paddle-boxes so that the weapon could be run out to port or starboard as necessary. It was reckoned by the crews that the turrets, the bucket-shaped crow's nests, the saloon areas and the wheelhouses were proof against small-arms fire at anything beyond 150 yards range. This was comforting news given the width of the Nile, provided that is the vessels were able to hold a course midstream.

Unfortunately the season dictated there were a great many stretches of river where sub-surface rock formations and sandbanks would oblige the *reises* (or pilots) to steer through narrow channels much closer to one bank than the other. In addition there were scores of islands, large and small, many of which sat squarely midstream and would likewise force vessels to port or starboard. Some of the larger islands were several miles in length. In places sub-surface rocks combined with islands to create well known choke-points, where the steamers' course would be pre-ordained and known to the enemy. It was not by chance that the Mahdīsts had established a battery at Wad Habeshi, an insignificant village located on the left or west bank (which is to say to starboard as the steamers plied their way upstream). The sandbanks at that point were so extensive that they left only a narrow channel within eighty yards of the riverbank. Khashm al-Mūs advised Sir Charles that they would have to run the gauntlet at Wad Habeshi late the following afternoon and told him about a ship-to-shore fight of some weeks earlier, on which occasion there had been two enemy guns emplaced there.[49] If the improvised armour-cladding of the steamers was of questionable utility even against short-range small arms fire, it would stand almost no chance of defeating a direct hit from an artillery piece. Moreover the hulls were not protected in any way, so that a hit below the waterline was almost certain to prove disastrous.

Assuming they could get past Wad Habeshi and then pass safely through the treacherous channels of the Sixth Cataract, the worst nightmare of all was likely to be running through the Sabalūka Gorge, where a range of precipitous hills sprang suddenly and spectacularly from an otherwise flat desert plain to constrict the Nile for a distance of between three and four miles. The crests and ridgelines towering over the river would permit enemy riflemen to see everybody on deck and render the armour-cladding irrelevant. Less than a mile into the gorge were the so-called 'Narrows of the Nile', where the channel was deep, but less than 150 yards wide. As if these were not perils enough, it was by no means clear how Wilson was going to get back from Khartoum. The expert advice of the captains and *reises* suggested that while it was going to be difficult enough to get *Bordein* and *Talahawiyeh* upstream at this time of year, bringing them back down again, this time with the current, when there would be every danger of the vessels being thrown against the sides of the narrowest passages, was certain to be even more hazardous.

The serenity of the voyage was disturbed at around 10.30 a.m. when a friendly Shā'iqī hailed the steamers from their port side. When the man came aboard *Bordein*, he warned that there was a Mahdīst battery at Gandattu,[50] just around the next bend in the river. The steamers pushed on, keeping close to the same bank as the battery so as to minimize its arcs of fire, until *Bordein* had the position in sight, at which point Wilson threw Gascoigne ashore at the head of a party of *bazingers*. Trafford and Stuart-Wortley followed up with some of their own men. It transpired that the battery had been abandoned, though fresh wheel-marks confirmed the recent presence of an artillery piece. Other friendly Shā'iqīa now approached and reported that Wad Hamza had taken the gun away to Shendy the previous day.[51] Through the good offices of Khashm al-Mūs, who evidently commanded great respect amongst the members of his tribe, Wilson sent off a note for Gordon to advise him that the steamers were on their way. Needless to say it never completed its journey.[52] Proceeding on their way, the steamers soon sighted 'a large body of horse and camel-men' to starboard. The *anṣār* opened a desultory long-range fire which mostly fell short or went sailing overhead. This it seems was the mounted component of the Faqī Muṣṭafa's force.

It will be helpful to the reader briefly to reprise the various Mahdīst contingents sent north from Omdurman to contest the advance of the British. The leading element had been the force commanded by Mūsā wad Ḥilū, consisting in the main of the powerful Kordofani contingent, which had borne the brunt of the fighting at Abu Klea. This had been followed by 2,000 men, under al-Nūr Bey Muḥammad 'Anqara, who arrived at Metemmeh on 18 January and fought at Abu Kru the following day. The Faqī Muṣṭafa, with about 3,000 men, left Omdurman two days after Nūr 'Anqara and should have reached Gubat on the 21st or the 22nd. What Wilson had learned from the various Shā'iqīa loyalists he had so far questioned was that this third body of *anṣār* had halted some twelve miles short of the British position, on running into parties of wounded returning from Abu Kru. It should also be noted in passing that following the fall of Khartoum, the Mahdī would order the Amīr 'Abd-al-Raḥmān wad al-Najūmi, who had commanded the assault on the city and was functioning pretty much as the rebel movement's senior military commander, to take a strong force north to attack the British.[53] In terms of our narrative, however, this fourth and last deployment would not be initiated for a number of days to come.

The steamers seem not to have returned fire at the Faqī Muṣṭafa's cavalry, nor did the horsemen give chase. About two hours after this encounter Wilson put in beside a deserted village to tear down the houses for firewood. He was appalled when the Sudanese found a stray camel and proceeded to dismember it for food. 'It was a horrible sight: the blacks wild with excitement, covered with blood, and running about with huge pieces of flesh, which they tore like wild beasts.'[54] Over the next few days taking on wood would invariably prove to be a tedious and time-consuming business, as the only means of obtaining it was by wrecking houses and *sakieh* wheels, while the handful of saws and axes available for chopping timber into boiler-sized lengths had been blunted and left unmaintained for some time.

There were several sniping incidents during the course of the day, all from the west bank. With night approaching the steamers pulled into the east bank and moored near a place called Gos-el-Basabir. That night Wilson lay awake for a long time, pondering how Gordon might react to the news of Wolseley's slow progress. Buller's calculations showed that General Earle and the River Column could not be expected to arrive at Shendy much before 5 March. 'More than another month to wait, and Gordon had given up hope in December,' he mused.

The outlook was not bright; my only hope was that, with the steamers and the few Englishmen, we might make a sortie before I left which would shake the enemy and bring in provisions. I try not to show anxiety. I do not know whether I succeed. Everyone else is in high spirits; they think all is finished or nearly so, and that the safety of Gordon and Khartoum is assured. I wish I could feel the same, but I do not see how he is to hold on till the middle of March.[55]

Sunday 25 January – Monday 26 January: The Sixth Cataract

Sunday began pleasantly enough with a 'delightfully fresh morning'. There was another stop to take on wood during the course of the morning, and it was a relief to get past Jabal Tanjur, an isolated hill not far from the riverbank, without encountering any opposition. Five miles further upstream the steamers readied themselves to fight their way past Wad Habeshi. They reached it at about 4.00 p.m.[56] The village lay to starboard, several hundred yards from the riverbank, where it was in large part concealed by a grove of date palms. It came as a great stroke of luck to find the position unoccupied. The mud-baked battery was close to the water's edge at the foot of a steep incline[57] and had three embrasures, one pointing upstream, another downstream and a third looking straight across the channel hard by the west bank, to the sand-clogged shallows beyond. At either end of the battery there were long shelter-trenches for riflemen.[58]

The approach to the Sixth Cataract lay four miles or so beyond Wad Habeshi. The cataract can perhaps best be characterized as a lengthy maze of part-submerged outcrops of rock, which much like icebergs are of uncertain dimensions, plus ninety-nine islands large and small, some of which one can cruise past quite happily, while others are best given a wide berth. In so hazardous an environment the steamer captains and *reises* would be worth their weight in gold, although it is clear that one or two members of the quartet understood the vagaries of the cataract rather better than the others. It is not uncommon for the badly mauled state of Beresford's Naval Brigade to be lamented in the context of the necessity to mount a river dash, but it is not to be imagined that British crews could have done better than Gordon's men. Indeed, as local knowledge was everything, there is every possibility that they would have fared a whole lot worse.

With the evening drawing nigh the captains grew anxious to call it a day, as they knew of no suitable anchorage they could gain before nightfall. Sir Charles, however, insisted that they could not afford to waste the remaining ninety minutes of daylight and demanded that they push on. The captain of the *Talahawiyeh*, an officer called Gibril, was said to be the most experienced of all the steamer captains and, pressed by the British officers to lead the way, duly eased his vessel ahead of *Bordein*. All went well until about 5.15 p.m. when *Bordein*, lagging behind by about 500–600 yards, ran hard aground. All efforts to shift her, whether by hauling, hawser or poling proved unavailing. After toiling for six hours by moonlight, it was decided to give up for the night and renew the attempt in the morning. *Talahawiyeh* meanwhile had moored safely at the north tip of Hassan Island.

With the coming of dawn the attempt to re-float *Bordein* began afresh. The first order of business was to shift all the hold cargo aft, so as to lift the bow as much as possible. The next job was to get the Sudanese troops moved across to a nearby island, so that they could haul on tow-lines from the starboard quarter. Unfortunately there was a nasty piece of water to cross and only two small boats to do it in. Getting everybody into position took a good deal of time, so that it was around 9.00 a.m. before all the preparations were complete. A first attempt using tow-lines alone was a failure, but a second attempt, this time with the engine running hard astern, at last eased the bow clear of the rocks. Re-embarking the troops was no less time-consuming than putting them ashore had been, but at length *Bordein* was able to steam upriver to join her consort off Hassan Island.

There were relatively broad channels running either side of the island, though the customary safe route lay up the left-hand or eastern one. It was agreed that Captain Gibril would go aboard *Bordein* to help get her through first, and then run back downstream in one of the small boats to re-join his own vessel. There was much broken water and a good many pointed rocks protruding from beneath the surface, but Gibril cautiously picked his way through and had all but come level with the southern tip of Hassan Island, when *Bordein* again ran aground, this time on a sandbank. The soldiers jumped into the shallow water and hauled on tow-lines with all their might, but once again to no avail. Gibril got into one of the small boats and rowed away with a sounding-pole. It soon became clear that there was a new sandbank across the channel and no obvious way through. He took the rowing boat back downriver to re-join *Talahawiyeh*, with the idea of bringing her up through the western channel to assist her sister-ship. He first lightened ship by disembarking the troops and leaving them to make their own way across Hassan Island. Eventually the bow of *Bordein* was once again worked free. She too disembarked her troops and then ran back the way she had come, to the north tip of Hassan, before then swinging up the western channel as *Talahawiyeh* had done.

Just beyond the point at which the two channels converged to become a single River Nile once again, there was what Sir Charles Wilson called 'a very awkward place – swift water between two rocks, and only just room for the steamer to pass; then we had some ugly turns between rocks in rapid water. Altogether it was very exciting, and one could not help admiring the way in which the captains and *reises* worked the boat.' I have myself travelled both upstream and downstream through these rapids in company with Ja'alī boatmen, in a much smaller vessel than the *Bordein*, and 'exciting' is certainly one of the adjectives one could use to describe the experience. By the time the two steamers were reunited in calm water they were peering into the mouth of the Sabalūka Gorge, but it was close to sunset and time to call a halt to the proceedings. Unhappily they had made precisely three miles during the course of 'a most unlucky day'.[59]

Tuesday 27 January

The following morning all eyes save those of the *reises* and helmsmen were fixed on the rocky crests high above the Sabalūka Gorge. 'Now we shall get slated,' thought Wilson. There was no shooting for the first mile. Neither did it come in the second mile, nor even the third. It was not very long before the steamers had laboured their way into much more familiar surroundings, a narrow green-belt of date-palms and standing crops, with vast expanses of golden desert beyond. The British could hardly believe their luck, for if ever one wanted to block a steamer-borne advance on Khartoum, Sabalūka was the place to do it. It was no less surprising, thirteen years later, that the advance of Kitchener's flotilla was not contested there either, although on that occasion there was an unfulfilled plan devised by Osman Digna to do so. A mile or two after emerging from the south end of the gorge, the steamers approached an isolated, flat-topped hill hard by the east bank. This was Jabal Royan, a truly commanding feature, which thankfully also proved to be unoccupied. The captains took the opportunity to pull in at the village of Gos Nefia on the opposite bank to gather in more firewood. It transpired that the villagers had not long since abandoned their homes, leaving a miscellany of plunder *in situ*. Observing many of the *bazingers* running in with goats, *angarebs* and all sorts of other loot, Sir Charles Wilson ran ashore to insist that they drop their ill-gotten gains and get on with the job in hand. Khashm al-Mūs and Muḥammad Effendi Ibrahim, Wilson's interpreter, were quickly into action with the *kourbash*, flaying anybody who hesitated to obey the angry British colonel. Towards the end of the foray there was some intermittent long-range rifle fire, but nothing to prevent the landing parties re-embarking without mishap.

From this point on the river became broad and the adverse current much less powerful, so that it proved possible to make much faster headway. During the course of the afternoon *Bordein* was hailed by a man standing on the west bank. He called across that a rider from the south had passed through his village that morning and spoken of Khartoum having fallen the previous day. Reassured by Khashm al-Mūs that such reports had been common currency for the past two months, Wilson chose to disregard it,[60] not that he had any other choice. There had been occasional sniping incidents throughout the morning, but from mid-afternoon onwards they became much more frequent. The Sudanese replied with their usual enthusiasm but little effect. Sir Charles Wilson had a lucky scrape when a bullet found its way into the wheelhouse and whirred past his cheek into the woodwork. Although a few splinters flew into his face, they failed to cause him injury.

After dark the steamers moored beside a deserted village on the west bank once again to tear down roofs and demolish *sakieh* wheels, as this would be the final opportunity to top up with wood. Trafford took his men out beyond the village and deployed them in a chain of four-man pickets, while Gascoigne and Stuart-Wortley alternately encouraged and belaboured the Sudanese to put their backs into their work. It was 1.00 a.m. before everybody had been re-embarked.

Wednesday 28 January – Khartoum in Sight

This was it then, the relief of Khartoum, as Lord Wolseley would later portray it – not that any of the officers present that day would have recognized the description, for the operation was to be conducted by Colonel Sir Charles Wilson and his batman, two other intelligence officers, twenty-one members of the Royal Sussex Regiment, three members of the Royal Navy, 250 semi-wild *bazingers* and *bāshi-būzuqs* and four antiquated brass cannon. This was the event which Lord Wolseley had predicted would cause Muḥammad Aḥmad and a 30,000-strong rebel host (a conservative estimate – the higher range is in the 50,000–60,000 bracket) to throw up their hands in despair and march quietly home to Kordofan, never again to breach the peace.

It was around 6.00 a.m. when *Bordein* and her consort set off on the final leg of the journey. An hour and a half later they passed a hill called Jabal Seg-et-Taib, where once there had been an enemy battery. Nothing happened. So far, so good. There were more and more sniping incidents of increasing severity as the morning wore on. By about 11.00 a.m. the officers could identify palm-fringed Tuti Island at the confluence of the Niles, beyond which were the indistinct but unmistakeable outlines of the Sudanese capital. Opposite the village of Fighailaia[61] (or 'Figeyeh'),[62] the enemy opened a 'regular fusilade [sic]'.[63] This was the cue for Sir Charles Wilson to take post in the gun turret above the paddle boxes, where the view was a good one and he would be able to shout instructions both to the wheelhouse and to the engine room below. With him were Fred Gascoigne, Khashm al-Mūs and Muḥammad Ibrahim. In anticipation of what was to come, the old Sudanese colonel sat down quietly in a corner and gave every indication of staying there. Inside the turret of course was one of the brass howitzers, served by a crew of black Sudanese and an enthusiastic Egyptian artillery officer called ʻAbd Allāh Effendi. Just below the turret, behind the funnel and down at deck level, the Royal Sussex lads were peering through their firing ports, waiting for Colour Sergeant Wellstead to give them their first fire-control order.

According to Lionel Trafford, *Talahawiyeh* was about fifty yards ahead of *Bordein* as the vessels drew near the east-bank village of Ḥalfaiya, once held by a contingent of Shāʼiqīa *bāshi-būzuqs* as Gordon's northernmost outpost. Wilson could see that the palm groves had been burned and the houses wrecked. There were a number of large boats moored in front of the village. Khashm al-Mūs was asked what he thought this meant and replied, 'Gordon's troops must be there as the Mahdī has no boats.' He was disabused of the notion when all of a sudden *Talahawiyeh* came under a heavy port-side fire from four guns and countless rifles. The engagement began at a range of about 800 yards and closed to 500 yards as the steamers drew level with a *sakieh* pit housing the first of the enemy guns. Trafford said that the riverbank was 'white with musketry', but that in accordance with Wilson's orders he and his men concentrated their fire only on the guns. One shell burst in the river only yards away from *Talahawiyeh*, throwing shards of shrapnel and a plume of water into the armour-clad deck-space occupied by the Royal Sussex detachment. Mercifully nobody was hurt. The burning fuze came clattering down on the deck with the shrapnel, but was quickly thrown overboard by Drummer Gilbert. *Bordein* now eased ahead to take the lead, but in passing *Talahawiyeh* to her port side managed to mask Trafford's fire at a critical moment.[64] *Bordein* quickly came into action against a pair of guns housed in a mud emplacement further up the riverbank.

Thus began one of the most iconic episodes of British military history, an affair which cannot be more authoritatively recounted than in the words of Sir Charles Wilson himself.

The guns were well placed, one in a sakieh pit, two in a little battery above, and one in the village. The bullets began to fly pretty thickly, tapping like hail against the ship's sides, whilst the shells went screeching overhead or threw up jets of water in the stream round us. Our men replied cheerily, and the gun in the turret was capitally served by the black gunners under their captain Abdullah Effendi, who laid the gun each time and fired it himself. The gunners who had nothing on but a cloth round their waists, looked more like demons than men in the thick smoke; and one huge savage was the very incarnation of savagery drunk with war. The shooting was fairly good, and we heard afterwards that we had dismounted one of the guns in the battery; but at the time we could not see the effect. After we had run the gauntlet and the fire was turned on our consort, the Sudanese sent up a wild cry of delight, raising their rifles in their hands and shaking then in the air. It was a strange weird sight, these black savages with their blood up, quivering with excitement.

I now had the leisure to watch the 'Talahawiyeh' coming through the thick of it, scathless as we had done, the red flag streaming bravely above the smoke, which hung in a dense cloud around her. The firing now ceased for a few minutes, and we could see the large Government House in Khartum plainly above the trees. Khashm was very anxious to know whether we could see the Egyptian flag, which he said Gordon always kept flying, but neither Gascoigne nor I could see a trace of one anywhere. Khashm now began to get anxious, and said he felt certain something must have happened at Khartum, and that the place must be in the Mahdi's hands, otherwise there would have been no boats at Halfiyeh, and the flag would be flying. I could not believe this; at any rate, we could not stop now until we were certain all was over.

We had only a short respite, for, directly after passing Shamba [a village to starboard], two guns on the right bank opened upon us, with a heavy rifle fire from both banks, and this was kept up until we came within range of the guns at Omdurman. When about halfway up Tuti I thought for a moment that the island was still in Gordon's hands. A sort of dike ran along the edge of the island, and behind this there was a long line of men firing away as hard as they could. I heard the bullets singing overhead, and saw them strike the sand amongst the enemy's sharpshooters on the opposite bank, and thought they were helping us. I then ordered the steamer to run in close to the bank, stop, cease firing and ask for news. This we did, getting within 60 or 70 yards. I felt so persuaded at first that they were Gordon's men that I got outside the turret, but the only reply to our shouts was a sharper and better directed fire, which soon drove me inside again.

It was clear that the enemy's riflemen were on Tuti; but Khartum might still be holding out – so after a delay of about a quarter of an hour we went on, old Khashm protesting that it was all up, and predicting terrible disaster to ourselves. No sooner did we start upwards than we got into such a fire as I hope never to pass through again in a 'penny steamer'. Two or more guns opened upon us from Omdurman fort, and three or four from Khartum or the upper end of Tuti; the roll of musketry from each side was continuous; and high above that could be heard the grunting of a Nordenfeldt or a mitrailleuse, and the loud rushing noise of the Krupp shells . . .

We kept on to the junction of the two Niles, when it became plain to everyone that Khartum had fallen into the enemy's hands; for not only were there hundreds of dervishes ranged under their banners, standing on the sand-spit close to the town ready to resist our landing, but no flag was flying in Khartum and not a shot was fired in our assistance; here too, if not before, we should have met the two steamers I knew Gordon still had at Khartum. I at once gave the order to turn and run full speed down the river. It was hopeless to attempt a landing or to communicate with the shore under such a fire.

The sight at this moment was very grand: the masses of the enemy with their fluttering banners near Khartum; the long rows of riflemen in the shelter-trenches at Omdurman; the numerous groups of men on Tuti; the bursting shells, and the water torn up by hundreds of bullets and occasional heavier shot, made an impression never to be forgotten. Looking out over the stormy scene, it seemed almost impossible that we should escape.

Directly we turned round, the Sudanese, who had been wild with excitement, and firing away cheerily, completely collapsed. Poor fellows! They had lost wives, families and all they possessed. Khashm el Mus sank into a corner of the turret with his mantle wrapped round his head, and even the brave gunner-captain forsook his gun. 'What is the use of firing?' he said, 'I have lost all.' For a few minutes we could get nothing out of him; but by dint of persuasion, and I am afraid some swearing – is it not Kinglake who notices this forcible character of Englishmen's language in action? – we got him at last to fire; and then, the devil once roused, he served his gun steadily until we had run the gauntlet again and were out of range of the guns of Halfiyeh.

As we passed the 'Talahawiyeh,' which had been aground off Tuti for a few minutes, we shouted to her to turn and follow; and just at this moment we saw a man on a white camel come down to the edge of the river below Omdurman with a flag of truce. He waved and beckoned to us, but as the firing kept up as briskly as ever, we took no notice of him. Whilst we were off Omdurman the small boat we were towing was struck by a shell, and a fragment of shell went through the funnel, cutting the stay and letting a rush of flame out, which soon set fire to the large wooden block left swinging in the air. I was rather anxious, as the sparks began to fly about, and the deck was littered with open ammunition boxes; but on calling for help, a plucky Sudan soldier jumped up, and after a few minutes managed to get down the flaming bit of wood and throw it overboard. If an Englishman, he would have had the Victoria Cross. He was afterwards shot, just as we were getting out of danger.

We all had narrow escapes. I was struck just above the knee by a spent shot which had got through a weak point in the turret; and my field glass, an old friend of twenty-five years, sent out to me in America, was broken in my hand as I was resting it on top of the turret. Gascoigne was as imperturbable as ever: he is about the coolest man under fire I have ever seen. Muhammed Ibrahim, the interpreter, was invaluable, always keeping the Sudanese up to the mark . . . and best of all, he did not lose heart when we turned to run down.[66]

By the time the steamers were safely outside Ḥalfaiya's arcs of fire it was gone 4.00 p.m. They had been continuously engaged with the enemy for more than four hours. That neither vessel had been sunk or disabled in the course of so protracted a fight was little short of miraculous. *Talahawiyeh* at least should have been lost, as she had been holed just above the waterline by a shell from Omdurman which must have sunk her had it not failed to detonate.[67] The armour-cladding notwithstanding two men had been killed and fifteen wounded.[68] Amongst the latter was Captain Gibril, shot in the arm but still on duty in his wheelhouse.[69]

Sir Charles Wilson and his gallant band had gained the confluence of the Niles, notwithstanding having twice run aground in transit and been left at the mercy of the enemy for extended periods. Yet still they had persisted in pushing on up a manifestly treacherous waterway. They had fought the enemy at Ḥalfaiya, Omdurman and on Tuti Island; they had observed a powerful enemy host arrayed beneath their banners on the south bank of the Blue Nile; and they had clapped eyes on both Government House and the Catholic cathedral. Famously there had been no flag. But this was by no means the only evidence of Gordon's demise, as is sometimes popularly portrayed. It had also been observed that the houses near the *sarāya* had been 'wrecked and half-destroyed', and that the armoured barges customarily deployed by Gordon as floating forts at the extremeties of the 'South Front' were now moored tamely beneath the guns at Omdurman.[70] At the point of confluence Wilson and his men had been caught squarely in a three-way crossfire from Omdurman Fort, Tuti Island and the city of Khartoum itself. Through it all not a shot had been fired to help them, so the idea that they were in any way uncertain as to the fate of Khartoum when they turned can safely be regarded as risible. Remarkably, it would not stop a despondent Wolseley suggesting to London that this was so. That they had pressed so hard and so far amounted to a collective act of valour no less creditable than the Defence of Rorke's Drift. Unlike Chard, Bromhead and the other heroes of that famous fight, Wilson and his officers had the means at their disposal to break free of their ordeal. And yet they chose not to turn until their duty had been more than amply fulfilled – until they reached a point when to proceed further would have been tantamount to suicide. How unreasonable, then, that for Garnet Wolseley this would still not be enough.

Retreat to Gubat

By nightfall the steamers had made fast to an island about twelve miles south of Jabal Royan. During the course of the following morning they would enter the twenty-mile-long Sixth Cataract. Navigating the maze at low-Nile was going to be difficult enough, but it was hardly to be imagined that the high ground above the Sabalūka Gorge would again be unoccupied. Beyond the gorge lay the tightest bottlenecks and worst stretches of cataract. To make matters worse the Sudanese crews were completely overwrought, none more so than the officers; Khashm al-Mūs had spent the afternoon curled up in a ball on the deck, while 'Abd al-Ḥamīd Bey's youthful petulance had quite run away with him. That there were so many Shā'iqīa aboard the steamers was a concern, as this was their home territory, where very plainly the new power in the land was Muḥammad Aḥmad. The traditional tribal tactic in such situations was to change sides. Wilson and his officers had to encourage the Shā'iqīa to believe that the Mahdīst ascendancy would be short-lived – that the great Wolseley was coming to chase the rebels back into Kordofan once and for all. That night Wilson dressed two of the Sudanese in Mahdīst *jibbehs* and sent them out as spies, one to make his way to Khartoum and ascertain the fate of General Gordon, the other to gather information locally. The second man came back some hours later to report that he had talked with a Ja'alī local who told him that Khartoum had fallen in the early hours of Monday 26 January, that the city had been given over to pillage and that Gordon Pasha had been killed in the fighting.

All three of these statements were correct. At the point at which Gordon met his end, *Bordein* was firmly aground in the Sixth Cataract.

The Ja'alī informant also added that the city had been taken through the perfidy of 'Faraj Pasha', more precisely Lieutenant General Faraj Pasha Muḥammad al-Zainī,[71] who was said to have thrown open the Masallamīya Gate to admit the rebels. Though this was evidently only a 'native rumour', it would nonetheless be reflected in a report written by Stuart-Wortley,[72] only to be immediately adopted as a certain fact by Gladstone and Wolseley, both of whom sensed that they might be able to derive a good deal of personal political comfort from the story. Some months later Major Kitchener would cast doubt on it in a comprehensive report entitled 'Notes on the Fall of Khartoum', but by then tales of treachery had outlived their immediate political utility.[73]

That Khartoum had been given over to rapine and slaughter cast an even deeper pall over the Sudanese. That night Wilson posted Royal Sussex sentries on top of the paddle-boxes, with orders to shoot any deserters on sight. Gascoigne and Stuart-Wortley spent the evening patching up the Sudanese wounded as best they could. It was fortunate that there were no serious surgical cases. Later on there was a long conference between the British officers and the ship's captains and *reises*, who foretold great difficulty in getting through the cataract in such heavily laden vessels. One easy fix was to jettison the hundreds of sacks of *dhura* which had been brought along to feed the famished garrison at Khartoum, but the real problem was the armour-cladding, the guns and ammunition and the quantity of people on board. Wilson thought that a cash incentive might help and promised that the captains would have £100 each and the *reises* £50, if they brought the steamers safely through the cataract.[74]

During the course of the 28th the news from Khartoum slipped past the British position at Gubat to reach the *anṣār* at Metemmeh. Harry Pearse of the *Daily News* reported:

. . . strange sounds and signs of rejoicing in and about the town of Metemmeh. On the plains, outside its walls, a kind of dervish dance was being performed to the ceaseless accompaniment of tom-toms. In an opposite quarter bombs were fired at intervals throughout the night, and an occasional volley of small-arms. Some said the people were celebrating a Mohammedan festival, others that they were working themselves into a state of fanatical frenzy for a night attack on our lines; but a few became apprehensive that the enemy must have received some news that gave them cause for joy, especially as it became known that an Arab on a swift trotting camel coming from the direction of Khartoum had passed within sight of our vedettes that morning.[75]

Thursday 29 January

The necessity to patch bullet-holes near the waterline and repair some minor damage to one of *Bordein*'s paddles meant that the steamers did not get under way until about 7.00 a.m. Ninety minutes later *Bordein* again grounded on a sandbank, but this time thirty minutes of hard toil sufficed to ease her free. By 12.30 p.m. most of the *dhura* had been thrown overboard and they were approaching the first dubious stretch of water south of Sabalūka. The captains and *reises* decided that all four of their number would be needed to take one steamer through at a time and that *Talahawiyeh* should go first. Just as she was pulling away ʿAbd al-Ḥamīd Bey jumped ashore and began walking in the direction of *Bordein*. It transpired that he was in a sulk because Stuart-Wortley had told him to get a grip of himself. All that happened now was that Sir Charles Wilson also pitched into him. It was evident that the late General Gordon's confidence had been more than a little misplaced. When *Bordein* had been brought up to join *Talahawiyeh*, the journey downriver resumed in good open water.

With Jabal Royan in sight, Sir Charles concluded that there was every prospect of being able to run the Sabalūka Gorge before nightfall. By about 4.30 p.m. they had drawn level with the *jabal*, with *Talahawiyeh* leading, *Bordein* just behind and a sandbank dead ahead. At this juncture Captain Gibril and his *reis*, who until now had done so well, failed to agree whether they should pass the sandbank through the channel to its left, or the one on the right. The bewildered helmsman steered ahead, waiting for them to make up their minds, and in so doing ran straight into a sub-surface rock-shelf. The obstruction was the best part of 300 yards in front of the sandbank,[76] so the mishap was in every sense an accident and might have occurred regardless of any difference of opinion between captain and pilot. Wilson had little inkling just how serious an accident it was until *Bordein* drew level and Stuart-Wortley shouted across that the ship was badly holed and foundering. All the readily accessible weapons, stores and equipment were quickly passed over the stern to be stowed in the *nuggar*. There was a scramble to save as much as possible from the flooding hold, but while a quantity of small-arms ammunition was retrieved, there was no time to save the artillery ammunition. *Bordein* stopped beside the sandbank while Fred Gascoigne put a party of oarsmen into the *felucca* and made his way back upstream. By the time he and his men arrived on the scene, Stuart-Wortley and Trafford had saved everything that could be saved, including the two howitzers. Gascoigne took a dozen souls aboard the *felucca* to ease the overcrowding in the *nuggar* and they all dropped downstream to join *Bordein*. Inevitably the loss of *Talahawiyeh* had put an end to any prospect of running through the gorge before nightfall.

During the course of the evening Wilson was notified that a messenger from the Mahdī wished to come aboard *Bordein* to deliver a letter from his master. It turned out to be the man on the white camel who had appeared under a flag of truce at Omdurman, a Dongolāwī known as the Faqī ʿAbd al-Raḥmān. Sir Charles Wilson remarked that he and his officers 'were much struck by his quiet manner, the business-like way in which he performed his mission, and his belief in the righteousness of the Mahdi's course'.[77] The letter was specifically addressed to the British and Shāʾiqīa officers aboard the steamers and, after several paragraphs of the Mahdī's habitual theological rhetoric, went on to demand that the latter change sides and that the former surrender and convert to Islam. In accordance with the usual formula the letter went on to imply that obeying the Mahdī would have a happy ending, while rejecting his overtures was certain to result in ruin and damnation. Wilson incorporates the full text of the letter as an appendix in *From Korti to Khartum*. He felt no compunction to reply, but was quickly ushered aside by Kha<u>sh</u>m al-Mūs who urged that he be permitted to send an ostensibly secret reply. He would say that it would not be safe to give himself up until such time as he was in possession of a special safe-conduct issued under the Mahdī's personal seal, but that if such a thing could sent to him he would deliver the British into the hands of the Faqī Muṣṭafa at Wad Habeshi. There was at least a hint of evil genius about the idea: anything that could buy them the time they required to run though the gorge and the rest of the cataract was worth trying. At first Sir Charles was held in check by his Anglo-Saxon upbringing, but then remembered that he was an intelligence officer and gave the wily old Shā'iqī fox the go-ahead. In a further prudent manifestation of his profession, he made sure that his trusty interpreter was looking over Kha<u>sh</u>m's shoulder as he was drafting his perfidious missive.

The British officers, meanwhile, did what they did best and engaged the Faqī 'Abd al-Raḥmān in polite conversation. Now that the 'divinely guided one' had taken Khartoum, the next stop in his campaign would be Cairo. The British nodded politely. After that would come Constantinople, then Rome, then all the other countries of the world. Stuart-Wortley could not help but observe in his faltering Arabic that all this might take quite a long time. Time is no object, insisted the *faqī*, when God is on your side. At some point in the proceedings one of the officers took the opportunity to enquire after the fate of Gordon Pasha, to be told by the mendacious *faqī* that he was now the Mahdī's prisoner. Having read the last volume of Gordon's journal, Wilson instantly rejected the assertion as a falsehood. Besides, even if it were true, he was powerless to do anything about it. The visitor concluded his diatribe by encouraging them to become Muslims and no longer contest the irresistible power of his master. It was high time to be rid of the *faqī*. As there is no source evidence describing quite how the deed was done, we can allow ourselves the luxury of imagining that just as the *faqī*'s handsome white camel was being brought up, he felt Kha<u>sh</u>m al-Mūs surreptitiously pressing a note into his hand.

'Abd al-Raḥmān was not the only visitor that night. Two or three Shā'iqīa notables also came on board and confided to Kha<u>sh</u>m al-Mūs and 'Abd al-Ḥamīd that they intended going over to the Mahdī. Ibrahim the interpreter once again proved invaluable, in wandering around ear-wigging all the conversations amongst the Shā'iqīa. Everything was reported to Sir Charles, who remained quietly confident in the fidelity of Kha<u>sh</u>m al-Mūs but more than a little suspicious of the temperamental boy-colonel.

Friday 30 January

After passing the last difficult stretch of water south of the high ground, *Bordein* took the *nuggar* in tow and paddled her way into the mouth of the Sabalūka Gorge. Once again all eyes were raised to the ridges above, but once again there was not a soul to be seen. Though this was both welcome and surprising, there were still plenty of pitfalls ahead. At the north end of the gorge, with the most treacherous stretch of the Sixth Cataract in sight, Wilson had *Bordein* pulled in to the bank and lightened ship by disgorging her passengers and throwing the last sacks of *dhura* overboard. The *nuggar* was sent on ahead to shoot the rapids and wait at the north tip of Hassan Island.

For *Bordein* there was another tortuous grounding incident of more than an hour's duration, before at last she was in a position to attempt the narrow gap in the rocks. When during the course of my fieldwork I ran the same gap, I was in a boat so narrow in the beam that there was very little chance of being dashed against the rocks to either side. Of course *Bordein* was (*and is yet*, for her hull lies in a North Khartoum dry-dock to this day), several times wider than the boat I chartered. Such was the torrent, roaring through so tight a gap, that if she simply ran the rapid, she was almost certain to be thrown against the rocks to one side or the other, with every prospect of being fatally holed in the process. The secret to success would be to ease her through the gap under control, for which purpose an ingenious system of hawsers, tow-ropes and anchor points was devised. Then she was turned stern on. With its engines running half-ahead to counteract the current and control her rate of descent, she was gently eased through the bottleneck, while all the while the disembarked troops hauled frantically on the ropes and anchor points to keep *Bordein* on a centre-line. It worked – it worked a treat – though inevitably the operation consumed a great deal of time. Sir Charles Wilson, who had been monitoring the proceedings from the top of the paddle boxes, was delighted and gathered the captains and *reises* around to compliment them on their skill and renew his promise of substantial cash rewards all round.

Before long the troops had been re-embarked and *Bordein* was able to steam down the western channel to join the *nuggar* below Hassan Island. By now the light was deteriorating. There was just enough time to take the *nuggar* in tow and make a little more progress before stopping for the night. Wilson chose to anchor midstream, both to avoid surprise attack and deter defections. Not far ahead of the anchorage was the narrow 'gate' where Bordein had run aground six days earlier. Just as they were coming to a stop Gascoigne's black servant, Sulaimān, approached his master to whisper that 'Abd al-Ḥamīd had tried to hatch a conspiracy amongst some of his fellow Shā'iqia to wreck *Bordein*. The rather more encouraging news was that K͟hashm al-Mūs had got wind of the plot and had taken action to thwart it. Try as they might the officers could elicit no details from a suddenly gormless Sulaimān. The absence of any details about the conspiracy, together with the glowing praise for 'Abd al-Ḥamīd in Gordon's journal, caused Wilson to doubt the accusation, though he resolved to keep an eye on the young Shā'iqī colonel all the same. It was just as well for 'Abd al-Ḥamīd that Sulaimān proved a poor informant, as the British would have had few qualms about summarily executing a traitor so heinous as to sabotage their only means of escape.

The Dubious Foundations of Doubt

Khashm al-Mūs seemed to have friends everywhere: that evening two more Shā'iqīa visitors came aboard. They too told a tale which, like the treachery of Faraj Pasha, would be duly incorporated into Stuart-Wortley's report of 1 February 1885. It was to the effect that Gordon had holed up in the Catholic cathedral with some fifty Greeks, including Nicola Leontides the consul, and a party of Shā'iqīa *bāshi-būzuqs*.[78] Wilson did not believe it, although it was known that Gordon had been using the stone-built church as a magazine and had stored all his munitions there.

The Shā'iqīa visitors did Sir Charles and his fellow Britons a favour with the rest of their news, notwithstanding the fact that none of it was true. First they spoke of how, after three days' fighting, the British had captured Metemmeh. Next they added that the recent British victories had dismayed the rebels to so great an extent that the *amīrs* were now refusing to lead their men against the infidels unless the Mahdī himself accompanied them. The British, it was said, were now 'swarming across the desert like ants'. Sir Charles could see that the news from the north had exerted an immediate uplifting effect on Khashm al-Mūs and the rest of the Sudanese officers. He later concluded that it had been a decisive development, in that it served at a critical juncture to confirm to them that their decision to remain loyal was the right one. Before the visitors went on their way, one of them undertook to go to Khartoum to try and discover the fate of Khashm al-Mūs's family.[79]

Saturday 31 January

The 'gate' ahead had caused trouble enough already but was bound to be an even more difficult proposition in the downstream direction. To make matters worse it incorporated a pronounced bend, which for a vessel of *Bordein*'s length would make the passage doubly hazardous. It was again decided to lower her down stern first, with the engines running half-ahead, and tow-lines and anchor points controlling her rate of progress and direction of travel. The laborious operation was accomplished without mishap and pretty much marked the end of the Sixth Cataract. The next problem would be Wad Habeshi, where, according to one of the Shā'iqīa visitors, the Faqī Muṣṭafa had just emplaced a number of guns, supported by 1,500 men.[80] If Khashm al-Mūs's deception plan had exerted any effect at all up to this point, it was at Wad Habeshi that the ruse would be exposed.

By now the supply of firewood was running extremely low, so that at about 10.00 a.m. Wilson had *Bordein* eased in to the bank to tear down two *sakieh* wheels. These would suffice to run past the battery at full speed and get about an hour beyond Wad Habeshi, before again having to find a source of firewood. While the troops ashore went about their business, various preparations were made for running the gauntlet, including stacking the hold cargo around the boiler to protect it. Noon had come and gone before all the wood had been brought on board and *Bordein* was again able to get under way. Not long afterwards Sir Charles was informed that during the course of the recent halt 'Abd al-Ḥamīd Bey had sent a man away with a letter. His suspicions aroused, he went to question the letter's author about its contents, but was given an assurance that it was only an enquiry after the fate of his family. Unable to perceive how the young colonel could possibly do any harm when the expedition appeared to be through the worst of its difficulties, Wilson let the matter rest. Three hours of easy steaming and quick progress ensued before, at around 3.00 p.m., the officers in the wheelhouse pointed out to Sir Charles that Wad Habeshi was in sight. Views can be alternately very long or very inhibited on this stretch of the Nile, but in this instance the river was fairly straight and there was still a good half-hour to run. Wilson had been on deck all day and decided to go and sit down in the cabin with the other British officers, for a few minutes' rest before the fight. He had been talking with them for about fifteen minutes, when all of a sudden the vessel was rocked by a violent impact. If it was apparent that *Bordein* had struck a rock, it was evidently a glancing blow which had done nothing to arrest her progress.[81] The sudden jolt had, however, separated the tow-line between steamer and *nuggar*.

Only Wilson felt the need to rush from the cabin to the bow to check for damage. Peering down through a hatch into the fore-hold, he could see water pouring in at a great rate. The irony was that this was a good, deep stretch of river, well beyond the northern extremities of the Sixth Cataract, but that in consequence there was every danger that, unlike *Talahawiyeh* which had bottomed out in relatively shallow water, *Bordein* would sink in the true sense of the word, leaving only her funnel above water. Wilson shouted to his interpreter to have the captain lay the vessel alongside the sandspit protruding from the northern tip of a long thin island lying to starboard. If one has not being paying close attention, it is easy in this stretch of the river to be tricked into thinking that the western edge of the island is the east bank of the Nile, but in fact there are two more channels on the far side. The first separates the midstream island from a much larger island called Mernat, while the second separates Mernat in its turn from the east bank and the open desert beyond.

During the course of my fieldwork I located the exact spot at which *Bordein* foundered, as can be seen from a comparison between a watercolour by Trafford and the modern photography in the plate section. I am reasonably sure that *Bordein* hit one of the two rocks identified in the photographs, as I could detect no other alternative candidates in broadly the right place. There is every chance that both rocks would have lain completely sub-surface at high-Nile and thus would not have represented known hazards. Their isolated position, some distance from the island in an otherwise apparently safe channel, renders them a particularly treacherous hazard to navigation. If in January 1885 the offending rock was showing above the water, then the accident can only have been attributable to inattention in the wheelhouse. If, however, it was submerged, then the accident was but the work of the Gods and a perfect demonstration of the treachery for which certain stretches of the Nile are notorious. Forced to hazard a guess it seems to me that the rock nearer the island is the more likely culprit, on the basis that the helmsman would in all likelihood have been trying to keep as much distance as possible between *Bordein* and potential enemy fire positions on the west bank.

Sir Charles ran back to the cabin to alert the other officers, to be greeted with stares of disbelief when he announced, 'It is all up; we are wrecked and the ship is sinking fast.' As improbable as the news might have appeared to a collectively stunned Trafford, Gascoigne and Stuart-Wortley, it was nonetheless perfectly true. Amidst all the excitement which then ensued, a strange and horrific incident occurred. For some unknown and inexplicable reason a black Shilluk soldier picked up an African youngster of about four or five years of age and threw the poor soul into the river. Of course the child was never seen again, but members of the Royal Sussex witnessed the affair and quickly seized and bound the brute responsible.[82] Quite what became of him subsequently is lost to history, but in the age of 'an eye for an eye' it is not beyond the realms of possibility that he faced some form of summary justice later the same day. In the meantime the captain had run the starboard bow onto the sandspit as Sir Charles had ordered, so that *Bordein* could bottom out but not sink. The British officers jumped into the shallows to inspect the damage, but the steamer was badly holed below the waterline, in a place that remained well under water even on the sandspit and was thus quite impossible to get at. An hour's work with the pumps and chains of men baling with buckets achieved nothing. By the time the stricken steamer had settled as low as she could go, the deck was only just above water.[83] *Bordein*, like *Talahawiyeh* before her, was finished.

Wilson and his party were still forty miles from Gubat and in the heart of enemy territory. At least they still had the *nuggar*. The Sudanese on board paddled the boat back upstream and wedged it in to the sand beneath *Bordein*'s stern. While the British officers were busy at the bow, supervising the unloading of the four howitzers, ammunition and other stores, some of the Sudanese from the *nuggar* swarmed aboard at the stern to loot what they could. The officers' servants were busily gathering their masters' kit together in the cabin but were caught by surprise and, as Wilson put it, 'allowed themselves to be hustled'. A number of items still lying about were stolen. When he realized what was afoot Sir Charles dashed along the sandspit to the stern, drew his revolver and promised to shoot the next man to step out of line. The ire of the ordinarily placid English colonel sufficed to restore a modicum of order.

Wilson's thoughts turned from the immediate crisis, to what to do next. There was always the option of marching downriver to Gubat along the east bank, although the proposition would be attended by three complications. First, there were a number of wounded to worry about; second, it would entail the abandonment of the guns; and third, Wilson had no idea where and in what strength the enemy might be deployed – only that Wad Hamza and his cavalry had last been seen riding into Shendy and might even now be prowling back to the south along the east bank. The safest bet was to minimize the length of the overland march by having one of the other steamers come upriver to pick them up somewhere north of Wad Habeshi. Calling Stuart-Wortley over, Sir Charles told him to pick out the best of the boats, man it with good men, four of whom could be members of the Royal Sussex, and prepare to set out after sunset to fetch help. If he was lucky he would be able to drift past Wad Habeshi in the dark without being seen. *Sāfia* and *Tawfīqiyeh* were still at Gubat: if the latter was small, all but unprotected and hence of little utility, the same could not be said of the sturdy *Sāfia*. As soon as Stuart-Wortley reached Gubat, he was to report to Colonel Boscawen and tell him to send *Sāfia* upriver to fetch them.

Sir Charles could see that the sandspit was commanded from a range of about seventy yards by steep-sided Mernat. The first order of business, then, was to get somebody across to the larger island to identify a good defensive position. Fred Gascoigne took a few men and set off in the *felucca*. Trafford and a handful of Royal Sussex men were the next to go across, followed by Wilson, Muḥammad Ibrahim and others. Khashm al-Mūs then followed on with a *nuggar*-load of disorderly Sudanese from the *Talahawiyeh*. In the meantime Gascoigne had scoured some little way across Mernat and located a few crude dwellings, where a handful of women were tending their crops. As soon as they clapped eyes on the Englishman, they fled to a small boat moored nearby and began paddling their way across the 300-yard channel separating Mernat from the east bank.[84]

Wilson conferred with Gascoigne and Trafford on his arrival and quickly concluded that Mernat was a 'miserable place for defence'. He decided that the optimal course of action would be to pass everybody across the second channel immediately and commence a forced night march along the east bank, leaving Gascoigne, a few sailors and an escort of soldiers aboard the *nuggar* to run downriver with the wounded and the guns. Wilson would stay on Mernat and begin ferrying the *Talahawiyeh* men over to the east bank in the *felucca*, while Trafford and Gascoigne returned to the smaller island in the *nuggar* to supervise the crossing of the howitzers, the stores and the main body of the troops. All well and good, except that when the time came for the *Talahawiyeh* men to start moving, Wilson was unable to get them to their feet. Such was the extent of the demoralization amongst the Sudanese that they could see no further than lighting fires and cooking up some food. When it came to breathing new life into the men, the officers proved 'worse than useless'. Sir Charles calculated that with the troops in such a state, the best he could hope to achieve was to have everybody on the east bank by midnight. So late a start to a night march would leave them anything up to twenty-five miles short of Gubat by the time the sun came up. By 6.30 p.m., at which point Stuart-Wortley and his crew rowed across to Mernat to see if there were any final instructions, Wilson had decided to abandon the idea of a forced night march in favour of allowing the troops a day's rest. If he was compelled to fight as a result, then so be it. Stuart-Wortley and a crew of twelve, four members of the Royal Sussex and eight Sudanese, rowed into the night about fifteen minutes later. Whether he went via the island to tell Gascoigne and Trafford to stay where they were for the night, or whether Sir Charles sent the *felucca* across is neither clear nor important. Either way, Stuart-Wortley's men were soon pulling their way into the main channel to chance their arm at Wad Habeshi.

It was a journey of about three miles along a straight stretch of river. Stuart-Wortley knew that he had to stay close to the west bank to hit the channel and avoid the great sandbank to starboard. When it became too dangerous to continue rowing, oars were shipped in favour of cradled rifles. They drifted silently with the current until at length the sound of voices told them they were level with the enemy battery. Stuart-Wortley strained his ears and realized to his horror that there was a conversation in progress as to whether that object on the water was a boat or not. A few moments later the moon put in a sudden appearance and the shooting started. Gascoigne and Trafford were standing on the sandspit three miles away willing Stuart-Wortley past the battery, but suddenly saw the darkness rent by the flashes of three distinct volleys.[85] Then it all went quiet again. Whether Stuart-Wortley had made it or not, there was no way of knowing.

Mernat Island: Sunday 1 February – Monday 2 February

Sunday morning was in large part consumed by moving the guns and the balance of the troops across to Mernat. A rearguard of twenty men was left behind on the first island to prevent enemy parties paddling across from the west bank and sniping across the channel at the *zariba* now being laid out by Wilson. The perimeter described a semi-circle, with its rear resting on the channel between the two islands. The position was well concealed behind the dense vegetation encircling Mernat and would be protected by the usual improvised barrier of thorn-bushes. When the defensive preparations were complete, Wilson had the troops stand to their arms and then toured the perimeter in company with Khashm al-Mūs, who was under instructions to address the men on the righteousness of their cause. The old colonel played his role admirably, making several fiery speeches in which he denounced the Mahdī and everything he stood for. Not long after they had returned to the command post, in reality simply a shaded spot under a tree, word was sent in that four Shā'iqīa notables had arrived and wished to speak with Khashm al-Mūs. Wilson agreed to them coming inside the perimeter, on the basis that betrayal was the greatest threat and it would be better for any such engagement to take place within earshot of Muḥammad Ibrahim.

The party were dressed as Mahdīsts but were evidently not the movement's most ardent members. Shaikh Abaluta, a relation of Khashm, acted as spokesman. He began by handing over two letters from the Mahdī, the first of which promised Khashm mercy if he would surrender, while the second threatened him with hellfire if he did not. Whether the first letter represented a direct response to Khashm's stratagem is not certain, albeit the circumstantial evidence that it was appears quite strong. Abaluta said that he and his compatriots had been left with no choice but to throw in their lot with the rebels and added that Khashm would be well advised to follow suit. Rather more helpfully he also imparted the welcome news that the small boat sent downriver the previous evening had passed Wad Habeshi safely. The Faqī Muṣṭafa, he went on, had two guns emplaced on the river (although it would turn out that in reality there were at least three and possibly four). Khashm thanked Abaluta and his companions for their visit, but brought the proceedings to an end by remarking that he had long been a government man and a government man he would stay. The rest of the day passed uneventfully. Overnight the British officers prowled the position, but by and large were impressed by the alertness of the Sudanese sentries.[86]

Not long after the morning stand-to, Wilson and Gascoigne made their way to the north tip of Mernat, which in those days was about three-quarters of a mile from the *zariba* position, although the ground has altered significantly since. When in 2009 I conducted my fieldwork on the river, I found that while Wilson's *zariba* position still survives, it now lies only a matter of a couple of hundred yards from a new north tip of Mernat Island. Beyond that point lies a fairly deep channel of 30–40 yards in width and then a small island which in 1885 would have been part of Mernat. When Wilson and Gascoigne reached the end of the island, they found that the mouth of the channel between Mernat and the east bank was too badly choked with rocks for the *nuggar* to be brought round to assist with any crossing they might have to make. With only the shallow-draught *felucca* available, passing the troops across to dry land was certain to require a good deal of time.

A little later in the morning the sentries reported that Khashm's sister had come from Ḥalfaiya to see him. Anxious for any news of events at Khartoum, Wilson agreed to the colonel going off to see her with Muḥammad Ibrahim and a small escort. They returned at about 2.00 p.m. The news from the city was much the same and again incorporated Faraj Pasha's treachery and great slaughter amongst the Shā'iqīa, though in this most recent version of events Gordon Pasha was again reported to have been killed in the fighting. Interestingly Wilson remarks in *From Korti to Khartum* that he disagrees with Kitchener's rebuttal of the Faraj Pasha story, but offers no compelling reason for doing so. Kitchener, by contrast, had some months to prepare his findings, during which period he interviewed many more survivors of the siege than Wilson ever did. It was particularly useful, when everything depended on Khashm's continued loyalty, that his sister had urged him on no account to surrender as he was certain to be executed. She was still waiting at the rendezvous for Khashm to return with some money, so that she could go back upriver and attempt to secure the release of other family members. Wilson gave him £110 and allowed him to return to his sister.

In the meantime another Shā'iqī had appeared on the riverbank and called across that two steamers had left Gubat at noon the previous day and were even now steaming south to the rescue. When, at about 5.00 p.m., Khashm and Ibrahim again returned to Wilson, it was with the dramatic news that they had spoken face-to-face with the Faqī Muṣṭafa. It transpired that although the *faqī* was a Ja'alī and not a Shā'iqī, he was married to a first cousin of Khashm al-Mūs. He too had advocated defection but met with canny and expedient obfuscation. Muḥammad Ibrahim reported to Sir Charles that he was unimpressed by the shifty *faqī*, who, he insisted, was evidently a mortal coward, as he had given a start at the sound of a rifle shot being fired at the *zariba* from the west bank. The palaver had broken up with an agreement that they would meet again the following morning to continue what the *faqī* had been led to believe were on-going surrender negotiations. By now Sir Charles had abandoned all the niceties of his Anglo-Saxon upbringing and resolved that if the enemy commander was indeed foolish enough to return, Muḥammad Ibrahim should pull a revolver on him and take him hostage. If there was little reason to doubt that Kha<u>sh</u>m al-Mūs would stay faithful to his salt, it now transpired that Gascoigne's man Sulaimān had been right all along about ʿAbd al-Ḥamīd Bey, who during the course of the afternoon had slipped away in company with a few other Shā'iqīa. If the British felt a sense of betrayal, it was as nothing to that of the pretty slave girl who had been at ʿAbd al-Ḥamīd's side throughout, but had now been abandoned to her fate. When Wilson, Trafford and Gascoigne sat down that evening to another indifferent supper they agreed that if in the morning there was no sign of a rescue party, they would forsake the *zariba*, cross the channel and begin marching north. They also made the desperate resolution that if any of the British officers or soldiers were wounded and unable to continue, they would have be shot dead rather than be allowed to seal the fate of their compatriots.[87] Whether three such fundamentally decent men could have brought themselves to carry through such a pledge is another matter.

Stuart-Wortley's Arrival at Gubat

Stuart-Wortley had picked his crew well. Rowing hard and riding the downstream current they completed a journey of about forty miles in less than eight hours. They arrived at Gubat at around 3.00 a.m. on Sunday 1 February. Stuart-Wortley went at once to find Boscawen. As he called out in the dark he woke Lieutenant Douglas Dawson, now employed as the colonel's ADC:

I jumped up and went out to see who it was, and then made out to my surprise Stuart-Wortley, whom we all thought at Khartoum. I looked towards the river, expecting in the faint light to see the steamers, then seeing nothing, and observing by his face that there was something wrong, I said, 'Why good heavens! Where are the steamers, what is the news?' He said, 'The very worst.'[88]

Boscawen was laid low with fever, so Dawson at once woke Colonel Percy Barrow, now acting as chief of staff.

Barrow heard out Stuart-Wortley's report and then pondered its implications with the stricken Boscawen and the rest of the staff. The first priority had to be the rescue of Sir Charles Wilson and his party. They inferred that the fall of Khartoum meant that there was a strong likelihood of the Mahdī bringing a powerful host downriver to attack Gubat. Boscawen was evidently in no fit state to remain in command and it was agreed that the next senior lieutenant colonel, Mildmay Willson of the Scots Guards, should take over. By the time the great and the good had completed their consultation it was just about light, at which point Stuart-Wortley was sent to brief Beresford aboard the *Sāfīa*. For the past few days Lord Charles had been patrolling the river in company with Willoughby Verner, trading for livestock, gathering intelligence from anybody who would talk to them and usually finding time to run downriver to shell either Shendy or Metemmeh. At first, Verner played the leading part, with Beresford resting on an *angareb* beside him. Eventually the surgeons had worked the senior naval officer's ailment into their waiting list and he was lanced, patched up and quickly back on his feet. Unfortunately Verner had now fallen ill and taken to the *angareb*. When Stuart-Wortley arrived to recount the events upriver, Verner sought to shrug off his illness and remain on board. Beresford could see that he was in no fit shape to participate in a serious operation of war and insisted he go ashore and report to the hospital.

Convoy Movements

Colonel Reggie Talbot and his convoy had returned from Jakdul Wells only the day before (31 January). The force at the river had stood to its arms in anticipation of having to fight in support of the convoy, but apart from a sixty-strong body of cavalry, the enemy at Metemmeh showed little interest in its arrival. When the convoy escort opened fire on the enemy cavalry with 7-pounders, it became clear to everybody at Gubat that Talbot had brought up Major Woodburn Hunter and the other half of 1st/1st Battery, Southern Division, RA (three officers and perhaps forty NCOs and men).[89] Also accompanying Talbot was Lieutenant Edmund Van Koughnet's 2nd Division of the Naval Brigade (four officers and fifty-two NCOs and men)[90] and a small detail of medics. These three components, minor details of sailors, gunners and medics, were the only reinforcements to have marched into Jakdul Wells since the departure of the Desert Column. The baggage camels were laden with more medical and commissariat supplies but, much to the surprise of the other colonels, Reggie Talbot brought neither fresh orders from Lord Wolseley, nor any news worth speaking of.

Beresford at least was happy. 'Never was reinforcement more timely,' he wrote.[91] Not only did he now have some officers to assist him, but he also had a second Gardner and a few dozen much more cheery naval ratings. In addition to Van Koughnet, the other newly arrived naval officers were Lieutenant Richard Poore, Sub-Lieutenants Colin Keppel and Edward Hardy and Surgeon Arthur May. The senior non-commissioned man was Chief Engineer Henry Benbow. They were a good crew: Keppel, May and Benbow would all subsequently rise by merit to be knights of the realm.[92]

Following the debriefing of Stuart-Wortley, the collective of colonels decided to evacuate all the wounded and sick who were fit to travel. Talbot would set out for Jakdul Wells at 7.00 p.m. that evening, taking all the available baggage camels and 300 of the riding camels – a hundred each from the Camel Corps regiments. During the course of the day Surgeon Major Ferguson identified five officers, forty-four NCOs and men and seven native workers who were strong enough to cope with the journey. The remaining four officers, forty-four NCOs and men and one native worker would not be up to it and would have to remain hospitalized at Gubat.[93] Talbot was also to pick up all the wounded who had been left at Abu Klea

Wells on his way through. The convoy would again be escorted by a contingent of 400 camel-mounted troops drawn from across all three camel regiments. As Marling mentions that C and D Companies of his regiment were detailed to this second convoy,[94] A and B Companies having gone with the first, it is probably safe to assume that the escort again comprised two companies from each regiment, and that the other two commanding officers would also have rotated their companies in the same fashion. Talbot was to drop off 100 men to reinforce Major Gern at Abu Klea and go on to Jakdul with a reduced escort of 300. This was a prudent measure as the wells at Abu Klea would be a vital staging post in any subsequent withdrawal back across the Bayūda and in the meantime would have to be held at all hazards. In the event Talbot would not get away until 9.00 p.m. that evening, having been delayed by the time-consuming process of loading fifty-six injured or fever-ridden men into litters and *cacolets*. The marching out state of the convoy was as follows:

	Officers/ORs	Camels (R)	Camels (B)	Horses
19th Hussars	0 & 9	0	0	9
HCR	8 & 135	244	0	0
GCR	4 & 149	253	2	0
MICR	7 & 129	245	0	0
C & T Corps	3 & 29	0	756	0
Medics	2 & 51	0	0	0
Total	24 & 502	742	758	9 [95]

It is interesting to note the following morning's parade-states for the units left behind at Gubat.[96] The figures are inclusive of the Royal Sussex men stranded upriver with Sir Charles Wilson and the members of Beresford's rescue party:

	Officers/ORs	Camels	Horses
19th Hussars	8 & 108	0	118
HCR	6 & 125	40	0
GCR	12 & 145	0	0
MICR	14 & 182	91	0
1st Royal Sussex	3 & 105	0	0
RN	9 & 99	94	0
RA	6 & 77	137	0
RE	2 & 22	109	0
C & T Corps	1 & 11	0	0
Medics	8 & 36	119	0
HQ Staff	4 & 2	10	1
Total	73 & 912	600	119

Stuart-Wortley's Report

When Stuart-Wortley had finished briefing Beresford, he sat down to write a long report on the events of the past few days, which he had been told was to go out with Talbot's convoy that night.[97] It is unsurprising given how tired he must have been that he failed to get the tone quite right. The principal problem was his first paragraph, where he set far too much store by unverified native rumour. His report began well, with an undoubted fact, flowed into a perfectly reasonable assessment, but then deployed uncorroborated hearsay altogether too prominently. Even worse it did so in respect of a mission-critical point of detail.

> The fall of Khartoum is without doubt. The fate of General Gordon is doubtful as reports are conflicting, but the general opinion is that he was killed; yet there is no preponderance of evidence one way or the other. He is either killed or besieged in the church at Khartoum.[98]

The unfortunately chosen words in the last sentence of the quotation, together with remarks about the purported treachery of Faraj Pasha, would pass through the hands of the C-in-C and be rapidly relayed to London. To a judgemental mind like Wolseley's it was inevitable that Stuart-Wortley's first paragraph would be interpreted to mean that the steamers had failed to press as far upriver as they ought to have done, far enough to be sure in other words, whereas in fact nothing could be further from the truth.

It is to some extent remarkable that Stuart-Wortley could write in such terms several days after the enemy was known to have broken into the city: even if Gordon *had* managed to make a stand in the cathedral, military common sense would dictate that an enemy equipped with Krupp artillery would have reduced such a position within hours. In fairness to him he was not an experienced intelligence officer, intended no harm by these words and was completely exhausted when he wrote them. If the notion that Gordon could still be fighting on the best part of a week later was little short of ridiculous, there was of course a much stronger possibility that he had been taken alive as the mendacious Faqī 'Abd al-Raḥmān had intimated.

By the time Wolseley received Stuart-Wortley's report he was already sneering, almost certainly quite unreasonably, at the letter sent by Wilson to Swaine after Abu Klea, and in addition had enjoyed a long talk with 'Bloody' Pigott, who had ridden into Korti in the early hours of Wednesday 28 January.[99] Pigott had proceeded to fuel Wolseley's scorn by speaking in less than glowing terms of Wilson's consultative command style. As we saw in the prologue, the journal entry written after this conversation included such remarks as, 'Wilson has proved a great failure as a soldier . . . On 21st instant Wilson made a foolish reconnaissance of Matammeh . . . a line of conduct that of course has encouraged enemy . . . During this silly operation . . .' and so on.

Thus the first few lines of Stuart-Wortley's report would do Sir Charles no favours in the eyes of a man pre-disposed to belittle and underestimate his endeavours.

Instead they served to reinforce Wolseley's worst prejudices. The truth was that while Wilson had consulted widely with the column's senior officers, he had inherited a bad tactical situation which was none of his making, had set things straight by winning a difficult battle and had not put a foot wrong since. Moreover he had displayed great moral and physical courage in pressing on to the confluence of the Niles. The irony was that far from unreasonably delaying the progress of Wolseley's operations, as was shortly to be suggested, he had actually adhered to a substantially unrealistic set of orders at grave risk to his own life and the lives of his men. That he and most of his compatriots were still alive could be more readily attributed to divine intervention than the quality of Lord Wolseley's plans.

Beresford to the Rescue

In the meantime the senior naval officer had thrown himself into readying *Sāfia* for a long voyage upriver and a hard fight at Wad Habeshi. He intended taking Van Koughnet, Keppel, Ingram and May, a picked crew of ratings, twenty marksmen from the Mounted Infantry and both of his machine guns. Chief Engineer Henry Benbow would look after the engine room with the help of a naval brigade chief stoker, two artificers called J. T. Garland and G. Woodman, the usual Egyptian engineer and six burly Sudanese boiler-men. There were two brass 4-pounder mountain guns aboard, one at the bow and one at the stern, both of which were mounted in the usual 'turrets' of timber and boiler plate. The two Gardners were emplaced amidships. Boatswain James Webber, until recently the acting commanding officer of the Naval Brigade, but now returned to an altogether more humble station in life, would turn his hand to the gunnery.[100] There was no way that Stuart-Wortley would permit himself to be left behind, besides which his knowledge of the river was bound to be invaluable. Interestingly Melton Prior also claims in his memoirs to have been on board, although the assertion is neither compelling nor substantiated by any other source.[101] The Sudanese *reis* was taken along in the wheelhouse, but would be passing his directions to a Royal Navy helmsman. In order to assist his concentration and sense of duty, Beresford first promised him a large cash reward, payable on the successful execution of his duties, then, less than subtly, had him handcuffed to a stanchion and proceeded to drop another kind of execution into the conversation. The presence of Quartermaster 'Punch' Olden, who took station behind the *reis* with a drawn revolver to hand, underscored the essence of Beresford's policy on treachery.[102]

After a while Lieutenant Bobby Bower KRRC led twenty members of A Company, MICR, up the gangplank. Sixteen of the soldiers were members of the 3rd KRRC section, which was unusual amongst the MI sections in that it had two officers – Marling, the senior of the pair, and the slightly younger Bower. When Marling fell sick and was unable to go with his company on Talbot's first run to Jakdul, he had not unnaturally thrown in his lot with Captain Dick Fetherstonhaugh's C (Rifles) Company, MICR, which included sections of 1st and 2nd KRRC. He had not been laid low for very long and, having made a tolerably rude recovery, soon found himself in the invariably risky position of being a 'spare' officer. By the time Bobby Bower and the rest of the section returned from Jakdul, Marling had for some days past been employed as the captain of *Tawfīqiyeh* and the commandant of 150 unloved Egyptian 'hens'.[103] For the foreseeable future, therefore, it was Bower who would have charge of the section.

With his intrepid crew aboard and all the ammunition he could ever need safely stowed in the hold, Beresford had one last preparation to complete: if *Sāfia* was to serve as a Royal Navy warship, it would be appropriate that she flew the White Ensign from her stern. With his battle ensign fluttering in a gentle river breeze, Beresford finally got under way at about 2.00 p.m. He made what could be best described as 'stately progress' for the rest of the day, at a speed of about 2½ miles per hour, the best that *Sāfia* could manage against an adverse current. With the onset of darkness Beresford ordered the anchor dropped midstream. The following day, Monday 2 February (the day on which Khashm al-Mūs was visited both by his sister and by the Faqī Muṣṭafa), proved equally uneventful for the crew of HMS *Sāfia*, although as usual it was necessary to stop from time to time and tear up *sakieh* wheels – an increasingly scarce resource on this stretch of the Nile. By his second night-time halt, Beresford had worked his way to within three or four miles of Wad Habeshi. It was time for a rousing naval address and Captain Lord Charles Beresford RN was just the man to give it. By the time it was over, 'The men were as cheery and steady as possible' – precisely the effect rousing naval addresses were meant to achieve.[104] Tuesday was set to be a somewhat less cheery affair.

The Battle of Wad Habeshi – Tuesday 3 February 1885

It was about 7.00 a.m. when Wad Habeshi came into sight off *Sāfia*'s starboard bow. Some considerable way upriver it was possible to make out the 'tilted hull and funnel of the stranded Bordein'.[105] After another thirty minutes' steaming the range to Wad Habeshi had closed to 1,200 yards, prompting Beresford to give the order for the bow-gun to open fire. On Mernat the sound of artillery fire was the cause of great rejoicing, at Wad Habeshi of great alarm and consternation. On the island the cry on everybody's lips was 'Ingliz! Ingliz!'[106] In the mud-baked battery downstream it was likely the same. Fred Gascoigne told Sir Charles that he would row out to *Bordein* and raise her flags to indicate their position to the rescuers. It had been agreed with Stuart-Wortley that they would fire three shots from the guns to indicate that they were still alright and that the rescue party should come on. Wilson gave the order to 'Abd Allāh Effendi, the officer who had fought his gun so well at the confluence of the Niles, but might as well have saved the ammunition as nobody aboard *Sāfia* was looking upriver for signal guns; instead, all eyes were on the enemy. Beresford's memoirs now pick up the story:

The only practicable channel ran within 80 yards of the fort. We could only crawl past the battery, and as we were defenceless against gun fire, our only chance was to maintain so overwhelming a fire upon the embrasures as to demoralise the gun's crews. It was an extreme instance of the principle that the best defence resides in gunfire rather than in armour; for we had no effective armour.

Accordingly the starboard Gardner and the two brass guns, the 20 soldiers and 14 bluejackets, poured a steady and an accurate fire into the fort, disregarding the parties of riflemen who were shooting at us from the bank. There were some 600 or 800 of these, and one gun opened fire from the side embrasure of the fort. Poor van Koughnet was shot in the leg, and second-class petty officer Edwin Curnow, number two of the crew of the starboard Gardner, fell mortally wounded and died that evening. But so deadly was the fire we poured into the embrasures of the fort, that the enemy could not fire the two guns bearing upon the Safieh while she was bore abeam of them. We passed the fort, and by the time we had left it about 200 yards astern, our fire necessarily slackened, as our guns no longer bore upon the battery.

Suddenly a great cloud of steam or smoke rose from the after hatchway. Instantly the fire of the enemy increased. Chief Engineer Benbow who was standing with me on the quarterdeck, ran to the engine room . . . I saw the black stokers rushing up from the stokehold hatchway. At the moment it was uncertain whether the ship was on fire or the boiler injured; but as she still had way upon her I ordered her to be headed towards the bank, away from the fort, and so gained another few yards. The carpenter's mate reported that there were three feet of water in the well, and that the vessel was sinking. Then she stopped.[107]

Sāfia was not sinking and Beresford knew it, as there was nothing like enough water beneath the keel for her to do so. There was, however, a sudden flood of casualties from below decks. Some of the Sudanese stokers came up scalded, one of whom was particularly badly hurt. Engine Room Artificers Garland and Woodman had be carried up to the deck and were 'so terribly scalded that the flesh of their hands, forearms and faces was hanging in strips, like the flesh of a boiled chicken'. It was clear that Surgeon May would have his work cut out for days to come. In all the confusion the worst hurt man amongst the Sudanese crawled under the fortified superstructure to die. Tragically he was not spotted doing so, was not missed subsequently and as a result would not be attended to by May.[108]

It was time for the captain to steady the ship. Instructing Bobby Bower to keep his riflemen blazing away at the enemy embrasures, lest *Bordein* be hit again, Beresford gathered his officers and bluejackets around him and addressed them once more. It is never a good idea for a British officer to resort to undue optimism in a crisis, for by definition this is the first resort of fools, and both 'Tommy' and 'Jack' tend to be far too bright to fall for it. Instead it is much more sensible to lay the truth before them, as it is grim reality which will bring out the best in them, and more often than not their best can turn the tide. Beresford was soon into his stride: the ship is alright; there is only a foot or two of water beneath the keel and we cannot sink; we will need to bring the ammunition and stores up from the hold lest they spoil in the water; no relief is possible; we are on our own and must get ourselves out of this; not a single dervish will come on board while one of us is still alive. There was an interjection from the back. 'It's all right sir, we'll make it 'ot for the beggars!'[109] Evidently such moments are not the preserve of wartime propaganda movies, but really do crop up in real life. Until the captain said otherwise, there was nothing to be done but shoot at Wad Habeshi. It had not long since turned 9.00 a.m.

Benbow now came on deck to make his report. The ship was certainly not sinking, nor was she even holed below the waterline, as the water below decks was hot and can only have gushed from the boiler. That much was a relief, but if the boiler was pierced *Sāfia* would be going nowhere. The captain duly posed the inevitable and vital question. 'Can you fix it?' Benbow was a consummate professional and had a good range of tools and other useful stores items at his disposal. 'I think I can do it,' he replied. The boiler was too hot for immediate examination; the fires would have to be drawn and water pumped in to cool it. It was not until 11.00 a.m. that the chief engineer was able to report that the hole in the boiler was about three inches in diameter. As is the way with kinetic penetration of metal plate, the inside lip was jagged and bound to preclude a hasty repair.[110]

On Mernat there had been a short fire-fight between the *zariba* position and *anṣār* riflemen secreted about the west bank. It had been initiated by Gascoigne's raising the flags on *Bordein*. Free at last to blaze away with their rifles, the loyalist Sudanese seemed suddenly to be revitalized. Nobody was happier than 'Abd Allāh Effendi, who was once again laying and firing his gun with obvious enthusiasm. The non-appearance of the steamers, in the plural, for they had every reason to believe there were two of them, told Wilson and his officers that something was amiss. Trafford went to take a look from the tip of the island and returned to report that there was a steamer enveloped in smoke in the middle of the channel. Gascoigne climbed a tree to look, while Wilson walked down to the end of the island as Trafford had done. Between them they concluded that one of the steamers had been crippled and that its consort had dropped anchor in the channel to cover it. Sir Charles decided to forsake Mernat and march down the east bank to support the steamers. When the order was given to abandon the *zariba* and form up in preparation for moving down to the north tip of the island, a 'scene of wild confusion' ensued, with many of the Sudanese rushing down to the *nuggar* with their personal belongings. It was necessary to send Gascoigne and four of the Royal Sussex lads to restore order and prevent the vessel being swamped. While the confusion was being gripped, a number of Sudanese soldiers and sailors were wounded by the incoming rifle fire from the west bank. Gascoigne was detailed to skipper the *nuggar* and told to move it down to the north tip of the island and wait there while everybody else crossed to the east bank in the *felucca*. He would keep Corporal Othen and Privates Cowstick, Paine and Dale with him, good men all, for the next twenty-four hours.[111] Also on board were the wounded, the stores, 'Abd Allāh Effendi's gun, two naval brigade artificers, the officer's servants, some Sudanese sailors and about fifty *bāshi-būzuqs* and *bazingers*. As everybody else was forming up for the march, one of Trafford's men was bowled over, apparently by a shot in the foot. It transpired that while the man's boot had two holes in it, the bullet had somehow been deflected from the entry point to the exit point without even breaking his skin. It came as a great relief to the officers that he was soon able to hobble along, albeit with a certain amount of discomfort, and that after a while the effects of the blow wore off altogether.[112]

Down at the crossing point Trafford deployed the rest of the C Company men to cover the first boatload of troops across the channel. It comprised a dozen *bāshi-būzuqs* under a reliable Kurdish officer called, by one account, Ali Agha, by another, Bakhit Agha, who hurried his men ashore to secure a nearby rise.[113] Not long afterwards Gascoigne came walking along the bank to report that he had secured a small hill a little further downstream. This tends to beg the question why the *nuggar* could not have made a number of such runs – along an oblique line between Mernat and the east bank – but it is clear from the sources that it was next to impossible for so large a boat to make headway against the current without the benefit of mast and sail. The best and bulk of the oars had gone with Stuart-Wortley, obliging the carpenter to spend most of the following day making four new oars for the *felucca*, using lengths of timber stripped from *Bordein*. Ferrying the rest of the command over the narrowest part of the channel in the *felucca* seemed to take an eternity. All the while the thunderous exchange of gunfire going on downriver continued without let-up. The distinctive five-round volleys of the naval Gardners told Wilson and his officers that their erstwhile rescuers were far from finished. In addition to sending Stuart-Wortley for help, Wilson had also despatched one of the Shā'iqīa soldiers to make his way to Gubat along the east bank, and it was now that the man returned. He reported that he had made it as far as Gandattu, where he had caught sight of two steamers coming upriver and turned back to re-join his comrades. His news sufficed to convince Wilson that one of the vessels must have been sunk under the guns at Wad Habeshi. Of course the truth was that there never had been two steamers, suggesting that the man had probably not been quite as faithful to his orders as he claimed. Wilson threw skirmishers out to his right and began marching downriver across cultivated land covered with a standing crop of ripe Indian corn.[114]

In the engine compartment of *Sāfia*, Henry Benbow was well into his stride, but as Beresford describes he had a great deal of work to get through:

Mr. Benbow, with no other assistance than that of the leading stoker, had to cut a plate, 16 inches by 14, drill the holes in it to receive the bolt, drill holes in the injured boiler plate corresponding to the first to a fraction, and cut the threads of the screws upon bolts and nuts. The new plate being too thin to take the pressure, he also had to bolt an iron bar across it, drilling the holes through the bar, through the new plate, and through the injured boiler plate.

During the whole time he was below in the stifling hot engine-room at work upon a task demanding at once great exertion and the utmost nicety, the fire from the fort never ceased. Bullets pattered continually upon the hull, some of them piercing it, and striking the wounded men who lay below. At any moment another shell might burst into the engine-room. But Mr. Benbow went on with his work.

On deck, we continued to maintain a steady fire, hour after hour, upon the fort. It was our only chance. The slightest cessation, and they would bring their gun to bear on us.[115]

The fire-fight was conducted over a range of less than 300 yards, with the enemy battery not quite directly astern. Sub-Lieutenant Colin Keppel and Boatswain James Webber had taken charge of the howitzer in the stern turret, but in order to be able to bring it to bear had been obliged to saw off a length of its trail. As a result the gun leapt into the air with each discharge, more often than not flipping itself onto its back. Keppel took to removing the gun-sight before firing, while re-laying the gun became back-breaking work. One of the Gardners was also moved from the twin battery amidships to the stern, where it was mounted on an improvised platform and served all day by Walter Ingram. Bobby Bower's riflemen added to the cacophony and by dint of the point accuracy of their fire might well have played the most important part in suppressing the enemy. From time to time, Surgeon May also took up a Martini and lent a hand.[116] As a result of the heavy British fire the Mahdīst gunners managed to get very few shots away, most of which fell short by a hundred yards or so, throwing up plumes of water on the sandbank to starboard.[117]

Although there were a few enemy horsemen galloping about the east bank, the skirmishers covering Wilson's right kept them in check with rifle fire, with the result that the shore party encountered no serious difficulty in drawing level with *Sāfia*. A few rudimentary huts dotted about the riverbank were put to the torch by the Sudanese as they passed.[118] Although the range across the river to Wad Habeshi was around 1,100 yards,[119] Wilson deployed his men to occupy a *sakieh* pit and its surrounds and quickly joined in the fire-fight. As soon as Gascoigne had brought up the *nuggar* and the *felucca*, 'Abd Allāh Effendi disembarked his gun and brought it into action. Although the range was long for so light a gun, he managed during the course of the afternoon to register two or three good hits on the Mahdīst emplacements.[120] It was about 2.00 p.m. when Beresford's signaller started spelling out a long signal with his flags. The message was to the effect that the boiler had been pierced, but that repairs were in hand and that Beresford would pick the shore party up as soon as he was able. Signalling by flag can be a tiresome business, so the indomitable Gascoigne volunteered to take a few men and row out in the *felucca* to speak with Beresford face-to-face.[121] Somebody had the eminently sensible idea that the two naval brigade artificers should go with him. As soon as they were aboard, they were ushered below to assist the hard-toiling Benbow.[122] Gascoigne returned to the east bank, again under a heavy but ineffective fire, to update Sir Charles on the situation aboard the steamer. He brought news that repairs would probably be complete by sunset and that in the meantime Beresford would be grateful for the continued fire support of the shore party. In addition to the rather wild fire of the Sudanese, the four best shots in the Royal Sussex took up fire positions on the riverbank and began sniping to good effect at the gun embrasures on the far bank.[123]

By about 5.00 p.m. Benbow and his helpers had finished preparing most of the parts, but were unable to fit them due to the heat inside the boiler. Eventually somebody was going to have to climb inside. Pumps were rigged so that over the course of the next hour the boiler could be flushed through with cold water a number of times.[124] Wilson, meanwhile, had decided to send Trafford and K͟hashm al-Mūs on ahead with the main body, so that they could identify a good pick-up point for the morning and secure a defensible overnight position. Sir Charles would stay behind with a rearguard consisting of 'Abd Allāh Effendi's gun crew and thirty riflemen, and continue lending fire support so long as there was light enough to see the far bank.[125] Gascoigne wondered whether he might not be able to get the *nuggar* and the *felucca* downriver by keeping close to the east bank. One of the *reises* was consulted and advised that it might conceivably be possible, but it was not long before the attempt had gone awry and the larger boat had grounded on the sandbank. Unhelpfully it had stuck squarely inside the enemy's arcs and soon came under a sharp fire.[126] In the meantime Trafford and K͟hashm al-Mūs had proceeded about a mile downriver, where they now had their men hacking away at the mimosa to throw up a thorn *zariba*.

At 6.00 p.m. Beresford's offer of a cash reward to any man prepared to climb inside the boiler attracted a willing young volunteer from amongst the Sudanese stokers. Although the lad had been smeared with tallow, the heat proved unendurable and he came flying out twice as fast as he had gone in. A little while later he tried again and this time was able to last long enough to pass the bolts through the side of the boiler.[127] By the time the patch had been secured, it was far too late in the day to re-lay and light the fires, get up steam, turn midstream and run down the channel in safety. Beresford decided to try and gain himself a breathing space by resorting to subterfuge.

With the realization that there was no viable channel under the east bank, Gascoigne resolved to take the *nuggar* back upriver and run the main channel under the cover of darkness. First he had to get the bows free of the sandbank. To lighten ship he made the walking wounded and the twenty-five women on board wade through the shallows to the east bank. It would be a simple enough matter for them to walk downriver to the new *zariba* position. The measure sufficed to free the *nuggar*, although pushing it back upstream and clear of the enemy's arcs proved hard going. In the meantime one of the Sudanese sailors, acting without orders, had pushed off downstream in the *felucca* with a few of the women. Gascoigne wanted the boat back, so as to have it available for laying out anchor points in the event the *nuggar* ran aground hard. One after the other his messengers returned to report that the current was too strong to move the boat back upstream. Convinced that none of them had actually been to the *zariba*, Gascoigne eventually despatched the trusty Private Paine.[128]

While there was still just enough light left for the enemy to see what he was about,

Beresford contrived a certain amount of bustle on deck and had *Sāfia*'s boats lowered, as if to suggest that the crew intended to abandon ship under the cover of darkness. Because the notion was so eminently plausible, the enemy fell for it hook, line and sinker. Aboard *Sāfia* all firing was stopped, all talking forbidden, all movement prohibited and all lights extinguished, except that is for the lamps required by Benbow in the battened down engine-room.[129] The steamer might look deserted, but not a single man had gone ashore. Unable any longer to see Wad Habeshi, Sir Charles Wilson and his rearguard set off downriver to join Trafford and Kha<u>sh</u>m al-Mūs. After a while manhandling the howitzer proved too much for the exhausted troops, so Wilson had it spiked, disassembled and thrown into the river piece by piece as they went.[130] After that they made good progress and soon gained the *zariba*. Nobody had any blankets or rations and the night had already turned bitterly cold. Fortunately the Sudanese had rounded up a few goats and managed to get some fires going. Wilson dined on goat meat and Indian corn, but like everybody else was quite unable to sleep for the cold.[131]

Gascoigne loitered in the shadows of the east bank for a couple of hours, waiting for Private Paine to return with the *felucca*, conscious that the evening was wearing on and that he needed to run the gauntlet before the moon rose.[132] Paine had reached the *zariba* and spoken to Sir Charles Wilson, who had at once given the order for the boat to be taken back upstream. Paine was given an escort of three Sudanese soldiers and sent to tell Captain Gascoigne that the *felucca* was on its way. But it was a lost cause; two separate efforts were made by different crews, the second of them incorporating members of the Royal Sussex, but no amount of effort could make headway against the current. In the meantime Gascoigne had decided to risk running the channel without the support of a second boat and set out before Paine could re-join him.[133] With him were Corporal Othen, Privates Cowstick and Dale, ten Sudanese sailors, Wilson's Arab servant, his own man Sulaimān and the most seriously hurt casualties. Drifting silently past the darkened *Sāfia*, they quickly drew level with the enemy embrasures. They were seen and fired on but not hit. They were all but clear of the channel when the *nuggar* suddenly grounded hard and swung broadside on to the current. Cursing his luck, Gascoigne clambered onto the offending rocks with a few men and tried to heave the bow free, but it proved far too seriously jammed to be freed by brute force alone. When at length the moon rose it became clear that the *nuggar* was about 400 yards below the enemy battery, but still squarely inside the arcs of the downstream embrasure.[134] The enemy tried a few more shots with the downstream gun but failed to register a hit.[135] Although Beresford and his crew had spotted Gascoigne drifting past, they remained oblivious to the fact that he had since run aground some 600–700 yards downstream of them.

There was a nasty moment for the crew of *Sāfia* some little while later, when the enemy manhandled a brace of guns into the open and again opened fire on the stranded steamer. Scores of riflemen also opened a sustained fusillade.[136] The British ducked low and made no reply. The silence and inactivity of the indistinct black shape on the water sufficed to convince the last of the Mahdīst doubters that the vessel had indeed been abandoned, at which point the guns fell silent and were wheeled back inside the battery. It was not long before most members of the Naval Brigade were fast asleep on the deck. Beresford paced the 'quarterdeck', as he liked to call it, for most of the night, receiving regular reports from the engine room. At one point it dawned on him that all his officers were lying in a row and might all be killed by one shot. He woke them to insist that they move well apart before going back to sleep.[137] The enemy, meanwhile, had broken out their *noggara* to celebrate their success and set about tom-tomming the night away.[138]

Gascoigne knew that if he was to free the *nuggar*, he had to obtain the services of a second boat. He called for a volunteer to swim across to the east bank to advise Sir Charles what had befallen them and plead for the despatch of the *felucca*. One of the Sudanese sailors declared himself a strong swimmer and lowered himself into the water. The position of the *zariba* was so well marked by watch fires that he experienced no difficulty finding it and was able to speak with Sir Charles at around 2.00 a.m.[139] The *felucca* duly started upriver for the third time. Although the crew had to battle against the current for up to three hours, they persevered like galley-slaves and reached Gascoigne's position not long before daybreak.

At around 5.00 a.m., roughly the same time that the *felucca* reached the *nuggar*, Chief Engineer Benbow re-lit *Sāfia*'s boiler. He was careful to keep the furnace doors only slightly ajar, so that the funnel would not give off any tell-tale sparks. Not everybody below decks, where there was a language barrier in play, was as wise a mariner or as expert a technician as Henry Benbow. At around 5.50 a.m., perhaps ten minutes shy of daylight, the Sudanese chief stoker put his head through the hatch of the engine compartment and spoke to one of his men in Arabic. Before Benbow or the artificers could grasp what had been said, the man had thrown the furnace open. Seconds later the funnel belched 'a fountain of hot ashes'. The game was up. The *noggara* started pounding a call to arms, but the British had been crouched behind their cover for some time, waiting on tenterhooks for the storm to break, and took only seconds to develop a storm of fire against the enemy's embrasures. For ten minutes the battle between ship and shore raged much as before. In that seemingly endless ten minutes, Benbow watched the gauge on the boiler gradually climb from 10 lb of pressure to 20. His repairs were not merely sound, but it was as if the boiler had never been holed in the first place. As the gallant *Sāfia* shuddered back into motion, 'a yell of rage went up from the Dervishes in the fort . . . Leaping and screaming on the bank, they took up handfuls of sand and flung them towards us.'[140] Bobby Bower and his men made a rather more pragmatic reply in lead. For six or seven minutes Beresford steamed well clear of the narrows until, content that he could turn in safety, he brought *Sāfia* about and began running downstream with the current. She was twice as fast as formerly. With the White Ensign flapping at her stern, the *Sāfia* stormed past the enemy battery belching flame and spitting lead. This time she did so without mishap. When in due course the ammunition fired at Wad Habeshi over the course of *Sāfia*'s long ordeal was tallied, it was found to amount to 5,400 machine-gun rounds, 2,150 rifle rounds and 126 artillery rounds.[141]

Given what was at stake, there could be no question of stopping in the narrow channel to assist the stranded Gascoigne and his crew. But neither was the Royal Navy in the habit of leaving its Army comrades in the lurch: a mile downstream, safely out of range of the enemy guns, Beresford dropped anchor and hurriedly sent a rowing boat back upstream under the command of Sub-Lieutenant Colin Keppel. Keppel had six burly bluejackets with him, but like everybody else soon realized that it was next to impossible to make headway against the current. He decided to land on the east bank, track his boat well upstream of the *nuggar* and then run back downstream to join it.[142] Over the course of the preceding two hours Gascoigne had been battling under fire to get an anchor point established, but even then had not been able to heave the bow free. When Keppel and his men arrived, it was agreed that the only thing to be done was to lighten ship by throwing the stores and baggage into the Nile, and then try heaving against the anchor point again with the benefit of the additional manpower.[143] The operation was carried out under brisk small-arms fire, from a range of about 400 yards. Covering fire was returned across the width of the river by a party of Sudanese regulars and *bāshi-būzuqs* under Bakhit Agha, sent back up the east bank to help by Sir Charles Wilson.[144] At one point Keppel was struck a painful blow in the groin by a spent round which, although it bruised him badly, failed to break the skin.[145] Remarkably nobody else was hit. When it again came to heaving, the six burly bluejackets made all the difference and this time the *nuggar* eased itself free. In a matter of minutes they drifted downstream to be taken in tow by *Sāfia*. It was just gone 9.00 in the morning on Wednesday 4 February. Not long afterwards Sir Charles Wilson and the rest of his party were taken aboard. Positively racing downstream with the current, *Sāfia* regained Gubat at 5.45 p.m. the same day.[146]

It is not known how many casualties the Mahdīsts took at Wad Habeshi, save in so far as the loss was heavy and must have run to at least a couple of hundred. The Faqī Muṣṭafa was not, as it turned out, the principal Mahdīst commander on the day. This role fell to the Amīr Aḥmad wad Faid who was killed in the battle. It seems likely that he joined the force after it had taken up its positions at Wad Habeshi. The commander of the rebel artillery is also believed to have been killed. When, some little while later, ʿAbd-al-Raḥmān wad al-Najūmi brought a fourth Mahdīst force northwards to do battle with the British, he concluded on the basis of the fight at Wad Habeshi that it would be unwise to operate in full view of the steamers and resolved only to do combat away from the river.[147]

Sir Charles Wilson's casualties during the course of his river dash and retreat amounted to two killed and twenty-five wounded.[148] Remarkably there were no casualties amongst his British personnel. Beresford for his part had lost two men killed – Petty Officer Curnow and the Sudanese stoker who had crawled into a hiding place to die – and one officer and six men injured. Lieutenant Van Koughnet had a flesh wound in the thigh,[149] while the injured sailors, four Sudanese and two British, had scald injuries of varying severity. Engine Room Artificers Garland and Woodman were badly injured.

Korti: Evening of 4 February 1885

About an hour and a quarter after *Sāfia* regained Gubat the couriers bearing Stuart-Wortley's bombshell arrived at Korti. Lord Wolseley was just about to sit down to dinner with his staff when the despatches of 1 February were laid before him. 'The fall of Khartoum is without doubt,' ran the first line of Stuart-Wortley's report. When later that evening the great man sat down with his journal he wrote, 'I was certainly knocked out of tune by the dreadful intelligence that Khartum was taken by Mahdi's troops on 26 January & that Gordon's fate was uncertain but he was said to have been killed.' A little further down the page, though, he lapsed into the same sort of cognitive dissonance which for the past two months had plagued his thinking:

Just as I may say my hand was ready to take hold of the prize, it has thus, by the decree of an inscrutable but wise Providence, been snatched from my grasp. If the traitors who admitted the Mahdi's troops into the city had but waited another few days, the arrival of Wilson at Khartoum would I believe have burst the whole siege up. The moral effect of English soldiers having reached the place, & brought in provisions, no matter how little, would have given such heart to the defenders & so depressed the besiegers, that the Mahdi's game would have been up.[150]

Thus, within two hours of the dread news arriving, did Wolseley begin rewriting the history of the Nile Campaign. By the time he went to bed that evening the relief of Khartoum was no longer an event which lay some six weeks in the future, as had been the case at breakfast time, but instead had already migrated miraculously into the past, where 'Providence', rather than stubborn adherence to an ill-conceived plan, had decreed that success be 'snatched' from his grasp. The new and convenient truth was that the relief of Khartoum had taken place on 28 January. If only he could wish away the two days intervening between the killing, decapitation and mutilation of General Gordon and the arrival at Khartoum of Sir Charles Wilson and twenty-seven Britons, the world would yet come to recognize that he had all but achieved the military miracle which had been asked of him. Unfortunately the only means by which the demons of ambition, pride and vanity could make his wish come true was by recourse to shameless calumny.

In truth the relief of Khartoum had not taken place on 28 January. What happened that day was the culmination of an extraordinarily resolute and gallant attempt to open communications with Gordon, precisely in accordance with the army commander's orders. Men have been showered with honours for deeds and endeavours far less worthy than those of Sir Charles Wilson. And yet this mild-mannered and intellectual colonel of engineers would be forced by his chief to defend his actions in writing. Only rarely in the history of the British Army can valour and dedication to duty have been so shamefully flouted.

Chapter 16

Too Late: Lies, Myth and Reality

Analysis and Conclusions

I take this opportunity of congratulating Her Majesty's Government upon having adopted the Nile route as the line of advance for this force on Khartum.

> General Lord Wolseley to Lord Hartington, 6 March 1885,
> some forty days after the fall of Khartoum

GETTING FEWER THAN THIRTY SERVICEMEN to Khartoum on the morning of Wednesday 28 January 1885 cost the British Empire hugely disproportionate quantities of blood and treasure. I have suggested that in contemplating the Gordon Relief Expedition, history has been tricked into a broadly superficial set of conclusions, not least in respect of its casual acceptance of the idea that Wolseley's campaign amounted to a near miss. I would venture that the preceding chapters have amply demonstrated that it was nothing of the sort. The expedition was a failure, a heroic failure perhaps, but a failure for all that. Moreover it cannot be said to have come remotely close to being a success. In essence a bad plan entirely of his own making had compelled Wolseley to enter the decisive phase of operations with way too little, far too late. Inexcusably he wasted a large part of his army. It is remarkable that he failed even to grasp that it was the advance across the Bayūda that would constitute the decisive phase of operations. If the Desert Column cannot be said to have been defeated in the conventional sense of the word, it was certainly fought to a standstill and by the end of the third week in January was in no sort of condition to effect the relief of Khartoum, even if by some miracle the opportunity to do so had been available for another fortnight. A hypothetical 1885 Battle of Omdurman, had it been fought against the full military might of Mahdīsm by fewer than a thousand British bayonets, would assuredly have resulted in a disaster on the scale of Isandlwana or Maiwand. The plain fact of the matter is that the salvation of Khartoum was never a matter of two days here or there and that the failure of the expedition was nothing whatever to do with Sir Charles Wilson. To endorse the notion that the timely arrival of Wilson's party would have saved the city, as too many historians have been wont to do, is merely to perpetuate Wolseley's great lie.

Few military failures are attributable to only one factor, to a single decision or to the deeds of one man. Neither is there much point in agonizing over military failure if the mission was unachievable. This final chapter will seek to demonstrate that the mission was not unachievable, but rather was rendered so by the adoption of the wrong course of action. Additionally it will seek to rise above the tactical nitty-gritty of the expedition to take a wider view of the Khartoum conundrum, with the object of establishing where the campaign planning went wrong, the interrelationship between mistakes and just who was to blame for what. There is a culpability issue in respect of the death of General Gordon and the slaughter, rape or enslavement of several thousand human souls who had been led to believe that the mighty British Empire would save them. The object must be to let the truth be told and to let the blame for these unhappy events be justly and properly apportioned. The preceding chapters will amply have served to exonerate Sir Charles Wilson. Wilson was falsely accused, but if there were failings at the tactical level of command, the level at which Wolseley unreasonably insisted on pointing an accusing finger of blame, these same chapters will also have served to leave Sir Herbert Stewart's reputation in a less exalted place than formerly. This is not to suggest that he was not a gallant and able officer, for he was assuredly both of these things. There is also a fundamental mitigating factor in play. He may have pressed too hard, both to the detriment of his fragile transport assets and ultimately to the continued battle-worthiness of his command, but at least he 'got it': that Khartoum simply had to be on its last legs and that the key operational-level imperative was time. Stewart, I believe, knew full well that he was Gordon's only chance. He got it as a tactical-level commander, in a way that the operational-level commander did not. Such was Wolseley's standing, however, that even Stewart, for all that he was regarded as a favoured son, did not dare press him to abort the wasteful and irrelevant advance into the Great Bend.

It will have been obvious from the outset that Gladstone's procrastination makes the strategic level of command somewhat simpler to dispense with than the operational and tactical levels. If in the course of this concluding chapter it can be shown that the same tactical-level outcomes achieved by Wolseley's operations could have been attained at a much earlier point in time, then it will follow that his criticism of Sir Charles Wilson was not merely inappropriate, but deeply unjust and highly unprofessional. It would also follow that such criticism was selfishly motivated and designed to deflect condemnation of Wolseley's judgement and generalship.

The vehemence of Wolseley's denunciation of Wilson in the privacy of his campaign journal tends to suggest that his views may have been genuinely delusional.[1] This may have been a function of stress and the 'loneliness of command', but must nonetheless exert a bearing on any assessment of his personal attributes and his quality as a general officer. The fact that his campaign journal also contains extremely harsh personal attacks on the personalities and professional competence of Wood, Buller, Butler and Brackenbury, amongst others, serves to illustrate just how far Wolseley's ego had run out of control by this point in his life. Also on the receiving end of his scorn were the Prime Minister, the Duke of Cambridge, Admiral Lord John Hay, the Royal Navy generally, Lieutenant General

Sir Frederick Stephenson, the heir to the throne and the Queen Empress herself.

This final episode in the story of the Wolseley Ring, in effect its decline and fall, demonstrates that the so-called 'personal' style of leadership, in which the army commander is the only man empowered to take significant decisions, is not amenable to large-scale, geographically dispersed operations. Such operations require the systematic approach and second-order thinking which can really only be conveyed by a structured general staff system and the adoption of a decentralized command philosophy, in which subordinate commanders are empowered to think and act for themselves within the context of a comprehensible and well-articulated master-plan.[2] Before moving on to discuss culpability and to contemplate alternative courses of action, we should reprise the essence of Wolseley's campaign plan and consider what would have happened had Khartoum not fallen when it did.

How Was Wolseley's Campaign Plan Meant to Culminate?

Wolseley's campaign had the appearance from the outset of being a great monolithic scheme but, as time wore on, events started to run away from him and he was forced to adapt his scheme of manoeuvre to changed circumstance. The necessity to adapt was driven primarily by two things: in the first instance, logistic delays and the inexorable passage of time; and in the second, as events moved towards a climax, messages from Gordon which projected how long he would be able hold out and which suggested that the power of the enemy was not to be sneezed at. There is no single, truly independent primary source from which we can derive a clear understanding of how the culminating phase of operations was meant to play itself out. In part this is a measure of just how far removed in time and space Wolseley was from attaining his goal when Khartoum fell, a matter to which we will return in due course. We can, however, piece things together from Colvile's *Official History* and from passing references in Wolseley's campaign journal, but in so doing should be careful to keep in mind that these are by no means impartial sources. Brackenbury's preface to Colvile's *History* makes it plain that the draft had to be circulated for comment and it is hard to imagine that Wolseley would not have insisted on seeing the manuscript and 'correcting' it wherever he thought it appropriate.

If the final phase of the military plan is vague, the desired political outcome, although slow to arrive, was in the end well articulated by Lord Hartington. HMG's strategic direction was that General Gordon and the Khedive's other soldiers and officials had to be safe, hence very decidedly not in Khartoum, by the time the expedition had run its course. We can also readily infer from the general thrust of the telegrams passing between London, Cairo and Korti that there was no stomach on the part of HMG for an extended occupation of central Sudan, or for sallying forth from the confluence of the Niles in order to defeat the rebels and restore a modicum of order in the region. This formed no part of the plan and as we shall see was wholly impracticable in any case.

It would be useful then to review exactly what we do know about the unfolding of the campaign plan, keeping in mind always that it may be overly generous to describe it as 'unfolding' if the rather more awkward truth is that it was never tenable in the first place and simply fell apart with the passage of time. Wolseley was not initially inclined, presumably on the basis of the ferocity of the fighting in the Rea Sea Littoral, to underestimate the enemy, nor was he a 'chancer' when it came to his career and reputation. Hence he sought to advance on Khartoum with the equivalent of two brigades of infantry and a brigade-sized camel corps, the latter also designed to fight in the infantry role. He intended from the outset to concentrate a minimum of 5,000 men at or near Shendy, before advancing the last 100 miles to Khartoum's salvation.[3]

The original target date for the relief of Khartoum, set by Wolseley in April 1884 when first he pondered the problem, was 15 November 1884.[4] HMG having failed to authorize any preparations before August 1884,[5] he settled subsequently on 31 January as his revised target.[6] At no point had Gordon projected that his food stocks would last into the New Year. Wolseley had no basis, therefore, either in known fact or assessed intelligence, for slipping the timeline to the right but did so anyway. Although he was always attuned to the possibility of having to send a wing of the army across the Bayūda Desert,[7] his original and preferred conception was that the unified command would follow the Great Bend in the Nile, with the infantry brigades in whalers and the Camel Corps paralleling them on land.[8]

Writing on 7 November 1884, Buller attempted to persuade Wolseley that the campaign had fallen behind schedule and that the best option to save Khartoum was a dash with the Camel Corps from Korti to Metemmeh, followed immediately by a direct overland advance across the last 100 miles to Khartoum.[9] At this 'early' date Wolseley rejected the proposal and for a further month persisted in the idea of advancing around the Great Bend to Berber, with the object of concentrating 5,000 men at Shendy.[10] By the time he left Dongola for Korti on 13 December he had accepted, but not yet promulgated, that an overland dash would now be necessary.[11] To his credit he was prepared to take the risk and intended taking personal command of a force of only 1,500 men (though in the event it was closer to 2,000). He did, as we have seen, ask HMG to express an opinion as to whether the fall of Khartoum and the death of Gordon would be a worse calamity than the possibility of a flying column meeting with a serious reverse,[12] stating that he presumed that the former was worse than the latter, though of course HMG replied vice versa, as he must always have known it would.[13] He might possibly have expected the government to prohibit a high-risk dash, thus mitigating any threat to his reputation. It did not do so. But perhaps it is more likely that the primary purpose of his message was to make it abundantly clear to posterity that he would be embarking on the adventure fully aware of the military risks entailed. This would serve in the event of a reverse to preserve his professional reputation, and in all likelihood actually enhance his standing as a heroic figure.

Everything changed on 31 December, the day after Stewart set out for Jakdul Wells, when authoritative news at last arrived from Khartoum.[14] Gordon's final message conveyed conflicting imperatives: first that the relief column should come quickly, but also that it should not leave an enemy-held Berber to its rear. This may have served to suggest to Wolseley that the enemy was in far greater strength at Berber than was actually the case: the message was oral of course but, from what we know of it, does not appear to have specified that this was so.[15]

In fact Wolseley had a tolerably accurate intelligence picture of the situation at Berber available to him, as every indigenous traveller who passed through the town was questioned by British officers, whether they gained government held-territory around Merowe or at Suakin. Suakin–Berber was of course an important pilgrim road in the journey to Mecca. It was travelled by many non-Sudanese Muslims and continued to be well used throughout the Mahdīst Uprising. It is curious that having already concluded that he could afford to leave Berber to the left flank and rear of the Desert Column until such time as Earle and the whaler-borne battalions came up to deal with the problem, that Wolseley should be so badly rattled by a simple and unexplained injunction not to do so. How could a long-besieged Gordon possibly understand the broader operational situation better than the commander of an approaching relief expedition? Any camel-borne operation for the capture of Berber which was required to jump-off from Metemmeh and return subsequently to its start-point, a round-trip of about 184 miles, could not fail to consume less than a fortnight and might well have taken three weeks. It seems likely, then, that Gordon imagined the operation being mounted by steamer, his own standard modus operandi. Such a foray would nonetheless still have eaten up six or seven days. One senses that the fundamental problem was that where Gordon imagined that the capture of Berber might be achieved relatively quickly by only a few hundred men, Wolseley envisaged the need for a much more deliberate operation involving a far more powerful force. The latter was probably the more realistic proposition.

The date 14 December, the day on which Gordon rehearsed his final courier, has added significance as the day on which he also drew his siege journal to a close. He sent it downriver aboard the steamer *Bordein* the following day. The final entry makes his oral injunction on Berber all the more peculiar, although of course it has no bearing on how Wolseley reacted to the arrival of the courier, as it was not until 21 January that a British officer (Wilson as it turned out) actually got to read the journal:

Now MARK THIS, if the Expeditionary Force, and I ask for no more than two hundred men, does not come in ten days, the town may fall; and I have done my best for the honour of our country. Good bye.

C. G. Gordon.

You send me no information, though you have lots of money.

C. G. G.[16]

We can only presume that Gordon thought that the relief expedition was within easy striking distance of Berber (as indeed it ought to have been if Khartoum was to be saved), and also that he expected his oral message to get to Wolseley much quicker than it did. But another nightmarish possibility also presents itself. It is surely not inconceivable, given the desperate tenor of the words he committed to paper the same day, that Gordon never actually said, 'Do not leave Berber in your rear.' Might something have been garbled in translation? Gordon had only a smattering of Arabic and so must have made use of an interpreter in briefing his courier. Similarly the debriefing at the other end of the journey would also have been conducted through an interpreter. Was the man confidently word perfect when he delivered the message? Did he struggle at all to remember what Gordon Pasha had said? Did Wolseley's interpreter prompt him with leading questions? These are things we simply do not know and, barring the highly improbable discovery of a private letter written by somebody who was present at the interview and felt compelled to describe its every twist and turn, are unlikely ever to know. One thing is certain: by New Year's Eve, the day on which the courier finally reached Wolseley, Gordon would have asked *only* for the best possible speed. Quite how he held out for another twenty-five days, without a mutiny or some other form of collapse amongst his starving troops, is a source of wonderment, as well as a tribute to his leadership, his strength of character and the generally unacknowledged resolve of his Sudanese and Egyptian soldiers.

What Gordon's advice on Berber did not do is seal his fate. It arrived with Wolseley far too late for that. By 31 December the die had been cast: Stewart had commenced his first journey into the Bayūda Desert and the fateful shuttle-run to Jakdul Wells was already afoot. Gordon had one chance and once chance only – if that is, the war correspondent Alex Macdonald was correct in suggesting that Wolseley had granted Stewart the discretion to push straight through to Metemmeh in the event the water-supply at Jakdul proved to be inadequate.[17] Although no other source reflects such a dispensation, there is more than likely to be a grain of truth in it. Wolseley could hardly give orders that Stewart should turn back without dropping the vital commissariat stores somewhere, as the entire plan of campaign would have been compromised. Of course there was more than enough water at Jakdul, which meant that to proceed Stewart would have had to out-Nelson Nelson in his disregard for orders. If, however, he had taken the bull by the horns, the river might have been gained by about 7/8 January without the sort of heavy fighting that later ensued.

Even so there was still the problem of the 2,000–3,000-strong enemy force reported by Kitchener and Colvile as present at Metemmeh. It is doubtful whether with only GCR, MICR and assorted details available to him, Stewart would have had sufficient assets both to secure a lodgement on the river adjacent to a hostile Metemmeh, and immediately throw several hundred men aboard the steamers. But if he was prepared to take the risk, assume the responsibility and deprive 'the Chief' of the glory he craved, there was at least a theoretical chance that Stewart could have gained Khartoum by about 12 January, almost a fortnight before it fell. The chances are that the near-approach of the British would still have triggered a major assault on Khartoum. Whether or not the garrison would have had the strength, courage and determination at that juncture to repel such an attack is not a question we can ever answer, but two weeks downstream it was reeling from starvation and stood next to no chance of doing so. According to Macdonald, Stewart thought hard about whether he could possibly be justified in pushing on, but the provisions of the dispensation were clear and he did not in the end feel able wilfully to disregard his orders. Given the factors in play, his decision to turn again for Korti in accordance with a doubtless very specific set of oral instructions from the army commander, cannot be considered in any way surprising, flawed or lacking in moral courage. Stewart was merely obeying his orders, as was expected of a good soldier in the High Victorian era. From the moment he turned back for Korti, however, the harsh realities of time and space compel the conclusion that there was no longer any hope for Gordon and Khartoum. In many ways the subsequent operations of the Desert Column were as irrelevant to the outcome at Khartoum as were the substantially pointless operations mounted by the River Column.

The real significance of Gordon's last message was that it caused Wolseley to wobble. When Stewart got back to Korti it was to find that the army commander would no longer be accompanying him on the return journey to Jakdul and that the intent was no longer to dash for Khartoum, but rather to send a fact-finding mission ahead of the fighting echelon. There would be no move on Khartoum by combat units until after Sir Charles Wilson had spoken with Gordon and returned to Korti to make his report. If Gordon felt able to hold on for a few more weeks, Stewart would be sent north from Metemmeh to cooperate with the River Column in the seizure of Berber. The unified force would then proceed south to Khartoum in full strength. Only if Wilson's report indicated that Gordon was *in extremis* would Wolseley go forward to Metemmeh and lead the Desert Column in a dash for Khartoum.[18]

The Hypothetical Relief of Khartoum: What Next?

In pursuit of a wider understanding of the challenges still ahead of Wolseley at the point at which Khartoum fell, and also perhaps of inherent flaws in his campaign plan, let us now imagine a hypothetical set of circumstances in which things have gone rather better in respect of time – the single most important factor in the military equation. Let us suppose that Gladstone had fired the strategic starting-gun some weeks earlier and that the seasonal fall in the Nile no longer presented quite the same array of problems as would later be the case. In other words, that at some point in early December the unified force, camel-borne and whaler-borne, having completed the 400-mile circuit around the Great Bend, taking Abū-Hamed and Berber en route, now reaches Metemmeh from the north. We will politely leave aside the inconvenient assumptions that a Kirbekan-type battle will have been fought, that gaining Metemmeh will entail a third successive assault on a defended urban area, that casualties are mounting and medical resources are already at full stretch.

Wolseley can field a fighting force, including the Egyptian and Sudanese troops aboard the steamers, of 5,000 men. Not less than one quarter of his strength would be lost to securing Abū-Hamed, Berber, Metemmeh and other key points on the lines of communication. He then advances 100 miles up the west bank of the Nile and fights some sort of winning engagement at or near Omdurman in much the same fashion as did Kitchener some thirteen years later – albeit, in the absence of the belt-fed and quick-firing weaponry yet to enter service, without anything like the same attendant slaughter of the enemy. Let us imagine, not unreasonably given precedents set elsewhere in the Sudan, the Mahdīsts attacking two brigade-sized squares and being repulsed with something around 2,000 casualties. Wolseley then passes his 3,750 troops across the White Nile in the steamers, marches in triumph up to the *sarāya*, where Gordon extends a hearty handshake in greeting. What then?

The city, still with around 14,000 loyalist citizens and a mixed Egyptian–Sudanese garrison of 8,000 men within its walls, is nearing the end of its food stocks. The surrounding countryside has been swept bare by Gordon in preparing for the siege and by the Mahdīst host subsequently: there is plainly no option to live off the land. Over the next month the Nile will fall dramatically and cannot be relied upon as an arterial line of supply. There are virtually no camels at Korti to sustain an overland line of supply across the Bayūda. Osman Digna and the Bīja rebels are still at large astride the Berber–Suakin road and there is no significant British field force at Suakin. Wolseley, with a dwindling stock of ammunition, and quite unable to feed his force at Khartoum for any length of time, has no option but to fall back to the north within a matter of days.

What then of General Gordon, whose purpose has been to draw British troops and a Sudanese figurehead fit to succeed him down the Nile, so that he can establish a self-governing state owing only nominal suzerainty to Egypt and at some later point withdraw with at least a semblance of honour? Wolseley is a general and Gordon a mere major general, which on the face of it seems straightforward enough, but the latter considers that he is exercising the delegated authority of the Khedive as Governor-General of the Sudan, outside the British military chain of command. In the circumstances he was not automatically bound to kow-tow to Wolseley's rank. Indeed technically the reverse would apply. Wolseley's trump-card, however, was the secret khedival *firman* which relieved Gordon of his duties and appointed Wolseley in his stead. Because it would have served to demolish Gordon's otherwise entirely lawful standing, this document, together with the mutual respect the two generals felt for one another, was bound ultimately to have precluded any unduly ugly scenes, such as any necessity to arrest Gordon, a scenario which Wolseley had half-joked about in his correspondence with Lady Louisa.

Gordon, then, could be dealt with and was only one man. But what would have become of the 22,000 Egyptian and Sudanese soldiers and civilians still bottled up in Khartoum? Wolseley could hardly steal out with the governor-general like a thief in the night; if nothing else this was inconsistent with his yearning for a crowning triumph to his career. Even if two-thirds of the citizenry were prepared to stay behind and throw themselves on the mercy of the Mahdī (an option they had already declined once, when Gordon threw open the gates of the city to those who wished to leave), how would a straggling convoy of several thousand refugees have fared in a great overland retreat? The famished Egyptian troops would have been in no condition either to march long distances or to fight in the open, and were of more than merely dubious quality to begin with. The civilian population was in an even worse state. Soldiers and citizens alike would have clustered themselves around the British troops for protection and, more likely than not, have flown into a panic when attacked. It is not difficult to imagine a hard-pressed retreat turning into a repetition of the Hicks disaster. Even if a retreat into Dongola had been unopposed, it seems certain that a great many people would have died of exhaustion or malnutrition along the way.

And what of events to Wolseley's rear: either the Mahdīsts occupy Khartoum and show clemency to the surrendered population, or the city is given over to rapine and slaughter in precisely the same fashion as occurred on the night of 25/26 January and the three succeeding days. Because it was the colonial capital city, full of what would have been seen by barefooted Kordofanis as treasure, it is unlikely that the Mahdī would even have attempted to impose restraint. The ultimate outcome, then, even if Khartoum had been relieved, is still a great slaughter of civilians, a Mahdīst plundering of the capital and the rise subsequently of a Dervish military state. This is what Cabinet ministers and military campaign planners alike should have been capable of foreseeing.

There is a strong hint in Wilson's orders that Wolseley may indeed have foreseen the insurmountable difficulties ahead. The only counter he had to offer was the gratuitous wishful thinking encapsulated within Wilson's orders:

It is always possible that when Mohammed Ahmed fully realises that an English Army is approaching Khartum he will retreat, and thus raise the siege. Khartum would, under such circumstances, continue to be the political centre of our operations, but Berber would become our military objective. No British troops would be sent to Khartum beyond a few red coats in steamers for the purpose of impressing upon the inhabitants the fact that it was to the presence of our army they owed their safety.

The siege of Khartum being thus raised, all our military arrangements would be made with a view to the immediate occupation of Berber, and to a march across the desert to Ariab on the Suakin road.[19]

Wishful thinking indeed, as the subsequent fierce resistance in the Bayūda was to demonstrate. It seems clear from this extract that the logistic difficulties of getting to Khartoum and of sustaining any sizeable force there were of such an order that Wolseley did not want to have to press south of Metemmeh in strength unless absolutely compelled to do so. In other words, by the time Sir Herbert Stewart set out from Korti on 8 January, Wolseley could already see the writing on the wall. He kept going because he had no other choice – precisely the same quandary with which Sir Charles Wilson would later be confronted.

It is difficult to conceive, even if Wolseley's wildest fantasies had come true and the Mahdists fell back say twenty-five miles up the White Nile, on the approach merely of two steamers, quite how he imagined the Khartoum garrison could then save itself *without* the assistance of British troops. Did he seriously imagine that Gordon would suddenly throw up his hands in joy, forsake his defences and march 8,000 malnourished soldiers and an unknowable number of starving civilian refugees out into the desert, to begin plodding 100 miles north to Metemmeh? The optimists and unfortunates left behind in Khartoum would have been put to the sword on the afternoon of the same day, while Gordon's straggling thousands would have been massacred by about lunchtime the day after. This was not even wishing thinking; this was nonsense.

The Alternative – A Suakin–Berber Hypothesis

With the starting gun having been fired in early August, it is inconceivable that a comparably sized and organized force as the Desert Column (making use of men shipped from England, stores shipped down from Cairo and camels shipped across the Red Sea from Aden and other parts of Arabia), could not have set out from Suakin by the end of September at the latest. Thus it would have been in a position to attack and secure Berber, which was no more strongly held than Metemmeh, but much more isolated from the support of the main Mahdist force at Omdurman, by no later than the middle of October. Berber was four or five days steaming from Khartoum. Having gained the river that much earlier, with the Nile still high, the passage of the Sixth Cataract would have been nothing like as difficult as would prove to be the case in the New Year.

Whilst it is true that such a plan would not have been a walk in the park and would not immediately have put 5,000 well-supplied men on the Nile, within striking distance of Khartoum, as Wolseley sought, neither did the whaler scheme do so, the 3,000 men of General Earle's River Column having been rendered completely irrelevant to the relief of Khartoum. It is a moot point quite how many infantry battalions could have marched to Berber in a month-long period following the capture of the town by a 1,500-strong advanced guard under Stewart, but since Wolseley's plan failed to bring a single additional infantryman to bear in a timely fashion, even if only two or three battalions been able to complete the march, the British hand would still have been much stronger.

The objection to the Suakin–Berber road that Wolseley always fell back on was shortage of water along the route. Let us then remind ourselves, by again referring to the orders given to Sir Charles Wilson, just how he intended to extricate his 5,000-man force from the depths of central Sudan: 'The siege of Khartum being thus raised, all our military arrangements would be made with a view to the immediate occupation of Berber, and to a march across the desert to Ariab on the Suakin road.' If there was sufficient water to sustain a force of several thousand men marching from Berber to Suakin, why was there not also sufficient water to sustain a force of the same size marching in the opposite direction? Let us not forget either that Suakin–Berber had for many years been the standard route by which the Egyptian military moved its units to and from Khartoum. In the summer of 1883, for example, Hicks Pasha and his staff had travelled that way with an escort of several hundred men and a train of baggage camels.[20] Gordon and Stewart would have travelled to Khartoum by the same route, or would have attempted to do so and most likely have been killed, had not Sir Evelyn Baring insisted they come via Cairo. In short Suakin–Berber was the Egyptian military's first choice route for travelling to Khartoum and yet Wolseley insisted on spurning it.

It transpires that the Intelligence Branch of the War Office was thoroughly conversant with the wells and watering holes along the way. A document called 'Report on the Egyptian Provinces of the Sudan, Red Sea, and Equator' was published by HMSO on behalf of the Intelligence Branch in July 1884, doubtless in anticipation of operations in the Sudan still to come. Amongst the subjects covered by the hard-backed, pocket-sized publication, intended evidently to be carried in the field, was leg-by-leg detail on all the major routes in Sudan including, on pages 176–7, the Suakin–Berber caravan road. These pages are headed, 'From report by Lieutenant Colonel D. H. Stewart, 11th Hussars, 12th January 1883'. The text of this report is incorporated below as Appendix H.

In terms of water supply, the critical part of the route was the last 100 miles. Ariab, to which Wolseley made reference in Wilson's orders, was about 140 miles from Suakin and was described by one traveller as 'the prettiest oasis between Suakin and Berber'.[21] Here, according to Colonel Hammill Stewart, there were 'two wells, revetted with stone, and about 50 or 60 feet deep'. This was not ideal for watering large numbers of animals quickly, but ease the rapidity with which a force is required to move and the problem is mitigated. It was about forty miles from Ariab to the wells at Obak, where Stewart tells us there were 'many wells with fair water, but they are constantly being filled up'. He was referring here to the nuisance of wind-blown sand, but this could readily have been dug out by the troops. After Obak came a harsh, waterless plain of about fifty-one miles, before one reached Bir Mahobeh where there was a 'large revetted well with good water'. Another seventeen miles brought the traveller to the Nile at Berber. In other words there was nowhere where camel-borne troops would have to go more than two days and one night without the opportunity to replenish their water. We have seen that the water-skins issued to the Camel Corps allowed individuals to carry up to seven gallons aboard their mounts alone. The Desert Column marched with a small number of reserve water tanks aboard the baggage train, the quantity of which could have been increased at the expense of the vast quantities of rations being carried out into the Bayūda. We have seen also that MICR marched from Korti to Jakdul Wells, a distance of ninety-eight miles, and arrived with a good deal of water left in their skins. If the troops could clearly take care of themselves for a week, without difficulty, we have also seen how the ponies and camels of the Desert Column marched from Korti to Abu Halfā, eighty miles into the Bayūda, without so much as a drop of water.

Wolseley always said that the idea of a column emerging from fifty miles of 'waterless' desert to fight for Berber rendered the Suakin–Berber route a non-starter.[22] The contention is not only belied by the performance of the Desert Column in the Bayūda, but also conveniently overlooks the water at Bir Mahobeh, which would offer a small force tasked with seizing a foothold on the Nile the opportunity to replenish a mere seventeen miles from the river. Most of the wells in the Nubian Desert could be drained if they were drawn upon by hundreds of men and animals at one sitting, but then generally recharged themselves within twenty-four hours. In a less frantic advance than Stewart was compelled to make in January, there would have been time in hand to allow this to happen. Of note is that Colonel John Colborne's account of Hicks Pasha's journey proves that a force of around 450 men could travel the route without a hint of difficulty. That being so it is a safe bet that 600 men could have done it with only a minimal amount of hardship.[23] Could 600 men have seized Berber? Possibly, but it would certainly represent a challenging and high-risk undertaking. Could 600 men have seized and held a lodgement on the Nile, within striking distance of Berber, until another 600 men came up 24–36 hours later, and then another 600 after that and so on? Provided they were on carefully chosen ground and well supplied with ammunition, the answer would have to be, yes, most certainly.

Writing in his journal on Thursday 15 January, by which time it must have been obvious to the slowest wit in the army that the whaler scheme had backfired, Wolseley comforted himself by remarking that marching 5,000 men to Berber from the coast would have required the support of 50,000 camels.[24] This was no more than vacuous hyperbole but, whatever the actual scale of the requirement, it would have been far easier for the world's greatest maritime power to assemble, say, 12,000 camels at Suakin, with the whole of Arabia just across the Red Sea, than it was to round up the 7,000 or so animals the transport officers eventually scraped together from Cairo and the Nile Valley. As it turned out 7,000 animals was nothing like enough to sustain the needs of the Nile Expedition, so here was another domain where Wolseley's preferred route would be found wanting. When, on 17 January, Earle telegraphed Buller to ask for forty baggage camels, he received the reply, 'I have not a camel or driver to send. They are in the desert.'[25]

What of the enemy though? What of Osman Digna and the rebellious Bīja in the Red Sea Littoral, and the Berberine rebels under Muḥammad al-Khair? The Bīja were impoverished hard-living desert nomads who had been whipped up on the back of skewed Islamist invective and the promise of rich pickings. After a difficult start they were rewarded with a succession of easy victories over the Egyptians. The opportunity to plunder Suakin, the littoral's 'county town' so to speak, represented the height of their military ambitions. They had come close to attaining this but, with the Graham intervention of February/March 1884, promptly received two hard drubbings at Second El Teb and Tamai. In the former action they fielded 6,000–8,000 men, of whom between a quarter and a third became casualties. At Tamai they deployed 9,000–12,000 men and took more than 2,000 casualties. They then melted away into the *khors* and hills and offered no further resistance to Graham. The Prime Minister's insistence that the expedition be withdrawn precluded a political settlement and final pacification of the littoral.

When, in the spring of 1885, in the aftermath of the fall of Khartoum, Sir Gerald Graham once again deployed, he fought a reconstituted Bīja host which did not at any point exceed 5,000 men. The British did the attacking at Hashīn, seven miles from Suakin, but the decisive action came two days later when the rebels fell upon Major General Sir John McNeill's force at Tofrek. While the enemy caught McNeill on the hop in thick scrub, almost gaining an improbable victory, the tide of battle quickly turned in favour of the British. Of the 5,000 rebels on the field, not fewer than 1,100, and possibly as many as 1,500, were killed.[26] A good many more were wounded and helped away. Such crippling casualties brought serious Bīja resistance to an end and once again cleared the way to political settlement and long-term pacification of the littoral. Unfortunately this second opportunity would also be squandered by British disengagement, but that part of Sudanese history lies well beyond the scope of this book. The key point about the two Suakin campaigns is that they showed that the British needed only to march a few miles into the desert to be attacked en masse by an unfailingly aggressive enemy. Graham did this three times from Suakin and on each occasion there was a heavy engagement within ten miles of the port. In other words, the Bīja enemy was inherently predictable. The campaign of March 1885, by which time Osman had been allowed a year to reconstitute his strength, usefully provides us with our worst-case parameters for a hypothetical campaign mounted six months earlier in September or October 1884.

It seems not at all unreasonable to infer that the six infantry battalions wasted in the whalers could have been put to much better use in the Red Sea Littoral. If Wolseley and Earle had marched from Suakin with a brigade-sized square of four battalions (or perhaps two three-battalion squares, as had been employed at Tamai), supported by Barrow's 19th Hussars and a battery of screw guns, they would in our worst-case scenario have been attacked within 24–48 hours by a force of about 5,000 rebels, the best that Osman could do after the cruel losses inflicted at Tamai some months earlier. With Wolseley in command, who would not have been so foolish as to entangle his force in close scrub like McNeill, the British would in all likelihood have gained a resounding victory in which another 1,500 rebels would have been killed or maimed.

Intelligence reports from Suakin, dated September 1884, serve to illustrate the real-world situation at precisely the point in time at which these hypothetical operations would have been taking place. Their gist makes it plain that the enemy were not only hungry, scattered and demoralized, but also outnumbered by Amarar 'friendlies'. This suggests that the actual threat would in all likelihood have fallen a long way short of our worst-case scenario. On 6 September Commodore Molyneux aboard HMS *Sphinx* reported to C-in-C Mediterranean that:

...the Hadendowas and others with Osman Digna are suffering great privation from want of food... and that many are sick and suffering from wounds. Getting no satisfaction from their appeals to Osman Digna, the following tribes, viz., Camerar, Garieb, Meshab, and Hamelab held a meeting, and decided that they would offer their submission to the Government on condition of a free pardon, but that they would go to Mahomed Ahmed (the Mahdi) if he came here.

... The Amarars [friendlies] have succeeded in making some important captures of cattle, grain &c. from the rebels along the Berber road; but Lieutenant Colonel Chermside[27] has discouraged their attacking Handoub, as the rebels are entrenched there, and as we cannot support them, a reverse might be fatal to the policy we are trying to pursue. Osman Digna is said to have reinforced the Handoub garrison, which may number 1,000 men, and has supplied them with two camel-loads of ammunition.

... the night attacks on Suakin during the last week or more have been fewer and have evidently been made by much smaller bodies of men than formerly, and with less spirit...[28]

On 11 September Molyneux reported to Hay in rather more detail.

The Amarars [friendly] and Hadendowas [hostile] are facing each other on the Berber road, the former with their headquarters at Essibil, the latter at Handoub. Both sides have been considerably reinforced, and according to the most recent accounts the enemy numbers about 2,000 and the Amarars about 3,000 men.

The force at Tamai, where I believe Osman Digna still remains, is reduced to about 400 men. Deserters from both of the rebel camps come in frequently, and all accounts agree that Osman Digna is losing his influence with the people, and the tribes have returned to their former custom of holding tribal meetings to discuss matters of importance instead of blindly obeying Osman Digna's orders...

... The night attacks on Suakin have almost entirely ceased and the rebels are rarely seen on the plain in the day-time.[29]

On 27 September 1884 Major General Fremantle telegraphed Sir Frederick Stephenson to report:

Events continue to appear satisfactory. Osman still at Tamai with weak force. Yesterday Karb Mohammed has sent by messenger to say enemy near Abat hungry, discouraged, encumbered with sick and wounded. Handoob empty, and plain clear of enemy at present.[30]

Following what would almost certainly have been an easy victory on the coastal plain, Wolseley could then have marched his infantry back to Suakin and forty-eight hours later have launched Sir Herbert Stewart and the Desert Column for Ariab, seven to ten days' march into the desert. A week after arriving at Ariab, Stewart would be reaching across the final leg of his march to secure a lodgement on the Nile south of Berber. Concurrent political operations in the littoral, mounted by somebody of Sir Charles Wilson's ilk, would have stood a better than even chance of securing the submission of the rebellious tribes, obliging the pestilential Osman to flee back to his master. Even if some Bīja clans remained hostile, the six infantry battalions and large numbers of Amarar friendlies would have been available for follow-up combat operations, convoy-escort duty on the road, or garrisoning wells and other staging posts on Stewart's line of communications.

Stewart's fighting echelon instead of being camel-borne, which greatly increased the amount of water required – water which could otherwise have been drunk by human beings – could have been infantry-based. If Egyptian infantry routinely marched to Berber as had been the case in former years, then so too could well-acclimatized British infantry, albeit not without some heatstroke cases. A Royal Engineer detachment could have done much to improve the water supply along the route, and if the same money, energy and ingenuity invested in the whaler scheme had been diverted into viable means of transporting water in the desert, a number of practical expedients would doubtless have been arrived at.

In short, forcing the Suakin–Berber road would not have been the impossibly difficult operation of war that Wolseley portrayed during the course of the 'Battle of the Routes'. Indeed, it is often overlooked that at the point at which it seemed the Nile route would be spurned by the Cabinet, Wolseley wrote to Hartington offering his services as the commander of a Suakin–Berber expedition.

And what of Muḥammad al-Khair, at the far end of the caravan road? The narrative chapters established that the Berberine rebels sent about 3,000 men to marry up with Mūsā wad Ḥilū and the Kordofani host from Omdurman, in resisting Stewart's advance across the Bayūda. But let us be generous and allow Muḥammad al-Khair a total fighting force of 4,000 men. In the scenario now postulated, Stewart's advance along the Suakin–Berber axis is taking place in the second half of October and on the opposite bank of the Nile. This means that Omdurman on the west bank is still securely held by Gordon, and the river, still high, is commanded effectively by his flotilla of steamers. News that the British are coming and have already beaten Osman on the coast has travelled down the Suakin–Berber road, in the apparently miraculous way that such news has of travelling across great distances. The Mahdī knows it and Gordon's spies detect it. Morale amongst the besieging Mahdīsts is damaged and that of the garrison boosted.

It seems not unreasonable to suggest that Muḥammad al-Khair, who in the real world of January 1885 sent his fighting men south to resist Stewart, will in the hypothetical world of late October/early November 1884 send them *east* to resist Stewart. Equally, if in January the Mahdīsts advanced one tactical bound into the desert to interpose themselves between the British and the wells at Abu Klea – twenty-five miles as it happened – would they not also have advanced seventeen miles east of Berber to the wells at Bir Mahobeh. Advancing from Obak, fifty miles to his rear (a direct parallel with the distance between Jakdul Wells and Abu Klea Wells), Stewart must again fight to secure the water ahead of him. What differentiates the real-world Battle of Abu Klea from the hypothetical 'Battle of Bir Mahobeh' is that crucially they are fought on opposite sides of the Nile. It would not have been possible, with Omdurman still in Gordon's hands, for the Mahdīsts to have detached so sizeable a force northwards. Nor would it have been possible to pass a large force over the river without it being detected and attacked by Nushi Pasha and the steamers. It seems almost certain, therefore, that the Battle of Bir Mahobeh would have been fought against a Mahdīst force safely less than half the size of the host at Abu Klea. Not only would it have been much smaller, but it would not have included any Kordofani shock troops. It follows that the probable outcome would have been a handsome British victory, free of the sort of mauling inflicted by the Kordofanis at Abu Klea. So small and roundly defeated a Mahdīst force would probably have been incapable of mounting a second round of resistance at the river. Berber might have been abandoned without a fight, but if not could have been attacked in concert by Stewart's column and Gordon's steamers.

Thus, without quibbling about a few days here or there, it seems perfectly apparent that the same result, which by river had taken until 21 January to achieve, could easily have been achieved overland from Suakin by the end of the first week in November. It would have been perfectly possible to put 500 British troops aboard the steamers, for them to have disembarked and attacked Ḥalfaiya about four days later, then to have continued steaming down the Nile in perfect safety, past the cheering garrison of Fort Omdurman, to land in front of the *sarāya* on or about 12/13 November. Between mid-November and the end of December large convoys could have moved along the Suakin–Berber road, bringing up more supplies and reinforcements. While the steamers returned to Berber to bring up another 500 men by the end of the third week of November, a tolerably strong force of around brigade strength could simultaneously have been advancing south along the east bank of the Nile, with the river interposing between it and the enemy's main body. It would thus have been possible to have had a minimum of 3,000–4,000 British troops operating in conjunction with a still well-nourished 8,000-strong Egyptian/Sudanese garrison and eight well-armed river steamers, against an enemy force of around 30,000 men. With a tenable overland line of communications, running along the line North Fort–Shendy– Berber–Obak–Ariab–Suakin–Royal Navy, the relief expedition would have had a much longer loiter time at Khartoum.

While the Mahdīst enemy would have been much weakened by its dispersal between the west bank of the White Nile and the south bank of the Blue Nile, Wolseley and Gordon would have enjoyed the advantage of operating on interior lines. There can be little doubt that they would have gained a swift victory which, at the very least, would have compelled an enemy withdrawal to El Obeid. It is unlikely that the inherently fractious rebel host would have held together in the wake of so great a reverse. Such a victory would have allowed the Egyptian soldiers and officials to be evacuated to Berber and points beyond in perfect safety. It would not immediately have solved the question of the Sudan's longer-term governance but, as had always been the case, that was a political matter. It is possible that HMG, having been driven to gaining a military victory at Khartoum, would have been sufficiently emboldened to allow Gordon to proceed with his plan to install Zubair as his successor. Large parts of the Sudan would inevitably have become 'un-

Time and Sustainability: The Key Factors

The Suakin–Berber expedition postulated above would undoubtedly have amounted to a challenging and complex operation of war. It could easily have derailed at some point, though almost certainly not fatally in the sense of time running out. The key point is that time dictated that this approach, or something like it, was the only way of achieving the military mission. Let us then demonstrate this by contemplating the constraints imposed by the 'all-important' time factor.

We have noted before that Wolseley's second memo to Hartington of April 1884, specifically identified 15 November as the latest date to which Khartoum could hold out.[31] This was the fundamental assumption on which Wolseley's advice to the Secretary of State, a strong preference for a Nile expedition ahead of all other options, was predicated. As it turned out Gordon somehow held on until the last week of January, although from the New Year onwards dozens of soldiers and scores of citizens were dying of starvation every day. Interestingly Gordon's final journal entry of 14 December records the quantity of food stocks left in his warehouses at that juncture. There were, he tells us, 546 'ardebs of dhoora' and 83,525 'okes' of biscuit.[32] *Ardebs* and *okes* are old Ottoman units of measure.

Dhoora or *dhura* is a sorghum or cereal grass, also known as 'Egyptian corn'. The kernels could be made into flour, while the green plants served as animal feed. An *ardeb* is the equivalent of 5.62 Imperial 'bushels', while a bushel is the equivalent of eight 'dry gallons'. There were therefore 24,548 dry gallons of *dhura* in stock. This quantity is probably best imagined, in very general terms, by thinking of a bushel as a round basket of about a foot deep and two feet in diameter. Thus there were some 3,050 such baskets in Gordon's warehouses. An *oke* is the equivalent of 2.75 lb or 1.24 kg. This means that there were 229,693 lb or 103,571 kg of biscuit left on 14 December. These quantities had to suffice for 22,000 people, around 8,000 of whom were under arms. If Gordon was feeding only his soldiers from 14 December, then there were only 10.44 lb of biscuit left per fighting man. One pound of biscuit would suffice as a standard biscuit ration for one day, but both the physical condition and the morale of men eating only biscuit day after day would deteriorate very quickly.

It seems evident, therefore, that the food warehouses would have been all but played out by Christmas and empty by the New Year. The timing of the final assault on Khartoum was determined in my view by three things: first, the reports of the Mahdī's spies in respect of the extent and effect of starvation; second, the precedent established by the costly Mahdīst attempt to storm El Obeid; and third, the British gaining the Nile at Metemmeh, an event which preceded the final assault on Khartoum by only five days.

The attack on a still hale and well-nourished Egyptian garrison at El Obeid on 8 September 1882 cost the rebels several thousand lives, including that of one of the Mahdī's brothers, but more importantly came close to shattering the faith of the *anṣār* in their leader. How could it be if Muḥammad Aḥmad was truly the Mahdī that his followers could suffer such a terrible mauling at the hands of apostate 'Turks'? The Mahdī slipped off the hook by angrily berating his commanders in public, insisting that he had told them to attack from the east, and that their failure to follow his instructions to the letter was tantamount to having disobeyed the will of the Prophet. The premature assault on El Obeid taught Muḥammad Aḥmad two things: first, that if he was to retain the blind obedience of the faithful he could ill afford serious military reverses, and second, that his prohibition on the use of captured firearms and artillery, as the unmanly weaponry of the godless, was unwise and should be reversed forthwith. Between September 1882 and January 1883 he played a waiting game before the walls of El Obeid. In the meantime a badly managed Egyptian relief expedition was defeated in the open by a detached wing of the rebel host. At length starvation drove the garrison to the verge of mutiny, compelling Major General Muḥammad Saʻīd Pasha to capitulate.

Thus, when it came to dealing with Gordon at Khartoum, the siege of El Obeid provided both a painful precedent and a recipe for success.[33] The Mahdī's self-anointed mission, to lead his host to Constantinople via Cairo and Mecca, in effect a conquest of the Islamic world, was in truth so grandiosely unrealistic that he can have been in no particular rush to extinguish Khartoum. The capture of the city may indeed have represented the true height of his ambitions, for the squabbling Mahdīst host was still encamped at the confluence of the Niles when, some five months later, the 'divinely guided one' died. It is clear, then, that it was the news of Abu Klea and the subsequent British march to the Nile that compelled the final assault of 25/26 January 1885. Had the relief column not been within a few days' steaming, Muḥammad Aḥmad would simply have waited for Gordon's troops to mutiny in the same way as Muḥammad Saʻīd Pasha's had. That they had still not done so the best part of a month after the food ran out, compelling them to survive on rats, cats and tree-gum, was testament both to their fear of the Mahdī and to their faith in Gordon's capacity to work miracles.

We have seen how a story to the effect that Faraj Pasha, one of Gordon's Egyptian officers, had thrown open the Masallamīya Gate to admit the Mahdīst attackers reached Wolseley's headquarters at Korti and was duly incorporated into London-bound reports. We have seen also that Major Kitchener would later compile a comprehensive report detailing what he had learned from locals and survivors about the fall of the Khartoum, in which he discredited the Faraj Pasha story.[34] Like a drowning man reaching for a lifebelt, however, Gladstone had immediately latched on to the notion. He talked constantly in his speeches about Khartoum falling through treachery, in the vain hope that this would absolve him of blame in the eyes of the electorate. In fact, whether the Masallamīya Gate was thrown open or not was in large part irrelevant, as the western end of the city's 'South Front' defences had been exposed by the seasonal fall of the White Nile, allowing thousands of rebels to pour into the city by that route alone. The plain fact of the matter was that a climactic assault could have been mounted against a garrison which was all but powerless to resist at any time after the New Year. This fact alone gives the lie to any suggestion that the Nile Expedition arrived a paltry two days too late. It was starvation that did for Khartoum. The game was up by the New Year and the timing of the *coup de grâce* lay squarely in the gift of the enemy. Just as Wolseley did not want to advance south of Metemmeh unless compelled to do so, neither did Muḥammad Aḥmad want to mount a direct assault until such time as he was left with no other choice.

Culpability

In addressing the issue of culpability it will be as well to be clear precisely what it is we are talking about: culpability for what? In essence it is simply this: who is to blame for the fact that the British Army should go to such extraordinary lengths to relieve Khartoum and yet fall so far short of the great object it had set itself?

If any one person was undeniably to blame, it would leap from the pages of history. To some extent the conventional interpretation of the Khartoum episode has demanded that William Ewart Gladstone be cast in the role of arch-villain, but it is unreasonable to assert that premiers are to blame for unsound military plans which founder in the field. Unworthy plans, both of a budgetary and operational nature, have been laid in recent times, only for unjust fingers of blame to be pointed at ministers subsequently, so the distinction between the strategic, operational and tactical levels of decision-making is not merely a key issue but also a topical one.

If Gladstone cannot be held solely responsible for Gordon's demise, it follows that culpability must be shared across various levels of decision making. Hence our poser becomes not merely who is to blame but, 'Which of the role-players are culpable, at what level, and in what measure?'

Culpability at the Strategic Level

That Prime Minister Gladstone delayed too long in assenting to a relief expedition is a given. He was angry that Gordon had not followed to the letter his instructions to extricate the Egyptian officials and soldiers from Khartoum and march them away in the direction of Cairo. He had certainly never intended that the loyalist citizenry of Khartoum should be regarded as part of the problem; they were simply to be left to shift for themselves. This whole premise was based on a misperception of what Mahdīsm represented. Gladstone understood it only as a substantially justifiable liberation movement and had formed the view that it could not possibly be worse for the Sudanese people than Egyptian colonial governance. That many thousands of Sudanese made their living on the back of the Egyptian administration and had no desire to see it withdrawn seems not to have dawned on him. That the Prime Minister had no real comprehension of fundamentalism and failed to understand what a serious threat it would pose to Upper Egypt, bespeaks great naiveté in the affairs of the Near East.

At no point did Gladstone make allowance for the slightly more refined solution advanced by Gordon while he was in transit to Khartoum, and to which he so stubbornly adhered subsequently. Gordon actually supported the idea of ending direct rule from Cairo and the consequent necessity to evacuate the Khedive's soldiers and officials. Indeed in *Modern Egypt* Lord Cromer asserts that Gordon inserted a clause into his own orders that the policy of evacuation should on no account be reversed.[35] He diverged from this strategy only in so far as he sought sufficient time and space to oversee an orderly transition of power to a Sudanese strong-man fit to contend with the powerful persona of the Mahdī. The only man he believed could play this role was Zubair who, having been mentored by Gordon for a few months, would be kept sweet subsequently by means of an annual subsidy, a standard tactic in retaining the fealty of the princes and nabobs of British India. In other words, Gordon sought only to provide the untainted Sudanese population with a sporting chance of not immediately falling under the sway of a fundamentalist theocracy, with all its attendant tyranny. If Gordon, a man of great compassion, cared how events in the Sudan played themselves out, Gladstone manifestly did not. Instead he sought only an immediate termination of Egyptian rule. The Prime Minister could not have chosen a man for the job with greater experience of the Sudan than Gordon and yet at the same time could not have chosen a candidate more likely to diverge from so callous a programme. Given the subsequent course of events, in essence the loss of many thousands of lives, with no real prospect of altering the outcome, the selection of Gordon for the mission was a serious error of judgement on Gladstone's part. Indeed, given a strategy of immediate abandonment, permitting any Briton to go to Khartoum amounted to a serious error of judgement.

What then of Gordon himself, the idiosyncratic but passionately committed Christian evangelical? If nothing else Charles Gordon was a man of honour. There can be no doubt that in seeking to broaden his mandate he believed he was acting in the best interests of the Sudanese people, for whom he harboured great sentimental attachment. That the citizenry of Khartoum held him in such great awe fuelled both his vanity and the righteousness of his cause. He openly stated his adapted plan in telegrams sent to Sir Evelyn Baring in the early days of the mission.[36] These communications had insisted that the exiled Zubair be sent down from Cairo post-haste to assist him and had outlined how the Gordon plan for a semi-autonomous Sudan, owing only nominal allegiance to Cairo, was to play itself out subsequently. Baring shared most if not all of Gordon's communications with Granville, but they had elicited no searing rebuke from Whitehall, instructing Gordon to get on and do what he been sent to do, as perhaps they ought to have done. Gordon had fallen into the trap in this same period of underestimating the fervour and military strength of the Mahdīst movement. He had dispersed disorganized Arab mobs using Egyptian troops during his first tour as governor-general, and arrived in Khartoum in February 1884 believing that he would still be able to do so. By the time he realized the extent of demoralization amongst the military and just how powerful the rebels had become, it was too late to get large numbers of people away to the north. Berber fell relatively early, on 26 May, from which point on he was hemmed in.

It might be fair to assert that Gordon was to blame for his own demise had HMG ever stipulated a timetable for evacuation. This it had not done, giving Gordon reason to believe that he had rather more say in the strategy for the Sudan than Gladstone had ever intended he should have. If the garrison was going to come out by river, an option which for want of direction to the contrary appeared to have been left open by HMG, then, given the rapidity of movement required for so few steamers to carry so many people, Gordon would have to wait for the Nile to rise. This could only occur from about July onwards – by which time Berber was in enemy hands. If Gordon marched out without waiting for the Nile to rise, then the only route open to him (the Berber–Suakin road having being closed by Osman Digna's rebellion) was down the west bank of the Nile to Metemmeh, followed by a crossing of the Bayūda Desert to Korti. Good hard-marching troops could have covered these 274 miles in something just shy of three weeks. An Egyptian army would have hampered itself with camp followers and baggage and would have been at least a week slower.

One of the real-world problems facing Gordon was that only a proportion of the Khartoum garrison was made up of Egyptian troops. Not only did he have 2,316 black Sudanese regulars under his command,[37] men who had no reason to march away for Egypt, but there was also an entire tribe of local Sudanese Arabs to worry about. For many years the Shā'iqīa had provided the Egyptian authorities with large numbers of irregular troops. As ardent collaborators and enthusiastic armed tax collectors, the Shā'iqīa were detested by most of the other Arab tribes. Some had been briefly won over to the rebel cause, but had since been rallied to the government side by Khashm al-Mūs and others. Some 2,330 members of the tribe were under arms as part of the Khartoum garrison.[38] Their territory lay just north of Khartoum and, like the black regulars from the south, they had absolutely no desire to march away in the direction of Egypt. These and other complexities were matters which Gladstone did not comprehend and to which he would have paid little heed in any case. Gordon, though, was in no position to magic such problems away.

It would be both unjust and unduly callous, in the absence of a clear-cut timetable for withdrawal, to hold Gordon to blame for his own demise. Besides, our object is to probe the culpability for the failure of the relief expedition, not to consider the reasons why such an operation became necessary.

Sir Evelyn Baring was by no means an enthusiastic supporter of the proposal to 'send Gordon', having no trust in the general's judgement. He only gave in to the public clamour in England, when pressed by the Foreign Secretary for a third time.[39] 'I gave a reluctant assent,' he wrote, 'in reality against my own judgment and inclination, because I thought that, as everybody differed from me, I must be wrong . . . In yielding I made a mistake which I shall never cease to regret.'[40] It was Baring who facilitated the transition of Gordon's role from an advisory one into an executive one, when he prevailed upon the Khedive to grant him a *firman* as Governor-General of the Sudan. Importantly the suggestion was Gordon's own and was directed in the first instance to Whitehall, while he was still in transit to Cairo.

It was Granville who forwarded the idea to Baring.[41] Baring was meticulous in communicating every nuance and development to the Foreign Secretary, but did not invariably receive carefully considered or thoughtful replies.

Once Gordon had gone south Baring remained consistently supportive, even when the telegraphic traffic from Khartoum started to ramble. As we have seen Gordon was much given to firing off telegrams at the drop of a hat, often failing to contextualize the interrelationship of his thoughts and ideas. In his memoirs Baring said that he considered 'impulsive flightiness' to be the general's principal character defect,[42] by no means an unfair assessment. Sensing that some of his telegrams were unsettling the Foreign Secretary, Baring telegraphed Granville to say, 'In considering Gordon's suggestions, please remember that his general views are excellent, but that undue importance must not be attached to his words. We must look to the spirit rather than the letter of what he says.'[43]

Baring read the deteriorating military situation around Khartoum accurately and kept Granville fully abreast of his views. In March 1884, when Sir Gerald Graham sought permission to open the Suakin–Berber road, Baring consulted with Generals Stephenson and Wood, who viewed the proposition as difficult but not impossible, and then telegraphed London lending strong support to the idea.[44] His recommendation was rejected by the Cabinet. As time wore on he sent more strongly disapproving messages to Granville, emphasizing that something had to be done to assist Gordon.[45] I detect no hint of strategic culpability in anything the consul-general did. On the contrary his advice to HMG was invariably intelligent, perceptive and timely. Unfortunately it was not always heeded, and was firmly rebuffed wherever it failed to fit with Gladstone's preconceptions.

As GOC of the Army of Occupation in Egypt and the senior British officer in the region, Sir Frederick Stephenson was also a strategic-level role-player. Gordon's operations in the Sudan were an 'Egyptian' matter, however, and as such were Baring's business not his. It was only when the consul-general turned to him for military advice that he was able to influence the conduct of government business. Baring was more inclined to turn to Sir Evelyn Wood for his military advice, as a result of which there was a certain amount of friction in play, though this was not a serious impediment to the trio coming together as an effective triumvirate.

In March 1884 Stephenson was initially hesitant about allowing Graham to advance on Berber. Having only just suffered extremely heavy punishment at Tamai (13 March 1884), the Bīja rebels would probably not have presented a serious threat to a further advance into the desert. It was shortage of water along the route that caused Stephenson to doubt the proposition. We have already established that this was a factor which dictated that the route could be used only by detachments of a few hundred men moving at intervals. Officially Graham sought merely to probe the road to Berber, not to march there in full strength to occupy the town permanently. Eventually Sir Herbert Stewart was instructed to prepare a plan for pushing the cavalry brigade through to Berber. Clearly Graham, as the man on the spot, had few doubts about the route's viability. In full cabal with Baring and Wood, and with the benefit of Graham's advice, Stephenson accepted that though Suakin–Berber would be difficult it was nonetheless viable. During the 'Battle of the Routes' he came down firmly in favour of Suakin–Berber. He also devised a workable plan for the river option, a plan which entailed immediately moving elements of his in-place force to Dongola without waiting for the whalers, a point to which we will return when we consider the operational level. Stephenson did nothing to impede the mounting of a relief expedition and provided consistently sound advice when asked to do so. When Hartington notified him that Wolseley was to be sent out,[46] Stephenson had the maturity and good grace to remain in post and support him as best he could. Writing to his wife on 13 September, Wolseley observed, 'I am on the best of terms with dear "Ben" Stephenson; he is "such a gentleman" in every way that it goes to my heart to be here superseding him in command of the troops.'[47] It is clear that Stephenson deserves no share in strategic-level culpability. On the contrary he deserves a good deal of credit for the quality of the advice he tendered to ministers. Unfortunately the advice was muscled aside in the War Office by Wolseley and senior members of the Ring.

What then of the key players at the War Office? As we have seen Wolseley presented his proposals for a river-borne expedition as early as 8 April 1884, cognizant that the seasonal rise and fall of the Nile was an important consideration. Where Lord Granville was inclined to a *laissez-faire* approach to strategy, Hartington was an altogether more practical-minded minister. It is doubtful whether public clamour alone would ever have compelled the Prime Minister to do something he was so determinedly against; it was the political instability which was certain to follow Hartington's resignation which left him no choice in the matter. Because Hartington and Wolseley grasped the need to act at the appropriate juncture, and laid tenable plans for doing so, no strategic-level blame can be attached to either of them. Of course they were also players at the operational level, where the picture is somewhat less rosy for both of them.

Culpability at the Operational Level

Gladstone delayed authorizing a relief expedition to the point where it necessarily became a touch and go affair. What he did not do, however, was tell the War Office in general or Lord Wolseley in particular how to go about executing the military task. Even so the Prime Minister cannot be entirely exonerated of operational-level blame, as it was his strategic-level inaction which squeezed the window in time and space to such an extent that it acted as a major contributory factor in the foundering of military decision-making.

The Prime Minster and the Secretary of State for War had the power to adjudicate against Wolseley's proposals for a Nile expedition and moreover had good grounds for doing so, given that both the Admiralty's agents on the spot and the GOC in Cairo had proffered advice to the contrary. Every conceivable argument for and against appeared in the letters pages of the national press. The politicians chose, however, to back the judgement of the man who had conquered Egypt.

Ultimately it was the wrong call. Thus Gladstone's culpability carries through into the operational level, while Hartington, free of any strategic-level blame, must now bear at least partial responsibility for giving Wolseley a free hand. The essential error perpetrated at the War Office was that of committing to a course of action without ever recognizing that in war the clock never stops – that time and space equations can only contract; that a good plan laid today might not hold water tomorrow.

When in early May the War Office telegraphed Sir Frederick Stephenson to seek his opinion on a preferred axis of advance, he urged adoption of the Suakin–Berber caravan road. The Sirdar was also entitled to an opinion and expressed a preference for using the river only as far as Korosko, at which point a 250-mile caravan route struck across the desert to Abū-Hamed at the northern tip of the Great Bend in the Nile. Because the Wood plan was never fully worked up, quite what was meant to happen thereafter is not altogether clear. The option of advancing from Kassala on the Red Sea was given short shrift by both the *in situ* generals: in this at least they were in full agreement with the Adjutant-General. Stephenson followed up his hasty reply of 4 May with a detailed memo dated the following day, in which he recognized the attendant difficulties of the Suakin–Berber road but dismissed the river axis. His rejection of the Nile did not consider the whaler scheme, of which he was still unaware, but was based on an 860-mile march along the riverbank from Wādī Halfā to Khartoum. He estimated that 4,500–5,000 camels would be required per 1,000 soldiers and that it would take four months to reach Gordon. Little wonder, then, that he dismissed the premise.[48] The Cabinet made no immediate decision on which route would be used. On 14 June Stephenson was notified that the government wanted to make preparations for laying a railway from Suakin to Berber.[49] All the while Wolseley was agitating in favour of a great Nile expedition and pouring scorn, rightly it must be said, on the proposed railway scheme. By the time the parliamentary Vote of Credit took place, Hartington had been won over by Wolseley and gave immediate instructions for Butler to proceed with commissioning the whalers.

Stephenson was only briefly in charge of the preparations for the relief of Khartoum. His tenure lasted from 8 August, the date on which Hartington telegraphed news of the parliamentary vote of credit, to 26 August, the date on which he telegraphed the news that he was despatching Wolseley to take command. In between these dates there was an exchange of traffic[50] in which Stephenson stated that he could immediately move around 3,000 British troops to Wādī Halfā, and then move them on as far as Dongola in steamers and *nuggars*, provided that the decision to pass the vessels up the Second Cataract (just to the south of Wādī Halfā) was made promptly, while the Nile was still high. Hartington's replies dealt in so much close military detail that it is safe to assume that they were drafted by Wolseley.

Stephenson insisted that a small-boat scheme was inappropriate. The Hartington–Wolseley combination countered by remarking that while Stephenson had a plan for getting troops to Dongola quickly, he had no follow-on boat plan to get to Khartoum, as *nuggars* and steamers would certainly not be able to get around the Great Bend once the river had started to fall. What was his plan, asked Whitehall, for getting troops to Khartoum and back again 'this season' – meaning the near side of Christmas 1884, from which point the insufferably hot weather would click in. Stephenson replied that getting to Khartoum and back in that sort of time-frame was impossible: of course subsequent events were to prove him right on this point. Because he could clearly foresee that the time and space equation surrounding a Nile expedition did not add up, he was tempted on 21 August to again express a preference for the Suakin–Berber axis.[51] On 27 August he was politely notified that he was to be superseded.

The advantage of an immediate high-Nile passage to Dongola by *nuggar* was demonstrated by the movements of 1st Royal Sussex. Sent initially by Stephenson to Aswan, to protect Upper Egypt, in mid-August the battalion received orders to proceed upriver to Wādī Halfā. It reached its destination on 26 August and a week or so later was then ordered forward to Dongola. It bypassed the Second Cataract by means of the short stretch of railway running south to Sarras, where on 6 September Colonel Vandeleur again embarked his men aboard *nuggars*. His first half-battalion gained Dongola in only thirteen days, whereas the same 210-mile journey took the whalers five weeks.[52] The officers and men of the Royal Sussex were fated to spend three months kicking their heels, with only an outbreak of smallpox to show for it, while the rest of the Nile Expedition caught up with them.

The battalion's movements show that it would have been perfectly possible to launch a force of comparable or greater size than the Desert Column (which given the easy going in the Bayūda need not have been camel-borne) from Korti to Metemmeh as early as late October. The whalers could have followed up in their own time, bringing up reinforcements and supplies to Korti, ultimately to serve as a means of *returning* downriver. Neither Wolseley nor Stephenson would have seen this as a complete plan, on the grounds that it might only have delivered 3,000 men to Metemmeh. This was what drove Stephenson, with his superior grasp of time and space, to prefer Suakin–Berber. What Wolseley seems not to have been able to see is that the long transit of the Great Bend was completely impracticable in the time available. In the event he left himself just enough time to mount a dash across the Bayūda, but even then ultimately fell prey to indecision.

If Sir Frederick Stephenson had been left to his own devices he would not have mounted a Nile expedition, but would have advanced along the Suakin–Berber axis. Accordingly no share of operational-level culpability can be attributed to him.

Wolseley's Novel Expedients: Success or Failure?

We have seen that when the whaler scheme became public, it triggered a furore in the newspapers. Much more importantly key military players such as C-in-C Mediterranean and GOC Cairo came out against it.[53] The so-called 'Battle of the Routes' then ensued. The extent and bitterness of the opposition to his scheme should have given Wolseley pause for thought. When challenged on the viability of the whaler scheme, Wolseley contrived a written submission to ministers by his old Red River comrades. No doubt the Red River had presented some formidable challenges, but to transpose directly the lessons learned on one river to an altogether different river on an altogether different continent, overthrowing all the best local and expert advice in the process, would seem to be the very epitome of dogmatic thinking.

The whalers did allow great logistic tonnages to be moved down the Nile with a minimum of effort, as the troops were sat amidst their food and ammunition and could never want for water. Logistically speaking the whaler scheme was an excellent one; in particular neutralizing water supply as an issue was a very compelling advantage indeed. But the real issue was not whether the whalers would get up the Nile, but *how quickly* they would get up the Nile.

When Wolseley devised and briefed his scheme in April 1884, in the reasonable expectation of being able to exploit high-Nile to good advantage, it may indeed have been the optimal way of attaining the object. What is clear, however, is that by August when Gladstone finally relented, it no longer represented the best option. Indeed it can be compellingly argued that it was no sort of option at all. Butler remained proudly unrepentant to the end of his days, but was much inclined to isolate the boat scheme, his direct responsibility, from its wider operational context. Illustratively it did not matter in the slightest if it took forty days to get from A to B, if it took sixty days to get the whalers to A in the first place; the total journey time to B is not forty days but 100 days. In his *Campaign of the Cataracts*, published two years after Gordon's death, he wrote:

Not only had the fleet equipped the whole Desert Column, and supplied it with food to last two months, but it had also brought to Korti three months' food for the River Column; and this result had been achieved in an average of forty days from start to finish, or at the rate of ten and a half miles per diem, cataracts included. One officer and six men had been drowned, a few boats had been lost, but nine-tenths of the fleet were in as sound condition as on the day they had left the English building yards. Standing on the high river bank at Korti, and looking down, day after day, upon scores of boats coming in, closing up their crews and cargoes, and giving out a vast surplus supply to feed the Desert Column, one could not help letting the mind run back to four months earlier, when the prophets of disaster had been loudest in their opposition. How many men were we not to have lost by sunstroke, by disease, by crocodile, and by cataract! What ignorance, what folly, what madness was this scheme of a boat expedition! And here, today, were these much abused boats piling out upon the shore at Korti box upon box of the best English provisions, equipping a desert force of 2000 men for a long campaign, and having still, for the use of another 3000 men, sufficient food supplies to last three entire months.

And the men whose labour under the sun and over the cataracts had achieved this result in these boats – were they the gaunt and sickly skeletons foretold by the wise ones? They were models of strength – pictures of health. Brown, sinewy and muscular, they sat at the oars or tramped the shore with the track-line in all the ease and freedom of a perfect knowledge of their work.[54]

All this was perfectly true but in an operational context it was also sublimely irrelevant. Elsewhere in his book Butler hit the nail on the head when he wrote:

> ...far better the long road which has water in the desert, than the short one which is without it. I have said that but for one consideration there could have been no hesitation between the routes to be followed from Korti. That consideration was, however, all important. It was time. The New Year had begun; the date to which Khartoum could hold out had been already passed, and if the place was to be succoured and Gordon saved, the attempt, cost what it might, must be made across the 180 miles of desert, and not by the 400 miles of river, to Metemma.[55]

Immediately after this passage Butler gives vent to the same sort of gratuitous wishful thinking as occurs in Wolseley's orders to Wilson.

> One month earlier at Korti, and there would have been no need of this desert dash. The entire force – horses, camels, and boats moving along the river and its shores – would have reached Metemma by the 10th of January and Khartoum ten days later. The Cataracts of Shaggieh, which we shall soon see, would have presented half the difficulties of passage they were now destined to oppose to us; and the line of the Nile taken along its loop, would have cleared every enemy before us, opened up at Abu Hamad the road to Korosko, and at Berber that to Suakin; and meeting Gordon's steamers at Berber would have carried to Khartoum the advanced guard of an army secure in its strength, its resources and its unmenaced base.[56]

Butler writes in this third passage as if the attainment of all these great objectives lay just around the corner. The truth, though, was that the presence of 3,000 whaler-borne troops at Korti was an operational irrelevance. On 30 December 1884, when the Desert Column was launched into the Bayūda, the whaler-borne battalions had not even started the transit of the 400-mile Great Bend. Only when they had gained Berber would they again have any bona fide relevance. The fact of the matter is that while Wolseley's appreciation and plan stipulated that a force of 5,000 men would be required to effect the relief of Khartoum, the slow progress of whaler-borne operations served to reduce his effective fighting strength to a paltry 1,800. The last whaler-borne troops did not embark at Gemai until 19 December.[57] In this seemingly insignificant footnote in the story of the campaign is to be found the true measure of just how slow and unsuited to its purpose the Nile route would prove in the end: troops which it had been intended would fight in a decisive battle just outside Khartoum did not get clear of 'Bloody Halfway' until the week before Christmas. If all that the whaler scheme achieved in the end was to hurl the Desert Column over a desert march of 174 miles against Metemmeh, then it achieved very little that could not have been achieved at a much earlier point in time – and time, as Butler rightly pointed out, was 'all important'. How much more difficult could it have been to march Stewart's command over 245 miles of desert from Suakin and hurl itself against Berber instead?

Let us turn now to the second of Wolseley's novel expedients. Conceptually speaking the Camel Corps was a brigade-sized force of mounted infantry. A doctrine note entitled 'Notes for the Use of Camel Regiments by the General Commanding in Chief in Egypt', which was conceived by Wolseley and signed by Buller, stated plainly in its fourth paragraph, 'The soldiers of the Camel Regiments will fight only on foot.' It went on to say:

> The men of the Camel Corps must therefore trust solely to themselves and their weapons when once they have dismounted for action.
>
> This cannot be too strongly impressed upon the men. If we have to fight in the Sudan, we must expect to meet an enemy far outnumbering us, and who may at first charge recklessly home, apparently regardless of the intense fire we bring to bear upon him. His arms are immeasurably inferior to ours, and to hurl back with heavy loss any such rush of undisciplined Arabs, we have only to keep in close formation that will give him no opening, while at the same time it enables us to give full development to our fire.[58]

That two of the four regiments in the brigade were made up of cavalrymen completely unversed in the 'infantry drill' was asking for trouble. In the event it was the Heavies who paid the price. The Guards and Mounted Infantry performed well, suggesting that the employment of composite regiments was not a particular hindrance per se. The real issue was using the wrong arm in the wrong role, when there was no necessity for it. The decision to do so was Wolseley's.

It might also be added that mounting large numbers of troops on camels proved in the end to be of little utility. The rate of advance for a camel-borne column was not determined by the riding camels but by the baggage train, and this moved no faster than a marching infantryman. It is probably true to say that marching rather than riding would have exacted a greater toll on the troops in terms of dehydration. On the other hand dismounting the Camel Corps for the crossing of the Bayūda would have provided an additional 2,000 baggage animals, so that a great deal more water could have been carried in any case. The measure would also have obviated the need for the shuttle-run to Jakdul Wells and thus have conveyed four significant advantages: first, British intent would not have been compromised in advance and there would not have been a strong enemy blocking force at Abu Klea; second, the transit of the Bayūda would have been completed a week earlier; third, Stewart would not have immobilized his command by driving his animals into the ground; fourth, there would have been sufficient baggage camels both to support a number of follow-on infantry battalions and still permit the maintenance of a reserve.

Writing in his journal on 11 January Sir Charles Wilson observed, 'It would be heresy to say the camelry is a mistake; but if Tommy Atkins cannot march in such a climate as this, we had better give up fighting.'[59] To prove his point the Royal Irish Regiment did indeed march across the Bayūda on foot, but by then the campaign had backfired. The Camel Corps: novel expedient or resource-intensive novelty? The answer is only too painfully apparent.

Execution of the Campaign Plan

Leaving aside the validity of a Camel Corps, it is clear that the Desert Column was provided with too few baggage camels. Traditionally this critical shortfall is fixed at around a thousand animals and is laid at the door of Sir Redvers Buller as chief of staff. We have seen, however, that Buller urged Wolseley to order a crossing of the Bayūda as early as the first week of November. It is perhaps no coincidence that the Ring's best brain, Brackenbury, was working under Buller as a DAAG at this juncture. If Buller's private correspondence is to be believed, Wolseley was so adamant that he intended going all the way to Khartoum by river that the army staff, from whom he separated himself for more than eight weeks, paid scant regard to the Korti–Metemmeh option. Remarkably Buller learned that an overland dash was in the offing only days before it was mounted, by which time it was far too late to procure any more camels. It is the commander's duty to convey his intent to the chief of staff, so the confusion and consequent shortage of camels was more of Wolseley's making than Buller's. An easy fix – dismounting the camel corps and marching across the Bayūda – was at hand but, as Sir Charles Wilson put it, advancing such a proposition would have been to speak heresy.

Wolseley had every right to expect that his chief of staff would be the master of the expedition's administrative nitty-gritty, although a good commander should always be sure that all is well with his logistics. The operation was critically dependent on the river steamers plying the lower reaches of the Nile. Unfortunately it did not dawn on Buller that such vessels do not run on thin air but coal. There was already a contract for its provision in place when Buller arrived on the Nile, but he failed to staff-check the quantities required and critical shortages duly occurred. It was estimated that the shortfalls imposed delays amounting to about ten to fourteen days in total. Buller, then, must bear some share of operational-level culpability.

Turning to the matter of key decision points, it is possible readily to identify two. Unfortunately Wolseley completely missed the first of them and fluffed the second. If it was obvious to Buller and Brackenbury as early as 7 November that proceeding via Abū-Hamed and Berber could not possibly effect the relief of Khartoum in time, then it should have been even more apparent to the C-in-C. In delaying as long as he did before finally deciding to launch Stewart across the Bayūda, Wolseley missed a critical decision point. A key part of generalship is not merely taking decisions, but working out in advance when they will have to be taken. It is a fundamental of military history that there have been no 'great captains' who were not masters of time and space. The second key decision point was not a natural one but, rather, was self-imposed. It occurred with the arrival on New Year's Eve of Gordon's last message. Wolseley wrote in his journal that he went to bed that night, 'with a heavy heart – Oh God how heavy!'[60] What he should have said was that he went to bed racked with uncertainty.

In the same entry he noted that he had made the decision to switch four battalions of infantry from the river route to the desert route, leaving only two battalions to proceed to Abū-Hamed and beyond in the whalers. This was predicated on Gordon's injunction, as Wolseley put it, 'not to advance unless I am strong'. It was by no means a bad precept, albeit bringing the infantry up would have been time-consuming. He envisaged leaving one battalion to garrison Metemmeh, and advancing on Khartoum with the Camel Corps and the other three infantry units. He observed that, 'This will be a safer plan of operation than I had previously determined upon but it will take more time & prevent me perhaps from being in Khartoum as I had hoped to be with a fighting force on the 31st Jany., at latest.' Importantly this new scheme of manoeuvre would have involved the infantry battalions in the plan, whilst at the same time retaining the ability to make a rapid advance with a leading echelon based around the Camel Corps. We should note in passing Wolseley's reiteration of his target date, noting that he would later feel no compunction about lambasting Wilson for gaining Khartoum on 28 January.

When Wolseley rose the next morning to meet with Buller and the rest of his staff he wavered. By the time the cabal had broken up Wolseley was no longer intent on commanding a do-or-die dash across the Bayūda, but had become fixated instead on another of Gordon's injunctions: do not leave Berber in your rear. His answer to this particular conundrum was to leave the infantry on the boats as originally intended and mount a much slower-moving pincer movement on Berber. The Desert Column would be tasked to gain Metemmeh as planned but instead of immediately dashing south for Khartoum would despatch Sir Charles Wilson to confer with Gordon. Only when Wilson returned to Korti would Wolseley decide whether to launch Stewart to the north or to the south. Earle's four battalions would be committed to rowing all the way to Berber after all. From being momentarily relevant, they had once again been consigned to manifest and permanent irrelevance. The key point, though, was that Wilson's mission represented a new and necessarily time-consuming phase in the Desert Column's scheme of manoeuvre.

Even more remarkable than the dithering was the fact that the orders subsequently issued to Stewart and Wilson made no provision for them deciding anything for themselves. Even if Wilson made it to Khartoum and back safely and, on disembarking at Metemmeh, reported that Gordon was indeed *in extremis*, Stewart did not have the authority either to march south immediately with the Camel Corps, or to throw troops aboard the steamers to make a second more powerful river dash. Whether or not he would have taken the responsibility upon himself is not something we can ever know. That a dire necessity to take urgent action might have been in play was surely obvious, yet Wolseley made no allowance for it. Instead of conceding some independence of action, he issued orders which expressly instructed Wilson to come back to Korti and make his report in person. Wolseley would then have had to cross the Bayūda in the opposite direction, if he was to assume personal command of the Desert Column's southwards advance. If everything had gone swimmingly for Wilson, the necessity for him to go to Khartoum, confer with Gordon and come back to Metemmeh at low-Nile would still have consumed a minimum of nine days. When at length he did cross the Bayūda to Korti, it took him four days.[61] Add the same again for Wolseley's crossing, plus a minimum of four or five days for him to give his orders and forge across the last 100 miles to the city, and we are safely three weeks from the date at which the Desert Column reached Metemmeh.

Lord Wolseley gave no orders which suggested that there was a not a second to be lost in getting Wilson to Khartoum. Indeed the orders issued to Stewart, Wilson and Beresford gave no guidance whatsoever on the urgency of the situation.[62] What Wolseley might have said to them face-to-face we do not know, but both Wilson and Beresford wrote comprehensive memoirs which make no mention of any separate exhortation to speed. Indeed if Wolseley had given any such orders we can be certain that he would have ranted about it in his campaign journal or his letters to his wife. Ultimately written orders are written orders and if Wolseley had intended to convey any dire necessity for speed, it was absolutely necessary that it be clearly articulated.

Culpability at the Tactical Level

Sir Herbert Stewart was a natural leader and a gallant soldier. Realizing the urgency of the situation he pressed his command extremely hard during his desert marches. However, in moving at such speed, with so little care and attention to the well-being of his animals, he ruined the very transport asset which was meant to convey his force to Khartoum.[63] He did not have enough camels to begin with and knew there were no more coming up the lines of communication.

At Abu Klea Stewart did not intentionally bypass the main enemy position as he claimed in his official despatch.[64] It was Burnaby who kept the square clear of the *khor*.[65] The use of skirmishers around the square was ordered by Stewart and was ill-advised. The skirmishers did not achieve anything that could not have been achieved by company volleys or independent fire directed from the sanctuary of the square.

Lord Charles Beresford has been unfairly blamed for the enemy breaking into the square. In fact it was Beresford who took it upon himself to sound the halt, who drew Stewart's attention to the disarray at the rear, and who set about putting things straight.[66] The Gardner was not outside the left-rear corner of the square as many secondary narratives have asserted, but not far from the centre of the left face,[67] only a matter of yards in front of the riflemen to its rear. The gun played no part in facilitating the enemy break-in, save in so far as it jammed at a particularly inopportune moment, something which it might have done at any point. Beresford did not break or meaningfully disrupt the British formation as has been suggested in some secondary accounts.[68]

It has always been portrayed that the square was broken into at its left-rear corner. Perceiving that this gap had in fact been created by the British themselves, I had for many years considered the assertion that the *anṣār* 'broke a British square' to be misleading. In the course of researching this book, however, it became clear that there was a second and slightly earlier penetration in the centre of the left face. This was brought about by direct shock action. Thus I conclude that the British square at Abu Klea was indeed broken. There are a number of reasons why this happened. First, Stewart's recourse to the use of skirmishers prevented the Heavies from developing their fire in the approved fashion. Second, there were too many camels in the centre of the square. This prevented the officers of the front-face companies from knowing whether the rear face was closed up or not. Third, the square was not halted on crossing a *khor*, resulting in the straggling rear face becoming detached from the other three sides. Then, just as the rear face was on the point of retrieving the situation, the officers of the front face advanced another thirty yards to improve their fields of fire. This disrupted the flanking faces and re-opened the gap at the rear.

All these things noted, the situation had again been retrieved, in the very nick of time, when the Heavies' feeble grasp on the infantry drill exerted a disastrous effect. As the enemy closed in, the cavalrymen in the left face not only failed to lock themselves in shoulder-to-shoulder, but began stepping backwards as they fired. This weakened the British line fatally, with the result that it was easily penetrated. Even worse, other members of the Heavies failed to take station in the rear face, but instead took it upon themselves to extend the left face. As we have seen, Lord Cochrane's account mentions the crass attitude of some of the cavalry officers to training for role.[69]

Although Fred Burnaby was not responsible for the ill-advised actions of members of the 1st Royal Dragoons, he did compound a gross tactical error by ordering at least one other half-company to conform to the movement. Whilst Burnaby is not directly or solely to blame for the fact that there was costly hand-to-hand fighting at Abu Klea, he did nothing to help the situation. In riding forward of the troops to fight at close quarters with his sword, he placed himself in acute danger and can be considered at that moment to have thrown up his rank and responsibilities. Gallant it may have been; the act of a professional officer it was not. It goes without saying that he died a hero's death but that is beside the point.

Sir Herbert Stewart's decision to march all night and keep pressing for the river in daylight exhausted his command and, even more crucially, meant that he had not secured his administrative echelon within a defended perimeter before the enemy closed in. As a result the advance of his fighting echelon was long delayed by the necessity to fortify the *zariba* under a heavy fire. This led to scores of unnecessary casualties. Sir Charles Wilson had attempted to forestall this unfortunate scenario by urging Stewart not to execute a night march in the first place, and later urging him to halt the march at a safe distance from Metemmeh.[70] In the former scenario the Battle of Metemmeh would have been fought on the morning of 20 January, to a deliberate battle plan prepared the previous afternoon and with the benefit of reconnaissance. In the latter scenario the Wilson plan would have seen a rested and revitalized British force fighting the Battle of Metemmeh at about 1.00 p.m. on the 19th, which is to say three hours before the real-world Battle of Abu Kru reached its climax. The costly delay prior to the advance at Abu Kru, laid by some of the Camel Corps bluebloods at Wilson's door, was not of his making but of General Stewart's.

Sir Charles Wilson was a surveyor by profession and had no command experience to draw upon. While he possessed many of the attributes of a good field soldier, not least courage, determination and intelligence, ultimately he was quite unqualified to command a field force. He was shrewd enough to know that this was so and at Abu Kru acted wisely in entrusting executive command of the fighting formation to Colonel Boscawen. During his short tenure in command he was also wise enough to consult with the other senior officers and with leading members of the staff. It is neither appropriate nor just that he be derided for 'command by committee', as suggested by Marling in *Rifleman and Hussar*.[71] While there was a future field marshal lurking in the background, there was nobody amongst the lieutenant colonels who leaps out of the historical record as an officer who would undoubtedly have done a better job. Indeed it is doubtful, when one delves into the detail, whether the job could actually have been done any better.

Wilson was right to terminate the 21 January assault on Metemmeh and focus instead on the arrival of Gordon's steamers. The badly mauled Desert Column could ill afford the potentially heavy casualties entailed in carrying a well-defended labyrinth of streets by storm. The lodgement on the Nile obviated the need to attack Metemmeh immediately. When Wilson took the decision to fall back on the camp it was because the steamer captains had sighted a powerful enemy force eighteen miles to the south, a development which manifestly posed a threat to the British rear.

The best available intelligence suggested that two enemy forces were converging on Gubat, one from Berber and one from Omdurman.[72] In addition there were still 2,000–3,000 enemy fighters in nearby Metemmeh. For the force commander to leave his command in so potentially dire a situation would have been quite wrong. Reconnaissance to confirm or disprove the near approach of the enemy was a militarily sound course of action. More than that, the failure to reconnoitre would have amounted to culpable negligence.

That Wilson and his party overcame all the obstacles posed by low-Nile and pressed within sight of Gordon's Palace in the face of an extremely heavy crossfire bespeaks great resolve, devotion to duty and valour. It is readily apparent that a number of VC citations could and should have followed the river dash and rescue. Such recommendations were in the gift of Lord Wolseley. None were awarded. Without the entirely contrived controversy, posterity would not have batted an eyelid if Sir Charles Wilson had been awarded the Victoria Cross.

Summary of Conclusions

Let us now, in concluding, condense these discussions into a few short paragraphs. Prime Minister Gladstone was to blame for the fact that the Army would have to race against the clock to save Khartoum and alone bears the responsibility for strategic failure. Lord Granville of course lurks in his shadow. Lord Hartington pressed the Prime Minister hard from the outset. Although he was the man who made the final decision to adopt the Nile route, in doing so he was merely endorsing the ardently proffered advice of the foremost military professional of the day. As a civilian minister he cannot be held unduly to blame for the fact that the 'best' military advice was deeply flawed. While no blame can be attached to Lord Hartington at the strategic level, the fact that he jumped in the wrong direction when confronted with conflicting military advice means that he cannot be regarded as entirely blameless at the operational level. Sir Evelyn Baring, Sir Frederick Stephenson and Sir Evelyn Wood, the men on the spot, did their duty faithfully and were in no sense responsible for the British failure.

When Khartoum fell the River Column was still approximately fifty-one days from Metemmeh, which is to say not less than sixty days from Khartoum. This means that even without making any allowance for enemy opposition at Abū-Hamed and Berber, the earliest date at which the re-unified Nile Expedition could have arrived at Khartoum was around 6/7 March. The truth is not that the Gordon Relief Expedition was two days too late, but that it was some sixty days too late.[73] If the troops, camels and stores required to mount an 1,800-man dash across the Bayūda had been moved upriver by *nuggar* while the Nile was still high, they could have been concentrated at Korti by mid-October. The whaler scheme served only to bring another 3,000 completely superfluous troops into terrain characterized by Wolseley himself as a 'howling wilderness'.

Crucially, the Desert Column was not engaged in a do-or-die attempt to save Khartoum when the city fell. Stewart's orders were to gain the river at Metemmeh, marry up with the steamers and despatch Sir Charles Wilson with a small escort of red-coated infantrymen to exchange situation reports with General Gordon. Wilson was under orders not to leave any troops in the city and was to return as rapidly as possible to report to Lord Wolseley at Korti.[74] In no sense was Wilson's 'river dash' meant to represent the relief of Khartoum.

Khartoum did not fall by treachery as was frequently asserted afterwards by Gladstone and Wolseley. It fell through an inevitably fatal combination of starvation and direct assault. It was the precedent established at El Obeid which determined the Mahdī's tactical approach to the siege. The final attack could have been mounted anything up to a fortnight earlier and would still have been made against an unhinged South Front and a garrison that was manifestly at the end of its tether.[75] It was never a question of two days here or there.

For Wolseley even to contemplate relieving Khartoum at any point between February and March 1885 was wholly unrealistic. In April 1884 he selected 15 November as his target date.[76] He should have stuck by this and, in August, have risen to the challenge, no matter how daunting such a timeline might have appeared. Having been forced to wait so long before he could finance any preparations, he should have resolved no longer to place all his eggs in the Nile basket, but rather immediately have adopted the Suakin–Berber axis instead. The river route was not merely time-consuming at the best of times, but was completely unworkable at low-Nile. It is remarkable that the Ring pushed so hard for the Nile route, when virtually nothing was known in Britain of the river's navigability between Berber and Korti. Montgomery's master principle of war, 'selection and maintenance of the aim', a precept every bit as valid in 1884 as 1944, would dictate that Wolseley should have launched a plan fit to bring a strong fighting force to bear on Khartoum by no later than mid-November. This he plainly failed to do. That he bullied Hartington and others into dismissing Suakin–Berber, subverting and dislodging the theatre commander in the process, does not rebound to his credit.

In addition to the fundamental misjudgement of proceeding with a Nile expedition so late in time and space, Wolseley made two other serious errors. First, he missed the optimal decision point to launch the Desert Column across the Bayūda by more than a month and even then failed to communicate his decision to his chief of staff for another week. Second, he over-reacted to the 31 December message, 'Do not leave Berber in your rear'. As a result he enacted measures which slowed the possibility of a dash to Khartoum by the Desert Column by something of the order of twenty-one days.

Wolseley's assertion that the blame for the fall of Khartoum could be attributed to decisions or actions taken at the tactical level is a manifest falsehood. The Vote of Credit came in August. There was no tactical level of operations prior to the New Year when Sir Herbert Stewart marched partway into the desert. His second march got under way on 8 January. By 20 January the Desert Column was no longer administratively capable of dashing to Khartoum, nor was it operationally capable of winning a final and decisive battle in the approach to Omdurman. The reasons for this flowed from conditions set at the operational level of command. The city fell on the night of 25/26 January. At no point during the long journey up the Nile had Wolseley ever counted on getting to Khartoum before 31 January. Even this date was untenable. He would not actually have been in a position to relieve Khartoum until early March, which is to say more than nine weeks after the food ran out and six weeks after the cats, rats and tree-gum ran out. The garrison had been physically and morally incapable of defending the city against direct assault since the second week of January. The assertion that Sir Charles Wilson had it in his power to save General Gordon is little short of risible. Wolseley behaved unreasonably and unprofessionally in casting spiteful and unwarranted slurs on Wilson's conduct.

Unfortunately the Nile Expedition was conceived not only as the means of General Gordon's salvation, but also as a crowning triumph to Lord Wolseley's career. It entailed a grandiose scheme to move a force of three brigades from Cairo to Khartoum and subsequently to Suakin. Wolseley's reluctance to see concurrent operations mounted in the Red Sea Littoral sprang from the fact that he intended to add to the lustre of saving Gordon by defeating Osman Digna and the eastern rebels on the way home. It was a good plan in April but an untenable one by August. If at that point he had executed his scheme of manoeuvre in reverse, it might just have worked. In the event the greater part of his deployed force was never brought to bear and he failed to attain any of his objectives. If the Nile Expedition proved nothing else, it was that in later life Wolseley had allowed his vanity and self-obsession to run out of control. The cruel irony of his last campaign was that in attempting to prove that he was to be counted amongst the 'great captains' of the nineteenth century, he laid out a testing course, only to then fail to compete it.

For all that the Gordon Relief Expedition was characterized by a small number of fundamental and irrecoverable errors of judgement on the part of the army commander (as well as by the incredible courage and determination of the men at the sharp end of the proceedings – British, Egyptian, loyalist Sudanese and Mahdīst Sudanese alike), it is only fair to reflect by way of a closing thought that what Wolseley was up against, ultimately, was the Sudan itself: and 'When God made the Sudan,' as the saying goes, 'he laughed.' Perhaps, faced with the same set of conundrums, Moltke, Lee, and Grant might also have struggled.

Epilogue

I never could understand the Nile campaign.

A. B. Wylde, *'83 to '87 in the Soudan*

'BLOODY-MINDED' PIGOTT ARRIVED at Korti bearing the news of Abu Kru and the fall of Sir Herbert Stewart at 3.30 in the morning of Wednesday 28 January, by which time Lord Wolseley was already propped up in bed reading the Psalms by candle-light.[1] Over the course of the next few hours Pigott poured scorn on Sir Charles Wilson's performance as the stand-in brigadier, an interpretation of recent events which Wolseley was only too ready to take at face value. It is ironic that, even as this conversation was taking place, Wilson was performing deeds of derring-do on the stretch of river between Tuti Island and Omdurman.

Wolseley's immediate response to the developments on the far side of the Bayūda was to appoint Sir Redvers Buller as the new commander of the Desert Column, and to designate Sir Evelyn Wood his new chief of staff. Before the day was out, Lieutenant Colonel Hugh Shaw VC had marched for the front with three companies of 1st Royal Irish. The rest of the battalion followed two evenings later under Shaw's second-in-command, Lieutenant Colonel Thomas Wray. General Buller, Major Kitchener and Lord Freddie Fitzgerald, Buller's ADC, set out on the 29th, the day in between the two detachments, and in due course overtook the leading half-battalion on the road. Buller had in his pocket a set of written orders from the C-in-C which began, 'Above all else don't get wounded. I can't afford to lose you.' The essence of his instructions was that he should 'clear the enemy out of the Metemmeh neighbourhood'. He could also attack Shendy, provided that he felt able to take it without significant loss. He was also told to husband his artillery ammunition; to be gentle with the Hassaniyeh tribe; to gather in as much *dhura* and grain as possible; and to ensure that Sir Charles Wilson came back to Korti to make his report, immediately he returned from his meeting with Gordon. The closing paragraph instructed Buller to, 'Keep me constantly informed of all you do and intend doing, and of all news from Khartoum and of the enemy.'[2] Hastening to the rescue of General Gordon did not so much as warrant a mention.

First Royal Irish marched mostly by night, accompanied by sufficient baggage camels for each man to be issued a gallon of water a day, a model which Wolseley might have done well to experiment with earlier. Colonel Shaw's shortest march was the first night out from Korti, during the course of which he asked only ten miles of his men. His longest was on the fourth night, during which the battalion made a commendable seventeen miles.[3] Sir Redvers and his party rode into Jakdul Wells, well ahead of the marching infantry, on the evening of Monday 2 February. The following day Lord Cochrane came in with despatches from Gubat and the unwelcome news that Khartoum was in the hands of the Mahdī.[4] Buller greeted him at the door of his tent and served the weary Household Cavalryman with a whisky and water, before sitting down to listen to the latest news from the Desert Column. Later in the day somebody handed Cochrane a letter addressed to the Earl of Dundonald – an ancient title dating to the seventeenth century – which contained the sad news that his father had died some weeks earlier and that he, Cochrane no longer, had succeeded as the 12th Earl. Before the day was out the new Lord Dundonald had been pronounced by the doctors to be heading for a fever.

Colonel Shaw and his battalion arrived at Jakdul Wells, ninety-eight miles into the Bayūda, without the loss of a single man, on Wednesday 4 February; the same day that Sir Charles Wilson and Lord Charles Beresford steamed back into Gubat aboard *Sāfia*. It was just as Wolseley was about to go into dinner with his staff that evening that the shocking news from Khartoum reached Korti.[5] Thinking through its implications, the C-in-C felt sure that the government would immediately order him to abandon the campaign and fall back into Egypt. He had, however, made insufficient allowance for the storm of public indignation that was about to break over Preme Minister Gladstone's head.

Sir Charles Wilson departed Gubat for Korti at 1.30 in the morning of Friday 6 February. He reached Jakdul Wells late on Saturday afternoon, to find that Buller and Kitchener had been in residence since Monday evening and had been aware of the fall of Khartoum since Tuesday. Also present was Colonel Reggie Talbot and a six-company convoy escort from the Camel Corps. During the course of the day Wilson had learned that he and his party had somehow crossed with 1st Royal Irish without ever clapping eyes on the battalion. It came as a relief to learn that the newly elevated Earl of Dundonald, who had earned something of a reputation as a desert navigator, was guiding Colonel Shaw and his men across the fifty-one miles to Abu Klea, in order that they would not have to march a single mile more than was strictly necessary. When, two days later, Dundonald's camel began lowering itself onto its haunches at Abu Klea, he was so weak with fever that he was unable to muster the strength to prevent himself being pitched over the animal's head. For the 12th Earl of Dundonald, the Nile Campaign had run its course.

On the morning of Sunday 8 February, Buller and Kitchener left for Abu Klea with Talbot's convoy, while Sir Charles Wilson set off in the opposite direction for Korti. He would arrive at Wolseley's headquarters on the evening of the 9th, having covered 174 miles in four days.[6] A letter from Wolseley, dated 5 February, caught up with Buller at Abu Klea on the 10th. It covered the anticipated lily-livered response of the government and included the news that the Light Camel Regiment had been despatched from Korti for the front; that General Earle had been told to halt the River Column where it was; and that no more supplies would be sent into the Bayūda. The most important injunction was that Buller should get all the wounded away from Gubat immediately and make all necessary preparations to retreat across the Bayūda. The worst possible thing that could happen now, Wolseley concluded, was for the force at Gubat to get itself besieged. Buller was not to hesitate to retreat to Jakdul, on his own responsibility, if communications with Korti were lost.[7] That part of Wolseley's letter dealing with HMG's likely response to the fall of Khartoum had in fact been obsolete for three days by the time Buller got to read it. On the evening of 7 February, Wolseley had been astonished to receive a telegram from Hartington which commenced:

Your military policy is to be based on the necessity, which we recognize on the state of the facts now before us, that the power of the Mahdi at Khartum must be overthrown. We leave it to you to decide the military measures best calculated to attain this object, and whether advance should be made this season or next. On this statement of our policy tell us at once what additional force you desire and when and where to be sent; also whether, on the plan you adopt under your instructions, you wish immediate despatch of force to attack Osman Digna.[8]

On the basis of the government's suddenly robust direction Wolseley decided to secure Berber, prior to entering an operational pause over the hot season. The breathing space would allow him to re-balance his force and move up re-inforcements and supplies, in preparation for mounting a powerful thrust through to Khartoum in the autumn. In the meantime a separate expedition would be mounted from Suakin, with the object of crushing Osman Digna and the rebellious Bīja tribes. He advised Hartington that the command in the Red Sea Littoral should go to Major General Sir George Greaves KCMG, who would have to be elevated to local lieutenant general.[9] Granting local rank to Wolseley's favourites was not a game the Duke of Cambridge was prepared to play, as a result of which he was forced into a swift re-think. His revised recommendation was that the command should go to the now Lieutenant General Sir Gerald Graham, with Sir George Greaves as chief of staff.[10] This was much a more amenable arrangement as far as the Duke was concerned and was duly enacted.

The orders to halt the River Column's advance on Abū-Hamed, pending the arrival of new political direction from London, reached Major General Earle on 5 February. Within hours of Hartington's no-holds-barred telegram of 7 February arriving at Korti, Earle received fresh instructions to press on upriver. The following morning 1st South Staffords and 1st Black Watch filed back into the whalers. Echeloned some way behind them were 2nd DCLI and 1st Gordons. The cavalry screen ashore was under the command of Colonel William Butler and consisted of a weak squadron of the 19th Hussars and a fifty-strong Egyptian Camel Corps. By sunset Butler had located and probed a strong enemy blocking position around a commanding high feature known as Jabal Kirbikān. The following day Earle moved his leading battalions to a bivouac within a mile of the rebels and went forward with the newly elevated Brigadier General Brackenbury to settle a plan of attack. At length Butler came riding in to report that he had identified an excellent right-flanking approach through dead ground, which would bring the assaulting troops to the right-rear of the lofty *jabal* and avoid any necessity for a potentially costly frontal attack. The enemy position was occupied by some 1,500 Robatab, Manāsir and Berberine *anṣār* under the overall command of the Amīr 'Abd-al-Mājid Nasr al-Din abū' l-Kailak, who it will be recalled had earlier led the Berber contingent at Abu Klea and been wounded in the arm.

On the morning of 10 February Butler's plan for the approach march was put into effect. Earle had ordered the assaulting infantry, six companies each of Lieutenant Colonel Philip Eyre's 1st South Staffords[11] and Lieutenant Colonel William Green's 1st Black Watch, into their red home-service frocks for the occasion. The highlanders also discarded the ragged trews they customarily wore in the whalers, in favour of a near full-dress rig of kilts, sporrans, white canvas gaiters and tartan hosetops. The approach march was the brilliant success Butler had planned for, though there was heavy fighting across the high ground subsequently, in which Eyre and Lieutenant Colonel Robert Coveny (one of the wing commanders in the Black Watch) both lost their lives. The *anṣār* were cleared from the position with a fatal loss of about 200 men. British casualties amounted to three officers and seven NCOs and men killed and four officers and thirty-eight NCOs and men wounded. Tragically, the third of the dead officers was none other than General Earle who, with his battle won, was unable to resist taking far too close an interest as the highlanders cleared a last few *anṣār* diehards from a stone-built hut. Despite being warned by a Black Watch sergeant not to come too close, and a subsequent apprehensive cry from Brackenbury to, 'Take care sir! The hut is full of men!' the general wandered within ten yards of a high window and was promptly shot in the head. He died within minutes. Never has the life of a British general officer been quite so needlessly lost.[12]

On Wednesday 11 February a tired and dejected Sir Charles Wilson was shown a telegram from the Secretary of State for War which instructed Lord Wolseley to, 'Express warm recognition of Government of brilliant services of Sir C. Wilson, and satisfaction at rescue of his party.'[13] Later the same day Buller marched into the River Fort at Gubat at the head of six companies of 1st Royal Irish (fifteen officers and 468 NCOs and men),[14] and Reggie Talbot's half-dozen Camel Corps companies. The arrival of a renowned fighting general did much to revitalize the flagging morale of the force. Buller brought with him the news that Her Majesty had been graciously pleased to approve Sir Herbert Stewart's immediate promotion to the rank of major general.[15] Kitchener set up camp with Verner and confided that the failure to capture Metemmeh had attracted a great deal of criticism amongst the headquarters staff. Buller, he added, was determined to storm the town without delay. Of course Kitchener was reflecting what had been said at Korti after Pigott had given vent to his no doubt stridently expressed opinions.

The following morning Buller sent for Verner and questioned him closely about the garrison and defences of Metemmeh. Verner recorded in his diary that, 'He appeared to think it would be a very ordinary affair to capture the place. Of this I have my own opinion but did not give it as I was not asked.'[16] Before the day was out the new GOC had acquired a much better understanding of the situation. Probably the most telling conversation he had was with Charlie Beresford, whom Buller both liked and admired. Beresford recorded the gist of the conversation in his memoirs: 'At his request I stated to him my view of the situation; which was, briefly, that unless we departed swiftly, we should be eaten up by the enemy, who were known to be advancing in immense force. I also reported officially that until the Nile rose, the two steamers remaining to us were practically useless.'[17] This latter remark referred to the fact that for the next few months the boats would be unable to proceed more than about twenty-five miles north of Metemmeh due to the state of the river.

Logistic factors were a particular cause for concern and made nonsense of any notion that the force had an option to stay where it was. With only twelve days' supply in hand at Gubat, twelve days' more at Abu Klea and no resupply coming up the lines of communication, Buller concluded that he had no choice but to give up all thought of attacking Metemmeh and immediately fall back on Abu Klea. He was confirmed in his decision by newly arrived intelligence to the effect that two days earlier the Mahdī had left Khartoum at the head of his main host and was even now marching for Metemmeh.[18] Buller lost no time in giving orders for a withdrawal, to commence first thing the following morning, Friday 13 February, with the evacuation of the sick, the wounded and the 300 Egyptian 'hens' and noncombatants taken off the steamers in advance of the river dash. There were seventy-five sick and wounded in all, made up of nine officers, sixty-one NCOs and men and five native workers.[19] The most seriously injured casualties, Major General Sir Herbert Stewart amongst them, would be carried by Egyptian stretcher parties in order to avoid their being jolted about on bearer-company litters. The escort would consist of a hundred men from each of the three camel regiments, with the hard-riding Reggie Talbot once again in command. Talbot was to parade his men at 5.45 on Thursday evening, bivouac just to the west of the Guards Fort and be ready to start from 4.00 a.m.

The numbers actually turned out by the camel regiments were six officers and 123 NCOs and men from the Heavies; three officers and 101 NCOs and men from the Guards; and seven officers and 100 NCOs and men from the Mounted Infantry. The GCR contingent, we know, was drawn from Nos. 2 and 4 Companies and was commanded by Captain Aylmer Pearson RMLI. The mainstay of the MICR contingent may have been found by the regiment's A Company, as the War Diary indicates that Lieutenant Bobby Bower was present. Additionally, the 19th Hussars provided an NCO's detail of five to act as Talbot's eyes and ears, there were three doctors, thirty-two medics and thirty-nine native drivers to take care of the wounded, and one officer and seven NCOs and men from the Commissariat &

Transport Corps to marshal the transport. Not including the hospital patients, the Egyptians or the native drivers, Talbot would have twenty officers and 368 NCOs and men available to him. Altogether there were probably something around 800 human souls and 732 camels in the convoy.[20]

In the event Talbot was not able to get away until 6.45 a.m.[21] The detail of hussars led the way, with a section- or possibly half-company-strength advanced guard of Coldstream Guardsmen under the command of Douglas Dawson not far behind them. Next came Captain Pearson and the main GCR contingent, comprised mostly of RMLI men. After that came the company of Heavies, followed by the convoy itself – an unruly procession of Egyptian stretcher parties, medics, drivers and baggage camels. The MICR company brought up the rear. Talbot made reasonable enough progress over the course of the morning, but after covering about eight miles halted the convoy for breakfast. It was not yet clear of the Shebacat bush. Douglas Dawson caught sight of General Stewart at one point and thought that he looked, 'dreadfully changed, but still able to recognise those around him'.[22] The convoy had been halted for some little while and was beginning to re-form in preparation for resuming the march, when all of a sudden one of the hussars came galloping in to report to Lieutenant Dawson that the bush ahead was alive with enemy cavalry. It was probably about 11.15 a.m. at this point. Dawson went forward to reconnoitre and sighted not only horsemen and spearmen, but donkeys too. He rode back in to report to Reggie Talbot, convinced in his own mind that they had bumped into an enemy convoy.

The colonel decided to throw the GCR company into an attack, while the Heavies and Mounted Infantry remained on the defensive to protect the convoy. After advancing 200 yards on its camels, Pearson's company came under a brisk fire and was obliged to dismount and form square. The bush was so thick that the soldiers could obtain only fleeting glimpses of the *anṣār* and were only able to return fire in the general direction of their rifle-smoke. If nothing else it was obvious that there were plenty of them and that the fight must soon spread to envelop the rest of the convoy. Amongst the wounded were the two engine-room artificers who had been so badly scalded aboard *Ṣāfia*, one of whom later told Beresford that, 'That was the first time my heart sank – when the bearers put down my litter, and the firing began.'[23] The baggage camels were rushed forward, arrayed around the outside of the wounded and lowered onto their haunches as a living barricade. While the Egyptians formed skirmish lines in front of the camels, the Heavies and Mounted Infantry shuffled into company squares to the front-right and left-rear of the position respectively.

It was not long before the main body had been pretty much surrounded on all sides. Concerned that Pearson's company was out on a limb and might be cut off, Talbot sent a messenger with instructions for it to fall back on the main body immediately. Pearson and Dawson worried that it would be wrong not to comply promptly, but realized that to do so would necessarily entail the abandonment of the company's camels. Sensibly they took the time to organize a scheme of withdrawal in which strings of half-a-dozen camels would be led to the rear by one of the men, while everybody else maintained a bold front to hold the enemy in check. An added complication was that there were already a number of wounded guardsmen and marines who would need to be carried to the rear. After what Dawson estimated as about fifteen minutes, the company was ready to make its move. The *anṣār* 'were now so close in the dense bush that it was necessary when retiring to halt, front, and fire a few volleys every few paces to prevent being rushed in the back'. Dawson was already helping one wounded guardsman along, when another man fell at his feet. As he stopped to help he saw smoke rising from a bullet-hole in the man's back. 'From so close a range had the shot been fired that I found his coat and hair on fire . . . but he died nearly directly.'

After a difficult few minutes, Pearson's men were able to form a merged square of something around 230 bayonets in concert with the Heavies. They volleyed into the scrub, all the time 'expecting to be charged, for their howls and signals for collecting for the charge could be heard on all sides'. Dawson felt that, 'It was the nastiest business in many ways that we had seen, for we were unable to act on the offensive for fear that if any of our small force left the convoy the niggers [*sic*] would charge down on our helpless wounded and spear every one of them.' As fraught an affair as it undoubtedly was, it is doubtful whether any of the Heavies would have acknowledged it as their worst experience of the campaign.

The fight lasted for about two hours in all and was brought to an end when Lieutenant Colonel John Brabazon came up with the leading company of the Light Camel Regiment. The panicked enemy broke off the engagement almost immediately, though for a few minutes Talbot and his men remained oblivious to their departure. Peering through a gap in the bush, Douglas Dawson glimpsed some suspicious movement about 700 yards away and called for a volley from his face of the square. He had already brought his men up into the aim with the word of command 'Present!', when on looking through his field glasses he discerned red saddlecloths and the distinctive profile of the foreign-service helmet. Under the old firing drill the men would by now have been counting a 'regulation pause' of two seconds before pulling the trigger. Fortunately the latest firing drill required the executive 'Fire!' to be given, allowing Dawson to avert a friendly-fire incident with, 'Come down! They are our fellows!'[24] Even so, one of the faces of the other square did loose a couple of volleys at Brabazon and his men before the MICR officers realized their mistake. Thankfully neither salvo did any harm.[25] The *Official History* states that the British loss in the engagement was two men killed and six men wounded. According to Willoughby Verner's *Diary*, however, the Heavies had 3 men killed and 8 wounded, the Guards 2 men killed and 4 men wounded, and the Egyptians 2 men killed – a total of 7 dead and 14 wounded in all.[26]

Two of the hussars who had gone out with the convoy came galloping into Gubat at about 2.00 p.m. to raise the alarm. Four companies of the Royal Irish and as many of the 19th Hussars whose ponies were up to it were quickly called to arms and despatched to assist the convoy. About two and a half hours later, a trio of riders, including Bobby Bower, arrived to report that the enemy had been driven off and that LCR had turned back to see the convoy safely in to Abu Klea.[27] Once the drama in the Shebacat bush had run its course, Colonels Clarke and Talbot marched their merged command two and half hours in the direction of Abu Klea, before halting for the night.

Back at the river, Buller's instructions for the next phase of the withdrawal were in circulation by mid-afternoon. The work of destroying anything which might be of use to the enemy, including surplus rations and the two remaining steamers, was to begin immediately in preparation for a 5.00 a.m. departure the following morning. It was not long before there were a number of raging bonfires burning. Beresford, meanwhile, had the six brass guns aboard the steamers spiked and thrown into the Nile. Below decks his artificers set about sabotaging the machinery in the engine rooms. At length the valves were opened and *Sāfia* and *Tawfīqiyeh* began gently lowering their keels onto the riverbed.[28]

The Royal Irish had marched about four miles into the desert by the time they learned that the convoy was safe and their services were no longer required. They returned to camp just as it was getting dark.[29] By then a surfeit of luxuries had been distributed around the troops including jam, marmalade, cocoa and milk. The balance of the unwanted rations had been loaded into boats and with the onset of darkness was rowed into midstream to be jettisoned in deep water. Gleichen reported that 19,000 lb of flour, 3,000 lb of biscuit, 21,220 lb of bully beef, 900 lb of bacon, 1,100 lb of tea and smaller quantities of oatmeal, preserved vegetables and coffee went into the river. It was doubly galling that the troops had subsisted on short commons for the past ten days.[30]

A new set of orders from the C-in-C had come up with LCR, which Buller got around to reading during the course of the evening. They were predicated on the new governmental declaration of intent and Wolseley's latest revision of his campaign plan. Buller's instructions required him to storm Metemmeh without delay, before then advancing northwards to cooperate with the River Column in a pincer movement against Berber. Unfortunately the orders were not grounded in reality. Nearby Metemmeh was well defended and unlikely to be a walkover. More fighting meant more casualties, whose evacuation would consume more precious transport assets. Buller had neither the supplies nor the camels to move his force a hundred miles to the north and, even if he had, such a manoeuvre would entail turning the rear of his command to the approaching enemy. It was already too late for the steamers. The greatest problem by far, though, was the growing threat to the British lines of communication. If a powerful Mahdist force was able to interpose itself between Gubat and Abu Klea, or even if the enemy commenced raiding vigorously into the desert, as Talbot's fight in the Shebacat bush suggested might now be likely, the Desert Column would very quickly require a relief expedition of its own. There were simply not the supplies for Buller's force to sustain itself at the River Fort for any length of time, nor anything like enough troops or transport at Korti to march to his relief. In the meantime the initiative was bound to rest with a much more mobile enemy.

In short the orders were not worth the paper they were written on and exerted no effect on Buller's settled resolve to get out of Gubat while he still could. He sat down and wrote to Wolseley to explain why in his view it was vitally necessary to retreat as least as far as Abu Klea forthwith. He left open the option of striking against Berber from Abu Klea, but cognizant of the state of his transport must have known that this would never come to pass. Over the next few days, there would be several more communications from Wolseley, all of which were at least one step behind the latest operational reality.

At 3.30 a.m. on Saturday 14 February the officers and men of the Desert Column were roused from their slumbers in preparation for the retreat. Willoughby Verner had once again been put in charge of navigation and led the British force back into the Bayūda at about 6.30 a.m. There were about 1,700 officers and men strung out behind him. With the exception of the 19th Hussars and the headquarters staff, everybody else was afoot, with one riding camel allowed to every four men for the carriage of their personal kit. Charlie Beresford recalled that very few soldiers still had a completely sound pair of boots and that many of his sailors marched barefoot. Lieutenant Gleichen had again drawn the short straw as GCR's baggage master, but consoled himself with the thought that it was a 'lovely morning' and 'first-rate weather for marching'.[31] Colonel Hugh Shaw had command of the rearguard, which consisted of 1st Royal Irish, a small party of hussars, two Royal Artillery 7-pounders and the 200 or so Sudanese troops from the steamers.[32]

After about an hour and a half on the march, Verner sighted a tell-tale cluster of scavenging birds and realized he was approaching the site of the 19 January *zariba* fight. The ground was 'thickly covered with dead camels' on which dozens of vultures were gorging themselves. He checked the place where Herbert and Cameron had been buried and was relieved to find that while the ground had been disturbed, the bodies had not. The stench from decomposing camels and horses was so bad that he felt no inclination to linger. By noon the column had covered about twelve miles and was roughly half-way to Abu Klea, at which point Buller gave orders to bivouac for the night.[33] The Clarke/Talbot column had reached Abu Klea about half an hour earlier. While LCR would remain *in situ* to marry up with Buller's force, Talbot would march his convoy for Jakdul Wells first thing the following morning.

After a lazy afternoon and a good night's rest, Buller started the main body at 5.30 a.m. and made it into Abu Klea at some point between 11.00 a.m. and noon, by which time Reggie Talbot had been on the road for some hours. Apart from a small party of horsemen who had tailed the retreat from a distance, the enemy had otherwise failed to put in an appearance. It was obvious to Buller that the wells at Abu Klea would be incapable of servicing the needs of so many men and animals for any length of time. More pressingly there was nothing with which to feed the camels and ponies and hence no option but to move them on as soon as possible.

The following day, Monday 16 February, Buller despatched a sizeable proportion of his force for Jakdul Wells, under the command of Percy Barrow. The 8.00 a.m. departures included the 19th Hussars, the remaining companies of HCR and GCR, the Commissariat & Transport Corps companies and the majority of the camels. A remarkable ninety-two animals died during the course of the day's march.[34]

Left behind at Abu Klea as the rearguard was MICR (minus the 100 men moving with Talbot), 1st Royal Irish, all four companies of 1st Royal Sussex, the artillery, the Naval Brigade with its brace of Gardners and LCR, the only Camel Corps regiment still functioning as a mounted unit. Finally, there was also a tiny detail of hussars consisting of Major John French, one NCO, six privates and eight ponies.[35] Verner asked Buller's permission to go and map the Abu Klea battlefield and was duly sent up the valley with one of the two remaining LCR companies, under Major Charles Beckett, acting as his escort. The rest of the rearguard busied itself with the construction of three mutually supporting biscuit-box forts. The nearby battlefield was still strewn with hundreds of decomposing Mahdist dead and was so poisonous that it made Verner 'uncommonly sick'. Nonetheless he made, 'a five foot contoured sketch of the field at a scale of 24 ins. to a mile'. He also had time to complete a pencil sketch of the stone cairn erected over Burnaby's grave by the Heavies.[36]

At about 4.30 p.m. Verner and Beckett were on their way back to the wells, when a heavy outbreak of firing gave notice that the enemy were approaching in force from the south. Beckett was able to hurry his company into the perimeter without any undue difficulty. There was enough high ground north and south of the wells for several hundred riflemen to take up commanding vantage points and subject the British positions to the usual galling long-range fire. Verner judged that the ensuing fire-fight was conducted over typical ranges of about 1,200 yards. It made sense at such extreme range for the Naval Brigade Gardners to lead the British response. Verner ran to gather in his kit from the overly exposed spot in which he and Kitchener had established their bivouac. As he did so he crossed with Captain Henry Walsh, the company commander of B Company, MICR, who Verner thought was walking rather strangely. He failed to realize until later that Walsh had taken a bullet through one of his lungs. The incoming fire slackened as the sun went down, but was afterwards resumed and maintained for much of the night. Mercifully, although the enemy's direction was good, their elevation was more often than not high. The Royal Irish, though, found themselves in an awkward spot on high ground and had one man killed and sixteen wounded during the course of the night.

It was just as the fighting was getting under way at Abu Klea that Reggie Talbot brought his convoy to a halt, seven miles north of the Jabal El Nus, and bivouacked for the night. Later that evening, after a month-long fight for life, the gallant General Stewart finally succumbed to his wounds. The following morning, Tuesday 17 February, Percy Barrow's column ran into Lieutenant Colonel Hugh McCalmont, who was riding despatches from Wolseley to Buller, escorted only by his batman and one of his sergeants. McCalmont broke the news of Stewart's demise and went on to talk of Kirbekan, the deaths of Earle, Eyre and Coveny, and of the fact that a second Suakin campaign was in the offing. General Stewart was held in such high esteem by the 19th Hussars that Barrow now made a forced march in an attempt to reach Jakdul Wells in time for his funeral.[37]

In the meantime the fighting had resumed at Abu Klea. At the beginning of the day Beresford's Gardners again did good work in suppressing the enemy's fire, although the limited amount of ammunition available prevented their being employed to their full potential. At 9.00 a.m. Buller sent Lieutenant Colonel John Brabazon on his way with a 100-strong company of LCR and 150 of the remaining 350 camels.[38] Around mid-morning Major Frederick Wardrop pulled off a brave and cunning ruse. Having taken out a small reconnaissance patrol consisting of Lieutenant Robert Tudway of B Company, MICR, and three private soldiers, Wardrop infiltrated his party onto the enemy's right flank and eventually came up behind a party of about thirty *anṣār* riflemen firing from rifle pits. By dashing back and forth, firing from a number of different positions as they went, they succeeded in creating the illusion that a new British force had come up, with the result that the *anṣār* bolted.[39] By about 1.00 p.m. the fight had temporarily tailed away. An hour later McCalmont rode in with his despatches. During the middle of the afternoon the enemy brought up a gun and opened fire from a range of about 2,000 yards. The piece fired three shots, none of which did any harm, before counter-battery fire from Major Hunter's 7-pounders silenced it. By late afternoon the enemy had broken off the action and withdrawn. The two-day skirmish had cost the British three men killed and four officers and twenty-three NCOs and men wounded.[40]

Reggie Talbot and his men rode into Jakdul at 3.00 p.m. that afternoon. No time was lost in preparing for the late GOC's funeral. Sir Herbert Stewart's mortal remains were borne to their final resting place by officers of the Camel Corps, with a crowd of several hundred soldiers in attendance at the graveside. Sadly the 19th Hussars rode in just too late to participate in the service.

Sir Evelyn Wood arrived at Jakdul the following day with four companies of the 1st Royal West Kents. Wolseley's latest idea called for Buller to march the Desert Column back across the desert to Merowe, while Wood supervised the evacuation of Jakdul Wells and all the other outposts on the Bayūda lines of communication. In the absence of both Wood and Buller, Colonel G. B. Wolseley, the C-in-C's younger brother, would stand in at Korti as the acting chief of staff. In the meantime a hard-riding Major Wardrop had left Abu Klea with a list of requirements which Buller wanted addressed if he was to march anywhere. Wardrop arrived with Wood to learn that Merowe was to be the destination.

The immediate problem, though, was to get Buller's force safely back to Jakdul Wells. Wardrop spent the next two days organizing administrative way-stations on the line of retreat. At the first he stockpiled 10,000 lb of *dhura* and 1,200 gallons of water. At the second, located only eight miles north of Abu Klea,[41] he positioned 15,000 lb of *dhura* and 2,500 gallons of water. Finally it was arranged that Colonel Brabazon would return to Abu Klea with as many camels as possible.

Sir Evelyn Wood busied himself with putting Wolseley's out-of-touch headquarters in the picture. In a memo dated 20 February he wrote,

It is desirable that it should be distinctly understood that in my opinion it is impossible for General Buller to march to Merowi, unless he gets the fresh camels mentioned in my letter of yesterday... I do not think the debilitated state of our transport is realised at Korti. The Heavy Camel Regiment now has 22 riding and 10 baggage-camels only. The Guards have 228, but they are in a wretched state.[42]

Fortunately the penny had at last dropped, not least because the operations of the River Column were also beginning to fall apart. Brackenbury had reported that a third of the biscuit aboard the whalers had spoiled and that he expected to make only slow progress around the Great Bend – so slow that he could not guarantee that there would be sufficient rations left to sustain a garrison at Berber. Concurrent communications from Buller and Wood about the state of the transport and the troops' boots made it clear that the Desert Column was administratively finished. Unless Buller got out of Abu Klea soon there was every danger that his command would be trapped and annihilated. On 20 February Wolseley's headquarters disseminated new orders which called for the River Column to put about and the Desert Column to extricate itself from the Bayūda and fall back on Korti. Wolseley's only object now was to break contact and reconstitute his forces in safe locations.

The energetic Wardrop got back to Abu Klea on Saturday 21 February, while Brabazon rode in the following day with a convoy of 9 officers, 104 NCOs and men, 220 native drivers and 782 camels.[43] Buller intended sending out all the casualties from the recent engagement on Monday, and to pull out the remainder of his force on Tuesday. The situation underwent a significant change at 11.00 a.m. on Monday when Captain William Morgan, commanding the Royal Irish picket on the high ground to the south of the wells, reported that there was a strong Mahdīst force approaching from the direction of Metemmeh. Verner permitted himself to be secretly pleased, as for some days past he had been predicting a powerful attack and had been baited by some of his brother officers over the enemy's non-appearance.[44]

Sir Redvers rode out with a party of other officers to take a closer look. There was indeed a very large force prowling across the desert. Somebody timed it moving across a gap and noted the pass-time as twenty minutes. The *anṣār* were observed to be marching roughly ten men abreast. Allowing two yards between ranks and a rate of advance of 3 mph, the calculation showed that there were around 8,000 men present. At length they moved into a *khor* and disappeared amidst the mimosa.[45]

At 2.00 p.m. Colonels Clarke and Brabazon were sent away with the wounded: the escort comprised all the LCR companies, two companies of 1st Royal Sussex and three of the 7-pounders.[46] Kitchener and Verner sought leave to sabotage the wells, so that the enemy would have difficulty following up across the waterless fifty-mile tract to the north. While poisoning the wells would certainly be an infringement of the 'rules of war', sabotaging them was a less clear-cut issue. Even so Buller hesitated to agree the measure. Wardrop pressed him on the matter, until at last he gave in and consented to the largest of the wells being filled in.

Wardrop, Kitchener and Verner each took a work party, went to look for a big well, and then each choked the largest they could find with camel saddles and sand. Once they had done for the first three, they checked the general was looking the other way and then each ruined the next largest they could find, and so on, until there were virtually no wells left which had not in some way been tampered with. As soon as darkness fell, the camp fires were stoked up. Next the units proceeded silently to abandon their positions and form up in column of route along the floor of the sandy *khor*. Amongst the last men away from the position were the buglers, who sounded the usual close of day calls before falling in with their regiments. By 9.00 that evening the Nile Expedition had broken contact with the enemy on all fronts. The Pendjeh Incident – or was it perhaps the projected cost to the Exchequer of a renewed bout of hostilities – would bring an end to the idea of an autumn campaign soon enough.

As the head of the column picked its way over the divide, to leave the 'Valley of the Shadow' behind, a senior officer was heard to say, 'We are damned well out of that.' There was no pursuit.

Appendix A

Composition of the Nile Expedition

River Column *Maj. Gen. William Earle* CB, CSI
  HQ Staff
  19th Hussars (1 squadron) — *Maj. J. C. H. Flood* — [91]
  2nd Bn., Duke of Cornwall's Light Infantry — *Col. W. S. Richardson* — [550]
  1st Bn., Black Watch (Royal Highlanders) — *Lt. Col. W. Green* CB — [550]
  1st Bn., South Staffordshire Regiment — *Lt. Col. P. H. Eyre* — [545]
  1st Bn., Gordon Highlanders — *Col. D. Hammill* CB — [550]
  26th Field Coy., RE (detachment) — *Capt. J. E. Blackburn* — [1 & 21]
  Egyptian Artillery Battery (camel-borne) — [120]
  Egyptian Camel Corps — *Maj. R. E. Marriott* — [90]
  Naval Detachment — [1 & 11]
  Field Hospital (dispersed 2 sects. per bn.)
  Medical Staff Corps
  11th Transport Company (elements) — *Capt. Lea* — [330 camels, 150 camel drivers]

Mudir of Dongola's 'Army' *Vakeel Jawdat Bey & Lt. Col. H. E. Colvile*
  Sudanese infantry — [350]
  1 brass mountain gun — *Maj. Aḥmad Sulaimān Effendi*
  Transport — [200 donkeys and 30 camels]

Total strength: British 2,500; Egyptians 210; Sudanese 350; Civilians 200

Desert Column* *Brig. Gen. Sir Herbert Stewart* KCB, ADC
  HQ Staff — [10 & 6, with 13 native workers]
  19th Hussars (2 squadrons) — *Lt. Col. P. H. S. Barrow* CB, CMG
    [8 & 127, 19 natives, 155 ponies, 73 camels]
  Heavy Camel Regiment — *Lt. Col. Hon. R. A. J. Talbot*
    [24 & 376, 5 natives, 420 camels]
  Guards Camel Regiment — *Lt. Col. Hon. E. E. T. Boscawen*
    [19 & 365, 4 natives, 406 camels]
  Mounted Infantry Camel Regiment — *Maj. Hon. G. H. Gough*
    [24 & 359, 4 natives, 424 camels]

* *The Desert Column is shown configured as it was on departure from Jakdul Wells.*

1st Bn., Royal Sussex Regiment	Maj. M. S. J. Sunderland	
		[4 coys. – 8 & 250, 4 natives]
1st Battery/1st Bde., Southern Div., RA	Capt. G. F. A. Norton	
	[½ battery, 3 x 7-pdr., 4 & 39 British, 1 & 7 Egyptians, 12 natives, 90 camels]	
1st Division, Naval Brigade	Capt. Lord C. Beresford RN	
		[5 & 53, 11 natives, 91 camels, 1 Gardner MG]
26th Field Coy., RE (detachment)	Maj. J. F. Dorward	[2 & 25, 4 natives, 40 camels]
9th & 11th Coys., C. & T. Corps	Asst. Commissary-General R. A. Nugent CB	
		[7 & 33, 202 natives, 1,118 camels]
No. 1 Moveable Field-Hospital (2 x sects.)	Surg. W. H. Briggs	[2 & 20, 12 natives, 54 camels]
Camel Bearer Company (2 x sects.)	Surg. A. Harding	[2 & 40, 57 natives, 146 camels]

Total Strength: 115 officers, 1,687 other ranks, 343 native workers, 162 ponies, 2,888 camels

Detached to Lines of Communication
Howeiyat Wells
2nd Bn., Essex Regiment	Capt. W. G. Carter	[1 coy., 3 & 55]

Korti–Jakdul
Light Camel Regiment	Col. S. de A. C. Clarke	[3 coys., 21 & 380]

Jakdul Wells
D, E and H Coys., 1st Royal Sussex	Col. J. O. Vandeleur	[8 & 150]

Committed Later
1st Bn., Royal Irish Regiment	Lt. Col. H. Shaw VC	
2nd Division, Naval Brigade	Lt. E. B. Van Koughnet	[3 & 50, 1 Gardner MG]
1st Battery/1st Bde., Southern Div., RA	Maj. W. Hunter	[½ battery, 3 x 7-pdr.]

Force Troops
1st Bn., Royal West Kent Regiment	Col. E. Leach
2nd Bn., Essex Regiment	Lt. Col. W. R. White
1st Bn., Queen's Own Cameron Highlanders	Col. H. H. St. Leger

Appendix B

Organization of the Camel Corps

Heavy Camel Regiment   **Lt. Col. Hon. R. A. J. (Reginald) Talbot, 1st Life Guards**   [24 & 376]

RHQ
  Adjt.   *Capt. Lord St. Vincent (John Jervis), 16th (The Queen's) Lancers*
  QM   *Lt. H. G. (Gerald) Leigh, 1st Life Guards*
  RMO   *Surg. J. J. (John) Falvey AMD*

No. 1 Company   *Maj. Hon. C. C. G. (Charles) Byng, 1st Life Guards*
  1st Life Guards   *Lt. Lord Rodney (George Dennett)*
  2nd Life Guards   *Capt. Lord Cochrane (Douglas Hamilton) & Lt. R. J. (Rowland) Beech*

No. 2 Company   *Maj. Lord H. A. G. (Arthur) Somerset, Blues*
  Royal Horse Guards (Blues)   *Lt. Lord (George) Binning*
  2nd Dragoon Guards (Queen's Bays)   *Capt. A. L. G. (Arthur) Gould & Lt. R. F. (Robert) Hibbert*

No. 3 Company   *Maj. W. H. (Walter) Atherton, 5th Dragoon Guards*
  4th (Royal Irish) Dragoon Guards   *Capt. J. W. W. (Joseph) Darley & Lt. C. W. A. (Charles) Law*
  5th (Princess Charlotte of Wales's) Dragoon Guards   *Lt. St. J. C. (St. John) Gore*

No. 4 Company   *Bvt. Maj. W. A. (Wilfred) Gough p.s.c., Royals*
  1st (Royal) Dragoons   *Lt. J. F. (John) Burn-Murdoch*
  2nd Dragoons (Royal Scots Greys)   *Capt. W. H. (William) Hippisley & Lt. R. (Richard) Wolfe*

No. 5 Company   *Maj. L. M. (Ludovick) Carmichael p.s.c., 5th Lancers*
  5th (Royal Irish) Lancers   *Lt. H. (Henry) Costello*
  16th (The Queen's) Lancers   *Maj. T. (Thomas) Davison & Lt. W. B. (William) Browne*

Theoretical strength of HCR's regimental detachments: 2 officers, 2 sergeants, 2 corporals, 1 trumpeter and 38 privates (or troopers in the case of the Household Cavalry).

518 • *Appendices*

Light Camel Regiment *Col. S. De A. C. (Stanley) Clarke* [21 & 380]
  Adjt. & QM *Capt. H. (Harold) Paget, 7th Hussars*
  RMO *Surg. P. B. (Paul) Connolly* AMD
  3rd (The King's Own) Hussars *Maj. C. E. (Charles) Beckett p.s.c., & Lt. J. S. R. (James) Scott*
  4th (The Queen's Own) Hussars *Capt. C. W. (Cecil) Peters & Lt. R. (Ronald) Kincaid-Smith*
  7th (The Queen's Own) Hussars *Bvt. Lt. Col. H. (Hugh) McCalmont*
    & Lt. Hon. R. T. (Richard) Lawley
  10th (The Prince of Wales's Own Royal) *Bvt. Lt. Col. J. P. (John) Brabazon*
    Hussars *& Lt. Hon. G. L. (George) Bryan*
  11th (Prince Albert's Own) Hussars *Maj. C. E. (Charles) Swaine & Lt. W. (William) Harrison*
  15th (The King's) Hussars *Capt. A. G. (Arthur) Holland & Lt P. K. H. (Percy) Coke*
  18th Hussars *Maj. C. O. (Charles) Gould & Lt. E. C. (Eustace) Knox*
  20th Hussars *Capt. E. R. (Edward) Courtenay*
    & Lt. R. M. (Robert) Richardson
  21st Hussars *Maj. W. G. C. (Walter) Wyndham and Lt. J. (John) Fowle*

Theoretical strength of LCR's regimental detachments: 2 officers, 2 sergeants, 2 corporals, 1 trumpeter and 38 privates. LCR is believed to have formed only three sub-units, probably by grouping the regimental detachments by threes in order of seniority. The sub-units are likely to have been called simply Nos. 1, 2 and 3 Companies, though there is one hint that they might have been termed 'squadrons'.

Guards Camel Regiment *Lt. Col. Hon. E. E. T. (Evelyn) Boscawen, Coldm. Gds.* [19 & 365, inc. 4 & 86 RMLI]
  RHQ
    Adjt. *Lt. C. (Charles) Crutchley, Scots Gds.*
    QM *Capt. E. M. S. (Eyre) Crabbe, Gren Gds.*
    Signals Officer *Lt. Col. H. W. M. (Harry) Bonham, Gren Gds.*
    RMO *Surg. J. (James) Magill* AMD
  No. 1 (Grenadier Guards) Company *Lt. Col. C. R. (Charles) Rowley, Gren Gds.*
    1st Bn., Grenadier Guards *Lt. Count A. E. W. (Edward) Gleichen*
    2nd Bn., Grenadier Guards *Lt. Col. I. J. C. (Ivor) Herbert p.s.c.,*
      & Lt. L. G. H. (Lionel) d'Aguilar
    3rd Bn., Grenadier Guards *Lt. R. G. (Robert) Wolrige-Gordon*
  No. 2 (Coldstream Guards) Company *Lt. Col. F. A. (Francis) Graves-Sawle, Coldm. Gds.*
    1st Bn., Coldstream Guards *Lt. V. J. (Vesey) Dawson & Lt. Hon. H. (Hugh) Amherst*
    2nd Bn., Coldstream Guards *Lt. D. F. R. (Douglas) Dawson p.s.c.*
  No. 3 (Scots Guards) Company *Lt. Col. M. W. (Mildmay) Willson, Scots Gds.*
    1st Bn., Scots Guards *Lt. Col. Sir W. G. (William) Gordon-Cumming Bart*
    2nd Bn., Scots Guards *Lt. F. W. (Frederick) Romilly p.s.c.*
  No. 4 (RMLI) Company *Bvt. Maj. W. H. (William) Pöe* RMLI [4 & 86]
    Royal Marine Light Infantry *Capt. A. C. (Aylmer) Pearson, Lt. C. V. (Charles) Townshend & Lt. H. S. N. (Herbert) White*

Theoretical strength of GCR's regimental detachments: 2 officers, 2 sergeants, 2 corporals, 1 bugler and 38 privates.

Organization of the Camel Corps • 519

Mounted Infantry Camel Regt. A/Lt Col. E. (Edward) Hutton KRRC*
[24 & 366]

RHQ
  2iC/Acting CO   *Bvt. Maj. Hon. G. H. (George) Gough p.s.c., 14th Hussars*
  Majors   *Maj. C. T. (Charles) Barrow, Scottish Rifles*†
                            & L/Maj. T. H. (Thomas) Phipps p.s.c., 7th Hussars
  Adjt.   *Capt. J. H. (John) Sewell, Norfolk Regt*
  QM   *Lt. R. A. (Robert) Grant, Gordons*

A Company   **L/Capt. C. H. (Charles) Payne, Gordons**
  No. 1 Sect.: 1st Bn., South   *Lt. C. O. (Charles) Hore*
    Staffordshire Regt
  No. 2 Sect.: 1st Bn., Black Watch   *Lt. C. P. (Charles) Livingstone*
    (Royal Highlanders)
  No. 3 Sect.: 3rd Bn., King's Royal   *Lt. P. S. (Percy) Marling VC & Lt. R. L. (Robert) Bower*
    Rifle Corps
  No. 4 Sect.: 1st Bn., Gordon Highlanders   *Lt. H. K. (Harry) Stewart*

B Company   **Capt. H. A. (Henry) Walsh, Somerset LI**
  No. 1 Sect.: 2nd Bn., Duke of   *Lt C. G. (Cyril) Martyr*
    Cornwall's Light Infantry
  No. 2 Sect.: 1st Bn., Royal Sussex Regt   *Lt. F. G. (Frederick) Todd-Thornton*
  No. 3 Sect.: 2nd Bn., Essex Regt   *Lt. R. J. (Robert) Tudway*
  No. 4 Sect.: 1st Bn., Queen's Own   *Capt. A. T. (Arthur) Morse*
    (Royal West Kent) Regt

C (Rifles) Company   **Capt. R. S. R. (Richard) Fetherstonhaugh KRRC**
  No. 1 Sect.: 1st Bn., KRRC   *Lt. W. P. (William) Campbell*
  No. 2 Sect.: 2nd Bn., KRRC   *Lt. A. E. (Archibald) Miles*
  No. 3 Sect.: 2nd Bn., Rifle Brigade   *Lt. W. M. (Max) Sherston*
    (The Prince Consort's Own)
  No. 4 Sect.: 3rd Bn., Rifle Brigade   *Capt. Hon. H. C. (Henry) Hardinge*
    (The Prince Consort's Own)

D Company   **Capt. C. B. (Charles) Pigott, 21st Hussars‡**
  No. 1 Sect.: 1st Bn., Prince Albert's   *Lt. T. D. (Thomas) Snow*
    (Somersetshire Light Infantry)
  No. 2 Sect.: 1st Bn., Royal Scots Fusiliers   *Lt. H. S. M. (Herbert) Stanuell*
  No. 3 Sect.: 2nd Bn., Queen's Own   *Lt. E. A. H. (Edwin) Alderson*
    (Royal West Kent) Regt
  No. 4 Sect.: 2nd Bn., Connaught Rangers   *Lt. C. J. (James) Carden*

Theoretical strength of MICR's regimental detachments: 1 officer, 5 NCOs and 25 privates.

* Sick from Nov. 1884.
† Acting CO, 17.1.85.
‡ Formerly KRRC.

Appendix C

Movement Plan to Ambukol and Korti

Leg	Distance (miles)	Conveyance	Notes
Cairo to Assiut	229	All by rail	
Assiut to Aswan	318	a. Troops – steamers and nuggars b. Whalers by barge as far as Aswan	Disembark Aswan (1st Cataract).
Aswan to Philae	9	a. Troops – rail (bypass 1st Cataract) b. Whalers through 1st Cataract with native labour	
Philae to Wādī Halfā	210	a. Troops – steamers and nuggars b. Whalers towed	Disembark Wādī Halfā (2nd Cataract). Camel regiments mounted at Wādī Halfā.
Wādī Halfā to Sarras/Gemai	33	a. Troops – rail (bypass 2nd Cataract) b. Whalers through 2nd Cataract with native labour, or portaged 1.5 miles by Egyptian troops c. Camel Corps by the riverbank from this point on	Marry up with whalers at Gemai. Canadian Voyageurs and West Indian kroomen employed from Wādī Halfā onward.
Sarras/Gemai to Dal Cataract	62	Infantry and supplies – whaler	
Dal Cataract to Kajbar Cataract	102	Infantry and supplies – whaler	
Kajbar Cataract		a. Infantry – overland. b. Supplies – camel transport	Portage required.
Kajbar Cataract to Hannek Cataract	31	Infantry and supplies – whaler	
Hannek Cataract		a. Infantry – overland. b. Supplies – camel transport	Portage required.
Hannek to Dongola	39	Infantry and supplies – whaler	
Dongola to Ambukol/Korti	100	Infantry and supplies – whaler	Bayūda Crossing (Korti to Metemmeh) – 174 miles.

Appendix D

Order of Battle: Abu Klea, 17 January 1885

British Forces — *Brig. Gen. Sir Herbert Stewart* KCB, ADC
  Brigade Major — *Capt. The Earl of Airlie*
Square — *Col. F. G. Burnaby*
  1st Division, Naval Brigade — *Capt. Lord Charles Beresford* RN [1 x Gardner MG, 5 & 40]
  Guards Camel Regiment — *Lt. Col. Hon. E. E. T. Boscawen* [4 coys., 19 & 365]
  Mounted Infantry Camel Regiment — *Maj. C. T. Barrow* [3½ coys., 19 & 315]
  Heavy Camel Regiment — *Lt. Col. Hon. R. A. J. Talbot* [5 coys., 24 & 376]
  C and G Coys., 1st Bn., Royal Sussex Regt — *Maj. M. S. J. Sunderland* [5 & 125]
  1st Battery/1st Bde., Southern Div., RA — *Capt. G. F. A. Norton* [½ bty., 3 x 7-pdr., 4 & 20]
  Transport [150 camels, 50 native drivers]
  Medical details
Flanks — *Lt. Col. P. H. S. Barrow* CB, CMG
  Left: 3 troops, 19th Hussars — *Maj. J. D. P. French* [5 & 90]
  Right: 1 troop, 19th Hussars — *Unknown* [1 & 30]
Zariba — *Maj. A. S. H. Gern*
  B & F Coys, 1st Bn., Royal Sussex Regt. — *Maj. A. S. H. Gern* [3 & 125]
  Nos. 1 & 3 Sections, B Company, MICR — *Capt. A. Morse* [2 & 45]
  26th Field Company, RE (detachment) — *Maj. J. F. Dorward* [2 & 25]
Administrative Details
  Nos. 9 and 11 Coys, C. & T. Corps [7 & 33, 300+ native drivers and 2,780 camels]
  Medics [4 & 60, minus some personnel with the square]

Notes
1. Casualties: 9 & 65 killed, 9 & 85 wounded (of whom 2 officers & 10 NCOs and men were mortally injured).
2. Strengths are in some cases estimates or calculations based on circumstance and available evidence.

Mahdīst Forces   *Amīr Mūsā wad Ḥilū*

Berber Contingent   *Amīr 'Abd-al-Mājid Nasr al-Din abū' l-Kailak*
   250 horse and 1,750 foot from the 'Abābda, Bisharin and Barabra tribes

Turncoat Egyptians   *Muḥammad Effendi Wahabi*
   60 riflemen from Berber

Metemmeh Contingent   *Amīr 'Ali-wad-Saad*
   2,000 townsmen (mostly Ja'līyīn and Awadiyeh)

Mahdīst Main Force   *Mūsā wad Ḥilū*
   4,000–6,000 Kordofani Arabs, Daghaim, Kināna and Hamr tribes (deployed from Omdurman), plus 600 spearmen from other Arab tribes and 400 riflemen (*jihādīya?*)

Total strength   9,000–11,000

Casualties   1,100 killed

Appendix E

Order of Battle: Abu Kru, 19 January 1885

British Forces *Brig. Gen. Sir Herbert Stewart* KCB, ADC
 [*then Bvt. Col. Sir Charles Wilson* KCMG, CB]

Square *Lt. Col. Hon. E. E. T. Boscawen*
  [approx. 1,000 officers and men]

    Guards Camel Regiment *Lt. Col. M. W. Willson* [4 coys., 19 & 350]
    Mounted Infantry Camel Regiment *Maj. C. T. Barrow* [4 coys., 19 & 320]
    ½ Heavy Camel Regiment *Lt. Col. Hon. R. A. J. Talbot* [2 coys., 8 & 132]
    1st Bn, Royal Sussex Regiment *Maj. M. S. J. Sunderland* [C & G Coys., 4 & 116]
    19th Hussars *Lt. E. S. Craven* [1 troop, 1 & 20]
    26th Field Coy., RE (detachment) *Lt. H. M. Lawson* [1 & 10]
    Transport [approx. 20 native drivers, 60 camels]

Zariba *Capt. Lord Charles Beresford* RN
    OC Troops *Lt. Col. P. H. S. Barrow* CB, CMG
    1st Division, Naval Brigade *Sub-Lt. E. L. Munro* RN [1 x Gardner MG, 1 & 30]
    19th Hussars *Maj. J. D. P. French* [3 troops, 6 & 100]
    1st Battery/1st Bde., Southern Div., RA *Capt. G. F. A. Norton* [3 x 7-pdr., 2 & 30]
    ½ Heavy Camel Regiment *Maj. T. Davison* [2 coys., 8 & 132]
    Balance of Royal Engineers *Maj. J. F. Dorward* [approx. 1 & 10]

Administrative Details
    Nos. 9 and 11 Coys., C. & T. Corps [7 & 33, 300+ native drivers, 2,750 camels]
    Medics [4 & 60, minus some personnel with the square]

Casualties 2 officers, 2 war correspondents and 22 men killed, 8 & 92 wounded

Strengths are in all cases estimates or calculations based on the Desert Column's start states and known events thereafter. Abu Klea casualties have been deducted from unit strengths. The strengths given for the units in the square make no allowance for casualties incurred prior to the advance to the Nile.

Mahdīst Forces   *al-Nūr Bey Muḥammad ʿAnqara*

Muḥammad ʿAnqara brought up 2,000 fresh troops from Omdurman on the day before the battle to reinforce the army which had fought at Abu Klea on 17 January (*see Appendix D, above*). The Daghaim, Kināna and Hamr Kordofanis had taken particularly heavy casualties in the first fight. Mūsā wad Ḥilū had been killed and the *amīrs* ʿAli-wad-Saad and ʿAbd-al-Mājid Nasr al-Din abū' l-Kailak wounded. Who succeeded the latter two in command of the Metemmeh and Berber contingents respectively is not known. It is likely that ʿAnqara's troops were also Kordofanis.

Total strength   7,000–8,000.

Casualties   Approx 250–300 killed in the charge, including five Baqqāra *amīrs*, plus an unknown number of additional fatalities and wounded around the *zariba* and axis of advance. It is not inconceivable that there were around 1,000 Mahdīst casualties in all.

Appendix F

Casualty Return: Abu Klea, 17 January 1885

Staff
Killed   Col. F. G. Burnaby, Royal Horse Guards (Blues).
Wounded   Maj. J. B. B. Dickson, 1st (Royal) Dragoons, Intelligence Department (severely);
            Capt. the Earl of Airlie (D. S. W. Ogilvy), 10th Hussars, Brigade Major (slightly).

1st Division, Naval Brigade
Killed   Lt. Cdr. A. Pigott RN; Lt. R. E. L. M. P. de Lisle RN; Chief Boatswain's Mate
            F. Rhoods; Gunner's Mate G. Webb; Armourer W. Miller; Able Seamen J. Burney,
            J. Nye and E. Soar.
Wounded   P.O. 1st Class C. Saysel (severely); Able Seamen A. Dredge (slightly), R. Legg
            (severely), A. H. March (severely), F. Moore (slightly) and J. Whitehead (slightly).

Heavy Camel Regiment
RHQ
Wounded   Capt. Viscount St Vincent (J. E. L. Jervis), 16th Lancers, mortally.

No. 1 Company   *1st Life Guards*
Killed   705 Tpr. W. Nicholson.
Wounded   1019 Tpr. F. Woodhouse (mortally, died 19.1.85).

                 2nd Life Guards
Wounded   Lt. R. J. Beech (slightly) and 1164 Tpr. J. Sellers (mortally).

No. 2 Company   *Royal Horse Guards (Blues)*
Wounded   Maj. Lord Arthur Somerset (slightly).

                 2nd Dragoon Guards (Queen's Bays)
Killed   Ptes. 2386 W. Beckwith, 1098 H. Cooper and 2537 J. Stenning.
Wounded   2499 Cpl. J. Hawley (severely).

No. 3 Company   *4th Dragoon Guards*
Killed   Capt. J. W. W. Darley; Lt. C. W. A. Law; Ptes. 2494 E. Blaine, 2722 J. Franklin and
            2534 H. Bunch.
Wounded   2499 Lance Sgt. T. Nix (mortally, died 3.2.85); Ptes. 2283 E. Brooks (severely),
            2074 F. Connolly (severely), 2839 W. Hayward (severely), 1726 W. Hewitt
            (mortally, died 18.1.85), 2630 F. Ryder (mortally, died 18.1.85), 2279 G. Rix
            (slightly), 2194 T. Simson (slightly, but died of enteric at Dongola 27.3.85) and 2715
            J. Steel (severely).

5th Dragoon Guards

Killed   Maj. W. H. Atherton; 1952 Sgt. J. Heverin; Ptes. 2099 C. Bates, 2116 B. Budd, 2202 J. Martin, 1787 B. Sargeant and 1942 J. Thompson.

Wounded   2014 Troop Sgt. Maj. Grant (slightly); Ptes. 1926 J. Brooks (mortally, died 18.1.85), 2090 G. Collins (mortally, died 18.1.85), 1404 A. Cook (slightly), 2321 W. Gibson (slightly), 1889 G. Martin (severely) and 1928 G. Roberts (slightly).

No. 4 Company — 1st (Royal) Dragoons

Killed   Maj. W. A. Gough; 1954 Sgt. H. Phillips; Ptes. 2223 R. Connell, 2087 A. Cordon, 1776 W. Cross, 2227 H. Johnson, 2275 P. Fox, 1302 W. Norman, 2202 A. Steadman, 2284 F. J. Read, 2230 C. Reed, 958 S. Robinson and 2220 G. Willis.

Wounded   2216 Cpl. A. Rogers (slightly); Ptes. 1800 E. East (severely), 1998 F. Moore (severely); 1533 M. Wagg (severely) and 2193 T. Ash (slightly).

2nd Dragoons (Royal Scots Greys)

Killed   Lt. R. Wolfe; 2276 L/Cpl. A. Sheals [possibly Shiels]; Ptes. 2283 R. Brannon, 2293 R. Campbell, 2187 D. Hall, 1507 J. Howitt, 2477 A. Hudson, 1988 E. Mealow, 2277 A. Nichol, 2155 J. Robb and 2082 A. Walton.

Wounded   Ptes. 2454 W. Begley (slightly), 2064 G. Hardy (slightly), 2141 G. Findlater, 2177 J. Kilorn (severely) and 2361 R. Reid (mortally, died 18.1.85).

No. 5 Company — 5th (Royal Irish) Lancers

Killed   Maj. L. M. Carmichael; 2344 Sgt. C. Percival; 2333 Cpl. S. Parker; Ptes. 1897 E. H. Bell and 2165 J. McGrath.

Wounded   Lt. H. Costello (slightly); 2130 Pte. G. Austin (slightly); 1833 Tptr. J. Coyne (slightly).

16th (The Queen's) Lancers

Killed   2034 Cpl. A. Jacques; Ptes. 3000 R. W. Osborne, 2044 H. Sylvester and 1823 J. Taylor.

Wounded   1987 Pte. H. Slack (slightly).

Guards Camel Regiment

RHQ

Wounded   Surg. J. Magill AMD (severely).

No. 1 (Grenadier Guards) Company

Killed   8056 Pte. G. Ormiston.

Wounded   Ptes. 5445 W. Davies (slightly), 7053 T. Hewitt (severely), 7123 G. Richardson (severely) and 6505 A. Rowlands (slightly).

No. 2 (Coldstream Guards) Company

Killed   5248 Pte. F. Taylor.

Wounded   5007 Lance Sgt. W. Pearson (severely).

No. 3 (Scots Guards) Company

Killed   5087 Pte. J. Donaldson.

Wounded   5335 Lance Sgt. W. Parker (severely); Ptes. 3317 J. Fox (severely) and 5020 W. Smith (severely).

No. 4 (RMLI) Company

Killed   4 Pte. W. Walters.

Wounded Ptes. 3 T. Kevin [possibly Kevan] (severely), 16 R. Luckin (mortally, died 28.1.85) and 35 H. Russell (severely).

Mounted Infantry Camel Regiment
RHQ
Wounded Maj. Hon. G. H. Gough, 14th Hussars (severely).

A Company   3rd KRRC
Killed 3476 Pte. G. Turner.

1st Gordon Highlanders
Wounded Ptes. 811 W. Penman (slightly) and 2186 G. Short (severely).

B Company   2nd Essex
Killed 381 Pte. C. Wilford (died 16.1.85).

1st Royal Sussex
Wounded 2027 Cpl. J. Virgo (slightly); Ptes. 908 J. Bennett (severely), 232 E. Botting (slightly) and 1772 D. Callaghan (dangerously).

2nd DCLI
Wounded Pte. 305 J. Smith (slightly).

C (Rifles) Company 1st KRRC
Wounded 4213 L/Cpl. H. Hobbs (mortally); Ptes. 1212 G. Mann and 3738 Tomkins (severely).

2nd KRRC
Killed 1923 Pte. J. Bowles.
Wounded 1152 Sjt. A. Leagett (mortally); Ptes. 1123 B. Fagan, 508 T. Hold (severely), 1102 C. Sanders [possibly Saunders], 3660 W. Thursden (severely) and 596 G. Tyler.

2nd Rifle Brigade
Wounded A/Cpl. 6162 W. Yetton (severely) and Pte. 4479 J. Payne (severely).

3rd Rifle Brigade
Wounded 2003 Cpl. W. Elliott (severely); Ptes. 3013 J. Finney (slightly), 3620 C. Augur (slightly), 3621 W. Franklin (slightly) and 3603 G. Wood (slightly).

D Company   1st Royal Scots Fusiliers
Wounded Ptes. 681 P. Rafferty (severely) and 545 J. White (mortally, died 12.3.85).

2nd Royal West Kents
Killed 2611 L/Cpl. G. Miles.
Wounded Pte. 2266 W. Neighbour (severely).

2nd Connaught Rangers
Killed 447 Pte. P. Cosgrave.
Wounded Ptes. 2660 P. McGinn (slightly), and 2630 B. Quinn (severely).

1st Royal Sussex
Killed Ptes. 26 J. McSorley and 37 W. Weston.
Wounded Ptes. 1094 D. Deadman (slightly) and 1793 H. Cloke [possibly Cloake] (slightly).

19th Hussars
Killed 2155 Cpl. S. Walker and Pte. W. Purton [possibly Perton].
Wounded 1061 Farrier QMS F. Short (mortally); Ptes. 1983 C. Ray (slightly), 1859 J. Whelan (slightly) and 1552 J. Whitfield (severely, but died of sunstroke at Dongola 28.4.85).

1st Battery/1st Brigade, Southern Division, RA

Wounded Lts. J. D. Guthrie (mortally, died 22.1.85) and C. N. Lyall (dangerously); 23609 Sgt. T. Lee (slightly); Gnr. J. Nicholson (slightly).

Miscellaneous

Wounded 2306 Sgt. R. Sheehan, 7th Hussars (severely).

The British Loss at Abu Klea

Unit	Officers Killed	Officers Wounded	Other Ranks Killed	Other Ranks Wounded
Staff	1	2	–	–
1st Division, Naval Brigade	2	–	6	6
Heavy Camel Regiment	7	3	51	24
RHQ	1	–	–	–
No. 1 Company, HCR	–	1	3	–
No. 2 Company, HCR	–	1	3	1
No. 3 Company, HCR	3	–	14	11
No. 4 Company, HCR	2	–	23	9
No. 5 Company, HCR	1	1	8	3
Guards Camel Regiment	–	1	5	10
RHQ	–	1	–	–
No. 1 Company, GCR	–	–	1	4
No. 2 Company, GCR	–	–	1	1
No. 3 Company, GCR	–	–	1	3
No. 4 Company, GCR	–	–	2	2
MI Camel Regiment	–	1	8	25
RHQ	–	1	–	–
A Company, MICR	–	–	–	2
B Company, MICR	–	–	1	5
C Company, MICR	–	–	4	14
D Company, MICR	–	–	3	4
1st Bn, Royal Sussex Regiment	–	–	2	2
19th Hussars	–	–	3	3
Royal Artillery	1	1	–	2
Miscellaneous	–	–	–	1
Total	11	8	75	73

The mortally wounded are tallied in the table as fatalities.

Source Documents

1. Casualty list in Brig. Gen. Sir Stewart's Official Despatch of 18 Jan. 1885 (*London Gazette*, 20 Feb. 1885).
2. Nominal roll of Naval Brigade casualties, Surg-Maj. T. F. O'Dwyer (*London Gazette*, 28 Apr. 1885).
3. Webb, J. V., *The Abu Klea Medal Rolls*.
4. Handwritten casualty returns submitted by commanding officers to Capt. Lord Airlie on 23 Jan. 1885 (National Archives of Scotland, 0204 GD16-52-57-10-A00118A).
5. Participant accounts (*see bibliography*).

Appendix G

Casualty Return: Abu Kru & Metemmeh, 19–21 January 1885

Staff
Wounded   Brig-Gen. Sir Herbert Stewart KCB, ADC, 3rd DG (mortally);
            Capt. the Earl of Airlie, 10th Hussars (slightly);
            Capt. A. G. Leonard, East Lancashire Regt. (Transport Staff).

1st Division, Naval Brigade
Wounded   Sub. Lt. E. L. Munro (severely).

Heavy Camel Regiment
No. 1 Company   *1st Life Guards*
Wounded   1557 Tpr. Godfrey.

                2nd Life Guards
Wounded   953 Tpr. W. Hodges (mortally).

No. 2 Company   *Royal Horse Guards (Blues)*
Wounded   Maj. Lord Arthur Somerset (slightly); Tprs. 1012 T. Proven (slightly) and 1020 J. McLeod (severely).

                2nd Dragoon Guards (Queen's Bays)
Wounded   2365 Sgt. E. Hare (mortally, died Jakdul Wells 17.2.85); Pte. 2308 W. Powell (mortally, died no later than 23.1.85).

No. 3 Company   *4th Dragoon Guards*
Wounded   1757 Pte. J. O'Brien (mortally, died 25.1.85).

                5th Dragoon Guards
Killed   2204 Cpl. J. Newton; 1410 Pte. G. Thornhill.
Wounded   1757 Pte. H. Randall.

No. 4 Company   *1st (Royal) Dragoons*
Killed   1446 Tptr W. Wilson.

No. 5 Company   *5th (Royal Irish) Lancers*
Killed   2139 Pte. A. Russell.
Wounded   2554 Pte. W. McDonald (slightly).

Guards Camel Regiment
RHQ
Wounded   Lt. & Adjt. C. Crutchley, Scots Guards

No. 1 (Grenadier Guards) Company
Killed   7712 Pte. W. Rogers.

Wounded   Ptes. 8587 D. Bailey (mortally, died no later than 23.1.85), 7224 P. Hickey (in square 19.1.85 – not Metemmeh 21.1.85 as stated in Webb – GCR casualty return of 23.1.85 refers), 8086 H. Lorraine, 5555 J. Vowles, 6908 J. Coyne, 7197 W. Purchase, 8099 R. Cragg, 7498 W. Burge and 7840 T. Button.

No. 2 (Coldstream Guards) Company
Wounded   2445 C/Sgt. G. Kekewich (mortally, possibly died same day, returned as dead on 23.1.85); Ptes. 4862 R. Smithborne, 4819 W. Dexter, 4911 E. Raynor (mortally, died 11.2.85), 5122 H. Page (slightly), 5137 A. Hobbs, 4829 T. Symons, 3399 J. Anscott (severely) and 5350 J. Harrison.

No. 3 (Scots Guards) Company
Killed   5074 Pte. W. West.

Wounded   5325 Cpl. W. Parker (severely); Ptes. 4962 H. Faithful (mortally), 4960 D. McKenzie (slightly), 5019 J. Clark, 4928 J. Reid (slightly), 5137 W. Redmond (mortally, 21.1.85 at Metemmeh); 5358 W. Greenwood and 2099 A. Calderbank (severely, Metemmeh 21.1.85).

No. 4 (RMLI) Company
Killed   37 Cpl. M. Carey; Ptes. 25 E. Arnold, 21 A. Holland, 24 W. Mitchell and 41 E. Meade.

Wounded   Maj. W H. Pöe (severely, 21.1.85 at Metemmeh); Sgt. C. Chislett (severely); Dmr. W. Shires; Ptes E. Pennington (slightly), Warner, J. North, J. Moran, J. Lister, H. Vickers and P. Goulding.

Mounted Infantry Camel Regiment

A Company   *1st South Staffordshires*

Killed   1732 Sgt. W. H. Hinton; Pte. 2000 J. Rose.

Wounded   Ptes. 524 A. Phillips (slightly), 1755 C. Jones and 46 F. Blythe.

                       1st Black Watch

Wounded   Lt. C. P. Livingstone (slightly).

                       3rd KRRC

Wounded   820 L/Cpl Thorward; Ptes 1751 Wareham (mortally, died 26.1.85), and 565 T. Winter (slightly).

                       1st Gordon Highlanders

Wounded   754 Ptes. J. Costello, 843 J. Studder (slightly) and 2073 W. Thompson.

B Company   *2nd DCLI*

Killed   1657 Pte. W. H. Jones.

Wounded   Ptes. 1517 J. Hart and 1350 T. Wickenden (slightly).

                       1st Royal Sussex

Killed   23 Sgt. L. M. Cowley (21.1.85 at Metemmeh).

Wounded   Ptes. 1607 J. Low (severely), 1668 P. Flynn and 1118 A. Durrant.

1st Royal West Kents
Wounded   2209 Pte. J. Gant.

C (Rifles) Company   2nd KRRC
Wounded   Ptes. 810 H. Holmes (severely) and 813 T. Basford.

2nd Rifle Brigade
Wounded   4479 Cpl. J. Payne (slightly).

D Company   1st Somersetshire Light Infantry
Wounded   Wounded: Lt. T. D. Snow; 1804 Pte G. Palmer.

2nd Royal West Kents
Wounded   2604/2644 Pte. S. Swinburne (mortally, died 27.1.85).

1st Royal Scots Fusiliers
Wounded   Ptes. 2762 G. Angus and 275 M. H. Carnegie (severely).

2nd Connaught Rangers
Wounded   Ptes. 1304 R. Blake (mortally, died no later than 23.1.85), 1912 W. Doyle (slightly), 2060 R. Jackson, 603 J. Moffatt (21.1.85 at Metemmeh), 2660 P. McGinn (slightly) and 2865 G. Dewart.

1st Bn. Royal Sussex Regiment
Killed   19 Dmr. E. Rogers; Ptes. 1769 J. Daly and 1763 R. Leppard.
Wounded   1803 Lance Sgt. J. Wright (slightly); 1340 Sgt. H. Sullivan (slightly); 683 L/Cpl H. Hollis; Ptes. 1331 W. Wingham, 1998 J. Johnson (severely), 862 C. Freeman, 1139 J. Taylor (slightly), 1 H. Horn (mortally, died 24.1.85); 638 J. Chandler and 51 T. Fogg (severely).

19th Hussars
Killed   QM A. G. Lima.
Wounded   Ptes. 1618 I. Pullan and 1698 A. Godfrey (severely).

1st Battery/1st Brigade, Southern Division, RA
Wounded   23654 Gnr J. Tucker (severely, 21.1.85 at Metemmeh).

26 Field Company, RE
Killed   16774 Spr. W. Chapman.
Wounded   16220 L/Cpl J. Dale (severely); Spr. 17848 F. Foster.

Miscellaneous
Killed   Mr John Cameron (*The Standard*); Mr St Leger Herbert (*Morning Post*); Conductor of Supplies A. C. Jewell, C & T Corps.
Wounded   Mr B. Burleigh (*Daily Telegraph*, slightly); Ptes. 1137 W. Pawley (No. 9 Coy., C. & T. Corps), 4392 J Johnston (No. 9 Coy., C. & T. Corps) and 4345 A. White (Medical Staff Corps)

The British Loss at Abu Kru and Metemmeh

Unit	Officers Killed	Officers Wounded	Other Ranks Killed	Other Ranks Wounded
Staff	1	2	–	–
1st Division, Naval Brigade	–	1	–	–
Heavy Camel Regiment				
RHQ	–	–		
No. 1 Company, HCR	–	–	1	1
No. 2 Company, HCR	–	1	2	2
No. 3 Company, HCR	–	–	3	1
No. 4 Company, HCR	–	–	1	–
No. 5 Company, HCR	–	–	1	1
Guards Camel Regiment				
RHQ	–	1	–	–
No. 1 Company, GCR	–	–	2	8
No. 2 Company, GCR	–	–	2	7
No. 3 Company, GCR	–	–	3	6
No. 4 Company, GCR	–	1	5	9
MI Camel Regiment				
A Company, MICR	–	1	3	8
B Company, MICR	–	–	2	6
C Company, MICR	–	–	–	3
D Company, MICR	–	1	1	8
1st Bn., Royal Sussex Regiment	–	–	2	9
19th Hussars	1	–	–	2
Royal Artillery	–	–	–	1
Royal Engineers	–	–	1	2
Miscellaneous	2	–	1	3
Total*	4	8	33	77

* Includes General Stewart (mortally wounded, died Jakdul Wells 16.2.85) and two war correspondents. Those named above as mortally wounded are tallied here as fatalities.

Source Documents
1. Attachment to Official Despatch, Wolseley to Hartington, Korti, 5.00 a.m. 23 January 1885 (published *The Standard*, 29 January).
2. Handwritten casualty returns submitted by commanding officers to Capt. Lord Airlie on 23 Jan. 1885 (Orders Book of the Desert Column, Airlie Papers, National Archives of Scotland, NAS 0204 GD16-52-57-10-A00118A).
3. Webb, J. V., *The Abu Klea Medal Rolls*.
4. Participant accounts (*see bibliography*).

Appendix H

Lt. Col. J. D. H. Stewart's Notes on the Suakin–Berber Route

Names of Places	Hours of March	Total hours of March	Description
Handub (1st night)	4½	4½	Leaving Suakin, the road crosses a gravelly plain covered with stunted acacias, and rises gently for some distance to Handub, where are several wells of rather brackish water. This is usually made the first halting place by caravans from Suakin. A short distance beyond this point the route enters the mountains, and, after crossing the first ridge, leads over a broad plain surrounded with hills of a volcanic origin. There are many indications of water below the surface and a plentiful supply could probaby be obtained by Abyssinian pumps.
Otao	4¾	9¼	Here are some wells with a small quantity of water full of surface impurities. In the rainy season there is a much larger supply. After leaving Otao, the road rises with a steep gradient and follows what appears to be the bed of a mountain torrent. It leaves the ordinary caravan track to Berber, and passes more directly through the mountains. It does not, however, present any difficulties to the passage of camels or travellers on foot.
3rd camp (2nd night)	8½	17¾	This camp was on the site of a barren hill where there was no water and little vegetation. The road then descends into a broad valley covered with green trees and shrubs. Water could no doubt be found beneath the surface. If the rain, which falls in the wet season was properly stored, the country could be made very fertile. Here and there the track crosses circular plains surrounded with volcanic hills, which appear to be the craters of extinct volcanos. The population is small, but possesses large flocks of sheep and goats, which crowd in thousands round the few small wells that have been dug.
Galuchi (3rd night)	5	22¾	There are good wells here and the water is excellent. The trees in the vicinity give a pleasant shade. The hills around are lofty and picturesque. The road from Galuchi is very good and could easily be

			made available for wheel traffic. There is a great deal of sameness about it, as it passes one broad valley after another, separated from each other by low cols.
Odros (4th night)	11½	34¼	Here are several wells with good water in a narrow gorge, surrounded by hills said to be infested with robbers, who, however, would not care to attack any party of moderate size. This is one of the highest points betweeen the Red Sea and the Nile, and has an altitude of rather more than 3,000 feet. Thence the general inclination of the road is downwards towards the Nile.
6th camp (5th night)	11¾	46	No water was obtainable here; it was necessary to bring a supply from the well at Odros.
7th camp	4½	50½	There was plenty of water at this camp in the bed of a torrent, which must be a stream at least 100 feet wide in the rainy season.
Mata (6th night)	4	54½	The road passes through a pleasant valley. The wells are surrounded by a group of fine trees, which give good shade and swarm with pigeons.
Sahol	4	58½	Here is a large pool of water, left after the rains. There are no signs of inhabitants.
10th camp (7th night)	6¼	64¾	No water at this camp. The road crosses a mountain range, steep and rocky in places, but passable for camels without any difficulty. There is but little vegetation; after passing the mountains the road descends into a comparatively fertile valley, in which is Roway, where there are wells with an abundant supply of good water.
Roway	8	72¾	The road again is steep, then crosses a sandy desert for two hours, and another range of hills.
12th camp (9th night)	9½	82¼	No water.
Obak (10th night)	10	92¼	The road crosses a wide desert before reaching these wells. The sand is light and unpleasant for marching. At Obak there are plenty of wells, but the water is brackish from passing through the salt sand. Here is joined the main road from Suakin to Berber.
14th camp (11th night)	9	101¼	No water. This part of the march is the most distressing. The sand is very deep in some places, and the camels march with difficulty.
Bir Mahobeh (12th night)	14¼	115½	Here is a good supply of water, which is very refreshing after the hot desert march. The wells are much frequented by shepherds with their flocks and by passing caravans, which take in a supply of water before crossing the sands to Obak.
Berber	2	117½	

Notes

Preface

1. Wolseley journal, 8 Jan. 85, Preston, *In Relief of Gordon*, p. 111.
2. Ibid., 14 Feb. 85, p. 145.
3. For the rise of the Mahdī, see Theobald, *The Mahdīya*, pp. 27–48; and Warburg, *Islam, Sectarianism and Politics in the Sudan*, pp. 22–30.
4. See Cromer's *Modern Egypt*, vol. i, pp. 351–2 for what he portrays as the contemporaneous 'official' Islamic theology on who and what the Mahdī would be. Cromer draws on a text called *The Conquests of Islam* written at Mecca in 1883. Importantly the Mahdī will be proclaimed against his will by the people, will not be the cause of strife amongst the faithful and will be acclaimed at Mecca. The event will coincide with the prophet Jesus descending again to join himself to the Mahdī. The text ran on '. . . whosoever shall, of his own will, declare himself to be the Mahdī and try to asert himself by force, is a pretender, such as have already appeared many times'.
5. Save in the case of the Royal Artillery, which later named a battery after the Battle of Abu Klea.
6. For a full biography see Jackson, *Osman Digna*.

Prologue

1. See for example Wolseley to his wife, 22 Feb. 85: 'You must tell me whether society is down on me for being too late to save Gordon . . .', Arthur, *Letters of Lord and Lady Wolseley*, p. 171.
2. Wolseley journal, 19 Oct. 84, Preston, *In Relief of Gordon*, p. 43.
3. For Wolseley's personal recollections of the campaign see *The Story of a Soldier's Life*, vol. ii, pp. 165–224.
4. Wolseley, *A Soldier's Life*, vol. ii, pp. 257–370.
5. Wolseley journal, 19 Oct. 84, Preston, *In Relief of Gordon*, p. 43.
6. Butler, *Campaign of the Cataracts*, p. 35.
7. See Maurice, *Military History of the Campaign in Egypt*.
8. Villiers, *Villiers: His Five Decades of Adventure*, vol. ii, p. 58.
9. Still technically at this juncture the 'General Commanding-in-Chief'. The foreshortened title was not formally adopted until 1887.
10. Wolseley to his wife, 11 Mar. 85, Arthur, *Wolseley Letters*, p. 206.
11. See Wolseley, *A Soldier's Life*, vol. ii, pp. 234–5.
12. Cromer, *Modern Egypt*, vol. ii, p. 17.
13. For a full biography see Watson, *The Life of Major-General Sir Charles Wilson*.
14. For a fresh appraisal of the foundation of the Intelligence Branch see Beaver, *Under Every Leaf*.
15. *Hart's Annual Army List for 1885*, vol. i, p. 205.
16. Sir A. H. Layard to the Marquess of Salisbury, 22 Mar. 1880; quoted in Watson, *Life of Wilson*, p. 162.
17. *Hart's Annual Army List for 1885*, vol. i, p. 205.
18. Ibid.
19. Watson, *Life of Wilson*, p. 224.
20. Wilson to his wife, Jan. 83, Watson, *Life of Wilson*, p. 232.
21. *Hart's Annual Army List for 1885*, vol. i, p. 205.
22. Watson, *Life of Wilson*, p. 270.
23. Wolseley journal, 6 Jun. 85, Preston, *In Relief of Gordon*, p. 222.
24. Ibid., 22 May 85, p. 217.
25. Wolseley was AG 1882–90, at which point he handed over to Buller. He was then obliged to go and kick his heels as GOC Ireland until 1895, when the Duke of Cambridge retired and he was at last able to succeed him as C-in-C. He handed Ireland over to Roberts at their first ever meeting.
26. Wolseley to his wife, 14 Feb. 85, Arthur, *Wolseley Letters*, p. 167.
27. Colvile, *Official History* (*OH*), vol. ii, p. 167.
28. See correspondence dated 22 Apr. 85, quoted in Watson, *Life of Wilson*, pp. 344–5.
29. Colvile, *OH*, vol. ii, p. 269.
30. Wilson to his wife, 23 Mar. 85, Watson, *Life of Wilson*, pp. 341–2.

31. Wolseley to his wife, 22 Feb. 85, Arthur, *Wolseley Letters*, pp. 173–4.
32. See for example Lady Wolseley to her husband, 9 Feb. 85, Arthur, *Wolseley Letters*, p. 183.
33. Lady Wolseley to her husband, 30 Jan. 85, Arthur, *Wolseley Letters*, pp. 179–80.
34. Colvile, *OH*, vol. ii, p. 166.
35. Egypt No. 13/1885, p. 31.
36. See for example, as a random sample at national and local level, the *Morning Post*, *London Evening Standard*, and *Sheffield Independent*, all dated 21 May 85.
37. Preston, *In Relief of Gordon*, p. 170.
38. Wolseley journal, 11 Mar. 85, Preston, *In Relief of Gordon*, p. 164.
39. Ibid., 28 Jan. 85, Preston, *In Relief of Gordon*, p. 127.
40. Ibid., p. 128.
41. *New York Times*, 10 Aug. 87 (which carries an article, incorporating biographical notes, heralding an imminent lecture tour by Williams).
42. See for example his *Daily Chronicle* report, quoted in *The Citizen*, 31 Jan. 85.
43. Wilson's interview of 22 Jun. 85. with a Press Asssociation representative; see *London Daily News*, Thu. 23 Jun. 85.
44. Watson, *Life of Wilson*, pp. 348–9. See for example *Hampshire Advertiser*, 30 May 85, which squarely rounded on Williams.
45. *Sheffield and Rotherham Independent*, 21 May 85.
46. Watson, *Life of Wilson*, p. 349.
47. *The Standard*, 21 May 85.
48. Watson, *Life of Wilson*, p. 354.
49. Colvile, *OH*, vol. ii, p. 177.
50. There was a story current at the time that he had been poisoned by one of his numerous wives or concubines; this was the version of his death cited in Wingate, *Mahdiism*, p. 228.
51. Watson, *Life of Wilson*, pp. 350–1.
52. Whose identity I have been unable to trace.
53. *London Daily News*, 23 Jun. 85.
54. See for example *Liverpool Mercury* of that date.
55. See for example *Edinburgh Evening News*, *Sheffield & Rotheram Independent*, *Liverpool Mercury*, and *Manchester Evening News*, all 24 Jun. 85, and *Abereen Journal* of the following day.
56. Preston, *In Relief of Gordon*, p. 113.
57. The accounts of Wilson, Gascoigne, Trafford and Stuart-Wortley are unanimously agreed that they fought their way past Ḥalfaiya, where there were a number of guns, and engaged enemy positions on Tuti Island and at Omdurman. The *Bordein* even hailed enemy riflemen on Tuti Island from a distance of 80 yards, in the mistaken belief that they were members of the garrison.
58. *Guernsey Star*, 28 Jun. 85, citing Colborne's 22 Jun. article for the *Daily News*.
59. Quoted in *Liverpool Mercury*, 24. Jun. 85.
60. A not altogether fair observation, as Wilson was only too keenly aware that in this instance his chief was doing his best to set him up as a scapegoat.
61. Cited in the *Birmingham Daily Post*'s coverage of the libel case, 28 Oct 1886.
62. I have identified the coverage through the medium of the 29 Jun. 85. edition of the *Edinburgh Evening News*, which in all likelihood would have been repeating an article carried by one of the London papers the same day.
63. *Edinburgh Evening News*, 6 Jul. 85.
64. Watson, *Life of Wilson*, p. 354.
65. Ibid., pp. 356–7.
66. Ibid.
67. Ibid., p. 357.
68. *Leeds Mercury*, 28 Oct. 85.
69. *London Gazette*, 10 Mar. 85, pp. 1026–8.
70. The case was well reported in the *Leeds Mercury* and *Birmingham Daily Post*, amongst other places, on 28 Oct. 86.
71. Hill, *Biographical Dictionary*, p. 379.
72. Wilson, *Korti to Khartum*, pp. 112–15.
73. Colvile, *OH*, vol. i, pp. 267–9.
74. Forbes, Archibald, 'The Failure of the Nile Campaign', *Contemporary Review*, January 1892, quoted in *Leicester Chronicle*, 9 Jun, 1892.
75. *The Nineteenth Century*, May 1892, p. 794.

Chapter 1: All Men Worship the Rising Sun

1. Later re-titled the First Sea Lord.
2. See Wood, *From Midshipman to Field Marshal*.
3. For Baker's role as a theorist see his, *The British Cavalry with Remarks on its Practical Organization*.
4. Ohrwalder and Wingate, *Ten Years' Captivity*, p. 25. While Ohrwalder asserts that Sa'id Pasha himself ordered that the three emissaries be hanged, Rudolf Slatin says that that they were shot at the insistence of another officer, Slatin, *Fire and Sword in the Soudan*, pp. 176–7.
5. The name by which the Prophet Muh.ammad's 'helpers' or 'followers' had been known.
6. Ohrwalder, *Ten Years' Captivity*, p. 122.
7. Also known as Kashgil. It is by no means certain whether the disaster occurred on 4 or 5 November, though the latter seems the more likely. For a full account of the Kordfofan Expedition and its culminating disaster see my *Go Strong into the Desert*.
8. Ohrwalder claimed to have elicted this through personal conversation with the Mahdi; see *Ten Years' Captivity*, pp. 106–7.
9. Cromer, *Modern Egypt*, vol. i, p. 423.
10. William Thomas Stead.

11. *Pall Mall Gazette*, 9 Jan. 1884, p.1. The Gordon interview ran on pp. 11–12.
12. Ibid., p.12.
13. Cromer, *Modern Egypt*, vol. i, p. 424.
14. Ibid., p. 437.
15. Ibid., p. 425.
16. Ibid., p. 448.
17. Ibid., p. 443–4.
18. Butler, *Sir William Butler: An Autobiography*, p. 269.
19. Cromer, *Modern Egypt*, vol. i, p. 440.
20. Gordon did it seems have some money of his own tucked away on his person. Sir Evelyn Wood describes him producing £300 in £10 notes from his wallet, while he was on the train from Port Said to Cairo on the afternoon of 24 Jan. 1884. According to Wood he remarked, 'This is the only money I have in the world, and my sister found some of it for me . . .', Wood, *From Midshipman to Field Marshal*, vol. ii, p. 163.
21. Cromer, *Modern Egypt*, vol. i, pp. 449–50.
22. Wood, *From Midshipman to Field Marshal*, vol. ii, p. 162.
23. Vetch, *Life, Letters, and Diaries of Lieutenant General Sir Gerald Graham*, p. 253.
24. Wood, *From Midshipman to Field Marshal*, vol. ii, p. 163.
25. Cromer, *Modern Egypt*, vol. i, p. 441.
26. Ibid., p. 460.
27. See Hill, *Biographical Dictionary*, pp. 390–1.
28. For a comprehensive account of the rising, based on Gessi's letters to Gordon, see Hill, *Gordon in Central Africa*, pp. 371–88.
29. For the full text of the note see Cromer, *Modern Egypt*, vol. i, p. 455–7.
30. By now a British possession.
31. Cromer, *Modern Egypt*, vol. i, p. 459.
32. At Baring's home.
33. A German in khedival service. Originally the director of telegraphs, Gordon elevated him to high political office in the Sudan. Giegler had in various interregnums been the acting governor-general. See Hill, *Biographical Dictionary*, p. 136.
34. An abridged transcript of the meeting was forwarded by Baring to Granville on 28 Jan. 84, Egypt No. 12/1884, pp. 38–41.
35. This it seems to me is probably linked to the naïve suggestion made by Gordon in his interview with W. T. Stead that Muḥammad Aḥmad was a mere puppet of the slavers.
36. Cromer, *Modern Egypt*, vol. i, pp. 459–60.
37. Ibid., p. 444–6.
38. For the text of the *firman* see Egypt No. 12/1884, p. 27.
39. Egypt No. 2/1884, p. 4.
40. Graham's biographer identifies the ADC as a Lt. W. A. Scott of the Cameron Highlanders. According to *Hart's Army List* for 1885, however, the only W. A. Scott in the regular army in 1884 was Captain William Augustus Scott of the Gordon Highlanders. There were no Scotts in the Camerons (with two 't's that is!).
41. Cromer, *Modern Egypt*, vol. i, p. 460.
42. Vetch, *Life of Graham*, p. 256.
43. Ibid., pp. 260–1.
44. Egypt No. 2/1884, pp. 27–9.
45. Ibid., p. 29.
46. See Snook, *Into the Jaws of Death*, pp. 240–2.
47. Cavalry: Gendarmerie 300, European Mounted Police 40, *bâshi-bûzuqs* 150. Infantry: Cairo Gendarmerie Battalion 500, Alexandria Gendarmerie Battalion 560, Massowah Sudanese Battalion 450, Senhit Sudanese Battalion 421, Zubair's Bazinger Battalion 678, 'Turkish' (*bâshi-bûzuq*) Battalion 429. Artillery: 2 x Krupp 75-mm, 2 x Gatling MG, 2 x rocket troughs.
48. Colvile, *OH*, vol. i, pp. 19–20.
49. Burleigh, *Desert Warfare*, pp. 16–17.
50. Hewett to the Secretary of the Admiralty, 3.30 p.m., 5 Feb. 1884, Egypt No. 12/1885, p. 30.
51. 'Report on the Egyptian Provinces of the Sudan, Red Sea and Equator', Intelligence Branch, War Office, p. 125.
52. For a full biography see Melville, *Life of the Right Hon. Sir Redvers Buller*.
53. For Wood's account of the operations of No. 4 Column see *From Midshipman to Field Marshal*, vol ii, pp. 24–71.
54. Colvile, *OH*, vol. i, p. 21.
55. For a comprehensive modern account of Second El Teb, including battlefield photography, see Snook, *Go Strong into the Desert*, pp. 44–58.
56. Graham to Hartington, 2 Mar. 1884, supplement to the *London Gazette*, 25 Mar. 1884; also cited in full in Vetch, *Graham, Life Letters and Diaries*, pp. 375–82. The despatch contains the disclaimer, 'Brigader-General H. Stewart CB showed himself, as he is known to be, a most able and daring leader of cavalry. My instructions to him were to avoid engaging the enemy until their formation was broken, and until they were in full retreat. The time of making the charge I left entirely to Brigadier-General Stewart as I wished him to keep well away from the square, not knowing on which side it might be attacked.'
57. Which is to say 600 killed outright and 1,200 wounded, of whom 200 were killed subsequently, leaving 1,000 wounded survivors.
58. Graham to Hartington, 3 Mar. 1884, and ditto 4 Mar. 1884; Hartington to Graham, 4 Mar. 1884: Egypt No. 12/1884, pp. 134–5.

59. Graham to Hartington, 3 Mar. 84 (official despatch on the Occupation of Tokar), *London Gazette*, 27 Mar. 84; or Vetch, *Graham, Life, Letters and Diaries*, pp. 383–6.
60. Burleigh, *Desert Warfare*, pp. 194–5.
61. For the official account of Tamai see Graham to Hartington, 15. Mar. 84, *London Gazette*, 3 Apr. 84; or Vetch, *Graham, Life, Letters and Diaries*, pp. 390–6. For a modern illustrated account see Snook, *Go Strong into the Desert*, pp. 59–75.

Chapter 2: Quandary

1. Undated memorandum from Gordon, including annotated map, received by Baring 4 Feb. 84, Egypt No. 12/1884, pp. 60–2.
2. 'With respect to the Slave Trade, I think nothing of it, for there will be Slave Trade always as long as Turkey and Egypt buy the slaves, and it may be Zobeir will or might see his interests to stop it in some manner.' Gordon to Baring, 25 Jan. 85, Cromer, *Modern Egypt*, vol. i, p. 455. Cromer also noted that Gordon's instructions from London said, 'You should pay especial consideration to the question of the steps that may usefully be taken to counteract the stimulus which it is feared may possibly be given to the Slave Trade by the present insurrectionary movement, and by the withdrawal of the Egyptian authority from the Interior.'
3. Gordon to Baring, 8 Feb. 84, Egypt No. 12/1884, pp. 132–3.
4. Egypt, No. 12/1885, p. 65.
5. Stewart to Baring, 13 Feb. 84, Cromer, *Modern Egypt*, vol. i, p. 469.
6. Egypt, No. 12/1885, p. 56.
7. See Map 2.
8. See Egypt, No. 12/1884, p. 190.
9. Gordon to Baring, 2 Mar. 84, Egypt No. 12/1884, p. 136.
10. Gordon to Baring, 3 Mar. 84, ibid., p. 156.
11. Gordon to Baring, 2 x untimed telegrams of 3 Mar. 84, ibid., p. 136.
12. Stewart to Baring, 4 Mar. 84, ibid., pp. 137–8.
13. Baring to Granville, 4 Mar. 84, ibid., p. 138.
14. Baring to Granville, 5 Mar. 84, ibid., p. 139.
15. Colvile, *OH*, vol. i, p. 43.
16. Gordon to Baring, 6 Mar. 84, Egypt, No. 12/1884, p. 170.
17. Baring to Granville, 9 Mar. 84, ibid., p. 146.
18. Sturge to Granville, 10 Mar. 85, ibid., p. 147.
19. Gordon to Baring, 9 Mar. 84, timed at 10.20 p.m., 11.00p.m., 11.30 p.m., 11.40 p.m. (which time appears on two separate telegrams), and 10 Mar. 84, timed at 8.00 a.m., 10.00 a.m.; ibid., pp. 160–2.
20. See Baring to Granville, 13 Mar. 84 (No. 243), ibid., p. 162.
21. See Baring to Granville, 13 Mar. 84 (No. 242), ibid., p. 160.
22. For Gordon's reports on events 13–16 Mar., ibid., pp. 10, 14–15.
23. Gordon to Baring, probably 23. Mar. 84, Egypt, No. 18/1884, p. 16.
24. Ohrwalder, *Ten Years' Captivity*, p. 111.
25. Gordon to Baring, 23 Mar. 84, Egypt, No. 18/1884, p. 16.
26. Graham to Hartington, 17 Mar. 1884, ibid., p. 176.
27. Granville to Baring, 21 Mar. 84, ibid., p. 181.
28. Baring to Granville, 21 Mar. 84, ibid., p. 183.
29. Baring to Granville, 24 Mar. 84, Egypt, No. 12/1884, p. 186.
30. Granville to Baring 28 Mar. 84, Egypt No. 13/1884 (Nos. 2 & 3), pp. 1–7.
31. Ibid., p. 4.
32. Gordon to Baring 7 Apr, Cromer, *Modern Egypt*, vol. i, p. 555.
33. See Morley, John, *The Life of William Ewart Gladstone* (London, 1903), vol. iii, pp. 156–60.
34. Granville to Baring, 8 Apr. 84, Egypt No. 13/1884, p. 9.
35. See Egerton to Granville, 30 May 84, Egypt No. 25/1884, p. 69.
36. Colvile, *OH*, vol. i, pp. 44–5.
37. Kitchener's personal attributes were such that although he ended up in precisely the same boat as Stuart-Wortley, nobody ever insisted on calling him Captain Kitchener.
38. Wingate, *Mahdiism*, p. 120.
39. Ibid., p. 119.
40. Ḥusain Pasha Khalifa to Baring, 14 Apr. 84; Egypt, No. 18/1884, p. 31.
41. Egypt, No. 18/1884, pp. 32–3.
42. Cromer, *Modern Egypt*, vol. i, p. 558.
43. Ibid., pp. 559–74.

Chapter 3: Novel Expedients

1. Colvile, *OH*, vol. i. pp. 26–30.
2. Sandes, *The Royal Engineers in Egypt and the Sudan*, p. 95. Also Gleichen, *With the Camel Corps*, p. 22.
3. Wolseley to Hartington, Colvile, *OH*, vol. i. p. 29.
4. Colvile, *OH*, vol. i. pp. 29–30.
5. Sandes, *RE in Egypt & Sudan*, pp. 100–1.
6. Stephenson to Hartington, 5 May 84, Colvile, *OH*, vol. i, pp. 32–4.
7. Hay to the Secretary for the Admiralty, 28 May 84, Egypt 25/1884, p. 70. Note that Colvile (vol. i, p. 37) is in error in implying that Hammill left on or about 18 May; it was 28 May.
8. Egerton to Granville, 12 May 84, enclosing 'Despatch addressed by the Officers of the Companies forming the Garrison of Dongola to the President of the Council, the Grand Master of

the Ceremonies and the Minister for War', dated 11 May. 84, Egypt, No. 25/1884, pp. 42–6.
9. Granville to Egerton, 13 May 84, Egypt No. 25/1884, p. 28.
10. Wingate, *Mahdiism*, p. 122.
11. See Egypt, No. 25/1884, pp. 31–4.
12. Bedford to Hay, 31 May 84, ibid., pp. 114–15.
13. Granville to Egerton, 20 May 84, ibid., p. 49.
14. Mudir of Dongola to the Egyptian Cabinet, 28 May 84, copied Egerton to Granville the same day; ibid.4, p. 68.
15. Wood to Watson, 23 Aug. 1884, Egypt No. 35.1884, p. 75.
16. Wingate, *Mahdiism*, p. 121.
17. Baker to Granville, and Egerton to Granville, both dated 1 Jun. 84, Egypt 25/1884, p. 70.
18. Kitchener to Wood, 29 May 84, ibid., p. 69.
19. Egerton to Granville, 30 May, ibid., p. 69.
20. Kitchener to Wood, 11 Jun. 84, ibid., p. 118.
21. Egerton to Granville, 26 Jun. 84, ibid., p. 26.
22. Stephenson to Hartington, 22 Jun. 84, ibid., p. 119.
23. Colvile, *OH*, vol. i, pp. 43–4.
24. Sandes, *RE in Egypt and Sudan*, pp. 67–8.
25. See Egerton to Granville, 6 May 84, Egypt No. 25/1884, p. 27. This telegram traces the intent to despatch Stuart-Wortley into the the desert, though he did not actually leave Assiut until 1 Jul.
26. Wingate, *Mahdiism*, pp. 122–4.
27. See Colvile, *OH*, Appendix 0 [zero] to vol. i., pp. 141–72, where Hammill's report is incorporated in full. Hammill gives the total length of the various cataracts he details as 22½ miles, not the 24½ miles that is their arithmetical total, though possibly one or more of the individual figures is incorrect.
28. For full details of Hay's message see Colvile, *OH*, vol. i, pp. 38–9.
29. Ibid., pp. 38–40.
30. For full career details see Butler's autobiography of 1911.
31. Wolseley to his wife, 5 Nov. 84, Arthur, *Wolseley Letters*, p. 128.
32. Butler, *Autobiography*, p. 269.
33. Ibid., p. 271.
34. Butler to Wolseley, 5 Aug. 84, Colvile, *OH*, vol. i, pp. 40–3.
35. Butler to Wolseley, 4 Aug. 84, ibid., p. 43.
36. Butler, *Campaign of the Cataracts*, p. 28.
37. Ibid., pp. 10–31; *Autobiography*, pp. 272–4.
38. Hartington to Stephenson, 7 Aug. 84, Egypt No. 35/1884, p. 13.
39. Hartington to Stephenson, 8 Aug. 84, ibid., pp. 16–17.
40. Stephenson to Hartington, 11 Aug. 84, ibid., p. 32.
41. Hartington to Stephenson, 12 Aug. 84, ibid., p. 34.
42. Wolseley journal, 22 Aug. 84, Preston, *In Relief of Gordon*, pp. 3–7. The entry of 22 Aug. 1884 is remarkable for its sustained spitefulness. The Duke of Cambridge, Stephenson and Wood were all subjected to character assassination.
43. Stephenson to Hartington, 16 Aug. 84, Egypt No. 35/1884, p. 45.
44. Hartington to Stephenson, 19 Aug. 84, ibid., p. 46.
45. Stephenson to Hartington, 21 Aug. 84, ibid., pp. 53–4.
46. Wolseley journal, 22 Aug. 84, Preston, *In Relief of Gordon*, pp. 3–4.
47. Ibid., pp. 5–6. For the text of Wolseley to Hartington, 18 May 84, see Holland, *Life of the Duke of Devonshire*, vol. 1, pp. 461–2.
48. Colvile, *OH*, vol. i, p. 63.
49. Wolseley journal, 23 Aug. 84, Preston, *In Relief of Gordon*, p. 8.
50. Ibid., 23–6 Aug. 84 inclusive, pp. 8–10.
51. Hartington to Stephenson, 26 Aug. 84, Egypt No. 35/1884, pp. 60–1.
52. Wolseley journal, 9 Sep. 84, Preston, *In Relief of Gordon*, p. 12.
53. Stephenson to Hartington, 29 Aug. 84, Egypt No. 35/1884, p. 63.
54. Wolseley journal, 13 Sep. 84, Preston, *In Relief of Gordon*, p. 16.
55. Wolseley to Hartington, 11 Sep. 84, Colvile, *OH*, vol. i, pp. 54–8.
56. Wolseley journal, 21 Sep. 84, Preston, *In Relief of Gordon*, p. 19.
57. See Colvile, *OH*, vol. i, pp. 176–7.
58. Ibid., appx. 4, 'Report on Canadian Voyageurs', pp. 187–90.
59. Ibid., p. 60.
60. Ibid., p. 61.
61. Ibid., pp. 68–73 (logistics and water transport) and pp. 73–6 (rail transport).
62. 'Report of the Director of Transport on the Formation and Working of the Land Transport of the Nile Expeditionary Force, 1884–5', Lt. Col. G. A. Furse, 12 Jul. 85, ibid., pp. 195–207.
63. Ibid., pp. 203–4.
64. Wolseley journal, 25 Sep. 84, Preston, *In Relief of Gordon*, p. 20.
65. Hartington's instructions to Wolseley, quoted in the *Standard*, 28 Oct. 1884.
66. Wingate, *Mahdiism*, p. 191. Following the Mahdi's death, the Faqi Medawi fell out with the Khalifa and defected to Egypt.
67. Hill, *Biographical Dictionary*, p. 11.
68. Colvile, *OH*, vol. i, p. 98.
69. Wolseley journal, 5 Oct. 84, Preston, *In Relief of Gordon*, p. 31.
70. Colvile, *OH*, vol. i, pp. 95–7.

71. Ibid., p. 105.
72. Ibid., p. 108.
73. Ibid., p. 109.
74. Ibid., p. 110.
75. Wolseley to his wife, 13 Sep. 85, Arthur, *Wolseley Letters*, p. 119.

Chapter 4: Delays and Decisions

1. Quoted in Melville, *Life of Buller*, p. 207.
2. Colvile, *OH*, vol. i, p. 249.
3. Wolseley to his wife, 17 Nov. 84, Arthur, *Wolseley Letters*, p. 130.
4. Butler, *Autobiography*, pp. 281–2.
5. Butler, *Campaign of the Cataracts*, p. 204.
6. Butler, *Autobiography*, p. 284.
7. Colvile, *OH*, vol. i, p. 124.
8. See Egypt No. 1/85, pp. 98–100.
9. This map is reproduced in Colvile, *OH*, vol. i, p. 122.
10. Colvile, *OH*, vol. i, p. 122.
11. Hartington to Wolseley, 5.00 p.m. 15 Nov 84; Egypt No. 1/1885, p. 100.
12. Wolseley to Hartington, 3.05 p.m. 22 Nov 84; ibid., p. 100.
13. Colvile, *OH*, vol i. pp. 129–30.
14. Wolseley journal, 17 Nov. 84, Preston, *In Relief of Gordon*, p. 67.
15. Colvile, *OH*, vol. i, p. 128.
16. Ibid., pp. 126–7.
17. Ibid., p. 127.
18. Wolseley journal, 19 Nov. 84, Preston, *In Relief of Gordon*, p. 68.
19. Prior, *Campaigns of a War Correspondent*, p. 204.
20. Wolseley journal, entries 19 & 20 Nov 84, Preston, *In Relief of Gordon*, pp. 68–9.
21. Prior, *Campaigns*, p. 204.
22. Wolseley journal, 23 Nov. 84, Preston, *In Relief of Gordon*, p. 71.
23. Ibid., 24 Nov. 84, p. 71.
24. Colvile, *OH*, vol. i, p. 130.
25. Butler, *Autobiography*, pp. 285–6.
26. Wolseley journal, 29 Nov. 84, Preston, *In Relief of Gordon*, p. 75.
27. Wolseley to Baring, 29 Nov. 84, Egypt No. 1/1885, p. 101.
28. Wolseley journal, 30 Nov. 84, Preston, *In Relief of Gordon*, pp. 76–7.
29. Ibid., p. 77.
30. Ibid.
31. Queen Victoria to Wolseley, 15 Dec. 84, Arthur, *Wolseley Letters*, p. 156.
32. Wolseley journal, 1 Dec. 84, Preston, *In Relief of Gordon*, p. 85.
33. With effect 29 Nov: Wolseley journal of the same day, Preston, *In Relief of Gordon*, p. 75.
34. Colvile, *OH*, vol. i, p. 133.
35. Quoted in Melville, *Life of Buller*, p. 208.
36. Colvile, *OH*, vol. i, p. 132.
37. Quoted in Melville, *Life of Buller*, pp. 208–9.
38. Colvile, *OH*, vol. i, p. 133.
39. Butler, *Campaign of the Cataracts*, p. 234.
40. Colvile, *OH*, vol. i, p. 135.
41. Ibid., p. 133.
42. Wolseley journal, 8 Jan. 85, Preston, *In Relief of Gordon*, p. 111.
43. McCalmont, *The Memoirs of Major General Sir Hugh McCalmont*, p. 236.
44. Colvile, *OH*, vol. i, p. 135.
45. Wolseley journal, 1 Dec. 84, Preston, *In Relief of Gordon*, p. 78.
46. Ibid., 24 Dec. 84, p. 98.
47. Colvile, *OH*, vol. i, pp. 138–9.
48. Grant, *Cassell's History of the War in the Soudan*, vol. iii, p. 46.
49. Colvile, *OH*, vol. i, p. 134.
50. Wolseley journal, 25 Dec. 84, Preston, *In Relief of Gordon*, p. 99.
51. Colvile, *OH*, vol. i, p. 270.
52. Colvile, *OH*, vol. ii, pp. 243–5.
53. Cameron, 28 Dec. 84, *The Standard*, 22 Jan. 85.

Chapter 5: Leap in the Dark

1. Wolseley journal, 27 Dec. 84, Preston, *In Relief of Gordon*, p. 100.
2. Colvile, *OH*, vol. i, pp. 135–6.
3. Ibid., p. 135.
4. Ibid., p. 136.
5. Cameron, 28 Dec. 84, *The Standard*, 22 Jan. 85.
6. Macdonald, *Too Late for Gordon and Khartoum*, p. 164.
7. Cameron, 28 Dec. 84, *The Standard*, 22 Jan. 85.
8. Macdonald, *Too Late*, pp. 165–6; see Wolseley, *Soldier's Pocket Book*, p. 225.
9. Ibid., p. 164.
10. Dawson, 'Sir Herbert Stewart's Desert March', *The Nineteenth Century*, Nov. 85, p. 723.
11. The War Diary of the Desert Column (Airlie Papers), 4 Jan. 85, identifies Craven as one of the pair, while Fanshawe is mentioned in a war correspondent's report, dated 5 Jan. 85, carried anonymously in *Aberdeen Journal*, 29 Jan. 85.
12. Lawson, 'Desert Notes from Korti to El Goubat', *RE Journal*, Vol. 15, 1885.
13. Assistant Commissary-General was the departmental equivalent of a lieutenant colonel.
14. The strengths cited here are drawn from the 30 Dec. entry in the War Diary. They differ slightly from the figures in the *OH*, Colvile, vol. ii, pp. 2–3.
15. Wolseley journal, 4 Jan. 85, Preston, *In Relief of Gordon*, p. 107.

16. Brackenbury, *Some Memories of My Spare Time*, p. 337.
17. Archer, *The War in Egypt and the Soudan*, vol. iv, pp. 62–3.
18. Marling, *Rifleman and Hussar*, p. 136.
19. Colvile, *OH*, vol. ii, p. 2.
20. Grant, quoting an unamed war correspondent, *Cassell's History*, vol. iii, p. 51.
21. Dawson, 'Stewart's Desert March', p. 724.
22. Cameron, *The Standard*, 31 Dec.
23. Grant, *Cassell's History*, vol. iii, p. 50.
24. War Diary, 30 Dec. 84. The *OH* times the halt at 07.30 a.m., Colvile, vol. ii, p. 3.
25. Dawson, 'Stewart's Desert March', p. 724.
26. Wolseley to his wife, 31 Dec. 84, Arthur, *Wolseley Letters*, p. 136.
27. Wolseley journal, 31 Dec. 84, Preston, *In Relief of Gordon*, p. 102.
28. Wolseley to his wife, 31 Dec. 84, Arthur, *Wolseley Letters*, p. 137.
29. Wolseley to Baring, 31 Dec 84, Egypt No.1/1885, p. 132.
30. Wolseley journal, 31 Dec. 84, Preston, *In Relief of Gordon*, p. 102.
31. Preston, *In Relief of Gordon*, p. 103.
32. Dawson, 'Stewart's Desert March', p. 724.
33. Colvile, *OH*, vol. ii, p. 3; Dawson, 'Stewart's Desert March', p. 725.
34. Snow, 'Mounted Infantry in the Desert Campaign'. Later a general officer, Snow was at the time the subaltern commanding the 1st Somerset Light Infantry section of D Coy., MICR.
35. Lawson, *Desert Notes*.
36. Dawson, 'Stewart's Desert March', p. 725.
37. Wolseley journal, 1 Jan. 85, Preston, *In Relief of Gordon*, p. 103.
38. Ibid., pp. 103–4.
39. Dawson, 'Stewart's Desert March', p. 725; Lawson, 'Desert Notes'.
40. Dawson, 'Stewart's Desert March', p. 725.
41. In the text I have given the timings quoted in the War Diary of the Desert Column. These are slightly at variance with those given in the *OH* (Colvile, vol. ii, pp. 2–4) but they are broadly in agreement with Dawson, 'Stewart's Desert March'.
42. Wolseley journal, 2 Jan. 85, Preston, *In Relief of Gordon*, pp. 104–5.
43. War Diary, 2 Jan. 85.
44. Or, according to Count Gleichen, 'Abu Loolah'.
45. Gleichen, *With the Camel Corps up the Nile*, p. 72.
46. Burleigh, *Daily Telegraph* report, 24 Jan. 85, quoted in *Leeds Mercury*, 6 Mar. 85.
47. Gleichen, *With the Camel Corps*, p. 82.
48. Ibid., pp. 80–1.
49. Dawson, 'Stewart's Desert March', p. 725.
50. Stewart's official despatch, dated 4 Jan. 85, Colvile, *OH*, vol. ii, pp. 246–7.
51. Colvile, *OH*, vol. ii, pp. 4–5.
52. War Diary, 2 Jan. 85.
53. Ohrwalder, *Ten Years' Captivity*, pp. 68–9.
54. See Gleichen's sketch, *With the Camel Corps*, p. 133.
55. Whitaker, *The Military Diary of Colonel W. W. C. Verner*, p. 26.
56. Ibid. p. 27.
57. Colvile, *OH*, vol. ii, p. 246.
58. Gleichen, *With the Camel Corps*, pp. 83–4.
59. Unit strengths and the overall total given here are drawn from the War Diary of the Desert Column, 2 Jan. 85, and are again slightly at variance with the figures given by Colvile.
60. Though Marling places the time of arrival not at 9.00 a.m., but 10.30 a.m., *Rifleman and Hussar*, p. 129.
61. Pronounced 'Fanshaw'.
62. War Diary, 4 Jan. 85.
63. The strength of the party left at Hambok is given in 'Sir H. Stewart's Report on his Second March to Jakdul', 14. Jan. 85, Colvile, *OH*, vol. ii, p. 250.
64. Marling, *Rifleman and Hussar*, p. 148.
65. Whitaker, *Verner Diary*, p. 29.
66. 'Sir H. Stewart's Report', Colvile, *OH*, vol. ii, p. 250.
67. Marling, *Rifleman and Husssar*, pp. 129–30.
68. War Diary, 4 Jan. 85; also Dundonald, *My Army Life*, p. 29, although Dundonald fails to name his travelling companions.
69. Cochrane says seven hours in his memoirs of 1926, but Wolseley's journal places his arrival at 8.00 p.m.
70. War Diary, 4 Jan. 85.
71. Macdonald states that Cochrane arrived at the hut with 'Lieutenant Hine' of the Mounted Infantry and two other officers, but the name occurs nowhere else in the sources and there is no officer of that name in the *Army Lists* of 1884–5, Macdonald, *Too Late*, p. 168.
72. Wilson, *Korti to Khartum*, pp. 297–9.
73. Wolseley journal, 3 Jan. 85, Preston, *In Relief of Gordon*, p. 107.
74. Whitaker, *Verner Diary*, p. 27.
75. Ibid.
76. Marling, *Rifleman and Hussar*, p. 130.
77. Colvile, *OH*, vol. ii, p. 5.
78. Dundonald, *My Army Life*, p. 30.
79. Turner, *Sixty Years of a Soldier's Life*, pp. 99–101.
80. Colvile, *OH*, vol. i, p. 266.
81. Wolseley journal, 5 Jan. 85, Preston, *In Relief of Gordon*, p. 108.
82. Colvile, *OH*, vol. ii, pp. 5–6.
83. For biographical details see Beresford, *Memoirs*.

84. Wolseley journal, 8 Jan. 85, Preston, *In Relief of Gordon*, p. 111.
85. Marling, *Rifleman and Hussar*, p. 130.
86. Wolseley journal, 8 Jan. 85, Preston, *In Relief of Gordon*, p. 109.
87. Whitaker, *Verner Diary*, pp. 27–8; Wilson, *Korti to Khartum*, p. xxi.
88. Colvile, *OH*, vol. ii, p. 6.
89. Macdonald, *Too Late*, p. 171.
90. Wolseley journal, 7 Jan. 85, Preston, *In Relief of Gordon*, p. 108.
91. Macdonald, *Too Late*, pp. 172–3.
92. The date of the orders is established in a letter from Stewart to Wolseley, dated Jakdul Wells, 14 Jan. 85, Colvile, *OH*, vol. i. p. 247.
93. Colvile, *OH*, vol. ii, pp. 6–8.
94. Ibid., p. 250.
95. Ibid., p. 246.
96. Macdonald, *Too Late*, p. 181, noting that the 'Colonel Featherstone' to whom Macdonald refers is in fact Capt. Fethersonhaugh.
97. Whitaker, *Verner Diary*, p. 29. Verner for some reason refers to the wells at Hambok as 'Abu Hasheen', but places them 47 miles from Korti, confirming that they are in fact one and the same.
98. Wilson, *Korti to Khartum*, pp. 300–3.
99. Colvile, *OH*, vol. ii, p. 9.
100. Wilson, *Korti to Khartum*, p. 303.
101. Wilson did not in the end get back to Korti until 9 Feb.
102. Wolseley to his wife, 15 Jan. 85, Arthur, *Wolseley Letters*, p. 155.
103. Colvile, *OH*, vol. ii, pp. 9–10.
104. War Diary, 8 Jan. 85.
105. Preston, *In Relief of Gordon*, pp. 108–12.
106. Wolseley journal, 8 Jan. 85, Preston, *In Relief of Gordon*, p. 111.

Chapter 6: Go Strong into the Desert

1. This time the overall totals of officers, men and animals are identical to the figures cited in the *OH*; see Colvile, vol. ii, p.6.
2. Stewart to Wolseley, 14 Jan. 85, Colvile, *OH*, vol ii. p. 250.
3. B to H Coys inclusive.
4. See for example the eyewitness watercolours and sketches by William S. Perry, a member of the Life Guards, in the collection of the Victoria and Albert Museum.
5. Gleichen, *With the Camel Corps*, Appendix II.
6. Ibid., pp. 60–1.
7. The 1871 pattern valise equipment was in the process of being superseded by a P1882 design, but Army-wide roll-out of such items was invariably slow, so that at this juncture the majority of units were still equipped with the old pattern.
8. Gleichen, *With the Camel Corps*, p. 107.
9. Trafford MS. A Trafford sketch shows officers of his battalion wearing red sashes in the right-rear corner of the square at Abu Klea. It is possible that they put them on specifically for the fight, so that their men could readily distinguish them. Equally they may have worn them by default.
10. Beresford, *Memoirs*, vol. i, pp. 252–3.
11. Gleichen, *With the Camel Corps*, p. 106.
12. Beresford, *Memoirs*, vol. i, p. 252.
13. Clowes, *The Royal Navy*, p. 359.
14. Snook, *Go Strong into the Desert*, p. 176.
15. Gleichen, *With the Camel Corps*, p. 106.
16. In fact Barrow died in Cairo in 1886, when his old wound reopened while he was tent-pegging.
17. See Wm S. Perry watercolours, V&A Collection.
18. Marling, *Rifleman and Hussar*, p. 121.
19. *Hart's AL* for 1885, vol. i, p. 307a, note 75.
20. Local captain, substantive lieutenant.
21. Walsh was the officer who carried despatches between Lord Chelmsford and Maj. John Dartnell on the night before Isandlwana.
22. Snow MS.
23. Snow MS.
24. Marling, *Rifleman and Hussar*, p. 124.
25. Ibid.
26. Wolseley journal, 26 Nov. 85, Preston, *In Relief of Gordon*, pp. 72–3.
27. Because Herbert is not mentioned in any of the participant accounts, it would be tempting to conclude that he had fallen sick at some earlier point in the campaign. However, the GCR casualty return of 23 Jan. 85, enclosed with the War Diary and orders book of the Desert Column, bears his signature. Ordinarily this would have fallen to the adjutant, but Lt. Crutchley had been seriously wounded four days earlier.
28. *Hart's AL 85*, vol. i, pp. 231–2.
29. Macdonald, *Too Late*, pp. 211–12.
30. *Hart's AL 85*, vol. i, p. 133.
31. This is a relatively small number of officers for a unit consisting of a battalion headquarters and seven companies. The established officer strength per company was a captain and two lieutenants, meaning that Vandeleur should have had twenty-one company officers alone.
32. Trafford MS.
33. According to Webb's *The Abu Klea Medal Rolls*, a Surgeon Charles Palmerston Turner was also eligible for the Abu Klea clasp. Webb lists him (p. 144) as having died during the course of the campaign, but attaches no date to his demise. I have found no primary source reference to Dr Turner.

34. Falvey is mentioned by Lord Dundonald, an HCR officer, as being at the rear of the square picking up wounded during the advance at Abu Klea. The rear face was composed of HCR companies.
35. Beresford, *Memoirs*, vol. i, p. 254.
36. War Diary, 8 Jan. 85.
37. Macdonald, *Too Late*, p. 175.
38. Turner, *Sixty Years of a Soldier's Life*, p. 103.
39. For a biography of Burleigh see Greaves, *Wild Bennet Burleigh*.
40. Turner, *Sixty Years of a Soldier's Life*, pp. 93–4.
41. Colvile, *OH*, vol. ii. p. 12.
42. Marling, *Rifleman and Hussar*, p. 130.
43. War Diary, 9 Jan. 85. In *Korti to Khartum* (p. 2), Wilson fixes reveille an hour earlier. Beresford also gives 12.30 a.m. in his *Memoirs* (vol. i, p. 254), but, as in many points of detail, is merely following Wilson's lead.
44. Wilson, *Korti to Khartum*, p. 4.
45. War Diary, 9 Jan. 85.
46. Ibid., 10 Jan. 85.
47. Wilson, *Korti to Khartum*, p. 5.
48. Whitaker, *Verner Diary*, p. 29.
49. Gleichen, *With the Camel Corps*, p. 103.
50. Wilson, *Korti to Khartum*, pp. 4–5.
51. Prior, *Campaigns*, p. 211.
52. War Diary, 10 Jan. 85.
53. Wilson, *Korti to Khartum*, pp. 5–6.
54. Colvile, *OH*, vol. ii. p. 250.
55. War Diary, 10 Jan. 85.
56. 'Sir H. Stewart's Report', Colvile, *OH*, vol. ii, pp. 247–50.
57. Whitaker, *Verner Diary*, p. 29.
58. War Diary, 11 Jan. 85.
59. Ibid.
60. 'Sir H. Stewart's Report', Colvile, *OH*, vol. ii, p. 250.
61. Wilson, *Korti to Khartum*, pp. 7–8.
62. Marling, *Rifleman and Hussar*, p. 130.
63. Whitaker, *Verner Diary*, p. 31.
64. War Diary, 11 Jan. 85.
65. The bottoms of which had been pierced with bayonets, Whitaker, *Verner Diary*, pp. 31–2.
66. Wilson, *Korti to Khartum*, pp. 8–9.
67. Ibid., p. 9.
68. Ibid., pp. 9–11.
69. Whitaker, *Verner Diary*, p. 32.
70. 'Sir H. Stewart's Report', Colvile, *OH*, vol. ii, p. 250.
71. Lawson, *Desert Notes*.
72. Report by Maj. James Dorward RE, 'Work Done at the Jakdul Wells', Colvile, *OH*, vol. ii, p. 252.
73. 'Sir H. Stewart's Report', Colvile, *OH*, vol. ii, p. 250.
74. Dorward, 'Work Done at the Jakdul Wells', Colvile, *OH*, vol. ii, p. 251.
75. Whitaker, *Verner Diary*, p. 34.
76. Reuters report, Jakdul Wells 3 Jan. 85, *The Standard*, 10 Jan. 85, p. 5.
77. Wilson, *Korti to Khartum*, p. 14.
78. Macdonald, *Too Late*, pp. 178–9.
79. *Pall Mall Gazette*, 12 Feb. 85.
80. Macdonald, *Too Late*, p. 197: 'The Mounted Infantry, however, had so economised their supply that they were able to continue their march, and reached the gorge, as already stated, shortly after I did.'
81. 'Sir H. Stewart's Report' itemizes all detached movements and makes no separate allowance for MICR, Colvile, *OH*, vol. ii, pp. 247–50. Neither is any such movement reflected in the War Diary. Marling's diary notes for 11 Jan. say, 'Got to Abu Halfa wells at 4.30 p.m. Not too much water and full of sand.' His notes for the following day say, 'Marched at 5.30 a.m. and got back to Gakdul wells at 11.00 a.m.' Marling was of course in A Coy., MICR; *Rifleman and Hussar*, p. 130.
82. War Diary, 12 Jan. 85.
83. Gascoigne, 'To Within a Mile of Khartoum', *Nineteenth Century*, July 85, p. 88.
84. War Diary, 12 Jan. 85.
85. 'Sir H. Stewart's Report', Colvile, *OH*, vol. ii, p. 248.
86. Whitaker, *Verner Diary*, p. 35. The passage in question refers to 13 Jan.
87. Trafford MS.
88. For the relative positions of the forts see Gleichen's sketch, *With the Camel Corps*, p. 92.
89. Dorward, 'Work Done at the Jakdul Wells', Colvile, *OH*, vol. ii, pp. 251–3.
90. Gleichen, *With the Camel Corps*, p. 93.
91. Macdonald, *Too Late*, p. 208.
92. Wright, *Life of Burnaby*, p. 267.
93. Dundonald, *My Army Life*, p. 30.
94. Gleichen, *With the Camel Corps*, p. 105.
95. Ibid.

Chapter 7: Approach to Battle

1. Wright, *Life of Burnaby*, p. 35.
2. Long-leave generally straddled Christmas and the New Year.
3. Wright, *Life of Burnaby*, p. 93.
4. Binning, Lt. Lord, *An Independent Account of the Battle of Abou Klea*; quoted in Wright, *Life of Burnaby*, pp. 304–5.
5. Dover to Envermeau, Nomandy.
6. Stuart-Menzies, *Memories Discreet and Indiscreet*, p. 55.
7. See Alexander, *The True Blue*, p. 162 (noting that Alexander gives the name incorrectly as 'Coffin'). The gun is now in the weapons collection at the Land Warfare Centre in Warminster, where a silver inscription on the butt gives 'Caffin' not 'Coffin'. The gun and inscription can also be seen

in Wilsey, Col. Robert, 'Burnaby's Weapons – Part 1: The Shotgun at El Teb', *Classic Arms and Militaria*, vol. xx, no. 1, Feb. 2013.
8. Alexander, *True Blue*, pp. 162–3.
9. All ranks and senority dates in the paragraphs above are derived from the 85 edition of *Hart's Army List*.
10. The figures cited are derived from the *OH*; see Colvile, vol. ii, p. 254.
11. They were brought up to Jakdul by Burnaby's convoy.
12. Stewart to Wolseley, 14 Jan. 85, Colvile, *OH*, vol. ii, pp. 10–11.
13. Wilson, *Korti to Khartum*, p. 16.
14. Whitaker, *Verner Diary*, p. 36.
15. Gleichen, *With the Camel Corps*, p. 108.
16. Ibid., p. 109.
17. Wilson, *Korti to Khartum*, p. 17.
18. Gleichen, *With the Camel Corps*, pp. 112–13.
19. War Diary, 14 & 15 Jan. 85.
20. Gleichen, *With the Camel Corps*, p. 113.
21. Dundonald, *My Army Life*, p. 31.
22. Gleichen, *With the Camel Corps*, pp. 110–14.
23. Whitaker, *Verner Diary*, p. 36.
24. War Diary, 15 Jan. 85.
25. Whitaker, *Verner Diary*, p. 37.
26. Wilson, *Korti to Khartum*, p. 17.
27. Binning, quoted in Wright, *Life of Burnaby*, p. 299.
28. Wilson, *Korti to Khartum*, p. 18.
29. Wilson (ibid., p. 19) describes the incident without identifying the officer . Gleichen (*With the Camel Corps*, p. 118) refers to what can only be the same incident but this time attributes it: 'Craven I think it was'. Gleichen, however, who self-evidently is not altogether sure, appears to have had it wrong. Alex Macdonald (*Too Late*, p. 213) also describes the incident but emphatically identifies the officer as Major John French; it is clear that he was told of the affair by French in person. Verner (*Diary*, p. 37) confirms that French pursued a party of camel-mounted Arabs across the divide and that in the course of the pursuit into the Abu Klea Valley, 'some spearmen rose out of the grass and attempted to cut them off'.
30. Williams, report of 18 Jan. 85, *Daily Chronicle*, 25 Feb. 85.
31. Macdonald, *Too Late*, p. 214.
32. Whitaker, *Verner Diary*, p. 37.
33. Gleichen, *With the Camel Corps*, p. 115.
34. See *Western Mail*, 23 Jan. 85, which cites Pearse's report.
35. Whitaker, *Verner Diary*, p. 37.
36. Macdonald, *Too Late*, pp. 215–16.
37. Stewart's 'Official Despatch', 18 Jan. 85, *London Gazette*, 20 Feb. 85, p. 755.
38. Macdonald, *Too Late*, p. 217; Colvile, *OH*, vol. ii, p. 15; Trafford MS.
39. Gleichen, *With the Camel Corps*, pp. 117–18.
40. Pearse, *Daily News* report, cited in *Western Mail*, 23 Jan. 85.
41. Prior, *Campaigns*, p. 212.
42. Ibid.; Wilson, *Korti to Khartum*, p. 19; Whitaker, *Verner Diary*, p. 37; Macdonald, *Too Late*, p. 218; Pearse, *Daily News/Western Mail*, 23 Jan. 85.
43. This was standard practice at this period. The existence of such a pennant is confirmed by Macdonald, see *Too Late*, p. 210.
44. Ibid., p. 218.
45. Dundonald, *My Army Life*, p. 38.
46. The only sources to state a number of flags are Jack Cameron's report for the *Evening Standard*, cited also in the *Yorkshire Gazette*, 23 Jan. 85, and Harry Pearse's report for the *Daily News*, cited in the *Western Mail* on the same date.
47. Marling, *Rifleman and Hussar*, p. 131.
48. Macdonald, *Western Morning News* report, quoted in the *Evening News*, 23 Jan. 85.
49. Verner sketch map, see *Diary*, p. 41.
50. Macdonald, *Too Late*, pp. 218–19.
51. Ibid., p. 219.
52. Lawson diagram, Macdonald, *Too Late*, p. 221.
53. Ibid.
54. The 150-yard dimension is fixed by a contemporaneous Reuters report. The 400-yard dimension I fixed myself on the basis of ground recce with Lawson's map.
55. Whitaker, *Verner Diary*, p. 38.
56. Wilson, *Korti to Khartum*, pp. 19–20; Whitaker, *Verner Diary*, p. 38.
57. Dundonald, *My Army Life*, p. 33.
58. Grant, *Cassell's History*, vol. iii, p. 64.
59. Gleichen, *With the Camel Corps*, p. 120.
60. Williams, report of 18 Jan. 85, *Daily Chronicle*, 25 Feb. 85.
61. Whitaker, *Verner Diary*, p. 38; Grant, *Cassell's History*, vol. iii, p. 64.
62. Marling, *Rifleman and Hussar*, p. 131.
63. Chaplin, *The Queen's Own Royal West Kent Regiment*, p. 34.
64. The second section can be identified by the fact that 381 Private C. Wilford of 2nd Essex is shown in the MICR casualty return of 23 Jan. 85 as being killed on a hilltop position on the night 16 Jan. See also Webb, *The Abu Klea Medal Rolls*, p. 126.
65. Trafford MS.
66. Ibid.
67. Beresford, *Memoirs*, vol. i, p. 258.
68. Lawson diagram, reference point G, Macdonald, *Too Late*, p. 221.
69. Wilson, *Korti to Khartum*, p. 21.

70. Gleichen, *With the Camel Corps*, p. 121.
71. Grant, *Cassell's History*, vol. iii, p. 67. Though Grant fails to cite sources, his account appears to be almost exclusively based on the copy of the war correspondents. Such an acute detail is certain to have been extracted from an eyewitness account.
72. Macdonald, *Too Late*, p. 220.
73. Snow MS.
74. Marling, *Rifleman and Hussar*, p. 131.
75. Macdonald, *Too Late*, p. 221. The most likely source of this information is the group of former Egyptian soldiers who came in from the hillside to surrender the following day.
76. Williams, report of 18 Jan. 85, *Daily Chronicle*, 25 Feb. 85.
77. Lawson, 'Desert Notes'.
78. Whitaker, *Verner Diary*, p. 39.
79. Burleigh, Bennet, *Daily Telegraph* report, quoted in Anon., *The English in Egypt*, p. 41.
80. Burleigh, quoted in *The English in Egypt*, p. 418.
81. Whitaker, *Verner Diary*, p. 39; Gleichen, *With the Camel Corps*, p. 122.
82. Wilson, *Korti to Khartum*, p. 22.
83. Wright, *Life of Burnaby*, p. 272.
84. Ibid.
85. Snow MS.
86. Wright, *Life of Burnaby*, p. 272.
87. Macdonald, *Too Late*, pp. 223–4.
88. Wright, *Life of Burnaby*, p. 273.
89. Marling, *Rifleman and Hussar*, p. 131.
90. Wright, *Life of Burnaby*, p. 300.
91. Dundonald, *My Army Life*, p. 33.
92. Macdonald, *Too Late*, p. 224.
93. Marling, *Rifleman and Hussar*, p. 131.
94. Gleichen, *With the Camel Corps*, p. 122.
95. Macdonald, *Too Late*, p. 224.
96. MICR casualty return, 23 Jan. 85.
97. Macdonald, *Too Late*, p. 224.

Chapter 8: Under Fire

1. Wilson, *Korti to Khartum*, p. 23.
2. In particular a very competent participant account contained in a letter sent by Sgt. William Stakings (2nd Royal West Kent section, D Coy., MICR) to his friend Sgt. Henry Charingbold at the regimental depot. The letter was dated Gakdul Wells 5 Feb. 85 and was published in *Chatham News*, 12 Mar. 85.
3. Whitaker, *Verner Diary*, p. 40.
4. Lawson, 'Desert Notes'.
5. Macdonald, *Too Late*, p. 220.
6. Gleichen, *With the Camel Corps*, p. 127.
7. Prior, *Campaigns*, p. 213.
8. Stakings to Charingbold, 5 Feb. 85; *Chatham News*, 12 Mar. 85.
9. Burleigh, quoted in *The English in Egypt*, p. 419.
10. Gleichen, *With the Camel Corps*, p. 123.
11. Burleigh, quoted in *The English in Egypt*, p. 419.
12. Christian name Richard: his familiar name is identified in Marling, *Rifleman and Hussar*, p. 129.
13. Nickname established in Marling, *Rifleman and Hussar*, p. 148.
14. Colvile, *OH*, vol. ii, p. 16.
15. Christened Archibald; his familiar name is established in Marling, *Rifleman and Hussar*, p. 140.
16. Williams, *Daily Chronicle* report, quoted in *Lloyd's Weekly London Newspaper*, 1 Mar. 85.
17. Whitaker, *Verner Diary*, p. 40.
18. Ibid.
19. Ibid.
20. In the later illustrated version of his diary, Trafford says that he left 25 men with Jones, which would have been roughly half the company. It is a direct contradiction and there is no way of knowing which of the two editions of the diary is correct.
21. Macdonald, *Too Late*, p. 220. Though he states that the post was held by the Mounted Infantry, Macdonald fails to specify a company. The deduction is driven by the absence of two sections of B Coy. from the advancing square.
22. Beresford, *Memoirs*, vol i, pp. 258–9.
23. Stewart to the Chief of the Staff, Abu Klea Wells, 18 Jan., 85, *London Gazette*, 20 Feb. 85, p. 755, and/or Colvile, *OH*, vol. ii, pp. 255–6.
24. Williams, report 18 Jan. 85, published *Daily Chronicle*, 25 Feb. 85.
25. Whitaker, *Verner Diary*, p. 40; Williams report, 18 Jan. 85, *Daily Chronicle*, 25 Feb. (and quoted in *Lloyd's Weekly London Newspaper*, 1 Mar.).
26. Williams, report 18 Jan. 85, published *Daily Chronicle*, 25 Feb. 85.
27. Wilson, *Korti to Khartum*, pp. 41–3.
28. Hill, *Biographical Dictionary*, p. 284.
29. Reid, 'The Mahdi's Emirs', p. 312.
30. The principal source upon which the Mahdist order of battle is based, Wilson's intelligence report of 18 Jan. 85, is in *London Gazette*, 20 Feb. 85, p. 758.
31. Gleichen, *With the Camel Corps*, p. 133.
32. See Snook, *Go Strong into the Desert*, pp. 201–9, for analysis and findings on Mahdist military dress at this period.
33. Colvile, *OH*, vol. ii, pp. 12–13.
34. Wylde, *'83 to '87 in the Soudan*, vol. i, pp. 6–7.
35. Herbert, *Morning Post*, 22 Jan. 85.
36. In amplification see Snook, 'The Myth of Native-Bashing', *BBC History*, vol. ix, No. 1, Jan. 2008.
37. See also Binning's *An Independent Account*, appended to Wright's, *Life of Burnaby* (p. 300): '... their main body advanced towards down the

centre of the valley, and then halted about a mile off'. In the captions to his *Sketches in the Soudan* Verner himself estimates the distance at 1,200 yards.
38. Burleigh, quoted in *The English in Egypt*, pp. 419–20.
39. Beresford, *Memoirs*, vol. i, p. 259. It is perhaps instructive to note that the attributed comment, 'I'm not in luck today', first appears in Macdonald's *Too Late*, p. 224, without any suggestion of it being addressed personally to Beresford. *Memoirs* would not be published for another 27 years.
40. Whitaker, *Verner Diary*, p. 40.
41. Gleichen, *With the Camel Corps*, p. 123.
42. Williams, *Daily Chronicle* report, quoted in *Lloyd's Weekly London Newspaper*, 1 Mar. 85.
43. Wright, *Life of Burnaby*, p. 271. Though his book is not a primary source, Wright corresponded with Marling in preparing it; it seems certain that this description of 'Moses' must have originated with Marling himself. Wright's grasp of military matters is generally feeble.
44. Marling, *Rifleman and Hussar*, pp. 125 & 133.
45. Wilson, *Korti to Khartum*, pp. 24–5.
46. Macdonald, *Too Late*, p. 227.
47. Colvile, *OH*, vol. ii, p. 16.
48. Burleigh, *Daily Telegraph* report, quoted in *The English in Egypt*, p. 420.
49. Williams, *Daily Chronicle* report, quoted in *Lloyd's Weekly London Newspaper*, 1 Mar. 85.
50. Macdonald, *Western Morning News* report, quoted in *Evening News*, 23 Jan. 85.
51. Macdonald, *Too Late*, p. 225.
52. Dundonald, *My Army Life*, p. 36.
53. Webb, *The Abu Klea Medal Rolls*, p. 73.
54. Wright, *Life of Burnaby*, p. 285.
55. Macdonald, *Too Late*, pp. 225–6.
56. Prior, *Campaigns*, p. 209.
57. Williams, *Daily Chronicle* report, quoted in *Lloyd's Weekly London Newspaper*, 1 Mar. 85.
58. Macdonald, *Too Late*, p. 226.
59. Wilson, *Korti to Khartum*, p. 24.
60. Macdonald, *Too Late*, p. 226. Macdonald fails to specify whether the man was a native employee or a soldier; theoretically either is possible. However, the handwritten casualty returns submitted to Lord Airlie and now archived in Edinburgh, include that of 1st Royal Sussex. Maj. Sunderland signed the return personally and reported that only two of his soldiers died at Abu Klea; both were with the square. This compels the conclusion that the mortally wounded groom was an Egyptian or Sudanese civilian in Sunderland's private employ.
61. Wilson, *Korti to Khartum*, p. 38.
62. Dawson, 'Stewart's Desert March', p. 727.
63. Burleigh, *Daily Telegraph* report, quoted in *The English in Egypt*, pp. 421–2.
64. Some explanation of the timings adopted in the text is appropriate. Most of the sources that touch on the subject of time agree that there was about an hour-long interval between Barrow leaving the zariba and the advance of the square. For example, in *Too Late for Gordon and Khartoum* (p. 231), Macdonald gives 9.00 a.m. for the departure of the 19th Hussars and 10.00 a.m. for the advance of the square. In his *Daily Telegraph* report Burleigh wrote, 'Precisely at 7.35 a.m. the troops marched forward . . .' This in my judgement, however definitively asserted it might sound, fails to allow sufficient time in daylight to accommodate the known events of the early morning. I have, accordingly, chosen to work backwards from 09.30 a.m., the time given for the advance of the square in the War Diary. Lord Airlie as brigade major was responsible for keeping the diary and, cognizant of this responsibility, will more than likely have specifically looked at his watch as the order to move was given. Even if he did not, he would have checked the recollection of the other staff officers when making his entry for the day of the battle. The time given in the War Diary seems to me to represent the authoritative or 'official' time for the British troops in the Bayūda and has the advantage of being directly contemporaneous.
65. Burleigh, quoted in *The English in Egypt*, p. 422.
66. Macdonald, *Too Late*, p. 227.
67. In confirmation of the number of men killed in or near the zariba, see also Verner's *Sketches in the Soudan*, where in one picture caption he states, 'It was not until then that we were able to form an estimate of our losses in the previous day's fighting. It was now found that in the zariba they amounted to 4 men killed and 4 officers and 13 men wounded.' This is the only source to state categorically what the casualties at the zariba were. For reasons explained later in the text, I conclude that a more accurate reflection might be 4 men killed and 3 officers and 16 men wounded.

Chapter 9: The Valley of the Shadow

1. The evolution of the High Victorian Army into the BEF of 1914 is traced in my *Into the Jaws of the Death: British Military Blunders 1879–1900*, London, 2008.
2. See for example Capt. Neill Malcolm's edited anthology of Henderson's work, *The Science of War: A Collection of Essays and Lectures* (London, 1908).

3. *Narrative of the Field Operations connected with the Zulu War of 1879* (War Office Official History), pp. 114–15.
4. Four ranks were usual in the old 'receive cavalry' square although, in reflecting the advent of the breech-loader, the 1877 manual now made allowance for two.
5. Dundonald, *My Army Life*, p. 28.
6. For participant comment see also the Snow MS, 'Mounted Infantry in the Desert Campaign'.
7. Trafford is in all likelihood referring to Lt. Col. Reggie Talbot as will later be explained.
8. Trafford MS.
9. Burleigh, *Daily Telegraph* report, quoted in *The English in Egypt*, p. 422.
10. Gleichen, *With the Camel Corps*, p. 124.
11. Colvile *OH*, vol. ii. p 16 (schematic), p. 256; Stewart to Buller, dated Abu Klea Wells, 18 Jan. 85 (Official Despatch), *London Gazette*, 20 Feb. 85, p. 755; Talbot, 'The Battle of Abu Klea', *The Nineteenth Century*, Jan. 86 (also cited in full in post-1886 editions of Wilson's *From Korti to Khartum*, and in *Aberdeen Journal*, 1 Jan. 86); Wilson, *Korti to Khartum*, p. 25; Whitaker, *Verner Diary*, p. 40 (schematic); Gleichen, *With the Camel Corps*, p. 128 (schematic); Trafford MS; Beresford, 'Report of Proceedings of the Naval Brigade from November 26 last to March 8, 85' (Official RN Despatch), *London Gazette*, 28 Apr. 85; Macdonald, *Too Late*, pp. 227–8; Royle, *The Egyptian Campaigns*, p. 342; Marling, *Rifleman and Hussar*, p. 132; War Diary of the Desert Column; Herbert, *Morning Post*, 22 Jan. 85, p. 5.
12. Beresford, 'Proceedings of the Naval Brigade', *London Gazette*, 28 Apr. 85, p. 1913.
13. Burleigh, quoted in *The English in Egypt*, p. 422.
14. Ibid., p. 419.
15. In his *With the Camel Corps up the Nile*, Gleichen estimates the number of camels accompanying the square as only 30 (p. 124). There is, however, an overwhelming weight of evidence in other accounts to show that he was well wide of the mark. See for example Burleigh, quoted in *The English in Egpt*, p. 420, who says, 'About one hundred beasts only were included in the fighting square.' See also Dundonald, *My Army Life*, p. 37, where he remarks, 'This was the first time that all our force had worked together in a square on the move and surrounding some 150 camels.' In *Too Late for Gordon and Khartoum*, p. 228, Macdonald proffers a figure of 120. See also Colvile, *OH*, vol. ii, p. 16, where a diagram of the square incorporates 150 camels.
16. Macdonald, *Too Late*, pp. 220–1, including inferences to be drawn from Lawson's map.
17. Though sourced as having been with Beresford overnight, Morse is not again specifically mentioned by any of the sources. It is the fact that Chaplin's regimental history talks of Lt. Alderson's 2nd Royal West Kents section being in the square, whilst failing to mention Morse's 1st Battalion section, that compels the inference that the latter was not present and *ipso facto* had been one of the two B Coy. sections left behind in the *zariba*.
18. Lawson, 'Desert Notes'.
19. Macdonald, *Too Late*, p. 230.
20. See *Hart's AL 85*, p. 279.
21. Macdonald, *Too Late*, p 278; also Dundonald, *My Army Life*, p. 23.
22. Burleigh, *Daily Telegraph* report, quoted in *The English in Egypt*, p. 424. See also Wright, *Life of Burnaby*, p. 286, for a purported verbatim rendition of the conversation. Burnaby's soldier-servant was 911 Trooper F. Buchanan, RHG (Blues). It is unlikely to have been Buchanan who got the shotgun, but rather an unknown native servant. According to Wright, Buchanan was in the square, probably marching, Martini in hand, with Lord Binning's detachment. Burleigh has assumed that it is the same gun at issue, whereas the gun used by Burnaby at El Teb was a borrowed one and had since been returned to its owner.
23. 'Smoke' features prominently in Snow, 'Mounted Infantry in the Desert Campaign'. Happily Snow reports that the dog survived the campaign.
24. Macdonald, *Too Late*, p. 211.
25. The *Morning Post*, 26 Nov. 85.
26. O'Malley's DCM citation refers to him bringing in an officer at this juncture (see *Morning Post*, 26 Nov. 85). We know from Binning's account (Wright, *Life of Burnaby*, p. 300), that Beech was wounded 'before the advance began'. As we know pecisely what happened to the other three officers wounded in or near the *zariba*, it follows that the officer brought in by O'Malley can only have been Beech. An emphatic statement by Verner in his *Sketches in the Soudan* to the effect that four wounded officers were brought up from the *zariba* when the column was reunited on the morning after the battle tends to support Binning, for if the first three were Dickson, Gough and Lyall who could the fourth have been if not Beech?
27. Macdonald, *Too Late*, p. 228.
28. Dundonald, *My Army Life*, p. 36.
29. Talbot, 'Battle of Abu Klea'; Macdonald, *Too Late*, p. 228.
30. Whitaker, *Verner Diary*, p. 41. 'Lock up their fours' probably reflects contemporary parade-ground jargon. As we have seen the formal battalion-sized 'receive cavalry' square was configured in four

ranks. At Abu Klea the square was certainly only two ranks deep: see Burleigh, quoted in *The English in Egypt*, p. 422, where he says, 'In lines two deep – not of four men as squares ordinarily are formed – our 1,400 or thereabouts of fighting men advanced.'
31. Burleigh, quoted in the *English in Egypt*, p. 422.
32. Whitaker, *Verner Diary*, p. 41.
33. Talbot, 'Battle of Abu Klea'; also cited in full in *Aberdeen Journal*, 1 Jan. 86.
34. Macdonald, *Too Late*, p. 232.
35. Trafford MS.
36. See *Hart's AL 85*, p. 158.
37. Dundonald, *My Army Life*, p. 37.
38. Sgt. Charles Williams MS, Toy Family Papers.
39. Talbot, 'Battle of Abu Klea'.
40. Macdonald, *Too Late*, pp. 242–3. Marling in his *Rifleman and Hussar*, p. 133, states that the man opposite St Vincent was a corporal major in the Blues. He cannot have seen this with his own eyes given his positon at the front of the square and examination of the HCR casualty roll fails to support the contention.
41. Dundonald, *My Army Life*, p. 23.
42. Talbot, 'Battle of Abu Klea'.
43. Dundonald, *My Army Life*, pp. 36–7.
44. See *Morning Post*, 26 Nov. 85. Parker was a member of the 1st Scots Guards contingent.
45. Trafford uses the defunct name for the corps of army medics; by Jan. 85 it had (not long since) changed its name to the Medical Staff Corps. Only later still would both doctors and medics be united as members of the Royal Army Medical Corps.
46. Trafford MS.
47. Pearse, *Daily News* report; also cited in *Western Mail*, 23 Jan. 85.
48. Whitaker, *Verner Diary*, p. 41.
49. Although Phipps is listed in *Hart's Annual Army List for 85* as a substantive captain, with no brevet indicated (vol. i, p. 149), he appears in a number of primary sources, including tellingly the War Diary of the Desert Column, in the next higher rank. It would be normal for an infantry wing commander to hold the rank of major, in order to be one grade above his captain company commanders. I have made the reasonably safe assumption, therefore, that Phipps had been granted local rank as a major for the duration of the campaign.
50. Whitaker, *Verner Diary*, p. 41.
51. Beresford, *Memoirs*, vol. i, p. 260.
52. Trafford MS.
53. Whitaker, *Verner Diary*, pp. 41 & 45.
54. Macdonald, *Too Late*, p. 233.
55. Dawson, 'Stewart's Desert March', p. 729.
56. Marling, *Rifleman and Hussar*, p. 132.
57. Whitaker, *Verner Diary*, p 41. Colvile states in the *OH* (vol. ii, p. 17) that the guns were 'dragged by the men', but on the basis of Verner's diary and the nature of the ground is evidently in error.
58. Macdonald, *Too Late*, p. 233.
59. Gleichen, *With the Camel Corps*, p. 126.
60. *The Morning Post*, 26 Nov. 85.
61. Pigott had actually been promoted to lieutenant commander but was unaware of the fact, Beresford, *Memoirs*, vol. i, p. 267.
62. Ibid., p. 260.
63. Talbot, 'Battle of Abu Klea'.
64. See for example Burleigh, quoted in *The English in Egypt*, p. 427: 'Our Aden camel-drivers, many of whom were killed and wounded, and who displayed a loyalty, courage and pluck conspicuous alongside the few cowardly Egyptians.'
65. Talbot, 'Battle of Abu Klea'.
66. Whitaker, *Verner Diary*, p. 41.
67. Dundonald, *My Army Life*, p. 37.
68. An allusion to the writing of Sir Walter Scott, extremely popular at this time.
69. Burleigh, quoted in *The English in Egypt*, pp. 422–3.
70. Ibid., p. 422.
71. Macdonald, *Too Late*, p. 231.
72. Trafford MS.
73. Verner's map shows at Letter K the point at which some 48 dead anṣār were later found. So heavy and concentrated a loss, at such a distance of the square, does not really accord with what we know of the main attack. It seems to me likely that they were killed in formation by a round from the 7-pounders which overshot the flags on the spur at this point.
74. Beresford, 'Proceedings of the Naval Brigade', *London Gazette*, 28 Apr. 85, p. 1914.
75. Macdonald, *Too Late*, p. 234.
76. Gleichen, *With the Camel Corps*, p. 129.
77. Though Gleichen, who makes no mention of Phipps, attributes the request to Campbell of the KRRC, *With the Camel Corps*, p. 129.
78. Marling, *Rifleman and Hussar*, p. 132.
79. Dawson, 'Stewart's Desert March', p. 729.
80. See the *London Gazette* dated 20 Feb. 85, p. 755.
81. Snow MS.
82. See Macdonald, *Too Late*, pp. 233–4, for an example of how a contemporary commentator, without the benefit of Snow's much later account to drawn upon, could be taken in by official despatches. At one point Macdonald observes, 'in fact he [Stewart] had completely outgeneralled the dervish commanders', arguably an overly generous statement.
83. For confirmation that a right oblique took place,

see Whitaker, *Verner Diary*, p. 42.
84. Macdonald, *Too Late*, p. 234.
85. Binning, 'An Independent Account', in Wright, *Life of Burnaby*, p. 301. He actually cites a distance of 60–80 yards.
86. Beresford, *Memoirs*, vol i., p. 262. For confirmatory evidence of the square being at the halt at this juncture see Gleichen, *With the Camel Corps*, p. 129, and Wilson, *From Korti to Khartum*, p. 26.
87. This would account for the mystified tone in respect of Burnaby's movements reflected in Lt. Snow's account. Just before the decisive moment, Snow saw Burnaby and Stewart talking at the left-front corner of the square and yet when the enemy appeared, only a few moments later, the colonel was already down at the left-rear, notwithstanding the crush of camels intervening between these two points. Snow had simply failed to observe Burnaby heading for the rear in response to Beresford's report.
88. Whitaker, *Verner Diary*, Nile Expedition Lecture Notes, p. xx.
89. Trafford MS.
90. Herbert, *Morning Post* report, 22 Jan. 85.
91. Dawson, 'Stewart's Desert March', p. 729.
92. Binning, 'An Independent Account', in Wright, *Life of Burnaby*, p. 301.
93. Wilson, *Korti to Khartum*, pp. 26–7.
94. *The Standard*, 30 Jan. 85. The report originated at Korti, where Capt. Pigott had come in with despatches. The anonymous correspondent states that his report is based on an interview with members of Pigott's escort.
95. Hare, *Annals of the King's Royal Rifle Corps*, vol. iv, pp. 342–3.
96. It was not merely for reasons of courtesy that Phipps was not identifed; he died of disease later in the campaign.

Chapter 10: England's Far and Honour a Name

1. This distance is specifically cited by Verner in his lecture notes on the Nile Expedition. As the man who surveyed and mapped the battlefield in Feb. 85, it seems to me that in matters of geography he is to be regarded as the most authoritative of the primary sources. Most other sources hover in the 400–500 yard bracket in any case. Having walked the battlefield myself I do not feel in any way tempted to dispute Verner's estimate/measurement.
2. *Western Mail*, 23 Jan. 85, citing Pearse.
3. Wilson, *Korti to Khartum*, p. 27.
4. *London Gazette*, 28 Apr. 85, p. 1914.
5. Wright, *Life of Burnaby*, p. 301.
6. Burleigh, quoted in *The English in Egypt*, p. 423.
7. Macdonald, *Too Late*, p. 236.
8. Colvile, *OH*, vol. ii, p. 257.
9. Gleichen, *With the Camel Corps*, p. 129.
10. Colvile, *OH*, vol. ii, p. 18.
11. Whitaker, *Verner Diary*, p. 42.
12. Beresford, *Memoirs*, vol. i, pp. 262–3.
13. Beresford, 'Proceedings of the Naval Brigade', *London Gazette* 28 Apr. 85, p. 1914.
14. Gleichen, *With the Camel Corps*, p. 132. In his first book Gleichen identified the officer only as 'R____', presumably at Rowley's request. Were it not for his later *Guardsman's Memories* (p. 32), we would be mystified as to whether he meant Rowley or Romilly, the only two officers in GCR whose name began with R. The identification of Rowley in Gleichen's later book is emphatic. For confirmation of the incident see also Dawson, 'Stewart's Desert March', pp. 729–30.
15. See *Morning Post*, 26 Nov. 85.
16. Gleichen, *With the Camel Corps*, p. 130. The MICR casualty return shows that only two KRRC men were killed with the square on 17 Jan. These were 1932 Pte. J. Bowles of the 2nd Bn. and 3476 Pte. J Turner of the 3rd Bn. As the 3rd KRRC section commanded by Marling was in A Coy., MICR, which did not send out skirmishers, the more likely eventuality is that the man overtaken and killed was Pte. Bowles. He would almost certainly have been the servant to either Capt. R. S. R. Fetherstonhaugh or Lt. A. E. Miles, rather than Lt. W. P. Campbell, as the first two were 2nd Bn. officers, while the last-named was a 1st Bn. man.
17. Marling, *Rifleman and Hussar*, p. 132. These are broadly the same words attributed to Campbell in the regimental history of the KRRC in connection with the incident with Phipps and the rallying square: see Hare, *Annals of the King's Royal Rifle Corps*, vol. iv, pp. 342–3. The two incidents would have occurred at opposite ends of a one-minute window in time and space. While there is no reason that Campbell could not twice have told his men to 'run like hell', it is unlikely in the circumstances that Marling could actually have heard what Campbell was saying. More probably Campbell 'dined out' on his injunction to his men in the aftermath of the battle and it became something of a standing joke amongst the KRRC officers. *Rifleman and Hussar* was not published until the early 1930s.
18. Talbot, 'Battle of Abu Klea'.
19. Trafford's estimate, Trafford MS.
20. Dundonald, *My Army Life*, p. 38.
21. Burleigh, quoted in *The English in Egypt*, p. 423.
22. Marling, *Rifleman and Hussar*, p. 133.
23. Burleigh, quoted in *The English in Egypt*, p. 424.

24. Colvile, *OH*, vol ii., p. 18.
25. Stakings to Charingbold, 5 Feb. 85, *Chatham News*, 12 Mar. 85.
26. Gleichen, *With the Camel Corps*, pp. 130–1.
27. That Dawson felt able at a very early stage to leave the Coldstreamers to their own devices seems to me to confirm that the Mahdist left wing posed no significant threat to the Guards companies deployed to the right of the guns.
28. Dawson, 'Stewart's Desert March', p. 730.
29. Whitaker, *Verner Diary*, Nile Expedition Lecture Notes, p. xviii.
30. Wilson, *Korti to Khartum*, p. 28.
31. Colvile, *OH*, vol. ii, p. 18. I have also verified the truth of this statment on the ground.
32. Ibid., vol. iii (map pack), for Intelligence Div. Map No. 685, dated Jan. 1888. This is a lithograph reproduction of 'Action at Abu Klea, 17th Jan. 85, surveyed by Capt. W. Verner Rif. Bde, DAAG Intell Br. N.E.F., Feb 16th 85'.
33. According to Burleigh this same Gardner had seen service at Tamai where, like all the other naval machine guns present on that occasion, it had been overrun by the enemy when they erupted from cover to break up Maj. Gen. Davis's square.
34. Although Beresford gives the chief boatswain's mate name as Rhodes in his *Memoirs* – indeed it may have been pronounced as such – it is noted on the Naval Brigade casualty return of 23 Jan. 85 as 'Rhoods'. (Airlie Papers). See also Webb, *The Abu Kleas Medal Rolls*, p. 152, where 'Rhoods' is again given. Both sources also give the man's only initial as 'F' not 'W'. In his official report (*London Gazette*, 28 Apr. 85, p. 1914), Beresford himself also uses Rhoods, suggesting a mere editing error in his *Memoirs* of 1914. However, in the same edition of the *London Gazette* (p. 1917), the name is rendered as Rhodes in the RN casualty return (compiled by Surgeon-Major T. F. O'Dwyer), appended directly beneath Beresford's report. In the case of Armourer 'Walter' Miller, Webb also gives his initial as 'F'. In the casualty return, however, there has been a contemporaneous pencil correction to Miller's initial which could well be a 'W'.
35. A reference to the Kordofani habit of wearing their white wrap-around robes over one shoulder much like a highland plaid. See Snook, *Go Strong into the Desert*, pp. 204–5.
36. Beresford, *Memoirs*, vol. i, p. 263.
37. Later KIA as the regiment's commanding officer during the Boer War.
38. Beresford, *Memoirs*, vol. i., p. 263.
39. Macdonald, *Too Late*, p. 235: 'The enemy were close at hand and Colonel Burnaby perceiving the dangerously exposed position of the Naval Brigade, ordered the company of the 4th and 5th Dragoons [*sic* – Dragoon Guards in both cases] to wheel out from the rear face in order to cover them.'
40. Trafford MS. For confirmation of such a move see also Colvile, *OH*, vol. ii, p. 19.
41. Dundonald, *My Army Life*, p. 38.
42. Binning, 'An Independent Account'; see Wright, *Life of Burnaby*, p. 302.
43. Snow MS: 'Our men on the left face of the square suddenly seemed to pull themselves together and shooting better mowed a lane through the dervishes . . .'
44. Wilson, *Korti to Khartoum*, p. 28.
45. Snow MS.
46. Whitaker, *Verner Diary*, p. 42. 'Several horsmen and men on foot with banners preceded them. These were all shot down in the advance . . .'
47. Wilson, *Korti to Khartum*, p. 34.
48. Marling, running letter to his father, commenced 28 Jan. 85, quoted in Emery, *Marching over Africa*, pp. 143–4.
49. Trafford MS.
50. Wilson, *Korti to Khartum*, p. 35.
51. The existence of such a rod is referred to in a report of November 1885 submitted by Brig. Gen. H. J. Alderson, Director of Artilery and Stores, to the Surveyor-General.
52. Beresford, *Memoirs*, vol. i, p. 267.
53. Macdonald, *Too Late*, p. 239.
54. Talbot, 'Battle of Abu Klea'.
55. Trafford MS.
56. Colvile, *OH*, vol. i, p. 18; Talbot, 'Battle of Abu Klea'.
57. Whitaker, *Verner Diary*, p 43; Lecture Notes, p. xix.
58. Pearse, *Daily News*, 29 Jan. 85, quoted in *Western Times*, 30 Jan. 85.
59. In his official report, Beresford stated that Rhoods was 'killed with a spear on my left': *London Gazette*, 28 Apr. 85, p. 1914.
60. Beresford, *Memoirs*, vol. i, pp. 263–4.
61. *London Gazette*, 28 Apr. 85, p. 1914.
62. Beresford, *Memoirs*, vol. i, p. 266. Though Beresford at no point directly identifies the man by name, the only able-bodied seaman listed in his official report as severely wounded at Abu Klea is a man called A. H. March. It should be noted, however, that Boatswain James Webber, who compiled the 23 Jan. casualty return for the Naval Brigade, renders what is evidently meant to be the same name very clearly as 'A. Marsh'. I tentatively identify Jumbo, therefore, as Able Seaman A. (H.?) Marsh.
63. Macdonald, *Too Late*, p. 238.
64. Binning, 'An Independent Account', Wright, *Life of Burnaby*, p. 302.

65. Laporte is named in Wright, *Life of Burnaby*, p. 290, though the author fails to source his remark. Laporte's regiment and other details are derived from Webb's, *The Abu Klea Medal Rolls*, p. 76.
66. Binning, 'An Independent Account', Wright, *Life of Burnaby*, pp. 290 & 303.
67. Burleigh, quoted in *The English in Egypt*, pp. 424–5.
68. Talbot, 'Battle of Abu Klea'.
69. Whitaker, *Verner Diary*, p. 45.
70. Beresford, *Memoirs*, vol. i, p. 265.
71. See Colvile, *OH*, vol. i, p. 19.
72. Some sources, such as Wilson, report Pigott and De Lisle as being cut down in defence of the Gardner: 'Their officers died, disdaining to move from their gun, as they did at Tamai' (*Korti to Khartum*, p. 36). Wilson was not in a position to see this for himself. Beresford, however, makes no mention of their near presence in his *Memoirs* and describes finding their bodies some 25 yards from the gun (vol. i, p. 267). In his earlier official report (*London Gazette* 28 Apr. 85, p. 1914), he says, 'After the fight I found the bodies of these officers [Pigott and De Lisle], of J. Burleigh and F. Nye, able seamen, together with most of the wounded, about 20 yards to the left-rear of the gun outside the square, which led me to believe they were borne away in the crush I have described, when the enemy turned away from the left flank, and headed across the rear of the square. This was corroborated by some of the wounded.' There were 40 members of the Naval Brigade in the square, only a fraction of whom were involved in crewing or towing the Gardner at any given moment. The remainder fought in the rear face of the square as riflemen. With Beresford having taken personal ownership of the Gardner, it seems likely that his lieutenants would have felt obliged to remain with the men in the centre of the rear face. Arguably Beresford's fixation with operating the Gardner himself improperly deprived the bulk of the Naval Brigade of their commanding officer, precisely when they needed him most.
73. Gleichen, *With the Camel Corps*, p. 131.
74. Wilson, *Korti to Khartum*, p. 36.
75. Dawson, 'Stewart's Desert March', p. 730.
76. Marling, letter to his father, quoted in Emery, *Marching over Africa*, pp. 143–4.
77. Talbot, 'Battle of Abu Klea'.
78. See *Western Mail*, 23 Jan. 85, where Pearse's report is cited in full.
79. Talbot, 'Battle of Abu Klea'.
80. Whitaker, *Verner Diary*, p. 45. Verner was given the 'slip [of paper]', as he calls it, by a corporal in the 4th Dragoon Guards, but lost it subsequently. Snow describes it as pages of the Islamic holy book and stated that they were still in his possession.
81. Wilson, *Korti to Khartum*, pp. 28–9.
82. Whitaker, *Verner Diary*, Nile Expedition Lecture Notes, p. xx. Verner separately identifies Yetton by name in a picture caption to his *Sketches in the Soudan*. He survived his injuries and on 25 Nov. 85 was presented with the DCM by the Queen; see the *Morning Post* of the following day. As a youth Yetton seems to have 'done time' aboard the 'Cornwall Reformatory Ship'. He was welcomed back to his *alma mater* a fortnight after receiving the DCM, to be presented by the captain with a watch and chain and be held up to the boys as a role model; *Manchester Courier and Lancashire General Advertiser*, 22 Dec. 85.
83. Beresford, *Memoirs*, vol. i, p. 265.
84. Ibid.
85. Marling, *Rifleman and Hussar*, p. 133.
86. Gleichen, *A Guardsman's Memories*, p. 25.
87. Dundonald, *My Army Life*, p. 39.
88. Beresford, *Memoirs*, vol. i, pp. 267–8.
89. *Morning Post*, 26 Nov. 85.
90. Macdonald, *Too Late*, p. 237.
91. For Smith's VC citation, see *London Gazette*, 12 May 85, p. 2156.
92. Dundonald, *My Army Life*, pp. 38–9.
93. Marling, *Rifleman and Hussar*, pp. 133–4.
94. *Morning Post*, 26 Nov. 85.
95. Trafford MS.
96. Whitaker, *Verner Diary*, p. 45.
97. Wilson, *Korti to Khartum*, p. 32. Though it is not emphatically stated, I infer that Wilson concluded this after looking at the corpses of the two majors in the aftermath of the battle. He must have been reasonably certain of his facts to have included the assertion in his book. Of note, however, is Verner's statement that he thought Carmichael had been killed just behind him during the initial break-in.
98. Macdonald, *Too Late*, p. 240.
99. Gleichen, *With the Camel Corps*, p. 132.
100. Dawson, 'Stewart's Desert March', p. 730.
101. *Morning Post*, 26 Nov. 85.
102. Wilson, *Korti to Khartum*, pp. 29–30.
103. Heazle Parke, Surg. Thomas, 'How General Gordon was Really Lost', *Nineteenth Century*, May 1892, p. 790.
104. Gleichen, *With the Camel Corps*, p. 132.
105. Dundonald, *My Army Life*, p. 39.
106. Though not mentioned in all the sources, reference to the cavalry charge on the right-rear is to be found in Dundonald, *My Army Life*, p. 39, Verner, *Diary*, p. 44, and in Colvile, *OH*, vol. i, p. 20. It is also plotted on Verner's map of the battle. Talbot makes the most extensive reference to it in his Jan. 86 article for *The Nineteenth Century*.

107. *Morning Post*, 26 Nov. 85.
108. Dawson, 'Stewart's Desert March', p. 730.
109. Ibid., pp. 730–1.
110. Wilson, *Korti to Khartum*, p. 30.
111. Burleigh, *Desert Warfare*, p. 165.
112. Trafford MS.
113. Wilson, *Korti to Khartum*, p. 30.
114. Gleichen, *With the Camel Corps*, p. 134.
115. Quoted in Knight, *Marching to the Drums*, p. 226.
116. Binning, 'An Independent Account', Wright, *Life of Burnaby*, p. 303.
117. Dawson, 'Stewart's Desert March', p. 731.
118. Report by Jack Cameron of the *Evening Standard*, quoted in *Yorkshire Gazette*, 23 Jan. 85; also Royle, *The Egyptian Campaigns*, p. 345.
119. Burleigh, quoted in *The English in Egypt*, p. 426.
120. Beresford's official report, *London Gazette*, 28 Apr. 85, p. 1914.
121. Gleichen, *With the Camel Corps*, p. 134.
122. Ibid., pp. 134–5.

Chapter 11: Walking Amongst Vipers

1. Burleigh, quoted in *The English in Egypt*, p. 427.
2. Whitaker, *Verner Diary*, p. 43. Since Atherton, Darley and Law were all dead, the 5th DG contingent was commanded by Lt. St John Gore, who was not a casualty, but makes no direct appearances in any of the sources. In order for Somerset's remark to be literally true, Gore would have to have been sick on the day of the battle. This is not impossible, for there one or two source references to fifty sick men being left at the *zariba* in the care of the doctors, though it is hard to conceive, in the absence of some sort of major outbreak of disease, how quite so many men had fallen by the wayside in so short a space of time. I am inclined to regard fifty as an inflated estimate. Heat exhaustions tends routinely only to strike down the unacclimatized, though it can afflict almost anybody during vigorous exercise.
3. *Morning Post*, 26 Nov. 85.
4. Whitaker, *Verner Diary*, p. 44.
5. Toy family papers.
6. Dundonald, *My Army Life*, p. 41.
7. *Morning Post*, 23 Jan. 85.
8. Binning, 'An Independent Account', Wright, *Life of Burnaby*, p. 303.
9. Macdonald, *Too Late*, p. 243.
10. Beresford, *Memoirs*, vol. 1, p. 266.
11. Macdonald, *Too Late*, p. 243.
12. Toy family papers.
13. Beresford, *Memoirs*, vol. i, pp. 266–7.
14. See *Hart's AL 85*, p. 379. Although there were three surgeon majors by the name of Ferguson/Fergusson in the Army at this time, Frederick Ferguson is the only one whose place of duty is identified as Egypt.
15. *The Standard*, 30 Jan. 85, quoting Capt. Pigott's oral account of the battle.
16. Wilson, *Korti to Khartum*, p. 38.
17. Trafford MS.
18. Wilson, *Korti to Khartum*, p. 32.
19. Whitaker, *Verner Diary*, p. 44.
20. Colvile, *OH*, vol. i, p. 20.
21. Interestingly, the 17 Jan. entry in the War Diary gives the casualties as 9 & 58 killed, and 2 & 69 men wounded, figures which do not quite dovetail with a straight subtraction of Verner's figures from the official figures. Airlie's War Diary figures show a deficit of 7 dead other ranks, 7 wounded officers and 16 wounded other ranks. It is clear, then, that the War Diary attempts to tally only those who were killed or wounded with the square. The marked discrepancy in the number of wounded officers can be accounted for by Airlie's omission of both the slightly wounded (himself included), and the three officers shot inside the *zariba* earlier in the morning. If he intended to count only the officers who were seriously injured with the square, then he has missed one from a cast consisting of St Vincent, Magill and Guthrie. The discrepancy of 7 too few dead soldiers is partly accounted for by the 4 men shot dead at the *zariba*, leaving 3 others still to be accounted for. The obvious conclusion is that these must be men who died of their wounds. As to the number of injured other ranks, if only 69 of the officially listed 85 wounded were with the square, then 16 must be accounted for elsewhere. Verner's figures for the *zariba* allow for 13 of the 16, suggesting that 3 mortally wounded men have been tallied as both dead and wounded and that the official number of wounded should be stated as 82 rather than 85. It is of course possible that the discrepancies can be accounted for by a straightforward inaccuracy embedded in one of the primary sources.
22. Costello was yet another member of the Anglo-Irish gentry. Interestingly, although he was a graduate of Trinity College, Dublin, he failed the Army entrance examination and chose to enlist in the ranks pending being picked out for a commission – a real-world example of one of Kipling's 'gentleman-rankers'.
23. HCR casualty return, dated 23 Jan. In Webb's *Abu Klea Medal Rolls* he is given as 2100 Cpl. G. Phillips.
24. Macdonald, *Too Late*, p. 248.
25. Ibid., p. 246.
26. Wilson, *Korti to Khartum*, pp. 42–3.
27. Macdonald, *Too Late*, pp. 246–7.

28. Marling, *Rifleman and Hussar*, p. 133.
29. Gleichen, *With the Camel Corps*, p 138.
30. *Morning Post*, 26 Nov. 85.
31. Beresford, *Memoirs*, vol. ii, p. 269.
32. Wilson, *Korti to Khartum*, p. 38.
33. Marling, *Rifleman and Hussar*, p. 133.
34. War Diary, 17 Jan. 85. Airlie gives the time of arrival specifically as 4.45 p.m.
35. Burleigh, quoted in *The English in Egypt*, p. 427.
36. Gleichen, *With the Camel Corps*, p. 139.
37. Dawson, 'Stewart's Desert March', p. 731.
38. Gleichen, *With the Camel Corps*, p. 140.
39. Dundonald, *My Army Life*, p. 42.
40. Burleigh, *Daily Telegraph* report, quoted in Grant, *Cassell's History*, vol. iii, p. 83.
41. Whitaker, *Verner Diary*, p. 46.
42. Burleigh, quoted in *The English in Egypt*, p. 428.
43. Trafford MS.
44. It is the War Diary (17 Jan.) that gives a hundred men from each of the camel regiments, and Burleigh (quoted in *The English in Egypt*, p. 428) who adds the detail on the *cacolets*. Burleigh diverges from Airlie by giving the strength of the force as only 250. They both agree that the time of departure was 8.00 p.m. Marling also corroborates this time; letter to his father quoted in Emery, *Marching over Africa*, p. 144.
45. Beresford, *Memoirs*, vol. ii, p. 270.
46. Dawson, 'Stewart's Desert March', p. 731.
47. Burleigh, quoted in *The English in Egypt*, p. 428.
48. Prior, *Campaigns*, pp. 215–16.
49. Beresford, *Memoirs*, vol. ii, p. 270–1.
50. Wilson, *From Korti to Khartum*, pp. 40–1.
51. Trafford MS.
52. Gleichen, *With the Camel Corps*, p. 141.
53. Ibid.
54. Macdonald, *Too Late*, p. 251.
55. Ibid., pp. 250–1.
56. Marling to his father, quoted in Emery, *Marching over Africa*, p. 144.
57. Burleigh, quoted in *The English in Egypt*, p. 428.
58. This is the same time that Stewart cites in his despatch, but half an hour later than Colvile places it in the *OH*.
59. Stewart's Official Despatch, Stewart to Buller, dated 18 Jan. 85; *London Gazette*, 20 Feb. 85, p. 755.
60. Williams, *Daily Chronicle* report, 18 Jan. 85, published 25 Feb. 85. See also *North-Eastern Daily Gazette* of the same date.
61. Macdonald, *Too Late*, p. 243.
62. Wilson, *From Korti to Khartum*, p. 37 n.
63. For the full text of Wilson's report see *London Gazette*, 20 Feb. 85, p. 755; or Colvile, *OH*, vol. ii, pp. 258–9.
64. Whitaker, *Verner Diary*, p. 47.
65. *London Gazette*, 20 Feb. 85, p. 755.
66. Whitaker, *Verner Diary*, p. 47.
67. Macdonald, *Too Late*, p. 255. There are no clues in the sources as to which of the COs this was.
68. Ibid., p. 256.
69. Burleigh, quoted in *The English in Egypt*, p. 427.
70. Wilson, *Korti to Khartum*, pp. 46–7.
71. Whitaker, *Verner Diary*, Nile Expedition Lecture Notes, pp. xx–xxi.
72. Macdonald, *Too Late*, p. 255.
73. Beresford, *Memoirs*, vol. ii, p. 271.
74. Villiers, *Peaceful Personalities and Warriors Bold*, p. 184.
75. *Hart's AL 85*, p. 279.
76. Or more accurately the headquarters clerk (probably) in whose hand the War Diary had been maintained since leaving Korti – Airlie was by now signing it off only, as opposed to keeping it personally as he had done during the journey up the Nile. The Orders Book is in the same anonymous hand, but again was signed off by Airlie, who as brigade major was responsible for the keeping and content of both books.
77. Burleigh, *Daily Telegraph* report 24 Jan. 85, quoted in *Leeds Mercury*, 6 Mar. 85.
78. Burleigh, quoted in *The English in Egypt*, p. 430.
79. Wolseley to his wife, dated 20 Jan. 85 (not despatched until 26 Jan.), quoted in Arthur, *Wolseley Letters*, pp. 159–61.
80. Both reports are in *London Gazette*, 20 Feb. 85, p. 758.
81. Gleichen, *With the Camel Corps*, p. 143.
82. Whitaker, *Verner Diary*, p. 47.
83. Dundonald, *My Army Life*, pp. 43–4.
84. Wilson, *Korti to Khartum*, p. 48.
85. Dundonald, *My Army Life*, pp. 42–3.
86. Lord Cochrane gives sunrise as 06.30 a.m., *My Army Life*, p. 43.
87. I have here preferred the time given by Airlie. A variety of times are to be found in the sources, but the War Diary wins out as the most authoritative among them. Sir Charles Wilson's official despatch for Abu Kru gives 3.30 p.m., Colvile, *OH*, vol. ii, p. 261. Verner gives 4.10 p.m., *Diary*, p. 47.
88. Colvile, *OH*, vol. ii, p 22.

Chapter 12: Endless Confusion

1. Colvile, *OH*, vol. ii, p. 21.
2. Whitaker, *Verner Diary*, p 48.
3. Gleichen, *With the Camel Corps*, p. 144.
4. Whitaker, *Verner Diary*, p. 47. Curiously Verner contradicts himself in the picture captions accompanying his *Sketches in the Soudan*, where he says that the column gained 6 miles before

nightfall. The latter estimate, whilst not impossible, flies in the face of what would appear to be a much more considered remark in his diary.
5. Wilson, *Korti to Khartum*, pp. 46–7. Also Colvile, *OH*, vol. ii, p. 21.
6. Whitaker, *Verner Diary*, p. 48.
7. There were two other night moves between Abu Klea and Metemmeh later in the campaign. These took place on 23 Jan. and 1 Feb. Avoiding the Shebacat bush, these marches were completed in around 10½ hours.
8. Burleigh, quoted in *The English in Egypt*, p. 430.
9. Wilson, *Korti to Khartum*, p. 49.
10. Ibid.
11. Macdonald, *Too Late*, p. 258.
12. Ibid., p. 259.
13. Ibid., p. 261.
14. Prior, *Campaigns*, p. 217.
15. Burleigh, quoted in Grant, *Cassell's History*, vol. iii, p. 99.
16. Burleigh, *Daily Telegraph* report, 24 Jan. 85, quoted in *Leeds Mercury*, 6 Mar. 85. For Dodd's service details see Webb, *Medal Rolls*, p. 106. Macdonald identifies the man killed at Metemmeh as a lance corporal in the Heavies, but fails to give his name and makes no reference to the native drivers. Peters is identified by name in Webb (p. 86), as 'Lost on March to Metemmeh'. In a letter to his father, Marling wrote that, 'One man in the Guards was lost altogether and strayed into Metemmeh and was killed.' It is more likely that Marling has the man's unit wrong than that a guardsman was also lost in like manner.
17. Whitaker, *Verner Diary*, p. 74.
18. Dawson, 'Stewart's Desert March', p. 732.
19. Whitaker, *Verner Diary*, pp. 47–8.
20. Wilson, *Korti to Khartum*, pp. 50–1.
21. Macdonald, *Too Late*, p. 261.
22. Wilson, *Korti to Khartum*, p. 60.
23. Whitaker, *Verner Diary*, p. 48.
24. Wilson, *Korti to Khartum*, p. 52.
25. A slip in Wilson's use of language; there were of course no bugle-calls 'sounded'.
26. Wilson, *Korti to Khartum*, pp. 53–5.
27. Whitaker, *Verner Diary*, p. 49.
28. Wilson, *From Korti to Khartum*, p. 55.
29. Whitaker, *Verner Diary*, p. 49.
30. Ibid., pp. 49–50.
31. Wilson, *Korti to Khartum*, p. 56.
32. Gleichen, *With the Camel Corps*, p. 148.
33. Whitaker, *Verner Diary*, p. 50.
34. Verner, *Sketches in the Soudan*.
35. Wilson, *Korti to Khartum*, pp. 56–7.
36. Macdonald, *Too Late*, p. 264.
37. Whitaker, *Verner Diary*, p. 50.
38. Prior, *Campaigns*, p. 218.
39. Macdonald, *Too Late*, pp. 264–5.
40. Wilson, *Korti to Khartum*, pp. 57–8.
41. Marling, *Rifleman and Hussar*, p. 134.
42. Verner, Lecture Notes, p. xxii.
43. Prior, *Campaigns*, p. 218.
44. Dundonald, *My Army Life*, p. 46. If Gleichen's temporary command of the previous night provides a standard model, there would have been three regimental baggage guards each of 8 men, to add to the 2 officers and 50 or so men of Trafford's C Coy., 1st Royal Sussex. Doubtless the 26 Field Coy. detachment and the Commissariat and Transport staff would also have been left behind.
45. Trafford MS.
46. Macdonald, *Too Late*, pp. 265–7.
47. Wilson, *Korti to Khartum*, pp. 58–9. Nowithstanding the strong case he makes against marching through the early hours of the morning, the contention that Metemmeh might have been taken by midday was overly optimistic. As it was, it would not now be attacked until 21 Jan.

Chapter 13: The Fight to the Nile

1. Burleigh, *Daily Telegraph* report, 24 Jan. 85, quoted in *Leeds Mercury*, 6 Mar. 85.
2. Beresford's official report, 10 Mar. 85, *London Gazette*, 28 Apr. 85, p. 1914.
3. Wilson, *Korti to Khartum*, sketch-map, p. 62. Also, Colvile, *OH*, vol. ii, sketch-map, p. 24.
4. Burleigh, *Daily Telegraph* report, 23 Jan. 85, quoted in *Western Times*, 31 Jan. 85.
5. Beresford, *Memoirs*, vol. ii, p. 273.
6. Burleigh, *Daily Telegraph* report, 24 Jan. 85, quoted in *Leeds Mercury*, 6 Mar. 85.
7. Macdonald, *Too Late*, p. 268; Burleigh, *Daily Telegraph* report, 24 Jan. 85.
8. Prior, eyewitness sketch for the *Illustrated London News*.
9. Burleigh, *Daily Telegraph* report, 23 Jan. 85, quoted in *Western Times*, 31 Jan. 85.
10. Macdonald asserts that the soldier hit in the head was a member of the 16th Lancers, but the 23 Jan. casualty returns compiled by Adjutant HCR (Maj. Byng) do not include any fatal casualties for that unit. The only member of HCR killed in the *zariba* was Trumpeter Wilson of the Royals; this does not necessarily imply that he was the man that Macdonald saw die. More likely the trooper was not actually killed by the shot.
11. Snow MS.
12. Payne was a substantive lieutenant, with the local rank of captain.
13. Whitaker, *Verner Diary*, p. 51.
14. Dawson, *Stewart's Desert March*, pp. 732–3.

15. Beresford, *Memoirs*, vol. ii, p. 273.
16. Burleigh, *Daily Telegraph* report, 24 Jan. 85, quoted in *Leeds Mercury*, 6 Mar. 85.
17. Interestingly one of the RMLI subalterns was Lt. Charles Townshend, later feted for the Defence of Chitral Fort (1895), but castigated as a general following the fall of Kut al Amara in 1915. While many members of Townshend's division failed to return from a savage captivity, their commander sat out his war in the comfort of a seaside villa.
18. Whitaker, *Verner Diary*, p. 51.
19. Ibid., p. 56.
20. Wilson, *Korti to Khartum*, p. 63. Macdonald (*Too Late*, p. 268) fixes the incident at some point between 8.30 and 9.00 a.m., but this seems far too early in the day to accomodate all the activity known to have preceded the general's fall. In the *OH*, Colvile differs only marginally from Wilson in placing the event at 10.00 a.m. Burleigh, however, differs markedly by placing the incident at 8.00 a.m. (*Daily Telegraph* report, 24 Jan. 85).
21. According to Macdonald (*Too Late*, p. 268), Stewart was standing with Rhodes when he made up his mind to give thirty minutes' notice of his intention to advance in square. He instructed Rhodes to move in one direction around the perimeter, advising the officers as he went, while he himself went round the position in the opposite direction. Stewart had taken barely a dozen strides before he was shot in the groin. Macdonald, however, was not an eyewitness to the general's wounding, whereas Villiers was. I have preferred his description accordingly.
22. Wilson, *Korti to Khartum*, p. 65.
23. Ibid., p. 64.
24. Whitaker, *Verner Diary*, pp. 51–2.
25. Ibid., p. 52.
26. Burleigh, *Daily Telegraph* report, 24 Jan. 85, quoted in *Leeds Mercury*, 6 Mar. 85.
27. In his *Abu Klea Medal Rolls*, Webb gives the name as 'Thouard'. Marling's version, as recorded in *Rifleman and Hussar*, looks the more credible. In his *Marching over Africa* (p. 145), Emery gives the man's name as 'Howard', presumably mis-transcribed from Marling's handwriting.
28. Marling, *Rifleman and Hussar*, pp. 134–5.
29. Macdonald, *Too Late*, pp. 272–3.
30. Prior, *Campaigns*, p. 219.
31. Toy family papers. The passage contains a number of errors of fact. Briggs was not the chief medical officer and his rank was surgeon not captain. In 1881 the Army Service Corps had been re-titled The Commissariat and Transport Corps. It was not until 1888 that the old name of the corps was resurrected.
32. Airlie papers.
33. 'Supplementary Despatch from Colonel Sir Charles Wilson to the Chief of the Staff', Korti, 14 Mar. 85, *London Gazette*, 10 Apr. 85, pp. 1677–8. Also Wilson, *Korti to Khartum*, p. 65.
34. Marling, *Rifleman and Hussar*, p. 135; Gleichen, *With the Camel Corps*, p. 152.
35. Williams, *Daily Chronicle* report, quoted in *The Citizen*, 31 Jan. 85.
36. Burleigh, *Daily Telegraph* report, 24 Jan. 85, cited in *Leeds Mercury*, 6 Mar. 85.
37. Wilson, *Korti to Khartum*, pp. 67–8.
38. Ibid., pp. 66–7.
39. *Morning Post*, 26 Nov. 85.
40. Wilson's 'Supplementary Despatch'; *London Gazette*, 10 Apr. 85, pp. 1677–8.
41. Gleichen, *A Guardsman's Memories*, p. 37.
42. In *With the Camel Corps up the Nile*, Gleichen renders the officer's name only as 'C___'. The officer's identity can, however, be inferred from his later *Guardsman's Memories*.
43. Gleichen, *With the Camel Corps*, p. 153.
44. Ibid.
45. Macdonald, *Too Late*, pp. 269–70.
46. Burleigh, *Daily Telegraph* report, 24 Jan. 85, quoted in *Leeds Mercury* 6 Mar. 85.
47. Prior, *Campaigns*, p. 219.
48. Burleigh, quoted in *The English in Egypt*, p. 431.
49. Beresford, *Memoirs*, vol. ii, p. 275.
50. Burleigh, *Daily Telegraph* report, 24 Jan. 85, quoted in *Leeds Mercury*, 6 Mar. 85.
51. Wilson, *Korti to Khartum*, p. 68.
52. Barrow was long since dead; though Evelyn Boscawen, by then the 7th Viscount Falmouth, did not die until 1918, and Col. Willoughby Verner, who may conceivably have been present, lived to 1922.
53. Verner, Lecture Notes, p. xxii.
54. Williams, *Daily Chronicle* report, quoted in *The Citizen*, 31 Jan. 85.
55. Dawson, 'Stewart's Desert March', p. 734.
56. Wilson, *Korti to Khartum*, p. 70.
57. Letter by Hibbert, quoted in Emery, *Marching over Africa*, pp. 150–1.
58. Macdonald, *Too Late*, p. 211. Jacky made it all the way to Metemmeh and at the end of the camapign returned north with the Grenadiers as far as Wādī Halfā, where sadly he was stolen from his British friends.
59. Gleichen, *With the Camel Corps*, p. 157; Dawson, 'Stewart's Desert March', p. 734.
60. *Leeds Mercury*, 6 Mar. 85.
61. For example, Sir George Colley's decision to use a composite battalion-strength force at Majuba Hill, rather than the battle-hardened Gordon

62. Trafford MS.
63. Wilson, *Korti to Khartum*, p. 70.
64. Quoted in Emery, *Marching over Africa*, p. 145.
65. It must at the same time be owned that Col. Evelyn Boscawen of GCR did not conform to the convention. This may have been to avoid offending the RMLI, who would otherwise always be in the junior position to the left of the Guards companies. Highlanders, newly arrived from Afghanistan, is commonly attributed to his desire to allow the other battalions in his force to avenge their defeats at Laing's Nek and Ingogo.
66. Snow MS.
67. Wilson, *Korti to Khartum*, p. 66.
68. Ibid., pp. 69–70. Lt. Edward Craven: see *Hart's AL for 1885*, p. 161.
69. *Morning Post*, 26 Nov. 85.
70. Trafford MS.
71. Conversely, Dawson portrays the Heavies more accurately than Gleichen.
72. The War Diary erroneously asserts that Major Davison was in command of the outpost, though clearly, with 150 Heavies under his command, his responsibilities were far wider. In *My Army Life*, Dundonald makes no reference to Davison and asserts that he was in command of the outpost.
73. Gleichen, *With the Camel Corps*, p. 156.
74. Prior, *Campaigns*, pp. 220–1.
75. Ibid., p. 221.
76. Dawson, 'Stewart's Desert March', pp. 733–4.
77. Wilson, *Korti to Khartum*, pp. 81–2.
78. Trafford MS.
79. Burleigh, *Daily Telegraph* report, 24 Jan. 85, quoted in *Leeds Mercury*, 6 Mar. 85.
80. Whitaker, *Verner Diary*, pp. 52–3.
81. Gleichen, *With the Camel Corps*, p. 156.
82. Wilson, *Korti to Khartum*, pp. 71–2.
83. Villiers, *Five Decades*, vol. ii. pp. 66–7. See also Wilson, *Korti to Khartum*, p. 68, and Macdonald, *Too Late*, p. 272. The latter states that Herbert 'was struck by a bullet in the head and instantly killed while beckoning to his servant to bring him his horse'. Neither Wilson nor Macdonald seem to have been eyewitnesses to Herbert's demise. I have preferred Villiers's account accordingly.
84. Wilson, *Korti to Khartum*, p. 71.
85. Marling, *Rifleman and Hussar*, p. 135.
86. Ibid., p. 137.
87. Macdonald, *Too Late*, p. 137.
88. Marling, *Rifleman and Hussar*, p. 137.
89. Whitaker, *Verner Diary*, p. 53.
90. Verner, Lecture Notes, p. xxiii.
91. See Wilson's official despatches of 22 Jan. and 14 Mar. 85, Colvile, *OH*, vol. ii, pp. 261 and 263; also Burleigh, *The English in Egypt*, p. 432; Beresford, *Memoirs*, vol. ii, p. 275; and Dundonald, *My Army Life*, p. 47. Gleichen gives 3.30 p.m. (*With the Camel Corps*, p. 156).
92. Macdonald, *Too Late*, p. 273.
93. It can be inferred from the 23 Jan. casualty return for GCR (Airlie papers), signed off by Lt. Col. Ivor Herbert, where Kekewich is returned as 'wounded (since died)', with no date of death given, that he must have lingered until at least the day after the battle. Webb's *Abu Klea Medal Rolls* lists him as killed on the 19th, but this is not what the directly contemporaneous GCR return suggests.
94. Trafford MS.
95. Ibid.
96. The only Household Cavalry field officers known to have been present with the square were Talbot and Somerset. Sunderland was senior to Somerset (see *Hart's Army List for 85*), who is in any case excluded by Trafford's second reference to the same officer, which occurs at a point by which Lord Arthur is known to have been incapacitated. Byng, now acting adjutant HCR, could very well have been with Talbot, but is nowhere definitively sourced as being present. He was a matter of five months senior to Sunderland as a major but had not been in the Army anything like as long. This would not have sufficed to supplant Sunderland, whose regiment provided two of three companies in the rear face.
97. Dawson, 'Stewart's Desert March', p. 735. Dawson may have got this from Beresford, with whom he was friendly, and who wrote, 'We judged their numbers to be greater than at Abou Klea' (*Memoirs*, vol. ii, p. 276).
98. Burleigh, quoted in *The English in Egypt*, p. 435.
99. Beresford, *Memoirs*, vol. ii, p. 276.
100. Macdonald, *Too Late*, p. 274.
101. Ibid.
102. Whitaker, *Verner Diary*, p. 54.
103. Villiers, *Five Decades*, vol. ii, p. 67.
104. This tends also to support the notion that D Company, MICR, was in reserve inside the square, for otherwise Pigott would surely have been busy supervising his command.
105. Macdonald, *Too Late*, p. 211.
106. Whitaker, *Verner Diary*, p. 54.
107. Letter by Hibbert, quoted in Emery, *Marching over Africa*, p. 150. Emery gives Hibbert's christian name as Charles, but this is not what is reflected in the 85 edition of *Hart's Army List*; see vol. i, p. 137.
108. Villiers, *Five Decades*, vol. ii, pp. 67–8.
109. That the square from time to time lay down to return fire, and that the volleys were fired by companies, is recorded in one of the picture

Notes to Pages 372–386 • 557

captions in Verner's *Sketches in the Soudan*. See also Wilson, *Korti to Khartum*, pp. 73–4.
110. Burleigh, quoted in *The English in Egypt*, p. 434.
111. Marling, *Rifleman and Hussar*, p. 136.
112. Ibid.
113. Whitaker, *Verner Diary*, p. 54.
114. Verner, *Sketches in the Soudan*.
115. Ibid.
116. Whitaker, *Verner Diary*, p. 54.
117. Wilson, *Korti to Khartum*, p. 76.
118. Verner, Lecture Notes, p. xxiii.
119. Whitaker, *Verner Diary*, p. 54.
120. Marling, *Rifleman and Hussar*, p. 135.
121. Verner, *Sketches in the Soudan*.
122. Marling, *Rifleman and Hussar*, p. 135.
123. Macdonald, *Too Late*, p. 275.
124. Verner, Lecture Notes, p. xxiv.
125. *The Standard*, 30 Jan. 85, p. 5. It is not clear who the eyewitness was, though it is stated that the description of the battle was written by an officer who arrived at Korti the day after Capt. Pigott.
126. Marling's *Rifleman and Hussar* (p. 135) establishes that the enemy attacked in two masses in the fashion here described.
127. Beresford, *Memoirs*, vol. ii, p. 276.
128. Macdonald, *Too Late*, p. 274; Villiers, *Five Decades*, vol. ii, p. 68.
129. Wilson, *Korti to Khartum*, p. 77. The range estimate is Wilson's and the estimate of elapsed time my own.
130. Wilson, *Korti to Khartum*, p. 77.
131. Gleichen, *With the Camel Corps*, p. 158.
132. Snow MS.
133. Villiers, *Five Decades*, p. 69.
134. Macdonald, *Too Late*, p. 276.
135. Villiers, *Five Decades*, p. 69.
136. Macdonald, *Too Late*, p. 276. See also Wilson's supplementary despatch, dated 14 Mar. 85 (Colvile, *OH*, vol. ii. p. 263) in which he says, 'On the defeat of the spearmen, a strong force of the enemy, which had been kept in check by a well-directed artillery fire from the zariba, dispersed in the direction of Metemmeh.' It is impossible to say for sure whether this is a reference to the second of the two *anṣār* masses which had been positioned on the gravel ridge, or whether it refers to a third body operating in the low ground.
137. Wilson, *Korti to Khartum*, p. 78.
138. Ibid.
139. Whitaker, *Verner Diary*, p. 55.
140. Wilson, *Korti to Khartum*, p. 80.
141. Marling to his father, running letter commenced 28 Jan. 85, quoted in Emery, *Marching over Africa*, p. 145. Marling also makes reference to the incident in his autobiography, but erroneously inserts Gough (who had not yet returned to duty after being 'knocked senseless' at Abu Klea), alongside Campbell in expostulating with Wilson; see *Rifleman and Hussar*, p. 136.
142. Whitaker, *Verner Diary*, p. 55.
143. Trafford MS.
144. Verner's intelligence; see *Diary*, pp. 72 & 75, noting that according to James Whitaker he renders Nūr 'Anqara as 'Nur Auga'; see also Slatin, *Fire & Sword*, p. 338.
145. Hill, *Biographical Dictionary*, p. 297.
146. Ohrwalder, *Ten Years Captivity*, p. 125. He is also said to have beheaded the Sultan Harun, a Dār Fūr rebel, in 1880, when he was still a government officer.
147. *London Gazette*, 20 Feb. 85, p. 758.
148. 'Ali-wad-Saad was reported by a spy in Verner's employ as being present in Metemmeh around 29/30 Jan; Whitaker, *Verner Diary*, p. 72.
149. Amīr 'Abd-al-Mājid Nasr al-Din abū'l-Kailak is known to have commanded the force which resisted Earle at Kirbekan on 10 Feb. This is by no means irreconcilable with his being in Metemmeh on about 30 Jan.
150. Slatin, *Fire and Sword in the Sudan*, p. 338.
151. Whitaker, *Verner Diary*, pp. 72 & 75.
152. Whitaker, *Verner Diary*, p. 75.
153. Wilson to Buller, 14 March 85. See Colvile, *OH*, vol. ii, p. 263.
154. In *From Korti to Khartum* Wilson consistently renders this name as 'Feki Mustafa'. In an official 'Report on Proceedings from January 24th to February 1st', however, Lt. Stuart-Wortley, Wilson's assistant on the intelligence staff, renders it as the 'Fakir Mustapha'. It is not inconceivable that this man was one and the same 'Sheikh Mustafa el Amin', referred to in evidence brought before the Intelligence Department in Cairo on 23 Feb. 1893; see Beresford, *Memoirs*, vol. ii, p. 310.
155. Wilson, *Korti to Khartum*, pp. 91–2.
156. Whitaker, *Verner Diary*, pp. 56–7.
157. Macdonald, *Too Late*, p. 283.
158. Burleigh, quoted in *The English in Egypt*, p. 435.
159. Colvile, *OH*, vol. ii, p. 27.
160. NAS 02024 GD 16–52–57–10–A-00116 to 00122 inclusive.
161. Webb, *Abu Klea Medal Rolls*, p. 132.
162. It is tempting to infer from the identities of the fatal casualties that the HCR companies present in the square might have been Nos. 3 and 5; on balance, however, there remain too many imponderables in play to sustain such a conclusion.
163. Sewart finally expired on 17 Feb. 85 and was buried at Jakdul Wells.
164. Gleichen, *With the Camel Corps*, pp. 159–60.

165. Ibid., p. 160.
166. Wilson, *Korti to Khartum*, p. 81.
167. Whitaker, *Verner Diary*, pp. 55–6.
168. Trafford MS.
169. Wilson, *From Korti to Khartum*, pp. 82–3.
170. Ibid., p. 83.
171. Snow MS.
172. The departmental equivalent of a major. Rainsford appears in *Hart's AL for 1885*, p. 366.
173. Macdonald, *Too Late*, pp. 278–9.
174. Beresford, *Memoirs*, vol. ii, pp. 277–8; Marling, *Rifleman and Hussar*, p. 141.

Chapter 14: The Fort of the Infidels

1. Trafford MS.
2. Gleichen, *With the Camel Corps*, p. 165.
3. Macdonald, *Too Late*, p. 282.
4. Whitaker, *Verner Diary*, p. 57.
5. Ibid., p. 58; Gleichen, *With the Camel Corps*, pp. 166–7.
6. Wilson, *Korti to Khartum*, p. 84.
7. Whitaker, *Verner Diary*, p. 58.
8. Marling, *Rifleman and Hussar*, p. 137.
9. Ibid.
10. Wilson, *Korti to Khartum*, p. 86.
11. Wilson's supplementary despatch of 14 Mar 85, Colvile, *OH*, vol. ii, p. 264.
12. Gleichen, *With the Camel Corps*, p. 163.
13. Wilson, *Korti to Khartum*, p. 86.
14. Gleichen, *With the Camel Corps*, p. 163.
15. Whitaker, *Verner Diary*, p. 58; see also the picture captions in his *Sketches in the Soudan*.
16. Wilson, *Korti to Khartum*, p. 87.
17. Ibid., pp. 88–9.
18. Ibid., p. 89.
19. Gleichen, *With the Camel Corps*, pp. 164–5.
20. Marling, *Rifleman and Hussar*, p. 138.
21. Dundonald, *My Army Life*, p. 49.
22. Macdonald, *Too Late*, p. 283.
23. Ibid.; Burleigh, *Daily Telegraph* report, 24. Jan. 85.
24. Macdonald, *Too Late*, p. 283.
25. Burleigh, *Daily Telegraph* report, 24. Jan. 85.
26. Wilson, *Korti to Khartum*, p. 89.
27. Snow MS.
28. Wilson, *Korti to Khartum*, p. 91.
29. Macdonald, *Too Late*, p. 285.
30. Marling, *Rifleman and Hussar*, p. 138.
31. War Diary, 20 Jan. 85, Airlie Papers.
32. The most likely candidate as the commander of the smaller square is Col. Talbot. Boscawen would have commanded the main fighting square, with which Wilson and the staff would also have travelled.
33. War Diary, 20 Jan. 85. See also Marling, *Rifleman and Hussar*, p. 138; Macdonald, *Too Late*, p. 285.
34. Burleigh, *Daily Telegraph* report, 24 Jan. 85.
35. Ibid.
36. Prior, *Campaigns*, p. 223.
37. Save apparently for their socks, Marling, *Rifleman and Hussar*, p. 138.
38. Wilson, *Korti to Khartum*, p. 91.
39. Macdonald, *Too Late*, p. 285. Curiously Wilson gives 'two or three', *Korti to Khartum*, p. 92.
40. Wilson, *Korti to Khartum*, p. 147.
41. Whitaker, *Verner Diary*, p. 58.
42. War Diary, 20 Jan. 85.
43. Wilson, *Korti to Khartum*, p. 93 (diagram).
44. Gleichen, *With the Camel Corps*, p. 166.
45. Macdonald, *Too Late*, p. 299.
46. Wilson, *Korti to Khartum*, pp. 93–7.
47. Ibid., p. 98.
48. Desert Column, Daily Orders by Col. Sir Charles Wilson, 20 Jan. 85, Airlie Papers.
49. Beresford, *Memoirs*, vol. ii, p. 281.
50. Whitaker, *Verner Diary*, p. 59; see also *Hart's AL for 1885*, vol. i, p. 229.
51. Trafford MS.
52. The dispositions of the HCR companies given at this point in the text is not emphatically stated in any of the sources, but is deduced from various passing references. That two unspecifed companies of HCR would go back to fetch Davison is stated in Column Daily Orders for 20 Jan. Alex Macdonald, who stayed at Gubat, tells us that the Royals, 4th DG and 5th DG detachments were present in the village after Wilson moved off (*Too Late*, p. 287). Whilst it is curious that Macdonald does not mention the Greys (ordinarily paired with the Royals in No. 4 Coy.), this data nonetheless enables the deduction that it was Nos. 3 and 4 Coys (which I assess to have been merged), which went back to fetch Davison. Although Macdonald does not mention the Greys, Verner's *Diary* tells us that Capt. William Hippisley was present at the village that morning and evidently in command of the detachments referred to by Macdonald. It is hard to know where the men of the Greys would have been if not with their officer. In all likelihood Macdonald simply failed to recognize them. Dundonald states specifically that he was now in command of No. 1 Coy., HCR (Maj. Charles Byng having become Adjutant, HCR, *vice* Lord St Vincent, mortally wounded), and that the company participated in the operation against Metemmeh (*My Army Life*, p. 50). It follows, if Davison and No. 5 Coy. were still in the desert, and the merged No. 3/4 Coy. was on standby to go and get them, that the company operating alongside Dundonald's Life Guards must be No. 2 (Blues and Bays).

53. War Diary, 21 Jan. 85.
54. Marling, *Rifleman and Hussar*, p. 138.
55. Gleichen, *With the Camel Corps*, p. 167.
56. Macdonald, *Too Late*, p. 286.
57. Whitaker, *Verner Diary*, p. 59.
58. Wilson, *Korti to Khartum*, p. 99.
59. Snow MS.
60. War Diary, 21 Jan. 85. It should be noted that in the text I have reversed the strengths given by Airlie for the Naval Brigade and the Royal Artillery. Clearly the Naval Brigade did not have three guns and the artillery only one.
61. Whitaker, *Verner Diary*, p. 60; Macdonald, *Too Late*, p. 290.
62. War Diary, 20 Jan. 85.
63. Colvile, *OH*, vol. ii, p. 28.
64. Gleichen, *With the Camel Corps*, p. 168; Dawson, 'Stewart's Desert March', p. 737.
65. Macdonald, *Too Late*, p. 287.
66. Ibid., p. 288.
67. Whitaker, *Verner Diary*, p. 71.
68. Gleichen, *With the Camel Corps*, p. 168, though this must be caveated by drawing attention to the confusion in Gleichen's account at this point.
69. Gleichen, *With the Camel Corps*, p. 169.
70. Whitaker, *Verner Diary*, p. 72.
71. Ibid., p. 72.
72. He led the assault on Khartoum on the night of 25/26 Jan.
73. Whitaker, *Verner Diary*, p. 59.
74. Ibid., p. 60.
75. Wilson, *Korti to Khartum*, p. 100.
76. Ibid., p. 101.
77. Macdonald, *Too Late*, p. 288.
78. Burleigh, quoted in *The English in Egypt*, p. 435: 'fugitives running towards the north'.
79. Gleichen, *With the Camel Corps*, p. 169.
80. Ibid., p. 169.
81. Wilson, *Korti to Khartum*, p. 101.
82. Ibid., pp. 101–2.
83. Macdonald, *Too Late*, p. 289.
84. Gleichen, *With the Camel Corps*, p. 170.
85. Wilson, *Korti to Khartum*, p. 102.
86. Dawson, 'Stewart's Desert March'; also Gleichen, *With the Camel Corps*, pp. 170–1.
87. Marling, *Rifleman and Hussar*, p. 138.
88. Gleichen, *With the Camel Corps*, p. 171.
89. Colvile, *OH*, vol. ii, p. 29.
90. Wilson, *Korti to Khartum*, pp. 102–3.
91. Ibid., p. 103.
92. Macdonald, *Too Late*, p. 290.
93. It is possible that Nushi Pasha may have been a major general.
94. Hill, *Biographical Dictionary*, p. 262.
95. Whitaker, *Verner Diary*, p. 60.
96. Ibid., p. 61.
97. Whitaker, *Verner Diary*, p. 60.
98. Ibid., p. 60.
99. Ibid., p. 61.
100. Macdonald, *Too Late*, p. 291.
101. Gleichen, *With the Camel Corps*, p. 171.
102. Marling, *Rifleman and Hussar*, p. 138.
103. Wilson, *Korti to Khartum*, p. 104.
104. Ibid., p. 105.
105. Whitaker, *Verner Diary*, p. 61.
106. Ibid., p. 62.
107. Gleichen, *With the Camel Corps*, p. 175.
108. Wilson, *Korti to Khartum*, p. 108.
109. Ibid., p. 105; Whitaker, *Verner Diary*, p. 62.
110. Wilson, *Korti to Khartum*, p. 110. While Wilson gives 14 Dec., Gordon's last journal suggests that he intended to send *Bordein* downriver the following day.
111. Macdonald, *Too Late*, p. 291.
112. Ibid., p. 292.
113. Dundonald, *My Army Life*, p. 51.
114. Ibid.
115. Whitaker, *Verner Diary*, p. 62.
116. Dundonald, *My Army Life*, p. 51.
117. Gleichen, *With the Camel Corps*, p. 174.
118. Wilson, *Korti to Khartum*, p. 109.
119. MICR casualty return, 23 Jan. 85.
120. Figures extracted from reports in the *Standard* of 29 Jan. 85, one of which was written by Melton Prior in lieu of his deceased friend Jack Cameron.
121. Wilson, *Korti to Khartum*, pp. 109–10.
122. Whitaker, *Verner Diary*, p. 62.
123. War Diary, 21 Jan. 85.
124. Wilson, *Korti to Khartum*, pp. 110–12. 'Watson' refers to Colonel Charles Watson, RE, a mutual friend, and later Wilson's biographer.
125. Ibid., p. 112.
126. Ibid., pp. 114–5.
127. Ibid., p. 115.
128. Whitaker, *Verner Diary*, p. 62.
129. Wilson, *Korti to Khartum*, p. 116.
130. Wolseley journal, 22 Jan. 85, Preston, *In Relief of Gordon*, p. 123.
131. Wolseley journal, 21 Jan. 85, ibid., p. 121.
132. Ibid., pp. 121–2.

Chapter 15: Boy's Own

1. Whitaker, *Verner Diary*, p. 63; and *Sketches in the Soudan*.
2. Whitaker, *Verner Diary*, p. 80.
3. The sources contain no clue as to which companies they were.
4. Wilson, *Korti to Khartum*, p. 116.
5. Whitaker, *Verner Diary*, p. 64.
6. Macdonald, *Too Late*, p. 300.

7. Ibid., p. 302.
8. Wilson gives the former name, Verner the latter.
9. Wilson, *Korti to Khartum*, pp. 117–18.
10. Whitaker, *Verner Diary*, p. 64.
11. Wilson, *Korti to Khartum*, p. 118.
12. Ibid., p. 120.
13. Ibid., p. 121.
14. *London Gazette*, 28 Apr. 85, p. 1915.
15. Macdonald, *Too Late*, p. 301.
16. Whitaker, *Verner Diary*, p. 67.
17. Macdonald, *Too Late*, p. 302.
18. Verner, *Sketches in the Soudan*. Towards the end of the occupation of Gubat, when the British were concerned that the enemy were bringing up artillery, Maj. Dorward and the engineers threw up a parapet along the water's edge, to enclose the position fully and protect the interior from snipers or guns on the right bank of the river; the excavation necessary to raise it smoothed out the floor of the fort and lowered the ground level inside by about 18 inches. Because this work was carried out so late, around about 12 Feb., it does not feature in the sketches of the River Fort drawn by Verner and Trafford, which show a three-sided earthwork only.
19. Verner, *Sketches in the Soudan*.
20. Burleigh, *Daily Telegraph* report, quoted in *Bristol Mercury and Evening Post*, 12 Feb. 85.
21. Whitaker, *Verner Diary*, p. 75.
22. Verner, *Sketches in the Soudan*.
23. Macdonald, *Too Late*, p. 299.
24. Prior, *Campaigns*, p. 224.
25. War Diary, 23 Jan.
26. Wilson, *Korti to Khartum*, p. 123.
27. Hart's AL for 1885, vol. ii, p. 532l.
28. Wright, *Life of Burnaby*, pp. 263–4.
29. Wilson, *Korti to Khartum*, p. 15.
30. Gascoine, 'To Within a Mile of Khartoum', *Nineteenth Century*, July 85, p. 97.
31. Wilson, *Korti to Khartum*, p. 142.
32. Ibid., p. 127.
33. Whitaker, *Verner Diary*, p. 65.
34. Arthur, *The Story of the Household Cavalry*, vol ii, p. 691: 'Twenty men of the Royal Sussex came up to Khartoum with us on the two steamers. Their red tunics had been sent up specially for them to wear on arrival at Khartoum, in order that the Khalifa's [sic – Mahdi's] men should realise the British had arrived. They did not wear their red tunics on the way up the river from Metemmeh – and as far as I can recollect – the tunics went to the bottom of the Nile when the steamers were wrecked coming down from Khartoum (Letter from Brig-Gen. The Hon. E. Stuart-Wortley, Jan. 19 1909).'
35. *Harts AL for 1885*, vol. i. p. 384.
36. Wolseley journal, 28 Jan., Preston, *In Relief of Gordon*, p. 127.
37. Dundonald, *My Army Life*, pp. 58–9.
38. Wolseley journal, 28 Jan., Preston, *In Relief of Gordon*, p. 127. Pigott left Jakdul at 10.30 a.m. on Mon. 26 Jan. and covered the remaining hundred miles to Korti in 29 hours, without further mishap.
39. Prior, *Campaigns*, p. 224.
40. Awarded DCM; Webb, *Abu Klea Medal Rolls*, p. 120.
41. Awarded DCM; ibid., p. 118.
42. It is of note that Trafford listed Pte. Ings as being present aboard both steamers. There was certainly only one soldier of that name in the battalion. Trafford records that 'I received orders to embark with 20 men.' Yet only 1 officer and 19 are identified in his journal (including Ings tallied twice). The possibility exists, therefore, that the name of one C Coy. man who was present on the steamers has been lost to history.
43. Archer, *The War in Egypt and the Soudan*, vol. iv, p. 104.
44. Although this man is often tallied separately, it seems to me more than likely that the signaller was actually one of the Royal Sussex men; it is worthy of note that Wingate says as much in his *Mahdiism and the Egyptian Sudan* (p. 173).
45. Awarded DCM; Webb, *Abu Klea Medal Rolls*, p. 118.
46. Awarded DCM; ibid., p. 120.
47. Wilson, *Korti to Khartum*, pp. 143–4.
48. Colvile, *OH*, vol. ii, p. 33.
49. Wilson, *Korti to Khartum*, p. 153.
50. Wilson to Wolseley, 23 Mar. 85, Colvile, *OH*, vol. ii, p. 269.
51. Ibid.
52. Wilson, *Korti to Khartum*, p. 146.
53. Slatin, *Fire and Sword*, pp. 351–2.
54. Wilson, *Korti to Khartum*, p. 149.
55. Ibid., pp. 151–2.
56. Gascoigne, 'To Within a Mile', p. 91.
57. Beresford, 'Proceedings of the Naval Brigade', *London Gazette*, 28 Apr. 85, p. 1915.
58. Wilson, *Korti to Khartum*, pp. 153–4.
59. Ibid., pp. 156–60.
60. Ibid., p. 167.
61. Ibid., p. 169.
62. Gascoigne, 'To Within a Mile', p. 93.
63. Wilson, *Korti to Khartum*, p. 169.
64. Trafford MS.
65. Wilson, *Korti to Khartum*, pp. 170–8.
66. Trafford MS.
67. Gascoigne, 'To Within a Mile', p. 93.
68. Wilson, *Korti to Khartum*, pp. 183–4.

69. Gascoigne, 'To Within a Mile', p. 93.
70. Hill, *Biographical Dictionary*, pp. 124–5.
71. *London Gazette*, 10 Mar. 85, pp. 1026–8. Stuart-Wortley wrote his report on 1 Feb., the date on which he returned to Gubat. It was sent through to London from Korti, under the cover of Wolseley to Hartington dated 9 Feb. 85. Thus the story of Khartoum having fallen through treachery was in the Prime Minister's hands from the moment the news of Gordon's death broke in Britain.
72. See Colvile, *OH*, vol. ii, pp. 270–6.
73. Wilson, *Korti to Khartum*, pp. 184–5.
74. Pearse, *Daily News*, 10 Mar. 85.
75. Gacoigne, 'To Within a Mile', p. 94.
76. Wilson, *Korti to Khartum*, p. 189.
77. Stuart-Wortley report, 1 Feb. 85, *London Gazette*, 10 Mar. 85, p. 1028.
78. Wilson, *Korti to Khartum*, pp. 198–200.
79. Stuart-Wortley report, 1 Feb. 85, *London Gazette*, 10 Mar. 85, p. 1028.
80. Wilson *Korti to Khartum*, pp. 200–2.
81. Ibid., pp. 205–6.
82. Stuart-Wortley report, 1 Feb. 85, *London Gazette*, 10 Mar. 85, p. 1028.
83. Gascoigne, 'To Within a Mile', p. 96.
84. Ibid.
85. Wilson, *Korti to Khartum*, pp. 211–29.
86. Ibid., pp. 229–36.
87. Dawson, 'Stewart's Desert March', p. 739.
88. A calculation based on the known strength of Norton's half-battery and the Desert Column parade-state of 2 Feb. which gives a total RA contingent of 6 officers and 77 NCOs and men.
89. Beresford, 'Official Report', 10 Mar. 85, *London Gazette*, d 28 Apr. 85, p. 1917.
90. Beresford, *Memoirs*, vol. ii, p. 291.
91. Ibid., p. 291.
92. War Diary, 2 Feb. 85. The figures given here for the wounded are drawn from the War Diary and are somewhat at variance with those given in Mildmay Willson's official despatch of 1 Feb. (*London Gazette*, 10 Mar. 85, p. 1026), where he cites 5 officers, 55 other ranks and 6 natives as having left with the convoy, and 7 officers, 35 other ranks and 2 natives still at Gubat. I have preferred the War Diary figures on the basis that they are a reflection of what actually happened, whereas Willson's figures appear to be a projection of what he had been told would happen.
93. Marling, *Rifleman and Hussar*, p. 142.
94. War Diary, 2 Feb. 85.
95. Ibid.
96. *London Gazette*, 10 Mar. 85, pp. 1026–8.
97. Stuart-Wortley report, 1 Feb. 85, *London Gazette*, 10 Mar. 85, p. 1026.
98. Wolseley journal, 28 Jan, Preston, *In Relief of Gordon*, p. 127.
99. Beresford, *Memoirs*, vol. ii, pp. 295–6.
100. Prior, *Campaigns*, p. 225.
101. Beresford, *Memoirs*, vol. ii, p. 296.
102. Marling, *Rifleman and Hussar*, pp. 139–43.
103. Beresford, *Memoirs*, vol. ii, p. 297.
104. Ibid.
105. Wilson, *Korti to Khartum*, p. 240.
106. Beresford, *Memoirs*, vol. ii, pp. 297–8.
107. Ibid., p. 299.
108. Ibid., p. 298.
109. Ibid., pp. 299–300.
110. Trafford MS.
111. Wilson, *Korti to Khartum*, pp. 242–5.
112. Ibid., pp. 245–6.
113. Ibid., pp. 246–8.
114. Beresford, *Memoirs*, vol. ii, p. 300.
115. Ibid., p. 307.
116. Ibid., pp. 300–1.
117. Wilson, *Korti to Khartum*, p. 248.
118. Ibid., p. 249.
119. Ibid., p. 250.
120. Ibid., p. 249.
121. Beresford, *Memoirs*, vol. ii, p. 303.
122. Wilson, *Korti to Khartum*, p. 249.
123. Beresford, *Memoirs*, vol. ii, p. 303.
124. Wilson, *Korti to Khartum*, p. 251.
125. Gascoigne, 'To Within a Mile', p. 99.
126. Beresford, *Memoirs*, vol. ii, p. 303.
127. Gascoigne, 'To Within a Mile', p. 99.
128. Beresford, *Memoirs*, vol. ii, pp. 303–4.
129. Wilson, *Korti to Khartum*, p. 252.
130. Ibid., p. 255.
131. Gascoigne, 'To Within a Mile', p. 99.
132. Wilson, *Korti to Khartum*, pp. 252–3.
133. Beresford, *Memoirs*, vol. ii, p. 306.
134. Gascoigne, 'To Within a Mile', p. 99.
135. Beresford, *Memoirs*, vol. ii, p. 304.
136. Ibid., p. 305.
137. Wilson, *Korti to Khartum*, p. 255.
138. Ibid., pp. 253–4.
139. Beresford, *Memoirs*, vol. ii, p. 305.
140. Beresford, 'Official Report', *London Gazette*, 28 Apr. 85, p. 1916.
141. Beresford, *Memoirs*, vol. ii, pp. 306–7.
142. Gascoigne, 'To Within a Mile', p 100.
143. Wilson, *Korti to Khartum*, p. 256.
144. Beresford, *Memoirs*, vol. ii, p. 306, quoting a personal account by Rear Adm. Sir Colin Keppel.
145. Beresford, 'Official Repor't, *London Gazette*, 28 Apr. 85, p. 1916.
146. Beresford, *Memoirs*, vol. ii, p. 310, citing evidence gathered for a meeting of the Intelligence Dept. in Cairo on 23 Feb. 1893. The same evidence refers

to the presence of a 'Sheikh Mustafa el Amin'. It is possible that this is another name for the Faqī Muṣṭafa.
147. Wingate, *Mahdiism*, p. 188.
148. Wolseley to Hartington, 9 Feb 1885, quoted in Watson, *Life of Wilson*, p. 333.
149. Wolseley journal, 4 Feb. 85, Preston, *In Relief of Gordon*, p. 135.

Chapter 16: Too Late: Lies, Myth and Reality

1. It should be noted, however, that Wolseley sent the pages of his journal home to his wife with his private letters and that she once remarked that he seemed to be writing for posterity. Adrian Preston, who transcribed the Nile journal in the mid-1960s, concluded that, 'Judging from the pencilled marginalia, occasional excisions and heavy overwriting, it would appear that Wolseley intended publishing these journals, in part or in whole, as a sequel to the *Story of a Soldier's Life* [his unfinished autobiography] which in fact ends where the journals begin.' It is hard to imagine that he would have published the Nile journal without a good deal more expurgation, for its tone would have done Wolseley's reputation no favours and, depending to some extent on the date of publication, would almost certainly have landed him in court. He was certainly vicious about Wood and unkind about Brackenbury, both of whom outlived him.
2. To some extent the careers of Marlborough and Wellington argue against this contention, but they were both bona fide military geniuses of a kind the British Army has never been blessed with since.
3. See the item of Buller's correspondence quoted in Melville, *The Life of General The Right Hon. Sir Redvers Buller*, p. 208.
4. Colvile, *OH*, vol. i, p. 31.
5. Ibid., p. 45.
6. Wolseley to his wife, 13 Sep. 85, Arthur, *Wolseley Letters*, p. 119.
7. Colvile, *OH*, vol. i, p. 133.
8. Melville, *Life of Buller*, p. 208.
9. See unspecified item of Buller's correspondence dated 8 Nov. 85, quoted in Melville, *Life of Buller*, p. 207.
10. Unspecified item of Buller's correspondence dated 24 Dec. 84, quoted in Melville, *Life of Buller*, p. 208.
11. Colvile, *OH*, vol. i, pp. 132–3.
12. Colvile, *OH*, vol. i, p. 139.
13. Wolseley journal, 3 Jan. 85, Preston, *In Relief of Gordon*, p. 107.
14. Wolseley journal, 30 and 31 Dec.; ibid., pp. 101–2.
15. Wolseley to Baring, 31 Dec. 84, see Egypt No. 1/1885, p. 132; also Colvile, *OH*, vol. i. p. 138.
16. Gordon's journal, 14 Dec. 84, Hake, *The Journals of Major-Gen. C. G. Gordon at Kartoum*, p. 395.
17. Macdonald, *Too Late*, pp. 203–4.
18. Wolseley journal, 2 Jan. 85, Preston, *In Relief of Gordon*, p. 105.
19. Colvile, *OH*, vol ii, p. 9.
20. Colborne, *With Hicks Pasha in the Soudan*, pp. 30–56, describes the journey from Suakin to Berber at great length.
21. Colborne, *With Hicks Pasha*, p. 40.
22. Wolseley to Hartington, 8 Apr. 84, Colvile, *OH*, vol. i, p. 29.
23. Colborne, *With Hicks Pasha*, p. 44. Colborne establishes the presence of 300 bāshi-būzuqs and 100 Egyptian soldiers: hence, with the staff officers and servants, not fewer than 450 men in all.
24. See Preston, *In Relief of Gordon*, p. 118.
25. Brackenbury, *River Column*, p. 61.
26. Snook, *Go Strong into the Desert*, p. 164.
27. Chermside was governor of Suakin, but had formerly been one of Sir Charles Wilson's subordinates in Anatolia.
28. Molyneux to Adm. Hay, 6 Sep. 84; Egypt No.1/1885, p. 1.
29. Ibid., p. 14.
30. Ibid., p.12.
31. Colvile, *OH*, vol. i, p. 31.
32. Gordon journal, 14 Dec. 84, Hake, *The Journals of Major-Gen. C. G. Gordon*, p. 395.
33. For an account of the siege of El Obeid, including a primary account of its fall, see Wingate, *Mahdiism*, pp. 22–3, and 54–6. See also Ohrwalder, *Ten Years' Captivity*.
34. See Colvile, *OH*, vol. ii, pp. 270–6 where Kitchener's report is cited in full.
35. Cromer, *Modern Egypt*, p. 445.
36. See various, Gordon to Baring, Egypt No. 12/1884.
37. Gordon journal, 19 Oct. 84, Hake, *The Journals of Major-Gen. C. G. Gordon*, p. 206.
38. Ibid., p. 206.
39. Cromer, *Modern Egypt*, vol. i, p. 437.
40. Ibid., pp. 437–8.
41. Ibid., pp. 447–52.
42. Ibid., p. 433.
43. Ibid., p. 434.
44. Ibid., pp. 535–42.
45. Ibid., pp. 543–4.
46. Hartington to Stephenson, 26 Aug. 84, Colvile, *OH*, p. 51.
47. Preston, *In Relief of Gordon*, pp. 119–20.
48. Stephenson to Hartington, 4 May 84; and Stephenson's memo of 5 May 84, Colvile, *OH*, vol. i, pp. 32–4.
49. Colvile, *OH*, vol. i, pp. 36–7.

50. Egypt No. 35/1884: Hartington to Stephenson 8 Aug. 84 [two telegrams of that date], pp. 14–17; 12 Aug, p. 34; 15 Aug, pp. 36–8; 19 Aug, p. 46; 22 Aug, p. 58; 23 Aug, p. 59; 26 Aug, pp. 60–1. Also Stephenson to Hartington, 11 Aug, p. 32; 14 Aug, p. 35; 16 Aug, p. 45; 21 Aug, pp. 53–4; 29 Aug, p. 63.
51. Stephenson to Hartington, 21 Aug. 84, Egypt No. 35/1884, pp. 53–4.
52. Macdonald, *Too Late*, p. 17.
53. Colvile, *OH*, vol. i, pp. 32 & 37.
54. Butler, *Campaign of the Cataracts*, pp. 266–7.
55. Ibid., p. 261.
56. Ibid., pp. 261–2.
57. Colvile, *OH*, vol. i, p. 132.
58. The document is cited in full in Colvile, *OH*, vol. i, pp. 240–3.
59. Wilson, *Korti to Khartum*, p. 11.
60. Preston, *In Relief of Gordon*, p. 103.
61. Wilson, *Korti to Khartum*, p. 274.
62. Colvile, *OH*, vol. ii, pp. 7–10.
63. See for example observations on the condition and treatment of the camels made by Wilson, *From Korti to Khartum*, pp. 95–7; and Marling, *Rifleman and Hussar*, pp. 131–2.
64. Colvile, *OH*, vol. ii, p. 257.
65. Snow MS.
66. Beresford, *Memoirs*, vol. i, p. 262.
67. Beresford, 'Proceeding of the Naval Brigade', *London Gazeette*, 28 Apr. 85.
68. See for example Keown-Boyd, *A Good Dusting*, p. 50.
69. Dundonald, *My Army Life*, p. 28.
70. Wilson, *Korti to Khartum*, pp. 48, 51–2 and 58–9.
71. Marling, *Rifleman and Hussar*, p. 137.
72. Wilson, *Korti to Khartum*, pp. 105–6; Colvile, *OH*, vol. ii, pp. 267–8.
73. The estimate is based on a projection made by Butler to the effect that when the River Column reached the furthest limit of its advance, on 24 Feb. 85, around a month after the fall of Khartoum, it was still at least three weeks shy of gaining Metemmeh. See Butler, *Campaign of the Cataracts*, p. 365.
74. Wilson, *Korti to Khartum*, pp. 300–2; further substantiaed by Colvile, *OH*, vol. ii, pp. 7–10.
75. Kitchener, 'Notes on the Fall of Khartum', cited in full in Colvile, *OH*, vol. ii, pp. 270–6.
76. Colvile, *OH*, vol. i, p. 31.

Epilogue

1. Wolseley journal, 28 Jan. 85, Preston, *In Relief of Gordon*, p. 127.
2. Melville, *Life of Buller*, pp. 221–2, where the instructions are given in full.
3. Colvile, *OH*, vol. ii. p. 52.
4. Dundonald, *My Army Life*, pp. 60–1.
5. Wolseley journal, 4 Feb. 85, Preston, *In Relief of Gordon*, p. 134.
6. Wilson, *Korti to Khartum*, pp. 266–270; Colvile, *OH*, vol. ii. p. 53.
7. Wolseley to Buller, 5 Feb. 85, Colvile, *OH*, vol. ii, pp. 53–5.
8. Hartington to Wolseley, 7 Feb. 85, ibid., p. 59.
9. Wolseley journal, 7 Feb. 85, Preston, *In Relief of Gordon*, p. 138.
10. Wolseley journal, 11 Feb. 85, ibid., p. 141.
11. Unusually for a battalion commander Eyre had come up from the ranks.
12. Colvile, *OH*, vol ii, pp. 102–9.
13. Wilson, *Korti to Khartum*, p. 275.
14. War Diary, 11 Feb. 85.
15. Wolseley had specifically asked Hartington to arrange the promotion with the Queen and the Duke of Cambridge.
16. Whitaker, *Verner Diary*, p. 79.
17. Beresford, *Memoirs*, vol ii, p. 318.
18. Colvile, *OH*, vol. ii, p. 57.
19. War Diary, 11 Feb. 85.
20. Colvile, *OH*, vol. ii, p. 66; Gleichen, *With the Camel Corps*, p. 212; Whitaker, *Verner Diary*, p. 78.
21. War Diary, 13 Feb. 85.
22. Dawson, 'Stewart's Desert March', p. 741.
23. Beresford, *Memoirs*, vol. ii, p. 320.
24. Ibid., p. 322.
25. War Diary, 13 Feb. 85.
26. Whitaker, *Verner Diary*, pp. 83–4.
27. War Diary, emtry 13 Feb. 85.
28. Beresford, *Memoirs*, vol ii, p. 323.
29. Whitaker, *Verner Diary*, p. 81.
30. Gleichen, *With the Camel Corps*, p. 213.
31. Ibid., p. 216.
32. Colvile, *OH*, vol. ii, pp. 67–8.
33. Whitaker, *Verner Diary*, pp. 82–3.
34. Gleichen, *With the Camel Corps*, p. 220.
35. War Diary, 16 Feb. 85.
36. Whitaker, *Verner Diary*, p. 84.
37. Gleichen, *With the Camel Corps*, pp. 220–2.
38. War Diary, 17 Feb. 85. It should be noted that the *OH* errs in placing this movement on 16 Feb; see Colvile, vol. ii, p. 70.
39. Whitaker, *Verner Diary*, p. 86.
40. Colvile, *OH*, vol. ii, p. 70.
41. Whitaker, *Verner Diary*, p. 92.
42. Colvile, *OH*, vol. ii, p. 71.
43. War Diary, 22 Feb. 85.
44. Whitaker, *Verner Diary*, p. 91.
45. Ibid.
46. War Diary, 23 Feb. 85.

Bibliography

Official Reports and Publications

Colvile, Col. H. E. *History of the Sudan Campaign* (3 vols.), compiled in the Intelligence Division of the War Office, London, 1889

Her Majesty's Government (Parliamentary Blue Books), Correspondence Respecting the Affairs of Egypt: No. 13 (1883) [C.-3693], No. 22 (1883) [C.-3802], No. 1 (1884) [C.-3844], No. 2 (1884) [C.-3845], No. 5 (1884) [C.-3852], No. 11 (1884), No. 12 (1884) [C.-3969], No. 13 (1884) [C.-3970], No. 15 (1884) [C.-3988], No. 16 (1884) [C.-3999], No. 18 (1884) [C.-4001], No. 20 (1884) [C.-4003], No. 21 (1884) [C.-4005], No. 22 (1884) [C.-4042], No. 25 (1884) [C.-4100], No. 26 (1884) [C.-4107], No. 32 (1884) [C.-4132], No. 33 (1884) [C.-4177], No. 34 (1884) [C.-4204], No. 35 (1884) [C.-4203], No. 1 (1885) [C.-4278], No. 20 (1885) [C.-4600], No. 2 (1886) [C.-4611], No. 5 (1886) [C.-4769]

HMSO. *Field Exercise and Evolutions of Infantry*, London, 1877

―――, *Field Exercise and Evolutions of Infantry*, London, 1884

―――, *Rifle & Field Exercises and Musketry Instructions for Her Majesty's Fleet*, London, 1877

―――, *Report on the Egyptian Provinces of the Sudan, Red Sea, and Equator, Compiled in the Intelligence Branch, Quartermaster General's Department, Horse Guards, War Office* (revised to July 1884), London, 1884

Hart, Lt. Gen. H. G. *The New Annual Army List*, London, 1879 and 1885 editions

London Gazette, editions dated: 20 Feb. 1885; 10 Mar. 1885; 27 Mar. 1885; 12 May 1885; 25 Aug. 1885

Stewart, Lt. Col. J. D. H. *Report on the Soudan* (Parliamentary Blue Book No. 11 of 1883, [C.-3670]), London, 1883

Unpublished Primary Sources

Airlie, David Ogilvy, 6th Earl of. Airlie Papers, National Archives of Scotland, War-Diary of the Desert Column (NAS GD16/52/57/10, Volume B); Orders Book of the Desert Column; Handwritten Casualty Returns of 23 Jan. 1885 (NAS 02024 GD-16-52-57-10-A-00118)

Trafford, Capt. Lionel, West Sussex Records Office, Royal Sussex Regiment Collection, Original MS Campaign Diary (RSR MS 1/85A); Illustrated (Retrospective) MS Campaign Diary (RSR MS 1/85).

Snow, Lt. T. D., MS Account, 'Mounted Infantry in the Desert Campaign', National Army Museum,

Williams, Sgt. Charles, MS Account, Toy Family Private Papers

Published Primary Sources

Abbas Bey, 'Diary', *Sudan Notes and Records*, Vol. XXXII, Pt. 2, Khartoum, 1951

Anon., 'From Gemai to Korti in a Whaler', *The Nineteenth Century*, Feb. 1885

Beresford, Lord Charles, *The Memoirs of Admiral Lord Charles Beresford*, London, 1914

Brackenbury, Maj. Gen. Henry, *The River Column*, London, 1885

―――, *Some Memories of My Spare Time*, London, 1909

Burleigh, Bennet, *Desert Warfare: Being the Chronicle of the Eastern Soudan Campaign*, London, 1884

―――, *Daily Telegraph* copy from the Sudan, 1884–5

Butler, Lt. Gen. Sir William F., *The Campaign of the Cataracts*, London, 1887

―――, *Charles George Gordon*, London, 1897

―――, *Sir William Butler: An Autobiography*, London, 1911

Colborne, Col. Hon. John, *With Hicks Pasha in the Soudan*, London, 1884

Cromer, Earl of, *Modern Egypt* (2 vols.), London, 1908

Dawson, Lt. Douglas, 'Sir Herbert Stewart's Desert March', *The Nineteenth Century*, Nov. 1885

De Cosson, Maj. E. A., *Fighting the Fuzzy Wuzzy: Days and Nights of Service with Sir Gerald Graham's Field Force at Suakin*, London, 1886
Dundonald, Lt. Gen. The Earl of, *My Army Life*, London, 1926
Gambier-Perry, Maj. E. (originally published anonymously as 'An Officer who was There'). *Suakin 1885: Being a Sketch of the Campaign of this Year*, London, 1885
Gascoigne, Capt. R. F. T., 'To Within a Mile of Khartoum', *The Nineteenth Century*, Jul. 1885
Gleichen, Major General Lord Edward, *With the Camel Corps up the Nile*, London, 1888
____, *A Guardsman's Memories: A Book of Recollections*, London, 1932
Gordon, John, *My Six Years with the Black Watch*, Boston, 1929
Greaves, George, *Memoirs of General Sir George Greaves*, London, 1924
Haggard, Lt. Col Andrew, DSO, *Under Crescent and Star*, London, 1896
Hamilton, Gen. Sir Ian, *Listening for the Drums*, London, 1944
Herbert, St Leger, *Morning Post* copy from the Sudan, 1884–5
Lawson, Lt. H. M., 'Desert Notes from Korti to El Goubat', *RE Journal*, Vol. 15, 1885
Marling, Col. Sir Percival, VC. *Rifleman and Hussar*, London, 1931
Macdonald, Alexander, *Too Late for Gordon and Khartoum: The Testimony of an Independent Eyewitness of the Heroic Efforts for their Rescue and Relief*, London, 1887
____, *Why Gordon Perished; or the Political and Military causes which led to the Sudan disasters*, London, 1896
McCalmont, Maj. Gen. Sir Hugh, KCB, CVO, The *Memoirs of Major General Sir Hugh McCalmont*, London, 1924
Neufeld, Charles, *A Prisoner of the Khaleefa: Twelve years Captivity at Omdurman* (Bell's Indian and Colonial Edition), London and Bombay, 1899
Ohrwalder, Fr. J., and Wingate, Maj. F. R. (ed.), *Ten Years Captivity in the Mahdi's Camp 1882–1892* (2 vols.), limited edition, London, 1893
Parke, Dr. Thomas Heazle, 'How General Gordon Was Really Lost', *The Nineteenth Century*, May 1892
Pearse, Harry, *Daily News* copy from the Sudan, 1884–5
Prior, Melton, *Campaigns of a War Correspondent*, London, 1912
Sartorius, Ernestine, *Three Months in the Soudan*, London, 1885
Slatin Pasha, Col. Sir Rudolf, *Fire and Sword in the Sudan* (4th edition), London, 1896
Talbot, Col. Hon. Reginald, 'The Battle of Abu Klea', *The Nineteenth Century*, Jan. 1886
Turner, Maj. Gen Sir Alfred E., *Sixty Years of a Soldier's Life*, London, 1912
Williams, Charles, 'How Gordon Was Lost', *The Fortnightly Review*, May 1885
Wilson, Col. Sir Charles, *From Korti to Khartum*, London, 1886
Wolseley, Field-Marshal Viscount, *The Story of a Soldier's Life* (2 vols.), London, 1903
Verner, Col. W. W. C., *Sketches in the Soudan*, London, 1885
Villiers, Frederic, *Pictures of Many Wars*, London, 1902
____, *Peaceful Personalities and Warriors Bold*, London, 1907
____, *Villiers: His Five Decades of Adventure* (2 vols.), New York & London, 1920
Wood, FM Sir Evelyn, VC, *From Midshipman to Field Marshal*, London, 1906
____, *Winnowed Memories*, London, 1918
Wylde, A. B., *'83 to '87 in the Soudan with an account of Sir William Hewett's Mission to King John of Abyssinia* (2 vols.), London, 1888

Published Compilations of Participants' Journals and Correspondence

Arthur, Sir George (ed.), *The Letters of Lord and Lady Wolseley 1870–1911*, London, 1922
Gordon, M. A. (ed.), *Letters of General Gordon to his Sister*, London, 1888
Hake, A. Egmont (ed.), *The Journals of Major-Gen. C.G. Gordon, CB., at Kartoum printed from the original MSS*, London, 1885
Power, Arnold (ed.), *Letters from Khartoum Written During the Siege* [Letters of Frank Power], London, 1885
Preston, Adrian (ed.), *In Relief of Gordon: Lord Wolseley's Campaign Journal*, London, 1967
Vetch, Col. R. H. (ed.), *Life, Letters and Diaries of Lieutenant General Sir Gerald Graham, VC, GCB*, London, 1901
Whitaker, James (ed.), *The Military Diary of Colonel W. W. C. Verner*, Leeds, 2003

Contemporary Illustrated Newspapers

Illustrated London News: eyewitness sketches by Melton Prior
The Graphic: eyewitness sketches by Frederic Villiers

Secondary Works

Aglen, E. F., 'The Sheikan Battlefield', *Sudan Notes and Records*, Vol. XX, Pt. 1, Khartoum, 1937
Alexander, Michael, *The True Blue: The Life and Adventures of Colonel Fred Burnaby*, London, 1957
Allen, Bernard, *Gordon and the Sudan*, London, 1931
Anglesey, The Marquess of, *A History of the British Cavalry 1816–1919*, Vols. II–IV, London, 1975, 1982 and 1986
Anon., *Pictorial Records of the English in Egypt, with a Life of General Gordon and other Pioneers of Freedom*, London, n.d
Archer, Thomas, *The War in Egypt and the Soudan* (4 vols.), London, 1887
Arthur, Capt. Sir George, *Life of Lord Kitchener* (3 vols.), London, 1920
――――, *The Story of the Household Cavalry* (2 vols.), London, 1909
Asher, Michael, *Khartoum: The Ultimate Imperial Adventure*, London, 2005
Baker, Anne, *A Question of Honour: The Life of Lieutenant General Valentine Baker Pasha*, London, 1996
Baker, Capt. Valentine, *The British Cavalry with Remarks on its Practical Organization*, London, 1858
Barthorp, Michael, *War on the Nile: Britain, Egypt and the Sudan 1882–1898*, Poole, 1984
Beatty, Charles, *His Country was the World: A Study of Gordon of Khartoum*, London, 1954
Beaver, William, *Under Every Leaf: How Britain Played the Greater Game from Afghanistan to Africa*, London, 2012
Bleby, Lt. Cdr. Arthur, *The Victorian Naval Brigades*, Glasgow, 2006
Brereton, J. M., *The 4th/7th Dragoon Guards (and their Predecessors) 1685–1980*, Catterick, 1982
Brook-Shepherd, Gordon, *Between Two Flags: The Life of Baron Sir Rudolf von Slatin Pasha*, London, 1972
Bullard, F. Lauriston, *Famous War-correspondents*, London, 1914
Chaplin, Lt. Col. H. D., *The Queen's Own Royal West Kent Regiment 1881–1914*, Maidstone, 1959
Chisholm, Cecil, *Sir John French: An Authentic Biography*, London, 1915
Clowes, Sir Wm. Laird, *The Royal Navy: A History from the Earliest Times to the Death of Queen Victoria*, London, 1903
De Ainslie, Gen. C. P., *Historical Record of the First or the Royal Regiment of Dragoons*, London, 1887.
Douglas, Sir George, *The Life of Major General Wauchope*, London, 1904
Elton, Lord, *General Gordon*, London, 1954
Emery, Frank (ed.), *Marching over Africa: Letters from Victorian Soldiers*, London, 1986
Everett, Sir Henry, *The Somerset Light Infantry (Prince Albert's) 1685–1914*, London, 1934
Farwell, Byron, *Prisoners of the Mahdi*, New York, 1967
――――, *Queen Victoria's Little Wars*, London, 1973
Field, Col. Cyril, *Britain's Sea Soldiers: A History of the Royal Marines* (2 vols.), Liverpool, 1924
Forbes, Archibald, *Souvenirs of Some Continents*, London, 1886
――――, *Memories and Studies of War and Peace*, London, 1895
――――, *The Failure of the Nile Campaign*, The Contemporary Review, Jan. 1892
French, Lt. Col. Hon. Gerald, DSO, *Gordon Pasha of the Sudan: The Life Story of an Ill-Requited Soldier*, London, 1958
Galloway, William. *The Battle of Tofrek*, London, 1887
Gardyne, Lt. Col. C. Greenhill, *The Life of a Regiment, The History of the Gordon Highlanders, Vol. II 1816–1898*, London, 1903 (2nd edition 1929)
Grant, James, *Cassell's History of the War in the Sudan* (6 vols.), London, c.1890
Greaves, Graeden, *Wild Bennet Burleigh; The Pen and the Pistol*, self-published, 2012
Green, Dominic, *Armies of God: Islam and Empire on the Nile 1869–1899: The First Jihad of the Modern Era*, London, 2007
Gretton, Lt. Col. G. de M, *The Campaigns and History of the Royal Irish Regiment from 1684 to 1902*, London, 1911
Hare, Maj. Gen. Sir Steuart, *The Annals of the King's Royal Rifle Corps*, London, 1929
Hill, G. Birkbeck, *Gordon in Central Africa 1874–79*, London, 1899
Hill, Richard, *A Biographical Dictionary of the Anglo-Egyptian Sudan*, Oxford, 1951
――――, 'Rulers of the Sudan 1820–1885', *Sudan Notes and Records*, Vol. XXXII, Pt. 1, Khartoum, 1951
――――, *Egypt in the Sudan 1820–81*, Oxford, 1959
Holland, Bernard, *Life of Spencer Compton, Eighth Duke of Devonshire* (2 vols.), London, 1911
Hutchinson, George Thomas, *Frank Rhodes: A Memoir*, printed for private circulation, 1908
Hutton, Lt. Gen. Sir Edward, *A Brief History of the King's Royal Rifle Corps 1755–1915*, Winchester, 1925
Hyde, H. Montgomery, *The Cleveland Street Scandal*, London, 1976
Jackson, H. C., *Osmán Digna*, London, 1926
James, Lawrence, *The Savage Wars: British Campaigns in Africa 1870–1920*, London, 1985
Jerrold, Walter, *Sir Redvers H. Buller VC: The Story of his Life and Campaigns*, London, 1900

Johnson, Peter, *Gordon of Khartoum*, Wellingborough, 1985
Keown-Boyd, Henry, *A Good Dusting: The Sudan Campaigns 1883–1899*, London, 1986
Knight, Ian, *Marching to the Drums*, London, 1999
Kochanski, Halik, *Sir Garnet Wolseley: Victorian Hero*, London, 1999
Lehmann, Joseph, *All Sir Garnet: A Life of Field Marshal Lord Wolseley*, London, 1964
Lidell, Col. R. S., *The Memoirs of the Tenth Royal Hussars*, London, 1891
MacGregor-Hastie, Roy, *Never to be Taken Alive: A Biography of General Gordon*, London, 1985
MacLaren, Roy, *Canadians on the Nile 1882–1898*, Vancouver, 1978
MacMichael, H. A., *The Tribes of Northern and Central Kordofan*, Cambridge, 1912
Mann, Michael, *The Regimental History of 1st The Queen's Dragoon Guards*, privately published by the regiment, 1993
Mansfield, Peter, *The British in Egypt*, Newton Abbot, 1973
Marlowe, John, *Mission to Khartum: The Apotheosis of General Gordon*, London, 1969
Maurice, Maj. Gen. Sir J. F., and Arthur, Sir George, *The Life of Lord Wolseley*, London, 1924
Maxwell, Col. Leigh, *The Ashanti Ring: Sir Garnet Wolseley's Campaigns 1870–1882*, London, 1985
McCourt, Edward, *Remember Butler: The Story of Sir William Butler*, London, 1967
Melville, Col C. H., *The Life of General Sir Redvers Buller* (2 vols.), London, 1923
Nicoll, Fergus, *The Sword of the Prophet*, Stroud, 2004
Nutting, Anthony, *Gordon: Martyr and Misfit*, London, 1966
Oxenham, Rev. H. N., *Memoir of Lieutenant Rudolph de Lisle RN*, London, 1886
Pimblett, W. Melville, *Story of the Soudan War*, London, 1885
Pomeroy, Maj. Hon. Ralph Legge, *History of the 5th Dragoon Guards*, London, 1924
Powell, Geoffrey, *Buller: A Scapegoat: A Life of General Sir Redvers Buller VC*, London, 1994
Reid, J. A., 'The Mahdi's Emirs', *Sudan Notes and Records*, Vol. XX, Pt. 2, Khartoum, 1937
Robson, Brian, *Fuzzy Wuzzy: The Campaigns in the Eastern Sudan 1884–85*, Tunbridge Wells, 1993
Ross-of-Bladensburg, Lt. Col., CB, *A History of the Coldstream Guards from 1815–1895*, London, 1896
Royle, Charles, *The Egyptian Campaigns 1882–1899* (2nd edition), London, 1900
Sandes, Lt. Col. E. W., DSO, MC, RE, *The Royal Engineers in Egypt and the Sudan*, London, 1937
Seymour, William W., *On Active Service*, London, 1939
Shibeika, Mekki, *British Policy in the Sudan 1882–1902*, Oxford, 1952
Small, E. Milton, *Told from the Ranks: Recollections of Service by Privates and NCOs of the British Army 1843–1901*, London, 1901
Snook, Lt. Col. Mike, MBE, *Into the Jaws of Death: British Military Blunders 1879–1900*, London, 2008
———, *Go Strong into the Desert: The Mahdist Uprising in Sudan 1881–5*, Nottingham, 2010
Spiers, Edward M., *The Late Victorian Army 1868–1902*, Manchester University, 1992
———, *The Victorian Soldier in Africa*, Manchester University, 2004
Stuart-Menzies, Mrs [Amy Charlotte], *Memories Discreet and Indiscreet by a Woman of No Importance*, London, 1917
Symons, Julian, *England's Pride: The Story of the Gordon Relief Expedition*, London, 1963
Theobald, A. B., *The Mahdiya: A History of the Anglo-Egyptian Sudan 1881–1899*, London, 1951
Thompson, Brian, *Imperial Vanities*, London, 2001
Verner, Col. Willoughby, *The Military Life of HRH George Duke of Cambridge* (2 vols.), London, 1905
Waller, John H., *Gordon of Khartoum: The Saga of a Victorian Hero*, New York, 1988
Warburg, Gabriel, *Islam, Sectarianism and Politics in the Sudan since the Mahdiyya*, University of Wisconsin, 2002
Warner, Philip, *Dervish: The Rise and Fall of an African Empire*, London, 1973
Watson, Col. Sir Charles M., *The Life of Major General Sir Charles William Wilson*, London, 1909
Webb, J. V., *The Abu Klea Medal Rolls*, London, 1981
Wingate, Maj. Francis Reginald, *Mahdiism and the Egyptian Sudan: Being an Account of the Rise and Progress of Mahdiism and of Subsequent Events in the Sudan to the Present Time*, London, 1891
Wilkinson-Latham, Robert, *From Our Special Correspondent: Victorian War Correspondents and their Campaigns*, London, 1979
Wright, Thomas, *The Life of Colonel Fred Burnaby*, London, 1908
Wortham, H. E., *Gordon: An Intimate Portrait*, London, 1933

Index

Abbas (steamer), loss of, 112–14, 122, 130
'Abd Allāh Effendi, 456, 458, 460, 461,
Abū-Hamed, 51, 64–5, 78–9, 84, 88, 105, 113, 120, 131, 133, 135, 140, 472–3, 489, 494, 495, 499, 504
abū'l-Kailak, Amīr 'Abd-al-Mājid Nasr al-Din, 113, 228–9, 269, 380, 405, 505
Abu Klea, Battle of:
  aftermath, 305–28
  'ambush' by Mahdīsts, 265
  British forces in, 521
  British loss in, 311–12, 525–8
  dead baggage camels, 308
  defence of *zariba*, 312–13
  hand-to-hand fighting, 295
  idea of night march, 323
  intelligence, decisions and doubt in, 321–2
  18 Jan. (Sunday), 318–21
  Mahdīst forces in, 522
  Mahdīst loss in, 309–10
  occupation of Abu Klea Wells, 313–18
  orders and intent during, 322–8
  phases of; *see below*
  Verner's map of, 268, 276
  Wolseley gets news of, 419–20
Abu Klea, phase I of, 222–40, 232
  anṣār positions, 222, 223
  British advance preparation, 237–40
  composition of Mahdīst force, 228–9
  early skirmishing, 224–5
  'gun-fort', 223
  infantry of C Coy, MICR, 225
  Mahdīst main body, advance of, 226–8
  Mahdīst minor tactics, 230–2
  stand-off distance from rebels, 232–3
  strengthening of defences, 223–4
  from Verner's diary, 225
Abu Klea, phase II of, 241–64
  casualties, 258–60
  crossing *khor*, 254–5
  defending *zariba*, 250–1
  enemy cavalry appear, 259–60
  incoming rifle fire, 254–5
  loss of soldiers, 255–6
  Magill injury during, 258
  necessity to halt, 256
  Qur'anic banners and, 260
  square advances, 251–6
  square formation, 246–50
  state of training in HCR, 244–6
  stop–start advance, 258–9
Abu Klea, phase III of, 265–304
  British musketry, 270–1
  British square, breaking, 279–84
  crisis during, 287–300
  decision-making in crisis, 271–4
  enemy receding, sudden, 300–4
  firing commencement, 274–8
  Mahdīst formation, 266–70
  Martini-Henry rifle battlefield performance, 284–7
  obscuration by smoke, 277
Abu Klea Valley, 141, 211, 217, 223, 226, 239, 244, 246, 271, 303, 329, 429
Abu Klea Wells:
  occupation of, 313–18
  Talbot's convoy at, 429
  water quality, 315
Abu Kru, Battle of, 339, 344–89
  ammunition expenditure, 347
  British forces, 523
  British loss in, 383–6, 532
  casualty returns, 351–2, 384–6, 529–31
  composition of square, 358–73
  decisiveness and delay issues, 355–8
  denouement of, 373
  enemy skirmishers, 346
  long-range shots, 345–6
  Mahdīst forces, 374–8, 379–82, 524
  Mahdīst loss in, 379
  Nur 'Anqara's battle plan, 382–3
  ordeal by fire, 347–52
  Prior struck by bullet, 354–5
  regiments move towards knoll, 345–7
  strengthening defence, 352–4
  uncertainty about *anṣār*, 404–5
  Verner's map of, 400
  war correspondents, 354–5
  'wounded viper' problem, 379
  at *zariba*, 388–9
'Achmet Mohamed', 381
Ali Agha, 459
Airlie, Earl of, 28, 145, 157, 185, 189, 191, 213, 260, 298, 311, 320, 342, 385–6, 404, 408, 415
  War Diary and papers of, 183, 208, 240, 313, 319, 323–4, 327, 384
Alderson, Edwin, 220
Alderson, H. J., 287
Alexandria, 13, 22, 32, 35, 52, 54, 87, 90, 100, 101, 104, 107, 108, 161, 172, 177, 180, 238
al-Heddai, Amīr Aḥmad, 87, 89–90, 103
Ali Loda, 153, 206, 339, 330, 333–5, 337–8
Alison, Sir Archibald, 180
Alleyne, James, 94–5
al-'Ubeid, Shaikh, 73, 112
Ambukol and Korti, movement plan to, 520
American Civil War, 6, 241, 243
angareb, 87, 391, 393, 422, 436, 452
anṣār, 35, 52, 58, 73, 74, 141, 155,

179, 188, 211, 216, 218, 222, 223, 231, 236, 258,, 216, 266, 267, 269, 273, 282, 284, 291, 296, 297, 300, 306, 307, 309, 310, 312, 313, 315, 316, 319, 340-2, 345, 357, 369–71, 373–9, 392, 396, 399, 404, 415, 416, 423, 424, 429, 432, 433, 441, 458, 483, 496, 505, 507, 508, 512, 513
  bodies of, 253
  flags and banners, 227
  massed formation of, 260
  respect for, 284
  retreating, 301
  riflemen, 222
Arab cavalry, 208, 378
Arabi Pasha (Aḥmad ʿUrābī), 52, 203, 370
  defeat and exile, 13
  expression of gratitude, 13–14
Arbuthnot, H. T., 287, 311
Army Medical Department (AMD)
  doctors, 187, 299, 311
Army of Occupation, 4, 32, 50, 54, 89, 96, 177, 487
  deployment of, 96–7, 98
  dissent in, 4
  units yielded by, 54
Ashanti campaign, 6, 8, 54
  uniform for, 172
Assiut, 72, 78, 86, 89, 101, 105, 107, 110, 123
  to Aswan, journey, 89, 105, 520
  boats arrived at, 107
Aswan, 50, 78, 82, 86, 88, 89, 105, 107, 109, 115, 116, 123, 126, 134, 184, 246, 490
Atherton, Walter, 287–9, 291, 311, 359
Atkins, Tommy, 128, 194, 311, 493
Austin, Shoeing-Smith, 288

Baggara cavalry, 235, 348,
Baker, Sir Samuel, 34, 40
Baker, Valentine, 34, 202
  Khedive's written instructions to, 52
  and Tokar Expedition, 52–4
Bakhit Agha, 459, 464
Baring, Sir Evelyn, 9, 11, 14, 32, 35, 38, 39, 43–52, 65, 66, 69, 70, 73, 75–80, 100, 101, 113, 122, 148, 152, 476, 485–7, 486, 499
  approves Gordon's orders, 48–9
  as Consul-General, 32

'exam question' on Berber, 76
and Gordon's plans for Zubair, 70–2
pleas of citizenry to, 79
reservations about Gordon, 42
Wolseley's telegram to, 148–9
Barrow, Charles, 247, 248, 256, 361
  at front-left corner of square, 275
  shelters Syrian greys, 223
Barrow, Percy, 177–8, 191, 206, 253, 265, 330, 359, 395, 404, 410, 428, 451, 511
'Battle of the Routes', 90–2, 119, 133, 480, 488, 490
Bayūda Desert, 58, 83, 90, 110, 118, 133, 138, 149, 251, 294, 339, 469, 471, 486
  advance across, 118, 324
  breeze in, 117
  crossing and Khartoum crisis, 119
  range of hills, 117–18
  surface of, 117
  as wilderness area, 117
bazingers, 46, 231, 413, 431, 432, 436, 458
Bedouin tribes, 78, 89
Beech, Rowland, 209, 252, 255, 311
Benbow, Henry, 452, 455, 457–63
Bengal Army mutiny, 6
Berber, 37, 50, 70, 72, 73, 79, 82, 112, 113, 115, 131, 132, 134–5, 148, 152, 158, 162, 167, 202, 228, 231, 302–4, 322, 380, 382, 397, 403, 418, 470–4, 485–7, 492, 495, 498, 499, 500, 509, 513
  camel-borne operation for, 470
  capture of, 470–1
  contingent, 228–9, 231, 380
  fighting force at, 115
  Gordon at, 64–5
  Gordon's advice on, 471
  investment of, 87–8
  March 1884 decision on, 75–8
Berber Egyptian garrison, 315
Berber–Suakin road, 71, 89, 97, 99, 133–6, 473, 475–82, 486–90
Beresford, Charles, 107, 160, 163, 177, 234–5, 248, 317–18, 349, 350, 355, 389, 424, 456, 496, 503
  command succession and, 350–1
  describes Mahdist formation, 266
  escape to relative safety, 295
  memoirs of, 289, 374–5
  to rescue, 455–6
  rescues party members, 453

rolls over 'Jumbo', 306
Wolseley's orders for, 163, 166–7
Beris, 89
Beshir Agha, 229
Binning, George, 185, 210, 221, 264, 267, 269, 290, 302, 306–7, 392
Bir Mahobeh, 476, 477, 480, 481
Bonham, Harry, 183, 195, 206, 401, 410, 412, 414
Bordein (steamer), 26, 411, 414, 417, 419, 421–3, 425, 427, 430–2, 437, 441–7, 456, 457, 459
  attempt to re-float, 434–5
  final leg of journey, 436–7
Boscawen, Evelyn, 145, 156, 183, 184, 196, 198, 206, 217, 248, 257, 292, 333, 349, 362, 370, 372, 375, 377, 407, 408, 413, 416, 419, 422, 427, 448
Bower, Bobby, 181, 347, 455, 457, 460, 463, 506, 509
Bowles, J., 273
Brackenbury, Henry, 103, 123, 137, 140, 161, 242, 467, 468, 494, 505, 513
  as first DMI, 11, 16
  memoirs, 146
breakfast:
  of fighting companies, 224
  of Marling, Percy, 347
Briggs, William, 187, 299, 316, 351, 352, 355
British Army, 49, 134, 137, 179, 186, 201, 241, 277, 374, 465, 484
  and Anglo-Zulu War, 243
  attacks in square, 244
  division of, 130–3
  failure to defeat Mahdist charge, 374
  'horse and musket' era and, 242–3
  Martini-Henry rifle for, 277
  musketry, 270–1
  regiments of dragoons, 179
British loss:
  in Battle of Abu Klea, 311–12
  in Battle of Abu Kru, 383–6
British square, at Abu Klea, 242–3, 247
  breaking, 279–84
  3½ company left face of, 280–1
  disarray, 244
  enemy's awareness and, 283
  formation of, 246–50
  front face of, 262–3
  left-front corner of, 281–2

principal commanders in, 248
British square, at Abu Kru, 359
  composition of, 358–73
  first halt, 368–9
  GCR and, 360–1
  HCR and, 359–61
  Lord Cochrane's troopers, 371
  movement in scrub, 371–2
  reached near ridge, 372–3
  reconstructing composition of, 360
  slow rate of advance, 372
  Verner joining, 367–8
British Tommies, 365, 374
British volley, 370, 373, 376
Buller, Sir Redvers, 54, 55, 59, 84, 90, 92, 97, 100, 115, 121–3, 126, 127, 135–7, 151, 156–61, 167, 199, 235, 251, 389, 419, 467, 469, 494, 495, 502, 503–6, 509, 510, 512,–14
  appointed as chief of staff, 97, 101
  on change of campaign plan, 119–20
  on contingency plan, 134
  at Korti, 131–2
  on poor passage of information, 132
  staff computations by, 142
  telegraph to Wood, 139–40
Burge, William, 302, 368
Burleigh, Bennet, 58, 153, 189, 190, 210, 219, 230, 232, 233, 235, 236, 239, 240, 248, 250, 251, 259, 260, 269, 270, 284, 287, 290, 301, 303, 307, 314, 315–17, 320, 326, 327, 332, 333, 344, 346, 348, 350, 353–6, 361, 363, 364, 367, 372, 395, 396, 404, 407, 408, 410, 412, 427
  account of Burnaby's last stand, 290–1
  British firing witness, 275–7
  experience of Sudanese battlefield crossing, 58
  introduction of spearmen, 235
  and 'vipers', 307
Burnaby, Frederick Gustavus, 52–3, 57, 165–7, 196, 199, 200–1, 210, 213–14, 219–21, 224, 227, 233, 234, 238, 248, 251, 262–4, 267, 271, 288–91, 293, 299, 302, 311, 320, 321, 420, 428, 496, 497
  blamed by Talbot, 293–4
  cross-Channel adventure, 202
  death of, 328

help to General Stewart, 271
horse of, 234
in Household Cavalry, 201–2
and Kordofan expedition, 203–4
at left-rear corner, 280
marriage of, 202
name in despatches, 204
patriotic political views, 201
recruitment for Nile Expedition, 204–5
return to England, 204
seniority, 205, 206
Tissot's portrait of, 200
Burn-Murdoch, John, 279, 289–91, 359–60, 412–13
Butler, William, 4, 16, 90, 91–3, 97, 104, 105, 107, 119, 121, 131, 133, 467, 489, 491, 492, 504, 505
Campaign of the Cataracts, 132–3
  career of, 91
  devotion to Wolseley, 91
  on poor passage of information, 132
  rebuke, 126–9
  on Red River memorandum, 92
  and whaler scheme, 94–6
Byng, Charles, 185, 238, 255, 257, 274, 288, 321

cacolets, 187, 250, 252, 255, 256, 297, 306, 307, 316, 331, 368, 370, 373, 402, 403, 453
Cairo to Assiut, railway, 105, 520
Camel Corps, 26, 81, 102, 104–5, 108, 110, 115–16, 124, 130, 134–6, 140, 143–4, 147, 150–1, 156, 159, 170, 172–5, 180, 183–7, 190, 198, 200, 223, 235, 237, 287, 295, 343, 345, 469, 494–5, 511–12
  detachments, 104
  dress and equipment, 173–4
  organization of, 517–19
  up the Nile, 174
camel transport, resourcing, 109–10
Cameron, John 'Jack', 52, 137–8, 142, 143, 146, 147, 189, 214, 219, 230, 238–9, 317, 326, 340, 348, 351, 383, 510
Campaign of the Cataracts, 16, 95, 132–3, 491
campaign plan, 3–4; see also Wolseley's plan of campaign
  adapting, 150–1
  change of, 119–20
  dividing the army, 130–3, 139–40

Campaigns of a War Correspondent, 238, 363, 396
Campbell, Johnny, 157, 158, 225, 256, 264, 378
Canadian officers, 104–5
Cardwell Reforms, 10–11
Carmichael, Ludovick, 273, 278, 283, 288, 298, 307, 308, 359
cavalry, 38, 52, 54–5, 57, 82, 88, 102, 123, 132, 173, 179, 185, 210, 217–18, 227, 235, 238, 240, 243–6, 259, 264, 284, 294, 300, 303, 334, 341, 364, 378, 380, 395, 399, 405, 410, 420, 447, 452, 487, 493, 497
Chamberlain, Joe, 202, 205
Chelmsford, Lord, 7, 100, 243
Christmas at Korti, 136–8
Chronicle, 320
Clarke, Stanley, 145, 162–3, 165, 192–3, 196, 207, 510
'Cleveland Street Scandal', 299
Cochrane, Lord, 157, 209, 221, 238, 249, 327–8, 342, 346, 361, 371, 415, 429, 503
  and baggage camels, 346, 352–3
  drink description by, 315
  Life Guards detachments under, 300
  troopers of, 371
Colborne, John, 24, 477
Coldstream Guards, 146, 182, 184, 206, 247–8, 306, 309, 360, 362–3, 507
Colley, Sir George, 32, 55, 56, 184, 238
Colvile, Henry, 16, 28, 89, 103, 105, 130, 141, 142, 156, 160, 167, 225, 229, 275, 383, 403–4, 426, 468, 471
  Christmas Day report by, 229
  official history of the campaign, 28
  on prisoners at Abu Halfa, 156
Commissariat & Transport Corps, 110, 137, 138, 250, 259, 318, 352–3, 384, 397, 511
Conservatives, 23, 32, 39, 94, 200, 202
Cook, J. R. M., 426
'County Waterford', 176, 259, 318, 375
Crabbe, Eyre, 184, 217, 354, 407–8
Crutchley, Charlie, 365, 385, 389, 396, 402, 419
culpability, 468, 484
  at operational level, 488–90

Index • 571

at strategic level, 484–8
at tactical level, 496–8
Curnow, Edwin, 457, 464
Cuzzi, Giuseppe, 79, 88

Daily Chronicle, 21, 189, 213, 225, 227, 352, 357
Daily News, 24, 29, 39, 189, 212, 256, 265, 293, 388, 441
Daily Telegraph, 28–9, 189, 232, 287, 315–16, 333, 348, 356, 361, 363, 396, 407, 412
Dār Fūr, 46, 50, 85, 87, 380
Darley, Joseph Watkins William, 257, 259, 278, 280, 281, 291, 311, 359
Davison, Thomas, 359–61, 363, 394–5, 401–2
Dawson, Douglas, 146, 151, 154, 195, 248, 258, 262, 264, 277, 292–3, 300–1, 315, 318, 333, 347, 360, 363–4, 369–70, 403–4, 451, 507–8
Debbeh, 85, 90, 104, 115, 119, 123, 130, 133
de Coëtlogon, Henry, 39, 67
de Lisle, Rudolph, 177, 221, 259, 292
Desert Column, march of, 16, 18, 20–1, 24, 29–30, 134–7,
from Bayūda to Metemmeh, 143
Camel Corps, 143
and camel-mounted Arabs, 210, 211
dress and equipment, 172–7
enemy in front, 211–14
to gain Metemmeh, 151–2
Guards Camel Regiment, 182–4
Heavy Camel Regiment, 184–6
19th Hussars, 177–9
and Jakdul Wells, 142–7, 149, 151, 153–61, 169–70, 187–97
and Korti, 171–2
Light Camel Regiment, 186
location of *zariba*, 214–21
logistic units, 143
marching-out state of, 206–11
Medical Sections, 187
MICR, 179–82
morning, 209–10
move via Jakdul to Metemmeh, 143
Royal Sussex Regiment, 186–7
seniority and command of, 205–6
single-phase crossing, 158

South Stafford Infantry, 142
tactical command of, 135
from Wādī Halfā to Ambukol, 142
Wolseley's written orders, 163–9
Desert Column, preparations for march of, 161–3
amount of water available, 141
final, 197–9
intelligence picture, 141–2
staff computations, 142
dhura, 408, 421, 482
Dickson, John, 239
Digna, Osman, 435, 477, 500
Distinguished Conduct Medal (DCM), 288, 296, 298, 305, 314
Dongola:
fighting force at, 115
force deployment in, 97–9
rebellion spreads to, 85–7
securing cooperation of, 120
telegraph office at, 127
Dorward, James, 145, 154–6, 160, 195, 198, 218, 219, 237, 250, 327, 352–3, 365, 395, 421
4th Dragoon Guards, 172, 280, 311
5th Dragoon Guards, 248, 289–91, 311
Du Boulay, Noel, 177, 369, 375, 377, 388
Dufferin, Earl of, 14, 30, 185, 337, 415, 503
Duke of Wellington, 3, 7–8, 34, 97, 100, 103–4, 136, 202, 420, 467, 504

Earle, William, 97, 101, 115, 135, 143, 477–8, 495, 504–5, 512
and Monassir tribe, 152
with River Column, 135, 140, 152, 155, 166, 433, 470, 504
telegram to Buller, 477
and Vandeleur, 125, 131
Egerton, Edwin, 80, 86–7, 89, 96, 101
and British consul in Suakin, 87
Egypt, military intervention in, 7
Egyptian army (EA), 13, 41, 177, 206, 486
British officers and NCOs, 33
transformation of, 33
El Fasher, 113
El Obeïd, 14, 36, 74, 155, 481, 499
Egyptian garrison at, 482–3
Mahdi's entry into, 38
siege of, 483

El Teb, 39, 53, 56, 116, 178, 203, 251
First Battle of, 51–4
Second Battle of, 234, 357
emancipation of slaves, 34, 66

Falvey, John, 187, 256, 316
Faqī Muṣṭafa, 396–7, 401, 403, 412, 414, 415, 417, 432–3, 443, 445, 449–50, 456, 464
Faraj Pasha; *see* Muḥammad al-Zainī
fellaheen, 52, 66, 74, 87, 166, 413
felucca, 105, 431, 442, 448, 458–63
Ferguson, Frederick, 145, 187, 256, 308, 315, 316,, 318, 346, 355, 401, 425, 452
Fetherstonhaugh, Richard, 157, 165, 191, 192, 225, 232, 277, 289
Field Exercise and Evolutions of Infantry, 242, 244, 257
Fighailaia, 437
Fire and Sword in the Sudan, 381
'flying column', 43, 140, 399, 469
Forbes, Archibald, 29, 190
Fortnightly Review, 21–3, 25, 352, 358
'Fourth Cataracts', 84, 133
Fox, J., 258
French, John, 178, 211–12, 252, 305, 345, 359, 403, 511
From Korti to Khartum, 28, 29, 266, 294, 308, 322, 324, 343, 356, 362, 377, 398, 408, 423, 431, 443

Gardner machine guns, 87, 126, 143, 176, 217–19, 226, 248–9, 255, 259, 273–5, 279, 281, 287–8, 309, 314, 345, 347, 350, 354, 360, 362, 369, 402, 452, 455, 457, 459, 461, 496, 511–12
Garland, J. T., 455, 457, 464
Gascoigne, Fred, 26, 426–8,, 436–9, 441–2, 447–51, 456, 458–63
on Williams's attack on Wilson, 26
Gemai, 81, 105, 107, 120–1, 123, 126, 131, 492
George, Duke of Cambridge:
and Battle of Isandlwana, 7
on despatch of regimental detachments, 104
private life, 8
respect for Wolseley's ability, 8
Gern, Arthur, 250–1, 318, 327
Gilligan, David, 295

Gizeh (vessel), 86–7, 108
Gladstone, William Ewart, 7, 9, 16–17, 22, 27, 29, 32, 35–8, 40–1, 43–4, 49, 60, 63–6, 76, 78–80, 86, 93–4, 99, 202, 204, 411, 441, 472, 483–6, 488, 491, 499
　abrogation of Sudanese affairs, 52–3
　criticism of, 16–17
　folly and ministerial incapacity, 15
　and 'Hicks Pasha' conspiracy, 37–8
　and Nile Expedition, 9
　political alliance, 94
　procrastination, 467
Gladstone administration:
　on British troops in Sudan, 71
　collapse of, 23
　domestic political affairs, 31–4
　on operation against Tamanieb, 76
　on proposal 'Send Gordon!', 40–5
　response to Mahdist rising, 36–7
　Sudan strategy, 64–5
　'Vote of Credit', 94
　Wolseley's appointment to Egypt, 99–100
Gleichen, Count Edward, 174–5, 185, 198–9, 211–12, 221, 223, 229, 247, 258, 292, 295, 298, 304, 314–15, 318, 338, 352–4, 360, 363, 376, 384, 392, 394, 397, 402–4, 407, 409, 416, 509, 510
Gordon, C. G., 134, 239, 313, 380, 411, 414, 417–18, 426–8, 433, 473, 484–7
　at Abū-Hamed and Berber, 64–5
　on al-ʿĀilafūn disaster, 112
　appointed governor-general of the Sudan, 41, 43–4, 46–7, 49, 51
　Cairo's orders to, 48–9
　culpability issue in death of, 467
　death knell of, 151–3
　defence of Khartoum, 37, 40
　departure of, 50–1
　estimates of enemy's strength, 150
　fate of, 440–1, 454
　groping for mature plan, 69–73
　'hearts and minds' offensive, 66
　khedival firman and, 110
　last message from, 147–9
　March 1884 decision on Berber, 75–8
　measures for evacuation, 70–1
　negotiating with Mahdī, 74–5

Pall Mall Gazette interview, 42–3
　plans for Zubair, 70–2
　proclamations wired to Granville, 45
　programme of operations, 61–3
　proposal 'Send Gordon!', 40
　rehearsed final courier, 470–1
　and Stewart, 113
　Wilson sends off note for, 432
　Zubair Pasha affair, 46–8
Gordon Relief Expedition, 3, 14, 466, 499, 501
　characterization of, 501
　outlines of, 15
　reasons of failure of, 15
Gordon's steamers, 399
　arrival of, 410–15
　commanders of, 411
　miscellany of infantry, 413
　in transit, 411–12
Gordon-Cumming, William, 183, 185, 196, 206, 351
Gos-el-Basabir, 433
Gos Nefia, 436
Gough, George Hugh, 120, 145, 158, 161, 181, 185, 247, 311
Gough, Wilfred Arbuthnot, 279, 298, 321, 359
Gould, Arthur, 371
Graham, Sir Gerald, 18, 33, 50, 55–60, 76, 78–9, 189, 204, 244, 326, 478, 487, 488
　close friendship with Gordon, 76
　infantry brigade of, 55
　operation against Tamanieb, 76
Great Bend of Nile, 50, 82–5, 89–90, 103, 105, 114, 117–19, 123–4, 130, 133–6, 144, 152, 382, 467, 469, 472, 489–90, 513
1st Grenadier Guards, 172
Grenadier Guards Company, 89, 124, 156, 172, 182–4, 206, 209, 248, 249, 252, 314, 315, 330, 354, 360, 363, 374, 376, 396, 401
Guards and Mounted Infantry, 141, 146, 256–7, 281, 359, 374, 392–3, 395, 409, 493
　deploying skirmishers from, 256
　HCR and, 359
　separate regimental squares, 392–3
Guards Camel Regiment (GCR), 20, 115, 124, 137, 139, 145, 156, 164, 174, 182–5, 190, 196–7, 207, 209, 212, 247–9, 255, 257, 274,

292, 306, 309, 311, 312, 329, 333, 345, 351–2, 360, 365, 368, 384–5, 389, 391, 392, 397, 402, 403, 409, 414, 417, 425, 453, 471, 507, 511, 518
　in Battle of Abu Kru, 360–1
　companies, 182
　deprived of targets, 292
　'double-rank' system, 182
　dress and equipment, 174–5
　formation of, 183
　job of leading, 184
　Private Burge of, 302
　in square at Abu Klea, 247–9
　status as Household troops, 182
'Guards Fort', 425
Gubat, 339–40
　halt behind, 408–9
　during 20–23 Jan. 1885, 390–420
　retreat, 440–1
　Stuart-Wortley's arrival at, 451–2
　Verner's map of, 400
Guthrie, James, 177, 272, 296

Ḥalfaiya, 24, 73, 437, 439, 440, 481
　counter-attack and regaining of, 74, 112
Hamley, Edward, 26
Harden, George, 327
Hardinge, Henry 'Punch', 157, 185, 225, 350, 391
Hardy, Edward, 56, 452
Hartington, Lord, 17–19, 27, 31, 44, 81, 93–4, 98, 122, 136, 140, 168, 480, 482, 488–9, 504
　disagreement between the generals, 96–9
　enquiries on second expedition, 136
　political direction, 110–12
　response to Wolseley's memo, 84, 93
　speech of, 27
　vetoes C-in-C's intentions, 140
　Wolseley's advice on route to, 83
　Wolseley's note to, 18–19
Hawkins-Whitshed, Elizabeth, 202–3
Hay, John, 85, 86, 90, 92, 101, 102, 467, 479
Heavy Camel Regiment (HCR), 115, 145, 157, 163–4, 172–3, 184–6, 191–2, 206–7, 212, 218, 220–1, 238, 240, 244–9, 252–3, 255, 257, 262, 271–3, 278–81,

Index • 573

283–4, 286, 291, 294–5, 297, 299, 300, 308, 311–12, 320, 328, 345–6, 358–62, 374, 378, 384–5, 391, 392, 395, 397, 402, 403, 405, 409, 414, 420, 428, 453, 497, 506–8, 511, 517
  as infantrymen, 245, 293
  in Battle of Abu Kru, 359–61
  composite regiment and, 244
  dress and equipment, 172–3
  regimental detachment, 185, 272
  and Reginald Talbot, 184–5
  skirmishers deployment, 257
  square at Abu Klea, 247–9
  state of training in, 244–6
  Talbot's instruction to divide, 358
Henderson, G. F. R., 242
Herbert, St Leger, 146, 231–2, 234, 326, 349, 365–7, 383
Hibbert, Robert, 359, 371
Hicks, William, 14, 39, 65, 228, 313, 474, 476–7
  civil and military superiors of, 37
  Kordofan expedition, 38
  long desert journey, 37
  Senaar expedition, 38
  telegraphic reports, 38
Highland battalions, inspection of, 57, 103
Hippisley, William, 220, 359–61, 405
Horse Guards Parade, 244
Household Cavalry, 102, 172, 185, 200–1, 203, 213, 244, 246, 299, 369, 428, 503
'How We Lost Gordon', 21
19th Hussars, 54, 57, 102, 115–16, 137, 139, 140, 143, 144, 149, 150, 153, 163, 172, 177–9, 190–2, 195, 206, 211, 216, 218, 230, 239–40, 253, 274, 304, 314, 315, 318, 321, 329–30, 338–9, 341, 345, 355, 358, 359, 362, 364, 369, 370, 383, 384, 395, 399, 401, 403, 405, 407, 412, 418, 421, 425, 453, 478, 504, 506, 508, 510–12
  armed with Martini-Henry carbine, 179
  captured letters brought by, 308
  detachment of, 339
  division of, 211
  encounter Mahdist cavalry, 406
  role as reconnaissance screen, 177
  scouting troop of, 274
  senior officers, 177–8

sheltering ponies, 237
supported by MICR, 345
troop supports Fetherstonhaugh's half-company, 232
Hutton, Edward 'Curly', 180–1

Ibrahim, Muḥammad Effendi, 229, 370, 430, 436, 437
Illustrated London News, 239, 348
imams, 375, 380
Ingram, Walter, 189, 364, 424, 455, 460
In Relief of Gordon, 30
Isandlwana, Battle of, 7, 243, 285, 466

Jabal Royan, 436, 440, 442
Jabal Seg-et-Taib, 436–7
Jabal Tanjur, 434
Jakdul Wells, 119, 141–7, 149, 151, 153–61, 166, 169, 171, 174, 184, 186–97, 200, 205, 206, 208, 229, 238, 316, 317, 326, 401, 419, 429, 452, 469, 471, 476, 480, 493, 503, 510–12
Jervis, J. E. L., 185, 255, 311
jibbeh, 75, 155, 162, 440
jihādiya, 231–32, 305, 348, 378, 381, 382
Jones, Rhys, 226, 384,
'Jumbo', 279, 289, 306, 316

Kane, Richard, 251
Kekewich, George, 306, 307, 368, 385
Keneh, 89, 109
Keppel, Colin, 452, 455, 460, 464
Key, Astley Cooper, 31, 90
Khartoum, 31, 37, 82, 325, 467
  attempt to save, 499
  fall of, 16
  'flying column' and, 399
  force deployment in, 97–9
  hearts and minds of people, 66
  hypothetical relief of, 472–5
  line of retreat bound for, 303
  march infantry detachment, 428
  marching north from, 321
  military position at, 67–9
  news from, 417–19
  order to push through to, 107
  riparian rebels north of, 155
  siege of, 73–4, 104
  in sight, 436–40
  tribes in, 228

Wilson departs for, 429–33
Wolseley's assertion and fall of, 500
Khartoum garrison, 15, 486
Khashm al-Mūs, Muḥammad, 410–14, 411, 412, 421, 426, 430, 432, 436, 437, 440, 443, 445, 449–50, 456, 461, 462, 486
khor(s), 59–60, 117, 192, 212–4, 216, 217, 218, 223, 224, 237, 239, 252, 253–6, 258, 260–69, 278, 279, 280, 281, 287, 291, 301–3, 309, 314, 318, 321, 478, 496, 497, 513, 514
  abandoned banners in, 262
  area around confluence of, 260–1
  crossing, 254–5
  feeder, 262
  parties of *anṣār* from, 291–2
  within range of screw guns, 258
Khor Ghob, 58
King's Royal Rifle Corps (KRRC), 54, 55, 56, 78, 157, 180–1, 225, 256–7, 273, 312, 314, 455
  free-thinking gentlemen of, 264
  skirmishers, 257, 261, 264, 271, 278,
Kirbekan, Battle of, 24, 512
  Kirbekan-type battle, 472
Kitchener, Herbert, 12, 78, 90, 103, 122, 125, 141, 146, 153, 156, 188, 195–6, 207, 229, 242, 441, 450, 471, 483, 502, 503, 505, 511, 513, 514
  report on news of Berber's fall, 88
  on siege of Khartoum, 104
Kordofan expedition, 24, 38, 74, 203, 228, 303
  and Hicks Pasha, 37–40
Kordofani contingent, 228, 229, 230, 233–4, 321, 433, 481
  at Abu Klea, 381
Kordofani tribes, 73, 229
Korosko, 50, 61, 64, 78, 88, 89, 90, 126, 135, 140, 152, 489
Korti, 17, 21, 22, 24, 89, 103, 107, 114, 119, 126, 130–3, 140–1, 142–3, 144, 145, 146, 147, 154, 156, 159, 160, 162, 166–9, 170, 174, 188, 190, 196–7, 199, 246, 317, 327, 370, 465, 472, 476, 490, 491–2, 499–500, 502–4
  and Ambukol, movement plan to, 520
  Christmas at, 135–8

as concentration area, 123
Desert Column march, 171–2
Korti–Metemmeh route, 310
kourbash, 33, 338, 436

Laker, A. S., 306
Law, Charles, 291, 311, 359
Lawson, Henry, 156, 216, 353, 354, 362, 392, 421
Leigh, Gerald, 355, 385
Life Guards detachments, 238, 300, 359, 363
Life of Colonel Fred Burnaby, The, 267
Light Camel Regiment (LCR), 115, 186, 503–4, 508, 518
90th Light Infantry, 5–6
Lima, Arthur, 178, 355, 383, 395
Little Big Horn, 285
London newspapers:
  on Baker disaster, 53
  Daily News, 29
  Morning Post, 22
  on Wilson controversy, 21–2

Macdonald, Alex, 143, 157, 162, 184, 189, 196–7, 212, 213, 219, 220, 235, 237, 238, 239, 240, 251, 252, 254, 260, 267, 269, 286–7, 312, 317, 318, 322–3, 326, 331, 332, 334, 340, 343, 346, 350, 354, 367, 370, 383, 374, 388, 390, 395, 397, 408, 415, 424, 471
  battlefield glimpses by, 319
  Mahdist formation description, 267–70
  and Martini-Henry myth, 286–7
  observing advance, 260
Magill, James, 187, 258, 311
Mahdi, The; *see* Muḥammad Aḥmad
Mahdi's emissaries, 36, 66, 86, 156
  Gordon's negotiation with, 74–5
  prisoners captured at Abu Halfâ, 156
Mahdi's 'uniform':
  portrayed by Verner and others, 156
  symmetrically patched *jibbeh*, 155
Mahdism, 23, 86, 404, 466, 484
Mahdist *amir*, 79, 86, 227, 373, 379, 380
  checked movement, 236
  tactics by, 230
Mahdist charge, 283, 306
  in Battle of Abu Kru, 374–8

view from Beresford Hill, 312
Mahdist contingents, 432–3
Mahdist force, in Battle of Abu Klea:
  Beresford's description, 266
  breakthrough, 294–5
  composition of, 228–9, 233
  exploiting breach in left face, 289
  formation, 266–70
  frontage, 283
  Kordofanis in, 233–4
  left wing, 269, 296
  Macdonald's description, 267–70
  main body advance, 226–8
  military commonality in, 230–1
  minor tactics of, 230–2
  at Omdurman, 228–9
  swordsmen, 298
  Wilson's description, 266–7
  Zulu comparison, 230
Mahdist force, in Battle of Abu Kru, 379–82
Mahdist loss:
  in Battle of Abu Klea, 309–10
  in Battle of Abu Kru, 379
  in Suakin expedition, 57–8
Mahdist threat, 64
  at Berber, 65
  estimation and Gordon's advice, 150
Mahdist uprising, 47, 470
  civil war about, 36–7
  course of, xxvii–xxx
  Kordofan expedition, 24, 37–40, 203, 228, 303
Mahmoudieh, 86–7
Majuba Hill, 32. 55–6, 180, 238, 347
Malet, Evelyn, 13, 14
Marling, Percy, 30, 157, 161, 180, 181, 190, 192, 213, 221, 235, 258, 261, 273, 275, 284, 306, 314, 341, 351, 352, 361, 363, 366–7, 372, 374, 378, 392, 395, 401–2, 429, 455
  breakfast of, 347
  interest in horseflesh, 394
  letter to father, 319
  state of health, 306–7
Marshall, William, 178
Martini-Henry rifle, 174, 175, 178–9, 243, 245
  battlefield efficacy of, 258, 284–7
  inexperienced riflemen and, 285–6
  Mark II pattern, 287
  myths around, 285–7

rounds, 285
  in service, 284–5
  Wilson's views on, 284
Martyr, Cyril, 261
Masallamiya Gate, 441, 483
Massowah battalions, 52
May, Arthur, 452, 455, 457, 460
McCalmont, Hugh, 135, 137, 145, 511–2
McNeill, Sir John, 90–1, 92, 478
McSorley, P. J., 256
Medical Staff Corps, 138, 187, 188, 250, 255, 298–9, 308, 388
Metemmeh, 136, 340
  British approach to, 336
  caravan route to, 332–3
  contingent, 381
  enemy force at, 471–2
  during 20–23 Jan. 1885, 390–420
  scanning, 407
  unit strengths to attack, 402
  Verner's map of, 400, 406
  walls of, 399–410
  Wilson's intention to attack, 324
Metemmeh, Battle of, 497
  British loss at, 532
  casualty return, 529–31
Miles, Archie, 157, 225, 256, 349, 385
Miller, Walter, 279, 288
Modern Egypt, 9, 485
Moncreiff, Lynedoch, 39
Montcalm, Marquis de, 186
Morning Post, 22, 146, 189, 231, 234, 298, 383
Mounted Infantry Camel Regiment (MICR), 115, 157, 171, 179–82, 519
  concept, 179
  formation of, 180
  veterans of Suakin Campaign, 179
MICR companies:
  in Battle of Abu Klea, 224–5, 278
  in Battle of Abu Kru, 360–2
  C Company, 180–1
  Rifle Company of, 225
  square formation at Abu Klea, 247–9
Mudir of Dongola, 85, 87, 88, 103, 104, 108, 109, 114, 142, 229
Muḥammad Aḥmad, the Mahdi, 23, 35, 37, 47, 65, 75, 79, 87, 149, 155, 187, 227, 262, 308, 380, 436, 440, 483, 484
Muḥammad 'Ali Pasha, 34, 112,

Index • 575

Muḥammad al-Khair, 79, 113, 150, 151, 158, 228
  Berberine rebels under, 477, 480
  investment in Berber, 87–8
Muḥammad al-Zainī, 441, 445, 450, 454, 483
Munro, Edward, 177, 356, 385, 401
Murad, force at, 88
Muṣṭafa Yāwar Pasha, 89, 115, 120, 125
  reports of Mahdist encroachment, 85–6
  talks with Mahdi's emissaries, 86
My Army Life, 29, 337

'Narrows of the Nile', 432
Naval Brigade, 143, 160, 173, 176, 191, 212, 217, 221, 248, 249, 262, 271, 280, 281, 292, 298, 307, 312, 345, 347, 356, 369, 401, 403, 404, 427, 430, 434, 455, 463, 511
  cutlass-bayonets, 295
  medical needs of, 299
  on right front, 226
  short-handed, 314
night march, 323, 325–6, 329–43
  breaking track, 334–7
  caravan routes, 332–3
  column halt during dawn, 337–9
  disarray during, 331–3
  Stewart discussion on route with Ali Loda, 330
  through Shebacat bush, 333–4
  view into Nile Valley, 339–43
Nile Delta, 118, 411, 413
Nile Expedition, 6, 104, 277, 490, 500–1, 503–14
  camel transport, 109–10
  commencement of, 73–4
  defeat of Shaikh al-'Ubeid, 112
  delay in sanctioning of, 9
  deployment of fighting force, 115–16
  'fighting base' of, 107
  historic reality, 15–16
  incentivizing progress of, 129–30
  loss of *Abbas* (steamer), 112–14
  operational originality, 3
  participant accounts of, 156
  railway and river journey, 105–6
  recapture of Ḥalfaiya, 112
  review of situation of, 120–4
  Stewart's death, 113–14
  Sudanese officers, 112
  support of civil power, 120
  Wolseley's prosecution of, 158
Nile river:
  lodgement on, 391–2
  reassurance patrols on, 86–7
  Sixth Cataract of, 433–5
  from Wādi Halfā to Dongola, 107
Nile Valley, 36, 41, 63, 72, 89, 93, 112, 118, 229, 345, 426, 477
  predominant tribes in, 228
  view into, during night march, 339–43
Nineteenth Century, The, 26, 29, 119, 248, 257, 283, 292
noggara, 219, 339, 463
Norton, Gilbert, 177, 218, 219, 223, 235, 248, 302, 350, 369, 388, 425
  back on knoll, 369
  gun-fort and, 223
  gunners, 224
  harassment of *anṣār*, 375
  response to crisis, 272
Nubian Desert, 117, 477
nuggars, 108, 431, 458, 460, 461, 490
Nūr 'Anqara, 381, 405, 433, 489–90
  battle plan, 382–3
  unsavoury character, 379–80
Nushi Pasha, 410, 411, 421, 481

O'Donovan, Edmund, 39
Official History, 29, 105, 130, 160, 167, 225, 275, 426, 468, 508
Ohrwalder, Josef, 38, 74, 380
Omdurman, 28, 69, 73, 136, 148, 155, 229, 230, 231, 233, 322, 381, 382, 396–7, 432–3, 439–40, 442, 473, 480, 500
  hypothetical battle of, 466
  Mahdist force at, 228, 475
  Mahdist camp at, 162

Parke, Thomas, 29, 187, 316, 299
Parliamentary Blue Book, 19, 28
Payne, Charles, 180, 181, 219, 347, 375
Payne, J. R, 220
Pearse, Harry, 24, 189, 213, 256, 265, 288, 293, 308, 354, 355, 363, 364, 384, 395, 441
'Pendjeh Incident', 17, 514
Phipps, Thomas, 153, 197, 256, 261–2, 264, 265, 273, 316–8, 422
Pigott, Alfred, 177, 259, 292, 311
Pigott, Charles Berkeley (Bloody Pigott), 20, 181, 219, 220, 251–2, 295–6, 358, 362, 370, 419, 425–6, 429, 454, 502
Poe, W. H., 139, 175, 213, 348, 361, 376, 396, 397, 402, 414, 416
Poore, Richard, 87, 452
Power, Frank, 39, 113, 114, 122
Prior, Melton, 53, 125, 134, 191, 213, 224, 230, 238, 239, 317, 320, 332, 340, 342, 350, 351, 354–5, 363–4, 376, 395, 396, 426, 429, 455

Qur'anic banners, 260, 262

Red River triumvirate:
  members, 90
  small-boat scheme, 92
  submission of, 91
Red Sea Littoral, 18, 33, 36, 38, 39, 52, 60, 61, 63, 71, 76, 89, 134, 146, 178, 203, 326, 477, 478, 500, 504
  Baker disaster in, 238
  Graham's force committed to, 244
  old hands from, 307
  veterans of, 254
Regimental Medical Officers (RMOs), 187, 256, 258, 305, 429
Remingtons, 56, 141, 230–1, 307
Rhodes, Frank, 145, 146, 188, 213, 298, 348, 349, 393, 422
Rhoods, William, 279
Rifleman and Hussar, 30, 361, 366, 498
'River Dash', 27, 421–65
  Beresford to rescue, 455–6
  convoy movements, 452–3
  downstream recce, 422–7
  final preparations, 427–9
  foundations of doubt, 445
  Friday 30 Jan., 443–5
  Khartoum in sight, 436–40
  Mernat Island, 449–51
  retreat to Gubat, 440–1
  Saturday 31 Jan., 445–9
  Sixth Cataract, 433–5
  Stuart-Wortley's arrival at Gubat, 451–2
  Stuart-Wortley's report, 454–5
  Talbot's convoy, 429
  Thursday 29 Jan., 441–3
  Tuesday 27 Jan., 435–6
  Wad Habeshi, Battle of, 456–64
  Wilson departs for Khartoum, 430–3
'River Fort', 425, 505, 509

Robertson, 187, 429
Romilly, Frederick, 257, 258, 273–4
Rorke's Drift, 223, 440
Rowley, Charles, 124–5, 183–4, 206, 273
Royal Artillery baggage camels, 413
Royal Artillery screw guns, 143, 345, 409
Royal Dragoons detachment, 279–80
Royal Marine Light Infantry (RMLI):
 in Battle of Abu Klea, 248, 249
 in Battle of Abu Kru, 360–1
 dress and equipment, 175
Royal Scots Greys, 253, 257, 279–80
Royal Sussex company
 defence of *zariba*, 250–1
 strength of, 249
 taking up fire positions, 460–1
 Trafford and, 281
Royal Sussex Regiment, 72, 91, 110, 140, 436
 1st Battalion, 186–7
 from Childers amalgamations, 186
 officers and NCOs, 186–7
 skirmishers, 258
Rundle, Henry, 78, 90, 135

Sabaluka Gorge, 414, 432, 435, 440, 442, 443
St Vincent, V., 185, 255, 297, 300, 311
Saturday Review:
 'War Correspondent, The', 25
 Williams v Beresford Hope libel case, 25, 27–8
Second Cataract, 83, 85, 90, 92, 98, 105, 107, 108, 121, 123, 160, 489, 490
Sāfia, 422, 423, 427, 448, 451, 455–60, 462, 463, 464, 465, 503, 509
 engine compartment of, 459–60
 Engine Room artificers of, 457
 serve as Royal Navy warship, 456
Shaikān, Battle of, 38, 39, 65, 228
shaikhs, 75, 132, 156, 227, 260, 274, 283, 373, 376, 396
 Bisharin, 78, 79, 88, 150, 228, 236, 269, 302, 380
 Dongolāwī, 156
 mounted, 376
Shaw, Hugh

instructions to, 502
 at Jakdul Wells, 503
 marched for the front, 502–3
Shebacat bush, 330, 507, 509
 march through, 333–4
Shebacat Wells, 333
Shendy, 79, 102, 119, 126, 135, 136, 142, 228, 229, 340, 422–4, 432, 433, 447, 452, 469, 502
 as concentration area, 82
 force to concentrate on, 115, 131
 force to fight at, 81
 routes to, 82–4
Sherston, Max, 157, 225, 350, 419, 521
Sibair, Shaikh Muḥammad, 410
Simmons, Lintorn, 23
Sixth Cataract, 91, 162, 313, 414, 432, 433–5, 440, 441, 444, 445, 446, 475
Sketches in the Soudan, 225, 278, 340, 368, 383, 410
skirmishers:
 deployment of, 257
 details of, 258
 from Guards and Mounted Infantry, 256
 KRRC, 261
 Royal Sussex, 258
 skirmishing tactics, 224–5
Smith, Albert, 296
Smith, C. H., 107
Smith, W. H., 23, 258
Snow, Thomas, 220, 262, 267, 281–2, 283, 346, 362, 376, 402
Somerset, Arthur, 185, 195, 299, 305, 311, 359, 370–1, 385, 392. 393
 staff planning and calculations, 101–3
Stakings, William, 275, 277
Stead, W. T., 45
 at Abū-Hamed, 64
 at Berber, 65
 interview of Gordon, 41
 and press campaign, 40–2
steamers:
 arrival of, 410–15
 conversion of, 431
 final preparations in, 427–9
 at Jabal Royan, 435–6
Stephenson, Sir Frederick, 5, 32, 81, 87, 101, 109, 116, 180, 468, 479, 487–90, 499
 demurs, 96–100

expedition to relieve Tokar, 54–6
 on force deployment in Dongola and Khartoum, 98–9
 Hartington's instruction to, 96–7
 objects to boat proposal, 96–7, 99
 proceedings reporting, 97
 and Suakin–Berber road, 84–5, 89
Stewart, Sir Herbert, 55, 149, 231, 234, 315, 396, 479
 advance to wells, 222
 brigade headquarters, 145
 and cavalry, 235–6
 command of mounted troops, 101
 Daily Orders, 323–4
 death of, 114
 deployment of skirmishers, 224–5, 257
 Desert March, 293
 experience at Majuba, 347
 generalship of, 237
 and Gordon, 113
 horse of, 298
 march into desert, 142–7, 149
 march to Jakdul Wells, 142–7, 149, 151, 153–61, 169–70
 order to strengthen defence, 223
 personal staff officers, 145
 private letter to Wolseley, 207–8
 seniority as a full colonel, 205
 task of recapturing Berber, 112
 Wolseley's orders for, 163–5
Stewart, J. D. H. (Hammill), 36, 37, 90, 431, 476, 533–4
Story of the Household Cavalry, The, 428
Stuart-Wortley, Edward, 23, 27–8, 78, 89, 167, 188, 219, 318, 330, 386, 387, 405, 412, 430, 432, 436, 441, 442, 443, 447–9, 465
 arrival at Gubat, 451–2
 debriefing of, 452–3
 report, 454–5
 travel with 'Abd al-Hamid Bey, 426
Suakin, 17, 37, 43, 45, 46, 52, 53, 82
Suakin–Berber road, 46, 99, 470, 475–82, 489
 Bija resistance and, 478
 Bir Mahobeh, 476
 and British government, 89
 convoys moved along, 481
 Desert Column march, 476
 forcing, 480
 intelligence reports on, 478–80

Index • 577

Mahdist enemy and, 481–2
Nubian Desert, wells in, 477
objections to, 475–6
time and sustainability, 482–4
water supply, 476
Suakin expedition, 54–60, 161
  advance on Tokar, 56
  battle near Tamai, 58–9
  Bija weapons of choice, 56
  Davis's brigade, 59
  divisional-sized force using, 54–5
  loss to Bija side, 57, 58, 60
  loss to British side, 57, 60
  pushing across the *khor*, 60
Sudan, 32
  Gordon's 'hearts and minds' offensive, 66
  rebellion in, 61–3
  theatre of operations, 2
  Egyptian occupation of, 34–7
  Balkan mercenaries and, 35
  civil war, 36–7
  collaboration in military domain, 35
  and Maḥmūd Ṭāhir Pasha, 39
  regime of pashas, 34–5
Senaar expedition, 38
Shāʾiqīa tribe, 36
Sulaimān, Shaikh, 114, 380, 430, 444, 451, 462
Sunderland, Marsden, 186–7, 197–8, 239, 248, 257, 263–4, 281, 316, 329, 342, 369, 391, 401, 402
Syrian greys, 223, 394

Talahawiyeh (steamer), 74, 410, 421–3, 425, 426, 427, 430–1, 432, 434, 435, 437–9, 442, 446, 447, 448
Talbot, Reginald, 184–5, 206, 248, 253, 254, 255, 257, 259, 263, 283, 290–1, 305, 359–61, 369, 378, 392, 401, 426–8, 452–3, 503, 506–8, 509, 510, 511, 512
  blaming Burnaby, 293–4
  convoy, 429
  defending conduct of his men, 292–3
  division of HCR, 358
tarbush, 411, 413
Tawfiqiyeh (steamer), 66, 410, 422, 425, 427, 448, 456, 509
Tawfiq Bey, Muḥammad, 31, 54
Ṭāhir Pasha, Maḥmūd, 39
Tel-el-Kebir, Battle of, 7

Tokar Expedition and First Battle of El Teb, 52–4
Too Late for Gordon and Khartoum, 165, 267, 280, 424
Topographical Department, 11
  serving officers in, 12
'To Within a Mile of Khartoum', 26
Trafford, Lionel, 28, 187, 198, 218, 226, 246, 255, 256, 257, 260, 279, 281, 284, 287, 297, 316, 342, 347, 368–9, 387, 390, 401, 428, 429–30, 431, 432, 437, 442, 446–9, 451, 458–9, 461, 462
  C Company, 342, 361
  deploys Royal Sussex, 288–9
  diary, 249, 327, 378
  recognizing courage of *anṣār*, 284
  uses his stature, 297
Trafford Hill, 250
Transit (troopship), 5–6
Transvaal Rebellion, 32, 55, 178, 180, 181
Trinkitat, 52, 53, 56, 58
Turner, Alfred, 159–60, 188, 190

Upper Egypt:
  EA battalions in, 78–9
  pleas of citizenry, 79–80
  relief expedition, 80
  Robatab Arabs and, 79

Van Koughnet, Edmund, 452, 455, 457, 464
Verner, Willoughby, 155–6, 188, 190, 191, 192, 208, 211, 213, 216, 217, 234, 272, 348, 370, 391
  Abu Klea battlefield map by, 268
  borrows troopers from Binning, 306
  as column's navigator, 329–30
  diary, 165, 198, 210, 225
  interrogation of prisoners, 162
  investigates enemy dead, 309–10
  issuing ammunition, 308
  lends hand to Talbot, 305
  manages intelligence, 405
  request for camels, 412
  sketches of, 176
  as supernumerary officer, 253
  tracking of Kitchener, 195
Victoria Cross, 32, 33, 55, 160, 178, 180, 296, 439, 498
Villiers, Frederick, 176, 189, 326, 327, 348, 349, 355, 364, 366, 371, 376, 377, 384–5, 395

Wad Habeshi, Battle of, 432, 434, 443, 445–9, 456–64
  C Company deployed, 459
  enemy horsemen, 460–1
  fire-fight conducted, 460
war correspondents, 25, 29, 52, 58, 190, 206, 212–13, 230, 326–7, 353–4, 354–5, 363–4, 383, 385, 395, 402
'War Correspondent, The', 25
Watson, Charles, 22, 27, 29, 48, 417
Wādī Halfā, 3, 70, 75, 82–3, 85, 86, 89–90, 97, 101, 105–8, 110, 120–4, 127, 131, 134, 155, 175, 181, 370, 489, 490
  to Berber, river route from, 82–3
  difficulties south of, 32
  fighting force at, 116
  to Khartoum, river route from, 83
  to Sarras, railway from, 83, 105
  sending troops to, 71–2, 78
  Wolseley at, 114–16, 120,
Webber, B. J., 401, 455, 460
Western Morning News, 143, 157, 189, 213, 320
whaler scheme, 4, 94–6, 105–8, 119, 126, 130, 475, 477, 480, 489–92, 499
Williams, Charles, 26–9, 210, 213, 219, 225, 227, 233–4, 239, 255, 293, 299, 306–7, 311, 316, 320, 33, 351, 352, 358, 368, 395
  criticism of, 25
  filibustering expedition, 21
  libel proceedings against Beresford Hope, 25, 27–8
  personal attack on Wilson, 21–3, 25
  as war correspondent, 21
Wilson controversy, 14
  and Conservative government, 23
  criticism after fall of Khartoum, 16
  cruel gossip, 26
  Gladstone's folly, 15
  'How We Lost Gordon', 21–2
  letters of support, 22, 23
  23 March report, 17–18, 28–9
  Press association interview, 23
  public criticism, 21–3, 25, 29–30
  Wolseley's recommendations, 17
  Wolseley's version of events, 15
Wilson, Sir Charles, 10–14, 16–30, 104, 165–6, 188, 192–3, 195, 206, 222, 229, 235, 246, 248, 264, 266, 270, 281–4, 292, 314, 321–2, 330,

335, 340–1, 343, 349–51, 356–8, 365–6, 373, 375, 376, 380, 387, 390–9, 401, 403, 407, 410, 413, 417–21, 423–4, 426–33, 436, 440–51, 458–62, 472, 495–6, 498–9
accusation of dawdling, 15–16
attack on Metemmeh, intention to, 324
and Arabi Pasha, 13
as chief of intelligence, 417–19
as column's navigator, 329–30
commissioned as a lieutenant, 10
departure for Dublin, 26
departure for Korti, 503
diplomacy and intelligence, 12–13
as Director of the Ordnance Survey, 12
education of, 10
feels pity for enemy, 278
first tour of duty overseas, 10
intelligence report, 327
interest in musketry, 408
letter to Lady Olivia, 14
Mahdist formation description, 266–7
against night march, 343
and problems with Martini-Henry, 284
re-joining headquarters, 391–2
reporting for duty in Ismailia, 13
seniority, 205, 206
service in Cairo, 13–14
sources of intelligence, 315–16
staff work at War Office, 10–12
summons to Buckingham Palace, 27
surveyor by profession, 498
upbringing of, 10
Wolseley's letter to, 14
Wolseley's orders for, 163, 165–6
Willson, Mildmay, 19–20, 183, 206, 257, 351, 360, 451
Wingate, Sir Reginald, 86, 87
With the Camel Corps up the Nile, 156, 174, 183, 223, 407
Wolfe, Richard, 134, 186, 311, 321, 359
Wolseley, Garnet, 3–10, 13–20, 22–3, 26, 28–30, 32, 43–5, 52, 54–5, 73, 75, 81–5, 89–94, 96–7, 99–104, 107, 109–10, 114–16, 119–37, 139–40, 142–52, 156–8, 161, 163, 165, 167–70, 172–3,

183, 186, 188, 190, 196, 204–5, 207–8, 235, 287, 324, 327, 418–20, 427, 433, 440–1, 454–5, 465–82, 484, 488–96, 499–504, 509–513
Abu Klea news, 419–20
appointment to Egypt, 99–100
arrival at Wādī Halfâ, 114
and Battle of Isandlwana, 7
bravery as young officer, 5
Christmas at Korti, 135–8
commission in 12th Regiment, 5
correspondence with his wife, 116
departure for Dongola, 115
and Duke of Cambridge, 8
ego and jealously, 9
family background of, 4
Gordon Relief Expedition, 3
grand conception, 133–5
and Hartington, 110–12
hostility to Wilson, 17–20
imperial strategy by, 75
inspects Highland battalions, 103
journal for Christmas Eve, 135–6
at Korti, 140–1
lambasts Stephenson, 99
limited role to Beresford, 351–2
novel expedients, 490–3
as 'our only general', 7
outline plan: despatch of additional men and material, 101–3; railway and river journey, 105–6; whaler-borne troops at Gemai, 105
on peace settlement with Kruger, 32–3
pompous General Order, 129–30
ponders change of plan, 150–1
promoted to captain, 5
rebels at Khartoum, 104
record of service, 8–9
response to Hartington, 84
response to the Bayūda developments, 502
returns home, 287
returns to Dongola, 124–6
rise to public renown, 6–7
and Second China War of 1860, 6
in Second Relief of Lucknow, 6
senior appointments, 101
in siege lines, 5
staff planning, 101–3
on Stewart's death, 114
at strategic and tactical level, 9
sudden burst of optimism, 128

taking command as Adjutant-General, 100
telegram to Baring, 148–9
version of events, 15
visit to Army of Northern Virginia, 242
youthful conviction of, 4
Wolseley's plan of campaign, 468–72
execution of, 494–6
and Gladstone, 93–4
new plan, 151–2
options for relief expedition, 81
proposed timetable, 135–6
Red River triumvirate, 90
resistance at Shendy, 81
routes for force, 82–4, 90–3
and Stephenson, 84–5, 96–100
unfolding of, 468–9
whaler scheme, 94–6
Wolseley Ring, 7, 32, 84, 468, 498
Wood, Sir Evelyn, 13, 28, 32–3, 42, 48, 52, 55, 76, 77, 88, 101, 102, 114, 136, 487, 499, 502, 512, 513
despatched to Port Said, 46
fighting record, 32–3
as GOC Lines of Communication, 107–8, 124, 131
logistic task facing, 108
as Sirdar, 33–4
'wounded viper' problem, 379
Woodman, G., 455, 457, 464
Wright, Thomas, 267, 278

zariba:
at Abu Klea, 214, 222–3, 390, 392
at Abu Kru, 388–9
burial of casualties at, 383–4
defending, 250–1
Fetherstonhaugh return to, 232
incoming fire and, 224
layout of, 215–16
line of march back towards, 393
main body advanced to, 227–8
map of, 215
al-Zubair, Pasha Raḥma Manṣūr, 46–8, 380
Gordon and, 70–2
Zulu army, 230, 243, 270, 283
Zulu commanders, 230
Zulu War, 32, 55, 178, 180, 184, 243